Fifth Edition

Understanding and Managing ORGANIZATIONAL BEHAVIOR

Jennifer M. George

Jesse H. Jones Graduate School of Management
Rice University

Gareth R. Jones

Mays Business School
Texas A & M University

Upper Saddle River, NJ 07458

Library of Congress Cataloging-in-Publication Data
George Jennifer M.
Understanding and managing organizational behavior Jennifer M. George,
Gareth R. Jones.—5th ed.
p. cm.
Includes bibliographical references and index.
ISBN 0-13-239457-X (alk. paper)
1. Organizational behavior. 2. Organizational effectiveness. I. Jones. Gareth R. II. Title.

HD58.7.G454 2007
658.3—de22

2006027396

Senior Acquisitions Editor: David Parker
VP/Editorial Director: Jeff Shelstad
Assistant Editor: Denise Vaughn
Editorial Assistant: Stephanie Kamens
Marketing Manager: Anne Howard
Marketing Assistant: Susan Osterlitz
Associate Director, Production Editorial: Judy Leale
Managing Editor, Production: Renata Butera
Production Editor: Kevin H. Holm
Permissions Coordinator: Charles Morris
Associate Director, Manufacturing: Vinnie Scelta
Manufacturing Buyer: Diane Peirano
Design/Composition Manager:
Christy Mahon
Art Director: Pat Smythe
Interior Design: Judy Allan
Cover Design: Jae Song
Manager, Visual Research: Beth Brenzel
Image Permission Coordinator: Robert Farrell
Photo Researcher: Melinda Alexander
Composition: GGS Book Services
Full-Service Project Management:
Jeanine Furino/GGS Book Services
Printer/Binder: R.R. Donnelley/Phoenix Color Corp.
Typeface: 10/12 Times

Credits and acknowledgments borrowed from other sources and reproduced, with permission, in this textbook appear on appropriate page within text, as well as on page 684.

Pearson Education LTD.
Pearson Education Singapore, Pte. Ltd
Pearson Education, Canada, Ltd
Pearson Education–Japan
Pearson Education Australia PTY, Limited
Pearson Education North Asia Ltd
Pearson Educación de Mexico, S.A. de C.V.
Pearson Education Malaysia, Pte. Ltd.

10 9 8 7 6 5 4 3 2 1
ISBN-13: 978-0-13-239457-4
ISBN-10: 0-13-239457-X

Brief Contents

Contents

Preface

Our challenge in revising *Understanding and Managing Organizational Behavior* has been to incorporate and integrate the latest advances in theorizing and research and provide a thorough and contemporary account of the factors that influence organizational behavior. Importantly, we strived to convey this knowledge to students in a very readable, applied, hands-on format to increase their understanding and enjoyment of the learning process.

Our intention has been to provide students with the most readable, succinct account of organizational behavior on the market. To accomplish this we have only drawn on the theories and concepts that have received the most empirical research support and acceptance by the academic community.

Once again, in terms of the way our book is organized, Chapter 1 discusses contemporary organizational behavior issues and challenges; it also provides an approach to understanding and managing organizational behavior that sets the scene for the rest of the book. In Part One, "Individuals in Organizations," we underscore the many ways in which people can contribute to organizations and how an understanding of factors such as personality, emotional intelligence, creativity, and motivation can help organizations and their members channel effort and behavior in ways that promote the achievement of organizational objectives and the well-being of all organizational stakeholders including employees. Chapters 2, 3, and 4 provide extensive coverage of personality, emotional intelligence, mood and emotion, values and ethics, and the proactive management of diversity; importantly, we link these factors to important behaviors and determinants of organizational effectiveness. Chapter 5 conveys the variety of ways in which organizational members can and do learn, with a new emphasis on continuous learning through creativity.

Our treatment of the important issue of work motivation is divided into two chapters. In Chapter 6, we provide an integrated account of work motivation and the latest development in motivation theory and research. Chapter 7 then focuses on how to create a motivating work environment through job design, organizational objectives, and goal setting. Chapter 8 addresses the changing nature of the employment relationship and the implications of factors such as outsourcing, pay differentials, boundaryless careers, and values for motivation and performance. Lastly, in Chapter 9, we focus on the very real stressors people face, how they can be effectively managed, and how to find a balance between work and other aspects of life. Overall, Part One reflects both contemporary theorizing and research and the challenges and opportunities facing organizations and their members.

In Part Two, "Group and Team Processes," we bring together the many ways in which organizational members work together to achieve organizational objectives, the challenges they face, and how to achieve real synergies. Chapters 10 and 11 focus on the key factors that lead to effective work groups and teams. Chapter 12 provides an updated treatment of leadership, particularly transformational leadership in organizations. Chapter 13 contains our discussion of power, politics, conflict, and negotiation. In Chapter 14, we discuss how the latest developments in information technology have changed the nature of communication in and between organizations. The final chapter in this part, Chapter 15, provides updated coverage of decision making, knowledge management, and innovation.

Part Three, "Organizational Processes," separates our treatment of organizational structure and organizational culture to allow for an integrated treatment of organizational culture and to underscore the importance of ethics. Chapter 16 focuses on organizational design, structure, and control and the factors that affect important organizational design choices. Chapter 17 presents an integrated treatment of organizational culture and ethical behavior. It focuses on the informal and formal social processes in organizations that affect the ways people behave, the sources of organizational culture, including organizational ethics, and the nature, causes, and consequences of ethical behavior. We also discuss the factors that can lead to unethical behavior. Finally, Chapter 18 provides updated coverage of organizational change and development to reflect current realities in the very dynamic environment in which organizations operate.

The combined result of all the changes we have made to our book is a fresh approach that builds on our cutting-edge coverage of organizational behavior topics and issues that our users have appreciated in prior editions. For students, we provide a treatment of organizational behavior that allows for self-assessment because it (1) is comprehensive, integrated, and makes important theories and research findings accessible and interesting to them; (2) is current, up-to-date, and contains expanded coverage of significant contemporary issues including ethics, diversity, globalization, and information technology; (3) uses rich, real-life examples of people and organizations to bring key concepts to life and provide clear managerial implications; and, (4) is experiential and applied. Our end-of-chapter experiential exercises contained in "Exercises in Understanding and Managing Organizational Behavior" give students the opportunity to catch the excitement of organizational behavior as a fluid, many-faceted discipline, and they allow students to develop and practice their own skills.

Pedagogical Structure

We believe that no other organizational behavior textbook has the sheer range of learning features for students that our book has. These features—some integrated into the text and some at the end of each chapter or part—engage students' interest and facilitate their learning of organizational behavior. The overall objective of these features is to help instructors actively involve their students in the chapter content.

What's New In This Edition

In response to the positive comments and support of our users and reviewers we have continued to refine and build upon the major revisions we made to the last edition of our book. The revised edition of *Understanding and Managing Organizational Behavior* mirrors the changes that are taking place in the world today, both on a global dimension, and in terms of the ways the changing nature of work is affecting organizational behavior.

First, we have extended our coverage of ethics, ethical behavior, and social responsibility because of the continuing controversies and scandals that have involved a growing number of well-known companies in the 2000s. We have more in-depth coverage of ethics both in terms of new content areas within chapters and in the many kinds of company examples we use to illustrate what organizations can do to curb individual self-interest and promote ethical organizational behavior. Many specific issues such as ethical dilemmas, ethical leadership, building a socially responsible culture, and the role of ethics officers are now included in the new edition.

Second, the increasing globalization of business and diversity of the workforce has led us to extend our coverage of the many opportunities and challenges globalization and diversity pose for understanding and managing organizational behavior today. In addition, we develop a new theme in this edition of global crisis management, which is carried on throughout the book. A new section in Chapter 1 defines the nature of natural, man-made, and geopolitical crises. Then in subsequent chapters specific organizational behavior issues are discussed in detail, such as problems in creating teams in crisis situations, crisis leadership issues, and communication and decision-making problems that arise under crisis. Finally, many of the *New York Times* cases at the end of each chapter were chosen because they help provide further insights into global and diversity themes developed in the chapters.

Third, this edition continues to be the leader in describing the multitude of ways in which continuing advances in information technology are affecting all aspects of behavior in organizations. We have expanded our already extensive coverage of the ways in which digital and wireless communication is transforming how people perform their jobs, how teams function, and how organizations achieve their goals. The continuing advances made by organizational behavior scholars and researchers as they develop new and improved theories and models to explain why and how people and teams behave as they do has led us to modify, update, and refine our coverage of many different aspects of organizational behavior. Concepts like personality, trust, creativity, mood, emotion, continuous learning, justice, virtual teams, transformational leadership, telecommuting, and knowledge management are now found in the central research areas of organizational behavior.

Finally, a major focus of this edition has been to build and extend the experiential exercises and instructor-support materials that come with our text. We have refined many of these exercises and now provide new *New York Times* cases at the end of each chapter. These articles provide instructors with the opportunity to discuss organizational behavior issues that are currently in the news. In addition, other experiential exercises can be found in the instructor's manual.

Teaching Support

Instructor's Resource Center

At www.prenhall.com/irc, instructors can access a variety of print, media, and presentation resources available with this text in downloadable, digital format. Registration is simple and gives you immediate access to new titles and new editions. As a registered faculty member, you download resource files and receive immediate access and instructions for installing Course Management content on your campus server.

If you ever need assistance, our dedicated technical support team is ready to help with the media supplements that accompany this text. Visit www.247.prenhall.com for answers to frequently asked questions and toll-free user support phone numbers.

The following supplements are available to adopting instructors (for detailed descriptions, please visit www.prenhall.com/irc):

- **Instructor's Resource Center with PPTs and TestGen test-generating software (available on the IRC Online or on CD-ROM**—CD-ROM ISBN: 0-13-239460-X)
- **Printed Instructor's Manual has been revised and includes inclusion of experiential exercises**—ISBN: 0-13-239459-6
- **Printed Test Item File has been completely updated and accuracy-checked**—ISBN: 0-13-239458-8
- **Videos on DVD**—ISBN: 0-13-239461-8

Student Supplements

Companion Website: www.prenhall.com/george is where students can access chapter quizzes and a student version of the PowerPoint Presentations.

SafariX eTextbooks Online—developed for students looking to save on required or recommended textbooks, SafariX eTextbooks Online saves students money off the suggested list price of the print text. Students simply select their eText by title or author and purchase immediate access to the content for the duration of the course using any major credit card. With a SafariX eText, students can search for specific keywords or page numbers, take notes online, print out reading assignments that incorporate lecture notes, and bookmark important passages for later review. For more information, or to purchase a SafariX eTextbook, visit www.safarix.com.

Acknowledgments

Finding a way to coordinate and integrate the rich and diverse organizational behavior literature is no easy task. Neither is it easy to present the material in a way that students can easily understand and enjoy, given the plethora of concepts, theories, and research findings. In writing *Understanding and Managing Organizational Behavior*, we have been fortunate to have the assistance of several people who have contributed greatly to the book's final form. We are very grateful to David Parker, our editor, and Denise Vaughn, assistant editor, for providing us with timely feedback and information from professors and reviewers that have allowed us to shape the book to meet the needs of its intended market; and to Kevin Holm, production editor, for ably coordinating the book's progress. We also appreciate the word-processing and administrative support of Patsy Hartmangruber, Texas A&M University, and Elaine Morris, of Rice University.

We are very grateful to the many reviewers and colleagues who provided us with detailed feedback on the chapters and for their perceptive comments and suggestions for improving the manuscript. A special thank you goes to the following professors who gave us feedback during the development of the 5th edition:

Nathan Podsakoff, University of Florida

Tracey Rockett, University of Texas at Dallas

Hannah Rothstein, Baruch College

Joseph Santora, New Jersey Institute of Technology

We would also like to acknowledge the following professors who have reviewed previous editions of our book:

Cheryl Adkins, Longwood University
Deborah Arvanites, Villanova University
Robert Augelli, University of Kansas
Regina Bento, University of Baltimore
Alicia Boisnier, University of Buffalo
Robert Bontempo, Columbia University
W. Randy Boxx, University of Mississippi
Dan Brass, Pennsylvania State University
Peggy Brewer, Eastern Kentucky University
Diane Caggiano, Fitchburg State University
Elena Capella, University of San Francisco
Russell Coff, Washington University
Jeanette Davy, Wright State University
Dave Day, Columbia College
Lucinda Doran
Stewart Edwards, Marymount University and NVCC
Mark Fearing, University of Houston
Dave Fearon, Central Connecticut State University
Dean Frear, Wilkes University
Steve Grover, University of Otago
Bob Gulbro, Jacksonville State University
Jennifer Halpern, Cornell University
Phyllis Harris, University of Central Florida
Sandra Hartman, University of New Orleans
Dave Hennessy, Mount Mercy College
Mary Hogue, Kent State University Stark Campus
Ronald Humphrey, Virginia Commonwealth University
Courtney Hunt, Northern Illinois University
Bruce Johnson, Gustavus Adolphus College
Eli Kass, Saint Joseph's University
Mary Kernan, University of Delaware
John Klocinski, Lourdes College
Deborah Litvin, Merrimack College
Rosemary Maellero, University of Dallas
Karen Maher, University of Missouri–St. Louis
Stephen Markham, North Carolina State University
Gary McMahan, University of Texas–Arlington
Jeanne McNett, Assumption College
Angela Miles, Old Dominion University
LaVelle Mills, West Texas A&M University
Janet Near, Indiana University
Margaret Padgett, Butler University
Tim Peterson, University of Tulsa
Allayne Pizzolatto, Nicholls State University

Peter Poole, Lehigh University
Nancy Powell, Florida International University
Asha Rao, California State University Hayward
Elizabeth Ravlin, University of South Carolina
Diana Reed, Drake University
Sandra Robinson, University of British Columbia
Chris Scheck, Northern Illinois University
James Schmidtke, California State University Fresno
William Sharbrough, The Citadel
Shane Spiller, Morehead State University
Christina Stamper, Western Michigan University
Eric Stephan, Brigham Young University
Charlotte Sutton, Auburn University
Brian Usilaner, University of Maryland University College
Sean Valentine, University of Wyoming
Betty Velthouse, University of Michigan Flint
Susan Washburn, Stephen F. Austin State University
Robert Whitcomb, University of Wisconsin Eau Claire
Frank Wiebe, University of Mississippi

Thanks are also due to Ken Bettenhausen, University of Colorado at Denver; David Bowen, Thunderbird; and Art Brief, University of Utah.

Finally, we are grateful to two incredibly wonderful children, Nicholas and Julia, for being all that they are and the joy they bring to all who know them.

J.M.G.-G.R.J.

About the Authors

Jennifer M. George is the Mary Gibbs Jones Professor of Management and Professor of Psychology in the Jesse H. Jones Graduate School of Management at Rice University. She received her B.A. in Psychology/Sociology from Wesleyan University, her M.B.A. in Finance from New York University, and her Ph.D. in Management and Organizational Behavior from New York University. Prior to joining the faculty at Rice University, she was a Professor in the Department of Management at Texas A&M University.

Professor George specializes in Organizational Behavior and is well known for her research on mood and emotion in the workplace, their determinants, and their effects on various individual and group-level work outcomes. She is the author of many articles in leading peer-reviewed journals such as the *Academy of Management Journal*, the *Academy of Management Review*, the *Journal of Applied Psychology*, *Organizational Behavior and Human Decision Processes*, *Journal of Personality and Social Psychology*, and *Psychological Bulletin*. One of her papers won the Academy of Management's Organizational Behavior Division Outstanding Competitive Paper Award and another paper won the *Human Relations* Best Paper Award. She is, or has been, on the editorial review boards of the *Journal of Applied Psychology*, *Academy of Management Journal*, *Academy of Management Review, Journal of Management*, *Organizational Behavior and Human Decision Processes, Administrative Science Quarterly, International Journal of Selection and Assessment,* and *Journal of Managerial Issues*, was a consulting editor for the *Journal of Organizational Behavior*, and was a member of the SIOP *Organizational Frontiers Series* editorial board. She is a Fellow in the American Psychological Association, the American Psychological Society, and the Society for Industrial and Organizational Psychology and a member of the Society for Organizational Behavior. Professor George is currently an Associate Editor for the *Journal of Applied Psychology.* She also has coauthored a leading textbook on *Contemporary Management*.

Gareth Jones received both his B.A. and Ph.D. from the University of Lancaster, U.K. He previously held teaching and research appointments at the University of Warwick, Michigan State University, and the University of Illinois at Urbana–Champaign. Professor Jones specializes in both organizational behavior and organizational theory and is well known for his research on socialization, culture, and applying transaction cost analysis to explain many forms of intraorganizational and interorganizational behavior. He also has published many articles in leading journals of the field and is one of the most prolific authors in the *Academy of Management Review*. One of his articles won the Academy of *Management Journal* Best Paper Award. He is, or has been, on the editorial review boards of the *Academy of Management Review*, the *Journal of Management*, and *Management Inquiry*.

Gareth Jones is a Professor of Management in the Mays Business School at Texas A & M University, where he is actively involved in teaching and research in Organizational Behavior and related fields.

CHAPTER 1

INTRODUCTION TO ORGANIZATIONAL BEHAVIOR

Learning Objectives

After reading this chapter you should be able to:

- Define organizational behavior and explain how and why it determines the effectiveness of an organization.
- Appreciate why the study of organizational behavior improves a person's ability to understand and respond to events that take place in a work setting.
- Differentiate between the three levels at which organizational behavior is examined.
- Appreciate the way changes in an organization's external environment continually create challenges for organizational behavior.
- Describe the four main kinds of forces in the environment that pose the most opportunities and problems for organizations today.

Opening Case

HOW JEFF BEZOS MANAGES AT AMAZON.COM

What are the keys to Amazon.com's success?

In 1994, Jeffrey Bezos, a computer science and electrical engineering graduate from Princeton University, was growing weary of working for a Wall Street investment bank. His computer science background led him to see an entrepreneurial opportunity in the fact that Internet usage was growing at an accelerating pace. Bezos decided that the online book-selling market offered an opportunity for him to take advantage of his technical skills in the growing virtual marketplace. Determined to make a break, he packed up his belongings and drove to the West Coast, deciding while on route that Seattle, Washington—a new Mecca for high-tech software developers, and the hometown of Starbucks's coffee shops—would be an ideal place to begin his venture.

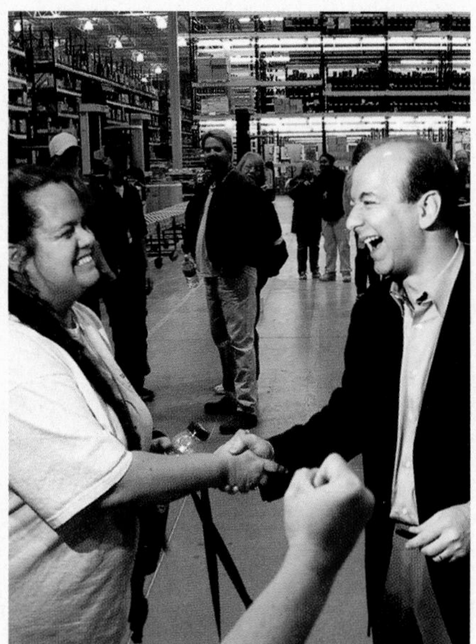

The world's largest Internet new-product retailer is Amazon.com. Here its founder and CEO Jeff Bezos is pictured joking with an employee in one of the company's many huge, state-of-the-art warehouses.

Bezos's plan was to develop an online bookstore that would be customer friendly, easy to navigate, and offer the broadest possible selection of books at low prices.[1] Bezos realized that, compared to a real "bricks and mortar" bookstore, an online bookstore could offer customers any book in print; his task was to provide online customers with an easy way to search for and learn about any book in print.

Working with a handful of employees and operating from his garage in Seattle, Bezos launched his venture online in July 1995 with $7 million in borrowed capital.[2] Within weeks he was forced to relocate to new, larger premises and hire additional employees, as book sales soared. The problem facing him now was how to best motivate and coordinate his employees to best meet his new company's goals. His solution was to organize employees into small groups and teams based upon the work tasks they needed to perform in order to satisfy his customers.

First, Bezos created the information technology (IT) team to continue to develop and improve the proprietary software that he had initially developed. Then he formed the operations group to handle the day-to-day implementation of these systems and to manage the interface between the customer and the organization. Third, he created the materials management/logistics group to devise the most cost-efficient ways to obtain books from book publishers and distributors and then to ship them quickly to customers. As Amazon.com grew, these groups have helped it to expand into providing many other kinds of products for its customers such as CDs, electronics, and gifts. By 2006, Amazon.com had 24 different storefronts, with operations in eight countries, and it sold its products to customers around the globe.

To ensure that Amazon.com strived to meet its goals of providing books quickly with excellent customer service, Bezos paid attention to the way he motivated and controlled his employees. Realizing that providing good customer service is the most vital link between customers and a company, he decentralized authority and empowered employees to search for ways to better meet customer needs. Also, from the beginning, Bezos socialized his employees into his company by encouraging them to adopt his values of excellent customer service; he also established strong norms about how employees' first task is to satisfy customers. All Amazon.com employees are carefully selected and recruited; they are then socialized by the members of their work groups so that they quickly learn how to provide excellent customer service. Also, to ensure his employees are motivated to provide excellent service, Bezos gives all employees stock in the company—today employees own over 10% of Amazon.com's stock.

Finally, as a leader, Bezos is a hands-on manager who works closely with employees to find innovative, cost-saving solutions to problems. Moreover, Bezos acts as a figurehead, and he behaves in a way that personifies Amazon's desire to increase the well-being of employees and customers. Indeed, he spends a great deal of his time flying around the world to publicize his company and its activities and he has succeeded because Amazon.com is one of the most well-recognized of any dot.com company. At Amazon.com, Jeff Bezos behaves in ways that help to improve employees' work attitudes and increase their performance, which improves the well-being of employees, customers, and his company.

Overview

Jeff Bezos has found a way to create a set of organizational behaviors that leads to a cooperative, win-win situation for the company and its employees. Amazon.com's employees work hard, are happy working for their company, and are less inclined to leave their jobs than employees in many other kinds of retail companies. This favorable work situation has been created because Amazon.com:

- Strives to increase employees' skills and knowledge and encourages them to take responsibility and to work in ways that lead to fast, helpful customer service.
- Provides employees with rewards to encourage high performance and makes sure that employees' contributions are recognized.
- Creates a work setting in which employees develop a longer-term commitment to their organization and are willing to cooperate and work hard to further their company's goals.

As Amazon.com's approach suggests, creating a favorable work situation in which people at all levels want to behave in ways that result in customers' receiving a high-quality product does not happen by chance. It is the result of careful planning and a solid understanding and appreciation of *how* people behave in organizations and *what* kinds of things cause them to behave the way they do. The best way to gain such an understanding of people at work, and the forces that shape their work behavior, is to study *organizational behavior*—the subject of this book.

In this chapter, we first define organizational behavior and discuss how a working knowledge of organizational behavior is essential for any person in today's complex, global world. We then examine how changes taking place *outside* an organization in the global, social, technological, and work or employment environments are changing the way people work together and cooperate *inside* an organization. The way rapid changes in an organization's environment have posed challenges for the behavior of all the people who work inside organizations is our focus. By the end of this chapter, you will understand the central role that organizational behavior plays in determining how effective an organization and all the men and women who are part of it are in achieving their goals.

What is Organizational Behavior?

To begin our study of organizational behavior, we could just say that it is the study of behavior in organizations and the study of the behavior of organizations, but such a definition reveals nothing about what this study involves or examines. To reach a more useful and meaningful definition, let's first look at what an organization is. An **organization** is a collection of people who work together and coordinate their actions to achieve a wide variety of goals. The goals are what individuals are trying to accomplish by being members of an organization (earning a lot of money, helping promote a worthy cause, achieving certain levels of personal power and prestige, enjoying a satisfying work experience, etc.). The goals are also what the organization as a whole is trying to accomplish (providing innovative goods and services that customers want; getting candidates elected; raising money for medical research; making a profit to reward stockholders, managers, and employees; being socially responsible and protecting the natural environment; etc.). An effective organization is one that achieves its goals.

ORGANIZATION
A collection of people who work together and coordinate their actions to achieve individual and organizational goals.

Police forces, for example, are formed to achieve the goals of providing security for law-abiding citizens and providing police officers with a secure, rewarding career while they perform their valuable services. Paramount Pictures was formed to achieve the goal of providing people with entertainment while making a profit, and in the process, actors, directors, writers, and musicians receive well-paid and interesting work.

Organizations exist to provide goods and services that people want, and the amount and quality of these goods and services are products of the behaviors and performance of an organization's employees—of its managers, of highly skilled employees in sales or research and development, and of the employees who actually produce or provide the goods and services. Today, most people make their living by working in or for some kind of company or organization. People such as a company's owners or managers—or company employees who desire to become future owners or managers—all benefit from studying organizational behavior. Indeed, people who seek to help or volunteer their time to work in nonprofit or charitable organizations also must learn the principles of organizational behavior. Like most employees today, volunteers attend training courses that help them understand the many kinds of issues and challenges that arise when people work together and cooperate in a company or organization to benefit others, such as when they seek to aid ill, distressed, or homeless people.

The Nature of Organizational Behavior

Organizational behavior (OB) is the study of the many factors that have an impact on how people and groups act, think, feel, and respond to work and organizations, and how organizations respond to their environments. Understanding how people behave in an organization is important because most people work for an organization at some point in their lives and are affected—both positively and negatively—by their experiences in it. An understanding of OB can help people to enhance the positive, while reducing the negative, effects of working in organizations.

ORGANIZATIONAL BEHAVIOR
The study of factors that affect how individuals and groups act in organizations and how organizations repond to their environments.

Most of us think we have a basic, intuitive, commonsense understanding of human behavior in organizations because we all are human and have been exposed to different work experiences. Often, however, our intuition and common sense are wrong, and we do not really understand why people act and react the way they do. For example, many people assume that happy employees are productive employees—that is, that high job satisfaction causes high job performance—or that punishing someone who performs consistently at a low level is a good way to increase performance or that it is best to keep pay levels secret. As we will see in later chapters, all these beliefs are either false or are true only under very specific conditions, and applying these principles can have negative consequences for employees and organizations.

The study of OB provides guidelines that help people at work to understand and appreciate the many forces that affect behavior in organizations. It allows employees at all levels in an organization to make correct decisions about how to behave and work with

EXHIBIT 1.1

What is Organizational Behavior

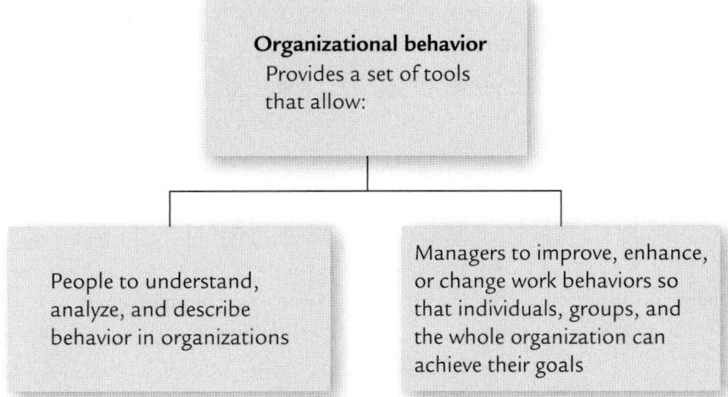

other people in order to achieve organizational goals. OB replaces intuition and gut feeling with a well-researched body of theories and systematic guidelines for managing behavior in organizations. The study of OB provides a set of tools—concepts and theories—that helps people to understand, analyze, and describe what goes on in organizations and why. OB helps people understand, for example, why they and others are motivated to join an organization; why they feel good or bad about their jobs or about being part of the organization; why some people do a good job and others don't; why some people stay with the same organization for thirty years and others seem to be constantly dissatisfied and change jobs every two years. In essence, OB concepts and theories allow people to correctly understand, describe, and analyze how the characteristics of individuals, groups, work situations, and the organization itself affect how members feel about and act within their organization (see Exhibit 1.1).

Levels of OB

In practice, there are three main levels at which OB is examined: the individual, the group, and the organization as a whole. A full understanding of OB is impossible without a thorough examination of the factors that affect behavior at each level (see Exhibit 1.2).

Much of the research in OB has focused on the way in which the characteristics of individuals (such as personality, feeling, and motivation) affect how well people do their

EXHIBIT 1.2

Levels of Analysis in Organizational Behavior

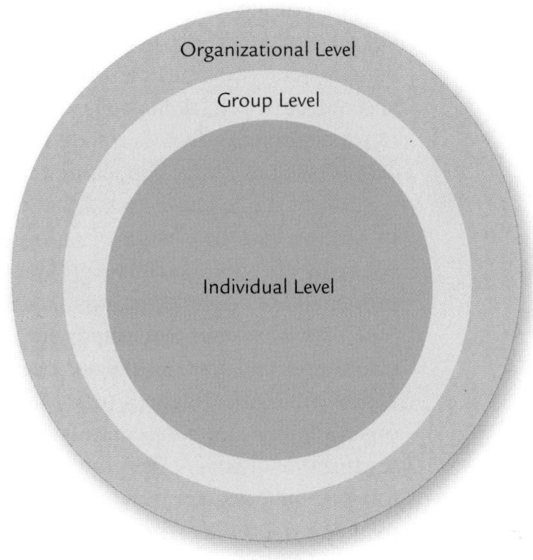

EXHIBIT 1.3

Components of Organizational Behavior

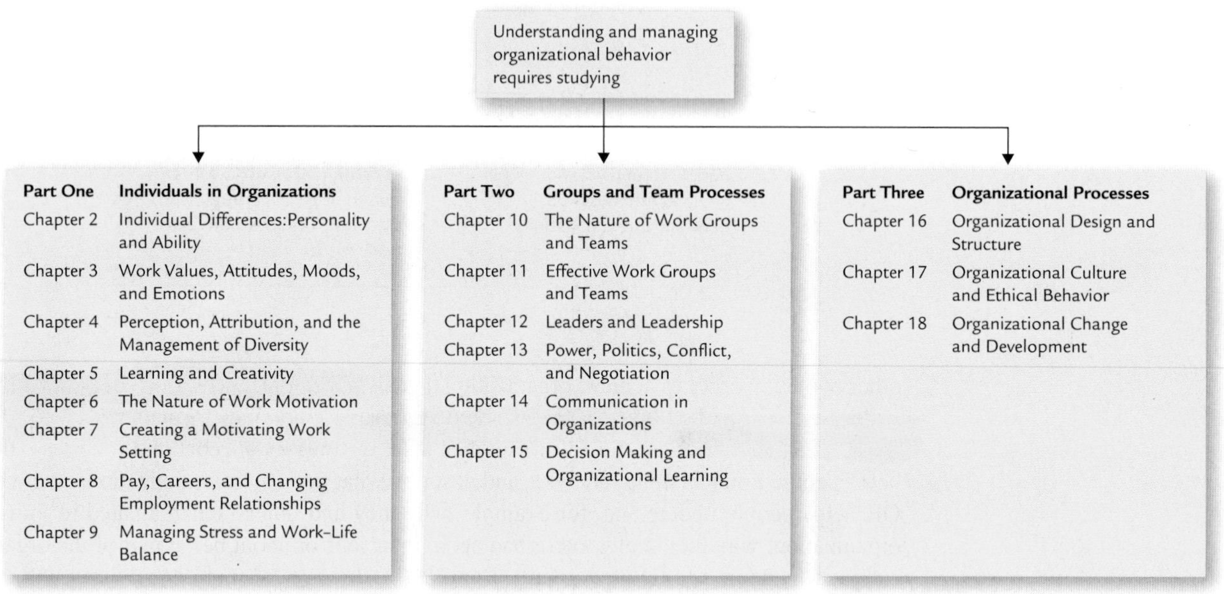

jobs, whether they like what they do, whether they get along with the people they work with, and so on. In Chapters 2 through 9 we examine individual characteristics that are critical for understanding and managing behavior in organizations: personality and ability; attitudes, values, and moods; perception and attribution; learning; motivation; and stress and work-life linkages. (see Exhibit 1.3).

GROUP
Two or more people who interact to achieve their goals.

TEAM
A group in which members work together intensively and develop team specific routines to achieve a common group goal.

VIRTUAL TEAM
A group whose members work together intensively via electronic mean, and who may never actually meet.

The effects of group or team characteristics and processes (such as communication and decision making) on OB also need to be understood. A **group** is two or more people who interact to achieve their goals. A **team** is a group in which members work together intensively and develop team-specific routines to achieve a common group goal. A **virtual team** is a group whose members work together intensively via electronic means using a common IT platform, and who may never actually meet. The number of members in a group, the type and diversity of team members, the tasks they perform, and the attractiveness of a group to its members all influence not just the behavior of the group as a whole but also the behaviors of individuals within the group. For example, a team can influence its members' decisions on how diligently they should do their jobs or how often they are absent from work, as happens at Amazon.com. Chapters 10 through 15 examine the ways in which groups affect their individual members and the processes involved in group interactions such as leadership, communication, and decision making.

Many studies have found that characteristics of the organization as a whole (such as its culture and the design of an organization's structure) have important effects on the behavior of individuals and groups. The values and beliefs in an organization's culture influence how people, groups, and managers interact with each other and with people (such as customers or suppliers) outside the organization. Organizational culture also shapes and controls the attitudes and behavior of people and groups within an organization and thus influences their desire to work toward achieving organizational goals. An organization's structure controls how people and groups cooperate and interact to achieve organizational goals. The principal task of organizational structure is to encourage people to work hard and coordinate their efforts to ensure high levels of organizational performance. Chapters 16 through 18 examine the ways organizational structure and culture affect performance, and they also examine how factors such as the changing global environment, technology, and ethics impact work attitudes and behavior.

OB and Management

The ability to use the tools of OB to *understand* behavior in organizations is one reason for studying this topic. A second reason is to learn how to *use* and *apply* these concepts, theories, and techniques to improve, enhance, or change behavior so that employees, groups, and the whole organization can all better achieve their goals. For example, a salesperson working in Neiman Marcus in Houston has the individual goal, set by his supervisor, of selling $5,000 worth of men's clothing per week. In addition, he and the other members of the men's clothing department have the group goals of keeping the department looking neat and attractive and of never keeping customers waiting. The store as a whole (along with all the other stores in the nationwide Neiman Marcus chain) has the goals of being profitable by selling customers unique, high-quality clothes and accessories and providing excellent service. If all these different goals are met, employees receive a large yearly pay bonus and Neiman Marcus makes a profit.

A knowledge of OB can help Neiman Marcus employees earn their bonuses. For example, OB research has found that organizations whose employees have been taught how to work as a team, and to take pains to be helpful, courteous, and agreeable to each other *and* to customers will be more effective than those organizations whose employees do not behave in this way. At Neiman Marcus, employees know what kinds of behaviors result in satisfied customers. They know that if they work hard to be courteous and agreeable to each other and to customers they will sell more clothes and so they (a) will achieve their personal sales goal, (b) their department's goal of never keeping customers waiting, and (c) the organization's goals of being profitable and providing excellent service.

A working knowledge of OB is important to employees at all levels in the organization because it helps them to appreciate the work situation and how they should behave to achieve their own goals (such as promotion or higher income). But knowledge of OB is particularly important to **managers**, people who direct and supervise the activities of one or more employees. For example, Sam Palmisano, chief executive officer (CEO) of IBM, and Anne Mulcahy, CEO of Xerox, have ultimate responsibility for all the hundreds of thousands of employees who work for these companies. The sales managers of IBM's or Xerox's southern region, who control hundreds of salespeople, are also managers, as are the managers (or supervisors) in charge of theses companies' technical service centers who supervise small teams of service technicians.

MANAGERS
Persons who supervise the activites of one or more employees.

Managers at all levels confront the problem of understanding the behavior of their subordinates and responding appropriately. Palmisano and Mulcahy have to manage

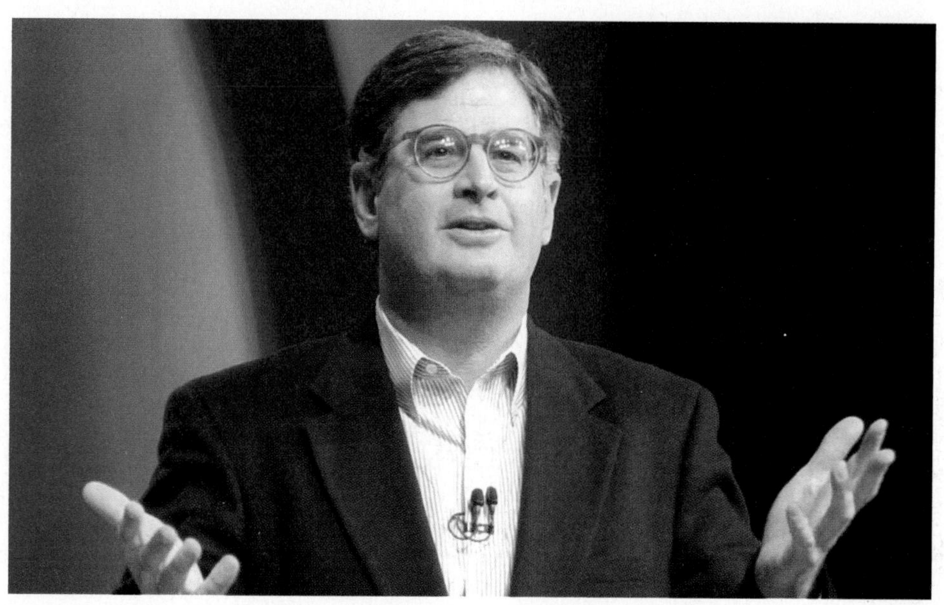
Sam Palmisano introduces the companies' new products to reporters and analysts at trade meetings.

TOP-MANAGEMENT TEAMS
High-ranking executives who plan a company's strategy so that the company can achieve its goals.

their companies' **top-management teams**, high-ranking executives who jointly plan the company's competitive strategy so that it can achieve its goals. The sales managers have to manage their sales forces so that they sell the mix of IT hardware, software, and services that best meets customers' information-processing needs. The service managers have to manage IT technicians so that they respond promptly and courteously to customers' appeals for help and quickly solve their problems. (And IBM and Xerox, like Amazon.com, both make providing customers high-quality customer service a principal goal.)

Each of these managers faces the common challenge of finding ways to help the organization achieve its goals. A manager who understands how individual, group, and organizational characteristics affect and shape work attitudes and behavior can begin to experiment to see whether changing one or more of these characteristics might increase the effectiveness of the organization—and the individuals and groups it consists of. **Organizational effectiveness** is the ability of an organization to achieve its goals. The study of OB helps managers meet the challenge of improving organizational effectiveness by providing them with a set of tools.

ORGANIZATIONAL EFFECTIVENESS
The ability of an organization to achieve its goals.

- A manager can work to raise an employee's self-esteem or beliefs about his or her ability to accomplish a certain task in order to increase the employee's productivity or job satisfaction.
- A manager can change the reward system to change employees' beliefs about the extent to which their rewards depend on their performance.
- A manager can change the design of a person's job or the rules and procedures for doing the job to reduce costs, make the task more enjoyable, or make the task easier to perform.

Recall from the chapter-opening case that Amazon.com's goal is to attract customers by providing them with high-quality, affordable books, CDs, and other products. To achieve this goal Amazon.com's founder created a work setting in which employees were taught what kinds of OBs result in economical, customer-friendly online operations. Amazon.com succeeded because it chose a way to motivate and reward employees that encourages them to work hard and well and behave in a way that benefits everyone. A key challenge for all organizations, and one that we address throughout this book, is how to encourage organizational members to work effectively for their own benefit, the benefit of their work groups, and the benefit of their organization.

Managerial Functions

MANAGEMENT
The process of planning, organizing, leading, and controlling an organization's human, financial, material, and other resources to increase its effectiveness.

The four principal functions or duties of **management** are the processes of planning, organizing, leading, and controlling an organization's human, financial, material, and other resources to increase its effectiveness.[3] And, as our previous examples showed, managers who are knowledgeable about OB are in a good position to improve their ability to perform these functions (see Exhibit 1.4).

PLANNING
Deciding how best to allocate and use resources to achieve organizational goals.

Planning. In **planning**, managers establish their organization's strategy—that is, they decide how best to allocate and use resources to achieve organizational goals. At Southwest Airlines, for example, CEO Gary Kelly and President Coleen Barrett's strategy is based on the goal of providing customers with low-priced air travel.[4] To accomplish this goal, Southwest uses its resources efficiently. For example, Southwest uses only one kind of plane, the Boeing 737, to keep down operating, training, and maintenance costs; employees cooperate and share jobs when necessary to keep down costs; and the company's website is state of the art and one of the easiest to use in the industry.

Planning is a complex and difficult task because a lot of uncertainty normally surrounds the decisions managers need to make. Because of this uncertainty, managers face risks when deciding what actions to take. A knowledge of OB can help improve the

EXHIBIT 1.4

Four Functions of Management

quality of decision making, increase the chances of success, and lessen the risks inherent in planning and decision making. First, the study of OB reveals how decisions get made in organizations and how politics and conflict affect the planning process. Second, the way in which group decision making affects planning, and the biases that can influence decisions, are revealed. Third, the theories and concepts of OB show how the composition of an organization's top-management team can affect the planning process. The study of OB, then, can improve a manager's planning abilities and increase organizational performance.

Planning
Decide on organizational goals and allocate and use resources to achieve those goals
Organizing
Establish the rules and reporting relationships that allow people to achieve organizational goals
Leading
Encourage and coordinate individuals and groups so that they work toward organizational goals
Controlling
Evaluate how well the organization is achieving its goals and take action to maintain and improve performance or take corrective action

ORGANIZING
Establishing a structure of relationships that dictates how members of an organization work together to achieve organizational goals.

Organizing. In **organizing**, managers establish a structure of relationships that dictates how members of an organization work together to achieve organizational goals. Organizing involves grouping workers into groups, teams, or departments according to the kinds of tasks they perform. At Southwest and IBM, for example, service technicians are grouped into a service-operation department, and salespeople are grouped into the sales department.

OB offers many guidelines on how to organize employees (the organization's human resources) to make the best use of their skills and capabilities. In later chapters we discuss various methods of grouping workers to enhance communication and coordination while avoiding conflict or politics. At Southwest Airlines, for example, although employees are members of particular departments (pilots, flight attendants, baggage handlers), they are expected to perform one another's nontechnical jobs when needed.

LEADING
Encouraging and coordinating individuals and groups so that all organizational members are working to achieve organizational goals.

SELF-MANAGED TEAMS
Groups of employees who are given the authority and responsibility to manage many different aspects of their *own* organizational behavior.

Leading. In **leading**, managers encourage workers to do a good job (work hard, produce high-quality products) and coordinate individuals and groups so that all organizational members are working to achieve organizational goals. The study of different leadership methods and of how to match leadership styles to the characteristics of the organization and all its components is a major concern of OB. Today, the way managers lead employees is changing because millions of employees work in **self-managed teams**—groups of employees who are given both the authority and responsibility to manage many different aspects of their *own* OB. These groups, for example, are often responsible for interviewing job applicants and for selecting new team members. Team members then train new recruits as well as help each other improve their own levels of job skills and knowledge. They also work together to develop new work methods and procedures that can increase their effectiveness.

The managers who used to actively supervise the team now play a different role—that of coaches or mentors. Their new role is to provide advice or support as needed and to champion the team and help it to obtain additional resources that will allow it to perform at a higher level and earn greater rewards as well. The way in which a small company called Dick's Drive-In Restaurant chose and followed this approach to managing OB illustrates many of these issues as the following OB Today suggests.

OB Today

Dick's Restaurants Understands Its Employees

Dick's Drive-In Restaurants is a five-store, family-owned hamburger chain based in Seattle, Washington. Founded in 1954, its owners have pursued an innovative approach to retaining hard-working employees in the fast-food industry—an industry known for its high level of employee turnover rates.[5] From the beginning, Dick's decided to pay its employees well above the industry average and offer them many benefits, too. Dick's pays its 110 part-time employees $8.75 an hour. It also covers 100 percent of the cost of its employees' health insurance and provides employees who have worked at Dick's for six months up to $10,000 toward the cost of their four-year college tuition! Dick's even pays its employees their regular wage if they perform four hours of voluntary work each month in the local community.

Dick's managers understand how to lead and motivate restaurant crews to obtain a high level of employee retention.

Dick's competitors, on the other hand—national hamburger chains like Wendy's and McDonald's—pay their part-time employees at the minimum wage of $5.85 an hour and offer them no health insurance and few other benefits—certainly nothing that can compare to Dick's. When asked why Dick's adopts this approach, Jim Spady, its vice-president, answered, "We've been around since 1954 and one thing we've always believed is that there is nothing more important than finding and training and keeping the best people you possibly can."[6]

Dick's approach to OB begins when it recruits new hires straight from high school. Its managers emphasize that they are looking for hard work and long-term commitment from employees. They stress further that in return Dick's will help and support employees by providing them with above-average pay, health-care insurance, and tuition money while they work their way through school. Dick's expects its employees to perform to the best of their abilities to get its burgers, and its customers, out the door as fast as they can. Employees are expected to be able to perform any of the tasks involved in the Burger restaurant such as taking orders, cooking the food, and cleaning up the premises. When performing their work, Dick's employees don't wait to be asked to do something; they know what to do to provide customers with the freshest burger Seattle has to offer.

Although Dick's does not expect its employees to remain with the company *after* they have graduated, it does, however, want them to stay with the company until they do. And here lies the reason why Dick's can afford to reward its employees with such generous salaries and benefits compared to its competitors. Employee turnover at large national burger chains is frequently more than 100 percent a year, meaning a typical burger restaurant has to replace all its employees at least once a year. As a result, large chains have to recruit and train new employees continually, which is very expensive and greatly increases the costs of operating a restaurant. High employee turnover also makes it difficult for managers to develop close working relationships with employees and find ways to encourage them to perform at a high level.

Dick's approach to OB leads to high performance and low turnover, which both keep operating costs low. Furthermore, Dick's managers have discovered that if employees stay for at least six months, its lower operating costs more than compensate for the extra pay and benefits employees receive. Dick's approach has therefore created a *win-win* situation for the company and its employees. If a person has to work their way through college then Dick's seems to be a good place to do it.

CONTROLLING
Monitoring and evaluating individual, group, and organizational performance to see whether organizational goals are being achieved.

Controlling. Finally, in **controlling**, managers monitor and evaluate individual, group, and organizational performance to see whether organizational goals are being achieved. If goals are being met, managers can take action to maintain and improve performance; if goals are not being met, managers must take corrective action. The controlling function also allows managers to evaluate how well they are performing their planning, organizing, and leading functions.

Once again, the theories and concepts of OB allow managers to understand and accurately diagnose work situations in order to pinpoint where corrective action may be needed. Suppose the members of a group are not working effectively together. The problem might be due to personality conflicts between individual members of the group, to the faulty leadership approach of a supervisor, or to poor job design. OB provides tools managers can use to diagnose which of these possible explanations is the source of the problem, and it enables managers to make an informed decision about how to correct the problem. Control at all levels of the organization is impossible if managers do not possess the necessary organizational-behavior tools.

Managerial Roles

ROLE
A set of behaviors or tasks a person is expected to perform because of the position he or she holds in a group or organization.

Managers perform their four functions by assuming specific roles in organizations. A **role** is a set of behaviors or tasks a person is expected to perform because of the position he or she holds in a group or organization. One researcher, Henry Mintzberg, has identified ten roles that manager's play as they manage the behavior of people inside and outside the organization (such as customers or suppliers).[7] (See Exhibit 1.5.)

Managerial Skills

SKILL
An ability to act in a way that allows a person to perform well in his or her role.

Just as the study of OB provides tools that managers can use to increase their abilities to perform their functions and roles, it can also help managers improve their skills in managing OB. A **skill** is an ability to act in a way that allows a person to perform well in his or her role. Managers need three principal kinds of skill in order to perform their organizational functions and roles effectively: conceptual, human, and technical skills.[8]

CONCEPTUAL SKILLS
The ability to analyze and diagnose a situation and to distinguish between cause and effect.

Conceptual skills allow a manager to analyze and diagnose a situation and to distinguish between cause and effect. Planning and organizing require a high level of conceptual skill, as do the decisional roles previously discussed. The study of OB provides managers with many of the conceptual tools they need to analyze organizational settings and to identify and diagnose the dynamics of individual and group behavior in these settings.

EXHIBIT 1.5

Types of Managerial Roles

Type of Role	Examples of Role Activities
Figurehead	Give speech to work force about future organizational goals and objectives; open a new corporate headquarters building; state the organization's ethical guidelines and principles of behavior that employees are to follow in their dealings with customers and suppliers.
Leader	Give direct commands and orders to subordinates; make decisions concerning the use of human and financial organizational resources; mobilize employee commitment to organizational goals.
Liaison	Coordinate the work of managers in different departments or even in different parts of the world; establish alliances between different organizations to share resources to produce new products.
Monitor	Evaluate the performance of different managers and departments and take corrective action to improve their performance; watch for changes occurring in the industry or in society that may affect the organization.
Disseminator	Inform organizational members about changes taking place both inside and outside the organization that will affect them and the organization; communicate to employees the organization's cultural and ethical values.
Spokesperson	Launch a new organizational advertising campaign to promote a new product; give a speech to inform the general public about the organization's future goals.
Entrepreneur	Commit organizational resources to a new project to develop new products; decide to expand the organization globally in order to obtain new customers.
Disturbance handler	Move quickly to mobilize organizational resources to deal with external problems facing the organization, such as environmental crisis, or internal problems facing the organization, such as strikes.
Resource allocatorr	Allocate organizational resources between different departments and divisions of the organization; set budgets and salaries of managers and employees.
Negotiator	Work with suppliers, distributors, labor unions, or employees in conflict to solve disputes or to reach a long-term contract or agreement; work with other organizations to establish an agreement to share resources.

HUMAN SKILLS
The ability to understand, work with, lead, and control the behavior of other people and groups.

TECHNICAL SKILLS
Job-specific knowledge and techniques.

Human skills enable a manager to understand, work with, lead, and control the behaviors of other people and groups. The study of how managers can influence behavior is a principal focus of OB, and the ability to learn and acquire the skills that are needed to coordinate and motivate people is a principal difference between effective and ineffective managers.

Technical skills are the job-specific knowledge and techniques that a manager requires to perform an organizational role—for example, in manufacturing, accounting, or marketing. The specific technical skills a manager needs depend on the organization the manager is in and on his or her position in the organization. The manager of a restaurant, for example, needs cooking skills to fill in for an absent cook, accounting and bookkeeping skills to keep track of receipts and costs and to administer the payroll, and artistic skills to keep the restaurant looking attractive for customers.

Effective managers need all three kinds of skills—conceptual, human, and technical. The lack of one or more of these skills can lead to a manager's downfall. One of the biggest problems that entrepreneurs who found their own businesses confront—a problem that is often responsible for their failure—is lack of appropriate conceptual and human skills. Similarly, one of the biggest problems that scientists, engineers, and others who switch careers and go from research into management confront is their lack of effective human skills. Management functions, roles, and skills are intimately related, and in the long run the ability to understand and manage behavior in organizations is indispensable to any actual or prospective manager.

Challenges For OB

In the last few decades, the challenges facing organizations to effectively utilize and develop the skills, knowledge, and "human capital" of their employees have been increasing. As we noted earlier, among these challenges, those stemming from changing pressures or forces in the social and cultural, global, technological, and work environments stand out. To appreciate the way changes in the environment affect behavior in organizations, it is useful to model an organization from an open-systems perspective. In an **open system**, an organization takes in resources from its external environment and converts or transforms them into goods and services that are sent back to that environment, where they are bought by customers (see Exhibit 1.6).

OPEN SYSTEM
Organizations that take in resources from their external environments and convert or transform them into goods and services that are sent back to their environments where customers buy them.

The activities of most organizations can be modeled using the open-systems view. At the *input stage*, companies such as Ford, General Electric, Ralph Lauren, Amazon.com, and Dick's Restaurants acquire resources such as raw materials, component parts, skilled employees, robots, and computer-controlled manufacturing equipment. The challenge is to create a set of OBs and procedures that allow employees to identify and purchase high-quality resources at a favorable price. An **organizational procedure** is a rule or routine an employee follows to perform some task in the most effective way.

ORGANIZATIONAL PROCEDURE
A rule or routine an employee follows to perform some task in the most effective way.

Once the organization has gathered the necessary resources, conversion begins. At the *conversion stage,* the organization's workforce, using appropriate skills, tools, techniques, machinery, and equipment, transforms the inputs into outputs of finished goods and services, such as cars, appliances, clothing, and hamburgers. The challenge is to develop the set of OBs and procedures that results in high-quality goods and services produced at the lowest possible cost.

At the *output stage,* the organization releases finished goods and services to its external environment where customers purchase and use them to satisfy their needs. The challenge is to develop the set of OBs and procedures that attract customers to a company's products and who come to believe in the value of a company's goods and services and thus become loyal customers. The money the organization obtains from the sales of its outputs

EXHIBIT 1.6

An Open System View of Organizational Behavior

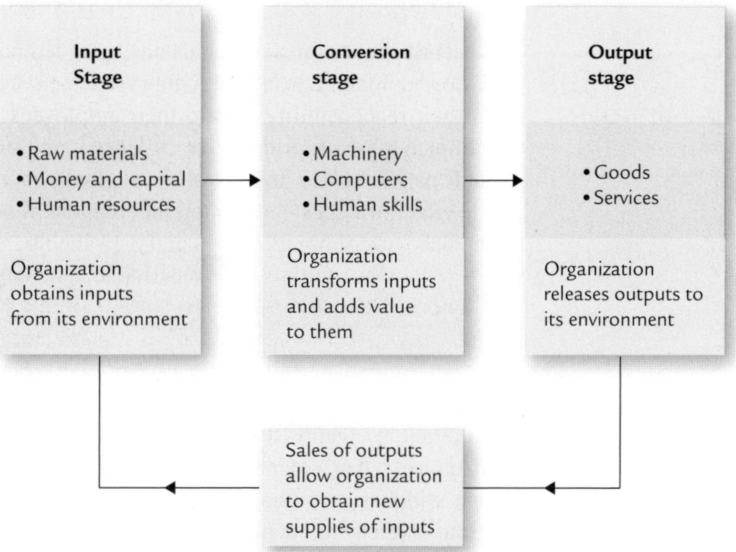

to customers allows the organization to acquire more resources so that the cycle can begin again.

The system just described is said to be open because the organization draws from and interacts with the external environment to secure resources, and then disposes of its outputs by selling its products to customers. Only by continually altering and improving its OBs and procedures to respond to changing environmental forces can an organization adapt and prosper over time. Organizations that fail to recognize the many changing forces in the environment lose their ability to acquire resources, to sell their products, and so they often disintegrate and disappear over time.

In the next sections, we introduce the four major OB challenges coming from a changing environment that the people who work in companies and organizations face today. We then examine these challenges in more depth throughout the rest of the book to reveal the many dramatic ways in which OB and procedures are changing today so organizations can adapt and prosper.

Challenge 1: The Changing Social and Cultural Environment

Forces in the social and cultural environment are those that are due to changes in the way people live and work—changes in values, attitudes, and beliefs brought about by changes in a nation's culture and the characteristics of its people. **National culture** is the set of values or beliefs that a society considers important and the norms of behavior that are approved or sanctioned in that society. Over time, the culture of a nation changes, and this affects the values and beliefs of its members. In the United States, for example, beliefs about the roles and rights of women, minorities, gays, and the disabled, as well as feelings about love, sex, marriage, war, and work, have all changed in each passing decade.

NATIONAL CULTURE
The set of values or beliefs that a society considers important and the norms of behavior that are approved or sanctioned in that society.

Organizations must be responsive to the changes that take place in a society, for these affect all aspects of their operations. Change affects their hiring and promotion practices, for one, as well as the forms of OBs and procedures that are seen as appropriate in the work setting. For example, in the last ten years the number of women and minorities assuming managerial positions in the work force has increased by over 25 percent. As we discuss in detail in later chapters, organizations have had to make enormous strides to prevent their employees from discriminating against others because of factors such as age, gender, or ethnicity, and to work to prevent sexual harassment. Two major challenges of importance to OB today are those that derive from a breakdown in ethical values and from the increasing diversity of the workforce.

Developing Organizational Ethics and Well-Being

Recently, huge ethical scandals have plagued hundreds of U.S. companies like Worldcom, Tyco, Adelphia, Enron, and Arthur Andersen, whose top managers put personal gain ahead of their responsibility toward their employees, customers, and investors. Many of these companies' stock prices have collapsed, and ordinary Americans have seen the value of their pension plans and investments plunge in value as a result. In light of these scandals, the effect of ethics—an important component of a nation's social and cultural values—on the behavior of organizations and their members has taken center stage.[9]

ETHICS
The values, beliefs, and moral rules that its managers and employees should use to analyze or interpret a situation and then decide what is the "right" or appropriate way to behave.

An organization's **ethics** are the values, beliefs, and moral rules that its managers and employees should use to analyze or interpret a situation and then decide what is the "right" or appropriate way to behave to solve an ethical dilemma.[10] An **ethical dilemma** is the quandary managers experience when they have to decide if they should act in a way that might benefit other people or groups, and that is the "right" thing to do, even though doing so might go against their own and their organization's interests. An ethical dilemma may also arise when a manager has to decide between two different courses of action, knowing that whichever course he or she chooses will inevitably result in harm to one person or group even while it may benefit another. The ethical dilemma here is to decide which course of action is the "lesser of two evils."

ETHICAL DILEMMA
The quandary managers experience when they have to decide if they should act in a way that might benefit other people or groups, and is the "right" thing to do, even though doing so might go against their own and their organization's interests.

Managers and employees know they are confronting an ethical dilemma when their moral scruples come into play and cause them to hesitate, debate, and reflect upon the "rightness" or "goodness" of a course of action. The ethical problem is to decide how a particular OB will help or harm people or groups—both inside and outside the organization—who will be affected by it.[11] Ethical OB is important because it can enhance or reduce the **well-being**—that is, the happiness, health, and prosperity—of a nation and its citizens in several ways.[12]

WELL-BEING
The condition of being happy, healthy, and prosperous.

First, ethics help managers establish the goals that their organizations should pursue and the way in which people inside organizations should behave to achieve them.[13] For example, one goal of an organization is to make a profit so that it can pay the managers, employees, suppliers, shareholders, and others who have contributed their skills and resources to the company. Ethics specify what actions an organization should take to make a profit. Should an organization be allowed to harm its competitors by stealing away their skilled employees or by preventing them from obtaining access to vital inputs? Should an organization be allowed to produce inferior goods that may endanger the safety of customers? Should an organization be allowed to take away the jobs of U.S. employees and transfer them overseas to employees in countries where wages are $5 per day? What limits should be put on organizations' and their managers' attempts to make a profit? And who should determine those limits?[14]

The devastating effect of a lack of organizational ethics is illustrated by the behavior of the company Metabolife International that made and sold the drug Ephedra, which used to be a widely used supplement taken for weight loss or body-building purposes. Although fears about this drug's side effects had been around for years, Metabolife resisted attempts by the Food and Drug Administration (FDA) to obtain a list of customer reports about the effects they had experienced from using its pills. After being threatened with a criminal investigation, Metabolife released over 16,000 customer reports about its Ephedra products that listed nearly 2,000 adverse reactions including 3 deaths, 20 heart attacks, 24 strokes, and 40 seizures.[15] Metabolife did not have to reveal this negative information about the side effects of its product because no laws existed to force supplement makers to do so, although pharmaceutical companies are governed by laws that require them to reveal side effects. Its actions might have been legal but they were unethical, and those who had suffered adverse reactions from using its pills began to sue the company and win large settlements.[16] A national lobbying campaign began to ban Ephedra from the market and in 2004 the FDA gained the power to ban the drug and did so.

In addition to defining right and wrong behavior for employees, ethics also define an organization's **social responsibility**, or its obligations and duty toward people or groups outside the organization that are directly affected by its actions.[17] Organizations and their managers must establish an ethical code that describes acceptable behaviors and they must create a system of rewards and punishments to enforce this ethical code.

SOCIAL RESPONSIBILITY
An organizations obligations toward people or groups that are directly affected by its actions.

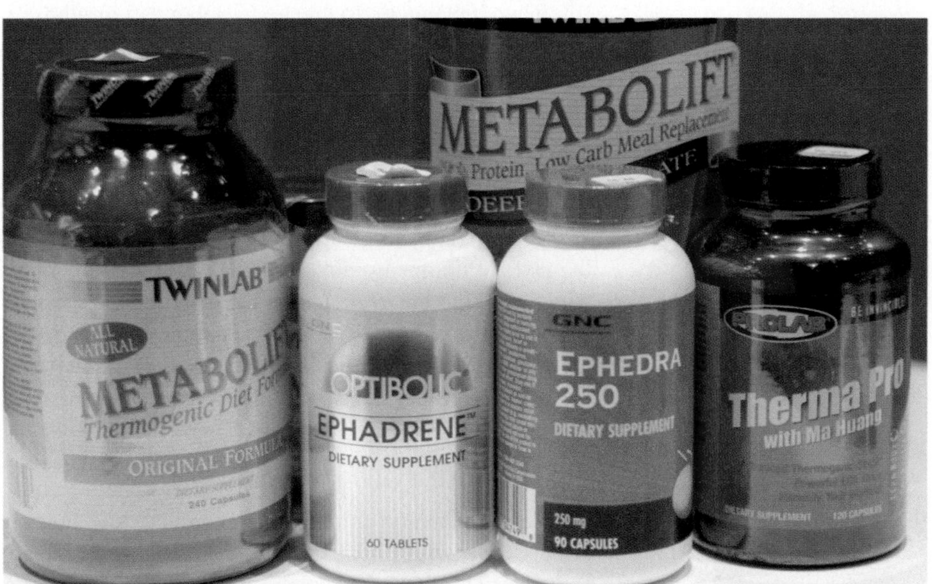

The ultimate goal of the firm is to make a profit. Suppose you were on the board of directors for Metabolife International. Would you have advised the company to warn consumers about the adverse effect of the company's diet pills if it weren't required by law?

Different organizations have different views about social responsibility.[18] To some organizations, being socially responsible means performing any action as long as it is legal. Other organizations do more than the law requires and work to advance the well-being of their employees, customers, and society in general.[19] Target, UPS, and Ben & Jerry's, for example, each contribute a significant percentage of their profits to support charities and community needs and expect their employees to be socially active and responsible. Starbuck's and Green Mountain Coffee Roasters seek out coffee-growing farmers and cooperatives that do not use herbicides and pesticides on their crops, that control soil erosion, and that treat their employees fairly and with respect in terms of safety and benefits. Starbuck's also signs contracts with small coffee growers abroad to ensure they receive a fair price for their coffee crop, even if world prices for coffee plunge—they want their growers to remain honest and loyal.

Not all organizations are willing or able to undertake such programs, but all organizations need codes of conduct that spell out fair and equitable behavior if they want to avoid doing harm to people and other organizations. Developing a code of ethics helps organizations protect their reputations and maintain the goodwill of their customers and employees. Today, many companies are strengthening their codes of ethics and making employees at all levels sign off that they understand them and will follow them, just as the Sarbanes-Oxley Act forces the CEO and chief financial officer (CFO) to sign a company's financial reports, indicating they are true and accurate.[20] Companies that have been found to act illegally are today often forced to agree to supervision from an outside ethics monitor, put in place to evaluate its managers' current decision making—as has happened to MCI and KPMG.[21]

It will also happen at Boeing, which has experienced major ethical problems in recent years. In 2006, for example, Boeing agreed to pay $615 million to end a three-year Justice Department investigation into reported defense-contracting scandals. The deal would allow Boeing to avoid criminal charges or any admission of wrongdoing. Boeing has been under investigation for improperly acquiring proprietary competitive information about rival Lockheed Martin's bidding intention for government rocket-launching contracts in order to win the auction. The government stripped Boeing of about $1 billion worth of rocket launches for its improper use of the Lockheed documents. Additionally, Boeing illegally recruited senior Air Force Procurement Officer Darleen Druyun while she still had authority over billions of dollars in other Boeing contracts. Druyun reportedly also championed Boeing's efforts to bypass normal procurement procedures in offering to provide refueling tankers to the Air Force through a controversial $20 billion leasing program. Druyun served nine months in prison in 2005 for violating federal conflict-of-interest laws. Michael Sears, formerly CFO at Boeing, was fired in 2003 and spent four months in federal prison for illegally recruiting her. The scandals also led to the resignation of Boeing Chairman Phil Condit. All this despite the fact that the Boeing supposedly had a strong code of ethics!

The challenge is to create an organization whose members resist the temptation to behave in illegal and unethical ways that promote their own interests at the expense of the organization or promote the organization's interests at the expense of people and groups outside the organization. Employees and managers have to recognize that their behavior has important effects not only on other people and groups inside and outside the organization but also on the organization itself.[22] The well-being of organizations and the well-being of the society of which they are a part are closely linked and are the responsibility of everyone.[23] (How to create an ethical organization is an issue that we take up throughout the text.) With this in mind, take a look at the ethical exercise in "A Question of Ethics," which is found in *OB in Action*, a collection of experiential exercises located at the end of every chapter of this book. For an example of the way the issue of social responsibility permeates global issues, and how we are all instrumental in determining well-being around the world, consider the issue of rose growing discussed in Ethics in Action.

DIVERSITY
Individual differences resulting from age, gender, race, ethnicity, religion, sexual orientation, and socioeconomic background.

Dealing With a Diverse Workforce

A second social and cultural challenge is to understand how the diversity of a workforce affects OB. **Diversity** results from differences in age, gender, race, ethnicity, religion, sexual orientation, socioeconomic background, and capabilities or disabilities. If an

Ethics in Action

Everything is *Not* Coming Up Roses

Every year on Valentine's Day tens of millions of roses are delivered to sweethearts and loved ones in the United States, and anyone who has bought roses knows that their price has been falling steadily. One of the main reasons for this is that rose growing is now concentrated in poorer countries in Central and South America. Rose growing has been a boon to poor countries where the extra income women earn can mean the difference between starvation or not for their families. Ecuador, for example, is the fourth biggest rose grower in the world, and the industry employs over 50,000 women who tend, pick, and package roses for above its national minimum wage. Most of these women are employed by Rosas del Ecuador, the company that controls the rose business in that country.

Some of the millions of bunches of roses sold each year are sold on Valentine's Day. Many of these roses are grown in less-developed countries that have low health and safety laws to protect the workers who grow them.

The hidden side of the global rose-growing business is that poorer countries tend to have lax or unenforced health and safety laws, something that lowers rose-growing costs in these countries. And, critics argue, many rose-growing companies and countries are not considering the well-being of their workers. For example, although the CEO of Rosas de Ecuador, Erwin Pazmino, denies workers are subjected to unsafe conditions, almost 60% of his workers have reported blurred vision, nausea, headaches, asthma, and other symptoms of pesticide poisoning.[24] Workers labor in hot, poorly ventilated greenhouses in which roses have been sprayed with pesticides and herbicides. Safety equipment such as masks and ventilators is scarce and the long hours women work adds to chemical overexposure. If workers complain, they may be fired and blacklisted, which makes it hard for them to find other jobs. So, to protect their families' well-being, workers rarely complain and so their health remains at risk.

Clearly, rose buyers worldwide need to be aware of these working conditions when deciding to buy roses, just as buyers of inexpensive clothing and footwear became concerned in the last few decades when they found out about the sweatshop conditions in which garment and shoe workers labored. Companies like Nike and Wal-Mart have made major efforts to stop sweatshop practices, and they now employ hundreds of inspectors who police the factories overseas that make the products they sell. In a similar way, the main buyers and distributors of flowers for the U.S. market also are beginning to consider the well-being of the workers who grow them.

organization or group is composed of people who are all of the same gender, ethnicity, age, religion, and so on, the attitudes and behavior of its members are likely to be very similar. Members are likely to share the same attitudes or values and will tend to respond to work situations (projects, conflicts, new tasks) in similar ways. By contrast, if the members of a group differ in age, ethnicity, and other characteristics, their attitudes, behavior, and responses are likely to differ as well.

In the last twenty years, the demographic makeup of employees entering the work force and advancing to higher-level positions in organizations has been changing rapidly. Partly because of affirmative action and equal-opportunity-employment legislation, the number of minority employees entering and being promoted to higher-level positions has increased.[25] By 2005, African-American and Hispanic employees made up over 22 percent of the work force, while the percentage of white males decreased from 51 percent to 46 percent.[26] At the same time, the number of women entering the work force has also been increasing dramatically and they are ascending to higher and higher positions in management.[27] Finally, because of increased globalization, the diversity of the U.S. population is increasing rapidly due to the large numbers of people born in other nations who immigrate to the United States to live and work.

The increasing diversity of the work force presents three challenges for organizations and their managers: a fairness and justice challenge, a decision-making and performance challenge, and a flexibility challenge (see Exhibit 1.7).

Fairness and Justice Challenge. Jobs in organizations are a scarce resource, and obtaining jobs and being promoted to a higher-level job is a competitive process. Managers are challenged to allocate jobs, promotions, and rewards in a fair and equitable manner. As diversity increases, achieving fairness can be difficult, at least in the short run, because many organizations have traditionally appointed white-male employees to higher organizational positions. Also, seniority plays a role and many minorities are recent hires.[28] Rectifying this imbalance by actively recruiting and promoting increasing numbers of women and minorities can lead to difficult equity issues because this attempt to fix the traditional imbalance reduces the prospects for white-male employees.[29] An increase in diversity can thus strain an organization's ability to satisfy the aspirations of its work force, creating a problem that, in turn, directly affects the work force's well-being and performance.[30] Organizations must learn to manage diversity in a way that increases

EXHIBIT 1.7

The Challenge Posed by Diverse Workplace

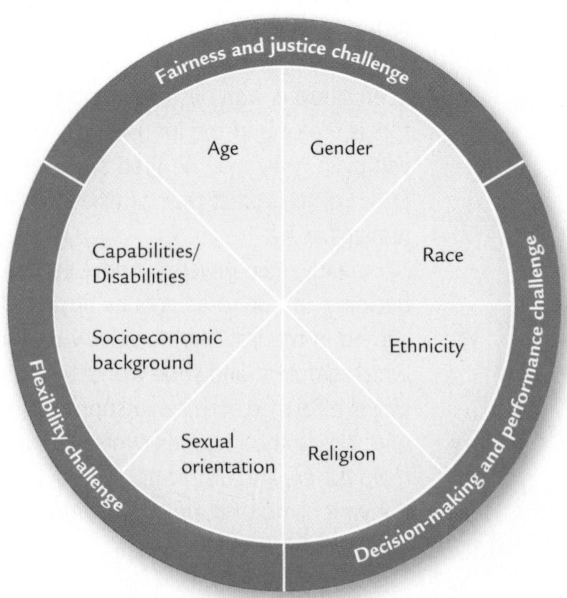

the well-being of all employees, but deciding how to achieve this goal can pose difficult ethical problems for managers.[31]

Decision-Making and Performance Challenge. Another important challenge posed by a diverse work force is how to take advantage of differences in the attitudes and perspectives of people of different ages, genders, or races, in order to improve decision making and raise organizational performance.[32] Many organizations have found that tapping into diversity, and taking advantage of the potential of diverse employees, leads to new and improved OBs and procedures.[33] Union Bank of California (UBC) is one example of a company that has enjoyed huge success because of the way it has developed an approach to diversity that reflects the needs of its employees, customers, and its environment.[34]

With assets of over $35 billion, UBC, based in San Francisco, is the third largest commercial bank in California and among the 25 largest banks in the United States.[35] California is one of the most diverse states in the nation and over half the population is Asian, Black, Hispanic, and/or gay. Recognizing this fact, the bank always had a policy of seeking to hire and recruit diverse employees. However, UBC also woke up to the fact that it could use the diversity of its employees to build its customer base. The process started when George Ramirez, a UBC vice president, suggested that the bank should create a marketing group to develop a plan to attract customers who were Hispanic like himself. So successful was this venture that a group of African-American employees decided that they should create a marketing group to develop a marketing campaign to attract new African-American customers. It was soon clear to UBC that it should use the diversity of its employees as a way of improving customer service so that, for example, if a customer walks into a bank branch in a predominately Latino neighborhood, they will be greeted by a substantial numbers of Latino employees.[36]

The bank, like many other organizations, also discovered that as its reputation as a good place for minorities to work increased, it began to attract highly skilled and motivated minority job candidates so that it helped itself. As Takahiro Moriguchi, its former CEO, said in accepting a diversity award for the company, "By searching for talent from among the disabled, both genders, veterans, all ethnic groups, and all nationalities, we gain access to a pool of ideas, energy, and creativity as wide and varied as the human race itself. I expect diversity will become even more important as the world gradually becomes a truly global marketplace."[37]

Flexibility Challenge. A third diversity challenge is to be sensitive to the needs of different kinds of employees and to try to develop flexible employment approaches that increase employee well-being. Examples of some of these approaches include the following:

- New benefits packages customized to the needs of different groups of employees, such as single employees with no children and families, gays in long-term committed relationships, and employees caring for aged parents
- Flexible employment conditions (such as flextime) that give employees input into the length and scheduling of their workweek
- Arrangements that allow for job sharing so that two or more employees can share the same job (to take care of children or aged parents, for example)
- Designing jobs and the buildings that house organizations to be sensitive to the special needs of handicapped employees (and customers)
- Creating management programs designed to provide constructive feedback to employees about their personal styles of dealing with minority employees[38]
- Establishing mentoring relationships to support minority employees[39]
- Establishing informal networks among minority employees to provide social support[40]

Managing diversity is an ongoing activity that has many important implications for organizations. We discuss diversity in depth in Chapter 4.

Challenge 2: The Evolving Global Environment

GLOBAL ORGANIZATIONS
Companies that produce or sell their products in countries and regions throughout the world.

The challenge of responding to social and cultural forces increases as organizations expand their operations globally and set up international operations in countries throughout the world. **Global organizations**, like GM, Toyota, Amazon.com, Nokia, PepsiCo, and Sony, are companies that produce or sell their products in countries and regions throughout the world. Each country has a different national culture, and so when they expand their operations abroad global organizations they encounter much greater differences in social and cultural values, beliefs, and attitudes. They therefore face the increased challenge of dealing with ethical and diversity-related issues across countries and national boundaries.[41] Two important challenges facing global organizations are to appreciate the differences that exist between countries and then to benefit from this new global knowledge to improve OBs and procedures.[42]

Understanding Global Differences

Companies must learn about many different kinds of factors when they operate globally.[43] First, there are the considerable problems of understanding OB in different global settings.[44] Evidence shows that people in different countries have different values, beliefs, and attitudes—not only about their work and organizations. It has been argued, for example, that Americans have an individualistic orientation toward work and Japanese people have a collectivist orientation. These different orientations to work reflect cultural differences, which affect people's behavior in groups and their commitment and loyalty to an organization.[45]

OB becomes especially complex at a global level because the attitudes, aspirations, and values of the work force differ by country. For example, most U.S. employees are astonished to learn that in Europe the average employee receives from four to six weeks paid vacation a year. In the United States, a comparable employee receives only one or two weeks. Similarly, in some countries, promotion by seniority is the norm, but in others, level of performance is the main determinant of promotion and reward. Understanding the differences between national cultures is important in any attempt to manage behavior in a global organization.[46]

Second, problems of coordinating the activities of an organization to match its environment become much more complex as an organization's activities expand across the globe.[47] Decision making, for example, must be coordinated between managers at home and those in countries abroad who are likely to have different views about what goals an organization should pursue. One of the most significant functions of global managers is the way they organize the company and decide how to allocate decision-making authority and responsibility between managers at home and abroad.[48]

Third, in many cases global organizations locate in a particular country abroad because this allows them to operate more effectively, but in doing so this also has major affects on their home operations. Today, for example, the need to reduce the costs of making and selling goods to stay competitive with companies from around the world has pushed many U.S. companies to make most of their products abroad. They contract with manufacturers in countries where labor costs are low to make their products, which are then shipped back to the U.S. for sale. In the last decade, for example, over 10 million jobs have been lost in the U.S. garment-making industry. Companies like Levi Strauss, which made all their clothing in the U.S. twenty years ago, now contract with foreign manufactures and virtually all their clothing is made abroad. The way IKEA has successfully met all these challenges using its global approach to OB is instructive for global companies, as the following Global View suggests.

GLOBAL LEARNING
The process of acquiring and learning the skills, knowledge, and organizational behaviors and procedures that have helped companies abroad become major global competitors.

Global Learning

Although the changing global environment has been a major threat to U.S. organizations and workers, it also offers them many opportunities to improve the ways they operate. By fostering **global learning**—the process of acquiring and learning the skills, knowledge,

Global View

IKEA's Worldwide Approach to OB

IKEA is the largest furniture chain in the world, and in 2006 the Swedish company operated over 231 stores in 33 countries.[49] In 2005 IKEA sales were almost $15 billion, over 20% of the global furniture market, but to its managers and employees this is just the tip of the iceberg. They believe IKEA is poised for massive growth throughout the world in the coming decade because it can provide what the average customer wants: well-designed contemporary furniture at an affordable price. IKEA's ability to provide customers with affordable furniture is very much the result of its approach to OB, that is, to the way it treats its employees and operates its global store empire. In a nutshell, IKEA's OB approach revolves around simplicity, attention to detail, cost-consciousness, and responsiveness in every aspect of its actions and behavior.

The origins of IKEA's successful approach derive from the personal values and beliefs of its founder Ingvar Kamprad, concerning how organizations should treat their employees and customers.[50] Kamprad, who is now in his 70s, was born in Smaland, a poor Swedish province whose citizens are well known for being entrepreneurial, frugal, and hard working. Kamprad definitely absorbed these values, for when he entered the furniture business he made them the core of his approach to OB. He teaches store managers and employees his values; his beliefs about the need to operate in a no-frills, cost-conscious way; and, that they are all in business "together," by which he means that every person in his company plays an essential role and has an obligation to everyone else.

Ingvar Kamprad, founder and CEO of IKEA, whose enthusiasm for managing his company and working with IKEA's associates to provide excellent customer service has never waned. Today, he is one of the richest people in the world.

What does Kamprad's frugal, cost-conscious approach mean in practice? All IKEA's members fly coach class on business, stay in inexpensive hotels, and work to keep traveling expenses to a minimum. It also means that IKEA stores operate on the simplest set of rules and procedures possible and that employees are expected to work together to solve problems on an ongoing basis to get the job done. Many famous stories exist about how the frugal Kamprad also always flies coach class, and about how, when he takes a coke can from the mini-bar in a hotel room, he replaces it with one bought in a store—and all this despite the fact that he is a multi-billionaire ranked in the top twenty on the Forbes list of the world's richest people![51]

IKEA's employees see what his approach to OB means as soon as they are recruited to work in one of its stores. Starting at the bottom of the ladder, they are quickly trained to perform all the various jobs involved in operating the stores. They also learn the

importance IKEA attaches to them learning to take the initiative and responsibility for solving problems and for focusing on the customer. Employees are rotated between departments and sometimes stores, and rapid promotion is possible for those who demonstrate the enthusiasm and togetherness that signifies they have bought in to IKEA's approach. Most of IKEA's managers rose from its ranks and, to make sure top executives are constantly in touch with stores, IKEA holds "breaking the bureaucracy weeks" when they are required to work in stores and warehouses for a week each year. Everyone wears informal clothes to work at IKEA, Kamprad has always worn an open-neck shirt, and there are no marks of status such as executive dining rooms or private parking places.

All employees believe that if they buy into IKEA's work values and behave in ways that will keep its operations simple and streamlined, and if they focus on being one step ahead of potential problems, that they will share in its success. Promotion, training, above-average pay, a generous store-bonus system, and also the personal well-being that comes from working in a place where people are valued by their coworkers are some of the rewards that Kamprad pioneered to build and strengthen IKEA's global OB approach.

Whenever IKEA enters a new country, or opens a new store in a new city, it sends its most experienced store managers to establish its global OB approach in its new stores. When IKEA first entered the U.S., the attitude of U.S. employees puzzled its managers. Despite their obvious drive to succeed and good education, employees seemed reluctant to take the initiative and assume responsibility. IKEA's managers discovered that their U.S. employees were afraid mistakes would result in the loss of their jobs, so they strived to teach employees the "IKEA way" and its approach to OB has prevailed. The U.S. has become its second-best market and it plans to open many more U.S. stores over the next decade.

and OBs and procedures that have helped companies abroad become major global competitors— U.S. companies have also prospered.[52] For example, U.S. companies have been able to gain access to many kinds of valuable resources present in companies abroad. Ford and GM have bought the design skills of Italian companies like Ferrari and Lamborghini, electronic components from Japanese companies like NEC and Matsushita (well known for their quality), and machine tools and manufacturing equipment from German companies like Daimler-Chrysler and BASF (well known for their excellent engineering skills). Through global learning, companies also learn how to better serve the needs of their customers and of course they can attract more customers for their goods and services. For example, the potential size of the U.S. market for hamburgers is 265 million people, but there are 3 billion potential burger-eaters in Asia alone. Thus it is not surprising that McDonald's has expanded globally, opening restaurants throughout Asia and the rest of the world in order to take advantage of the huge global appetite for hamburgers, french fries, and milk shakes.[53]

EXPATRIATE MANAGERS The people who work for a company overseas and are responsible for developing relationships with organizations in countries around the globe.

To respond to the global challenge, more and more companies are rotating their employees and moving them to their overseas operations so they can learn firsthand the problems and opportunities that arise when working in countries overseas. **Expatriate managers** are those who live and work for companies in countries abroad. There are many ways they can help their companies develop improved OBs and procedures. First, expatriate managers can learn about the sources of low-cost inputs and the best places to assemble their products throughout the world. Second, expatriate managers in functions such as research and development, manufacturing, and sales can take advantage of their presence in a foreign country to learn the skills and techniques those companies in that country use. They can apply this knowledge to improve the performance not only of their operations abroad but also of their domestic or home operations. Many companies also use global virtual teams to increase global learning.[54]

After World War II, for example, many of Toyota's manufacturing managers visited the U.S. car plants of GM and Ford to learn how these companies assembled cars. Those Japanese managers took that manufacturing knowledge back to Japan, where they improved on the American techniques and developed the lean manufacturing technology that gave Toyota and other Japanese automakers their competitive advantage over U.S. companies in the 1980s. Recognizing the lead Japanese companies had gained in quality manufacturing techniques, GM, Ford, Xerox, Motorola, and many other U.S. companies sent their managers to Japan in the 1980s and 1990s to learn about the new techniques. These U.S. companies then incorporated the Japanese techniques into their manufacturing operations, often improving on them in the process, so that in the 2000s companies like GM and Ford have substantially narrowed the efficiency gap. In this way, global learning continually takes place as global organizations compete with one another worldwide for customers. Organizational effectiveness increases because all global companies are forced to learn about recent advances in technology and adopt the best OBs and procedures if they are to survive and prosper.

Global Crisis Management

Today, global learning is also important to tackle another challenging issue, global crisis management. Extensive global learning allows for more effective responses to the increasing number of crises or disasters that are occurring from natural or man-made causes or because of international terrorism and geopolitical conflicts. Crises that arise because of natural causes include the wave of hurricanes, tsunamis, earthquakes, famines, and diseases that have devastated so many countries in the 2000s—hardly any country has been left untouched by their effects. Man-made crises, such as those that are the result of global warming, pollution, and the destruction of the natural habitat or environment, also seem to be increasing. For example, pollution has become an increasingly important problem for companies and countries to deal with. Companies in heavy industries such as coal and steel have polluted millions of acres of land around major cities in Eastern Europe and Asia, and huge cleanups are necessary. Disasters such as the Chernobyl nuclear power plant meltdown released over 1540 times as much radiation into the air as occurred at Hiroshima, and over 50,000 people have died from this while hundreds of thousands more have been affected.[55] The need to avoid crises of this kind is of paramount importance.

Man-made crises, such as global warming due to emissions of carbon dioxide and other gases, may have made the effects of natural disasters more serious. For example, increasing global temperatures and acid rain may have increased the intensity of hurricanes, led to unusually strong rains and lengthy droughts, and caused the destruction of coral reefs, forests, and the natural habitat in many parts of the world. The shrinking polar icecaps are expected to raise the sea level by a few, but vital, inches.

Finally, increasing geopolitical tensions that are the result of the speed of the process of globalization itself have upset the global balance of power as different countries or world regions try to protect their own economic and political interests. Rising oil prices, for example, have strengthened the bargaining power of major oil-supplying countries, which has led the United States to adopt global political strategies, including its war on terrorism, to secure the supply of oil that is vital to protect the national interest. In a similar way, countries in Europe have been forming contracts and allying with Russia to obtain its supply of natural gas as Japan and China have been negotiating with Iran and Saudi Arabia.

OB has an important role to play in helping people and organizations respond to such crises, for it provides lessons as to how to manage and organize the resources needed to respond to a crisis. As we discuss in later chapters, crisis management involves important decisions such as (1) creating teams to facilitate rapid decision making and communication, (2) establishing the organizational chain of command and reporting relationships necessary to mobilize a fast response, (3) recruiting and selecting the right people to lead and work in such teams, and (4) developing bargaining and negotiating strategies to manage the conflicts that arise whenever people and groups have different interests and objectives. How well managers make these decisions determines how quickly an effective response to a crisis can be implemented, and sometimes can prevent or reduce the severity of the crisis itself.

WORLD WIDE WEB
A global store of information that contains the products of most kinds of human knowledge such as writing, music, and art.

INTERNET
The global network of interlinked computers.

INFORMATION
A set of data, facts, numbers, and words that has been organized in such a way that it provides its users with knowledge.

KNOWLEDGE
What a person perceives, recognizes, identifies, or discovers from analyzing data and information.

INFORMATION TECHNOLOGY
The many different kinds of computer and communications hardware and software, and the skills of their designers, programmers, managers, and technicians.

ORGANIZATIONAL LEARNING
The process of managing information and knowledge to achieve a better fit between the organization and its environment.

INTRANETS
A network of information technology linkages inside an organization that connects all its members.

Challenge 3: Advancing Information Technology

One kind of technology that is posing a major challenge for organizations today is information technology (IT). Just decades ago, science-fiction writers like Robert Heinlein and Isaac Asimov imagined devices such as wrist-held videophones; virtual reality machines, and speech-programmed, hand-held computers. Today, companies like Palm, HP, Nokia, Sony, and Microsoft are offering these devices to their customers. Even science-fiction writers did not imagine the development of the **World Wide Web** (WWW), a global store of information that contains the products of most kinds of human knowledge such as writing, music, and art. Such knowledge can be accessed and enjoyed by anyone connected to the global network of interlinked computers that is the **Internet**. We live in a different world than just a mere decade ago; advances in IT have changed the way people think and the very nature of OB. To understand how IT has changed OB and the way companies operate it is necessary to understand the concept of information.

Suppose you add up the value of the coins in your pocket and find you have $1.36 in change. You have been manipulating basic data, the numerical value of each individual coin, to obtain information, the total value of your change. You did so because you needed to know, for example, if you have enough change to buy a coke and a candy bar. **Information** is a set of data, facts, numbers, and words that has been organized in such a way that they provide their users with knowledge. **Knowledge** is what a person perceives, recognizes, identifies, or discovers from analyzing data and information. Over time, the result of acquiring more and better information and knowledge is learning. In an organization, the issue is to use and develop IT that allows employees to acquire more and better information that increases an organization's ability to respond to its environment.

Information technology (IT) is the many different kinds of computer and communications hardware and software, and the skills of their designers, programmers, managers, and technicians. IT is used to acquire, define, input, arrange, organize, manipulate, store, and transmit facts, data, and information to create knowledge and promote organizational learning. **Organizational learning** occurs when its members can manage information and knowledge to achieve a better fit between the organization and its environment. In the following, we examine the effect IT has on two important kinds of OB. First, those behaviors that increase effectiveness by helping an organization improve the quality of its products and lower their cost. Second, those behaviors that increase effectiveness by promoting creativity and organizational learning and innovation.

IT and Organizational Effectiveness

The Internet and the growth of **intranets**—a network of information technology linkages inside an organization that connects all its members—dramatically changed OB and procedures. With information more accurate, plentiful, and freely available, IT allows for the easy exchange of know-how and facilitates problem solving.[56] And as computers increasingly take over routine work tasks, employees have more time to engage in constructive, work-expanding kinds of activities such as finding better ways of performing a task or providing customers better service.[57]

As an example of how IT can improve organizational effectiveness consider what happened at the textile fibers division of Dupont, the giant chemical company. To reduce costs, Dupont offered early retirement incentives to reduce its workforce, and over half its middle managers decided to take the early retirement package. At first, the division's top managers panicked, wondering how work could get done if everyone left at the same time. But the division had recently installed an e-mail system and a corporate intranet that supplied its remaining employees with most of the information they needed to perform their tasks. Employees began to use it heavily, and learned to make their own decisions and over time the intranet actually speeded communication and decision making.[58]

IT has allowed organizations to become much more responsive to the needs of their customers. Organizations like retail stores, banks, and hospitals depend entirely on their employees performing behaviors that result in high-quality service at reasonable cost. And, as the United States has moved to a service-based economy (in part because of the loss from manufacturing jobs going abroad), advances in IT have made many kinds of service organizations more effective. Developing IT has also opened new opportunities for entrepreneurs to found small dot.com's to better satisfy customers as the following OB Today suggests.[59]

Finally, inside companies, integrating and connecting an organization's employees around the world through electronic means such as video teleconferencing, e-mail, and intranets, is becoming increasingly important. Because the success of a global company depends on communication between employees in its various business operations both at home and abroad, the importance of real-time communication through the use of personal digital assistants such as smartphones (like the popular Blackberry, tablet PCS, and laptops) and by video teleconferencing has grown. For example, teleconferencing allows

OB Today

Entrepreneurs Found "Relationship" Dot.com's

The speed at which IT is changing the way people interact is nowhere more apparent than in the way "dot.com" businesses come and go. The early success of industry leaders such as Amazon.com and Yahoo! led entrepreneurs to start up thousands of new kinds of virtual companies in the search-engine, retailing, and service businesses. Most of these collapsed and went bankrupt during the dot.com crisis of the early 2000s. Only those dot.coms like Amazon.com that enjoyed brand-name recognition and loyal customers were able to hang on. Of course bricks and mortar companies such as Barnes & Noble and J.C. Penny that had established virtual storefronts had the resources to withstand this crisis, but online grocers like Webvan, that had invested billions of dollars in building a food-distribution network, had totally underestimated the costs involved in delivering food to customers and thus went bankrupt.

Pictured are MySpace founders, Chris DeWolfe and Tom Anderson who sold their fast-growing company to Fox for $580 million in 2005

By the mid-2000s, entrepreneurs began to take advantage of the growth in broadband internet service to start sophisticated kinds of relationship-building websites to better meet customer needs. These websites aim to satisfy people's needs to talk, share, collaborate, and swap stories and images; the goal is to satisfy social facilitation—not just person-specific—needs. These websites have proved to be wildly successful. Some of the most notable of these newcomers are myspace.com, the website hosting and social-group facilitator; YouTube.com, the video hosting provider; Flickr, the picture sharing and swapping website; and Rottentomatoes.com, an interactive movie-review site.[60] For example, myspace.com, founded by Chris DeWolfe and Tom Anderson, which employs only 919 people, provides its users with the facility to post their personal bios, pictures, links, and so on.[61] Within a few years it had over 60 million users! Similarly, YouTube has 30 million visitors a day who watch videos and post over 50,000 new videos as well. All these sites took advantage of the fact that their users supply the content, whether it be personal pages, pictures, or videos. All these dot.coms do is provide the web servers to host this content and then charge companies to place adds on their site where they will be seen by their millions of users. The key to the phenomenal success of these companies is that they provide their users with IT that allows them to meet, view, talk to one another, and collaborate and learn as they share their experiences, knowledge, and beliefs.

managers in different countries to meet face-to-face through broadband hookups. It reduces communication problems, allows decisions to be made quickly, and facilitates learning when managers in domestic and overseas divisions meet to confront important issues and to solve mutual problems. For example, Hitachi uses an online teleconferencing system to coordinate its twenty-eight R&D laboratories worldwide, and Ford uses one to coordinate the activities of its worldwide car-design activities.

IT, Creativity, and Organizational Learning

Today, using new IT to help people, groups, and organizations to be creative and enhance organizational innovation and learning is a major challenge. *Creativity* is the generation of novel and useful ideas. One of its outcomes is *innovation*, an organization's ability to make new or improved goods and services or improvements in the way they are produced. The United States is home to some of the most innovative companies in the world, and innovation is the direct result or outcome of the level of creativity in an organization.

IT plays a major role in fostering creativity and innovation because it changes OBs and procedures. Innovation is an activity that requires constant updating of knowledge and a constant search for new ideas and technological developments that can be used to improve a product over time. Typically, innovation takes place in small groups or teams and IT can be used to create virtual teams that can enhance creativity and cooperation between employees. Developing an IT system that allows scientists and engineers from all parts of a company to cooperate by way of bulletin boards, chatrooms, or teleconferencing is also a way to use IT to speed creativity and innovation. One good example of a company using IT to promote creativity and innovation is IBM.

IBM's thousands of consultants are experts in particular industries such as the automotive, financial services, or retail industries. They have a deep understanding of the particular problems facing companies in those industries and how to solve them. Palmisano asked IBM's consultants to work closely with its software engineers to find ways to incorporate their knowledge into advanced software that can be implanted into a customer's IT system. IBM has developed 17 industry "expert systems," which are industry-specific, problem-solving software organizations that researchers and scientists can use to improve their abilities to innovate new products. One of these expert systems was developed in the pharmaceutical industry. Using IBM's new software, a company can use IBM's expert system to simulate and model the potential success of its new drugs under development. Currently only 5 to 10 percent of new drugs make it to the market; IBM's new software will increase scientists' ability to develop innovative new drugs, for they will now know better where to focus their time and effort.

As this example suggests, there are many, many ways in which IT can be used at all levels in the organization, between departments, and between its global divisions to enhance learning, speed decision making, and promote creativity and innovation. Throughout this book, you will find many more examples of the importance of facilitating learning and creativity in OB today.

Challenge 4: Shifting Work and Employment Relationships

In the last few decades, the relationship between an organization and its members has been changing because of increasing globalization and the emergence of new information technologies.[62] The effects of these changes on OB have taken many forms, and important developments include a shortening employment relationship because of downsizing, the growth in the number of contingent or temporary employees, and outsourcing.[63]

In the past it was quite common for many people to spend their whole careers at a large company like IBM, Microsoft, or Ford, often moving up the organizational hierarchy over time to higher seniority and better-paying jobs. Throughout the 1990s, most companies have been pressured by global competition to find ways to reduce operating costs and the result has been that tens of millions of employees have found themselves laid off by their companies and forced to search for new jobs.

DOWNSIZING
The process by which organizations lay off managers and workers to reduce costs.

Downsizing is the process by which organizations lay off managers and workers to reduce costs. The size and scope of these downsizing efforts have been enormous. It is estimated that, in the last few decades, Fortune 500 companies have downsized so much that they now employ about 15–20 percent fewer employees than they used to. The drive to reduce costs is often a response to increasing competitive pressures in the global environment.[64] While companies often realize considerable cost savings by downsizing, the remaining employees in downsized organizations often work under stress, both because they fear they might be the next employees to be let go and because they are forced to do the work that was previously performed by the lost employees—work that oftentimes they cannot cope with.[65]

The increasing tendency of companies to layoff hard-working, loyal employees when the need arises seems to be changing the employment relationship between employees and the companies they work for.[66] Today, employees realize that to keep their jobs and to advance to better ones they need to invest more in themselves and make sure that they keep their job skills and knowledge up to date. The also need to search for new job opportunities. Some experts argue that people starting their careers today can expect to make at least six to eight job and organizational changes over the course of their working lives—some because of their own personal choice but also some because of layoffs.[67]

EMPOWERMENT
The process of giving employees throughout an organization the authority to make important decisions and to be responsible for their outcomes.

Other important trends that go hand in hand with downsizing are the increasing use of empowered self-managed teams, contingent or temporary workers, and outsourcing. **Empowerment** is the process of giving employees throughout an organization the authority to make important decisions and to be responsible for their outcomes. Self-managed teams are work groups who have been empowered and given the responsibility for leading themselves and ensuring that they accomplish their goals.[68]

CONTINGENT WORKERS
People employed for temporary periods by an organization and who receive no benefits such as health insurance or pensions.

As organizations have downsized, there has also been an increasing trend for companies to employ contingent workers to keep costs down. **Contingent workers** are people who are employed for temporary periods by an organization and who receive no benefits such as health insurance or pensions. Contingent workers may work by the day, week, or month performing some functional task, or they may contract with the organization for some fee to perform a specific service to the organization. Thus, for example, an organization may employ ten temporary accountants to "do the books" when it is time or it may contract with a software programmer to write some specialized software for a fixed fee.

The advantages an organization obtains from contingent workers are that they cost less to employ since they receive no benefits and they can be let go easily when their services are no longer needed. It has been estimated that 20 percent of the U.S workforce today consists of part-time employees who work by the day, week, month, or even year for their former employ-

You're the Management Expert

Moving to Self-Managed Teams

Tony Norris is the owner of a large building-products supply company. He has decided that he could operate more effectively if he organizes his 30 employees into three self-managed work teams. Previously his employees worked separately to stock the shelves, answer customer questions, and checkout customers under the supervision of five department managers. Norris believes this system did not encourage employees to find ways to improve operating procedures and raised costs. He believes he can offer better customer service if he changes to team-based OBs and procedures.

Norris has asked you, one of his best managers, to think about the kinds of opportunities and problems this shift to teams might cause. He also wants your frank opinion of his idea and whether you think it will increase the effectiveness of the company. When you meet with him tomorrow, what will be your response to his ideas? Why?

ers. Part-time employees pose a new OB challenge because they cannot be motivated by the prospect of rewards such as job security, promotion, or a career within an organization.

OUTSOURCING
The process of employing people, groups, or a specialist organization to perform a specific type of work activity or function that was previously performed inside an organization.

FREELANCERS
People who contract with an organization to perform specific services.

Finally, also as a way to reduce costs, organizations are also engaging in an increasing amount of outsourcing. **Outsourcing** is moving a specific type of work activity, process, job, or function that was performed inside an organization to outside, where it is carried out by another person or company. At the individual level, for example, companies may outsource particular kinds of jobs such as bookkeeping, computer support, and website design to **freelancers**—independent specialists who contract with an organization to perform specific tasks. They often work from their homes and are connected to an organization by computer, phone, fax, and express package delivery. Freelancers are similar to contingent workers except that they do not physically work inside a company.

Sometimes an organization outsources a whole value-creation activity such as manufacturing, marketing, or the management of its IT to a specialist company that can perform it at a lower cost than the organization itself. In this case, an organization stops performing the value-creation itself. For example, a company may hire a specialist IT company to manage its computer network or a national distributor to deliver its products to stores or a specialist in customer service to manage its customer call center. Dell, for example, employs 10,000 people in India to manage requests from customers around the world for help with purchasing or operating their computers. It announced in 2006 that it would be adding 5,000 more.[69] The huge wave of outsourcing by U.S. companies has resulted in the loss of hundreds of thousands of call-center jobs at home. Millions more jobs have been lost as companies have outsourced their manufacturing operations to companies in countries like Mexico, China, and Malaysia.

While outsourcing has helped to change the nature of the employment relationship in the United States, it is also having dramatic effects abroad. Today, many of the countries that gained the jobs lost by U.S. workers are experiencing the same problem themselves as other countries use their *still lower* labor costs to compete for manufacturing contracts. Take the example of Mauritius, a tiny island off the coast of South-East Africa famous for its white sand beaches. In the 1980s to alleviate its enormous poverty, Mauritius created a low-tax export zone to encourage foreign clothing companies to locate there and employ its citizens who at that time worked for 10 cents an hour or less. For many years this worked well for the island, the income of its people climbed steeply, and it became one of the most prosperous countries in Africa. More and more companies such as Gap and The Limited had their clothing made in Mauritius, and by 2000 it exported over $1 billion of low-cost clothing to the United States.

After 2000, however, the picture was not so rosy on Mauritius because its labor costs had increased and countries like India and China, whose billions of people still are paid some of the lowest wages in the world, now had the lowest costs. The result was that U.S. clothing companies shifted their business to India and China and unemployment increased

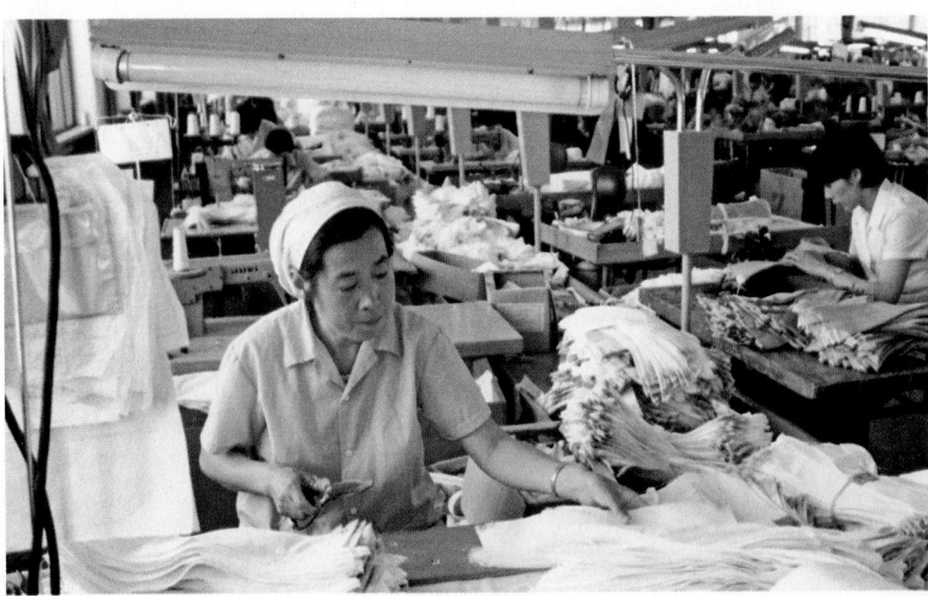

Free-trade around the globe cuts both ways, as the people of Mauritius, a tiny island off the coast of Africa, discovered. For two decades, Mauritius' citizens manufactured clothing for U.S. clothing labels outsourcing the work. But the country's prosperity unraveled when lower-cost producers like China and Vietnam captured much of the business.

dramatically in Mauritius, which has learned the hard way that global competition is a fierce process. And, unlike the United States, whose vibrant economy creates new jobs, its people are struggling to cope with the new reality of a low-cost global economy.

Downsizing, empowered self-managed teams, the employment of part-time contingent workers, and outsourcing are ways in which organizations are changing OBs and procedures to battle effectively against domestic and global competitors. Several OB researchers believe that organizations in the future will increasingly become composed of a "core" of organizational employees who are highly trained and rewarded by an organization and a "periphery" of part-time employees or freelancers who are employed when needed but will never become true "organizational employees." The challenge facing people today is to continually improve their skills and knowledge and build their human capital so that they can secure well-paying and satisfying employment either inside or outside an organization.

Summary

OB is a developing field of study. Changes in the environment constantly challenge organizations and their owners', managers', and employees' abilities to adapt and change work behaviors and procedures to increase the effectiveness with which they operate. In this chapter, we made the following major points:

1. Organizations exist to provide goods and services that people want, and the amount and quality of these goods and services are products of the behaviors and performance of an organization's employees.
2. OB is the study of the many factors that have an impact on how people and groups act, think, feel, and respond to work and organizations and how organizations respond to their environments. OB provides a set of tools—theories and concepts—to understand, analyze, describe, and manage attitudes and behavior in organizations.
3. The study of OB can improve and change individual, group, and OB to attain individual, group, and organizational goals.
4. OB can be analyzed at three levels: the individual, the group, and the organization as a whole. A full understanding is impossible without an examination of the factors that affect behavior at each level.
5. A significant task for an organization's managers and employees is to use the tools of OB to increase organizational effectiveness—that is, an organization's ability to achieve its goals.
6. The activities of most organizations can be modeled as an open system in which an organization takes in resources from its external environment and converts or transforms them into goods and services that are sent back to that environment, where customers buy them.
7. Changing pressures or forces in the social and cultural, global, technological, and employment or work environment pose many challenges for OB, and organizations must respond effectively to those challenges if they are to survive and prosper.
8. Two major challenges of importance to OB today from the social and cultural environment are those that derive from a breakdown in ethical values, social responsibility, and from the increasing diversity of the workforce.
9. Three important challenges facing organizations from the global environment are to appreciate the differences that exist between countries; to benefit from this new global knowledge to improve OBs and procedures; and to use global learning to find better ways to respond to global crises.
10. Changes in the technological environment, and particularly advances in information technology (IT), are also having important effects on OB and procedures. IT has improved effectiveness by helping an organization improve the quality of its products, lower their costs, and by promoting creativity and organizational learning and innovation.
11. Many changes have also been taking place in the employment or work environment, and important developments that have affected OB include a shortening employment relationship because of downsizing, the growth in the number of contingent or temporary employees, and global outsourcing.

Exercises in Understanding and Managing OB

Questions for Discussion and Review

1. Why is a working knowledge of OB important to organizations and their employees?
2. Why is it important to analyze the behavior of individuals, groups, and the organization as a whole in order to understand OB in work settings?
3. What is an open system and why is it important for an organization to be open to its environment?
4. Select a restaurant, supermarket, church, or some other familiar organization, and think about which kinds of OBs and procedures are the most important determinant of its effectiveness.
5. What are organizational ethics, and why is ethics such an important issue facing organizations today?
6. Why is diversity an important challenge facing organizations today?
7. What special challenges does managing behavior on a global scale pose for organizations?
8. In what ways does IT change OBs and procedures?
9. Why has the employment relationship been shortening?

OB: Increasing Self-Awareness

Behavior in Organizations

Think of an organization—a place of employment, a club, a sports team, a musical group, an academic society—that provided you with a significant work experience, and answer the following questions.

1. What are your attitudes and feelings toward the organization? Why do you think you have these attitudes and feelings?
2. Indicate, on a scale from one to ten (with one being not at all and ten being extremely), how hard you worked for this organization or how intensively you participated in the organization's activities. Explain the reasons for your level of participation.
3. How did the organization communicate its performance expectations to you, and how did the organization monitor your performance to evaluate whether you met those expectations? Did you receive more rewards when you performed at a higher level? What happened when your performance was not as high as it should have been?
4. How concerned was your organization with your well-being? How was this concern reflected? Do you think this level of concern was appropriate? Why or why not?
5. Think of your direct supervisor or leader. How did this person's leadership style affect your attitudes and behaviors?
6. How did the attitudes and behaviors of your coworkers affect yours, particularly your level of performance?
7. Given your answers to these questions, how would you change OBs and procedures to make this organization more effective?

Small Group Breakout Exercise

Identifying an Open System

Form groups of three or four people and appoint one member as the spokesperson who will communicate your conclusions to the rest of the class.

1. Think of an organization you are all familiar with, such as a local restaurant, store, or bank. Once you have chosen an organization, model it from an open-systems perspective. For example, identify its input, conversion, and output processes.
2. Identify the specific forces in the environment that have the greatest opportunity to help or hurt this organization's ability to obtain resources and dispose of its goods or services.
3. Using the three views of effectiveness discussed in the chapter, discuss which specific measures are most useful to managers in evaluating this organization's effectiveness.

A Question of Ethics

Ethical versus Unethical Behavior

What factors determine whether behavior in organizations is ethical or unethical? Divide up into small groups, and each person think of some unethical behaviors or incidents that you have observed in organizations. The incidents could be something you experienced as an employee, a customer, or a client, or something you observed informally.

Discuss these incidents with other group members. Then, identify three important criteria to use to determine whether a particular action or behavior is ethical. These criteria need to differentiate between ethical and unethical OB. Be ready to describe the incidents of unethical behavior and criteria with the rest of the class.

Topic for Debate

Now that you understand the nature of OB and management, and the kinds of issues they address, debate the following topic:

Team A. The best way to increase organizational effectiveness is to clearly specify each employee's job responsibilities and then to closely supervise his or her work behavior.

Team B. The best way to increase organizational effectiveness is to put employees in teams and allow them to work out their own job responsibilities and supervise each other.

Experiential Exercise

Ethical Issues in Globalization

There are many laws governing the way companies in the United States should act to protect their employees and to treat them in a fair and equitable manner. However, many countries abroad do not have similar laws and treat employees in ways that would be seen as unacceptable and unethical in the United States.

Either individually or in small groups, think about the following issues and answer the questions they raise.

1. In Pakistan and India it is common for children as young as eight years old to weave the hand-made carpets and rugs that are exported to Western countries. Many of these children work for a pittance and are losing their eyesight because of the close attention they have to devote to their tasks, often for twelve hours a

day. Do you think these children should be employed in such occupations? Do you think it is ethical to buy these rugs?

2. Millions of U.S. workers in manufacturing industries have lost their jobs because companies have moved their operations to low-cost countries overseas. There, many women and children work long hours every day for low wages, performing the jobs that used to be done by workers in the United States. Do you think it is ethical for multinationals to operate just on the basis of where they can obtain low-cost resources? Do you think laws should be passed to prevent global companies from relocating abroad to protect the relatively high-paying jobs of U.S. workers?

New York Times *Cases in the News*

The New York Times

For the Avon Lady, A World Beyond Ringing Doorbell's

By Julie Bosman, NYT, May 1, 2006, p. F.10.

LUZ STELLA BONGIOVI has a job that many people would envy. After 12 years in the same business, she supervises more than 100 employees and logs about 50 hours a week, coming into work at 10 a.m. and often working at home. She has been sent on junkets to Hawaii, Las Vegas and Puerto Rico. Her earnings total nearly $170,000 a year.

Her job title: Avon lady.

The folks at Avon, however, would call her a sales representative, the updated term for the 468,000 people in the company's work force generating more than 95 percent of sales revenue. But to the public, "Avon lady" has stuck, ever since the company's sales representatives began ringing doorbells in 1886.

Ms. Bongiovi is an example of how to succeed the old-fashioned way: she started small, worked hard and took advantage of her natural business sense to build a living slowly by selling Avon to her extended network of family, friends and acquaintances. But now, Avon is trying to force itself to step into the future—and bring the sales reps with it, turning its distinctly mid-20th-century sales model into a 21st-century version.

In fact, Avon will announce a new initiative this month to encourage more business to move to the Internet, said Thomas Kelly, Avon's senior vice president for direct selling in the United States. "We really are guns blazing with our excitement about the Internet," he said. "We're moving from just ordering online to supporting their efforts to sell online."

The company is teaching its sales reps to file customer orders online; before, reps would phone in their orders. Now, more than 80 percent use the Internet to do business. Avon is also encouraging its sales reps to set up individual pages on the company's Web site for customers to make online purchases. For instance, by typing in their ZIP code, customer will be directed to their sales rep's page.

But Avon is still holding on to the fundamental part of its business model—a sales force that is paid only by commissions, without salaries, health care or benefits. Signing up is simple: a potential rep pays a $10 fee, fills out a form and receives a starter kit. Then it's up to the newly minted representative to go out and garner sales. That person is also responsible for day-to-day operating expenses and promotions.

Ms. Bongiovi pays for print advertising from her own budget. For example, if a rep wants business cards printed with her name, she pays for them herself. Asked to define the employment status of sales reps, an Avon spokeswomen responded, "Self-employed."

On a recent morning, Ms. Bongiovi was sitting behind a desk in her office in Bushwick, which doubles as a retail space with a storefront on Myrtle Avenue, where she sells Avon products and performs occasional walk-in makeovers. Avon began for her as it had for many women—a side job for stay-at-home mothers who want to earn a little extra money. (The reps are predominantly female.) Ms. Bongiovi grew up in Colombia. Her father owned a supermarket, and she often watched him working in the store and fantasized about her own future.

"I used to dream, 'Oh, I want to have a business when I grow up,' " she said.

Marriage and three children intervened, but one day she signed up for Avon on an whim, getting her first order mostly from family and friends in her neighborhood.

"My first order was $500, and I thought, 'Hmm, this is good,' " said Ms. Bongiovi, who wore a neatly cut blazer, violet-framed eyeglasses and gleaming red nail polish.

Soon, she began recruiting other people to become sales representatives in her "downline," Avon's term for sales reps' own staff members whom they personally recruit and supervise.

Ms. Bongiovi's sales pitch to potential reps reflects her own life story. When she first started selling Avon, she had children at home and no income of her own. Now she owns a six-unit apartment building in Brooklyn and is going through a divorce, divide up assets and income.

When talking to potential reps, she said, "I tell them: 'What about if your husband leaves you? What if you don't have a husband anymore?' I like to help them, I like to give them support. I teach them how to earn money with Avon."

It is a pitch that falls on welcome ears to Mr. Kelly, the Avon executive. It may be partly a company pitch with a feminist slant, but fundamentally, he said, the business will always be about serving the needs of women.

"Initially, what drove us to this place is that women would like a significantly greater earning opportunity," he said.

But the ability to earn money through Avon may be getting more difficult as the one-on-one sales model goes out of style. How many women today would buy cosmetics from a door-to-door seller? And in an era when many women buy makeup at superstores like Sephora or buy online, how does the Avon sales rep stand a chance?

Mary Lou Quinlan, the chief executive of Just Ask a Woman, a marketing company in New York, said she thought that many women were too busy to sit down and talk to sales representatives.

Still, "it's amazing how women will make the time for face-to-face, woman-to-woman events when they want to," she said. "You do tend to buy more when you're buying face to face with someone."

Mr. Kelly said that the individual sales representative was a retro image that Avon was not willing to let go of.

"I really feel an obligation, like we're a public institution," he said.

Besides making itself more tech-proficient, Avon has also tried to shed its fusty image by taking on the college market. In 2003, the company introduced Mark, a cosmetics line aimed at teenagers and women in their 20's.

The plan was twofold: to introduce Avon to younger women who considered the brand grandmother territory; and, after these women were established customers, encouraging them to become sales reps themselves.

Gyda Arder, 26, an actress who lives in Manhattan, is one such woman. She became aware of Avon through a television commercial for Mark. While visiting avon.com, and buying more than $150 in Mark merchandise, she noticed an online ad on the site that offered 40 percent off a purchase, if you signed up to be an Avon sales representative. Ms. Arber signed up.

"Living in Manhattan, you don't run into a lot of Avon ladies," she said. But after she began pitching products to her friends and colleagues in local theater, she found herself with a part-time job.

"There have been periods where it's been 100 percent of my income," Ms. Arber said, citing the unpredictability of her acting work.

Ms. Arber also gives home parties once or twice a month, inviting friends and acquaintances.

It is a technique that has been borrowed by retailers much more fashionable than Avon. The Body Shop (recently acquired by L'Oreal) has a feature on its Web site, thebodyshop.com, allowing customers to host a "girls' nite out" to sell products to friends at home. The Body Shop has also begun a service encouraging customers to sign up as "independent consultants," a sales model like Avon's.

Getting advice from Avon sales representatives could be described as the one-on-one consultation that many women want, albeit from a friend or acquaintance who is considered more trustworthy than a stranger in a lab coat at a cosmetics counter.

"In an industry often focused on buzz, the service that Avon offers is still about trust between sellers and consumers," said Andy Sernovitz, chief executive of Word of Mouth Marketing Association, a trade group in Chicago.

Questions for Discussion

1. How has the job of an Avon Lady been changing? For example, how have changing customer needs, demographics, IT, and so on affected the job?
2. As a result of these changes, what kinds of OB issues must Avon's managers deal with to motivate and coordinate its 486,000-strong salesforce today?
3. How would you describe the kind of employment relationship that exists between Avon and its salesforce?

The New York Times

"Outsourcers Struggling to Keep Workers in the Field"

By Saritha Rai, NYT, November 12, 2005, p. C13.

Not long ago, Sierra Atlantic, an outsourcing company specializing in writing business software, did something unusual.

It invited employees at its Hyderabad unit to bring their spouses to work. There, counselors offered sessions on better relationship, being better parents and work-home balance.

Sierra Atlantic's "Bring Your Spouse to Work" and "Bring Your Parents to Work" programs are among the new benefits and strategies outsourcing firms in India are using to hold on to workers in an increasingly competitive market for skilled English speakers.

Annual raises of 10 percent or more are now the norm in India's $17.2-billion-a-year outsourcing industry. It supplies workers who write software code, answer customer service calls, do legal and equity research and engineering design, among other jobs, for overseas corporate customers.

But despite rising pay, outsourcing firms face annual attrition rates of 15 to 30 percent in their Indian labor force, compared with 10 percent in outsourcing companies in Eastern Europe and 7.5 to 15 percent in China, according to industry experts.

Labor shortages and turnover problems are affecting India's other high-growth industries like financial services, retail and airlines, but nowhere is it as pronounced as in outsourcing.

Employee churn in now one of the biggest challenges for the Indian outsourcing industry, said Nandan M. Nilekani, chief executive of Infosys Technologies, one of India's largest outsourcing companies. "Talent acquisition, transformation and management are critical anchors for the growth of the industry," said Mr. Nilekani, whose company added 8,026 employees in the quarter ended in September. Infosys has 46,196 employees.

Competition has become more intense as demand rises faster than the supply of trained workers. Even with pay increasing, Indian engineers are paid a quarter of what their American counterparts earn, which feeds the outsourcing boom.

According to Nasscom, the outsourcing industry trade group in India, the country produces three million college graduates every year, and 350,000 of them are engineers. "It is great raw material, but only 30 percent of this pool is ready to plunge straight in and deliver," said Kiran Karnik, president of Nasscom. Improving the quality of that pool, Mr. Karnik said, is on the industry's "A-list of challenges."

The problem of churn is even more acute for outsourcing companies offering lower-skilled back-office work like call center services. Once trained, those workers tend to hop from job to job. Some outsourcing companies in that field are reporting a complete turnover of employees in the span of a year. "Employees could leave because the chicken curry at the place next door is better or the girlfriend has moved to another company," said Saurav Adhikari, vice president for corporate strategy at HCL Technologies, based in New Delhi, another large outsourcing firm. While growth in outsourcing will continue in the near future, said Frances Karamouzis, research director at Gartner, the attrition problem "will be looked upon as the early signs of the limits and boundaries around the India model."

Even for companies that are successful in attracting new workers, attrition is a challenge. Patni Computers, another leading outsourcing company, based in Mumbai, for example, has grown from 6,000 employees two years ago to nearly double that number now. "We especially feel the pain when employees in critical projects and positions decide to leave," said Milind Jadhav, senior vice president for human relations at Patni.

Smaller operations feel the squeeze particularly severely. In Hyderabad, bigger outsourcing businesses like the Indian unit of the Oracle Corporation have an advantage in attracting employees. So Sierra, with nearly 1,000 workers worldwide and headquarters in Fremont, Calif., has had to try more innovative programs to attract and retain workers.

Sierra Atlantic has adopted retention strategies like permitting crucial employees to change jobs across departments within the company. The company also offers top performers bonuses and flexibility in work arrangements. As a result, it has cut attrition to 16 percent this year from 22 percent last year, company executives said.

Other companies, too, are embracing novel approaches. The Calcutta office of Acclaris, which has headquarters in Tampa, Fla., has a "cheif fun officer" whose job is to arrange employee parties and come up with ideas to liven up the workday. One recent event was a rossogolla-eating competition (rossogollas are a local dessert made from milk). At HCL Technologies, which is based in New Delhi and has 26,000 employees, Shiv Nadar, the chief executive, said the company followed an employee-first philosophy. A few months ago, the new president, Vineet Nayar, flew to HCL offices across India to shake hands with 10,000 of the company's employees. To celebrate reaching a revenue milestone recently, the company had a party for more than 900 employees in the New Delhi suburbs at a nightclub that advertised having the country's biggest dance floor.

At top outsourcing companies like Infosys, benefit packages and retention approaches have become more sophisticated. Infosys, which was the first Indian company to start an employee stock option plan, now offers variable compensation packages as well as what it says are cutting-edge training programs.

Questions for Discussion

1. Why are Indian outsourcing companies having a difficult time recruiting and retaining employees?
2. What are some of the ways in which they have used OB to reduce employee turnover?
3. What are some possible implications for the way U.S. companies will organize their outsourcing activities in the future?

Appendix 1

A Short History of OB

The systematic study of OB began in the closing decades of the nineteenth century, after the industrial revolution had swept through Europe and America. In the new economic climate, managers of all types of organizations—political, educational, and economic—were increasingly turning their focus toward finding better ways to satisfy customers' needs. Many major economic, technical, and cultural changes were taking place at this time. With the introduction of steam power and the development of sophisticated machinery and equipment, the industrial revolution changed the way goods were produced, particularly in the weaving and clothing industries. Small workshops run by skilled employees who produced hand-manufactured products (a system called crafts production) were being replaced by large factories in which sophisticated machines controlled by hundreds or even thousands of unskilled or semiskilled employees made products. For example, raw cotton and wool that, in the past, families or whole villages working together had spun into yarn was now shipped to factories where employees operated machines that spun and wove large quantities of yarn into cloth.

Owners and managers of the new factories found themselves unprepared for the challenges accompanying the change from small-scale crafts production to large-scale mechanized manufacturing. Moreover, many of the managers and supervisors in these workshops and factories were engineers who had only a technical orientation. They were unprepared for the social problems that occur when people work together in large groups (as in a factory or shop system). Managers began to search for new techniques to manage their organizations' resources, and soon they began to focus on ways to increase the efficiency of the employee-task mix. They found help from Frederick W. Taylor.

F. W. Taylor and Scientific Management

Frederick W. Taylor (1856–1915) is best known for defining the techniques of scientific management, the systematic study of relationships between people and tasks for the purpose of redesigning the work process to increase efficiency. Taylor was a manufacturing manager who eventually became a consultant and taught other managers how to apply his scientific-management techniques. Taylor believed that if the amount of time and effort that each employee expends to produce a unit of output (a finished good or service) can be reduced by increasing specialization and the division of labor, the production process will become more efficient. Taylor believed the way to create the most efficient division of labor could best be determined using scientific-management techniques, rather than intuitive or informal rule-of-thumb knowledge. Based on his experiments and observations as a manufacturing manager in a variety of settings, he developed four principles to increase efficiency in the workplace:[70]

- *Principle 1: Study the way employees perform their tasks, gather all the informal job knowledge that employees possess, and experiment with ways of improving how tasks are performed.*

  To discover the most efficient method of performing specific tasks, Taylor studied in great detail and measured the ways different employees went about performing their tasks. One of the main tools he used was a time and motion study, which involves the careful timing and recording of the actions taken to perform a particular task. Once Taylor understood the existing method of performing a task, he then experimented to increase specialization; he tried different methods of dividing up and coordinating the various tasks necessary to produce a finished product. Usually this meant simplifying jobs and having each employee perform fewer, more routine tasks, as at the pin factory or on Ford's car-assembly line. Taylor also sought to find ways to improve each employee's ability to perform a particular task—for example, by reducing the number of motions employees made to complete the task, by changing the layout of the work area or the type of tool employees used, or by experimenting with tools of different sizes.
- *Principle 2: Codify the new methods of performing tasks into written rules and standard operating procedures.*

  Once the best method of performing a particular task was determined, Taylor specified that it should be recorded so that the procedures could be taught to all employees performing the same task. These rules could be used to further standardize and simplify jobs—essentially, to make jobs even more routine. In this way efficiency could be increased throughout an organization.
- *Principle 3: Carefully select employees so that they possess skills and abilities that match the needs of the*

task, and train them to perform the task according to the established rules and procedures.

To increase specialization, Taylor believed employees had to understand the tasks that were required and be thoroughly trained in order to perform the task at the required level. Employees who could not be trained to this level were to be transferred to a job where they were able to reach the minimum required level of proficiency.[71]

- *Principle 4: Establish a fair or acceptable level of performance for a task, and then develop a pay system that provides a reward for performance above the acceptable level.*

  To encourage employees to perform at a high level of efficiency, and to provide them with an incentive to reveal the most efficient techniques for performing a task, Taylor advocated that employees benefit from any gains in performance. They should be paid a bonus and receive some percentage of the performance gains achieved through the more efficient work process.

By 1910, Taylor's system of scientific management had become nationally known and in many instances faithfully and fully practiced.[72] However, managers in many organizations chose to implement the new principles of scientific management selectively. This decision ultimately resulted in problems. For example, some managers using scientific management obtained increases in performance, but rather than sharing performance gains with employees through bonuses as Taylor had advocated, they simply increased the amount of work that each employee was expected to do. Many employees experiencing the reorganized work system found that, as their performance increased, managers required them to do more work for the same pay. Employees also learned that increases in performance often meant fewer jobs and a greater threat of layoffs, because fewer employees were needed. In addition, the specialized, simplified jobs were often very monotonous and repetitive, and many employees became dissatisfied with their jobs.

From a performance perspective, the combination of the two management practices—(1) achieving the right mix of employee–task specialization and (2) linking people and tasks by the speed of the production line—resulted in the huge savings in cost and huge increases in output that occur in large, organized work settings. For example, in 1908, managers at the Franklin Motor Company using scientific-management principles redesigned the work process, and the output of cars increased from 100 cars a month to 45 cars a day; employees' wages, however, increased by only 90 percent.[73]

Taylor's work has had an enduring effect on the management of production systems. Managers in every organization, whether it produces goods or services, now carefully analyze the basic tasks that employees must perform and try to create a work environment that will allow their organizations to operate most efficiently. We discuss this important issue in Chapters 6 and 7.

The Work of Mary Parker Follett

Much of Mary Parker Follett's (1868–1933) writing about management, and the way managers should behave toward employees, was a response to her concern that Taylor was ignoring the human side of the organization.[74] She pointed out that management often overlooks the multitude of ways in which employees can contribute to the organization when managers allow them to participate and exercise initiative in their everyday work lives.[75] Taylor, for example, never proposed that managers should involve employees in analyzing their jobs to identify better ways to perform tasks, or even ask employees how they felt about their jobs. Instead, he used time and motion experts to analyze employees' jobs for them. Follett, in contrast, argued that because employees know the most about their jobs, they should be involved in job analysis and managers should allow them to participate in the work-development process.

Follett proposed that "Authority should go with knowledge . . . whether it is up the line or down." In other words, if employees have the relevant knowledge, then employees, rather than managers, should be in control of the work process itself, and managers should behave as coaches and facilitators—not as monitors and supervisors. In making this statement, Follett anticipated the current interest in self-managed teams and empowerment. She also recognized the importance of having managers in different departments communicate directly with each other to speed decision making. She advocated what she called "cross-functioning": members of different departments working together in cross-departmental teams to accomplish projects—an approach that is increasingly utilized today.[76] She proposed that knowledge and expertise, and not managers' formal authority deriving from their position in the hierarchy, should decide who would lead at any particular moment. She believed, as do many OB researchers today, that power is fluid and should flow to the person who can best help the organization achieve its goals. Follett took a horizontal view of power and authority, rather than viewing the vertical chain of command as being most essential to effective management. Thus, Follett's approach was very radical for its time.

The Hawthorne Studies and Human Relations

Probably because of its radical nature, Follett's work went unappreciated by managers and researchers until quite recently. Most continued to follow in the footsteps of

Taylor and, to increase efficiency, they studied ways to improve various characteristics of the work setting, such as job specialization or the kinds of tools employees used. One series of studies was conducted from 1924 to 1932 at the Hawthorne Works of the Western Electric Company.[77] This research, now known as the Hawthorne studies, was initiated as an attempt to investigate how characteristics of the work setting—specifically the level of lighting or illumination—affect employee fatigue and performance. The researchers conducted an experiment in which they systematically measured employee productivity at various levels of illumination.

The experiment produced some unexpected results. The researchers found that regardless of whether they raised or lowered the level of illumination, productivity increased. In fact, productivity began to fall only when the level of illumination dropped to the level of moonlight, a level at which presumably employees could no longer see well enough to do their work efficiently.

As you can imagine, the researchers found these results very puzzling. They invited a noted Harvard psychologist, Elton Mayo, to help them. Mayo proposed another series of experiments to solve the mystery. These experiments, known as the relay assembly test experiments, were designed to investigate the effects of other aspects of the work context on job performance, such as the effect of the number and length of rest periods and hours of work on fatigue and monotony.[78] The goal was to raise productivity.

During a two-year study of a small group of female employees, the researchers again observed that productivity increased over time, but the increases could not be solely attributed to the effects of changes in the work setting. Gradually, the researchers discovered that, to some degree, the results they were obtaining were influenced by the fact that the researchers themselves had become part of the experiment. In other words, the presence of the researchers was affecting the results because the employees enjoyed receiving attention and being the subject of study and were willing to cooperate with the researchers to produce the results they believed the researchers desired.

Subsequently, it was found that many other factors also influence employee behavior, and it was not clear what was actually influencing Hawthorne employees' behavior. However, this particular effect—which became known as the Hawthorne effect—seemed to suggest that the attitude of employees toward their managers affects the level of employees' performance. In particular, the significant finding was that a manager's behavior or leadership approach can affect performance. This finding led many researchers to turn their attention to managerial behavior and leadership. If supervisors could be trained to behave in ways that would elicit cooperative behavior from their subordinates, then productivity could be increased. From this view emerged the human relations movement, which advocates that supervisors be behaviorally trained to manage subordinates in ways that elicit their cooperation and increase their productivity.

The importance of behavioral or human relations training became even clearer to its supporters after another series of experiments—the bank wiring room experiments. In a study of employees making telephone-switching equipment, researchers Elton Mayo and F. J. Roethlisberger discovered that the employees, as a group, had deliberately adopted a norm of output restriction to protect their jobs. Other group members subjected employees who violated this informal production norm to sanctions. Those who violated group-performance norms and performed above the norm were called "ratebusters"; those who performed below the norm were called "chisellers."

The experimenters concluded that both types of employees threatened the group as a whole. Ratebusters threaten group members because they reveal to managers how fast the work can be done. Chisellers are looked down on because they are not doing their share of the work. Work-group members discipline both ratebusters and chisellers in order to create a pace of work that the employees (not the managers) think is fair. Thus, the work group's influence over output can be as great as the supervisors' influence. Since the work group can influence the behavior of its members, some management theorists argue that supervisors should be trained to behave in ways that gain the goodwill and cooperation of employees so that supervisors, not employees, control the level of work-group performance.

One of the main implications of the Hawthorne studies was that the behavior of managers and employees in the work setting is as important in explaining the level of performance as the technical aspects of the task. Managers must understand the workings of the informal organization, the system of behavioral rules and norms that emerge in a group, when they try to manage or change behavior in organizations. Many studies have found that, as time passes, groups often develop elaborate procedures and norms that bond members together, allowing unified action either to cooperate with management in order to raise performance or to restrict output and thwart the attainment of organizational goals.[79] The Hawthorne studies demonstrated the importance of understanding how the feelings, thoughts, and behaviors of work-group members and managers affect performance. It was becoming increasingly clear to researchers that understanding behavior in organizations is a complex process that is critical to increasing performance.[80] Indeed, the increasing interest in the area of management known as OB, the study of the factors that have an impact on how individuals and groups respond to and act in organizations, dates from these early studies.

Theory X and Theory Y

Several studies after the Second World War revealed how assumptions about employees' attitudes and behavior affect managers' behavior. Perhaps the most influential approach was developed by Douglas McGregor. He proposed that two different sets of assumptions about work attitudes and behaviors dominate the way managers think and affect how they behave in organizations. McGregor named these two contrasting sets of assumptions Theory X and Theory Y.[81]

Theory X

According to the assumptions of Theory X, the average employee is lazy, dislikes work, and will try to do as little as possible. Moreover, employees have little ambition and wish to avoid responsibility. Thus, the manager's task is to counteract employees' natural tendencies to avoid work. To keep employees' performance at a high level, the manager must supervise them closely and control their behavior by means of "the carrot and stick"—rewards and punishments.

Managers who accept the assumptions of Theory X design and shape the work setting to maximize their control over employees' behaviors and minimize the employees' control over the pace of work. These managers believe that employees must be made to do what is necessary for the success of the organization, and they focus on developing rules, SOPs, and a well-defined system of rewards and punishments to control behavior. They see little point in giving employees autonomy to solve their own problems because they think that the workforce neither expects nor desires cooperation. Theory X managers see their role as to closely monitor employees to ensure that they contribute to the production process and do not threaten product quality. Henry Ford, who closely supervised and managed his workforce, fits McGregor's description of a manager who holds Theory X assumptions.

Theory Y

In contrast, Theory Y assumes that employees are not inherently lazy, do not naturally dislike work, and, if given the opportunity, will do what is good for the organization. According to Theory Y, the characteristics of the work setting determine whether employees consider work to be a source of satisfaction or punishment; and managers do not need to closely control employees' behavior in order to make them perform at a high level, because employees will exercise self-control when they are committed to organizational goals. The implication of Theory Y, according to McGregor, is that "the limits of collaboration in the organizational setting are not limits of human nature but of management's ingenuity in discovering how to realize the potential represented by its human resources."[82] It is the manager's task to create a work setting that encourages commitment to organizational goals and provides opportunities for employees to be imaginative and to exercise initiative and self-direction.

When managers design the organizational setting to reflect the assumptions about attitudes and behavior suggested by Theory Y, the characteristics of the organization are quite different from those of an organizational setting based on Theory X. Managers who believe that employees are motivated to help the organization reach its goals can decentralize authority and give more control over the job to employees, both as individuals and in groups. In this setting, individuals and groups are still accountable for their activities, but the manager's role is not to control employees but to provide support and advice, to make sure they have the resources they need to perform their jobs, and to evaluate them on their ability to help the organization meet its goals.

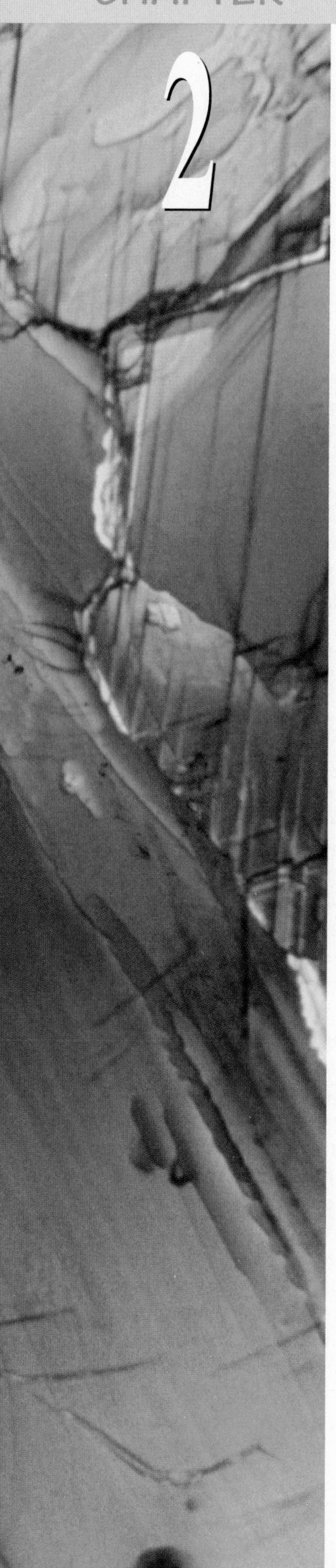

INDIVIDUAL DIFFERENCES: PERSONALITY AND ABILITY

Learning Objectives

After studying this chapter, you should be able to:

- Understand the nature of personality and how it is determined by both nature and nurture.
- Describe the Big Five personality traits and their implications for understanding behavior in organizations.
- Appreciate the ways in which other personality traits, in addition to the Big Five, influence employees' behaviors in organizations.
- Describe the different kinds of abilities that employees use to perform their jobs.
- Appreciate how organizations manage ability through selection, placement, and training.

Opening Case

FORGING INTO CHINA

What does it take to establish a new manufacturing facility in China?

Gary Heiman, CEO of the privately held Standard Textile Co., is no stranger to taking on new opportunities and challenges with a determination and dedication to make them succeed. Around thirty years ago when the small business founded by his grandfather was still selling bed sheets out of an apartment in Chicago, Heiman convinced his father to increase Standard's wholesale operations and open a new factory in Israel near the Negev desert.[1] Fast forward to 2006 and Standard—a manufacturer and distributor of textiles and apparel to hotels, hospitals, and factories—has over $500 million in annual revenues, operates in 49 countries, and has over 3,000 employees.[2] Standard manufactures and sells an array of products ranging from scrubs, surgical gowns, and high-strength insulated coveralls for heavy industry to bed linens, towels, and decorative bedspreads and pillows.[3] Not only is Standard committed to researching and developing new products to meet its customers' needs but it is also keeping apace of the global economy.[4]

Many textile manufacturers and distributors like Standard Textile have opened manufacturing facilities in China and other Asian countries to take advantage of relatively low labor costs and a booming Asian economy.

Around 5 years ago, Heiman was convinced that Standard should open a new manufacturing facility in Asia given the area's booming economic growth and relatively low-cost labor. True to his openness to new experiences and his conscientious determination to find the ideal location for the facility, Heiman spent a year traveling through Pakistan, India, the Philippines, and neighboring countries, before deciding to open the facility in Linyi, China, a relatively remote noncoastal city of 4 million halfway between Beijing and Shanghai. Heiman committed $23 million to open the Linyi facility and he has overcome numerous challenges in this new venture with persistence, determination, and dedication. When he was struggling to get the facility up and running, Heiman indicates that "Nothing, absolutely nothing, went right."[5] Problems ranged from a heating system that didn't work for two weeks, custom machine parts made to order in China that did not fit machines imported from the United States, and polluted water to an over 15% increase in utility charges to run the plant. Unshaken by these challenges, Heiman was convinced that China was the place to be and he was determined to make this new venture a success.[6]

Heiman's adventurousness and hard work seem to be paying off and bed sheets manufactured in Linyi are now being shipped to the United States and also will soon be sold in China. In addition to relatively low labor costs in Linyi (about 40% less than they would be in Shanghai and more than 80% less than they would be in the United States), Standard's Chinese employees are proving to be quick learners, becoming highly skilled after just a few weeks of training. For example, new employees with no prior textile-weaving experience, have so excelled at tying nearly imperceptible weavers' knots when threads snap during high-speed weaving that they do not need to carry scissors with them as weavers normally do to snip off loose threads.

Heiman has found that Standard's Chinese employees are motivated to learn and perform well, though they are not always comfortable taking the initiative, which may be due to China's history of state-controlled factories.[7]

Of course, expansions into China like Standard's are not without their critics who fear that ultimately jobs will be lost in the United States. And while Standard has not laid off U.S. employees and does not plan on doing so, it is estimated that, over the next five years, the U.S. garment and textile industry will lose around 30% of its 450,000 jobs.[8] While Heiman acknowledges that textile manufacturing based in the United States is likely to decline, he suggests that textile manufacturers need to focus their efforts on R&D while at the same time being in step with the global economy.[9]

Interestingly enough, while Heiman's investment in establishing a manufacturing facility in Linyi has been both his largest investment and also the one that has caused him the most problems along the way as booming China moves from a state-controlled to a market economy, he is convinced that overcoming all the hurdles along the way was well worth the effort. As he puts it, "I know the potential is simply awesome."[10]

Overview

Each member of an organization has his or her own style and ways of behaving. Effectively working with others requires an understanding and appreciation of how people differ from one another. Gary Heiman, for example, is persistent and determined, qualities that have contributed to his success as CEO of Standard Textile. In order to effectively work with Heiman, it is important that Heiman's subordinates and colleagues understand what he is like and what is important to him.

INDIVIDUAL DIFFERENCES
The ways in which people differ from each other.

In this chapter, we focus on **individual differences**, the ways in which people differ from each other. Managers need to understand individual differences because they have an impact on the feelings, thoughts, and behaviors of each member of an organization. Individual differences affect, for example, job satisfaction, job performance, job stress, and leadership. Organizational members interact with each other on a daily basis, and only if they understand each other are their interactions likely to result in high levels of satisfaction and performance.

Individual differences may be grouped into two categories: personality differences and differences in ability. We focus on the nature, meaning, and determinants of personality and on the ways that personality and situational factors combine to influence feelings, thoughts, and behavior in organizations. We discuss specific personality traits that are particularly relevant to organizational behavior. We then turn our attention to differences in ability. After describing various types of ability, we discuss the key issue for managers: how ability can be managed to ensure that employees can effectively perform their jobs.

The Nature of Personality

People's personalities can be described in a variety of ways. Some people seem to be perfectionists; they can be critical, impatient, demanding, and intense. Other kinds of people are more relaxed and easygoing. You may have friends or co-workers who always seem to have something to smile about and are fun to be around. Or perhaps you have friends or coworkers who are shy and quiet; they are hard to get to know and may sometimes seem dull. In each of these examples, we are describing what people are generally like without referring to their specific feelings, thoughts, and behaviors in any given situation. In formulating a general description of someone, we try to pinpoint something that is relatively enduring about the person, something that seems to explain the regularities or patterns we observe in the way the person thinks, feels, and behaves.

PERSONALITY
The pattern of relatively enduring ways that a person feels, thinks, and behaves.

Personality is the pattern of relatively enduring ways that a person feels, thinks, and behaves. Personality is an important factor in accounting for why employees act the way they do in organizations and why they have favorable or unfavorable attitudes toward their jobs and organizations.[11] Personality has been shown to influence career choice, job satisfaction, stress, leadership, and some aspects of job performance.

Determinants of Personality: Nature and Nurture

Why are some employees happy and easygoing and others intense and critical? An answer to this question can be found by examining the determinants of personality: nature and nurture.

NATURE
Biological heritage, genetic makeup.

Personality is partially determined by **nature**, or biological heritage. The genes that you inherited from your parents influence how your personality has unfolded.[12] Although specific genes for personality have not yet been identified, psychologists have studied identical twins in an attempt to discover the extent to which personality is inherited.[13]

Because identical twins possess identical genes, they have the same genetic determinants of personality. Identical twins who grow up together in the same family have the same permissive or strict parents and similar life experiences. If the twins have similar personalities, it is impossible to identify the source of the similarity because they have not only the same genetic makeup but also similar life experiences.

In contrast, identical twins who are separated at birth and raised in different settings (perhaps because they are adopted by different families) share the same genetic material but often have very different life experiences. Evidence from research on separated identical twins and other studies suggests that approximately 50 percent of the variation we observe in people's personalities can be attributed to nature—to genetic factors (see Exhibit 2.1).[14] Thus, about half of the variation we observe in employees' personalities in organizations reflects the distinctive ways of thinking, feeling, and behaving they inherited from their parents. The other 50 percent reflects the influence of **nurture**, or life experiences.

NURTURE
Life experiences.

Personality develops over time, responding to the experiences people have as children and as adults. Factors such as the strictness or permissiveness of a child's parents, the number of other children in the family, the extent to which parents and teachers demand a lot from a child, success or lack of success at making friends or getting and keeping a job, and even the culture in which a person is raised and lives as an adult are shapers of personality.

Because about half of the variation in people's personalities is inherited from their parents and, thus, is basically fixed at birth, it comes as no surprise that personality is quite stable over periods of time ranging from 5 to 10 years. This does not mean that personality cannot change; it means that personality is likely to change only over many years. Thus, the impact of any specific work situation or crisis on an employee's personality is likely to be felt only if the situation continues for many years. An important outcome of this fact is that managers should not expect to change employees' personalities. In fact, for all practical purposes, managers should view employees' personalities as relatively fixed in the short run.

EXHIBIT 2.1

Nature and Nurture: The Determinants of Personality

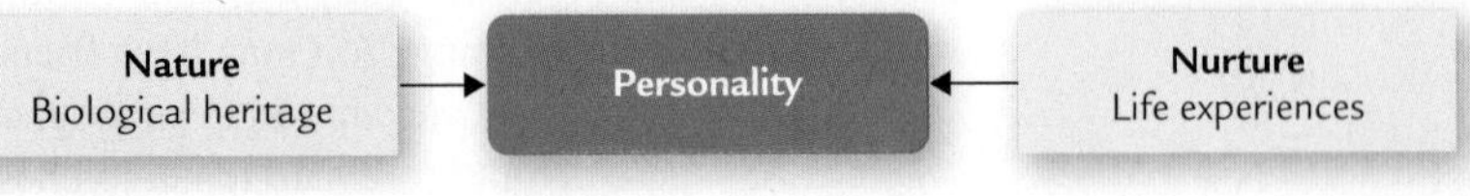

Personality, nevertheless, is an important individual difference that managers and other organizational members need to take into account in order to understand why people feel, think, and act as they do in organizations. For example, realizing that an employee complains a lot and often gets upset because of his or her personality will help a manager deal with this type of employee, especially if the employee's job performance is acceptable.

Personality and the Situation

Because personality accounts for observable regularities in people's attitudes and behaviors, it would seem reasonable to assert that it would account for such regularities at work. A substantial body of literature in psychology and a growing set of studies in organizational behavior suggest that personality useful for explaining and predicting how employees generally feel, think, and behave on the job.[15] Personality has been shown to influence several work-related attitudes and behaviors, including job satisfaction (Chapter 3), the ability to handle work-related stress (Chapter 8), the choice of a career (Chapter 8), and leadership (Chapter 12).[16] Because of personality, some people, like Gary Heiman in the opening case, are very conscientious about most things they do and, thus, perform at a higher level than do those who are not so conscientious, as we discuss later in this chapter.[17]

However, in addition to personality, the organizational situation also affects work attitudes and behaviors. In some organizations, there are strong situational constraints and pressures (such as job requirements or strict rules and regulations) that force people to behave in a certain way, regardless of their personalities.[18] For example, an employee on an assembly line manufacturing bicycles must put handlebars on each bicycle that passes by. A bike passes by every 75 seconds, and the employee has to be sure that the handlebars are properly attached to each bicycle within that time frame. It doesn't matter whether the employee is shy or outgoing; regardless of his or her personality, the employee has a specific task to perform day in and day out in the same manner. Because the employee is not free to vary his or her behavior, personality is not useful for understanding or predicting job performance in this situation.

Consider another example. Employees at McDonald's and other fast-food restaurants follow clearly specified procedures for preparing large quantities of burgers, fries, and shakes and serving them to large numbers of customers. Because each employee knows exactly what the procedures are and how to carry them out (they are spelled out in

When there are strong situational pressures to perform specific behaviors in a certain manner, as is the case on this assembly line, personality may not be a good predictor of on-the-job behavior.

a detailed manual), the food is always prepared in the same manner, regardless of the employees' personalities.

As these two examples show, in organizations in which situational pressures on employees' behaviors are strong, personality may not be a good predictor of on-the-job behavior. When situational pressures are weak, however, and employees have more choice about how to perform a job, personality plays a more important role, and what a person can put into his or her job performance will sometimes depend on the kind of person he or she is. For instance, a statewide English curriculum requires English teachers to teach Shakespeare's *Macbeth* to high-school seniors, but the curriculum does not specify exactly how the play is to be taught. A teacher who is outgoing and has a flair for the dramatic may bring the play and its themes to life by dressing up in period costumes and acting out scenes. A teacher who is less outgoing may simply ask students to take turns reading aloud from the play or ask them to write a paper on how Shakespeare reveals a certain theme through the play's dialogue and action. Both teachers are following the curriculum but, as you can see, their individual personalities affect *how* they do so.

By now it should be clear to you that both personality and situational factors affect organizational behavior.[19] It is the interaction of personality and situational factors that determines how people think, feel, and behave in general and, specifically, how they do so within an organization (see Exhibit 2.2). Robert Greene, for example, is an executive in an advertising agency who is responsible for coming up with advertising campaigns and presenting them to the agency's clients. Greene is a creative, achievement-oriented person who has good ideas and has developed the agency's most successful and lucrative campaigns. But Greene is also shy and quiet and cannot always effectively communicate his ideas to clients. Greene's personality and the situation combine or interact to determine his overall performance. He performs well when working on his own or with his team to develop advertising campaigns, but in interpersonal situations, such as when he presents his campaigns to clients, he performs poorly. A manager who understands this interaction can capitalize on the personality strengths (creativity and achievement orientation) that propel Greene to develop successful advertising campaigns. The manager can also guard against the possibility of clients having a negative reaction to Greene's shyness by teaming him up for presentations with a gregarious executive whose strong suit is pitching campaigns to clients. If Greene's manager did not understand how Greene's personality and the situation interacted to shape Greene's performance, the advertising agency might lose clients because of Greene's inability to relate to them effectively and convince them of the merits of his campaigns.

Effective managers recognize that the various situations and personality types interact to determine feelings, thoughts, attitudes, and behaviors at work. An understanding of employees' personalities and the situations in which they perform best enables a manager to help employees perform at high levels and feel good about the work they are doing. Furthermore, when employees at all levels in an organization understand how personality and the situation interact, good working relationships and organizational effectiveness are promoted.

As profiled in the following Focus on Diversity, the interactions of personality and situational factors often influence the kinds of positions and organizations people are attracted to and, ultimately, their effectiveness.

EXHIBIT 2.2

The Interaction of Personality and Situational Factors

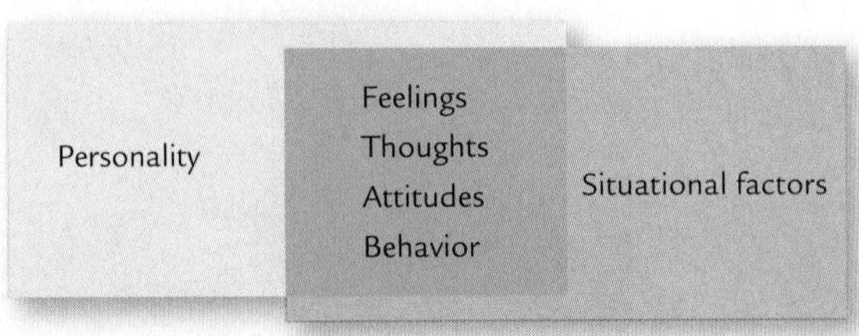

Focus on Diversity

Liane Pelletier Transforms Alaska Communications

When a recruiting firm contacted Liane Pelletier to see if she was interested in becoming CEO of Alaska Communications Systems (ACS), Pelletier wavered, but not for long.[20] At the time, Pelletier was a senior vice president at Sprint where she had worked for the past seventeen years.[21] Why was Pelletier attracted to the position at ACS? And why would this Connecticut-born executive who loves to travel consider moving to Alaska, which makes travel a time-consuming endeavor since it can take over 3 hours just to fly from Anchorage to Seattle?[22]

Lianne Pelletier's love for adventure, in combination with her skills and expertise gained from years of experience in the telecommunications industry, have contributed to her effectively transforming Alaska Communications Systems to better serve its customers and expand its range of products.

The combination of Pelletier's love for adventure and new experiences, the opportunity to leverage her industry experience, and the challenge of remaking ACS actually made the decision to head up ACS a relatively easy one for Pelletier. Pelletier has always had an adventuresome side—hiking along the Appalachian trail, venturing down the Amazon River, and, now, snowshoeing in Alaska[23] are the kinds activities she seeks out and enjoys—so moving to Alaska appealed to this aspect of her personality.

As a seasoned manager in the telecommunications industry, the position at ACS represented an exciting opportunity to revamp Alaska's largest local exchange carrier and the only local provider who has its own local, long distance, wireless, and Internet infrastructure.[24] When Pelletier came to ACS, she discovered that the company was organized around products rather than customers. Different divisions would provide different kinds of services to customers without regard to how these same customers might be using other products provided by other divisions. Pelletier restructured ACS to focus on the customer—how to better serve customers through the multiple products and services that ACS provides. Now, sales and service to customers are integrated across product lines, and employees receive training so that they are knowledgeable about all of ACS's products.[25] Customer-focused growth and improving wireless service are priorities for ACS and Pelletier's efforts to transform ACS have paid off in terms of increases in ACS's earnings and stock price.[26] Clearly, the combination of Pelletier's love of adventure, her skills and expertise as a seasoned telecommunications executive, and the opportunity to transform ACS to better serve its customers and expand its range of products and services have all contributed to her effectively transforming ACS.[27]

Personality: A Determinant of the Nature of Organizations

Ben Schneider, a prominent organizational researcher at the University of Maryland, has come up with an interesting view of the way in which personality determines the nature of whole organizations. He calls his schema the **attraction-selection-attrition (ASA) framework**.[28] Schneider proposes that the "personality" of a whole organization is largely a product of the

ATTRACTION-SELECTION-ATTRITION (ASA) FRAMEWORK
The idea that an organization attracts and selects individuals with similar personalities and loses individuals with other types of personalities.

personalities of its employees. He suggests that individuals with similar personalities tend to be attracted to an organization (*attraction*) and hired by it (*selection*), and individuals with other types of personalities tend to leave the organization (*attrition*). As a result of the interplay of attraction, selection, and attrition, there is some consistency or similarity of personalities within an organization, and this "typical" personality determines the nature of the organization itself.[29]

ASA processes operate in numerous ways. When organizations hire new employees, they implicitly size up the extent to which prospective hires fit in with the organization—that is, the extent to which their personalities match the personalities of current members. This sizing up is especially likely to occur in small organizations. Larry Pliska, who heads up Planterra, a Michigan company that sells plants and trees, hires all new managers himself so that he can be sure they relate to and support his philosophy for the company. John Schaeffer, founder of the California company Real Goods Trading, conducts most of the final interviewing and does most of the hiring for his company in an attempt to find what he calls "even-tempered" employees.[30]

What are the implications of the ASA framework? We would expect, for example, that people who are creative and like to take risks would be attracted to entrepreneurial organizations and would be likely to be hired by such organizations. Individuals who do not have this orientation either would not seek jobs with these organizations or would be likely to leave them. Over time, ASA processes may result in these organizations being composed of large numbers of creative risk takers who, in turn, give the organization its entrepreneurial nature. The entrepreneurial nature of the organization, in turn, influences employees' feelings, thoughts, and behaviors and reinforces their own propensity for risk taking. It is important to realize that although ASA processes can strengthen an organization, they can also lead an organization to perform poorly or even fail. This negative outcome occurs when most members of the organization view opportunities and problems in the same way and, as a result of their shared point of view, are resistant to different points of view and making needed changes.

The Big Five Model Of Personality

When people describe other people, they often say things like "She's got a lot of personality," meaning that the person is fun loving, friendly, and outgoing, or "He's got no personality," meaning that the person is dull and boring. In fact, there is no such thing as a lot of personality or no personality; everyone has a specific type of personality.

Because personality is an important determinant of how a person thinks, feels, and behaves, it is helpful to distinguish between different types of personality. Researchers have spent considerable time and effort trying to identify personality types. One of the most important ways that researchers have found to describe a personality is in terms of traits. A **trait** is a specific component of personality that describes the particular tendencies a person has to feel, think, and act in certain ways, such as in a shy or outgoing, critical or accepting, compulsive or easygoing manner. In the opening case, Gary Heiman of Standard Textile was described as being conscientious and open to new experiences; as you will learn, conscientiousness and openness to experience are actually two personality traits. Thus, when we speak of a person's personality, we are really referring to a collection of traits that describes how the person generally tends to feel, think, and behave.

TRAIT
A specific component of personality.

Researchers have identified many personality traits, and most psychologists agree that the traits that make up a person's personality can be organized in a hierarchy.[31] The Big Five model of personality places five general personality traits at the top of the trait hierarchy: extraversion, neuroticism, agreeableness, conscientiousness, and openness to experience (see Exhibit 2.3).[32] Each of the Big Five traits is composed of various specific traits. Extraversion (the tendency to have a positive outlook on life), for example, consists of specific traits such as positive emotions, gregariousness, and warmth. The Big Five and the specific traits lower in the hierarchy are universal. They can be used to describe the personalities of people regardless of their age, gender, race, ethnicity, religion, socioeconomic background, or country of origin.

Each of the general and specific traits represents a continuum along which a certain aspect or dimension of personality can be placed. A person can be high, low, average, or anywhere in between on the continuum for each trait. Exhibit 2.4 shows a profile of a person

EXHIBIT 2.3

The Hierarchical Organization of Personality

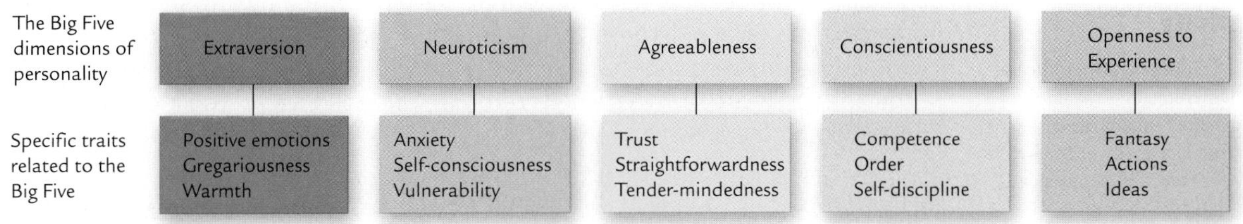

Source: Adapted from R.R McCrae and P.T. Costa "Discriminant Validity of NEO-PIR Facet Scales." *Educational and Psychological Measurement* 52: 229-237. Copyright © 1992. Reprinted by Sage Publications, Inc.

who is low on extraversion, high on neuroticism, about average on agreeableness and conscientiousness, and relatively high on openness to experience. To help you understand what a Big Five personality profile means, we describe the extremes of each trait next. Keep in mind that a person's standing on the trait could be anywhere along the continuum (as in Exhibit 2.4).

Extraversion

EXTRAVERSION
The tendency to experience positive emotional states and feel good about oneself and the world around one; also called positive affectivity.

Extraversion, or **positive affectivity**, is a personality trait that predisposes individuals to experience positive emotional states and feel good about themselves and about the world around them. Extraverts—people high on the extraversion scale—tend to be sociable, affectionate, and friendly. Introverts—people low on the extraversion scale—are less likely to experience positive emotional states and have fewer social interactions with others. At work, extraverts are more likely than introverts to experience positive moods, be satisfied with their jobs, and generally feel good about the organization and those around them. Extraverts also are more likely to enjoy socializing with their coworkers. They may do particularly well in jobs requiring frequent social interaction, such as in sales and customer-relations positions.

Of course, people who are low on extraversion can succeed in a variety of occupations. For example, Steve Case, former chairman and CEO of America Online and AOL Time Warner, is often described as not being high on extraversion.[33] An example of a personality scale that measures a person's level of extraversion is provided in Exhibit 2.5.

Neuroticism

NEUROTICISM
The tendency to experience negative emotional states and view oneself and the world around one negatively; also called negative affectivity.

In contrast to extraversion, **neuroticism**—or **negative affectivity**—reflects people's tendencies to experience negative emotional states, feel distressed, and generally view themselves and the world around them negatively. Individuals high on neuroticism are more likely than individuals low on neuroticism to experience negative emotions and stress over time and across situations. Individuals who are high on neuroticism are more likely to

EXHIBIT 2.4

A Big Five Personality Profile

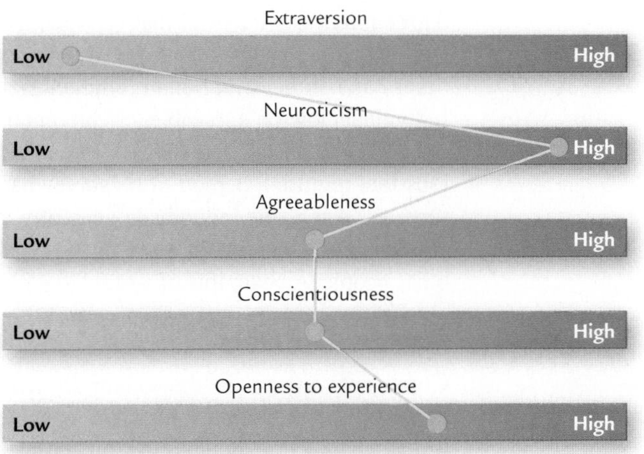

EXHIBIT 2.5

A Measure of Extraversion or Positive Affectivity

Source: A. Tellegen, "Brief Manual for the Differential Personality Questionnaire," unpublished manuscript, University of Minnesota, 1982. Reprinted with permission.

Instructions: Listed below is a series of statements a person might use to describe her or his attitudes, opinions, interests, and other characteristics. If a statement is true or largely true, put a "T" in the space next to the item. If the statement is false or largely false, mark an "F" in the space.

Please answer *every statement*, even if you are not completely sure of the answer. Read each statement carefully, but don't spend too much time deciding on the answer.

_____ 1. It is easy for me to become enthusiastic about things I am doing.

_____ 2. I often feel happy and satisfied for no particular reason.

_____ 3. I live a very interesting life.

_____ 4. Every day I do some things that are fun.

_____ 5. I usually find ways to liven up my day.

_____ 6. Most days I have moments of real fun or joy.

_____ 7. I often feel sort of lucky for no special reason.

_____ 8. Every day interesting and exciting things happen to me.

_____ 9. In my spare time I usually find something interesting to do.

_____ 10. For me, life is a great adventure.

_____ 11. I always seem to have something pleasant to look forward to.

Scoring: Level of extraversion or positive affectivity is equal to the number of items answered "True."

experience negative moods at work, feel stressed, and generally have a negative orientation toward the work situation.[34] Often, the term *neurotic* is used in the media and popular press to describe a person who has a psychological problem. Neuroticism, however, is a trait that all normal, psychologically healthy individuals possess to a certain degree.

Individuals high on neuroticism are sometimes more critical of themselves and their performance than are people low on neuroticism. That tendency may propel them to improve their performance. As a result, they may be particularly proficient in certain situations, such as ones that require a high degree of quality control, critical thinking, and evaluation. Individuals high on neuroticism may also exert a needed "sobering" influence during group decision making by playing devil's advocate and pointing out the negative aspects of a proposed decision. Individuals low on neuroticism do not tend to experience negative emotions and are not as critical and pessimistic as their high-neuroticism counterparts. An example of a personality scale that measures neuroticism is provided in Exhibit 2.6.

Agreeableness

AGREEABLENESS
The tendency to get along well with others.

Agreeableness is the trait that captures the distinction between individuals who get along well with other people and those who do not. Likability in general and the ability to care for others and to be affectionate characterize individuals who are high on agreeableness. Individuals low on agreeableness are antagonistic, mistrustful, unsympathetic, uncooperative, unsympathetic, and rude. A low measure of agreeableness might be an advantage in jobs that require a person to be somewhat antagonistic, such as a bill collector or a drill sergeant. Agreeable individuals generally are easy to get along with and are team players. Agreeableness can be an asset in jobs that hinge on developing good relationships with other people. An example of a scale that measures agreeableness is provided in Exhibit 2.7.

Conscientiousness

CONSCIENTIOUSNESS
The extent to which a person is careful, scrupulous, and persevering.

Conscientiousness is the extent to which an individual is careful, scrupulous, and persevering. Individuals high on conscientiousness are organized and have a lot of self-discipline.[35] Individuals low on conscientiousness may lack direction and self-discipline.

EXHIBIT 2.6

A Measure of Neuroticism or Negative Affectivity

Source: A. Tellegen, "Brief Manual for the Differential Personality Questionnaire," unpublished manuscript, University of Minnesota, 1982. Reprinted with permission.

Instructions: Listed below is a series of statements a person might use to describe her or his attitudes, opinions, interests, and other characteristics. If a statement is true or largely true, put a "T" in the space next to the item. If the statement is false or largely false, mark an "F" in the space.

Please answer every statement, even if you are not completely sure of the answer. Read each statement carefully, but don't spend too much time deciding on the answer.

_____ 1. I often find myself worrying about something.

_____ 2. My feelings are hurt rather easily.

_____ 3. Often I get irritated at little annoyances.

_____ 4. I suffer from nervousness.

_____ 5. My mood often goes up and down.

_____ 6. I sometimes feel "just miserable" for no good reason.

_____ 7. Often I experience strong emotions—anxiety, anger—without really knowing what causes them.

_____ 8. I am easily startled by things that happen unexpectedly.

_____ 9. I sometimes get myself into a state of tension and turmoil as I think of the day's events.

_____ 10. Minor setbacks sometimes irritate me too much.

_____ 11. I often lose sleep over my worries.

_____ 12. There are days when I'm "on edge" all of the time.

_____ 13. I am too sensitive for my own good.

_____ 14. I sometimes change from happy to sad, or vice versa, without good reason.

Scoring: Level of neuroticism or negative affectivity is equal to the number of items answered "True."

Being open to new experiences and willing to take risks has paid off handsomely for billionaire Mark Cuban, the colorful owner of the Dallas Mavericks. Cuban made his first million founding a computer company after college—without ever having taken an information systems class.

Conscientiousness is important in many organizational situations and has been found to be a good predictor of performance in many jobs in a wide variety of organizations.[36] Roger Salquist, entrepreneur and CEO of the successful Calgene Inc. (now part of Monsanto Corporation), is known for his attention to details. When trying to win U.S. Food and Drug Administration (FDA) approval for his genetically altered tomato, for instance, Salquist made over 25 trips to Washington, DC, and was relentless in his efforts to provide the FDA and other agencies with all the scientific data he could in support of the safety of his tomato. Salquist's conscientiousness paid off because the FDA agreed that no special labeling or testing would be necessary for genetically engineered foods such as Calgene's new tomato.[37] In the opening case, it is also clear that Gary Heiman of Standard Textile is high on conscientiousness.

Of course, in order for conscientiousness to result in high performance, employees need to have the capabilities or skills needed to be high performers. For example, a recent study found that when job performance depends on being effective interpersonally, conscientiousness was only positively related to performance among those employees who had high social skills.[38] An example of a scale that measures conscientiousness is provided in Exhibit 2.7.

Openness to Experience

The last of the Big Five personality traits, **openness to experience**, captures the extent to which an individual is original, open to a wide variety of stimuli, has broad interests, and is willing to take risks as opposed to being narrow-minded and cautious. Recall Gary Heiman's openness to experience in the opening case. For jobs that change frequently, require innovation, or involve considerable risk, individuals who are open to experience may have an

EXHIBIT 2.7

Measure of Agreeableness, Conscientiousness, and Openness to Experience

Listed below are phrases describing people's behaviors. Please use the rating scale below to describe how accurately each statement describes **you**. Describe yourself as you generally are now, not as you wish to be in the future. Describe yourself as you honestly see yourself, in relation to other people you know of the same sex as you are, and roughly your same age.

1	2	3	4	5
Very inaccurate	**Moderately inaccurate**	**Neither inaccurate nor accurate**	**Moderately accurate**	**Very accurate**

_____ 1. Am interested in people.
_____ 2. Have a rich vocabulary.
_____ 3. Am always prepared.
_____ 4. Am not really interested in others.*
_____ 5. Leave my belongings around.*
_____ 6. Have difficulty understanding abstract ideas.*
_____ 7. Sympathize with others' feelings.
_____ 8. Pay attention to details.
_____ 9. Have a vivid imagination.
_____ 10. Insult people.*
_____ 11. Make a mess of things.*
_____ 12. Am not interested in abstract ideas.*
_____ 13. Have a soft heart.
_____ 14. Get chores done right away.
_____ 15. Have excellent ideas.
_____ 16. Am not interested in other people's problems.*
_____ 17. Often forget to put things back in their proper place.*
_____ 18. Do not have a good imagination.*
_____ 19. Take time out for others.
_____ 20. Like order.
_____ 21. Am quick to understand things.
_____ 22. Feel little concern for others.*
_____ 23. Shirk my duties.*
_____ 24. Use difficult words.
_____ 25. Feel others' emotions.
_____ 26. Follow a schedule.
_____ 27. Spend time reflecting on things.
_____ 28. Make people feel at ease.
_____ 29. Am exacting in my work.
_____ 30. Am full of ideas.

*Items reverse scored: 1=5; 2=4; 4=2, 5=1

Scoring: Sum responses to items for an overall scale

Agreeableness = Sum of items 1, 4, 7, 10, 13, 16, 19, 22, 25, 28

Conscientiousness = Sum of items 3, 5, 8, 11, 14, 17, 20, 23, 26, 29

Source: http://ipip.ori.org/ipip/ Lewis R. Goldberg, Oregon Research Institute.

OPENNESS TO EXPERIENCE The extent to which a person is original, has broad interests, and is willing to take risks.

advantage. For openness to experience to be translated into creative and innovative behavior in organizations, however, the organization must remove obstacles to innovation. Moreover, jobs and tasks must not be too closely defined so that job holders are able to use their openness to experience to come up with new ideas.[39] Entrepreneurs, who are often characterized as risk takers,[40] frequently start their own businesses because the large organizations that employed them placed too many restrictions on them and gave them too little reward for innovation and risk taking. Although openness to experience clearly is an advantage for entrepreneurs and those performing jobs that require innovation, organizations also need people to perform jobs that do not allow much opportunity for originality. In addition, organizations are sometimes afraid to take the risks that employees high on openness to experience may thrive on. An example of a personality scale that measures openness to experience is provided in Exhibit 2.7.

Sometimes the combination of high openness to experience and high conscientiousness can be beneficial when employees need to make difficult decisions in uncertain times. This has proven to be the case for Fujio Mitarai, CEO of Canon, Inc., as profiled in the accompanying Global View.

Global View

Fujio Mitarai Cuts Costs and Develops New Products at Canon

Fujio Mitarai, Chairman and CEO of Canon, Inc., has turned around Canon's fortunes and more than tripled its net profits since assuming top management positions at this global camera, printer, fax, and copier maker over a decade ago. Mitarai has made many changes at Canon—changes that reflect his high levels of conscientiousness and openness to experience. Mitarai realized that to revitalize Canon he needed to cut costs and boost profitability. His conscientiousness helped him to take the steps needed to make this happen: shutting down weak businesses and divisions, pushing employees to always be on the lookout for ways to cut costs, and rewarding employees for increasing sales and profitability.[41]

Whereas Mitarai's discipline has served Canon well, so has his high level of openness to experience, which has influenced him throughout his life. As a child who only knew the Japanese language and culture, he longed to go overseas. After a few years at Canon in Japan, in 1966 he transferred to the company's New York office, where he remained for 23 years, building the camera and copier business for Canon in the United States. In 1989, he returned to Japan as managing director prior to assuming the CEO position.[42]

Fujio Mitarai, president and CEO of Canon Inc., has turned around Canon's fortunes and more than tripled its net profits. The many changes he has made at Canon reflect his high levels of conscientiousness and openness to experience.

Mitarai's openness to both the Japanese and the American ways of managing has led him to become somewhat of a role model for other executives, and he was recently named one of *BusinessWeek's* "Best Managers."[43] For example, consistent with American practices, he believes in merit pay to reward high performers; consistent with Japanese practices, he values loyalty and, thus, is an advocate of lifetime employment. Rather than appoint outsiders to the board of directors to keep top management on track, he prefers the value-added contributions insiders on the board can make. However, he also recognizes the need for the oversight of management that is accomplished by empowering auditors to play a more active role in corporate governance.[44]

Mitarai's openness to experience has even changed the way that Canon manufactures its cameras and copiers. In Japan, Mitarai replaced its traditional assembly lines used for production with a "cell" system. Each cell is made up of six workers who assemble products in a small area rather than on a long assembly line. Cell production has proven to be much more efficient than assembly lines in Japan, and Canon is now implementing the new method in its production facilities outside of Japan. Looking to the future, Mitarai

has increased Canon's spending on research and development to take advantage of the latest scientific developments in technology to create new and better products.[45] Canon commits around 8% of sales to R&D, has filed over 17,000 patents since 1995, and is developing new products ranging from SED TV panels (a new type of flat screen TV) to OLEDs (organic light-emitting displays that are brighter and consume less power than LCDs).[46] Clearly, high levels of conscientiousness and openness to experience have helped Mitarai get Canon back on track.

Conclusions

Research suggests that the Big Five traits are important for understanding work-related attitudes and behaviors and, thus, our understanding of organizational behavior. As we discuss in more detail in Chapter 9, for example, neuroticism or negative affectivity is useful in understanding stress in the workplace.[47] Researchers have found that individuals high on negative affectivity are more likely to indicate that there are significant stressors in the workplace and to experience stress at work. Research has also shown that individuals high on extraversion or positive affectivity are more likely to feel good at work and be satisfied with their jobs. These people are likely to perform well in jobs such as sales and management, which require social interaction.[48]

As you have undoubtedly recognized from our discussion of the Big Five traits, there is no such thing as a good or bad personality profile. Each person is unique and has a different type of personality that may be suited to different kinds of organizational situations. Good managers need to understand and learn to deal with people of all personality types.

You're the Management Expert

Understanding a New Employee

Marty Feldman owns a music store that caters to all kinds of musicians ranging from beginners to professionals. The store sells many varieties of music for different instruments and takes special orders for hard-to-find music and instruments. Located in the heart of New York City, Feldman prides himself not only on the store's extensive musical offerings but also on his very knowledgeable staff, many of whom are, themselves, practicing musicians. Feldman recently added a new member to his staff, Paul Carvacchio. Carvacchio is a pianist who plays in a local symphony, gives piano lessons to children and adults, tunes pianos, and works part-time in the store as its specialist pianist. Feldman continues to be impressed with Carvacchio's knowledge and expertise. Recently, Feldman observed Carvacchio helping a customer who was a first-time piano buyer; Feldman was impressed with how Carvacchio helped the customer identify a piano that would best suit her needs and budget, and the customer recently placed a special order to purchase the piano through the store. Moreover, she signed up for the store's maintenance and piano-tuning service. However, Feldman continues to be puzzled by Carvacchio's seeming dissatisfaction with the job. Carvacchio periodically complains about small things and tends to be quite critical when mishaps occur in the store. Feldman recently asked Carvacchio how things were going and if he liked working at the store, and Carvacchio indicated that everything was fine and he had no complaints. Yet Feldman is afraid that Carvacchio didn't tell him the whole story. As an expert in organizational behavior, Feldman has come to you for help. Why does Carvacchio sometimes act like he is dissatisfied with working at the store when he has indicated he likes his job and he is performing well?

Other Organizationally Relevant Personality Traits

Several other specific personality traits are relevant to understanding and managing behavior in organizations (see Exhibit 2.8).

Locus of Control

People differ in how much control they believe they have over situations they are in and over what happens to them. Some people think they have relatively little impact on their surroundings and little control over important things that happen in their lives. Others believe that they can have a considerable impact on the world around them and on the path their lives take. The locus-of-control trait captures this difference among individuals.[49]

EXTERNAL LOCUS OF CONTROL
Describes people who believe that fate, luck, or outside forces are responsible for what happens to them.

INTERNAL LOCUS OF CONTROL
Describes people who believe that ability, effort, or their own actions determine what happens to them.

"Externals," or individuals with an **external locus of control**, tend to believe that outside forces are largely responsible for their fate, and they see little connection between their own actions and what happens to them. "Internals," or individuals with an **internal locus of control**, think that their own actions and behaviors have an impact on what happens to them. When people with an internal locus of control perform well, they are likely to attribute their performance to qualities within themselves, such as their own abilities or efforts. When people with an external locus of control perform well, they are likely to attribute their performance to external forces such as luck, the effects of powerful people, or simply the fact that the task was easy. In organizations, internals are more easily motivated than externals. Internals do not need as much direct supervision because they tend to believe their work behaviors influence important outcomes such as how well they perform their jobs and the pay increases, praise, job security, and promotions they receive.

Self-Monitoring

SELF-MONITORING
The extent to which people try to control the way they present themselves to others.

Self-monitoring is the extent to which people try to control the way they present themselves to others.[50] High self-monitors want their behavior to be socially acceptable and are attuned to any social cues that signal appropriate or inappropriate behavior. They strive to behave in a situationally appropriate manner. For example, if they are in a meeting and see others making suggestions, they will try to make suggestions as well. They are also good at managing the impressions that others have of them. In contrast, low self-monitors are not particularly sensitive to cues indicating acceptable behavior, nor are they overly concerned about behaving in a situationally appropriate manner. For example, they may act bored in a meeting with the president of an organization or they might voice their concerns in a job

EXHIBIT 2.8

Personality Traits Specifically Relevant to Organizations

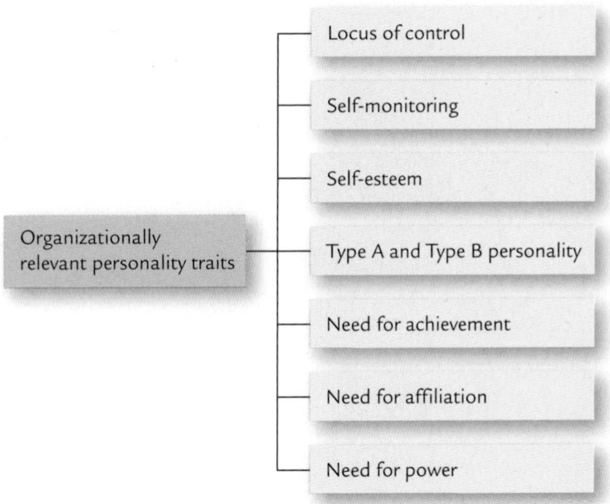

interview about working long hours. People who are low self-monitors are guided by their own attitudes, beliefs, feelings, and principles and are not too concerned about what others think of their behaviors.

High self-monitors are more likely than low self-monitors to tailor their behavior to fit a given situation. Thus, high self-monitors may perform especially well in jobs such as sales or consulting, which require employees to interact with different types of people on a regular basis. In addition, because high self-monitors can modify their behavior to approximate what individuals or groups expect of them, they are particularly effective when an organization needs someone to communicate with an outside group whose support is being sought, such as when a nonprofit organization tries to secure donations from wealthy individuals.

Low self-monitors are more likely than high self-monitors to say what they think is true or correct and are not overly concerned about how others will react to them. Thus, low self-monitors may be especially adept at providing organizational members with open, honest feedback (particularly when it's negative) and playing devil's advocate in decision-making groups. A scale that measures self-monitoring is provided in Exhibit 2.9.

EXHIBIT 2.9

A Measure of Self-Monitoring

Source: S. Gangestad and M. Snyder, "'To Carve Nature at Its Joints': On the Existence of Discrete Classes in Personality," Psychological Review 92 (1985): 317–49. Copyright © 1985 by the American Psychological Association. Reprinted with permission.

Instructions: Please indicate the extent to which each of the following statements is true or false for you personally.

____ 1. I find it hard to imitate the behavior of other people.

____ 2. At parties and social gatherings, I do not attempt to do or say things that others will like.

____ 3. I can only argue for ideas that I already believe.

____ 4. I can make impromptu speeches even on topics about which I have almost no information.

____ 5. I guess I put on a show to impress or entertain others.

____ 6. I would probably make a good actor.

____ 7. In a group of people, I am rarely the center of attention.

____ 8. In different situations and with different people, I often act like very different persons.

____ 9. I am not particularly good at making other people like me.

____ 10. I'm not always the person I appear to be.

____ 11. I would not change my opinions (or the way I do things) in order to please someone or win their favor.

____ 12. I have considered being an entertainer.

____ 13. I have never been good at games like charades or improvisational acting.

____ 14. I have trouble changing my behavior to suit different people and different situations.

____ 15. At a party I let others keep the jokes and stories going.

____ 16. I feel a bit awkward in public and do not show up quite as well as I should.

____ 17. I can look anyone in the eye and tell a lie with a straight face (if for a right end).

____ 18. I may deceive people by being friendly when I really dislike them.

Scoring: Individuals high on self-monitoring tend to indicate that questions 4, 5, 6, 8, 10, 12, 17, and 18 are true and that questions 1, 2, 3, 7, 9, 11, 13, 14, 15, and 16 are false.

Self-Esteem

SELF-ESTEEM
The extent to which people have pride in themselves and their capabilities.

Self-esteem is the extent to which people have pride in themselves and their capabilities.[51] Individuals with high self-esteem think they are generally capable and worthy people who can deal with most situations. Individuals with low self-esteem question their self-worth, doubt their capabilities, and are apprehensive about their ability to succeed in different endeavors.

Self-esteem has several implications for understanding behavior in organizations.[52] Self-esteem influences people's choices of activities and jobs. Individuals with high self-esteem are more likely than individuals with low self-esteem to choose challenging careers and jobs. Once they are on the job, individuals with high self-esteem may set higher goals for themselves and be more likely to tackle difficult tasks. High self-esteem also has a positive impact on motivation and job satisfaction. Clearly, Gary Heiman's high self-esteem has contributed to his success at Standard Textile. It must be kept in mind, however, that people with low self-esteem can be just as capable as those with high self-esteem, in spite of their self-doubts.

Type A and Type B Personalities

TYPE A
A person who has an intense desire to achieve, is extremely competitive, and has a strong sense of urgency.

TYPE B
A person who tends to be easygoing and relaxed.

In the popular press, you will often hear someone referred to as a "Type A" or read that "Type A personalities" are prone to high blood pressure. Individuals who are **Type A** have an intense desire to achieve, are extremely competitive, have a sense of urgency, are impatient, and can be hostile.[53] Such individuals have a strong need to get a lot done in a short time period and can be difficult to get along with because they are so driven. They often interrupt other people and sometimes finish their sentences for them because they are so impatient. More relaxed and easygoing individuals are labeled **Type B**.

Because they are able to accomplish so much, Type A's would seem to be ideal employees from the organization's perspective, especially in situations in which a lot of work needs to be done in a short amount of time. However, because they can be difficult to get along with, Type A's may not be effective in situations that require a lot of interaction with others. Consistent with this observation, one study found that Type A managers were more likely to have conflicts with their subordinates and with coworkers than were Type B managers.[54] Type A employees are not particularly good team players and often work best alone. In addition, Type A's may get frustrated in long-term situations or projects because they like to see results quickly.

Another important difference between Type A and Type B individuals has received a lot of attention in the popular press. Type A individuals are more likely than Type B's to have coronary heart disease. In fact, two heart doctors identified this trait after they realized that many of their heart-attack patients were very impatient, sometimes hostile, and always in a hurry and watching the clock. Some research suggests that a tendency toward hostility is particularly responsible for Type A's heart problems.

Needs for Achievement, Affiliation, and Power

David McClelland has done extensive research on three traits that are present in all people to varying degrees: the need for achievement, the need for affiliation, and the need for power.[55]

NEED FOR ACHIEVEMENT
The desire to perform challenging tasks well and to meet one's own high standards.

Individuals with a high **need for achievement** have a special desire to perform challenging tasks well and to meet their own personal standards for excellence. They like to be in situations in which they are personally responsible for what happens, like to set clear goals for themselves, are willing to take personal responsibility for outcomes, and like to receive performance feedback. Not surprisingly, such individuals are often found in jobs that help them to satisfy their strong desire to excel. Indeed, McClelland has found that entrepreneurs and managers are especially likely to have a high need for achievement. In one study, for example, McClelland found that 10 years after graduation, undergraduates who had shown a high need for achievement were more likely to be found in entrepreneurial occupations than were those who had shown a low need for achievement.[56] In addition, effective managers often have a strong goal orientation and tend to take moderate risks, a finding that is consistent with the profile of an individual with a high need for achievement.

It is not surprising, therefore, that a high need for achievement often goes hand in hand with career success. This has been the case for Flight Operations Vice-President Captain Deborah McCoy, who oversees more than 8,700 flight attendants and 5,200 pilots at Continental Airlines.[57] As a teenager, McCoy worked at a grocery store to earn money to take flying lessons. She joined Continental as a pilot in 1978 and has since been promoted many times, leading up to her current high-ranking position.[58]

NEED FOR AFFILIATION
The desire to establish and maintain good relations with others.

Individuals with a high **need for affiliation** are especially concerned about establishing and maintaining good relations with other people. They not only want to be liked by others but they also want everyone to get along with everyone else. As you might expect, they like working in groups, tend to be sensitive to other people's feelings, and avoid taking actions that would result in interpersonal conflict. In organizations, individuals with a high need for affiliation are especially likely to be found in jobs that require a lot of social interaction. Although they make good team players, a manager might not want a group to be composed primarily of individuals with a high need for affiliation because the group might be more concerned about maintaining good interpersonal relations than about actually accomplishing its tasks. Individuals with a high need for affiliation may also be less effective in situations in which they need to evaluate others because it may be hard for them to give negative feedback to a coworker or a subordinate—a task that might disrupt interpersonal relations.

NEED FOR POWER
The desire to exert emotional and behavioral control or influence over others.

Individuals with a high **need for power** have a strong desire to exert emotional and behavioral control or influence over others.[59] These individuals are especially likely to be found in managerial jobs and leadership positions, which require one person to exert influence over others. Individuals with a high need for power may actually be more effective as leaders than those with a low need for power. In a study of the effectiveness of former presidents of the United States, for example, Robert House of the University of Pennsylvania and his colleagues found that a president's need for power was a good predictor of his performance and effectiveness in office.[60] The power-level needs of a president were assessed by analyzing his inaugural speeches for thoughts and ideas indicative of the need for power. From the opening case, it is clear that Gary Heiman has a high need for power, which contributes to his effectiveness as CEO of Standard Textile.

What combination of the needs for achievement, affiliation, and power results in higher managerial motivation and performance? Although it might seem that high levels of all three are important for managerial effectiveness, research by Michael Stahl suggests that managers should have a high need for achievement and power.[61] A high need for affiliation might not necessarily be a good quality in managers because they may try too hard to be liked by their subordinates instead of trying to lead them to higher performance levels. Stahl's findings on managerial effectiveness primarily apply to lower- and middle-level managers.[62] For top executives and managers, the need for power appears to be the need that dominates all others in determining their success.[63]

How Personality Is Measured

We have been discussing the various traits that make up an individual's personality without much mention of how to determine an individual's standing on any of these traits. By far the most common and cost-effective means of assessing the personality traits of adults is through scales developed to measure personality. To complete these scales, individuals answer a series of questions about themselves.[64] Exhibits 2.5, 2.6, 2.7, and 2.9 provide examples of scales that measure the Big Five personality traits and self-monitoring. Personality scales like these are often used for research purposes, for example, to determine how people who vary on these traits respond to different work situations. Although the use of such scales always runs the risk of respondents intentionally distorting their answers to portray themselves in a desirable fashion, research suggests that this is not a significant problem.[65]

The Nature of Ability

When looking at individual differences and the way they affect the attitudes and behaviors of employees, we must look not only at each employee's personality but also at the *abilities, aptitudes*, and *skills* the employee possesses. Those terms are often used interchangeably. In

ABILITY
The mental or physical capacity to do something.

our discussion, however, we focus on **ability**, which has been defined as "what a person is capable of doing."[66] Ability has important implications for understanding and managing organizational behavior. It determines the level of performance an employee can achieve and, because the effectiveness of an organization as a whole depends on the performance levels of all individual employees—from janitors and clerks to upper managers and the CEO—ability is an important determinant of organizational performance. Two basic types of ability affect performance: cognitive or mental ability and physical ability.

Cognitive Ability

Psychologists have identified many types of cognitive ability and grouped them in a hierarchy. The most general dimension of cognitive ability is *general intelligence*.[67] Below general intelligence are specific types of cognitive ability that reflect competence in different areas of mental functioning (see Exhibit 2.10). Eight types of cognitive ability identified and described by psychologist Jum Nunnally, whose work was based in part on the pioneering work of L. L. and T. G. Thurstone in the 1940s, are described in Exhibit 2.11.[68]

Research suggests that cognitive ability predicts performance on the job, as long as the ability in question is relied on in performing the job.[69] For example, numerical ability is unlikely to predict how well a writer or comedian will perform on the job. To understand the relation between cognitive ability and job performance, one needs to identify the abilities that are required to effectively perform the job.[70] In the previous example, verbal ability is especially likely to be important for a writer or comedian. Thus, this is the cognitive ability most likely to predict success in these jobs.[71] Cognitive ability also is an important contributor to group or team performance.[72] It is important to keep in mind, however, that other things in addition to cognitive ability determine performance.

Physical Ability

People differ not only in cognitive ability but also in physical ability. Two types of physical abilities are motor and physical skills.[73] A *motor skill* is the ability to physically manipulate objects in an environment. A *physical skill* is a person's fitness and strength. E. A. Fleishman has devoted considerable attention to identifying and studying physical ability and has concluded that there are 11 basic motor skills (such as reaction time, manual dexterity, and speed of arm movement) and nine physical skills (such as static strength, which includes the ability to lift weights and stamina).[74]

Where Do Abilities Come from and How Are They Measured?

Like personality, both cognitive ability and physical ability are determined by nature and nurture (see Exhibit 2.12). General intelligence is determined by the genes we inherit from our parents (nature)[75] and by situational factors (nurture). Standardized tests such as the GMAT (General Management Aptitude Test) or the SAT (Scholastic Aptitude Test) are designed to measure certain basic aptitudes and abilities that people are probably born with, but we know that people's scores on these tests change over time and that situational changes such as repeated training on practice exams can improve performance. Moreover, an individual may be genetically endowed with superior intelligence, but if that person grows up in a severely impoverished environment (characterized by poor nutrition, irregular school attendance, or parents who are drug abusers), his or her scores on standard intelligence tests will probably suffer.

EXHIBIT 2.10

Types of Cognitive Ability

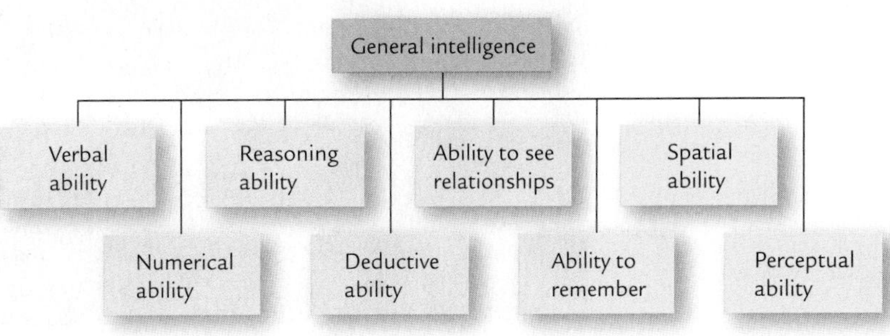

EXHIBIT 2.11

Cognitive Abilities

Ability	Description	Examples of jobs in which the ability is especially important
Verbal ability	Ability to understand and use written and spoken language	Comedians, teachers, lawyers, writers
Numerical ability	Ability to solve arithmetic problems and deal with numbers	Waiters, investment bankers, engineers, accountants
Reasoning ability	Ability to come up with solutions for problems and understand the principles by which different problems can be solved	Therapists, interior designers, car mechanics, computer software designers
Deductive ability	Ability to reach appropriate conclusions from an array of observations or evaluate the implications of a series of facts	Medical researchers, detectives, scientists, investigative reporters
Ability to see relationships	The ability to see how two things are related to each other and then apply this knowledge to other relationships and solutions	Anthropologists, travel agents, consultants, wedding planners
Ability to remember	Ability to recall things ranging from simple associations to complex groups of statements or sentences	Translators, salespeople, managers, researchers
Spatial ability	Ability to determine the location or arrangement of objects in relation to one's own position and to imagine how an object would appear if its position in space were altered	Air traffic controllers, architects, clothing designers, astronauts
Perceptual	Ability to uncover visual patterns and see relationships within and across patterns	Professional photographers, airplane pilots, cruise ship captains, landscape designers

Source: Based, in part, on J. C. Nunnally, Psychometric Theory, 2nd ed. (New York: McGraw-Hill, 1978).

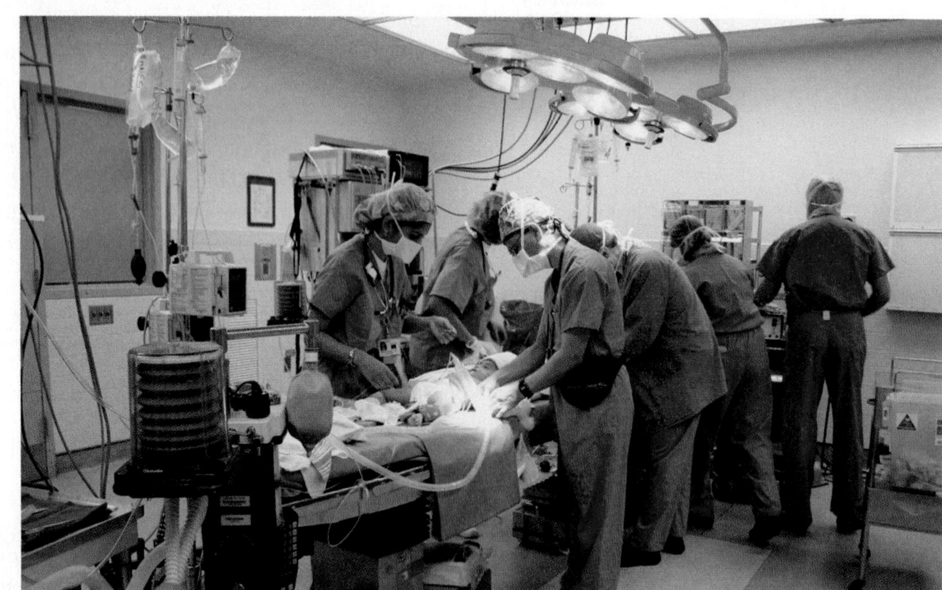

Surgeons like those who separated Ahmed and Mohamed Ibrahim—Egyptian twins conjoined at the head—need both cognitive and physical skills. The delicate, intricate procedure required a year of planning and 26 hours of prior surgery to complete. The twins were separated in 2003.

EXHIBIT 2.12

Nature and Nurture: The Determinants of Cognitive and Physical Abilities

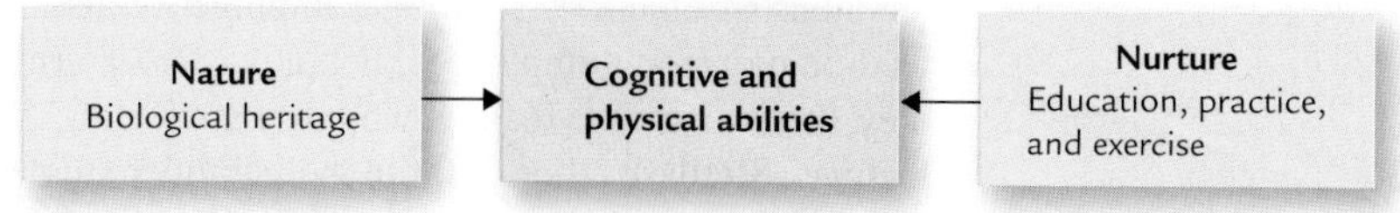

Both nature and nurture also determine physical ability. Height, bone structure, limb length, and relative proportions are genetically determined and cannot be changed. Through practice and training such as weight-lifting and aerobic exercise, however, people can enhance some of their physical and motor skills.

Researchers have developed many accurate paper-and-pencil measures of cognitive ability; managers can often rely on the results of these tests as useful indicators of the underlying ability they are measuring. The tests can be used to ensure that prospective employees have the types of ability necessary to perform a job, to place existing employees in different jobs in an organization, to identify individuals who might need additional training, and to evaluate how successful training programs are in raising ability levels (we discuss each of these issues in the next section). Before using any of these tests, however, managers have to make sure that the tests are ethical and do not unfairly discriminate against different kinds of employees. Some tests of cognitive ability have been criticized for being culturally biased. Critics say that they ask questions that, because of differences in the test takers' ethnic backgrounds, may be relatively easy for members of certain groups to answer and more difficult for members of other groups to answer.

Physical ability can be measured by having a person engage in the activity he or she would have to do on the job. For example, managers who need to see whether a prospective employee is strong enough to deliver, unpack, and set up heavy appliances could ask the individual to lift progressively heavier weights to determine the level of his or her static strength. New York City Sanitation Department evaluates the physical ability of prospective employees by having them pick up trash bags and toss them into garbage trucks.

Although organizations spend considerable time and effort to ensure the people they hire have the abilities they need to be effective in their jobs, sometimes people are not given the opportunity to use their abilities on the job. A recent study of over 600 managers and 700 hourly employees found that two thirds of the managers and employees surveyed thought that their companies used only about 50 percent of their employees' cognitive abilities.[76] Even some IT professionals believe that their abilities are not being effectively utilized. A recent study of over 200 IT professionals found that over 40 percent of them were so bored at work that they thought about quitting their current jobs.[77] Hence, in addition to ensuring that employees have the abilities needed to perform at a high level, organizations should also strive to give them the opportunity to use them.

Cognitive and physical abilities can degenerate or become impaired because of disease, drug or alcohol abuse, excessive levels of stress, or fatigue. In many organizations, it is important to accurately assess the ability level of an employee to know what he or she is capable of doing, but it is also necessary to know when and why that ability may become impaired. Organizations have traditionally responded to impairment by testing employees for substance abuse. This has, indeed, been found to reduce illegal drug use.[78]

Drug testing can detect the presence of drugs and alcohol, but it does not tap into impairment due to other factors like excessive fatigue or disease. Another problem with conducting a drug test is that it usually takes at least two to three days to get back the results. In response to those problems, some firms have developed "fitness for duty" performance tests to determine whether employees can safely perform their jobs. Some of these tests involve the use of computer terminals and games that measure accuracy and reaction time against an employee's baseline score.[79]

EMOTIONAL INTELLIGENCE
The ability to understand and manage one's own feelings and emotions and the feelings and emotions of other people.

Emotional Intelligence: A New Kind of Ability

Psychologists have identified a new kind of ability that is not so much concerned with cognitive or physical capabilities but rather with emotional capabilities. **Emotional intelligence** is the ability to understand and manage one's own feelings and emotions and the feelings and emotions of others.[80] Emotional intelligence also helps promote effective functioning and well-being among employees. People differ in terms of the extent to which they know how they, themselves, are feeling, why they are feeling that way, and their ability to manage those feelings. Similarly, they differ in their ability to understand what other people are feeling and why, and their ability to influence or manage the feelings of others. Emotional intelligence describes these individual differences.[81] An example of a scale that measures emotional intelligence is provided in Exhibit 2.13.

Research on emotional intelligence is in its early stages. However, it is plausible that emotional intelligence may facilitate job performance in a number of ways and a low level of emotional intelligence may actually impair performance. For example, psychologist Martin Seligman found that salespeople at Metropolitan Life who were high on optimism (an aspect of emotional intelligence) sold considerably more insurance policies than salespeople who were less able to manage their feelings and think positively.[82] As another example, a recent study conducted by Kenneth Law and colleagues found that emotional intelligence predicted levels of life satisfaction among students and levels of job performance among employees in Hong Kong and the People's Republic of China.[83]

EXHIBIT 2.13

A Measure of Emotional Intelligence

Please indicate the extent to which you agree or disagree with each of the following items using the 1–7 scale below.

1 Totally Disagree	2 Disagree	3 Somewhat Disagree	4 Neither Agree nor Disagree	5 Somewhat Agree	6 Agree	7 Totally Agree

_____ 1. I have a good sense of why I have certain feelings most of the time.
_____ 2. I always know my friends' emotions from their behavior.
_____ 3. I always set goals for myself and then try my best to achieve them.
_____ 4. I am able to control my temper so that I can handle difficulties rationally.
_____ 5. I have good understanding of my own emotions.
_____ 6. I am a good observer of others' emotions.
_____ 7. I always tell myself I am a competent person.
_____ 8. I am quite capable of controlling my own emotions.
_____ 9. I really understand what I feel.
_____ 10. I am sensitive to the feelings and emotions of others.
_____ 11. I am a self-motivating person.
_____ 12. I can always calm down quickly when I am very angry.
_____ 13. I always know whether or not I am happy.
_____ 14. I have good understanding of the emotions of people around me.
_____ 15. I would always encourage myself to try my best.
_____ 16. I have good control of my own emotions.

Scoring: Self-Emotions Appraisal = sum of items 1, 5, 9, 13
Others-Emotions Appraisal = sum of items 2, 6, 10, 14
Use of Emotion = sum of items 3, 7, 11, 15
Regulation of Emotion = sum of items 4, 8, 12, 16

Source: K. Law, C. Wong, and L. Song, "The Construct and Criterion Validity of Emotional Intelligence and Its Potential Utility for Management Studies," *Journal of Applied Psychology*, 2004, 89(3), p. 496; C. S. Wong and K. S. Law, "The Effects of Leader and Follower Emotional Intelligence on Performance and Attitude: An Exploratory Study," *Leadership Quarterly*, 2002, 13, pp. 243–274.

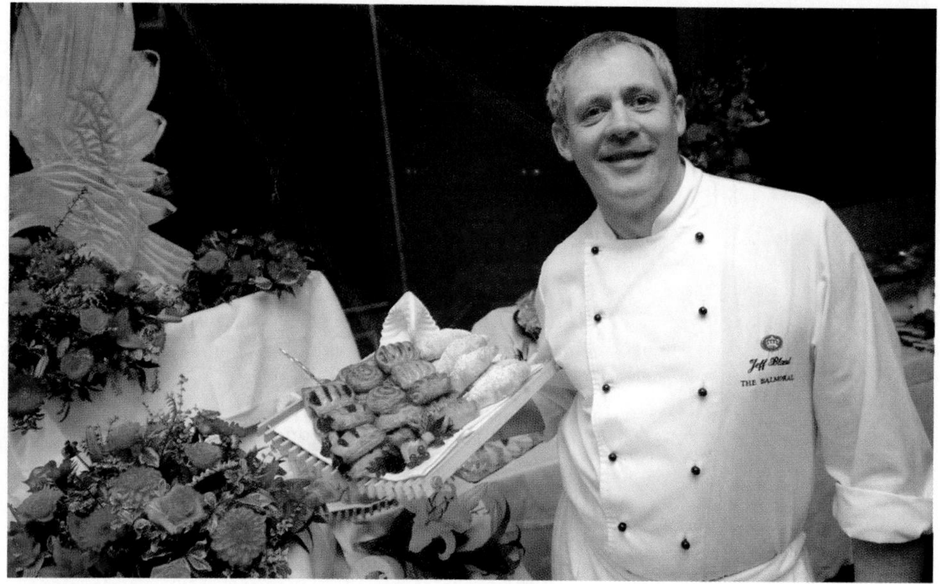

Emotional intelligence led Sir Rocco Forte to create a leading luxury hotel management company in Europe by helping him understand what customers want. Despite his expertise and success, Forte says the real asset of his hotels is its employees.

Recent theorizing and research suggest that emotional intelligence is an especially important ability for leaders and managers, enabling them to understand and relate well to others as well as understand themselves.[84] Emotional intelligence also helps leaders and managers maintain their enthusiasm and confidence and communicate a vision to followers that will energize them to work toward organizational goals.[85] Jing Zhou and Jennifer George, professors at Rice University, have theorized that leaders' emotional intelligence might be especially important for awakening employee creativity.[86] For Sir Rocco Forte, CEO of Forte Hotels, the ability to understand how customers feel and determine what they want is the key to excellent customer service.[87]

Emotional intelligence sometimes plays a subtle but important role in effective workplace behaviors. For example, consider the case of Jane, who was hired by George McCown of McCown Dee Leeuw, a buy-out company in Menlo Park, California, to help determine which companies are good purchase opportunities. Jane was highly intelligent with excellent numerical skills and a top-notch educational background. McCown sent Jane to visit a company he was interested in purchasing. After visiting the company and performing various calculations, Jane advised McCown to buy the company because the numbers looked good. McCown, however, decided to visit the company himself, and he was glad he did. As he puts it, "I could tell in the first two minutes of talking to the CEO that he was experiencing serious burnout. The guy was being overwhelmed by problems. On paper, things looked great. But he knew what was coming down the line. Jane had missed those cues completely."[88] Evidently, Jane's low level of emotional intelligence prevented her from understanding how the CEO of the targeted company was feeling and why—cues her boss was able to pick up on. Jane is no longer with McCown Dee Leeuw.[89]

Andrea Jung, CEO and chair of Avon Products, is a firm believer in the importance of emotional intelligence. As she puts it, "Emotional intelligence is in our DNA here at Avon because relationships are critical at every stage of our business."[90]

Understanding people and relationships clearly has paid off for Christine Poon, Vice Chairman of Johnson & Johnson (J&J) and Worldwide Chairman for J&J's Medicines and Nutritionals.[91] While holding one of the highest-ranking positions in J&J, Poon doesn't act like a "celebrity manager"; she believes that all employees make a company successful, not just those at the very top.[92] Poon's high level of emotional intelligence is reflected in her philosophy, management style, and how she interacts with people. Poon has an easygoing demeanor and seems down to earth, yet she is a careful and deliberate decision maker. Equally important to her is fostering a work environment where respect for employees, customers, and the general public is valued.[93] She has the confidence and emotional stamina to take on what might seem to be insurmountable challenges and conquers them in an easygoing manner. Poon is intelligent and creative and encourages those around her to be equally inquisitive and ask questions.[94] Being results oriented and driven to succeed, Poon realizes that her employees drive that success, so she treats them as equal members of her team.[95]

The Management of Ability in Organizations

Although we have mentioned the many types of ability that people possess, only a few abilities are likely to be relevant for the performance of any particular job. Managerial work, for example, requires cognitive ability, not very many physical abilities, and probably some degree of emotional intelligence, whereas being a grocery-store shelf stocker or a car washer requires mainly physical ability. A brain surgeon, for instance, must rely on cognitive and physical abilities when performing highly complicated and delicate operations.

For managers, the key issue regarding ability is to make sure that employees have the abilities they need to perform their jobs effectively. There are three fundamental ways to manage ability in organizations to ensure that this match-up happens: selection, placement, and training.

Selection

Managers can control ability in organizations by selecting individuals who have the abilities they need. This first involves identifying the tasks they want the employees to accomplish and the abilities they need to do them. Once these abilities are identified, managers then have to develop accurate measures of them. The key question at this point is whether a person's score on an ability measure is actually a good predictor of the task that needs to be performed. If it isn't, there is no point in using it as a selection device. Furthermore, it would be unethical to do so. An organization that uses an inappropriate measure and rejects capable applicants leaves itself open to potential lawsuits for unfair hiring practices. But if the ability measure does predict task performance, then managers can use it as a selection tool to ensure that the organization has the mix of abilities it needs to accomplish its goals.

Placement

Once individuals are selected and become part of an organization, managers must accurately match each employee to a job that will capitalize on his or her abilities. Again, managers need to identify the ability requirements of the jobs to be filled, and they need accurate measures of these abilities. Once these measures are available, the aim is to place employees in positions that match their abilities. Placement, however, involves more than just assigning new employees to appropriate positions. It also becomes an issue in horizontal moves or promotions within the organization. Obviously, an organization wants to promote only its most able employees to higher-level positions.

Training

Selection and placement relate to the *nature* aspects of ability. Training relates to the *nurture* aspects of ability. Training can be an effective means of enhancing employees' abilities. We often think that the goal of training is to improve employees' abilities beyond the minimum level required. Frequently, however, organizations use training to bring employees' skills up to some minimum required level. Extensive research suggests that job-appropriate training is effective in increasing employees' skills and abilities and, ultimately, their performance.[96]

To gain a competitive advantage, organizations often need to use new and advanced technology to lower costs and increase quality, efficiency, and performance. Companies that use advanced technology often find that their employees' abilities and skills are deficient in a number of ways. In the factories of the past, most employees could get by with sheer physical strength and stamina, but those days are largely gone. In today's technical world, higher levels of skill are generally needed. Companies like General Electric, Motorola, The Container Store, and Milliken have found that investments in training more than payoff in terms of high performance.[97] At Oregon-based Umpqua Bank, employees receive training in all banking areas so everyone is qualified to help customers in their banking needs and customers are not kept waiting.[98] Interestingly enough, in China's booming economy where skilled employees are in short supply and high demand, companies are finding that providing training and learning opportunities can be an effective means of recruiting and retaining employees.[99]

Training can also be used to increase the emotional intelligence of employees. In order for emotional intelligence training to succeed, however, employees must recognize the importance of emotional intelligence and be motivated to improve their own emotional capabilities. Emotional intelligence training typically begins with an accurate assessment of the employee's strengths and weaknesses. Someone who is very familiar with the employee's on-the-job behaviors and is trusted by the employee should provide this assessment. Employees then need to practice handling different situations and reflect on what went well and what didn't. Throughout the process, the support of a trusted confidant or coach can help them realistically analyze their own feelings and behaviors and the feelings and behaviors of others. As employees begin to develop more effective ways of interacting with others, their emotional intelligence has the potential to increase. Today, emotional intelligence training is becoming more commonplace. Avon and Metropolitan Life are among the many companies that offer emotional intelligence training to their employees.

Summary

The two main types of individual differences are personality differences and ability differences. Understanding the nature, determinants, and consequences of individual differences is essential for managing organizational behavior. Because people differ so much from each other, an appreciation of the nature of individual differences is necessary to understand why people act the way they do in organizations. In this chapter, we made the following major points:

1. Personality is the pattern of relatively enduring ways that a person feels, thinks, and behaves. Personality is determined both by nature (biological heritage) and nurture (situational factors). Organizational outcomes that have been shown to be predicted by personality include job satisfaction, work stress, and leadership effectiveness. Personality is not a useful predictor of organizational outcomes when there are strong situational constraints. Because personality tends to be stable over time, managers should not expect to change personality in the short run. Managers should accept employees' personalities as they are and develop effective ways to deal with people.
2. Feelings, thoughts, attitudes, and behaviors in an organization are determined by the interaction of personality and situation.
3. The Big Five personality traits are extraversion (or positive affectivity), neuroticism (or negative affectivity), agreeableness, conscientiousness, and openness to experience. Other personality traits particularly relevant to organizational behavior include locus of control, self-monitoring, self-esteem, Type A and Type B personalities, and the needs for achievement, affiliation, and power.
4. In addition to possessing different personalities, employees also differ in their abilities, or what they are capable of doing. The two major types of ability are cognitive ability and physical ability.
5. Types of cognitive ability can be arranged in a hierarchy with general intelligence at the top. Specific types of cognitive ability are verbal ability, numerical ability, reasoning ability, deductive ability, ability to see relationships, ability to remember, spatial ability, and perceptual ability.
6. There are two types of physical ability: motor skills (the ability to manipulate objects) and physical skills (a person's fitness and strength).
7. Both nature and nurture contribute to determining physical ability and cognitive ability. A third, recently identified, ability is emotional intelligence.
8. In organizations, ability can be managed by selecting individuals who have the abilities needed to accomplish tasks, placing employees in jobs that capitalize on their abilities, and training employees to enhance their ability levels.

Exercises in Understanding and Managing Organizational Behavior

Questions for Review

1. Why is it important to understand that both nature and nurture shape an employee's personality?
2. What are some situations in which you would *not* expect employees' personalities to influence their behavior?
3. What are some situations in which you would expect employees' personalities to influence their behavior?
4. Is it good for organizations to be composed of individuals with similar personalities? Why or why not?
5. A lawyer needs to score high on which of the Big Five personality traits? Why?
6. What are some jobs or situations in which employees who are high on agreeableness would be especially effective?
7. When might self-monitoring be dysfunctional in an organization?
8. What levels of the needs for achievement, power, and affiliation might be desirable for an elementary school teacher?
9. What types of abilities are especially important for an upper-level manager (such as the president of a division) to possess? Why?
10. What are the three ways in which ability can be managed in organizations?

OB: Increasing Self-Awareness

Characteristics of People and Jobs

Choose a job that you are very familiar with—a job that you currently have, a job that you used to have, or the job of a close family member or friend. Or the job could be one that you have been able to observe closely during your interaction with an organization as a customer, client, or patient. For the job of your choosing, respond to the following items.

1. Describe the job, including all the tasks that the jobholder must perform.
2. Choose two of the Big Five personality traits that you think would have the most impact on the jobholder's feelings, thoughts, attitudes, and behaviors. Explain why you think these traits might be particularly important for understanding the jobholder's reactions.
3. Identify three of the organizationally relevant personality traits that you think would affect performance on this job and explain why you think they are likely to be important.
4. Which of the jobholder's behaviors are primarily determined by the situation and not personality?
5. What cognitive abilities must the jobholder possess?
6. What physical abilities must the jobholder possess?
7. How can selection and placement be used to ensure that prospective jobholders have these abilities?
8. How can an organization train jobholders to raise levels of these abilities?

A Question of Ethics

Emotional intelligence—the ability to understand and manage one's own and other people's moods and emotions—can be increased through training. When people are high on emotional intelligence, they are better able to understand and use emotions to influence others. However, people can be influenced in positive and negative ways. As an example of the latter, historical atrocities and cult tragedies have been attributed to the ability of certain individuals to have high levels of influence over others.

Questions

1. What are the ethical implications of emotional intelligence training?
2. What steps can organizations take to ensure that employees' emotional intelligence is put to good use and not used for personal gain or unethical purposes?

Small Group Break-Out Exercise

Understanding Situational Influences

Form groups of three or four people and appoint one member as the spokesperson who will communicate your conclusions to the rest of the class.

1. Take a few minutes to think about a recent incident in which you behaved in a manner that was inconsistent with your personality and/or abilities.
2. Take turns describing these situations and why you behaved the way you did.
3. As a group, develop a list of the characteristics of situations in which people's behavior is primarily determined by the context or situation and in which individual differences play a very minor role.
4. Think of reasons why it is important for employees and managers to be aware of situational influences on work behavior.

Topic for Debate

Personality and ability have major implications for how people feel, think, and behave in organizations. Now that you have a good understanding of these individual differences, debate the following issue:

Team A. Organizations should select or hire prospective employees on the basis of their personality traits.

Team B. Organizations should *not* select or hire prospective employees on the basis of their personality traits.

Experiential Exercise

Individual Differences in Teams

Objective

In organizations like Merck & Co., the pharmaceuticals giant, and Microsoft Corporation, the leading producer of computer software, research scientists or computer programmers often work together in small teams on complex, path-breaking projects to create new drugs or computer software. Team members interact closely, often over long time periods, in order to complete their projects. Individual differences in personality and ability provide teams not only with valued resources needed to complete their projects but also potential sources of conflict and problems. Your objective is to understand how individual differences in personality and ability affect people's behavior in teams.

Procedure

The class divides into groups of three to five people, and each group appoints one member as spokesperson to present the group's findings to the whole class. Each group discusses how the personalities and abilities of team members may affect team performance and may cause conflict and problems. Using the knowledge of personality and ability gained in this chapter, each group answers the following questions.

1. Do certain personality traits make people good team members? If so, what are they and why are they important? If not, why not?
2. Is it more effective for teams to be composed of members who have different personality types or similar personality types?
3. What kinds of abilities make people good team members?
4. Should team members have similar or different kinds and levels of abilities?

When all the groups are finished discussing these issues, the spokespersons take turns presenting the groups' findings to the rest of the class, and the instructor lists the findings on the board.

New York Times *Cases in the News*

The New York Times

"The Math Whiz vs. the Media Moguls in a Battle for Millions,"

By Richard Siklos, April 3, 2006, p. C1, C5.

Henry C. Yuen is in a protracted legal struggle with Rupert Murdoch, over Mr. Yuen's management of Gemstar and its troubled accounting.

Amid the flash of the Internet bubble, Henry C. Yuen, the chairman and chief executive of **Gemstar-TV Guide International**, did things his way.

Despite running a company worth more than $20 billion in early 2000 and being partners with **Rupert Murdoch's News Corporation**, he operated out of low-rent offices in Pasadena, Calif. A visitor to the headquarters recalls that using a fax machine required unplugging the telephone because there was only one line. A former Gemstar employee recalled Mr. Yuen driving to lunch four blocks from the office, but then parking two blocks away to avoid paying a valet charge.

But even as Mr. Yuen was pinching pennies, he was manipulating hundreds of millions in revenue to make the company look more profitable, according to prosecutors and investors.

Mr. Yuen was forced out as Gemstar's chairman and chief executive more than three years ago, after the company acknowledged that revenue had been inflated and the stock price collapsed. News Corporation's involvement with Mr. Yuen—it owns 41 percent of Gemstar—resulted in 2002 in a $6 billion writedown, the biggest such hit Mr. Murdoch has taken in his storied career.

An investigation into Mr. Yuen's conduct by the Securities and Exchange Commission, and a tangle of other litigation, show that Mr. Yuen, a mathematician and lawyer who built Gemstar by developing and aggressively defending patents for television viewing, still casts a long shadow over the News Corporation and Mr. Murdoch.

News Corporation, through Gemstar, has pursued Mr. Yuen with unusual vigor, going so far as to file a victim statement asking a court to overturn Mr. Yuen's plea agreement in a criminal case. In addition to his other legal troubles, including a class-action lawsuit, Mr. Yuen faces an arbitration dispute with Gemstar, in which Mr. Murdoch seeks to force Mr. Yuen to return earnings totaling some $100 million, including $2 million in annual salary he still receives under the severance agreement.

Neither Mr. Murdoch nor Mr. Yuen would comment for this article. But several people who work closely with Mr. Murdoch say Gemstar's tough stance has been a response to Mr. Yuen's hardball tactics.

"Rupert doesn't look back, he doesn't spend a lot of time thinking about Henry," Lawrence A Jacobs, group general counsel for the News Corporation, said in an interview. He added, however, "This is one of the few people we've ever dealt with who clearly committed fraud."

Ripples from the Gemstar debacle go beyond financial losses. Gemstar represented the beginnings of a partnership between News Corporation and the media billionaire John C. Malone that has become hotly contentious.

Last month, in a civil action brought by the S.E.C., a federal district judge in Los Angeles ruled that Mr. Yuen had committed accounting fraud while running Gemstar by misrepresenting some $200 million worth of revenue in seven transactions from 1999 to 2002. At a hearing Wednesday, the judge, Mariana R. Pfaeizer, will deliberate on the S.E.C.'s request that Mr. Yuen pay more than $60 million in restitution. Mr. Arkin said his client intended to appeal. Separately, a spokesmen for the United States attorney in Los Angeles said a criminal inquiry on Mr. Yuen was continuing.

Mr. Yuen, who is 57, has maintained that he was the target of an orchestrated effort by Mr. Murdoch's allies to commandeer the business he had built.

His lawyer, Stanley S. Arkin, asserted: "To some extent, this company, News Corporation, set out to blow up my guy and they did it. It's too bad it came to this. I think we have severely diminished our opportunity to benefit from the genius of Henry Yuen and his vision and entrepreneurship."

Gemstar's early chapters were far more promising for Mr. Yuen. The son of a Hong Kong lawyer, he moved to the United States when he was 17 to study mathematics at the University of Wisconsin and then at the California, Institute of Technology in Pasadena. At Caltech, he became friends with another doctoral student, Daniel Kwoh, with whom he would found Gemstar in 1989 "He played soccer very well, even though he was kind of smallish—he was very fast, very decisive," Mr. Kwoh recalled in an interview.

Mr. Yuen went on to gain a law degree from Loyola University. He put his knowledge of math and law together with Mr. Kwoh to invent VCR Plus, a patented system for simplifying the way people program their videocassette recorders. Although relatively few people used VCR Plus, Gemstar was able to persuade both hardware makers and publishers of TV listings, including Mr. Murdoch's TV Guide, to pay license fees for it.

Mr. Yuen's next innovation was to buy up companies that had developed interactive programming guides that would help navigate the growing numbers of TV options.

Mr. Yuen could be ruthless. Outside Gemstar, he acquired the nickname "patent terrorist" for his willingness to sue potential partners like Thomson Electronics or Time Warner. Framed copies of the company's patents decorated the conference room.

Within the company, he was abrupt and secretive as a chief executive, and former colleagues say his only confidant was Elsie M. Leung, Gemstar's longtime chief financial officer. Three Gemstar employees said Mr Yuen would suddenly turn to Ms. Leung in meetings with other executives and begin speaking with her in Cantonese. "I would not say of Henry that sweetness and diplomacy were his strong suit," Mr. Arkin said.

In another of Mr. Yuen's many legal tangles, he has been in lengthy litigation with his ex-wife, Molly Yuen, the mother of two of his four children. She contended in a 1996 lawsuit that Mr. Yuen forged her signature on divorce documents a decade earlier and that she was not aware of the faked divorce for years. She argued that the divorce was intended to deprive her of a claim on Mr. Yuen's growing fortune. Mr. Yuen denied the accusations and, although the divorce matter was settled in 2000, the couple remains in litigation over payments Mr. Yuen stopped making to her two years later.

Mr. Kwoh left the company in 1997 after what he described as a dispute over business strategy, which he declined to elaborate on. Although he and Mr. Yuen both live in Pasadena, they have not spoken since, Mr. Kwoh said.

Mr. Malone and Mr. Murdoch had tried separately and together to buy out Mr. Yuen. They both coveted Gemstar's rich profit margins from licensing; in 1998 the company had a profit of $38.7 million on revenue of $126 million. Indeed, amid the hoopla over convergence at the time, Mr. Yuen thought that his on-screen guide would be the ultimate toll-keeper for the media and told colleagues that Gemstar would someday be bigger than Microsoft.

After his efforts to buy Gemstar failed, Mr. Malone became a big shareholder in TV Guide by merging a company with his own on-screen guide business into it. Then in 1999, Mr. Murdoch proposed to Mr. Yuen that Gemstar acquire TV Guide for $9.2 billion in stock. This time, he agreed, with conditions: Mr. Murdoch would end up the biggest shareholder, but he would get an employment contract putting him firmly in charge for five years. Mr. Yuen next turned to buying companies to produce so-called electronic-book readers. Mr. Murdoch hailed Mr. Yuen in Business Week magazine as a brilliant strategist."

But cultures and strategies clashed, Mr. Murdoch felt that TV Guide was being neglected in favor of Mr. Yuen's electronic ventures. He began convening weekly management meetings at TV Guide's offices in New York that Mr. Yuen would attend by teleconference. According to one person who attended, Mr. Yuen would often put the meeting on hold after only a few minutes, leaving the sound of Muzak coming through the speaker as his contribution.

In private meetings, Mr. Murdoch and Peter Chernin, News Corporation's president, pressed Mr. Yuen to replace Ms. Leung as chief financial officer. Mr. Yuen refused. Mr. Yuen's lawyers described this as "a campaign to take over Gemstar and oust Dr. Yuen" in court filings, but News Corporation officials and lawyers deny this. They say they became increasingly concerned that Gemstar, under Mr. Yuen and Ms. Leung's direction, was overstating the growth prospects for the electronic publishing guides.

The Gemstar board began an internal investigation that led to revenue restatements that would total some $330 million. As the accounting issues became public in 2002. Gemstar's stock withered and the boardroom turned venomous, Mr. Yuen and Mr. Murdock met several times—accompanied only by Mr. Arkin on Mr. Yuen's side or Mr. Chernin with Mr. Murdoch—to negotiate a graceful exit for Mr. Yuen.

Those negotiations led to Mr. Yuen's and Ms. Leung's departures in November 2002. But to Mr. Yuen's surprise, a nearly $30 million severance negotiated with Mr. Murdoch was placed in escrow by Gemstar at the behest of the S.E.C.

Mr. Yuen has admitted that shortly after Gemstar received a broad subpoena from the S.E.C., he deleted information from a hard drive in his Gemstar office, including e-mail and corporate documents. Then, the day before he was scheduled to testify before the S.E.C., Mr. Yuen installed a program that erased other files. A week later, he had the hard drive removed from his office, according to the criminal plea he entered into last year.

Mr. Yuen's lawyers say this was an error in judgment, not an admission that he had committed fraud. In pleading guilty to the obstruction charge last October, Mr. Yuen had agreed to serve six months of home detention and spend two years on probation. But both the S.E.C. and Gemstar in its victim's brief, petitioned a federal district judge, John Walter, to reject the deal.

Richard L. Stone, a lawyer for Gemstar with Hogan & Hartson in Los Angeles, argued that as a result of the conduct by Mr. Yuen and others, Gemstar had already paid more than $70 million to settle shareholder lawsuits, plus a $10 million fine to the S.E.C.

In addition to the billions of dollars in market value Gemstar's shareholders had lost, Mr. Stone said, Gemstar has incurred more than $100 million in legal fees related to investigating and pursuing Mr. Yuen.

In December 2005, Judge Walter rejected the terms of the plea and Mr. Yuen withdrew it.

Last year Mr. Yuen struck a deal with the S.E.C. under which he would have paid some $14 million and avoided trial. But Mr. Yuen insisted that the money come from the frozen $30 million severance. When the judge rejected that request, Mr. Yuen told his lawyer, "I have no other funds." This was unexpected, given that, among other earnings, Mr. Yuen had sold $59 million of Gemstar stock in the spring of 2002.

The S.E.C.'s case against Mr. Yuen proceeded to trial, where he and Ms. Leung testified that he did not knowingly order or commit any accounting fraud. In her ruling against Mr. Yuen on March 20, Judge Pfaeizer wrote that she "did not find the testimony of either Yuen or Leung to be persuasive or credible."

All the others implicated in the Gemstar troubles, including Ms. Leung; Gemstar's auditor, KPMG; and three other former Gemstar executives have agreed to settle the S.E.C. claims against them. KPMG had paid $10 million, and Ms. Leung has agreed to pay $1.35 million.

For Mr. Murdoch's company, one of the scars from its involvement with Mr. Yuen is a deal it concluded with Mr. Malone shortly after the merger, in September 2000. Mr. Malone traded his 21 percent interest in Gemstar-TV Guide for a roughly 12 percent nonvoting interest in the News Corporation that, combined with 6 percent he already held, made him the conglomerate's largest shareholder outside the Murdoch family Given the coming collapse in Gemstar shares, that proved to be a brilliant move for Mr. Malone. Two years ago, he surprised Mr. Murdoch by converting his stock into voting shares. Last year, Mr. Murdoch put in place a poison pill to stave off his erstwhile friend and partner.

Gemstar now occupies a relatively quiet corner of the News Corporation. Mr. Murdoch's and Mr. Yuen's vision for the electronic programming guide as a major money maker has yet to materialize. Gemstar shares closed on Friday at $3.06, down from $41 in 2000.

Mr. Yuen has spent much of his time since Gemstar at a house in the Pasadena hills and at another house in Laguna Beach, Calif. People close to Mr. Yuen wonder why he did not move on from Gemstar while he had the chance. Had he taken the buyout offers for the company in the late 1990's he would have walked away with $300 million.

Another former member of Gemstar's management team, who, like others interviewed for this article asked not to be identified because of the litigation surrounding Mr. Yuen, recalled asking Mr. Yuen shortly after the merger with TV Guide why he had not cashed out. Mr. Yuen's response: "Sitting at the beach with all that money is my idea of hell."

Questions for Discussion

1. Based on the material in the case and the chapter content, how would you describe Henry Yuen's personality?
2. How might his personality and the situation he was in have contributed to his actions at Gemstar?
3. How would you characterize his abilities?
4. Based on the information in the case, do you think he is high or low on emotional intelligence? Why? Be specific.

The New York Times

Served as King of England, Said the Résumé

By Matt Villano, March 19, 2006, Section 3, p. 9

Q. *You need to update your résumé. To what degree is it acceptable to embellish your skills and experience?*

A. A résumé is your best shot at persuading prospective employers to meet you in person and learn more about you, but if you veer from the truth, you're out of line.

"A résumé can be attention-grabbing, startling, interesting, intriguing, provocative, entertaining, wry, amusing or funny," said Barry A. Liebling, president of Liebling Associates, a management consulting firm in New York. "But all of that means nothing if the content isn't real."

Q. *How often do people falsify résumés?*

A. Evidently, fairly often Nick Fishman, executive vice president of Background Information Services, a pre-employment screening company in Cleveland, said his organization found that 56 percent of résumés contained falsehoods of some kind. "When you consider these numbers," Mr. Fishman said. "if you're not the one who's falsifying something, your neighbor probably is."

Even high-level employees sometimes engage in false advertising. Last month, for example, David J. Edmondson, the former chief executive of Radio Shack, the electronics retail chain based in Fort Worth, resigned after acknowledging that he had claimed to have two college degrees but actually had none.

Q. *Why do people lie on their résumés?*

A. "Most applicants do it because they are insecure about their experiences and want to seem more qualified," said Robert S. Feldman, professor of psychology at the University of Massachusetts in Amherst. "When we want to try to be likable, we shade things to put them in the best possible light," Mr. Feldman said. "Unless people are pretty sure that résumé is going to be checked, it's tempting to shade reality and make one's prior experiences more flowery."

Rachel Weingarten, president of GTK Marketing Group, an entertainment marketing firm in Brooklyn, says one lie begets another. "With a lot of people, when they first put in something that's untrue, it's not a grandiose lie, but instead a minor detail," she said. "Over time, they add to it until they've got a completely different experience, and they believe every word."

Q. *Which facts are commonly misrepresented?*

A. You name it, people have made it up. A 2003 survey by the Society of Human Resource Management, a trade association in Alexandria, Va., found that 44 percent of 2.6 million respondents said they had misstated their work experience on their résumés. And a 2004 report by the Federal Bureau of Investigation estimated, based on a sampling, that 500,000 people in the United States had listed false college degrees on their résumés and work applications.

Donna Flagg, a principal of the Krysalis Group, a human resources consulting firm in New York, said grade point averages were often liberally rounded upward, turning a 3.6 into a 4.0.

Then there's the nebulous timeline, which Michelle Roccia, vice president of Human Resources at Authoria, a staffing company in Waltham, Mass., described as stretching the duration of employment to eliminate gaps.

"A candidate might say they worked at a company 'from 2004–2005,' but in fact, that person only worked at the company from November 2004 to January 2005, which is hardly a full year," Ms. Roccia said.

People also tend to exaggerate their skills. Anna Ivey, author of "The Ivey Guide to Law School Admissions" (Harcourt, 2005), says unscrupulous applicants may falsely claim knowledge of a language or a computer program.

"All it takes is one interviewer who happens to speak the language to call your bluff, and that one fudge undermines the credibility of everything else you say about yourself," Ms. Ivey, who lives in Orlando, Fla., said.

Q. *Is it wrong to omit certain facts or experiences to disguise age?*

A. If the information on your résumé is accurate, you are free to leave in or take out whatever you like. George F. Brenila, a partner at the New York law firm Clifton Budd & DeMaria, said it was perfectly acceptable to list a degree that you earned from a particular school without revealing when you received it. Under the Civil Rights Act and the Age Discrimination in Employment Act, "he said, the only age-related question employers are legally allowed to ask is whether an applicant is over 18."

"Disguising age might look suspicious," he said, "but it's perfectly within an employee's rights under the law."

Q. *What precautions should you expect an employer to take against fraud?*

A. The federal Fair Credit Reporting Act allows employers to verify everything on an applicant's résumé. Many managers run simple background checks on the Internet before the hiring process concludes. On rare occasions, a company will retain a screening company to verify a résumé after an employee has been hired.

Vance, an investigation and security firm in Oakton, Va., requires its new hires to sign documents indicating that everything on their résumé and job application is true. Drew McKay, senior vice president and deputy general counsel, said that a later discovery that an employee had violated this contract was clear grounds for termination.

"Our system is all about the facts," Mr. McKay said. "If you tell the truth from the beginning, you have nothing to worry about."

Questions for Discussion

1. How is the management of ability in organizations affected when job applicants lie on their résumés?
2. In what ways can lying on resumes hurt job applicants?
3. How does lying on resumes affect employers?
4. Why do some people feel the need to lie on their resumes?

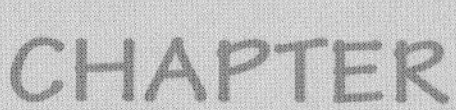

VALUES, ATTITUDES, AND MOODS AND EMOTIONS

Learning Objectives

After studying this chapter, you should be able to:

- Describe the nature of work values and ethical values and why they are of critical importance in organizations.
- Understand why it is important to understand employees' moods and emotions on the job.
- Appreciate when and why emotional labor occurs in organizations.
- Describe the nature, causes, theories, and consequences of job satisfaction.
- Appreciate the distinction between affective commitment and continuance commitment and their implications for understanding organizational behavior.

Opening Case

A WINNING FORMULA AT VALERO ENERGY

How can an old-economy company transform itself, prosper, and be good to its employees?

A decade ago, no one would have thought that San Antonio, Texas-based Valero Energy—with a single oil refinery processing low-cost, sour crude oil—would become the powerhouse it is today. In the ensuing years, Valero CEO and now chairman, Bill Greehey, proceeded to buy up unwanted refineries from other companies at a fraction of their replacement costs. Today, Valero is the largest oil refiner in the United States with 18 refineries, mostly focused on sour crude oil.[1] Valero's revenues and profits have soared.[2] And while this success is clearly driven by a combination of good business decisions and market conditions, it is also driven by the important values and attitudes that pervade the company and all it does.

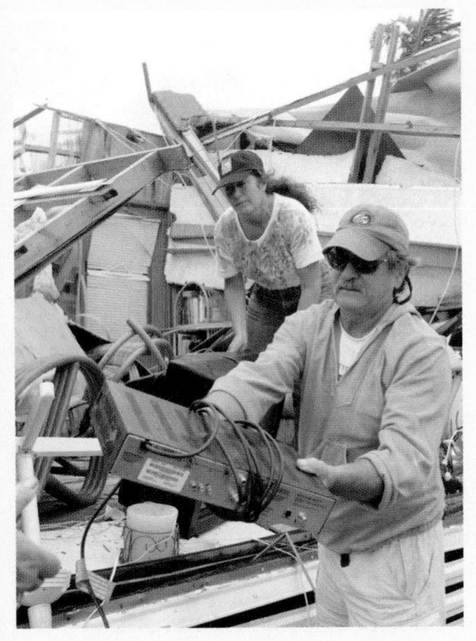

Valero Energy demonstrated its commitment to its employees in the wake of Hurricane Katrina, which hit the Louisiana coastline in 2005. In addition to delivering supplies, water, and food to employees, Valero brought in mobile homes for those employees and their families whose homes were unlivable.

Greehey values his employees—so much so, that they come first, before shareholders and customers. As he puts it, ". . . the more you do for your employees, the more they do for shareholders and the more they do for the community."[3] While devastating accidents have plagued some other oil companies in recent years, Valero ranks safety among one of its core values. The company installed new safety equipment in the refineries it purchased and pursues safety relentlessly; any intentional violation of safety rules on the part of managers or employees results in dismissal.[4]

Greehey realizes that employees are the backbone of Valero and is committed to doing right by them. Not only does Valero provide employees with generous benefits, it also has a no-layoff policy. Managers are expected to treat employees with respect and like they would want to be treated themselves; managers who show a lack of respect for their subordinates, treat them with condescension, or, for example, curse at them can lose their jobs.[5]

The values and attitudes that pervade Valero were put to the test in the wake of Hurricane Katrina, which hit the Louisiana coastline in 2005. The remarkable ways in which employees stood by each other and the company, and the ways in which Valero stood by its employees, literally brought long-time employee and plant manager for Valero's St. Charles oil refinery near New Orleans, Jonathan Stuart, to tears when he was briefing Greehey and other key executives on how the refinery and its employees had fared a few days after the hurricane had wrought its destruction. Stuart headed up a 50-person crew that rode out the storm in the shut-down refinery.[6]

The crew stood by Valero and Valero stood by its employees. For example, the day before the hurricane hit, a supervisor used his own personal credit card to purchase supplies and stayed up all night cooking meals for the crew. Crew members worked twenty-hour days, replacing motors, putting up new power poles, and repairing power lines. Within eight days, the plant was up and running (while a neighboring Shell refinery was still shut down); at the same time, the crew had determined the whereabouts of all the plant's 570 employees.[7]

Back in San Antonio, headquarters arranged for supplies to be delivered to employees whose homes were devastated and trucks brought in water, food, chain saws, generators, refrigerators, shovels, and Nextel phones (the only cell phone system that remained operable). For employees whose homes were unlivable, 60 mobile homes were brought in. The company provided free fuel to employees and law enforcement personnel and the Valero SAFE fund provided employees with up to $10,000 in aid. Valero continued to pay its employees while other refineries stopped issuing pay checks. Melvin Edgar, a security supervisor, who spent two days on the roof of his house in the Gentilly section of New Orleans before being rescued and brought to the over-crowded Superdome, lined up for a bus there to take him to San Antonio. When he arrived, he called Valero, and office services manager Robert Pena picked him up, took him shopping for clothes, took him for a meal, and then took Edgar to his own home to shower and get some sleep. The next day, Pena drove Edgar back to St. Charles so Edgar could find his family. Recalling the experience, Edgar says, "I wanted to get back to find my family and get back to work. If it wasn't for Valero, Lord knows where I'd be."[8]

Clearly, Valero and Greehey came through for employees and the community during the aftermath of Katrina with flying colors. And the company's commitment to its employees shows through in their commitment to the company and high levels of job satisfaction. Not surprisingly, in 2006, Valero Energy ranked number 3 in *Fortune's 100 Best Companies to Work For.*[9] In explaining why Valero is a great company, Fortune wrote "When disaster strikes, this team pulls together. After hurricanes Katrina and Rita hit, Valero dispatched semis filled with supplies, set up temporary housing for employees, fed volunteers—and donated $1 million to the Red Cross."[10]

Overview

What people think and feel about work in general, and about their jobs and organizations in particular, affects not only how they behave at work but also their overall well-being—how happy, healthy, and prosperous they are. From the opening case, it is clear that employees at Valero are not only satisfied with their jobs and committed to the organization, but that Valero stands by and is committed to its employees and their own well-being. In this chapter, we focus on the thoughts and feelings that determine how people experience work and the ways in which these thoughts and feelings affect organizational behavior. We discuss values, attitudes, and moods and emotions—the different types of thoughts and feelings people have about work in general and about their jobs and organizations in particular. We describe the nature and consequences of two of the most widely studied work attitudes: job satisfaction and organizational commitment. By the end of this chapter, you will have a good appreciation of the range of thoughts and feelings central to the experience of work and the implications of these thoughts and feelings for understanding and managing organizational behavior.

Values, Attitudes, and Moods and Emotions

The thoughts and feelings people have about work, their jobs, and their organizations determine how they experience work. Some thoughts and feelings are fundamental and broad; they are concerned not so much with aspects of a particular job or organization but more with the meaning and nature of work itself. These thoughts and feelings, called *values*, are relatively long lasting. Other thoughts and feelings are more specific. Those that are focused directly on a person's current job or organization, called *work attitudes*, are not as long lasting as values. *Work moods and emotions*—that is, how people feel while they are performing their jobs from day to day, hour to hour, and even minute to minute—also determine how they experience work. Next we describe each of these determinants of how people experience work.

The Nature of Values

VALUES
One's personal convictions about what one should strive for in life and how one should behave.

Values are one's personal convictions about what one should strive for in life and how one should behave.[11] From the opening case, it is clear that Bill Greehey's values include providing a safe working environment for Valero's employees, putting them first, and looking out for them and their communities in times of need. While researchers have identified multiple values ranging from a world at peace and a world of beauty to a comfortable life and social recognition, two kinds of values that are especially relevant to organizational behavior are work values and ethical values (see Exhibit 3.1; in Chapter 17, we describe another type of important values: national values).

WORK VALUES
An employee's personal convictions about what outcomes one should expect from work and how one should behave at work.

Work Values. **Work values** are an employee's personal convictions about what outcomes one should expect from work and how one should behave at work. Outcomes that people might expect to obtain through work include a comfortable existence with family security, a sense of accomplishment and self-respect, social recognition, and an exciting life.[12] Ways people think they should behave at work include being ambitious, imaginative, obedient, self-controlled, and respectful to others.[13] Work values are general and long-lasting feelings and beliefs people have that contribute to how they experience work.

Why are work values important for understanding and managing organizational behavior? They reflect what people are trying to achieve through and at work. An employee who thinks that he or she should learn new things on the job, for example, will be unhappy working as a cashier in a supermarket because, once he or she has learned how to use the cash register, there will be little opportunity for any further learning. His or her unhappiness may, in turn, cause him or her to be less helpful to customers or more likely to look for another job.

The work values that researchers in organizational behavior have identified generally fall into two broad categories: intrinsic work values and extrinsic work values (see Exhibit 3.2).[14]

EXHIBIT 3.1

Values in the Workplace

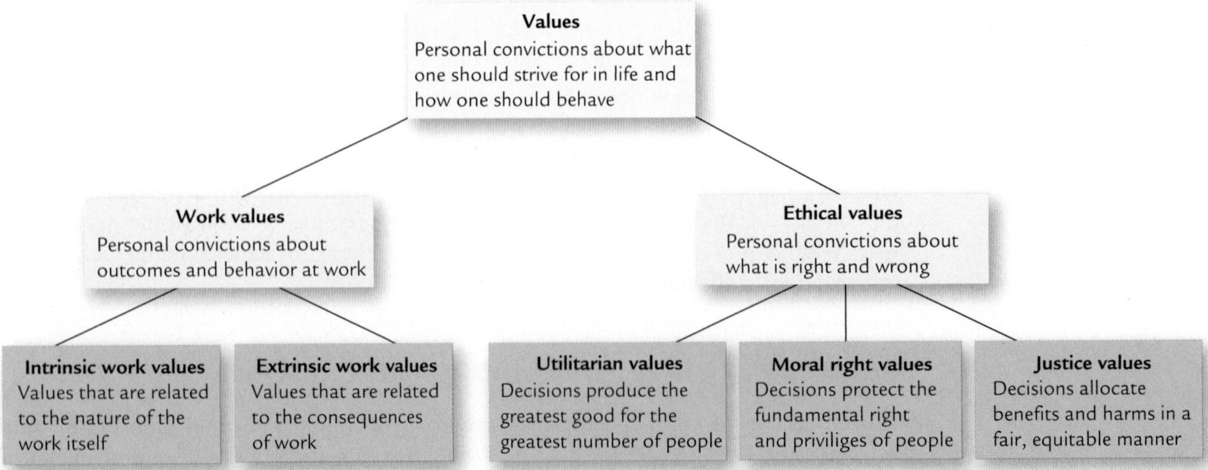

EXHIBIT 3.2

A Comparison of Intrinsic and Extrinsic Work Values

Intrinsic Work Values	Extrinsic Work Values
Interesting work	High pay
Challenging work	Job security
Learning new things	Job benefits
Making important contributions	Status in wider community
Reaching full potential at work	Social contacts
Responsibility and autonomy	Time with family
Being creative	Time for hobbies

INTRINSIC WORK VALUES
Work values that are related to the nature of work itself.

Intrinsic work values are values that are related to the nature of the work itself. Employees who desire to be challenged, learn new things, make important contributions, and reach their full potential on their jobs have intrinsic work values. These employees want challenging jobs that use all of their skills and abilities and provide them with responsibility and autonomy (the ability to make decisions), while at the same time giving them opportunities for personal growth. Employees who desire adventure, being creative, or helping other people also are satisfying intrinsic work values because the work they perform, whether it be building new businesses, composing a new symphony, or helping a troubled teen, is what is important to them.

EXTRINSIC WORK VALUES
Work values that are related to the consequences of work.

Rather than valuing features of the work itself, some employees have **extrinsic work values**, values that are related to the consequences of work. Employees whose primary reason for working is to earn money, for example, have extrinsic work values. They see work primarily as a means of providing economic security for themselves and their families. These employees value their work not for its own sake but for its consequences. Other extrinsic work values include a job's status in the organization and in the wider community, social contacts provided by the job, and the extent to which a job enables an employee to spend time with his or her family, pursue a hobby, or volunteer for a worthy cause.

Because working is the way most people make a living, there is an extrinsic element to most people's work values, but many people have both extrinsic and intrinsic work values. Extrinsic and intrinsic work values differ in their relative importance from one person to another. An elementary schoolteacher who likes teaching but quits her job to take a higher-paying position as a sales representative for a computer company has stronger extrinsic than intrinsic work values. A social worker who puts up with low pay and little thanks because he feels that he is doing something important by helping disadvantaged families and their children has stronger intrinsic than extrinsic work values.

When making changes in the workplace, managers need to take into account employees' values. Managers may try to increase employees' motivation by making their work more interesting, giving them more freedom to make their own decisions, or expanding the number of activities they perform (see Chapters 6, 7, and 8 for details on motivation). A manager might try to increase the motivation of a computer sales representative by requiring her to call on different types of customers and by giving her the responsibility for setting up the equipment a customer purchases.

The success of such approaches to increasing motivation, however, depends on the extent to which the change in an employee's job relates to the employee's values. Making the work of the computer sales representative more interesting and challenging may do little to increase her motivation if her strong extrinsic work values result in her being motivated primarily by the money she earns. Indeed, these efforts may actually backfire if the sales representative thinks she is working harder on her job but not receiving any additional financial compensation. Employees who are extrinsically motivated may be much more responsive to financial incentives (such as bonuses) and job security than to changes in the work itself.

Because work values reflect what employees are trying to achieve through working, they hold the key to understanding how employees will react to different events in the workplace and to understanding and managing organizational behavior. Managers need to be especially sensitive to the work values of their subordinates when making changes in jobs, working hours, or other aspects of the work situation.

ETHICAL VALUES
One's personal convictions about what is right and wrong.

Ethical Values **Ethical values** are one's personal convictions about what is right and wrong. Ethical values help employees decide on the right course of action and guide their decision making and behavior.[15] Especially in situations in which the proper course of action is unclear, ethical values help employees make moral decisions. Some ethical values are focused on an individual's conduct and whether it is right or wrong, such as being honest or trustworthy.[16]

Other kinds of ethical values come into play when a person must decide how to make decisions that have the potential to benefit or harm other individuals or groups. These ethical values are especially important guides for behavior when a decision may benefit one individual or group to the detriment of another.[17] For example, when major corporations like Eastman Kodak announce plans to layoff thousands of employees due to lower demand for their products and services, the stock price of shares in these companies often rises.[18] Fewer employees means fewer costs and greater profitability. The workforce reduction benefits shareholders of the corporation because the value of their stock has increased, but it hurts those employees whose jobs have been or will be cut.

UTILITARIAN VALUES
Values that dictate that decisions should be made that generate the greatest good for the greatest number of people.

Utilitarian, moral rights, and justice values are complementary guides for decision making and behavior when a decision or action has the potential to benefit or harm others.[19] **Utilitarian values** dictate that decisions should be made that generate the greatest good for the greatest number of people. **Moral rights values** indicate that decisions should be made in ways that protect the fundamental rights and privileges of people affected by the decision, such as their freedom, safety, and privacy. **Justice values** dictate that decisions should be made in ways that allocate benefit and harm among those affected by the decision in a fair, equitable, or impartial manner.[20]

MORAL RIGHTS VALUES
Values that dictate that decisions should be made so that the decisions produce the greatest good for the greatest number of people.

JUSTICE VALUES
Values that dictate that decisions should be made in ways that allocate benefit and harm among those affected by the decisions in a fair, equitable, or impartial manner.

Each kind of ethical value should be taken into account when evaluating whether or not a course of action is an ethical one. Even with these values as guides, employees are often faced with ethical dilemmas because the interests of those who might be affected by the decision are often in conflict and it is not always clear how to determine, for example, how to weigh the benefits and costs of different groups to determine the greatest good, which rights and privileges must be safeguarded, and what is a fair or ethical decision.[21] For example, what sort of job security do loyal and hardworking employees deserve? What does the corporation owe its shareholders in terms of profits?

People develop their own individual ethical values over time based on influences from family, peers, schooling, religious institutions, and other groups.[22] As employees, these ethical values guide their behavior in the workplace. Sometimes different groups of employees or people holding certain kinds of jobs or professions develop what are called professional ethics.[23] Physicians, lawyers, and university professors have professional ethics that dictate appropriate and inappropriate behaviors. Societal ethics, embodied in laws, customs, practices, and values, apply to a society as a whole.

CODE OF ETHICS
A set of formal rules and standards, based on ethical values and beliefs about what is right and wrong, that employees can use to make appropriate decisions when the interests of other individuals or groups are at stake.

Individual ethics, professional ethics, and societal ethics all contribute to an organization's code of ethics. A **code of ethics** is the set of formal rules and standards, based on ethical values and beliefs about what is right and wrong, that employees can use to make appropriate decisions when the interests of other individuals or groups are at stake.[24] Recent corporate scandals, allegations of wrongdoing, and fraud at companies such as WorldCom, Enron, Tyco, Adelphia, and ImClone[25] have resulted in many organizations taking active steps to ensure that employees behave in an ethical manner and their codes of ethics are followed. However, some of the organizations in which the most egregious instances of fraud have recently occurred actually did have codes of ethics.[26] The problem was that they were not followed, and outside parties such as auditors, bankers, analysts, and lenders did not intervene when they should have. Rather, as in the case of Enron, it took the courageous action of a whistleblower (Sherron Watkins) to bring the wrongdoing to light.[27] A **whistleblower** is a person who informs people in positions of authority and/or the public of instances of wrongdoing, illegal behavior, or unethical behavior in an organization.[28] As the accompanying Managing Ethically feature illustrates, having a code of ethics only results in ethical behavior when it is followed and enforced.

WHISTLEBLOWER
A person who informs people in positions of authority and/or the public of instances of wrongdoing, illegal behavior, or unethical behavior in an organization.

Managing Ethically

When Codes of Ethics Fail

Enron had a code of ethics and a conflict-of-interest policy that, if followed, should have prevented the downfall of this once high-flying company. However, its board of directors waived the code and policy to allow Enron managers to form the off-balance-sheet partnerships that destroyed the company.[29] At Tyco, one of the lawyers in charge of compliance with ethics policies has been accused of falsifying records. Arthur Andersen LLP, Enron's auditing firm, was convicted of obstruction of justice for destruction of documents pertaining to Enron's audits. Ironically, prior to the conviction, Arthur Andersen routinely performed ethics consulting services for clients.[30]

The former chief financial officer of Enron Corp., Andrew S. Fastow is escorted in the custody of the FBI to the federal courthouse Wednesday, Oct. 2, 2002 in Houston. Fastow surrendered to FBI agents as prosecutors were expected to file.

"Ethical failures usually are not the result of people not knowing the law or regulations. It is because they felt a variety of other pressures," explains Barbara Lee Toffler, an ethics expert and professor at Columbia University's business school. [31] It is because of these pressures that the federal government passed the Sarbanes-Oxley Act of 2002, which has dramatically increased the reporting and accountability obligations of public companies and also requires independence on the part of a company's audit committees.[32] The act also provides protections for whistleblowers and has increased the criminal penalties for those engaging in white-collar crime. The act has been called, "the most dramatic change to federal securities laws since the 1930s."[33]

Does passage of the Sarbanes-Oxley Act override the need for an organization to have a code of ethics? Absolutely not. Rather, the act not only requires a code of ethics be enacted, but it also mandates strict adherence to it. It also requires that organizations have ethics programs in place.[34] If a company is convicted of fraud, the penalties might be reduced if the firm can document it had implemented programs to encourage ethical behavior and detect fraud. Many organizations such as Ford Motor Co. and Johnson & Johnson are stepping up their ethics training for all employees through the use of Web-based programs offered by companies such as Integrity Interactive Corp. and Legal Knowledge Co.[35] A number of nonprofit organizations, such as the National Whistleblower Association, formed in 1988, provide assistance to would-be whistleblowers.[36] Hopefully, heightened public awareness of the potential for corporate wrongdoing, penalties for those convicted of white-collar crimes, enforcement of the Sarbanes-Oxley Act, and protection for would-be whistleblowers will reduce the incidence of unethical behavior in organizations.

The Nature of Work Attitudes

WORK ATTITUDES Collections of feelings, beliefs, and thoughts about how to behave in one's job and organization.

Work attitudes are collections of feelings, beliefs, and thoughts about how to behave that people currently hold about their jobs and organizations. Work attitudes are more specific than values and not as long lasting because the way people experience their jobs often changes over time. For example, a person's work situation might be altered due to a job transfer or being given or denied a promotion. As a result, his or her work attitudes might change, too. Values, in contrast, can and often do remain constant from job to job and organization to organization. Two work attitudes that have especially important implications for organizational behavior are job satisfaction and organizational commitment.

JOB SATISFACTION The collection of feelings and beliefs that people have about their current jobs.

Job satisfaction is the collection of feelings and beliefs that people have about their current jobs. People's levels or degrees of job satisfaction can range from extreme satisfaction to extreme dissatisfaction. In addition to having attitudes about their jobs as a whole, people also can have attitudes about various aspects of their jobs such as the kind of work they do; their coworkers, supervisors, or subordinates; and their pay.

ORGANIZATIONAL COMMITMENT The collection of feelings and beliefs that people have about their organization as a whole.

Organizational commitment is the collection of feelings and beliefs that people have about their organization as a whole. Levels of commitment can range from being extremely high to extremely low, and people can have attitudes about various aspects of their organization such as the organization's promotion practices, the quality of the organization's products, and the organization's stance on ethical issues.

Work attitudes, like job satisfaction and organizational commitment, are made up of three components: feelings, the affective component; beliefs, the cognitive component; and thoughts about how to behave, the behavioral component (see Exhibit 3.3).[37] For example, the *affective component* of an employee's attitude is the employee's *feelings* about his or her job or organization. The *cognitive component* is the employee's *beliefs* about the job or organization—that is, whether or not he or she believes the job is meaningful and important. The *behavioral component* is the employee's *thoughts* about how to behave in his or her job or organization. Each component of a work attitude influences and tends to be consistent with the other components.

Because job satisfaction and organizational commitment are key determinants of the experience of work and central to understanding and managing organizational behavior, we explore these two work attitudes in depth later in the chapter.

The Nature of Moods and Emotions

WORK MOOD How people feel at the time they actually perform their jobs.

Work mood describes how people feel at the time they actually perform their jobs. Some employees tend to feel excited and enthusiastic at work, whereas others feel anxious and nervous, and still others feel sleepy and sluggish. Much more transitory than values and attitudes, work moods can change from hour to hour, day to day, and sometimes minute to minute. Think about how your own moods have varied since you

EXHIBIT 3.3

Components of Work Attitudes

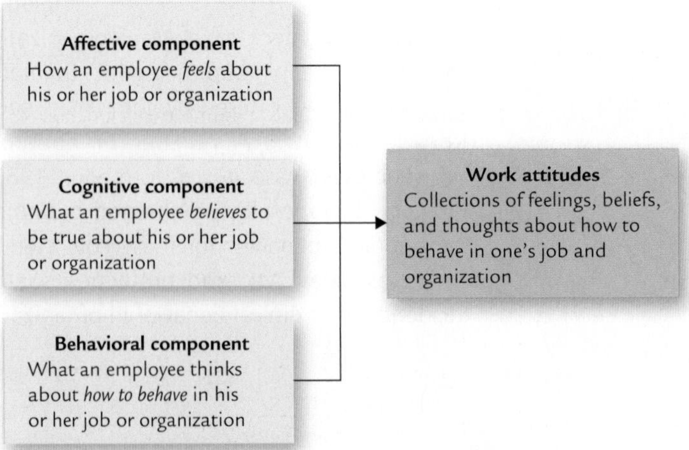

A wide range of situational factors can result in employees such as these experiencing positive moods ranging from pleasant interactions with coworkers to receiving positive feedback and successfully completing a project.

woke up today or about how your moods today differ from how you felt yesterday. Then you will have some idea about the fluctuating nature of work moods.

Although people can experience different moods at work, moods can be categorized generally as positive or negative. When employees are in *positive moods*, they feel excited, enthusiastic, active, strong, peppy, or elated.[38] When employees are in *negative moods*, they feel distressed, fearful, scornful, hostile, jittery, or nervous.[39] Sometimes employees' feelings are neither strongly positive nor strongly negative; they may simply experience less intense feelings such as being drowsy, dull, and sluggish or calm, placid, and relaxed.[40] The extent to which employees experience positive, negative, and less intense moods at work is determined by both their personalities and the specific situation.

Recall from Chapter 2 that employees who are high on the personality trait of *positive affectivity* are more likely than other employees to experience positive moods at work, and employees who are high on the trait of *negative affectivity* are more likely to experience negative moods at work. A wide range of situational factors also affects work mood—major events and conditions, such as receiving a promotion (or a demotion) and getting along well with one's coworkers, and relatively minor conditions, such as how pleasant the physical surroundings are.[41] If you stop and think a minute about the different factors that influence your own moods—weather, pressures of school or family life, your love life, and so on—you will see that many of them, though unrelated to work, nonetheless have the potential to influence an employee's mood on the job. Getting engaged, for example, may put an employee in a very good mood both on and off the job, but having a big argument with one's spouse may put an employee in a very bad mood.

WORKPLACE INCIVILITY Rude interpersonal behaviors reflective of a lack of regard and respect for others.

Preliminary research suggests that **workplace incivility**, rude interpersonal behaviors reflective of a lack of regard and respect for others, may be on the rise, which can lead to more negative moods being experienced by organizational members.[42] The increasing use of e-mail and phone conversations in place of face-to-face communications and mounting workloads and pressures on many employees has resulted in some managers and employees being uncivil to each other and just plain rude.[43] Office incivility can range from ignoring a coworker or subordinate, making rude comments, or never having the time for even a brief conversation to raising one's voice, being sarcastic, refusing requests for help, and verbal belittlement. When organizational members are uncivil toward each other, there can be potentially numerous negative consequences in addition to the recipients of such behavior feeling bad, such as reduced job satisfaction and lower organizational effectiveness.[44]

Research suggests that mood at work has important consequences for understanding and managing organizational behavior.[45] Employees in positive moods at work, for example, are more likely to be helpful to each other and those around them, including clients and customers, and they may also be less likely to be absent from their jobs.[46] One study found that salespeople who were in positive moods at work provided higher-quality service to customers in a department store than did salespeople who were not in positive moods.[47] Another study found that the extent to which leaders (in this case, managers of small retail stores) experienced positive moods was related to the performance levels of their subordinates (the salespeople in the stores).[48] (Leadership is the subject of Chapter 12.) Research has also found that moods influence important behaviors such as creativity, decision making, and the accuracy of judgments.[49]

Recent studies suggest that the influence that moods have on behaviors is likely to depend on the situation or context, too.[50] For example, some studies have found that people in positive moods are more likely to come up with unusual word associations, which has been used to index creativity.[51] The reasoning in these studies is that positive moods result in people thinking more broadly or expansively. However, other studies have found that being in a negative mood sometimes fosters creativity. For example, when employees are striving to be creative on the job, and have to determine for themselves how well they are doing or when they have to come up with a creative idea under pressure, people in negative moods tend to demand more of themselves and put forth more effort to be creative.[52] Whether positive moods, negative moods, or both lead to creativity appears to depend on situational factors such as the goals or objectives that are being sought, the extent to which people receive clear feedback about how they are doing, and the nature of the tasks they are working on.[53] Similarly, we know that positive and negative moods influence decision making. Again, however, the exact nature of that influence depends on situational factors such as the kind of decision being made, the goals of the decision maker, and the kinds of information available to the decision maker.

Clearly, work moods can have important effects on organizational behavior. Moreover, because managers and organizations can do many things to promote positive moods—for example, giving people attractive offices to work in, giving praise when it is deserved, providing employees with opportunities for social interaction, and incorporating fun and humor into the workplace—work moods are receiving more attention from researchers and managers alike. Additionally, since all employees are likely to experience negative moods at some time or another on the job, it is important to understand the consequences of those bad feelings and how they might be channeled into effective behaviors. (For more on understanding and managing moods, see the discussion of emotional intelligence in Chapter 2.)

Moods tend to be general and pervasive feelings that do not interrupt employees' thoughts or behaviors. Emotions, by contrast, are much more intense than moods. **Emotions** are intense, short-lived feelings that are linked to a specific cause or antecedent and interrupt thought processes and behaviors. Emotions have adaptive, evolutionary value in that they signal to people that something has happened or will happen that has implications for personal well-being.[54] Thus, emotions alert us to things we need to pay attention to and things we need to do. For example, the fear a newly hired office worker experiences upon hearing that her company has had a really bad fourth quarter and is about to layoff employees interrupts her ongoing work as she thinks about how she should deal with this potential threat (e.g., try to find out more information, update her résumé, start looking for other jobs). Researchers have identified basic emotions that have universal nonverbal expressions such as anger, disgust, sadness, fear, surprise, and happiness.[55] Preliminary research suggests that certain other emotions such as pride also have universal nonverbal expressions.[56]

EMOTIONS
Intense short-lived feelings that are linked to a specific cause or antecedent.

Over time, emotions can feed into moods.[57] For example, if a manager engages in workplace incivility by berating a subordinate in front of coworkers, the subordinate may initially feel strong emotions of anger or shame. As time goes by, the intense emotion may subside and feed into a less intense negative mood that the subordinate experiences for the remainder of the day, coloring his or her thoughts, feelings, and behaviors. As another example, take the case of Mary and Paul Putnam, a dual-career couple who work in different states and have been commuting on weekends to see each other. Both of the Putnams have been trying to relocate to eliminate their long-distance marriage, and they have agreed that whoever finds an acceptable position first will make the move. Recently, Paul received a phone call indicating that he was offered a position in a company close to where Mary is working. It is just what he has been looking for. Paul is ecstatic and puts what he has been working on aside. He is thrilled and calls Mary, and the two count their blessings for their good fortune. A short while later, Paul realizes he must get back to work and finish a report that is due to his boss the following day; throughout the day, Paul is in a great mood, even when he is not thinking about his new job.

For Sir Richard Branson, the flamboyant founder and chief executive of Virgin Group Ltd., positive emotions and moods stem from pursuing his love of adventure, starting new businesses, and enjoying his family life, as profiled in the following Global View.

Global View

Richard Branson Thrives on Excitement

Richard Branson, the maverick founder and chief executive of Virgin Group Ltd., describes his own experience of work as follows, "I don't think of work as work and play as play. It's all living I'm living and learning every day."[58] Living and learning for Branson means indulging his endless curiosity, being adventuresome, having fun, and filling each day with a seamless integration of work and family life.

British-born Branson, a high-school dropout, has grown the Virgin Group into an over $7 billion global collection of over 200 companies, each with its own CEO and board of directors. These companies are truly a diverse lot ranging from records (Virgin Records) and airlines (Virgin Atlantic) to retail goods, cell phones, and consumer electronics.[59] Potential new ventures range from grape fermenting and oil refining to space travel (Virgin Galactic is taking reservations for space travel planned to lift off in 2008).[60] Some of his companies are very successful and others not so successful, but Branson clearly has had enough success to continue to pursue new businesses that strike his fancy; his net worth is estimated to be over $2.5 billion.[61]

Sir Richard Branson, founder and chief executive of Virgin Group Ltd., thrives on excitement, adventure, living life to its fullest, and starting new businesses.

Branson thrives on adventure, taking risks, and enjoying life to its fullest. He can't stand being bored and always likes to be doing something. In terms of his career, that means building new businesses in diverse locations around the globe.[62] Of course, he wants these businesses to be successful but not so much for financial gain as to enable him to keep doing what he loves—learning about new businesses and diving in head-first.[63] Branson also values his family time and often works from home when he is not traveling. He typically wakes up early in the morning and does some work, then has time with his family, then works some more—work and family life are often intertwined. He seems to thrive on a relentless stream of activity including hot air ballooning and tennis.[64] For all his love of adventure and fun, Branson also keeps a close eye on his businesses.[65] Perhaps it is the combination of intense involvement and commitment with a love of surprise and adventure that explains Branson's accomplishments. One thing is certain—he has enjoyed every minute of it.

On certain kinds of jobs, it is important that employees express certain kinds of moods and emotions and refrain from expressing other kinds. For example, waiters, flight attendants, and cheerleaders are expected to display positive moods and emotions, like enthusiasm and pleasure, and refrain from experiencing negative moods and emotions, like anger and hostility. Thus, no matter how distressed these employees might be for a variety of reasons—say, being forced to deal with a difficult customer, experiencing flight delays, or having problems at home—they are expected to be cheerful and pleasant. Sometimes this is very hard to do and can be quite stressful. We have all been in situations in which we tried to hide how we really felt and express an emotion other than our true feelings. This can be quite challenging on occasion. Now imagine having to do this day in and day out as part of your job. **Emotional labor** is the work that employees perform to control their experience and expression of moods and emotions on the job.[66]

EMOTIONAL LABOR
The work that employees perform to control their experience and expression of moods and emotions on the job.

Emotional labor is governed by *display rules*.[67] There are two types of display rules: feeling rules and expression rules. *Feeling rules* dictate appropriate and inappropriate feelings for a particular setting.[68] For example, funeral directors are not supposed to feel delighted in the presence of grieving families, and managers are not supposed to feel angry when letting subordinates know that they have just received promotions. As another example, professors are expected to be enthusiastic when they teach classes and not be bored. *Expression rules* dictate what emotions should be expressed and how they should be expressed in a particular setting.[69] For example, professors are expected to be enthusiastic via their facial expressions and tone of voice, but they are not expected to jump up and down and hoot and holler. Employees who are high on emotional intelligence (see Chapter 2) are likely to be better able to follow feeling and expression rules.

Emotional labor takes place in many organizations and in a variety of kinds of jobs. For example, many employees believe that they should not cry in the workplace in front of coworkers, no matter how badly they might be feeling. However, jobs do differ in terms of the extent to which emotional labor is required on a day-to-day basis. Jobs that involve high levels of interpersonal interaction (whether with the public, students, coworkers, clients, customers, or patients) typically require more emotional labor than jobs that entail less frequent interactions with others.

EMOTIONAL DISSONANCE
An internal state that exists when employees are expected to express feelings that are at odds with how the employees are actually feeling.

Emotional dissonance occurs when employees are expected to express feelings that are at odds with how the employees are actually feeling.[70] For example, a waiter who is angry after dealing with a particularly difficult customer is nonetheless expected to act pleasant and helpful. Emotional dissonance can be a significant source of stress for employees,[71] especially when it occurs frequently or on a day-to-day basis. (We discuss stress in more detail in Chapter 9.) In a recent study, Steffanie Wilk and Lisa Moynihan found that when call-center employees' supervisors place heavy emphasis on employees expressing positive emotions and being pleasant and polite to callers no matter how rude the callers might be to the employees, the employees were much more likely to feel emotionally exhausted from their work.[72]

Of course, emotional labor is often part and parcel of high-quality customer service and does not necessarily need to lead to high levels of stress if it is managed appropriately. Take the case of the restaurant at the Inn at Little Washington, famous for its exceptional food and perhaps even more famous for its high-quality customer service.[73] Cofounder and chef, Patrick O'Connell, believes it is his obligation and the obligation of his staff to provide such a superior dining experience that people leave the restaurant feeling much better than when they entered it.[74] Not only is the staff expected to manage their own emotions, but they are also expected to manage the emotions of their customers.

When a dining party enters the restaurant, the captain assigns the party a mood rating gauging their current state of mind from a low of 1 to a high of 10. Ratings of 7 and lower suggest that the party seems unhappy or displeased. The mood ratings are placed on the table's order and also hung in the kitchen. O'Connell insists that guests leave his restaurant with a mood rating of 9 or 10, and staff members are encouraged to do whatever they can to see that this happens. Tours of the kitchen, tableside visits from the chef, and complimentary drinks or desserts all are used to try to ensure that everyone leaves the restaurant feeling great.[75] And it is up to the staff to figure out how to improve the moods of customers who might have just gotten into an argument or had a very rough day.

The restaurant staff also is required to be very knowledgeable about a variety of topics ranging from different kinds of foods and wines to the likes and dislikes of important food and restaurant critics. Staff members are admonished never to say "no" or "I don't know."[76] O'Connell provides them with the training and experience before they actually begin serving customers, so they never need to plead ignorance. New wait staff receive several months of training, which includes being asked every kind of question that a customer might pose to them. Only when they are able to satisfactorily answer these questions do they receive their portion of the tip pool. O'Connell indicates that his almost fanatical approach to providing high-quality customer service essentially reflects his gratitude to his customers, without whom the restaurant would cease to exist. And employees seem to like the emphasis on customer service; turnover at the Inn is much lower than at many other restaurants.[77]

Relationships Between Values, Attitudes, and Moods and Emotions

Values, attitudes, and moods and emotions capture the range of thoughts and feelings that make up the experience of work. Each one of these determinants of the experience of work has the potential to affect the other two (see Exhibit 3.4). Because work values are the most stable and long lasting, they can strongly affect work attitudes, moods, and emotions. A person whose work values emphasize the importance of being ambitious, for example, may have negative work attitudes toward a job that offers no possibility of promotion.

Work attitudes can affect work moods and emotions in a similar fashion. A salesperson who is very satisfied with his or her job and loves interacting with customers may often be in a good mood at work. In this case, work attitudes (job satisfaction) affect work moods and emotions (positive feelings).

In the long run—over the course of a few years—a person's work values might change in response to his or her more fleeting attitudes, moods, and emotions toward work. A person who values work as merely a way to make a living and not as a source of personal fulfillment might find a nursing job so rewarding and exciting that he or she is usually in a good mood while on the job and finds it satisfying. Eventually, the person's work values may change to include the importance of doing something to help other people. By contrast, an employee who frequently experiences bad moods at work and often feels angry (perhaps because of a dishonest or unpleasant supervisor) may be less satisfied and decide the job isn't meeting his or her expectations. Persistent moods and emotions, in other words, can have an impact on long-held attitudes and values.[78]

When members of an organization share important values, have positive attitudes, and experience positive moods, they may be more likely to trust each other.[79] **Trust** is an

TRUST
An expression of confidence in another person or group of people that you will not be put at risk, harmed, or injured by their actions.

EXHIBIT 3.4

Relationships Between Values, Attitudes, and Moods and Emotions

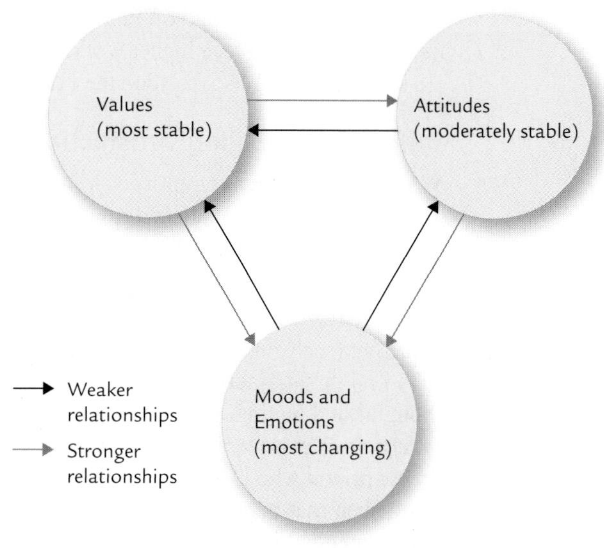

Trust is not only important among members of an organization but also between an organization and its customers or clients. For example, it is important for airline passengers to trust pilots and flight attendants to look out for their safety and well-being.

expression of confidence in another person or group of people that you will not be put at risk, harmed, or injured by their actions.[80] Trust, in turn, can enhance cooperation and the sharing of information necessary for creativity and innovation. A lack of trust between employees and managers is often symptomatic of more widespread problems in an organization.[81] At a minimum, managers must ensure that employees can be confident that their well-being will not be jeopardized by their jobs. From the opening case, it is clear that trust levels are high at Valero Energy. Unfortunately, this is not always the case.

Job Satisfaction

Job satisfaction (the collection of feelings and beliefs that people have about their current jobs) is one of the most important and well-researched work attitudes in organizational behavior. Why do managers and researchers think it's so important? Job satisfaction has the potential to affect a wide range of behaviors in organizations and contribute to employees' levels of well-being. Interestingly enough, research suggests that levels of job satisfaction in the United States have declined in the past decade.[82] According to a Conference Board survey, job satisfaction levels have decreased across all income levels and employees tend to be least satisfied with their companies' promotion and bonus policies and pension and health plans.[83] And, after many companies have laid off employees to cut costs, those who have been fortunate to keep their positions often face higher workloads, which has the potential to decrease their levels of job satisfaction and also question the extent to which their employers are committed to them.[84]

Determinants of Job Satisfaction

What causes different employees to be satisfied or dissatisfied with their jobs? Four factors affect the level of job satisfaction a person experiences: personality, values, the work situation, and social influence (see Exhibit 3.5).

Personality. Personality, the enduring ways a person has of feeling, thinking, and behaving (see Chapter 2), is the first determinant of how people think and feel about their jobs or job satisfaction.[85] An individual's personality influences the extent to which thoughts and feelings about a job are positive or negative. A person who is high on the Big Five trait of extroversion, for instance, is likely to have a higher level of job satisfaction than a person who is low on this trait.[86]

Given that personality helps to determine job satisfaction and that personality is, in part, genetically determined, researchers have wondered whether genetics influence job

EXHIBIT 3.5

Determinants of Job Satisfaction

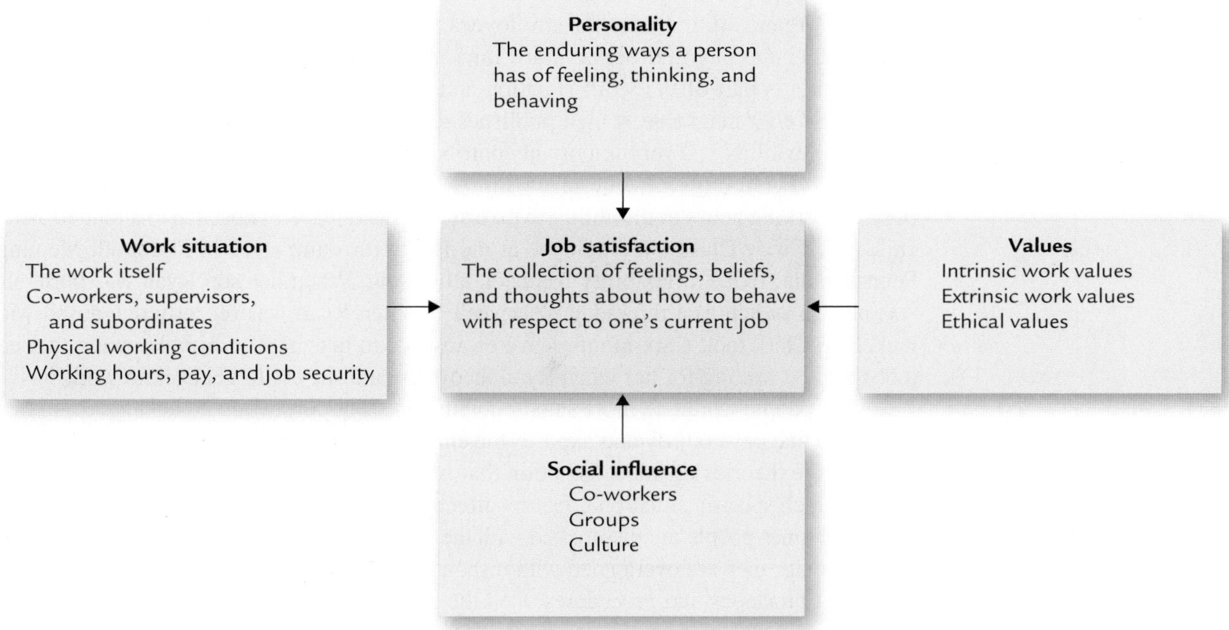

satisfaction. Richard Arvey of the University of Minnesota and his colleagues explored the extent to which employees' levels of job satisfaction were inherited from their parents.[87] They studied 34 identical twins who were raised apart from an early age. The twins shared the same genetic makeup but were exposed to different situational influences in their developmental years and later in life. For each pair of twins, the researchers measured the degree to which one twin's level of job satisfaction was the same as the other twin's level.

The researchers found that genetic factors accounted for about 30 percent of the differences in levels of job satisfaction across the twins in their study. Another interesting finding was that the twins tended to hold jobs that were similar in complexity, motor skills needed, and physical demands required. This suggests that people seek out jobs that are suited to their genetic makeup. In other words, people's personalities (which are partially inherited) predispose them to choose certain kinds of jobs.

What do these findings mean for managers? Essentially, they suggest that part of job satisfaction is determined by employees' personalities, which an organization or manager cannot change in the short run. Does this mean that managers should not worry about the job satisfaction levels of their subordinates or that it is pointless to try to improve levels of job satisfaction? Definitely not. Although it certainly is impressive that genetic factors account for 30 percent of the differences in levels of job satisfaction, 70 percent of the variation in job satisfaction remains to be explained. It is this 70 percent that managers can influence. Thus, managers should be concerned about job satisfaction because it is something that is within their power to influence and change.

Values. Values have an impact on levels of job satisfaction because they reflect employees' convictions about the outcomes that work should lead to and how one should behave at work. A person with strong intrinsic work values (those related to the nature of the work itself), for example, is more likely than a person with weak intrinsic work values to be satisfied with a job that is interesting and personally meaningful (such as social work) but that also requires long working hours and doesn't pay well. A person with strong extrinsic work values (those related to the consequences of work) is more likely than a person with weak extrinsic work values to be satisfied with a job that pays well but is monotonous.

WORK SITUATION
The work itself, working conditions, and all other aspects of the job and the employing organization.

The Work Situation. Perhaps the most important source of job satisfaction is the **work situation** itself—the tasks a person performs (for example, how interesting or boring they are), the people a jobholder interacts with (customers, subordinates, and supervisors), the surroundings in which a person works (noise level, crowdedness, and temperature), and the way the organization treats its employees (such as the job security it offers them and whether the pay and benefits are fair). Any aspect of the job and the employing organization is part of the work situation and can affect job satisfaction.[88] According to *Working Mother* magazine, which publishes a list of the top 100 companies for working mothers, flexibility is a very important contributor to the job satisfaction levels of working mothers.[89] Flexibility can take many forms, ranging from compressed workweeks and flexible working hours to the ability to take an extended leave of absence to attend to a sick child. For Cindy Clark, an employee at the IKEA furniture store in Plymouth Meeting, Pennsylvania, IKEA's flexibility has been a blessing. When her son Ryan was born, she was able to switch to a three-day workweek.[90] When Ryan was recently diagnosed with leukemia, Clark took a six-month leave of absence to take care of him, knowing that her job would be waiting for her when Ryan recovered and she could get back to work.[91]

Most people would be more satisfied with a job that pays well and is very secure than with a job that pays poorly and exposes the employee to the ever-present threat of a layoff. Some of the theories of job satisfaction that we consider later in the chapter focus on the way in which specific situational factors affect job satisfaction.

Sometimes people are dissatisfied with their jobs because of real problems in the workplace. Perhaps they are overloaded with responsibilities. Or perhaps they are required to use inefficient processes and procedures, lack the autonomy to expediently solve problems or institute more efficient and effective ways of doing things, or feel frustrated that their organization is not taking a more proactive approach to seizing opportunities. Recent research suggests that dissatisfaction can actually be an impetus for change and improvement in an organization to the extent that an organization provides a supportive environment. For example, Jing Zhou and Jennifer George of Rice University found, in a study of 149 office employees of a company that makes petroleum drilling equipment, that experienced job dissatisfaction was positively related to creativity on the job (i.e., coming up with new and useful ideas to improve things) when employees were committed to remain with the organization and either received useful feedback from their coworkers, had coworkers who were helpful and supportive, or perceived that their organization was supportive of employees' creativity.[92] Interestingly enough, when Pepsi Cola had virtually lost the "cola wars" to rival Coca Cola over a decade ago, dissatisfaction with that state of affairs led managers and employees to rethink their business. As a result, they redefined their business as focusing on

Some job holders, like this pediatrician, derive their job satisfaction from the kind of work that they do.

foods and beverages, not just soft drinks, and today, Pepsi has a best-selling bottled water in Aquafina, its Gatorade has 80% of the market for sports drinks, and Pepsi has 60% of the U.S. snack-food market with products like Frito-Lay chips. Today, Pepsi is outperforming Coke on several financial indicators such as share price and profitability. Clearly, the proactive response that Pepsi managers and employees had to the dissatisfaction they experienced from losing the cola wars lead to far bigger wins for Pepsi.[93]

SOCIAL INFLUENCE
The influence that individuals or groups have on a person's attitudes and behavior.

Social Influence. The last determinant of job satisfaction is **social influence**, or the influence that individuals or groups have on a person's attitudes and behavior. Coworkers, the groups a person belongs to, and the culture a person grows up and lives in all have the potential to affect employees' levels of job satisfaction.

Social influence from *coworkers* can be an important determinant of an employee's job satisfaction because coworkers are always around, often have similar types of jobs, and often have certain things in common with an employee (such as educational background). Coworkers can have a particularly potent influence on the job-satisfaction levels of new hires. New hires are still likely to be forming an opinion about the organization and the job. They might not yet know what to make of it or whether or not they will ultimately like it. If they are surrounded by coworkers who are dissatisfied with their jobs, they are more likely to be dissatisfied themselves than if they are surrounded by employees who enjoy and are satisfied with their jobs.

The groups he or she belongs to also influence an employee's level of job satisfaction. The family in which a child grows up, for example, can affect how satisfied the child is with his or her job as an adult. An employee who grows up in a wealthy family might be dissatisfied with a job as an elementary schoolteacher because the salary places out of reach the high standard of living he or she enjoyed while growing up. A teacher raised under more modest circumstances might also desire a higher salary but might not be dissatisfied with his or her teaching job because of its pay level.

A wide variety of groups can affect job satisfaction. Employees who belong to certain religious groups are likely to be dissatisfied with jobs that require working on Saturdays or Sundays. Unions can have powerful effects on the job-satisfaction levels of their members. Belonging to a union that believes managers are not treating employees as well as they should be, for example, might cause an employee to be dissatisfied with a job.

The *culture* a person grows up and lives in may also affect an employee's level of job satisfaction. Employees who grow up in cultures (such as the American culture) that emphasize the importance of individual achievement and accomplishment are more likely to be satisfied with jobs that stress individual accomplishment and provide bonuses and pay raises for individual achievement. Employees who grow up in cultures (such the Japanese culture) that emphasize the importance of doing what is good for everyone may be less satisfied with jobs that stress individual competition and achievement. (We discuss national culture in more depth in Chapter 17.)

In fact, cultural influences may shape not just job satisfaction but also the attitudes employees have about themselves. An American may introduce a lecture with a joke that displays both his knowledge and his wit, but a Japanese lecturer in the same position would more likely start off apologizing for his lack of expertise. According to Dr. Hazel Markus of the University of Michigan and Dr. Shinobu Kitayama of the University of Oregon, these two contrasting styles reflect how Americans and Japanese view themselves, which is, in turn, based on the values of their respective cultures.[94]

Consistent with American culture, the American lecturer views and portrays himself as independent, autonomous, and striving to achieve; this makes him feel good and makes his American audience comfortable. In contrast, Japanese culture stresses the interdependence of the self with others; the goal is to fit in, meet one's obligations, and have good interpersonal relations. The Japanese lecturer's more self-effacing style reflects these values; it demonstrates that he is but one part of a larger system and emphasizes the connection between himself and the audience.

Markus and her colleagues have been conducting some interesting research that further illuminates the effects of culture on attitudes about the self. They have asked Japanese and

American students to describe themselves using what the researchers call the "Who Am I" scale. Americans tend to respond to the scale by describing personal characteristics (such as being athletic or smart). Japanese students, however, tend to describe themselves in terms of their roles (such as being the second son). These responses again illustrate that Americans view themselves in terms of personal characteristics, and Japanese view themselves in terms of social characteristics such as their position in their family.[95] This is a simple yet powerful demonstration of how the culture and society we grow up in influences our attitudes, even attitudes as fundamental as our attitudes about ourselves!

Theories of Job Satisfaction

There are many theories or models of job satisfaction. Each of them takes into account one or more of the four main determinants of job satisfaction (personality, values, the work situation, and social influence) and specifies, in more detail, exactly what causes one employee to be satisfied with a job and another employee to be dissatisfied. Here, we discuss four of the most influential theories: the facet model, Herzberg's motivator-hygiene theory, the discrepancy model, and the steady-state theory. These different theoretical approaches to job satisfaction are complementary. Each helps us understand the various aspects of job satisfaction by highlighting the factors and issues managers need to consider in order to enhance the satisfaction levels of their subordinates.

The Facet Model of Job Satisfaction

JOB FACET
One of numerous components of a job.

The facet model of job satisfaction focuses primarily on work situation factors by breaking a job into its component elements, or **job facets**, and looking at how satisfied employees are with each facet. Many of the job facets that researchers have investigated are listed and defined in Exhibit 3.6. An employee's overall job satisfaction is determined by summing his or her satisfaction with each facet of the job.

As Exhibit 3.6 indicates, employees can take into account numerous aspects of their jobs when thinking about their levels of job satisfaction. The facet model is useful because it forces managers and researchers to recognize that jobs affect employees in multiple ways. However, managers who use this model to evaluate the work situation's effect on job satisfaction always need to be aware that, for any particular job, they might inadvertently exclude an important facet that strongly influences an employee's job satisfaction.

The extent to which an employing organization is "family friendly," for example, is an important job facet for many employees. Given the increasing diversity of the workforce and the increasing numbers of women, dual-career couples, and single parents who need to balance their responsibilities on the job and at home, family-friendly organizational policies and benefits are becoming important to more and more employees.[96]

Amgen, a biotechnology company and drugmaker, was listed in *Fortune* magazine's 100 Best Companies to Work for in 2004.[97] Amgen recently opened one of the biggest on-site child care facilities in the United States. The child care center can accommodate up to 430 children ranging in age from 6 weeks to 5 years old. Although employees must pay for their children to come to the center, it is less expensive than other child care facilities and provides a safe and educational environment. Bright Horizons, headquartered in Massachusetts, manages the center for Amgen. Before the new center opened, Amgen had a much smaller on-site facility with a long waiting list.[98]

Another issue that must be considered by managers using facet models of job satisfaction is that some job facets may be more important than others for any given employee.[99] Family-friendly policies, for example, are generally valued by employees with dependents, but they clearly are less important for employees who are single and intend to remain so. Telecommuting (see Chapter 9) and work-at-home arrangements might be facets that appeal to working parents and those with long commutes, but they might not appeal to younger employees who enjoy social interaction with their coworkers. Compensation and security might be key job-satisfaction facets for a single woman who has strong extrinsic work values. At the other end of the spectrum, a high-ranking military retiree receiving a generous pension

EXHIBIT 3.6

Job Facets That Play a Part in Determining Job Satisfaction

Source: D. J. Weiss et al., Manual for the Minnesota Satisfaction Questionnaire, 1967. Minnesota Studies in Vocational Rehabilitation: XXII. © 1967 University of Minnesota. Reproduced by permission of Vocational Psychology Research.

Job Facet	Description
Ability utilization	The extent to which the job allows one to use one's abilities
Achievement	The extent to which an employee gets a feeling of accomplishment from the job
Activity	Being able to keep busy on the job
Advancement	Having promotion opportunities
Authority	Having control over others
Company policies and practices	The extent to which they are pleasing to an employee
Compensation	The pay an employee receives for the job
Co-workers	How well one gets along with others in the workplace
Creativity	Being free to come up with new ideas
Independence	Being able to work alone
Moral values	Not having to do things that go against one's conscience
Recognition	Praise for doing a good job
Responsibility	Being accountable for decisions and actions
Security	Having a secure or steady job
Social service	Being able to do things for other people
Social status	The recognition in the wider community that goes along with the job
Human relations supervision	The interpersonal skills of one's boss
Technical supervision	The work-related skills of one's boss
Variety	Doing different things on the job
Working conditions	Working hours, temperature, furnishings, office location and layout, and so forth

For employees with children, family friendly policies and on-site child care facilities, such as this one at the SAS Institute, can be important contributors to job satisfaction.

might have strong intrinsic work values; he might be more satisfied with a postretirement job offering high levels of ability utilization, achievement, and creativity.

Frank Courtney, a Harvard University graduate, was the butt of jokes when he accepted a position with U.S. Steel while many of his classmates were accepting positions with more prestigious and glamorous companies.[100] Working in heavy industry, however, provided Courtney with a job facet he truly desired: responsibility. At U.S. Steel, he was responsible for overseeing the production and shipping of hundreds of tons of steel while his buddies in the more glamorous legal and financial industries were spending a lot of their time making photocopies.[101]

Herzberg's Motivator-Hygiene Theory of Job Satisfaction

One of the earliest theories of job satisfaction, Frederick Herzberg's motivator-hygiene theory, focuses on the effects of certain types of job facets on job satisfaction. Herzberg's theory proposes that every employee has two sets of needs or requirements: motivator needs and hygiene needs.[102] *Motivator needs* are associated with the actual work itself and how challenging it is. Job facets such as how interesting the work is, autonomy on the job, and the responsibility it affords satisfy motivator needs. *Hygiene needs* are associated with the physical and psychological context in which the work is performed. Job facets such as the physical working conditions (for example, the temperature and pleasantness of the surroundings), the nature of supervision, amount of pay, and job security satisfy hygiene needs.

Herzberg proposed the following theoretical relationships between motivator needs, hygiene needs, and job satisfaction:

1. When motivator needs are met, employees will be satisfied; when these needs are not met, employees will not be satisfied.
2. When hygiene needs are met, employees will not be dissatisfied; when these needs are not met, employees will be dissatisfied.

According to Herzberg, an employee could experience job satisfaction and job dissatisfaction at the same time. An employee could be *satisfied* because *motivator needs* are being met. For example, the employee might find the work interesting and challenging yet be *dissatisfied* because his or her *hygiene needs* are not being met. (Perhaps the position offers little job security.) According to the traditional view of job satisfaction, satisfaction and dissatisfaction are at opposite ends of a single continuum, and employees are either satisfied or dissatisfied with their jobs. Exhibit 3.7(a) illustrates the traditional view. Herzberg proposed that dissatisfaction and satisfaction are two *separate dimensions*, one ranging from satisfaction to no satisfaction and the other ranging from dissatisfaction to no dissatisfaction. Exhibit 3.7(b) illustrates Herzberg's view. An employee's location on the satisfaction continuum depends on the extent to which motivator needs are met, and an employee's location on the dissatisfaction continuum depends on the extent to which hygiene needs are met.

Many research studies have tested Herzberg's formulations. Herzberg himself conducted some of the early studies that supported the theory. He relied on the *critical incidents technique* to collect his data. Herzberg and his colleagues interviewed employees and

EXHIBIT 3.7

Two Views of Job Satisfaction

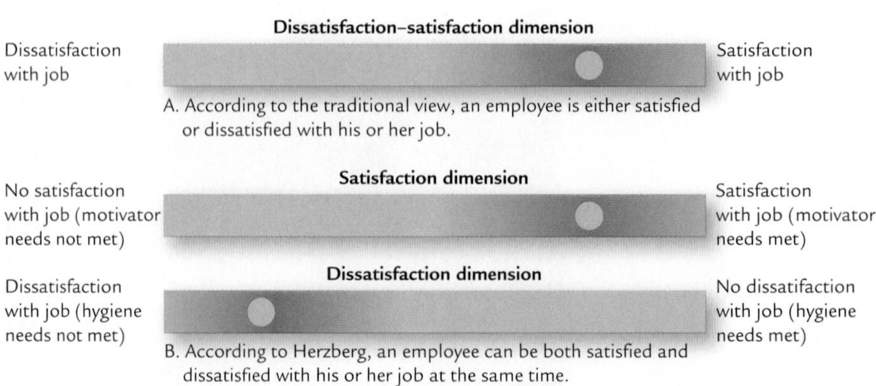

asked them to describe a time when they felt particularly good about their jobs and a time when they felt particularly bad about their jobs. After collating responses from many employees, they made the following discovery: Whenever employees related an instance when they felt good about their job, the incident had to do with the work itself (it was related to their *motivator needs*). Whenever they described an instance when they felt bad about their job, the incident had to do with the working conditions (it was related to their *hygiene needs*). These results certainly seemed to support Herzberg's theory.

When other researchers used different methods to test Herzberg's theory, however, the theory failed to receive support.[103] Why did studies using the critical incidents technique support the theory? As you will learn in Chapter 4, people have a tendency to want to take credit for the good things that happen to them and blame others or outside forces for the bad things. This basic tendency probably accounts for employees' describing good things that happened to them as being related to the work itself, because the work itself is something an employee can take direct credit for. Conversely, working conditions are mostly outside the control of an employee, and it is human nature to try to attribute bad things to situations beyond one's control.

Even though research does *not* support Herzberg's theory, the attention Herzberg paid to motivator needs and to work itself as determinants of satisfaction helped to focus researchers' and managers' attention on the important topic of job design and its effects on organizational behavior (discussed in detail in Chapter 7). Nevertheless, managers need to be aware of the lack of research support for the theoretical relationships Herzberg proposed.

The Discrepancy Model of Job Satisfaction

The discrepancy model of job satisfaction is based on a simple idea: To determine how satisfied they are with their jobs, employees compare their job to some *ideal job*.[104] This ideal job could be what one thinks the job should be like, what one expected the job to be like, what one wants from a job, or what one's former job was like. According to the discrepancy model of job satisfaction, when employees' expectations about their ideal job are high, and when these expectations are not met, employees will be dissatisfied. New college graduates may be particularly prone to having overly high expectations for their first jobs.[105] According to discrepancy models of job satisfaction, they are bound to experience some job dissatisfaction when their new positions fail to meet their high hopes.

Some researchers have combined the facet and discrepancy models of job satisfaction.[106] For each of the job facets described in Exhibit 3.6, for example, we could ask employees "how much" of the facet they currently have on the job compared to what they think their jobs should have. The difference between these two quantities would be the employees' level of satisfaction with the facet. For example, an employee who indicates that she thinks she should have a lot of autonomy on her job but reports that she currently has limited autonomy would be dissatisfied with the autonomy facet of her job. After determining satisfaction levels for each of the job facets in this manner, the total of all of the responses would yield an overall satisfaction score.

Discrepancy models are useful because they take into account that people often take a comparative approach to evaluation. It is not so much the presence or absence of job facets that is important but rather how a job stacks up against an employee's "ideal job." Managers need to recognize this comparative approach and should ask employees what they want their jobs to be like. This information can help them make meaningful changes to increase the level of job satisfaction their subordinates are experiencing.

The Steady-State Theory of Job Satisfaction

The steady-state theory suggests that each employee has a typical, or characteristic, level of job satisfaction, called the steady state or equilibrium level. Different situational factors or events at work may move an employee temporarily from this steady state, but the employee will return eventually to his or her equilibrium level[107] (see Exhibit 3.8). For example, receiving a promotion and raise may temporarily boost an employee's level of job satisfaction, but it eventually will return to the equilibrium level. The finding that job satisfaction tends to be somewhat stable over time[108] supports the steady-state view. The

EXHIBIT 3.8

Job Satisfaction as a Steady State

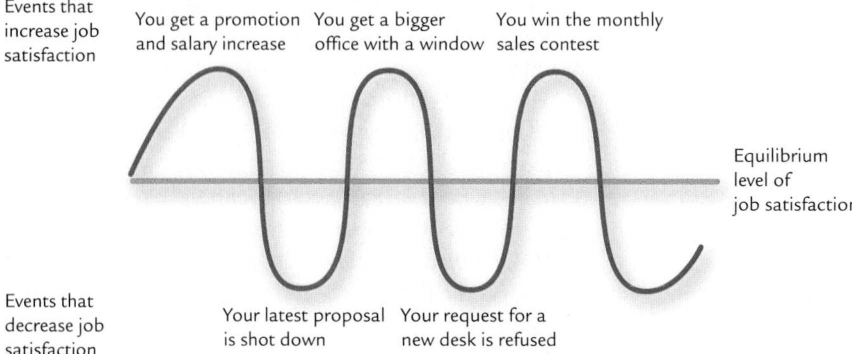

influence of personality on job satisfaction also is consistent with the steady-state approach. Because personality, one of the determinants of job satisfaction, is stable over time, we would expect job satisfaction to exhibit some stability over time.

The steady-state theory suggests that when managers make changes in the work situation in an effort to enhance job-satisfaction levels, they need to determine whether the resulting increases in satisfaction are temporary or long lasting. Some researchers have found, for example, that when changes are made in the nature of the work itself (such as making jobs more interesting), levels of job satisfaction increase temporarily (e.g., for six months) but then return to their former levels.[109] To decide on the most effective ways to sustain an increase in job satisfaction, it is also important for managers to determine *how long* it takes employees to return to their equilibrium levels. Changes in some job facets, for example, may lead to longer-lasting changes in job satisfaction than changes in other facets.

Measuring Job Satisfaction

There are several measures of job satisfaction that managers can use to determine job-satisfaction levels. A manager who discovers that most employees are dissatisfied with the same few job facets and that overall levels of job satisfaction are low as a result can use this information to determine where to make changes in the work situation. Researchers can also use these measures to learn more about the causes and consequences of job satisfaction. Most of these measures ask employees to respond to a series of questions or statements about their jobs. Among the most popular scales are the Minnesota Satisfaction Questionnaire (based on a facet approach),[110] the Faces Scale,[111] and the Job Descriptive Index.[112] Sample items from the first two of these scales appear in Exhibit 3.9.

EXHIBIT 3.9

Sample Items from Popular Measures of Job Satisfaction

Source: (A) D. J. Weiss et al., Manual for the Minnesota Satisfaction Questionnaire, 1967. Minnesota Studies in Vocational Rehabilitation: XXII. Copyright 1967 University of Minnesota. Reproduced by permission of Vocational Psychology Research. (B) R. B. Dunham and J. B. Herman, "Development of a Female Faces Scale for Measuring Job Satisfaction." *Journal of Applied Psychology* 60 (1975): 629–31. Copyright © 1975 by the American Psychology Association. Reprinted with permission.

A. Sample items from the Minnesota Satisfaction Questionnaire

Employees respond to each of the items by checking whether they are:

- ☐ Very dissatisfied
- ☐ Dissatisfied
- ☐ Can't decide whether satisfied or not
- ☐ Satisfied
- ☐ Very satisfied

On my present job, this is how I feel about . . .

1. Being able to keep busy all the time.
2. The chance to be "somebody" in the community.
3. The way my job provides for steady employment.
4. My pay and the amount of work I do.
5. The freedom to use my own judgment.
6. The chance to work by myself.
7. The chance to develop close friendships with my co-workers.
8. The way I get full credit for the work I do.
9. The chance to help people.
10. My job security.

B. The Faces Scale

Employees select the face that best expresses how they feel about their job in general.

11 10 9 8 7 6 5 4 3 2 1

Potential Consequences of Job Satisfaction

Earlier, we said that job satisfaction is one of the most important and most studied attitudes in organizational behavior. One reason for the interest in job satisfaction is that whether or not an employee is satisfied with his or her job has consequences not just for the employee but also for coworkers, managers, groups, teams, and the organization as a whole. In this section, we consider several potential consequences of job satisfaction: job performance, absenteeism, turnover, organizational citizenship behavior, and employee well-being.

Does Job Satisfaction Affect Job Performance?

Intuitively, most people (including managers) believe that job satisfaction is positively associated with job performance—that is, that employees who are more satisfied with their jobs will perform at a higher level than those who are less satisfied. Many studies have been conducted to see whether this piece of conventional wisdom holds true. Surprisingly, the results indicate that job satisfaction is *not* strongly related to job performance; at best, there is a very weak positive relationship. One recent review of the many studies conducted in this area concluded that levels of job satisfaction accounted for only about 2 percent of the differences in performance levels across employees in the studies reviewed.[113] Another recent review found somewhat similar results: Job satisfaction accounted for, on average, about 3 percent of the differences in performance levels across employees.[114] For all practical purposes, then, we can conclude that job satisfaction is *not* meaningfully associated with job performance.

Although this finding goes against the intuition of many managers, it is not that surprising if we consider when work attitudes such as job satisfaction *do* affect work behaviors. Research indicates that work attitudes (such as job satisfaction) affect work behaviors only when employees are free to vary their behaviors and when an employee's attitude is relevant to the behavior in question.

Are most employees free to vary their levels of job performance to reflect how satisfied they are with their jobs? Probably not. Organizations spend considerable time and effort to ensure that members perform assigned duties dependably regardless of whether they like their jobs or not. As you will see in later chapters, organizations develop rules and procedures that employees are expected to follow. To ensure the rules are followed, they reward employees who perform at acceptable levels and punish or dismiss employees who do not. Such rules, procedures, rewards, and punishments are situational pressures that compel employees to perform at acceptable levels.

If chefs in a restaurant, for example, lower the quality of the meals they prepare because they are dissatisfied, customers will stop coming to the restaurant, and the restaurant will either go out of business or the owners will replace the chefs. Similarly, firefighters will not keep their jobs if, because of their levels of job satisfaction, they vary the number of emergencies they respond to. And a secretary who, because of dissatisfaction, cuts back on the quality or quantity of letters he or she types is likely to be reprimanded or even fired and certainly will not be offered a promotion.

In order for a work attitude (job satisfaction) to influence behavior, the attitude must be relevant to the behavior in question (job performance). Sometimes employees' levels of job satisfaction are not relevant to their job performance. Suppose a security guard is satisfied with his job because it is not very demanding and allows him to do a lot of outside reading while on the job. Clearly, this employee's job satisfaction is not going to result in higher levels of performance because the reason for his satisfaction is that the job is not very demanding.

Because of strong situational pressures in organizations to behave in certain ways and because an employee's level of job satisfaction may not be relevant to his or her job performance, job satisfaction is *not* strongly related to job performance. Some research, however, suggests that the direction of influence between these two factors (satisfaction and performance) may be reversed: Job performance may lead to job satisfaction if employees are fairly rewarded for a good performance. The relationship between job performance and

EXHIBIT 3.10

Determinants of Absence from Work

Motivation to Attend Work Is Affected by	Ability to Attend Work Is Affected by
Job satisfaction	Illness and accidents
Organization's absence policy	Transportation problems
Other factors	Family responsibilities

rewards, the importance of equity or fairness, and the implications of these issues for understanding and managing organizational behavior are covered in more detail in Chapters 6, 7, and 8 on motivation.

Absenteeism

Absenteeism can be very costly for organizations. It is estimated that approximately 1 million employees a day are absent from their jobs. In a year, absenteeism costs companies in the United States approximately $40 billion.[115] Not surprisingly, in an effort to reduce absenteeism, many researchers have studied its relationship to job satisfaction. Research focusing on this question has indicated that job satisfaction has a weak negative relationship with absenteeism: Employees who are satisfied with their jobs are somewhat less likely to be absent.[116]

Richard Steers and Susan Rhodes have provided a model of absenteeism that helps explain these results.[117] They propose that employee attendance is a function not only of their motivation to go to work but also of their ability to attend (see Exhibit 3.10). An employee's *ability* to go to work is influenced by illness and accidents, transportation problems, and family responsibilities. Because of the variety of situations and factors that affect work absences, it's not surprising that the relationship between satisfaction and absenteeism is relatively weak. Job satisfaction is just one of many factors that affect the *motivation* to attend.[118]

Absenteeism is a behavior that organizations can never eliminate, but they can control and manage it. Attendance policies should not be so restrictive, however, that they literally force employees to come to work even if they are ill. A certain level of absenteeism—perhaps from a high-stress job—can be functional. Many companies, such as General Foods Corporation, have acknowledged this possibility by including "mental health days" or "personal days" in their absence policies. General Foods employees can take a mental health or personal day at their discretion. They aren't penalized for these absences, and the absences don't count toward the numbers of sick and vacation days they're allowed.

Turnover

TURNOVER
The permanent withdrawal of an employee from the employing organization.

Turnover is the permanent withdrawal of an employee from the employing organization. Job satisfaction shows a weak-to-moderate negative relationship to turnover—that is, high job satisfaction leads to low turnover. Why is this relationship observed? Employees who are satisfied with their jobs are less likely to quit than those who are dissatisfied, but some dissatisfied employees never leave, and others who are satisfied with their jobs eventually move on to another organization. Moreover, unlike absenteeism, which is a *temporary* form of withdrawal from the organization, turnover is *permanent* and can have a major impact on an employee's life. Thus, the decision to quit a job is not usually made lightly but is instead the result of a carefully thought-out process.

When, in the turnover process, does job satisfaction play an important role? According to a model of the turnover process developed by Bill Mobley, job satisfaction triggers the whole turnover process (see Exhibit 3.11).[119] Employees who are very satisfied with their jobs may never even think about quitting; for those who are dissatisfied, it is the dissatisfaction that starts them thinking about quitting.

EXHIBIT 3.11

Mobley's Model of the Turnover Process

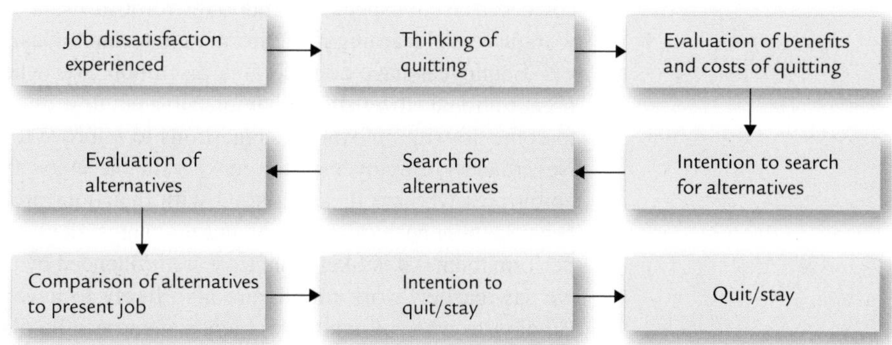

Source: Adapted from W. H. Mobley, "Intermediate Linkages in the Relationship Between Job Satisfaction and Employee Turnover," *Journal of Applied Psychology 6* (1977): 237-40. Copyright © 1977 by the American Psychological Association. Reprinted with Permission.

As indicated in Exhibit 3.11, job dissatisfaction will cause an employee to begin thinking about quitting. At this point, the individual evaluates the benefits of searching for a new job versus the costs of quitting. These costs could include any corporate benefits that are linked to seniority (such as vacation time and bonuses), the loss of pension and medical plans, and a reduced level of job security (which is often based on seniority in the organization). On the basis of this cost/benefit evaluation, the individual may decide to search for alternative jobs. The person evaluates and compares these alternatives to the current job and then develops an intention to quit or stay. The intention to quit eventually leads to turnover behavior. Hence, although job satisfaction or dissatisfaction is an important factor to consider because it may trigger the whole turnover process and start an employee thinking about quitting, other factors come into play to determine whether or not an employee actually quits. (Mobley's model applies neither to employees who impulsively quit their jobs nor to employees who quit their jobs before even looking for alternatives.)

Just as in the case of absenteeism, managers often think of turnover as a costly behavior that must be kept to a minimum. There are certainly costs to turnover, such as the costs of hiring and training replacement employees. In addition, turnover often causes disruptions for existing members of an organization; it may result in delays on important projects; and it can cause problems when employees who quit are members of teams.

Although these and other costs of turnover can be significant, turnover can also have certain benefits for organizations. First, whether turnover is a cost or benefit depends on who is leaving. If poor performers are quitting and good performers are staying, this is an ideal situation, and managers may not want to reduce levels of turnover. Second, turnover can result in the introduction of new ideas and approaches if the organization hires newcomers with new ideas to replace employees who have left. Third, turnover can be a relatively painless and natural way to reduce the size of the workforce through *attrition*, the process through which people leave an organization of their own free will. Attrition can be an important benefit of turnover in lean economic times because it reduces the need for organizations to downsize their workforces. Finally, for organizations that promote from within, turnover in the upper ranks of the organization frees up some positions for promotions of lower-level members. Like absenteeism, turnover is a behavior that needs to be managed but not necessarily reduced or eliminated.

Organizational Citizenship Behavior

ORGANIZATIONAL CITIZENSHIP BEHAVIOR
Behavior that is not required but is necessary for organizational survival and effectiveness.

Although job satisfaction is not related to job performance, new research suggests that it is related to work behaviors that are of a more voluntary nature and not specifically required of employees. **Organizational citizenship behavior** (OCB) is behavior that is above and beyond the call of duty—that is, behavior that is not required of organizational members but is nonetheless necessary for organizational survival and effectiveness.[120] Examples of OCB include helping coworkers; protecting the organization from fire, theft, vandalism, and other misfortunes; making constructive suggestions; developing one's skills and capabilities; and spreading goodwill in the larger community. These behaviors are seldom required of organizational members, but they are important in all organizations. Helping coworkers is an especially important form of OCB when it comes to computing in the workplace and learning new information technologies.

Employees have considerable discretion over whether or not they engage in acts of organizational citizenship behavior. Most employees' job descriptions do not require them to come up with innovative suggestions to improve the functioning of their departments. Nevertheless, employees often make valuable innovative suggestions, and it may be that employees who are most satisfied with their jobs are most likely to do so. Once again, because these behaviors are voluntary—that is, there are no strong situational pressures to perform them—it is likely that they are influenced by attitudes such as job satisfaction. As we saw earlier, work moods are also likely to have some impact on these behaviors. Employees who are in positive moods are especially likely to perform forms of OCB, such as helping customers or suggesting new ideas.[121]

Dennis Organ of Indiana University suggests that satisfied employees may be likely to perform these behaviors because they seek to give something back to an organization that has treated them well.[122] Organ notes that most people like to have fair exchanges with the people and organizations for which they work. Because of this desire, employees who are satisfied may seek to reciprocate or give something back to the organization by engaging in various forms of OCB.

Because the various forms of organizational citizenship behavior are not formally required of employees, they may not be formally recognized by the organization's reward and incentive systems. Often managers may not even be aware of these behaviors or may underestimate their occurrence (as in the case of employees helping others with their PC problems). This lack of awareness does not mean, however, that managers cannot recognize and acknowledge OCB that does occur.

John Brady, president of John Brady Design Consultants, developed a simple yet innovative method to acknowledge OCB. At the start of each year he gives each of his 18 employees a jar containing 12 marbles. Throughout the year, employees give marbles to others who have helped them in some way or have accomplished some out-of-the-ordinary feat. In this way, employees are recognized for the OCB that occurs and are proud of the marbles they accumulate over the year, even though they may receive no more tangible rewards (such as a bonus) for performing these behaviors.[123]

Similarly, Texas A&M University recognizes OCB by publishing accounts of OCB in the *Human Resources Newsletter* distributed periodically to all employees of the university. A special section of the newsletter titled "We Caught You Doing Something Right" chronicles instances of OCB that have taken place during the past few months. Here is a

When employees voluntarily help each other out on the job, they are engaging in organizational citizenship behavior.

sample entry: "Michael Jackson, who works in the Library, was caught coming in on his own time to review work for a cooperative grant-funded project involving 18 Texas academic libraries. By voluntarily contributing his time, Michael has enabled the Texas Documents to the People Project to stay on schedule."[124]

Employee Well-Being

EMPLOYEE WELL-BEING
How happy, healthy, and prosperous employees are.

Employee well-being—how happy, healthy, and prosperous employees are—is the last potential consequence of job satisfaction we consider. Unlike absenteeism and turnover, this consequence focuses on the employee rather than the organization. If you count the number of hours of their adult lives that employees spend on the job, the number is truly mind-boggling: An employee who puts in an eight-hour day, works five days a week, and has two weeks off a year for vacation works approximately 2,000 hours a year. Over a 40-year period (from age 25 to 65), this employee clocks in some 80,000 hours on the job. (These figures don't even touch on the amount of time employees spend thinking about their jobs during their time off.) Being dissatisfied with one's job for a major portion of one's working life almost certainly adversely affects well-being and general happiness. Consistent with this observation, research suggests that job satisfaction contributes to overall well-being in life.[125] According to Benjamin Amick, a professor at the University of Texas, "More satisfaction leads to improved physical and mental health and saves money through reduced health-care costs and improved productive time at work."[126]

Organizational Commitment

AFFECTIVE COMMITMENT
The commitment that exists when employees are happy to be members of an organization, believe in and feel good about the organization and what it stands for, are attached to the organization, and intend to do what is good for the organization.

CONTINUANCE COMMITMENT
The commitment that exists when it is very costly for employees to leave an organization.

Whereas job satisfaction relates to feelings and beliefs that individuals have about specific jobs, organizational commitment relates to feelings and beliefs about the employing organization as a whole. Researchers have identified two distinct types of organizational commitment: affective commitment and continuance commitment.[127] **Affective commitment** exists when employees are happy to be members of an organization, believe in and feel good about the organization and what it stands for, are attached to the organization, and intend to do what is good for the organization. **Continuance commitment** exists when employees are committed not so much because they want to be but because they have to be—when the costs of leaving the organization (loss of seniority, job security, pensions, medical benefits, and so on) are too great.[128] As you might imagine, affective commitment generally has more positive consequences for employees and organizations than continuance commitment.

Determinants of Affective Commitment

A wide range of personality and situational factors has the potential to affect levels of affective commitment. For example, employees may be more committed to organizations that behave in a socially responsible manner and contribute to society at large. It is easier to believe in and be committed to an organization that is doing good things for society rather than causing harm, such as polluting the atmosphere. Ben & Jerry's Homemade, the ice cream company, encourages employee commitment through socially responsible corporate policies and programs that support the community and protect the environment.[129] The Body Shop, which manufactures and sells organic beauty products, engenders commitment in its employees by supporting the protection of the environment and animal rights. Employees may also be more likely to be committed to an organization that shows that it cares about its employees and values them as individuals. Managers cannot expect employees to be committed to an organization if the organization is not committed to employees and society as a whole.

Potential Consequences of Affective Commitment

Managers intuitively believe that employees who are committed to an organization will work harder, and research has found affective commitment to have a weak positive relationship with job performance.[130] However, affective commitment (like job satisfaction) may be more highly related to organizational citizenship behavior (OCB). Because these behaviors are voluntary, they tend to be more directly related to employees' attitudes toward an organization.

You're the Management Expert

Increasing Affective Commitment

Juan Quintero is a division manager in a large consumer products firm. Quintero's division recently underwent a restructuring, which resulted in 10 percent of the division's employees being laid off. Quintero did everything he could to help those employees who were laid off find other positions by, for example, giving them advance notice of the layoff, enabling them to use office space at the company until they found a new job, hiring career counselors to help them figure out their best options and prepare résumés, and so forth. He also honestly explained to all employees why the restructuring and resulting layoffs were a business necessity. Prior to the layoff, Quintero felt pretty good about satisfaction and commitment levels in his division. On prior annual surveys the company had conducted, Quintero's division always came out on top in terms of employee satisfaction and commitment. However, he is beginning to worry that things might have changed, and he has data to support his fears. After informal chats with some of the division's employees, Quintero sensed diminished levels of job satisfaction and affective commitment to the company. On the latest annual survey conducted one month ago, Quintero's division scored in the lowest quartile in affective commitment. Quintero is concerned, to say the least. He cannot understand why attitudes have changed so much over the year. Even more worrisome, he does not know how to address this problem. Looking for an expert in organizational behavior, Quintero has come to you for help. Why have levels of affective commitment deteriorated in this division, and how can he bring them back up to their prior highs?

When affective commitment is high, employees are likely to want to do what is good for the organization and, thus, perform OCBs.[131] However, when continuance commitment is high, employees are not expected to go above and beyond the call of duty because their commitment is based more on necessity than a belief in what the organization stands for.

Affective commitment also shows a weak, negative relationship to absenteeism and tardiness.[132] A stronger, negative relationship exists between affective commitment and turnover. Employees who are committed to an organization are less likely to quit; their positive attitude toward the organization itself makes them reluctant to leave.[133]

Summary

Values, attitudes, and moods and emotions have important effects on organizational behavior. Values (an employee's personal convictions about what one should strive for in life and how one should behave) are an important determinant of on-the-job behavior. Job satisfaction and organizational commitment are two key work attitudes with important implications for understanding and managing behaviors such as organizational citizenship behavior, absenteeism, and turnover. Work moods and emotions also are important determinants of behavior in organizations. In this chapter, we made the following major points:

1. Two important kinds of values that influence organizational behavior are work values and ethical values. Work attitudes, more specific and less long lasting than values, are collections of feelings, beliefs, and thoughts that people have about how to behave in their current jobs and organizations. Work moods and emotions, more transitory than both values

and attitudes, are people's feelings at the time they actually perform their jobs. Values, attitudes, and moods and emotions all have the potential to influence each other.

2. Work values are employees' personal convictions about what outcomes they should expect from work and how they should behave at work. There are two broad types of work values: intrinsic work values and extrinsic work values. Intrinsic work values are values related to the work itself, such as doing something that is interesting and challenging or having a sense of accomplishment. Extrinsic work values are values related to the consequences of work, such as having family security or status in the community.
3. Ethical values are an employees' personal convictions about what is right or wrong. Three types of ethical values are utilitarian values, moral rights values, and justice values. Utilitarian values dictate that decisions should be made so that the decision produces the greatest good for the greatest number of people. Moral rights values indicate that decisions should be made in ways that protect the fundamental rights and privileges of people affected by the decision. Justice values dictate that decisions should be made in ways that allocate benefit and harm among those affected by the decision in a fair, equitable, or impartial manner.
4. Two important work attitudes are job satisfaction and organizational commitment. Job satisfaction is the collection of feelings and beliefs that people have about their current jobs. Organizational commitment is the collection of feelings and beliefs that people have about their organization as a whole. Work attitudes have three components: an affective component (how a person feels about his or her job), a cognitive component (what a person believes about his or her job), and a behavioral component (what a person thinks about how to behave in his or her job). People can have work attitudes about specific aspects of their jobs and organizations and about their jobs and organizations as a whole.
5. People experience many different moods at work. These moods can be categorized generally as positive or negative. When employees are in positive moods, they feel excited, enthusiastic, active, strong, peppy, or elated. When employees are in negative moods, they feel distressed, fearful, scornful, hostile, jittery, or nervous. Employees also experience less intense moods at work, such as feeling sleepy or calm. Work moods are determined by both personality and situation and have the potential to influence organizational behaviors ranging from absence to being helpful to customers and coworkers to creativity to leadership. Emotions are intense, short-lived feelings that are linked to a specific cause or antecedent. Emotional labor is the work that employees perform to control their experience and expression of moods and emotions on the job.
6. Job satisfaction is one of the most important and well-researched attitudes in organizational behavior. Job satisfaction is determined by personality, values, the work situation, and social influence. Facet, discrepancy, and steady-state models of job satisfaction are useful for understanding and managing this important attitude.
7. Job satisfaction is not strongly related to job performance because employees are often not free to vary their levels of job performance and because sometimes job satisfaction is not relevant to job performance. Job satisfaction has a weak, negative relationship to absenteeism. Job satisfaction influences turnover; employees who are satisfied with their jobs are less likely to quit them. Furthermore, employees who are satisfied with their jobs are more likely to perform voluntary behaviors, known as organizational citizenship behavior, that contribute to organizational effectiveness. Job satisfaction also has a positive effect on employee well-being.
8. Organizational commitment is the collection of feelings and beliefs that people have about their organization as a whole. Affective commitment exists when employees are happy to be members of an organization and believe in what it stands for. Continuance commitment exists when employees are committed to the organization because it is too costly for them to leave. Affective commitment has more positive consequences for organizations and their members than continuance commitment. Affective commitment is more likely when organizations are socially responsible and demonstrate that they are committed to employees. Employees with high levels of affective commitment are less likely to quit and may be more likely to perform organizational citizenship behavior.

Exercises in Understanding and Managing Organizational Behavior

Questions for Review

1. How would you describe a person you know who has strong intrinsic and extrinsic work values?
2. Why might two employees with the same job develop different attitudes toward it?
3. On what kinds of jobs might the moods that employees experience be particularly important for understanding why they behave as they do?
4. Why are attitudes less long lasting than values, and why are moods more transitory than attitudes?
5. What specific standards might people use to determine their satisfaction with different facets of their jobs?
6. Why is job satisfaction not strongly related to job performance?
7. Should managers always try to reduce absenteeism and turnover as much as possible? Why or why not?
8. In what kinds of organizations might organizational citizenship behaviors be especially important?
9. What specific things can an organization do to raise levels of affective commitment?
10. In what kinds of organizations might affective commitment be especially important?

OB: Increasing Self Awareness

Understanding Your Own Experience of Work

1. Describe your work values. Are they predominantly extrinsic or intrinsic?
2. How would your work values affect your reactions to each of these events at work?
   a. Getting promoted
   b. Being reassigned to a position with more responsibility but receiving no increase in pay
   c. Having to work late at night and travel one week a month on a job you find quite interesting
   d. Having a stressful job that pays well
   e. Having an exciting job with low job security
3. Describe your mood over the past week or two. Why have you felt this way? How has your mood affected your behavior?
4. What facets of a job are particularly important determinants of your level of job satisfaction? What standards do you (or would you) use to evaluate your job on these dimensions?
5. Toward what kind of organization are you most likely to have affective commitment? Toward what kind of organization are you most likely to have continuance commitment?
6. How might your affective commitment to an organization affect your behavior?
7. What forms of organizational citizenship behavior are you especially likely to perform, and why? What forms of organizational citizenship behavior are you least likely to perform, and why?

A Question of Ethics

On some jobs, employees are expected to perform emotional labor most of the time. Salespeople, for example, are often required to be cheerful and polite, even to the most unpleasant customers. However, this can create high levels of stress for employees to the extent that they often have to hide their true feelings. Additionally, to the extent that a customer is rude or abusive, demands for emotional labor might be questionable on ethical grounds.

Questions

1. Are there limits to the extent to which an employer should require employees to perform emotional labor? If so, what are these limits? If not, why not?
2. Under what condition do you think it would be unethical to require emotional labor from employees? Be specific.

Small Group Break-Out Exercise

Identifying Unethical Behavior

Form groups of three or four people, and appoint one member as the spokesperson who will communicate your conclusions to the rest of the class:

1. Take a few minutes to think about instances in which you observed unethical behavior taking place in an organization (as an employee, customer, client, or observer).
2. Take turns describing these instances.
3. Each person then should take a few minutes to write down criteria that helps to distinguish ethical behavior from unethical behavior.
4. Using input from Step 3, as a group, come up with the key criteria that you think should be used to determine whether behavior is ethical or unethical.

Topic for Debate

Values, attitudes, and moods and emotions have important implications for understanding and managing organizational behavior. Now that you have a good understanding of values, attitudes, and moods and emotions, debate the following issue.

Team A. Because job satisfaction is not related to job performance, managers do not need to be concerned about it.

Team B. Managers *do* need to be concerned about job satisfaction even though it is not related to performance.

Experiential Exercise

Promoting Organizational Citizenship Behavior

Objective

Organizations work most effectively when their members voluntarily engage in organizational citizenship behaviors. It is likely that you have witnessed some kind of organizational citizenship behavior. You may have seen this behavior performed by a coworker or supervisor where you work. You may have seen this behavior when you were interacting with an organization as a customer or client. Or someone in your university (a faculty or staff member or a student) may have gone above and beyond the call of duty to help another person or the university as a whole. Your objective is to identify instances of OCB and think about how managers can promote such behavior.

Procedure

Each member of the class takes a few minutes to think about instances of organizational citizenship behavior that he or she has observed and makes a list of them. The class then divides into groups of three to five people, and each group appoints one member as spokesperson to present the group's conclusions to the whole class. Group members do the following:

1. Take turns describing instances of organizational citizenship behavior they have observed.
2. Discuss the similarities and differences between each of these instances of organizational citizenship behavior and suggest some reasons why they may have occurred.
3. Compile a list of steps that managers can take to promote organizational citizenship behavior.

Spokespersons from each group report the following back to the class: four examples of organizational citizenship behavior that group members have observed and three steps that managers can take to try to promote OCB.

New York Times *Cases in the News*

The New York Times

"Here's an Idea: Let Everyone Have Ideas,"

By W. C. Taylor, New York Times, March 26, 2006, Section 3, p. 3.

Like many top executives, James R. Lavoie and Joseph M. Marino keep a close eye on the stock market. But the two men, co-founders of **Rite-Solutions**, a software company that builds advanced—and highly classified—command-and-control systems for the Navy, don't worry much about Nasdaq or the New York Stock Exchange.

Instead, they focus on an internal market where any employee can propose that the company acquire a new technology, enter a new business or make an efficiency improvement. These proposals become stocks, complete with ticker symbols, discussion lists and e-mail alerts. Employees buy or sell the stocks, and prices change to reflect the sentiments of the company's engineers, computer scientists and project managers—as well as its marketers, accountants and even the receptionist.

"We're the founders, but we're far from the smartest people here," Mr Lavoie, the chief executive, said during an interview at Rite-Solutions headquarters outside Newport, R.I. "At most companies, especially technology companies, the most brilliant insights tend to come from people other than senior management. So we created a marketplace to harvest collective genius."

That's a refreshing dose of humility from a successful C.F.O. with decades of experience in his field. (Mr. Lavoie, 59, is a Vietnam War veteran and an accomplished engineer who has devoted his career to military-oriented technologies.)

Most companies operate under the assumption that big ideas come from a few big brains; the inspired founder, the eccentric inventor, the visionary boss. But there' a fine line between individual genius and know-it-all arrogance. What happens when rivals become so numerous, when technologies move so quickly, that no corporate honcho can think of everything? Then it's time to invent a less top-down approach to innovation, to make it everybody's business to come up with great ideas.

That's a key lesson behind the rise of open source technology, most notably Linux. A ragtag army of programmers organized into groups, wrote computer code, made the code available for anyone to revise and, by competing and co-operating in a global community, reshaped the market for software. The brilliance of Linux as a model of innovation is that it is powered by the grass-roots brilliance of the thousands of programmers who created it.

According to Tim O'Reilly, the founder and chief executive of O'Reilly Media, the computer book publisher, and an evangelist for open source technologies, creativity is no longer about which companies have the most visionary executives, but who has the most compelling "architecture of participation." That is, which companies make it easy, interesting and rewarding for a wide range of contributors to offer ideas, solve problems and improve products?

At Rite-Solutions, the architecture of participation is both businesslike and playful. Fifty-five stocks are listed on the company's internal market, which is called Mutual Fun. Each stock comes with a detailed description—called an expect-us, as opposed to a prospectus—and begins trading at a price of $10. Every employee gets $10,000 in "opinion money" to allocate among the offerings, and employees signal their enthusiasm by investing in a stock and, better yet, volunteering to work on the project. Volunteers share in the proceeds, in the form of real money, if the stock becomes a product or delivers savings.

Mr. Marino, 57, president of Rite-Solutions, says the market, which began in January 2005, has already paid big dividends. One of the earliest stocks (ticker symbol: VIEW) was a proposal to apply three-dimensional visualization technology, akin to video games, to help sailors and domestic security personnel practice making decisions in emergency situations. Initially, Mr. Marino was unenthusiastic about the idea—"I'm not a joystick jockey"—but support among employees was overwhelming. Today, that product line, called Rite-View, accounts for 30 percent of total sales.

"Would this have happened if it were just up to the guys at the top?" Mr. Marino asked. "Absolutely not. But we could not ignore the fact that so many people were rallying around the idea. This system removes the terrible burden of us always having to be right."

Another virtue of the stock market, Mr. Lavoie added, is that it finds good ideas from unlikely sources. Among Rite-Solutions' core technologies are pattern recognition algorithms used in military applications, as well as for electronic gambling systems at casinos, a big market for the company. A member of the administrative staff, with no technical expertise, thought that this technology might also be used in educational settings, to create an entertaining way for students to learn history or math.

She started a stock called Win/Play/Learn (symbol: WPL), which attracted a rush of investment from engineers eager to turn her idea into a product. Their enthusiasm led to meetings with Hasbro, up the road in Pawtucket, and Rite-Solutions won a contract to help it build its VuGo multimedia system, introduced last Christmas.

Mr. Lavoie called this innovation an example of the "quiet genius" that goes untapped inside most organizations. "We would have never connected these dots," he said. "But one employee floated an idea, lots of employees go passionate about it and that led to a new line of business."

The next frontier is to tap the quiet genius that exists outside organizations—to attract innovations from people who are prepared to work with a company even if they don't work *for* it. An intriguing case in point is **InnoCentive**, a virtual research and development lab through which major corporations invite scientists and engineers worldwide to contribute ideas and solve problems they haven't been able to crack themselves.

InnoCentive, based in Andover, Mass., is literally a marketplace of ideas. It has signed up more than 30 blue-chip companies, including Procter & Gamble, Boeing, and DuPont, whose research labs are groaning under the weight of unsolved problems and unfinished projects. It has also signed up more than 90,000 biologists, chemists and other professionals from more than 175 countries. These "solvers" compete to meet thorny technical challenges posted by "seeker" companies. Each challenge has a detailed scientific description, a deadline and an award, which can run as high as $100,000.

"We are talking about the democratization of science," said Alpheus Bingham, who spent 28 years as a scientist and senior research executive at Eli Lilly & Company before becoming the president and chief executive of InnoCentive. "What happens when you open your company to thousands and thousands of minds, each of them with a totally different set at life experiences?"

InnoCentive, founded as an independent start-up by Lilly in 2001, has an impressive record. It can point to a long list of valuable scientific ideas that have arrived with surprising speed, from faraway places. In addition to the United States, the top countries for solvers are China, India and Russia.

Last month InnoCentive attracted a $3 million infusion of venture capital to accelerate its growth. "There is a 'collective mind' out there," Dr. Bingham said, "The question for companies is, what fraction of it can you access?"

That remains an unanswered question at many companies, whose leaders continue to rely on their own brainpower as the key source of ideas. But there's evidence that more and more top executives are recognizing the limits of their individual genius.

Back at Rite-Solutions, for example, one of the most valuable stocks on Mutual Fun is the stock market itself (symbol: STK) So many executives from other companies have asked to study the system that team championed the idea of licensing it is a product—another unexpected opportunity.

"There's nothing wrong with experience," said Mr. Marino, the company's president. "The problem is when experience gets in the way of innovation. As founders, the one thing we know is that we don't know all the answers."

Questions for Discussion

1. What values does Rite-Solutions' approach to innovation appeal to? Why?
2. How might work attitudes be influenced by their approach?
3. How might work moods and emotions be affected?
4. How might suggesting a new idea that gets implemented affect levels of employee commitment at Rite-Solutions?

The New York Times

"Trying Out for Life's Second Act,"

By D. Gill, New York Times, April 11, 2006, p. E11.

Notorious for high financial risk and grueling work hours, entrepreneurship sounds like just the sort of venture a retirement-minded person would shun. But more people at or near retirement age are going into business for themselves, sometimes living out their senior years far differently than they ever would have imagined.

Separate studies in the past two years from the Ewing Marion Kauffman. Foundation and the Center on Aging and Work at Boston College indicate that Americans are increasingly becoming entrepreneurs at age 50 or later, a trend researchers expect to intensify as baby boomers expand the age group. Even the over-65 age group is becoming self-employed more often now, according to the Kauffman Foundation research.

While many of these self-employed workers are independent contractors—often operating a one-person business like a consultancy—research also indicates that older workers are opening or buying full-fledged businesses more than in the past. A study published by AARP in 2004, using research from the nonprofit RAND Corporation, shows an upward trend in the number of people over age 50 who own incorporated businesses.

As much as these unlikely entrepreneurs are drawn by the challenge of succeeding in business, experts say, many are pushed into the effort by difficult circumstances.

For 57-year-old Howard DuBrow, the decision to buy a business came from a company merger that left him jobless in 2002. After 30 years of climbing corporate ladders, he found himself in a quandary; he was too young to retire, too old to do it again.

"I knew I couldn't just retire," said Mr. DuBrow, who as a vice president of a major computer-leasing company oversaw some $2.5 billion in accounts before the layout "I didn't have enough money for that. But I had just had it with corporate work. I was tired and burned out. I didn't think I had the drive anymore to go back in and fight my way up again."

Instead, he left Chicago and dipped into his collected bonuses and 401(k)'s to buy a small, struggling hardware store in New Port Richey, Fla. Today, he spends about 50 hours a week stocking shelves, helping customers and running Davis Hardware along with his five employees. It hasn't worked out exactly as he had planned—Mr. DuBrow had envisioned profits and three-day work-weeks—but he said he was happy, "It's fun," he said, "I still like it a lot better than anything I did before."

Certainly, people generally want to work later in life than ever before, said Marcie Pitt-Catsouphes, director of the Boston College Center on Aging and Work. "Almost every single survey makes that loud and clear," she said. "In contrast to the past, people don't want to quit."

Yet despite some companies' recent efforts to retain senior workers, corporate downsizing has left many older workers out of jobs before they wanted to leave, said Sara Rix, senior policy adviser at AARP. Also, as retirement looms, she said, they take a harder look at how much they have accrued toward retirement, and if it will support the quality of life they had expected. If someone wants to begin to earn more, entrepreneurship can seem easier or more attractive than finding good-paying salaried employment after 50.

Clarence Wildes, who worked for 22 years in engineering jobs at Sprint, said he applied for dozens of jobs and even drove a school bus awhile after he was forced into early retirement at age 52. At the time, he was surprised to find his bank account short of a retirement living, he said, in part because his company stock had lost much of its value. "I had expected the position I was in to give me a whole lot more toward retirement than what I got," he said.

Two years later, he took a crash course in starting a business at the Kauffman Foundation, which promotes entrepreneurship. In 2003, he opened Rolling Wheels Training Center, a motorcycle driving school in Kansas City. Long before leaving Sprint, Mr. Wildes had dreamed of starting Rolling Wheels—in retirement. "I was forced into it before I was ready," he said.

Unemployment is a powerful motivator for entrepreneurship, said the economist Rob Fairlie, an associate professor at the University of California, Santa Cruz, and author of the "Kauffman index of Entrepreneural Activity." He said his research shows that people who lost jobs are more likely to start businesses than others. Of those who do, he said, the average age is 50.

Kathryn Morrison said she never envisioned herself as an entrepreneur until she found herself unemployed at age 50, after a career in broadcasting and a stint as a press go-between for a financial trade association. "I couldn't find a job," she said. "I was terrified."

But she landed a contract to produce a brochure for one mutual fund company and then another. She opened SunStar, based in Alexandria Va., as a media relations company for investment advisers, which has grown to 12 employees with about $2.5 million in annual revenues. Ms. Morrison, now 65, said she had no intention of retiring any time soon.

Of course, some late-in-life entrepreneurs are simply fulfilling longtime dreams that could be fulfilled only after decades of wage or salary work. Early retirement packages or hetty 401(k)'s sometimes make those goals possible.

"All of my life I had wanted to go into business for myself," said Wally Blume, 67, one of the inventors of the formula for Moose Tracks ice cream. In his 30's and 40's, Mr. Blume looked into numerous entrepreneurial opportunities, including a franchise cheese store. "But I never had the money to make it work," he said. He eventually resigned himself to a long career at the supermarket giant Kroger Corporation in new product development, followed by a stint as an ingredients salesman for a smaller company.

But when Moose Tracks, an ice cream flavoring he and a few colleagues invented on the side became an unexpected hit, Mr. Blume discovered he had both the opportunity and the product to finally start a business. He was 62 when he built a home in Wayland, Mich, with an entire floor dedicated to turning the brand into a full-fledged business.

His business, Denali Flavors, now sells ingredients for 30 copyrighted flavors, including Moose Tracks. While he wouldn't disclose Denali's financial condition, he said its flavors were included in products that generate roughly $85 million a year in sales. The company is expanding the use of its products in cakes and cookies, as well as in ice cream in foreign countries.

As an entrepreneur, Mr. Blume said he has worked a lot longer hours than he did in his youth, particularly in the first couple of years. "But you just love it," he said. "This was my business, and this was my passion."

Sometimes, older workers look into buying a business as a way to ease into retirement. But there are very few successful companies that allow the owners to work half-days, business brokers typically tell clients. "There are none—they're all broke," said Bob Hough, president of Sunbelt Business Brokers in Clear water, Fla. Entrepreneurship, they warn, requires long hours.

Regardless, older entrepreneurs tend to be more satisfied than their counterparts in salaried jobs, according to research at the Boston College center. In an unpublished study this year, some 90 percent of small business owners over age 50 that the center surveyed were more likely than wage and salaried workers to want to stay in the same job.

Like any other population in business, older entrepreneurs report a variety of success. Mr. DuBrow said he was still putting more money into his hardware store than he got out of it. He said he hoped to make a profit of about $2,000 to $3,000 a month from it within a couple of years. Mr. Wildes, the motorcycle school owner, said he did not expect to get rich. "But we'll make a living," he said.

Mr. Blume and Ms. Morrison both said they were financially far happier and more successful than they ever expected. "I drive expensive cars and vacation around the world," Ms. Morrison said. "My life is better than my best dreams."

Questions for Discussion

1. Why are some older workers becoming entrepreneurs?
2. What work values drive would-be entrepreneurs?
3. Why are some entrepreneurs more satisfied with their work as entrepreneurs than in their prior jobs, despite putting in longer work hours?
4. What might cause moods and emotions to fluctuate for entrepreneurs?

Opening Case

EFFECTIVELY MANAGING DIVERSITY IS AN ONGOING CHALLENGE

How can organizations meet the challenge of effectively managing diversity?

Some people believe that discrimination is a thing of the past. They acknowledge that discrimination in the workplace was a serious problem in earlier times but feel that today, heightened awareness of the problem, as well as the significant legal and financial consequences that can result from it, has eliminated most forms of discrimination.

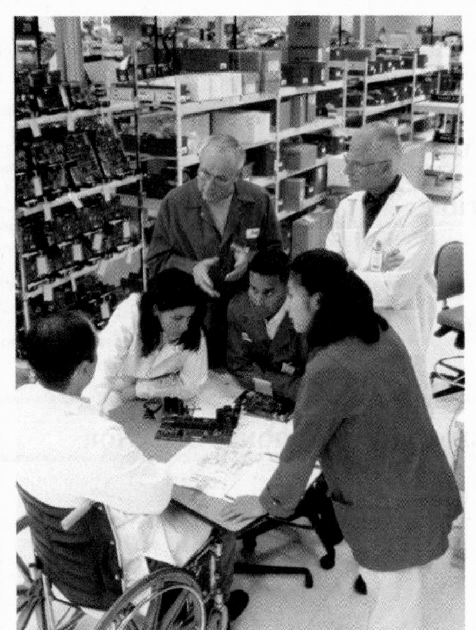

Effectively managing diversity is critical for all organizations, large and small.

Unfortunately, discrimination is not a thing of the past. Class-action discrimination lawsuits are still being settled every day to the tune of millions of dollars. For example, over the past 10 years, the Adam's Mark chain of luxury hotels agreed to pay \$8 million to settle a racial discrimination lawsuit;[1] Texaco settled a \$176.1 million racial discrimination lawsuit involving 1,400 employees;[2] Ford Motor Company agreed to pay \$3 million to settle allegations that women and minority applicants were discriminated against in the hiring process at several Ford plants;[3] and Coca-Cola settled a racial discrimination lawsuit for \$192.5 million.[4] Currently, unsettled suits alleging workplace discrimination are pending at organizations ranging from Johnson & Johnson and BellSouth to the National Football League, General Electric, and Wal-Mart.[5]

When managers become aware of evidence of potential discrimination, they need to pay immediate attention and act proactively both to address the potential problem and perhaps change the organization's policies and practices. How problems were addressed at General Motors when its minority dealership program was in trouble is a case in point. Problems with the program became apparent in a report prepared by civil rights attorney Weldon Latham. The report addressed alleged problems ranging from minority dealers being overcharged for their dealerships and given undesirable locations to being inadequately trained and having their life savings depleted as a result. GM's program was originally designed to eliminate discrimination, but it seemed to be hurting rather than helping minority dealers.

Eric Peterson, who had recently become head of the minority dealership program when Latham's report came out, took quick proactive steps and implemented 213 of Latham's 215 recommendations to solve the problems he had documented. General Motors now responds to minority dealers' complaints within 30 days; 80 percent of minority dealers are now earning a profit compared to only 50 percent before the changes, and approximately 16 percent of minority dealerships are earning more than \$1 million, which compares favorably with statistics for GM dealerships overall.[6]

Unfortunately, the fact that discrimination lawsuits continue to be filed in U.S. courts signals that at least some organizations are not meeting the challenge of effectively managing diversity.[7] Recently, the National Urban League (a nonprofit organization) conducted a large-scale study of over 5,500 U.S. workers in a variety of jobs, organizations, and positions ranging from entry level employees to top managers and CEOs to determine how employees themselves view the diversity initiatives of their employers.[8] The results of the survey (which was funded by Enterprise rent-a-car) underscore how challenging effectively managing diversity can be. Only 32 percent of employees felt that that their employers effectively managed diversity; only 47 percent of top managers felt that their companies effectively managed diversity. Interestingly enough, of the top managers surveyed, 59 percent indicated that they were partly to blame for their companies not doing a better job of hiring, promoting, and fairly treating diverse employees because they themselves were not as active in diversity initiatives as they could have been.[9]

The study also identified eight companies ("Effective Diversity Practices" companies or "EDP" companies) whose employees indicated were actually doing a good job of effectively managing diversity. How do the EDP companies meet the challenge of effectively managing diversity? While each company has a somewhat different approach, the study identified some consistent themes that set these companies apart.[10] First, there is genuine top-management commitment to the effective management of diversity as an actionable goal, the attainment of which is regularly reviewed. Second, diversity training and recognition and rewards for successful diversity initiatives take place on an ongoing basis at all levels in the organizations. Third, recruiting and hiring diverse employees is a top priority. And lastly, EDP companies' diversity initiatives are not just internally focused, but rather they reach out to the communities in which the companies operate by, for example, seeking diversity in the suppliers of goods and services, marketing to diverse customers, and utilizing external advisory boards to provide guidance as to how the companies can effectively meet the diversity challenge vis-à-vis their own employees, their suppliers and their customers, and the communities in which they operate. Interestingly enough, the growth in productivity of the EDP companies over a recent four-year period was over 15 percent higher than the growth in the productivity of the U.S. economy at large.[11] All in all, while discrimination is definitely not a thing of the past, at least some organizations appear to be meeting the challenge of effectively managing diversity.

Overview

Often two people in an organization with the same qualifications are viewed differently. One may be seen as much more capable than another, even though there is no objective basis for this distinction—the "more capable" person doesn't perform at a higher level. The opening case shows, for example, that African Americans and other minorities in business settings are sometimes seen as less capable and competent than nonminority employees, even when they have identical qualifications.

As another example of the way people can view things differently, think of the last group meeting you attended and the different ways in which people in the group interpreted what went on in the meeting. One person might have seen the final decision as the result of an impartial consideration of all alternatives, but another person might have seen it as the result of a powerful member imposing her or his will. Similarly, what might have appeared to be a reasonable, lively discussion to one person was a noisy, incomprehensible free-for-all to a second, and deeply offensive to a third. The fact is that each of us sees and interprets the same people, objects, and events differently.

In this chapter, we look at how perception and attribution help people organize, make sense of, and interpret what they observe. We discuss why equally qualified members of an organization or equally well intentioned customers are perceived differently, why people who attend the same meeting might have different interpretations of what went on, and even why two people who watch the same movie might come away with very different opinions about it. A major focus of this chapter is the role of perception and attribution in the effective management of diverse employees. Throughout the chapter, we give examples of how managers can enhance their abilities to manage diverse employees by paying attention to the ways they perceive and judge other people.

Perception and attribution are of fundamental importance in understanding and managing organizational behavior because all decisions and behaviors in organizations, such as the management of diversity, are influenced by how its members interpret and make sense of the people and events around them. Decisions about who should be hired, fired, transferred, or promoted and decisions about how to encourage organizational members to be more productive, to be more helpful to coworkers, or to perform otherwise desirable organizational behaviors are all based on managers' interpretations of the situations they face. Managers at all levels of an organization who understand how perception and attribution shape such interpretations are in a good position to try to ensure that their decisions help rather than harm the organization and its members. Understanding perception and attribution can actually help people at all levels of an organization interact with others and be more effective in their jobs.

The Nature of Perception

PERCEPTION
The process by which individuals select, organize, and interpret the input from their senses.

Perception is the process by which individuals select, organize, and interpret the input from their senses (vision, hearing, touch, smell, and taste) to give meaning and order to the world around them. Through perception, people try to make sense of their environment and the objects, events, and other people in it. Perception has three components (see Exhibit 4.1):

1. The *perceiver* is the person trying to interpret some observation that he or she has just made, or the input from his or her senses.
2. The *target of perception* is whatever the perceiver is trying to make sense of. The target can be another person, a group of people, an event, a situation, an idea, a noise, or anything else the perceiver focuses on. In organizational behavior, we are often concerned with *person perception*, or another person as the target of perception.
3. The *situation* is the context in which perception takes place—a committee meeting, the hallway, in front of the office coffee machine, and so on.

Characteristics of all three components influence what is actually perceived.

People tend to think that perception is a simple phenomenon. They believe that there is an objective reality—a reality that exists independent of who observes or describes it—and that as long as their senses are not impaired (as long as they see clearly, hear well, are not intoxicated, and so forth), perception is simply the understanding of this objective reality. People who believe in objective reality tend to believe that their own perceptions are

EXHIBIT 4.1

Components of Perception

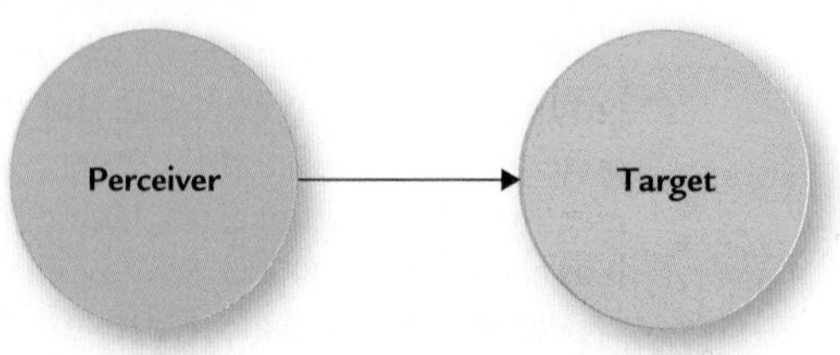

Situation or context in which perception takes place

ACCURATE PERCEPTIONS
Perceptions that are as close as possible to the true nature of the target of perception.

accurate depictions of that reality. They believe that they perceive the true nature of the target (see Exhibit 4.1) and behave as if this were the case.

The perceptual process, however, does not always yield **accurate perceptions**—perceptions that are as close as possible to the true or objective nature of the target. Even people who are trying to be totally "objective" often base their decisions and act on an interpretation of reality that is subjective—that is, one that is based on their own thoughts, feelings, and experiences. As a result, interpretations of reality vary among individuals. What is seen depends on who is doing the looking.

The fact that perception is not always accurate has significant implications for understanding and managing organizational behavior. Virtually every decision that a manager makes—whether it be about hiring, firing, compensating organizational members, and so on—depends on the perceptions of the decision maker, so accurate perceptions are the prerequisite for good decisions. When perceptions are inaccurate, managers and other members of an organization make faulty decisions that hurt not only the employees involved but also the organization. Why are accurate perceptions of such fundamental importance in organizational behavior in general and in managing diverse employees in particular? The answer to this question touches on issues of motivation and performance, fairness and equity, and ethical action.

Motivation and Performance

Recall from Chapter 1 that a major responsibility of managers at all levels is to encourage organization members to perform to the best of their abilities in ways that help the organization achieve its goals. In essence, managers need to make sure that subordinates are motivated to perform at a high level. Because motivation and performance are of such fundamental importance in organizations, in Chapters 6 and 7 we discuss them in detail and the OB tools that managers can use. However, in order to use these tools and motivate their subordinates, managers need to first have an understanding of their diverse subordinates and see them as they really are. The more accurately managers perceive subordinates, the better able they are to motivate them. For example, a manager who accurately perceives that a subordinate is independent and resents close supervision will be more likely to give the subordinate the breathing room he or she needs. Similarly, if a manager accurately perceives that a subordinate who shies away from difficult tasks has the ability to do them but suffers from low self-esteem (one of the personality traits discussed in Chapter 2), the manager will be more likely to assign to the subordinate tasks of an appropriate level of difficulty while at the same time provide the encouragement and support the subordinate needs. Accurate perceptions also help managers relate to each other and enable members at all levels to work together to achieve organizational goals.

Fairness and Equity

Suppose a manager supervises a diverse group of 20 subordinates and every six months the manager has to decide how well each subordinate performed and how big a bonus each deserves. When the manager makes these decisions, it is extremely important that his or her perceptions of each subordinate's performance are as accurate as possible. If the manager's perceptions are inaccurate, the wrong decisions will be made, and some employees are likely to believe they are not being fairly treated and perhaps are even being discriminated against. If some of the high performers receive lower bonuses than some of the mediocre performers, for example, the high performers might feel they are not being treated fairly. As you will see in Chapter 6, fair and equitable treatment is important when it comes to motivating employees. Consequently, inaccurate perceptions on the part of the supervisors of these high performers may breed resentment and cause them to minimize their efforts: Why should they bother to try so hard when their efforts are not being recognized? Similarly, as suggested by the opening case, if African Americans are passed up for promotions because they are mistakenly perceived to be less competent, this unfair treatment hurts not only these employees but also the organization as a whole because it won't fully be utilizing the talents of all of its members. Ultimately, some minority employees

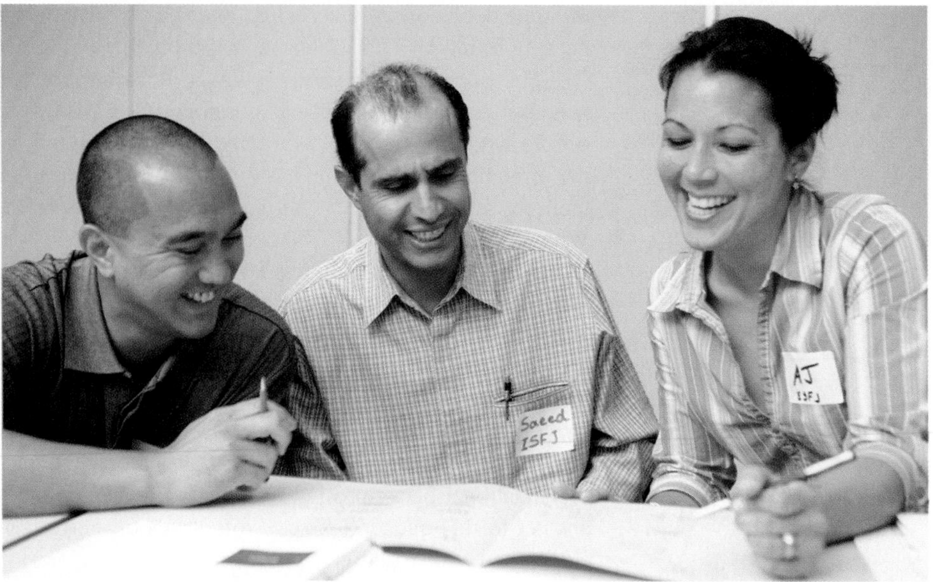

In today's global economy, attracting and retaining a global workforce is a top priority for many organizations.

may leave the organization to seek fairer treatment elsewhere; this turnover will further weaken the organization. It is, therefore, extremely important that managers' perceptions be accurate because their decision making and ultimate effectiveness depend on it.[12]

In today's global economy, it is increasingly important for organizations to be able to attract and retain a global workforce. Just as companies headquartered in the U.S. are hiring employees from around the globe, so too are companies in China and India hiring—for example, hiring American and European employees.[13] Attracting and retaining a global workforce necessitates that employees' contributions, accomplishments, and capabilities are accurately perceived regardless of the employees' nationality or country of origin. Essentially, in order to have an effective global workforce, all members of an organization need to be treated fairly. For example, take the case of an American manager in a Japanese company who is a superior performer and seeks to advance to a top management position. If this manager believes that regardless of her capabilities and contributions, she will never be promoted to such a position because she is not Japanese and all top managers in her company have always been Japanese, she will likely seek to leave the organization. For some reason, managers in her company inaccurately perceive the capabilities and contributions of employees who are not Japanese and thus, do not promote them into high-ranking positions. As another example, a Latino working in an Indian outsourcing company recently decided to change employers when he realized the likelihood of his advancing in the ranks were slim, regardless of his performance and contributions.[14] Thus, regardless of what country a company is based in, attracting and retaining a global workforce requires that employees' capabilities and performance are accurately perceived and that all employees are treated fairly, regardless of their countries of origin.

Ethical Action

We mentioned in Chapter 1 that the workforce is becoming increasingly diverse and members of an organization often interact with others who may be different from them in age, race, gender, ethnicity, and other characteristics. Accurately perceiving diverse members of an organization and their abilities, skills, and performance levels is not only a legal requirement but also an ethical necessity. To give these individuals the opportunities and rewards they deserve, avoid illegal discrimination, and act in an ethical manner, a manager's perceptions must therefore be accurate. Managers and others who understand what perceptions are, how they are formed, and what influences them are in a better position to ensure this happens and that the organization benefits from it.

Characteristics of the Perceiver

Have you noticed that several people can observe the same person or event and come away with different interpretations of what they saw? That suggests that something about the perceiver may influence his or her perception.

Perceivers do not passively process information. Their experience or knowledge (*schemas*), their needs and desires (*motivational states*), and their feelings (*moods*) filter information into their perceptions of reality (see Exhibit 4.2). We now consider the way each of these characteristics of the perceiver affects perception.

Schemas: The Perceiver's Knowledge Base

When John Cunningham, a project manager at the engineering firm Tri-Systems Inc., was assigned to a new supervisor (a retired Air Force colonel), he did not gather a lot of information before forming an impression of him. Instead, he took whatever information was at hand (however incomplete) and developed his own view or perception of his new boss. Simply knowing that his new supervisor used to be in the military was enough to convince Cunningham that he had a pretty good handle on what the retired colonel was like. Cunningham's supervisor in his last position had served in the armed forces, and Cunningham had found him bossy and opinionated. To a neutral observer, such limited information (the supervisor's military background) hardly seems sufficient to support an assessment. But for Cunningham, the equation was simple: His new ex-military supervisor would be opinionated and bossy just as his other one had been.

Like Cunningham, we all interpret the world around us on the basis of limited information. In large part, we rely on past experience and the knowledge we have gathered from a variety of sources to interpret and make sense of any new person or situation (the *target of perception*) we encounter. Our past experiences are organized into **schemas**, abstract knowledge structures that are stored in memory and allow people to organize and interpret information about a given target of perception.[15] Once an individual develops a schema for a target of perception (such as a former military person), any new target related to the schema activates it, and information about the target is processed in a way consistent with information stored in the schema. Thus, schemas determine the way a target is perceived.

SCHEMA
An abstract knowledge structure that is stored in memory and makes possible the organization and interpretation of information about a target of perception.

Schemas help people interpret the world around them by using their past experiences and knowledge. Think about the last time you went to a party where there were many people you didn't know. How did you decide whom to talk to and whom to try to avoid? Without realizing you were doing so, you probably relied on your schemas about what different types of people are like to form your perceptions and then decided with whom you wanted to spend some time.

John Cunningham's schema for *ex-military supervisor* indicates that "ex-military supervisors are bossy and opinionated." Because his new boss was in the military, Cunningham perceives him as bossy and opinionated. All perceivers actively interpret reality so that it is consistent with their expectations, which are, in turn, determined by their schemas.[16]

Schemas also influence the sensory input we pay attention to and the input we ignore. Once a schema is activated, we tend to notice information that is consistent with the schema and ignore or discount information that is inconsistent. Because of his schema, Cunningham is especially attuned to any information that indicates that his new supervisor is bossy and

EXHIBIT 4.2

Characteristics of the Perceiver That Affect Perception

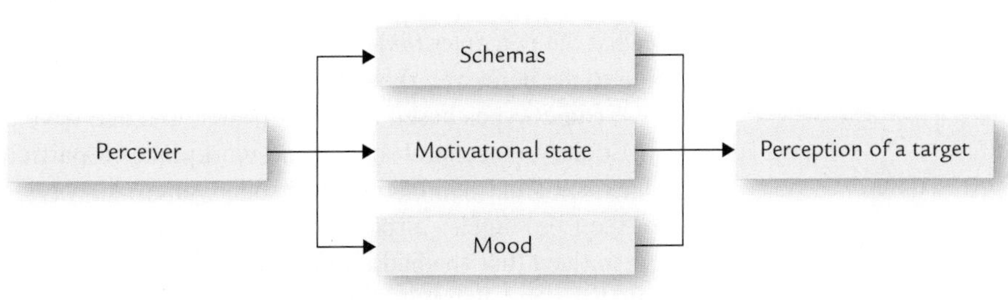

opinionated (the boss has already rearranged the office layout), but Cunningham tends to ignore information to the contrary (the boss solicits and listens to other people's suggestions).

By selecting sensory input consistent with existing schemas and discounting or ignoring inconsistent input, schemas are reinforced and strengthened. It is not surprising, then, that schemas are resistant to change.[17] Resistance does not indicate that schemas are immutable; if they were, people would be unable adapt to changes in their environment. Schemas are, however, slow to change. A considerable amount of contradictory information must be encountered before a person's schemas are altered, and he or she is able to perceive a target differently.

Are Schemas Functional? Many times we jump to the wrong conclusions and form inaccurate perceptions of other people based on our schemas, especially when we have limited information about the target. Schemas, nevertheless, are functional for perceivers. We are continually bombarded with so much sensory input, so many potential targets of perception, that we cannot possibly take them all in and make sense of each one. Schemas help us make sense of this confusing array of sensory input, help us choose what information to pay attention to and what to ignore, and guide our perception of often ambiguous information. In this way, schemas help members of an organization learn about and adapt to the complex environment inside and outside the organization.

Schemas can be dysfunctional, however, if they result in inaccurate perceptions. Cunningham's new supervisor may not be at all bossy or opinionated but may instead be an accessible, competent, and talented manager. Cunningham's schema for *ex-military supervisor*, however, causes him to perceive his boss in a different—and negative—light. Thus, Cunningham's schema is dysfunctional because his inaccurate perceptions color his interactions with his new boss.

Inaccurate perceptions can also be dysfunctional for the target of perception. Some men in business have schemas that fit successful female professionals into a pigeonhole marked "wife, mother, daughter."[18] When a man with such a schema encounters a woman in an organization, the schema is activated, and the man perceives the woman as less competent and capable in a business context than she actually is. This incorrect perception can hurt the woman's future prospects when she is passed up for promotion or denied access to financing to start her own business.

Schemas can guide perceptions in a functional way, but we have to guard against the common tendency to jump to incorrect conclusions based on our past experiences.[19] John Cunningham clearly did not have enough information to have an accurate perception of his supervisor, and he should have refrained from making a judgment until he saw how his supervisor actually behaved on the job.

STEREOTYPE
A set of overly simplified and often inaccurate beliefs about the typical characteristics of a particular group.

Stereotypes: An Example of a Dysfunctional Schema. A **stereotype** is a set of overly simplified and often inaccurate beliefs about the typical characteristics of a particular group. We all are familiar with stereotypes based on highly visible characteristics, such as race, gender, nationality, or age, and we are aware of the damage they can do.[20] Stereotypes are dysfunctional schemas because they are often based on inaccurate information about individuals' interests, beliefs, capabilities, behaviors, and so on. Stereotyped individuals are assigned to the schema only because they possess a single distinguishing characteristic.

As soon as a person is encountered and stereotyped, the perceiver assumes that the person has the characteristics associated with the stereotype.[21] The perceiver pays attention to information consistent with the stereotype and ignores inconsistent information. Because objective reality (what the person is really like) rarely matches subjective reality (what the perceiver *thinks* the person is like), stereotypes can be dysfunctional and damaging to the perceiver, the target, and the organization.

Stereotypes based on race, gender, and age have been responsible for discrimination in society in general and in the workplace in particular. For example, when Margaret Jackson, chairman of the Australian Qantas Airways, was going through airport security at the Los Angeles airport recently, a security guard stopped her and had her frisked after he noticed that she had aircraft designs in her carry-on bag.[22] Jackson told the guard that she was the Chairman of Qantas and in disbelief, he said, "But you're a woman."[23]

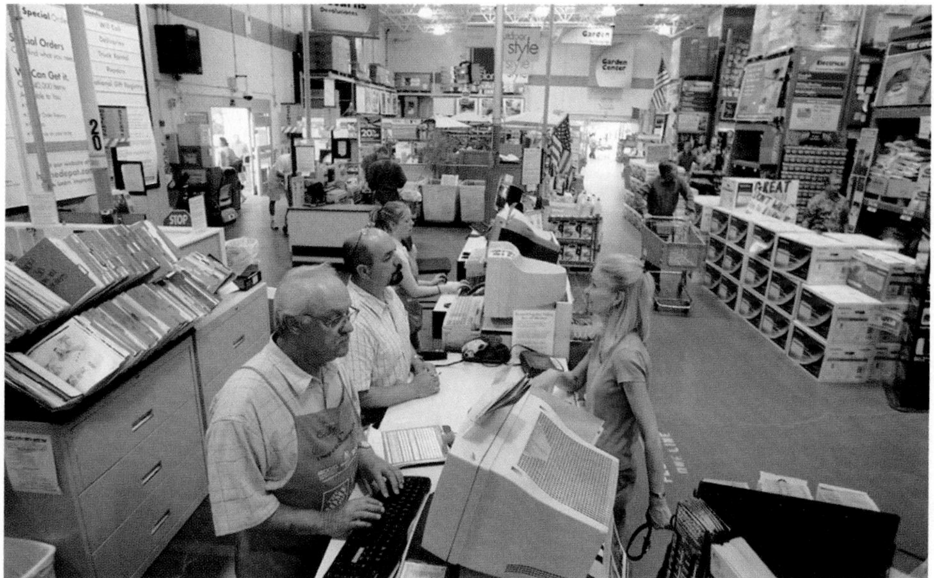

In an effort to recruit and retain older workers, Home Depot offers employees the option of working during the winter months in stores in Florida and during the summer months in stores in states like Maine and Pennsylvania.

As a result of the negative effects of such stereotypes, it is illegal to discriminate against people because of their race, gender, or age, and organizations that do so may face lawsuits, as indicated in the opening case. The aging of the workforce, combined with increases in average life expectancy, has lead to an increase in the number of age discrimination lawsuits being filed by laid-off older workers who believe that they lost their jobs because of their age.[24] At the same time, some organizations are actively recruiting and hiring older employees, as profiled in the following Focus on Diversity.

Employees have to guard against thinking stereotypically about different types of organizational members. One way to do so is to encourage members of an organization to think about the characteristics that really affect job performance and not irrelevant characteristics like age, race, or gender. Discriminating against or treating employees differently because of their gender, age, or race is not only illegal but also unethical. Moreover, it is unethical to discriminate against employees based on any characteristic unrelated to performance whether it is sexual orientation, religion, disabilities, or country of origin. In the years since the fateful September 11 terrorist attack that felled the World Trade Center in New York City, some Arab Americans and others of Middle Eastern descent have been victims of discrimination in the workplace.[25]

The Perceiver's Motivational State

PERCEIVER'S MOTIVATIONAL STATE
The needs, values, and desires of a perceiver at the time of perception.

The **perceiver's motivational state**—the perceiver's needs, values, and desires at the time of perception—influences his or her perception of the target. Perceivers see what they want to see, hear what they want to hear, and believe what they want to believe because of their motivational state. A simple yet ingenious experiment has demonstrated the effects of the perceiver's motivational state. Participants are shown a series of meaningless abstract pictures and are asked what objects and shapes they perceive in them. The images they see depend on their motivational states. Those who are hungry, for example, are motivated to see food and actually do indicate that they perceive images of food in the abstract pictures.[26]

Like schemas, motivational states can result in inaccurate perceptions and faulty decision making. Suppose a manager does not get along with a hardworking, productive subordinate. The subordinate is a thorn in the manager's side, and the manager would welcome any opportunity to justify recommending that the subordinate be transferred to another position or even dismissed. What is likely to happen when the manager must evaluate the subordinate's performance on some relatively subjective dimensions such as cooperation and being a good team player? Even if the subordinate actually deserves to score high, the manager may rate the person low.

Organizational members need to be aware that their own needs and desires influence their perceptions and can result in faulty decisions that have negative consequences for the

Focus on Diversity

Some Older Workers Lose Jobs, Others Find Them

A growing number of companies are facing age discrimination lawsuits filed by laid-off employees who believe that their age was the reason they were let go. Lynette Steuck was a 51-year-old software project manager when she was laid off from Best Buy. Steuck and 45 of other laid-off employees are suing Best Buy for age discrimination. Stephen Snyder, the attorney handling the case, indicates that age was a factor in the lay-off decisions and that "The people in their 30s were at greater risk of termination than those in their 20s, the 40's more than the 30s, the 50's more than the 40s. And the people in their 60s and up were at the greatest risk of all."[27] Hugh Juergens, a plaintiff in the Best Buy case, indicated that he received exemplary performance evaluations from his boss prior to being laid off by the company. Best Buy denies that age discrimination took place and it will be up to the courts to decide the outcome of the case.[28]

Best Buy is not alone in being faced with charges of age discrimination. For example, both Sprint and IBM face similar charges (which they also refute). In the Sprint case, 2,300 employees were laid off and those filing the age discrimination suit claim a forced ranking system was used to categorize older workers as low performers. Sharon Louk, a plaintiff in the Sprint case, recalls her boss telling her that "We need to get young people."[29] Bonnie Hoopes, another plaintiff, said that her boss told her in an email that the best employees have a variety of characteristics including "lots of runway ahead of them."[30] Again, the outcomes of these and other age discrimination lawsuits will be decided by the courts. Law Professor Howard Eglit at the Chicago-Kent School of Law estimates that less than one third of age discrimination lawsuits actually are settled in favor of the employees alleging age discrimination.[31]

Ironically, just as these lawsuits are increasing, other organizations like Home Depot, Borders Bookstores, and Wal-Mart are actively trying to recruit older workers.[32] Home Depot offers employees the option of working during the winter months in stores in Florida and during the summer months in stores in states like Pennsylvania and Maine. Borders Bookstores recruits retired teachers and other older employees by providing them with free books and other benefits that appeal to them. Wal-Mart recruits older workers in senior centers and has over 200,000 employees over the age of 55.[33] However, it is generally harder for older workers to find new jobs than younger ones and it takes them longer to do so.[34] In any case, when companies do discriminate against older employees, not only do they risk having to fight costly lawsuits, but they also risk losing the contributions of valuable employees.

organization. One way managers can guard against this outcome is to base perceptions on actual behaviors they have observed a person performing. In sum, managers need to be aware of their own motives, concentrate on perceiving how people actually perform, and refrain from assuming how someone probably behaved when they did not directly observe his or her behavior.

PERCEIVER'S MOOD
How a perceiver feels at the time of perception.

The Perceiver's Mood

The **perceiver's mood**—how the perceiver feels at the time of perception—can also influence perception of the target. In Chapter 3, we discussed how work moods (people's feelings at the time they perform their jobs) influence organizational behavior. People's moods also affect their perception of a target.[35]

Marie Flanagan, a fashion designer for a clothing manufacturer, was so excited about the new line of women's suits she finished designing late one afternoon that she could hardly wait to show her sketches to her supervisor Phil Kraus the next day. But when Flanagan saw Kraus in the hallway the next morning, he barely grunted "hello," and later that morning his secretary told Flanagan that Kraus was in a terrible mood. Despite her eagerness to find out what Kraus thought of her new line, Flanagan decided to wait until he was in a better mood before showing him her sketches. She reasoned that even if the new line was a potential winner, Kraus was likely to find fault with it because of his bad mood. She realized that people's moods influence their perceptions and judgments. When employees are in a positive mood, they are likely to perceive their coworkers, supervisors, subordinates, and even their jobs in a more positive light than they would when they are in a negative mood.[36]

Characteristics of the Target and Situation

We defined *perception* as the process whereby people select, organize, and interpret the input from their senses to give meaning and order to the world around them. This input comes from the targets of perception in the situations in which they are perceived. Thus, just as characteristics of the perceiver influence perceptions, so, too, do the characteristics of the target and the situation (see Exhibit 4.3).

How do characteristics of the target influence perception? Consider two job applicants (the targets of perception) who have similar qualifications and are equally capable. An interviewer (the perceiver), however, perceived one applicant much more positively than the other because of the way each acted during the interview. One applicant tried to make a good impression by volunteering information about his past accomplishments and achievements and behaving in a confident and businesslike fashion. The other was low key and mentioned his achievements only when he was specifically asked about them. The difference in behavior caused the interviewer to perceive one applicant as more capable than the other.

Here is an example of how the situation influences perception. Suppose you (the perceiver) see one of your friends (the target) wearing a bathing suit at the beach (the situation). You might perceive that he is relaxed and enjoying himself. Now suppose you see the same friend wearing a bathing suit at work (another situation). You perceive that he is psychologically disturbed.

In this section, we consider the ambiguity and social status of the target and impression management by the target. We then discuss how characteristics of the situation influence perception by providing additional information for the perceiver to use to interpret the

EXHIBIT 4.3

Factors That Influence Perception

Characteristics of the Perceiver	Characteristics of the Target	Characteristics of the Situation
Schemas: The perceiver's knowledge base	Ambiguity: A lack of clearness or definiteness that makes it difficult to determine what a person, place, or thing is really like	Additional information: Situational information that the perceiver uses to interpret the target
Motivational state: The perceiver's needs, values, and desires at the time of perception	Social status: A person's real or perceived position in society or an organization	Salience: The extent to which a target stands out among a group of people or things
Mood: The perceiver's feelings at the time of perception	Use of impression management: A person's efforts to control others' perceptions of him or her	

target. Managers and other members of an organization who are aware of the ways in which various target- and situation-related factors influence perception are well positioned to ensure that their perceptions of people, things, and events are as accurate as possible.

Ambiguity of the Target

The word *ambiguity* refers to a lack of clearness or definiteness. It is difficult for a perceiver to determine what an ambiguous target is really like. As the ambiguity of a target increases, it becomes increasingly difficult for perceivers to form accurate perceptions. It is also more likely that different perceivers will differ in their perceptions of the target.

Four managers are jointly responsible for choosing new locations for fast-food restaurants for a national chain. Certain locations (for example, those across the street from a large university) are sure winners and others (for example, those difficult to enter and leave because of traffic congestion) are sure losers. Such locations are relatively unambiguous targets of perception. Each of the four managers perceives them accurately, and they agree with each other about the desirability of those locations.

When the nature of a target is clear, different perceivers have little difficulty forming similar perceptions of the target that are close to its real nature. But when a target is ambiguous, the perceiver needs to engage in a lot more interpretation and active construction of reality to form a perception of the target. The suitability of some of the locations that the four managers must evaluate is ambiguous. Will a restaurant located in a once prosperous but now failing shopping mall that is being renovated do well? Will a restaurant located on the outskirts of a small town in a rural area attract enough customers to earn a profit? The managers' perceptions of the desirability of such locations tend to be less certain than their perceptions of less ambiguous locations, and they often find themselves disagreeing with each other.

The more ambiguous a target is, the more potential there is for errors in perception. Thus, when targets are ambiguous, members of an organization should not be overly confident about the accuracy of their perceptions, and they should acquire as much additional information as they can to help them form an accurate perception. When looking at ambiguous restaurant locations (to continue our example), the four managers should collect a lot of information—estimates of the performance levels of other fast-food restaurants in the vicinity, traffic patterns at mealtimes, population growth in the area, spending patterns of likely patrons, and so on—to be sure their perceptions are accurate before they make a decision.

Social Status of the Target

SOCIAL STATUS
A person's real or perceived position in society or in an organization.

Social status is a person's real or perceived position in society or in an organization. In the minds of many people, targets with a relatively high status are perceived to be smarter, more credible, more knowledgeable, and more responsible for their actions than lower-status targets. Organizations often use a high-status member to make an important announcement to other members of the organization or to the public at large because the audience is likely to perceive the announcer as credible. A lower-status member of the organization who is more knowledgeable than anyone else about the issue at hand is likely to lack credibility because of his or her status.

To ensure that women and members of minority groups enjoy equal footing with white men, and have the social status they deserve in an organization and to conform to legal requirements, many organizations have adopted affirmative-action programs. These programs, however, sometimes perpetuate the perception problems and stereotypes they were meant to overcome. Women and minority group members are sometimes perceived as having relatively low status in the organization because they were affirmative-action hires—people hired not because of their own merits but because of their gender or minority status. Their affirmative-action status causes other members of the organization to perceive and treat them as second-class citizens.

U.S. courts have been increasingly restricting affirmative-action programs in universities on the grounds that they are unconstitutional. The Business-Higher Education Forum, a recently formed cooperative consisting of 25 corporations, 36 universities, and 7 nonprofit organizations, is nonetheless seeking to promote diversity in the college admissions process. CEOs of major corporations support the Forum because in the years to come they want to be able to hire and maintain a diverse workforce reflecting the broader diversity of their customer bases.[37]

Impression Management by the Target

IMPRESSION MANAGEMENT
An attempt to control the perceptions or impressions of others.

Impression management is an attempt to control the perceptions or impressions of others.[38] Just as a perceiver actively constructs reality through his or her perceptions, a target of perception can also play an active role in managing the perceptions that others have of him or her.

People in organizations use several impression-management tactics to affect how others perceive them. They are especially likely to use these tactics when interacting with perceivers who have power over them and on whom they are dependent for evaluations, raises, and promotions.[39] Subordinates, for example, use impression-management tactics on their supervisors to a greater extent than supervisors use them on subordinates. Nevertheless, impression management is a two-way street engaged in by people at all organizational levels as they interact with superiors, peers, and subordinates as well as with suppliers, customers, and other people outside the organization. Exhibit 4.4 describes five common

EXHIBIT 4.4

Impression Management Tactics

Tactic	Description	Example
Behavioral matching	The target of perception matches his or her behavior to that of the perceiver.	A subordinate tries to imitate her boss's behavior by being modest and soft-spoken because her boss is modest and soft-spoken.
Self-promotion	The target tries to present herself or himself in as positive a light as possible.	An employee reminds his boss about his past accomplishments and associates with co-workers who are evaluated highly.
Conforming to situational norms	The target follows agreed-upon rules for behavior in the organization.	An employee stays late every night even if she has completed all of her assignments, because staying late is one of the norms of her organization.
Appreciating or flattering others	The target compliments the perceiver. This tactic works best when flattery is not extreme and when it involves a dimension important to the perceiver.	A co-worker compliments a manager on his excellent handling of a troublesome employee.
Being consistent	The target's beliefs and behaviors are consistent. There is agreement between the target's verbal and nonverbal behaviors.	A subordinate whose views on diversity are well known flatters her boss for her handling of a conflict between two co-workers of different racial backgrounds. When speaking to her boss, the target looks her boss straight in the eye and has a sincere expression on her face.

Source: C. N. Alexander, Jr., and G. W. Knight, "Situated Identities and Social Psychological Experimentation," *Sociometry* 34 (1971): 65–82; S. T. Fiske and S. E. Taylor, *Social Cognition* (Reading, MA: Addison-Wesley, 1984); K. J. Gergen and M. G. Taylor, "Social Expectancy and Self-Presentation in a Status Hierarchy," *Journal of Experimental Social Psychology* 5 (1969): 79–92; D. Newston and T. Czerlinsky, "Adjustment of Attitude Communications for Contrasts by Extreme Audiences," Journal of Personality and Social Psychology 30 (1974); 829–37; B. R. Schenkler, *Impression Management: The Self-Concept, Social Identity, and Interpersonal Relations* (Monterey, CA: Brooks/Cole, 1980); M. Snyder, "Impression Management," in L. S. Wrightsman (Ed.), Social Psychology in the Seventies (New York: Wiley, 1977).

impression-management tactics: behavioral matching, self-promotion, conforming to situational norms, appreciating or flattering others, and being consistent.

Conforming to situational norms—the informal rules of behavior that most members of an organization follow—is a particularly important impression-management tactic.[40] Situational norms can pertain to working past the traditional 5 P.M. quitting time to impress the boss, disagreeing with others in meetings to be seen as important, or even dressing to make a good impression.

People differ in the extent to which they conform to situational norms and engage in other forms of impression management. In Chapter 2, we discussed how people who are high on the trait of self-monitoring are especially concerned about behaving appropriately. It is likely, therefore, that people who are high on self-monitoring are more likely than individuals who are low on self-monitoring to engage in impression-management tactics such as conforming to situational norms.

Conforming to situational norms can often be difficult for people operating in the international arena. Common courtesies and gestures that are taken for granted in one culture or country may be frowned on or downright insulting in another. The common hand signal for "Okay" that is used in the United States, for example, is considered obscene in Brazil, Ghana, Greece, and Turkey and means "zero" or "worthless" in France and Belgium. As another example, in the United States it is considered polite to ask a man how his wife is, but in Arab countries this inquiry is considered indiscreet.[41]

Outright deceit can be used in impression management but is probably not very common. Ingrained moral or ethical codes prevent most people from deliberately misrepresenting themselves or lying.[42] In addition, the chances of being found out are often pretty high. Claiming on an employment application, for example, that you attended a certain school or worked for a company though you never did is neither honest nor smart. Most impression management is an attempt to convey as positive an impression as possible without lying about one's capabilities, achievements, and experiences. People are especially likely to engage in impression management when they are likely to benefit from it. The reward may be desirable job assignments, promotions, raises, or the good opinions of others.

Information Provided by the Situation

The situation—the context or environment surrounding the perceiver and the target—provides the perceiver with additional information to use in interpreting the target. Consider the situation Marci Sloan was in when she started a new job as supervisor of salespeople in a large department store. The department store had just begun a push to increase the quality of customer service, and Sloan's boss impressed on her that improved service to customers should be a major priority for her department. On her first day on the job, Sloan decided to spend as much time as she could unobtrusively observing her salespeople in action so she could get a good idea of the level of service they were routinely providing.

The levels of service offered by the four salespeople she was able to observe varied considerably. In forming her perceptions of these salespeople, however, she relied not only on the behavior she observed but also on the situation in which the behavior occurred. One key factor was how busy the department was when she observed each salesperson. She observed two of them in the morning when business was slow. Each person handled only two customers, but one salesperson provided significantly more service than the other. She observed the other two salespeople in the late afternoon—the busiest time of day for the department. Both had a continual stream of customers. One salesperson handled more customers than the other, but the slower salesperson gave each customer more personal attention. Clearly, Sloan could not rely solely on the behavior of the salespeople in forming her impression of the customer service they were providing. She also had to consider all the additional information that the situation provided.

Standing Out in the Crowd: The Effects of Salience in a Situation

SALIENCE
The extent to which a target of perception stands out in a group of people or things.

In considering how the situation affects perception, we need to focus on one factor that is particularly important: the **salience** of the target in the situation—that is, the extent to which the target stands out in a group of people or things. We have all experienced the effects of salience.

The decisions of Justice Sandra Day O'Connor, the first woman to serve on the U.S. Supreme Court, were closely watched following her appointment in 1981 by President Ronald Reagan. Justice O'Connor's first major case came in 1982. She wrote an opinion holding that a male student could not be rejected from a nursing school because of his gender.

Have you ever been the only student in a room full of professors, the only man in a group of women, or the only African-American person in a room full of white people? A salient individual is very conspicuous and often feels self-conscious. He or she believes that everyone is watching his or her every move. That assessment is pretty accurate too. The other people in the group or room do pay more attention to the salient person, for he or she indeed does stand out. Salience, in and of itself, *should not affect* how a target is perceived. After all, a man is the same person regardless of whether he is in a room full of men or women. But remember that perception is a subjective process and, because of that subjectivity, salience *does affect* how a target is perceived. Exhibit 4.5 lists some situational factors that cause a target to stand out.

EXHIBIT 4.5

Causes of Salience

Cause	Description	Examples
Being novel	Anything that makes a target unique in a situation	Being the only person of a particular age, sex, or race in a situation; wearing jeans when everyone else is dressed in business clothes
Being figural	Standing out from the background by virtue of being bright or illuminated, changing, moving, sitting or standing in a prominent place, or seeming to be complex	Being in a spotlight; moving more than others in a group; sitting at the head of the table; wearing bright clothes
Being inconsistent with other people's expectations	Behaving or looking in a way that is out of the ordinary	A normally shy person who is the life of the party; a salesperson who insults a customer; a man or woman who is exceptionally attractive

Source: S. T. Fiske and S. E. Taylor, *Social Cognition* (Reading, MA: Addison-Wesley, 1984); R. M. Kanter, *Men and Women of the Corporation* (New York: Basic Books, 1977); L. Z. McArthur and E. Ginsberg, "Causal Attribution to Salient Stimuli: An Investigation of Visual Fixation Mediators," *Personality and Social Psychology Bulletin 7* (1981); 547–53; L. Z. McArthur and D. L. Post, "Figural Emphasis and Person Perception," *Journal of Experimental Social Psychology* 13 (1977); 520–35; C. Wolman and H. Frank, "The Solo Woman in a Professional Peer Group," *American Journal of Orthopsychiatry* 45 (1975): 164–71.

What are the consequences of salience for perception in organizations? Consider the experiences Mary Schwartz has had as the only female partner in a small consulting firm. Her male colleagues treat her as their equal, and she gets along well with each of them, but she still feels the effects of her salience. These effects take the form of extreme evaluations and stereotyping.

Extreme Evaluations. Schwartz noticed that her male colleagues' reactions to her various accomplishments and mishaps on the job seemed to be extreme. She recently landed a major new account for the firm and received such lavish praise that she became embarrassed. Likewise, when she was unable to attend an important meeting because of a family problem, it was made clear to her that she had lost favor in everyone's eyes.

Schwartz's experience is not unique. Individuals who are salient are often perceived in more extreme terms (positive or negative) than inconspicuous members of a group. They are also seen as being especially influential or responsible for what happens to them and to the groups they belong to.[43]

Stereotyping. On several occasions Schwartz felt that her male colleagues were unintentionally stereotyping her as a "typical woman." They frequently called on her to enlighten them about the "woman's point of view" on various matters such as how to deal with a female client or subordinate. On several occasions, Schwartz was tempted to tell her colleagues that all women are not alike and to point out that she had more in common with them even though they were men than she had in common with their female subordinates or clients.

Individuals who are salient, like Schwartz, are often perceived in terms of whatever is causing their salience: They are stereotyped.[44] Perceivers consider the thoughts, feelings, and behaviors of salient individuals to be more consistent with their distinguishing feature than would be the case if they were not salient. Perceivers often also view them as being representative of all people who are like them with regard to the salient characteristic.

Being salient and stereotyped in a situation can actually result in a target's performance being adversely affected.[45] Research by Claude Steele, a psychologist at Stanford University, has found that when people who are salient think about stereotypes that are relevant to task performance, their performance might actually be impaired.[46] Performance impairment occurs because salient, stereotyped individuals become concerned that others will perceive them based on the stereotype, which distracts them and diverts some of their attention away from task performance.[47] This phenomenon, called *stereotype threat,* can affect the performance of individuals who are salient for a variety of reasons.[48]

Salience due to race has particularly powerful effects on perception. Although there are more African Americans and minorities in management positions today than there were several years ago, African-American managers still experience the effects of their relative salience and stereotyping. A recent study found that 45 percent of minority senior executives had been the butt of cultural or racial jokes while on the job, and 44 percent reported that they had to control their anger resulting from differential treatment at work. More than half of the executives felt that their organizations gave less-challenging assignments to minorities.[49] Other research suggests that a little less than half of minority employees believe that their organizations are not trying hard enough to provide opportunities for nonwhite employees. Thus, it may not be surprising that African-American employees see less of a connection between their levels of performance and the pay they receive and are less likely to feel that they are paid well than their white counterparts.[50] Fortunately, the situation is improving and more and more organizations are taking concrete steps to reduce the negative effects of salience and stereotyping on minority employees. One such step that seems to be effective is linking managers' bonuses to diversity goals and initiatives. According to Fortune magazine, 38 of the 50 best companies for minorities to work for do this, and it is helping provide more opportunities and a fairer workplace for all employees.[51]

Another that has employees who have felt the negative effects of salience and stereotyping are people with disabilities. There are over 20 million people of working age with disabilities in the United States and only about 37.5 percent of them are working.[52] Of those who are not working, many wish they had a job.[53] The percentage of working-age Americans with disabilities is projected to increase due to a variety of factors including the aging of the population, medical advances, and U.S. involvement in the war in Iraq.[54] The Americans with Disabilities Act (ADA), passed by Congress in 1990 and put into effect in 1992, requires that organizations make their buildings and workplaces accessible to the disabled and provide accommodations to enable disabled employees to do their jobs.[55]

Ethics in Action

Disabled Employees Key to Success at Habitat International

Habitat International, a manufacturer and contractor of indoor-outdoor carpet and artificial grass and supplier to major home-improvement companies such as The Home Depot and Lowe's, was founded over 20 years ago by CEO David Morris, and his father Saul.[57] Habitat has an enviable track record of success. Over the past 10 years, profits have increased every year, the factory's defect rate is lower than one-half percent, and there have been only about 10 carpets that have been cut incorrectly in the company's entire history, even though during its peak months from January to June, some 15,000 rugs are produced daily.[58]

Morris is the first to acknowledge that Habitat's employees are responsible for his company's success. Interestingly enough, about 75 percent of Habitat's employees (including some managers) have either a mental or physical disability or both kinds of disabilities.[59] When plant manager Connie Presnell recently filled a rush order by assigning it to a team of her fastest workers, each of them had some sort of disability (e.g., Down's syndrome, schizophrenia, cerebral palsy).[60] Throughout the years, Habitat also has provided employment opportunities to the homeless, alcoholics who are recovering, and refugees from other countries who do not speak English. Habitat's employees are paid competitive wages for the kind of work they do and absence and turnover

Habitat International's commitment to social responsibility and diversity has provided numerous employment opportunities for disabled working-age people in Chattanooga, TN, and has enabled the company to flourish. Approximately 75% of Habitat's employees have some kind of disability.

rates at Habitat are very low. The company is sensitive to its employees' needs and provides them with the accommodations that they need to perform their jobs effectively, which results in a win-win situation.[61]

While Habitat has gained some accounts due to its commitment to diversity, the company's ethical values and social responsibility have also led it to forego a major account. In terms of the latter, Morris became very angry several years ago when representatives of a distribution company made disparaging comments about his employees (out of their earshot). While the head of the company called and apologized, the same thing happened again (after the apology was made) and Morris dropped the account. It took Habitat two years to regain the revenues it lost from that account and Morris has no regrets.[62] All in all, Habitat's commitment to diversity and social responsibility has enabled the company to flourish and has provided employment opportunities for people with disabilities in Chattanooga, Tennessee.[63]

However, employment rates of people with disabilities have actually declined in recent years. As profiled in the following Ethics in Action, Habitat International's commitment to social responsibility and diversity has both provided employment opportunities for disabled working age people in Chattanooga, Tennessee, while at the same time enabling the company to flourish.[56]

Biases and Problems in Person Perception

BIAS
A systematic tendency to use or interpret information in a way that results in inaccurate perceptions.

We have been describing what perception is, how and why perceptions are formed, and the powerful effects they have on organizations and their members. Throughout this discussion, we emphasized the importance of accurate perceptions. Accurate perceptions enable managers to evaluate subordinates' performance correctly and make fair and ethical decisions about whom to hire and promote. They also enable members of an organization to understand and get along with each other and with clients, customers, and other people outside the organization.

You might think that once members of an organization are armed with this knowledge of perception (as you are now), their perceptions would be greatly improved, and they would do a better job of seeing other people (targets) as they really are. Unfortunately, biases and problems in person perception limit the accuracy of perception,[64] and dramatic improvement does not always come about.

Primacy effects are common problems in interviews. An interviewer who falls victim to the primacy effect may turn down qualified interviewees who fail to perform well in the first minute or two of an interview because they are nervous.

A **bias** is a systematic tendency to use or interpret information about a target in a way that results in inaccurate perceptions. When bias and problems in person perception exist, perceivers form inaccurate perceptions of a target. In turn, when perceptions are inaccurate, decisions are likely to be inappropriate: An incompetent subordinate gets promoted, or a competent job candidate receives a negative rating from an interviewer. Managers, coworkers, and subordinates who are aware of biases and problems in person perception are in a good position to prevent them from affecting their subsequent behavior and decisions. We have already examined how stereotypes can bias perception. In this section, we look at primacy, contrast, and halo effects and other common biases (see Exhibit 4.6).

Primacy Effects

Despite the old saying "You can't judge a book by its cover," you have probably heard or learned firsthand how important first impressions are. Scientific evidence, however,

PRIMACY EFFECT
The biased perception that results when the first information that a perceiver has about a target has an inordinately large influence on the perceiver's perception of the target.

supports the folk wisdom of the adage. **Primacy effect** is the biased perception that results when the first pieces of information that people have about some target have an inordinately large influence on their perception of the target.

Primacy effects are common problems in interviews. Research has found that many interviewers decide in the first few minutes of an interview whether a job candidate is a good prospect and then spend the rest of the interview confirming their initial judgment by selectively paying attention to information that is consistent with that judgment and discounting or ignoring inconsistent information. An interviewer who falls victim to the primacy effect may turn down qualified interviewees who fail to perform well in the first minute or two of an interview because they are nervous.

Primacy effects can also be a problem in the perception and evaluation of long-time members of an organization. The manager of a subordinate who starts out on the fast track but then begins to slide downhill may fail to perceive the subordinate's performance problems because of the primacy effect. The manager's perception of the subordinate's current level of performance is biased by the subordinate's early success. As a result of this faulty perception, the manager will fail to give the subordinate the feedback and coaching necessary to get the subordinate back on track. Organizational members who are aware of

EXHIBIT 4.6

Biases and Problems in Person Perception

Source of Bias	Description	Example
Primacy effects	The initial pieces of information that a perceiver has about a target have an inordinately large effect on the perceiver's perception and evaluation of the target.	Interviewers decide in the first few minutes of an interview whether or not a job candidate is a good prospect.
Contrast effect	The perceiver's perceptions of others influence the perceiver's perception of a target.	A manager's perception of an average subordinate is likely to be lower if that subordinate is in a group with very high performers rather than in a group with very low performers.
Halo effect	The perceiver's general impression of a target influences his or her perception of the target on specific dimensions.	A subordinate who has made a good overall impression on a supervisor is rated as performing high-quality work and always meeting deadlines regardless of work that is full of mistakes and late.
Similar-to-me effect	People perceive others who are similiar to themselves more positively than they perceive those who are dissimilar.	Supervisors rate subordinates who are similar to them more positively than they deserve.
Harshness, leniency, and average tendency	Some perceivers tend to be overly harsh in their perceptions, some overly lenient. Others view most targets as being about average.	When rating subordinates' performances, some supervisors give almost everyone a poor rating, some give almost everyone a good rating, and others rate almost everyone as being about average.
Knowledge of predictor	Knowing how a target stands on a predictor of performance influences perceptions of the target.	A professor perceives a student more positively than she deserves because the professor knows the student had a high score on the SAT.

primacy effects can be on guard not to let their first impressions distort their perceptions. For example, if a new hire comes to work with visible tattoos or body piercings, this personal appearance choice should not influence perceptions of how capable or conscientious the new hire might be.

Contrast Effects

CONTRAST EFFECT
The biased perception that results when perceptions of a target person are distorted by the perceiver's perception of others.

A **contrast effect** is the biased perception that results when perceptions of a target person are distorted by the perceiver's perception of others in the situation. A manager's perception of a subordinate whose performance is average is likely to be less favorable if that subordinate is in a group of very high performers than it would be if that subordinate were in a group of average or low performers. An average job applicant will be perceived more favorably by an interviewer if he or she is preceded by two or three below-average applicants rather than by two or three above-average applicants. Both the manager and the interviewer in those examples are victims of the contrast effect. The subordinate's and the job applicant's performance and capabilities are not changed at all by the behavior of other employees and applicants.

Halo Effects

HALO EFFECT
The biased perception that results when the perceiver's general impression of a target distorts his or her perception of the target on specific dimensions.

A **halo effect** occurs when the perceiver's general impression of a target distorts his or her perception of the target on specific dimensions.[65] A subordinate who has made a good overall impression on a supervisor, for example, may be rated as performing high-quality work and always meeting deadlines (specific dimensions of performance) even though the person's work is full of mistakes and is usually late. Because of the halo effect, the subordinate will not receive the feedback necessary to improve performance on the specific dimensions in question. Halos can be negative too: A supervisor who has a negative overall impression of a subordinate may mistakenly perceive that the subordinate is uncooperative and spends too much time on the telephone.

Similar-to-Me Effects

It is a fact of life that people tend to like others who are similar to themselves. In organizations, this "birds of a feather"/"like likes like" tendency can create problems because people tend (often unconsciously) to perceive those who are similar to themselves more positively than they perceive those who are dissimilar. During a performance appraisal, for example, supervisors may rate subordinates who are similar to them more positively than they deserve.[66] Likewise, interviewers may evaluate potential candidates who are similar to themselves more positively than they rate candidates who are dissimilar. Similar-to-me effects can be particularly problematic for women and minority group members trying to climb the corporate ladder. For example, similar-to-me effects may lead male CEOs to groom as their successors men who are like themselves and thus not perceive a woman as a viable successor.[67]

The similar-to-me bias is especially important to overcome today given the increasing diversity in organizational membership. In a work force that includes many women, members of minority groups, and increasing numbers of people with disabilities, managers and subordinates have more frequent contact with people unlike themselves. When evaluating others who are different, people must try to be as objective as possible and avoid the similar-to-me trap.

Members of an organization also have to be on the lookout for the similar-to-me bias when interacting with people from other cultures. For example, when researchers from three global organizations—Siemens AG of Germany, Toshiba Corporation of Japan, and IBM—joined forces at IBM's East Fishkill, New York, facility to work together to develop a revolutionary computer chip, the similar-to-me bias struck. Some of the researchers tried to interact primarily with people from their own cultures. Some of the Japanese researchers, for instance, tried to work mainly with other Japanese researchers, rather than with the German or American researchers, whom they perceived as "so different."[68]

Harshness, Leniency, and Average Tendency Biases

When rating a subordinate's performance, some supervisors tend to be overly harsh, whereas some are overly lenient. Others tend to rate everyone as being about average. Any of these tendencies is problematic for two reasons. First, the supervisor does not correctly perceive the variations in the performance of his or her subordinates. As a result, high performers do not receive appropriate recognition and rewards for their superior accomplishments, and low performers do not receive the constructive feedback they need to improve performance.

The second reason why these biases are problematic is that they make it difficult to evaluate and compare the performance of subordinates who have different supervisors. A subordinate who has received relatively poor ratings from a harsh supervisor may be just as accomplished as a subordinate who has received average or high ratings from a lenient one. Evaluations biased in this manner can result in faulty decision making about pay raises and promotions. These biases can also operate in classroom settings. One professor, for example, gives mostly A's in a course in which another professor maintains a C+ class average. Students in the first professor's class may be content, but those in the other professor's class are likely to feel that they are not being fairly treated.

Knowledge-of-Predictor Bias

To decide whom to hire, how to assign jobs to newly hired and existing members of an organization, and whom to promote, organizations measure people's standing on different predictors of performance. Depending on the job in question, the indicators used to determine how well a person will be able to accomplish work activities in the future can range from educational background and prior work experiences, to standardized tests scores, and performance on certain critical job-related tasks.

If coworkers, managers, or others in the organization know a person's standing on a predictor of performance, the information may bias their perceptions of the person. This problem is known as **knowledge-of-predictor bias**. If a professor knows, for example, that a student has scored highly on some predictor of academic performance such as the Scholastic Aptitude Test (SAT) or the Graduate Management Admission Test (GMAT), this knowledge may lead the professor to perceive the student more positively than he or she deserves. This bias could also work to the disadvantage of a person who scored poorly on the predictor.

KNOWLEDGE-OF-PREDICTOR BIAS
The biased perception that results when knowing a target's standing on a predictor of performance influences the perceiver's perception of the target.

SELF-FULFILLING PROPHECY
A prediction that comes true because a perceiver expects it to come true.

Sometimes, knowledge-of-predictor bias results in a **self-fulfilling prophecy**—a prediction that comes true because a perceiver expects it to come true.[69] The classic demonstration of this phenomenon took place in a classroom setting in the 1960s. At the beginning of the school year, teachers were told that a few of their students were potential "late bloomers" who, given the proper encouragement, should excel. In fact, these students had been randomly selected from the class rosters and were no different from their peers. Later on in the school year, however, the "late bloomers" were indeed doing better and had even improved their scores on standardized IQ tests compared to their earlier performance and the performance of the other children in the class.[70] What was responsible for the change? The teachers in the study probably gave the "late bloomers" more attention, encouragement, and feedback and had higher expectations of them, all of which resulted in their improved performance. The teachers may have also looked more at these students and made encouraging body gestures toward them. In this way, knowledge of a predictor (in this case, a false predictor) resulted in behavior changes that caused that prediction to become true. Research has also shown that when an interviewer conveys negative expectations to a job applicant simply through nonverbal body language, the applicant performs poorly.[71] This situation hurts both the applicant and the organization; the applicant won't get the job, and the organization may lose a potentially capable member.

Sometimes, self-fulfilling prophecies can occur in an entire work group. A group of construction workers, for example, may be very responsible and perform highly when their supervisor has high expectations and treats them with respect. The same workers, however, may act lazy and perform at a low level when they have a supervisor who has low expectations and a derogatory attitude toward them.

Attribution Theory

Through the process of perception, people try to make sense of their environment and the people in it. Sometimes, however, just making sense of a target does not produce good understanding. To return to an earlier example, if you see your friend drinking beer before a 9 A.M. class, you perceive that he has a drinking problem. This perception may lead you to wonder why he has the drinking problem. To answer the question of "why," you attribute your friend's behavior to a certain cause. Your explanation of his behavior is an **attribution**.

ATTRIBUTION
An explanation of the cause of behavior.

ATTRIBUTION THEORY
A group of theories that describes how people explain the causes of behavior.

Attribution theory describes how people explain the causes of their own and other people's behavior. Attribution theory is interested in why people behave the way they do and what can be done to change their behavior. Consider the case of Martin Riley, a newly hired production worker at Rice Paper Products. Riley worked at a much slower pace than his coworkers; he always seemed to be lagging behind the other members of his production team. The big question in his supervisor's mind was why. Attribution theory focuses on how the supervisor and how Riley himself explain the cause of Riley's lackluster performance.

In organizations, the decisions that are made and the actions that are taken are based on attributions for behavior. Only when these attributions are accurate (that is, only when the real cause of a behavior has been determined) are good decisions likely to be made and appropriate actions taken. In a job interview, for example, whether a qualified applicant who is quiet and fails to ask questions receives an offer often depends on the interviewer's attributions for this behavior. Is the applicant a shy person who takes a while to warm up to new people? Was the applicant suffering from a bad case of nerves? Is the applicant not really interested in the job? If the interviewer makes the last attribution for the applicant's behavior, an offer will probably not be forthcoming. If that attribution is inaccurate, however, and the applicant was simply nervous, then the organization may be missing an opportunity to hire one of the best applicants for the job.

Similarly, supervisors' reactions to high or low performance by subordinates often depend on the attributions the supervisors make. A supervisor who attributes a subordinate's high performance to exceptional ability may give the subordinate increasingly challenging assignments and eventually recommend a promotion. If the subordinate's high performance is attributed to luck, however, no changes may be made in the subordinate's assignments. In either case, if the attributions are incorrect, problems are likely to result: The subordinate will be overwhelmed by challenging assignments or will not receive the challenges he or she thrives on. When subordinates perform poorly, supervisors are likely to provide additional on-the-job training if they attribute poor performance to a lack of knowledge rather than to laziness. If laziness is the real cause, however, training is not likely to improve performance.

Smooth day-to-day interactions among members of an organization often hinge on the extent to which people's attributions are accurate.[72] If a coworker snaps at you a couple of times one day, and you correctly attribute the coworker's behavior to the personal problems he is having at home, these small incidents are not going to damage your relationship. If you incorrectly attribute this behavior to the coworker's dislike for you, however, you may start avoiding him and treating him in a cold and distant manner, which will cause your relationship to deteriorate.

Internal and External Attributions

INTERNAL ATTRIBUTION
An attribution that assigns the cause of behavior to some characteristic of the target.

People generally attribute someone's behavior to internal and external causes (see Exhibit 4.7). An **internal attribution** assigns the cause of behavior to some characteristic of the target and assigns credit or blame to the individual actor. Martin Riley's supervisor at Rice Paper Products might attribute Riley's poor performance to personal limitations: (1) Riley lacks the ability to perform at a higher level; (2) Riley is not making an effort to work faster; (3) Riley has a low need for achievement. Attributions to ability, effort, and personality are the most common internal attributions that people make.

EXHIBIT 4.7

Types of Attributions

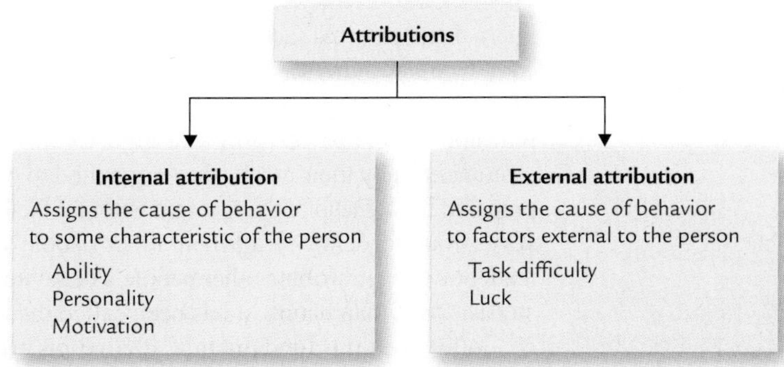

EXTERNAL ATTRIBUTIONS
An attribution that assigns the cause of behavior to outside forces.

However much people like to feel that they are in control of what happens in their lives, outside forces often play a decisive role in determining behavior. **External attributions** assign the cause of behavior to factors outside the individual. The most common external attributions relate to task difficulty and luck or chance. A salesperson who has just landed a major contract, for example, may have been successful because her company is the sole provider of a particular product in a certain geographic region or because the customer was in a particularly good mood at the time of negotiations. In the first case, the salesperson's success is attributed to the easiness of the task; in the second case, it is attributed to luck.

Whether attributions for a behavior are internal or external is an important determinant of how people respond to the behavior. If the supervisor of the salesperson mentioned previously correctly attributes the landing of the major contract to external causes such as an easy task or luck, getting this contract may have little impact on the supervisor's decisions about the salesperson's job assignments and suitability for promotion. But if the supervisor incorrectly attributes the behavior to an internal cause such as ability, the supervisor might promote this salesperson instead of another one who is more deserving but covers a more difficult territory.

The attributions people make for their own behavior also influence their own subsequent actions. An employee who fails on a task and attributes this failure to a lack of ability may be likely to avoid the task in the future or exert minimal effort on it because he or she feels that his or her lack of ability will almost certainly guarantee a negative outcome. Conversely, attributing failure to a lack of effort may lead the employee to try harder in the future on the same task. As another example, an employee who succeeds on a task and attributes the outcome to luck is unlikely to be affected by his or her success, whereas attributing the success to his or her ability or effort will increase his or her confidence.

Attributional Biases

The attributions people make to their own behaviors and those of others can have a profound impact on their subsequent actions. Like perceptions, however, attributions may sometimes be inaccurate because of certain biases. Here we consider three of these biases: the fundamental attribution error, actor-observer effect, and self-serving attributions (see Exhibit 4.8).

EXHIBIT 4.8

Attributional Biases

Bias	Description
Fundamental attribution error	The tendency to overattribute behavior to internal rather than to external causes
Actor–observer effect	The tendency to attribute the behavior of others to internal causes and to attribute one's own behavior to external causes
Self-serving attribution	The tendency to take credit for successes and avoid blame for failures

The Fundamental Attribution Error. Behavior is often caused by a combination of internal and external factors, but situational factors are the sole determinants of behavior in certain circumstances. Regardless of how capable and motivated an employee might be, for example, if the employee does not have the proper resources to accomplish a task, she or he will not be able to perform at a high level. No matter how hard a waiter tries to have customers enjoy their meals, they are bound to be dissatisfied if the restaurant serves poorly prepared food. Despite the fact that external factors often determine behavior, people have a very strong tendency to attribute other people's behavior to internal factors. Because this tendency to overattribute other people's behavior to internal rather than to external causes is so basic to human nature, it has been called the **fundamental attribution error**.[73]

FUNDAMENTAL ATTRIBUTION ERROR
The tendency to overattribute behavior to internal rather than to external causes.

Why does the fundamental attribution error occur? Researchers have offered two explanations. According to the first, which concentrates on perception of the target's behavior, when we observe a person behaving, we focus on the person, and the situation is simply the background for the behavior. Because the person is the focus of our thinking and the situation receives little attention, we tend to think that something about the person prompted the behavior. According to the second reason for the occurrence of the fundamental attribution error, we often are simply unaware of all the situational factors that may be responsible for the behavior we observe.

Because of the tendency to overattribute other people's behavior to internal causes, managers are likely to think that a subordinate's behavior is due to some characteristic of the subordinate rather than to the situation. Similarly, subordinates are likely to think that their supervisor's behavior is determined by internal rather than external causes. Suppose a manager must lay off 30 percent of his or her staff because of a major decline in the organization's performance. Those who are laid off (and those who remain) may be likely to attribute this action to the manager's hardheartedness and lack of concern for the well-being of others rather than to economic necessity.

People who manage diverse employees need to be especially aware of the fundamental attribution error and try to avoid it. Just as perceptions can be inaccurate as a result of stereotypes, so, too, can attributions. Inaccurate stereotypes about women, older workers, or African Americans, for example, may cause members of an organization to inappropriately attribute behavior to internal causes such as gender, age, or race when the behavior is actually caused by an external factor. If an older worker has difficulty getting new computer software to run, the worker's supervisor may fall victim to the stereotype that older workers have difficulty learning new things and inaccurately attribute this behavior to the worker's age, even though the real cause of the problem is that the computer has insufficient memory to handle the new software (an external cause).

The Actor-Observer Effect. We make attributions not only for the behavior of other people but also for our own behavior. Researchers comparing these two types of attributions uncovered an interesting phenomenon: the **actor-observer effect**. The actor-observer effect is the tendency to attribute the behavior of others to internal causes (the fundamental attribution error) and to attribute one's own behavior to external causes.[74] We tend to think that other people's behavior is relatively stable from situation to situation because it is due to their very nature, but we think that our own behavior varies from situation to situation.

ACTOR-OBSERVER EFFECT
The tendency to attribute the behavior of others to internal causes and to attribute one's own behavior to external causes.

What causes this bias? According to one explanation, when we are behaving, we focus not on our behavior but rather on the situation we are in. Because we are totally aware of the external, situational pressures that we face, we see them as key. Because we are less aware of external pressures or factors that another person is dealing with, we are likely to see his or her behavior as internally driven.

Self-Serving Attribution. Suppose you get promoted at work. Chances are you attribute this outcome to your superior abilities and the excellent job you have been doing. Now suppose that one of your coworkers gets the promotion that you have been expecting. You probably think that your supervisor has been unfair or that some political maneuvering has taken place. This example illustrates **self-serving attribution**, the tendency to take credit for successes and avoid blame for failures.[75] The considerable

SELF-SERVING ATTRIBUTION
The tendency to take credit for successes and avoid blame for failures.

You're the Management Expert

Helping a Coworker

Juan Coto works closely with one of his coworkers Roger Brice. Coto and Brice work in the customer service department of Diamond Furniture and do everything from taking payments, approving credit, and arranging for furniture deliveries to responding to customer complaints and handling returns. Coto and Brice both work the same hours and often are the only full-time employees handling customer service at any one time. Periodically, the store manager will receive a complaint from a customer about Brice; the manager talks to Brice about it, Brice gets annoyed, and the matter is forgotten. Coto realizes that these incidents are probably not doing anyone any good, so he has decided to try to figure out why customers occasionally complain about Brice but very rarely about him, even though they both seem to be doing an equally good job. So, Coto has started watching Brice when he deals with customers who are having a problem and notices that Brice typically approaches these situations by essentially "blaming" the customer. For example, when a customer called to complain that her furniture had not been delivered on the day it was promised, Brice looked up her record and then told her that she must have made a mistake because the delivery had been scheduled for a different date than she thought. As an expert in OB, Coto has come to you for help. Why is Brice blaming customers for their problems, and how can he help Brice provide better customer service?

amount of research conducted on this phenomenon suggests that accepting the credit for success is more common than avoiding blame for failure.[76] Furthermore, people are most likely to accept the blame for failure when it is due to something they can control in the future, such as by working harder or planning their time better.[77]

Self-serving attribution can also bias one's perception of friends and spouses and even organizations.[78] People are more likely to attribute the good things that happen to their spouses to internal causes and the bad things that happen to their spouses to external causes.[79] When your organization makes a record contribution to the United Way, you are likely to attribute this generosity to the organization's being socially responsible (an internal cause). But when your organization is cited for polluting the environment, you may attribute its problems to external circumstances such as the unavailability or high cost of alternative ways to dispose of waste (an external cause).

Effectively Managing a Diverse Workforce

Throughout this chapter, we have discussed how accurate perceptions and attributions are necessary to effectively manage a diverse workforce and the many issues involved with it. Effective management of a diverse workforce is necessary for an organization to make fair and ethical decisions, perform at a high level, and gain a competitive advantage. In this section, we explore four steps organizations can take to promote accurate perceptions and attributions and effectively manage diverse employees: securing the commitment of top management to diversity, diversity training, education, and mentoring. We also discuss the steps organizations can take to eliminate and prevent sexual harassment.

Securing Top-Management Commitment to Diversity

Applied Materials, a $4 billion semiconductor equipment company in Silicon Valley, California, is a good example of an organization whose top management is committed to diversity. Applied Materials has made *Fortune* magazine's "America's 50 Best Companies

Applied Materials is well known for its commitment to diversity. Fifty-one percent of new hires at Applied Materials are minorities, as are 28.4 percent of the company's officials and managers and 26 percent of its highest-paid executives.

for Minorities" list for five years in a row.[80] This commitment is shown in numerous ways, ranging from a financial commitment to promoting diversity and a commitment to hiring and giving diverse employees equal opportunities, to a commitment to helping minorities in the Silicon Valley area. Fifty-one percent of new hires at Applied Materials are minorities, as are 28.4 percent of the company's officials and managers and 26 percent of its highest-paid executives.[81]

Applied Materials has committed $1 million to help open up opportunities for minorities in Silicon Valley by, among other things, funding a center in East Palo Alto, California, devoted to teaching computer skills to community members and minority students. Another one of the company's program's links up employees with high-school students in a nearby school district comprised largely of minority adolescents.[82] Applied Materials stands out among other Silicon Valley high-tech firms as one of a select few that have demonstrated a commitment to diversity in multiple ways and are taking active steps both internally and externally to support it.[83]

Glen Toney, group vice president for corporate affairs, is an African American who has been with Applied Materials for more than 20 years. He is a mentor for several minority employees of various racial and ethnic backgrounds and provides career counseling, personal insights about how the company works, and positive feedback for a job well done. As Toney puts it, "People who come aboard here have to move faster than they ever have before, and the organization is complex and can be frustrating."[84] Toney and other top managers at Applied Materials really care that all employees are treated fairly and given the opportunities that they deserve. This benefits Applied Materials because it is able to capitalize on the many talents of its diverse workforce.

What is the likely outcome when top managers are committed to diversity? Their commitment helps ensure they will perceive and attribute the behavior of all of their employees in as accurate a light as possible and that they will understand and see them as they really are. Top-management commitment to diversity also helps to promote accurate perceptions and attributions of people throughout the organization. When supervisors support diversity, subordinates are more likely to be committed to it, too, and less likely to rely on stereotypes.

One way to demonstrate and reinforce top-management commitment to diversity is the creation of an active and influential chief diversity officer. When she was chief diversity officer for PricewaterhouseCoopers (PwC), Toni Ricarrdi sat on the U.S. Management Committee, a 12-person group that oversees global operations. Riccardi's responsibilities included managing the diversity and work-life initiatives for over 100,000 employees working in more than 140 countries. The U.S. Management Committee must approve any task forces that are formed, and Riccardi made sure that the task forces reflected the diversity in PwC not only to increase their effectiveness but also to give the diverse members of the firm important leadership experience and visibility.[85] Riccardi recently retired from PwC and Chris Simmons took her place as chief diversity officer.[86]

Many other global organizations have diversity-designated director or officer positions to ensure that diversity is effectively managed throughout the countries in which an organization operates. For example, Leslie Jones is the director of ethnicity and diversity at Ernst & Young. Jones strives to make the work environment at Ernst & Young attractive to minorities because they are key contributors to the success of the organization.[87] Sharon Hall, who focuses on senior executive placements at the Chicago search firm, Spencer Stuart, indicates that demand for chief diversity officers is strong and relatively recession-proof as more and more global organizations acknowledge how important it is to have a workforce that is as diverse and multicultural as their customers and consumers.[88] As Riccardi put it, "The challenge is to make sure people view diversity and work-life as positive pieces of this new world rather than add-ons that you don't have time for."[89]

Diversity Training

Diversity training can facilitate the management of a diverse workforce. There are many diversity training programs that have a variety of objectives, including the following:

- making explicit and breaking down organizational members' stereotypes that result in inaccurate perceptions and attributions
- making members aware of different kinds of backgrounds, experiences, and values
- showing members how to deal effectively with diversity-related conflicts and tensions
- generally improving members' understanding of each other

Diversity training programs can last hours or days and can be run by consultants or existing members of an organization with diversity expertise. Small organizations are more likely to rely on consultants; larger organizations often have diversity managers. More than 50 percent of Fortune 500 organizations, for example, have diversity managers on staff.[90]

Diversity training can include but is not limited to:

1. Role-playing, in which participants act out appropriate and inappropriate ways to deal with diverse employees.
2. Self-awareness activities, in which participants' own prejudices and stereotypes are revealed.
3. Awareness activities, in which participants learn about others who differ from them in lifestyle, culture, sexual orientation, gender, and so on.

Cardiac Concepts Inc., a Texas medical laboratory that performs cardiovascular tests, helped to reduce conflict among employees with diverse ethnic backgrounds by using a training program in which pairs of participants from different ethnic backgrounds made lists of the stereotypes held about each other.[91] Prudential, the largest U.S. life insurance company, has its managers participate in other organizations in which they will be a minority so they can understand the challenges that minorities experience.[92] Simmons Associates, based in New Hope, Pennsylvania, provides diversity consulting services including a "Special Sensitivities" session. This session educates participants about words, phrases, situations, and scenarios that might be disturbing to certain groups due to their backgrounds and histories. For example, male African-American teens might take offense at being referred to as "boys." The goal of the sessions is to help avoid blunders whereby one person says something that is highly offensive to another, sometimes without realizing it.[93]

Many diversity programs are successful, but others do not change the ways that people perceive and treat each other in organizations. It appears that diversity training is most likely to be successful when it is ongoing or repeated (rather than a single session), when there are follow-up activities to see whether the training has accomplished its objectives, and when it is supplemented by other diversity-related activities in an organization, such as events focused on celebrating diversity. IBM's Systems Storage Division in San Jose, for example, sets aside one day a year as Diversity Day. On that day, employees dress in traditional ethnic clothing and share authentic dishes with their coworkers.[94]

Education

Sometimes effectively managing diversity requires that members of an organization receive additional education to make them better able to communicate and work with diverse employees and customers. The Kentucky state government, for example, realized that it was unable to provide employment opportunities for people with hearing impairments and could not provide high-quality service to hearing-impaired citizens wanting to use state-provided services and programs. The Americans with Disabilities Act requires organizations to be responsive to and accommodate people with disabilities (including deafness or hearing impairments).[95]

After considerable research, the Kentucky state government developed a three-stage program to improve its responsiveness to people (both customers and potential employees) who are hearing impaired or deaf. First, state employees chosen for the program participate in a one-day workshop that educates them about deaf culture and background. Second, employees attend a four-day workshop in which they learn some of the basics of American Sign Language (the most often used form of signing and a visual language that deaf people use to communicate). Finally, employees attend a week-long workshop on advanced American Sign Language.[96]

MENTORING
A process through which an experienced member of an organization (the mentor) provides advice and guidance to a less-experienced member (the protégé) and helps the less-experienced person learn the ropes and do the right things to advance in the organization.

Mentoring Programs

Mentoring is a process through which an experienced member of an organization (the mentor) provides advice and guidance to a less-experienced member (the protégé) and helps the less-experienced person learn the ropes and do the right things to advance in the organization. Due to the similar-to-me effect and stereotyping, some young minority managers find that white senior colleagues aren't mentoring them. Ilene Wasserman, of the Cincinnati-based Kaleel Jamison Consulting Group, which specializes in helping organizations manage a diverse workforce, says that senior managers typically try to mentor someone who reminds them of themselves when they were younger—someone who, as she puts it, is a "clone."

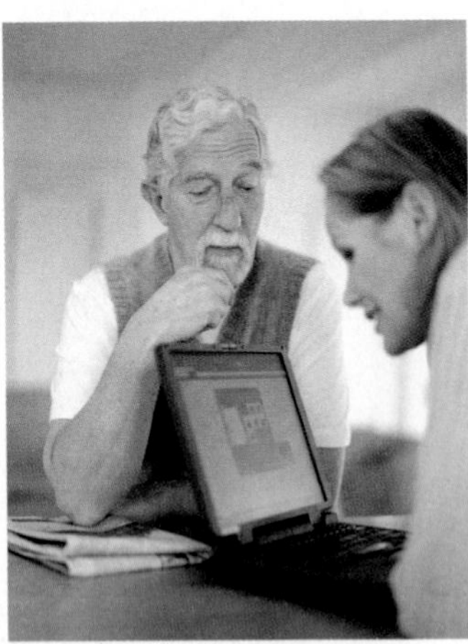

Mentoring—both formal and informal—can help entry-level employees develop the skills they need to excel on the job. Seventy percent of minority executives, for example, say informal mentors helped them early in their careers.

Mixed-race mentor-protégé relationships are rare. Benson Rosen, a management professor at the University of North Carolina at Chapel Hill, indicates that white managers sometimes feel uncomfortable dealing with minorities and may slight them (often unintentionally) in various ways such as failing to invite them to functions and giving them performance feedback that is less constructive than the feedback they give white subordinates. LaVon Stennis, a young African-American lawyer who worked for a large corporation in Nebraska, found it difficult to relate to her white male superiors, so it was unlikely that any of them would serve as her mentor. These observations do not mean that white men cannot mentor minorities or that minorities do not want to receive help from white managers. Rather, they suggest that all members of an organization (regardless of race, gender, or other characteristics) need to be aware that the similar-to-me bias might predispose them to help members who are similar to them. In his study, Rosen found that white women were more likely than white men to mentor minorities of either gender.[97]

A recent study of minority executives found that more than 70 percent of the executives had informal mentors, and they generally believe that mentors helped them in their careers.[98] Lloyd David Ward, CEO of the Maytag Corporation and one of a handful of African Americans to head a major U.S. corporation, was mentored by older African-American engineers when he was an employee at Procter & Gamble as well as by Dr. Price Cobbs, a psychiatrist and consultant who helped him deal with the anger he felt from being treated differently because of the color of his skin.[99] Former Coca-Cola president Donald R. Keough mentored Carl Ware, head of global public affairs and a senior African-American manager at Coca-Cola. Keough is currently chairman of Allen & Company (an investment bank).[100]

Mentors are not only important for managers and executives. The United Parcel Service relies on mentors to help entry-level employees develop basic skills and habits such as being punctual and dressing appropriately.[101] Mentors are also key for entrepreneurs trying to start their own businesses. African-American Bernadette Williams, who founded i-strategy.com Inc., believes that mentors are particularly important for minority women trying to start a business, and her beliefs are confirmed by many surveys. Williams cofounded the Women's New Media Alliance to help young women interested in technology connect with a woman experienced in the area they wish to pursue.[102] Clearly, mentoring can be beneficial for all kinds of employees but it may be especially important for women and minorities trying to overcome the effects of the similar-to-me bias, stereotypes, and potential discrimination.[103]

Mentoring programs can be formal or informal. And protégés can benefit from mentors who are different from them as well as from mentors who are similar to them. What must exist for successful mentoring to take place is an atmosphere of mutual respect and understanding and for the mentor to have the protégé's best interests in mind. Maureen Giovanni, a multicultural consultant with J. Howard & Associates, suggests that when mentors and protégés are diverse or differ from each other on one or more salient dimensions, there can be enhanced opportunities for mutual learning. The mentor can learn about the background and experiences of the protégé, and the protégé can learn the ropes in the organization and how to be successful from the mentor.[104] Through this process, both the mentor and the protégé become more skilled in developing effective interpersonal relations with different kinds of people. At Prudential, managers are paired with mentors who are different from them to help them learn about differences between groups and the issues various groups face. Managers, in turn, are evaluated on their attention to diversity in multiple ways (on the amount of money they spend on ethnic marketing, for example, and how well they incorporate diversity issues into their meetings and speeches).[105]

Visible top-management commitment, training, education, and mentoring are just some of the ways in which organizations can effectively manage a diverse workforce. As we have discussed throughout this chapter, effectively managing diversity begins by recognizing that the perceptions and attributions of the organization's members need to be as accurate as possible, regardless of the age, race, gender, ethnic background, religion, sexual orientation, or other characteristic of the target of perception.

Sexual Harassment

After extensive study, the U.S. Army has indicated that sexual harassment exists throughout its ranks.[106] A recent study commissioned by Congress and the Pentagon and conducted by the Defense Task Force on Sexual Harassment and Violence at the Military Service Academies concluded that sexual harassment is a problem at the U.S. Military Academy and the Naval Academy.[107] Unfortunately, sexual harassment is not just an Army problem but also a problem that many other organizations, such as Chevron Corporation and Ford Motor Company, have had to face.[108] There are two distinct types of sexual harassment: quid pro quo sexual harassment and hostile work environment sexual harassment. **Quid pro quo sexual harassment** is the most obvious type. It occurs when the harasser requests or forces an employee to perform sexual favors in order to receive some opportunity (such as a raise, a promotion, a bonus, or a special job assignment) or to avoid a negative consequence (such as a demotion, dismissal, a halt to career progress, or an undesired assignment or

QUID PRO QUO SEXUAL HARASSMENT
Requesting or forcing an employee to perform sexual favors in order to receive some opportunity(such as a raise, a promotion, a bonus, or a special job assignment) or avoid a negative consequence (such as demotion, dismissal, a halt to career progress, or an undesired assignment or transfer).

HOSTILE WORK ENVIRONMENT SEXUAL HARASSMENT
Creating or maintaining a work environment that is offensive, intimidating, or hostile because of a person's sex.

transfer).[109] **Hostile work environment sexual harassment** is more subtle and occurs when organizational members are faced with a work environment that is offensive, intimidating, or hostile because of their sex.[110] Pornographic pictures, sexual jokes, lewd comments, sexually oriented comments about a person's physical appearance, and displays of sexually oriented objects are all examples of hostile work environment sexual harassment. Hostile work environments interfere with organizational members' abilities to perform their jobs effectively and are illegal. Chevron settled a $2.2 million lawsuit with four employees who experienced a hostile work environment by, for example, receiving violent pornography through the company's mail system and being asked to deliver pornographic videos to Chevron employees in Alaska.[111] As another example, Ford settled a $17.5 million lawsuit involving employees at two factories in Illinois. The employees claimed they endured years of unwanted touching and massaging, being called sexually explicit names, having pornography and sexual graffiti displayed in the workplace, and other forms of hostile work environment harassment.[112] Hostile work environment sexual harassment can also take place electronically when employees send or receive sexually oriented e-mails or pornography over the Internet. For example, Dow Chemical, Xerox, the New York Times, Edward Jones, and First Union Bank have all fired employees for using company e-mail systems to send sexually oriented messages.[113] According to a recent study, 70 percent of the employees surveyed indicated that they have viewed or sent e-mails at work that would be considered adult oriented. Moreover, over 60 percent admitted that they have sent e-mails that were either personally offensive or inappropriate.[114]

Research suggests that sexual harassment continues to occur in a wide variety of organizations[115] and has adverse effects on victims' job satisfaction, stress levels, life satisfaction, and psychological well-being. Victims of harassment may also be more likely to try to withdraw from the workplace, for example, by being late or absent, trying to avoid certain tasks or situations, or thinking about quitting and looking for another job.[116] They also tend to have negative attitudes about their supervisors and their coworkers.[117] Interestingly, a recent study found that regardless of whether employees experience sexual harassment themselves, being in a work group in which sexual harassment occurs results in employees being more dissatisfied with their work, their coworkers, and their supervisors and experiencing higher levels of stress.[118]

Organizations have a legal and ethical obligation to eliminate and prevent sexual harassment, which can occur at all levels in an organization. Many organizations, such as NBC, include segments on sexual harassment in their diversity training and education programs.[119] At a minimum, there are several key steps that organizations can take to combat the sexual harassment problem.[120]

- *Develop a sexual harassment policy supported by top management.* This policy should (1) describe and prohibit both quid pro quo and hostile work environment sexual harassment, (2) provide examples of types of behaviors that are prohibited, (3) outline a procedure employees can follow to report sexual harassment, (4) describe the disciplinary actions that will be taken in instances of sexual harassment, and (5) describe the organization's commitment to educating and training its members about sexual harassment.
- *Clearly communicate the organization's sexual harassment policy throughout the organization.* All members of an organization should be familiar with its sexual harassment policy.
- *Investigate charges of sexual harassment with a fair complaint procedure.* A fair complaint procedure should (1) be handled by a neutral third party, (2) be dealt with promptly and thoroughly, (3) protect victims and treat them fairly, and (4) treat alleged harassers fairly.
- *Take corrective action as soon as possible once it has been determined that sexual harassment has taken place.* The nature of these corrective actions will vary depending on the severity of the sexual harassment.
- *Provide sexual harassment training and education to all members of the organization.* Many organizations have such training programs in place, including Du Pont, NBC, Corning, Digital Equipment, and the U.S. Navy and Army.[121] A growing number of

organizations are taking steps to ensure that new hires and interns are aware of their organization's sexual harassment policy. For example, the Katz Media Group, which helps to sell advertisements for television and radio stations, includes a 25-minute video on sexual harassment in its orientation program for new hires.[122] According to Christine Walters, sexual harassment prevention and resolution director at Johns Hopkins University, all new hires of that organization are educated about the behaviors that constitute sexual harassment.[123]

Summary

Perception and attribution are important topics because all decisions and behaviors in organizations are influenced by how people interpret and make sense of the world around them and each other. Perception is the process by which individuals select, organize, and interpret sensory input. Attribution is an explanation of the cause of behavior. Perception and attribution, thus, help to explain how and why people behave in organizations and how and why they react to the behavior of others. In this chapter, we made the following major points:

1. Perception is the process by which people interpret the input from their senses to give meaning and order to the world around them. The three components of perception are the perceiver, the target, and the situation. Accurate perceptions are necessary to make good decisions and to motivate employees to perform at a high level, to be fair and equitable, and to be ethical.
2. The perceiver's knowledge base is organized into schemas—abstract knowledge structures stored in memory that allow people to organize and interpret information about a given target of perception. Schemas tend to be resistant to change and can be functional or dysfunctional. A stereotype is a dysfunctional schema because stereotypes often lead perceivers to assume erroneously that targets have a whole range of characteristics simply because they possess one distinguishing characteristic (e.g., race, age, gender). In addition to the perceiver's schemas, his or her motivational state and mood also influence perception.
3. Characteristics of the target also influence perception. Ambiguous targets are subject to a lot of interpretation by the perceiver; the more ambiguous the target, the more likely perceivers are to differ in their perceptions of it. The target's social status also affects how the target is perceived. Through impression management, targets can actively try to manage the perceptions that others have of them.
4. The situation affects perception by providing the perceiver with additional information. One particularly important aspect of the situation is the target's salience—that is, the extent to which the target stands out in a group of people or things.
5. Biases and problems in person perception include primacy effects; contrast effects; halo effects; similar-to-me effects; harshness, leniency, and average tendencies; and knowledge-of-predictor bias. Inaccurate perceptions resulting from these biases can lead to faulty decision making.
6. Attributions are important determinants of behavior in organizations because how members of an organization react to other people's behavior depends on what they think caused the behavior. Attribution theory focuses on understanding how people explain the causes of their own and others' behavior. Common internal attributions for behavior include ability, effort, and personality. Common external attributions for behavior include task difficulty and luck or chance.

   Like perceptions, attributions can be inaccurate as a result of several biases, including the fundamental attribution error, the actor-observer effect, and self-serving attribution.
7. Three ways in which organizations can promote accurate perceptions and attributions and effectively manage diverse employees are securing top management's commitment to diversity, diversity training, education, and mentoring programs. Organizations also need to take steps to eliminate and prevent both quid pro quo and hostile work environment sexual harassment.

Exercises in Understanding and Managing Organizational Behavior

Questions for Review

1. How do schemas help members of an organization make sense of each other and of what happens in the organization?
2. Are stereotypes ever functional for the perceiver? Why or why not?
3. Why might a supervisor be motivated to perceive a subordinate's performance as being poor when it really is not?
4. How might managers' moods affect organizational decision making?
5. In what ways might impression management be functional in organizations? In what ways might it be dysfunctional?
6. Can and should employees who are salient try to reduce their salience?
7. Why do perceptual biases exist?
8. Why might a supervisor make internal attributions for a subordinate's poor performance?
9. Why are attributions important determinants of behavior in organizations?
10. Why might members of an organization disagree about the nature of hostile work environment sexual harassment?

OB: Increasing Self-Awareness

Understanding Perceptions and Attributions in Group Meetings

Think about the last meeting or gathering that you attended. It could be a meeting that took place at the organization you are currently working for, a meeting of a club or student organization you are a member of, a meeting of a group you have been assigned to for a project in one of your classes, or any other recent gathering that involved more than two people.

1. Describe your perceptions of what took place during the meeting and explain why events unfolded as they did.
2. Describe the characteristics and behavior of the other people who were present at the meeting and explain why they acted the way they did.
3. Describe how you think you were perceived by other people during the meeting and explain why you behaved as you did.
4. After you have completed activities 1 through 3, pick another person who participated in the meeting and arrange to meet with her or him for around 15 minutes. Explain to the person that you want to ask a few questions about the meeting for one of your classes.
5. When you meet with the person, ask her or him to be as accurate and honest as possible. Remind the person that your get-together is part of an assignment for one of your classes and assure that person that answers to your questions are confidential. While the person is answering you, take careful notes, and do not attempt to correct anything that is said. Just listen and take notes. Ask the person to respond to each of these questions (one by one):
   a. How would you describe what took place during the meeting, and why do you think it took place?
   b. How would you describe the characteristics and behavior of the other people who were present at the meeting, and why do you think they behaved as they did?
   c. How would you describe the reasons why I behaved as I did during the meeting?
6. Compare your own descriptions from activities 1 through 3 with the descriptions you obtained from activities 4 and 5. In what ways were your perceptions and attributions similar to those of the other person? In what ways were they different?
7. Use the knowledge you have gained from this chapter to explain why there were differences in your and the other person's perceptions and attributions and why there were similarities. Be specific.

A Question of Ethics

Given perceptual problems and biases, such as stereotyping and the similar-to-me effect, proponents of affirmative action argue that organizations need to take proactive steps to ensure that minorities and women are given the opportunities they deserve. Opponents, on the other hand, argue that these policies can inadvertently result in more discrimination rather than less.

Questions

1. Think about the ethical implications of affirmative action programs.
2. What obligation do organizations have to ensure that all members of the organization are treated fairly?

Small Group Break-Out Exercise

Dealing with Salience

Form groups of three or four people and appoint one member as the spokesperson who will communicate your conclusions to the rest of the class.

1. Take a few minutes to think about situations in which you were salient (i.e., you stood out in a group of people).
2. Take turns describing these situations and how you felt.
3. Then take turns describing what other people in these situations did to make the situation better or worse for you.
4. As a group, come up with ways that (a) individuals who are salient in a situation can effectively deal with their salience, and (b) those who are not salient in a situation can avoid paying undue attention to others who stand out and avoid forming extreme evaluations of them and stereotyping.

Topic for Debate

Perception and attribution have major effects on the decisions that are made in organizations and on how members of an organization respond to each other's behavior. Now that you have a good understanding of perception and attribution, debate the following issue.

Team A. There is not much that managers can do to reduce the negative effects of problems and biases in perception and attribution in organizations.

Team B. Managers can take active steps to reduce the negative effects of problems and biases in perception and attribution in organizations.

Experiential Exercise

Managing Diversity

Objective

Your objective is to gain firsthand experience in some of the issues involved in managing diversity.

Procedure

The class divides into groups of three to five people, and each group appoints one member as spokesperson to present the group's recommendations to the whole class. Each group plays the role of a team of diversity consultants who have been called in by a high-tech company in the computer industry to help effectively manage diverse employees. Here is the scenario.

Nick Hopkins is the team leader of a group of 10 programmers who are developing innovative software to be used in architectural design. The team is composed of seven men and three women. Hopkins thought that everything was going pretty smoothly in his team until the following two recent events. First, one of the women, Cara Lipkin, informed him that she would be resigning to work for a competing organization. Hopkins asked Lipkin why she decided to make this change, and she answered at length.

"I can't exactly explain it," she said, "but I never really felt that my contributions were valued by the team. I know you always appreciated the work I did and appraised my performance highly, but somehow I didn't really feel a part of things. In the long run, I was afraid that my prospects in the company might not be as good as other people's because I didn't seem to be included in certain activities and discussions. To give you what will probably sound like a real silly example, last month I overheard several of my team members planning a deep-sea fishing trip; I kept waiting to be included but never was. As another example, I sometimes feel like the last person people will come to for help with a programming problem."

The second event troubling Hopkins was as follows: Bob Risoto, another team member who at the time was unaware of Lipkin's resignation, complained that the women on the team always seemed to stick together.

"It's like they've got their own little clique going," Risoto said. "They go to lunch together. They talk to each other but not really to the rest of the team. When I have a programming problem that I think one of the women on the team would be able to help me with, for some reason I often feel hesitant to seek out her advice. Maybe it's just my fault. I don't know."

Hopkins has met with you (in your role as a team of diversity consultants) and asked you to help him effectively manage diversity as a team leader. He has indicated that he thought everything was going smoothly, but it evidently isn't and he wants to take some concrete steps to improve matters. Develop a plan of action to help Hopkins effectively manage diversity in his team.

Once your group has developed a plan, the spokesperson for the group will present the group's recommendations and the rationale behind them to the rest of the class.

New York Times *Cases in the News*

The New York Times

Up the Down Staircase: Why Do So Few Women Reach the Top of Big Law Firms?

By T. L. O'Brien, The New York Times, March 19, 2006, Section 3, pp. 1, 4.

HUNDREDS of feet above Manhattan, the reception area of Proskauer Rose's headquarters boasts all of the muscular, streamlined ornamentation that symbolizes authority and power in a big city law firm.

Bettina B. Plevan, a 60-year-old specialist in labor and employment law, has spent more than three decades at Proskauer navigating the professional riptides and intellectual cross-currents of firm life on her way to reeling in one of the legal world's most storied and most lucrative prizes: a partnership.

"I decided I wanted to be a partner shortly after I got here—by nature I have a lot of drive. I'm competitive and I have a lot of energy," she says. "For me, being a partner was a way in which my talents and skills could be recognized. And I wanted that recognition."

Ms. Plevan has that recognition. Besides the handsome salary and bragging rights accompanying the grueling hours and emotional juggling that constitute a partnership, she has earned ample plaudits from peers outside Proskauer. According to a small plaque, one among many stacked along her window, other lawyers around the country have voted her one of the "Best Lawyers in America" in each of the last 13 years.

Following in the footsteps of Elihu Root, Charles Evans Hughes, Whitney North Seymour Jr. and Cyrus R. Vance, Ms. Plevan is president of the New York City Bar Association, only the second woman to hold that position since the organization's founding in 1870. She has a job that makes her happy and reflects her sense of herself. She is an accomplished lawyer. She has arrived.

She also is an anomaly.

Although the nation's law schools for years have been graduating classes that are almost evenly split between men and women, and although firms are absorbing new associates in numbers that largely reflect that balance, something unusual happens to most women after they begin in climb into the upper tiers of law firms. They disappear.

According to the National Association for Law Placement, a trade group that provides career counseling to lawyers and law students, only about 17 percent of the partners at major law firms nationwide were women in 2005, a figure that has risen only slightly since 1995, when about 13 percent of partners were women.

Even those who have made it to the top of their profession say that the data shows that women's legal careers involve distinct, often insurmountable hurdles and that those hurdles remain misunderstood or underexamined.

"You have a given population of people who were significantly motivated to go through law school with a certain career goal in mind," says Ms. Plevan, who notes that Proskauer has always provided her with a welcoming professional home. "What de-motivates them to want to continue working in the law?"

For years, one pat response to that question was that once law school graduation rates substantially equalized between men and women, that pipeline would fuel firm diversity and cause partnerships to equalize as well. Yet the pipeline has been gushing for about two decades and partnership disparity remains.

Although women certainly leave firms to become more actively involved in child-rearing, recent detailed studies indicate that female lawyers often feel pushed into that choice and would prefer to maintain their careers and a family if a structure existed that allowed them to do so. Some analysts and many women who practice law say that having children isn't the primary reason most women leave law firms anyhow; most, they say, depart for other careers or for different ways to practice law.

"Firms want women to stay. Men at the firms want women to stay, and women want to stay. So why aren't they?" asks Karen M. Lockwood, a partner at Howrey in Washington. "Law firms are way beyond discrimination—this is about advancement and retention. Problems, with advancement and retention are grounded in biases, not discrimination."

With law firms courting major corporations that demand diversity within the ranks of those advising them, and with women increasingly dominating the top tiers of law school graduates, veteran lawyers say that promoting women's legal careers is not just a matter of good-will or high-mindedness. It's also a winning business strategy.

"Forget about skin color or gender or whatever, if you want to run a great business, you need great, talented people. And I don't care if I'm hiring Martians if it makes good business sense," says Michael M. Boone, a founding partner of Haynes and Boone in Dallas. "Even the largest firms are at risk if they don't do this."

Ms. Plevan said that male partners at Proskauer had worked actively as her mentors. "I was given opportunities to be the lead lawyer and demonstrate what I could do professionally very early here." she recalls. "I think the opportunity to prove yourself is part of what puts someone on the partnership track. Of course, you have to seize the opportunity as well."

Proskauer anointed Ms. Plevan as a partner in 1980, shortly before law firms around the country began embarking on a broad consolidation wave that transformed the profession. Large firms became even larger; expanded their global reach and practice areas; focused more tightly on benchmarks such as "billable hours" to assess the performance of individual lawyers; and competed voraciously for coveted spots in news media reports that ranked them by financial yardsticks such as profit per partner. Those forces gained momentum in the 1990's and continue today.

Women entering this environment discovered that men enjoyed some distinct advantages, largely deriving from the simple facts that there were more men in most firms and that they had their hands on the levers of power. Although Ms. Plevan benefited from strong male mentoring, most women who practice law do not, according to analysts and female lawyers. Women lawyers also enjoy less access to the networking and business development opportunities that flourish in largely male playgrounds—think golf courses or football games—or through an invitation for a casual after-work drink with a male boss.

"Women aren't being adequately mentored, but I think male associates aren't particularly well mentored at all firms either, and there's pretty widespread dissatisfaction with that," said Merudith Moore, director of the office for diversity at the New York City Bar. "Having said that, I do think that superstar male associates are identified more clearly for informal mentoring than superstar female associates."

Some of this give-and-take enters gray areas that may have as much to do with caution as it does with biases. Is a male boss reluctant to invite a younger female lawyer out for a drink because water cooler chatter might spark rumors of an affair or give rise to a sexual harassment suit? Is a female associate hesitant to address a male partner informally in a hallway because it will be derided as flirting?

Still, the sexes have been mingling in the workplace for some time now, and professionals, in all their adaptational glory, have found ways to manage these situations. Anyhow, female lawyers say, why is a woman who hunts down her male boss for a chat seen as overly aggressive or possibly flirtatious, while a male doing the same thing is seen as merely ambitious?

Lauren Stiller Rikleen, a 52-year-old partner in the Framingham, Mass., office of the Worcester, Mass., firm of Bowditch & Dewey, details the hurdles facing female lawyers in her recently published book "Ending the Gauntlet: Removing Barriers to Women's Success in the Law" (Thomson Legalworks, $25). In her book she writes that law firms need to reorganize if they want to encourage and retain women as partners, and that roadblocks—whether they be errant mentoring, opaque networking opportunities, low-grade case assignments or arbitrary male control of key management committees—should all be reviewed.

"Law firms like to talk about running the firm like a business and looking at the numbers, but they're running on an institutional model that's about 200 years old," she says. "Most law firms do a horrible job of managing their personnel, in terms of training them and communicating with them."

Ms. Rikleen, as well as many of the women she interviewed for her book, note how lonely life at a law firm can feel for women if they stay on the partnership track and find fewer women around them as they ascend. In her book, she writes about her early career. "I had very little help and no mentors. I saw other women arrive at the firm, struggle, and leave." Although she established a thriving environmental law practice and now finds her firm more welcoming, in the early days, "I never felt like I belonged," she writes.

Others have had similar experiences. Jennifer L. Bluestein says she enjoys her career as head of professional development for Baker & McKenzie, the Chicago monolith that is the country's largest law firm. But Ms. Bluestem, a 35-year-old dean's list graduate of the Northwestern University School of Law, said that at her two previous employers, she felt like an undervalued and unwanted outsider. She describes her experiences at those law firms as lonely, degrading, and akin to journeys through halls of mirrors.

"Women are held to higher standards, and if they don't jump up and down like a man would at a meeting they aren't seen as partnership material," she says "Women are less likely to get the attention than men. Some of this is left over from the sexual harassment cases from the 90's but I think that it's more because of the fact that we don't look like men."

To be sure, some big firms have already recognized the benefits of keeping women on the partnership track and have made concerted efforts to address the issue. Ms. Lockwood, the Howrey partner, is also president of the Women's Bar Association of the District of Columbia, and she is spearheading an effort with that group, her firm and the Georgetown University Law Center to find practical solutions. Some at the country's biggest firms are backing her initiative, including Latham R. Watkins, Kirkland & Ellis and Covington & Burling.

In addition to "glass celling" issues that work against women in law firms, Ms. Lockwood's initiative—which she says has benefited from the backing of Howrey's managing partner, Robert F. Ruyak—is also exploring the impact of what she describes as the "material wall" on female lawyers. She says that this wall is built on the unstated assumption among male partners that women who return to firms after having children will automatically be less willing to work hard or will be less capable than they were prior to that—resulting in less-choice assignments or less-senior postings.

Jane DiRenzo Pigott, a former Winston & Strawn lawyer who now runs a Chicago consulting firm, the R3 Group, that advises law firms on diversity issues, says the dynamics surrounding female lawyers in the Midwest mirror trends elsewhere in the country.

"People explain it simply as the fact that women have children, but so many other factors play into it," she says. "Women self-promote in a different way than men, and because women don't get their success acknowledged in the same way as men who more aggressively self-promote, it creates a high level of professional dissatisfaction for women.

"Saying these two words, 'I want,' is not something many women are used to doing," she adds. "They are not saying, 'I want the top bonus,' or 'I want that position.' They have a different style of self-promotion. But women need to learn how to be comfortable saying, 'I want,' and how to say it effectively"

According to "Women in Law," a 2001 study by Catalyst, a New York research firm that tracks women's experiences in a wide range of workplaces, most male lawyers don't see a lack of mentoring and networking opportunities—or commitments to family and personal responsibilities—as significant barriers to women's advancement. Those biases, says Catalyst, are more pronounced in the legal world than in other industries and professions. Ms. Plevan agrees.

"As long as firms are male-dominated, it's much less likely that firms will make changes to accept the challenges of work-life balance" she says "It's not that men aren't receptive to these issues, it's that they're not aware."

Research conducted by the project for Attorney Retention, a program sponsored by the University of California's Hastings College of the Law, has identified an inflexible, billable-hours regime as an obstacle to job satisfaction for both sexes, a trend that is more pronounced among the most recent crop of law school graduates. Some veteran lawyers witness this dissatisfaction firsthand and say that it tugs more powerfully at women than men because of social expectations about household roles and child-rearing.

"We are very accommodating with leaves and flexible schedules, and even with that we still lose women," says Edith R. Matthai, who founded a Los Angeles law firm, Robie & Matthai, with her husband in 1987. "I think the pressures on women from spouses, family, peers, schools and others is huge.

"I think the real solution is a re-assessment of the role that women play in the family," adds Ms. Matthai, who is president of the Los Angeles County Bar Association. "One thing we need is a sense of shared responsibilities for the household and most importantly, shared responsibilities for taking care of the kids."

Ms. Matthai said that conditions for women had improved a good deal over the last 30 years, but added; "We have a long way to go. It's my dream that more women will stick it out in the law until they get to the fun part, and it just breaks my heart to see them giving up the dream."

Research conducted by the New York City Bar Association and other groups indicates that women who temporarily give up their professional dreams to pursue child-rearing of other personal goals have a difficult, if not impossible, time finding easily available on-ramps when they choose to re-enter the legal world.

"I don't think we're thinking very clearly about how to help people do that," Ms. Plevan says. "Firms need to keep in touch with those people and those people need to keep in touch with firms so they don't become marginalized."

She also remains firmly aware of the challenges that partnerships entail.

"I have found my legal work and public service enormously satisfying, and I would never want to be without that, but I won't kid you—at times it's very, very tiring and very, very demanding," Ms. Plevan said. "I truly believe that lawyers make a huge difference in society, and I think it's a loss when women decide to leave firms.

"I think diversity is a beneficial thing in an organization," she adds. "Without it, you have a loss of different points of view."

Questions for Discussion

1. Why do some women face struggles in large law firms?
2. Why do female lawyers tend to receive less mentoring than male lawyers?
3. How and why might the same behaviors be perceived and interpreted differently if they are performed by a male lawyer than if they are performed by a female lawyer, and vice versa?
4. What is the "maternal wall," and how can it lead to inaccurate perceptions and attributions?

The New York Times

"Looking at the Free Market, and Seeing Red"

By R. Stross, The New York Times, April 9, 2006, Section 3, p. 3.

LOU DOBBS is a master of the Sinister tease. Last month, he was in top form. Previewing a story, he told viewers of his nightly CNN newscast that when the State Department seeks secure network communications, it "turns to Communist China," and thus renders the United States "perhaps more vulnerable than ever."

The story turned out to be another Lou Dobbs exercise in bashing immigrants, or, more precisely, bashing a single immigrant. Lenovo, the PC maker originally based in China that last year acquired I.B.M.'s PC division and is now based in Raleigh, N.C. Lenova recently won a competitive bid to sell the State Department $13 million worth of personal computers. Mr. Dubbs like some politicians on Capitol Hill, suggests that those PC's could provide shadowy spooks in the Chinese government with an ideal means of conducting espionage.

Merely hinting at such a possibility is enough to hurt Lenovo's reputation. This is a potentially serious impairment in the highly competitive, commoditized PC business. What is happening to Lenovo, the most internationalized company in the industry, is a drive-by smearing.

Mr. Dobbs is not the only practitioner of the hit-and-run attack. In his segment about Lenovo he called upon Michael R. Wessel, a member of the U.S-China Economic and Security Review Commission, an advisory body to Congress. Mr. Wessel said that the State Department would use the Lenovo computers in offices around the world, potentially providing China access to "some of our deepest secrets," a "treasure trove of information they could use against us."

Mr. Wessel's segment was too brief to explain how China's agents would be able to grab hold of the machines to install the software for clandestine data transmission back to the party's Central Committee. The Lenovo desktops headed for the State Department will be assembled in facilities in North Carolina, not a People's Liberation Army compound in China. Also unexplained was how infected machines would meet General Services Administration security standards and get past the State Department's two computer security groups, which oversee the administration of their own test suites and install firewalls and other security software.

Last week, I spoke with Mr. Wessel to learn more about the basis for his alarm. It turned out that he was not able to describe how Chinese agents could gain access to the Lenovo machines, undetected, while they were being assembled.

When I asked why he thought the State Department's security procedures were inadequate he suggested that he could not say because the State Department had been less than forthcoming with him. "We don't fully know" what the procedures are, he said. But when I asked him if he had requested information from the department about its protocols before he publicly voiced his concerns about the Lenovo deal, he said he had not.

Larry M. Wortzel, the chairman of the security review commission on which Mr. Wessel serves, was even more animated in asserting that there were security risks in the Lenovo sale to the State Department. When I spoke with him, he professed to be mystified as to "why the State Department would take the risk." What had the State Department told him about its security procedures? He, too, had yet to speak with anyone there; the commission's the commission's request for a briefing had been drafted but not yet sent.

Both commissioners assume that Lenovo is managed by puppets whose strings are pulled in Beijing. Mr. Wessel said he was certain that "a major portion" of Lenovo was "controlled by the Chinese government." State enterprises are placed in the hands of "princelings," who are the children of government leaders, he began to explain before I interrupted.

Princelings installed at the meritocratic Lenovo? When I asked Mr. Wessel to identify a Lenovo princeling, he said, "I haven't done a research of Lenovo." He said he had merely "raised questions" and had "never purported to have answers." This was similar to the reply from Mr. Wortzel when he was asked to substantiate his allegations with details.

The fact is that Lenovo is a living repudiation of the system that these critics assume it represents. It was born in 1984 from unCommunist entrepreneurial impulses among a group of Chinese computer scientists who wanted to start their own company. Their employer, the Chinese Academy of Sciences, gave them $25,000 in venture capital, and off they went. It was among the first Chinese companies to issue employee stock options.

The Academy of Sciences retains a minority ownership position, but so do I.B.M. and three American private-equity firms. The largest block of shares is owned by public shareholders. (Its shares are traded on the Hong Kong exchange.) Lenovo is headed not by a princeling but by an American, William J. Amelo—a former senior vice president for Dell, as it happens.

Perhaps the security concerns could be validated by an authority on China's military. I spoke with James C. Mulvenon, deputy directory of the Center for Intelligence Research and Analysis, which is based in Washington and run by Defense Group Inc.

Dr. Mulvenon said he had many concerns about China's state-sponsored espionage activities but Lenovo was not on his list. He described the controversy about Lenovo as "xenophobia and anti-China fervor dressed up as a technology concern."

Rob Enderle of the Enderle Group, a technology consulting firm in San Jose, Calif., said he also saw the criticism of Lenovo as lacking in substance. With an executive staff split between Chinese and Americans, Lenovo is the most global company in the PC industry, he said. The real story, he said, was that these critics were "really torqued that China is out-executing the U.S."

Lenovo is an inviting magnet for all sorts of free-floating American anxieties about global competition. The visceral nature of these concerns can be seen in other remarks by Mr. Wortzel of the U.S-China Economic and Security Review Commission. He said, "As a taxpayer, I have a serious concern about why my tax money is spent on a computer made by a company owned by the government of the People's Republic of China." Why, he asked, couldn't the State Department place its order with a "100 percent American-owned company"?

The cold-war template of us versus them, capitalist versus Communist, does not fit the geography of the globalized supply chain that underpins the computer industry. All players, even the "100 percent American-owned" vendors, have a major presence in China. Roger I. Kay, the president of Endpoint Technologies Associates, a consulting firm in Natick, Mass., said China had attracted so many companies based in the United States that the PC ecosystem there had reached a critical mass. Low-cost production is not the draw. "Now the reason you want to be in China," he said, "is because that's where everyone else is."

Wishing wistfully for a return to the past—in which I.B.M. was still in the PC business—is not likely to improve American competitiveness here and now. Mr. Enderle said that ignoring the discomfiting fact that technology companies based in the United States are losing leadership positions to their counterparts in east Asia—not just China, but also Taiwan and South Korea—does not make the problem go away. "It's still going to hit us," he said.

Nevertheless, Mr. Dobbs and members of the U.S.-China Economic and Security Review Commission have tarred Lenovo with suspicion of espionage—and the State Department with being their willing dupe. Mr. Kay says the damage to Lenovo has been done, even if the State Department purchase proceeds.

"The next time," Mr. Kay predicted, "the government bureaucrat will say: 'Do I want to go through this? No, I'll go with the company that is perceived as American.' "

The smears will linger, he fears. "Facts don't matter," he said. "Perception matters."

Questions for Discussion

1. Why were some people concerned about Lenovo winning a State Department competitive bid?
2. Were their perceptions and attributions accurate or inaccurate?
3. How might the CNN Newscast by Lou Dobbs lead to inaccurate perceptions in viewers?
4. Do you believe discrimination or stereotyping is an issue in this case? Why or why not?

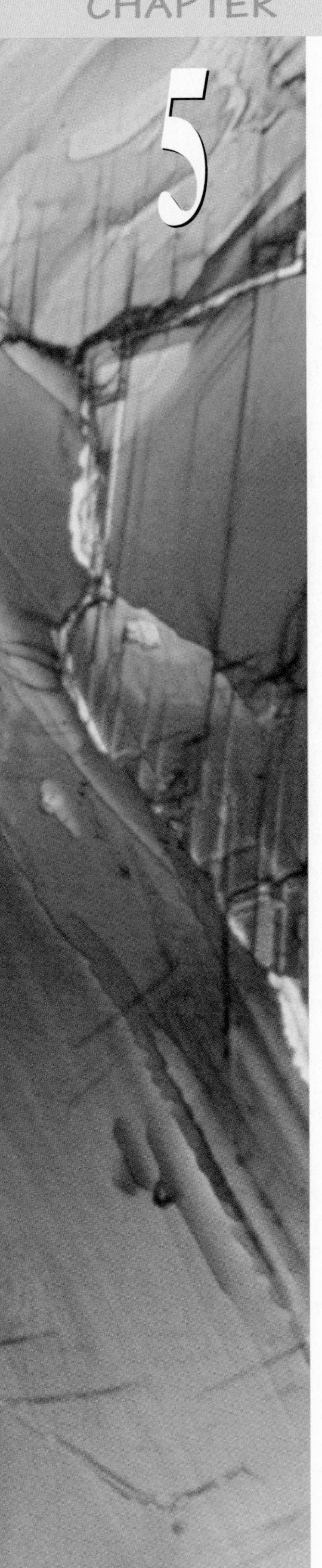

5

LEARNING AND CREATIVITY

Learning Objectives

After studying this chapter, you should be able to:

- Describe what learning is and why it is so important for all kinds of jobs and organizations.
- Understand how to effectively use reinforcement, extinction, and punishment to promote the learning of desired behaviors and curtail ineffective behaviors.
- Describe the conditions necessary to determine if vicarious learning has taken place.
- Appreciate the importance of self-control and self-efficacy for learning on your own.
- Describe how learning takes place continuously through creativity, the nature of the creative process, and the determinants of creativity.
- Understand what it means to be a learning organization.

Opening Case

CONTINUOUS LEARNING AND THE GLOBAL CREATIVITY ADVANTAGE

Why is continuous learning a necessity in today's business environment?

In today's global economy, more and more kinds of jobs are being outsourced to countries with lower labor costs. Outsourcing has moved beyond the manufacture of products to skilled, technical, knowledge-based work with countries like China, India, Russia, Czech Republic, and Hungary increasing their presence as a source of skilled, relatively low-cost labor. Thus, jobs in engineering, accounting, software design, and customer service are also being outsourced. In order to remain competitive, a growing number of companies and their managers are realizing that improving efficiency, cutting costs, and keeping abreast of the latest technological developments are not enough. Rather, what is essential is continuous learning through creativity that enables organizations to create new concepts, products, and services and reinvent old ones.[1]

Rudy Krolopp, lead designer of the first cell phone, poses with Motorola's first cellular phone the DynaTAC8000X and their new Razr cell phone April 5, 2005, in Schaumburg, Ill. Dubbed "the brick," the DynaTAC weighed in at 2 pounds, sold for $3,995, and would give you about a half-hour of talk time before recharging.

A key ingredient in this continuous learning is learning from consumers and customers—watching them as they go about their daily routines, imagining how they experience goods and services, and learning what appeals to them even though they themselves might not be able to articulate it.[2] This kind of continuous learning entails experimentation—trying out new things and seeing how people react to them. And when they react well, an organization has the opportunity to create a whole new market for itself. In creating new markets, workers also continuously learn from each other, whether it be an engineer working along side a factory worker to solve a technical problem in the manufacture of a new product, or a product designer and a marketing expert sharing insights.[3]

There are countless examples of companies that have successfully reinvented old products, created new concepts, or changed the nature of the consumer experience. Just as Cirque du Soleil has transformed the circus experience through its breathtaking performances, original music, and outlandish costumes, so too has Starbuck's reinvented the coffee shop and Apple the electronics store.[4]

Interestingly enough, large corporations like Motorola, General Electric, and Procter & Gamble are also recognizing the importance of continuous learning through creativity and seeking to promote it in numerous ways.[5] In order to facilitate continuous learning and creativity, some organizations are creating separate workspaces called innovation labs to bring people from different backgrounds together to learn from each other and create. Motorola's smash hit Razr cell phone was developed in Motorola's innovation lab, Moto City, in an office building in Chicago rather than at the company's R&D center in Libertyville, Illinois. Designers, marketers, engineers, and managers were brought to Moto City to develop the Razr, bypassing traditional hurdles that new ideas typically have to go through at Motorola, such as having regional managers sign-off on new products.[6]

At Fisher-Price, the preschool toy unit of Mattell, new products are developed in an innovation lab called the Cave, a separate space at company headquarters in East Aurora, New York. In developing new products, employees continuously learn from going out and observing how families and parents interact with their children and then coming back and learning from each other to develop new products. This is how the Laugh and Learn, Learning Home line of toys was developed—by watching families, employees learned that parents spend a lot of time teaching very young children about ordinary household objects like doorbells, lights, and drawers. Engineers, marketers, and product designers then learned from each other in the Cave to develop a model home made of plastic that infants can crawl through and experiment in while seeing the alphabet, making noises, and playing with numbers.[7]

Employees at Proctor & Gamble learn from consumers by watching how they go about cleaning their houses, and then they come back and brainstorm ideas for new products, build prototypes, and then go test them with consumers to learn how they react to them. This was how the Mr. Clean MagicReach product was created—pairing an old brand (Mr. Clean) with a new concept (cleaning hard to reach spots with a detachable pole).[8]

Top managers at large corporations are increasing recognizing that continuous learning through creativity is key to remaining competitive in today's global economy. As Jeffrey Immelt, CEO of General Electric, recently said, "Imaginative leaders are the ones who have the courage to fund new ideas, lead teams to discover better ideas, and lead people to take more educated risks."[9] Embracing continuous learning through creativity, and learning from others and experimentation, are enabling companies in a variety of industries to meet the challenges of the global economy in new ways.[10]

Overview

Learning is an ongoing process in everyone's life, both on and off the job. In organizations, employees need to learn how to perform the tasks and duties that make up their jobs, how to effectively interact with others, and how things work in the wider organization. Although learning is particularly important to newcomers (discussed in more detail in Chapter 10), it is also important for experienced members at all levels in an organization because they are frequently called on to do things they haven't done before. Moreover, rapid rates of change in organizational environments require that employees continually learn on the job. Changes in knowledge, technology, markets, competition, and customer preferences are among the forces in the environment that necessitate ongoing learning. In the opening case, we described how continuous learning through creativity is a key to remaining competitive in today's global economy.

In this chapter, we discuss the many ways in which learning takes place in organizations. We describe how to use reinforcement effectively to promote learning and how organizational members can "unlearn" undesired behaviors. Additionally, we explain how organizational members can learn from watching others, can learn on their own, and can learn "by doing." Finally, we discuss how organizations can promote continuous learning through creativity. By the end of this chapter, you will have a good appreciation of why multiple kinds of learning are essential for an organization to be effective.

The Nature of Learning

LEARNING
A relatively permanent change in knowledge or behavior that results from practice or experience.

Learning is a relatively permanent change in knowledge or behavior that results from practice or experience.[11] There are several key points in this definition. First, with learning comes *change*. For example, when you learn a second language, your knowledge about how to communicate evolves, and your behavior changes when communicating with native speakers of the language. Second, the change in knowledge or behavior has to be *relatively permanent* or long lasting. If you attempt to communicate with someone in another language by looking up words in a dictionary that you quickly forget once the interaction is complete, learning did not take place because there was no permanent change in your knowledge of the second language. The third key aspect of the definition is that learning takes place as a result of practice or through *experience*. Learning a second language requires much practice in pronunciation, word usage, and grammar. Similarly, through practice or experience, secretaries learn how to use new software packages, financial analysts learn the implications of new tax laws, engineers learn how to design more fuel-efficient automobiles, and flight attendants learn how to serve meals on airplanes. In this chapter, we discuss the multiples ways in which organizational members can and do learn.

Learning Through Consequences

OPERANT CONDITIONING
Learning that takes place when the learner recognizes the connection between a behavior and its consequences.

One of the most fundamental ways in which people learn throughout their lives is through the consequences they receive for their behaviors and actions. Psychologist B. F. Skinner was fascinated by the power of consequences to influence behavior, and his **operant conditioning** approach describes how learning takes place through consequences.[12] Operant conditioning is learning that takes place when the learner recognizes the connection between a behavior and its consequences (see Exhibit 5.1).[13] An individual learns to engage in specific behaviors (such as being responsive to customers' needs) in order to receive certain consequences (such as a bonus). This type of learning is called *operant* conditioning because individuals learn to operate in their environment in a certain way to achieve certain consequences.

You have probably learned that if you study hard you will receive good grades, and if you keep up with your reading throughout the semester, you will not be overburdened

EXHIBIT 5.1

Operant Conditioning

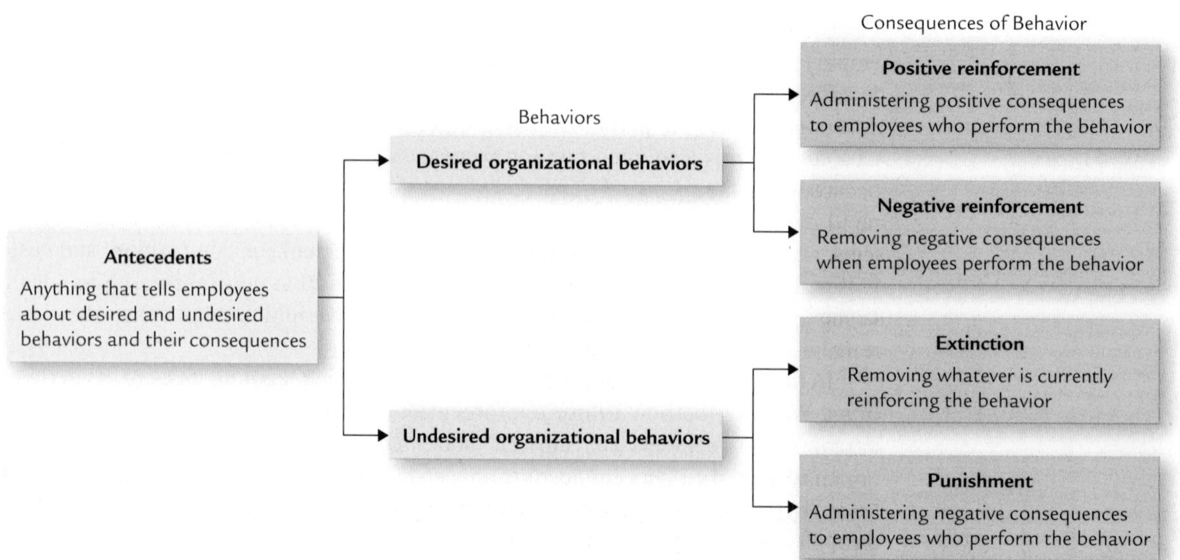

during finals week. Thus, you have learned how to *operate* in your environment to achieve your desired goals. In organizations, operant conditioning focuses on associating work behaviors (such as job performance, absenteeism, and lateness) with the consequences that will ensue in the employee's environment. These include *desired* consequences, such as pay and verbal praise, and *undesired* consequences, such as reprimands.

In addition to making the connection between a behavior and its consequences, antecedents play an important role in operant conditioning. Antecedents are instructions, rules, goals, advice from other members of an organization, and anything else that helps employees realize what behaviors they should and should not perform and what the consequences are for different behaviors. Antecedents play an educational role by letting employees know the organizational consequences (such as a pay raise or a promotion) for different behaviors (performing at a high level or impressing the division president during a presentation) and, thus, what behaviors they should perform.[14] For example, a rule (the antecedent) that three incidences of tardiness result in the loss of one vacation day (the consequence) lets employees know what will happen if they are continually late (the behavior).

Operant conditioning focuses on how organizations can use consequences to achieve two outcomes. One is increasing the probability that employees perform desired behaviors such as satisfying customers and coming to work on time. The other is decreasing the probability that employees perform undesired behaviors such as excessive Web surfing and making lengthy personal telephone calls at work. In the next section, we focus on the use of operant conditioning to promote desired behaviors in organizations; then we describe how operant conditioning can be used to discourage undesired behaviors.

Encouraging Desired Behaviors Through Positive and Negative Reinforcement

REINFORCEMENT
The process by which the probability that a desired behavior will occur is increased by applying consequences that depend on the behavior.

In operant conditioning, **reinforcement** is the process by which the probability that a desired behavior will occur is increased by applying consequences that depend on the behavior in question. One of a manager's major responsibilities is to ensure that subordinates learn and continue to perform desired behaviors consistently and dependably. In operant conditioning terms, managers need to increase the chances that this will occur. For example, they may want to encourage their subordinates to sell more products; assemble computer components faster; attend work more regularly; make more consistent use of safety equipment such as helmets, earplugs, and goggles; or provide higher-quality customer service.

Identifying Desired Behaviors. The first step in the use of reinforcement is to identify desired behaviors that the organization wants to encourage or reinforce, such as using safety equipment or giving customers good service (see Exhibit 5.1). Surprisingly, correctly identifying these behaviors is not as easy as it might seem.

To an outside observer, for example, paying a commission on sales seems like a logical way to encourage salespeople to learn to satisfy customers. In this example, making sales is the behavior that is the focus of the reinforcement effort. However, this approach may result in short-run sales but not necessarily satisfied, loyal customers. It might lead to salespeople adopting a hard-sell approach, pushing customers to buy items that do not really meet their needs. Thus, the behaviors that result in satisfied long-term customers—behaviors such as building long-term relationships and making sure customers buy what is right for them—have not been identified correctly. What has been identified is the amount of actual sales.

Similarly, a professor who wants to encourage students to participate in class might reason that students have to regularly attend class in order to participate. The professor might, therefore, decide to reinforce attendance by making it worth 5 percent of a student's grade. Most students do come to class, but they do not actively participate

Companies frequently use award walls and plaques as positive reinforcers to motivate their employees. But reinforcers differ from person to person. A money-motivated employee, for example, may be less than pleased if presented with a plaque versus a bonus check.

because the behavior the professor has reinforced is attendance, not actual participation. The professor has not correctly identified the desired behavior.

When desired behaviors are identified correctly, the second step in the reinforcement process is to decide how to reinforce the behavior. In operant conditioning, there are two types of reinforcement: positive and negative.[15]

POSITIVE REINFORCEMENT
Reinforcement that increases the probability of a desired behavior by administering positive consequences to employees who perform the behavior.

Positive Reinforcement. **Positive reinforcement** increases the probability that a behavior will occur by administering positive consequences to employees who perform the behavior. These positive consequences are known as *positive reinforcers*. To use positive reinforcement to facilitate the learning of desired behaviors, managers need to determine what consequences a given employee considers positive. Potential positive reinforcers include rewards such as higher pay, bonuses, promotions, job titles, interesting work, verbal praise, time off from work, and awards. Managers can determine whether these rewards are positively reinforcing for any given employee by seeing if that employee performs desired behaviors in order to obtain them.

It is important to keep in mind that individuals differ in what they consider to be a positive reinforcer. An employee who is independently wealthy, for example, may not view financial rewards as a positive reinforcer but may consider interesting work very reinforcing. In contrast, an employee with many financial needs and few financial resources may have exactly opposite preferences. Similarly, getting 5 percent credit for attending class regularly might be a powerful positive reinforcer for a student who is hoping to earn an A but not a positive reinforcer for a student who is content with a B or C in the course. Thus, managers need to take into account employees' individual preferences for different consequences.

With a little creative thinking, organizations can use reinforcement to promote the learning and performance of a wide variety of desirable behaviors. Many companies, for example, are trying to encourage their employees to give equal opportunities to an increasingly diverse workforce, yet are having a hard time getting a specific handle on the best ways to accomplish this objective. Positive reinforcement for diversity efforts may be one strategy that organizations can use. At Colgate-Palmolive, for example, a manager's pay is linked to diversity initiatives through the firm's Executive Incentive Compensation Plan. According to the plan, incentive compensation (such as a yearly bonus) depends on the extent to which a manager achieves certain predetermined objectives—one of which is supporting diversity. Colgate's diversity efforts in the United States have focused primarily on giving equal opportunities to women, African Americans, and Hispanics by having managers recruit and hire these employees, and once hired, giving them meaningful job assignments and opportunities for advancement and promotion.[16]

Negative Reinforcement. As in the case of positive reinforcement, subordinates experiencing negative reinforcement learn the connection between a desired organizational behavior and a consequence; however, the consequence is not a positive one that an employee wants to obtain but a negative one that the employee wishes to remove or avoid. **Negative reinforcement** increases the probability that a desired behavior will occur by removing, or rescinding, a negative consequence when an employee performs the behavior desired. The negative consequence that is removed is called a *negative reinforcer*. For example, if a manager complains every time an accountant turns in a report late, the complaints are a negative reinforcer if they result in the accountant learning to turn in the reports on time. By turning in reports when they are due, the accountant is able to "remove" the negative consequence of the complaints. Just as with positive reinforcement, managers need to take into account that individuals differ in what they consider to be a negative reinforcer.

NEGATIVE REINFORCEMENT
Reinforcement that increases the probability of a desired behavior by removing a negative consequence when an employee performs the behavior.

When positive and negative reinforcement is used to promote learning, it is important for the consequences to be equivalent in magnitude to the desired behavior.[17] For example, even if pay is a positive reinforcer for an employee, a small increase in pay (a $5 weekly bonus) might not be significant enough to cause the employee to perform a desired behavior (say, make follow-up calls to all new customers). In the same way, 5 percent of the course grade might not be a big enough reinforcer to cause chronically absent students to come to class, and a professor's complaints in class might not be a big enough negative reinforcer to get some students to participate in class discussions (and by doing so, stop the professor from complaining).

Using Reinforcement Appropriately. In general, positive reinforcement is better for employees, managers, and the organization as a whole than negative reinforcement. Negative reinforcement often has unintended side effects and makes for an unpleasant work environment. For example, a supervisor who continually complains may be resented and disliked. Even if positive reinforcement and negative reinforcement are equally successful in encouraging desired behaviors, the person or organization providing the reinforcement is likely to be viewed much more positively when positive reinforcement is consistently used.

When using reinforcement to promote the learning of desired behaviors in organizations, managers need to exercise some caution: When certain behaviors receive extensive reinforcement and others do not, employees may tend to focus on the former and ignore the latter. For example, if salespeople are paid solely on a commission basis, they may focus on making quick sales, and in doing so, may not perform the behaviors necessary for building long-term customer satisfaction (like making follow-up calls and service reminders, for example). Similarly, managers have to be careful to identify the right behaviors to reinforce.

Reinforcement Schedules. Managers using reinforcement to encourage the learning and performance of desired behaviors must choose whether to use continuous or partial reinforcement. When reinforcement is *continuous*, a behavior is reinforced every time it occurs. When reinforcement is *partial*, a behavior is reinforced intermittently. Continuous reinforcement can result in faster learning than can partial reinforcement. But if the reinforcement for some reason is curtailed, continuously reinforced behaviors will stop occurring more quickly than will partially reinforced behaviors.

Practical considerations often dictate whether reinforcement should be continuous or partial. A manager who is trying to encourage employees to use safety equipment, for example, may find continuous reinforcement infeasible: If she has to continually monitor her subordinates' use of safety equipment, she will never be able to get any work done herself.

Managers who decide to use partial reinforcement can choose from four schedules of partial reinforcement.[18] With a *fixed-interval schedule*, the period of time between the occurrence of each instance of reinforcement is fixed or set. An insurance agent whose supervisor takes him out to lunch at a fancy restaurant on the last Friday of the month if he has written a large number of policies during that month is being reinforced on a fixed-interval schedule. Once the supervisor has taken the agent out to lunch, a month will pass before the supervisor takes him out again for performing well. If in any given month the agent writes only a few policies, the supervisor does not treat him to lunch.

With a *variable-interval schedule*, the amount of time between reinforcements varies around a constant average. The owner of a car wash company who every so often watches each employee work on a car and praises those who do a good job is following a variable-interval schedule. The owner may watch and reinforce a given employee once a week, once every three weeks, or once a month, but over a six-month period the average amount of time between reinforcements is two weeks.

With a *fixed-ratio schedule*, a certain number of desired behaviors must occur before reinforcement is provided. Employees who are paid $5 for every three circuit boards they assemble are being reinforced on a fixed-ratio schedule. Many piece-rate pay plans currently in use at companies such as Lincoln Electric follow a fixed-ratio schedule.[19]

With a *variable-ratio schedule*, the number of desired behaviors that must occur before reinforcement varies around a constant average. A manager who allows an employee to leave early after she has stayed late for several evenings is following a variable-ratio schedule of reinforcement. Sometimes the manager allows the employee to leave early after working two late evenings, at other times after four late evenings, but over time the average is three evenings.

The choice of a schedule of partial reinforcement often depends on practical considerations: the particular behavior being encouraged, the type of reinforcer being used, or the nature of the employee's job. The specific type of schedule chosen is not as important as the fact that reinforcement is based on the performance of desired behaviors: Learning takes place only when the provision of a reinforcer depends on performance of a desired behavior.

Stimulating learning involves reinforcing good performance bit-by-bit as employees learn the skills they need to do their jobs.

Shaping

Sometimes a desired behavior is unlikely to occur on its own or at any given point in time because an individual does not have the skills and knowledge necessary to perform the behavior or because the behavior can only evolve out of practice or experience. Consider, for example, a trainee who is learning to drive a bus in New York City. At the beginning of her training conducted by the firm's driving instructor, the trainee is unlikely to drive the bus properly and, thus, cannot be reinforced for this desired behavior. The instructor can use reinforcement to *stimulate* learning, however, by reinforcing successively closer approximations to the desired behavior (in this case, the proper handling of the bus in city traffic). Suppose the trainee initially jumps the curb when making left turns but after her sixth trip finally makes a turn that is still too wide but does not jump the curb. Even though the behavior was not at its ideal level, because the turn was a bit wider than it should have been, this improved behavior is positively reinforced by verbal praise from the instructor to increase the probability that it will occur again.

SHAPING
The reinforcement of successive and closer approximations to a desired behavior.

The reinforcement of successive and closer approximations to a desired behavior is known as **shaping**.[20] Shaping is particularly effective when employees need to learn complicated sequences of behavior. When it is unlikely that employees will be able to perform the desired behaviors all at once, managers reinforce closer and closer approximations to the desired behavior to encourage employees to gradually acquire the skills and expertise needed to perform at an adequate level.

Discouraging Undesired Behaviors Through Extinction and Punishment

Just as managers need to ensure that employees learn to perform desired behaviors dependably, they also need to ensure that employees learn *not* to perform undesired behaviors. Examples of undesired behaviors in organizations include (among hundreds of others) excessive absenteeism, excessive Web surfing on company time, operating heavy equipment such as bulldozers and cranes in a dangerous fashion, and sexual harassing other employees. Two main operant conditioning techniques reduce the probability of undesired behaviors: extinction and punishment (see Exhibit 5.1).

Extinction. According to the principles of operant conditioning, all behaviors—good and bad—are controlled by reinforcing consequences. Thus, any behavior that occurs is performed because the individual is receiving some form of reinforcement for it. If managers wish to lessen the probability that an undesired behavior will occur, they need to first determine what is currently reinforcing the behavior and then remove the source of reinforcement. Once the undesired behavior ceases to be reinforced, its frequency diminishes until it no longer occurs. This process is called **extinction**.

EXTINCTION
The lessening of undesired behavior by removing the source of reinforcement.

Suppose every time a manager has a meeting with one of her subordinates, Sam, he always tells jokes and fools around. At first, the manager thinks Sam's joking is harmless, but soon she realizes that the meetings are taking twice as long as they should, that certain items on the agenda are getting short shrift, and that Sam is having a hard time remembering the important points made during the meeting. After attending a management development seminar on operant conditioning, the manager realizes that she is actually positively reinforcing Sam's behavior by laughing at his jokes. At the next meeting, she treats Sam cordially but refrains from laughing at his jokes. Sam looks a little perplexed but soon stops joking and takes the meetings more seriously.

This example illustrates that extinction can be a relatively painless way to reduce the occurrence of undesired behaviors. The supervisor had considered talking directly to Sam or criticizing his behavior at their next meeting. Eliminating Sam's positive reinforcement for horsing around probably did less to hurt his feelings and disrupt their otherwise good relationship.

Punishment. Managers do not have the time to wait for extinction to lessen or eliminate some undesired behaviors. Certain behaviors are so detrimental or dangerous they need to stop immediately. Just as a parent cannot rely on extinction to stop a child from touching a hot stove, a manager cannot rely on extinction to eliminate highly undesirable behaviors in the workplace such as sexual harassment or operating heavy equipment in a dangerous fashion. Under such circumstances, a manager can try to eliminate undesired behavior by using **punishment**—administering a negative consequence when the undesired behavior occurs.

PUNISHMENT
The administration of a negative consequence when undesired behavior occurs.

In operant conditioning, punishment and negative reinforcement are often confused. Students, employees, and managers alike think that these two techniques for managing behavior are similar or have the same result. However, they differ from each other in two important ways. First, punishment *reduces* the probability of an *undesired* behavior; negative reinforcement *increases* the probability of a *desired* behavior. Second, punishment involves *administering* a negative consequence when an *undesired* behavior occurs; negative reinforcement entails *removing* a negative consequence when a *desired* behavior occurs. Exhibit 5.2 summarizes the effects of the different operant conditioning techniques that managers can use to encourage the performance of desired behaviors and eliminate undesired behaviors.

Managers need to take into account the fact that people differ in what they consider to be punishment. If being scolded by a supervisor after coming to work late is a source of punishment for one employee, then that employee will try as hard as possible not to be late after receiving a scolding. But an employee who hardly gives the scolding a second thought will come to work late again the next day. Some forms of punishment that organizations typically use are verbal reprimands, reductions in pay, elimination of privileges (such as personal days an employee can take off at his or her discretion), and temporary suspension. Organizations sometimes use a system of progressive punishment to try to curtail undesired behavior: the more an employee engages in the behavior, the stricter the punishment becomes.

Punishment can have some unexpected side effects and should be used only when necessary. It not only has the potential to threaten the employee's self-respect but can also

EXHIBIT 5.2

Operant Conditioning Techniques

Technique	How Consequence Is Administered	Effect on Behavior	Example
Positive reinforcement	Positive consequence is given when desired behavior is performed	Increases probability of desired behavior	Employee is praised for cleaning up work station
Negative reinforcement	Negative consequence is removed when desired behavior is performed	Increases probability of desired behavior	Supervisor complains about messy work station and stops only when worker cleans it
Extinction	Positive consequence is removed when undesired behavior is performed	Decreases probability of undesired behavior	Manager refrains from laughing at a subordinate's disruptive jokes when the two have important matters to discuss
Punishment	Negative consequence is given when undesired behavior is performed	Decreases probability of undesired behavior	Manager criticizes subordinate for telling disruptive jokes when the two have important matters to discuss

create so much resentment and negative feelings toward the punisher and organization as a whole that the employee might want to retaliate. Thus, when punishment is used, managers need to be very careful that, while eliminating the undesired behavior, they do not create excessive hostility or negative feelings.

The following guidelines can help to ensure that punishment has its intended effect and does not generate negative side effects:

- Try to downplay the emotional element involved in punishment. Remember that you are punishing the person's undesirable behavior, not the person.
- Make sure the chosen negative consequence is indeed a punishment for the individual, and punish the undesired behavior immediately.[21] Make sure employees know why they are being punished.
- Try to avoid punishing an employee in front of others. Although public punishment might seem like a good idea because it serves as a warning to others, it is likely to humiliate the individual being punished, reduce his or her esteem, and make coworkers uncomfortable. Remember: The key goal is to eliminate a person's undesirable behavior, not his or her self-respect.
- When possible, provide employees with a desired behavior in place of the undesired behavior.

When a manager does not follow those guidelines, not only is the individual who is being punished likely to suffer, but so too are his or her coworkers, the manager, and the whole organization.

ORGANIZATIONAL BEHAVIOR MODIFICATION (OB MOD) The systematic application of the principles of operant conditioning for teaching and managing important organizational behaviors.

Organizational Behavior Modification

The systematic application of the principles of operant conditioning for learning desired behaviors is called **organizational behavior modification (OB MOD)**. OB MOD has been successfully used to improve productivity, attendance, punctuality, safe work practices, customer service, and other important behaviors in a wide variety of kinds of organizations such as banks, department stores, factories, hospitals, and construction sites.[22]

EXHIBIT 5.3

Steps in Organizational Behavior Modification

Source: Adapted from F. Luthans and A. D. Stajkovic, "Reinforce for Performance: The Need to Go Beyond Pay and Even Rewards," *Academy of Management Executive* 13(2) (1999): 49–57.

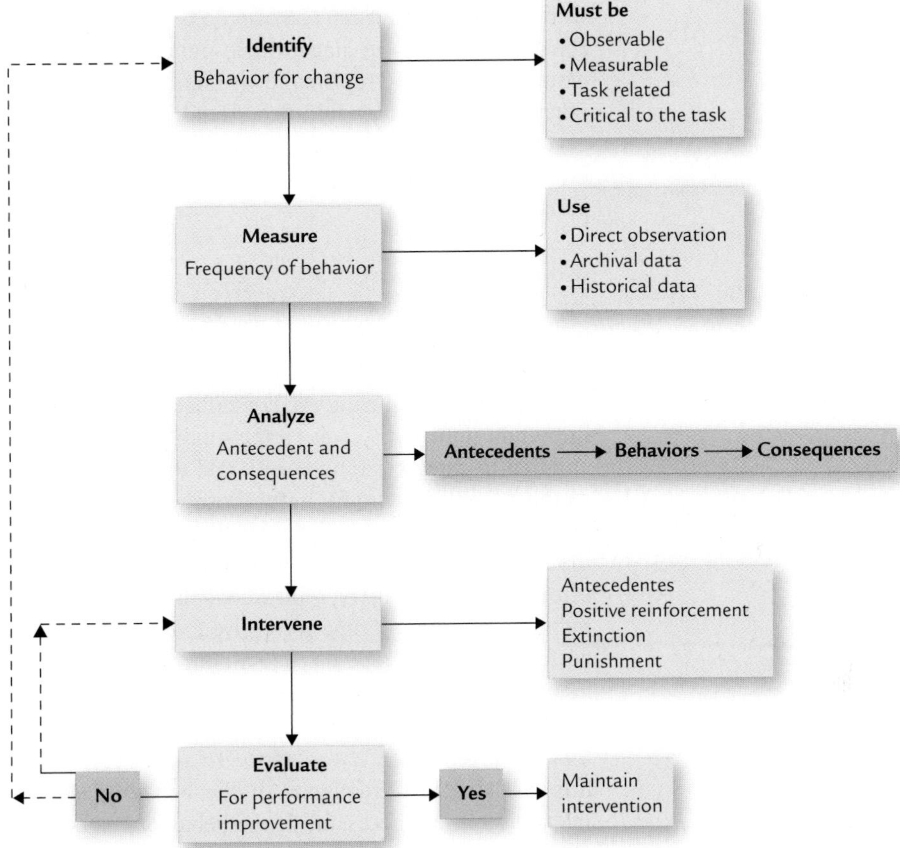

OB MOD can be used to encourage the learning of desired organizational behaviors as well as to discourage undesired behaviors.

Organizations that successfully use OB MOD follow a five-step process: identify, measure, analyze, intervene, and evaluate (see Exhibit 5.3).[23]

Identify *the behavior to be learned.* OB MOD should be used to encourage behaviors that can be observed by others (and can, therefore, be reinforced), are important for task performance, and can be measured. Examples include attendance, punctuality, the use of safety equipment, sales goals, customer service levels, productivity, and quality control.[24] The work behaviors also should be relevant to the job and to organizational performance. For example, at the Treehouse Day Care Center in Chicago, the director of the center has identified punctuality as a critical behavior in need of improvement. OB MOD has been successfully used to promote desired behaviors ranging from safe driving by city bus drivers and timely and error-free registration and admittance procedures performed by hospital administrators to safe mining practices followed in open pit mines. It has also been used to encourage bank tellers to establish eye contact with their customers and greet them by name, to improve the productivity of vineyard pruners, and to improve the output of factory workers.[25]

Measure *the frequency of the behavior.* Before any actions are taken, it is important to get a baseline measure of how often the identified behavior occurs. For example, the director of Treehouse measured the punctuality of the center's staff over a two-week period and discovered that each staff member was late around three times per week.

Analyze *the antecedents and consequences of the behavior.* Once the frequency of the behavior has been determined, it is important to identify the current antecedents and consequences of the behavior. At Treehouse, the director realized that while it was assumed that staff would come to work on time for their shifts, there were no actual antecedents in place to cue punctuality. In terms of consequences, the director would occasionally reprimand workers who were excessively late for their shifts, and other staff members would occasionally complain when they had to remain on the job past their own quitting time because staff members on the next shift were late. However, the director realized there were no positive reinforcers in place to actually promote punctuality.

Intervene *to change the frequency of the behavior.* Interventions can include introducing antecedents and applying operant conditioning techniques including positive reinforcement, negative reinforcement, punishment, and extinction. Remember, whenever feasible, positive reinforcement is preferred to negative reinforcement and extinction is preferred to punishment. At Treehouse's next staff meeting, the director stressed how important punctuality was to the quality of child care, how important state-mandated children-to-caregiver ratios were, and the importance of being considerate to other staff members (who have to fill in for those who are late). The director also had a plaque made that summarized the reasons why "Punctuality Benefits Us All," which was hung next to the center's bulletin board. In addition to cuing punctuality with these antecedents, the director also positively reinforced punctuality in two ways. First, each week, staff members arriving on time were given verbal praise from the director. Second, staff with perfect punctuality records each month were allowed to take a half-day off the following month.

Evaluate *whether the intervention was successful in changing behavior.* At this last step, the frequency of the behavior is again measured to determine if the intervention was successful. If the behavior has been successfully modified, then all that needs to be done at this step is to maintain the intervention (for example, continue to use the antecedents and positive reinforcers from the prior step to encourage the behavior). If the behavior has not been successfully modified, then managers need to reconsider their intervention methods and modify them accordingly and/or reconsider the behavior they originally identified. At Treehouse, the director measured the punctuality of the staff over a two-week period following the intervention and was delighted to discover that no staff members were late for their shifts during the entire two weeks.

Research suggests that when OB MOD is appropriately used, it can be highly effective when it comes to promoting desireable organizational behavior.[26] For example, a recent review of research on OB MOD showed that it improved employee performance by 17 percent on average. In a recent field experiment conducted by Alexander Stajkovic and Fred Luthans in a division of a large organization that processes credit card bills, it was found that OB MOD resulted in a 37 percent increase in performance when the reinforced behavior included financial incentives.[27] Interestingly, when performance was positively reinforced by simple supervisory feedback, the performance of employees increased by 20 percent. When social recognition and praise were used, performance increased by 24 percent.[28]

Ethical Issues in OB MOD

There is some controversy surrounding the use of OB MOD in organizations. Proponents rightfully claim that OB MOD is a useful way to manage important organizational behaviors. Research indicating that OB MOD can be successfully used to increase productivity and cut down on accidents, waste, and absenteeism is certainly consistent with this view. Opponents of OB MOD, however, complain that it is overly controlling. These critics believe that managers who explicitly manipulate consequences to control behavior strip employees of their dignity, freedom of choice, and individuality. They also believe that treating employees in such a cut-and-dried fashion may, over time, rob them of the initiative they might otherwise have had to respond appropriately to changing conditions.

Moreover, employees who are managed in such a fashion may refrain from performing important organizational behaviors that are not specifically part of their job duties, such as helping coworkers or coming up with new and good ideas, because these behaviors often cannot be assigned in advance and appropriately reinforced. These voluntary behaviors are essential for organizational survival and effectiveness but may not be covered by an organization's formal system of rewards because they are performed voluntarily. When employees are managed according to the principles of operant conditioning, they may become so reinforcement oriented that they refrain from doing anything that is *not* reinforced.

There is no clear-cut answer to the ethical dilemma posed by OB MOD, and there are counterarguments to each of the anti–OB MOD positions. In response to the criticism that OB MOD strips employees of their freedom of choice and individuality, for example, OB MOD proponents might assert that whether an employee performs a behavior or not is ultimately his or her own choice and that operant conditioning takes individuality into account when the individual preferences of different reinforcers are considered. Nonetheless, as a manager, it is important to be aware of the issues raised by this debate and think through their implications from one's own perspective. Additionally, any use of OB MOD must conform to employment laws. For example, in California and many other states, labor laws require that employers compensate employees for overtime work, even if they are paid on a piece-rate basis, to encourage them to produce products as quickly as possible.[29]

Learning From Others

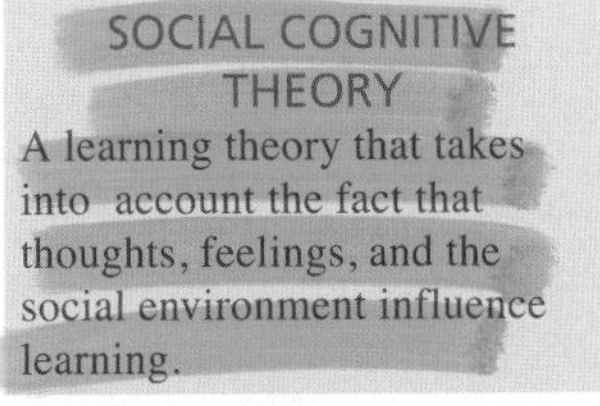

SOCIAL COGNITIVE THEORY
A learning theory that takes into account the fact that thoughts, feelings, and the social environment influence learning.

Although operant conditioning accurately describes some of the major factors that influence learning in organizations, certain aspects of learning are not covered in this theory. To get a more complete picture of how members of an organization learn, we now turn to **social cognitive theory** (also referred to as social learning theory). Albert Bandura, one of the principal contributors to social cognitive theory, suggests that any attempt to understand how people learn must also take into account a person's feelings and thoughts (cognitions) and their observations of the world around them (that is, their social environment; see Exhibit 5.4). Social cognitive theory acknowledges the importance of the person in the learning process by taking cognitive processes into account.[30]

COGNITIVE PROCESSES
Thought processes.

Cognitive processes are the various thought processes that people engage in. When people form attributions (see Chapter 4), for example, they are engaging in a cognitive process to determine why a person has performed a specific behavior. From the perspective

EXHIBIT 5.4

Social Cognitive Theory

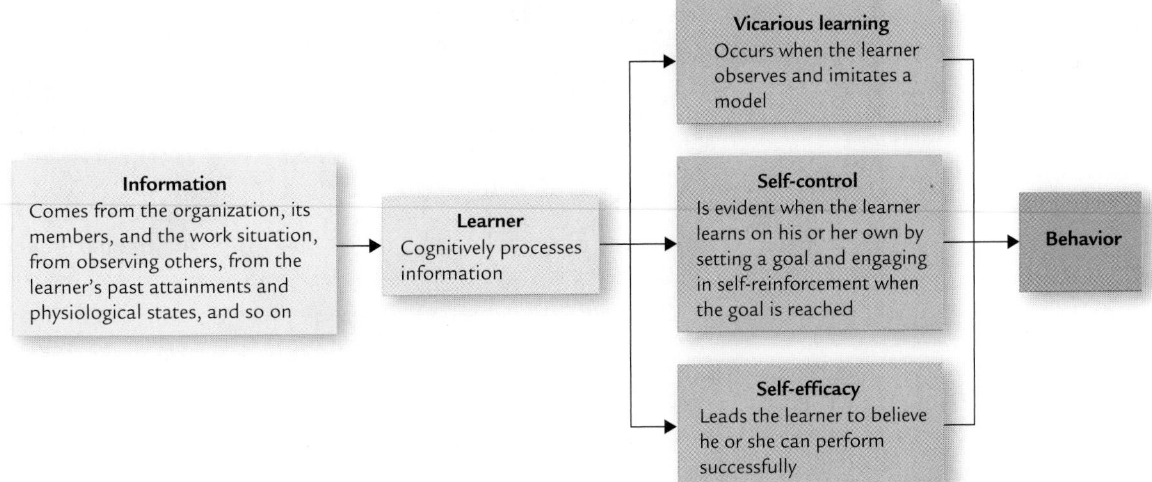

Is evident when the learner learns on his or her own by setting a goal and engaging in self-reinforcement when the goal is reached

of social cognitive theory, employees actively process information from the social environment and those around them when they learn.[31]

Suppose you study hard yet are doing poorly in one of your classes. A friend of yours doesn't seem to put in as much time as you do yet is maintaining a B+ average in the class. You think you are just as smart as your friend and notice how your friend studies for the class: He or she takes detailed notes in class, highlights the chapters, and then summarizes the key points, and goes to see the professor whenever he or she is confused. You start doing this yourself, your grades improve, and you think you can salvage a B in the course after all. This example demonstrates how you have learned from observing another person. In learning how to do well in the class, your thoughts about your poor performance and about your friend's relatively good performance, your observations of how your friend studies for the class, your belief that you are just as smart as your friend, and your decision to copy your friend's approach to studying were the steps you took to learn how to perform well in the class.

VICARIOUS LEARNING
Learning that occurs when one person learns a behavior by watching another person perform the behavior.

In social cognitive theory, learning from observing others perform a behavior is called **vicarious learning**. When vicarious learning occurs, a person (the learner) observes another person (the model) perform a behavior. The learner observes the effect of the model's behavior on the environment (is it reinforced?), and when an appropriate situation arises, the learner imitates the model's behavior.

Several conditions must be met for vicarious learning to take place:[32]

- The learner must observe the model when he or she is performing the behavior.
- The learner must accurately perceive the model's behavior.
- The learner must remember the behavior.
- The learner must have the skills and abilities necessary to perform the behavior.
- The learner must see that the model receives reinforcement for the behavior in question. If the model is not reinforced (or is punished) for the behavior, there is obviously no incentive for the learner to imitate the behavior.

A substantial amount of the learning that takes place in organizations occurs vicariously. Training new recruits, for example, involves considerable amounts of vicarious learning. Formal training sessions often rely on demonstrations of appropriate behaviors by experienced employees and role playing during which employees observe others performing appropriate and inappropriate behaviors. Retail organizations sometimes use films showing experienced salespeople giving customers good service in an effort to train new salespeople to do the same. For these films to be effective, it is essential for the model (the experienced salesperson) to be reinforced for the high-quality service behaviors. Often the reinforcement is the customer's decision to purchase something. Similarly,

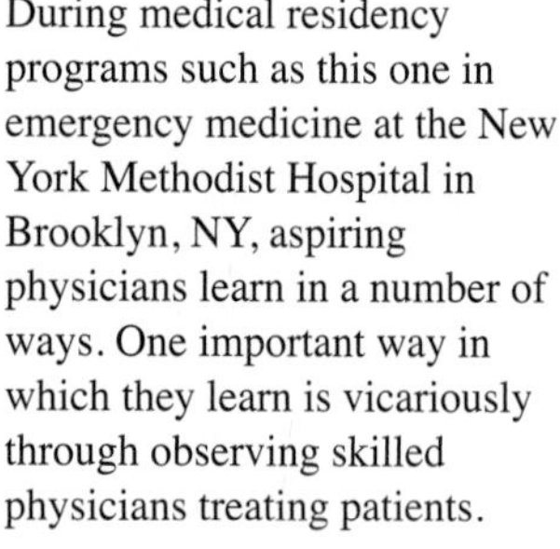

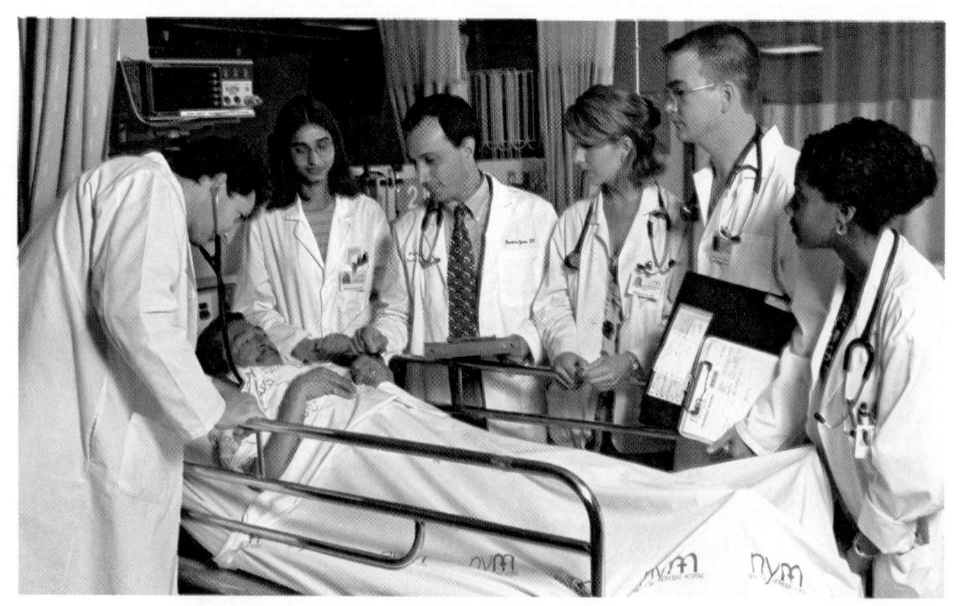

During medical residency programs such as this one in emergency medicine at the New York Methodist Hospital in Brooklyn, NY, aspiring physicians learn in a number of ways. One important way in which they learn is vicariously through observing skilled physicians treating patients.

restaurants often have inexperienced waiters and waitresses follow and observe the behaviors of an experienced coworker for a few days prior to serving their first customers. By watching others, new recruits learn appropriate on-the-job behaviors, such as those desired by the Ritz-Carlton, which is profiled in the accompying Global View.

Global View

Vicarious Learning at the Ritz-Carlton

The Ritz-Carlton luxury hotel chain is a global organization with 28,000 employees and 59 hotels scattered in more than 20 countries worldwide ranging from Bahrain, Turkey, and the United Arab Emirates to Italy, Japan, and China. Currently, five new hotels are planned to open in China alone.[33] In order to appeal to its global customers around the world, the Ritz-Carlton recently partnered with NewspaperDirect, giving its guests access to over 150 daily newspapers from 40 countries.[34]

Providing high-quality customer service is the hallmark of the Ritz-Carlton, and it is embodied in the first sentence of its credo: "The Ritz-Carlton Hotel is a place where the genuine care and comfort of our guests is our highest mission."[35] In order to ensure that each new employee learns how to provide "the finest personal service" to Ritz-Carlton guests—whether in Osaka, Japan, or Philadelphia, Pennsylvania—the Ritz-Carlton relies on vicarious learning.[36]

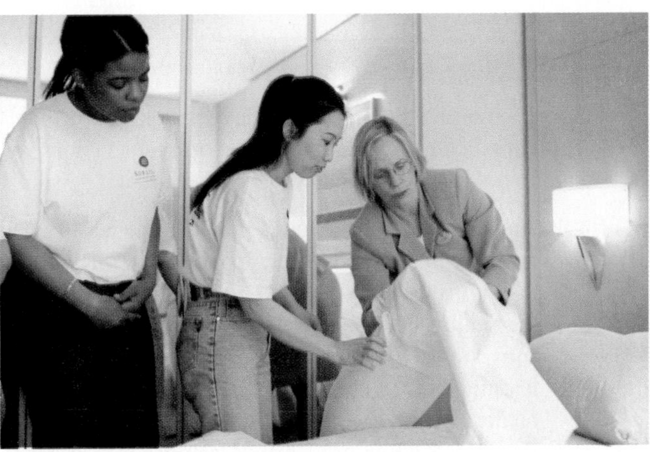

The Ritz-Carlton is renowned for its outstanding service. New hires learn "vicariously" how to give guests great service by accompanying experienced staff members and emulating their behavior.

Take the case of a new employee who will be a room-service waiter at the Ritz-Carlton in Boston.[37] After a two-day orientation program, the new employee is teamed up with an experienced room-service waiter and literally follows the experienced waiter around for the next few days, observing what the waiter says and does and how customers react. The newcomer picks up certain tips along the way, such as the importance of trying to anticipate what customers might want even if they don't ask for it. For example, a guest ordering one dinner and a bottle of wine might need two glasses. If he or she orders dinner along with ice cream, the dinner needs to stay hot while the ice cream needs to stay cold. After observing the experienced waiter model appropriate behavior, the newcomer starts playing a more active role by talking to customers or opening a bottle of wine, but the model waiter is never far from sight until the newcomer has learned all he or she needs to pass a test administered by the manager in charge of in-room dining services.[38] Clearly, vicarious learning has paid off handsomely for the Ritz-Carlton. It has won the prestigious Malcolm Baldrige National Quality Award, ranked first in *Business Travel News'* Top U.S. Hotel Chain survey, and has been ranked as the most prestigious brand by The Luxury Institute's Luxury Brand Status Index Survey.[39]

Vicarious learning also plays an important role in the day-to-day functioning of most organizations. Organizational members continually observe others and often try to remember behaviors that result in reinforcement. These behaviors can range from relatively routine matters, such as when to arrive at work, how long to take for lunch, the best way to present a report to upper-level management, or how to conduct oneself in a business meeting. Moreover, recent research suggests that employees can even learn how to be creative by observing the behavior of creative coworkers.[40]

Vicarious learning is also an important means of acquiring behaviors that are complicated and have a high cost of failure. Much of the learning that takes place through operant conditioning is the result of trial and error: The learner engages in a variety of behaviors and learns to repeat those that are reinforced and abandon those that are not. For some kinds of work, however, an organization simply cannot afford the costs of trial-and-error learning. No one would want to be at the mercy of a medical intern who is learning open-heart surgery by means of trial and error; the costs (a few dead patients) of learning in this manner are just too high. In such situations, vicarious learning is essential. A learner who has all the necessary knowledge, skills, and abilities can learn quite complicated sequences of behavior by carefully observing the behaviors and outcomes of others with more experience.

In organizations there are many potential models available for members to imitate. However, only a few of these models will be used to acquire new behaviors vicariously. To take advantage of vicarious learning in organizations, managers should ensure that good performer models are available for newcomers and existing organizational members to learn from. Models that are most likely to be imitated by others tend to be provided by (1) members of the organization who are highly competent in the modeled behavior and may even have a reputation for being an expert, (2) individuals with high status in the organization, (3) employees who receive reinforcers the learner desires, and (4) individuals who engage in desired behaviors in a friendly manner.[41]

SELF-CONTROL
Self-discipline that allows a person to learn to perform a behavior even though there is no external pressure to do so.

SELF-REINFORCERS
Consequences or rewards that individuals can give to themselves.

Learning On Your Own

Social cognitive theory acknowledges that people can learn on their own by using **self-control**—that is, by learning to perform a behavior even though there is no external pressure to do so. Several conditions indicate that a person is using self-control:[42]

1. An individual must engage in a low-probability behavior. A low-probability behavior is a behavior that a person would ordinarily not want to perform. This condition distinguishes individuals exhibiting self-control from those engaging in activities they enjoy. For example, Sylvia Crano, an administrative secretary, has had a new software package for graphics sitting on her desk for the past six months. She hates learning how to use new software and, fortunately, her boss hasn't put any pressure on her to learn the new software. Taking the initiative to learn how to use the new software is a low-probability response for Crano. If she bites the bullet and comes in one Saturday to learn it, Crano will be exhibiting self-control.
2. Self-reinforcers must be available to the learner. **Self-reinforcers** are any consequences or rewards that individuals give to themselves. Potential self-reinforcers include buying oneself a present, eating a favorite food, going out to a movie, getting some extra sleep, and going out with friends. Sometimes self-reinforcement comes simply from a feeling of accomplishment or achievement. In the past, when Sylvia Crano has accomplished a particularly difficult task, she has rewarded or reinforced herself by buying a new CD or having lunch with a friend.
3. The learner must set goals that determine when self-reinforcement takes place. When self-control takes place, people do not indiscriminately reward themselves but set goals that determine when they will self-reinforce. How do people determine these goals or standards? Essentially, they rely on their own past performance, the performance of others on similar kinds of tasks, or some socially acquired performance standard. Crano's goal was to complete the software's tutorial and use the new program to reproduce some graphs she had done previously.

When employees care about their work and doing a good job, they often engage in self-control. When employees engage in self-control, managers should avoid closely supervising their work.

4. The learner must administer the reinforcer when the goal is achieved. Crano allowed herself to have lunch out with her friend only when she was able to use the new software to reproduce her existing graphs.

All people engage in self-control and self-reinforcement to learn behaviors on and off the job. These activities can range from the relatively mundane (such as cutting short a lunch hour to catch up on e-mails) to the more involved (learning how to appropriately give subordinates negative feedback). Managers need to be aware that self-control takes place at work, especially when individuals are interested in and care about their work. When opportunities for self-control are present and employees engage in it, managers do not need to take as active a role in controlling behavior and consequences because employees are taking responsibility for learning and performing desired behaviors themselves. In such cases, the managers' efforts at control may be not only redundant but counterproductive because they may irritate and anger those who are self-controlled. Instead of trying to control individuals like this, managers would be wise to focus their efforts on those who need more guidance.

Employees who manage their own behavior through self-control are often said to be self-managing. Sometimes, however, employees may need a bit of coaching and guidance to become truly self-managing. Managers can provide the training and support employees need to develop self-management skills and put them to use. Some organizations such as National Semiconductor explicitly recognize this need and have formal programs in place to teach self-management.[43]

Beliefs About One's Ability to Learn: The Role of Self-Efficacy

SELF-EFFICACY
A person's belief about his or her ability to perform a particular behavior successfully.

Social cognitive theory also emphasizes the importance of **self-efficacy**—a person's belief about his or her ability to perform a particular behavior successfully—in the learning process.[44] One secretary may believe that she can learn how to use a new software package on her own, and another may have strong doubts about his ability to learn new software without taking a formal training course. Self-efficacy has powerful effects on learning because people try to learn only those behaviors that they think they will be able to perform successfully.[45] Self-efficacy affects learning in three ways:[46]

1. *Self-efficacy influences the activities and goals that individuals choose for themselves*: Employees with a low level of self-efficacy may never try to learn how to perform challenging tasks because they think they will fail at them. Such employees tend to set relatively low goals for themselves. Conversely, an individual with high self-efficacy is likely to try to learn how to perform demanding tasks and set high personal goals. Consistent with this reasoning, research has found that individuals not only learn but also perform at levels consistent with their self-efficacy beliefs. Employees learn what they think they are able to learn.
2. *Self-efficacy affects learning by influencing the effort that individuals exert on the job*: Employees with high self-efficacy generally work hard to learn how to perform new behaviors because they are confident that their efforts will be successful. Employees with low self-efficacy may exert less effort when learning how to perform complicated or difficult behaviors, not because they are lazy but because they don't think the effort will pay off. Their lack of confidence in their ability to succeed causes them to think that exerting a lot of effort is futile because they are likely to fail anyway.
3. *Self-efficacy affects the persistence with which a person tries to master new and sometimes difficult tasks*: Because employees with high self-efficacy are confident that they can learn how to perform a given task, they are likely to persist in their efforts even in the face of temporary setbacks or problems. Conversely, employees with low self-efficacy who think they are unlikely to be able to learn a difficult task are likely to give up as soon as an obstacle appears or the going gets a little tough. Consistent with this reasoning, in a recent review of the extensive literature on self-efficacy, Albert Bandura and Ed Locke concluded that self-efficacy is a powerful determinant of job performance.[47]

Sources of Self-Efficacy

Because self-efficacy can have such powerful effects on learning and performance in organizations, it is important to identify where it comes from. Bandura has identified four principal sources.[48]

Past performance is one of the most powerful sources of self-efficacy. Employees who have succeeded on job-related activities in the past are likely to have higher self-efficacy for such activities than employees who have failed. Managers can boost low levels of self-efficacy by ensuring that employees can and do succeed on certain tasks. "Small successes" boost self-efficacy and enable more substantial accomplishments in the future.

Vicarious experience or observation of others is another source of self-efficacy. Seeing coworkers succeed at a particular task may heighten the observer's self-efficacy. Conversely, seeing coworkers fail is likely to discourage the observer.

Verbal persuasion—that is, trying to convince people that they have the ability to learn and succeed at a particular task—can give rise to self-efficacy. Research has shown that when managers are confident that their subordinates can succeed at a particular task, the subordinates actually perform at a higher level.[49]

An individual's reading of his or her internal physiological states is the fourth source of self-efficacy that Bandura identified.[50] A person who expects to fail at some task or to find something too demanding is likely to experience certain physiological symptoms: a pounding or racing heart, feeling flushed, sweaty hands, headaches, and so on. The particular symptoms vary from individual to individual but over time become associated with doing poorly. If the symptoms start to occur in any given situation, self-efficacy for dealing with that situation may plummet.

Consider the case of Michael Pulinski, who was facing an important job interview. Pulinski really wanted to get this job and had spent a considerable amount of time preparing for the interview. He was familiar with the company and had prepared good questions to ask the interviewer about the job. He also had thoroughly rehearsed answers to typical interview questions (such as "Where do you see yourself in five years?") and had bought a new suit for the occasion. The day of the interview, Pulinski got up feeling quite good and was actually looking forward to the interview and to demonstrating that he was the right candidate for the job. He arrived to the interview a little early and paged through a recent copy of *Business Week* in the reception area. As he was thinking about how much this job meant to him, he started getting nervous. He could feel his face getting flushed, his hands were sweaty, and his heart started pounding in his chest. Pulinski's self-efficacy plummeted. Because of these physical symptoms, he decided that he was much too nervous to make a good impression in the interview. Unfortunately, his low self-efficacy resulted in his not doing well in the interview and failing to get a job offer.

Learning By Doing

EXPERIENTIAL LEARNING
Learning that occurs by the direct involvement of the learner in the subject matter being learned (that is, learning by doing).

Some learning takes place by actually engaging in a new or different activity. Often referred to as **experiential learning**, this learning occurs by the direct involvement of the learner in the subject matter being learned—learning by doing, in other words.[51] Consider, for example, how people learn to be air traffic controllers. They, of course, can read reference books on air traffic patterns, study Federal Aviation Administration rules and regulations, learn how to communicate with pilots who are flying planes, and study the configurations of different airports. However, if they only rely on these kinds of activities, they will never be an effective and safe air traffic controller. What's missing? Learning by doing. In order to master air traffic controlling, it is essential that prospective controllers learn their jobs by doing them. Clearly, it would be too dangerous for them to learn how to be an air traffic controller while directing real traffic in airspace. But they can and do learn by performing realistic simulations of actual air traffic controllers' jobs using the same equipment they will be using on the job.

On some jobs, learning by doing through performing actual work tasks on the job is too dangerous. Aspiring air traffic controllers, for example, learn their jobs by performing realistic simulations of actual air traffic controllers' jobs using the same equipment they will be using on the job.

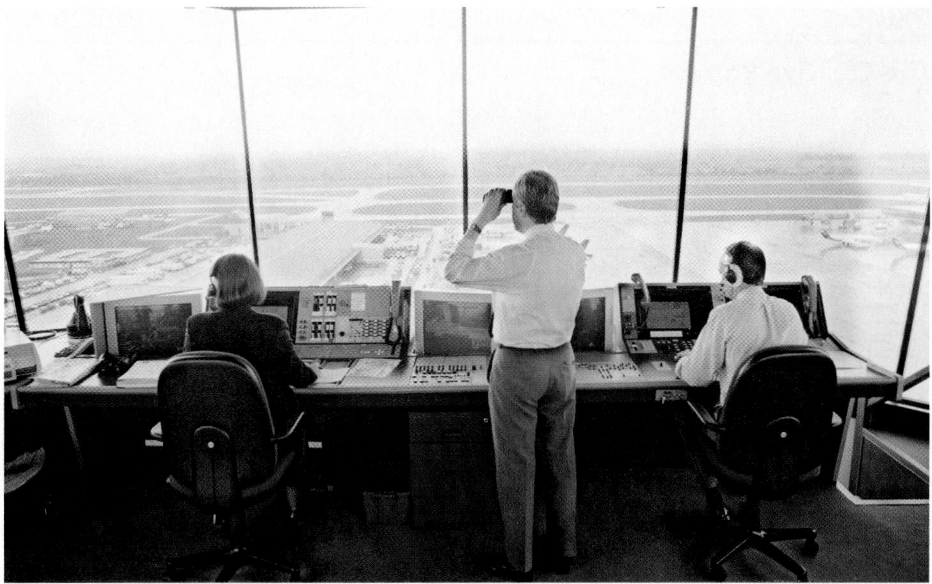

Learning by doing is an important component of many kinds of jobs and occupations ranging from landscape architecture and nursing to sports, acting, and surgery. Moreover, learning by doing it not just important in order to be able to be able to execute technical, physical, or artistic tasks well—it is also important for interpersonal skills. In the opening case, when engineers, product designers, and marketers work together in innovation labs on new products, they are not only developing new products but learning valuable interpersonal skills for effective teamwork.

Continuous Learning Through Creativity

CREATIVITY
The generation of novel and useful ideas.

Creativity is the generation of novel and useful ideas.[52] By *novel* we mean ideas that represent new ways of thinking. By *useful* we mean ideas that have the potential to contribute to the performance and well-being of individuals, groups, and organizations. When people are being creative, they are engaged in continuous learning, whether it is to discover a vaccine for the HIV virus that causes AIDS, develop a new design for kitchen cabinets, or successfully revive a classic car model such as the Volkswagon Beetle. The idea of easy-to-use stick-on notes (Post-it Notes™), the idea of offering healthy foods like salads in fast-food restaurants such as McDonald's, and the idea of flexible work schedules—all are examples of the results of creativity. Creative ideas such as these are novel and useful responses to problems and opportunities and result from continuous learning. From the opening case, it is clear that continuous learning through creativity is key to remaining competitive in today's global economy.

INNOVATION
The successful implementation of creative ideas.

Innovation is the successful implementation of creative ideas.[53] The 3M™ Corporation innovated when it successfully manufactured and marketed Post-it Notes™; Apple Computer innovated when it designed and built the first personal computer, and it continues to innovate today with its new product offerings and new ways to enhance consumers' shopping experience in its Apple Stores.

The Creative Process

Each instance of creativity seems unique because an individual or group has come up with something that seems totally new or different. The creative process, however, usually entails a number of learning steps (see Exhibit 5.5).[54] The first two steps are recognizing a problem or opportunity and gathering information. Sometimes the first step entails learning that something people think is a problem really isn't. Decades ago, some

EXHIBIT 5.5

The Creative Process

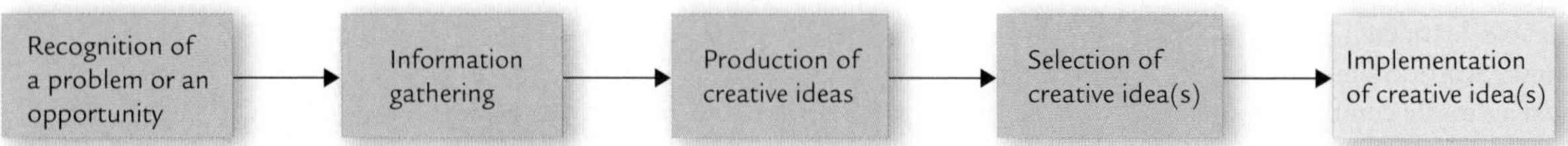

well-intentioned, but misinformed, educators thought it was a problem to be left-handed; so when left-handed children were learning how to write, they were urged to use their right hands no matter how awkward or difficult it was. Sometimes the problem needs redefining, in other words. Tooth decay in toddlers, for example, is not so much a function of what toddlers eat and drink but how and when they do it. (The real culprit is drinking from a bottle, especially right before bedtime.) Identifying a problem is also part of this first step—for example, recognizing that excessive exposure to the sun can lead to cancer—as is recognizing a potential opportunity—for example, that reality shows appeal greatly to today's TV viewers.[55]

An important part of learning about a problem or opportunity is involved in the second step—gathering information. Here, too, learning takes place as the learner figures out what kind of information to gather. In the process of gathering information, the learner might decide the problem or opportunity has been defined too broadly or too narrowly. He or she may then go back to step one and redefine the problem or opportunity before proceeding to learn about which information to gather and how to find it.

The third step in the creative process is the production of ideas. Once learners have gathered information, they need to come up with potential responses to problems or opportunities. During the production of ideas, it is important that learners feel free to come up with ideas that seem far-fetched or off the wall.

Once the ideas have been produced, learners are then ready for the fourth step of the creative process: selecting the idea or ideas they think will be useful. Sometimes learners assess each idea according to some criterion they may have previously determined to be important, such as the estimated annual sales of a new type of digital camera or the amount of computer memory needed to run a program. At this step, the information gathered during the second step can be helpful in evaluating the usefulness of each idea generated.

Once one or more ideas have been selected, it is time for implementation. At this stage in the creative process, innovation kicks in. Can the organization successfully implement the creative ideas it has developed and chosen to pursue? Although the steps in the creative process are described previously and are shown in Exhibit 5.5 as if they always occur in a certain sequence, the order in which they occur is not fixed, nor does each step have to take place for creativity to occur.

As profiled in the Opening Case, many organizations are relying on innovation labs with open spaces and comfortable surroundings to bring teams together to create new products and services. South Korean consumer electronics giant, Samsung Electronics, has taken this concept one step further with its VIP Center,[56] as profiled in the following Global View.

Creativity and the creative process, by their nature, are hard to predict. It is difficult to tell in advance, for example, which decision makers will come up with creative ideas. Some people are naturally more creative than others, but, under the right circumstances, a person who is not very creative may come up with a creative solution. Evidence also shows that creativity is more likely to occur in some groups and organizations than in others. Researchers who have tried to identify some of the determinants of creativity have found that characteristics of individual decision makers and of the situations in which they make decisions contribute to creativity.

Global View

Creating New Products at Samsung

Samsung Electronics has grown to be the dominant and most profitable company in the global consumer electronics industry, surpassing even Sony.[57] Creating new products at rapid-fire speed is key to Samsung's success. Many of these products are developed in Samsung's Value Innovation Program Center (VIP Center) located in a five-story building in Suwon, South Korea. Researchers, engineers, and product designers are brought to the Center to brainstorm new ideas for products, solve design problems, cut costs, and create and innovate.[58]

The Center boasts training rooms; work rooms for teams; a kitchen; a relaxation center in the basement with a sauna, gym, billiards, and ping-pong (though apparently, employees are often too busy to relax); and a dormitory with 42 rooms on the fifth floor. The presence of the dormitory speaks to the intense, round-the-clock creating that takes place in the VIP Center. In fact, when employees are working on a project or trying to solve a problem, they are often expected to stay at the Center until their problem is solved or their project has progressed. As long-time team leader Song indicates, "When people are told they have to come here, they know they have to come up with results in a very, very short time."[59]

Samsung Electronics has grown to be the dominant and most profitable company in the global consumer electronics industry by creating new and innovative products at breakneck speed.

Samsung's commitment to continuous learning through creativity is a global phenomenon.[60] For example, Samsung allocates a higher percentage of its annual revenues to R&D than Sony, Microsoft, and Intel, employs close to 27,000 researchers, and operates 17 research centers around the world.[61] In the highly competitive global economy, Samsung emphasizes the importance of speed—rapidly solving problems, detecting defects, coming to market with a new product. Hence, there is a real sense of urgency to the work that is performed in the Center. Teamwork is emphasized and encouraged by common work areas as is rapid decision making and communication. There is also a sort of crisis mentality—if problems aren't detected and solved quickly enough, or if a new product takes too long to develop—failure could be a step away. Thus, Samsung expects total commitment from its employees, who often work round the clock. As Vice Chairman and CEO Jong-Yong Yun puts it, ". . . we stand at the crossroads to [be]coming a world leader or a major failure."[62] Clearly, this sense of urgency has paid off handsomely for Samsung.

Characteristics of Employees that Contribute to Creativity

Numerous characteristics of employees have been linked to creativity, but the ones that seem to be most relevant to understanding creativity in organizations are personal characteristics or individual differences, task-relevant knowledge, and intrinsic motivation (see Exhibit 5.6). These characteristics contribute to creativity whether employees work individually or in groups.

Although these factors contribute to creativity, they do not, of course, guarantee that any given employee or group of employees will be creative. And the lack, or low level, of any of these factors does not mean that a person or group will not or cannot be creative. Creativity is determined by the interaction or joint effects of a number of factors.

Individual Differences. In Chapter 2, we described a variety of ways in which people differ from each other and some of the personality traits and abilities especially relevant to understanding and managing organizational behavior. At least three of the personality traits we discussed earlier are likely to contribute to creativity.[63]

Recall that one of the Big Five general personality traits is *openness to experience*, which captures the extent to which an individual is original, is open to a wide variety of stimuli, has broad interests, and is willing to take risks. How does openness to experience contribute to creativity? It helps employees come up with new ideas and ways of doing things, and it helps to ensure that employees are willing to take the risks involved in proposing unusual ideas.

Two specific personality traits that are likely to contribute to creativity are *locus of control* and *self-esteem* (see Chapter 2). Locus of control captures the extent to which people think that their own actions and behaviors are important in determining what happens. *Internals* believe they have a lot of control over their environments and what happens to them. *Externals* believe that outside forces determine their fates. An *internal* locus of control contributes to creativity because it results in employees' feeling responsible for coming up with new ideas and being creative.[64] An *external* locus of control hinders creativity because employees believe that their own efforts are unimportant.[65]

Self-esteem is pride in oneself and in one's capabilities.[66] Self-esteem contributes to employees' confidence that they can come up with creative ideas, and it gives them the confidence to take risks and suggest ideas that may seem outlandish.

In addition to personality, it also is likely that ability contributes to creativity. At the broadest level, intelligence contributes to creativity because it helps employees come up with new ideas, see connections between things that other people do not see, view things from different perspectives, and synthesize a lot of information. Other cognitive abilities

EXHIBIT 5.6

Determinants of Creativity

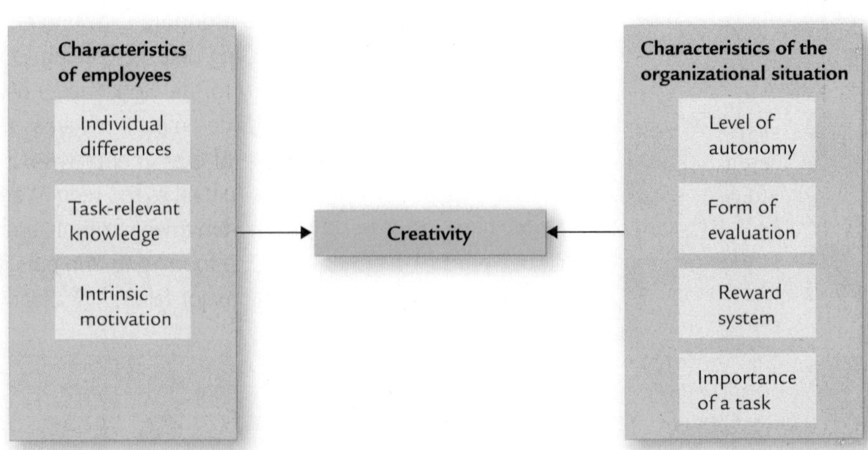

also contribute to creativity, especially when they are relevant to the kind of work an employee is engaged in. Numerical ability (the speed and accuracy with which a person can solve arithmetic problems), for example, is likely to contribute to creativity in a group of people who are looking at the overall cost implications of various changes to a manufacturing process.

Task-Relevant Knowledge. Task-relevant knowledge is all of the information, skills, and expertise that an individual or group has about the kind of work being performed.[67] Without task-relevant knowledge, it would be difficult for an architect to come up with a creative design for a new building, for a doctor to find a new way to treat arthritis, or for a secretary to discover a unique and useful filing system. To generate creative responses, the architect needs a good understanding of building design and architectural principles, the doctor needs knowledge pertaining to medicine in general and to arthritis in particular, and the secretary needs to be familiar with the kinds of information to be filed, the ways in which it needs to be accessed, and how frequently it's accessed.

Intrinsic Motivation. In Chapter 6, we distinguish between intrinsic and extrinsic motivation. For intrinsically motivated employees, the source of motivation is the work itself. These employees enjoy performing their jobs, often love their work, and get a sense of personal satisfaction when they do a good job or come up with a creative idea. Extrinsically motivated employees may perform at a high level, but the source of their motivation is external; they are motivated by, for example, the pay they receive and the chances of receiving a bonus, raise, or promotion—positive reinforcers provided by others, in other words.

In general, employees are more likely to be creative when they are intrinsically motivated.[68] The high level of involvement in the work that intrinsic motivation brings seems to spur creativity.

Characteristics of the Organizational Situation that Contribute to Creativity

Although certain individuals may be more likely than others to be creative, creativity is also more likely to occur in certain situations than in others. Four situational characteristics are likely to affect creativity: level of autonomy, form of evaluation, reward system, and the importance of a task or problem (see Exhibit 5.6).

Level of Autonomy. More than 70 percent of the research and development (R&D) scientists who participated in a study of creativity indicated that autonomy was an important factor in instances of creativity that they were involved in or observed in their organizations.[69] Autonomy is the freedom and independence to make decisions and have personal control over one's work on a day-to-day basis. A high degree of autonomy is good for creativity. And when autonomy is low, creativity is unlikely.

Form of Evaluation. Imagine how William Shakespeare would have felt when he was writing some of his masterpieces if a supervisor had been standing over his shoulder critiquing scenes or bits of dialogue that didn't sound quite right ("A hero who believes in ghosts, talks to himself a lot, and kills his girlfriend's father? I don't think so, Will") and criticizing him when he took too long to complete a play. In all likelihood, these kinds of actions would have hampered some of Shakespeare's creativity.

Creative people and employees like to know how they are doing and to receive feedback and encouragement. But overly evaluative feedback and criticism can hamper creativity because it can make employees afraid to take risks.[70] If there is a strong likelihood that your boss will criticize the far-out idea you come up with, you may not risk expressing it. However, if your boss is interested in your ideas, provides constructive comments about how they may be improved, and points out some of their pros and cons, you may be encouraged to come up with an even better idea.

Reward System. People who come up with creative ideas like to be rewarded for them. But what happens if employees think that their salaries, bonuses, and chances for promotion hinge on their almost always being right, rarely or never making mistakes, and always being efficient in their use of time? Their creativity may be hampered, and they may be unlikely to take risks to come up with and choose creative responses to problems and opportunities.[71] By definition, creative responses are new, and there is always the potential that they may fail.

To help promote creativity, an organization's reward system should recognize and reward hard work and creativity. Creative employees and others in the organization need to see that hard work and creativity are recognized, appreciated, and rewarded—for example, through bonuses and raises. It is important, however, that these rewards not be seen as an attempt to control behavior and that employees do not feel they are being closely watched and rewarded based on what is observed.[72] It also is important that employees are *not* punished when some of their creative ideas do not pan out. Indeed, if employers want creativity, they need to encourage organizational members to take reasonable risks and be willing to accept failure.

By now it should be clear to you that OB Mod should *not* be used for behaviors that involve creativity or when creativity is desired. OB Mod assumes that desired behaviors can be objectively determined in advance; this is impossible for any kind of creative activity, which, by definition, is novel or new. Moreover, the relatively rigid matching of behavior and consequences in OB Mod ensures that any out-of-the-ordinary behavior (which could be creative) is discouraged. More generally, principles of operant conditioning, which are useful for learning desired behaviors that can be determined in advance, should not be used for creative kinds of work and tasks. However, even when creativity is desired, principles from operant conditioning can be used to promote the learning of certain kinds of behavior, such as using safety equipment, which can be objectively specified in advance. For example, suppose a welder is trying to come up with a way to join thin steel cylinders so that the place where they are joined together is invisible to the naked eye. In order to come up with the new procedure or process, the welder should have autonomy to experiment, and consequences such as rewards should not be directly linked to his or her current behaviors or else his or her creativity will be hampered. However, a priori, her supervisor knows that she must wear safety goggles and follow certain safety procedures—for these kinds of behaviors, operant conditioning can be beneficial.

Importance of a Task. Being creative is intrinsically rewarding, but it also can be hard work. Creativity is enhanced when members of an organization feel that what they are working on is important.[73]

The Interaction of Personality and Situational Factors

Recall from Chapter 2 how behavior is often the result of the interaction of personality and the situation. Recent research suggests that this is the case for creativity. For example, a recent study found that whether or not openness to experience was related to creativity in jobs that do not necessarily entail creative work depended on the extent to which the employees' tasks provided them with the opportunity to be creative, or entailed some degree of flexibility and uncertainty, and the extent that the employees received positive feedback.[74] Results from this study and others are encouraging, as they suggest that all personality types have the potential to be creative if the situation they are in and those around them provide them with the right kinds of encouragement and support.[75]

You're the Management Expert

Encouraging Independent Thinking

Susan Armstrong, the owner and operator of a chain of nail salons in the southeastern United States, has recently hired a store manager, Marcy Cook. Cook is not only very qualified for the job but also has many creative ideas that can increase the visibility of the salons and their sales. In fact, Cook runs circles around Armstrong's other store managers, who are good at keeping the stores running but do not seem that interested in doing much else. Since Cook took over as store manager, revenues at her salon have increased by 20 percent, and none of her staff members have quit. (The salons have generally been plagued by high turnover rates in the past.) After visiting the salons, Armstrong concluded that part of Cook's success as a store manager is due to her independent thinking—she takes the initiative to solve problems on her own, seeks and develops new opportunities, and creates a positive atmosphere in her salon both for clients and the staff. The other store managers are effective in terms of ensuring smooth operations, adequate staffing, and salon appearance, but they just don't take the initiative to go beyond the basics. Because your are an expert in OB, Armstrong has come to you for help. How can she foster the kind of independent thinking and creativity among her other store managers that Cook exhibits?

The Learning Organization

ORGANIZATIONAL LEARNING
The process through which managers instill in all members of an organization a desire to find new ways to improve organizational effectiveness.

Not only is it important that individuals learn to perform behaviors that contribute to organizational effectiveness but also that the organization as a whole adopts a learning mentality. **Organizational learning** involves instilling all members of the organization with a desire to find new ways to improve its effectiveness.[76] Moreover, learning organizations make sure their members actually have the knowledge and skills to learn continuously. They also take steps to ensure that new ideas are acted upon and knowledge is shared throughout the organization.[77]

Learning theorist Peter Senge has identified five key activities central to a learning organization.[78]

- *Encourage personal mastery or high self-efficacy*. In order for members of an organization to strive to find new ways of improving organizational effectiveness, they must have confidence in their abilities to do so.
- *Develop complex schemas to understand work activities*. Recall from Chapter 4 that schemas are abstract knowledge structures. In order for the members of an organization to learn new ways to cut costs or increase revenues, they must have an appreciation of not only their own jobs but also how the work they do affects the work of others and the organization as a whole.
- *Encourage learning in groups and teams*. New discoveries often take place in groups and teams.[79] Members of groups and teams need to strive to find new ways of doing things and manage the learning process by, for example, increasing the self-efficacy of group members who may question their own capabilities.
- *Communicate a shared vision for the organization as a whole*. Members of an organization need guidance in terms of what they should be striving for. For example, should they be striving to cut costs, or should they focus more on improving customer satisfaction even at the expense of higher costs? As indicated in the Opening

Case, more and more managers and companies are finding that cutting costs and improving efficiency are not enough to remain competitive in today's global economy. What are really needed are creativity and innovation to develop new products, concepts, and experiences that customers don't even know they want and then realize they can't live without.

- *Encourage system thinking*. Organizations are systems of interrelated parts. What one part of the organization does or learns affects other parts of the organization. Organizational members must be encouraged to think in these terms and address how their individual actions and their actions in groups and teams influence other parts of the organization.

Organizational learning is especially important for organizations in environments that are rapidly changing. As John Browne, CEO of British Pretoleum, puts it, "Learning is at the heart of a company's ability to adapt to a rapidly changing environment. It is the key to being able both to identify opportunities that others might not see and to exploit those opportunities rapidly and fully."[80]

An important ingredient for a learning organization is *knowledge management*—being able to capitalize on the knowledge members of the organization have that might not be written down or codified in formal documents. As employees do their jobs, they gain knowledge about the tasks they perform and learn the best ways to get certain things done and solve specific problems. Through knowledge management, this information can be shared and used by others. This knowledge is not necessarily contained in job descriptions or written down in rules, standard operating procedures, or manuals. Rather, it is knowledge that has evolved from actually performing work tasks.[81] By disseminating and sharing this knowledge in an organization, other members will be able to take advantage of it.

A recent study of customer service representatives who repair Xerox machines confirms the importance of knowledge management. Repairing machines seems pretty straightforward—error codes on the machines indicate what the problems are, and written documents and manuals specify how to fix the problems. When anthropologist Julian Orr observed the representatives performing their jobs, however, their work didn't seem straightforward at all.[82] In a typical workday, the representatives came across many idiosyncratic breakdowns and problems and solutions that weren't predictable or detailed in the manuals. By actually performing their jobs, the representatives learned about the idiosyncrasies of the machines they repaired, how to solve a variety of problems not covered in the manuals, and how a variety of factors ranging from air temperature to the age of a certain part may affect their operation. Moreover, the representatives got together regularly over breakfast, coffee, lunch, or at the end of the workday and also at other times to share their knowledge while joking, playing games, or chatting. In these informal get-togethers, the representatives discussed problems they had encountered and how they were solved and shared their insights gleaned on the job.[83] Clearly, the people performing a certain job are likely to learn the most about it. Knowledge management seeks to share this learning and knowledge throughout an organization.

Summary

Organizational members can learn from multiple sources and in multiple ways. In this chapter, we made the following major points:

1. Learning is a relatively permanent change in knowledge or behavior that results from practice or experience.
2. In operant conditioning, the learner behaves in a certain way to achieve certain consequences. Antecedents let employees know which behaviors are desired, which should be avoided, and what the consequences are for performing different behaviors.

3. In operant conditioning, there are two ways to promote the learning of desired behaviors in organizations: positive reinforcement and negative reinforcement. Positive reinforcement increases the probability that a behavior will occur by administering positive consequences to employees who perform the behavior. Negative reinforcement increases the probability that a desired behavior will occur by removing a negative consequence if an employee performs the behavior. Positive reinforcement is generally preferred over negative reinforcement.
4. Reinforcement can be continuous or partial. Partial reinforcement can be administered according to one of four schedules: fixed interval, variable interval, fixed ratio, and variable ratio. The choice of reinforcement schedules in organizations is often influenced by practical considerations such as the nature of the behavior, job, and reinforcer in question. Shaping, or reinforcing progressively closer approximations to a desired behavior, can be used to encourage behaviors that are unlikely to occur on their own.
5. In operant conditioning, there are two ways to reduce the probability of undesired behaviors in organizations: extinction and punishment. Extinction, removing the source of reinforcement for an undesired behavior, can take time. Punishment, administering a negative consequence when an undesired behavior occurs, is sometimes needed to eliminate detrimental behaviors quickly. Punishment can have some unintended negative side effects (such as resentment) and should be used with caution.
6. The systematic application of the principles of operant conditioning to managing organizational behavior is known as organizational behavior modification (OB MOD). OB MOD works best for managing behaviors that are observable, important for task and organizational performance, and measurable.
7. In order for vicarious learning to take place, the learner must pay attention to the model, accurately perceive the model's behavior, remember the behavior, and have the skills and abilities necessary to perform the behavior; the model must also receive reinforcement for the behavior. Models who are most likely to be imitated by employees are competent or expert, have high status, receive positive reinforcers that the learner desires, and model behaviors in a friendly manner.
8. In order for self-control (taking the initiative to learn desired behaviors on one's own) to take place, the following conditions must be satisfied: An individual must engage in a low-probability behavior, self-reinforcers must be available, the learner must set performance standards or goals, and reinforcers must be self-administered when the goal is attained. Self-efficacy (beliefs about one's ability to perform particular behaviors successfully) influences the tasks employees choose to learn and the goals they set for themselves. Self-efficacy also affects employees' levels of effort and persistence when learning difficult tasks. Past performance, observations of others, verbal persuasion, and physiological states are determinants of self-efficacy.
9. Continuous learning takes place through creativity. Creativity is the generation of novel and useful ideas and innovation is the successful implementation of creative ideas. The steps in the creative process are recognition of a problem or opportunity, information gathering, productions of ideas, selection of ideas, and implementation. Learners who are high on openness to experience have an internal locus of control, have high self-esteem, have task-relevant knowledge, and are intrinsically motivated are especially likely to be creative. Situational characteristics that are likely to impact creativity are employees' levels of autonomy, the evaluation and reward system used in an organization, and the perceived importance of a decision.
10. Organizational learning is the process through which managers instill in all members of an organization a desire to find new ways to improve organizational effectiveness. Knowledge management is important for organizational learning.

Exercises in Understanding and Managing Organizational Behavior

Questions for Review

1. Why might an organization prefer to use positive reinforcement rather than negative reinforcement?
2. How can a manager use the principles of operant conditioning to stop employees from bickering and fighting with each other?
3. Why do some organizations use punishment more often than others?
4. Is OB MOD ethical? Why or why not?
5. In what ways are the behaviors of taxi drivers controlled by the principles of operant conditioning?
6. On what kinds of jobs might vicarious learning be especially prevalent?
7. When might employees be especially likely to engage in self-control?
8. Why do some capable members of an organization have low levels of self-efficacy?
9. Why do organizations desiring creativity need to be willing to accept a certain level of failure?
10. What steps can organizations take to promote organizational learning and knowledge management?

OB: Increasing Self-Awareness

Learning Difficult Behaviors

Think about the last time you finally succeeded at something that had been giving you trouble. It could be a particularly troublesome class that you managed to pull through with a decent grade or a difficult project at work that you finally were able to finish satisfactorily.

1. Describe the specific behaviors that gave you trouble.
2. What antecedents prompted you to perform these behaviors?
3. What were the reinforcing consequences for performing these behaviors successfully?
4. Would you have been punished if you had not finally succeeded? If you had been punished, how would you have felt about being punished?
5. Did you use vicarious learning to try to solve your problem? If you did, who did you imitate and why? If you did not, why not?
6. Did you use self-control to try to solve your problem? If you did, what goal did you set for yourself, and what was your self-reinforcer? If you did not use self-control, why not?
7. Describe your level of self-efficacy when you first started out, when you were having a particularly troublesome time, and when you finally succeeded.
8. What do you think your level of self-efficacy will be for similar tasks in the future? Why do you think your self-efficacy will be at this level?

A Question of Ethics

Positive reinforcement can be used to promote the learning of desired behaviors in organizations. Commission pay plans, for example, reinforce salespeople for selling by paying them a percentage of their actual sales. However, sometimes these plans can be taken to extremes and may result in unethical behavior.

Questions

1. Think about the ethical implications of pay plans that link an employee's current pay to his or her current performance.
2. Under what conditions might linking pay to performance be questionable on ethical grounds?

Small Group Break-Out Exercise

Raising Self-Efficacy

Form groups of three or four people and appoint one member as the spokesperson who will communicate your conclusions to the rest of the class:

1. Take a few minutes to think about something that you are currently trying to learn and having trouble with—it could be a subject that you are having trouble with in school, learning a musical instrument, excelling in a sport, or learning a foreign language.
2. Take turns describing what you are trying to learn and how you have gone about it. After each person describes his or her "current learning challenge," as a team develop ways for this person to boost his or her self-efficacy for the challenge in question.
3. Each person then should take a few minutes to write down specific steps he or she can take based on the group's suggestions in step 2.
4. Take turns describing the specific action steps generated in step 3.

Topic for Debate

Creativity is the generation of new and useful ideas. Now that you have a good understanding of creativity, debate the following issue.

Team A. Creativity is only important in certain kinds of jobs and organizations.

Team B. Creativity is important in most jobs and organizations.

Experiential Exercise

Managing the Learning Process

Objective

Your objective is to gain experience in applying learning principles and theories and understanding the challenges involved in managing the learning process.

Procedure

The class divides into groups of three to five people, and each group appoints one member as spokesperson to present the group's findings to the whole class. Here is the scenario.

You are members of a group of supervisors that is responsible for teaching production workers how to operate a new, computerized production process. The new process requires employees to work in small teams, and each team member's performance influences the performance of the team as a whole. Prior to this major change, employees did not work in teams but performed simple, repetitive tasks that required few skills.

To operate the new production process, employees are required to learn new skills to perform their now more complicated jobs, and they are currently receiving formal training in a classroom setting and on-the-job instruction in their teams. Some employees are responding well to the changes, are doing well in training and instruction, and are performing up to expectations in their teams. Other employees are finding it difficult to adapt to their changed jobs and to teamwork and have been slow to acquire the necessary new skills. In addition, there have been reports of high levels of conflict among members of some teams. As a result, the overall performance of the teams is suffering and below expectations.

As the group of supervisors responsible for ensuring a smooth transition to the new production process and high performance in the production teams, do the following:

1. Develop a plan of action based on the principles of operant conditioning to facilitate learning and high team performance. Be specific about how operant conditioning techniques (positive reinforcement, negative reinforcement, punishment, and extinction) could be used to promote team members' learning of desired behaviors, working well together, and performing at a high level.
2. Develop a plan of action based on the principles of social cognitive theory (vicarious learning, self-control, and self-efficacy) to facilitate learning and high team performance. Be specific about how social cognitive theory could be used to promote team members' learning of desired behaviors, working well together, and performing at a high level.
3. Decide whether the two plans of action that you developed should be combined for the most effective learning to take place. Explain why or why not.

New York Times *Cases in the News*

The New York Times

"Running Away from the Pack in Japan"

By M. Fackler, The New York Times, March 22, 2006, pp. C1, C5.

OSAKA, Japan—In corporate Japan, companies have long preferred to run with the pack. But some are now learning to act like lone wolves.

Take **Sharp**, which for decades looked like other big Japanese electronics makers, producing every device under the sun from rice cookers to semi-conductors. But when the company faced collapse eight years ago, its newly installed president, Katsuhiko Machida, jettisoned unprofitable products and bet Sharp's future on a single, then unproven new product; flat-panel televisions using a screen technology called liquid crystal display.

The gamble paid off. Sharp now reaps record profits as a leader in the booming global market for L.C.D. televisions. "Survival today means innovating and doing things that no one else does," Mr. Machida said. "This is a lesson not only for Sharp but for all of Japan."

It is a lesson that the business world here has apparently taken to heart, as a wave of corporate revamping and innovation breathes new life into Japan's long-moribund economy. And as these lone wolves multiply, they may help Japan play a stronger role in global growth as the world's second-largest economy.

Companies from supermarket chains to camera makers are moving away from traditional conformity. They have gotten more aggressive about containing costs after spending Japan's lost decade of stagnant economic growth closing factories, shrinking payrolls and writing off debt. More companies are also acting like Sharp, trying to set themselves apart from rivals with unique products and services.

The changes are rewriting the rules of Japan's business culture, where for decades after World War II companies marched in lock step to advance the nation's economy. That collectivist system broke down when Japan's economy stalled and even contracted in the 1990's after the collapse of twin bubbles in the real estate and stock markets.

"It's a new era for Japanese business," said John C. Beck, president of the business consulting company North Star Leadership and co-author of "Japan's Business Renaissance." "Japan has become much more entrepreneurial and innovative. Companies are taking new risks, going into new areas, making new products."

At Sharp, Mr. Machida said he had learned to take risks because the company had no choice. Sharp had thrived during the postwar years with products like hand-held calculators. But when Mr. Machida took the helm in 1998, weak domestic sales and cheaper Asian competition had plunged the 94-year-old company into its worse crisis since an earthquake flattened its original factory in 1923.

As profit plummeted, Mr. Machida decided to shrink or halt production of semiconductors, computer monitors and tube televisions, which were major product lines where Sharp could no longer compete on price. Mr. Machida said he decided the only way to beat cheaper manufacturers was to stay ahead technologically. He said he chose flat-panel televisions to take advantage of L.C.D. technology that Sharp had originally developed in the 1970's for calculator screens.

"The old way of doing things was just spreading us too thin," Mr. Machida said in an interview at Sharp's headquarters in this industrial city in western Japan.

While Sharp does not break out earnings by product, it said L.C.D. TV's will account for a hefty chunk of the record profit of 87 billion yen ($737 million) it expects in the current fiscal year, ending March 31. That is up from a profit of 4.6 billion yen ($39 million) in 1998, when Mr. Machida took over. Sharp's profit margin is also higher at 5.5 percent, up from 1.5 percent over the same time period.

Demand is so strong for the TV's that the company is investing 350 billion yen ($2.97 billion) to expand annual production capacity to about 20 million in two years, up from about 5 million sets now. It is also stepping up hiring, with plans to add 615 new employees next year, double the number it hired in 2003.

Economists say turnaround stories like Sharp's are fueling the current revival in Japan's $4.6 trillion economy, the second-largest after the United States. As companies hire more employees and build new factories, the recovery has found a firm footing in domestic consumption, unlike previous, short-lived up-turns here that relied on exports. Many economists now predict that Japan will expand as much as 3.6 percent this year, rivaling and perhaps even surpassing growth in the United States.

To be sure, some specialists say Japan has not changed enough. They point out that levels of productivity and earning power still tend to lag behind those in the United States. The problem, they say, is that fundamental change is limited to a small number of companies, while most remain too timid to leave the pack.

"I don't see enough differentiating," said William Swinton, an assistant dean in the business school at the Tokyo campus of Temple University. "Some companies are using more focused strategies, but many still have a long way to go."

Still, most agree that change has reached even the cobweb-filled corners of Japan's domestic economy. Aeon, Japan's largest supermarket operator, has shaken up the country's retailing industry by erecting sprawling, Wal-Mart-style supercenters even more aggressively than Wal-Mart's own local subsidiary, Seiyu. Customers are flocking to its low-cost stores, helping Aeon forecast record profit for this year.

Orix, an auto and aircraft leasing company, has gotten even more creative, seeking to turn itself into a global investment bank with acquisitions like the $500 million purchase in October of Houlihan Lokey Howard & Zukin, the Los Angeles-based mergers and acquisition advisory firm.

But nowhere are the changes in corporate behavior more apparent than in Japan's electronics industry, where companies compete in what the Japanese business press has dubbed a new "era of winners and losers." The former include **Canon**, the camera maker; **Matsushita Electric**, maker of Panasonic; and Sharp, all thriving. Meanwhile, other well-known companies like **Sanyo Electric, Pioneer** and **Sony** have floundered.

"Everything changes much faster now than 10 years ago," said Kesanobu Yamagishi, a spokesman at Pioneer.

But this new era of competition also bears some distinctly Japanese flourishes. One is the relatively small number of layoffs, which companies still shun here for fear of ruining morale. Mr. Machida, for one, is proud of the fact Sharp did not release any of its 49,000 employees during its turnaround, instead cutting costs by dropping product lines.

He spent his first year as president making almost daily trips to Sharp offices and factory floors around Japan, exhorting employees to work extra hard to make his plan a success.

"If we don't do this, Sharp has no future," Mr. Machida repeatedly said, according to employees. Many listened sullenly, unwilling to contradict their boss in public.

Mr. Machida faced a particularly tough sell at Sharp's computer panel division, whose products he was scrapping. In town-hall-style meetings with 50 to 100 employees at a time, he said South Korean and Taiwanese manufacturers could make the same panels and he challenged his engineers to raise the quality of L.C.D. screens high enough to work for televisions. He set technical goals, such as tripling the contrast ratio, a way of measuring picture sharpness, within three years.

Employees said they were skeptical at first that L.C.D.'s could work, particularly for large televisions. But support quickly grew as they reached targets ahead of schedule.

Sharp gained an early lead in L.C.D. televisions that it still strives to maintain. In October, it will open the first factory in the world to use so-called eighth-generation L.C.D. production technology, which increases production by using glass panels as large as a king-size bed but only as thick as a postcard. Sharp now competes in the global L.C.D. market with companies more than 10 times its size, like Sony and **Samsung Electronics**.

"We are constantly telling employees to push ahead," said Shigeaki Mizushima, head of Sharp's L.C.D. division. "We can't stand still for a moment."

Questions for Discussion

1. What are corporations in Japan like Sharp learning?
2. What forces are prompting them to learn to do things differently than they have in the past?
3. How can managers and employees in other Japanese organizations learn vicariously from corporations like Sharp?
4. How did Katsuhiko Machida boost employees' levels of self-efficacy to implement dramatic changes at Sharp?

The New York Times

"Going Off the Beaten Path for New Design Ideas"

By L. Chamberlain, The New York Times, March 12, 2006, Section 3, p. 28.

When most other design firms were still using the same old focus-group techniques, **IDEO** invented the unfocus group, in which side conversations among participants are also recorded—to hear what they were really thinking. Finding out not just what people really think, but also how they really live, is the lifeblood of IDEO's innovative design work.

The firm made its name in designing products, including the Palm V hand-held organizer, but it has been turning its attention to spaces, or environment design. IDEO, founded in San Francisco in 1991, is delving into the psychology of space and coming up with unusual approaches for companies like **Marriott International** and **Forest City Enterprises**, two of the largest real estate businesses in the country.

Although IDEO has grown to 400 employees, it has retained its research techniques and small-firm attitude.

No one has a formal title, including Fred Dust, who might he described as the team leader of Smart Space, the company's real estate division. With a bachelor's degree in art history from Reed College in Oregon and a master's in architecture from the University of California, Berkeley, Mr. Dust is much like the firm itself: studied yet unpretentious, casually hip, optimistic by nature—and very hard-working.

Smart Space takes on 45 projects a year. They range from designing a better office cubicle to a project to redevelop commercial ventures within an African-American neighborhood in Kansas City. "We design for activity as much for space," Mr. Dust said.

To achieve this, the team starts with a "deep dive," during which Smart Space designers, anthropologists and researchers spend days—sometimes weeks—shadowing people to observe how they live: when and where they eat, what time they go to bed, what their hobbies are, how they spend their money. The results of this research are often quite different from the conventional wisdom.

An example is a project that Smart Space recently completed for a Marriott's extended-stay hotel chain, TownePlace Suites. The prevailing wisdom about travelers who need extended-stay accommodations is that they want all their needs to be met by the hotel itself. IDEO researchers found this assumption to be incorrect after spending weeks talking with TownPlace guests.

What they found was that people on extended stays do not talk about "staying" in the hotel but "living" in the city. They want to get to know the community around them, and they do not want to spend a lot of time hanging around the hotel. And because they have fewer chores—like mowing the lawn or walking the dog—they also want to use their spare time on such things as learning a new language or taking piano lessons.

IDEO translated those results into a design concept. In the new lobby, instead of the traditional couch, coffee table and television set that nobody is watching, there are "10-minute perches"—benches, stools and places to stand and lean—where a guest can flip through a magazine while finishing a cup of coffee.

More significantly, the Smart Space team designed a map wall: a huge rendering of the immediate area, with notations about local shopping, restaurants, parks and recreation areas. But it is more than just a map. It can be annotated by guests who find their own hidden treasures in the community, and it serves as a conversation starter.

The team also found that because guests often need the equivalent of a home office, they may turn their bedrooms into work spaces. So it came up with a highly flexible modular wall unit where there had previously been only a large dining table; guests can adapt the elements to use them as an office as well as a place to eat.

The client, of course, has to buy into a design concept. So the Smart Space team built a life-size lobby and suite out of white foam core and invited Marriott executives, hotel managers and even guests to interact with the new design and to make suggestions.

"We've never gone through anything like this," said Laura Bates, senior vice president for extended-stay brands at Marriott. "We have built sample rooms, but it's more of a décor approach. This was fundamentally changing the space layout and the architecture. Not only did we get a strategy based on the anthropology of the guest, but we got very quickly to tangible design."

Marriott hired an architecture firm to carry out the redesign, which will be rolled out at all 122 TownePlace Suites sites starting in April.

One of IDEO's biggest clients is Forest City Enterprises, the real estate development company based in Cleveland.

For most residential projects, "the typical developer programs the number of one-, two- and three-bedroom units based on some kind of research of the area, and then hires an architect," said Gregory Vilkin, president of Forest City Residential West. "That's not very sophisticated," he added. "We wanted to really understand—what is urban housing and who lives there? They conducted extensive research and came up with five different prototypes of the urban dweller, and we tested that against our clients, and it was remarkably accurate."

For example, Smart Space researchers identified one group as "explorers"—curious and investigative people who like to explore the neighborhood and are attracted to old commercial buildings converted into housing and other creative living spaces. Another group is "modern romantics," who tend to be highly educated, want comfort and seek to live in traditional apartment buildings.

Because of the researchers' work, the Smart Space team recommended scrapping the old-fashioned leasing office and replacing it with a "welcoming center." One will open soon at University Park Living, a four-building development in Cambridge, Mass.

Rather than just selling units, the welcoming center will also showcase the surrounding area with a "Five, Five, Five" map that shows neighborhood amenities within five minutes, five blocks and five miles. Potential residents are also offered a selection of postcards that include facts about the development and the neighborhood; one card, for example, might have a picture of a dog with information about nearby veterinary clinics. People take the cards that interest them and essentially create their own brochures, instead of being handed general ones by sales agents.

An interactive area will have computers where people can take a tongue-in-cheek personality test to find out which of the four Forest City buildings—all very different in design—will best suit them.

"It's a whole different way to experience leasing," said Adam Siegal, vice president for strategic marketing at the Forest City Enterprises residential group.

Though Forest City Enterprises and IDEO have worked together for only a little more than a year, the company expects the relationship to have a significant impact on how developments are ultimately designed, not just marketed. Forest City Enterprises has signed an exclusive contract with IDEO, which now has a team that works solely on Forest City projects, focusing on its high-end urban rental housing.

"When you're building a new space, the client has to own it," Mr. Dust said. "So we are at our best when we're teaching our clients how to be their own design advocates."

Questions for Discussion

1. How does learning take place at IDEO?
2. Why is it important to listen to and observe people to learn what appeals to them?
3. What process does IDEO follow to come up with creative new ideas?
4. Why do most corporations approach design in a very different way from IDEO?

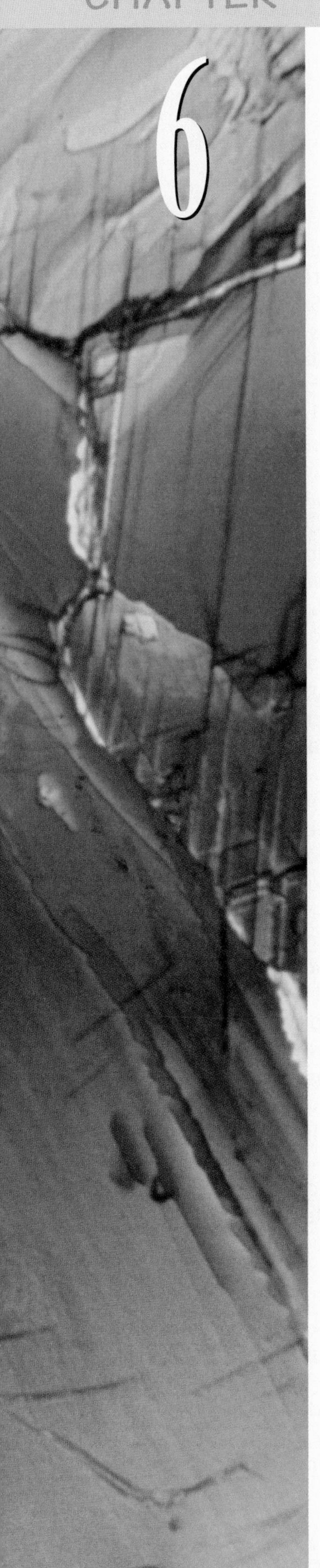

6 THE NATURE OF WORK MOTIVATION

Learning Objectives

After studying this chapter, you should be able to:

- Appreciate why motivation is of central importance in organizations and the difference between intrinsic and extrinsic motivation.
- Understand what we can learn about motivation from need theories.
- Describe why expectancy, valence, and instrumentality are of central importance for work motivation.
- Appreciate the importance of equity and the dangers of inequity.
- Understand why organizational justice is so important and how to promote it.

Opening Case

MOTIVATING EMPLOYEES AT THE SAS INSTITUTE: A GLOBAL SUCCESS STORY

How can organizations continue to grow and have satisfied employees in the hard times as well as the good times?

With over 10,000 employees, the SAS Institute is the largest privately owned software company in the world.[1] Annual revenues at the SAS Institute have increased for 29 years in a row; in 2005, SAS's annual revenues were over $1.6 billion and 24 percent of these revenues were reinvested in research and development.[2] SAS's customers can be found in 110 different countries and, in addition to its headquarters and offices in the United States, SAS has offices in Europe, the Middle East, Africa, Canada, Asia Pacific, and Latin America.[3]

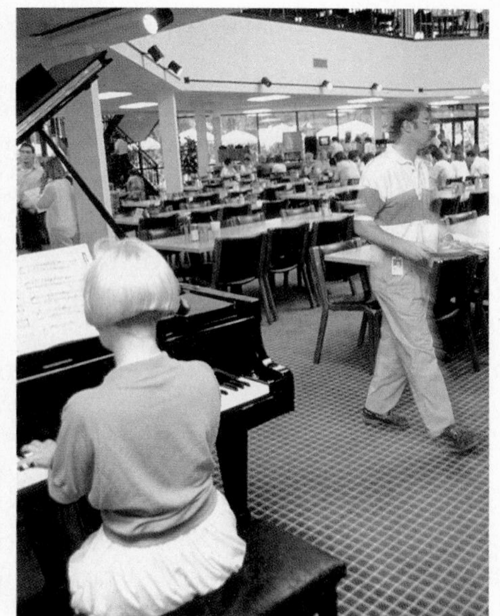

The SAS Institute motivates its employees in numerous ways which has enabled it to achieve an enviable track record of success.

Moreover, the SAS Institute continues to win accolades for the way it treats its employees. For nine years in a row, it was included in *Fortune* magazine's "100 Best Companies to Work for in America," and it has been cited 13 times as one of the "100 Best Companies for Working Mothers."[4] Moreover, SAS is well known for its ability to attract and retain top talent in the software industry; employee turnover rates at SAS are much lower than in many other large organizations.[5] How does the SAS Institute maintain this win-win situation of sustained growth and satisfied employees, even in economic downturns? Essentially, by the way it goes about motivating its workforce.

The SAS Institute, founded in 1976, has always strived to ensure its employees enjoy their work and are motivated by the work they perform. Managers believe that employees should be interested and involved in the work they are doing and feel that they are making meaningful contributions. For example, whereas some software companies seeking to expand into new markets, such as video games or educational software, buy companies that have already developed these products, the SAS Institute does all its new product development internally. Although this approach might take longer, SAS believes it is beneficial because employees find that developing new products is interesting work. Moreover, SAS encourages its employees to change jobs within the company (getting additional training if needed) so they continue to be interested in their work and don't grow bored with what they're doing.[6]

Whereas the work itself is a major source of motivation for SAS employees, managers at SAS are also concerned with fairly and equitably rewarding employees for a job well done. Pay and bonuses are linked to performance, and the company emphasizes fair treatment in numerous ways. For example, all employees have private offices. As another example, Jim Goodnight, one of SAS's cofounders and its current CEO and chairman, says that a founding and enduring principle of the company is that managers should treat employees the way the managers want to be treated themselves.[7]

The SAS Institute also cares about its employees and their families' well-being both on and off the job. Some of the many other benefits employees receive in addition to interesting work and equitable financial rewards include an attractive work environment, with atriums overlooking rolling hills and artwork adorning the walls, access to the latest technology, 35-hour workweeks, two low-cost on-site child care facilities, a 77,000-square-foot fitness and recreation center,[8] on-site medical care, a putting green, and high chairs in the company cafeteria so employees can eat lunch with their children. The corporation's headquarters is located on 200 idyllic acres in Cary, North Carolina. Employees and their families can walk or jog around the campus's scenic trails or picnic on its grounds.[9] And, in 2006, *Fortune* magazine ranked SAS No. 1 in childcare.[10]

Goodnight has been committed to motivating employees to develop creative and high-quality products that are responsive to customers' current and future needs since SAS's founding days; currently, 96 percent of the top 100 companies in the Fortune 500 list use SAS products for any number of purposes including risk management, monitoring and measuring performance, managing relationships with customers and suppliers, and detecting fraud.[11] SAS also provides educational software for schools and teachers through SAS in Schools.[12] At the SAS Institute, motivating employees really is a win-win situation.

Overview

As the SAS Institute case suggests, motivating employees to make important contributions to their jobs can have a profound impact on organizational effectiveness. Motivation is central to understanding and managing organizational behavior because it explains why people behave as they do in organizations.[13] Just as your own motivation determines how many classes you take, how hard you study for exams, and the amount of time and effort you spend on research projects, similarly, motivation determines how hard members in an organization will work to help achieve its goals. Motivation explains, for example, why one employee wants and tries to do a good job while another employee with the same abilities couldn't care less. Motivation also explains why some students strive for A's and study much harder than others, who are content with maintaining a solid B average.

In this chapter, we examine work motivation. We focus on the important distinctions between motivation and performance and between intrinsic and extrinsic motivation. We discuss several specific theories of work motivation: need theory, expectancy theory, equity theory, and organizational justice theory. Each theory seeks to explain why people behave as they do in organizations and suggests ways of increasing employee motivation and performance. An understanding of motivation is of utmost importance for organizational effectiveness. Managers need to ensure that employees choose to act in ways that help the organization achieve its goals and avoid behaving in ways that hinder the pursuit of organizational objectives.

What is Work Motivation?

Motivation is a frequently used but poorly understood term. Over 140 definitions have been provided over the years,[14] and noted scholars of work motivation have said that trying to define *motivation* often gives them "a severe stomachache."[15] This remark may be a bit of an exaggeration, but it underscores the need to get a firm grasp on what motivation is before we try to understand its role in understanding and managing organizational behavior.

WORK MOTIVATION
The psychological forces that determine the direction of a person's behavior in an organization, a person's level of effort, and a person's level of persistence.

Motivation is important because it explains why employees behave as they do. **Work motivation** can be defined as the psychological forces within a person that determine the direction of that person's behavior in an organization, effort level, and persistence in the

EXHIBIT 6.1

Elements of Work Motivation

Element	Definition	Example
Direction of behavior	Which behaviors does a person choose to perform in an organization?	Does an engineer take the time and effort to convince skeptical superiors of the need to change the design specifications for a new product to lower production costs?
Level of effort	How hard does a person work to perform a chosen behavior?	Does an engineer prepare a report outlining problems with the original specifications, or does the engineer casually mention the issue when he or she bumps into a supervisor in the hall and hope that the supervisor will take the advice on faith?
Level of persistence	When faced with obstacles, roadblocks, and stone walls, how hard does a person keep trying to perform a chosen behavior successfully?	When the supervisor disagrees with the engineer and indicates that a change in specifications is a waste of time, does the engineer persist in trying to get the change implemented or give up despite his or her strong belief in the need for a change?

face of obstacles.[16] Because motivation involves psychological forces within a person, many of the topics that we cover in prior chapters are relevant to understanding motivation: personality and ability (Chapter 2); values, attitudes, and moods (Chapter 3); and perception and attribution (Chapter 4).

The three key elements of work motivation are direction of behavior, level of effort, and level of persistence (see Exhibit 6.1).

Direction of Behavior

Which behaviors does a person choose to perform? On any job, there are many behaviors (some appropriate, some inappropriate) that the jobholder can engage in. *Direction of behavior* refers to the behavior employees *choose* to perform from the many potential behaviors they *could* perform. If a stockbroker in an investment banking firm illegally manipulates stock prices, if managers advance their own careers at the expense of their subordinates, or if an engineer convinces skeptical superiors to change the design specifications of a new product in order to lower production costs—all of these actions reflect behaviors these employees chose to perform.

As the examples illustrate, employees can be motivated in *functional* ways that help an organization achieve its goals or in *dysfunctional* ways that hinder an organization from achieving its goals. In looking at motivation, managers want to ensure that the direction of their subordinates' behavior is functional for the organization. They want employees to be motivated to come to work on time, perform their assigned tasks dependably, come up with good ideas, and help others. They do not want employees to come to work late, ignore rules concerning health and safety, or pay lip service to quality.

Level of Effort

How hard does a person work to perform a chosen behavior? It is not enough for an organization to motivate employees to perform desired functional behaviors; the organization must also motivate them to work hard at these behaviors. If, for example, an engineer decides to try to convince skeptical superiors of the need for design changes, the engineer's

Starbucks is a model of employee learning, ownership, involvement, and motivation. Even part-time Starbucks employees, or "partners," as they are called, get stock options, full healthcare benefits, and extensive training.

level of motivation determines the lengths to which he or she will go to convince them. Does the engineer just mention the need for the change in casual conversation, or does he or she prepare a detailed report outlining the problems with the original specifications and describing the new, cost-saving specifications that are needed?

Level of Persistence

When faced with obstacles, roadblocks, and stone walls, how hard does a person keep trying to perform a chosen behavior successfully? Suppose the engineer's supervisor indicates that a change in specifications is a waste of time. Does the engineer persist in trying to get the change implemented or give up even though he or she strongly believes it's necessary? Likewise, if a factory employee's machine breaks down, does the employee simply stop working and wait for someone to come along to fix it, or does the employee try to fix the machine or at least alert others about the problem?

The Distinction Between Motivation and Performance

Because motivation determines what employees do and how hard and diligently they do it, you might think that an employee's motivation to do a job is the same as the employee's job performance. In fact, motivation and performance, though often confused by employees and managers alike, are two distinct aspects of behavior in an organization. *Performance* is an evaluation of the results of a person's behavior: It involves determining how well or poorly a person has accomplished a task or done a job.[17] *Motivation* is only one factor among many that contributes to an employee's job performance. The performance of a screenwriter for a television series, for example, is the extent to which viewers find his scripts to be informative, entertaining, and engaging. Similarly, a research scientist's performance is the extent to which her research advances knowledge, and a physician's performance is the extent to which he provides high-quality care to patients.

What is the relationship between motivation and performance? All else being equal, one would expect a highly motivated screenwriter to write better scripts than those written by a poorly motivated screenwriter.[18] All else, however, is not always equal because so many other factors affect performance—factors such as personality and ability (see Chapter 2), the difficulty of the task, the availability of resources, working conditions, and chance or luck. A screenwriter who is highly creative, for example, may quickly turn out high-quality scripts, even though his or her motivation to do so is not high. And a physician in Somalia who is highly motivated to provide high-quality medical care may have difficultly providing it due to inadequate facilities or a lack of supplies.

In summary, because motivation is only one of several factors that can affect performance, a high level of motivation does not always result in a high level of performance. Conversely, high performance does not necessarily imply that motivation is high: Employees with low motivation may perform at a high level if they have a great deal of ability. Managers have to be careful not to automatically attribute the cause of low performance to a lack of motivation or the cause of high performance to high motivation (see Chapter 4). If they incorrectly assume that low performance stems from low motivation, managers may overlook the real cause of a performance problem (such as inadequate training or a lack of resources) and fail to take appropriate actions to rectify the situation. Similarly, if managers assume that employees who perform at a high level are highly motivated, they may inadvertently fail to take advantage of the talents of exceptionally capable employees: If employees perform at a high level when their motivation levels are low, they may be capable of making truly exceptional contributions to the organization if managers devote their efforts to boosting their motivation.

Intrinsic and Extrinsic Motivation

INTRINSICALLY MOTIVATED WORK BEHAVIOR
Behavior that is performed for its own sake.

Another distinction important to a discussion of motivation is the difference between the intrinsic and extrinsic sources of work motivation. **Intrinsically motivated work behavior** is behavior that is performed for its own sake; the source of motivation actually comes from performing the behavior itself, in other words.[19] A professional violinist who relishes playing in an orchestra regardless of relatively low pay and a millionaire CEO who repeatedly puts in twelve-hour days because she enjoys her work are both intrinsically motivated. From the opening case, it is clear that employees at the SAS Institute are intrinsically motivated; they really enjoy their work. Employees who are intrinsically motivated often remark that their work gives them a sense of accomplishment and achievement or that they feel that they are doing something worthwhile. For young professionals in China, learning and having the opportunity to develop new skills on the job are important sources of intrinsic motivation. After surveying Chinese managers, Grace Cheng, the managing director of Korn Ferry's search firm in Beijing, concluded that "money is a less important reason to change jobs than the potential to grow. . ."[20]

As indicated in the accompanying Managing Ethically feature, protecting the natural environment is a source of intrinsic motivation that benefits us all.

EXTRINSICALLY MOTIVATED WORK BEHAVIOR
Behavior that is performed to acquire material or social rewards or to avoid punishment.

Extrinsically motivated work behavior is behavior that is performed to acquire material or social rewards or to avoid punishment.[21] The behavior is performed not for its own sake but rather for its consequences. The operant conditioning theory of learning discussed in Chapter 5 essentially deals with how consequences (positive and negative reinforcers and punishment) can be used to generate extrinsically motivated behavior. Examples of rewards that may be a source of extrinsic motivation include pay, praise, and status (discussed in detail in Chapter 8).

An employee can be extrinsically motivated, intrinsically motivated, or both.[22] When employees are primarily extrinsically motivated and doing the work itself is not a source of motivation, it is especially important for an organization and its managers to make a clear connection between the behaviors the organization wants employees to perform and the outcomes or rewards employees want.

You may be wondering whether there is any connection between intrinsic and extrinsic motivation and the intrinsic and extrinsic work values we described in Chapter 3. Employees who have intrinsic work values want challenging assignments, the opportunity to make important contributions to their jobs and organizations, and the opportunity to reach their full potentials at work. Employees with extrinsic work values desire some of the consequences of working, such as earning money, having status in the community, social contacts, and time off from work for family and leisure. It stands to reason that employees with strong intrinsic work values are likely to want to be intrinsically motivated at work and those with strong extrinsic work values are likely to want to be extrinsically motivated at work.

Theories of Work Motivation

We have explored what motivation is, where it comes from, and how it is related to the performance of behaviors in an organizational setting. But we have not considered what motivates people, why they become motivated, and how they sustain their motivation.

Managing Ethically

Protecting the Environment

William McDonough is on a mission to save the planet, get rid of waste, and make large corporations believe it is worthwhile to take part in these efforts.[23] And his mission is paying off. McDonough is an environmental designer who, along with partner Michael Braungart, are developing methods for organizations to make products in ways that do not result in waste and harm the natural environment. For example, McDonough and Braungart helped make a new material for the soles of Nike athletic shoes that biodegrades without toxic chemicals being released. They also helped Herman Miller design a factory that relies on solar heating and cooling, which reduced energy consumption at the facility by around 30 percent.[24]

McDonough is so intrinsically motivated to protect the environment that he believes even recycling does too much harm. Products that are made out of recycled substances still contain some of the toxic substances in the original products. For example, plastic bottles are often recycled, but the heavy metals and carcinogens in the bottles still make their way into the recycled products. And those products eventually make their way into landfills.[25]

William McDonough designed this building for Herman Miller.

McDonough and Braungart introduced the concept of "cradle-to-cradle design" in their book entitled *Cradle to Cradle: Remaking the Way We Make Things*, published by Northpoint Press and translated into Chinese, Korean, German, Italian, and Spanish.[26] Cradle-to-cradle design means developing products using biodegradable raw materials in ways so that when a product is no longer useful, either the materials it is made of can be used over and over again in other products or they organically decompose. McDonough recently developed a new carpet for the Shaw Industries unit of Berkshire Hathaway according to this design principle.[27] The carpet, called "A Walk in the Garden," is made of nylon pellets and polymers that can be used over and over again to make new carpets, once an original carpet wears out. Typically, even material from recyclable carpets ends up being used to make other products that find their ways to landfills once they are no longer useful. Not so with A Walk in the Garden, which has manufacturing costs that are 10 percent lower than some of Shaw's other carpet lines.[28] McDonough is currently working with the China Housing Industry Association to help them design sustainable housing in seven new cities with materials that contain no harmful chemicals and in ways that require minimal energy costs for cooling and heating.[29] Clearly, social responsibility and protecting and preserving the natural environment are ethical concern's that should be on all of our minds.

EXHIBIT 6.2

The Motivation Equation

Inputs	Performance	Outcomes
Effort Time Education Experience Skills Knowledge Job behaviors	Quantity of work Quality of work Level of customer service	Pay Job security Benefits Vacation Job satisfaction Feeling of accomplishment Pleasure of doing interesting work

Theories about work motivation provide answers to such questions by explaining why employees behave as they do in organizations. The key challenge facing managers in terms of motivation is how to encourage employees to contribute inputs to their jobs and to the organization. Managers want employees to be motivated to contribute inputs (effort, specific job behaviors, skills, knowledge, time, and experience) because inputs influence job performance and, ultimately, organizational performance. Employees are concerned with obtaining outcomes from the organization—both extrinsic outcomes (pay and job security) and intrinsic outcomes (a feeling of accomplishment from doing a good job or the pleasure of doing interesting work). These key concerns for managers and their employees lie at the heart of motivation. As indicated in Exhibit 6.2, we can graphically depict these concerns in an equation: Inputs→Performance→Outcomes.

The four theories that we describe in this chapter—need theory, expectancy theory, equity theory, and organizational justice theory—are *complementary* perspectives. Each theory addresses different questions about motivation in organizations and the relationships between inputs, performance, and outcomes, shown in Exhibit 6.2. Note that each of the four theories has its own merits—there is no "best" theory, in other words. To get a good understanding of organizational motivation, we need to consider all four.

Need Theory

Need theory focuses on the outcome side of the equation in Exhibit 6.2 and on this question: *What outcomes are individuals motivated to obtain from their jobs and organizations?* The principal message of need theory is that employees have needs that they are motivated to satisfy in the workplace.[30] In order to determine which outcomes motivate employees the most, managers must first learn which needs employees are trying to satisfy.

Once an employee's needs are determined, the manager must make sure that she or he can control—either administer or withhold—the outcomes satisfying those needs. The manager should make it clear to the employee that receiving the outcomes depends on the desired behaviors being performed. Then the manager must administer the outcomes contingent upon that performance. In this way, the employee satisfies her or his needs while also contributing important inputs to the organization.

NEED THEORY
A group of theories about work motivation that focuses on employees' needs as the sources of motivation.

Although we just described need theory as if it is only one theory, **need theory** is actually a group of theories about work motivation. Collectively, these theories explain what motivates employees to behave in certain ways by focusing on employees' needs as the sources of motivation. Need theories propose that employees seek to satisfy many of their needs at work and that their behavior at work is, therefore, oriented toward need satisfaction.

NEED
A requirement for survival and well-being.

A **need** is a requirement for survival and well-being. To determine what will motivate an employee, a manager first must determine what needs an employee is trying to satisfy on the job because needs will vary from person to person. The manager then must ensure that the employee can satisfy his or her needs by engaging in behaviors that contribute to the organization's effectiveness. The two theories that we discuss next by Abraham Maslow and Clayton Alderfer describe several specific needs employees try to satisfy through their work behaviors and the order in which they try to satisfy them. In previous chapters, we discussed two other need-based approaches to understanding behavior in organizations: David McClelland's work on achievement, affiliation, and power needs (see Chapter 2) and Frederick Herzberg's motivator-hygiene theory (Chapter 3).

Maslow's Hierarchy of Needs

Psychologist Abraham Maslow proposed that human beings have five universal needs they seek to satisfy: physiological needs, safety needs, belongingness needs, esteem needs, and self-actualization needs. These needs and examples of how they can be satisfied are described in Exhibit 6.3. Maslow proposed that these needs can be arranged in a hierarchy of importance, with the most basic or compelling needs—physiological and safety needs—at the base.[31] These basic needs must be satisfied before an individual seeks to satisfy needs higher up in the hierarchy. Maslow argued that once a need is satisfied, it is no longer a source of motivation.

There are many ways that organizations can help employees who are at different levels in Maslow's hierarchy satisfy their needs while at the same time also help the organization achieve its goals and a competitive advantage. Some organizations, for example, help satisfy employees' esteem needs by providing special recognition for their outstanding accomplishments and achievements.[32]

EXHIBIT 6.3

Maslow's Hierarchy of Needs

Need Level	Description	Examples of How Needs Are Met or Satisfied in an Organization
Highest-Level Needs		
Self-actualization needs	Needs to realize one's full potential as a human being	By using one's skills and abilities to the fullest and striving to achieve all that one can on a job
Esteem needs	Needs to feel good about oneself and one's capabilities, to be respected by others, and to receive recognition and appreciation	By receiving promotions at work and being recognized for accomplishments on the job
Belongingness needs	Needs for social interaction, friendship, affection, and love	By having good relations with co-workers and supervisors, being a member of a cohesive work group, and participating in social functions such as company picnics and holiday parties
Safety needs	Needs for security, stability, and a safe environment	By receiving job security, adequate medical benefits, and safe working conditions
Physiological needs	Basic needs for things such as food, water, and shelter that must be met in order for an individual to survive	By receiving a minimum level of pay that enables a worker to buy food and clothing and have adequate housing
Lowest-Level Needs (most basic or compelling)		

According to Maslow's theory, unsatisfied needs are the prime motivators of behavior, and needs at the lowest levels of the hierarchy take precedence over needs at higher levels.[33] At any particular time, however, only one set of needs motivates behavior, and it is not possible to skip levels. Once an individual satisfies one set of needs, he or she tries to satisfy needs at the next level of the hierarchy, and this level becomes the focus of motivation.

By specifying the needs that contribute to motivation, Maslow's theory helps managers determine what will motivate any given employee. A simple but important lesson from Maslow's theory is that employees differ in the needs they try to satisfy at work and that what motivates one employee may not motivate another. What does this conclusion suggest? To have a motivated workforce, managers must identify which needs each employee is seeking to satisfy at work, and once these needs have been identified, managers must ensure that the employee's needs are satisfied if he or she performs the desired behaviors.

Alderfer's ERG Theory

Clayton Alderfer's existence-relatedness-growth (ERG) theory is also a need theory of work motivation. Alderfer's theory builds on some of Maslow's thinking but reduces the number of universal needs from five to three and is more flexible in terms of movement between levels.[34] Like Maslow, Alderfer also proposes that needs can be arranged in a hierarchy. The three types of needs in Alderfer's theory are described in Exhibit 6.4.

Whereas Maslow assumes that lower-level needs must be satisfied before a higher-level need is a motivator, Alderfer lifts this restriction. According to ERG theory, a higher-level need can be a motivator even if a lower-level need is not fully satisfied, and needs at more than one level can be motivators at any time. Alderfer agrees with Maslow that as lower-level needs are satisfied, an employee becomes motivated to satisfy higher-level needs. But Alderfer breaks with Maslow on the consequences of need frustration. Maslow says that once a lower-level need is satisfied, it is no longer a source of motivation. Alderfer proposes that when an individual is motivated to satisfy a higher-level need but has difficulty doing so, the person's motivation to satisfy lower-level needs will increase.

EXHIBIT 6.4

Alderfer's ERG Theory

Need Level	Description	Examples of How Needs Are Met or Satisfied in an Organization
Highest-Level Needs		
Growth needs	Needs for self-development and creative and productive work	By continually improving skills and abilities and engaging in meaningful work
Relatedness needs	Needs to have good interpersonal relations, to share thoughts and feelings, and to have open two-way communication	By having good relations with co-workers, superiors, and subordinates and by obtaining accurate feedback from others
Existence needs	Basic needs for human survival such as the need for food, water, clothing, shelter, and a secure and safe environment	By receiving enough pay to provide for the basic necessities of life and by having safe working conditions
Lowest-Level Needs		

To see how this process works, let's look at the case of a middle manager in a manufacturing firm whose existence and relatedness needs (lower-level needs) are pretty much satisfied. Currently, the manager is motivated to try to satisfy her growth needs but finds this hard to do because she has been in the same position for the past five years. She is very skilled and knowledgeable about all aspects of the job, and the wide variety and number of her current responsibilities leave her no time to pursue anything new or exciting. Essentially, the manager's motivation to satisfy her growth needs is being frustrated because of the nature of her job. According to Alderfer, this frustration will increase the manager's motivation to satisfy a lower-level need such as relatedness. As a result of this motivation, the manager becomes more concerned about interpersonal relations at work and continually seeks honest feedback from her colleagues.

The Research Evidence

Because Maslow's and Alderfer's theories were among some of the earliest approaches to work motivation, they have received a considerable amount of attention from researchers. Although they seem logical and intuitively appealing and many managers like them, by and large these theories have tended *not* to receive support from research.[35] There appear to be at least two major difficulties with the theories. First, it may be unreasonable to expect a relatively small set of needs ordered in a particular fashion to apply to all human beings. Second, it may be unrealistic to expect that all people become motivated by different types of needs in a set order (that is, that the satisfaction of higher needs is sought *only* when lower-level needs have been satisfied).

Studies of American employees generally do not support the main tenets of Maslow's and Alderfer's theories, and it is likely that international studies conducted in other cultures would yield even less support. Even though the conclusions of the theories have not been supported, we can still learn some important lessons about motivation from the work of Maslow and Alderfer.

EXPECTANCY THEORY
A theory about work motivation that focuses on how employees make choices among alternative behaviors and levels of effort.

Expectancy Theory

Need theories try to explain *what* motivates employees. Expectancy theory focuses on *how* employees decide which specific behaviors to perform and *how much* effort to exert. In other words, **expectancy theory** is concerned with how employees make choices among alternative behaviors and levels of effort.[36] With its emphasis on choices, expectancy theory focuses on employees' perceptions (see Chapter 4) and thoughts or cognitive processes (Chapter 5).

According to expectancy theory, employees like this oil field worker in Texas must believe that high levels of effort will lead to high levels of performance in order for their motivation to be high.

Expectancy theory addresses two questions about motivation and the equation in Exhibit 6.2. One question is: *Does an individual believe that his or her inputs (such as effort on the job) will result in a given level of performance?* Expectancy theory proposes that regardless of which outcomes are available, employees will not be motivated to contribute their inputs to the organization unless they believe it will result in achieving a given level of performance. Employees' beliefs about the relationship between their inputs (such as effort) and the performance level they reach are, thus, central to understanding motivation. Put simply, if employees do not think they are capable of performing at an adequate level even with maximum effort, their motivation to perform at that level will be zero.[37]

The other question that expectancy theory addresses is: *Does an individual believe that performing at this level will lead to obtaining the outcomes he or she wants (pay, job security, a feeling of accomplishment, and so forth)?* The second key part of expectancy theory indicates that employees will be motivated to perform at a given level only if that level leads to the desired outcomes.[38]

Only when the answer to both of these questions is "yes" will the individual be motivated to contribute effort and other inputs on the job. According to expectancy theory, a manager who wants to motivate an employee to perform at a certain level must first make sure the employee believes he or she can achieve the performance level. Then the manager must make sure the employee believes he or she will receive, and actually does receive, the desired outcomes once the performance level has been achieved.

To understand the overall focus of expectancy theory, consider the *direction of behavior* of an experienced nurse who has just taken a job at a new hospital. Which behaviors could she choose to perform? Does she spend time casually chatting with patients, or does she limit her interactions to those directly pertaining to medical care? Does she discuss her patients' symptoms and complaints with their physicians in detail, or must doctors rely on her written records? Does she readily help other nurses when they seem to have a heavy load, or does she provide assistance only when asked?

Once the nurse chooses what she will do, she also needs to decide how much *effort* to exert on the job. Should she push herself to do as much as she can, even if doing so means forgoing some of her authorized breaks? Should she do just enough to adequately perform her job requirements? Should she minimize her efforts by taking longer breaks, referring her most difficult patients to her supervisor, and avoiding conversations with patients and physicians?

Also, with what level of *persistence* should she report her fears that a junior doctor has made a misdiagnosis? Should she mention it to some of her more senior coworkers? Should she tell her supervisor? If her supervisor does nothing about it, should she raise the issue with the head nurse in charge of her unit? If the head nurse is unconcerned, should she discuss her fears with a more senior doctor?

Expectancy theory seeks to explain how employees go about making these various decisions. Because these choices determine what employees do on the job and how hard they work, they have profound effects on organizational effectiveness. By describing how employees make these choices, expectancy theory provides managers with valuable insights on how to get employees to perform organizationally functional behaviors and how to encourage employees to exert high levels of effort when performing these behaviors.

Because of its profound organizational implications, expectancy theory is among the most popular theories of work motivation. The theory, which was originally developed by Victor Vroom in the 1960s, assumes that employees are essentially pleasure seeking[39]—that is, they are motivated to receive positive outcomes (such as a weekly paycheck, a bonus, or an award) and to avoid negative outcomes (such as getting reprimanded, fired, or demoted). It also assumes that employees are rational, careful processors of information and use information about their jobs, abilities, and desires to decide what they will do on the job and how hard they will do it.

Expectancy theory identifies three major factors that determine an employee's motivation: valence, instrumentality, and expectancy.[40]

Valence: How Desirable Is an Outcome?

> **VALENCE**
> In expectancy theory, the desirability of an outcome to an individual.

Employees can obtain a variety of outcomes from their jobs—pay, job security, benefits, feelings of accomplishment, the opportunity to do interesting work, good relationships with coemployees, and promotions. For any individual, the desirability of each outcome is likely to vary. The term **valence** refers to the desirability of an outcome to an individual employee. Valence can be positive or negative and can vary in size or magnitude. If an outcome has *positive valence*, an employee prefers having the outcome to not having it. If an outcome has *negative valence*, an employee prefers not having the outcome. For most employees, getting a raise is likely to have positive valence, and being fired is likely to have negative valence. The magnitude of valence is how desirable or undesirable an outcome is for an employee.[41] Maslow's and Alderfer's need theories suggest that employees will find outcomes that satisfy their needs to be especially attractive or valent. In the opening case, some highly valent outcomes for the SAS employees include the opportunity to do interesting and creative work, develop new products, and access the latest technology. Other valent outcomes at SAS include being fairly rewarded financially, working in a pleasant environment, and having access to a company-provided day care and gym.

Some motivation problems occur because highly valent outcomes are unavailable to employees. To determine what outcomes might motivate an employee, managers must determine what outcomes an employee desires or the valence of different outcomes for the employee.

Instrumentality: What Is the Connection Between Job Performance and Outcomes?

In our discussion of learning and operant conditioning in Chapter 5, we emphasized how important it is for outcomes (or *consequences,* as they are called in operant conditioning) to be given to employees on the basis of their performance of desired behaviors. Like operant conditioning, expectancy theory proposes that outcomes should be directly linked to desired organizational behaviors or to overall levels of job performance.

Instrumentality, the second key determinant of motivation according to expectancy theory, is an employee's perception about the extent to which performing certain behaviors or performing at a certain level will lead to the attainment of a particular outcome. In organizations, employees are going to engage in desired behaviors and be motivated to perform them at a high level only if they perceive that high performance and desired behaviors will lead to positively valent outcomes such as a pay raise, a promotion, or sometimes even just a pat on the back.[42]

INSTRUMENTALITY
In expectancy theory, a perception about the extent to which performance of one or more behaviors will lead to the attainment of a particular outcome.

Just like valence, instrumentality can be positive or negative and varies in size or magnitude. Instrumentality, the *perceived* association between a certain level of job performance (or the performance of certain behaviors) and the receipt of a specific outcome, can be measured on a scale from −1 to +1. An instrumentality of −1 means that an employee perceives that performing a certain behavior, or performing it at a certain level, definitely *will not result* in obtaining the outcome. An instrumentality of +1 means that the employee perceives the performance *definitely will result* in obtaining the outcome.

An advertising executive, for example, perceives that if she obtains three new major corporate accounts this year (and holds on to all of her existing accounts), her performance definitely *will result* in her receiving a hefty year-end bonus (an instrumentality of +1) and definitely *will not result* in her being asked to relocate to one of the agency's less prestigious locations (an instrumentality of −1). The magnitude of instrumentalities between the extremes of −1 and +1 indicates the extent of the perceived association or relationship between the performance and the outcome. An instrumentality of zero means that an employee perceives *no* relationship between performance and outcome. Let's continue with the example of the advertising executive. She perceives that there is some possibility that if she performs at a high level she will be given a promotion (an instrumentality of .3) and a larger possibility that she will obtain a bigger office (an instrumentality of .5). She perceives that her medical and dental benefits will be unaffected by her level of performance (an instrumentality of zero).

In trying to decide which behaviors to engage in and how hard to work (the level of job performance to strive for), the advertising executive considers the *valences* of the outcomes that she perceives will result from different levels of performance (how attractive the outcomes are to her) and the *instrumentality* of performing at a certain level for attaining each outcome (how certain it is that performing at that level will result in that outcome). In this way, both instrumentality and valence influence motivation.

Instrumentalities that are, in fact, high and that employees believe are high are effective motivators. Managers need to make sure that employees who perform at a high level do in fact receive the outcomes that they desire—outcomes with high positive valence. In the opening case, the SAS Institute maintains high instrumentalities by linking employees' pay and bonuses to their performance. Managers also need to clearly communicate instrumentalities to employees by letting them know what outcomes will result from various levels of performance.

Sometimes employees are not motivated to perform at a high level because they do not perceive that high performance will lead to highly valent outcomes (such as pay raises, time off, and promotions). When employees think that good performance goes unrecognized, their motivation to perform at a high level tends to be low.

Expectancy: What Is the Connection Between Effort and Job Performance?

Even though an employee perceives that a pay raise (a highly valent outcome) will result directly from high performance (high instrumentality), he or she still may not be motivated to

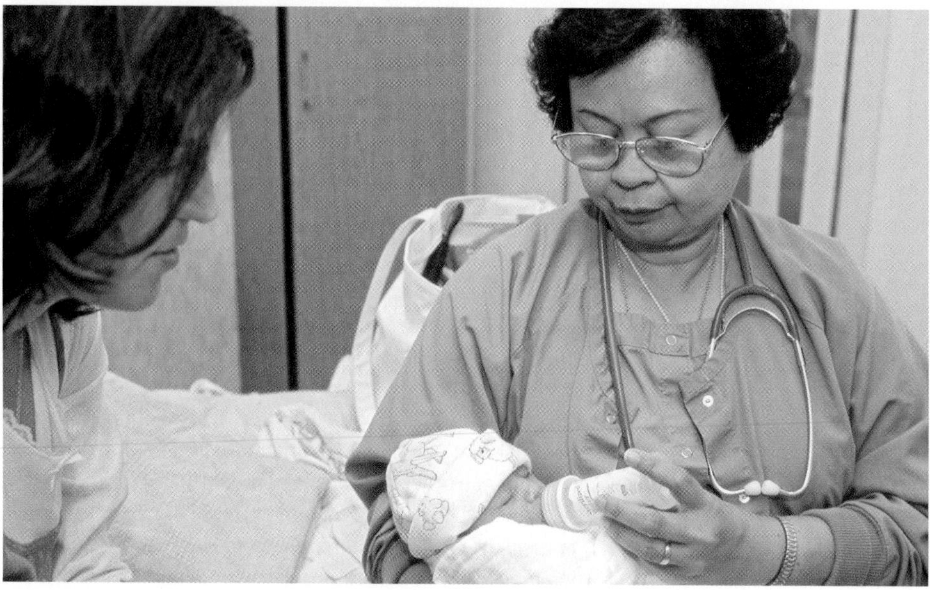

In order for workers like this pediatric nurse to be highly motivated, expectancy, instrumentality, and valence must all be high.

perform at a high level. To understand why motivation is low even when instrumentalities and valences are high, we need to consider the third major factor in expectancy theory: expectancy.

EXPECTANCY
In expectancy theory, a perception about the extent to which effort will result in a certain level of performance.

Expectancy is an employee's perception about the extent to which his or her effort will result in a certain level of job performance. Expectancy varies from 0 to 1 and reflects the chances that putting forth a certain amount of effort will result in a certain level of performance. An expectancy of 0 means that an employee believes there is no chance that his or her effort will result in a certain level of performance. An expectancy of 1 signifies that an employee is absolutely certain that his or her effort will lead to a certain level of performance. Expectancies between 0 and 1 lie along the continuum between the two.

Employees are going to be motivated to perform desired behaviors at a high level only if they think they can do so.[43] If they think they actually *will perform* at a high level when they work hard, their expectancy is high. No matter how much the advertising executive in our earlier example wants the pay raise and promotion that she thinks will result from high performance, if she thinks she cannot possibly perform at the necessary level, she will not be motivated to do so. Similarly, no matter how much a student wants to pass a course, if she thinks she will flunk no matter how hard she studies, she will not be motivated to study. Expectancy is similar to the concept of self-efficacy, discussed in Chapter 5, which captures the idea that employees are not always certain that their efforts will be successful or result in a given level of performance.

If motivation levels are low because employees do not think their efforts will pay off with improved performance, managers need to reassure them that they are capable of performing at a high level if they try hard. In addition, organizations can boost employees' expectancies by helping them improve their skills and abilities. Organizations ranging from the SAS Institute to the Container Store and Southwest Airlines are great believers in training to boost expectancies.[44]

The Combined Effects of Valence, Instrumentality, and Expectancy on Motivation

In order for an employee to be motivated to perform desired behaviors and to perform them at a high level, the following conditions are necessary (see Exhibit 6.5):

- *Valence* must be high: The employee wants outcomes the organization has to offer.
- *Instrumentality* must be high: The employee perceives that she or he must perform the desired behaviors at a high level to obtain these outcomes.
- *Expectancy* must be high: The employee thinks that trying hard will lead to performance at a high level.

EXHIBIT 6.5

Expectancy Theory

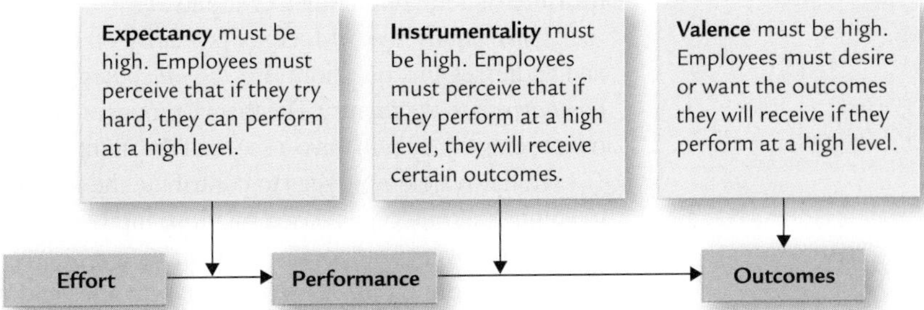
In order for employees to be motivated to perform desired behaviors at a high level . . .
Expectancy must be high. Employees must perceive that if they try hard, they can perform at a high level.
Instrumentality must be high. Employees must perceive that if they perform at a high level, they will receive certain outcomes.
Valence must be high. Employees must desire or want the outcomes they will receive if they perform at a high level.
Effort
Performance
Outcomes

If just one of these three factors—valence, instrumentality, or expectancy—is zero, motivation will be zero. In addition to believing that performing certain behaviors at a high level will result in obtaining outcomes (positive instrumentality), our advertising executive must perceive that (1) she is likely to receive desired (positively valent) outcomes if she performs at a high level and (2) she can perform at a high level if she tries (has a high expectancy).

High performance depends on what an employee does and how hard he or she does it. According to expectancy theory, in trying to decide what to do and how hard to do it, employees ask themselves questions such as these:

- Will I be able to obtain outcomes I want? (In expectancy theory terms: Is the valence of outcomes that the organization provides high?)
- Do I need to perform at a high level to obtain these outcomes? (In expectancy theory terms: Is high performance instrumental for obtaining these outcomes?)
- If I try hard, will I be able to perform at a high level? (In expectancy theory terms: Is expectancy high?)

Only when employees answer "yes" to each of these three questions are they motivated to perform as best they can. Expectancy theory suggests not only that rewards should be based on performance and that employees should have the abilities necessary to perform at a high level but also that managers must make sure that employees accurately perceive this to be the case.

Expectancy theory is a popular theory of motivation and has received extensive attention from researchers. Some studies support the theory, and others do not,[45] but by and large the theory has been supported.[46]

Equity Theory

EQUITY THEORY
A theory about work motivation that focuses on employees' perceptions of the fairness of their work outcomes and inputs.

OUTCOME/INPUT RATIO
In equity theory, the relationship between what an employee gets from a job (outcomes) and what the employee contributes to the job (inputs).

The equity theory of work motivation was developed in the 1960s by J. Stacy Adams (*equity* means "fairness"). Equity theory is based on the premise that an employee perceives the relationship between the *outcomes*—what the employee gets from a job and organization—and his or her *inputs*—what the employee contributes to the job and organization.[47] Outcomes include pay, fringe benefits, job satisfaction, status, opportunities for advancement, job security, and anything else the employees wants from the organization. Inputs include special skills, training, education, work experience, effort on the job, time, and anything else that employees believe they contribute. According to **equity theory**, however, it is *not* the objective level of outcomes and inputs that is important in determining work motivation. What is important to motivation is the way an employee perceives his or her outcome/input ratio compared to the **outcome/input ratio** of another person.[48]

This other person, called a *referent* by Adams, is simply another employee or group of employees perceived to be similar to oneself. The referent could also be oneself at a different place or time (for example, in a previous job), or it could be one's expectations (for example, one's beliefs about what the outputs and inputs of an entry-level accountant's job should be). Regardless of the referent an employee chooses, it is the *employee's perceptions* of the referent's outcomes and inputs that are compared—not any objective measure of actual outcomes or inputs.

Thus, equity theory focuses primarily on the relationship between inputs and outcomes and addresses this question: *Are the outcomes perceived as being at an appropriate level in comparison to the inputs?* The theory proposes that from past experience or the observation of others, employees will have a sense of the input levels that should result in certain outcomes.[49]

To motivate employees to contribute the inputs the organization needs, managers need to administer outcomes based on those inputs. Moreover, managers need to ensure that different employees' outcome-input *ratios* are approximately equal so that employees who contribute more inputs receive more outcomes and vice versa.

Equity

Equity exists when an individual's outcome/input ratio equals the outcome/input ratio of the referent (see Exhibit 6.6). Because the comparison of the ratios is what determines the presence or absence of equity (not the comparison of absolute levels of outcomes and inputs), equity can exist even if the referent receives more than the individual who is making the comparison.

Consider the case of two financial analysts who have been working at the same corporation for two years. At the end of the two years, analyst A gets promoted, but analyst B does not. Can both analysts consider this situation to be equitable? The answer is yes: Equity exists if analyst A and analyst B perceive that that their respective outcome/input ratios are equal or proportional and that analyst A generally worked more hours than analyst B. Perhaps, for example, added input, or overtime, accounts for analyst A's additional outcome (the promotion).

When an employee perceives that the employee's and the referent's outcome/input ratios are proportionally equal, the employee is motivated either to maintain the status quo or to increase his or her inputs to receive more outcomes.

OVERPAYMENT INEQUITY
The inequity that exists when a person perceives that his or her outcome/input ratio is greater than the ratio of a referent.

UNDERPAYMENT INEQUITY
The inequity that exists when a person perceives that his or her outcome/input ratio is less than the ratio of a referent.

Inequity

Inequity, or lack of fairness, exists when outcome/input ratios are not proportionally equal. Inequity creates tension and unpleasant feelings for an employee and motivates the individual to try to restore equity by bringing the two ratios back into balance.

There are two basic types of inequity: overpayment inequity and underpayment inequity (see Exhibit 6.6). **Overpayment inequity** exists when an individual perceives that his or her outcome/input ratio is greater than that of a referent. **Underpayment inequity** exists when a person perceives that his or her outcome/input ratio is less than that of a referent.

EXHIBIT 6.6

Conditions of Equity and Inequity

	Individual / Referent	Example
Equity	$\frac{\text{Outcomes}}{\text{Inputs}} = \frac{\text{Outcomes}}{\text{Inputs}}$	A financial analyst contributes more inputs (time and effort) to her job and receives proportionally more outcomes (a promotion and a pay raise) than her referent receives.
Overpayment inequity	$\frac{\text{Outcomes}}{\text{Inputs}} > \frac{\text{Outcomes}}{\text{Inputs}}$ (greater than)	A financial analyst contributes the same level of inputs to her job as her referent but receives more outcomes than the referent receives.
Underpayment inequity	$\frac{\text{Outcomes}}{\text{Inputs}} < \frac{\text{Outcomes}}{\text{Inputs}}$ (less than)	A financial analyst contributes more inputs to her job than her referent but receives the same outcomes as her referent.

Consider the case of Steve and Mike, who are janitors in a large office building. Steve is a conscientious employee who always gets to work on time and keeps his areas of the building spotless. Mike is often late, takes long lunch hours, and often "forgets" to clean some of his areas. Steve and Mike receive the same level of pay, benefits, and other outcomes from their employer. According to equity theory, if both employees have accurate perceptions and choose each other as a referent, Mike should perceive *overpayment inequity*. This perception creates tension within Mike (perhaps it makes him feel guilty), and so he's motivated to restore equity. Steve, in contrast, perceives *underpayment inequity*. Because Steve is contributing more than Mike yet receiving the same level of outcomes, he, too, experiences tension (perhaps anger) and is motivated to restore equity.

Ways to Restore Equity

There are several ways by which equity can be restored in situations like the one involving Steve and Mike.[50]

1. *Employees can change their inputs or outcomes.* When employees perceive underpayment inequity, for example, they can restore equity by reducing their inputs. In the case of the two janitors, Steve could restore equity by cutting back on his inputs—by coming to work late, taking longer breaks, and working less conscientiously. An underpaid employee could also try to change his or her outcomes by asking for a raise.
2. *Employees try to change their referents' inputs or outcomes.* Steve might complain to his supervisor about Mike's coming to work late and not doing a very good job in the hope that the supervisor will alter Mike's inputs (perhaps by getting him to show up on time or do a better job) or his outcomes (cutting his pay or threatening his job security). On the other hand, Mike might encourage Steve to relax and take it easy on the job.
3. *Employees change their perceptions of inputs and outcomes (either their own or the referents').* Mike could restore equity by changing his perceptions about his inputs. He could start to think that his area is larger or harder to clean than Steve's or that he works faster, so his and Steve's ratios are really proportional after all. As this example illustrates, employees who perceive overpayment inequity are especially likely to change their perceptions (rather than their actual inputs or outcomes) to restore equity. This is why overpaid employees often do not feel guilty for very long.
4. *Employees can change the referent.*[51] An employee may decide that the original referent does not allow for an appropriate comparison and, thus, select another one. Steve might recall hearing that Mike is a relative of one of the managers in the company and conclude that he is not the most suitable basis for comparison. Conversely, Mike might decide that Steve is clearly an extraordinary, almost superhuman janitor and select someone else to compare himself to.
5. *Employees leave the job or organization or force the referent to leave.* The most common example of this approach is employee turnover and, not surprisingly, leaving the organization is most prevalent in situations of underpayment inequity. Thus, Steve might be motivated to look for a job elsewhere, or he might try to get Mike fired.

Employees who belong to labor unions sometimes go on strike to protest when they think they are being unfairly treated and other methods of trying to restore equity have proved to be futile.

The Effects of Inequity and the Research Evidence

Both underpayment inequity and overpayment inequity are dysfunctional for organizations, managers, and employees. In the case of overpayment, although employees are sometimes motivated to increase their inputs to restore equity (an effort that is functional for the organization), they are more likely to be motivated to change their perceptions of inputs or outcomes (an effort that is dysfunctional because there is no *actual* increase in the level of inputs contributed by the overpaid employees). In the case of underpayment, capable and deserving employees may be motivated to reduce their inputs or even leave the organization, both of which are dysfunctional for the organization. Moreover, sometimes when employees feel very unfairly treated, they engage in unethical behaviors such as stealing from the organization.[52]

All in all, motivation is highest when equity exists and outcomes are distributed to employees on the basis of their inputs to the organization. Employees who contribute a high level of inputs and receive, in turn, a high level of outcomes are motivated to continue to contribute inputs. Employees who contribute a low level of inputs and receive a low level of outcomes know that if they want to increase their outcomes, they must increase their inputs.

Like expectancy theory, equity theory is a popular theory of motivation and has received extensive research attention. Also, as in the case of expectancy theory, although there have been some nonsupportive results, by and large the research supports the main ideas of the theory.[53]

ORGANIZATIONAL JUSTICE
An employee's perception of overall fairness in his or her organization.

Organizational Justice Theory

Organizational justice, employees' perceptions of overall fairness in their organizations, is increasingly being recognized as an important determinant of employee motivation, attitudes, and behaviors.[54] Organizational justice theory does not refer to a single theory

You're the Management Expert

When Equal Treatment Backfires

Tom Li manages the order processing department of a large catering company in New York City. Times have been tough, and he has been told that he will have very limited funds available for annual salary increases. In an effort to be fair, he has decided to take his entire pool of funds for raises and distribute a flat, 3 percent salary increase equally to each of his subordinates. At the end of the last department meeting, he announced the 3 percent raise and noted that, given the decrease in the company's revenues over the past year, he was pleasantly surprised that any funds were available for raises. A few days after the meeting, one of Li's subordinates, Sebastian Saltado, came by his office and complained about his measly raise and asked why he was receiving the same percentage increase as everyone else in the department. Li told him that he knew that Saltado processed orders more quickly than other members in the department and was more responsive to customers, and he wished he could do something more to recognize his contributions. But, Li explained, because very limited funds were available for raises, he thought it only fair to share the raise pool equally. Two weeks later Saltado gave notice that he would be leaving the company because he found a better job working in a large department store. Li is concerned and confused—he thought Saltado really liked his work at the catering company and was satisfied with his job; in fact, Saltado had mentioned that a friend of his would be interested in a job in the same department if a position opened up. And Li is really going to miss having Saltado around; he could always count on Saltado to placate a disgruntled customer and somehow arrange for changes or replacements on an order to be processed and delivered in record time. As an expert in OB, Li has come to you for help. Why did Saltado quit, and was there anything that Li should have done differently?

per se, but rather describes a group of theories that focus on the nature, determinants, and consequences of organizational justice. Based on this group of theories, researchers have identified four forms of organizational justice: distributive justice, procedural justice, interpersonal justice, and informational justice.[55]

Organizational justice theory addresses this question about motivation: *Are the procedures used to assess inputs and performance and distribute outcomes perceived to be fair, are employees treated with dignity and respect, and do managers provide adequate explanations of their decisions and the procedures used to arrive at them?* Organizational justice theory proposes that employees will not be motivated to contribute their inputs unless they perceive that fair procedures will be used to distribute outcomes in the organization and that they will be treated fairly by managers. These procedures include those used to assess input levels, determine the level of performance achieved, and then actually distribute the outcomes.

When these procedures are perceived to be unfair and employees feel unfairly treated, motivation suffers because *all* the relationships in the motivation equation (see Exhibit 6.2) are weakened: assessing the inputs, determining the performance, and ultimately distributing the outcomes.

Forms of Organizational Justice

DISTRIBUTIVE JUSTICE
The perceived fairness of the distribution of outcomes in an organization.

PROCEDURAL JUSTICE
The perceived fairness of the procedures used to make decisions about the distribution of outcomes in an organization.

Because equity theory focuses on the fair distribution of outcomes across employees to encourage high levels of motivation, it is often called a theory of distributive justice.[56] **Distributive justice**, the perceived fairness of the distribution of outcomes in organizations, such as pay, promotions, and desirable working conditions and assignments, is an important contributor to more general perceptions of organizational justice.[57] An example of a scale that measures distributive justice is provided in Exhibit 6.7.

Procedural justice is concerned with the perceived fairness of the procedures used to make decisions about the distribution of outcomes. It is *not* concerned about the actual distribution of outcomes.[58] Procedural decisions pertain to how performance levels are evaluated, how grievances or disputes are handled (if, for example, an employee disagrees with a manager's evaluation of his or her performance), and how outcomes (like raises) are distributed. Like equity theory, employees' *perceptions* are of fundamental importance for procedural justice. That is, employees' reactions to procedures depend on how fair they *perceive* the procedures to be rather than how fair they actually are.[59]

Procedural justice theory holds that employees are going to be more motivated to perform at a high level when they perceive that the procedures used to make decisions about the distribution of outcomes are fair.[60] In other words, they'll be more motivated if they think their performance will be accurately assessed. Conversely, if employees think their performance will not be accurately assessed because the supervisor is not aware of their contributions to the organization or lets his or her personal feelings affect appraisals, employees will not be as strongly motivated to perform at high levels.

Employees are likely to perceive that procedural justice is high when they are able to have input into procedures that are used to determine the distribution of outcomes in an organization and when they have the opportunity to express their own views and opinions.[61] Take the case of a subordinate who has worked very hard to attain the goal of reducing inventory levels by 20 percent to cut costs. On the surface it seems as if the goal has not been met, as the dollar value of inventory has remained unchanged. However, the subordinate knows that she has actually reduced physical inventory levels by 20 percent; the dollar value of inventory on hand does not reflect this reduction since prices have increased by about 20 percent. Having the opportunity to explain to her supervisor why inventory costs appear to be unchanged despite all her hard work to successfully reduce inventory quantities by 20 percent will increase the subordinate's perceptions of procedural justice.

Procedural justice is also likely to be high when employees perceive that procedures are used consistently across employees (e.g., all employees with the same job have their performance appraised through the same process); accurate information is

EXHIBIT 6.7

A Measure of Four Forms of Organizational Justice

Please respond to each item using the 1–5 scale below.

1	2	3	4	5
To a small extent		**To a moderate extent**		**To a large extent**

The following items refer to your outcomes. To what extent:

1. Do your outcomes reflect the effort you have put into your work?
2. Are your outcomes appropriate for the work you have completed?
3. Do your outcomes reflect what you have contributed to the organization?
4. Are your outcomes justified, given your performance?

The following items refer to the procedures used to arrive at your outcomes. To what extent:

5. Have you been able to express your views and feelings during those procedures?
6. Have you had influence over the outcomes arrived at by those procedures?
7. Have those procedures been applied consistently?
8. Have those procedures been free of bias?
9. Have those procedures been based on accurate information?
10. Have you been able to appeal the outcomes arrived at by those procedures?
11. Have those procedures upheld ethical and moral standards?

The following items refer to (the authority figure who enacted the procedure). To what extent:

12. Has he/she treated you in a polite manner?
13. Has he/she treated you with dignity?
14. Has he/she treated you with respect?
15. Has he/she refrained from improper remarks or comments?

The following items refer to the authority figure who enacted the procedure. To what extent:

16. Has he/she been candid in his/her communications with you?
17. Has he/she explained the procedures thoroughly?
18. Were his/her explanations regarding the procedures reasonable?
19. Has he/she communicated details in a timely manner?
20. Has he/she seemed to tailor his/her communications to each individual's specific needs?

Scoring: Distributive justice = sum of items 1–4.
Procedural justice = sum of items 5–11.
Interpersonal justice = sum of items 12–15.
Informational justice = sum of items 16–20.

Source: J. A. Colquitt, 2001, "On the Dimensionality of Organizational Justice: A Construct Validation of a Measure." *Journal of Applied Psychology*, 86: 386–400. Reprinted with permission.

relied on (e.g., numerical data such as sales figures are free of errors); and procedures are unbiased (e.g., supervisors do not let their personal likes and dislikes influence their judgments).[62] Additionally, having the opportunity to appeal judgments and decisions that have been made as well as knowing that procedures used in an organization adhere to the organization's code of ethics promotes procedural justice.[63] An example of a scale that measures procedural justice is provided in Exhibit 6.7.

When managers are courteous and polite and treat employees with dignity and respect, they are promoting interactional justice.

INTERPERSONAL JUSTICE
The perceived fairness of the interpersonal treatment employees receive from the distributors of outcomes or their managers.

INFORMATIONAL JUSTICE
Employee perceptions of the extent to which managers explain their decisions and the procedures they used to arrive at these decisions.

Interpersonal justice is concerned with the perceived fairness of the interpersonal treatment employees receive from the distributors of outcomes (usually their managers).[64] It is important for managers to be courteous and polite and to treat employees with dignity and respect to promote interpersonal justice.[65] Additionally, managers should refrain from making disparaging remarks or belittling subordinates.[66] An example of a scale that measures interpersonal justice is provided in Exhibit 6.7.

Informational justice captures employee perceptions of the extent to which managers explain their decisions, and the procedures used to arrive at them, to employees.[67] For example, managers can explain to employees (1) how they assess inputs (including time, effort, education, and previous work experience); (2) how they appraise performance; and (3) how they decide to distribute outcomes. When managers describe the procedures they use to distribute outcomes in an honest, forthright, and timely manner, when their explanations are thorough, and when subordinates perceive these explanations to be well-reasoned, perceptions of informational justice are likely to be high.[68] An example of a scale that measures informational justice is provided in Exhibit 6.7.

Organizational justice is important for all kinds of organizations and employees, even those intrinsically motivated by their work, as profiled in the following OB Today.

Consequences of Organizational Justice

Perceptions of organizational justice (i.e., distributive justice, procedural justice, interpersonal justice, informational justice) can have widespread ramifications for employee motivation, attitudes, and behaviors.[69] One can get a good handle on some of the possible consequences of organizational justice by considering the implications of procedural justice for the expectancy and equity theories of motivation.

Recall that expectancy theory asserts that individuals are motivated to work hard when they believe that (1) their efforts will result in their achieving a satisfactory level of performance (expectancy is high) and (2) their performances will lead to desired outcomes such as pay or a promotion (instrumentality and valence of outcomes are high). Suppose, however, that an organization has a problem with procedural justice, and its employees do *not* perceive that the procedures used to distribute outcomes are fair. More specifically, suppose employees believe that the performance appraisal system is inaccurate and biased, so that performing at a high level does *not* ensure a good performance appraisal, and performing poorly has been known to result in an average performance rating. In this organization, employees may believe that they are capable of performing at a high level (their expectancy

OB Today

Organizational Justice at Genentech

Genentech, the San Francisco biotechnology company that researches, develops, and manufactures new drugs to combat life-threatening conditions and diseases such as cancer was named the Number 1 "Best Company to Work For" in 2005 by *Fortune* magazine.[70] Founded in 1976, Genentech has been called "the first biotech company" and has developed drugs such as Avastin® to treat colon cancer, Raptiva® to treat psoriasis, and Activase® to treat blood clots. Genentech's operating sales in 2005 were over $5.4 billion (representing a 46 percent increase over 2004), and it has over 10,000 employees.[71]

Researchers and scientists at Genentech thrive in a culture that embodies organizational justice.

The researchers and scientists at Genentech are truly intrinsically motivated by their work, developing new drugs to save lives and cure diseases. They also thrive in a culture that embodies organizational justice. All employees, regardless of position or rank, are treated with respect and dignity. There are no special offices, parking spots, or dining rooms for top managers like CEO Art Levinson (who also happens to be an exceptionally talented scientist) and all employees are addressed by their first name (regardless of whether or not they have a PhD or an MD).[72]

An outcome that is very important to the researchers and scientists is funding for their projects, and Genentech ensures that organizational justice is served when these funding decisions are made. Around once or twice a year, the Research Review Committee (composed of 13 expert PhD's) makes decisions about where the company's research funds will be allocated.[73] Scientists and researchers seeking funding for their projects have the opportunity to discuss the progress and merits of their work with the committee, and the committee considers multiple sources of information to make sure that all R&D allocations are based on the scientific merits of the projects under consideration and are not subject to any bias or favoritism. When a project is not funded, scientists know why, do not lose their jobs, and move on to another project. As Levinson puts it, "At the end of the day, we want to make drugs that really matter. That's the transcendent issue."[74] And Genentech's commitment to organizational justice contributes to ensuring its scientists and researchers are motivated to do just that.

is high), but they cannot be sure that they will receive a high performance rating because the appraisal system is unfair (procedural justice is low). Employees will *not* be motivated to exert a lot of effort on the job if they think their performance will *not* be accurately and fairly assessed and they will *not* receive the outcomes they think they deserve.

From the perspective of equity theory, motivation will also suffer when perceptions of procedural justice are low. Employees may believe that their inputs to the organization are not going to be fairly assessed or that outcomes will not be distributed based on relative inputs. Under these circumstances, employees will not be motivated to contribute inputs, for there is no guarantee that they will result in the outcomes they think they deserve.

It appears that perceptions of procedural justice are especially important when outcomes, like pay and benefits, are relatively low—that is, when there are few rewards to distribute to employees. When individuals obtain high levels of outcomes, they may view them as fair *regardless* of whether or not the procedures in place to distribute them are really fair. However, they view low outcome levels—assuming they're the ones receiving them—as equitable only when the procedures used to distribute them really *are* fair.[74]

More generally, organizational justice has been found to be positively associated with job satisfaction, organizational commitment, job performance, and organizational citizenship behavior and negatively associated with absenteeism and turnover intentions.[75] Research also suggests that when perceptions of organizational justice are low, there might be increased potential for the occurrence of counterproductive work behaviors.[76] **Counterproductive work behaviors** are those behaviors that violate organizational values and norms and have the potential to harm individuals and the organization as a whole.[77] Such behaviors can range from relatively minor infractions such as wasting time and resources to much more major infractions such as theft, sabotage, and verbal and physical abuse.[78]

COUNTERPRODUCTIVE WORK BEHAVIORS
Behaviors by an employee that violate organizational values and norms and that can potentially harm individuals and the organization.

Summary

Work motivation explains why employees behave as they do. Four prominent theories about work motivation—need theory, expectancy theory, equity theory, and organizational justice theory—provide complementary approaches to understanding and managing motivation in organizations. Each theory answers different questions about the motivational process. In this chapter, we made the following major points:

1. Work motivation is the psychological forces within a person that determine the direction of the person's behavior in an organization, the person's level of effort, and the person's level of persistence in the face of obstacles. Motivation is distinct from performance; other factors besides motivation (for example, ability and task difficulty) influence performance.
2. Intrinsically motivated behavior is behavior performed for its own sake. Extrinsically motivated behavior is behavior performed to acquire material or social rewards or to avoid punishment.
3. Need theory, expectancy theory, equity theory, and organizational justice theory are complementary approaches to understanding motivation. Each answers different questions about the nature and management of motivation in organizations.
4. Need theories of motivation identify the needs that employees are motivated to satisfy on the job. Two major need theories of motivation are Maslow's hierarchy of needs and Alderfer's existence-relatedness-growth theory.
5. Expectancy theory focuses on how employees decide what behaviors to engage in on the job and how much effort to exert. The three major concepts in expectancy theory are valence (how desirable an outcome is to an employee), instrumentality (an employee's perception about the extent to which a certain level of performance will lead to the attainment of a particular outcome), and expectancy (an employee's perception about the extent to which effort will result in a certain level of performance). Valence, instrumentality, and expectancy combine to determine motivation.
6. Equity theory proposes that employees compare their own outcome/input ratio (the ratio of the outcomes they receive from their jobs and from the organization to the inputs they contribute) to the outcome/input ratio of a referent. Unequal ratios create tension inside the employee, and the employee is motivated to restore equity. When the ratios are equal, employees are motivated to maintain their current ratio of outcomes and inputs or raise their inputs if they want their outcomes to increase.
7. Organizational justice theory is concerned with employees' perceptions of overall fairness in their organizations. Four forms of organizational justice are distributive justice, procedural justice, interpersonal justice, and informational justice. Perceptions of organizational justice can have widespread ramifications for employee motivation, attitudes, and behaviors.

Exercises in Understanding and Managing Organizational Behavior

Questions for Review

1. Why might a person with a very high level of motivation perform poorly?
2. Why might a person with a very low level of motivation be a top performer?
3. Why do people differ in the types of needs they are trying to satisfy at work?
4. Why might employees differ in their valences for the same outcomes?
5. Why might perceptions of instrumentality be relatively low in an organization?
6. Why might a very capable employee have low expectancy for performing at a high level?
7. How does the choice of a referent influence perceptions of equity and inequity?
8. Is inequity always dysfunctional for an organization? Why or why not?
9. Why might fair procedures be perceived as being unfair by some employees?
10. What steps can organizations take to encourage organizational justice?

OB: Increasing Self-Awareness

Peak Motivation Experiences

Think about the last time you felt really motivated to do well at some activity: in one of your classes, at work, or in some kind of hobby or leisure activity (such as playing golf, running, or singing).

1. Describe the activity and indicate how you felt while engaged in it.
2. Was your motivation extrinsic, intrinsic, or both?
3. What needs were you trying to satisfy by this activity?
4. What outcomes did you hope to obtain by performing this activity well?
5. Did you think it was likely that you would attain these outcomes if you were successful?
6. How would you characterize your expectancy for this activity? Why was your expectancy at this level?
7. Did you ever compare what you were putting into the activity and what you were getting out of it to the input and outcome of a referent? If not, why not? If so, how did you feel about this comparison, and how did it affect your behavior?
8. Did thoughts of procedural justice ever enter your mind and affect your motivation?

A Question of Ethics

Employees often differ in their needs for time off from work. Employees with small children, single parents, employees with health problems, and employees who are the primary caregiver for an elderly or infirm relative may need more time off, for example, than employees who are single with no dependents and in good health. And one could argue that organizations should be responsive to these differing needs on ethical grounds. However, some might feel that the same expectations should apply to all employees regardless of their needs.

Questions

1. Why should organizations take employees' personal needs into account in providing benefits such as time off from work?
2. How can organizations take employees' personal need into account while at the same time ensuring that organizational members perceive that they are being fairly treated?

Small Group Break-Out Exercise

Promoting Procedural Justice

Form groups of three or four people and appoint one member as the spokesperson who will communicate your conclusions to the rest of the class:

1. Take a few minutes to think about a time in your life when you felt that you were really being treated unfairly and it was because of the procedures that were being used.
2. Take turns describing each of your experiences and the nature of the procedures that were unfair.
3. Then, as a group, come up with a list of the causes of a lack of procedural justice in the examples in your group.
4. Based on step 3, develop specific recommendations for promoting procedural justice.

Topic for Debate

Motivation explains why members of an organization behave as they do and either help or hinder the organization from achieving its goals. Now that you have a good understanding of motivation, debate the following issue:

Team A. Equity and justice cannot be achieved in the workplace.

Team B. Equity and justice can be achieved in the workplace.

Experiential Exercise

Motivating in Lean Economic Times

Objective

Your objective is to gain experience in confronting the challenges of (1) maintaining high levels of motivation when resources are shrinking and (2) developing an effective motivation program.

Procedure

The class divides into groups of three to five people, and each group appoints one member as spokesperson to present the group's recommendations to the whole class. Here is the scenario.

Each group plays the role of a team of top managers in a magazine publishing company that has recently downsized and consolidated its businesses. Now that the layoff is complete, top management is trying to devise a program to motivate the remaining editorial and production employees, who range from rank-and-file employees who operate printing presses to upper-level employees such as magazine editors.

As a result of the downsizing, the workloads of most employees have been increased by about 30 percent. In addition, resources are tight. A very limited amount of money is available for things such as pay raises, bonuses, and benefits. Nevertheless, top management thinks the company has real potential and that its fortunes could turn around if employees could be motivated to perform at a high level, be innovative, and work together to regain the company's competitive advantage.

Your group, acting as the top-management team, answers the following questions:

1. What specific steps will you take to develop a motivation program based on the knowledge of motivation you have gained from this chapter?
2. What key features will your motivation program include?
3. What will you do if the program you develop and implement does not seem to be working—if motivation not only fails to increase but also sinks to an all-time low?

When your group has completed those activities, the spokesperson will present the group's plans and proposed actions to the whole class.

New York Times *Cases in the News*

The New York Times

"Career Switchers Add New Depth to Talent Pool in Real Estate"

By S. Siwolop, The New York Times, March 15, 2006, p. C8.

When John McCarthy, a treasury manager at Toys "R" Us, started looking for a new job in July 2005, he was not looking at commercial real estate per se, merely for a position in which he might be able to improve a company's business more directly—and be rewarded for the effort.

At Toys "R" Us, Mr. McCarthy spent considerable time evaluating the real estate potential of the individual stores as the company was in the process of being acquired. But he felt that his credentials—which included an M.B.A. in finance and corporate accounting—were most suited to a job in investment banking.

He did get an offer in that field, but in the end opted for a job at Cushman & Wakefield of New Jersey, a commercial real estate firm, where he is now working on leasing both office and industrial properties.

Commercial brokerage teams used to consist mainly of people who had spent their entire careers in real estate, but lately they have grown to be surprisingly diverse, according to many industry executives.

At Cushman & Wakefield, for example, Mr. McCarthy joined several other recently hired brokers who started in other fields; they included two former lawyers, two certified public accountants and a former saleswoman for Microsoft, said Gualberto Medina, the executive managing director.

Mr. Medina himself started out as a lawyer and as a certified public accountant. Before joining Cushman & Wakefield in 2002, he also served as secretary of commerce for the State of New Jersey, handled business development for an Internet telecommunications company and was president of a biotech start-up.

In August, Mr. Medina took the helm of Cushman & Wakefield's New Jersey operations, and since then he has looked for both seasoned professionals and industry newcomers as a way of providing specialized experience or expertise to his company's clients. Lately, Mr. Medina has also been receiving more unsolicited résumés from other types of professionals who think commercial real estate offers both more interesting challenges and better compensation.

Executives at other companies confirm the interest. Some of it, they say, can be pegged to the greater number of universities that now offer course work in real estate, as well as the career restlessness that seemed to course through many industries after the Sept. 11 terrorist attacks.

But executives say that many job switchers also seem convinced that commercial real estate offers less drudgery and deskwork than other careers, like law, as well as the potential to earn large commissions, rather than simply bringing home a salary.

Michael Bush, the executive director of the Real Estate Associate Program, an industry-backed program that recruits and trains minority candidates for careers in commercial real estate, said that about a third of the 33 students who started the inaugural program in New York in

January had come from either law firms or Wall Street firms.

The program, which already exists in Washington and Atlanta, meets for three hours a week in the evening and lasts for 24 weeks. Mr. Bush said the typical participant was 25 to 35 years old with several years of business experience.

Marisa Manley, the founder and principal of Commercial Tenant Real Estate Representation in Manhattan, said that when her company recently had an opening for a transaction manager, she interviewed four lawyers for the job, as well as an accountant who held both a law and a business school degree.

"The talent pool is stronger, and I'm seeing stronger professional backgrounds than I would have seen 10 years ago," said Ms. Munley, who was first trained as both an architect and as a lawyer.

Robert A. Knakal, co-founder of Massey Knakal Realty Services in Manhattan, agreed that the pool of applicants today had a wider range of talents. "The people coming into the field now have tremendous credentials," he said. "For about a year after Sept. 11, we found, to our great surprise, that the quality of people looking to get into the business had changed dramatically. In the 80's and 90's, it's very unlikely that people would have left other careers to go into commercial real estate."

Still, making the jump is not always easy, some real estate executives caution. Mr. Knakal said that while his company's efforts to bring in other professionals had allowed it to grow substantially over the last five years, his firm has also had to make a "substantial commitment" to training programs, which are taught by the company's current employees and generally run two or three months each.

Even with training, newcomers usually take a while to establish themselves in the field. "Commercial real estate is not a quick and easy game, and we are always stressing the long-term nature of this business." Ms. Manley said. "This is a business where lease negotiations can take 12 weeks or more and where 18 months is usually the minimum amount of time" to close projects of 20,000 square feet and more.

Still, some recent careers switchers say they relish the change.

Earl L. Segal spent more than 30 years practicing real estate law before he joined the Washington office of Newmark Knight Frank in January as a business adviser. Last week, Mr. Segal said that while he was not necessarily reading fewer stacks of legal documents these days, he had "moved up the line" to working on a broader range of issues.

At Massey Knakal, John Barrett, one of the company's newest brokers, said he hoped eventually to use his love of problem-solving to generate high prices for properties that he is asked to represent. Before joining the company. Mr. Barrett, 42, spent more than 20 years running his own corporate and group travel services firm and then spent six months getting his real estate license.

He recently completed a two-month training program and planned to spend the next two months learning everything he could about the area that he would eventually cover—a sizable segment of Westchester County.

"I had done one thing since graduating from college, and I thought it was time for a new challenge," Mr. Barrett said last week.

So did Marjorie L. Torres, the founder and chief executive of Concrete Stories, a Manhattan company that offers real estate advice as well as brokerage and development services. Ms. Torres, 38, worked as an industrial engineer and then as a Wall Street investment banker before she was sent to Latin America in 1995 to turn around distressed properties.

There, she discovered that she preferred some of the more tangible rewards of commercial real estate. "In investment banking you do a lot of deals, but very rarely can you build something that you can actually touch," she said.

Questions for Discussion

1. What are some sources of intrinsic motivation for real estate brokers?
2. What are some sources of extrinsic motivation for real estate brokers?
3. From an expectancy theory perspective, why do some people find real estate work more motivating than their prior jobs?
4. How can specialized training in real estate enhance the motivation of real estate brokers?

The New York Times

"Airline Pilots Still Flying, but No Longer Quite So High"

By M. L. Wald, The New York Times, March 10, 2006, p. C3.

WASHINGTON, March 9—Within the world of aviation, airline pilots used to be one step down from astronauts. Now they feel one step up from bus drivers.

With half the seats in the nation's airliners run by companies either in bankruptcy or limping out of it, even the pilots at the top—the ones who are within a few years of mandatory retirement at 60, flying the big planes and earning top dollar—are facing a new world.

Their pay and pensions have been cut, and they work more hours to earn them. In another concession to the airlines, their days are interrupted more than ever by long hours of unpaid idleness.

They say they try hard not to let these things break their concentration or interfere with their work, flying passengers by the scores or hundreds, flawlessly, around the country and the world. They have piloted their planes to a record 40 million safe takeoffs and landings across the country in the last five years, whether the airline was solvent, bankrupt or just squeaking by.

Still, the boardroom blues are working their way into the cockpit.

"My philosophy right now is, I just go to work," said an American Airlines captain who, before his company's troubles, loved to fly. On one recent trip, he flew a 6 a.m. flight from Newark to Miami, then piloted a plane from Miami to Los Angeles the next evening, then a flight back to Newark, accumulating 15 paid hours for three days on the road.

The Federal Aviation Administration limits commercial pilots on domestic flights to eight hours a day, measured from pushback until arrival at the gate. The limits are 30 hours in seven days, 100 hours a month and 1,000 hours a year. The airlines do not exceed those limits but many now schedule much closer to them.

The F.A.A. rules do not address the amount of time between flights, so a pilot could be in uniform 12 hours or more to accumulate the day's hours. Eight hours of rest time every 24 hours is required, however. And pilots feel acutely the difference between getting a month's work in 14 days versus 18 days.

"They kind of bleed us out," the American Airlines captain said, on condition he not be identified for fear of losing his job. Pilots for major airlines said they expected to be fired if they were publicly candid on the new challenges of their jobs.

One veteran United Airlines captain, who laments that when he retires in a few years his pension will be about one-fourth what he expected, said he had to shut it out of his mind to prevent the distraction from affecting his work.

After a recent takeoff from California for the long flight across the Pacific, that was all his first officer wanted to talk about. The captain said he snapped back: "You know what, can we not talk about United Airlines? All it does is cause me frustration and anger and there's nothing I can do about it. It churns my stomach."

So the two, flying in one of the world's most automated, advanced airplanes, talked about a hobby they had in common: flying single-engine planes on their days off.

The dissatisfaction at the top has not changed some basics of the field: young people still dream of flying, and people who fly small planes still aspire to fly bigger ones. Legions of laid-off pilots hope to be hired back, even at reduced pay levels.

"They must love it," said Arnold I. Barnett, a professor of management science at the Sloan School of Management at the Massachusetts Institute of Technology. He said airline pilots were reacting with more fortitude than other professionals might in the same circumstances.

"I cannot fathom how faculty would react if M.I.T. abolished tenure, increased reaching loads and cut salaries by 35 percent because market conditions had changed," he said.

But senior airline pilots, in dozens of interviews, spoke about feeling depressed and struggling not to let it affect their performance.

Academics have noticed a change. "The pilots are not a happy group right now," said Paul S. Fischbeck, a professor of engineering and public policy at Carnegie Mellon University in Pittsburgh.

Dr. Fischbeck, who flew in the Navy and has colleagues who went on to fly for the airlines, said that the change in financial circumstances and job security were good reasons to be unhappy.

But Dr. Fischbeck and others pointed out that the industry culture is such that pilots must face the hardship on their own. Other workers with health plans might seek professional counseling. With pilots licensed by the F.A.A., however, "as soon as you sign up for it, it's on your record, and you're toast."

A US Airways pilot echoed that sentiment: "If it gets reported to the F.A.A., you can forget it, you're not coming back to work, until you go through a lot. The system requires us to deal with it ourselves. That makes it very difficult to go through what we just went through."

Maxine E. Lubner, director of the Aviation Institute of York College, at the City University of New York, said that eroding morale, along with problems like "the distraction of not knowing where your pension is," could not help safety.

Neither could working longer hours, which pilots for many major airlines are now doing because of contract concessions both in the number of hours flown and the number of hours they can be made to wait on the ground between flights. Some are also flying more hours to offset their pay losses.

"I would say morale and attitude are all in that mix," Dr. Lubner said. The morale effect is probably small, she said, but "we know fatigue in itself will create poor attitude and lack of motivation and irritability."

"And there's no question that something that's a distraction is a safety threat," she said.

But she agreed there was no empirical evidence supporting that theory. Statistically, the airlines are in one of their safest periods ever, with about one fatal accident for every 15 million flights.

"With the economic turbulence that's being experienced by U.S. carriers, bankruptcy, the price of oil on every page, it's a testament to the aviation industry stakeholders and the U.S. government that we are reaching those safety levels despite enormous challenges," said Marion C. Blakey, the F.A.A. administrator, in a speech to an aviation safety conference that her agency organized last fall.

There are some warning signs, however. NASA recently told the F.A.A. of numerous reports of errors by ground personnel, a category of worker that has had heavy turnover. It also warned of reports of planes loading too little fuel.

A Northwest pilot described his own forgetfulness. "There are certain things I'm supposed to do to set up my part of the cockpit," he said. "We do the stuff first, then go back with the checklist and double-check it," he said. And in double-checking, he once found a set of switches he was certain he had set, but had not. "I though I had turned those on," he recalled thinking. "I hadn't, I just wasn't as sharp. I'd lost my edge."

Airline executives say they do not know how to measure the effect of morale. At US Airways, Carlo Bertolini, a spokesman, said, "No one's going to deny that US Airways employees have been through a tough time, with layoffs, changes in work rules and steps lowering costs. A lot of these sacrifices came from employees."

But "we all have a stake in the safety of the airline," he added. "We're definitely confident that all employees always have safety at the top of their mind."

Pilots say the same but add that the change in schedules often means more fatigue. "You can feel yourself getting to a point where you're beginning to make more little mistakes," a senior captain at US Airways said.

"Most of the mistakes are caught very quickly, and most are very minor errors," he said. But "at that level of fatigue, after weeks or months of this without a break, it's easy to make a major mistake."

Not everyone agrees that the longer working schedule is a problem.

"It's hard for me to feel sorry for them," said Capt. Jeffrey R. Hefner, the safety chairman of the union that represents pilots at Southwest Airlines, who have always flown longer hours than pilots at older airlines.

"They're a bunch of spoiled brats," he said. "Historically, this has been a really cushy job once you get to the majors. You make a lot of money and you don't have to fly a lot. But there had to be a market balancing at some point."

Questions for Discussion

1. In what ways are pilots intrinsically motivated and extrinsically motivated by their work?
2. Why might pilots' levels of motivation be declining from a need theory perspective?
3. Why might pilots' levels of motivation be declining from an expectancy theory perspective?
4. Why might pilots' levels of motivation be declining from an organizational justice perspective?

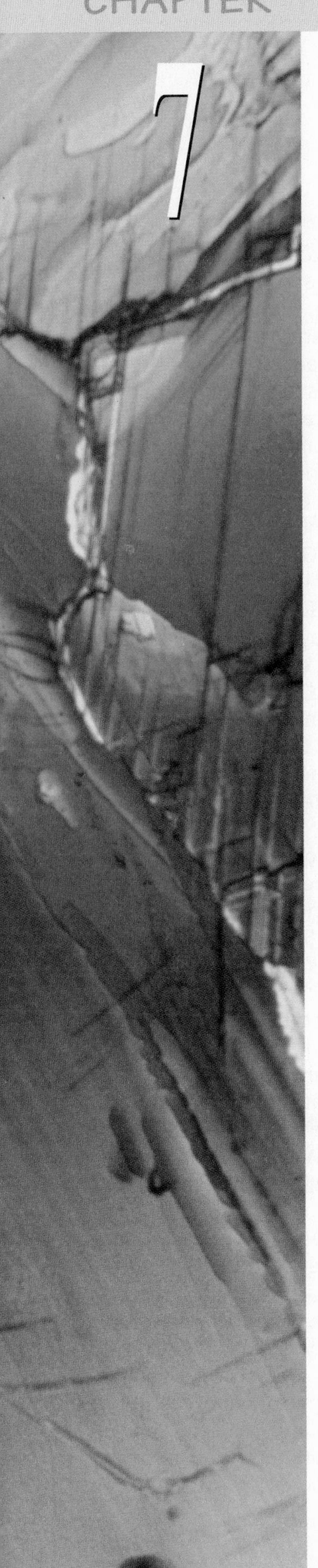

7

CREATING A MOTIVATING WORK SETTING

Learning Objectives

After studying this chapter, you should be able to:

- Appreciate the advantages and disadvantages of the scientific management approach to job design.
- Describe the job characteristics model and its implications for using job design to create a motivating work setting.
- Understand the implications of the social information processing model.
- Appreciate how and why organizational objectives can motivate employees.
- Describe goal setting theory and the kinds of goals that contribute to a motivating work setting.

Opening Case

MOTIVATING EMPLOYEES AT GOOGLE

How can organizations create a motivating work setting?

Google is the largest search engine on the Internet today and the most popular search engine in not only the United States but also in Argentina, Brazil, Australia, Belgium, Denmark, France, the United Kingdom, Germany, India, Italy, Mexico, Spain, Sweden, Switzerland, and Canada.[1] Its popularity is due, in no small part, to Google, Inc.'s steadfast objective to provide the best search results possible to its users and "organize the world's information."[2] Google's organizational objective dictates that users' experiences are paramount. Consequently, employees are continually collecting data on what users like and don't like and what will improve that experience.[3] Over 5,600 people work at Google, many of them top-notch engineers.[4] Creating algorithms that make searches on Goggle the most efficient in the industry while keeping costs low is a consuming passion for Google's employees (known as Googlers).[5]

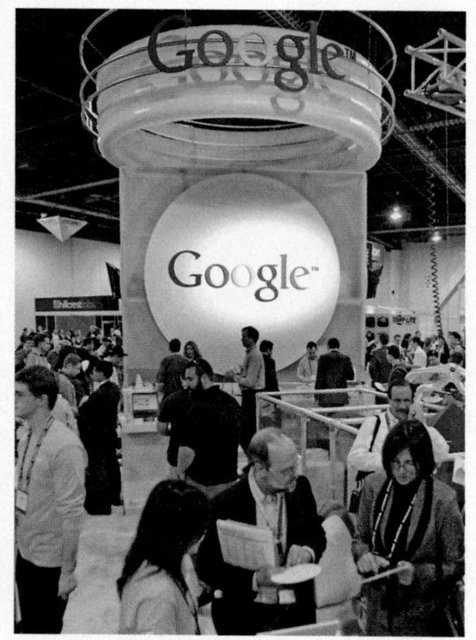

A general view of the google booth at the 2006 International Consumer Electronics Show in Las Vegas. Google was giving prizes to show-goers who correctly answered a quiz.

Google's founders, Larry Page and Sergey Brin, who met as graduate students in computer science at Stanford University in 1995, collaborated on a search engine called BackRub back in 1996.[6] They continued to work on the search engine from Larry's dorm room, and in 1998, sought funding to found their own company, Google, Inc. in Menlo Park, CA. The rest has been literal history as Google, now located in the Googleplex in Mountain View, CA, has grown at a phenomenal rate.[7] And Google continues to grow. For example, in the first quarter of 2006, Google's revenues were $2.25 billion (a 79 percent increase over the first quarter of 2005) and earnings for the quarter increased 60 percent over the prior year's quarter to $592.3 million.[8] Google is now a truly global corporation with offices in Europe, Australia, South America, Canada, India, and Korea.[9]

A key ingredient for Google's ongoing success story is the way in which Google creates a motivating work setting for its employees. Fueled by the overarching objective of providing users with the ultimate search, Googlers concentrate on giving users exactly what they want at breakneck speed.[10] To achieve results like these, employees at Google are given the flexibility and autonomy to experiment, take risks, and sometimes fail. They are encouraged to learn from their failures, however, and apply what they've learned to subsequent projects.[11]

Google's engineers are provided with one day a week to work on their own projects that they are highly involved with, and new products such as Google News often emerge from these projects.[12] Managers, including founders Page and Brin, believe that good ideas can be found from anyone anywhere in the company and all Googlers are encouraged to come up with the next big idea. Googlers can post proposals for new projects on a mailing list that circulates throughout the company. Top managers have office hours during which employees can drop in, discuss new ideas and projects, and receive feedback. These projects often call upon a variety of employee skills. For example, Google's international webmaster who comes up with the site's holiday logo translated the whole site into Korean and the chief operations engineer is also a neurosurgeon.[13] Engineers collaborate with each other on their projects and with managers.

While Google has grown exponentially since its founding, it still has an aura of an informal, small company where highly motivated Googlers work on projects to achieve organizational objectives of speed and cost-containment, projects that they have the autonomy to pursue and a sense of ownership to have succeed.[14] Marissa Mayer, Vice President of Search Projects & User Experience, is involved in many of these projects and interfaces between engineers with PhDs and managers with MBAs to ensure that the best projects see the light of day.[15] Mayer, whose office with glass walls is purposely located next to the snack area frequented by engineers and programmers, not only holds office hours for Googlers but also is typically at work from 9 A.M. to midnight and available for engineers to stop by and discuss their ideas. Just as speed is essential to Internet searches, so too is it to new product development, according to Mayer. As she puts it, "I like to launch [products] early and often. That has become my mantra."[16] And having such a mantra is motivational for Googlers as they know their ideas will be listened to and heard and what they are doing is important not only for the company but also for users around the globe.

Overview

Changes in the design of jobs and work processes are dramatically altering the nature of work. Employees are being required to develop and use more skills than ever before. They are also experiencing more autonomy as is the case at Google in the Opening Case.

In Chapter 6, we examined the nature of work motivation and four approaches to understanding motivation in organizations. Building from this foundation, in this chapter we focus on how an organization can create a motivating work setting by the way it designs its jobs and the objectives and goals it sets for its employees.[17] Job design can have a profound effect on employee motivation. The specific goals employees strive for and the more general corporate objectives that an organization pursues over time (such as Google's commitment to organizing information and providing the best and fastest Internet search capabilities for users around the world) are important sources of motivation for employees. In terms of the motivation equation, introduced in Chapter 6 (see Exhibit 6.2) and restated in Exhibit 7.1, job design and goal setting are key factors that motivate employees to contribute inputs to the organization.

Job Design: Early Approaches

JOB DESIGN
The process of linking specific tasks to specific jobs and deciding what techniques, equipment, and procedures should be used to perform those tasks.

Job design is the process of linking specific tasks to specific jobs and deciding what techniques, equipment, and procedures should be used to perform those tasks. The tasks that make up a secretary's job, for example, include answering the telephone, filing, typing letters and reports, and scheduling meetings and appointments. The techniques, equipment, and procedures the secretary uses to accomplish these tasks may include using a personal computer and one or more word-processing software packages to type documents and prepare graphs, using an answering machine to take calls, and keeping a weekly appointment book to schedule and keep track of meetings.

In general, managers try to design jobs to motivate employees to perform well, enjoy their work, and receive the outcomes they deserve. Job design also influences the motivation

EXHIBIT 7.1

Motivation Tools

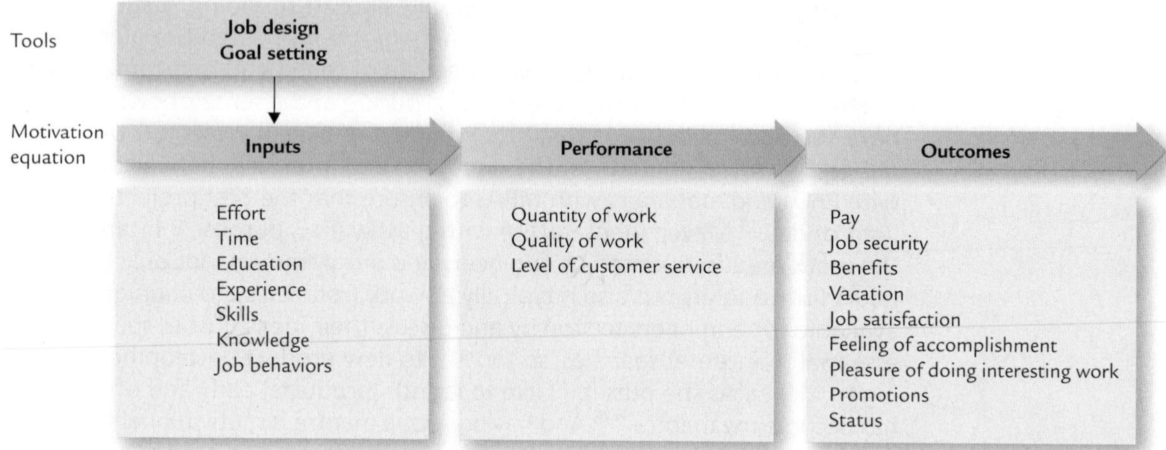

of employees and their input levels (see Exhibit 7.1). When employees are motivated to contribute inputs at a high level (to work harder, more efficiently, and more creatively) and perform their jobs more effectively, organizational effectiveness increases.

In the next sections, we examine scientific management, job enlargement, and job enrichment—three early approaches to job design. Each has implications not only for how *new* jobs should be designed but also for how *existing* jobs can be redesigned to improve motivation and performance. Some of the approaches can be used to design a job so the employee doing it gets more satisfaction from it (discussed in Chapter 3) along with the outcomes (pay, promotion, or other rewards) he or she desires.

Scientific Management

In 1911, Frederick W. Taylor published one of the earliest approaches to job design, *The Principles of Scientific Management*.[18] Taylor was concerned that employees were slacking off and not performing as highly on the job as they should be. **Scientific management**, a set of principles and practices stressing job simplification and specialization, was developed by Taylor to increase the performance of individual employees. Taylor started with this premise: There is one best way to perform any job, and management's responsibility is to determine what that way is. He believed that following the principles of job simplification and specialization would help managers make this determination. **Job simplification** involves breaking up the work that needs to be done into the smallest identifiable tasks. Jobs are then designed around these narrow tasks. **Job specialization** results when employees are assigned to perform small, simple tasks and focus exclusively on them.

SCIENTIFIC MANAGEMENT
A set of principles and practices designed to increase the performance of individual employees by stressing job simplification and specialization.

JOB SIMPLIFICATION
The breaking up of the work that needs to be performed in an organization into the smallest identifiable tasks.

JOB SPECIALIZATION
The assignment of employees to perform small, simple tasks.

Many fast-food restaurants employ the principles of job simplification and specialization. The way food preparers at Subway (the sandwich shop chain) do their jobs illustrates the principles of simplification and specialization. One person puts the meat on a sandwich, another person puts on the trimmings (like lettuce, tomatoes, and condiments), and another person collects the money from customers. Because of simplification and specialization, Subway restaurants can make a large number of "custom" sandwiches in a short period. The effectiveness of this job design is easily illustrated by watching what happens when one or more employees are unavailable (because, for example, they are on the telephone or are replenishing supplies). When this occurs, the other Subway employees must do their own work plus the work of the temporarily absent employee(s). As a result, it generally takes much longer to serve a customer. A cashier who fills in for the "trimmings" employee, for example, must wash his or her hands after handling a customer's money before trimming another sandwich (in keeping with Subway's cleanliness policy).

Frederick W. Taylor, a pioneer in job design, envisioned the specialization of Henry Ford's first automobile assembly line. Taylor's time and motion studies led to dramatic productivity improvements, but they were criticized for dehumanizing employees.

TIME AND MOTION STUDIES
Studies that reveal exactly how long it takes to perform a task and the best way to perform it.

Advocates of scientific management conduct time and motion studies to determine the one best way to perform each narrow task. **Time and motion studies** reveal exactly how long it takes to perform a task and the best way to perform it—for example, what body movements are most efficient for performing the task. Employees are then instructed in precisely how to perform their tasks.

Employees at Subway, for example, learn exactly how to slice the roll for a sandwich, how to place the meat on a sandwich, and how to add the trimmings. Because these tasks are simple, employees quickly learn to perform them correctly. Because managers know (from time and motion studies) exactly how long it should take to perform each task, they know how much output, on average, they can expect from an employee. Subway knows, for example, how many sandwiches can be made and how many customers can be served in each shop per hour. By clearly specifying exactly what an employee should do on the job, exactly how a task should be done, and exactly how long the task should take, scientific management ensures that employee inputs result in acceptable performance levels.

In the scientific management approach to job design, pay is the principal outcome used to motivate employees to contribute their inputs. Pay is often linked closely to performance by a piece-rate pay system in which employees are paid a set amount of money for performing a certain number of tasks. For example, an employee might be paid $5 for every eight sound mufflers that he or she attaches to computer printers.

Scientific management has been instrumental in helping organizations improve employee effectiveness and productivity. The early assembly lines that made the mass production of affordable automobiles possible reflected scientific management principles. These principles still guide some mass-production assembly lines in use today. Eventually, however, some disadvantages of designing jobs according to the principles of scientific management became apparent. Many problems stemmed from the fact that employees are intelligent human beings who have the capacity to be intrinsically as well as extrinsically motivated and who also like to have control over their work.

Recall from Chapter 6 that *extrinsically* motivated behavior is behavior performed to acquire rewards (such as pay) or to avoid punishment, and *intrinsically* motivated behavior is behavior performed for its own sake. Employees who are intrinsically motivated enjoy performing their jobs; the motivation comes from the work itself. However, scientific management focuses exclusively on extrinsic motivation and ignores the important role of intrinsic motivation. This narrow focus results in several disadvantages for employees and the organizations trying to motivate them.

First, employees may feel that they have lost control over their work behaviors. With its careful, exact specification of how a simple, repetitive, specialized task should be performed, and how long it should take, scientific management leaves no room for employees to feel that they have control over their actions. Second, employees tend to feel as if they are part of a machine and are being treated as such. Because they view their work as depersonalized, meaningless, and monotonous, their job satisfaction may decline. This decline, in turn, can lead to lower work-life quality and potential increases in absenteeism and turnover. Finally, employees have no opportunity to develop and acquire new skills with job simplification and specification. These three drawbacks are part of the reason Subway and other fast-food restaurants experience high turnover levels: Employees leave to find more interesting and demanding work.

Job Enlargement and Job Enrichment

JOB ENLARGEMENT
Increasing the number of tasks an employee performs but keeping all of the tasks at the same level of difficulty and responsibility; also called horizontal job loading.

The first widespread attempt to counteract some of the disadvantages related to the scientific management approach was job enlargement, a movement that started in the late 1940s and continued through the 1950s.[19] **Job enlargement** involves increasing the number of tasks an employee performs but keeping all of the tasks at the same level of difficulty and responsibility. Job enlargement is often referred to as *horizontal job loading* because the content of a job is expanded, but the difficulty remains constant. For example, one might enlarge the job of assembly-line workers who attach the paper tray to a computer printer by also requiring them to attach the sound muffler and the toner cartridge. The employees now do more tasks of equal difficulty with no increase in the level of responsibility.

Proponents of job enlargement thought that increasing the number of tasks performed on a job might increase intrinsic motivation. The job enlargement approach to job design was put into effect at a number of companies including IBM, Maytag, and AT&T.[20] Some companies reported increased employee productivity and satisfaction from job enlargement, but at other companies the effects were not as clear-cut. This mixed success is not surprising because jobs that are "enlarged" may still be simple and limited with regard to how much control and variety employees have. Even though they no longer do one simple task, employees performing several simple tasks (each of which may quickly lose its appeal) may still be bored.

JOB ENRICHMENT
Increasing an employee's responsibility and control over his or her work; also called vertical job loading.

In response to the limited effects of job enlargement on work motivation, job enrichment emerged in the 1960s. **Job enrichment** involves designing jobs to provide opportunities for employee growth by giving employees more responsibility and control over their work. Job enrichment is often referred to as *vertical job loading* because employees are given some of the responsibilities that used to belong to their supervisors, such as planning for how to go about completing a project or checking the quality of one's work. Herzberg's motivator-hygiene theory (discussed in Chapter 3) was a driving force in the movement to enrich jobs. Recall that Herzberg's theory suggested that employees' motivator needs are satisfied by things such as having autonomy on the job and being responsible for one's work, and that employees are satisfied with their jobs only when these needs are met.

Managers can enrich jobs in a variety of ways. The following are some of the most common:[21]

- *Allow employees to plan their own work schedules.* For example, when possible, allow a secretary to determine when he or she does various tasks, such as typing, filing, and setting up meetings, and how much time to allow for each activity.
- *Allow employees to decide how the work should be performed.* If a manager wants a secretary to prepare a new company brochure or filing system, the manager may let the secretary decide how to design the brochure or filing system.
- *Allow employees to check their own work.* Instead of insisting that the secretary give a draft of the brochure to the manager to check for errors, the manager holds the secretary responsible for producing a top-quality, error-free brochure.

- *Allow employees to learn new skills.* A secretary may be given the opportunity to learn bookkeeping and some basic accounting procedures.

Like job enlargement, job enrichment is aimed at increasing intrinsic motivation so that employees enjoy their jobs more. When employees are given more responsibility, they are more likely to feel competent and like they have control over their own work behaviors. Job enrichment can also lead to efficiency gains, as indicated in the accompanying OB Today.

OB Today

Cutting Costs and Increasing Efficiency at General Mills

When Randy G. Darcy, Chief Technical Officer of General Mills, set out to dramatically reduce costs and improve efficiency at plants making Cheerios cereal, Betty Crocker cake mixes, and Hamburger Helper, he realized that much of his cost-cutting efforts would revolve around redesigning jobs.[22] As part of this effort, he enriched employees' jobs by making them responsible for thinking of ways to do their jobs more efficiently.

Darcy and other General Mills employees subsequently studied all kinds of different work groups ranging from U.S. SWAT teams and Air Force mechanics to mountain-climbing teams. By studying all kinds of high-performing, efficient groups and organizations, they hope to find new ways to lower costs at General Mills.[23] Being challenged to think about new and better ways to do their jobs has, in itself, been job enriching.

Studies of NASCAR teams helped food manufacturer General Mills speed up food manufacturing. General Mills employees used the NASCAR studies to figure out how to quickly change products on their assembly lines.

For example, by studying how racing car pit crews at NASCAR change tires in split seconds, General Mills employees figured out how to cut the amount of time it takes factories making Betty Crocker mixes to switch from one kind of mix to another. The employees managed to cut the process down from 4.5 hours to just 12 minutes, resulting in real cost savings and increases in efficiency. Essentially, they realized that by replacing traditional bolts with bolts that only need to be turned one quarter and by equipping employees with tool boxes containing all the equipment they need to change over a production line, what was once a slow and tedious process could be accomplished in less than 15 minutes. Efficiency gains like these are essential if Darcy is to reach his goal of dramatically cutting costs at General Mills.[24] Thus far, he has appeared to be successful and he was recently named Executive Vice President overseeing Worldwide Supply Chain Operations, Engineering Technology, R&D, and Quality and Regulatory Operations.[25]

Not all employees, however, want the additional responsibility that job enrichment brings, and it can sometimes have disadvantages for the organization as a whole. Enriching some jobs can be expensive for an organization and may be impossible to do. Enriching other jobs may result in less efficiency. One of the reasons why Subway shops are able to make large numbers of customized sandwiches is because of job simplification and specialization. Enriching the jobs of Subway employees might increase the time it takes to serve customers, an outcome that would reduce organizational effectiveness.

Research evidence on the effects of job enrichment has been mixed. Although employees seem to be more satisfied with enriched jobs, it is not clear whether employees with enriched jobs are actually more motivated and perform at higher levels.

Job Design: The Job Characteristics Model

The job enlargement and job enrichment movements came about in part because of some of the negative effects observed when jobs were designed according to the principles of scientific management. Both movements attempted to increase employees' levels of intrinsic motivation to perform their jobs, in the hope that employees who found their jobs more interesting and meaningful would be more motivated to perform at higher levels and be more satisfied. Satisfied employees would mean less turnover and absenteeism. The **job characteristics model** proposed by Richard Hackman and Greg Oldham in the 1970s was built on these early approaches but went further.[26] Based on the work of A. N. Turner and P. R. Lawrence, Hackman and Oldham attempted to identify exactly which job characteristics contribute to intrinsically motivating work and what the consequences of these characteristics are.[27]

JOB CHARACTERISTICS MODEL
An approach to job design that aims to identify characteristics that make jobs intrinsically motivating and the consequences of those characteristics.

The job characteristics model is one of the most popular approaches to job design. Hackman and Oldham sought to provide a detailed and accurate account of the effects of job design on motivation, performance, job satisfaction, and other important aspects of organizational behavior. Like the job enlargement and enrichment approaches, the job characteristics model focuses on what makes jobs intrinsically motivating. When employees are intrinsically motivated, Hackman and Oldham reasoned, good performance makes them feel good. This feeling motivates them to continue to perform at a high level, so good performance becomes self-reinforcing.[28]

Core Job Dimensions

According to the job characteristics model, any job has five core dimensions that affect intrinsic motivation: skill variety, task identity, task significance, autonomy, and feedback. The higher a job scores on each dimension, the higher the level of intrinsic motivation.

SKILL VARIETY
The extent to which a job requires an employee to use different skills, abilities, or talents.

1. **Skill variety** is the extent to which a job requires an employee to use a number of different skills, abilities, or talents. Employees are more intrinsically motivated by jobs that are high on skill variety.
   High variety: In the opening case, we described how Googlers use a variety of skills to perform their jobs. Today, even factory jobs, which traditionally have had relatively low levels of variety, are increasing in skill variety due to the prevalence of sophisticated and computer-based technology. Factory employees now use a variety of skills, including computer skills, mathematics, statistical control, and quality control, in addition to skills related to whatever they are producing, such as metal products.
   Low variety: The jobs of employees in a Subway restaurant have a low level of skill variety. All the employees need to know is how to slice rolls and put meat and trimmings on them.

This carpenter has a high level of task identity. He makes furniture like this chair from start to finish.

2. **Task identity** is the extent to which a job involves performing a whole piece of work from its beginning to its end. The higher the level of task identity, the more intrinsically motivated an employee is likely to be.
   High identity: At Google, engineers and programmers working on new projects have a high level of task identity, as they are responsible for their projects from start to finish. Similarly, a carpenter who makes custom wood cabinets and furniture has high task identity. The carpenter designs and makes cabinets and furniture from start to finish.
   Low identity: For a factory worker assembling computer printers, task identity is low if the worker only attaches the paper tray.
3. **Task significance** is the extent to which a job has an impact on the lives or work of other people in or out of the organization. Employees are more likely to enjoy performing their jobs when they think their jobs are important in the wider scheme of things. Recall from the opening case how Googlers view their work as highly significant for users around the globe.
   High significance: Medical researchers and doctors experience high levels of task significance because their work promotes the health and well-being of people.
   Low significance: The job of an employee who dries cars off after the cars go through a car wash has low task significance because the employee doesn't think it has much impact on other people.
4. **Autonomy** is the degree to which a job allows an employee the freedom and independence to schedule work and decide how to carry it out. High autonomy generally contributes to high levels of intrinsic motivation.
   High autonomy: From the opening case, it is clear that employees at Google have high autonomy.
   Low autonomy: An employee at the Internal Revenue Service who opens tax returns and sorts them into different categories has a low level of autonomy because she or he must work at a steady, predetermined pace and follow strict guidelines for sorting the returns.
5. **Feedback** is the extent to which performing a job provides an employee with clear information about his or her effectiveness. Receiving feedback has a positive impact on intrinsic motivation.
   High feedback: Computer-based technology in factories often gives factory workers immediate feedback on how well they are doing, and this information contributes to their intrinsic motivation.
   Low feedback: An employee who reshelves books in the New York City Public Library rarely receives feedback as he or she performs the job and is often unaware of when he or she makes a mistake or does a particularly good job.

TASK IDENTITY
The extent to which a job involves performing a whole piece of work from its beginning to its end.

TASK SIGNIFICANCE
The extent to which a job has an impact on the lives or work of other people in or out of the organization.

AUTONOMY
The degree to which a job allows an employee the freedom and independence to schedule work and decide how to carry it out.

FEEDBACK
The extent to which performing a job provides an employee with clear information about his or her effectiveness.

According to the job characteristics model, when managers consider the five core dimensions of a job, it is important for them to realize that *employees'* perceptions of the core dimensions (not the actual reality or a manager's perceptions) are the key determinants of intrinsic motivation. As we discussed in Chapter 4, two people can watch the same movie or take part in the same group meeting and have very different perceptions of what they have experienced. One person might hate a movie that another person loved, and one group member might perceive that a group meeting was a noisy, incomprehensible, free-for-all while another perceives that a reasonable and lively discussion took place. In a like manner, two employees may have the same job yet perceive it differently. For example, one employee might perceive the job to be high on task significance while another perceives it to be low on this dimension.

The Motivating Potential Score

To measure employees' perceptions of their jobs on each of the core dimension, Hackman and Oldham developed the *Job Diagnostic Survey*. The scales used to measure the five dimensions are shown in Exhibit 7.2. Once an employee completes each of these

MOTIVATING POTENTIAL SCORE (MPS)
A measure of the overall potential of a job to foster intrinsic motivation.

scales for his or her job, it is possible to compute the job's motivating potential score. The **motivating potential score (MPS)** is a measure of the overall potential of a job to foster intrinsic motivation. MPS is equal to the average of the first three core characteristics (skill variety, task identity, and task significance) multiplied by autonomy and feedback, as indicated in Exhibit 7.2. Each of the three core dimensions is assigned a score ranging from a low of 1 to a high of 7. The lowest MPS possible for a job is 1 (1 × 1 × 1), and the highest MPS possible is 343 (7 × 7 × 7). The lowest actual MPS score that Hackman and Oldham observed was 7 for a typist in an overflow typing pool; the typist waited at her typewriter all day for the occasional jobs she received when the regular pool got overloaded. The highest score was 300 for a management consultant. Hackman and Oldham suggest that an average motivating potential score for jobs in U.S. corporations is around 128.[29]

The *Job Diagnostic Survey* can be used to identify the core dimensions that are most in need of redesign in order to increase a job's motivating potential score and, thus, an employee's intrinsic motivation. Exhibit 7.3 shows a survey profile for a gardener who

EXHIBIT 7.2

Measures of the Five Core Characteristics from Hackman and Oldman's *Job Diagnostic Survey*

Skill variety

1. How much *variety* is there in your job? That is, to what extent does the job require you to do many different things at work, using a variety of your skills and talents?

1	2	3	4	5	6	7
Very little; the job requires me to do the same routine things over and over again.			Moderate variety			Very much; the job requires me to do many different things, using a number of different skills and talents.

2. The job requires me to use a number of complex or high-level skills.

How accurate is the statement in describing your job?

1	2	3	4	5	6	7
Very inaccurate	Mostly inaccurate	Slightly inaccurate	Uncertain	Slightly accurate	Mostly accurate	Very accurate

3. The job is quite simple and repetitive.*

How accurate is the statement in describing your job?

1	2	3	4	5	6	7
Very inaccurate	Mostly inaccurate	Slightly inaccurate	Uncertain	Slightly accurate	Mostly accurate	Very accurate

Task identity

1. To what extent does your job involve doing a *"whole" and identifiable piece of work?* That is, is the job a complete piece of work that has an obvious beginning and end? Or is it only a small part of the overall piece of work, which is finished by other people or by automatic machines?

1	2	3	4	5	6	7
My job is only a tiny part of the overall piece of work: the results of my activities cannot be seen in the final product or service.			My job is a moderate-sized "chunk" of the overall piece of work; my own contribution can be seen in the final outcome.			My job involves doing the whole piece of work, from start to finish; the results of my activities are easily seen in the final product or service.

2. The job provides me with the chance to completely finish the pieces of work I begin.

How accurate is the statement in describing your job?

1	2	3	4	5	6	7
Very inaccurate	Mostly inaccurate	Slightly inaccurate	Uncertain	Slightly accurate	Mostly accurate	Very accurate

3. The job is arranged so that I do not have the chance to do an entire piece of work from beginning to end.*

How accurate is the statement in describing your job?

1	2	3	4	5	6	7
Very inaccurate	Mostly inaccurate	Slightly inaccurate	Uncertain	Slightly accurate	Mostly accurate	Very accurate

Task significance

1. In general, how significant or important is your job? That is, are the results of your work likely to significantly affect the lives or well-being of other people?

1	2	3	4	5	6	7
Not very significant; the outcomes of my work are not likely to have important effects on other people.			Moderately significant			Highly significant; the outcomes of my work can affect other people in very important ways.

2. This job is one where a lot of people can be affected by how well the work gets done.

How accurate is the statement in describing your job?

1	2	3	4	5	6	7
Very inaccurate	Mostly inaccurate	Slightly inaccurate	Uncertain	Slightly accurate	Mostly accurate	Very accurate

3. The job itself is not very significant or important in the broader scheme of things.*

How accurate is the statement in describing your job?

1	2	3	4	5	6	7
Very inaccurate	Mostly inaccurate	Slightly inaccurate	Uncertain	Slightly accurate	Mostly accurate	Very accurate

Autonomy

1. How much *autonomy* is there in your job? That is, to what extent does your job permit you to decide on *your own* how to go about doing your work?

1	2	3	4	5	6	7
Very little; the job gives me almost no personal "say" about how and when the work is done.			Moderate autonomy; many things are standardized and not under my control, but I can make some decisions about the work.			Very much; the job gives me almost complete responsibility for deciding how and when the work is done.

2. The job gives me considerable opportunity for independence and freedom in how I do the work.

How accurate is the statement in describing your job?

1	2	3	4	5	6	7
Very inaccurate	Mostly inaccurate	Slightly inaccurate	Uncertain	Slightly accurate	Mostly accurate	Very accurate

3. The job denies me any chance to use my personal initiative or judgment in carrying out the work.*

How accurate is the statement in describing your job?

1	2	3	4	5	6	7
Very inaccurate	Mostly inaccurate	Slightly inaccurate	Uncertain	Slightly accurate	Mostly accurate	Very accurate

(Continued)

Feedback

1. To what extent does *doing the job itself* provide you with information about your work performance? That is, does the actual *work itself* provide clues about how well you are doing—aside from any "feedback" coworkers or supervisors may provide?

1	2	3	4	5	6	7
Very little; the job itself is set up so I could work forever without finding out how well I am doing.		Moderately; sometimes doing the job provides "feedback" to me; sometimes it does not.		Very much; the job is set up so that I get almost constant "feedback" as I work about how well I am doing.		

2. Just doing the work required by the job provides many chances for me to figure out how well I am doing.

How accurate is the statement in describing your job?

1	2	3	4	5	6	7
Very inaccurate	Mostly inaccurate	Slightly inaccurate	Uncertain	Slightly accurate	Mostly accurate	Very accurate

3. The job itself provides very few clues about whether or not I am performing well.*

How accurate is the statement in describing your job?

1	2	3	4	5	6	7
Very inaccurate	Mostly inaccurate	Slightly inaccurate	Uncertain	Slightly accurate	Mostly accurate	Very accurate

Scoring: Responses to the three items for each core characteristic are averaged to yield an overall score for that characteristic.

Items marked with an "*" should be scored as follows: 1 = 7; 2 = 6; 3 = 5; 5 = 3; 6 = 2; 7 = 1

$$\text{Motivating potential score} = \left(\frac{\text{Skill variety} + \text{Task identity} + \text{Task significance}}{3}\right) \times \text{Autonomy} \times \text{Feedback}$$

Source: J. R. Hackman and G. R. Oldham, *Work Redesign*, copyright © 1980 Addison-Wesley Publishing Co., Inc., Reading, Mass. Reprinted with permission.

works for a landscape company. The gardener is a member of a three-person crew that provides landscape services to residential and commercial customers. The crew is headed by a landscape supervisor who assigns individual tasks (such as cutting grass, preparing flower beds, or planting trees) to crew members at each job site. As indicated in Figure 7.3, the gardener's levels of task identity and autonomy are especially low and should be the main focus of any redesign efforts. Currently, the supervisor assigns very specific and unrelated tasks to each crew member: At a particular site, the gardener might plant some flowers, cut some borders, and plant a tree. The supervisor also tells the crew members exactly how to do each task: Put the daisies here and the marigolds around the border.

To increase task identity and autonomy, the supervisor could change the way he assigns tasks to crew members: The supervisor could make each crew member responsible for a major aspect of a particular landscaping job and, after providing some basic guidelines, give the crew member the autonomy to decide how to accomplish this aspect of the job. On one job, for example, the gardener might be responsible for preparing and arranging all of the flower beds (resulting in high task identity). After the supervisor tells the gardener about the customer's likes and dislikes, the gardener would be free to design the beds as he sees fit and work on them in the order he wants (resulting in high

EXHIBIT 7.3

Sample Job Diagnostic Survey Profiles

Before job redesign
Profile of a gardener
MPS + [(3.5 + 1 + 4)/3] × 1.2 × 6 = 20.4

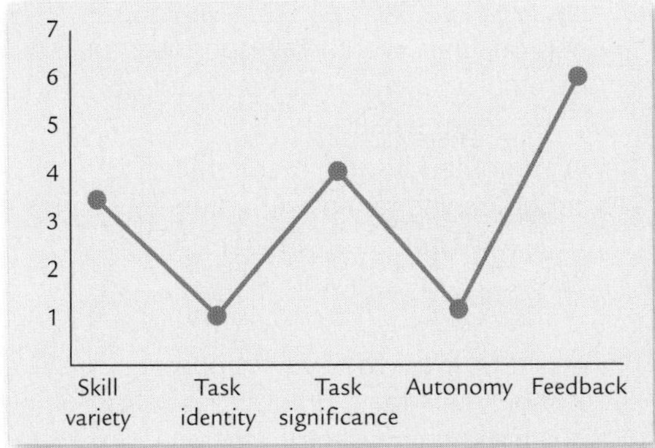

After job redesign
Profile of a gardener
MPS = [(3.5 + 5 + 4)/3] × 4 × 6 = 100

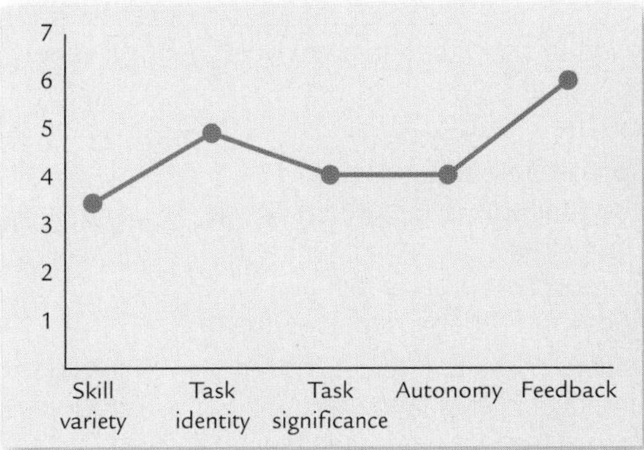

autonomy). As a result of these changes, the MPS of the gardener's job would rise from 20.4 to 100 (see Exhibit 7.3).

Jobs can be redesigned in a variety of ways to increase levels of the five core dimensions and the MPS. Common ways to redesign jobs are described in Exhibit 7.4.

Critical Psychological States

Hackman and Oldham proposed that the five core job dimensions contribute to three critical psychological states that determine how employees react to the design of their jobs: experienced meaningfulness of the work, experienced responsibility for work outcomes, and knowledge of results.

First, employees who perceive that their jobs are high in skill variety, task identity, and task significance attain the psychological state of experienced meaningfulness of the work. **Experienced meaningfulness of the work** is the degree to which employees feel their jobs are important, worthwhile, and meaningful as do many employees at Google in the opening case. The second critical psychological state, **experienced responsibility for work outcomes**, is the extent to which employees feel they are personally responsible or accountable for their job performance. This psychological state stems from the core dimension of autonomy. The third critical psychological state, **knowledge of results**, is the degree to which employees know how well they perform their jobs on a continuous basis; it stems from the core dimension of feedback. Exhibit 7.5 summarizes the relationships among the five core dimensions, the three critical psychological states, and work and personal outcomes (discussed next).

EXPERIENCED MEANINGFULNESS OF THE WORK
The degree to which employees feel their jobs are important, worthwhile, and meaningful.

EXPERIENCED RESPONSIBILITY FOR WORK OUTCOMES
The extent to which employees feel personally responsible or accountable for their job performance.

KNOWLEDGE OF RESULTS
The degree to which employees know how well they perform their jobs on a continuous basis.

Work and Personal Outcomes

Hackman and Oldham further proposed that the critical psychological states result in four key outcomes for employees and their organizations: high intrinsic motivation, high job performance, high job satisfaction, and low absenteeism and turnover (see Exhibit 7.5).

1. *High intrinsic motivation.* One of the major outcomes of job design is intrinsic motivation. When jobs are high on the five core dimensions, employees experience the three critical psychological states and are intrinsically motivated. When

EXHIBIT 7.4

Ways to Redesign Jobs to Increase MPS

Change Made	Core Job Dimensions Increased	Example
Combine tasks so that an employee is responsible for doing a piece of work from start to finish.	Skill variety Task identity Task significance	A production worker is responsible for assembling a whole bicycle, not just attaching the handlebars.
Group tasks into natural work units so that employees are responsible for performing an entire set of important organizational activities rather than just part of them.	Task identity Task significance	A computer programmer handles all programming requests from one division instead of one type of request from several different divisions.
Allow employees to interact with customers or clients, and make employees responsible for managing these relationships and satisfying customers.	Skill variety Autonomy Feedback	A truck driver who delivers photocopiers not only sets them up but also trains customers in how to use them, handles customer billing, and responds to customer complaints.
Vertically load jobs so that employees have more control over their work activities and higher levels of responsibility.	Autonomy	A corporate marketing analyst not only prepares marketing plans and reports but also decides when to update and revise them, checks them for errors, and presents them to upper management.
Open feedback channels so that employees know how they are performing their jobs.	Feedback	In addition to knowing how many claims he handles per month, an insurance adjustor receives his clients' responses to follow-up questionnaires that his company uses to measure client satisfaction.

Source: Based on J. R. Hackman, "Work Redesign," in J. R. Hackman and J. L. Suttle, eds., *Improving Life at Work* (Santa Monica, CA: Goodyear, 1976).

intrinsic motivation is high, employees enjoy performing a job for its own sake. Good performance makes employees feel good, and this positive feeling further motivates them to continue to perform at a high level. Poor performance makes employees feel bad, but this feeling may motivate them to try to perform at a high level. In other words, because good performance is self-reinforcing (performance is its own reward), the motivation to perform well comes from inside the employee rather than from an external source like praise from a supervisor or the promise of pay.

2. *High job performance.* Jobs high in the five core dimensions, which lead to high levels of the three critical psychological states, motivate employees to perform at a high level.
3. *High job satisfaction.* Hackman and Oldham reasoned that employees are likely to be more satisfied with their jobs when the critical psychological states are high because they will have more opportunities for personal growth and development on the job.
4. *Low absenteeism and turnover.* When employees enjoy performing their jobs, Hackman and Oldham reasoned, they will be less likely to be absent or quit. (Also, recall from Chapter 3 that satisfied employees are less likely to be absent or quit.)

EXHIBIT 7.5

The Job Characteristics Model

Source: Adapted from J. R. Hackman and G. R. Oldham, *Work Redesign*, copyright © 1980 Addison-Wesley Publishing Co., Inc., Reading, MA.

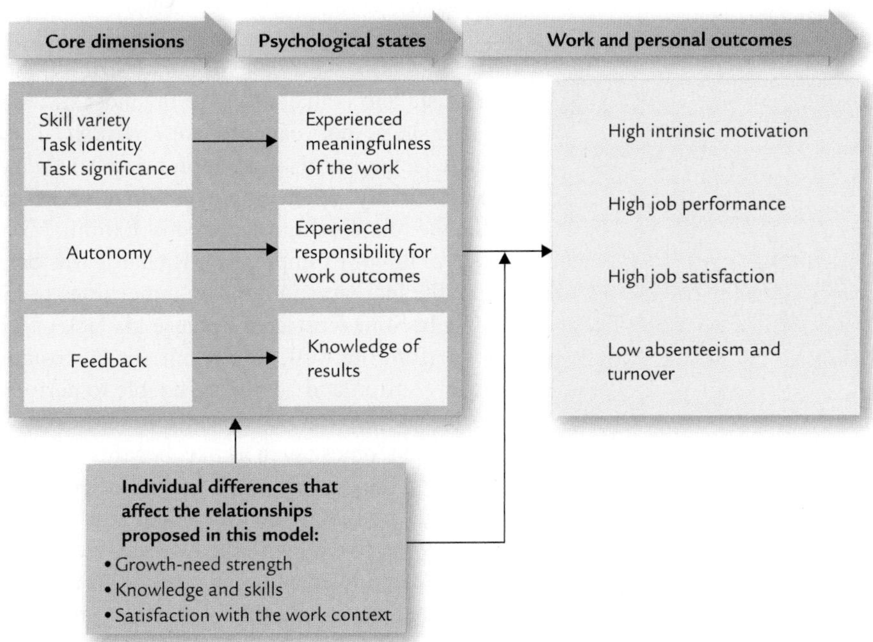

The Role of Individual Differences in Employees' Responses to Job Design

The job characteristics model acknowledges the role that individual differences play in determining how employees respond to the design of their jobs. To see how individual differences interact with job design, let's look at the case of three sales managers, each of whom manages a different department in a department store. Mary Catalano, the manager of women's shoes, is a competent manager, eager to learn more about different aspects of retailing, and is serious about her career. Ron Richards, the manager of men's shoes, is still mastering the responsibilities of his first supervisory position and is having a rough time. Roberta Doran, who has an MBA in marketing, manages the china department. Doran is a competent manager but always complains about how low retailing salaries are compared to salaries she could be making in other organizations.

To increase the motivating potential score of each manager's job, the department store has recently redesigned each job. In the past, a manager's main responsibility was to supervise the sales teams in his or her respective departments. After the redesign, managers also became responsible for purchasing merchandise (an increase in skill variety and task significance), hiring and firing salespeople (also an increase in skill variety and task significance), and the profitability of their respective departments (an increase in task identity, autonomy, and feedback).

As you might expect, Catalano, Richards, and Doran have responded in different ways to their redesigned jobs. The job characteristics model helps explain why employees may respond somewhat differently to an increase in some of the core characteristics of their jobs. It identifies three types of individual differences that affect the relationships between the core dimensions and the psychological states and the relationships between the psychological states and the outcomes (see Exhibit 7.5). The nature of those relationships depends on the growth-need strength, knowledge and skills, and satisfaction with the work context of the individual employee.

1. *Growth-need strength* is the extent to which an individual wants his or her work to contribute to personal growth, learning, and development. When an individual wants his or her job to fuel personal growth, both relationships in the model (core

dimensions–psychological states and psychological states–outcomes) are stronger. Such individuals are expected to be especially responsive both to increased levels in the core dimensions and to the critical psychological states. In our example, Mary Catalano is likely to have the most favorable response to the job redesign because she is most eager to learn what she can about her chosen career.

2. *Knowledge and skills* at an appropriate level enable employees to perform their jobs effectively. When employees do not have the necessary knowledge and skills, the relationships depicted in Exhibit 7.5 may be weak, nonexistent, or even negative. In our example, Ron Richards was barely keeping his head above water before the increases in the core dimensions of his job. Once the job is redesigned, he may become frustrated because his lack of knowledge and skills prevents him from performing well. As a result, his intrinsic motivation and job satisfaction will probably suffer, and he will be unable to perform the more complicated job.
3. *Satisfaction with the work context* describes how satisfied employees are with extrinsic outcomes (such as pay, benefits, job security, and good relationships with coworkers) they receive from their jobs. Hackman and Oldham reasoned that when employees are dissatisfied with their work contexts, they spend much of their energy trying to deal with their dissatisfaction with the contexts and are not able to appreciate and respond to the potential for intrinsic motivation on their jobs.[30] When satisfaction with the work context is high, the relationships depicted in Exhibit 7.4 are expected to be strong; when context satisfaction is low, they are expected to be weak. In our example, Roberta Doran's dissatisfaction with her pay is intensified by the job redesign because she must now take on additional responsibilities but will receive no extra pay. (In terms of the equity theory that we discussed in Chapter 6, Doran sees her outcome/input ratio as being more unfavorable than it was before the job redesign because her inputs are going up but she is not receiving any additional outcomes.) Instead of increasing intrinsic motivation and job satisfaction, the changes in Doran's job make her even more dissatisfied with her pay, and she spends much of her time complaining, thinking about how to improve matters, and looking for another job.

Although the job characteristics model focuses on the relationships between the core job dimensions and psychological states and, in turn, psychological states and outcomes, cultural differences may also have an impact on these relationships. American employees are used to a certain amount of autonomy at work, but employees in other countries like China have traditionally had very little freedom and independence on the job. Chinese employees, for example, may be motivated by core job dimensions such as autonomy, but it might take a little time and effort to convince them that they can really make decisions on their own. This proved to be the case at Minneapolis-based H. B. Fuller Company, which owns and runs a joint venture factory in China that makes adhesives used in products ranging from cardboard boxes to packages of cigarettes. The Chinese employees were originally reluctant to make decisions on their own but now find autonomy to be a source of motivation.[31]

The Research Evidence

Many research studies have tested different components of the job characteristics model since Richard Hackman and Greg Oldham originally proposed it. A recent review of this literature conducted by Fried and Ferris identified almost 200 studies. Fried and Ferris's overall conclusion from their review is that there is modest support for the model.[32] Some of their specific findings are as follows:

1. It is not clear that exactly five dimensions (the five core job dimensions outlined by Hackman and Oldham) best describe the job design of all jobs.
2. Research shows that job dimensions have the most significant effects on intrinsic motivation and on job satisfaction; the effects on actual work behaviors (such as job performance, absenteeism, and turnover) are not as strong.

You're the Management Expert

Redesigning Jobs

Marcia Long has recently been hired as the manager of a group of five employees who process mortgage applications for a bank in West Hempstead, New York. When Long was interviewing for the position, her boss told her there were certain morale problems in the group. This was confirmed during Long's first week on the job when her boss shared the results of an employee attitude survey with her. The employees in her group were very dissatisfied with the work they did—they found it monotonous and boring. They were actually satisfied with extrinsic factors such as pay, benefits, and their coworkers. But the nature of their actual jobs was a real problem. In Long's group there are basically three different kinds of jobs. Two employees focus on the beginning of the process of granting a mortgage; they interact with home buyers, provide them with applications, and make sure their applications are complete with all supporting documents attached. They also run credit and background checks. Two employees focus on the next stage of the process—getting surveys and appraisals conducted, interacting with builders in the case of new homes, and arranging for title searches and a title policy. The remaining employee focuses on arranging closings, making sure everything is complete and in good order beforehand, and interacting with customers once they have been approved for a mortgage. Much to Long's surprise, the employees were about equally dissatisfied with their jobs, regardless of which of the three positions they had. Because you are an expert in OB, Long has come to you for help. She wants to redesign her employees' jobs so that they are more motivated and satisfied, but she has no idea where to start and what to focus on. What should she do?

3. Simply adding the scores for the job characteristics might be a better way of calculating the motivating potential score than using the multiplicative formula proposed by Hackman and Oldham.

The results of this review of the job characteristics model as well as other reviews and studies[33] lead to these overall conclusions: Employees tend to prefer jobs that are high in the five core dimensions in the model, they tend to be more satisfied with these types of jobs, and they have higher levels of intrinsic motivation. Thus, job design can contribute to the quality of work life and may also have some indirect effects on absenteeism and turnover rates. In addition, when the intrinsic motivation of employees is high, they are internally motivated to perform well. As a result, managers do not need to supervise them as closely as they do when their intrinsic motivation is low. The need for less supervision may free up some management time for other activities. Nevertheless, it is not clear that job performance will actually be higher when core dimensions are high.

SOCIAL INFORMATION PROCESSING MODEL
An approach to job design based on the idea that information from other people and employees' own past behaviors influence employees' perceptions of and responses to the design of their jobs.

Job Design: The Social Information Processing Model

The job characteristics model is complemented by another approach to job design: the social information processing model developed in 1978 by Gerald Salancik and Jeffrey Pfeffer.[34] According to the **social information processing model**, factors other than the core dimensions specified by Hackman and Oldham influence how employees respond to the design of their jobs. Salancik and Pfeffer propose that how employees perceive and respond to the design of their jobs is influenced by *social information* (information from other people) and by employees' own past behaviors. The following example highlights the social information processing model.

Joseph Doherty and Robert Cantu have recently received their law degrees from Columbia University and accepted associate positions with the same prestigious Wall Street law firm. They work in different sections of the corporate law department and report to different partners in the firm, for whom they do a lot of research and grunt work. The design of their jobs and the extrinsic outcomes (pay and perks) that they receive are similar. About half of their work is interesting and challenging, and the other half is tedious. They are expected to put in between 60 and 70 hours each week and are well paid, receiving $100,000 a year.

Despite these and other similarities, Doherty's and Cantu's reactions to their jobs are different. Doherty still can't believe his luck at landing a job that is so interesting and challenging. He enjoys his work and thinks nothing of the long hours; his high salary is the icing on the cake. Cantu complains that he didn't spend four years in college and three years in law school (never mind the year spent studying to pass the bar exam) to spend half of his time at work running errands for the partners of a law firm. He resents the fact that he is not able to deal directly with corporate clients (this job is reserved for the partners) even though he is the one who does most of the work on their cases. In his view, his high salary barely makes up for the long working hours.

Doherty is both intrinsically motivated by and very satisfied with his job. The opposite is true for Cantu, whose motivation (both intrinsic and extrinsic) is low and dissatisfaction is high. Why do they have such different reactions to jobs that are similar on most dimensions?

The Role of the Social Environment

Salancik and Pfeffer's social information processing model suggests several reasons why Doherty's and Cantu's reactions are so different. First, the model proposes that the social environment provides employees with information about which aspects of their job design and work outcomes they should pay attention to and which they should ignore. Here, *social environment* means the other individuals with whom employees come into contact at work. An employee's social environment, thus, includes his or her coworkers,

The social environment provides employees with information about how they should evaluate their jobs and work outcomes.

supervisors, and other work group members. Second, the model suggests that the social environment provides employees with information about how they should evaluate their jobs and work outcomes.

Doherty and Cantu belong to two different work groups, each of which has three other associates in it. In Doherty's work group, there is one other new associate and two experienced associates who have been with the firm for several years. Rumor has it that the experienced associates are soon to be promoted to the position of managing attorney. From day one, these two associates impressed on Doherty and the other newcomer to the group the valuable experience they would obtain if they did their jobs well. They acknowledged the dullness of the grunt work but made light of it and instead stressed the considerable autonomy the new associates had in conducting their research. These two associates are very satisfied with their jobs and are intrinsically motivated. Interestingly enough, the long hours expected of all the associates never became a topic of conversation in this group. Doherty's social environment emphasizes the importance of the valuable experience he is obtaining from his job, points out the considerable autonomy he has, and suggests that this job provides high levels of intrinsic motivation and satisfaction.

Cantu's work group is also composed of one other newcomer and two experienced associates who have been with the firm for several years. These two associates, however, do not expect to be promoted, and both are on the job market. They are bitter about their experiences in the law firm and warn Cantu and the other newcomer that they can look forward to being "the personal slaves" of the partners for the next several years. They also complain that most of the work they had to do when they first joined the firm didn't require someone with a law degree and that the long hours were simply inhumane. Given the type of social environment Cantu encountered, his dissatisfaction with his new job and his lack of intrinsic and extrinsic motivation are hardly surprising. If two seasoned veterans evaluate the job so negatively, why should he think any differently?

The different social environments that Doherty and Cantu encounter cause them to focus on different aspects and outcomes of their jobs and how they should evaluate these factors.

CONTINGENT WORKERS
Employees whom organizations hire or contract with on a temporary basis to fill needs for labor that change over time.

The increasing reliance of organizations on contingent employees has some interesting implications for social environments at work. **Contingent workers** are employees organizations hire or contract with on a temporary basis to fill needs for labor, which change over time.[35] Contingent workers have little job security and loyalty toward their organizations because they know their employment is on a temporary, as-needed basis.[36] Contingent workers often face a different social environment on the job than do regular employees.

Contingent workers, like those hired by temporary employment agencies, are motivated by different factors than full-time employees with more job security.

The Role of Past Behaviors

The social information processing model proposes another reason why Doherty and Cantu view their similar jobs so differently: Employees' past behaviors have implications for how they view their current jobs and work outcomes. Doherty made considerable sacrifices to get through law school. He worked at night as a waiter to supplement the $60,000 worth of student loans he took out to pay his tuition and living expenses over the three-year period. His hectic schedule made his social life practically nonexistent. Cantu, in contrast, did not have to take out any loans or work to pay for law school. His father, an attorney, always assumed that Cantu would follow in his footsteps. In fact, Cantu was not overjoyed by the prospect of going to law school but couldn't find a decent job with his BA in anthropology. His parents were pleased that he decided to attend the Columbia law school and thought nothing of paying the high tuition and living expenses involved.

Because Doherty freely chose to become a lawyer, made a lot of sacrifices to attend law school, and will be paying off his debts from law school for the next several years, his intrinsic motivation is high, and his attitude toward his job is extremely positive. Having such a good job justifies all the sacrifices he has made. Cantu, who didn't have many options after graduating from college, was pressured by his parents to become a lawyer and didn't have to sacrifice much at all to attend law school. In terms of his past behaviors, Cantu has much less to justify because he didn't have much choice, nor was he required to make many sacrifices.

The social information processing model, thus, identifies a second factor that affects employees' reactions to the design of their jobs: Employees' past behaviors have implications for their evaluations of their current jobs, their levels of intrinsic motivation, and their levels of job satisfaction, especially when these behaviors are freely chosen and involve certain personal sacrifices.

To sum up, the social information processing model points to the importance of the social environment and past behaviors for an understanding of how employees react to the design of their jobs.[37] It helps explain why two employees with the same job and outcomes may have very different levels of motivation and satisfaction. As you might expect, research has found that both the objective features of a job (its actual design in terms of the five core dimensions of the job characteristics model) and an employee's social environment and past behavior all interact to affect motivation levels and satisfaction.[38] Research has found that the social environment is an especially potent source of information when employees with limited information and experience are new to a job or to an organization. Once employees have gained firsthand experience with their jobs, the social environment may play less of a decisive role in molding reactions, and the actual design of the job itself may become more important.

Job Design Models Summarized

Scientific management, job enlargement, job enrichment, the job characteristics model, and the social information processing model—each theory highlights different aspects of job design that are important to consider when it comes to understanding work motivation. The main features and motivational focus of each approach are recapped in Exhibit 7.6.

Scientific management advocates job simplification and job specialization, and its key goal is maximizing performance. Scientific management implicitly assumes that extrinsic motivation is the primary determinant of performance and provides no opportunity for intrinsic motivation. Proponents believe employees can be motivated to contribute inputs to their jobs and organizations if pay is closely linked to performance by means of piece-rate pay systems. Jobs designed according to the principles of scientific management tend to be boring, monotonous, and dissatisfying.

Job enlargement and *job enrichment* focus on expanding the simple jobs created by scientific management (enlargement through horizontal loading; enrichment through vertical loading) to promote intrinsic motivation.

In response to some of the problems related to designing jobs according to the principles of scientific management, Hackman and Oldham proposed the *job characteristics model*. The job characteristics model outlines the job dimensions that lead to high levels of intrinsic motivation. When employees are intrinsically motivated, they contribute inputs to their jobs because they enjoy the work itself. According to this model, how jobs are designed along five core dimensions can affect intrinsic motivation, job performance, job satisfaction, and absenteeism and turnover rates.

The *social information processing model* makes the important point that how employees view their jobs and their levels of intrinsic and extrinsic motivation is affected not just by the objective nature of the job but also by the social environment at work and the employees' own past behaviors.

As we mentioned at the beginning of this chapter, the primary aim of the different approaches to job design is to try to ensure that employees are motivated to contribute their inputs (time, effort, knowledge, and skills) to their jobs and organizations.

EXHIBIT 7.6

Approaches to Job Design

Approach	Main Features	Motivational Focus
Scientific management	Work simplification Specialization Time and motion studies Piece-rate pay	Extrinsic
Job enlargement	Horizontal job loading (increase number of tasks with no increase in difficulty and responsibility)	Intrinsic
Job enrichment	Vertical job loading (increase responsibility and provide employee with opportunities for growth)	Intrinsic
Job characteristics model	Core job dimensions Skill variety Task identity Task significance Autonomy Feedback Motivating potential score Critical psychological states Experienced meaningfulness of the work Experienced responsibility for work outcomes Knowledge of results Work and personal outcomes Intrinsic motivation Job performance Job satisfaction Absenteeism and turnover	Intrinsic
Social information processing model	Emphasis on social environment (what aspects to consider, and how to evaluate a job) Emphasis on implications of past behaviors (on how jobs and outcomes are perceived)	Extrinsic and intrinsic

Approaches such as scientific management, which stress extrinsic motivation, advocate designing jobs from an efficiency standpoint and closely linking pay and performance to them. Approaches such as the job characteristic model, which stress intrinsic motivation, suggest designing jobs to make them interesting and enjoyable. Regardless of whether the motivational focus is intrinsic, extrinsic, or both, job design affects motivation levels primarily by influencing the level and amount of inputs employees contribute to their jobs and organizations.

Organizational Objectives

ORGANIZATIONAL OBJECTIVES
The overarching purpose of an organization, what it stands for, and what it seeks to accomplish.

Organizational objectives describe the overarching purpose of an organization—what it stands for and what it seeks to accomplish. From the opening case, it is clear that a key objective of Google is providing users with the best possible Internet search experience. Organizational objectives contribute to creating a motivating work setting because they can provide employees with a sense of meaning and purpose. Just as a hospital's objective of providing high-quality patient care can be motivating, so, too, can Google's objective of protecting the environment and playing a positive role in the communities in which it operates. Take the case of a janitor in a not-for-profit teaching hospital known for its superior patient care and the fact that needy patients are never turned away. A key source of motivation for the janitor might be knowing he is contributing to an organization that really helps people regardless of their financial means.

Organizational objectives can focus on the wider environment in which an organization operates, its products and services, and various stakeholder groups including employees. This is true at Hydro, Norway's biggest industrial company, as profiled in the accompanying Global View.

SOCIAL IDENTITY THEORY
A theory that describes how individuals use the groups and organizations they are members of to define themselves.

Social identity theory explains how and why an organization's objectives can serve to motivate its employees. **Social identity theory** postulates that people tend to classify

Global View

Hydro's Commitment to the Environment and Its Employees

Hydro has operations in 40 countries and 33,000 employees globally.[39] The company operates in a variety of sectors, including oil and energy, aluminum, and agricultural industries.[40] A fundamental premise underlying Hydro's business model is social responsibility and corporate sustainability.[41] Corporate sustainability reflects a long-term commitment to protecting the environment and solving environmental problems and a commitment to social well-being.[42] Hydro was recently added to the prestigious Dow Jones Sustainability Index, a select list of companies that excel in sustainability in the industries in which they operate.[43] These companies are proactive in terms of integrating environmental and social concerns into their operations around the world.[44]

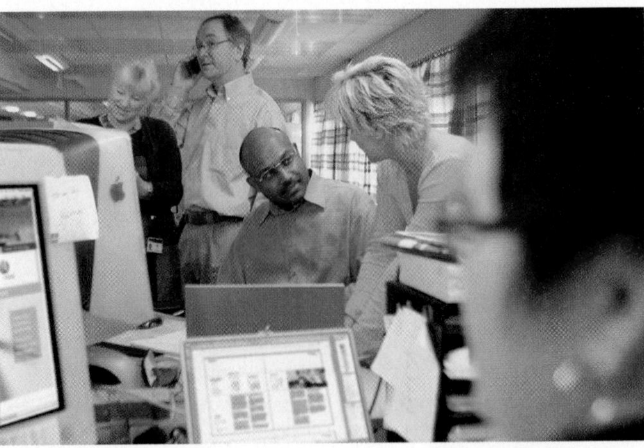

Hydro, Norway's biggest industrial company, is committed to social responsibility, corporate sustainability, and the well-being of its employees.

In Norway, Hydro is known for its many initiatives to promote the job satisfaction and well-being of its employees. These initiatives revolve around Hydro's organizational objective of being a responsible employer.[45] Key to these initiatives is providing employees with interesting, meaningful, and intrinsically motivating work while allowing them to achieve a sense of balance between work and their personal lives.

Employees at Hydro are given considerable amounts of autonomy and feel personally responsible for the quality of their work. Whereas in the United States employees are putting in ever longer hours, in Norway most people end the workday around 4:00 or 4:30 P.M., and women receive between seven and eight months of paid maternity leave (men can receive up to four weeks of paid paternity leave). Balance between work and personal life is a strong societal value in Norway and at Hydro.[46] Thus, not only are employees granted autonomy when it comes to the tasks they perform but also when and where they perform them.

Morten Lingelmen owns a farm an hour and a half away from his job at Hydro in Oslo. Although he has demanding responsibilities as a manager and an engineer, he is still able to be back at his farm with his family by 6:00 P.M.; the commuter train he rides has an "office car" where he can work and use his laptop computer. Atle Taerum also lives on a farm an hour and a half away from his job; he comes to the office three days a week and stays home with his young daughter the remaining two days. When Unni Foss's father was dying, she worked full time from her parents' house so she could be there for both of them and help them out. Managers at Hydro gave Foss the autonomy to decide where she worked. They knew she was a responsible person and would ensure her work was coordinated with others. Allowing employees to have balance in their lives, according to Hydro, helps them perform better, contributes to their job satisfaction and organizational commitment, and contribute's to Hydro's organizational objective of being a responsible employer.

themselves and others into social categories, such as being members of a certain group or team, religion, political party, or organization. When people identify with an organization, they define themselves in terms of being a member and see their destiny as being connected to it.[47]

Identification helps people answer the "who am I?" question.[48] People also prefer positive identifications to negative ones. Thus, for example, most employees would prefer to work for and identify with an organization that makes safe, life-improving products for consumers rather than for an organization whose products have a questionable safety record. When individuals identify with an organization, they are motivated to make positive contributions to it because their organizational membership is one way in which they see themselves.[49] At Google, as engineering director Peter Norvig puts it, "There are people who think they are creating something that's the best in the world . . . And that product is changing people's lives."[50]

Identifying with an organization can also help employees keep things in perspective when doing tedious or unpleasant tasks or when they're frustrated by a persistent work-related problem. Knowing they are adding real value to society can help them get through tough times and prop up their motivation. Although individual employees typically focus on achieving their goals tied to their own jobs, they are more likely to realize that by meeting their individual or group goals, they are helping the organization to reach its objectives, too. Thus, in addition to general organizational objectives, the individual goals employees work toward play an important role in creating a motivating work setting. Goal-setting theory (discussed in the next section) describes when, how, and why goals contribute to creating a motivating work setting.[51]

Increasing numbers of organizations are turning to outsourcing, or offshoring, of business functions and jobs to other countries such as China and India, to meet their objectives of cutting costs. However, as profiled in the following Global View, offshoring can also be viewed as a way to fuel growth and efficiency.

Global View

Offshoring Is Here to Stay

Offshoring is increasingly being relied on by organizations to reduce costs. According to estimates by Gartner Inc., offshoring of information technology and business process functions alone are valued at more than $34 billion per year.[52] And while offshoring manufacturing to low-cost countries like China has a relatively longer history, offshoring of services is much less capital-intensive and thus has the potential to achieve more cost reductions per dollar invested in offshoring than manufacturing, which typically entails significant capital expenditures to get plants up and running overseas.[53]

General Electric (GE) and McKinsey & Co. are two companies who have been at the forefront of offshoring.[54] Managers at both companies have learned that offshoring is more than just a way to cut costs. Rather, offshoring also can enable companies to grow while increasing efficiency. GE Capital set up an office in Delhi, India called GE Capital Investment Services with around 300 employees in the late 1990s because it was having a hard time filling positions in its growing business of mortgage refinancing. Less than a decade later, Genpact (as the company, which is now owned by GE and two private equity firms, is called) has over 20,000 employees, over $490 million in revenues, and offices in Mexico, Romania, Hungary, India, China, and the United States.[55]

Outsourcing or offshoring of business functions and jobs to other countries like India and China is increasingly being relied on to cut costs and fuel efficiency and growth.

McKinsey also was a pioneer within the offshoring movement, setting up a Knowledge Center in New Delhi in the mid 1990s to analyze data, perform statistical work, and help in the preparation of reports and presentations.[56] In fact, many former McKinsey and GE employees are now top managers at outsourcing companies. For example, former GE employee Pramod Bhasin is President and CEO of Genpact.[57] As another example, Rizwan Koita was a 29-year-old associate with McKinsey in London and New Delhi when he left the firm in 1999 to start his own outsourcing company, TransWorks Information Services LTD, which performs back-office functions and operates call centers for high-tech companies and banks. Koita sold TransWorks in 2003 to AV Birla Group, a conglomerate based in India, and started another new outsourcing business named Citius Tech Inc., which provides services for companies in the healthcare technology industry.[58] Additionally, as some former employees of GE and McKinsey assume top jobs in other large organizations (e.g., Robert Nardelli, CEO of Home Depot Inc., was a former top manager at GE), they bring with them the knowledge and experience with how offshoring can help a company reach its growth and efficiency objectives. For example, Home Depot relies on the India outsourcing company Tata Consultancy Services Ltd. for back-office functions in merchandising and management and call-center operations.[59] Clearly, it appears as if offshoring is here to stay.

Goal Setting

GOAL
What an individual is trying to accomplish through his or her behavior and actions.

A **goal** is what an individual is trying to accomplish through his or her behavior and actions.[60] Goal-setting theory, like the different approaches to job design, focuses on how to motivate employees to contribute inputs to their jobs[61] (see Exhibit 7.1). The theory also stresses the importance of ensuring their inputs result in acceptable job performance levels.

Edwin Locke and Gary Latham, leaders in goal-setting theory and research, suggest that the goals employees try to attain at work have a major impact on their levels of motivation and performance. Just as you might have a goal to get an A in this course or to find a good job or nice apartment upon graduation, employees likewise have goals that direct their behaviors in organizations. Salespeople at Dillard's department stores, for example, have weekly and monthly sales goals they are expected to reach, and telephone operators have goals for the number of customers they should assist each day. CEOs of organizations such as IBM, Chrysler, and Acme Metal strive to meet growth, profitability, and quality goals.

Goal setting is used in organizations not just to influence input levels employees are motivated to contribute but also to ensure the inputs are directed toward furthering organizational goals.[62] **Goal-setting theory** explains what types of goals are most effective in producing high levels of motivation and performance and why goals have these effects.

GOAL-SETTING THEORY
A theory that focuses on identifying the types of goals that are most effective in producing high levels of motivation and performance and why goals have these effects.

What Kinds of Goals Lead to High Motivation and Performance?

According to goal-setting theory, there are two major characteristics of goals that, together, lead to high levels of motivation and performance. One is specificity; the other is difficulty.

Specific goals lead to higher performance than do vague goals or no goals. Specific goals are often quantitative, such as a salesperson's goal of selling $600 worth of merchandise in a week, a telephone operator's goal of assisting 20 callers per hour, or a CEO's goal of increasing monthly and annual revenues by 10 percent. Vague goals are much less precise than specific goals. A vague goal for a salesperson might be to "sell as much as you can." A vague goal for a CEO might be to "increase revenues and quality."

Difficult goals lead to higher motivation and performance than do easy or moderate goals. Difficult goals are hard (but not impossible) for most employees to reach. Practically all employees can achieve easy goals. Moderate goals can be achieved, on average, by about half of the people working toward the goal.

The theory states that specific and difficult goals lead to higher motivation and performance than do easy, moderate, or vague goals or no goals at all. Goal-setting theory is supported by research studies conducted in a wide variety of organizations.[63] Although most of the studies have been conducted in the United States, research conducted in Canada, the Caribbean, England, Israel, and Japan suggests that specific, difficult goals lead to high levels of motivation and performance in different cultures as well.[64]

Specific, difficult goals lead to high motivation and performance whether the goals are set by managers for their subordinates, by employees themselves,[65] or by managers and employees together. When managers set goals for subordinates, it is important that the subordinates accept the goals—that is, agree to try to meet them.[66] It is also important that employees are committed to attaining goals—that is, want to attain them. Sometimes managers and employees may set goals together (a process often referred to as allowing subordinates to *participate* in goal setting) to boost subordinates' acceptance of and commitment to the goals. High self-efficacy also helps ensure that employees will be motivated to try to reach difficult goals. Recall from Chapter 5 that self-efficacy is a person's belief that she or he can successfully perform a behavior. Employees with high self-efficacy believe that they can attain difficult goals, and this belief contributes to their acceptance, commitment, and motivation to achieve them. Sometimes providing employees with flexibility to achieve their difficult goals can increase their self-efficacy and performance. For example, at TechTarget, an interactive media company in Needham, Massachusetts, employees are given specific, difficult goals on a quarterly basis, but they are then given the flexibility to set their own hours and schedules to meet them.[67] Finally, goal setting seems to work best when employees are given feedback about how they are doing.[68]

Why Do Goals Affect Motivation and Performance?

Why do specific, difficult goals lead to consistently higher levels of motivation and performance than easy or moderate goals or vague goals such as "do your best"? There are several reasons, and they are illustrated in the case of Mary Peterson and Allison Rios, who are the division managers of the frozen desserts and frozen vegetables divisions, respectively, of a food-processing company. Both divisions overran their operating budgets the previous year. One of the priorities for the current period is to cut operating expenses. When Peterson and her supervisor, the vice president who oversees the dessert division, met to decide Peterson's goals for the year, they agreed that she should aim to cut operating expenses by 10 percent. Rios met with the vice president of the vegetables division on the same issue, and they decided on a goal of reducing operating expenses by 25 percent. At year end, even though Peterson met her goal of reducing expenses by 10 percent and Rios failed to meet her goal, Rios's performance was still much higher than Peterson's because she had reduced expenses by 23 percent.

Why did Rios's more difficult goal motivate her to perform at a level higher than Peterson? First, Rios's difficult goal prompted her to direct more attention toward reducing expenses than Peterson felt she needed to expend. Second, it motivated her to put forth more effort than Peterson felt she had to put forth. Consequently, Rios spent a lot of time and effort working out ways to reduce expenses; she developed more efficient inventory and product distribution systems and upgraded some of her division's production facilities. Peterson, on the other hand, devoted much less attention to reducing expenses and focused exclusively on cutting back inventories. Third, Rios's difficult goal motivated her to create a plan for achieving her goal. The plan outlined the cost savings from each change she was proposing. By contrast, Peterson, confident that she could reach her goal through improved inventory management, didn't do much planning at all. Fourth, Rios's difficult goal made her more persistent than Peterson. Both Rios and Peterson changed their inventory-handling procedures to try to cut costs, and they originally decided to focus on reducing their inventories of both raw materials and finished products. The former, however, was much easier than the latter to cut back. Peterson, confident that she could attain her easy goal, decided to maintain her finished-product inventories as they were and focus solely on reducing the raw-materials inventories. Rios also encountered problems in reducing her finished-product inventory but persisted until she was able to come up with a viable plan to do so.

To sum up, specific, difficult goals affect motivation and performance by

- directing employees' attention and action toward goal-relevant activities
- causing employees to exert higher levels of effort
- causing employees to develop action plans to achieve their goals
- causing employees to persist in the face of obstacles or difficulties[69]

It is important to note that research shows that goal setting affects motivation and performance even when employees are *not* given any extra extrinsic rewards for achieving their goals. Not surprisingly, however, specific, difficult goals tend to have more powerful effects on performance when some financial reward *is* given for goal attainment. Goal setting can operate to enhance both intrinsic motivation (in the absence of any extrinsic rewards) and extrinsic motivation (when employees are given extrinsic rewards for achieving their goals).

Because goals work so well, setting them may lead employees to *not* perform activities *not* related to the specific goals they're supposed to attain (recall the discussion of organizational citizenship behavior in Chapter 3). Research has found, for example, that employees with specific, difficult goals may be less likely to help a coworker who is having a problem because it might interfere with the achievement of their own goals.[70] A telephone operator who spends time explaining how to use a new electronic directory to a coworker, for example, might fail to meet her own goal of assisting 20 callers per hour because of the 15 minutes she spent helping her coworker. Some of these unassigned goals, however, may be paramount to the organization's overall effectiveness.

Moreover, it's important that employees do not so single-mindedly purse their goals that they behave in questionable or unethical ways. Clearly, no goal is so important that a person's or an organization's ethics should be compromised.

Limits to Goal-Setting Theory

Although goal-setting theory has received extensive research support for a variety of jobs and organizations, some recent research suggests that there may be certain limits on the theory's applicability. Research suggests that there are three circumstances under which setting specific, difficult goals will not lead to high motivation and performance:

1. *When employees lack the skills and abilities needed to perform at a high level.* Giving an employee the goal of writing a computer program to calculate production costs will not result in high levels of motivation and performance if the employee does not know how to write computer programs.
2. *When employees are given complicated and difficult tasks that require all of their attention and require a considerable amount of learning.* Good performance on complicated tasks depends on employees being able to direct *all* of their attention to learning the task at hand. When employees are given difficult goals for such tasks, some of their attention will be directed toward trying to attain the goal and not toward actually learning about the task. Under these circumstances, assigning a specific, difficult goal actually *reduces* performance.[71] Once the task has been mastered, goal setting will then have its customary effects.

   Ruth Kanfer and Philip Ackerman of the University of Minnesota explored the effects of goal setting on the performance of Air Force personnel who were learning the complicated, difficult tasks involved to become air traffic controllers.[72] During the early stages of learning, assigning goals to the recruits resulted in lower levels of performance because it distracted some of their attention away from learning how to direct air traffic and toward trying to achieve the goal. Once the recruits had developed a certain level of mastery over the task, setting specific, difficult goals did enhance performance.
3. *When employees need to be creative.* As we discussed in Chapter 5, creativity is the generation of new and useful ideas whether they be products, services, or processes.[73] Given that creativity involves coming up with something that is novel and has not been thought of before, it is often not appropriate to provide employees with specific, difficult goals as the outcome of their creative efforts is unknown. If they are coming up with something that is really new, a specific, difficult goal cannot be set a priori because managers do not yet know what it is that they will create. Additionally, if creativity is desired and employees are given specific, difficult goals, it is likely they will focus on achieving the goals rather than being creative. However, this does not mean that more general kinds of goals cannot help motivate creativity. Indeed, research has found that giving employees the general goal to be creative can help encourage creativity. And, clearly, creative pursuits are driven by organizational objectives and group goals, such as providing new services that will meet clients' needs.

MANAGEMENT BY OBJECTIVES (MBO)
A goal-setting process in which a manager meets with his or her supervisor to set goals and evaluate the extent to which previously set goals have been achieved.

Management by Objectives

Some organizations adopt formal systems to ensure that goal setting actually takes place on a periodic basis.[74] **Management by objectives (MBO)** is a goal-setting process in which a manager meets periodically with his or her supervisor to set goals and evaluate

EXHIBIT 7.7

Basic Steps in Management by Objectives

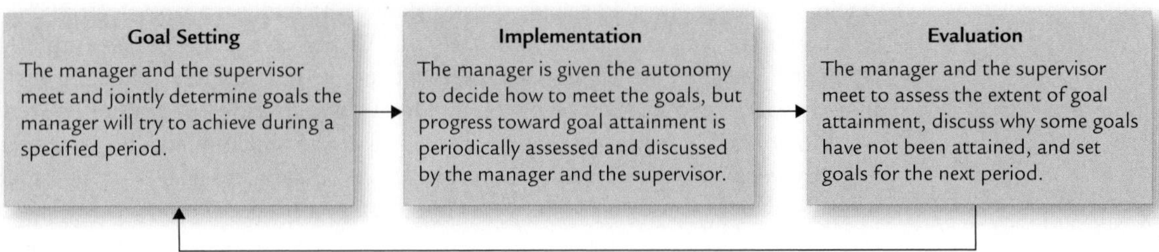

how well previously set goals have been met.[75] The objective of MBO is to make sure that all goal setting contributes to the organization's effectiveness. Most MBO programs are usually reserved for managers, but the programs can also be used as a motivational tool for nonmanagers. Although the form and content of MBO programs vary from organization to organization, most programs have three basic steps: goal setting, implementation, and evaluation (see Exhibit 7.7).[76]

1. *Goal setting*. The manager and the supervisor meet and jointly determine the goals the manager will try to achieve during a specific time period, say, 6 or 12 months. In our earlier example, Allison Rios, the division manager for frozen vegetables, met with the vice president to whom she reports, and together they decided that she should work throughout the coming year toward the goal of reducing operating expenses by 25 percent.
2. *Implementation*. The manager is given the autonomy to decide how to meet the goals in the specified time period. Progress toward goal attainment is periodically assessed and discussed by the manager and her or his supervisor. In our example, Rios came up with several ways to cut expenses, including the development of more efficient inventory and product distribution systems and upgrading the production facilities. Rios made and implemented these decisions on her own and periodically met with her supervisor to review how her plans were working.
3. *Evaluation*. At the end of the specified time period, the manager and supervisor again meet to assess the extent of goal attainment, discuss why some goals may not have been attained, and set goals for the next period.

The success of an MBO program depends on the appropriateness and difficulty of the goals that are set. Clearly, the goals should focus on key dimensions of a manager's performance such as cutting operating expenses, expanding sales, or increasing the profitability of a division's product line that are under the manager's control. And, as we've seen, goals should be specific and difficult. Finally, for MBO to work, a certain amount of rapport and trust must exist between managers and their supervisors. A manager who doesn't trust her supervisor, for example, might fear that if some unforeseen, uncontrollable event prohibits her from attaining a difficult goal, the supervisor will penalize her (for example, by not giving a raise). To avoid this situation, the manager may try to set easy MBO goals. Managers and supervisors must be committed to MBO and be willing to take the time and effort needed to make it work. Moreover, when conditions change, a willingness to change objectives in midstream can be important; if an objective is no longer appropriate, there is no point in continuing to work toward it.

Goal Setting and Job Design as Motivation Tools

Recall from Chapter 6 that motivating employees to contribute their inputs (which include their time, effort, and skills) to their jobs is a key challenge in an organization. Goal-setting theory suggests that one way to meet this challenge is to set specific, difficult goals.

Employees exert more effort for such goals than they do for easy or vague goals, and they are more likely to persist in the face of obstacles. In addition to motivating employees, goals focus employee inputs in the right direction so that the inputs result not only in acceptable levels of job performance but also in the achievement of organizational goals.

Together, job design and goal setting address some of the many questions managers face in the realm of motivation: How can I make my subordinates more interested in doing a good job? What is the best way to assign specific tasks to each of my subordinates? How can I get my subordinates to care about their work? How can I achieve increases in performance and quality necessary for the organization to achieve its goals? In terms of the motivation equation (Inputs → Performance → Outcomes), job design and goal setting focus primarily on how to motivate employees to contribute their inputs to their jobs and organizations (see Exhibit 7.1).

Summary

Job design and goal setting are the foundations of a motivating work setting. The ways in which jobs are designed and the types of goals that are set can have profound effects on employee motivation and performance and the extent to which an organization is able to achieve its goals. In this chapter, we made the following major points:

1. One of the earliest systematic approaches to job design was scientific management, which stresses job simplification and job specialization. Scientific management focuses on extrinsic motivation and can result in an efficient production process. It also may result in high levels of job dissatisfaction.
2. Job enlargement and job enrichment focus, respectively, on the horizontal and the vertical loading of jobs. Each attempts, by raising levels of intrinsic motivation, to overcome some of the problems that arise when jobs are designed according to the principles of scientific management.
3. The job characteristics model also focuses on intrinsic motivation. The model proposes that five core dimensions (skill variety, task identity, task significance, autonomy, and feedback) lead to three critical psychological states (experienced meaningfulness of the work, experienced responsibility for work outcomes, and knowledge of results) that in turn lead to several outcomes (intrinsic motivation, job performance, job satisfaction, and low absenteeism and turnover). Individual differences (growth-need strength, knowledge and skills, and satisfaction with the work context) affect the key relationships in the model. Research suggests that intrinsic motivation and job satisfaction do tend to result from the core characteristics and psychological states as proposed by the model; however, job performance is not necessarily affected.
4. The social information processing model suggests that the social environment provides employees with information about which aspects of their job design and work outcomes they should pay attention to and how they should evaluate them. This information influences motivation. In addition, employees' past behaviors have implications for how they view their current jobs and current levels of motivation, particularly when these past behaviors were freely chosen or entailed personal sacrifices.
5. Goal-setting theory and research suggest that specific, difficult goals lead to higher motivation and performance than do easy goals, moderate goals, vague goals, or no goals. Specific, difficult goals influence motivation and performance by directing employees' attention toward goal-relevant activities, influencing effort expenditure, influencing levels of persistence, and causing employees to develop action plans. When employees are performing very complicated and difficult tasks that require all of their attention and a considerable amount of learning, specific, difficult goals should not be set until the employees have mastered the tasks.

Exercises in Understanding and Managing Organizational Behavior

Questions for Review

1. Why might an organization want to design jobs according to the principles of scientific management?
2. Why might some employees not want their jobs enriched?
3. How might a manager redesign the job of a person who delivers newspapers to raise levels of the core job dimensions identified by the job characteristics model?
4. Can principles of scientific management and the job characteristics model both be used to design a job? Explain why or why not.
5. Why do individual differences affect the relationships in the job characteristics model?
6. Why does the social environment influence employees' responses to the design of their jobs?
7. Why should organizations clearly communicate organizational objectives to their employees?
8. What kinds of goals should be set for a supermarket cashier?
9. Why do people try to attain difficult goals?
10. When might specific, difficult goals result in low levels of performance?

OB: Increasing Self-Awareness

Extrinsic and Intrinsic Motivation

Pick two people you know pretty well who are working (such as friends or relatives). Try to pick one person who is primarily extrinsically motivated by his or her job and another person who is primarily intrinsically motivated (or both intrinsically and extrinsically motivated). Informally meet with each of these people and ask them about their jobs (especially what their jobs entail, the social environment at work, and their work goals, if any). Then do the following:

1. Describe each person's job.
2. Is either job designed according to the principles of scientific management? If so, how?
3. Describe each job in terms of the five core dimensions of the job characteristics model.
4. Describe each person in terms of the individual differences in the job characteristics model.
5. How are the people's social environments at work similar? How are they different?
6. Is either person assigned goals? If so, what kinds of goals?
7. What do you think accounts for the extrinsic motivation and the intrinsic motivation of the people you have chosen?

A Question of Ethics

Some employees are given specific, difficult goals and their very livelihood depends on how well they perform. For example, salespeople who are paid strictly on a commission basis have all their earnings hinging on the extent to which they are successful in selling to customers. This can sometimes cause salespeople considerable stress, especially when they are very dependent on their earnings to support themselves and/or loved ones.

Questions

1. Think about the ethical implications of assigning specific, difficult goals to employees.
2. Is it ethical to have employees' earnings based entirely on the extent to which they attain their goals?

Small Group Break-Out Exercise

The Power of Social Influence

Form groups of three or four people and appoint one member as the spokesperson who will communicate your conclusions to the rest of the class.

1. Take a few minutes to think about a situation in which your opinion differed from the general consensus of the group of people you were with.
2. Write down a brief description of the situation, how you felt, whether or not you expressed your opinion, and whether or not you or anyone in the group changed their opinions.
3. Take turns describing these situations and the information you wrote down for step 2.
4. As a group, try to come up with explanations for why sometimes people who disagree with a majority fail to express their opinions and/or end up changing them.

Topic for Debate

Job design and goal setting are two major motivational tools that managers can use to increase motivation and performance. Now that you have a good understanding of job design and goal setting, form two teams and debate the following issue.

Team A. Managers should try to avoid designing jobs according to the principles of scientific management whenever possible.

Team B. Designing jobs according to the principles of scientific management can help an organization achieve its goals and should be used whenever appropriate.

Experiential Exercise

Increasing Autonomy

Objective

Your objective is to gain experience in redesigning a job to increase employee autonomy.

Procedure

Assume the role of a manager in charge of a group of artists that draws pictures for greeting cards. You currently assign the artists their individual tasks. Each artist is given a particular kind of card to work on (one works on birthday cards for female relatives, one on birthday cards for children, and so on). You inform each artist of the market research that has been done on his or her particular category of cards. You also communicate to each artist your ideas about what you would like to see in the cards he or she creates. The artists then produce sketches based on this information. You review the sketches, make changes, sometimes make the decision to abandon an idea or suggest a new one, and eventually give the artists the go-ahead to proceed with the drawing.

You thought everything was working pretty smoothly until you accidentally overheard one of your subordinates complaining to another that you are stifling his creativity. This exchange brought to mind another troubling incident. One of your artists who had drawn some of the company's best-selling cards quit a few months ago to work for a competitor. You began to wonder whether you have designed the artists' jobs in the best way possible.

You decide to administer the *Job Diagnostic Survey* to your subordinates. They complete it anonymously, and you are truly shocked by the results. Most of your subordinates indicate that their jobs are low on autonomy. Being an artist yourself, you are disturbed by this outcome because you see autonomy as being a necessary ingredient for creativity.

1. Develop an action plan to increase levels of autonomy in the artists' jobs. Although you want to increase autonomy, you also want to make sure that your group creates cards that are responsive to market demands and customer taste.
2. The class divides into groups of three to five people, and each group appoints one member as spokesperson to present the group's recommendations to the whole class.
3. Group members take turns describing their own specific action plans for increasing autonomy in the artists' jobs while making sure the cards are responsive to market demands and customer taste.
4. Discuss the pros and cons of the different alternative action plans and create an action plan that group members think will best increase autonomy while at the same time meet the organizational goal of creating best-selling cards.

When your group has completed those activities, the spokesperson will present the group's action plan to the whole class.

New York Times *Cases in the News*

The New York Times

"DuPont Looking to Displace Fossil Fuels as Building Blocks of Chemicals"

By C. H. Deutsch, The New York Times, February 28, 2006, p. C1, C15.

Nestled away in a small room on DuPont's 150-acre research center in Wilmington, Del., robotic arms fill tiny tubes with gelatinous material that was extracted from corn and soybean plants. Other metallic arms will soon dip and measure and deconstruct each sample, spewing forth a list of its attributes and traits.

Only a fistful—maybe one of every 50—will move on to the fermentation lab, a few buildings away. There, researchers will see how the samples react to different mixtures of air, glucose and microbes. Down the hall, other researchers will tinker with the microbes themselves.

All of them are chasing the same holy grail: bio-based substances that can replace oil and gas as building blocks for chemicals. "We figure out what works in theory, and then we see what works in practice." Alexander D. Kopatsis, a research associate, said.

E. I. du Pont de Nemours & Company, unlike most chemical companies, has moved the quest for bio-based raw materials off the wish list and onto the to-do agenda. The company has allocated nearly 10 percent of its $1.3 billion research budget to extracting ingredients from carbohydrates—things that grow and can be infinitely replaced—rather than from hydrocarbons, which are mined or drilled and readily depleted.

DuPont already makes 10 percent of its products from nonpetrochemical substances, and Charles O. Holliday Jr., DuPont's chief executive, expects to increase that to 25 percent by 2010. By then, he says, such products will yield the equivalent of $3 billion in revenue in current dollars. The way Mr. Holliday sees it, so-called industrial biotechnology can solve myriad problems. It can insulate DuPont from the relentless rise in gas and oil prices. It can win kudos from environmentalists and share-holders who worry about the harmful effect of extracting and burning oil. It can play well in Washington, particularly since a quest for alternate energy sources was a crucial point in President Bush's State of the Union message. But during a nearly two-hour conversation in his spacious office above the Hotel DuPont, Mr. Holiday stressed his real motive in pushing for bio-based materials: his belief that they yield better products. He notes, for example, that the corn-based propane diol, a product used in carpet fibers that DuPont will begin selling this spring, offers better dye absorption and stain resistance than the petrochemical version DuPont now sells.

"We're using biology to solve problems that chemistry can't." he said.

It is not just bombast. DuPont is working with the Energy Department to turn corn plants—the husks, the ears, the stems, everything—into the vehicular fuel. DuPont is close to developing plant-based hair dyes and nail polishes that will not adhere to skin, surgical bin-glues that can stanch internal bleeding and a textile fiber made from sugar that will act and feel like cotton.

This spring DuPont will open a factory in London, Tenn., that will make propane diol—trademarked as Sorona—from glucose. For now the output is earmarked for carpet fiber, but DuPont is exploring whether it can work in rigid plastics for automobile interiors or de-icing compounds for airplanes.

The company has already converted many labs that once worked on pharmaceuticals or textiles—two businesses DuPont has shed—to now search for ingredients to replace oil and gas. Next year, it plans to cluster them all in one building and move a marketing staff in with them.

"Industrial biotechnology is an area in which we can differentiate ourselves, so we're spending a lot more than any other company on it," said Thomas M. Connelly, DuPont's chief science officer.

DuPont's optimism has other chemical industry executives scratching their heads. Dow Chemical pulled out of a joint venture with Cargill to make polylactic acid, a component of food packaging, from corn. Eastman Chemical sold its stake in Genencor International, a leader in industrial biotechnology.

"We really do believe that industrial biotech is critical to our evolution, but the technologies of the foreseeable future just do not give the returns we expect from our research dollar," said Andrew N. Liveris, chief executive of Dow, which is looking for ways to make polyurethane from soybean oil, but has put a higher priority on extracting ingredients from coal.

Friedhelm Balkenhohl, senior vice president for bio-catalysis research at the BASF Corporation, echoes that view. "Raw material change is one of our hot topics, but even 10 years from now, renewables will account for less than 10 percent of our ingredients," he said.

Some companies are shrugging off bio-based ingredients entirely, and concentrating solely on using petroleum ingredients more efficiently. "I'm glad that larger companies are spending their time, talent and money in such exotic areas, because they have left a wide-open field for us that we are fully exploiting." said Jeffrey M. Lipton, chief executive of the Nova Chemicals Corporation, which makes building-block chemicals like styrene and polyethylene.

The skeptics do not faze Mr. Holliday. He points to the thriving business that DuPont—and even more so, Monsanto—has built from genetically engineered crops. "Ten years ago it didn't seem logical to go after insect-resistant crops, either," he said. "We're not betting the company on bio-based materials, but we do think they have the potential to have the same impact on us that long-chain polymers once did," he said, referring to the scientific discoveries that led to nylon.

Industrial biotechnology is not a new concept, of course. As far back as the 1970's, companies experimented with turning crops and agricultural waste into fuels. In most cases, the processes were costly and polluting. Even worse, it often took more oil to transport the alternate fuels from farm to factory than was saved by eliminating petrochemicals.

The economics work better today. Prices for oil and gas remain persistently high, and few industry prognosticators predict steep plunges. Moreover, fermentation technologies have improved, as has the ability to isolate and manipulate plant genes. And the growing clamor from environmentalists and environmentally conscious shareholders has given companies an added impetus to invest in "green" technologies like renewable resources.

Still, of the chemical companies, DuPont seems to have the most immediate need for the advantages that industrial biotechnology can provide. In the late 1990's it paid more than $9 billion to buy the seed company Pioneer Hi-bred, a price that many analysts still insist was too high. If DuPont can use more of Pioneer's biotechnology expertise, it can perhaps allay the criticism.

Moreover, DuPont's once-steller reputation for scientific innovation has flagged of late. Although DuPont portrays itself as a new-product mill—Mr. Holliday says that a third of last year's revenues came from products that were less than five years old—analysts say too many of the new products represent incremental improvements. They note, for example, that DuPont's new hybrid corn seeds do yield more corn, but not enough to gain share back from Monsanto.

"In the last three, four years, nothing has stood out as a really breakout product," said William R. Young an analyst at Credit Suisse who has a neutral rating on DuPont shares. Goldman Sachs has an outperform rating on DuPont stock, yet Edlain Rodriguez, a Goldman analyst, agrees. "DuPont has always prided itself on being a science company, and it has to find a way to regain that leadership," he said.

It is under severe time pressure. Like many chemical companies, DuPont's costs soared when high energy prices were made worse by Hurricanes Rita and Katrina. Teflon, one of DuPont's workhorse products, contain perfluorooctanoic acid, or PFOA, which has been linked to cancer and strokes, and which the Environmental Protection Agency has asked manufacturers to eliminate.

And about 18 percent of DuPont's pretax earnings stem from sales of Cozaar and Hyzaar, two hypertension drugs it developed before it sold its pharmaceutical business to Bristol-Myers in 2002. The patents on the drugs expire in 2010, and so will DuPont's $751 million in annual royalties.

Analysts are divided on DuPont's prospects. According to Thomson Financial, of the 16 analysts that follow the company, 11 rate it a buy while five rate it a hold. Shares of DuPont, which were trading in the $50 range in the first half of 2005, fell 27 cents, to $40.05 yesterday.

Clearly, DuPont hopes that biochemistry will pump the stock up. "If we can make this integrated science game work, it will be ours to lose," said John Pierce, director of biochemical sciences and engineering.

It will still be a hard game to play. Oil and gas remain easier to transport than solids like corn and soybeans, and do not degrade with harsh weather. Plants also vary widely in shape and composition, making it harder to control the quality of distillates made from them.

"The corn crop, the sugar crop, either can be good or bad, and that makes the market inherently volatile," said David N. Weidman chief executive of the Celanese Corporation, which has temporarily shelved a patented process for getting micro-organisms to excrete acetic acid. "We are not saying that biotechnology will never result in chemicals, but it is a long, arduous and risky road."

Then, again, so is the prospect of relying on foreign oil. Albert, H. Segars, professor of technology management at the Kenan-Flagler Business School at the University of North Carolina, notes that against the backdrop of political instability in so many oil-producing regions, DuPont's biotechnology strategy seems almost safe. "If a war breaks out with Iran," he said, "your biology-based fuels will look at lot better than your petro-based ones.

Questions for Discussion

1. What organizational objectives are being pursued at E. I. du Pont de Nemars & Company?
2. Why are these organizational objectives being pursued?
3. How might these organizational objectives be motivational for du Pont employees?
4. How do these objectives influence the goals scientists and researchers are striving to achieve?

The New York Times

"Finding Happiness In the Pursuit"

By M. P. Dunleavey, The New York Times, April 8, 2006, p. B6.

One of the great puzzles of human nature is why humans strive for more material things—money, jobs, homes, cars, flat-screen televisions—when they do not seem to make them any happier in the long run.

Philosophers have pondered this conundrum for centuries, and modern economists have been examining it over several decades in a multitude of cultures. Not only does greater wealth not guarantee happiness—even when you get what you want—research indicates that you will not find it as satisfying as you had hoped, and you will want something else.

Richard A. Easterlin, professor of economics at the University of Southern California, is a seminar researcher in this area. In effect, his work shows that if you think buying a three-bedroom condo and a Honda Element will make you happy, you had better think twice. In a few years, a) you're not likely to report being any happier, and b) you're likely to say that, now, finding a good private school for your children and buying a vacation home will really make you happy.

In Dr. Easterlin's view, this cycle of desire and dissatisfaction tends to keep people on an endless treadmill. This may sound self-defeating, but that is Dr. Easterlin's point. Why not get off the treadmill and pursue a life with fewer material ambitions? You would probably be happier.

Or would you? If material achievements tend to leave people only momentarily fulfilled, why do so many keep reaching for that next goal?

Claudia Senik, professor of economics at the Sorbonne, believes that the struggle for a certain achievement may offer a peculiar reward all its own. Although many people seem quite goal-oriented—especially when it comes to money, homes, cars, new kitchens and other goods that have become stand-ins for status—maybe it's not so much *having* the stuff that people really enjoy, but the struggle to obtain it.

In an unpublished paper called "Is Man Doomed to Progress?" which she presented at a symposium, "Economics and Happiness," last month at U.S.C., Dr. Senik examined the impact of anticipating future gains on a person's current level of well-being.

Researchers have noted that, for example, given the opportunity to schedule a fancy meal, many people tend to postpone the feast—to savor the anticipation of it. In fact, Dr. Senik found that when people aspire to a better quality of life within the next 12 months, the attempt to reach that goal alone—the anticipation independent of the outcome—seems to bestow happiness in the present.

"For the basic person there is pleasure in progress." Dr. Senik said, "We are proud to aim at something—to earn a degree, buy a house. So when I work to reach a higher position or earn a higher income, I'm already happy today."

Dr. Senik compares it somewhat humorously to being invited to a fabulous party. "Once you get there, maybe you enjoy the party or maybe you don't—but that doesn't matter because you've already spent the last few days looking forward to it."

Of course, that is not how most people view the quest for a better job, nicer car or bigger home. The glory is in getting what you want. Yet we have all experienced the phenomenon—behavioral economists call it adaptation—whereby once you attain whatever you most covet, it quickly loses its luster. Dr. Senik's research suggests that it's fine to crave the condo and the car as long as you realize there may be more pleasure in striving for those goals than in actually achieving them.

I find this oddly comforting, because like many people I am well acquainted with materialistic tread-mills, and they are exhausting. You can feel like Sisyphus, pushing a boulder uphill over and over again to get the things you want.

It may seem that people are all hapless consumers, at the mercy of greed and needs (or cursed by Zeus). But Dr. Senik offers a more positive view. You can let go of the rather iffy rewards of getting and spending, and look for everyday pleasure while struggling to advance, improve, progress, achieve and attain.

As Dr. Easterlin said, "If you recognize that the striving can be of value in itself, then instead of taking a job that pays you the most, you may be better off taking work you'll enjoy." In other words, choose your treadmills carefully. Like Sisyphus, they're where most of us will spend our time.

Questions for Discussion

1. What are the implications of this case for job design?
2. How can jobs be designed to be more motivating?
3. What are the implications of this case for the use of goal setting in organizations?
4. Why might difficult goals be especially motivating?

CHAPTER 8

PAY, CAREERS, AND CHANGING EMPLOYMENT RELATIONSHIPS

Learning Objectives

After studying this chapter, you should be able to:

- Describe the determinants and types of psychological contacts and what happens when they are broken.
- Appreciate the two major roles of performance appraisal.
- Understand the different kinds and methods of performance appraisal.
- Appreciate the importance of merit pay and the choices organizations face in using pay to motivate employees.
- Understand the importance of careers, different kinds of careers, and effective career management.

Opening Case

VALUING EMPLOYEES AT COSTCO

Can organizations treat their employees very well and still remain competitive?

When large corporations in the discount retailing industry like Wal-Mart come under fire for paying low wages and being less than generous when it comes to providing employees with benefits like health insurance, the customary response is that such measures are necessary for these organizations to remain competitive. Costco Wholesale Corporation, the fifth largest retailer and the top warehouse retailer in the United States, challenges this conventional wisdom. Costco treats its employees very well, and these employees, in return, are satisfied, committed, loyal, and motivated.[1]

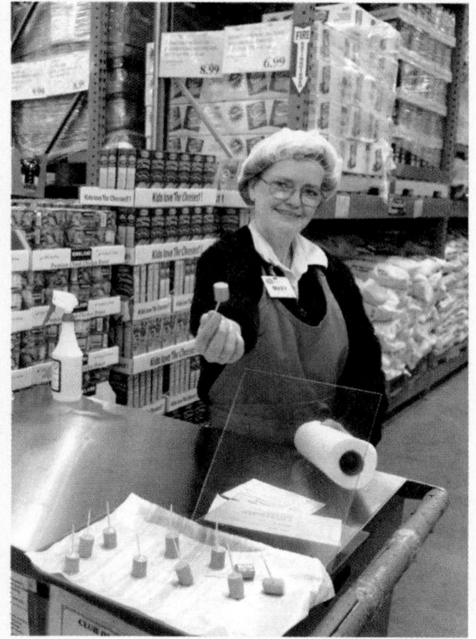

Costco Wholesale Corporation, the fifth largest retailer and the top warehouse retailer in the US, treats its employees very well. Costco employees, in return, are satisfied, committed, loyal, and motivated.

Hourly wages at Costco average $17 an hour, which are over 40 percent greater than the average hourly wage at Wal-Mart, Costo's biggest competitor.[2] Costco covers the majority of health insurance costs for its employees (employees pay around 8 percent compared to an industry average of about 25 percent), part-time employees receive health insurance once they have remained with Costco for six months, and around 85 percent of its employees have health insurance at any point in time (in contrast, less than 45 percent of Wal-Mart and Target employees have health insurance). Costco employees also have a generous 401-K pension plan for their retirement.[3]

According to Costco CEO Jim Sinegal, treating employees well makes good business sense. Costco's financial performance and growth bears this out. For example, for the first half of fiscal 2006, Costco's net sales of $26.45 billion were 11 percent higher than for the same period in fiscal 2005 and net earnings were $512 million.[4] Costco, which started out with a single warehouse store in Seattle, Washington in 1983, now has 457 stores, including stores in South Korea, Taiwan, Japan, Canada, and Britain. Costco has over 44 million members who pay $45 a year to shop in Costco stores.[5]

While treating employees well is an ethical imperative for Costco and a principle in its Code of Ethics ('Take care of our employees'), these employees, in turn, are highly committed to Costco and motivated to perform at high levels.[6] Costco's turnover rate is much lower than industry averages, which yields major cost savings; employee theft rates are also very low.[7] Traditionally, turnover in the retail industry is high and costly since for every employee who quits, a replacement hire needs to be recruited, tested, interviewed, and trained. Compared to Sam's Club (Wal-Mart's warehouse unit), Costco has lower labor costs as a percentage of sales and higher sales per square foot of store space.[8]

While Costco's customers love the bargains and low prices that come with shopping in a warehouse store, they also like the fact that Costco treats its employees well. Costco's customers are very loyal and part of this loyalty stems from the fact that they know that their bargains are not coming at the expense of employees' paychecks and benefits. Customer loyalty also comes from both the relatively high quality of the goods Costcos stock and the company's commitment to not marking up prices by more than 14 percent or 15 percent (relatively low mark-ups for retail), even if the goods will sell with higher mark-ups.[9]

CEO Jim Sinegal, who opened the first Costco store with an entrepreneur in Seattle, has a long-term approach to management. Treating employees well is a key part of this approach. As John Matthews, Senior Vice President for Human Resources indicates, 'When Jim talks to us about setting wages and benefits, he doesn't want us to be better than everyone else, he wants us to be demonstrably better.'[10] Take the case of Cesar Martinez who works in the Redwood City, California, Costco warehouse store. Martinez earns over $19 an hour and has been with Costco for over 10 years. Martinez indicates that he has stayed with Costco so long because he feels fairly treated, likes his job, and has a good salary and pension.[11]

Fair treatment at Costco also means that top managers are not paid hundreds times more than entry-level employees. Sinegal's salary is $350,000 (and he has received annual bonuses of around $200,000), which is very low by CEO standards, with some CEOs making hundreds of million dollars per year.[12] For example, while Costco is among the top 30 U. S. companies in terms of revenues, Sinegal's pay is less than 10 percent of what many other CEOs make. Sinegal says, 'I just think that if you're going to try to run an organization that's very cost-conscious, then you can't have those disparities. Having an individual who is making 100 or 200 or 300 times more than the average person working on the floor is wrong.'[13] Clearly, the ways in which Costco treats its employees and the company's performance and growth demonstrate that an organization can both treat employees very well *and* remain competitive.

Overview

Building off of Chapters 6 and 7, in this chapter we focus on the broader context in which employee motivation takes place. Although it is important to understand what motivates people, how they are motivated, and why, it is also important to understand how key aspects of the employment relationship can serve to encourage and maintain high levels of motivation. If mismanaged, these factors can lower motivation. In the opening case, it is clear that how Costco treats its employees contributes to their motivation, satisfaction, and loyalty.

The nature of the relationship between employees and organizations is changing. Organizations in the United States are increasingly outsourcing not only manufacturing jobs but also white-collar jobs, such as computer programming, engineering, and consulting, to countries with lower labor costs.[14] Recent waves of layoffs have changed U. S. workers' expectations about their careers and how they might unfold. In this chapter, we discuss these changes in depth. We describe the nature of the psychological contract an individual has with an organization and factors that cause psychological contracts to change over time. Psychological contracts and the motivation equation, explained in Chapter 6, all underscore the fact that the relationship between an organization and its employees is an exchange relationship: Employees make certain contributions to the organization and, in exchange, expect to receive certain outcomes.[15] We then discuss three factors that play a central role in this exchange relationship: performance appraisal, pay, and careers. In order to have a meaningful, reciprocal exchange, organizations need to be able to accurately assess the nature of the contributions employees make through performance appraisals. Given that pay is one of the most important outcomes for employees, regardless of the kinds of jobs they hold and organizations they belong to, we focus on pay and how it can be used to enhance motivation. Lastly, we take a longer-term perspective on the employment relationship and address the careers of the organization's employees.

Psychological Contracts

PSYCHOLOGICAL CONTRACT
An employee's perception of his or her exchange relationship with an organization, outcomes the organization has promised to provide to the employee, and contributions the employee is obligated to make to the organization.

A good way to think about the exchange relationship between an employee and an organization is in terms of a psychological contract.[16] A **psychological contract** is an employee's perception of his or her exchange relationship with an organization: outcomes the organization has promised to provide and contributions the employee is obligated to make.[17] There are a few key points worth emphasizing in this definition. First, psychological contracts are perceptual in nature[18] (see Chapter 4). Hence, they can be subject to errors and biases and also can be somewhat idiosyncratic. Having said this, though, does little to diminish the impact psychological contracts have on employee motivation. Second, psychological contracts refer to the perceived exchange relationship between an employee and an organization in terms of reciprocal promises or obligations.[19] Given the prevalence of reciprocity norms in the United States and other countries, such as China, Singapore, and Belgium,[20] organizations and the people within them generally seek to abide by psychological contracts. (The belief that making a contribution should lead to a commensurate outcome is an example of one such norm.)

Determinants of Psychological Contracts

How do individuals form their psychological contracts? Essentially, by piecing together information from a variety of sources to determine what is expected of them and what they can expect from the organization in return. Three sources of information are particularly influential in helping individuals form their psychological contracts: direct communication from coworkers and supervisors; observations of what actually transpires in the organization, including how similar employees behave and are treated; and written documents (see Exhibit 8.1).[21]

Direct communication. Psychological contracts can begin to form before a prospective employee even joins an organization. For example, when managers try to

EXHIBIT 8.1

Determinants of Psychological Contracts

Direct communication
- During recruitment of prospective employees
- On-the-job information from co-workers and supervisors

Observation
- How employees behave and how they are treated by the organization
- The nature of, and manner in which, important decisions are made

Written documents
- Employee handbooks, organizational policies, human resource documents
- Company Web site

Psychological contract
- Perceived exchange relationship between an employee and organization
- Includes reciprocal promises and obligations

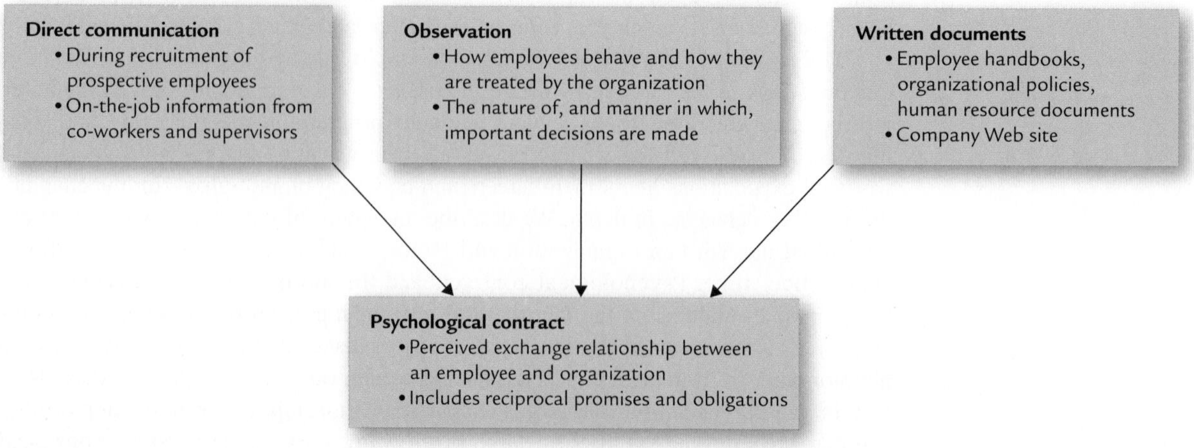

To promote motivation, job satisfaction, and retention of employees, during interviews, managers should provide prospective employees with realistic job previews.

REALISTIC JOB PREVIEW
An honest assessment of the advantages and disadvantages of a particular job and working in a particular organization.

recruit new employees, they often focus on the advantages of joining the organization and accepting a particular job. Take the case of Maria Gomez who was recruited to be a marketing assistant for a large consumer products firm. Gomez has a BA in marketing and was attracted to the position because she hoped it would put her on track for eventually assuming the position of brand manager. When she was recruited, she was told that upward mobility at the firm was encouraged, and if she performed well and proactively sought to advance, she would have opportunities. This promise was one of the reasons she accepted the position.

Once employees are on the job, they continue to receive direct communication from organizational members that form the basis of their psychological contracts.[22] In Gomez's case, however, two coworkers who held similar positions to hers complained they were stuck in dead-end, glorified clerical positions. This upset Gomez because of her own aspirations and what she was told when she was recruited. She began to wonder to what extent she might have been misled by the recruiter. Gomez's experience is, unfortunately, not uncommon. Organizations often seek to hire the best applicants by making lofty promises. However, this strategy often backfires once employees are on the job and realize how things really are. Thus, research suggests that to promote motivation, satisfaction, and retention of employees—as well as create more accurate psychological contracts—organizations should provide prospective employees with realistic job previews. A **realistic job preview (RJP)** is an honest assessment of the advantages and disadvantages of a particular job and working in a particular organization.[23] RJPs enable employees to make informed decisions and form realistic expectations and more accurate psychological contracts.

Observation. Although the adage, 'actions speak louder than words,' is somewhat of a cliché, it certainly rings true when it comes to psychological contracts. Essentially, employees observe how they are treated, how their coworkers are treated, what kinds of decisions are made and in what manner, how their managers behave, and how outcomes are distributed in an organization to form their psychological contracts.[24] In Gomez's case, she observed that two of the current brand managers in her division had started out as marketing assistants and also that her boss made the effort to explain the kinds of things she (the boss) did and how it fit in with the plan for the brand.

Written documents. Written documents are also used in forming psychological contracts. For example, documents describing compensation and benefit policies, performance appraisal processes, and career development become the basis for forming psychological contracts.[25] During her first few weeks on the job, Gomez periodically would consult her company's Web-site and online human resources and career development programs to get a better understanding of what to expect and see if the promises made to her were likely to be fulfilled. Fortunately for her, all signs pointed to a good potential for advancement to the brand manager position—except for the complaints of two of her coworkers. The pair had been passed over for a promotion a few months earlier, but because of the information Gomez had garnered, she was able to dismiss those complaints as 'sour grapes.'

Types of Psychological Contracts

There are two major types of psychological contracts: transactional and relational (see Exhibit 8.2).[26]

Transactional contracts. Transactional contracts tend to be short term and very specific.[27] They are narrow in focus and relatively flexible given their short-term nature. If either party terminates the relationship, a replacement can be found.[28] In transactional contracts, individuals focus primarily on extrinsic outcomes such as pay. Recall the discussion of contingent workers. Contingent workers have transactional kinds of psychological contracts—they transact with an organization to provide some good or service (for example,

EXHIBIT 8.2

Types of Psychological Contracts

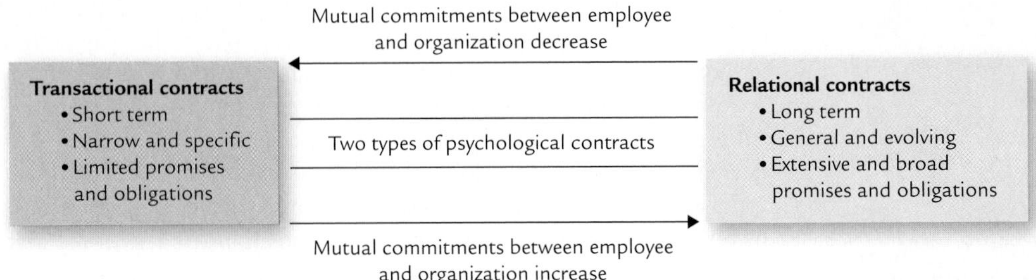

extra help during a busy time of year or clerical services to fill in for an employee on medical leave) for a set economic return (say, hourly pay). The employing organization expects adequate performance on the part of the contingent worker but not much else, and the contingent worker expects pay for the hours worked but little more of the organization. Of course, sometimes organizations decide that they want a longer-term relationship with a valued contingent worker and may seek to employ that individual on a more permanent basis. Another example of a transactional contract is an employment situation in which there is an initial probationary period during which either party can terminate the relationship.

Relational contracts. Relational contracts are longer term, more general, and evolve more gradually over time. They imply a mutual commitment on the part of both parties.[29] Employees are affectively committed to their organizations (see Chapter 3), and the organization is committed to promoting the well-being of the employees.[30] Relational contracts cover much more ground than transactional contracts and are also more subjective because they entail more intangible kinds of factors, such as, for example, opportunities for career development. Although extrinsic outcomes like pay are still important to relational contracts, so too are intrinsic factors such as making an important contribution to the organization and a sense of achievement. University professors who are tenured have relational kinds of psychological contracts.

The previous scenarios involving contingent workers and tenured professors are relatively clear-cut examples of transactional and relational contracts. For other jobs, however, the distinction becomes a bit murkier. One way to think about the distinction is in terms of the extent to which the employment relationship is more transactional (short term) or more relational (long term; see Exhibit 8.2). Indeed, theories and research suggest it is useful to think of psychological contracts as varying along a continuum, with transactional contracts falling at one end of the continuum and relational contracts falling at the other. Of course, the nature of the psychological contract is essentially determined by an employee's perceptions of it.

A number of recent developments have caused researchers to question to what extent psychological contracts are undergoing some sweeping changes. Massive layoffs by both major corporations and smaller start-ups and high-tech companies have caused employees to question how committed their organizations are to them. Today, it is probably more the exception than the rule to expect to spend one's entire career in a single organization. Moreover, the outsourcing of work to countries with lower-cost labor such as China and India is becoming pervasive in more and more industries.[31] The trend also leads one to wonder to what extent psychological contracts are undergoing fundamental changes. While outsourcing is not a new phenomenon, what *is* new is a dramatic increase in the outsourcing of white-collar jobs.[32] Jobs for financial analysts, telemarketers, accountants, engineers, computer programmers, claims adjusters, loan processors, and architectural drafters are among

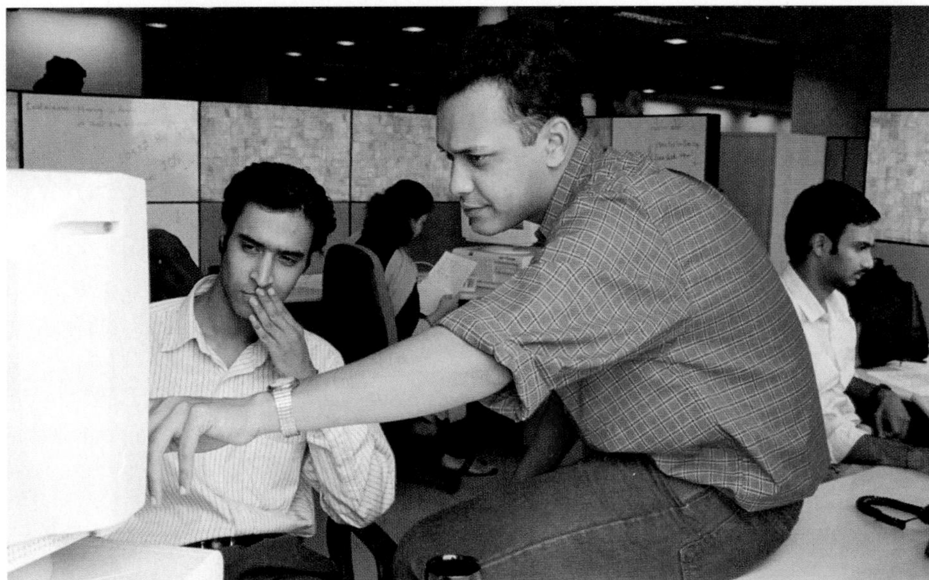

Not only are manufacturing jobs outsourced today, so are many white collar jobs. India, for example, has carved out a niche for itself handling computer programming work for other countries.

those being outsourced to China, India, and other countries with low labor costs. Even mainstay American organizations such as IBM, Microsoft, and Procter & Gamble are outsourcing their white-collar jobs.[33] Although outsourcing has resulted in less job security for U. S. workers, many multinational organizations believe they must outsource at least some white-collar work to reap the benefits of low labor costs and remain competitive.[34]

When Psychological Contracts Are Broken

When employees perceive that their psychological contracts have been breached or broken due to the failure of the organization to live up to its promises, their motivation and performance can suffer. Breached contracts can also result in employees experiencing more negative moods and emotions, being more dissatisfied with their jobs, and looking for employment elsewhere. The larger the perceived violation, the more intense the potential negative reaction. When contracts are intentionally breached by an organization in significant ways, employees' levels of trust in the organization plummet.[35] In our prior example, had Maria Gomez found out that there was no chance of ever being promoted to the position of brand manager (even though she was promised this when she was recruited), in all likelihood, her commitment to the company would plummet, and she would have started looking for another job.

Sometimes observing other employees having their psychological contracts breached can cause people to be concerned about their own futures in an organization.[36] For example, if an organization is outsourcing more and more jobs, a computer programmer who is still employed might fear that his job, too, will eventually be outsourced and might act on this fear by finding another job. However, if the programmer was a valued member of the organization, and his job was not actually in jeopardy, both parties stand to lose. The organization has lost a valued member and the programmer has lost a good job. Thus, whenever organizations take actions that have the potential to affect their members' psychological contracts, care must be taken to accurately and honestly communicate what the action was, why it was taken, and what the future is likely to hold. Moreover, how an organization treats workers whose contracts have been broken is important.[37] For example, during a layoff, whether or not workers are given adequate advance notice, given help in finding other positions, provided with additional training to make them more employable, and whether or not the organization is doing all it can to help them through a tough time and transition out of it can have profound effects on how survivors of the lay-off view their own psychological contracts.

Sometimes, when psychological contracts are broken repeatedly, employees' whole lives can be disrupted as indicated in the following Ethics in Action.

Ethics in Action

GM Gypsies and Other Displaced Workers Face On-Going Struggle

Over the past 10 years, North Carolina has lost 250,000 jobs in manufacturing. On one single day, 6,500 employees of Pillowtex (a textile manufacturer) lost their jobs when their organization closed all of its manufacturing facilities.[38] Unfortunately, this is not an isolated story as employees around the country and the world find their psychological contracts broken when their employers engage in massive lay-offs. For example, IBM recently announced that it would lay off around 12,500 employees (predominantly in Europe) to lower costs and increase earnings.[39]

Tom Hoppe has worked at GM plants for 28 years, and moves around the country in the hopes of holding on to his job.

Workers in the auto industry have been hit especially hard, and continue to face broken psychological contracts as big automakers like Ford and GM struggle to remain competitive. Amid mounting losses, GM recently announced that it would reduce health benefits for retired GM employees. Glenn Shock worked for GM for over 30 years in production and driving fork-lifts and is now retired. Upon hearing his health benefits were going to be cut, he indicated 'That was my contract with them when I retired. Now they're reneging on it, and when you make a contract you should be liable for it.'[40]

Knowing of GM's plans to cut at least 25,000 more jobs over the next several years, some GM employees find themselves moving around the country to hold on to a job as plants are closed in one location and they transfer to another. Over the past 20 years, 300,000 jobs have been cut at GM and the parts supplier it spun-off, Delphi Corporation.[41] As GM closes plants, and opens new ones, still-employed GM workers find themselves moving time and time again to keep their jobs; so many times, in fact, that they call themselves the 'GM Gypsies.'[42] Tom Hoppe has worked at GM plants for 28 years, and moves around the country in the hopes of holding on to his job. As he puts it, 'I'm always getting ready to leave. Some GM workers just keep their stuff in boxes.'[43] Moving around so much and the threat of job loss takes its toll not only on the GM gypsies but also their families and home lives as they face the bind of trying to build a life in one location while knowing they might be moving again next year.[44] Production workers are not the only ones hard-hit by U. S. automakers' mounting troubles. Ford, for example, is planning on significant reductions in white-collar jobs.[45] As these and other companies face difficult decisions in their quest to remain competitive, the consequences of psychological contract breaches for their current and former employees are ongoing ethical concerns as these employees struggle to provide for themselves and their loved ones.

Performance Appraisal

Psychological contracts and almost all of the theories and approaches to motivation we have covered so far assume that managers can accurately *appraise*—that is, evaluate—their subordinates' performance and contributions to their jobs and to the organization. In expectancy theory (see Chapter 6), two of the main determinants of motivation are *expectancy* (the perceived connection between effort and performance) and *instrumentality* (the perceived connection between performance and outcomes such as pay, praise, and career opportunities). Employees are likely to have high levels of expectancy, instrumentality, and, thus, motivation only if their managers can accurately appraise their performances.

According to equity theory, employees will be motivated to perform at a high level only if they perceive that they are receiving outcomes in proportion to their inputs or contributions. Accurately appraising performance is necessary for determining employees' contributions. From the perspective of equity theory, then, employees will be motivated to perform at a high level only if their performance can be and is accurately appraised.

Procedural justice theory suggests that the procedures that are used to appraise performance must be perceived as fair in order for motivation to be high. If employees think managers' appraisals are biased or that irrelevant information is used to evaluate performance, their motivation is likely to suffer. In that sense, procedural justice theory is similar to equity theory. No matter which approach managers use to motivate employees, employees will be motivated to contribute their inputs to the organization and perform at a high level only if they think that their managers can and do appraise their performances accurately.

Because motivation and performance have so great an impact on organizational effectiveness, many researchers have focused on how to appraise performance in organizations. **Performance appraisal** has two overarching goals:

PERFORMANCE APPRAISAL
Evaluating performance to encourage employee motivation and performance and to provide information to be used in managerial decision making.

- to encourage high levels of employee motivation and performance
- to provide accurate information to be used in managerial decision making[46]

Encouraging High Levels of Motivation and Performance

As we mentioned earlier, all the approaches to motivation we discussed in Chapter 6 depend on the accurate assessment of an employee's performance. An accurate appraisal gives employees two important pieces of information: (1) the extent to which they are contributing the appropriate level of inputs to their jobs and the organization and (2) the extent to which they are focusing their inputs in the right direction on the right set of tasks. Essentially, performance appraisal gives employees *feedback* that contributes to intrinsic motivation.

A positive performance appraisal lets employees know that their current levels of motivation and performance are both adequate and appreciated. In turn, this knowledge makes employees feel valued and competent and motivates them to sustain their current levels of inputs and performance. Many employees consider a good performance appraisal an important outcome or reward in itself.

An inadequate performance appraisal tells employees that their performance is unacceptable and may signal that (1) they are not motivated to contribute sufficient inputs to the job, (2) they cannot contribute certain inputs that are required (perhaps because they lack certain key abilities), or (3) they are misdirecting their inputs, which in and of themselves are at an adequate level.

The case of Susan England, Ramona Michaels, and Marie Nouri, salespeople in the women's clothing department of a large department store, illustrates the important role of performance appraisals in encouraging high levels of motivation and performance. England, Michaels, and Nouri have just met individually with the department supervisor, Ann Rickels, to discuss their latest performance appraisals. The performances of all three sales clerks were assessed along four dimensions: quality of customer service, dollar amount of sales, efficient handling of transactions (for example, processing sales and returns quickly to avoid long lines), and housekeeping (returning clothing from dressing rooms to display racks and shelves and keeping the shelves and racks neat).

England received a very positive evaluation on all four dimensions. This positive feedback on her performance helps sustain England's motivation because it lets her know that her efforts are appropriate and appreciated.

Michaels received a positive evaluation on the customer service dimension but a negative evaluation on sales, efficiency, and housekeeping. Michaels tried very hard to be a good performer and provided exceptionally high levels of service to the customers she served. Rickels noted, however, that even though her shifts tended to be on the slow side in terms of customer traffic, there was often a long line of customers waiting to be served and a backlog of clothes in the dressing room to be restocked. Rickels judged Michaels's sales performance to be lackluster. She thought the problem might be that Michaels' attempts to help individual customers arrive at purchase decisions were consuming most of her time. Discussions with Michaels confirmed that this was the case. Michaels indicated that she was working as hard as she could, yet she knew that her performance was lacking on three of the four dimensions. She confessed to feeling frustrated that she couldn't get everything done even though she always seemed to be busy. Michaels's negative performance evaluation let her know that she was misdirecting her inputs. The time and effort she was spending to help customers were preventing her from performing her other job duties. Even though Michaels's performance evaluation was negative, it helped sustain her level of motivation (which had always been high) because it showed her how she could become a good performer.

Nouri received a negative evaluation on all four dimensions. Because Nouri was an experienced salesperson who had the necessary skills and abilities, the negative evaluation signaled Nouri and her manager that Nouri's level of motivation was unacceptable and in need of improvement.

Providing Information for Decision Making

As mentioned earlier, the second goal of performance appraisal is to provide information for managerial decision making. Part of Rickels's job as supervisor of the women's clothing department, for example, is training the salespeople in her area and making decisions about pay raises and promotions.

On the basis of the performance appraisals, Rickels decides that England should receive a pay raise and is most deserving of a promotion to the position of senior sales associate. The performance appraisals let Rickels know that Michaels needs some additional training in how to provide an 'appropriate' level of customer service. Finally, Rickels decides to give some counseling to Nouri because of the negative evaluation of her performance. Rickels knows that Nouri is looking for another job and doesn't expect to remain with the department store for long. Rickels lets Nouri know that as long as she remains in the department, she must perform at an acceptable level to receive the outcomes she desires—pay, not having to work in the evenings, and good working relationships with the other members of the department.

In this example, performance appraisal is used to decide how to distribute outcomes such as pay and promotions equitably and how to improve the performance of employees who are not performing as well as they should be. Performance appraisal can also be useful for other aspects of decision making. For example, information from performance appraisals may allow managers to more effectively use the talents of employees, assign them specific tasks, and group them into high-performing work teams. Performance appraisals also can alert managers to problems in job design or shortcomings in an organization's approach to motivating employees and distributing outcomes.

Finally, performance appraisals provide employees and supervisors with career planning information. By helping managers identify an employee's strengths and weaknesses,[47] the performance appraisal sets the scene for meaningful discussions about the employee's career aspirations and how he or she can best progress toward those goals. The performance appraisal can also signal areas of improvement for the employee and the skills he or she needs to develop.

Developing a Performance Appraisal System

Managers can use the information gained from performance appraisals for two main purposes:

- *Developmental purposes* such as determining how to motivate an employee to perform at a high level, evaluating which of an employee's weaknesses can be corrected by additional training, and helping an employee formulate appropriate career goals
- *Evaluative, decision-making purposes* such as deciding whom to promote, how to set pay levels, and how to assign tasks to individual employees

Regardless of which purpose is most important to a manager, there are a number of choices he or she needs to make when it comes to developing an effective performance appraisal system. In this section, we discuss four of these choices: the extent to which formal and informal appraisals are to be used, what factors are to be evaluated, what methods of appraisal are to be used, and who is to appraise performance (Exhibit 8.3).

Choice 1: The mix of formal and informal appraisals. When a performance appraisal is formal, the performance dimensions and the way employees are evaluated on them are determined in advance. IBM, GE, ExxonMobil, and most other large organizations use formal appraisals, which are usually conducted on a fixed schedule (such as every six months or once a year).[48] In a meeting between the employee whose performance is being appraised and the person doing the evaluating, the employee is given feedback on his or her performance. Feedback contributes to intrinsic motivation.

Sometimes employees want feedback on a more frequent basis than that provided by the formal system. Similarly, managers often want to use performance feedback to motivate subordinates on a day-to-day basis. If an employee is performing poorly, for example, a manager might not want to wait until the next six- or twelve-month performance review to try to rectify the problem. In these situations, an informal performance appraisal, in which managers and subordinates meet informally to discuss ongoing progress, can meet the needs of both employees and managers. Informal appraisals vary in form and content and range from a supervisor commending an employee for doing an outstanding job on a project to criticizing an employee for slacking off and missing a deadline.

Informal performance appraisals are beneficial. Because they often take place right after desired or undesired behaviors occur, employees immediately have a good idea of what they are doing right or wrong. As you learned in Chapter 5, employees will learn to perform desired behaviors and learn not to perform undesired behaviors only when it is clear to them that consequences such as praise (for a desired behavior) or a reprimand (for an undesired behavior) result from performing the behavior in question. The smaller an organization is, the more likely it is to rely exclusively on informal performance appraisals.

Ideally, an organization should rely on both formal and informal performance appraisals to motivate its members to perform at a high level and to make good decisions. The formal appraisal ensures that performance gets assessed periodically along the dimensions important

EXHIBIT 8.3

Choices in Developing an Effective Performance Appraisal System

Choosing the mix of formal and informal appraisals

Choosing what factors to evaluate (traits, behaviors, or results)

Choosing methods of appraisal (graphic rating scales, BARS, or BOS)

Choosing who appraises performance (supervisors, peers, subordinates, workers themselves, or customers/clients)

Performance appraisal system

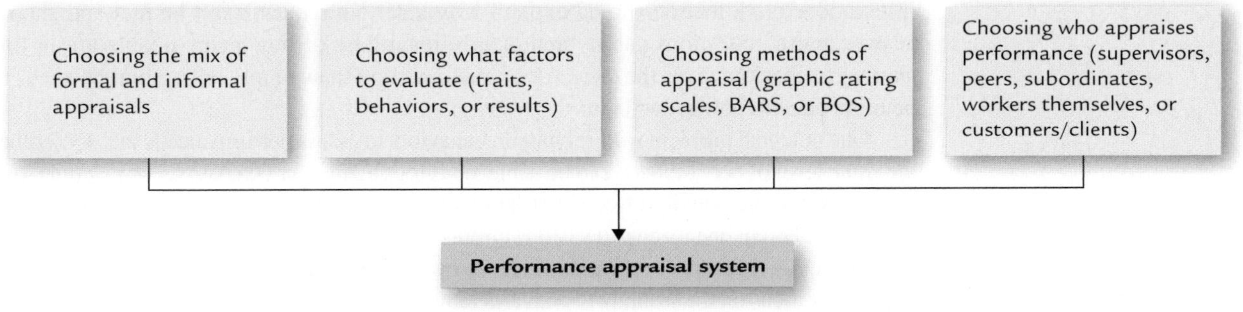

to the organization. Because many managers and employees believe that formal performance appraisals should not yield any 'surprises,' however, ongoing informal appraisals should be part of an organization's performance appraisal system. An employee who is performing poorly should not have to wait six months or a year to find out about it; likewise, good performers should frequently be told that they are on the right track. Informal performance appraisals are important for motivation and performance on a day-to-day basis because they identify and rectify problems as they arise. Although managers in small organizations may not want to spend time and money on the development of a formal system, and managers of large organizations may spend less time than they should appraising performance informally, in most cases the motivational benefits of using formal and informal appraisals outweigh the costs.

Choice 2: What factors to evaluate. In addition to varying in degree of formality, performance appraisals can also vary in content. Traits, behaviors, and results are the three basic types of information that can be assessed.[49]

When traits are used to assess performance, personal characteristics (such as personality, skills, or abilities) that are deemed relevant to job performance are evaluated. A division manager of a large corporation may be evaluated on personal initiative, forecasting skills, and the ability to identify and promote managerial talent. A hotel reservations clerk may be evaluated on patience, politeness, and the ability to remain calm under pressure.

Using traits to assess performance has several disadvantages. First, recall from Chapter 2 that the *interaction* of individual differences such as personality traits or abilities and situational influences usually determines behavior. For this reason, traits or individual differences *alone* are often poor predictors of performance because the possible effects of the situation are not taken into account. Traits may be good indicators of what an employee is like but not very good indicators of what the employee actually does on the job.

Second, because traits do not necessarily have clear-cut relationships with actual behaviors performed on the job, employees and law courts involved in cases of potential employment discrimination are likely to view trait-based performance appraisals as unfair. To avoid the negative effects of perceived unfairness on employee motivation, as well as costly litigation, organizations should use trait-based approaches only when they can clearly demonstrate that the traits are *accurate* indicators of job performance.

Finally, the use of traits to assess performance does little to help motivate employees because it focuses on relatively enduring characteristics that cannot be changed in the short term, if at all. For example, telling a division manager that she lacks initiative or a hotel reservations clerk that he is impatient does not give either employee much of a clue about how to do the job differently.

When *behaviors* are used to appraise performance, the focus is on the actual behaviors or actions an employee displays on the job: What an employee does is appraised, not what the employee is like. A division manager's behavior might be appraised in terms of the extent to which she has launched successful new products and scrapped unprofitable existing products. A hotel reservations clerk might be assessed on his ability to make accurate reservations accommodating guests' requests and the extent to which he satisfactorily explains unmet requests to guests.

Relying on behaviors to assess performance is especially useful because it lets employees know what they should do differently on the job. For example, telling a hotel reservations clerk that he should explain why a certain request can't be met and should answer guests' questions calmly and clearly regardless of how many people are in line waiting to check in gives the clerk a lot more direction than simply telling him he needs to be more patient, polite, and calm.

One potential problem with relying on behaviors to assess performance is that sometimes the *same* level of performance can be achieved through *different* behaviors. For example, two managers may be equally effective at launching new products and scrapping unprofitable ones, even though one reaches decisions through careful, long-term research and deliberation while the other relies more on gut instincts. To overcome this problem, performance appraisals sometimes focus on the results of behaviors rather than on the behaviors themselves.

When *results* are used to appraise performance, the focus is not on what employees do on the job but on the *effects* of their behaviors, or their actual output. The performance of a hotel clerk might be assessed in terms of the number of reservations handled per day and on guests' satisfaction ratings with their check-in experience. When there are many ways to achieve the same result, and the avenue the employee chooses is inconsequential, the result itself can be a useful way of assessing performance.

Just like the other two approaches, however, using results alone to assess performance has its disadvantages. Sometimes results are not under an employee's control: A division's profitability might suffer because sales were lost when foreign trade regulations changed unexpectedly. A day's worth of reservations might be lost because of a computer malfunction. Employees may also become so results oriented that they engage in unethical practices such as overcharging customers or failing to perform important organizational citizenship behaviors such as helping their coworkers.

Sometimes organizations can use both behaviors and results to appraise employee performance, as is the case at USAA, an insurance and investment management firm.[50] It is a good idea to appraise both behavior and results when both dimensions of performance are important for organizational effectiveness. In most sales jobs, for example, the results of a salesperson's behavior (number of items sold) are crucial, but the kinds of behaviors employed (treating customers courteously and politely and processing transactions efficiently) are often equally important. Because traits generally bear less directly on many kinds of jobs, they are not as useful in performance appraisals.

You're the Management Expert

Promoting High-Quality Customer Service

Mark Milstein is the manager of an upscale sporting goods store. There are fifteen full-time sales associates in the store who are paid, in part, based on commissions. The store is more expensive than its competitors in the local market it serves, but it also stocks higher-quality items that are difficult to find for the sports enthusiast. The store also prides itself on outstanding customer service. When customers enter the store, they are approached by a sales associate who helps them find what they are looking for and actually stays with them until they are ready to check out. The sales associates then escort their customers to the checkout counter where they pay for their purchases, and the cashier enters the ID numbers of the sales associate who helped them. Although sales associates are paid the minimum wage per hour, the commissions on their sales can double or triple their actual earnings. Milstein uses weekly sales per associate to appraise their performances and works with new sales associates and those with relatively low sales to improve their performances. Lately, however, Milstein has noticed a troubling trend. Fall sales are up compared to fall sales a year ago, but so are returns. In fact, taking returns into account, sales are actually down from a year ago. Milstein is concerned that perhaps the sales associates are encouraging customers to buy items they may not need or want; thus, the relatively high volume of returns results. Given that high-quality, individualized customer service is the distinguishing competitive advantage of the store, Milstein is worried that his sales associate are perhaps too overzealous in their attempts to 'perform' at a high level. And he wonders if the way he appraises their performances and compensates them might have something to do with it. Because you are an expert in OB, Milstein has come to you for help. Does he need to change the way he appraises the sales associates' performances to promote high-quality customer service?

OBJECTIVE MEASURES
Measures that are based on facts.

SUBJECTIVE MEASURES
Measures that are based on individual perceptions.

GRAPHIC RATING SCALE
A subjective measure on which performance is evaluated along a continuum.

Choice 3: Methods of appraisal. Regardless of the approach to performance appraisal (formal or informal) and the types of information assessed (traits, behaviors, or results), the measures managers use to appraise performance can be of two types: objective or subjective. **Objective measures** such as numerical counts are based on facts. They are used primarily when results are the focus of performance appraisal. The number of televisions a factory worker assembles in a day, the dollar value of the sales a salesperson makes in a week, the number of patients a physician treats in a day, and the return on capital, profit margin, and growth in income of a business are all objective measures of performance.

Subjective measures are based on individuals' perceptions and can be used for appraisals based on traits, behaviors, and results. Because subjective measures are based on perceptions, they are vulnerable to many of the biases and problems that can distort person perception (discussed in Chapter 4). Because for many jobs there is no alternative to subjective appraisal measures, researchers and managers have focused considerable attention on the best way to define these measures.

Typically, when subjective measures are used, managers identify specific dimensions of performance (traits, behaviors, or results) that are important in a job. Then they develop some kind of rating scale or measure to assess an individual's standing on each dimension. Various rating scales can be used. Three of the most popular types are graphic rating scales, behaviorally anchored rating scales, and behavioral observation scales (see Exhibit 8.4). Graphic rating scales can be used to assess traits, behaviors, or results. Behaviorally anchored rating scales and behavioral observation scales focus exclusively on behaviors.

When a **graphic rating scale** is used, the rater—the person responsible for the performance appraisal—assesses the performance of an employee along one or more continua with clearly specified intervals. As indicated in Exhibit 8.4(a), for example, level of customer service may be assessed by rating a salesperson in terms of how courteous she or he is to customers on a five-point scale ranging from 'very discourteous' to 'very courteous.' Graphic rating scales are popular in organizations because they are relatively easy to construct and use.[51] One potential disadvantage of these scales is that different raters may

EXHIBIT 8.4

Examples of Subjective Measures of Performance

a. Graphic rating scale

How courteous is this salesperson toward customers?

●	●	●	●	●
Very discourteous	Discourteous	Neither discourteous nor courteous	Courteous	Very courteous

b. Behaviorally anchored rating scale

1	2	3	4	5	6	7
Ignores customers who need help	Keeps customers waiting unnecessarily	Fails to thank customers for purchases	Answers customers' questions promptly	Completes transactions in a timely manner	Greets customers pleasantly and offers assistance	Always tries sincerely to help customers locate items to suit their needs

c. Behavioral observation scale

	Almost never				Almost always
Sincerely thanks customers for purchases	1	2	3	4	5
Pleasantly greets customers	1	2	3	4	5
Answers customers' questions promptly	1	2	3	4	5

disagree about the meaning of the scale points. For example, what is 'very discourteous' behavior to one rater may be only 'discourteous' to another.

BEHAVIORALLY ANCHORED RATING SCALE (BARS)
A subjective measure on which specific work-related behaviors are evaluated.

A **behaviorally anchored rating scale (BARS)** attempts to overcome that problem by carefully defining what each scale point means. Examples of specific work-related behaviors correspond to each scale point.[52] Exhibit 8.4(b) is an example of a BARS rating for a salesperson on the courtesy dimension. One potential problem with behaviorally anchored rating scales is that sometimes employees exhibit behaviors corresponding to more than one point on the scale. For example, a salesperson may thank customers for their purchases but otherwise tend to ignore them. BARS can also take a considerable amount of time and effort to develop and use.

BEHAVIORAL OBSERVATION SCALE (BOS)
A subjective measure on which the frequency with which an employee performs a behavior is indicated.

A **behavioral observation scale (BOS)** overcomes the BARS problem of employees exhibiting behaviors corresponding to more than one scale point by not only describing specific behaviors (as does BARS) but also asking raters to indicate the frequency with which an employee performs the behaviors, as shown in Exhibit 8.4(c).[53] BOS, however, tends to be even more time consuming than BARS for raters to complete.

These are just a few of the types of scales that are available for subjective appraisals of performance. As we indicated, each scale has its advantages and disadvantages, and it is not clear at this point that any one type is better to use than another. BARS and BOS can be a lot more time consuming to develop and use than graphic rating scales, but they can be more beneficial for giving feedback to employees because they appraise more precise behaviors.

Choice 4: Who appraises performance? We have been assuming that supervisors are the people who appraise their subordinates' performance. This is usually a fair assumption. In most organizational settings, supervisors are responsible for performance appraisals because they are generally the most familiar with their subordinates' behavior and are responsible for motivating them to perform at acceptable levels. Sometimes, however, self-appraisals, peer appraisals, subordinate appraisals, customer/client appraisals, and multiple raters are also used to appraise performance.[54]

Self-appraisal may offer some advantages because an employee is likely to be familiar with his or her own level of performance. But most people consider themselves to be above average, and no one likes to think of him or herself as a poor performer, so a self-appraisal is likely to be inflated.

Peer appraisals are appraisals given by an employee's coworkers. Peers are often very familiar with performance levels, yet they may be reluctant to provide accurate appraisals. An employee may not want to give his friend a poor rating. An employee may not want to give her coworker a high rating if she thinks it will make her look bad in comparison. Nevertheless, peer evaluations can be useful, especially when employees are members of a team, and the team's performance depends on each member being motivated to perform at a high level. Under these circumstances, team members are motivated to provide accurate peer ratings because the whole team suffers if one member performs poorly. By accurately appraising one another's performance, members can motivate each other to perform well and ensure everyone does their share of the work. It is for this reason that many professors who assign group projects have the members appraise each other's performance. Peer ratings help to ensure that no group member gets a 'free ride' or takes advantage of the other hardworking students in the group.

Subordinate appraisals are appraisals given to a manager by the people he or she supervises. Subordinates rate the manager on, for example, his or her leadership behaviors. In order for subordinates to feel free to give an accurate appraisal (especially a negative one), it is often desirable for the appraisals to be anonymous so they need not fear retaliation from their supervisors. Many universities use anonymous student evaluations to appraise the quality of their teachers.

Customer/client appraisals are another source of performance information. Recall from Chapter 5 that some health maintenance organizations, such as U.S. Healthcare and AvMed–Sante Fe, evaluate their physicians' performance, in part, on the basis of scores they receive on patient surveys. These surveys measure whether the doctors are available for emergencies, provide clear explanations of treatments, and show concern for patients' needs.

The advantage of using other sources of information, such as customers, subordinates, or peers, is that each of these sources is likely to be familiar with a different dimension of an employee's performance. But because each source has considerable disadvantages if used exclusively, some organizations rely on 360-degree appraisals. In a **360-degree appraisal**, an employee's performance is evaluated by a variety of people who are in a position to evaluate the employee's performance. A 360-degree appraisal of a manager, for example, may include evaluations made by peers, subordinates, superiors, and clients or customers who are familiar with the manager's performance. The manager would then receive feedback based on evaluations from each of these sources. When 360-degree appraisals are used, managers have to be careful that each evaluator is familiar with the performance of the individual he or she is evaluating. Although 360-degree appraisals can be used for many different kinds of employees, they are most commonly used for managers.

360-DEGREE APPRAISAL
A performance appraisal in which an employee's performance is evaluated by a number of people who are in a position to evaluate the employee's performance such as peers, superiors, subordinates, and customers or clients.

The growing popularity of 360-degree appraisals attests to the need for more feedback in organizations. And who is in a better position to give employees feedback than all the different individuals they come into contact with on the job? An employee's peers, for example, may have a different perspective on his or her performance than the boss. A manager who lacks assertiveness when dealing with superiors may be too assertive and dictatorial when dealing with subordinates. Receiving feedback based on evaluations from these multiple sources has the potential to provide employees with a richer picture of their strengths, weaknesses, and areas for improvement.

The lending cooperative, Farm Credit Service Southwest, relies on 360-degree appraisals for about 50 percent of its annual performance appraisal process. Although the company's chief financial officer, John Barkell, found the process a bit intimidating, he did receive useful feedback that he has subsequently acted upon, including the need to communicate more with his subordinates. Barkell subsequently instituted weekly meetings with his staff to open lines of communication and answer questions.[55]

At Public Service Electric & Gas in Newark, New Jersey, manager Gordon Smouther's 360-degree appraisal indicated he was too controlling and defensive, which resulted in him dismissing other people's ideas without giving them a chance. As a result of the appraisal, Smouther and his boss put together a plan that included his taking a course at a center specializing in creative leadership and giving him private lessons with an executive coach. Smouther's ratings improved dramatically.[56]

Experiences such as these point to the advantages of 360-degree appraisals—they can provide managers and other employees with valuable feedback they can use to improve their performances. However, there are also certain potential problems with 360-degree appraisals. Some managers fear that 360-degree appraisals might turn into popularity contests, with managers who are well liked being rated more highly than those who may be less popular but produce better results. Others fear that managers will be reluctant to make unpopular decisions or difficult choices because they may have a negative effect on how their subordinates evaluate them. On the one hand, if appraisals are anonymous, disgruntled subordinates may seek revenge by giving their bosses negative evaluations. On the other hand, some bosses coach their subordinates and sometimes even threaten them to get positive ratings.[57]

A manager at Citibank indicated that he received a very negative appraisal from a subordinate that was almost like a personal attack; he was pretty sure it came from a poor performer.[58] At Baxter International, although employees in the information technology unit were very familiar with each other's performances, they were reluctant to provide any negative evaluations and gave each other positive ratings because they knew the ratings were being used for pay raise decisions and the evaluations were not anonymous. Baxter decided to continue using the peer evaluations but more for developmental purposes rather than decision making.[59]

Clearly, 360-degree appraisals have both advantages and disadvantages. In order to reap the benefits of 360-degree appraisals, research suggests the appraisals should focus on behaviors rather than traits or results and that much care be taken to ensure appropriate raters are chosen. The research also suggests that appraisals are more likely to be honest when they are anonymous, and raters should receive training in how to use the rating form.[60]

Regardless of whether a formal 360-degree appraisal system is in place, organizations need to be careful that managers and all employees are accurately appraised by individuals who are knowledgeable about their behaviors. Subordinates can be particularly knowledgeable about their supervisors' behaviors but sometimes lack the means to communicate this knowledge in ways that can motivate their supervisors to improve. The Web-site ImproveNow.com provides a potential solution to this problem.[61] The site contains a 60-item questionnaire subordinates can complete to appraise the performance of their supervisors. After multiple subordinates complete the form independently online, the results are tabulated, and the supervisor receives specific feedback about how he or she is doing in different areas. Those areas might include standing up for their subordinates and being supportive, rewarding them, or having a good sense of what the organization or work group should strive for in the future.[62]

Lee Burnley and eight of her coworkers at Alliance Funding, a mortgage lending unit of Superior Bank FSB located in Orangeburg, New Jersey, completed the appraisals online for their supervisor Sonia Russomanno. Russomanno received an overall score of B on the appraisal, based on specific dimensions in the rating form. Her reaction? At first, she was grateful that her rating wasn't worse but then let down that it wasn't better. More importantly, she realized the value of getting honest feedback from her subordinates to help her

EXHIBIT 8.5

Problems and Biases in Person Perception That May Result in Inaccurate Performance Appraisals

Problem or Bias	Description	Example of Problem or Bias Leading to an Inaccurate Performance Appraisal
Stereotype	A type of schema (abstract knowledge structure stored in memory) built around some distinguishing, often highly visible characteristic such as race, gender, or age.	A 35-year-old supervisor gives a 60-year-old engineer a negative performance appraisal that indicates that the engineer is slow and unwilling to learn new techniques although this is not true.
Primacy effect	The initial pieces of information that people have about a person have an inordinately large effect on how that person is perceived.	A subordinate who made a good first impression on his supervisor receives a better performance appraisal than he deserves.
Contrast effect	People's perceptions of a person are influenced by their perception of others in an organization.	A subordinate's average level of performance is appraised more harshly than it should be by her supervisor because all the subordinate's co-workers are top performers.
Halo effect	People's general impressions of a person influence their perceptions on specific dimensions.	A subordinate who has made a good overall impression on a supervisor is appraised as performing high-quality work and always meeting deadlines although this is not true.
Similar-to-me effect	People perceive others who are similar to themselves more positively than they perceive those who are dissimilar.	A supervisor gives a subordinate who is similar to her a more positive performance appraisal than the subordinate deserves.
Harshness, leniency, and average tendency biases	When rating their subordinates' performance, some supervisors tend to be overly harsh, some overly lenient. Others tend to rate everyone as about average.	An exceptionally high-performing secretary receives a mediocre performance appraisal because his supervisor is overly harsh in rating everyone.
Knowledge-of-predictor bias	Perceptions of a person are influenced by knowing the person's standing on a predictor of performance.	A computer programmer who scored highly on cognitive and numerical ability tests used to hire programmers in an organization receives a more positive performance appraisal than she deserves.

improve her performance. For example, as a result of the feedback she received, Russomanno realized that she needs to work on using rewards to motivate her subordinates. She plans to have her subordinates evaluate her again at the ImproveNow.com Web site in the future to see how she is doing.[63]

Potential Problems in Subjective Performance Appraisal

Recall from Chapter 4 that a number of problems and biases can result in inaccurate perceptions of other people in an organization. These problems and biases (recapped in Exhibit 8.5) can be particularly troublesome for subjective performance appraisals. Awareness of these perception problems can help prevent these problems and biases from leading to an inaccurate appraisal.

Pay and the Employment Relation

The accurate assessment of performance is central to the goals of motivating employees to perform at acceptable levels and improving the effectiveness of managerial decision making. One area of decision making that often has profound effects on the motivation of all members of an organization—managers and employees alike—is the distribution of outcomes, such as pay, benefits, vacations, perks, promotions and other career opportunities, job titles, offices, and privileges. In this section, we focus on the outcome that is one of the most powerful of all motivation tools: pay. Pay can be used not only to motivate people to perform highly but also to motivate them to join and remain with an organization. Thus, pay is a central aspect of psychological contracts and a key component of the exchange relationship between employees and an organization.

The principles of operant conditioning discussed in Chapter 5 and all of the approaches to motivation covered in Chapter 6 suggest that outcomes should be distributed to employees *contingent* on their performing desired organizational behaviors:

- Operant conditioning theory suggests that to encourage the learning of desired organizational behaviors, positive reinforcers or rewards should be distributed to employees contingent on performance.
- Need theory suggests that when pay is contingent on performance, employees are motivated to perform because doing so will help satisfy their needs.
- Expectancy theory takes into account the fact that pay is an outcome with high valence (highly desirable) for most employees and that instrumentality (the association between performance and outcomes) must be high for motivation to be high.
- Equity theory indicates that outcomes (pay) should be distributed in proportion to inputs (performance).
- Procedural justice theory suggests that the methods used to evaluate performance and distribute pay need to be fair.

From a learning and motivational perspective, the message is clear: Whenever possible, pay should be based on performance.[64]

Merit Pay Plans

MERIT PAY PLAN
A plan that bases pay on performance.

A plan that bases pay on performance is often called a **merit pay plan**.[65] When pay is not based on merit, it might be based on the particular job an employee has in an organization or on an employee's tenure in the organization. Merit pay, however, is likely to be much more motivational than pay that is not based on performance.

Merit pay plans tend to be used most heavily at the upper levels in organizations,[66] but basing pay on performance has been shown to be effective for employees at lower levels in an organization's hierarchy as well. Many organizations are increasingly using merit pay to attract, motivate, and retain employees. Manufacturing companies, accounting firms, law offices, and investment banks have all stepped up their use of merit pay to motivate employees at all levels.[67] Additionally, merit pay is an important motivation tool not only in the United States but in many other countries as well such as Great Britain, Japan, and Germany.[68]

Should Merit Pay Be Based on Individual, Group, or Organizational Performance?

One of the most important choices managers face in designing an effective merit pay plan is whether to base merit pay on individual, group, or organizational performance. The following guidelines, based on the theories of learning and motivation discussed in previous chapters, can be used to make this choice:

1. When individual performance can be accurately assessed (for example, the number of cars a salesperson sells, the number of insurance policies an insurance agent writes, a lawyer's billable hours), the maximum motivational impact is obtained from basing pay on individual performance.[69]
2. When employees are highly interdependent—when what one employee does affects the work of others—and individual performance levels cannot be accurately assessed, an individual-based pay-for-performance plan is not a viable option. In this case, managers can implement a group or organization-level pay-for-performance plan. Under such a system, employees' pay levels depend on how well their group or the organization as a whole performs. It is impossible, for example, to accurately assess the performance of individual members of a group of carpenters who jointly design and construct large, elaborate pieces of custom furniture. Together they produce pieces of furniture that none of them could construct alone.
3. When organizational effectiveness depends on individuals working together, cooperating with each other, and helping each other out, group- or organization-based pay-for-performance plans may be more appropriate than individual-based plans.[70] When a team of research scientists works together in a laboratory to try to come up with a cure for a disease such as AIDS, for example, it is essential for group members to share their insights and findings with each other and build upon each other's findings.

Sometimes it is possible to combine elements of an individual and group or company-wide plan to get the benefits of both. Lincoln Electric, for example, uses a combination of individual- and organization-based plans.[71] Each year, Lincoln Electric establishes a bonus fund, the size of which depends on the whole organization's performance that year. Money from the bonus fund is then distributed to employees on the basis of their individual levels of performance. Lincoln Electric employees are motivated to cooperate and help each other because when the firm as a whole performs well, everybody benefits by receiving a larger bonus at year-end. Employees are also motivated to perform at a high level individually not only because their individual performances determine their share of the fund but also because they are paid on piece-rate basis, which is discussed next.

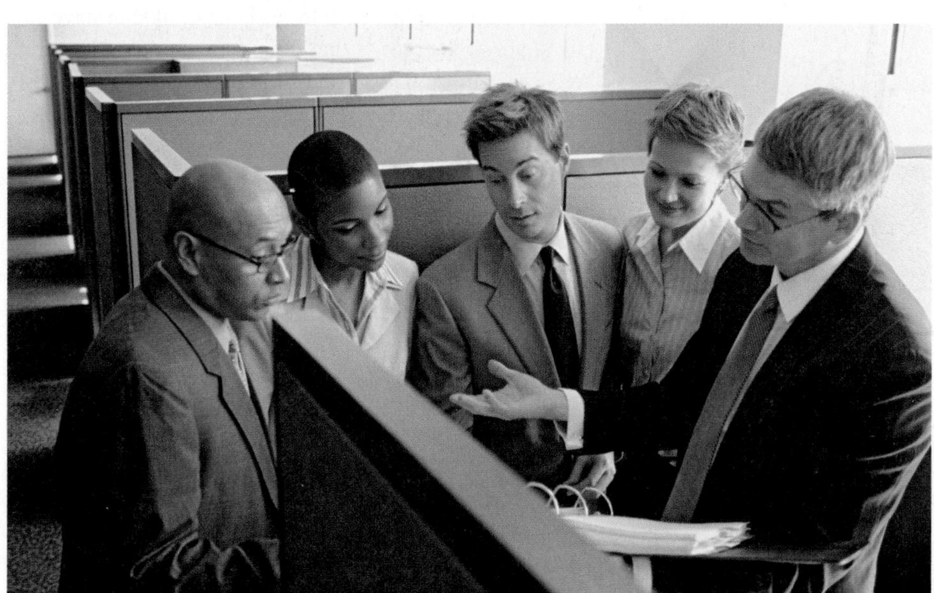

When employees are highly interdependent in work teams and individual performance levels cannot be accurately assessed, managers can implement a team or organization-level pay-for-performance plan.

Should Merit Pay Be in the Form of a Salary Increase or a Bonus?

There are two major ways to distribute merit pay: salary increases and bonuses. When salary increases are used, individual salaries are increased by a certain amount based on performance. When bonuses are used, individuals receive a lump-sum amount (in addition to their regular salary) based on performance. Bonus plans such as the one used by Lincoln Electric tend to have a greater impact on motivation than do salary increase plans, for three reasons.

First, an individual's current salary level is based on performance levels, cost-of-living increases, and so on, from the day the person started working in the organization; thus, the absolute level of one's salary is based largely on factors not related to current performance. Increases in salary levels based on current performance tend to be small (for example, 6 percent) in comparison to total salary amounts. Second, current salary increases may be only partially based on performance. This occurs when, for example, across-the-board, cost-of-living raises are given to all employees. Third, organizations rarely cut salaries, so salary levels across employees tend to vary less than performance levels. Bonus plans overcome some of the limitations of salary increases because a bonus can be tied directly and exclusively to performance and because the motivational effect of a bonus is not mitigated by the other factors mentioned previously. Bonuses can vary considerably from time period to time period and from employee to employee, depending on performance levels.[72] When organizations want all employees to cooperate and work together for an organizational objective, bonuses can be based on organizational performance.

Examples of Merit Pay Plans

Two clear examples of individual-based merit pay plans are piece-rate pay and commission pay. In a *piece-rate pay plan*, an employee is paid for each unit he or she produces, as in the case of a tailor who is paid for each piece of clothing he sews or alters, or a factory worker who is paid for each television she assembles. With commission pay, often used in sales positions, salaries are a percentage of sales. Salary levels in *full commission plans* fluctuate directly in proportion to sales that are made. Salary levels in a *partial commission plan* consist of fixed salaries plus an amount that varies with sales levels. The maximum motivational impact is obtained when pay is based solely on performance, as in a full commission plan. Employees operating under such a plan, however, are not likely to develop any kind of team spirit.

When pay is based solely on individual performance, employees are motivated to perform at a high level, and organizations may be able to attract and retain top performers because they will receive maximum levels of pay. But such plans can also cause employees to adopt a highly individualized approach to their jobs and not work together as a team.

Pay plans that are linked strictly to organizational performance are often called *gain-sharing plans*. Employees in organizations that have these kinds of plans are given a certain share of the profits that the organization makes or a certain share of the expenses that are saved during a specified time period. Gain sharing is likely to encourage camaraderie and a team spirit among employees because all of the organization's members stand to benefit if it does well. But, because pay is based on organizational rather than on individual performance, each individual may not be so motivated to perform at the high level he or she would have achieved under a pay plan based on individual merit.

One kind of gain-sharing plan is the *Scanlon plan*, developed by Joseph Scanlon, a union leader at a steel and tin plant in the 1920s.[73] The Scanlon plan focuses on reducing costs. Departmental and organization-wide committees are established to evaluate and implement cost-saving suggestions provided by employees. Employees are motivated to make suggestions, participate on the committees, and help implement the suggestions because they get a portion of the cost savings realized.

Another kind of gain-sharing pay plan is *profit sharing*. Employees participating in profit-sharing plans receive a certain share of an organization's profits. Approximately 16 percent of employees in medium and large companies and 25 percent of employees in small firms receive some form of profit sharing. Rutgers University economist Douglas Kruse estimates that productivity tends to increase from 3 to 5 percent when companies institute profit sharing. Profit-sharing plans that give employees their share of profits in cash tend to be more successful than programs that use some sort of deferred payment (such as contributing employees' shares of profits to their retirement funds).[74] If an organization has a bad year, then no money may be available for profit sharing regardless of individual or group performance levels.

The Ethics of Pay Differentials and Comparable Worth

It is well established that women earn less money than men. Women earn approximately 74 cents for every dollar earned by men.[75] Some of the gender gap in rates of pay may be due to overt discrimination or to the fact that some men have more experience or better qualifications. But there is another reason for these discrepancies in pay.[76] This subtle form of discrimination works as follows: Jobs that women have traditionally held (as nurses, teachers, secretaries, librarians, and so forth) have lower pay rates than jobs that men have traditionally held (as carpenters, managers, doctors, and construction workers, for example), even though the jobs require similar skill levels, and the organization values them equally.

Pay differentials between men and women have the potential to adversely affect the motivation of high-performing women who perceive they are not receiving as much pay as the job is worth. From the perspective of equity theory, women who perceive themselves as contributing levels of inputs equivalent to those of their male counterparts but receiving lower levels of outcomes (in particular, pay) may be motivated to reduce their inputs (perhaps by exerting less effort) to restore equity. More critical than their effects on motivation, pay differentials based on gender, age, race, ethnic background, or any other nonperformance characteristic are unethical.

COMPARABLE WORTH
The idea that jobs of equivalent value to an organization should carry the same pay rates regardless of differences in the work and the personal characteristics of the employee.

The principle of **comparable worth** suggests that jobs of equivalent value to an organization should carry the same pay rates regardless of differences in the nature of the work itself and the personal characteristics of the people performing the work.[77] Pay rates should be determined by factors such as effort, skill, and job responsibility—not by the type of person who usually performs the job. The gender, race, or ethnic background of jobholders is an irrelevant input that managers should not consider when they establish pay rates for different positions. When pay rates are determined by comparable worth, it is more likely that all members of an organization will be motivated to perform at a high level because they are more likely to perceive they are being paid on an equitable basis.

Although comparable worth makes a lot of sense in principle, it has been hard to put into practice. Organizations have resisted basing salaries on comparable worth because pay levels for some jobs would have to be raised (organizations rarely lower pay rates). On a more fundamental level, however, determining what the value or worth of a job is to an organization and comparing this value to that of other very different types of jobs is difficult. Such comparisons are often value laden and the source of considerable disagreement. Even so, comparable worth is an ethical issue that managers need to be aware of and a goal worth striving for.

Another pay differential that has been receiving increasing attention is the difference between the pay received by those at the very top of an organization and the many employees under them. Today, the average CEO earns over 430 times what the average hourly worker earns.[78] While some employees are actually seeing their pay being cut and raises eliminated, CEOs, on the other hand, seem to be earning ever more money.[79] For example, the average annual compensation package for CEOs of large public companies is around $10 million with some CEOs earning many times this amount.[80] From the opening case, this is clearly not the case at Costco where CEO Jim Sinegal believes that being cost-conscious does not go hand-in-hand with vast pay differentials.[81] Huge pay differentials between those at the top of the corporate hierarchy and those lower down raise concerns about distributive justice, especially when lay-offs take place, salaries are cut, or raises are minimal.

Careers

There are outcomes in addition to pay that are part of many employees' psychological contracts and central to their exchange relationships with their employers. One of these outcomes, career opportunities, is related not just to the specific job a person holds today but also to the jobs a person expects to perform or advance to over the course of his or her entire career.

Career opportunities often include things such as being in a fast-track management program or getting a promotion, but they can include other specific career-related outcomes such as having the opportunity to do the kind of work you really want to do, receiving career-relevant experiences and training, and having exposure to people who can help you advance your own career. Many of these career opportunities affect intrinsic motivation levels because they help people pursue the kind of work they enjoy.

Sometimes it is possible to give employees the chance to do what they love, even when they are performing a job that is not directly related to their career aspirations. At a restaurant called Applause in New York City, many aspiring singers and actors take what they hope are temporary jobs waiting tables to support themselves because Applause allows waiters and waitresses to sing and entertain customers while serving meals. The restaurant, thus, gives aspiring singers and actors the chance to do what they love, to gain experience performing in front of a live audience, and meet customers who might be talent scouts, directors, and producers who, of course, can further their careers.

Both organizations and individual employees should engage in career management. When careers are effectively managed, organizations make the best use of their members' skills and abilities, and employees are motivated to perform at high levels and tend to be satisfied with their jobs, all of which help the organization achieve its goals. To use career opportunities as a motivational tool, managers must understand what careers are, how people progress through them, and how they can be managed by both employees and organizations.

The Nature of Careers

CAREER
The sum of work-related experiences throughout a person's lifetime.

A **career** can be defined as the sum of work-related experiences throughout one's lifetime.[82] A career includes the number and types of jobs a person has had as well as the different organizations a person has worked for.

Why are individuals concerned about their careers? A career can have major effects on a person's economic and psychological well-being. At a basic economic level, work provides most people in modern society with the income they need to support themselves and their loved ones and pursue their personal interests such as their hobbies and leisure activities. From this economic perspective, career opportunities are an important source of *extrinsic motivation* for employees.[83] As a source of psychological well-being, work can provide personal fulfillment and give a sense of meaning and purpose to people's lives. From this psychological perspective, career opportunities are an important source of *intrinsic motivation*.

Why are organizations concerned with the careers of their members? Effectively managing careers helps an organization motivate its members to achieve individual and organizational goals and perform at a high level. Effective career management in an organization means that there will be well-qualified employees at all levels who can assume more responsible positions as needed to help the organization achieve its goals. Organizations can help motivate their members through career management by helping them develop the knowledge, skills, abilities, and other inputs needed for high levels of performance[84] and by rewarding high performers with career opportunities such as valuable experience and training, choice job assignments, and promotions.

Types of Careers

Although every individual's career is unique, careers fall into four general categories: steady-state careers, linear careers, spiral careers, and transitory careers.[85]

Steady-state careers. A steady-state career reflects a one-time commitment to a certain kind of job that is maintained throughout one's working life.[86] Employees with steady-state careers can become very skilled at, and intrinsically motivated by, the work they do and often see themselves as experts. A family doctor who sets up a medical practice in her hometown when she finishes her medical training and keeps the same practice throughout her career until she retires at age 70 has a steady-state career.

Linear careers. In a linear career, a person progresses through a sequence of jobs, and each job entails progress over the prior one in terms of responsibility, skills needed, level

Some postal workers have steady-state careers.

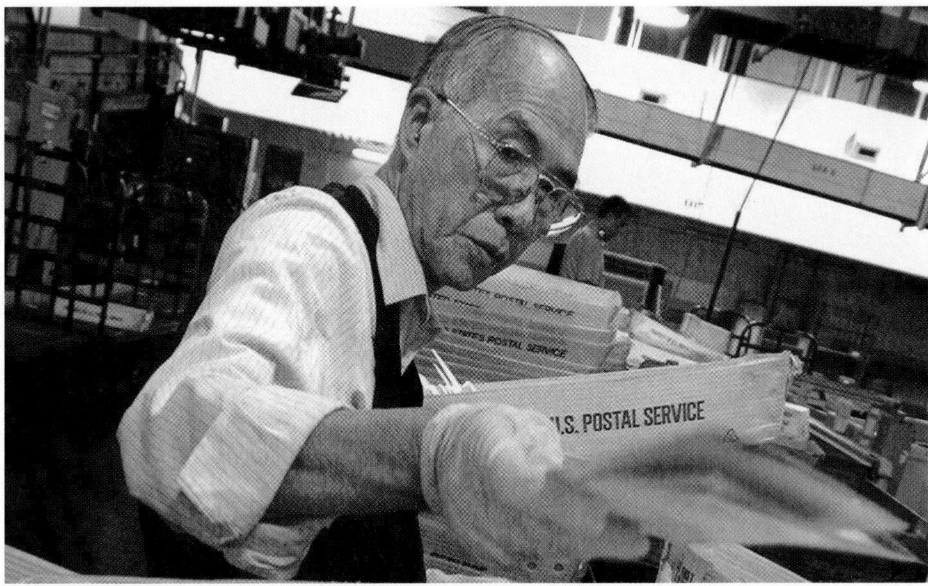

in the hierarchy of an organization, and so on.[87] Employees can stay with the same organization or move from company to company as they pursue linear careers. Edwin L. Artzt, former chairman of Procter & Gamble, started working for Procter & Gamble over 40 years ago in a low-level job and worked his way up the corporate ladder through each of the corporate divisions to assume the top position.[88]

Spiral careers. In a spiral career, a person holds different types of jobs that build on each other but tend to be fundamentally different.[89] An associate professor of management with a spiral career leaves university teaching and research to head up the human resources department at a large company, then, after working at that job for 10 years, leaves to start a consulting company.

Transitory careers. A person with a transitory career changes jobs frequently, and each job is different from the one before it.[90] After graduating from college, Paul Jones worked as the manager of a hardware store for two years, then worked in a bank for a year, and is currently training to become a police officer.

Career Stages

Although each person's career is unique, there are certain career stages that at least some people seem to progress through. And even if a person does not progress through each stage, he or she experiences some subset of the stages. Each stage is associated with challenges to be met and tasks to be tackled. Researchers disagree about the exact number of career stages; here, we discuss five stages that are useful to understand a person's career, even if each of these stages is not experienced to the same extent (see Exhibit 8.6).[91]

More often than not, these career stages are experienced in different organizations. As we have said, given the high levels of uncertainty in the environment, lay-offs, outsourcing, and increased global competition, many people's psychological contracts do not include expectations of a lifelong career with a single organization or even a relatively long-term relationship. The **boundaryless career** captures the idea that careers are not tied to (or bound to) a single organization and that people will have a variety of work

BOUNDARYLESS CAREER
A career that is not tied to a single organization and in which a person has a variety of kinds of work experiences in different organizations.

EXHIBIT 8.6

Career Stages

Preparation for work → Organizational entry → Early career → Midcareer → Late career experiences in different organizations over the course of their careers.[92] Boundaryless careers are becoming increasingly prevalent in the United States.[93]

Preparation for work. During the first stage, individuals must decide what kind of career they want and learn what qualifications and experiences they need to obtain a good career-starting job.[94] Critical tasks faced in the preparation stage involve acquiring the necessary knowledge, skills, education, and training either from formal classroom education or from on-the-job apprenticeships or other programs.

Personality, ability, attitudes, and values are among the factors that affect initial career choice.[95] Individuals who are high on the Big Five dimension of extraversion (see Chapter 2), for example, may tend to gravitate toward careers such as sales that require a lot of social interaction with others. Individuals with exceptional numerical abilities may lean toward a career in engineering. A person who has extrinsic work values (Chapter 3) and values work for its consequences may choose a law career earning him or her a high income. By contrast a person who has intrinsic work values and values work for its own sake may choose a nursing career leading to feelings of personal accomplishment and fulfillment.

A recent study by researchers Jacquelynne Eccles and Mina Vida sought to understand why young men and women who desired science careers tended to concentrate on different subjects, with women being more likely to focus on the biological sciences (including social science, environmental science, and medicine) rather than mathematically based sciences such as physics, engineering, astronomy, and information technology.[96] Evidently, it seems that the young women in the study were more people oriented and saw areas such as medicine as more social and important for society. Young men who were more people oriented also were more likely to go into the biological sciences, but on the whole, young men were more interested in the mathematical sciences than young women.[97] Eccles suggests that educators need to focus more on communicating to young people how different kinds of careers contribute to society. For example, engineers design many things that help people, ranging from safe, functional buildings, to wheelchairs and other medical equipment that improve the quality of life for the disabled.[98] By having more information about how different jobs and careers contribute to society and help people, young women and men will be able to make more informed career choices.

Organizational entry. During the second stage, people try to find a job that will be a good start to their chosen careers. People in the entry stage find out as much as they can about potential jobs and organizations from various sources, including business newspapers and magazines, college placement offices and career/job fairs, company-sponsored information and seminars, and personal contacts.

Once job seekers have gathered this information, they want to become jobholders. Getting an interview with an organization you're interested in is sometimes as simple as signing up with a company representative visiting on campus or getting 'the friend of a friend' to put in a good word for you with his wife, who is a manager at the company.

Once an interview is scheduled, it is crucial to make the most of it. Finding out as much as possible about the company, doing practice interviews, and thinking of interesting questions to ask the interviewer and good answers to frequently asked questions (for example, 'Where do you see yourself in five years?' or 'Why do you want to be an accountant?') are things job applicants can do to increase their prospects. In Chapter 4, we discussed many of the factors that affect perception and, thus, both how interviewers perceive job applicants and how job applicants can actively influence the perception process through impression management. We also explained how perception is distorted by biases such as the primacy effect, which leads interviewers to make an initial decision about someone in the first few minutes of the interview and then spend the rest of the interview selectively hearing and seeing things that confirm that initial impression. In an interview, then, job applicants must make a good impression from the minute they walk in the door.

In addition to selling themselves to an organization, applicants also need to find out as much information as they can about the job they are seeking, their career prospects with the organization, and the organization as a whole to make a good choice. Sometimes what people think a job or an organization will be like is very different from what they actually experience on the job. A new assistant to the division president might find, to her dismay, that her job is really a secretarial position and not the start to the management career she envisions.

Organizations should provide applicants with accurate information about the jobs they apply for, their career prospects, and the organization as a whole. Sometimes, in an effort to attract outstanding applicants who might have several job offers, members of an organization might be tempted to paint a rosy picture of what their organization has to offer. This practice can lead new hires to experience disappointment and negative attitudes, both of which might prompt them to quit. Research has found that organizations that disseminate realistic job information can reduce turnover.[99]

Early career. The early career stage starts once a person has obtained a job in a chosen career. There are two distinct steps in this stage. The first step is *establishment*, during which newcomers are motivated to learn how to perform their jobs, what is expected of them, and more generally how to fit in (see Chapter 10).[100] The second step is *achievement*.[101] Once newcomers have mastered their jobs and 'know' the organization, they are motivated to accomplish something worthwhile and make a significant contribution to the organization. Achievement can mean different things to different people. For some, achievement is synonymous with moving up the corporate ladder; for others, it can mean becoming an expert in a certain area or devising creative solutions to difficult problems.

Organizations can do several things to help ensure members are motivated to achieve individual, group, and organizational goals. In Chapters 6 and 7, we discussed how organizations motivate members to perform at high levels and how jobs should ideally be designed. In addition, managers need to convince employees they are able to achieve difficult goals (have high expectancy) and will receive the outcomes they desire when they do (have high instrumentality).

According to equity theory, managers must also distribute outcomes (pay, status, choice job assignments, promotions, and other career opportunities) to employees based on their inputs to the organization (ability, education, experience, time, and effort). Earlier in this chapter, we saw the important role that performance appraisals can play by providing employees with feedback to motivate them. Accurate performance appraisals help employees assess their own levels of achievement, determine how to improve in the future, and more generally assess their career progress.

In addition to identifying where and how they can make the most valuable contributions to an organization, individuals can advance their careers during the achievement step by seeking out a mentor (see Chapter 4) and setting their own career goals. Getting help from a mentor has been found to increase levels of pay and pay satisfaction and the rate of promotion for protégés.[102] Although it has commonly been assumed that mentors seek out protégés, protégés can and do seek out mentors. One recent study found that employees who had an internal locus of control, were high on self-monitoring, and were low on negative affectivity (Chapter 2) were most likely to seek out and obtain help from a mentor. Moreover, the mentoring clearly benefited the employees in terms of salary levels and the extent to which the protégés felt good about their accomplishments and the progress they were making.[103]

Some organizations have formal mentoring programs that assign experienced members to newcomers. Often, however, mentoring is an informal process in which mentors and protégés seek each other out because of some common interest or bond. One researcher who interviewed successful working women found that 77 percent of them had received help from a mentor. Jennie Coakley received extensive help from her mentor, Ronnie Andros, when she began teaching the fifth grade at Columbia Elementary School in Fairfax County, Virginia. Andros helped Coakley cope with many of the challenges new teachers face. For example, Andros clarified official rules and procedures, introduced Coakley to important school administrators, and gave Andros tips about how to obtain textbooks.

Mentors are often in the same organizations as their protégés, but sometimes protégés can obtain help from mentors outside their organizations. For example, Lee Cooke was the office manager of the American Automobile Association in Washington, DC, when he met his mentor at a local Rotary Club meeting. Lee's mentor was an orchid breeder, and their relationship eventually led Lee to land a position with the American Orchid Society in West Palm Beach, Florida.[104]

In addition to seeking out the help of a mentor, employees can also advance their careers by formulating career goals. In Chapter 7, we said that goals are useful motivational tools because they help to focus employees' attention and effort in the right direction. Career goals are the experiences, positions, or jobs that employees would like to have in the course of their careers.[105] **Career goals** are good guides for achievement because they help employees decide what activities to concentrate on to advance their careers.

CAREER GOALS
The experiences, positions, or jobs that employees would like to have in the course of their careers.

Midcareer. Employees in the midcareer stage have generally been in the workforce between 20 and 35 years and face the challenge of remaining productive. Many employees achieve the height of career success during the midcareer stage, as exemplified by current or one-time CEOs Scott McNealy of Sun Microsystems, Steve Jobs of Apple Computer, John Chambers of Cisco Systems, Carly Fiorina of Hewlett Packard, and Pat Russo of Lucent Technologies. Many other midcareer employees, however, need to come to terms with career plateaus, obsolescence, and major career changes.

CAREER PLATEAU
A position from which the chances of obtaining a promotion or a job with more responsibility become very small.

A person is said to have reached a **career plateau** when the chances of being promoted within his or her own organization or another organization are slim.[106] There are several reasons why employees reach a career plateau. First, because of the hierarchical nature of most organizations, there are fewer and fewer positions to be promoted into as employees advance. Second, competition for upper-level positions in organizations is intense, and the number of these positions has been reduced because of downsizing.[107] Third, if some employees delay retirement past the traditional age of 65, their positions do not open up for midcareer employees to assume.[108] Finally, changes in technology or the lack of important new skills and abilities may limit the extent to which employees can advance in organizations.[109]

How can organizations help 'plateaued' employees remain satisfied, motivated, and productive? Encouraging lateral moves and job rotation is often an effective means of keeping plateaued employees motivated when they no longer have the prospect of a major promotion to work toward. Chevron is one of many organizations using this strategy.[110] At the SAS Institute (see the opening case for Chapter 6), all employees are encouraged and have the opportunity to make lateral moves and learn new skills.[111]

What steps can plateaued employees take to remain valuable, motivated members of the organization who are satisfied with their jobs? They might take on the role of mentor. They might become 'good citizens' of their organizations by suggesting changes, improvements, and generally engaging in the various forms of organizational citizenship behavior discussed in Chapter 3. Employees in early career stages often concentrate on activities that advance their careers and do not take the time to do things that help the organization as a whole. Plateaued employees, who often have a good understanding of their organization, are sometimes in an especially good position to help start a major company-wide recycling program, establish an outreach program to encourage members of an organization to volunteer time to community causes, or organize social activities such as company picnics, for example.

Employees face obsolescence when their knowledge and skills become outmoded and prevent them from effectively performing their organizational roles. Obsolescence is caused by changes in technology or in an organization's competitive environment that alter how jobs are performed. Organizations can help prevent obsolescence by providing their members with additional training whenever possible and allowing employees time off from work to take courses in their fields to keep them up-to-date. Whenever possible, employees should seek out additional training to keep their skills current.

Late career. The late-career stage extends as long as an individual's career is active. Obsolescence and other potential midcareer problems also carry over into the late-career stage, and it is important for employees and organizations to take some of the steps discussed earlier to overcome these problems and help older employees remain motivated, productive, and satisfied. Unfortunately, age-related stereotypes sometimes cause members of an organization to perceive older employees as slower, resistant to change, or less productive than younger employees, although this characterization is simply not true. Organizations need to dispel these myths by educating their members about the capabilities and contributions of their most senior members. Some older employees choose to continue working at their current occupations, others switch occupations, and still others choose to volunteer in nonprofit organizations. As indicated in the following Focus on Diversity, as the 'baby boom' generation enters their 60s, more and more of them are choosing to continue working and making significant contributions to their organizations, communities, and society as a whole.

Focus on Diversity

Older Workers Continue to Make Valuable Contributions

Approximately seventy-seven million Americans are classified as baby boomers, meaning that they were born in the post World War II period of economic posterity between the years of 1946 and 1964.[112] As baby boomers begin to enter their 60s, more and more of them are planning on continuing to work past traditional retirement ages. According to studies conducted by AARP (American Association of Retired Persons), only 20 percent of baby boomers plan to retire when they reach age 65.[113]

And many companies are seeking to retain the valuable contributions of their older workers by providing them with training opportunities and benefits. Take the case of Frederick Simms, who at 68, works for Consolidated Edison Inc., a power company in New York.[114] Simms is an emergency field manager who has been with Consolidated Edison for 49 years and has a vast array of experience dealing with emergencies both large and catastrophic (such as the tragic 2001 collapse of the World Trade Center) and more minor (such as broken pipes and water mains). Simms is willing to work sixteen-hour days when an emergency warrants it, and his good working relations with Fire Dept. brass and other emergency personnel in New York City are invaluable.

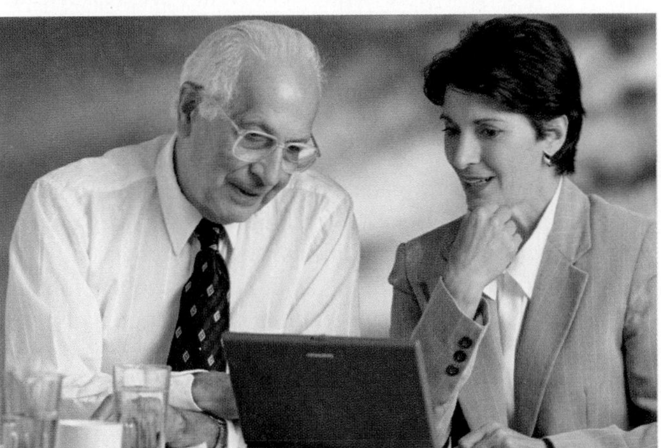

Many older workers continue to make valuable contributions to their jobs and organizations.

United Technologies Corporation (UTC) spends over $60 million a year for its employees (of any age) to learn new things through courses and training programs taken during their free time through its Employee Scholar Program.[115] Many older workers take advantage of this program to learn new skills such as Ed Perez. Perez, 62 years old and a lead mechanic at the Hamilton Sundstrand unit of UTC in Miramar, Florida, is going to school in his spare time to obtain his bachelor's degree in legal studies and plans to eventually go to law school.[116] Based on the experience of social worker Emma Shulman, he's got many more productive years ahead of him. At 93, Shulman not only put in a full work week recruiting Alzheimer's patients for a clinic at New York University's School of Medicine, but does it with so much energy that her boss, Dr. Steven H. Ferris, says 'We'd definitely have to hire two or three people to replace her.'[117] Clearly, older workers have much to contribute to organizations and society.

All in all, organizations and individual employees can do many things to manage careers. When careers are effectively managed, employees are satisfied with their jobs and careers and are motivated to perform at high levels and thereby help organizations achieve their goals.

Contemporary Career Challenges

In Chapter 1, we discussed contemporary challenges for organizational behavior and management. Some of these challenges are very relevant to the motivation of organizational members as they pursue their careers. When career management is effective, employees are given a series of motivating job assignments that they value and that contribute to their own development. In this case, the organization makes good use of its human resources to accomplish its goals. In this section, we discuss three career challenges that organizations face: ethical career management, career management that supports diversity, and career management in an era of dual-career couples. In Chapter 9, we discuss in more detail some of the specific steps organizations can take to meet these challenges as well as the challenges that arise when organizations downsize and lay off some of their members.

Ethical career management. In Chapter 1, we defined *ethics* as rules, beliefs, and values that outline the ways that managers and employees should behave when confronted with a situation in which their actions may help or harm other people inside or outside an organization. A key challenge for organizations and their managers is to ensure that career practices are ethical and that members of the organization pursue their own careers in an ethical manner.

Ethical career practices are practices built on honesty, trust, and open communication. Honesty means that managers are frank with employees concerning their career prospects, their strengths and weaknesses, and their progress to date. As we saw earlier, honesty begins before an employee actually joins an organization, when an organization informs job applicants about the good and not-so-good things in various positions and in the organization itself. Honesty continues when managers appraise performance and give employees clear and accurate feedback, which contributes to employees' being motivated to perform at high levels. To motivate subordinates, managers should also provide honest feedback concerning how subordinates' careers are progressing and information about future career opportunities and prospects. Honesty continues into the later career stages when organizations follow through on their commitments regarding provisions for retirement.

Trust is also built on organization members following through on their commitments to each other. If a manager or an organization motivates an employee by promising a certain type of career progression given adequate job performance, the opportunities should be forthcoming whenever possible. Likewise, if an employee promises his or her supervisor to remain on the job and vows that the organization will benefit by, say, enrolling him or her in an expensive course to learn a new technology, trust results when the employee follows through on this commitment.

Ethical career management cannot take place without open communication between managers and subordinates. Open communication leads to a clear and shared understanding of the development of careers, career prospects, and mutual expectations.

When careers are managed in an ethical fashion, promotions are based on performance. When employees understand the link between performance and promotion and other career opportunities (such as receiving challenging assignments and special training), they are more likely to be motivated to perform at high levels. Moreover, ethical career management means that supervisors do not abuse their power to make career decisions and provide career opportunities to their subordinates. An extreme case of a supervisor abusing his or her power happens, for example, when sexual harassment occurs, and a subordinate is led to believe he or she can't advance without tolerating inappropriate behavior or language. To advance their careers, employees should not be coerced to do things compromising their own ethical standards or those of the organization. Exhibit 8.7 contains a short ethics quiz that provides some examples of behaviors that supervisors may request subordinates to perform that may be unethical.[118]

EXHIBIT 8.7

Ethics Quiz

Source: Adapted from G. Graham, 'Would You Lie for Your Boss or Would You Just Rather Not,' *Bryan-College Station Eagle*, October 24, 1994, p. C3. Reprinted with permission.

Supervisors sometimes ask subordinates to do things that may be questionable on ethical grounds. Ethical career management means that subordinates do not have to engage in unethical behaviors to advance their own careers. Which of the following behaviors would you feel comfortable performing, and which do you think are basically unethical?

1. Your supervisor asks you to sign her name on some letters.
2. Your supervisor asks you to respond to a request and send it under her name.
3. Your supervisor asks you to tell callers that she is with a customer when you know that this is not true.
4. Your supervisor asks you to delay recording expenses until the next quarter.
5. Your supervisor asks you to tell others that she hasn't made a decision yet even though you know she has.
6. Your supervisor tells you to record the purchase of office equipment as an advertising expense.
7. Your supervisor asks you to backdate invoices to last quarter.
8. Your supervisor requests that you tell people you don't know certain things that you do know.
9. Your supervisor tells you to tell top management that she is working on a project that she hasn't begun yet (if top management happens to ask you).
10. Your supervisor tells you not to report sexist language you overheard if anyone asks about it.

According to Gerald Graham, Dean of the W. Frank Barton School of Business at Wichita State University, most people would consider items 3, 4, 5, 6, 7, 8, 9, and 10 to be deceptive or unethical and probably should not be agreed to.

Career management that supports diversity. The increasing diversity of the workforce means that managers have to make sure the organization's diverse members are given the career opportunities they deserve. Although progress has certainly been made with regard to diversity and hiring, somewhat less progress has been made when it comes to motivating diverse employees and making sure they're given equal career opportunities.

In Chapter 4, we discussed several reasons why people have a tendency to perceive others who are similar to themselves in gender, race, age, or cultural background more favorably than they perceive those who are different, and we described ways to overcome these biases. Problems such as the similar-to-me bias can result in certain members of an organization not receiving the career opportunities they deserve because they are dissimilar to managers making the career-related decisions. This inequity can result in a lack of motivation among employees who think they won't receive their 'due.' Managers who are aware of these biases and problems and ways to overcome them are in a good position to motivate their employees and promote career management diversity.

Organizations, too, can take specific steps to ensure equal career opportunities to their diverse members. Pacific Bell, for example, has undertaken a number of initiatives to promote the careers of minorities—in particular, Hispanics. Summer internships and scholarships are offered to minorities even before they join Pacific Bell, to help seek out minority applicants with the college degrees necessary for management positions. Minorities without college degrees are hired into nonmanagement positions, but these employees nonetheless can eventually advance into management. One of the ways Pacific Bell does this is by holding efficacy seminars, which prepare minority employees for future promotions. The company has also instituted a special two-year development track for minority managers to support their career development, help them develop their knowledge and skills, and provide them with access to mentors.[119]

Xerox Corporation is another organization that supports diversity via career management. Xerox is careful to place women and minorities in positions that will give them the experiences they need for future promotions. Minority and female caucus groups at Xerox provide guidance to diverse employees on how to manage their careers. Because managers often make important decisions that affect the careers of women and minorities, Xerox's Balanced Work Force process links the performance appraisals and compensation managers receive to their efforts to provide women and minorities with career opportunities.[120] The Balanced Work Force process thereby motivates managers to support diversity at Xerox and use career opportunities to motivate their diverse subordinates.

Career management in an era of dual-career couples. In managing careers, organizations have to take into account the fact that the dual-career couple is now the norm rather than the exception. Individual employees cannot make career decisions such as relocating, accepting a promotion, and transferring to another state without considering the preferences and careers of their spouses. When dual-career couples have children, the needs of the entire family have to be taken into account as the couple's careers unfold. To help dual-career couples, employees who are single parents, and those caring for elderly parents effectively manage their careers, organizations can take several steps:

1. *Organizations can limit unnecessary moves and travel as much as possible.* When employees do need to relocate in the course of their careers, relocation programs can be used to help their partners find new jobs and the families adjust to their new surroundings.
2. *Organizations can use flexible working arrangements to allow their members time off when needed.* Sometimes these arrangements may entail simply changing the hours worked (for example, from 6 A.M. to 2 P.M. instead of from 9 A.M. to 5 P.M.) like Xerox does. Sometimes that may mean that employees perform some of their assigned tasks at home. At other times, that may mean managers accommodate employees who need to take time off to, for example, take care of sick children or parents.
3. *Organizations can have on-site day care centers.* One of the most pressing concerns for dual-career couples with small children and for single parents is finding quality day care for their children. On-site day care centers are growing in popularity and give working parents the peace of mind that comes from knowing that their children are in good hands.

These are just a few of the steps that organizations can take to help members manage their careers in light of the many other demands and constraints that employees face from

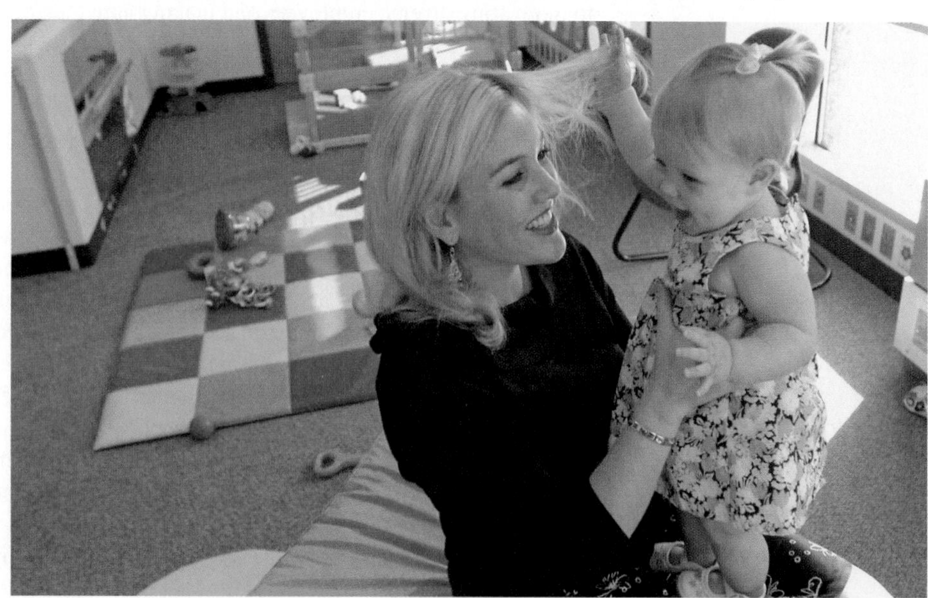

One of the most pressing concerns for parents of small children is finding quality day care. On-site day care centers, like this one at General Mills headquarters in Golden Valley, MN, give working parents like public relations manager Kirstie Foster peace of mind.

their personal lives. Rather than ignoring these demands and constraints, as some organizations have tried to do in the past, organizations should take steps to help employees effectively meet them.

Summary

The relation between employees and an organization is an exchange relationship that is embodied in the employees' psychological contracts. Accurate performance appraisals are essential for the fulfillment of psychological contracts and a motivated workforce. Pay and career opportunities are two of the most important outcomes in the exchange relationship between employees and an organization and have important implications for motivation. In this chapter, we made the following major points:

1. A psychological contract is an employee's perception of his or her exchange relationship with an organization, outcomes the organization has promised to provide to the employee, and contributions the employee is obligated to make to the organization. The determinants of psychological contracts include direct communication, observation, and written documents. The two major types of psychological contracts are transactional contracts and relational contracts.
2. The goals of performance appraisal are to encourage high levels of employee motivation and performance and to provide accurate information to be used in managerial decision making. Performance appraisal can focus on the assessment of traits, behaviors, or results, be formal or informal, and rely on objective or subjective measures. Supervisors most often appraise the performances of their subordinates.
3. Pay is an important outcome for most employees. Motivation and learning theories suggest that pay should be based on performance. When individual performance can be accurately assessed, the maximum motivational impact is obtained from basing pay on individual performance. When employees are highly interdependent, individual levels of performance cannot be accurately appraised, or high levels of cooperation across employees are desired, it can be advantageous to base pay on group or organizational performance.
4. Merit pay in the form of bonuses generally is preferable to salary increases because salary levels have multiple determinants in addition to current performance. The ethics of pay differentials and comparable worth are important issues that managers face in using pay as a motivational tool and striving for the equitable distribution of pay in organizations.
5. A career can be defined as the sum of work-related experiences throughout a person's lifetime. Effective career management helps to ensure that members of an organization are motivated to perform at high levels and receive the career opportunities they should while also ensuring that the organization is making the best use of its human resources.
6. Four general types of careers are steady-state careers, linear careers, spiral careers, and transitory careers. Increasingly, careers are boundaryless meaning that people have a variety of kinds of work experiences in different organizations during their careers. Careers can be thought of as progressing through stages, although each individual's career is somewhat unique and these stages are not necessarily experienced by all people. At each stage, organizations and individuals can take steps to ensure high levels of employee motivation and effective career management. The five stages are (1) preparation for work, (2) organizational entry, (3) early career, (4) midcareer, and (5) late career. The early career stage is made up of two steps: establishment and achievement. Mentors and career goals can be especially helpful to employees during the achievement step.
7. Contemporary career challenges include ethical career management (built on honesty, trust, and open communication), career management that supports diversity (ensures that diverse members of an organization are given the career opportunities they deserve), and career management in an era of dual-career couples (acknowledges the many demands on employees arising from their jobs and personal lives).

Opening Case

GLOBALIZATION HEIGHTENS WORK STRESS

Is work stress out of control?

Uncertainty in the world today is creating heightened levels of anxiety for more and more people. The sources of this anxiety are varied. They include a challenging global economy; layoffs; international terrorism, geopolitical conflicts, and war; natural disasters such as hurricanes and tsunamis; pollution and destruction of the natural environment; as well as a series of high-profile scandals at corporations such as Enron, WorldCom, and Tyco.[1]

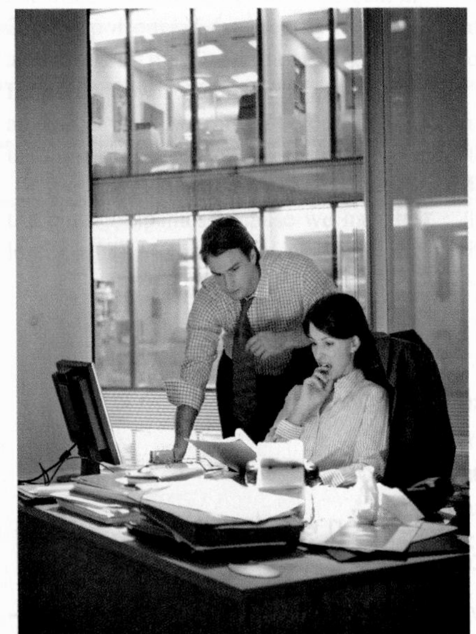

Globalization has increased workloads and time demands for some employees who instead of relaxing at home with their families in the evenings, find themselves engaged in conference calls and emails back and forth to employees in other countries like India who are beginning their work days.

Work stress, moreover, is at an all-time high. Employees at all levels of organizations are being asked to accomplish more with less.[2] Our ability (and sometimes our need) to stay electronically connected to the job twenty-four hours a day, seven days a week has also contributed to mounting levels of stress. Increasingly, employees with laptops and company-provided cell phones are taking work home at night and on their vacations. Based on a recent poll, Travelocity concluded that around 40 percent of workers traveling on vacation check their work e-mails, over 30 percent have work-related cell phone conversations while vacationing, and 25 percent of travelers take their laptops with them.[3]

The fact is employees are trying to juggle myriad responsibilities, including responsibilities related to their jobs, raising their children, and caring for their elderly parents. Maintaining a balance between work and the rest of one's life is becoming a huge challenge. Increasing globalization has the potential to heighten levels of stress for multiple reasons. Clearly, the outsourcing of both manufacturing and white-collar jobs to low-cost countries like India, China, and Russia is a major source of stress for workers who face the constant threat of losing their jobs, or who actually do lose their jobs when companies shut down manufacturing facilities or outsource white-collar jobs.

And when companies do outsource work, employees who retain their jobs often face mounting workloads and ever-increasing demands on their time, never mind the fear of one day having their own positions off-shored. Consider the case of PortalPlayer, a Santa Clara, California, company that develops software and chips for music players like the iPod and has outsourced around 90 positions to Hyderabad, India.[4] Given the twelve-and-a-half-hour time difference between India and California, instead of relaxing at home with their families in the evenings, engineers and managers in California are increasingly finding themselves engaged in conference calls and e-mails back and forth to employees in India who are beginning their work days.[5] And while this round the clock global workday contributes to PortalPlayer's efficiency, effectiveness, and competitiveness, it has the potential to take a heavy toll on employees. As Christopher Lochhead, a marketing executive in a consulting firm that operates in 35 countries puts it, "You can't even get a rest on the weekend . . . The reality is that when you do business globally, somebody working for you is always on the clock."[6]

A key challenge for organizations is to ensure that efficiency, quality, and innovation do not suffer and their members retain their sanity and well-being. Not meeting this challenge not only hurts employees but also organizational effectiveness. A recent study conducted by the nonprofit Families and Work Institute based in New York suggests that over 30 percent of workers in the United States have chronically high workloads.[7] Moreover, as work overload increased, workers indicated that they were more likely to make errors, get angry with coworkers and managers, feel more stressed, and not take care of their health and have it suffer.[8]

Some organizations have been able to address this problem by examining work processes and making creative changes to improve effectiveness.[9] For example, Debbie DeGabrielle, a top marketing manager at WRQ, a software integration company based in Seattle, Washington, recently had her staff of 50 reduced to 22 while she was aiming to increase sales. DeGabrielle took a proactive approach to her dilemma, and with the help of her staff, came up with creative ways to do more with less by developing things such as an online "toolbox" to help staff members during sales calls and presentations. However, she also recognizes the need to make sure she doesn't push her staff too hard, so after strenuous periods of nonstop work, she encourages them to take a day off. As she puts it, "You have to make sure that you don't push so hard that you burn out."[10]

John Seiple, a top manager at ProLogis, a distribution facilities company based in Denver, Colorado, was similarly challenged when the volume of his operations increased 40 percent while his workforce was reduced by 5 percent. Seiple met this challenge by eliminating unnecessary activities and paperwork. Rather than worrying about getting their paperwork done, employees are urged to remain focused on customers and give customers their undivided attention.[11]

Clearly, mounting levels of stress and overload is an important issue that many organizations need to proactively address. For example, a recent study by the National Institute for Occupational Safety and Health (OSHA) found that over 50 percent of the employees surveyed considered job stress to be a big problem for them personally, and over 40 percent of the employees believed that their coworkers required some kind of assistance to manage their job stress.[12] A study by Marlin Company, a research firm specializing in the workplace, found that 29 percent of the employees surveyed categorized their stress levels as being high.[13] According to research conducted by the American Institute of Stress, job stress and its consequences, such as absenteeism and mental health deterioration, carry a heavy price tag for corporate America-estimated at over $300 billion annually, in fact.[14] Moreover, job stress appears to be a global problem. The European Community proclaimed job stress to be among the top work-related health problems in Europe. Unfortunately, stress is not going to go away, so what is important, stress management experts say, is helping employees change how they respond to and cope with stress.[15]

Overview

In previous chapters, you learned about many of the ways in which working in an organization affects individuals. In Chapter 3, you learned how people's experiences in organizations shape important attitudes they have, such as their job satisfaction and organizational commitment.

In Chapters 5, 6, 7, and 8, you learned how and why different aspects of an organization—the way it designs jobs, sets goals, appraises performance, and administers rewards such as pay and praise—affect motivation and performance. In this chapter, we continue to explore how working in an organization affects individuals by focusing on stress and work-life balance (the relationships between people's work and their lives as a whole).

Stress affects how people feel and behave both on and off the job. Stress is a national and global concern and unfortunately an all-too-familiar problem.[16] Most of us at one time or another have experienced some of the consequences of too much stress: sleepless nights, anxiety, nervousness, and headaches or stomachaches. A recent study found that around 40 million Americans experienced stress during a two-week period.[17] And, as indicated in the opening case, stress costs organizations billions of dollars a year in lost productivity, absenteeism, turnover, and healthcare costs for stress-related illnesses. Understanding and managing stress is important not only for the well-being of the members of an organization but also for the effectiveness of the organization itself.

In this chapter, we describe the nature of stress and the consequences it has for individuals and organizations. We discuss the sources of stress and the steps that employees and their organizations can take to help employees cope effectively with stress. By the end of this chapter, you will have a good understanding of how stress affects people and how employees and organizations can manage stress effectively.

The Nature of Stress

When was the last time you felt particularly stressed? Maybe you had a paper due in a couple of days, but you hadn't even started it. Perhaps you had three big exams on the same day, and you weren't getting along with your roommate, or you were worried about not being able to find a good job when you graduate. You might have had a sense of being overwhelmed, of facing a problem that seemed insurmountable, or of being expected to do too many things at once. Or you may have felt uncertain about how to respond to an opportunity that had the potential to benefit you but also was very challenging.

STRESS
The experience of opportunities or threats that people perceive as important and also perceive they might not be able to handle or deal with effectively.

Stress is the experience of opportunities or threats that people perceive as important and also perceive they might not be able to handle or deal with effectively.[18] Several significant aspects of stress are highlighted in this definition. First, stress can be experienced because of both opportunities and threats. An *opportunity* is something that has the potential to benefit a person. A *threat* is something that has the potential to harm a person.[19] Opportunities such as learning new skills or getting a new job can be stressful if employees lack self-efficacy (see Chapter 5) and fear that they will not be able to perform at an acceptable level. When an organization reduces the size of its workforce, employees experience stress because their financial security, psychological well-being, and career development are threatened. From the opening case, it is clear that having to work long hours causes employees to experience stress because it threatens their family lives.

A second aspect of stress is that the threat or opportunity experienced is important to a person. By *important* we mean that it has the potential to affect a person's well-being or the extent to which someone is happy, healthy, or prosperous. Many of the things that people encounter in their daily lives could be classified as opportunities or threats, but usually only the important ones result in stress. Driving through traffic on the way to work is a threat, for example, but for many people it is not significant enough to result in stress. The threat of heavy traffic may become important enough to cause stress, however, if you are caught in a traffic jam at 7:50 A.M. and are scheduled to make a crucial presentation to upper management at 8:00 A.M. In this situation, heavy traffic has the potential to affect your well-being negatively—being late for your own presentation will not make you look good in the eyes of your superiors.

Clearly, workplace violence is one of the most life-threatening sources of stress. How real is the threat, and what can be done to overcome it? Managing Ethically discusses this.

A third key aspect of stress is *uncertainty*: The person who is experiencing an important opportunity or threat is not sure that he or she can effectively deal with it. When people

Managing Ethically

Violence in the Workplace

A Xerox employee in Honolulu shoots and kills seven coworkers; two employees of a Seattle boat repair business are shot and killed by a man dressed in camouflage clothing; a troubled employee of a Lockheed Martin aircraft plant in Meridian, Mississippi, shoots and kills five of his coworkers and then kills himself.[20] Unfortunately, these examples of workplace violence underscore a national problem.

In the 1990s, widely publicized tragedies involving violence by postal workers[21] led people to believe that violence in the U.S. Postal Service was more prevalent than elsewhere. The truth is postal employees are only about one-third as likely as employees in general in the United States to be killed on the job.[22] That said, approximately 2 million employees in the United States are victims of workplace violence (ranging from threats and verbal abuse to physical attacks and homicide). Workplace violence, believe it or not, is one of the major causes of work-related deaths.[23]

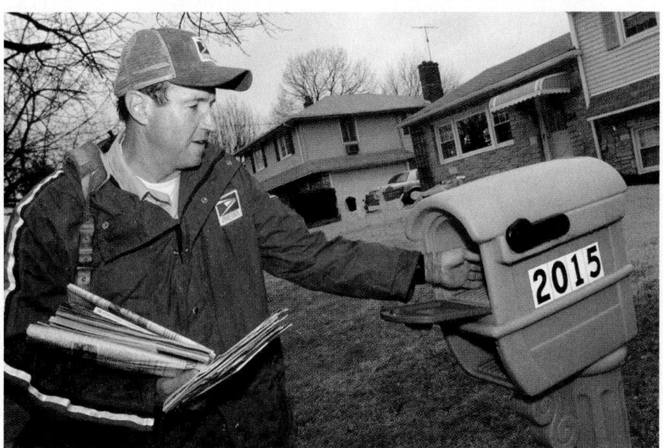

Despite heightened publicity about violence in the 1990s, U.S. Postal Service employees are only about one-third as likely to be killed on the job as other employees in the United States. Nonetheless, the postal service has instituted a workplace violence awareness program along with a hotline employees can call to report hostile situations.

The threat of violence on the job is highest for employees in service jobs whose work hours or places of employment put them particularly at risk, and for employees whose interactions with the public entail the exchange of money.[24] Overall, employees in retail settings are more than five times more likely to be victims of homicides at work than post-office workers. Taxicab drivers and chauffeurs tend to be at most risk for homicide while on the job, followed by sheriffs and police officers; gas station, convenience store, and garage workers; and security guards. More often than not, the perpetrators of these crimes are not current or former coworkers and do not know their victims. Sometimes domestic violence spills over into the workplace such as when an abusive partner attacks his or her estranged spouse in the spouse's place of employment.[25] Nonetheless, current or former coworkers continue to commit acts of workplace violence as well. In 2005, a former post-office employee shot five employees at a large mail-processing center in Goleta, California, and then shot herself.[26]

It is an ethical imperative that managers and organizations take whatever steps they can to minimize the threat of workplace violence. When a former employee of Intel Corporation made violent threats, managers decided to take swift action to ensure that the work environment was safe. They instituted a multipronged program that includes guidelines, training, and awareness programs for employees. At each Intel location in the United States, a workplace violence team composed of members from security, human resources, and nursing helps employees deal with threats and responds to any incidents that might occur.[27]

According to the Occupational Health and Safety Administration (OSHA), all organizations should have a "zero-tolerance policy" toward violence in the workplace.[28] Organizations should also take specific steps to ensure that employees are aware of the policy and what it covers. Additionally, pragmatic steps should be taken to make the workplace as safe as possible so that employees are not put in risky situations. These steps can range from installing security systems, surveillance cameras, and locked drop safes to limiting the amount of available cash in stores and providing employees with safety equipment such as handheld alarms and cell phones. It might also include security officers escorting employees to their cars at night.[29]

are confident that they can effectively handle an opportunity or threat, they usually do not experience stress. An orthopedic surgeon performing a routine knee operation is not likely to experience stress if he or she has performed similar operations in the past and feels confident about doing a good job. Performing a complicated hip replacement on an elderly patient who is in poor health, however, might be stressful for the surgeon if he or she is uncertain about the outcome. Similarly, employees experience stress from the uncertainty of being able to have a good family life while still advancing their careers.

The last aspect of stress emphasized in our definition is that stress is rooted in perception. Whether people experience stress depends on how they *perceive* potential opportunities and threats and how they *perceive* their capabilities to deal with them. One person might perceive a job change or a promotion as an opportunity for learning and career advancement, and another person might perceive the same job change or promotion as a threat because of the potential for failure. Similarly, a person with high self-efficacy might feel well equipped to take on additional responsibility. However, an equally capable employee with low self-efficacy might perceive that he or she can't handle any more responsibility.

Individual Differences and Stress

Our definition emphasizes that an individual's experience of stress depends on a number of factors such as how important a person thinks a given opportunity or threat is and the extent to which a person thinks he or she can deal effectively with the opportunity or threat. Above all else, stress is a very personal experience. Although it may be terrifying for some students to make a presentation in front of class, others enjoy being in the spotlight and having a chance to display their knowledge and wit. Similarly, some nurses who care for AIDS patients find this duty highly stressful because of the threat of accidental infection or the emotional pain caused by the death of their patients. But other nurses consider caring for AIDS patients a professional opportunity that they have the skills and knowledge to deal with. Members of an organization must realize that individuals may respond differently to the same potential source of stress and that what might seem trivial to one employee might be a real source of stress for another.

In Chapter 2, we discussed the two major ways in which people differ from each other, in personality and ability, and their implications for understanding and managing organizational behavior. Individual differences also play a significant role in determining how members of an organization perceive and think about potential sources of stress, their ability to deal with stress effectively, and ultimately the extent to which they experience stress.

Personality. Several of the personality traits we discussed in Chapter 2 are important for understanding why employees exposed to the same potential source of stress may differ in the extent to which they actually experience stress. Employees who are high on the Big Five personality dimension of *neuroticism*, or *negative affectivity*, for example, have a general tendency to view themselves, their organizations, their jobs, and the people they work with in a negative manner. These employees are likely to view ambiguous conditions and changes at work as potential threats and feel ill-equipped to deal with both threats and opportunities. Consistent with this reasoning, employees high on negative affectivity tend to experience more stress than those low on negative affectivity.[30]

As another example, employees who are high on the Big Five dimension of *extraversion*, or *positive affectivity*, tend to be outgoing and enjoy interacting and socializing with other people. In the classroom, extraverts are less likely than introverts to experience stress when making presentations. Similarly, extraverts are less likely to experience stress in jobs requiring frequent presentations or meeting with new people on a day-to-day basis. Sales and service jobs are examples.

Openness to experience, which captures the extent to which employees are daring and open to a wide range of experiences, is a final example of a personality trait from the Big Five model that is likely to affect the extent to which employees experience stress. For most people, taking risks and making frequent changes can be stressful. Even entrepreneurs are stressed by the risks of starting their own companies and the frequent changes needed to be innovative. Nevertheless, it is likely that employees who are high on openness to experience may find risk taking and frequent change less stressful than those who are low on openness to experience.

In Chapter 2, we also discussed some other, more specific personality traits that are relevant to understanding and managing organizational behavior, and it is likely that these traits also affect stress. Employees who are high on *self-esteem*, for example, are less likely to experience stress from challenging work assignments and are also more likely to think they can deal effectively with sources of stress. As another example, *Type A employees* have stress experiences different from those of *Type B employees*. Type A's, as you recall, have a strong desire to achieve, are competitive, have a sense of time urgency, are impatient, and can be hostile. They have a strong desire to get a lot done in a short period of time. The more relaxed Type B's are not so driven. Initially, researchers thought that Type A's would experience more stress than Type B's; however, recent research suggests that only Type A's who are very hostile experience high levels of stress. A final example of a personality trait that is likely to play a role in the extent to which employees experience stress is *locus of control*. Employees with an internal locus of control may experience less stress than those with an external locus of control because they feel that they can influence what happens to them. However, when events are largely beyond an employee's control (for example, when his or her company goes bankrupt), internals may experience stress because they are not in control of the situation.

Ability. In addition to having different personalities, employees also differ in their abilities, which can affect stress levels. Stress can be experienced when employees lack the abilities necessary to perform their jobs. Employees at the Collins & Aikman carpet factory in Dalton, Georgia, for example, experienced stress when the factory was computerized. Some of the employees were not able to read or perform the calculations necessary to work with the new computers and felt that their jobs were threatened. Collins & Aikman helped employees deal with this source of stress by providing extensive additional training. The training itself was a source of stress for some employees who were afraid that they would not be able to improve their skills because of other time demands at work and at home.[31]

Somewhat related to ability is another factor that affects whether employees feel stressed or not: experience. People are more likely to feel stressed when they lack experience at doing something, and they are less likely to feel stressed as they gain experience. This explains why employees starting new jobs often feel stressed and nervous—their lack of on-the-job experience breeds uncertainty. A new supervisor in a bank, for example, is uncertain about how to settle work-scheduling conflicts among his subordinates, how to run a group meeting most effectively, how to get help from his boss without seeming incompetent, and how to motivate a capable but poorly performing subordinate. These sources of uncertainty create stress for the supervisor, but the stress diminishes over time as he gains experience.

Consequences of Stress

Because what an employee considers to be stressful is highly personal, employees differ in the extent to which they experience the consequences of stress, even when they are exposed to the same sources of stress (such as making a presentation or getting laid off).

At some point in their lives, however, all employees experience some of the consequences of stress. These consequences are of three main types: physiological, psychological, and behavioral. Each consequence has the potential to affect well-being, performance, and effectiveness at the individual, group, and organizational levels.

Physiological consequences. Were you ever unable to fall asleep or stay asleep at night when you were experiencing particularly high levels of stress during the day? Such sleep disturbances are just one of the many potential physiological consequences of stress. Other potential physiological consequences range from sweaty palms, feeling flushed, trembling, a pounding heart, elevated blood pressure, headaches, dizziness, nausea, stomachaches, backaches, and hives to heart attacks and impaired immune system functioning. Rock singer Stevie Nicks, for example, says that when she experiences stress before a live performance, her stomach gets upset, she breaks out in a sweat, and her asthma bothers her.[32]

The relationship between stress and physiological consequences is complicated, and researchers are still struggling to understand the dynamics involved.[33] Two individuals experiencing the same high levels of stress may have different physiological reactions. Moreover, some people seem to experience more physiological consequences than others do. People also differ in the extent to which they complain about physical symptoms of stress such as headaches and stomach aches.[34] The most serious physiological consequences of stress are likely to occur only after considerably high levels of stress are experienced for a prolonged period of time. High blood pressure, cardiovascular disease, and heart attacks, for example, may result from excessive levels of prolonged stress.

Psychological consequences. One of the major psychological consequences of stress is the experience of stressful feelings and emotions. Stressful feelings and emotions can range from being in a bad mood, feeling anxious, worried, and upset to feeling angry, scornful, bitter, or hostile. Any or all of these feelings will detract from employees' well-being.[35]

Another psychological consequence of stress is that people tend to have more negative attitudes when they experience stress. Employees who are highly stressed tend to have a more negative outlook on various aspects of their jobs and organizations and are more likely to have low levels of job satisfaction and organizational commitment. Stressed employees may feel underappreciated, feel a lack of control, and also feel that their work is interfering with their personal lives. Marlin Company and the American Institute of Stress developed a short quiz that measures the extent of stress based on the severity of its psychological consequences (see Exhibit 9.1).

Difficulties falling asleep at night or staying asleep are one of many potential physiological consequences of stress.

EXHIBIT 9.1

A Stress Quiz

Source:

This quiz was adapted from a stress scale developed by Marlin Company and the American Institute of Stress. Employees respond to each of the items based on the following scale:

1	2	3	4	5
Never	Rarely	Sometimes	Often	Very Often

1. Conditions at work are unpleasant or sometimes even unsafe. _____
2. I feel that my job is making me physically or emotionally sick. _____
3. I have too much work or too many unreasonable deadlines. _____
4. I can't express my opinions or feelings about my job to my boss. _____
5. My work interferes with my family or personal life. _____
6. I have no control over my life at work. _____
7. My good performance goes unrecognized and unrewarded. _____
8. My talents are underutilized at work. _____

TOTAL _____

Responses to each item are summed to yield an overall stress score. Scores at or below 15 are indicative of low stress whereas those above 25 are indicative of high stress. The higher the score, the higher the level of stress.

BURNOUT
Psychological, emotional, or physical exhaustion.

Burnout—psychological, emotional, or physical exhaustion—is a special kind of psychological consequence of stress that afflicts some employees who experience high levels of work stress day in and day out for an extended period of time. Burnout is especially likely to occur when employees are responsible for helping, protecting, or taking care of other people.[36] Nurses, doctors, social workers, teachers, lawyers, and police officers, for example, can be at risk for developing burnout due to the nature of their jobs.

Three key signs of burnout are feelings of low personal accomplishment, emotional exhaustion, and depersonalization.[37] Burned-out employees often feel that they are not helping others or accomplishing as much as they should be. Emotionally, they are worn out from the constant stress of dealing with people who are sometimes in desperate need of assistance. Burned-out employees sometimes depersonalize the people they need to help, thinking about them as objects or things rather than as feeling human beings. A burned-out social worker, for example, may think about a foster child in need of a new home as a case number rather than as a very scared 12-year-old. This psychological consequence may lead to a behavioral consequence when the burned-out social worker treats the child in a cold and distant manner.

Behavioral consequences. The potential consequence of stress on job performance is perhaps of most interest to managers. One way to summarize the relationship between stress and performance is in terms of an inverted U (see Exhibit 9.2). Up to a certain point (point A in the figure), increases in stress enhance performance. Beyond that point, further increases in stress impair performance. Stress up to point A is *positive stress* because it propels employees to perform at a high level. Stress beyond point A is *negative stress* because it impairs performance. Dr. Allen Elkin, who works at the Stress Management Counseling Center in New York City, suggests that each person has to find the right level of stress for himself or herself—enough to feel productive and fulfilled but not too much to be overwhelming. Dr. Elkin likens finding the optimal level of stress to tuning the strings on a violin or guitar. If the strings are too loose, there is no sound; if they are too tight, they break; when they are tuned correctly, they can make beautiful music.

The fact that stress can be positive is illustrated by considering the motivational theories and tools we discussed in Chapters 6, 7, and 8. These theories and tools can be used to raise levels of motivation and job performance, but they also have the potential to increase

EXHIBIT 9.2

An Inverted U Relationship Between Stress and Performance

Stress up to point A is positive because it prompts a worker to perform at a high level. Stress beyond point A is negative because it impairs performance.

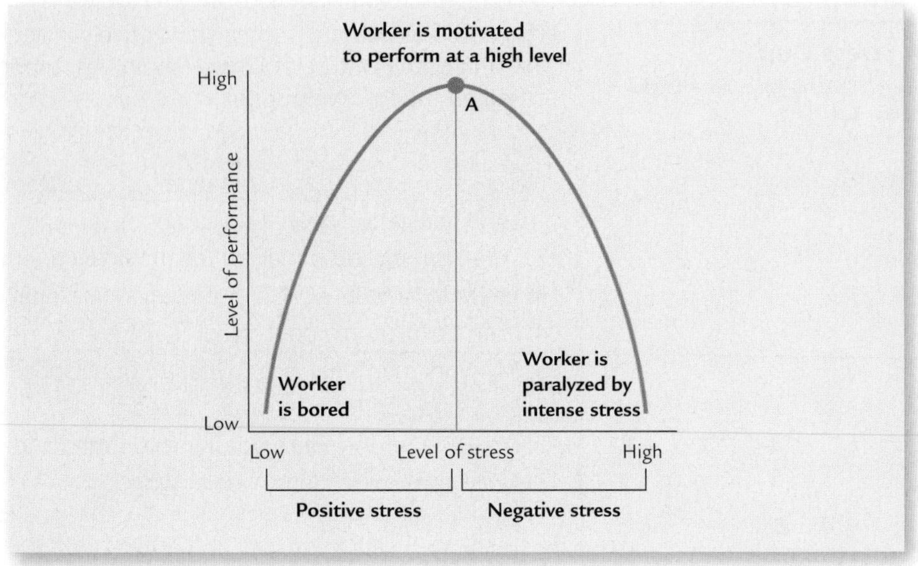

levels of stress. For example, giving an employee a difficult goal to reach and then telling the employee that he or she will receive a hefty bonus only if the goal is attained is likely to result in a certain level of stress. In this case, however, the stress is positive because it energizes the employee to try to reach the goal. Similarly, the stress that most students experience as exams approach is positive because it propels them to study. As a final example, many performers and athletes find that a certain amount of stress (or stage fright) gets their adrenaline pumping and helps them do their best. As singer Stevie Nicks indicates, "If I wasn't really nervous before walking on stage, I'd be really worried."[38] The expression "I work best under pressure" captures the feeling that positive stress can propel people to reach their goals and perform at high levels.

Stress levels that are too high, however, can impair performance and, thus, are negative. Students who suffer from serious test anxiety cannot remember material they may have known quite well the day before the test. Their stress and anxiety interfere with their

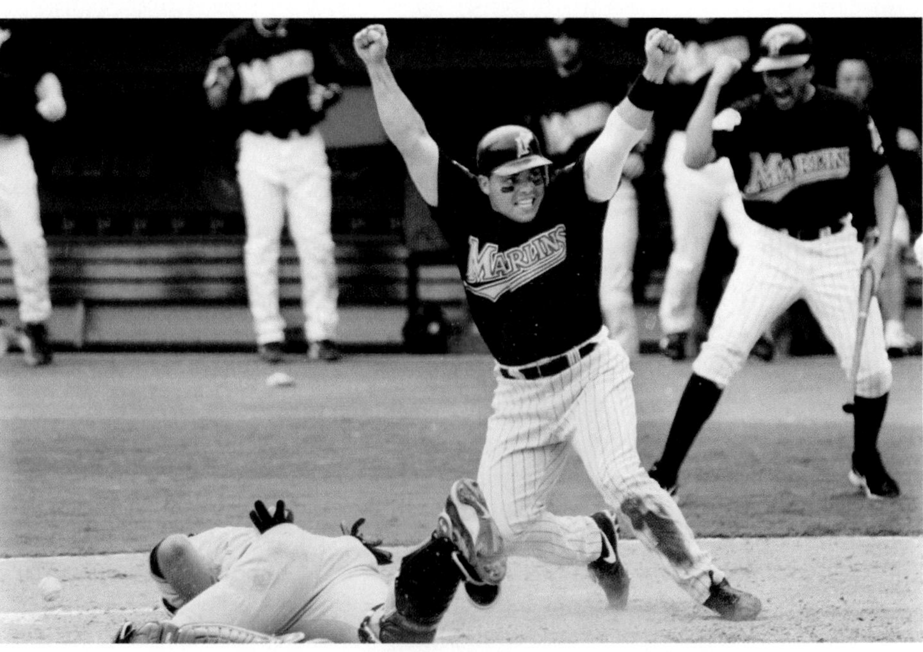

On-the-job stress can be good, if it's kept at an optimal level. Sports teams like the New York Yankees and the Florida Marlins can actually use stress to enhance their performance in high-stakes games like the World Series.

ability to take the test, and thoughts of how poorly they are going to do prevent them from concentrating on the questions being asked. Similarly, excessively high levels of stress may prevent employees from effectively performing their jobs. Entertainers who experience excessive levels of negative stress may avoid live performances altogether, as Barbra Streisand did for 27 years.[39] In 1994, world-renowned speed skater Dan Jansen was able to win the gold medal that had eluded him for three previous Olympic Games only when he was able to relax and control his dysfunctional level of stress with the help of sports psychologist James E. Loehr.[40]

Individual differences also affect the relationship between stress and performance. Some employees, because of their personalities and abilities, are able to withstand high levels of stress that seem to propel them on to even higher levels of performance; for such employees, high levels of stress are positive. The performance levels of other employees suffer when stress becomes too high. For each employee, the point at which increases in levels of stress result in decreases in performance depends on the employee's personality traits and abilities.

Besides enhanced or diminished job performance, other potential behavioral consequences of stress include strained interpersonal relations, absenteeism,[41] and turnover. When employees are experiencing excessively high levels of stress (negative stress), it is often hard for them to be as caring and understanding with others (coworkers, subordinates, superiors, customers) as they normally would be. A normally agreeable employee who suddenly flies off the handle may be experiencing a very high level of stress. Joseph Strickland, a vice president in charge of Amoco's Dallas plant, realized that stress levels were getting out of hand when one of the managers at the plant started giving everyone a hard time. "He was yelling at the secretaries, he was screaming at the human resources people," Strickland recalled. "It was very unlike him."[42] Employees experiencing high levels of stress may also have strained relationships with their spouses and families. This was found to be the case with some employees who were laid off at Phillips Petroleum Company.[43]

Excessively high levels of stress may also lead to absenteeism and turnover, especially when employees have other employment options. A recent study found that many nurses experience so much stress and burnout they are planning to quit their jobs or leave nursing altogether.[44]

In Japan, where work overload is a significant source of stress for many employees, an extreme behavioral consequence of negative stress is what the Japanese call *karoshi*, death from overwork.[45] A study conducted by the Japanese government found that in 1993 about one out of six men worked a minimum of 3,100 hours a year (60 hours a week, 52 weeks a year), a schedule that physicians suggest can lead to karoshi. Karoshi is not limited to Japan; the British Medical Association has investigated claims that karoshi took the life of a young doctor who worked 86 continuous hours in England.[46] Unfortunately, if anything, it appears that work overload is on the rise—in Japan and around the globe. According to Japan's Health, Labor, and Welfare Ministry, 317 deaths in Japan in 2002 could directly be associated with excessive working hours.[47] However, experts believe the actual figure is many times higher than this, especially among professional workers.[48] A recent study conducted by the Japanese Trade Union Confederation estimates that around 33 percent of male employees in Japan in their early thirties work approximately 58 hours per week.[49] England, Australia, and the United States also appear to be trending toward increasingly long working hours.[50] And, as illustrated in the opening case, excessive working hours can be not only a significant cause of stress but can also lead to health problems.

Sources of Stress

STRESSOR
A source of stress.

What causes stress? Five major potential **stressors**, or sources of stress, are one's personal life, one's job responsibilities, membership in work groups and organizations, work-life balance, and environmental uncertainty. Whether potential stressors become

EXHIBIT 9.3

Sources and Consequences of Stress

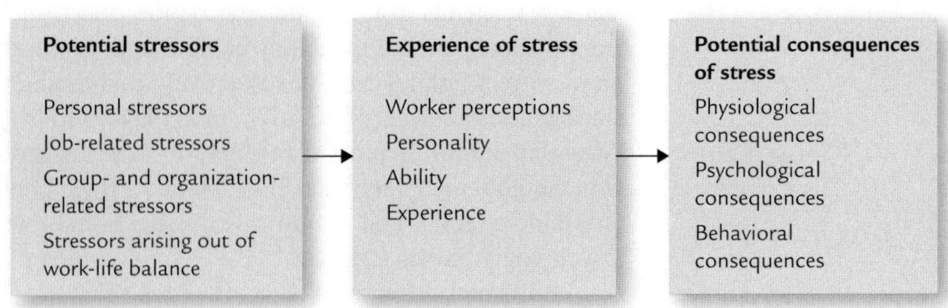

actual stressors and produce stress and whether the stress an employee experiences is positive or negative depend on individual differences and how the individual perceives and interprets the stressors. Between the five categories of potential stressors (discussed next), a nearly infinite combination of them can lead to the physiological, psychological, and behavioral consequences of stress (see Exhibit 9.3). The effects of these stressors combine to determine the overall level of stress a person experiences. Each stressor contributes to or influences how stressed a person generally feels.

Personal Stressors

Why are we bothering to discuss stressors from one's personal life in a book on organizational behavior? What happens to employees off the job can affect their attitudes, behaviors, and performance on the job as well as their own well-being. A normally polite and helpful salesperson may lose his temper with a disgruntled customer because he is preoccupied with the fight he had with his wife that same morning. Similarly, a marketing manager who normally has an open-door policy may avoid interacting with her colleagues because she can't get her mind off her teenage son's drug problem. Marriott International found that personal and family problems are a significant cause of the high turnover rates of employees in some of its restaurants and hotels.[51] From the opening case, it is clear that family responsibilities and home life are an important concern for employees both on and off the job.

One way of viewing these and other personal sources of stress is in terms of major and minor life events.[52] *Major life events* can have serious implications for stress and well-being and include the death of a loved one, divorce, serious illness of oneself or a loved one, and getting arrested. These are all sources of stress involving emotional or physical "threats" and are negative. Other major life events are positive "opportunities" that can be stressful, such as getting married, buying a house, having or adopting a baby, and moving to another state. Relatively *minor life events* also can be sources of stress, such as getting a speeding ticket, having trouble with your in-laws or child care provider, and even going on vacation.

How stressed a person generally feels appears to depend not only on the extent to which the stressors occur and how significant they are for the person but also on how many of them occur simultaneously during any given period.[53] New college graduates, for example, sometimes experience high levels of stress because many potentially stressful life events (both positive and negative) occur in a short period of time—moving, losing old friends, making new friends, getting married, and becoming financially independent while at the same time starting or looking for a job. Although each event might be only mildly stressful by itself, the fact that they are all happening together results in a high level of stress.

Researchers have developed questionnaires that contain checklists of stressful life events and their perceived impact. Overall stress levels are determined by the number of events that have occurred during a certain period (such as the past three years) and their significance to a person. Overall stress levels, in turn, have been shown to be related to the extent to which some of the negative consequences of stress we discussed earlier occur.[54] Items from one of these questionnaires are listed in Exhibit 9.4.

EXHIBIT 9.4

Sample Items from a Life Event Checklist

	Happened in Last Three Years?		Current Impact on You?		
	No	Yes	Negative	None	Positive
1. Started school or a training program after not going to school for a long time	No	Yes	−3 −2 −1	0	+1 +2 +3
2. Started work for the first time	No	Yes	−3 −2 −1	0	+1 +2 +3
3. Changed jobs for a better one	No	Yes	−3 −2 −1	0	+1 +2 +3
4. Changed jobs for a worse one	No	Yes	−3 −2 −1	0	+1 +2 +3
5. Changed jobs for one that was no better or no worse than the last one	No	Yes	−3 −2 −1	0	+1 +2 +3
6. Had trouble with boss	No	Yes	−3 −2 −1	0	+1 +2 +3
7. Demoted at work	No	Yes	−3 −2 −1	0	+1 +2 +3
8. Found out was not going to be promoted at work	No	Yes	−3 −2 −1	0	+1 +2 +3
9. Conditions at work got worse, other than demotion or trouble with boss	No	Yes	−3 −2 −1	0	+1 +2 +3
10. Had significant success at work	No	Yes	−3 −2 −1	0	+1 +2 +3
11. Fired from previous job	No	Yes	−3 −2 −1	0	+1 +2 +3
12. Promoted on present job	No	Yes	−3 −2 −1	0	+1 +2 +3
13. Started a business or profession	No	Yes	−3 −2 −1	0	+1 +2 +3
14. Suffered a business loss or failure	No	Yes	−3 −2 −1	0	+1 +2 +3
15. Sharply increased workload	No	Yes	−3 −2 −1	0	+1 +2 +3
16. Sharply reduced workload	No	Yes	−3 −2 −1	0	+1 +2 +3
17. Had trouble with a co-worker or peer	No	Yes	−3 −2 −1	0	+1 +2 +3
18. Had trouble with a subordinate	No	Yes	−3 −2 −1	0	+1 +2 +3
19. Had trouble with a customer or client	No	Yes	−3 −2 −1	0	+1 +2 +3
20. Spouse started work for the first time	No	Yes	−3 −2 −1	0	+1 +2 +3
21. Spouse changed jobs for a worse one	No	Yes	−3 −2 −1	0	+1 +2 +3
22. Spouse promoted	No	Yes	−3 −2 −1	0	+1 +2 +3
23. Spouse demoted at work	No	Yes	−3 −2 −1	0	+1 +2 +3
24. Spouse fired	No	Yes	−3 −2 −1	0	+1 +2 +3
25. Took out a mortgage	No	Yes	-3 −2 −1	0	+1 +2 +3
26. Started buying a car, furniture, or other large purchase on an installment plan	No	Yes	−3 −2 −1	0	+1 +2 +3
27. Foreclosure of a mortgage or loan	No	Yes	−3 −2 −1	0	+1 +2 +3
28. Did not get an expected wage or salary increase	No	Yes	−3 −2 −1	0	+1 +2 +3
29. Took a cut in wage or salary without a demotion	No	Yes	−3 −2 −1	0	+1 +2 +3
30. Spouse did not get an expected wage or salary increase	No	Yes	−3 −2 −1	0	+1 +2 +3

(Continued)

31. Robbed	No	Yes	−3 −2 −1	0	+1 +2 +3
32. Got involved in a court case	No	Yes	−3 −2 −1	0	+1 +2 +3
33. Acquired a pet	No	Yes	−3 −2 −1	0	+1 +2 +3
34. Pet died	No	Yes	−3 −2 −1	0	+1 +2 +3
35. Was not able to take a planned vacation	No	Yes	−3 −2 −1	0	+1 +2 +3
36. Remodeled a home	No	Yes	−3 −2 −1	0	+1 +2 +3
37. Became engaged	No	Yes	−3 −2 −1	0	+1 +2 +3
38. Engagement was broken	No	Yes	−3 −2 −1	0	+1 +2 +3
39. Spouse was physically ill	No	Yes	−3 −2 −1	0	+1 +2 +3
40. Expecting a baby	No	Yes	−3 −2 −1	0	+1 +2 +3
41. Child started college	No	Yes	−3 −2 −1	0	+1 +2 +3
42. Serious family argument other than with spouse	No	Yes	−3 −2 −1	0	+1 +2 +3

Source: Adapted from R. S. Bhagat, S. J. McQuaid, H. Lindholm, and J. Segouis. "Total Life Stress: A Multimethod Validation of the Construct and Its Effects on Organizationally Valued Outcomes and Withdrawal Behaviors," *Journal of Applied Psychology* 70 (1985): 202–14; A. P. Brief, M. J. Burke, J. M. George, B. S. Robinson, and J. Webster, "Should Negative Affectivity Remain an Unmeasured Variable in the Study of Job Stress?" *Journal of Applied Psychology* 73 (1988): 193–98: B. S. Dohrenwend, L. Krasnoff, A. R. Askenasy, and B. P. Dohrenwend, "Exemplification of a Method for Scaling Life Events: The PERI Life Events Scale," *Journal of Health and Social Behavior* 19 (1978): 205–29; J. H. Johnson and I. G. Sarason, "Recent Developments in Research on Life Stress." In V. Hamilton and D. M. Warburton (eds.), *Human Stress and Cognition: An Information Processing Approach* (New York: Wiley, 1979), 205–36.

Job-Related Stressors

Just as a wide variety of life events can be potentially stressful, a wide variety of potential stressors arise from a person's job. Here we consider six job-related stressors: role conflict, role ambiguity, overload, underload, challenging assignments, promotions, and conditions that affect employees' economic well-being.

ROLE CONFLICT
The struggle that occurs when the behaviors or tasks that a person is expected to perform are at odds with each other.

In Chapter 1, we defined a *role* as a set of behaviors or tasks a person is expected to perform because of the position he or she holds in a group or organization. **Role conflict** occurs when expected behaviors or tasks are at odds with each other.[55] A social worker experiences role conflict when he is told to (1) spend more time and effort to determine whether children in foster care should be returned to their parents and (2) double the number of cases he handles each month. A middle manager experiences role conflict when her supervisor expects her to increase production levels, and her subordinates complain they are being overworked.

ROLE AMBIGUITY
The uncertainty that occurs when employees are not sure what is expected of them and how they should perform their jobs.

Role ambiguity is the uncertainty that occurs when employees are not sure about what is expected of them and how they should perform their jobs.[56] Role ambiguity can be an especially potent source of stress for newcomers to an organization, work group, or job. Newcomers are often unclear about what they are supposed to do and how they should do it. Most employees, however, experience some degree of role ambiguity at one time or another because organizations frequently change job responsibilities to adapt to changing conditions in the competitive environment. Ford Motor Company, for example, realized it needed to adapt to increased customer demands for high-quality automobiles and workers' demands for more autonomy. To address the need for change, Ford reorganized some of its factories so that employees performed their jobs in teams rather than individually. Some team members experienced role ambiguity because they were unsure about their new responsibilities in the teams.

OVERLOAD
The condition of having too many tasks to perform.

Sometimes employees experience job-related stress not because of conflicting demands (role conflict) or uncertain expectations (role ambiguity) but because of **overload**—the condition of having too many tasks to perform.[57] Robert Kakiuchi, vice president of human resources at the U.S. Bank of Washington, often works nights, weekends, and holidays to accomplish all of the tasks he is assigned. Layoffs reduced Kakiuchi's department from 70 employees to six, but the number of human resource services that he is expected to provide to other departments in the bank has not been reduced at all.[58] Kakiuchi is experiencing overload because his organization expects the remaining human resource workers to perform the tasks that used to be performed by laid-off workers.[59] Nadine Billard, a manager of export sales for the book publisher HarperCollins, experiences so much overload that she typically works fifteen-hour days and takes work home on weekends.[60] According to a recent study conducted by the Families and Work Institute, dual-career couples worked, on average, 91 hours per week in 2003, compared to an average of 81 hours per week in 1977.[61] Whether the high level of stress an overloaded employee experiences is negative and impairs performance depends on the employee's personality traits and abilities.

Overload is particularly prevalent among middle and top managers.[62] A recent study conducted by the American Management Association found that 41 percent of the middle managers surveyed had more work to do than time in which to do it. Another study conducted by the Seattle consulting firm Priority Management found that many middle managers are working much longer hours because of the extent of their overload.[63] Earlier we discussed how overload is a significant problem in Japan and sometimes leads to karoshi (death by overwork).

UNDERLOAD
The condition of having too few tasks to perform.

Underload, not having enough work to do, can also be a source of stress for employees. When was the last time you were really bored? Maybe it was a slow day at work, or you were doing research for a paper at the library. Perhaps you were bored while studying for an exam or watching a bad movie. Now imagine that you were truly bored for eight hours a day, five days a week. You would probably experience stress just because you were bored. As we know from the job characteristics model (see Chapter 7), most employees like to use different skills on the job and feel like they're doing something worthwhile. More generally, a certain level of stress is positive and leads to high levels of motivation and performance, as indicated in Figure 9.1.

Promotions and challenging assignments can be a source of stress for employees who are not sure that they can perform effectively or who have low self-efficacy. An employee promoted to a supervisory position who has never before had subordinates reporting to him may experience stress because he is not sure that he will be able to be assertive enough. Barbra Streisand was so negatively stressed by the challenge of performing in front of 125,000 people in New York's Central Park in 1967 that she forgot the lyrics to three of her songs and avoided live performances for the next 27 years. Madonna found the opportunity of singing at the 1991 Oscar presentation (which is broadcast to billions of television viewers) so stressful that her hand shook.[64]

Stressors that affect employees' *economic well-being and job security* are also powerful sources of stress.[65] When job-related income is very low or threatened by layoffs and downsizing, a lack of job security, or pay cuts, the well-being of employees and their families is put in jeopardy.

Numerous studies have shown that when organizations lay off employees, unemployment stress can be very damaging to employees and their families and may result in physical and mental illness, including depression, suicide, family violence, and even a family's breakup.[66] Layoffs can also be stressful for members of an organization who do not lose their jobs or are survivors of the layoff.[67] Layoff survivors can feel guilty, angry, unhappy, lonely, or fearful that they will be the next to lose their jobs. Sometimes they become physically ill from their high levels of stress. A 46-year-old geologist who has worked for a Houston oil company for the past 11 years survived a layoff and was promoted to be the leader of a group of 12 of her close colleagues. One of her first assignments in her new supervisory role was to lay off half of the geologists in the group. Her stress levels were so high that she started to go to bed earlier and earlier at night so that she would not have to think about work.[68] As indicated in the accompanying Managing Ethically, extensive layoffs and resultant financial difficulties are significant sources of stress for increasing numbers of employees in the United States.

Given how important job income is to employees and their families, opportunities for increasing pay levels also can be stressful to employees who are not sure that they can meet

Managing Ethically

Laid Off and On Your Own

Increasing numbers of employees in the United States are being laid off[69] and given little assistance to deal with the sudden loss of income and challenges of finding another job. According to a recent study conducted by the John J. Heldrich Center for Workforce Development at Rutgers University, one out of five employees randomly interviewed was laid off in the period from 2000 to 2003.[70] Less than half of those laid off received unemployment insurance, less than one-third had their health insurance coverage extended by their employer during their unemployment period, and less than one-fifth received any help from their former employer when it came to retraining or finding another job. Furthermore, approximately one-third of those laid off received no advance warning that their jobs were being terminated, and another third received only one or two weeks' notice.[71]

Unfortunately, for those laid off, finding another job is often a real challenge. Many workers are being forced to take part-time work or jobs for which they are overeducated and overskilled just to try to make ends meet. For example, John Wilkins was a software specialist with many years of work experience who was laid off from his job. After his search for another job in the computer industry was unsuccessful, he now works two part-time jobs (unloading packages for UPS in Palatine, Illinois, and counseling teenagers in a family service agency). And he is only making 25 percent of what his salary used to be.[72] Greg Fuller is in a similar bind. He used to be the director of program management for Motorola's cell phone division prior to being laid off. Now he sells cell phones at Best Buy, earns 15 percent of what he used to at Motorola, and is thinking about selling his house and finding less-expensive housing.[73]

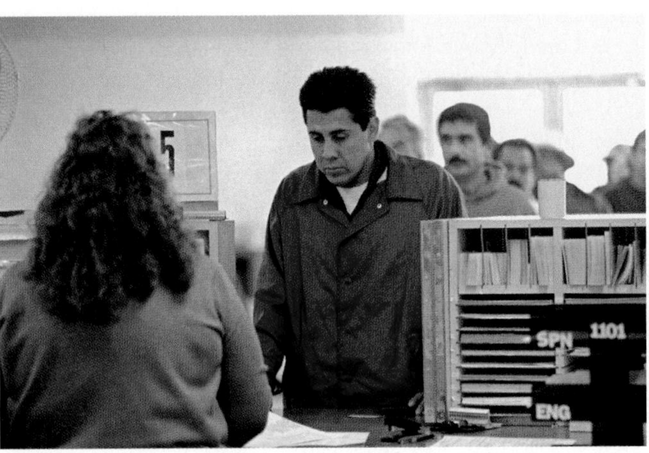

Job loss can be one of life's most traumatic experiences. Sometimes the effects of a job loss on a person's emotional outlook can be so severe that it interferes with his or her finding another job.

Unemployment and underemployment are growing problems in the United States. An estimated 4.8 million Americans are working at part-time jobs because they have been unable to find full-time work.[74] While extended mass layoffs were actually lower in 2005 than in recent prior years, according to the U. S. Bureau of Labor Statistics (BLS), in 2005 there were 4,780 extended mass layoffs that affected over 850,000 workers.[75] The BLS defines an extended mass layoff as one in which there are at least 50 claims for unemployment insurance benefits from a company during a 5-week period and at least 50 employees are laid off for more than 30 days.[76] While CEOs and top managers continue to take home record salaries, many laid-off, lower-level employees are struggling to find other jobs or make ends meet on a fraction of the pay they used to earn. This is a troubling ethical concern for corporate America that does not appear to be resolving itself.

the requirements for pay increases.[77] A car salesman working strictly on a commission basis experiences considerable stress every day because his ability to support his family and buy them the things they need depends on how many cars he sells. He likes his job because he has a lot of autonomy and is given the opportunity to earn high commissions by his hard work. But the job is stressful because so much is riding not only on what he does but also on things that are beyond his control, such as the economy, company-sponsored discounts, and advertising.

The previous examples constitute just a few of the potential stressors people face. But there are still many others, some of which we discussed in previous chapters. For example, being a victim of discrimination or sexual harassment (see Chapter 4) is typically very stressful for employees.[78]

Although we discuss how employees and organizations can cope with stressors in general later in the chapter, at this point it is useful to list some of the steps managers can take to make sure that job-related stressors do not cause employees to experience stress levels so high that their well-being and performance are impaired:

- To make sure that role conflict does not get out of hand, managers should be sure not to give employees conflicting expectations. They should try to ensure that what they expect of subordinates does not conflict with what others (customers, coworkers, and other managers) expect from them.
- Role ambiguity can be kept to a manageable level by telling employees clearly what is expected of them, how they should do their jobs, and what changes are being made.
- Managers should try to avoid overloading their subordinates and redesign jobs with too many tasks and responsibilities.
- When underload is a problem, managers should consider redesigning jobs so they score higher on the five core dimensions in the job characteristics model (skill variety, task identity, task significance, autonomy, and feedback).
- When employees experience stress from promotions or challenging job assignments, managers should take steps to raise their self-efficacy—their belief that they can be successful. We discussed several ways to boost self-efficacy in Chapter 5, such as encouraging small successes, letting subordinates know that others like themselves have succeeded in similar kinds of situations, having high expectations, and expressing confidence in subordinates' abilities.
- Organizations should do whatever they can to minimize the negative effects of layoffs and downsizing on their employees' economic well-being by giving employees advance notice of layoffs, fair and equitable severance pay, and providing them with counseling services. Similar steps can also be taken to reduce the stress of layoff survivors.
- When employees are experiencing stress due to, for example, a pay-for-performance plan, managers should actively work on boosting employee's self-efficacy.

Group- and Organization-Related Stressors

Potential stressors that can cause too high a level of stress also can arise at the work group and organizational levels. At the work group level, for example, misunderstandings, conflicts, and interpersonal disagreements can be sources of negative stress for group members. In Chapters 10 and 11, we discuss the benefits of using groups in organizations, some of the specific problems they face, and ways to alleviate them.

Given increasing globalization, more and more organizations are assembling cross-cultural teams whose members come from different countries. Misunderstandings and conflicts due to cultural differences sometimes are sources of stress in these teams. For example, in an impressive cross-cultural business venture, researchers from three competing companies—Siemens AG of Germany, Toshiba Corporation of Japan, and IBM—worked together at IBM's East Fishkill, New York, facility to build a new computer memory chip. The more than 100 scientists from the three different cultures working on the project called themselves the Triad. The managers (from all three companies) who organized the effort were initially concerned the scientists might encounter problems working together because of their different cultural backgrounds. Their concerns were borne out: Misunderstandings and conflicts became a significant source of stress for many of the scientists. For instance, the German scientists from Siemens were aghast when their Japanese counterparts from Toshiba closed their eyes during meetings and appeared to be sleeping. (Apparently, overworked scientists and managers frequently do this in Japan during parts of meetings that don't relate to them.) As another example, the American scientists from IBM experienced stress because they thought that the Germans spent too much time on planning, the Japanese spent too much time reviewing ideas, and neither spent enough time actually getting the project done.

Working through potential misunderstandings such as these in cross-cultural teams is important because international joint ventures have many advantages: Participants get different perspectives on a project or problem, a wide variety of skills and expertise is represented, and participants are able to benefit from their exposure to new ways of doing things. To take advantage of the benefits of diversity without experiencing too much stress from *culture shock*, individuals and groups need to be sensitive to the role that national culture plays when it comes to behavior in groups and organizations.

Uncomfortable working conditions are another source of stress for groups and entire organizations. Excessive noise, temperature extremes, and poorly designed office equipment and machinery can be very stressful when employees are exposed to them day in and day out. In recent years, more than 2,000 lawsuits have been filed by employees who claim that poorly designed computer keyboards—some made by well-known companies such as Eastman Kodak, IBM, and AT&T—have resulted in high levels of stress and painful, sometimes crippling, injuries to the employees' hands and wrists.[79]

Uncomfortable working conditions took on new meaning at Jim Beam's Clermont, Kentucky, bourbon distillery when a new policy prevented workers from using the rest room whenever they needed to. Bottling-line employees at the plant complained to the United Food and Commercial Workers Union when they were restricted to four breaks to use the restroom during their 8 ½-hour shifts, with only one of the breaks being unscheduled.[80] Employees found enforcement of this policy highly stressful, uncomfortable, and for some, a medical challenge. Employees who received notes from their doctors did not have to follow the policy and were able to use the rest room whenever nature called.[81]

Potentially *unsafe* or dangerous jobs that involve, say, working in nuclear power plants, with toxic chemicals or dangerous machinery, or with people who have communicable diseases such as AIDS, can cause stress and injuries.[82] A recent study by Circadian Technologies Inc. found that pilots who fly for United Parcel Service face dangerous working conditions between 15 percent and 31 percent of the time. The pilots' union attributes these dangerous working conditions to flights that cross several time zones, and flight schedules that cause pilots to alternate between flying at night and flying during the day.[83] Dangerous working conditions can also lead to on-the-job injuries. A recent study conducted by the University of Michigan School of Public Health found that employees in Michigan missed 8.9 million days of work in a year for injuries they received while performing their jobs.[84]

Mergers and acquisitions are often an organizational source of stress, particularly for employees in the acquired firm. Employees in the acquired firm often feel like second-class citizens and fear being laid off. Such fears are often justified because once an acquisition is completed, the acquiring firm or parent company typically restructures the organization it has acquired to capitalize on synergies across the two companies and eliminate duplication of effort.[85] Some employees in the acquired firm may be likely to lose their jobs. Others will be required to do more with less. This is what happened at Kentucky Fried Chicken when PepsiCo acquired the franchise.[86] Employees in the newly merged firm might experience stress from heightened uncertainty about the future and potential culture clashes between the two organizations.

We discuss what individuals and organizations can do to cope with stressors in general later in the chapter, but at this point it is useful to consider what managers and organizations can do to try to make sure that group- and organizational-level stressors do not get out of hand. First, members of work groups can be trained to work together as a team and communicate effectively with each other. (In Chapter 19, we discuss some team-building strategies.) Second, organizations should make sure that employees have comfortable working conditions whenever possible. Third, organizations should ensure that employees are not exposed to any unnecessary risks on the job and that all safety precautions are in place to limit the risk of injury on the job. Fourth, when organizations are undergoing major changes such as mergers and acquisitions,[87] they should provide employees with accurate and timely information about how the change will proceed and how it may affect them. This is just a sampling of the steps managers and organizations can take to try to limit the extent to which these potential stressors have negative effects on the employees exposed to them.

Stressors Arising Out of Work-Life Balance

People employed as factory workers, receptionists, managers, nurses, and truck drivers are also often parents, spouses, children of elderly parents, volunteers in community organizations, and hobbyists. A recent study conducted by the nonprofit Families and Work Institute based in New York found that 85 percent of U. S. employees are responsible for family members living at home.[88] In light of the fact that employees are working longer hours than they did 20 years ago, this suggests that achieving a balance between work and life outside of work can be a real challenge.[89] When work roles conflict with one's personal life, stress is often the result. New accountants and attorneys working in major accounting and law firms, for example, are expected to put in very long hours. Although working long hours can be stressful in its own right, it can be even more stressful when it conflicts with demands from one's personal life. Many employees have young children at home and a spouse who is putting in equally long hours. Add in the responsibility of taking care of an ill parent or being president of a local charity and the stress can be overwhelming. Single parents often feel even more burdened because they do not have a spouse to help them deal with family problems and responsibilities.[90]

Even when employees do not have children, family responsibilities often cause stress when they conflict with work demands. Faith Merrens, a manager of software designers at U. S. West Communications Inc., indicates that "elder care is the biggest personal issue we face in maintaining productivity from day to day."[91] Most of her subordinates have been forced to take time off from work to care for elderly relatives. Even Merrens and her boss had to take time off when their parents were hospitalized.

Additionally, many employees fall into what has been called the "sandwich generation."[92] These employees are responsible for not only taking care of their own children, but also taking care of their aging parents.[93] Responsibilities for children and infirm parents often conflict with heavy workloads, significantly increasing stress for those caught in the middle. Later in the chapter, we discuss some of the steps organizations can take to help prevent these kinds of conflicts from overwhelming their employees.

Another form of conflict between work and personal life occurs when employees are asked to do things that conflict with their personal values or when they work in organizations with ethics different from their own. It is very stressful, for example, for some emergency room personnel at private hospitals to turn away potential patients because they lack medical insurance. Likewise, it is sometimes stressful for loan officers at banks to foreclose on a family's mortgage because the family can't keep up the payments. Similarly, it may be difficult for insurance agents to cancel medical insurance or deny coverage to patients for certain kinds of ailments. An environmentalist may feel stressed out working for an organization that fails to recycle; salespeople may experience stress selling products they know are low quality.

Environmental Uncertainty

Just as employees can experience stress from their personal lives, so too can they experience stress from uncertainty and crises in the wider environment in which organizations operate. The tragic and devastating terrorist attacks on the United States on September 11, 2001, shocked the nation and the world. Research suggests the attacks were a significant source of stress for the employees directly affected by the attacks and those people in the vicinity of the attacks. But the attacks were also deeply distressful to people living and working hundreds of miles away who didn't know anyone personally affected. This is a stressor that unfortunately continues to be present as heightened security at airports and public venues. We hear it in governmental warnings, and security lapses contribute to a sense of threat and vulnerability over which many people feel they have little control. Although the threat of terrorism continues to be a potential source of stress around the world, research suggests that it does not appear to have changed employees' attitudes about their jobs and organizations.[94]

Other examples of contemporary stressors stemming from the wider environment include global instability and wars in Afghanistan, Iraq, and elsewhere. The outbreak of a deadly disease in Asia (SARS), fears of a potential bird flu pandemic, a growing number of corporate scandals in which top managers engaged in deception and fraud,[95] tragic accidents such as an explosion at a BP oil refinery in Texas City that killed 15 employees and injured 100,[96] and pollution of the natural environment and exposure to toxins are just a few examples. Stressors like these that stem from uncertainty in the wider environment can affect the well-being and stress levels of employees in organizations—whether or not they have a close connection to the stressor. Such stressors can be particularly troubling because many individuals feel they have little personal control over the stressors.

Although people may have little control over terrorism, war, or contagious diseases, there are steps they can take to manage how they feel about, think about, and deal with environmental stressors. The accompanying Global View explains how.

Global View

Coping with Grief and Loss

When machinery exploded at a Texas City BP oil refinery, 15 employees were killed and over 100 were injured. Grief counselors helped survivors cope with their feelings of loss and guilt.

Psychologists Dr. James Gordon, director of the Center for Mind-Body Medicine in New York, and Dr. Barrie Cassileth, a medical social worker and director of Integrative Medicine at Memorial Sloan-Kettering Cancer Center, both have helped people manage stress resulting from traumatic events.[97] Dr. Cassileth helps patients and their families deal with life-threatening diseases. Dr. Gordon helps people in countries such as Bosnia, Macedonia, and Kosovo return to a sense of normalcy in the aftermath of war. He also helped New York City firefighters in the wake of September 11, 2001. *New York Times* reporter Jane E. Brody recently spoke with these caregivers about the steps people can take to deal with the stress caused by traumatic environmental events. Here are some of their recommendations.[98]

Gordon and Cassileth say that, first of all, a person needs to try to maintain a healthy balance between knowing what is going on in the world and avoiding overexposure to it. Thus, it might be beneficial for you to be cognizant of the events that are occurring around you and how you might deal with them—perhaps by volunteering or expressing your feelings to others—but it is not a good idea to spend excessive amounts of time dwelling on trauma (say, watching endless news reports and films, reading articles, listening to reports on the radio, and so forth). Second, if you feel overwhelmed, try to take things one day at a time and focus on your key priorities. Gordon and Cassileth suggest you also maintain some kind of routine on a daily or weekly basis. Last, but not least, try to take care of yourself physically and emotionally. Exercise, relaxation techniques, meditation, and seeking help and support from others are all beneficial ways to try to maintain your physical and emotional balance.[99]

In 2005, when machinery exploded at a Texas City BP oil refinery killing 15 employees and injuring over 100, grief counselors were brought in to help survivors cope with their feelings of loss and guilt.[100] Some survivors feel guilty because they didn't do anything to prevent a major tragic accident (even though they couldn't have and it was out of their control), others feel guilty because they perhaps weren't as nice as they could have been to a coworker that died or was injured, and others just feel guilty that they are alive. Ian McDougall, a grief counselor who met with BP employees after this tragic explosion indicates that "Fatalities make people feel very reflective. I encourage them to live today and enjoy the day and not live in the past or the future."[101]

Research done a few months after September 11, 2001, suggests that sometimes people respond to traumatic environmental events by altering their values and priorities. A significant number of employees who participated in one survey indicated they had changed their values and priorities.[102] Some employees were struck by how very important their families had become to them and that they should spend more time with their families and tell them how important they are.[103] Lauren Howard, a psychotherapist in New York City, had this to say following September 11: "There is . . . a greater sense of community in New York. We care more about other people," Howard explained.[104] Indeed, the city mourned the deaths of the 2,792 people who died at the World Trade Center, and 265 others who perished just two months later in a plane crash in Queens.[105] The tragic events caused the citizens to pull together like never before.

The accompanying Global View clearly suggests that how people deal or cope with stressors can have important effects on how they react to them. While we have discussed coping in reaction to certain specific preceding stressors, we now turn to a more general discussion of ways of coping with stress.

Coping with Stress

Ultimately, the extent to which stress is experienced and whether it is positive or negative depends on how people *cope*—that is, manage or deal with stressors. There are two basic types of coping: problem-focused coping and emotion-focused coping. **Problem-focused coping** relates to the steps people take to deal directly with and act on the source of stress.[106] For example, employees facing the threat of a layoff may cope in a problem-focused manner by looking for other jobs in organizations that are not downsizing. When problem-focused coping is successful, it helps employees deal with opportunities and threats that are causing stress.

PROBLEM-FOCUSED COPING
The steps people take to deal directly with and act on the source of stress.

Emotion-focused coping relates to the steps people take to deal with and control their stressful feelings and emotions.[107] For example, some employees facing the threat of a layoff may try to alleviate some of their stressful feelings and emotions by exercising regularly or meditating. When emotion-focused coping is successful, stressful feelings and emotions generated by threats and opportunities do not get out of hand.

EMOTION-FOCUSED COPING
The steps people take to deal with and control their stressful feelings and emotions.

Research suggests that most of the time people engage in both kinds of coping when dealing with a stressor.[108] Individuals cope with stressors in a variety of problem- and emotion-focused ways, and there are steps organizations can take to help employees cope with the many stressors they face.

Problem-Focused Coping Strategies for Individuals

Problem-focused coping is coping directly tailored to the stressor being experienced. A college senior experiencing stress due to an upcoming job interview copes in a problem-focused way by finding out as much information as possible about the company and doing some practice interviews with a friend. When Dale Morley moved his family from London to New York so that he could assume the position of vice president of sales and marketing for Avis International, he and his family coped with the stress of being away from relatives by periodically making audiocassettes and sending them back home.[109] In addition to problem-focused coping strategies devised to manage a very specific source of stress, such as preparing for a job interview or relocating, more general strategies can be used to deal with several kinds of stressors. Here we consider three: time management, getting help from a mentor, and role negotiation.

> TIME MANAGEMENT
> Prioritizing and estimating techniques that allow employees to identify the most important tasks and fit them into their daily schedule.

Time management. One strategy for coping with overload is **time management**, a series of techniques that can help people accomplish more with the limited amount of time they do have. Time management usually entails these steps:

- Employees make lists of all the tasks they need to accomplish during the day.
- The tasks are then prioritized in terms of those that are most important and must be done and those that are less important and can be put off, if need be.
- Employees estimate how long it will take to accomplish these tasks and plan their workdays accordingly.[110]

Time management is a coping strategy for individuals, but organizations can help their members learn effective time management techniques. Valerie Nossal is employed as a time management expert at MeadWestvaco Consumer and Office Products in Stamford, Connecticut, to help employees better manage their time.[111] She suggests that employees need to be proactive and also set priorities and limits. Given the high volumes of work many employees are faced with, they could work around the clock and not get everything done. Thus, employees need to set priorities not only in terms of what is more and less important to get done at work but also in terms of making sure they have a balance between work and the rest of their lives. Nossal advises employees to schedule time to exercise and be with their families because these are important activities that should not be neglected due to work pressures.[112] Moreover, not paying attention to one's priorities and achieving a work-life balance may actually make employees less efficient.

Given pressures to get more done in less time, some employees engage in multitasking—doing two or more things at once—such as writing a report during a meeting, answering e-mails while talking on the telephone, or opening mail while listening to a coworker. Does multitasking save time? Preliminary research suggests that rather than saving time, multitasking might actually make people become less, rather than more, efficient, especially when they are working on complex tasks or activities.[113] Multitasking that relies on the same parts of the brain makes a person especially vulnerable to efficiency losses.[114] For example, if you are trying to compose an e-mail while carrying on a conversation with your boss over your speaker phone, both of these tasks require you to use and process language. One will likely interfere with the other, resulting in lower efficiency. However, photocopying documents while talking with a coworker might be more feasible, though the coworker is probably receiving a bit less of your attention than he or she would have received if you weren't multitasking.[115]

Getting help from a mentor. Recall from Chapter 4 that more-experienced members of an organization (mentors) can offer advice and guidance to less-experienced members (protégés). Getting help from a mentor can be an effective problem-focused coping strategy for dealing with stressors such as role conflict, role ambiguity, overload, and challenging assignments and promotions. A mentor can advise an overloaded protégé, for example, about how to prioritize tasks so the important ones get accomplished, how to determine what tasks can be put aside, and when to say "no" to additional assignments or requests.

Like time management, getting help from a mentor is an individual-based, problem-focused coping strategy, but organizations can take steps to help ensure that mentors are available to protégés. For example, some organizations have formal mentoring programs to help new employees get the guidance and advice they need to achieve their goals.

ROLE NEGOTIATION
The process through which employees actively try to change their roles in order to reduce role conflict, role ambiguity, overload, or underload.

Role negotiation. **Role negotiation** is the process through which employees actively try to change their roles in order to reduce role conflict, role ambiguity, overload, or underload.[116] Sometimes simply saying "no" to additional assignments can be an effective means of role negotiation for overloaded employees.

Role negotiation can also be an effective problem-focused coping mechanism for employees experiencing stress due to work-life linkages. Blake Ashdown, a consultant based in East Lansing, Michigan, helps resorts develop and manage exercise programs and facilities. He has engaged in role negotiation by being more selective about the assignments he takes and by turning down some resorts. Ashdown has found this strategy to be an effective means of coping with the conflict between his demanding work schedule and his responsibilities at home. By negotiating his role, Ashdown is able to spend more time with his wife and five children and avoid high levels of stress from his work.[117]

Emotion-Focused Coping Strategies for Individuals

In addition to trying to manage problems and opportunities that are stressful, employees also have to learn to manage the feelings and emotions they give rise to. Here we consider four emotion-focused coping strategies for individuals: exercise, meditation, social support, and clinical counseling.

Exercise. One of the reasons why exercise is so popular today is that it is an effective means of emotion-focused coping. Jogging, aerobics, swimming, tennis, and walking are just a few of the types of exercise that employees ranging from entry-level employees to CEOs and even American presidents use to cope with stressors in an emotion-focused way. Regular exercise can reduce stress, improve cardiovascular functioning, and enhance well-being.

Yoga is growing in popularity as a means to alleviate stress and can also increase people's ability to concentrate. According to the magazine *Yoga Journal,* 15 million adults in the United States engage in yoga, and over 35 million say they want to try it in the next 12 months.[118] Yoga involves practicing certain postures and poses, controlling breathing, and achieving a sense of calm and alleviating stress. Some organizations are actually providing optional yoga classes to help their employees combat stress. For example, Katz Media Company in New York and Lomangino Studio, a Washington, D.C., graphic design company, both offer on-site yoga classes for their employees.[119] And some counselors in the New York City fire department who worked 80-hour weeks after September 11 found yoga helped them cope with the stress of helping firefighters and their families deal with the deaths of 343 fellow firefighters. Bill Crawford, who has over 30 year's experience with the department and heads its counseling group, is a yoga devotee himself. As he puts it, yoga "makes me focus and put aside all the stray thoughts of the day that overwhelm us and cause us stress."[120]

Meditation. Some employees deal with stressful emotions through meditation. There are various forms of meditation, and some of them require professional training to learn.

EXHIBIT 9.5

A Measure of Satisfaction with Social Support

Instructions: The following questions ask about people in your environment who provide you with help or support. Each question has two parts. For the first part, list all the people you know, excluding yourself, whom you can count on for help or support in the manner described. Give the persons' initials, their relationship to you (see example). *Do not list more than one person next to each of the numbers beneath the question.*

For the second part, circle how *satisfied* you are with the overall support you have.

If you have had no support for a question, check the words "No one," but still rate your level of satisfaction. Do not list more than nine persons per question.

Please answer all the questions as best you can. All your responses will be kept confidential.

Example

Who do you know whom you can trust with information that could get you in trouble?

____ No one	1 T.N. (brother)	4 T.N. (father)	7
	2 L.M. (friend)	5 L.M. (employer)	8
	3 R.S. (friend)	6	9

How satisfied?

6	(5)	4	3	2	1
very satisfied	fairly satisfied	a little satisfied	a little dissatisfied	fairly dissatisfied	very dissatisfied

1. Whom can you really count on to be dependable when you need help?

____ No one	1	4	7
	2	5	8
	3	6	9

2. How satisfied?

6	5	4	3	2	1
very satisfied	fairly satisfied	a little satisfied	a little dissatisfied	fairly dissatisfied	very dissatisfied

3. Whom can you really count on to help you feel more relaxed when you are under pressure or tense?

____ No one	1	4	7
	2	5	8
	3	6	9

4. How satisfied?

6	5	4	3	2	1
very satisfied	fairly satisfied	a little satisfied	a little dissatisfied	fairly dissatisfied	very dissatisfied

5. Who accepts you totally, including both your worst and best points?

____ No one	1	4	7
	2	5	8
	3	6	9

6. How satisfied?

6	5	4	3	2	1
very satisfied	fairly satisfied	a little satisfied	a little dissatisfied	fairly dissatisfied	very dissatisfied

7. Whom can you really count on to care about you, regardless of what is happening to you?

____ No one	1	4	7
	2	5	8
	3	6	9

8. How satisfied?

6	5	4	3	2	1
very satisfied	fairly satisfied	a little satisfied	a little dissatisfied	fairly dissatisfied	very dissatisfied

9. Whom can you really count on to help you feel better when you are feeling generally down in the dumps?

____ No one	1	4	7
	2	5	8
	3	6	9

10. How satisfied?

6	5	4	3	2	1
very satisfied	fairly satisfied	a little satisfied	a little dissatisfied	fairly dissatisfied	very dissatisfied

(Continued)

11. Whom can you count on to console you when you are very upset?

____ No one	1	4	7
	2	5	8
	3	6	9

12. How satisfied?

6	5	4	3	2	1
very satisfied	fairly satisfied	a little satisfied	a little dissatisfied	fairly dissatisfied	very dissatisfied

Scoring: Satisfaction with social support is measured by averaging responses to the even-numbered questions (2, 4, 6, 8, 10, and 12).

Source: Scale obtained from I. G. Sarason, Psychology Department NI-25, University of Washington, Seattle, WA 98195. Reprinted with permission. Scale described in I. G. Sarason, B. R. Sarason, E. N. Shearin, and G. R. Pierce, "A Brief Measure of Social Support: Practical and Theoretical Implications," *Journal of Social and Personal Relationships* 4 (1987): 497–510.

Generally, however, meditation entails being in a quiet environment, sitting in a comfortable position, and tuning out everyday cares and worries by focusing mentally on some visual image or verbal phrase.[121].

Buddhist monks are masters of the practice of meditation and excel at the kind of trained introspection that meditation involves. In fact, neuroscientists at MIT have met with the Dalai Lama to understand how meditation works and what it can reveal about the workings and power of the brain.[122] The French monk Matthieu Ricard met with neuroscientists at the University of Wisconsin for similar reasons. Not only do the scientists hope to learn from the Buddhists but the Buddhists hope to learn from the scientists as well.[123].

Social support. People naturally seek help from others—social support—when they are having problems or feeling stressed. The social support of friends, relatives, coworkers, or other people who care about you and are available to discuss problems, give advice, or just be with you can be an effective means of emotion-focused coping.[124] Both the number of people you can turn to and the quality of the relationships you have with those people are important in helping to alleviate stress. A sample measure that is used to determine the extent to which a person is satisfied with the social support available to him or her is provided in Exhibit 9.5.

Clinical counseling. Sometimes employees have difficulty coping on their own and seek professional help or clinical counseling. Trained psychologists and psychiatrists can help employees learn how to cope with stressors that may seem overwhelming and at times unbearable.

Nonfunctional strategies. The four emotion-focused coping strategies that we have discussed are functional for individuals because they generally help alleviate stressful feelings and emotions without creating new problems or sources of stress. Unfortunately, however, there are other emotion-focused ways of coping that are less functional for employees. Some people react to high levels of stress by eating too much, drinking too much, or taking drugs. Some employees employed by Phillips Petroleum Company, for example, started having problems with alcohol when they experienced high levels of stress from a big layoff.[125] These ways of coping are never effective in alleviating stressful feelings and emotions in the long run, and they create more problems, such as being overweight, being addicted to alcohol or drugs, and being unable to function to one's fullest capacity.

Problem-Focused Coping Strategies for Organizations

Managers and organizations can do several things to deal with problems and opportunities that are sources of stress for employees. Some problem-focused coping strategies for organizations are job redesign and rotation, reduction of uncertainty, job security, company day care, flexible work schedules, job sharing, and telecommuting.

You're the Management Expert

Coping with the Stress of a Challenging New Job

Pamela Perkins recently took a new job as the managing director of a chain of day care centers in the northeastern United States. After three weeks on the job, she already feels burned out. She has been putting in 15 hour days, five days a week and spending her weekends catching up on paperwork and visiting individual centers. Perkins feels pressure from all sides: The relatively low-paid teachers and aides who staff the centers have a high absenteeism and turnover rate that creates logistical nightmares. Each day, there is at least one parent who calls on Perkins with a concern at one of the centers. Her own staff members lack initiative, and she does not feel comfortable delegating tasks to them. And as a single parent of a toddler who is enrolled in one of the centers, she feels guilty she's not spending more time with her son in the evenings and on weekends. The owner of the centers recently complimented Perkins on her swift adjustment to the new job and the seamless way in which she seems to have gotten up to speed. He remarked that Perkins has actually become much more adept at managing the centers than her predecessor, who never seemed quite on top of things and took too long to address problems and make changes. Perkins was pleased that her boss recognized the fruits of her labor, but it was a bittersweet kind of feeling because she was feeling so stressed out at the time. Perkins has come to the realization that something must change if she is to keep this job. Because you are an expert in OB, Perkins has come to you for help. How can she effectively cope with the excessive levels of stress she is experiencing?

Job redesign and rotation. Sometimes it is possible to redesign jobs to reduce negative stress caused by high levels of role conflict, role ambiguity, overload, or underload, or to improve working conditions. The job characteristics model (see Chapter 7) outlined the aspects of the job especially important to consider—namely, skill variety, task identity, task significance, autonomy, and feedback. Increasing autonomy can be useful to combat role conflict, and providing feedback can help cut down on role ambiguity. When overload is a problem, reducing the number of tasks a jobholder must perform is a viable option. Underload can be remedied by raising the skill levels, variety, task identity, and task significance related to the job. Uncomfortable and dangerous working conditions should be remedied whenever possible. Redesigning jobs to reduce unnecessary travel and job relocations can also help reduce levels of stress, particularly for dual-career couples and single parents.

JOB ROTATION
Assigning employees to different jobs on a regular basis.

When job redesign is not a viable option, **job rotation**, assigning employees to different jobs (which themselves do not change) on a regular basis, can sometimes alleviate stress. Physicians, for example, often rotate on-call duty for hospital emergency rooms and thereby reduce the level of stress that any one physician experiences from this job assignment.

Reduction of uncertainty. Often employees experience stress because they are uncertain about how to perform their assigned tasks, how to deal with conflicting goals or expectations, or how to prioritize assignments. Uncertainty also can cause stress when employees are unsure about how an organization expects or wants them to deal with competing demands at work and home. Whatever gives rise to it, uncertainty often results in stress.

One way to reduce uncertainty in organizations is by allowing employees to participate in making decisions that affect them and their jobs. When employees participate in decision making, they often have a lot more information about changes an organization can make and how to adjust to them. We discuss participation in decision making in more detail in Chapters 12 and 14. As we discuss in Chapter 14, participation can be taken one step further by empowering employees—giving them the authority to make decisions and be responsible for the outcomes of those decisions.

Another way to reduce uncertainty is to improve communication throughout an organization. Employees need clear, accurate information on a timely basis, and steps should be taken to ensure that employees understand what this information essentially means for them as well as the organization as a whole. Good communication is so important in understanding and managing organizational behavior that it is the focus of Chapter 13.

Job security. Whenever possible, providing employees with job security so that they know they will be able to support themselves and their loved ones helps to eliminate stressors related to the economic functions of work. Employees in Japan and Europe typically have higher levels of job security than do employees in the United States.

In lean economic times, it may be hard for organizations to guarantee job security. IBM and other companies that in the past prided themselves on high levels of security have been forced to lay off employees. Nevertheless, organizations can take steps to reduce the impact a layoff has on employees and their families. If a layoff is a real possibility, managers should provide employees with clear, honest information about their prospects in the organization. When laying off employees is necessary, it is best to give them as much advance notice as possible so they can prepare themselves and explore their options. Whenever possible, outplacement counseling should be made available to help employees find other positions or obtain additional training to increase their employment options. Employees should also receive fair severance packages.

Company day care. The problem of finding good, safe, affordable day care for young children is well known to many working parents. So is the problem of knowing what to do with their children when they get sick. Many organizations are coming up with innovative ways to help employees cope with stressors arising out of this work-life linkage. For example, Tallahassee Memorial Hospital in Florida spends around $300,000 a year to run a child care center for its employees. The facility is open from 7 A.M. to midnight.[126] As another example, when four staff members, three of whom were supervisors, at the San Jose National Bank became pregnant, bank president James Kenny and human resources director Laura Graves gave the women the option of taking the standard 12 week maternity leave allowed by the San Jose National Bank or coming back to work after eight weeks with their babies in tow. Bank employees are allowed to bring their babies to work until they are six months old or are crawling.[127]

Organizations can also help employees cope with the problem of what to do when children become ill. Such assistance not only helps reduce employees' stress but also can reduce absenteeism. Schering-Plough, a pharmaceutical company in Memphis, Tennessee, has a special sick room in its child care center (run by a pediatrician), so employees' children receive proper care when they are ill. In its first six months of operation, the sick room reduced employee absenteeism by 133 days. The money the company saves in six months from lower absenteeism covers the cost of operating the sick room for a whole year.[128] Time Warner has an emergency child care service for its employees. Babysitters take care of employees' sick children in their homes. They also step in to care for children should an employee's regular babysitter miss work.[129]

Flexible work schedules and job sharing. Many organizations use flexible work schedules to help their employees cope with conflicts between work and personal life. Stride Rite, a shoemaker, and eight other organizations have joined together to find ways to promote flexibility in the workplace. Companies such as Du Pont and Corning train their supervisors to manage employees on flexible schedules.[130] Flexible schedules allow employees to take time off when they need to take care of a sick child or an elderly parent. Employees at Xerox have this option and keep records of how they make up for their absences.[131] (For more information on flexible work schedules, see the closing case for this chapter.)

When job sharing is used, two or more employees are responsible for a single job and agree on how to divide job tasks and working hours. One employee might perform the job

Telecommuting is growing at a brisk pace. A recent study estimates that over 45 million people in the United States work from their homes at least part of the time.

in the mornings and another in the afternoons; employees might alternate days; one might work on Mondays, Wednesdays, and Fridays and the other on Tuesdays and Thursdays; or each employee might be accountable for particular tasks and assignments. Job sharing helps employees cope with the competing demands they face at work and home. In order for job sharing to be effective, however, good communication and understanding between the organization and its employees are necessities.

The prospect of increased flexibility leads some people to become contingent workers, hired on a temporary basis by organizations. If a contingent worker is finished with an assignment at one company and wants to take some time off before the next job, he or she is free to do so. However, this increased flexibility comes at the expense of job security, and a lack of job security can be a source of stress in and of itself. Art director David Debowski works on a freelance basis out of San Francisco, choosing the projects he wants to work on from ad agencies. Although he enjoys the flexibility of freelance work, he initially found it stressful to not know if he would have a new project to work on when he finished his current project. He coped with this source of stress by listing himself with a temporary employment agency that specializes in his kind of work.[132]

TELECOMMUTING
A work arrangement whereby employees are employed by an organization and have an agreement that enables them to work out of their homes regularly but not necessarily all the time.

Telecommuting. When **telecommuting** is used, employees are employed by an organization and have an agreement that enables them to work out of their homes regularly but not necessarily all the time.[133] Some employees' telecommuting arrangements may entail working three days at home and two days in the office. Other employees may work primarily at home but come to the office for meetings on an as-needed basis. Still others have the option of working from home as the need arises. New advances in information technology offer telecommuters multiple ways to communicate and stay in constant contact with their coworkers, bosses, customers, and clients.

Telecommuting can help employees cope with stress by providing them with more flexibility, freeing up time that would ordinarily be spent commuting, and giving them more autonomy. However, some telecommuters feel isolated, and others think that they end up working longer hours than they would have because their work is always "there"—at home, that is. Telecommuting also has potential advantages and disadvantages for the employing organization. On the plus side, telecommuting can help organizations attract and retain valuable employees. It can also lead to higher productivity and less time lost due to absences. On the downside, telecommuting can result in coordination problems and tensions between employees who telecommute and those who don't.[134]

Research suggests that employees tend to appreciate the opportunity to telecommute. For example, one recent study found that telecommuters were generally satisfied with telecommuting.[135] Another study found that telecommuters perceived lower levels of role conflict and ambiguity, had higher levels of organizational commitment, and were more satisfied with their supervisors than employees who did not telecommute. However, the telecommuters were less satisfied with their coemployees and opportunities for promotions.[136] Research also suggests that telecommuting may be more likely to reduce stress levels when telecommuters perceive that their organizations are supportive and really care about their well-being.[137]

Clearly, more organizations are making telecommuting an option for employees, and more employees are choosing to telecommute. A recent study estimates that over 45 million people in the United States work from their homes at least part of the time.[138]

Emotion-Focused Coping Strategies for Organizations

Organizations can help employees cope effectively with stressful feelings and emotions through such things as on-site exercise facilities, organizational support, employee assistance programs, and personal days and sabbaticals.

On-site exercise facilities. Realizing the benefits of exercise, many organizations such as General Foods Corporation and the SAS Institute have exercise facilities and classes that employees can use before and after work and during their lunch hours.

ORGANIZATIONAL SUPPORT
The extent to which an organization cares about the well-being of its members, tries to help them when they have a problem, and treats them fairly.

Organizational support. **Organizational support** is the extent to which an organization cares about the well-being of its members, listens to their complaints, tries to help them when they have a problem, and treats them fairly.[139] Feeling and knowing that an organization cares about and is committed to its members are likely to help reduce employees' stressful feelings and emotions.[140] Research has found, for example, that nurses who perceive high levels of organizational support are less likely to experience negative feelings and emotions when they take care of AIDS patients.[141] Organizational support is also likely to help mitigate some of the negative feelings and emotions generated by downsizing and layoffs. An example of a measure of employees' perceptions of how supportive their organizations are is provided in Exhibit 9.6.

EXHIBIT 9.6

A Measure of Perceived Organizational Support

Workers indicate the extent to which they agree or disagree with each of the following statements about their organizations using the following scale:

1	2	3	4	5	6	7
Strongly disagree	***Disagree***	**Slightly *disagree***	**Neither agree nor *disagree***	**Slightly agree**	**Agree**	**Strongly agree**

1. The organization values my contribution to its well-being.	1	2	3	4	5	6	7
2. If the organization could hire someone to replace me at a lower salary, it would do so.*	1	2	3	4	5	6	7
3. The organization fails to appreciate any extra effort from me.*	1	2	3	4	5	6	7
4. The organization strongly considers my goals and values.	1	2	3	4	5	6	7
5. The organization would ignore any complaint from me.*	1	2	3	4	5	6	7
6. The organization disregards my best interests when it makes decisions that affect me.*	1	2	3	4	5	6	7
7. Help is available from the organization when I have a problem.	1	2	3	4	5	6	7
8. The organization really cares about my well-being.	1	2	3	4	5	6	7
9. Even if I did the best job possible, the organization would fail to notice.*	1	2	3	4	5	6	7
10. The organization is willing to help me when I need a special favor.	1	2	3	4	5	6	7
11. The organization cares about my general satisfaction at work.	1	2	3	4	5	6	7
12. If given the opportunity, the organization would take advantage of me.*	1	2	3	4	5	6	7
13. The organization shows very little concern for me.*	1	2	3	4	5	6	7
14. The organization cares about my opinions.	1	2	3	4	5	6	7
15. The organization takes pride in my accomplishments at work.	1	2	3	4	5	6	7
16. The organization tries to make my job as interesting as possible.	1	2	3	4	5	6	7

Scoring: Responses to items are averaged for an overall score.

Items marked with a "*" should be scored as follows: 1 = 7, 2 = 6, 3 = 5, 5 = 3, 6 = 2, 7 = 1.

Source: Copyright © 1977 by the American Psychological Association. Reprinted with permission.

EMPLOYEE ASSISTANCE PROGRAMS (EAPS)
Company-sponsored programs that provide employees with counseling and other kinds of professional help to deal with stressors such as alcohol and drug abuse and family problems.

Employee assistance programs. Many organizations realize that employees sometimes face stressors that they simply cannot handle on their own. IBM, General Motors, Caterpillar, and many other organizations use **employee assistance programs (EAPs)** to provide their members with professional help to deal with stressors. According to the Society for Human Resource Management, approximately 70 percent of organizations have EAPs. Some EAPs simply provide employees with free professional counseling by trained psychologists. Others are structured to deal with particular types of stressors and problems, such as alcohol or drug abuse by employees or members of their families or problems with troubled teens. Champion International Corporation, for example, offers workshops to its employees on how to deal with potential drug abuse in their families.[142]

In order for EAPs to be effective, however, employees must be guaranteed confidentiality so they're not afraid their jobs and careers will be jeopardized by seeking help.

Employee health management programs (EHMPs) are a special kind of EAP designed to promote the well-being of members of an organization and encourage healthy lifestyles. These programs focus on helping employees improve their well-being and abilities to cope with stressors by, for example, controlling their weight, quitting smoking, improving their eating habits and nutrition, and detecting potential health problems such as high blood pressure early.[143] Eighty-one percent of large organizations have at least one kind of EHMP in place.[144] Du Pont, for example, offers classes ranging from 4 to 10 weeks long that are held during lunch and before and after work. How to stop smoking, control one's weight and eat a healthy diet, and deal with back-related problems are among the topics discussed.[145]

Personal days, time off, and sabbaticals. Providing personal days, time off from work, and sabbaticals can help reduce stressful feelings and emotions by allowing employees to put their work-related stress aside for a day or two (in the case of personal days) or for a more extended period (in the case of sabbaticals). Personal days are common at many large and small organizations and are available to all employees. Realizing the mounting pressures employees face, some organizations are setting aside days when all employees take off. For example, in 2005, PriceWaterhouseCoopers gave all of its employees 10 consecutive days off from work during the December holiday season.[146]

People usually cope with stressors in both problem-focused and emotion-focused ways. When coping is successful, it helps employees effectively deal with stressful opportunities and threats without experiencing too many stressful feelings and emotions. Exhibit 9.7 summarizes the various coping strategies available to individuals and organizations.

EXHIBIT 9.7

Coping Strategies

Summary

Stress affects individual well-being and has the potential to affect the extent to which individuals and organizations achieve their goals and perform at high levels. Stress is bound up with employees' personal lives; thus, the study of stress also entails exploring the nature of work-life linkages. In this chapter, we made the following major points:

1. People experience stress when they face opportunities or threats that they perceive as important and also perceive they might not be able to handle or deal with effectively. An opportunity is something that has the potential to benefit a person. A threat is something that has the potential to harm a person. Stress is a highly personal experience influenced by an individual's personality, abilities, and perceptions; what is stressful for one person might not be stressful for another.
2. Stress can have physiological, psychological, and behavioral consequences. The relationship between stress and physiological consequences is complicated, and the most serious physiological consequences (for example, cardiovascular disease and heart attack) result only after considerably high levels of stress have been experienced for a prolonged period of time. Psychological consequences of stress include negative feelings, moods, and emotions; negative attitudes; and burnout. Potential behavioral consequences of stress include poor job performance, strained interpersonal relations, absenteeism, and turnover.
3. Employees who are responsible for helping others sometimes experience burnout. The three key signs of burnout are feelings of low personal accomplishment, emotional exhaustion, and depersonalization.
4. A certain level of stress is positive in that it can result in high levels of job performance. When stress levels are excessively high, negative stress is experienced, and performance suffers. Other potential behavioral consequences of high stress include strained interpersonal relations, absenteeism, and turnover.
5. Potential stressors can arise from employees' personal lives, job responsibilities, membership in work groups and organizations, work-life balance, and environmental uncertainty. Stressors from employees' personal lives include major and minor life events. Job-related stressors include role conflict, role ambiguity, overload, underload, challenging assignments and promotions, and conditions that affect employees' economic well-being. Group- and organization-related stressors include misunderstandings, conflicts, and interpersonal disagreements; uncomfortable working conditions; and dangerous or unsafe working conditions. Stressors arising out of work-life balance result when work roles conflict with people's personal lives. Stressors arising out of environmental uncertainty result from events and conditions in the wider environment in which organizations function, such as the threat of terrorism, pollution of the natural environment, and infectious diseases.
6. Coping methods are the steps people take to deal with stressors. Problem-focused coping involves steps people take to deal directly with the source of stress. Emotion-focused coping involves steps people take to deal with their stressful feelings and emotions. Most of the time, people engage in both types of coping when dealing with a stressor.
7. Some problem-focused coping strategies that individuals can use are time management, getting help from a mentor, and role negotiation. Some emotion-focused coping strategies for individuals are exercise, meditation, social support, and clinical counseling. Some problem-focused coping strategies that organizations can use are job redesign and rotation, reduction of uncertainty, job security, company day care, flexible work schedules and job sharing, and telecommuting. Some emotion-focused coping strategies for organizations are on-site exercise facilities, personal days and sabbaticals, organizational support, and employee assistance programs.

Exercises in Understanding and Managing Organizational Behavior

Questions for Review

1. Why are opportunities such as a job promotion stressful for some people?
2. Why might excessively high levels of stress lead to turnover?
3. Should managers try to eliminate all or most role conflict and ambiguity? Why or why not?
4. Is underload as stressful as overload? Why or why not?
5. Do organizations have an ethical obligation to guarantee their members job security? Why or why not?
6. How can managers help their subordinates learn how to cope with stressors in a problem-focused way?
7. What should a manager do if he or she thinks a subordinate is using a dysfunctional form of emotion-focused coping (such as abusing drugs)?
8. Is a certain level of stress necessary to motivate employees to perform at a high level? Why or why not?
9. Why might some employees be reluctant to use an employee assistance program?
10. Why should an organization care whether its members eat well or exercise regularly?

OB: Increasing Self-Awareness

The Nature of Stressful Experiences

Think about the last significant stressful experience that you had on the job or at school. For the experience you have chosen, do the following:

1. Describe the experience and the surrounding circumstances.
2. Explain whether the experience was stressful because it entailed an opportunity or a threat. What was the opportunity or threat?
3. Describe your feelings when you first encountered the source of stress.
4. Describe the (a) physiological, (b) psychological, and (c) behavioral consequences of the stress.
5. Describe how you actually coped with the stressor in a problem-focused manner.
6. Describe how you actually coped with the stressor in an emotion-focused manner.
7. Describe how your employing organization or university helped you cope with the stressor. If your employing organization or university did not help you cope with the stressor, do you think it should have? How?
8. Describe the extent to which your coping efforts were successful in helping you deal with the source of stress and with your stressful feelings and emotions.

A Question of Ethics

As many organizations continue to lay off employees, CEOs and top managers are taking home record salaries. In the United States, the differences between what employees at the very top of an organization make and those at the very bottom tend to be much greater than they are in other countries. When layoffs take place, CEOs and top managers typically indicate that they are an economic necessity. Yet these very same people might be earning millions of dollars a year. There are many cases of a major layoff taking place in the same year that a CEO of the company laying off employees earned a record salary.

Questions

1. Are there ethical implications of organizations laying off hundreds of employees in the same year that the CEOs earn record salaries? If so, what are these ethical implications? If not, why not?
2. What ethical obligations do organizations have when they are considering laying off employees?

Small Group Break-Out Exercise

Emotion-Focused Ways of Coping

Form groups of three or four people, and appoint one member as the spokesperson who will communicate your conclusions to the rest of the class.

1. Take a few minutes to think about the emotion-focused ways of coping that you personally rely on to cope with stressful feelings and emotions.
2. Take turns describing your emotion-focused ways of coping and have the spokesperson list them on a piece of paper.
3. Now go through the list and determine as a group to what extent each way of coping is likely to be effective/functional or ineffective/dysfunctional.
4. As a group, come up with a list of effective emotion-focused coping strategies. (This list may include but is not limited to the list that was generated previously in step 2.)

Topic for Debate

Stress can have major impacts on people and their organizations. Now that you understand how stress affects individual employees as well as organizations, debate the following issue:

Team A. The primary responsibility for managing work-related stress lies with the employing organization.

Team B. The primary responsibility for managing work-related stress lies with the individual employee.

Experiential Exercise

Developing Effective Coping Strategies

Objective

Your objective is to gain experience in developing effective strategies for helping members of an organization cope with stress.

Procedure

Assume the role of a supervisor of a group of 12 financial analysts for a petroleum company. Your subordinates tend to be in their late twenties and early thirties. Although some of them are single, others are married and have young children, and one is a single parent. Because of their job demands, they often work late and take work home on weekends.

Your company has fallen on hard times and has recently downsized. You were forced to lay off three subordinates. The layoff has really shaken up the survivors, who fear that they may be next to get a "pink slip." Workloads have increased, and lately your subordinates always seem to be on edge.

Recently, four of the financial analysts got into a serious and loud argument over a project they were working on. One of the participants in this fight came to you practically in tears. She said that things had gotten so bad that members of the group always seemed to be at each other's throats, whereas in the past they had helped each other. This incident, along with your recent observations, suggested the need to take steps to help your subordinates cope effectively with the stress they seem to be experiencing.

1. Describe the steps you, as the supervisor, should take to determine which problem-focused and emotion-focused coping strategies might be effective in helping the financial analysts deal with the stress they are experiencing.
2. The class divides into groups of three to five people, and each group appoints one member as spokesperson to present the group's recommendations to the whole class.
3. Group members in the role of supervisor take turns describing the steps each would take to determine effective problem-focused and emotion-focused coping strategies to help subordinates deal with the stress they are experiencing.
4. Group members develop an action plan that the group as a whole thinks would best lead to the development of effective problem-focused and emotion-focused coping strategies.

When your group has completed those activities, the spokesperson will present the group's action plan to the whole class.

New York Times *Cases in the News*

The New York Times

"Nine to Five, and Then Some"

By M. Villano, The New York Times, April 16, 2006, p. BU 9.

Q. *Your boss expects you to work long hours, and your personal life is suffering. What can you do to keep both your job and your sanity intact?*

A. As soon as your professional life over-shadows your personal one, speak up. Cali Williams Yost, president of Work + Life Fit, a strategic consulting company in Madison, N.J., said that even if employees were not upset about how much they were working, dwindling personal time would breed disillusionment down the road. "If you don't put a stop to it early on, you become so burned out, unproductive and overwhelmed that eventually you leave without even trying to salvage the situation," said Ms. Yost, author of "Work + Life: Finding the Fit That's Right for You" (Riverhead, 2004).

Q. *Whatever happened to the eight-hour workday?*

A. It may seem that the average workday has lengthened considerably since the 1980 film "Nine to Five." Many industries are downsizing and workplace tasks have become more complicated, placing a greater burden on fewer employees. Jim Murphy, founder and chief executive at Afterburner, a management consulting firm in Atlanta, calls this phenomenon "task saturation," and he notes that in areas like consulting, financial services and law, it's not uncommon for junior staff members to work 12- or 14-hour days.

But the federal Bureau of Labor Statistics says the average American employee is still working close to an eight-hour day. Last year, companies employing a total of 48 million workers reported that more than 72 percent of them worked about 8.25 hours a day. In a 2002 report, the Families and Work Institute in New York reported that 67 percent of roughly 3,500 salaried employees said they worked 35 to 50 hours a week.

Q. *Is it legal for companies to expect employees to work long days?*

A. It depends on the workplace and the job. Federal law mandates overtime pay after 40 hours a week for most workers, but there are important exemptions for executives, administrative personnel and outside sales employees, among others. And mandatory overtime may be routine for some workers—certain hospital employees, for example. Companies do not typically advertise that they expect employees to work 12-hour days; instead, they nurture a corporate culture of overachieving and leave employees to make scheduling choices on their own.

Julie Jansen, author of "You Want Me to Work with Who?" (Penguin, 2006), experienced this firsthand as a business consultant. Her bosses encouraged her to work harder, she said, even though she was already putting in 70- and 80-hour weeks. "I remember pleading with them at one point for an assistant or someone to help," said Ms. Jansen, who lives in Stamford, Conn. The situation was never resolved, she said, and it finally drove her to quit.

Q. *How do you request a lighter schedule without looking like a slacker?*

A. The best way to get a reprieve is to demonstrate that you deserve one. First, chart your hours over a two-week period, and try to quantify the projects you have handled over that time. Then, meet with the boss and cite the list as proof of your contributions to the firm. Armed with these facts, you should be able to make your case without being viewed as an underachiever.

Nevertheless, be tactful. The boss is probably overworked as well. Christine M. Riordan, professor of management and associate dean of the M. J. Neeley School of Business at Texas Christian University in Fort Worth, says it is important to avoid sounding like a complainer. "You need to put yourself in your boss's shoes," Ms. Riordan said. "What are the market conditions? What demands and pressures might he be facing?"

Q. *What practical moves might reduce the number of hours you spend at work?*

A. Improve your time management. Offer to take work home or to telecommute. Look into alternate work schedules —some companies give employees every other Friday off if they work nine 10-hour days in between. There's also flextime—a customized schedule that lets an employee incorporate personal needs like child care into a workday.

Several studies shows that these approaches to scheduling can be effective. In a 2005 study titled "Making Flexibility Work; What Managers Have Learned About Implementing Reduced-Load Work," professors at Michigan State University in East Lansing found that productivity and team effectiveness soared at companies that responded creatively to the demand for flexible schedules.

"Just because an employee works long hours doesn't necessarily mean that he or she is productive," said Ellen Ernst Kossek, a professor of labor and industrial relations at the university and one of the authors of the study. "Sometimes a flexible work schedule or slightly fewer hours can do wonders for an employee's effectiveness and desire to get involved."

Q. *What should you do if the boss is unwilling to compromise?*

A. If you ask for a lighter workload, be prepared for all possible outcomes, including rejection, said Ken Siegel, president of the Impact Group, an organizational consulting firm in Beverly Hills, Calif.

"Ultimately, everybody, including your boss, has a job to do," Mr. Siegel said. "If the boss promises you that the light at the end of the tunnel is not a train bringing you more work," maybe you should keep going. "Otherwise," he added, "It might be time to start looking for a less demanding job."

Questions for Discussion

1. What sources of stress does this case focus on?
2. Why are some workers being required to work longer and longer hours?
3. How can workers cope with these sources of stress?
4. Why is work-life balance important for both employees and employers?

The New York Times

"An Ugly Side of Free Trade: Sweatshops in Jordan"

By S. Greenhouse and M. Barbaro, The New York Times, May 3, 2006, pp. C1, C7.

Propelled by a free-trade agreement with the United States, apparel manufacturing is booming in Jordan, its exports to America soaring twentyfold in the last five years.

But some foreign workers in Jordanian factories that produce garments for Target, Wal-Mart and other American retailers are complaining of dismal conditions—of 20-hour days, of not being paid for months, and of being hit by supervisors and jailed when they complain.

An advocacy group for workers contends that some apparel makers in Jordan, and some contractors that supply foreign workers to them, have engaged in human trafficking. Workers from Bangladesh said they paid $1,000 to $3,000 to work in Jordan, but when they arrived, their passports were confiscated, restricting their ability to leave and tying them to jobs that often pay far less than promised and far less than the country's minimum wage.

"We used to start at 8 in the morning, and we'd work until midnight, 1 or 2 A.M., seven days a week," said Nargis Akhter, a 25-year-old Bangladeshi who, in a phone interview from Bangladeshi said she worked last year for the Paramount Garment factory outside Amman. "When we were in Bangladesh they promised us we would receive $120 a month, but in the five months I was there I only got one months's salary—and that was just $50."

The advocacy group, the National Labor Committee, which is based in New York, found substandard conditions in more than 25 of Jordan's roughly 100 garment factories and is set to release a report on its findings today. Its findings were supported in interviews with current and former workers.

Such complaints have dogged the global apparel industry for years, even as it has adopted measures intended to improve working conditions in factories that produce clothing for American and European consumers. But the abusive conditions that the guest workers described show how hard it is to control sweat-shops as factories spring up in new places, often without effective monitoring in place.

In recent years, Jordan has become a magnet for apparel manufacturers, helped by the privileged trade position that the United States has given it, first because of its 1994 peace accord with Israel and then because of a free trade agreement signed with Washington in 2001.

Jordan's apparel industry, which exported $1.2 billion to the United States last year, employs tens of thousands of guest workers, mainly from Bangladesh and China.

In interviews this week, five Bangladeshis who used to work in Jordanian apparel factories and four who still do had similar tales of paying more than $1,000 to work in Jordan, of working 90 to 120 hours a week, of not being paid the overtime guaranteed by Jordanian law, of sleeping 10 or 20 to a small dorm room. The National Labor Committee helped arrange interviews with the Bangladeshi workers.

The largest retailer in the United States, Wal-Mart, and one of the largest clothing makers, Jones Apparel, confirmed yesterday that they had discovered serious problems with the conditions at several major Jordanian factories.

In addition, a factory monitor for a major American company confirmed that Jordanian factories routinely confiscated their guest workers' passports, doctored wage and hour records and coached employees to lie to government and company inspectors about working conditions. The monitor asked not to be identified because the company had not given authorization to speak publicly.

Beth Keck, a spokeswoman for Wal-Mart, said the company did not own or manage factories, but tried to improve working conditions in Jordan and elsewhere. "It is a continuous challenge, not just for Wal-Mart but for any company," she said, noting that the most commonly observed problems included failure to pay proper wages, "egregious hours," and "use of false or insufficient books or documentation."

Charles Kernaghan, executive director of the National Labor Committee, which has exposed mistreatment in factories in Central America and China, said he was shocked by what he discovered in Jordan.

"These are the worst conditions I've ever seen," he said. "You have people working 48 hours straight. You have workers who were stripped of their passports, who don't have ID cards that allow them to go out on the street. If they're stopped, they can be imprisoned or deported, so they're trapped, often held under conditions of involuntary servitude."

Mr. Kernaghan said Bangladeshi workers had contacted his organization to complain about working conditions in Jordan. He then traveled to Jordan and met quietly with dozens of workers. He said American companies, despite their monitoring efforts, were often slow to uncover workplace abuses because workers were coached to lie to them or were scared to speak out. Moreover, factories often send work out to substandard subcontractors without notifying American retailers.

Several factory owners in Jordan insisted that they treated their workers properly.

"Some people are always making allegations," said Karim Saifi, the owner of United Garment Manufacturing, a factory near Amman that workers criticized for long hours and wage violations. "As far as we know, we follow all the labor laws here. If we were not abiding by all of the local Jordan laws, we would not be able to operate."

Several foreign apparel workers said that while their factories required them to stay until midnight, the Jordanian workers were usually allowed to leave at 4 P.M.

Two large industrial zones outside Amman are thriving, having geared themselves to the American apparel market. They have attracted dozens of garment manufacturers, some with 200 workers, some with 2,000, that say they produce clothes for J. C. Penney, Sears, Wal-Mark, Gap and Target.

"It would be wrong to think that problems at a few places are representative of the 102 apparel factories in my country," said Yanal Beasha, Jordan's trade representative in Washington.

Jordan's ambassador to the United States, Karim Kawar, said "If there are any violations of our labor laws, we certainly take it seriously."

Mr. Beasha said Jordanian government inspectors monitor the working conditions in factories. But several guest workers said factory managers hid abuses by coaching workers to lie. Mr. Beasha said the Jordanian government cared about the welfare of foreign guest workers, noting that it enforced overtime laws and recently increased the minimum wage for citizens and guest workers.

But Mohammed Z., who has worked for more than a year at the Paramount Garment Factory, said that even though he worked more than 100 hours a week—normally from 7 to midnight seven days a week—the company refused to pay him overtime when he did not meet production targets. He asked that his last name be withheld for fear of retribution.

Having paid $2,000 to work in Jordan, he said, in an interview from Amman, "I'm not earning enough to repay my loan or to support my wife and son."

Unhappy that his passport has been confiscated, he said; "My identity has been taken by the company. I have no freedom because I have no freedom to move to other places."

Mohammed Saiful Islam, 30, a Bangladeshi who was production manager at Western Garment, said that several times the workers had to work until 4 A.M., then sleep on the factory's floor for a few hours, before resuming work at 8 A.M.

"The workers got so exhausted they became sick," he said. "They could hardly stay awake at their machines."

Mr. Saiful, who is in the United States to highlight poor working conditions in Jordan, pointed to a yellow and black fleece sweatshirt that he said his factory made. It had an Athletic Works label made for Wal-Mart selling for $9.48.

"Sometimes when companies sent in monitors, the workers were instructed what to say," Mr. Saiful said.

Mohamed Irfan, who in a telephone interview from Jordan said, he was Western' owner, said. "The workers get the minimum wage, and all times, there is no problem in out factory."

Mohamed Kasim, Paramount's owner, said his factory also paid its workers properly. Mr. Kasim and other factory managers said workers received free room and board and sometimes medical care.

But several workers said that when they were sick they did not receive medical care, but were instead punished and had their pay docked.

Several Bangladeshis said there were terrible conditions at factories that made clothes for Wal-Mart and Jones Apparel, which owns brands like Gloria Vanderbilt and Jones New York.

Ms. Keck, the Wal-Mart spokeswoman, said company inspectors recently identified "serious violations" of its labor rules at three Jordanian factories. At Honorway Apparel Jordan, for example, which manufactures sleepwear for Wal-Mart, inspectors found employees working off the clock, managers who refused to pay overtime and wages that "could not be verified," Ms. Keck said. At the Ivory Garment Factory, which Wal-Mart ceased working with two years ago, inspectors found "egregious working hours."

Joele Frank, a spokeswoman for Jones Apparel, said the company had also found "serious problems," at the Ivory Garment Factory, which produces Gloria Vanderbilt clothing, and said it would "monitor the situation closely." A spokesman for Sears Holding said the company was investigating potential problems at Honorway, which produces clothes for Kmart, a division of Sears Holding.

A Kohl's spokeswoman denied workers' accusations that clothing sold by the company was made at several Jordanian factories with poor conditions. Target said it worked with only one such factory, Al Safa Garments, which Wal-Mart recently cited for labor violations.

Many retailers said their policy was, after discovering violations, to work with a factory to improve conditions, rather than automatically withdraw their business. Wal-Mart says it gives factories a year to fix serious problems, reinspecting them every 120 days.

"Our business with the factory is the only leverage we have to push for improvement," Ms. Keck said.

After *The New York Times* asked about the accusations on Monday, Wal-Mart dispatched two inspectors to Jordan.

Hazrat Ali, 25, who worked from September 2004 to March 2005 at the Al Shahaed factory, said he sometimes worked 48 hours in a row and received no pay for the six months.

"If we asked for money, they hit us," he said.

Nasima Akhter, 30, said that the Western factory gave its workers a half-glass of tea for breakfast and often rice and some rotten chicken for lunch.

"In the four months I was in Jordan, they didn't pay us a single penny," she said. "When we asked management for our money and for better food, they were very angry at us. We were put in some sort of jail for four days without anything to eat. And then they forced us to go back to Bangladesh."

Questions for Discussion

1. Why do foreign workers go to Jordan to work in the apparel manufacturing industry?
2. What sources of stress do they encounter there?
3. What are the ethical obligations of firms like Wal-Mart and Jones Apparel who have products manufactured in factories in Jordan?
4. What can and should be done to rectify this situation?

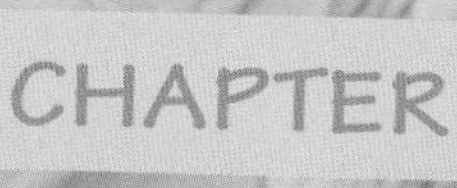

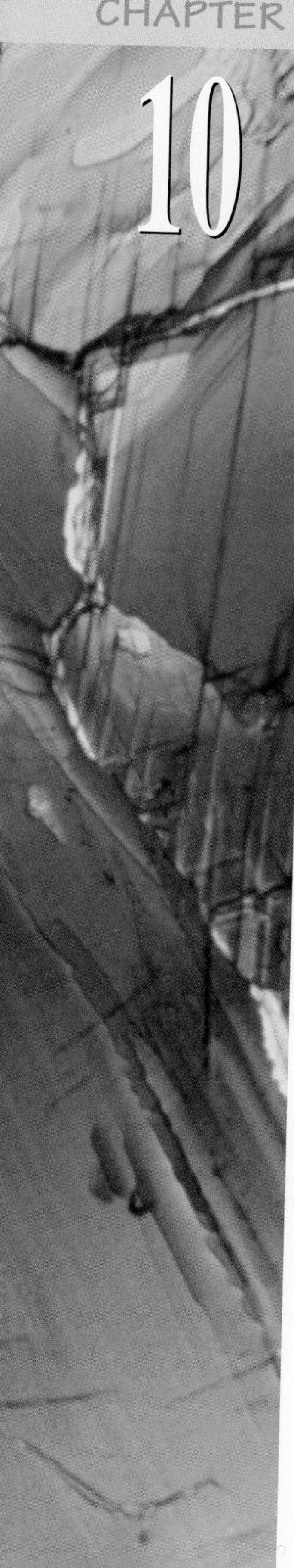

CHAPTER 10

THE NATURE OF WORK GROUPS AND TEAMS

Learning Objectives

After studying this chapter, you should be able to:

- Describe the different types of work groups and the difference between a group and a team.
- Appreciate the characteristics of work groups and the effects on the behavior of group members.
- Describe how groups control their members through roles, rules, and norms.
- Appreciate the need for conformity and deviance in groups and why and how group goals need to be aligned with organizational goals.
- Understand the socialization process and how socialization tactics can result in an institutionalized or an individualized role orientation.

Opening Case

TEAMS FUEL GLOBAL INNOVATION AT WHIRLPOOL

How can teams fuel innovation?

These days, Whirlpool Corporation is a leading global manufacturer and marketer of innovative home appliances.[1] Based in Benton Harbor, Michigan, Whirlpool has more than 80,000 employees and almost 60 production and research centers around the world.[2] Typically, one would not think of a manufacturer of refrigerators, dishwashers, and washers and dryers as a global innovator, but Whirlpool has become just that. While a strong commitment to innovation pervades the company and its culture, so too does the realization that cross-functional global teams that bring together diverse perspectives and areas of expertise are central to innovation.[3]

Cross-functional teams fuel global innovation at Whirlpool. Team members gain valuable insights by observing volunteer consumers trying out and interacting with products in specially designed rooms in Whirlpool's Global Consumer Design Division.

Bringing together different areas of expertise in cross-functional teams was central to Charles L. Jones's approach when he was hired by Whirlpool to build the Global Consumer Design division, of which he is currently the vice president. In the past, the actual design of appliances was more of an afterthought rather than an integral part of new product development. As a consequence, Whirlpool would churn out appliances that were high quality yet very similar to those of key competitors and competition was based on price; thus the Whirlpool appliance prices were falling by around 3 percent a year though demand kept pace with a housing boom. At that point, top management realized that innovation was the key to the company's future.[4]

When Jones came on board, he created cross-functional teams composed of engineers, graphic artists, usability researchers, human factors experts, marketers, and industrial designers to develop new products. The top-selling and award-winning Whirlpool brand Duet® Fabric Care System (also referred to as the Dreamspace® Fabric Care System in Europe), a high-end matching washer and dryer set with a novel, attractive design, was the result of the efforts of a global cross-functional team.[5] The Duet® features a front-loading washer with a porthole and can be raised off the ground on a pedestal so consumers don't have to stoop as much as they ordinarily would to load and unload clothes from a front-loading washer. It also has a large cleaning and drying capacity, and is efficient in terms of saving on water and energy usage. In designing the Duet system, the interests and desires of consumers in both the United States and Europe were taken into account, as were the perspectives of industrial design, usability, human factors, visual appeal, marketing, and engineering; hence, the need for a truly global cross-functional team. The Duet® dryers are manufactured in Ohio, while the washers are produced in Germany. Thus, much coordination was required between both locations to ensure that materials and colors matched perfectly.[6] As Ruben Castano, an employee in the Whirlpool Global Consumer Design division in Cassinetta, Italy, indicates, "It was just a matter of small adjustments in terms of colors, graphics and labeling of programs in order to make the product fit perfectly in each market . . . the core processes and work methods inside Whirlpool are truly global. This makes it very easy to create teams with members from all over the world."[7]

Cross-functional teams at Whirlpool learn a lot by actually observing consumers interacting with products. Thus, it is not uncommon to see team members huddled behind two-way mirrors in specially designed rooms watching volunteer consumers trying out the products.[8] This is in contrast to the traditional focus-group approach to product development where consumers are brought together in a group and asked questions about their needs and reactions to products. By actually watching consumers, team members can gauge how useable their products are and how they will actually be used (something consumers might not be able to articulate themselves).[9]

Groups are used in other ways at Whirlpool to spark innovation. For example, employees in the Global Consumer Design division can devote about 20 percent of their time to developing new ideas, which are then presented to a group of about 8 or 10 employees in studio critique fashion.[10] The division is organized around brands rather than products and often employees working on one brand such as Roper will critique a new idea that employees working on another brand such as KitchenAid come up with to get a diversity of perspectives with the overall objective of giving those with new ideas honest and helpful feedback.[11]

Using teams and groups to spark innovation has paid off handsomely for Whirlpool.[12] In 2005, the company estimates that $760 million of its sales were from new products and Chairman and CEO Jeff Fettig predicts that in 2006, $1.2 billion in revenues will come from new products. With over 560 new projects in the pipeline, innovation appears to be alive and well at Whirlpool Corporation.[13]

Overview

In previous chapters, we focused on how various traits an individual has (his or her personality, ability, values, attitudes, moods, perceptions, and attributions) and the traits of the organization (its rewards, punishments, promotion practices, goals, and so on) determine how employees feel, think, and behave and ultimately how well the organization achieves its goals. Of course, organizations don't consist of individuals working alone. Employees are usually assembled or clustered into groups or teams. Organizations use groups or teams because they can sometimes accomplish things that no one individual could accomplish working alone, such as designing, manufacturing, and marketing a new washer-dryer set like the Whirlpool brand Duet®. For example, in a group, individuals can focus on particular tasks and become better at performing them. Performance gains that result from the use of groups have led to the popular saying, "A group is more than the sum of its parts."

Groups are the basic building blocks of an organization. Just as the effective functioning of a university depends on the performance of the various groups in the university (departments such as management and psychology; student groups and athletic teams; and governing bodies such as the university's student council and the faculty senate), so, too, does the effectiveness of GM, Yahoo!, and other organizations depend on the performance of groups.

Using groups in organizations, however, can sometimes be very challenging for organizations.[14] People behave differently when they work in groups than when they work alone.[15] And although groups can sometimes work wonders for an organization, they can also wreak havoc if they function improperly.[16]

Given the important role groups play in all organizations, in this and the next chapter we concentrate on the nature and functioning of work groups and teams. We start by describing what a group is, how work groups develop, key characteristics of work groups, and how being a member of a group affects individual behavior. We describe how groups control their members' behavior and turn newcomers into effective group members through the socialization process. Essentially, in this chapter we explain what work groups are like and why they are this way. In the next chapter, we build on this foundation and explore what causes some groups to perform at a high level and help an organization achieve its goals.

Introduction to Groups

Is any gathering of individuals a group? If not, what distinguishes a group from a mere collection of individuals? Two basic attributes define a group:

1. Members of a group interact with each other: what one person does affects everyone else and vice versa.[17]
2. Members of a group believe there is the potential for mutual goal accomplishment—that is, group members perceive that by belonging to the group they will be able to accomplish certain goals or meet certain needs.[18]

GROUP
A set of two or more people who interact with each other to achieve certain goals or to meet certain needs.

A **group**, then, is a set of two or more people who interact with each other to achieve certain goals or meet certain needs.

It is important to note at the outset that although group members may have one or more goals in common, this does not mean that all their goals are identical. For example, when a person from each of four different departments in an organization (research and development, sales, manufacturing, and engineering) is assigned to a group to work on a new product, all members of the group may share the common goal of developing the best product they can. But the person from research and development might define the *best product* as the one that has the most innovative features; the person from sales might define it as the one that most appeals to price-conscious customers; the representative from manufacturing might define it as one that can be produced the most inexpensively; and the person from engineering might define it as one that will be the most reliable. Although they agree on the common goal—giving the customer the best product they can devise—deciding what *best product* means can be a difficult task. A **group goal** is one that all or most members of a group can agree on.

GROUP GOAL
A goal that all or most members of a group can agree on as a common goal.

Types of Work Groups

FORMAL WORK GROUP
A group established by management to help the organization achieve its goals.

There are many types of groups in organizations, and each type plays an important role in determining organizational effectiveness. One way to classify groups is by whether they are formal or informal. Managers establish **formal work groups** to help the organization achieve its goals. The goals of a formal work group are determined by the needs of the organization. Examples of formal work groups include a product quality committee in a consumer products firm, the pediatrics department in a health maintenance organization (HMO), and a task force created to end sex discrimination in a law firm. Managers establish each of these groups to accomplish certain organizational goals—increasing product quality in the case of the product quality committee, providing health care to children who belong to the HMO in the case of the pediatrics department, and ending discrimination at the law firm in the case of the task force.

EXHIBIT 10.1

Types of Work Groups

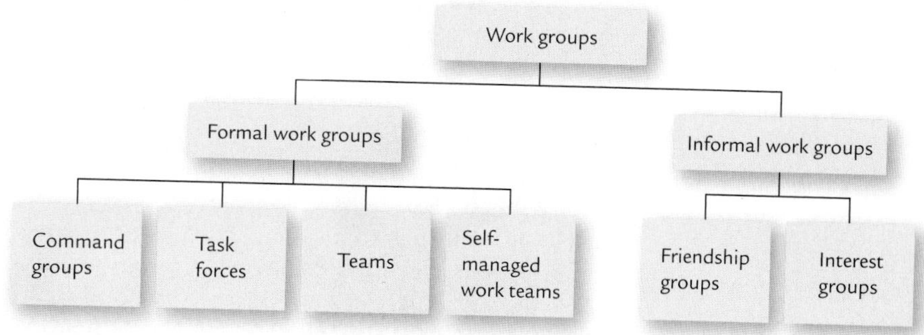

INFORMAL WORK GROUP
A group that emerges naturally when individuals perceive that membership in a group will help them achieve their goals or meet their needs.

Informal work groups emerge naturally in organizations because members believe that working together in a group will help them achieve their goals or meet their needs. A group of five factory workers who go bowling every Thursday night to satisfy their common need for affiliation and friendship is an example of an informal group.

COMMAND GROUP
A formal work group consisting of subordinates who report to the same supervisor.

Types of formal work groups. Four important kinds of formal work groups are command groups, task forces, teams, and self-managed work teams (see Exhibit 10.1). A **command group** is a collection of subordinates who report to the same supervisor. Command groups are based on the basic reporting relationships in organizations and are frequently represented on organizational charts as departments (marketing, sales, accounting, and so on). The pediatrics department in an HMO, the research and development department in a pharmaceutical company, and the financial aid department in a university are all examples of command groups. Command groups are the vehicle through which much of the work in an organization gets accomplished. Thus, they have a huge impact on the extent to which an organization is able to achieve its goals. The supervisors or leaders of command groups play such an important role in determining the effectiveness of these groups that we devote Chapter 12 to the topic of leadership.

TASK FORCE
A formal work group consisting of people who come together to accomplish a specific goal.

A **task force** is a collection of people who come together to accomplish a specific goal. Once the goal has been accomplished, the task force is usually disbanded. The group established to end sex discrimination in a law firm and the product quality committee in a consumer products firm are examples of task forces. Sometimes, when task forces address a goal or problem of long-term concern to an organization, they are never disbanded, but their membership periodically changes to offer new insights about the goal or problem as well as to relieve existing task force members of their duties so they can focus on their regular jobs. These kinds of task forces are sometimes referred to as *standing committees* or *task groups*. The consumer products firm, for example, may always have a standing committee assigned to product quality to ensure that feature is a foremost consideration as new products are developed and existing ones modified.

TEAM
A formal work group consisting of people who work intensely together to achieve a common group goal.

A **team** is a formal group of members who interact at a high level and work together intensely to achieve a common group goal. When teams are effective, they draw on the abilities and experiences of their members to accomplish things that could not be achieved by individuals working separately or by other kinds of work groups. Boeing, for example, uses *cross-functional teams* (described earlier) to design and build new kinds of airplanes. Some organizations run into trouble effectively managing teams because their members spend too much time trying to come to an agreement on important issues. This, as we explained, is precisely what happened at Digital Equipment.

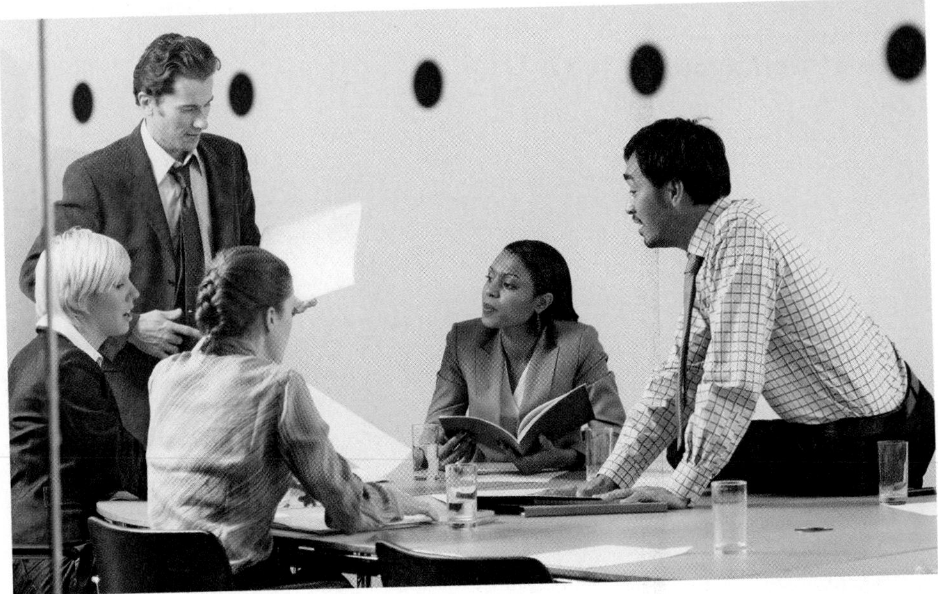

In work teams such as this one, members have high levels of interaction and work together intensely to achieve common goals.

Just because people work in a group does not mean they work as a *team*, which is further characterized by *intense* interaction and a strong commitment to its goals.

SELF-MANAGED WORK TEAM A formal work group consisting of people who are jointly responsible for ensuring that the team accomplishes its goals and who lead themselves.

A team with no manager or a team member assigned to lead the team is called a **self-managed work team**. Members of a self-managed work team are responsible for ensuring the team accomplishes its goals and for performing leadership tasks such as determining how the group should go about achieving its goals, assigning tasks to individual group members, disciplining group members who are not performing at an adequate level, coordinating efforts across group members, and hiring and firing.[19] Self-managed work teams are becoming increasingly popular because they can have a dramatic impact on organizations and their members. We discuss them in detail in the next chapter.

FRIENDSHIP GROUP An informal work group consisting of people who enjoy each other's company and socialize with each other on and off the job.

INTEREST GROUP An informal work group consisting of people who come together because they have a common goal or objective related to their organizational membership.

Types of informal work groups. Two important types of informal work groups are friendship groups and interest groups. A **friendship group** is a collection of organizational members who enjoy each other's company and socialize with each other (often both on and off the job). A group of factory workers who go bowling or a group of accountants at a Big Four firm who frequently have lunch together can be described as friendship groups. Friendship groups help meet employees' needs for social interaction, are an important source of social support (see Chapter 9), and can contribute to job satisfaction and employees' experiencing positive moods.

Members of an organization form **interest groups** when they have a common goal or objective (related to their organizational membership) that they are trying to achieve by uniting their efforts. Interest groups are often formed in response to pressing concerns that certain members of an organization have. Those concerns might include lobbying the company to sponsor a day care or elder care center, extend the amount of time allowed for maternity leave, actively protect the environment, or improve conditions in the community at large. Interest groups help members of an organization voice their concerns and can be an important impetus for needed organizational changes.

Although many of the concepts we discuss in the rest of this chapter and in the next apply to both formal and informal work groups, we mainly focus on the formal side of the organization because this is where managers can have the most impact.

EXHIBIT 10.2

Tuckman's Five-Stage Model of Group Development

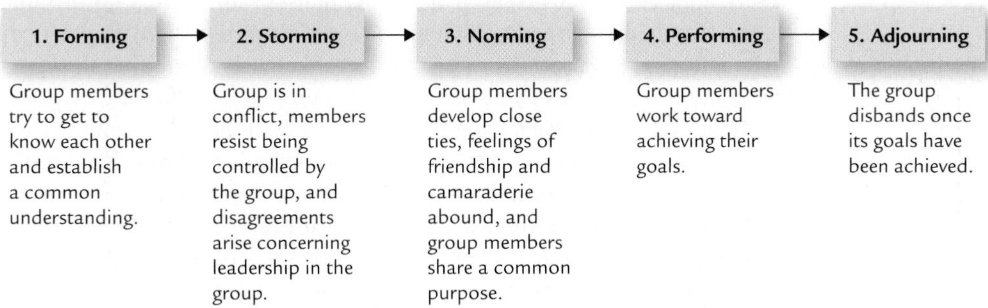

1. Forming
Group members try to get to know each other and establish a common understanding.
2. Storming
Group is in conflict, members resist being controlled by the group, and disagreements arise concerning leadership in the group.
3. Norming
Group members develop close ties, feelings of friendship and camaraderie abound, and group members share a common purpose.
4. Performing
Group members work toward achieving their goals.
5. Adjourning
The group disbands once its goals have been achieved.

Group Development over Time: The Five-Stage Model

All groups change over time as group members come and go (because of turnover, hiring, and promotions, among other things); group tasks and goals change; and group members gain experience as they interact with one another. Some researchers have tried to determine the stages groups normally go through over time. Understanding how groups change is important because, as we discuss later in the chapter, groups and their members face different challenges at different stages of development. In order for groups to be effective and perform at high levels, it is important for these challenges to be effectively managed. Think back to the last group project you worked on for one of your classes. It is likely that your first group meeting was dramatically different from your last group meeting or from the meetings that took place in between. At each point, the group faced different challenges. Likewise, as work groups evolve from their initial inception, they too undergo important changes.

One well-known model of group development is Bruce W. Tuckman's five-stage model, outlined in Exhibit 10.2.[20] During stage 1, which Tuckman called *forming*, group members try to get to know each other and establish a common understanding as they struggle to clarify group goals and determine appropriate behavior within the group. Once individuals truly feel they are members of the group, the forming stage is completed.

Stage 2, called *storming*, is characterized by considerable conflict, as its name implies. In the storming stage, members resist being controlled by the group and might disagree about who should lead the group or how much power the leader should have. This stage is completed when members no longer resist the group's control, and there is mutual agreement about who will lead the group. Members usually complete this stage because they see it is in their best interests to work together to achieve their goals.

In stage 3, *norming*, members really start to feel like they belong to the group, and they develop close ties with one another. Feelings of friendship and camaraderie abound, and a well-developed sense of common purpose emerges in the group. By the end of this stage, group members agree on standards to guide behavior in the group.

By the time stage 4, *performing*, is reached, the group is ready to tackle tasks and work toward achieving its goals. This is the stage at which the real work is done, so ideally, it shouldn't take long to reach it. Sometimes, however, it can take as long as two or three years to get to the performing stage, especially when the groups are self-managed work teams. Saturn Corporation, for example, experienced such a slowdown when it started using self-managed work teams.[21]

In the last stage of group development—*adjourning*—identified by Tuckman as stage 5, the group disbands after having accomplished its goals. Ongoing work groups in organizations do not go through this stage and often remain at the performing stage. In contrast, a task force is likely to be adjourned after it has achieved its goals.

The five-stage "forming-norming-storming-performing-adjourning" model is intuitively appealing, but research indicates that not all groups go through each of the stages. Nor do they go through them one at a time or in the order specified by Tuckman. Some groups are characterized by considerable levels of conflict throughout their existence, in fact,[22] and always experience elements of the storming stage. Organizational researcher Connie Gersick's studies of task forces found that groups with deadlines for goal accomplishment did not go through a series of stages. Rather, they alternated between periods of inertia in which little was accomplished and periods of frenzied activity in which the group rapidly progressed toward its goals.[23] Interestingly enough, these studies found that the timing of these stages depended on how long the group was given to achieve its goals. All of the groups studied experienced inertia for approximately the first half of their duration. For example, a group given six months to accomplish its goal might experience an initial stage of inertia for its first three months, and a group given three months to accomplish its goals may be in an initial stage of inertia for its first month and a half.

As research into group development continues, it is probably safest to conclude that although all groups change over time, there doesn't seem to be a single set of stages all groups go through in a predetermined sequence.

Characteristics of Work Groups

Work groups vary in many other respects in addition to type. Here we examine five characteristics of groups that profoundly affect the way members behave and the group's overall performance. Those characteristics are the group's size, composition, function, status, and efficacy. We also discuss a characteristic that groups have on their members: social facilitation.

Group Size

The size of a group is measured by the number of full-time members who work together to achieve the group's goals. Groups may be composed of just three people or more than 20.[24] Group size is an important determinant of the way group members behave. When groups are small, members are likely to know one another and interact regularly with each other on a day-to-day basis. When groups are small, it is relatively easy for members to share information, recognize individual contributions to the group, and identify with the group's goals. Strong identification with the group and its goals may lead to increased motivation and commitment to group goals and higher levels of satisfaction.

In large groups, members are less likely to know one another and may have little personal contact with each other on a day-to-day basis. The lower level of interaction between members of large groups makes sharing information difficult. In addition, because of the many members, individuals may consider their own contributions to the group unimportant, and this can reduce their motivation and commitment to the group. For all these reasons, people generally tend to be less satisfied in large groups than in smaller ones.[25]

The disadvantages of large groups have to be weighed against their advantages, however. On the advantage side, larger groups have a greater number of resources at their disposal to accomplish their goals. These resources include the skills, abilities, and accumulated work experience and knowledge of their members. A second advantage of larger groups are the benefits that come from the **division of labor**—dividing up work assignments to individual group members. When individual members focus on particular tasks, they generally become skilled at performing these tasks at a high level. In fact, one of the

DIVISION OF LABOR
Dividing up work and assigning particular tasks to specific workers.

One of the primary reasons groups are used in organizations is to achieve the benefits of a division of labor.

primary reasons why groups (as well as whole organizations) exist is to make the division of labor possible.

When making a decision about group size, an organization needs to balance the skill and resource advantages that large groups offer against certain disadvantages. Chief among these disadvantages are the communication and coordination problems that occur as the number of members increases. For example, as a group gets bigger, it is much more difficult to let group members know about a change in procedures. Imagine communicating complex procedural changes to each member of a 40-member group versus each member of a group of four. It also gets more difficult to coordinate members as the size of the group increases. If, for example, a group of 20 students (versus, say, five) is doing a joint research project, it is much more likely that two students will inadvertently cover the same material, that the project report the group is submitting will be disjointed, and that some students will not do their share of the work. In general, the larger a group is, the greater is the potential for conflict, duplication of effort, and low motivation. Some of these problems are discussed in detail in the next chapter. Exhibit 10.3 summarizes some of the potential advantages of small and large group size.

Group Composition

Group composition refers to the characteristics of members of a group.[26] In the opening case, recall how members of the teams that Charles Jones created in the Global Consumer Design division of Whirlpool were cross-functional and global in that their members came from different functional areas such as engineering, marketing, industrial design, human factors, and usability and also from different countries. One way to think about group composition is in terms of how similar or different the members are from each other.

HOMOGENEOUS GROUP
A group in which members have many characteristics in common.

Members of a **homogeneous group** have many characteristics in common. These characteristics can be demographic characteristics (such as gender, race, socioeconomic background, cultural origin, age, educational background, or tenure with an organization), personality traits, skills, abilities, beliefs, attitudes, values, or types of work experience. A group of white men from the northeastern United States who all attended Ivy League colleges, place a great deal of importance on their careers, and

EXHIBIT 10.3

Group Size Advantages

Potential Advantages of Smaller Groups	Potential Advantages of Larger Groups
Interactions among group members are more frequent. Information is more easily shared among group members. Group members recognize their contributions to the group. Group members are motivated and committed to the group's goals. Group members are satisfied.	Group has many resources at its disposal to accomplish its goals, including members' skills, abilities, knowledge, and experience. Group can have a greater division of labor, so group members focus on particular tasks. When group members focus on particular tasks, they generally become skilled at performing them.

work for the same New York law firm is a homogeneous group. In contrast, a group of men and women of diverse races and cultural origins who possess degrees from both large and small state and private universities, have differing beliefs about the centrality of work in their lives, and work for the same New York law firm constitutes a heterogeneous group. Members of a **heterogeneous group** do not have many characteristics in common. Heterogeneous groups are characterized by diversity, homogeneous groups by similarity.

HETEROGENEOUS GROUP
A group in which members have few characteristics in common.

The relationships between group composition, members' behaviors, and the group's performance are complex. On the one hand, people tend to like and get along well with others who are similar to themselves. Thus, members of homogeneous groups may find it easier to share information, have lower levels of conflict, and fewer communication and coordination problems than members of heterogeneous groups. On these grounds you might expect the performance and goal attainment of homogeneous groups to be higher than that of heterogeneous groups. Because group members are more likely to get along with each other in homogeneous groups, you might also expect their motivation and satisfaction to be high as well.

On the other hand, a group that is composed of people with different backgrounds, experiences, personalities, abilities, and "views of the world" may be better able than a homogeneous group to make good decisions because more points of view are represented in the group. A heterogeneous group may also be able to perform at a high level because the group has a variety of resources at its disposal. Because of their differences, group members may be more likely to challenge each other and existing ways of doing things, and the outcome may be valuable and needed changes. The homogeneous group of lawyers, for example, might have few disagreements and little trouble communicating with one another but have difficulty dealing with female clients or clients from different ethnic or racial backgrounds. The more heterogeneous group of lawyers might have more disagreements and communication problems but fewer problems interacting with clients from different races and cultural backgrounds.

To reap the advantages of heterogeneity, it is important for group members to understand each others' differences and points of view and use these diverse perspectives to enable the group to perform at a high level and achieve its goals.[27] Exhibit 10.4 summarizes some of the potential advantages of homogeneous and heterogeneous groups.

Toyota used heterogeneous groups, called *oobeyas,* to facilitate the design, manufacturing, marketing, and sales of the Matrix. In Japanese, *oobeya* means "big, open office." However, the term pertains more to what goes on in the big, open space rather

EXHIBIT 10.4

Group Composition Advantages

Potential Advantages of Homogeneous Groups	Potential Advantages of Heterogeneous Groups
Group members like and get along well with each other.	Group makes good decisions because diverse points of view are represented.
Group members share information, have low levels of conflict, and have few coordination problems.	Group performs at a high level because the group has a variety of resources at its disposal.

than the actual physical environment. An oobeya is a meeting of a heterogeneous group (that can be large) including people from all parts of an organization to work on a project in new and different ways. Takeshi Yoshida, Toyota's chief engineer for the Toyota Matrix, utilized oobeyas including employees from design, engineering, manufacturing, marketing, logistics, and sales around the globe to design and bring the Matrix to market.[28]

With millions of baby-boomers in their 60s, a thin rank of middle managers due to downsizing, and large numbers of young, relatively inexperienced employees, many large organizations are utilizing heterogeneous groups so that older, more experienced managers can share their knowledge with younger employees before they retire, as profiled in the following Focus on Diversity.

Group Function

GROUP FUNCTION
The work that a group performs as its contribution to the accomplishment of organizational goals.

Group function is the work that a group contributes to the accomplishment of organizational goals. A manufacturing department, for example, is a command group that has the responsibility for producing the goods (automobiles, televisions, etc.) that an organization sells. The manufacturing department's function is to produce these goods in a cost-effective manner and maintain appropriate levels of quality.

Within the manufacturing department are small groups of employees responsible for performing a specific aspect of the manufacturing process. In an automobile-manufacturing plant, for example, one group's function might be to make the automobile bodies, another's to attach the transmission to the body, and another's to paint the body. In fact, we can think of an entire organization as a series of groups linked together according to the functions they perform.

The function of a group affects the behavior of its members by letting them know how their work contributes to the organization achieving its goals. A group's function gives its members a sense of meaning and purpose.[29] When members see how the work of their group influences the work of other groups, they may become motivated to perform at a high level. Just as task significance—the extent to which a job affects the lives and work of other people (see Chapter 7)—affects the intrinsic motivation of individuals, so, too, does a group's function. To motivate members, managers should remind them that their activities, behaviors, and the group's function all are important contributions to the organization.

Group Status

GROUP STATUS
The implicitly agreed upon, perceived importance for the organization as a whole of what a group does.

The work that some groups in an organization do is often seen as being more important to the organization's success than the work of other groups. **Group status** is the implicitly agreed upon, perceived importance of what a group does in an organization. The status of a top management team is likely to be very high because it sets the organization's goals

Focus on Diversity

Heterogeneous Groups Combat Knowledge Drain

With many seasoned employees retiring or nearing retirement age, fewer experienced middle managers than in the past due to downsizing, and a relatively large cadre of young, inexperienced employees, many large organizations are realizing that it is important that the knowledge and expertise that older employees have gained over decades of work be passed on to younger generations.[30] While it is easy to pass along some kinds of knowledge, called explicit knowledge, through written documents, manuals and instructions, and websites and company intranets, other kinds of knowledge, called tacit knowledge, are harder to capture. Scott Schaffar, director of knowledge management at Northrop Grumman, describes tacit knowledge this way, "It's what is held in our heads and includes facts, stories, biases, misconceptions, insights, and networks of friends and acquaintances, as well as the ability to invent creative solutions to problems . . . tacit knowledge tends to accumulate over years of experience."[31]

In order to promote the sharing of this tacit knowledge throughout an organization before it is lost when older employees retire, some organizations are creating heterogeneous groups composed of employees from different areas and generations to share their expertise with each other.[32] Northrop Grumman, for example, has formed communities of practice bringing together employees from diverse functional areas and divisions to share ideas and expertise. A community of practice with new hires in it might bring in retired project managers to share their expertise with the group, and engineers fresh out of college might be given the opportunity to spend time following experienced engineers as they go about performing their jobs to absorb both explicit and tacit knowledge on-the-job.[33]

In order to promote the sharing of tacit knowledge throughout an organization, some organizations are creating heterogeneous groups composed of employees from different areas and generations to share their expertise with each other.

General Electric has created what it refers to as action learning teams: groups of employees from different functional areas such as sales, marketing, finance, production, and legal affairs with varying levels of experience that are formed to address specific issues, problems, or projects.[34] While an action learning team works on a particular project, its members gain know-how in areas they might not be familiar with, feedback on their performance, and experience addressing relatively "big" projects.[35] As Bob Corcoran, chief learning officer at General Electric, puts it, action learning teams "encourage people to learn a lot about a lot of things . . . It reduces the likelihood that when boomers do retire, you'll be left saying, 'Gee, old Alex was the only person here who knew how

to do this'"[36] And of course, older employees also have the opportunity to learn from their younger team members. All in all, heterogeneous groups seem to be one way to combat knowledge drain and encourage the sharing of tacit knowledge in organizations.[37]

and determines how it will achieve them. The work performed by a group of accountants who prepare quarterly profit-and-loss statements and balance sheets is certainly important. However, it is often seen as less central to the organization's performance as a whole than the work performed by the top management team. Thus, the status of the group of accountants is lower than that of the top management team. The more important the task performed by a work group or a group's function is, the higher is the group's status in the organization. Members of groups with high status are likely to be motivated to perform at high levels because they see their work as especially important for the success of the organization as a whole.

Group Efficacy

GROUP EFFICACY
The shared belief group members have about the ability of the group to achieve its goals and objectives.

Recall from Chapter 5 how self-efficacy is a powerful determinant of employees' behavior in an organization. Groups and teams have a sense of collective efficacy.[38] **Group efficacy** is the shared belief group members have about the ability of the group to achieve its goals and objectives.[39] How do members come to share a belief about the group's ability to coordinate and mobilize its members to perform effectively? By taking into account many of the factors that contribute to the group's effectiveness, such as its composition (including the ability, knowledge, and skills of its members), members' willingness to work together and share information, the resources the group has to work with, and the extent to which the group is able to develop effective strategies to achieve its goals.[40]

Thus, group efficacy develops over time as members come to understand each other, how the group functions, the tasks it needs to accomplish, and the group's capabilities.[41] We know from the stages of group development discussed earlier that it takes time for groups to perform up to their capabilities. Efficacy is not something that exists when a group is initially formed but rather a shared belief that emerges over time as members work together. Just as a newly formed soccer league comprised of members who have never played together before will not have a sense of group efficacy until the

Top management teams typically have very high status because of the perceived importance of what the team does for the organization.

league practices and competes with other leagues, so too will a newly formed group of computer programmers developing a novel software package lack a sense of what the group will be able to accomplish when it is first formed. However, as the soccer league practices and wins and loses games and as the group of programmers share their ideas, develop a strategy, and start writing code, both groups' collective sense of efficacy begins to emerge.

Once members come to share a sense of group efficacy, this will also play an important role in the future of the group.[42] For example, group efficacy can influence the aspirations members have for the group, their effort levels, how they approach tasks, and their persistence when the going gets tough.[43] A group of computer programmers with high group efficacy are likely to put forth more effort, be more persistent when problems arise, and have higher aspirations for what the group can achieve than a group of programmers with low efficacy.

When a group has low efficacy, there are a number of things that can be done to improve it. For example, if certain skills or capabilities are lacking in the group, there are a variety of ways to get them. That might mean adding new members with the requisite skills to the group, training existing members, or seeking outside help. If members are not able to effectively work together, group training and development might be in order (see Chapters 11 and 18). If the group is having trouble developing appropriate task strategies, members can reexamine the strategies they do rely on, reevaluate what seems to work and what doesn't, explicitly consider their strategies before they begin their tasks, and evaluate how effective the new strategies they utilized were upon completing their tasks. If communication problems exist, there are steps group members can take to become better communicators (see Chapter 14). Just as self-efficacy is an important determinant of individual accomplishments, group efficacy is an important determinant of group accomplishments.[44]

Social Facilitation

Does a secretary type more or fewer letters when placed in a room with three other secretaries or in a private office? Does a computer programmer take more or less time to find an error in a complex program when working on the program in the presence of other computer programmers or when working alone? Research on social facilitation provides answers to questions such as these.

SOCIAL FACILITATION
The effects that the presence of others has on performance, enhancing the performance of easy tasks and impairing the performance of difficult tasks.

Social facilitation is the effect the physical presence of others has on an individual's performance. The presence of other group members tends to arouse or stimulate individuals, often because the individuals feel that others will evaluate their performance and give them positive or negative outcomes dependent on how well or poorly they do.

Two types of social facilitation effects have been studied. *Audience effects* are the effects of passive spectators on individual performance. In this case, other group members are not engaged in the task itself but are present as an audience. *Co-action effects* are the effects of the presence of other group members on the performance of an individual when the other group members are performing the same task as the individual.

Research on both types of social facilitation has produced some contradictory results, summarized in Exhibit 10.5. A typist might type more letters in the presence of other group members than when typing alone. But a computer programmer might take more time to find an error in a complex program when working in a group. Why?

When individuals are stimulated by the presence of other group members, their performance of well-learned tasks and behaviors they have performed repeatedly in the past is enhanced.[45] Typing letters is a well-learned behavior for a secretary. She or he knows exactly how to do it—it doesn't require much thought. The presence of other group members enhances the secretary's performance, and she or he types more letters. More generally, when individuals are stimulated or aroused, their performance of well-learned tasks tends to be enhanced.

EXHIBIT 10.5

Social Facilitation

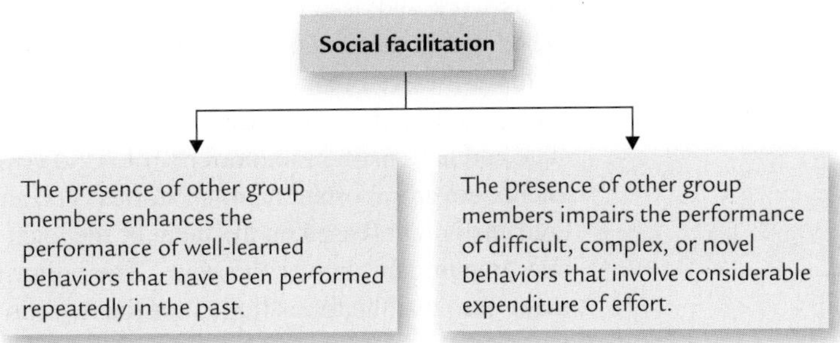

However, when individuals are stimulated by the presence of other group members, their performance of difficult, complex, or novel tasks and behaviors is impaired.[46] Finding an error in a complex computer program is a difficult task. The programmer will need to spend a considerable amount of attention, time, and effort to detect the error. It will probably take longer to locate it working in the presence of others, who might create distractions. More generally, when individuals are stimulated or aroused, their performance of difficult tasks tends to be impaired.

When people realize the presence of others is distracting them or interfering with their performance, they often try to isolate themselves by closing office doors, letting the answering machines take their calls, or finding quiet places to work alone.

Organizations can actually buy special furniture to maximize the benefits of social facilitation and minimize the drawbacks. Furniture and the arrangement of it can provide members with the space they need to work alone yet still provide the opportunity they need to meet together as a group. For example, Aetna Life & Casualty's employees in its home office are organized into self-managed work teams. Team members need to be able to meet with one another and coordinate their efforts. At the same time, they need to be alone to concentrate on complicated tasks, such as calculating the projected risks and returns for different types of insurance policies. Aetna's solution to the problem was to purchase some new "team" furniture manufactured by Steelcase.[47] The furniture divides the total work space into areas called "neighborhoods." In each neighborhood, a central work space is created with a table where members can meet. Individual work areas that are clustered around the central work space give employees the privacy they need to perform their tasks.[48]

How Groups Control Their Members: Roles and Rules

In order for any group (formal or informal, command group or self-managed work team, large or small, homogeneous or heterogeneous) to accomplish its goals, the group must *control*—that is, influence and regulate—its members' behavior. Controlling members' behavior is crucial whether a group is charged with writing superior computer programs, providing excellent customer service, raising quality levels, or cutting costs. Effective groups are groups that control their members' behavior and channel it in the right direction. A group of waiters and waitresses in a restaurant, for example, needs to ensure customers are promptly and courteously waited on, that staff members do not wait on each other's tables or grab each others' food orders, and that customers are given their checks in a timely fashion. Three mechanisms through which groups control their members' behavior are roles, rules, and norms. We discuss each next.

Roles

The division of labor that occurs in groups and organizations necessitates the development of roles. Recall from Chapter 9 that a *role* is a set of behaviors or tasks a person is expected to perform by virtue of holding a position in a group or organization. When a group divides up its work and assigns particular tasks to individual members, different roles are established within the group. For example, there are four roles in a group of employees responsible for the evening news program at a small television station. The local news reporter's role is to compile local stories of interest and provide on-the-scene reports as needed. The state and national news reporter's role is to cover statewide news stories and help the news anchor cover important national stories. The anchor's role is to select the stories to be covered each night (based on the input of the local reporter and the state and national reporter) and prepare and deliver the news. The editor's role is to oversee this entire process and make sure that the time allotted for the news is efficiently and effectively used, that important stories are covered in a meaningful order, and that there is the right amount of on-the-scene reporting.

As we mentioned earlier, sometimes organizations form cross-functional teams. In a cross-functional team, a member's role is likely to be representing his or her function's perspective on the group's project.

Associated with each role in a group are certain responsibilities and rights. All of the behaviors expected of a role occupant (the individual assigned to a role) are the role occupant's *responsibilities*. On a news team, for example, the anchor's responsibility is to prepare and deliver the news. Each role occupant also has *rights or privileges*, such as the right to use resources assigned to the role. Resources can include people, money, specialized equipment, or machinery. The local news reporter on a news team has the right to use the local camera crew and its equipment and has a monthly budget at his or her disposal for tracking down stories.

Roles facilitate the control of group members' behaviors for several reasons. First, roles tell members what they should be doing. Second, roles not only enable a group to hold its members accountable for their behavior but also provide the group with a standard by which to evaluate the behavior. Finally, roles help managers determine how to reward members who perform the behaviors that make up their various roles.

> ROLE RELATIONSHIPS
> The ways in which group and organizational members interact with one another to perform their specific roles.

Members or managers also define the **role relationships** within the group. Role relationships dictate the way members should interact with one another to perform their specific roles. Role relationships may be formally specified in a written job description or emerge informally over time (for example, at the storming or norming stage of group development) as members work out methods for getting the job done.

On a news team, the anchor's role relationships with the local reporter and state and national reporter are formally specified in all three group members' job descriptions: The two reporters and the anchor are to work together to decide what stories will be covered each night, but the final decision is ultimately up to the anchor. The anchor has also developed an informal role relationship with the local reporter, who is given considerable autonomy to determine what local news gets covered. This informal role relationship developed when the anchor realized how skilled and motivated the local news reporter was.

A large part of a person's role in a group may not be specified but may emerge over time as members interact with one another. For example, one member of a group may assume a significant number of responsibilities for the group and emerge as an informal leader when she handles those responsibilities well. Sometimes a manager notices that an informal leader performs certain tasks effectively and then promotes the informal leader to become the new formal leader, should the formal leader of the group leave, be promoted, or replaced. The process of taking the initiative to create a role by assuming certain responsibilities that are not part of one's assigned role is called **role making**. In contrast, **role taking** is the process of performing one's responsibilities associated with an assigned role. Role taking is the common process of assuming a formal organizational role.

> ROLE MAKING
> Taking the initiative to create a role by assuming responsibilities that are not part of an assigned role.

> ROLE TAKING
> Performing the responsibilities that are required as part of an assigned role.

On the news team, for example, the local news reporter did such a good job covering the local scene for the evening news that the anchor always followed her suggestions for stories. Station managers recognized her initiative and high performance, and when the anchor left for a better position in a larger city, the local reporter was promoted to become the new anchor. Role making can be an important process in self-managed work teams where members are jointly trying to find innovative ways to accomplish the group's goals.

Written Rules

Effective groups sometimes use written rules to control their members' behaviors. Written rules specify behaviors that are required and those that are forbidden. The news team, for example, developed a rule that requires members to determine at the beginning of each year when they will take their allotted three weeks of vacation. Other rules require them to arrange their schedules so that only one person is on vacation on any given day, and no one can take more than one week off at a time. The rules help the group cover and present each day's news thoroughly and maintain the continuity of the news from the viewer's perspective. Over time, groups should experiment with their rules and try to find better ones to replace those that currently exist.

Some rules groups develop, often called *standard operating procedures*, specify in writing the best way to perform a particular task. Standard operating procedures help ensure that the group's tasks will be performed correctly and efficiently. For example, a rule specifies exactly when and in what form the news anchor should communicate his or her plans for the evening news each night to the editor so that the editor has enough time to review the format and make any needed changes before the program airs. Zingerman's Community of Businesses (ZCoB) has developed its own unique standard operating procedures. ZCoB's procedures have been so effective that other companies send their employees to its training center to learn them, as profiled in the accompanying OB Today.

OB Today

Zingerman's "Steps" to Success

Zingerman's Delicatessen was founded in 1982 by Ari Weinzweig and Paul Saginaw in Ann Arbor, Michigan.[49] Weinzweig and Saginaw are food aficionados. From the start, they have prided themselves on making wonderful sandwiches and tracking down unique, traditional foods. Finding tasty treasures from around the world and endless selections of the best condiments, including exotic oils, vinegars, and olives, has been a labor of love for the two.[50] In order to expand their business yet maintain high-quality service and an intimate atmosphere, Weinzweig and Saginaw expanded their deli concept to encompass a community of related businesses that they call ZCoB. ZCoB now includes the original deli, a mail-order unit, a

Zingerman's Delicatessen, founded in 1982 by Ari Weinzweig and Paul Saginaw in Ann Arbor, MI, trains employees and manages its businesses through its unique brand of standard operating procedures.

bakery, a caterer, and a creamery.[51] The founders' persistent emphasis on great food, high-quality service, and commitment to people and community are part and parcel to their savvy business expertise.[52]

A primary tool that ZCoB uses to manage its businesses and train employees is its unique brand of standard operating procedures. These procedures encapsulate the key steps necessary to accomplish important objectives at ZCoB. During training, new employees learn the "Four Steps to Selling Great Food." Step 1 is "know the food"—whether it's how a certain artisan bread rises or how olives are cured.[53] There are also distinct steps for particular food groups. For example, "Six Steps to Selecting Superior Cheese" include a primary emphasis on taste, choosing handmade cheeses, and getting your cheese cut to order.[54] Having trouble with a coworker? "Four Steps to Productive Resolution of Your Differences" suggests you speak directly to the coworker about your concerns.[55] And not forgetting the need to make a profit, ZCoB's "Three Steps to Great Finance" suggests you should understand how finance works, measure your financial performance on a weekly basis, and make sure all employees benefit from good financial performance.[56]

As word of ZCoB's success spread, other organizations sought to emulate it. Enter Zing Train, ZCoB's training, development, and consulting business. Hospitals, restaurants, banks, and grocery store chains have all sent employees to Zing Train in Ann Arbor to learn ZCoB's steps to success in different business areas.[57] The steps not only seem to work, but they also seem to lead to satisfied employees who love what they do.

Rules have several advantages that help groups control and manage behavior and performance:

- Rules help groups ensure members will engage in behaviors that contribute to the effectiveness of the group and the organization and avoid behaviors that hinder performance and goal attainment.
- Rules facilitate the control of behavior because members and managers know how and when role occupants are expected to perform their assigned tasks.
- Rules facilitate the evaluation of individual group members' performance levels because their behavior can be compared to the behavior specified by the rules.
- When the membership in a group changes, rules help newcomers learn the right way to perform their roles.

A group can develop rules at any stage of its development. Rules developed at early stages are often changed or abandoned as the nature of the group's work, group goals, or organizational goals change. A healthy group recognizes the need for change and is willing to alter its rules (and roles) when warranted.

How Groups Control Their Members: Group Norms

Roles and rules help group members and managers control the behavior in groups because they specify the behaviors members should engage in. Norms serve the same purpose.[58] Norms signal members about the behaviors expected of them. Unlike written rules, however, which are *formal* descriptions of actions and behaviors required by a group or organization, **group norms** are *informal* rules of conduct. Often they are not put in writing.

GROUP NORMS
Informal rules of conduct for behaviors considered important by most group members.

When members share a common idea of acceptable behavior, they can monitor each other's behavior to make sure everyone is following the group's norms. This is key to controlling the group. Groups enforce their norms by rewarding members who conform to the norms by behaving in the specified manner and punishing members who deviate from the norms.[59] Rewards for conforming to group norms can include being treated in a friendly manner by other group members, verbal praise, receiving help from others when needed, and tangible rewards, such as bonuses or perks. Punishments for deviations can include being ignored by other members, criticized or reprimanded, stripped of certain privileges, or expelled from the group.

A group of waiters and waitresses in a busy restaurant may develop informal norms to the effect that members should not steal each other's tables or orders in the kitchen and should always inform others when they observe that customers at another member's table are ready for their check. These norms help the group effectively accomplish its goals of providing good service to customers and earning the best tips possible. A group member who does not follow the norm (a waiter, for example, who steals an order in the kitchen on a particularly busy day) might be reprimanded. If deviation from the norm continues, the individual might even be expelled from the group. A waitress who continually steals tables to earn more tips, for example, might be brought to the attention of the restaurant manager and eventually fired. Waiters and waitresses who conform to the group's norms are rewarded with continued membership in the group and other perks. Those perks might include verbal praise from the restaurant manager and other members and bigger tips from customers.

Like formal roles and rules, norms develop to channel the behavior of members in a direction that leads to the achievement of group and organizational goals.[60] When norms exist, members do not have to waste time thinking about what to do in a particular situation; norms guide their actions and specify how they should behave. Furthermore, when people share common norms, they can predict how others will behave in certain situations and thus anticipate one another's actions. This improves the interaction among members and results in fewer misunderstandings between them.

Why Do Group Members Conform to Norms?

COMPLIANCE
Assenting to a norm in order to attain rewards or avoid punishment.

Individuals conform to group norms for three main reasons. The first and most widespread basis for conformity to group norms is **compliance**—assenting to a norm in order to attain rewards or avoid punishment.[61] When individuals comply with norms, they do not necessarily believe the behavior specified by the norm is important for its own sake. However, they know that abiding by the norm will result in certain benefits and ignoring it will result in certain costs. Consider how norms operate in the following example. The internal auditing department of a chemical company annually solicits contributions for the United Way, a charitable organization. Mary Kelly is a group member who doesn't really like the United Way because she has read some articles questioning the way the charitable organization uses its funds. Nevertheless, Kelly always contributes to the United Way because she is afraid her coworkers will think less of her and perhaps avoid her if she does not.

IDENTIFICATION
Associating oneself with supporters of a norm and conforming to the norm because those individuals do.

The second reason for conformity is **identification**—associating oneself with supporters of a norm and conforming to the norm because those individuals do. John Bickers, one of the newest members of the auditing department, really looks up to Ralph Diaz and Steve Cashion, who have been in the department for several years and are ripe for promotion. Around the time of the United Way campaign, Bickers casually asks Diaz and Cashion over lunch how they feel about the United Way. Both Diaz and Cashion indicate they think it's a worthy cause, and both tell Bickers they contributed to it during the annual fund drive. This information causes Bickers to decide to contribute as well.

INTERNALIZATION
Believing that the behavior dictated by a norm is truly the right and proper way to behave.

The third and potentially most powerful basis for conformity to group norms is **internalization**—believing that the behavior dictated by the norm is truly the right way to behave. Diaz and Cashion's basis for conformity is internalization: They wholeheartedly believe in the United Way's cause. Norms have the most influence on group members when the basis for conformity is internalization.

Idiosyncrasy Credit

Although most group members are expected to conform to group norms, one or a few group members sometimes are allowed to deviate from the norms without being punished. These privileged individuals are generally group members who have contributed

IDIOSYNCRASY CREDIT
The freedom to violate group norms without being punished that is accorded to group members who have contributed a lot to the group in the past.

a lot to the group in the past. Their above-average contributions to the group give them what has been termed **idiosyncrasy credit**—the freedom to violate group norms without being punished.[62]

In the restaurant described earlier, John Peters, the waiter who has been with the restaurant for the longest period of time, generally takes on the responsibility of training new waiters and waitresses and settling conflicts that arise in the group. On very busy days, Peters sometimes "mistakes" other group members' orders in the kitchen for his own. However, he is never reprimanded for stealing orders. His beyond-the-call-of-duty contributions to the group give him idiosyncrasy credit, which allows him to deviate from the group's norms. Similarly, a highly skilled developer in a group of computer programmers might frequently fight with other group members and with the supervisor yet never be reprimanded. Although her behavior violates the group's norm of members' being polite and considerate to one another, the behavior is tolerated because this programmer is the one who always finds the bug in a program.

The Pros and Cons of Conformity and Deviance

From our discussion of group norms, you probably get the impression that conformity is good in all situations. Conformity *is* good when norms help a group control and influence its members' behaviors so that the group can accomplish its goals. But what if a group's norms are inappropriate or unethical? Or what if a norm that was once appropriate is no longer appropriate because the situation has changed? Many norms, such as always behaving courteously to customers or always leaving a work area clean, promote organizational effectiveness, but some group norms do not.

Studies have shown that groups of employees can develop norms that actually hurt the group's performance. A group of employees on an assembly line might develop norms to control the speed at which the work is performed. An employee who works very quickly (and, thus, produces "too much") may be called a "rate buster." An employee who works very slowly (or below the group norm) may be called a "goldbricker," a "slacker," or a "chiseler."[63] Other members of the group may reprimand slackers and rate busters alike. In the case of a rate buster, the reprimand may hinder group performance, because rate busters generally tend to lower their levels of performance to fall more in line with the group norm.

This same kind of process can occur at all levels in an organization. A group of middle managers may adopt a don't-rock-the-boat norm that signals managers to agree with whatever top management proposes, regardless of whether they think the ideas are right or wrong. A new middle manager soon learns that it doesn't pay to rock the boat because this behavior will incur the wrath of not only the top manager but his or her comanagers, too. When such a norm exists, all middle managers might be reluctant to speak up even when they all realize that a change is sorely needed for the organization's success. In cases like this, conformity maintains dysfunctional group behaviors, and deviance from the norm is appropriate.

DEVIANCE
Deviation from a norm.

Deviance—deviation from a norm—occurs when a member of a group violates a norm. Groups usually respond to deviance in one of three ways.[64] First, the group might try to get the deviant to change by, for example, explaining to the deviant why the norm is so important, pointing out that he or she is the only member of the group violating the norm, or reprimanding and punishing the deviant for violating the norm. Second, the group might reject[65] or try to expel the deviant, as the group of restaurant employees did when a waitress violated the norm of not stealing tables. Third, the group might actually change the norm in question to be more in line with the deviant's behavior. When group norms are inappropriate, deviance can spark a needed change within the group.

Balancing Conformity and Deviance

As illogical as it might sound, groups need both conformity and deviance to accomplish their goals and perform at a high level. In our restaurant example, conformity to the group norms of not stealing tables or food orders and of informing members when customers are ready for their checks helps the group meet its goals. A group norm for handling customer complaints, however, has recently changed.

In the past, whenever customers complained about a meal, the norm was to refer the complaint to the restaurant manager. The manager would talk to the customer and invariably offer him or her an alternative selection. Then, on a particularly busy day, one of Sally Schumaker's customers had a complaint. Rather than seek out the manager, Schumaker decided to handle the problem herself. She offered the customer another meal because that was how the manager always solved such a problem. After that, Schumaker continued to take matters into her own hands whenever one of her customers had a complaint. Over time, other members of the group noticed Schumaker's behavior and asked her why she was circumventing the restaurant manager. She explained her reasons for violating the group norm, and they made sense to the other members: Handling problems themselves would enable them to please dissatisfied customers more quickly and avoid bothering the manager with every problem.

John Peters, the senior waiter, decided to check with the manager to make sure it was all right with him if the wait staff offered a new meal for a customer who had a complaint about the food. The manager thought this was a great idea and was surprised he hadn't thought of it himself. He informed the wait staff that from then on they should handle complaints themselves (as Schumaker was already doing), but that they should be sure to let the cook know about the nature of the complaints.

The norm of referring all complaints to the restaurant manager was dysfunctional for the group of waiters and waitresses for two reasons: (1) It meant keeping dissatisfied customers waiting (which prevented the group from achieving its good-service goal); and (2) it meant seeking out the manager, which took time that could have been used to serve other customers (preventing members from earning the maximum amount of tips they could). Deviance from this norm was functional for the group because it stimulated the group to reexamine the norm and change it.

As this story shows, *conformity* ensures that a group can control members' behaviors to get tasks accomplished, and *deviance* forces group members to reexamine the appropriateness of norms. Exhibit 10.6 depicts the relationship between levels of conformity and deviance in a group and the group's goal accomplishment. The group at point A has a low level of conformity and a high level of deviance. This group has difficulty controlling members' behaviors and fails to attain its goals. The group at point B has achieved just the right balance: Conformity helps the group direct members' behaviors toward its goals, and deviance forces it to periodically reexamine the appropriateness of it norms. In the group at point C, conformity is so high that it is stressed at the expense of the group achieving its goals. Because group members are extremely reluctant to deviate from its norms, this group retains dysfunctional norms and resists any sort of change.

Because deviance can be an impetus for change and improvement, how groups respond to deviance can be an important determinant of group effectiveness. For example, research has found that groups can benefit by allowing members who deviate from the norms or hold a position at odds with the majority to air their views.[66] Sometimes the deviant or dissenter is justified, and the norm or majority position is ineffective or unwarranted. In this case, by listening to the deviant and thinking through his or her arguments, the group might improve how it functions. Even if the deviant's position is not justified, listening to him or her and discussing his or her perspective is likely to lead the group to a better understanding of the issues at hand, including the deviant.[67] Additionally, when the group's tasks require creativity[68] (see Chapter 5), it is especially important that all views are expressed and heard, regardless of how outlandish or deviant they might seem.

Some national cultures promote high levels of conformity. In cultures such as these, group members are likely to abide by the norms at all costs and fear change. This phenomenon is prevalent in Japan. In Japan, young children are taught the importance of conforming to group norms at an early age because the Japanese tend to see

EXHIBIT 10.6

The Relationship Between Levels of Conformity and Deviance in a Group and Group Goal Accomplishment

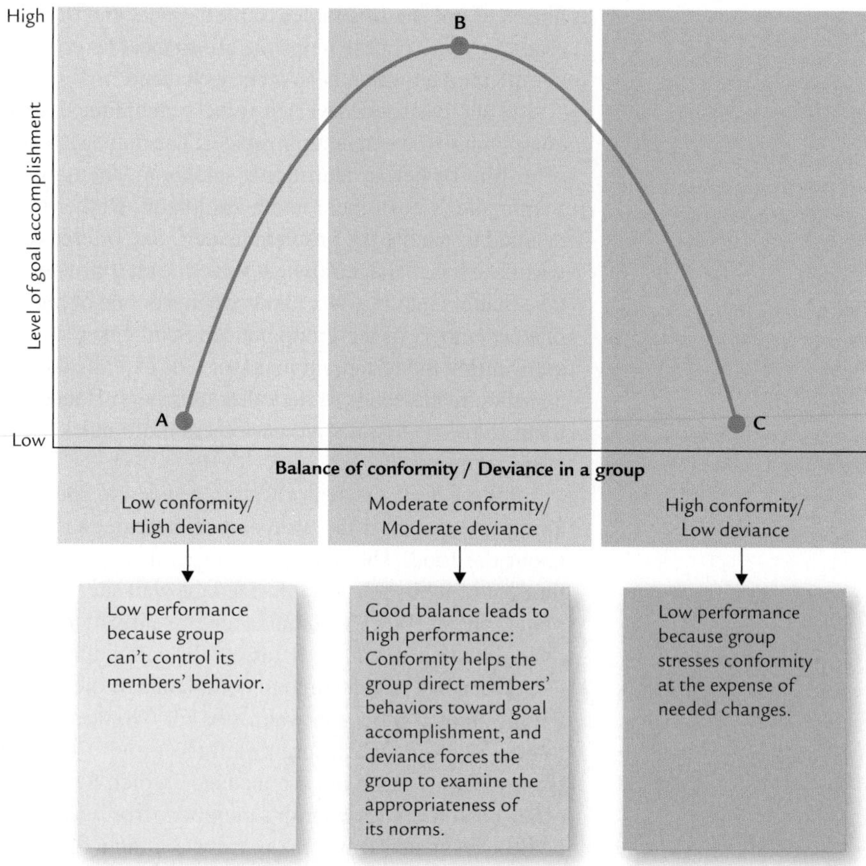

conformity as desirable and change as threatening. For example, JAL Coordination Service Company, a Japanese company, teaches its female office employees the proper ways to bow and smile, per the norm. Proper bowing and smiling are deemed to be so important, in fact, other companies send hundreds of their members to JAL each year for a two-day, bowing-and-smiling training seminar. The cost is about $240 per employee. The Japanese stress conformity to group norms to such a great extent that harmony is sometimes valued over needed change. Sociologist Akira Fujitake suggests that change in Japan may be slow because of "a barrier called 'the group.'"[69] The use of oobeyas, profiled earlier in Global View, can be an effective way of alleviating the pressures related to conformity. In an oobeya, everyone is on equal footing, has a voice, and is listened to, and all issues are open for discussion and potential disagreement.

Ensuring that Group Norms Are Functional for the Organization

In our restaurant example, because the group's goals are aligned with the restaurant's goals, the norms that are functional for the group are also functional for the organization. Similarly, the norms that are dysfunctional for the group (such as referring all customer complaints to the manager) are dysfunctional for the organization. When group and organizational goals are closely aligned, groups are inclined to develop norms that help the groups achieve its goals and are also functional for the organization. Likewise, they are inclined to discard norms that are dysfunctional for the group and the organization.

Group goals, however, are not always congruent with organizational goals. The goal of a group of employees that assembles radios, for example, might be to *minimize* the amount of effort each member exerts on the job. To achieve this goal, the employees develop the norm of assembling no more than 50 radios per day. The group could easily assemble 75 radios each day, but this performance level would entail additional effort on the part of members. In this case, the group norm is clearly dysfunctional for the organization because group goals are inconsistent with organizational goals. The norm, however, is functional for the group because it helps members achieve their goal of not having to work too hard.

How can managers ensure that group norms are functional and aligned with those of the organization? One way is by making sure members are rewarded when the organization achieves its goals. In our restaurant example, members benefitted from the restaurant achieving its goal of providing good service because good service leads to bigger tips. Another way is by rewarding group members on the basis of individual or group performance.

The group of employees assembling radios, on the other hand, receives no tangible benefits when the organization reaches its performance goal. Members are paid on an hourly basis and receive the same amount of money regardless of how many radios they assemble. Their group goal (minimizing effort expenditure) is not aligned with their

You're the Management Expert

Aligning Goals

Marcy Long heads a diagnostic laboratory that performs a wide variety of blood tests in a large city. When physicians give their patients medical orders to have certain blood tests performed, Long's lab is one of many in the city patients have the option to use. The laboratory accepts most major insurance plans in the area and has a close relationship with many of the nearby medical practices. Some of these practices direct their patients exclusively to Long's lab. Patients, of course, can choose to go elsewhere, but often they do not. Although Long is generally satisfied with the performance of her employees, several physicians recently complained to her that the staff are inflexible in terms of making exceptions and being responsive to special requests. For example, if a certain blood test typically takes three days but can be performed in one or two days if needed, staff members are unwilling to do the test sooner, even when the reasons for doing so are compelling. As another example, when a patient has multiple tests performed and some take longer than others, the lab typically waits until all or most of the test results are in before faxing them over to the physicians. In some cases, physicians and/or patients are anxious to get the results as they become available, and the lab's policy is to accommodate these requests. However, some physicians have told Long they've repeatedly had to request partial results before receiving them. Long has always told her staff members that they the need to be sensitive to the needs of patients and their doctors and be as responsive as possible while maintaining the highest standards in the field. While her staff excels at the latter, she has come to realize they are not as responsive as they could be. Although she has emphasized this point repeatedly in staff meetings, the complaints from physicians and their patients have not stopped. In one instance, Long herself had to intervene to satisfy a special request.

Because you are an expert in OB, Long has come to you for help. How can she get her staff to be flexible and responsive to the special requests and needs of physicians and their patients?

organization's goal (performance) because they do not benefit if the organizational goal is met. The norms the group has developed (restricting production) are functional for its members but dysfunctional for the organization.

The need to align group and organizational goals has a very clear implication for how outcomes (such as pay) should be distributed to members of the group when their individual contributions or performance levels cannot be readily identified or evaluated. Essentially, the outcomes members receive should be based on the group's levels of performance. In other words, members should be rewarded when the group is effective and contributes to the attainment of the organization's overall goals. When members are rewarded for their high performance, this then becomes a group goal, and norms develop toward that end. If our radio employees were able to increase their earnings by assembling more radios, it is likely the group's goal would be to increase production rather than to limit it, and new norms would probably develop toward this end.

Socialization: How Group Members Learn Roles, Rules, and Norms

The ability of a group to control its members' behaviors depends on the extent to which newcomers learn the group's roles, rules, and norms. Newcomers do not initially know what is expected of them and what they can and cannot do.[70] A newcomer to a group of secretaries, for example, does not know whether it is all right to take a long lunch one day and make up the time the next day or whether it is acceptable to work from 8:30 to 4:30 instead of from 9:00 to 5:00. Newcomers are outsiders, and only when they have learned the group's roles, rules, and norms do existing group members accept them as insiders. The process by which newcomers learn the roles, rules, and norms of a group is **socialization**.

SOCIALIZATION
The process by which newcomers learn the roles, rules, and norms of a group.

A newcomer can learn how the group controls members' behavior by simply observing how existing members behave and inferring from this behavior what is appropriate and what is inappropriate. This might be perfectly acceptable to the newcomer, but from the group's point of view, it could be risky because the newcomer might observe and learn bad habits that are unacceptable to the group. In one of our earlier examples, a computer programmer gets away with argumentative behavior that violates the group norm of being cooperative because of her idiosyncrasy credit. A newcomer to the group observing her combative behavior, however, might mistakenly assume that this behavior is acceptable—that it is in conformity with a group norm.

Socialization and Role Orientation

John Van Mannen and Edgar Schein developed a model of socialization describing the different ways in which groups socialize their members. How groups socialize newcomers, in turn, influences the role orientation that newcomers adopt.[71] **Role orientation** is the characteristic way in which members of a group respond to various situations. For example, do members react passively and obediently to commands and orders? Are they creative and innovative when it comes to finding solutions to problems?

ROLE ORIENTATION
The characteristic way in which members of a group respond to various situations.

Van Mannen and Schein identified six pairs of contrasting socialization tactics that influence a newcomer's learning and role orientation. The use of different combinations of these tactics leads to two different role orientations: institutionalized and individualized. In an **institutionalized role orientation**, newcomers are taught to respond to situations in the same way that existing group members respond to similar situations. An institutional orientation encourages obedience and conformity to existing roles, rules, and norms. Newcomers who have an institutionalized orientation are more likely to engage in role taking rather than in role making because this orientation emphasizes the importance of following existing ways of doing things.

INSTITUTIONALIZED ROLE ORIENTATION
A role orientation in which newcomers are taught to respond to situations in the same way that existing group members respond to similar situations.

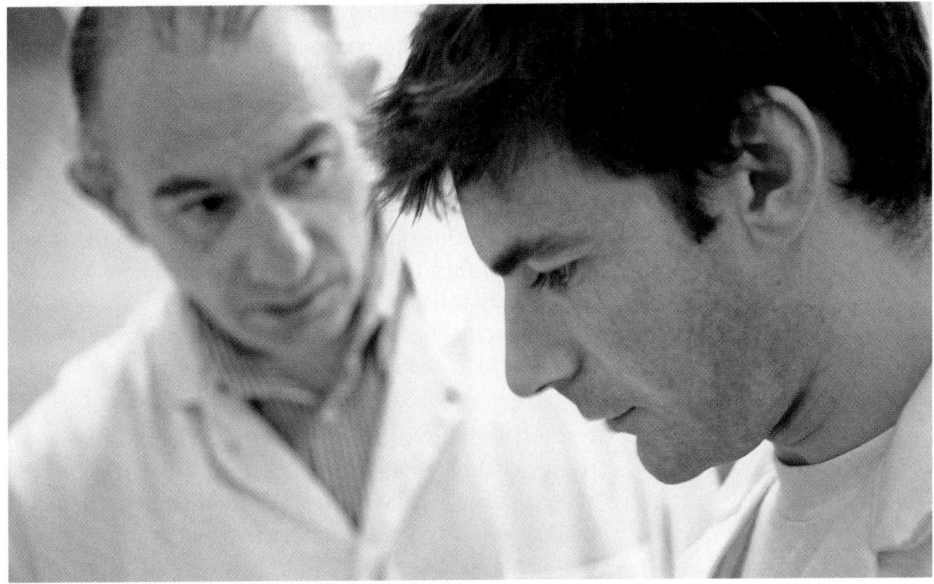

When an individualized role orientation is desired, newcomers still need to learn and follow existing roles, rules, and norms but also are taught that it is acceptable and desirable to be creative and to experiment with changing how the group does things.

INDIVIDUALIZED ROLE ORIENTATION A role orientation in which newcomers are taught that it is acceptable and desirable to be creative and to experiment with changing how the group does things.

In an **individualized role orientation**, individuals are taught that it is acceptable and desirable to be creative and to experiment with changing how the group does things.[72] Although group members with an individualized orientation still need to learn and follow existing roles, rules, and norms, they realize that these ways of controlling behavior are not cast in stone and that the group will consider changing them if a more effective way of behaving is identified. Members with an individualized orientation tend to engage more in role making rather than in role taking.

Socialization Tactics

The socialization tactics identified by Van Mannen and Schein are discussed next and summarized in Exhibit 10.7. Groups or organizations can use all six tactics or a subset of the six tactics, depending on their needs and goals. Each of the six tactics actually represents a pair of contrasting tactics from which a choice can be made.

Collective versus individual tactics. When *collective* tactics are used, newcomers go through a common learning experience designed to produce standardized or highly similar responses to different situations. For example, all of the new sales associates hired by a department store receive collective socialization by participating in the same two-week

EXHIBIT 10.7

Socialization Tactics That Shape Group Members' Role Orientations

Tactics That Lead to an Institutionalized Orientation	Tactics That Lead to an Individualized Orientation
Collective tactics	Individual tactics
Formal tactics	Informal tactics
Sequential tactics	Random tactics
Fixed tactics	Variable tactics
Serial tactics	Disjunctive tactics
Divestiture tactics	Investiture tactics

training program. They watch videotapes showing the proper way to greet customers, process a sale or returned item, and deal with customer complaints.

When *individualized* tactics are used, newcomers are taught individually how to behave. Because learning takes place on an individual basis, each newcomer's learning experiences are somewhat different, and newcomers are encouraged to behave differently in the various situations they may encounter on the job. For example, newcomers to a group of cosmetics salespeople, each of whom is responsible for a different line (Estée Lauder, Lancôme, and so on), are socialized individually by company representatives to ensure that they develop the appropriate knowledge about the line and the type of customers it appeals to.

Collective tactics tend to lead to an *institutionalized* orientation; *individual* tactics tend to lead to an *individualized* orientation.

Formal versus informal tactics. When tactics are *formal*, newcomers are segregated from existing group members during the learning process. For example, new sales associates receive their two-week training in the department store's training room. During this period, they never interact with members of the groups they are to join once their training is complete.

When tactics are *informal*, newcomers learn on the job. For example, many restaurants socialize new waiters and waitresses by having them work alongside experienced waiters and waitresses.

Formal tactics tend to lead to an *institutionalized* orientation; *informal* tactics tend to lead to an *individualized* orientation.

Sequential versus random tactics. When *sequential* tactics are used, newcomers are provided with explicit information about the sequence in which they will perform new behaviors. For example, a new assistant in a veterinarians' office is told that during her first two weeks she will assist the vets with routine checkups. After that, she will also weigh the animals and administer injections. After one month on the job she will also assist the vets in surgery.

When *random* tactics are used, the order in which socialization proceeds is based on the interests and needs of the individual newcomer, and no set sequence is followed. For example, an apprentice woodworker who has just joined a group of custom furniture makers might be told that the order in which he learns to make the different types of furniture is up to him.

Sequential tactics tend to lead to an *institutionalized* orientation; *random* tactics tend to lead to an *individualized* orientation.

Fixed versus variable tactics. *Fixed* tactics give newcomers precise knowledge about the timetable for completing each stage in the learning process. The socialization of the assistant in the veterinarians' office relies on fixed tactics. The assistant knew that two weeks would have to elapse before she moved on to the next stage in her training.

Variable tactics provide no information about when newcomers will reach a certain stage in the learning process; the speed of socialization depends on the individual newcomer. The woodworker was socialized with variable tactics; he was never told how long it should take him to learn how to make different types of furniture.

Fixed tactics tend to lead to an *institutionalized* orientation; *random* tactics tend to lead to an *individualized* orientation.

Serial versus disjunctive tactics. When *serial* tactics are used, existing group members socialize newcomers. (Waiters and waitresses training newcomers is one example.)

When *disjunctive* tactics are used, newcomers must figure out and develop their own ways of behaving. They are not told what to do by experienced group members. For example, many new professors learn how to teach and do research through disjunctive socialization. Experienced professors in the groups or department they join often do not give them training or guidance in how to teach and do research.

Serial tactics tend to lead to an *institutionalized* orientation; *disjunctive* tactics tend to lead to an *individualized* orientation.

Divestiture versus investiture tactics. With *divestiture* tactics, newcomers receive negative interpersonal treatment from other members of the group. For example, they are ignored or taunted. Existing group members refrain from treating newcomers kindly and with respect until they learn existing roles, rules, and norms. The classic example of divestiture is in military boot camp, where new recruits are insulted and subjected to a wide variety of abuse until they learn the ropes.

With *investiture* tactics, newcomers immediately receive positive social support from other group members. For example, a group of nurses might go out of its way to teach a new member how things are done in the group and make the member feel welcome.

Divestiture tactics tend to lead to an *institutionalized* orientation; *investiture* tactics tend to lead to an *individualized* orientation.

To summarize, collective, formal, sequential, fixed, serial, and divestiture tactics tend to lead newcomers to develop an institutionalized orientation. Individual, informal, random, variable, disjunctive, and investiture tactics tend to lead newcomers to develop an individualized orientation.[73] What is the significance of this model for socialization in organizations?

Consider the use of socialization tactics by the military. New recruits are placed in platoons with other new recruits (*collective*), are segregated from existing group members (*formal*), go through preestablished drills and learning experiences (*sequential*), know exactly how long basic training will take and what they have to do (*fixed*), have superior officers such as platoon sergeants who socialize them (*serial*), and are treated with little respect and tolerance until they have learned their duties and "gotten with the program" (*divestiture*). As a result of their socialization experiences, new recruits develop an institutionalized role orientation in which obedience and conformity to group roles, rules, and norms are signs of success. New members who cannot, or will not, perform according to these standards either leave the military or are asked to leave.

Few groups exert the same amount of control over its members as the military, but other groups do use similar tactics to socialize their members. For example, Disneyland prides itself on visitors having a fun-filled experience in a wholesome, clean, cheerful, and friendly theme park. How does an organization that employs over 30,000 people ensure its employees will behave in accordance with these standards? A careful socialization process geared toward developing an institutionalized role orientation is one important means for Disney.

Disney wants all its employees to carefully follow its roles (such as their individual job duties), rules (such as refraining from growing mustaches or wearing dangling earrings), and norms (such as always going the extra mile to help guests have a good time). The institutionalized orientation helps employees do their jobs the Disney way and helps the company succeed in its quest to maintain its competitive advantage.

New recruits, or "cast members" as they are called at Disney, receive formal training at Disney University in groups of around 45. Their collective socialization follows a set sequence of activities. During the Traditions I program, which lasts for a day and a half, newcomers learn the Disney language and the four Disney guiding principles: safety, courtesy, show or entertainment, and efficiency. They also receive training in how to answer guests' questions no matter how difficult the questions may be.

Once cast members complete Traditions I, they move on to further socialization in the attraction areas (Adventureland, Fantasyland, and so on) that they will be joining. This session, which can last as long as a day and a half, covers the rules for each specific

Disney socializes its thousands of employees, or "cast numbers," by sending them to Disney University. Careful socialization and training ensures new cast members learn how to act the Disney way.

area. Last, but not least, is on-the-job training the newcomers will be given by the experienced cast members in the groups they're joining (a serial tactic). This part of the socialization process can take up to two and a half weeks to complete and includes new cast members' learning their roles and their accompanying responsibilities, privileges, and role relationships. All in all, careful socialization ensures new cast members learn how to do things the Disney way.[74]

Should a group encourage an institutional role orientation in which newcomers accept the status quo? Or should it encourage an individual role orientation whereby newcomers are allowed to develop creative and innovative responses to the tasks required of them? The answer to this question depends on the goals of the group and organization.

The main benefit of an institutionalized orientation is also its main danger: the homogeneity it produces among group members. If all members of a group have been socialized to share the same way of looking at the world and have the same strong allegiance to existing roles, rules, and norms, the group may become resistant to change and lack the wherewithal to come up with creative solutions to problems. As we discuss in Chapter 19, however, the very survival of groups and organizations depends on their willingness and ability to change as needed in response to changes in the environments in which they exist. Such changes include changes in customer demands, in the nature and diversity of the workforce, and changes in economic conditions or technology. Groups such as marketing departments, self-managed work teams, and research and development teams, and organizations such as consumer products firms, auto companies, and computer manufacturers are likely to have to respond to frequent changes in the business climate. These groups and organizations can benefit from an individualized orientation and should try to use individual, informal, random, variable, disjunctive, and investiture tactics whenever feasible. Microsoft, for example, tends to rely on many of these tactics to promote individualized role orientations. Microsoft takes this approach because the effectiveness of the various groups in the organization depends not on standardized individual behavior (like at Disneyland) but on encouraging members to come up with new and improved solutions to software problems.

Socialization helps groups achieve whatever goals they have established—to provide consistently high quality audits, to assemble 75 radios a day, and to develop new software—by helping them control their members' behaviors. Whether a group wants its members to closely follow established ways of doing things or offer suggestions for ways to do things differently, it needs to exert control over its members' behaviors and actions in order to make this happen.

Summary

Work groups are the basic building blocks of an organization. Work groups use roles, rules, and norms to control their members' behaviors, and they use several socialization tactics to turn newcomers into effective group members. Groups contribute to organizational effectiveness when group goals are aligned with organizational goals. In this chapter, we made the following major points:

1. Two attributes separate work groups from random collections of individuals in an organization. Members of a work group (a) interact with each other and (b) perceive the potential for mutual goal accomplishment. Work groups vary in whether they are formal or informal. Formal work groups include command groups, task forces, teams, and self-managed work teams. Informal work groups include friendship groups and interest groups. Teams are characterized by intense interactions between team members to achieve team goals.
2. Groups develop and change over time. The five-stage model of group development proposes that groups develop in five sequential stages: forming, storming, norming, performing, and adjourning. Research, however, has not indicated that there is a universal set of stages that all groups experience in the same order.
3. Five important characteristics of groups are size, composition, function, status, and group efficacy. Each has the potential to affect the extent to which a group achieves its goals, performs at a high level, and ultimately is effective in helping an organization attain its goals. Social facilitation is a characteristic effect that the presence of other group members has on individual performance such that having others present enhances performance of well-learned tasks and impairs performance of difficult tasks.
4. All groups, regardless of their type or characteristics, need to control their members' behaviors to be effective and attain their goals. Roles and rules can be used to control behavior in groups.
5. A role is a set of behaviors or tasks that a person is expected to perform by virtue of holding a position in a group or organization. Roles have rights and responsibilities attached to them. Role relationships are the ways in which group and organizational members interact with each other to perform their specific roles. Group members acquire roles through role making and through role taking.
6. Written rules specify behaviors that are required of group members or are forbidden. They also specify how particular tasks should be performed.
7. Groups also control their members' behaviors by developing and enforcing group norms. Group norms are shared expectations for behavior within a group. There are three bases for conformity to group norms: compliance, identification, and internalization.
8. To accomplish goals and perform at a high level, groups need both conformity to and deviance from norms. Whether group norms result in high levels of group performance depends on the extent to which group goals are consistent with organizational goals. To facilitate goal alignment, group members should benefit or be rewarded when the group performs at a high level and contributes to the achievement of organizational goals.
9. Group members learn roles, rules, and norms through the process of socialization. Collective, formal, sequential, fixed, serial, and divestiture socialization tactics tend to lead to an institutionalized role orientation. Individual, informal, random, variable, disjunctive, and investiture socialization tactics tend to lead to an individualized role orientation.

Exercises in Understanding and Managing Organizational Behavior

Questions for Review

1. At what stage in the five-stage model of group development might groups exert the most control over their members' behaviors?
2. Do most members of an organization want to work in teams? Why or why not?
3. In what situations might the advantages of large group size outweigh the disadvantages?
4. In what kinds of situations might it be especially important to have heterogeneous groups?
5. Why are roles an important means of controlling group members' behaviors in self-managed work teams?
6. Why do groups need rules?
7. How are rules that specify how to perform a particular task developed?
8. Why might a group keep following a dysfunctional norm or a norm that prevents the group from achieving its goals?
9. Do all groups socialize their members? Do all groups need to socialize their members? Why or why not?
10. Is socialization ever completely finished, or is it an ongoing process?

OB: Increasing Self-Awareness

Analyzing a "Real" Group

Choose a work group featured in a television series (e.g., *Gray's Anatomy, Boston Legal, CSI Miami, CSI New York, Numbers, Criminal Minds, House*). For the group you have chosen, answer these questions:

1. Is this a formal or an informal group? What kind of formal or informal group is it?
2. What stage of development is this group at according to the five-stage model of group development?
3. What can you say about the size, composition, function, and status of this group?
4. What are the roles and role relationships in this group?
5. What rights and responsibilities are attached to each role in the group?
6. What rules does this group use to control its members' behaviors?
7. What norms does this group use to control its members' behaviors?
8. How does the group react to deviance from its norms?
9. Do any members of this group have idiosyncrasy credit?

A Question of Ethics

In many organizations, some groups of employees typically have higher status than others. And sometimes the groups with the lower status feel that they are not appreciated and are "second-class citizens." For example, in hospitals, physicians generally have higher status than nurses; in universities, faculty typically have higher status than staff; and in law firms, partners have higher status than attorneys who are not partners and paralegals.

Questions

1. Think about the ethical implications of these kinds of status differences in organizations.
2. To what extent should groups with different status in an organization be treated differently, and to what extent should they receive equal treatment? Why?

Small Group Break-Out Exercise

Encouraging Dissenting Views

Form groups of three or four people, and appoint one member as the spokesperson who will communicate your conclusions to the rest of the class.

1. Take a few minutes to think about groups that you were a member of in which there was a high level of conformity to group norms.
2. Think about how someone who openly disagreed with the majority would feel and be treated in these groups.
3. Take turns describing these groups and the bases for conformity in them. And then discuss how deviants would likely be treated in these groups.
4. As a group, come up with ways that groups in which conformity is emphasized at the expense of deviance can encourage group members to express dissenting views.

Topic for Debate

Groups are the basic building blocks of organizations. Now that you have a good understanding of the nature and types of groups and how groups control and socialize their members, debate the following issue.

Team A. In most organizations, an institutionalized role orientation is more desirable than an individualized role orientation.

Team B. In most organizations, an individualized role orientation is more desirable than an institutionalized role orientation.

Experiential Exercise

Developing Roles, Rules, and Norms

Objective

Your objective is to gain experience in developing roles, rules, and norms that contribute to group effectiveness.

Procedure

The class divides into groups of three to five people, and each group appoints one member as spokesperson, to present the group's findings to the whole class. Here is the scenario.

eliminate social loafing on group projects by having students evaluate each other's contributions to a group project and assigning grades to individual students based, in part, on these evaluations.

Making individuals feel that they are making valuable contributions to a group. In some kinds of groups, it is impossible for supervisors or group members to monitor individual behavior or make individual contributions identifiable. In a professional singing group that provides background music for commercials and movies, for example, it is very difficult to assess the effort of any individual singer. Indeed, each singer's contribution (the quality of a person's singing) cannot be distinguished from the performance of the group as a whole.

In situations in which each employee's contribution cannot be separated from the performance of the group as a whole, managers can reduce social loafing by making each individual feel that he or she makes an important and worthwhile contribution to the group.[28] Making individuals feel valued is the second way to reduce social loafing and increase work-group effectiveness. This goal could be accomplished in the group of singers by periodically reminding each of them of their special talents and the contributions they make to the group. A singer with a very deep and resonant voice, for example, could be reminded that his singing adds unique richness to the group's overall sound. Another way to stress the importance of each member's value and contributions is to let individual members know that the success or failure of the group sometimes hinges on his or her efforts.

Bill Walsh, celebrated former coach of the San Francisco 49ers and the Stanford University football team, tried to make each football player feel that he made an important contribution to team performance in order to motivate him to do his best and eliminate any potential for social loafing. As Coach Walsh put it, "You develop within the organization and the players an appreciation for the role each athlete plays on the team. You talk to each player and let each one know that, at some point, he will be in a position to win or lose a game. It may be one play in an entire career for a certain player or many plays each game for a Joe Montana. But the point is that everyone's job is essential. Everyone has a specific role and specific responsibilities. . . You talk to each player and indicate the importance of everyone's participation in the process—that it is important for everyone to express himself, to offer ideas, explanations, solutions, formulas."[29] Walsh's ability to make each member feel like his or her unique contributions are important to the team's success comes from his years of experience as a football coach. Still, they are important for managers of teams in small and large companies alike to have.

Another way to reduce social loafing is by reminding each employee why their individual talents led them to be chosen as a member of the group. In forming task forces, for example, managers typically select individuals with different kinds of expertise and experience to get the full range of perspectives a heterogeneous group provides (see Chapter 10). By reminding members that they were selected for the task force because of the unique contributions they can make, managers can drive home the message that members can (and are expected to) make an important and worthwhile contribution to the group.

Keeping the group as small as possible. The third way to reduce social loafing is to keep the group as small as possible.[30] Social loafing is more likely as groups get bigger because individuals perceive that their own efforts and performance levels are unidentifiable, unnecessary, or likely to be duplicated by others in the group. In Levi Strauss's factories, work groups were originally as large as 35 members. This resulted in the motivation and coordination problems discussed in the opening case. To prevent problems like these, managers should try to identify the optimal size of a group, given the tasks members are performing. If managers sense that process losses are increasing as a group gets larger, they should take steps to reduce the group's size.

One way to do this is to divide the work so that two smaller groups perform it. In the menswear department, for example, rather than have six different salespeople interacting to manage the whole department, two people could be given the responsibility to manage men's designer clothes like Polo and Tommy Hilfiger, and the other four could manage the lower-priced clothing section. Indeed, one reason why organizations consist of so many different groups is to eliminate the process losses that occur because of social loafing inherent in larger-sized groups. The following OB Today illustrates an example of this.

OB Today

How GlaxoSmithKline Used Groups to Boost Productivity

The need to develop new kinds of prescription drugs is a continual battle for pharmaceutical companies. In the last few years, many of these companies have been merging to try to increase their research productivity. In 2001, GlaxoSmithKline was created when Glaxo Wellcome and SmithKline Beechum merged.[31] Prior to the merger, both companies had seen steep declines in the number of new prescription drugs their scientists had been able to deliver. How could the newly formed company combine the talents of its scientists and researchers to quickly create exciting new drugs?

High-tech research and development teams whose members work closely together and depend on each other for decision-making input need to be kept small so their members can communicate easily.

GlaxoSmithKline's top managers realized that after the merger there would be enormous problems associated with coordinating the activities of the thousands of research scientists who were working on hundreds of different kinds of drug programs. Understanding the problems associated with large size, top managers decided to group researchers into eight smaller groups so they could focus on particular clusters of diseases such as heart disease or viral infections. Each of the groups was instructed to behave like a company in its own right, and they were told that they would be rewarded based upon the number of new prescription drugs they were able to invent, and the speed with which they could bring them to market.

To date, GlaxoSmithKlein's new group approach to research seems to have worked. The company claims that research productivity has more than doubled since it reorganized its scientists into teams: The number of new drugs moving into clinical trials doubled from 10 to 20, and the company has over 130 new drugs currently being tested. Moreover, the company claims that the morale of its researchers has increased, and turnover is down because the disease-focused groups enjoy working and collaborating together. The company expects to have the best new-drug "pipeline" in its industry in the next three to four years.[32]

How the Nature of Tasks Affects Group Performance

Process losses, particularly those that result from social loafing, are most prevalent when group members feel their individual contributions are not identifiable or important. In some groups, however, process losses occur because of the types of tasks that members perform. Process losses are especially likely to occur when the nature of the task itself makes it difficult to identify individual performance levels and reward employees on that basis.

To determine how to assign outcomes to the individual members in the group, the kinds of tasks it performs must be taken into account. James D. Thompson's model of group tasks helps managers identify (1) task characteristics that can lead to process losses and (2) the most effective ways to distribute outcomes or rewards to group members to generate high motivation. Thompson's model is based on the concept of **task interdependence**—the extent to which the work performed by one member affects what other group members do.[33] As task interdependence within a group increases, the degree and intensity of the interactions among group members who are required to perform the tasks also increase.[34] Thompson identifies three types of task interdependence: pooled, sequential, and reciprocal.[35]

TASK INTERDEPENDENCE
The extent to which the work performed by one member of a group affects what other members do.

Pooled Interdependence

If a group task involves **pooled task interdependence**, each member of the group makes a separate and independent contribution to group performance. Because each member's contribution is separate, it can be readily identified and evaluated. On group tasks that involve pooled interdependence, group performance is determined by summing up the contributions or performances of the individual members.[36] Pooled interdependence is depicted in Exhibit 11.2A. Members A, B, and C make independent contributions to group performance, and their contributions are added together to measure the group's performance.

POOLED TASK INTERDEPENDENCE
The task interdependence that results when each member of a group makes a separate and independent contribution to group performance.

Examples of tasks with pooled interdependence include the work performed by the members of a typing pool, by the waiters and waitresses in a restaurant, by a group of physicians in a health maintenance organization, and by a group of sales representatives for a book publisher. In each of these examples, group performance is the result of adding up the performances of individual group members: the amount of correspondence typed, the number of customers served, the number of patients treated, or the number of books sold.

One common source of process losses on tasks with pooled interdependence is duplication of effort, such as when two waiters inadvertently take orders from the same table or two typists mistakenly type the same report. This coordination problem can usually be solved by carefully and clearly assigning tasks to group members.

Motivation problems can easily be avoided on tasks with pooled interdependence by evaluating the performance levels of the individuals in the group and rewarding them on that basis. Distributing rewards based on individual performance is likely to result in high levels of motivation, as theories of learning and motivation suggest. In fact,

EXHIBIT 11.2

Three Types of Task Interdependence

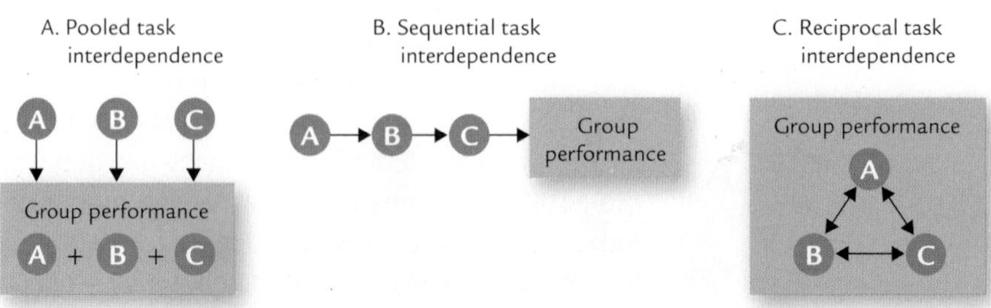

because pooled interdependence allows each member's contribution to be gauged and rewarded, the potential for process losses due to a lack of motivation is relatively low. When Levi's used a piece-rate system to reward employees, it was using pooled task interdependence.

Sequential Interdependence

SEQUENTIAL TASK INTERDEPENDENCE
The task interdependence that results when group members must perform specific behaviors in a predetermined order.

A group task based on **sequential task interdependence** requires specific behaviors to be performed by the group's members in a predetermined order. The level of each member's performance therefore affects the performance of other members down the line. The output of one employee depends upon another employee, in other words. In Exhibit 11.2B, for example, the performance of member A affects the ability of member B to perform her task; in turn, the activities of member B affect the ability of member C to perform his task. Examples of sequential interdependence include all types of assembly-line work—from the production of cars, to televisions, or Subway sandwiches—where the finished product is the result of the sequential inputs of group members. One company that failed to anticipate the problems the move from using pooled to sequential task interdependence would cause is Levi-Strauss. In the 1990s, Levi-Strauss's competitors outsourced their manufacturing activities to low-cost Asian companies; Levi Strauss, being more committed to its employees, decided it would instead try to increase the productivity of its U. S. factory employees by moving to use work groups. The company abandoned its piece-rate plan whereby each employee worked separately on a specific task and was paid according to how many tasks, or pieces, he or she completed. Instead, employees were assigned to work groups of up to 35 people who were now jointly responsible for all the jean-making tasks such as sewing on pockets, zippers, and belt loops. They were paid according to the number of pairs of jeans the whole team made.

But after the new team system was implemented, productivity plunged. In part, this was because employees weren't used to the new issues and problems the groups created. Levi's most skilled employees, for example, found that they could only work as fast as the slowest members of their teams and that their paychecks were falling. On the other hand, the paychecks of less-skilled employees were increasing because they were benefitting by being teamed up with the faster, more highly skilled workers. Soon, the fastest employees began to feel that some team members were not pulling their weight, in-fighting between team members increased, and employee morale fell.[37]

To improve the situation Levi's began to group employees according to their skill levels, and they reduced the size of the teams so employees had more control over each other. Supervisors also gave more training to slower employees and helped group members develop new team skills to improve their group performance. Even after it made these changes, however, Levi's found that team production had not increased productivity; in fact, productivity was just 93 percent of what it was when employees worked separately. With its attempts to increase productivity failing, Levi's was forced to close down more of its U. S. manufacturing plants.[38] Its final plant was closed in 2004.[39] When Levi's decided to group its employees into teams, it switched from using pooled to sequential task interdependence.

As Levi's found out, sequential interdependence makes identifying the individual performances of group members difficult because each member contributes to the same final product. (In contrast, when task interdependence is *pooled*, each member contributes his or her own final product, and group performance depends on the sum of these contributions.) Identification of individual performance is also difficult because an error made by a group member at the beginning of a work sequence can affect how well members later in the sequence perform their tasks. If an employee on a car assembly line fails to align the axle correctly, for example, employees farther down the line will have a hard time aligning the wheels and making the brakes work properly. Similarly, if one employee sews the waist of the jeans improperly, a second will have difficulty attaching belt loops.

When the activities of group members are sequentially interdependent, the performance level of the least capable or poorest-performing member of the group determines group performance. In a plant that produces televisions on an assembly line, for example, televisions move along the line at a set speed, and employees stationed along the line complete their required tasks on each television that passes by. The assembly line can move only at the speed of the slowest employee along the line; thus, the number of televisions produced by the group of assembly-line employees is limited by the performance capabilities of the group's poorest performer.

For these reasons, the potential for process losses is higher with sequential interdependence than with pooled interdependence. Motivation and social-loafing problems are also encountered more often because all of the group's members work on the same product, and so it's hard to discern what individual performance levels are. This was the problem Levi's encountered; its most skilled workers could only work as fast as its less-skilled workers.

How can organizations try to overcome the motivation and social-loafing problems associated with sequential interdependence? One way is by closely monitoring the on-the-job behaviors of group members. Assembly lines, for example, usually employ a relatively large number of supervisors to do this. A second way to counteract the negative effects of sequential task interdependence is to form work groups consisting of individuals with similar levels of ability—as Levi Strauss subsequently did. When that is done, the talents and motivation of high performers will not be hampered by the presence of a low performer in the group.

In some situations, a third way to overcome motivation problems in sequentially interdependent groups is to reward group members on the basis of the group level of performance. Since social loafing by one member impairs group performance and reduces the rewards received by all members of the group, this leads members to monitor and control each others' behaviors. The most skilled employees are also more likely to help the less skilled learn how to perform at a high level, too, so that over time the group's performance as a whole increases. Since rewards based on group performance can lead to hostility among team members, however, supervisors must be willing to help train the team's members, and the most skilled workers should be guaranteed their old rates of pay until the group's performance is brought up to speed. Japanese companies have long recognized how to take advantage of sequential interdependence to continuously improve group performance over time—a process called *Kaizen* that we discuss in Chapter 18.

Process losses arising from coordination problems also occur when tasks are sequentially interdependent. If an employee at the start of an assembly line comes to work late or needs to stop working during the day, for example, the whole line must be shut down until a replacement can be found. How can managers try to overcome coordination difficulties? They can reward employees for good attendance and punctuality, and they can have a pool of multiskilled employees on hand who can step in at different points in production for those who are absent.

Thousand of companies now organize their employees into groups and teams to make and sell their goods and services because teamwork can significantly improve employee productivity and efficiency. Whether or not a company succeeds in creating high-performing teams depends crucially on the way managers and supervisors structure and control team members' behaviors.

The experience of Hickory Springs Manufacturing Co., based in Hickory, North Carolina, illustrates many of the issues associated with creating effective groups and teams. Hickory Springs is a leading supplier of mattress components, such as bedsprings, foam pads, wire, and fabrics, to mattress makers.[40] Competition between suppliers for mattress makers' business is fierce, and suppliers have been unable to raise their prices for several years for fear of losing business. As a consequence, Hickory Springs was forced to take a close look at the way it makes its products. Edward Weintraub, its owner, has searched for ways to reduce costs and increase productivity in its factories and one of his major innovations was to change how its employees worked together.

Making a bed frame involves taking angle iron, cutting it to size, punching holes, inserting rivets, painting the bed frame, and then putting the frame and casters into a cardboard box for shipping. Hickory Springs employees used to work separately and in sequence to perform the different activities necessary to make and pack each bed frame. Often, bottlenecks arose during production because employees at one stage of the process could perform their jobs faster than those at other stages. To encourage employees to help each other out when this occurred, Weintraub decided to organize them into work groups.

Employees were grouped into teams that are responsible for all the activities necessary to make and pack bed frames. In the new group-work system, in addition to the $12 an hour each employee receives for performing his or her own specific task, he or she also receives a $3 or 25 percent bonus if the group as a whole hits its assigned production target. To obtain the bonus employees must not only achieve the performance target associated with their own jobs, they must also cooperate and help other employees who are falling behind for whatever reason. So, for example, if riveters or packers are falling behind, those employees responsible for punching holes quickly move to help their team members out to achieve the group bonus.

Team members have learned to think for themselves in the new group system and self-manage their teams to control their own activities. This change has freed up supervisors to think about new ways to increase productivity, like improving the design of the machines used to make the frames and finding better ways to physically organize the production process to save time and effort.[41] Hickory Springs's use of self-managed teams has resulted in substantial and continuing gains in productivity, thereby enabling the company to prosper despite its inability to increase prices.

Reciprocal Interdependence

RECIPROCAL TASK INTERDEPENDENCE
The task interdependence that results when the activities of all work-group members are fully dependent on one another.

Group tasks are characterized by **reciprocal task interdependence** when the activities of all work-group members are fully dependent on one another so that each member's performance influences the performance of every other member of the group. Figure 11.2C shows that not only do member A's actions affect B's, and member B's actions affect C's (as would be the case with sequential interdependence), but member C's actions also affect A's and B's, member A's actions affect C's, and member B's actions affect A's. Examples of work groups whose tasks are reciprocally interdependent include high-tech research and development teams, top management teams, emergency room personnel, and an operating room team in a hospital. In all these cases, team members work very closely together, communicate frequently, and each member of the team depends on the others for decision-making input.

The potential for process losses is highest when tasks are reciprocally interdependent because motivation and coordination problems can be particularly troublesome. Motivation problems like social loafing ensue because it is difficult, if not impossible, to identify an individual's level of performance when the final product is the result of the complex interplay of the contributions made by everyone.

How can managers try to minimize process losses when a group's activities are reciprocally interdependent? They should keep groups relatively small, emphasize that each member can make an important and distinct contribution to the group, and encourage members to feel personally responsible for meeting the group's goals.[42] To reduce the tendency for social loafing, managers should reward the members for the group's performance and encourage them to continuously improve their own performances over time by offering them increased pay and incentives for doing so.

An example of a group characterized by reciprocal interdependence is the top management team of a small company that manufactures toys. On the team are the vice presidents in charge of marketing and sales, production, research and development, and

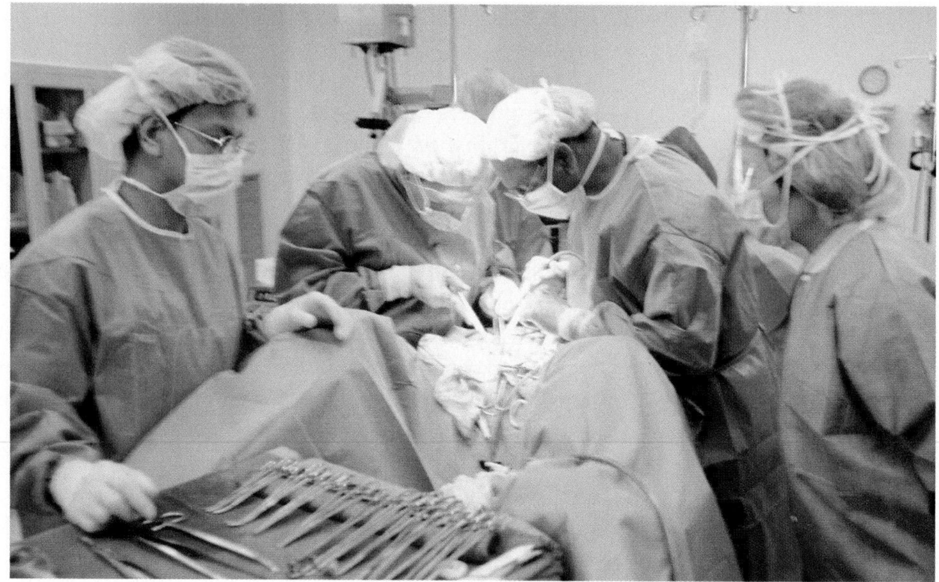

The members of a surgical team need to be reciprocally interdependent to make it possible for them to engage in the intense interactions necessary to keep patient operations as short as possible and error free.

finance. Leading the team is the president of the company. How well the company as a whole does depends on the complex interplay between those various functions, but at any point in time it is difficult to evaluate the performance of any one of the top managers. Under these circumstances, there is a high potential for social loafing, but it does not often occur because (1) the group is relatively small, (2) each vice president thinks that his or her contributions are indispensable to the success of the company because each is an expert in a particular function, and (3) group members' salaries depend on how well the firm does.

Work groups performing tasks characterized by reciprocal interdependence experience considerable coordination problems because of the inherent unpredictability of group relations and interactions. There is no set ordering of the group's activities when its tasks are organized reciprocally, unlike when its tasks are organized in a sequential fashion. The top management team previously described experiences coordination problems on a day-to-day basis. When sales of a new dinosaur board game greatly exceeded expectations, for example, the managers in charge of marketing, production, and finance had to work out a plan to increase production runs for the game while keeping costs down and not interfering with the production of other products. But the production manager was on a month-long trip to Taiwan, China, and Singapore to evaluate the feasibility of moving some of the firm's manufacturing facilities overseas, so the group had difficulties coming up with a viable plan, and sales were lost.

How can managers alleviate coordination problems when it comes to complex tasks? Again, one way is to keep group sizes relatively small to limit the number of individuals who must coordinate their efforts. Another way is to locate group members close to one another so that whenever one member needs input from another, the input is readily available. With the electronic forms of communication available today, team members in different locations can now keep in constant communication with one another. If the production manager scouting out factory sites in East Asia had been electronically in touch with other members of the group, for example, the manufacturing problem at the plant might have been averted. Finally, coordination difficulties can be reduced if groups develop norms encouraging members to help one other when needed.

As task interdependence moves from pooled to sequential to reciprocal interdependence, the potential for *process losses* increases because identifying individual performances becomes increasingly harder and because coordination becomes more difficult. The potential for *process gains* also increases as task interdependence becomes more complex. As the level

You're the Management Expert

What Kinds of Groups and Tasks?

You have just completed your degree in computer science. You have decided to refurbish and upgrade used PCs and then rent them to college students for a low monthly fee. As a part of this service you will also repair them as the need arises.

To get your business off the ground, you'll need to hire about 20 college students on a part-time basis to buy used PCs, bring them to the workshop for servicing, deliver them to customers, and make on-site repairs as necessary. You know that your ability to provide good customer service is vital in the rental business and your problem is how to group employees to get the best out of them—to get them to increase and realize their performance potential.

Using the previous material in the chapter, and given the tasks that your business requires, what kind of task interdependence do you think is most appropriate for your business? Also, do you think you should organize employees into just one large group, or would you divide them into several smaller groups? If so, how many? What kinds of motivation and coordination problems are you trying to prevent with your decisions?

SYNERGY
A process gain that occurs when members of a group acting together are able to produce more or better output than would have been produced by the combined efforts of each person acting alone.

and intensity of group members' interactions increase and the expertise and skills of group members are brought to bear on the group's tasks, the potential for synergy increases. **Synergy** (a type of process gain) occurs when members of a group acting together are able to produce more or better output than would have been produced by the combined efforts of each person acting alone.

For example, the top management team of the toy company recently developed a new line of compact travel toys that were an instant success with children and very profitable for the company. The managers in charge of marketing, production, research and development, and finance worked closely throughout the development and launch of the new line. As a result, their reciprocally interdependent interactions enabled them to come up with a winner in record time. If each of the managers had worked independently, the new line would never have been developed successfully or launched so quickly. Employees at Hickory Springs in the previous OB Today were able to achieve much more by working as a team than they did when each employee worked alone.

In sum, the potential for process gains often increases as the level of task interdependence increases, but so too does the potential for process losses. Thus, the actual performance gains an organization achieves depend on its managers' abilities to choose the form of task interdependence that best matches the products being produced and then create a work setting minimizing motivation and coordination problems related to them.

Group Cohesiveness and Performance

GROUP COHESIVENESS
The attractiveness of a group to its members.

Regardless of the kinds of tasks performed, work groups also differ in another important respect—how *attractive* they are to their members. When groups are very attractive to their members, the individuals within them value their membership and strongly want to remain in them. The attractiveness of a group to its members is called **group cohesiveness**.[43] Groups high in cohesiveness are very appealing to their members; those low in cohesiveness are not appealing to their members and may even repulse them to the point where they try to leave the team. An important property of work groups, group cohesiveness affects group performance and effectiveness.

Factors that Contribute to Group Cohesiveness

A variety of factors influence a group's level of cohesiveness.[44] Here, we examine five: group size, similarity of group members, competition between groups, success, and the exclusiveness of the group (see Exhibit 11.3).

Group size. As you learned in Chapter 10, as groups get bigger, their members tend to be less satisfied. For this reason, large groups do not tend to be cohesive. In large groups, a few members of the group tend to dominate group discussions, and the opportunities for participation by other group members are limited. Large groups have the greatest potential for conflict, and members find it difficult to form close ties with one other. A small or medium group size (between 3 and 15 people), on the other hand, tends to promote cohesiveness.

Similarity/diversity of group members. People generally like, get along with, and most easily communicate with others who are similar to themselves. Moreover, people tend to perceive others who are similar to themselves more positively than they perceive those who are different (due to the similar-to-me bias discussed in Chapter 4). Groups tend to be most cohesive when group members are homogeneous or share certain attitudes, values, experiences, and so on. For example, a task force composed of individuals (such as engineers) with the same educational background and work experiences will tend to be more cohesive than a task force whose members (an engineer, an accountant, a financial analyst, and a biochemist) have dissimilar backgrounds. One caveat, however, needs to be made about the similarity or homogeneity of group members. As you saw in Chapter 10, diversity (or heterogeneity) can be beneficial because it offers the group varied resources and perspectives (a wider range of skills, abilities, experiences, and so forth) upon which to draw.[45] If the diversity of the group's members helps it achieve its goals, then *diversity,* rather than similarity, is likely to facilitate group cohesiveness.[46]

Competition between groups. Competition between groups in an organization increases group cohesiveness when it motivates members of each group to band together to achieve its goals.[47] For this reason, organizations often promote group cohesiveness by having work groups compete against each other.[48] Groups of salespersons compete to see which can sell the most each month, groups of production employees compete to see which can maintain the highest quality standards, and groups of maintenance employees compete to achieve the best attendance record. Healthy competition is also encouraged by naming groups and recognizing

EXHIBIT 11.3

Determinants of Group Cohesiveness

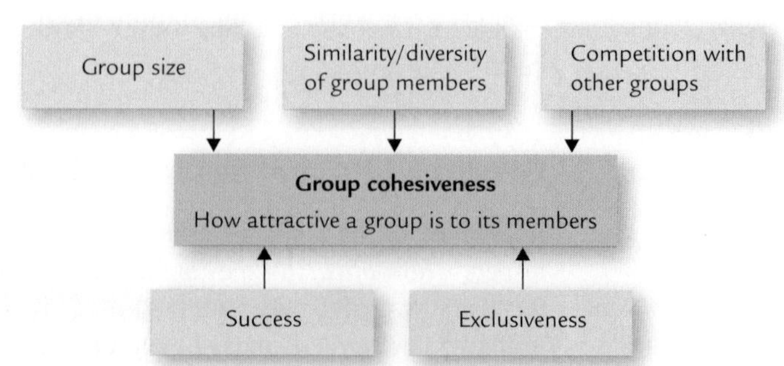

Globalization has increased the need for and use of virtual teams linked together by fax, phone, e-mail, and videoconferencing. Technologies allowing instant communication and the growing complexity of multinational organizations are likely to lead to more virtual teams in the future.

the ones doing especially well. Sometimes, groups compete not so much with groups inside their organization, but with groups from other organizations.

Although a certain level of competition across groups can help each group be cohesive, too much competition can be dysfunctional and impair effectiveness. When competition is too intense, groups sometimes try to sabotage each other. They become more concerned with "winning the battle" than achieving the organization's goals, in other words. If an organization is to achieve its goals, the different groups within it must be willing and able to work together and cooperate, even when they are competing with one another.[49]

Success. "Nothing breeds success like success," according to an old adage. When groups are successful, they become especially attractive to their members and others, and the cohesiveness of the groups increases.

Exclusiveness. A group's exclusiveness is indicated by how difficult it is to become a member of the group, the extent to which outsiders look up to the group's members, the group's status within the organization (see Chapter 10), and the special rights and privileges accorded its members. When group members must undergo a very tough initiation process or are required to undertake extensive training to join the group, being a member becomes more highly prized.[50] For example, individuals who want to become firefighters must meet stringent physical criteria and engage in extensive training exercises. Groups of firefighters tend to be highly cohesive, in part because of how difficult it is to become a member of the group. Fraternities, sororities, football teams, and cheerleading squads at universities also tend to be high on cohesiveness. It is often difficult to become a member of these groups. These groups tend to have high status as a result, and outsiders look up to the members, who often have special rights and privileges.

Consequences of Group Cohesiveness

Is cohesiveness a group property that managers should encourage? Is there such a thing as too much cohesiveness? As we saw when discussing group norms in Chapter 10, the consequences of group cohesiveness for an organization depend on the extent to which group goals are aligned with organizational goals. Recall from the restaurant example in Chapter 10 how the goals of the group of waiters and waitresses (providing good service and getting good tips) were aligned with the restaurant's goal of having satisfied customers. In examining the consequences of group cohesiveness, we first focus on the case in which group and organizational goals are aligned, and then we look at the case in which they are not.

Consequences when group goals are aligned with organizational goals. The first major consequence of group cohesiveness when group and organizational goals are aligned is *the level of participation and communication within the group*.[51] As cohesiveness increases, members become more active participants in the group, and the level of communication within it increases. This outcome can be beneficial for the organization. Members will be more likely to perform behaviors necessary for the group and organization to achieve its goals, and information will be readily shared among members. (As we discuss in Chapter 15, an exception to this consequence occurs in cohesive decision-making groups that fall victim to groupthink.)

The group of waiters and waitresses, for example, was moderately cohesive. As a result, its members performed a variety of behaviors to ensure that customers received good service. They kept the salt and pepper shakers and sugar bowls on the tables filled, helped each other with especially large tables, and kept the restaurant clean and tidy. Moreover, information flowed through the group very quickly. When the group changed its norm of always referring complaints to the manager, for instance, the change was communicated to all group members on the very same day that it was discussed with the manager.

Although good communication within groups is important, too much communication can be dysfunctional if members waste a lot of time talking to each other, especially about nonwork matters such as the Monday night football game or last night's episode of "CSI." Thus, a moderate amount of group cohesiveness is functional for the group and the organization when it encourages members to participate in the group and share information. Too much cohesiveness, however, can be dysfunctional if members waste time chitchatting.

The second major consequence of cohesiveness when group and organizational goals are aligned is *the level of conformity to group norms*.[52] As group cohesiveness increases, conformity to the group's norms tends to increase as well. Increased conformity can be functional for groups and the organization because it enables the groups to control and direct their members' behaviors toward achieving those goals. Too much conformity, however, can be dysfunctional if a group eliminates all deviance. As we discussed in Chapter 10, deviance can benefit a group by helping it recognize and discard dysfunctional norms, but excessive conformity can make a group resistant to change.

A moderate amount of cohesiveness gives groups the level of conformity they need to achieve their goals but still allows for some deviance. Too much cohesiveness can stifle opportunities for change and growth. There was enough conformity within the restaurant group that it was able to control its members' behavior, but there wasn't so much that members were afraid to deviate from a dysfunctional norm (like referring all food complaints to the manager, when they were able to handle some of the complaints themselves).

The third major consequence of cohesiveness when group and organizational goals are aligned is *group goal accomplishment*.[53] Cohesive groups tend to be very effective at achieving their goals. Group members who value their memberships are motivated to help the group achieve its goals. Such members generally work well together, help each other when needed, and perform the behaviors necessary for the group to be effective. This consequence certainly seems to be effective for the organization, and for the most part it is. If groups become too cohesive, however, the members may be so driven toward group goal accomplishment that they lose sight of the fact that the group is part of a larger organization. When this happens one group may fail to cooperate with another because the members are solely loyal to their own groups. Once again, a moderate amount of group cohesiveness is functional for groups and organizations because it facilitates goal accomplishment. Too much cohesiveness is dysfunctional because it can lead members to fail to cooperate with people outside the group.

By now it should be clear that a certain level of cohesiveness contributes to group effectiveness. When that level is insufficient (1) group members are not motivated to participate in the group, (2) do not effectively communicate with each other, (3) the group has difficulty influencing its members' behaviors, and (4) the group often fails to achieve its goals. When that level is excessive—when groups are *too* cohesive—(1) time is wasted by members socializing on the job, (2) conformity is stressed at the expense of needed change, and (3) group goal accomplishment becomes more important than cooperation with other groups to achieve the organization's goals.

A *moderate* amount of group cohesiveness results in the most favorable group and organizational outcome. A moderately cohesive group has (1) the appropriate level of communication and participation between members, (2) the ability to influence members' behaviors to ensure conformity while still allowing for some deviation, and (3) the capacity to stress the importance of the group's accomplishments but not at the expense of other groups and the organization. Indicators or signs of the level of cohesiveness in a work group are as follows:

- *Signs that a group has a moderate level of cohesiveness.* Members work well together, there is a good level of communication and participation in the group, the group is able to influence its members' behaviors, and it tends to achieve its goals.
- *Signs that a group has a low level of cohesiveness.* Information flows slowly within the group, the group has little influence over its members' behaviors, and it tends not to achieve its goals.
- *Signs that a group has a very high level of cohesiveness.* Group members socialize excessively on the job, there is a very high level of conformity in the group and intolerance of deviance, and the group achieves its goals at the expense of other groups or the organization as a whole.

Exhibit 11.4 summarizes some of the advantages and potential disadvantages of a *high level* of cohesiveness when group goals are aligned with organizational goals. The way in which Nokia has achieved this balancing act is profiled in the following Global View.

EXHIBIT 11.4

Consequences of High Cohesiveness When Group Goals Are Aligned with Organizational Goals

Consequences of High Cohesiveness	Advantages	Potential Disadvantages
A high level of participation and communication within the group	Group members are more likely to perform behaviors necessary for the group and organization to achieve their goals, information flows quickly in the group, and turnover may be relatively low.	Group members may waste time socializing on the job and chatting about nonwork matters.
A high level of conformity to group norms	The group is able to control its members' behavior to achieve group goals.	Excessive conformity within the group may result in resistance to change and failure to discard dysfunctional norms.
Group goal accomplishment	The group achieves its goals and is effective.	Group members may not cooperate with other groups as much as they should.

A Global View

Teams, Teams, and More Teams at Nokia

Nokia Corporation, headquartered in Espoo, Finland, employs 60,000 people around the world and is the market leader in the global wireless communications industry.[54] Nokia has research and development (R&D) units in 14 countries, to which it dedicates one-third of its workforce.[55] The company's success and competitive advantage is the result of its use of teams throughout the organization. In fact, it has been said that any task or project that is of any significance in the company is assigned to a team. This commitment to teams starts at the top of the organization, where managers work together as a team to make all of Nokia's important business decisions.[56] The number of teams cascades on down through the organization, with almost all its employees mirroring the model set by the company's top managers.

Why does Nokia get good results from its teams? Teams are given high levels of autonomy and encouraged to be creative. High emphasis is placed on letting those people who are most knowledgeable about a problem or opportunity make decisions concerning it regardless of their position in the hierarchy (which by nature is very flat at Nokia).[57] Teams and their members take personal responsibility for decisions and believe that their efforts and contributions are important for Nokia's continued success. Good communication, mutual respect, and a high regard for the members of one's team are its central values and norms. Annual meetings, referred to as the Nokia Way, also help keep teams on track as well provide a vehicle for teams throughout the organizations to help actualize Nokia's vision for the future.[58] Through these means, Nokia ensures that team goals are aligned with organizational goals and that its cohesive groups work to benefit the organization as a whole.

Consequences when group goals are not aligned with organizational goals. Our conclusions about the consequences of cohesiveness apply only when the group's goals are aligned with the organization's goals. What are the consequences when group goals are *not* aligned with the organizational goals?

When group goals are not aligned with organizational goals (recall from Chapter 10 the radio assemblers whose goal was to minimize effort expenditure), the consequences for the organization are almost always negative. In this case, group cohesiveness is dysfunctional for the organization because it helps the group achieve its goals at the expense of organizational goals.

Like the group of restaurant employees, the group of radio assemblers was moderately cohesive. However, the radio assemblers' group goal to minimize the expenditure of effort was inconsistent with the organization's performance goal. Consequently, the moderate level of cohesiveness within the group was dysfunctional for the organization. There was a high level of communication within the group, but it usually revolved around nonwork concerns like football and baseball scores. There also was a sufficient amount of conformity to group norms, which resulted in members restricting their output so that the group never produced more than 50 radios a day, even though it could have produced 75. Finally, the group was very effective at achieving its goal of producing no more than 50 radios.

Exhibit 11.5 summarizes the consequences of a *high level* of cohesiveness when group goals are not aligned with organizational goals.

EXHIBIT 11.5

Disadvantages of High Cohesiveness When Group Goals Are Not Aligned With Organizational Goals

Consequences of High Cohesiveness	Disadvantages
A high level of participation and communication within the group	Group members waste time socializing on the job and chatting about nonwork matters.
A high level of conformity to group norms	Group members behave in ways that are dysfunctional for the organization.
Group goal accomplishment	The group achieves its goals at the expense of organizational goals.

Important Organizational Groups

Now that you understand some of the problems and challenges that groups face in organizations and the factors that influence work-group effectiveness, we turn to a discussion of four types of work groups: top management teams, self-managed work teams, research and development teams, and virtual teams. Although we could discuss other important types of groups in organizations (such as whole departments, assembly-line groups, or task forces), we concentrate on these four because they have the potential to dramatically affect an organization's performance.

The Top Management Team

TOP MANAGEMENT TEAM
The team of managers who report to the chief executive officer (CEO) and determine what an organization is trying to accomplish and develop plans for goal attainment.

An organization's **top management team** is the team of managers who report to the chief executive officer (CEO). Top management teams (chosen by an organization's CEO and its board of directors) profoundly affect organizational performance because they decide which overall goals should be pursued, and they establish the plan of action or means to achieve these goals. Because the complex nature of top management activities requires intensive interaction among team members, top management teams are characterized by reciprocal task interdependence.

What steps can a CEO take to reduce process losses associated with reciprocal task interdependence? First, team size should be kept relatively small (most top management teams average between five and seven members). Second, members of the team need to be assured that their individual input to the group is important for the team's and the organization's success. Third, group members need to be persuaded to be honest and open in their communication with one another. Finally, a CEO should make sure that members are readily available and accessible whenever other group members need their input and expertise.

The quality of decision making in the top management team is a function of the personal characteristics and backgrounds of team members.[59] It has been found, for example, that the best decisions are made by top management teams that are diverse or heterogeneous, consisting of managers from different functions (such as marketing, finance, and production). Diversity in team membership ensures that the team will have the adequate complement of skills, knowledge, expertise, and experience to guide the activities of the organization as a whole. Also, when managers bring different points-of-view and information to the table, an organization can avoid the dangerous problem of *groupthink*, a pattern of faulty decision making that occurs when like-minded people reinforce one another's tendencies to interpret events and information in similar ways (see Chapter 15).[60] Finally, the top management team affects its company's performance by the way the team uses human resource practices such as performance appraisal and rewards to encourage performance.[61]

Self-Managed Work Teams

In a self-managed work team, team members have the autonomy to lead and manage themselves and determine how the team will perform its tasks (see Chapter 10). Self-managed teams can be found at all levels in an organization.

Some organizations use self-managed work teams, rather than more traditional types of groups or individuals working separately. The idea is to enhance job satisfaction and motivate members to perform at higher levels.[62] In a self-managed work team, separate tasks normally performed by individual employees and managed by a supervisor fall under the responsibility of a group of employees empowered to ensure they get done and get done well.[63]

As an example of how a self-managed work team operates, consider the following situation. Requests for credit from AT&T Credit Corporation used to be processed by individuals. Extending or denying credit to customers involved a number of steps: reviewing the application, verifying the customer's credit rating, notifying the customer of whether his or her request for credit had been accepted or rejected, preparing a written contract, and collecting payments from the customer. Individuals were assigned to one of these steps. Some employees focused exclusively on reviewing applications, others on checking credit ratings, others on collecting payments, and so on. As a result, with this grouping of tasks, employees had little sense of how their individual jobs contributed to AT&T's organizational goal of first-class customer service. To remedy this situation, AT&T decided to combine these individual tasks and give teams of employees the responsibility for all activities, ranging from the initial review of an application to collecting payments from approved customers. The switch to the use of self-managed work teams resulted in customers' being notified of the acceptance or rejection of their applications several days sooner than under the old system and the daily processing of twice as many applications.[64]

The job characteristics model of job design (see Chapter 7) provides a good framework for understanding why the use of self-managed work teams can lead to higher levels of motivation, performance, and satisfaction. Recall that this model suggests that jobs will be motivating and result in high levels of performance and satisfaction when they are high in skill variety, task identity, task significance, autonomy, and feedback.[65] Often, it is difficult to design individual jobs that are high on each of these dimensions. The job of reviewing applications at AT&T Credit Corporation, for example, required a limited number of skills, was low on task identity because the employee often did not know whether the

Self-managed work team members have the autonomy to lead and manage themselves and determine how they will jointly perform the tasks necessary for the team to achieve its goals. Here a team of Toyota workers work to assemble a car body.

application was eventually accepted or rejected, low on task significance because the employee did not have a sense of how the job affected the customer, and low on autonomy. Combining the tasks of this job with the tasks of other jobs involved in the process, and then giving a group of employees responsibility for performing all of these tasks, heightens the job characteristic levels for *each group member*. Skill variety increases because members use a full array of skills to perform all of the various activities. Task identity and task significance are heightened because the groups perform all the activities necessary to provide credit to customers and have a real sense of how their activities impact customer satisfaction.

A number of conditions must be present for self-managed work teams to be effective.[66]

1. The group must be truly self-managing. The group itself must have the autonomy and authority to do many of the things traditionally reserved for managers, like setting the group's goals, determining how the group should go about reaching them, and assigning individual tasks to members. Some managers are reluctant to give up these responsibilities. One of the advantages of using self-managed teams is that the number of middle managers needed in an organization may decrease.
2. Self-managed work teams appear to be most effective when the work performed by group members is sufficiently complex and results in some sort of finished end product. By "complex," we mean that a number of different steps and procedures must be performed to accomplish the group's goals. By "finished end product," we mean some identifiable group output such as extending or rejecting credit to customers and collecting payments.
3. Managers in the organization must support and be committed to utilizing self-managed work teams. Sometimes self-managed teams fail because managers are reluctant to relinquish their authority to the teams, or they don't support the teams by giving them the guidance and coaching they need. Managers need to be available to the groups in an advisory capacity and provide coaching when needed as well as help groups that veer off course to get back on track. When members of a self-managed work team have serious disagreements, for example, managers should be available to help team members settle their differences fairly.[67]
4. Members of successful self-managed work teams must be carefully selected to ensure that the team has the right complement of skills and expertise to get the job done.[68]
5. Team members need to be able to work with one another and want to be part of the team. Not all employees want to work closely with others on a team or want the responsibility that goes along with being a member of a self-managed team.[69]

Self-managed work teams have been used successfully by a number of organizations, such as General Mills, Federal Express, Chaparral Steel, 3M, Aetna Life & Casualty, and Johnsonville Foods.[70] However, more research is needed to understand why they have been successful as well as why they are sometimes not so successful. One study suggests that members of self-managed work teams may be somewhat reluctant to discipline each other (for example, withhold rewards or punish a member who is not performing acceptably).[71] This can result in some members performing at a lower level in self-managed teams. Other studies suggest that the success of a self-managed team depends on the extent to which its members value being part of the team and the status the group has within the organization.[72] In any case, additional research is needed to explain why some self-managed teams succeed and others fail.

RESEARCH AND DEVELOPMENT (R&D) TEAM
A team that is formed to develop new products, may be cross-functional, and is often used in high-tech industries.

Research and Development Teams

Organizations often use **research and development (R&D) teams** to develop new products, especially in high-tech industries such as electronics, pharmaceuticals, and computers.[73] Some R&D teams are cross-functional; team members represent each of the different

EXHIBIT 11.6

A Cross-Functional Research and Development Team

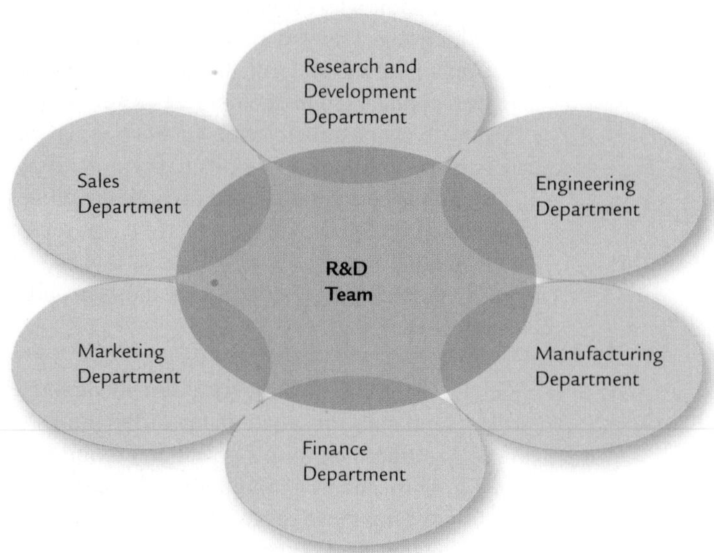

functions or departments necessary to develop and launch a new product. An R&D team trying to develop a sophisticated electronic notepad, for example, might include members from research and development, engineering, manufacturing, finance, marketing, and sales (see Exhibit 11.6). A team on which each of these capabilities is represented is in a good position to develop a successful new product.

SKUNK WORKS
An R&D team that is created to expedite new product design and promote innovation in an organization.

An R&D team that is created to expedite new product designs and promote innovation in an organization is known as a **skunk works**. The group consists of members of the engineering and research departments and other support functions like finance and marketing. Skunk works often meet and work in facilities that are separated from the rest of the organization. Having their own facilities gives group members the opportunity for the intensive interactions necessary for innovation (or other process gains) and ensures the group will not be interrupted or distracted by the day-to-day problems of the organization. Members of skunk works often become very possessive of the products they are developing and feel completely responsible for the success or failure of them.

Ford Motor Company established a skunk works to develop a new Mustang coupe and convertible. Interestingly enough, when Ford managers projected that developing the new Mustang would cost approximately $1 billion, top executives almost abandoned the project. However, the project was ultimately spared and turned over to a skunk works. When all was said and done, developing the new Mustang cost Ford only about $700 million and was accomplished in 25 percent less time than Ford usually takes to develop a new model. This helped Ford in its quest to regain its competitive advantage.

John Coletti, one of the champions of the Mustang and founders of the skunk works, along with other team members, realized that to develop the new Mustang in a timely fashion while at the same time lowering costs, the team would need the freedom to make its own decisions and not follow Ford's usual development process. Will Boddie, the engineer who led the team, recognized the need to have everyone working on the project in close proximity to one another but distanced from Ford itself so that they would not be encumbered by the company's prevailing procedures and norms. A furniture warehouse in Allen Park, Michigan, was converted to become the home of the skunk works, and team members—everyone from drafters to engineers and stylists to "bean counters"—moved into cramped offices to work on the Mustang.

A turning point in the team's development occurred when an unexpected problem arose during the testing of the prototype for the Mustang convertible. When chief engineer Michael Zevalkink test-drove the prototype, the car shimmied and shook.

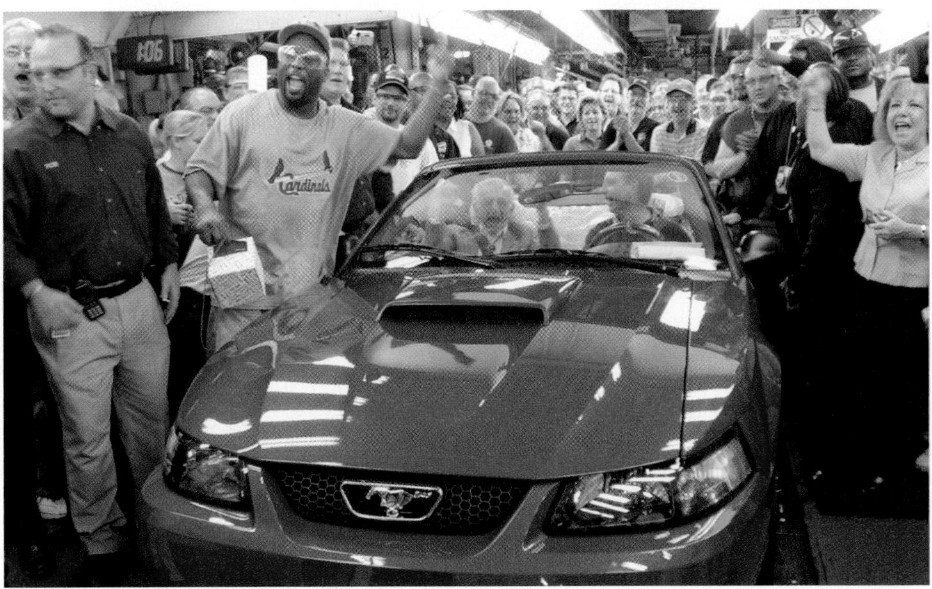

Ford created an "extreme" team to develop a new version of its classic Mustang coupe and convertible. Members of the group—also know as the "skunk works"—literally barricaded themselves in an empty furniture warehouse until they got the job done.

Engineers worked for a year to resolve the problem, but when Zevalkink test-drove the "corrected" model, the car still shook. Senior executives at Ford were aware of the problem but did not renege on their promise to preserve the independence and autonomy of the skunk works.

During an eight-week period, the convertible was furiously reengineered (the engineers working on it even slept on the floor of the warehouse at night), and the problem was solved by installing braces in the car and redesigning its mirrors. Will Boddie, however, wasn't satisfied with these changes. When he saw a new Mercedes convertible in a parking lot, he thought, "Why shouldn't the Mustang convertible have as smooth a ride as a Mercedes convertible?" He told the skunk works engineers to purchase a Mercedes convertible and take it apart to learn the key to its smooth ride. The consequence of this research was the attachment of a 25-pound cylinder behind the front fender of the Mustang (a similar attachment on the Mercedes contributes to its smooth ride).[74]

The skunk works was successful in developing the new Mustang in record time and at a lower-than-usual cost because the team members closest to the issues involved not only had the autonomy to make decisions and changes as circumstances warranted but also a high level of commitment to the team's goal of keeping the Mustang alive. The skunk works's autonomy and relative isolation enabled it to respond to problems and make needed changes quickly and efficiently.

A skunk works approach to R&D can be very successfully used to develop new and innovative products. Even when new-product development requires the involvement of many different people in an organization, skunk works can still be effective. The skunk works that developed the Mustang, for example, included about 400 people grouped into what were called "chunk teams," each of which worked on developing a particular aspect, or "chunk," of the car.[75]

Virtual Teams

VIRTUAL TEAM
A team in which a significant amount of communication and interaction occurs electronically rather than face to face.

Virtual teams are teams in which a significant amount of communication and interaction among members occurs electronically, using computer hardware and software.[76] Organizations use virtual teams to help people in different places and/or time zones work together.[77]

Members of virtual teams use a variety of new information technologies to share information, interact with one another, and achieve their goals. More specifically, there are two types of information technologies that virtual teams rely on. Synchronous technologies enable team members to communicate with each other in real time and simultaneously. These technologies include videoconferencing, teleconferencing, instant messaging, and electronic meetings.[78] When asynchronous technologies are used, communication among team members is delayed rather than instantaneous. For example, using e-mail, electronic bulletin boards, and websites often results in some communication delays.[79] Many virtual teams rely on both kinds of technologies, depending on the tasks they are performing. The kind of technologies teams use also hinges on levels of task interdependence in a virtual team. For example, teams whose members are reciprocally interdependent have greater need for synchronous technologies than teams characterized by pooled interdependence. For this reason the development of relationship-building, web-based software that allows for much more team interaction and contact is becoming increasingly important today, and many organizations are taking advantage of its power to facilitate group interaction (see the *New York Times* case at the end of the chapter).[80]

According to researcher Lee Sproull, who studies virtual teams, organizations will increase their reliance on virtual teams because of increasing levels of globalization. When team members live and work in different countries, virtual teams are often a necessity.[81] Virtual teams allow organizations to keep their members apprised of the knowledge, expertise, and experience they need to accomplish the task at hand, regardless of where they are located.

Virtual teams face all the challenges that members of ordinary teams face, such as curbing social loafing and maintaining a good balance between conformity and deviance. They also face the additional challenge of building trust and cohesiveness among people who rarely interact with one another in person.[82] To meet this additional

OB Today

The Challenges of Being a Virtual Team Member

Hewlett-Packard, the electronics and computer technology giant, prides itself on taking advantage of the latest development in information technology to support flexibility and diversity.[83] Thus, telecommuting, using new information technology to facilitate working from the home, and virtual teams are all realities at Hewlett-Packard. Take the case of Barbara Recchia, who is a member of a team in the company's human resources department. The other members of Recchia's team work at corporate headquarters in Palo Alto, California, while Recchia works from her home in Santa Rosa, California (which is north of San Francisco), and communicates with the team by phone and e-mail.[84]

Although Recchia likes her virtual arrangement, she also sometimes gets lonely and feels isolated from the other members of her team. She recalls when she first started working from her home, she used to come to the office in Palo Alto around once a month. She soon realized, however, that she was feeling very disconnected from her team and the organization as a whole. Now, she comes to headquarters about once a week, and she tries to attend important meetings on site. She also finds that it is important to sometimes meet face to face with her supervisor to get some sense of how her supervisor really feels about key issues and decisions.[85]

Equally important is making time to socialize with members of her team when she comes to Palo Alto. Getting together for lunch after a morning meeting helps to build a sense of camaraderie and enables Recchia to feel connected with her team and the company. These occasions also help satisfy her need for social interaction.[86]

challenge, some virtual teams make it a point to schedule group recreational activities like skiing trips so that their members can get to know, understand, and trust each other.[87] Many virtual teams also schedule periodic face-to-face meetings to supplement electronic forms of communication, which can be especially important for newly formed virtual teams.[88]

Research on virtual teams is at an early stage, but preliminary studies suggest that while some virtual teams can perform as well as teams whose members meet face to face, team members may be less satisfied with the experience, and cohesiveness may be lower in virtual teams.[89] Periodic face-to-face meetings and scheduled recreational and social activities can improve the cohesiveness of virtual teams.

In some virtual teams, some members are located in the same physical location and often interact in person, whereas other members of the same team work in a different location and interact with the rest of the team primarily through electronic forms of communication.[90] While this kind of arrangement has the benefits of increased flexibility, it also presents some special challenges as indicated in the following OB Today.

Summary

Group and organizational effectiveness hinges on minimizing process losses, achieving process gains, aligning group goals with organizational goals, and having the appropriate level of group cohesiveness. Four types of groups that are especially important in many organizations include the top management team, self-managed work teams, research and development teams, and virtual teams. In this chapter, we made the following major points:

1. Actual group performance often falls short of potential performance because of process losses due to coordination and motivation problems in groups. Process gains cause the potential performance of a group to rise, and they enhance group effectiveness.
2. Social loafing, a motivation problem that leads to process losses, is the tendency of individuals to exert less effort when they work in a group than when they work alone. Social loafing occurs for two reasons: (a) Individuals in a group think that they will not receive positive outcomes for performing at a high level or negative outcomes for substandard performance because individual levels of performance cannot easily be identified and evaluated; also, (b) Individuals think that their own efforts are unimportant or not really needed. Social loafing can be eliminated or reduced by making individual performance levels identifiable, making each individual feel that he or she can make an important and worthwhile contribution to the group, and by keeping group size down.
3. Group tasks can be characterized in terms of the nature of interdependence between group members. Thompson describes three types of task interdependence: pooled, sequential, and reciprocal. The nature and causes of process losses and process gains depend on the type of task involved and the degree of interdependence among group members.
4. Group cohesiveness is the attractiveness of a group to its members. Group size, the similarity/diversity of group members, competition with other groups, success, and the exclusiveness of the group help to determine the level of group cohesiveness. Consequences of group cohesiveness are the level of participation and communication within a group, the level of conformity to group norms, and group goal accomplishment. When group goals are aligned with organizational goals, there is an optimal level of group cohesiveness that results in high levels of performance. When group goals are not aligned with organizational goals, group cohesiveness is dysfunctional for an organization.
5. Four kinds of work groups that have the potential to affect organizational performance dramatically are top management teams, self-managed work teams, research and development teams, and virtual teams.

Organizational Behavior in Action

Questions for Review

1. Give an example of (a) a process gain in a research and development team and (b) a process loss in a research and development team.
2. Give an example of (a) a process gain in a self-managed work team and (b) a process loss in a self-managed work team.
3. Why do some individuals engage in social loafing while others do not?
4. Can managers change the type of task interdependence in a work group, or is task interdependence a relatively fixed characteristic? If managers can change it, how might they do so?
5. Why is it sometimes hard to manage groups that are reciprocally interdependent?
6. Is social loafing a problem in top management teams? Why or why not?
7. What kinds of employees would probably prefer to work in a virtual team rather than in a team that meets face to face?
8. How can excessive group cohesiveness result in low levels of performance?
9. How can too little group cohesiveness result in low levels of performance?
10. In what kinds of organizations might it be especially important for work groups to be cohesive?

OB: Increasing Self-Awareness

Group Effectiveness

Think of a group that you are currently a member of—a work group, a club, or any other group that you belong to and actively participate in. Briefly describe the group. Then answer each of these questions:

1. What process losses are experienced in this group? Why?
2. What process gains are experienced in this group? Why?
3. Does the actual performance of this group equal its potential performance? Why or why not?
4. How might this group raise its potential performance?
5. Is social loafing a problem in this group? Why or why not?
6. How would you characterize the major tasks performed by this group in terms of Thompson's model of task interdependence?
7. Is this a cohesive group? Why or why not?
8. Does cohesiveness help or hinder the group's performance?
9. Are group goals aligned with any larger organizational goals?

A Question of Ethics

Group Processes and Ethics

As the chapter notes, sometimes when groups or teams become too large the problem of social loafing arises as some employees withhold their own efforts and let other members of the team bear the work burden. If this happens, the members of a group are likely to come into conflict because they do not think this is fair, and that some people are putting their own self-interests above those of other group members. With this in mind think about the following issues:

- To what extent should the members of a group attempt to correct and change the behavior of a group member they feel is shirking?
- At what point is it appropriate to inform their supervisor about this behavior?
- At what point does conflict between group members become unethical?

Small Group Break-Out Exercise

When and How to Use Groups

After reading the following scenario, break up into groups of three or four people and discuss the issues involved. Be prepared to share your thinking with the rest of the class.

You are the managers who are in charge of the operations of a large building-products supply company. In the past you each were responsible for a different department and each of you were responsible for managing ten employees who worked separately to stock the shelves, answer customer questions, and check out customers. You have decided that you can operate more efficiently if you organize these employees into work teams. You believe that the old system did not encourage your employees to behave proactively. Indeed, you think that the way the work situation was designed prevented them from finding ways to improve operating procedures and this is why you have chosen to use work teams.

Teams will change how employees perform their tasks in many ways. You are meeting to decide how to change the way you motivate employees to encourage other employees in the new work groups to perform at a higher level. Using the chapter material:

1. Identify the kinds of process gains and losses associated with this change to work groups and discuss ways to solve potential motivation and coordination problems.
2. Discuss how to change the incentive system to encourage employees to cooperate and work together in their new teams to improve performance.
3. Discuss some steps you can take to smooth the transition to teams and help employees become used to working in their new teams.

Topic for Debate

Organizational effectiveness hinges on the effectiveness of the groups that make up an organization. Now that you have a good understanding of what makes for effective work groups, debate the following issue.

Team A. Process losses in work groups are more common than process gains.

Team B. Process gains in work groups are more common than process losses.

Experiential Exercise

Curtailing Social Loafing

Objective

Your objective is to gain experience in developing a strategy to reduce social loafing in an ongoing group.

Procedure

Assume the role of a manager of a home improvements/building supply store that sells a wide range of products—including lumber, plumbing fixtures, windows, and paint—to both commercial accounts and individual customers. The store is staffed by three types of employees who work in three different groups: (1) a group of six cashiers who check out purchases made by individuals on site; (2) a group of five floor employees who help customers locate items they need, stock merchandise, and reshelve returns; and (3) a group of four employees who handle commercial accounts. All the employees are paid on an hourly basis. The cashiers and floor employees earn the minimum wage; the commercial account employees earn one and a half times the minimum wage.

You are pleased with the performance of the cashiers and the commercial account employees. The floor employees, however, seem to be putting forth less effort than they should. On several occasions, customers have complained about not being able to find items, and you personally have located the items for them even though there were ample floor employees on duty. The floor employees do not seem busy, and their workloads have not increased recently, yet they have a backlog of work to be done, including stocking of new merchandise and reshelving. Despite their backlog, you often see members of this group chatting with each other, taking cigarette breaks outside the back of the store, and making personal telephone calls—all outside their regularly scheduled breaks.

1. Individually develop a plan of action to reduce social loafing in the group of floor employees.
2. The class divides into groups of three to five people, and each group appoints one member as spokesperson to present the group's action plans to the whole class.
3. Group members take turns describing their action plans for reducing social loafing among the floor employees.
4. After discussing the pros and cons of each different approach, the group develops a plan of action to reduce social loafing among the floor employees.

When your group has completed these activities, the spokesperson will present the group's action plan to the whole class.

New York Times *Cases in the News*

The New York Times

"Surgical Teams Found Lacking"

Eric Nagourney, NYT, May 9, 2006, p. F6.

They call it a surgical team, but there may be a lot of teamwork left to be desired, a new study finds. The researchers surveyed more than 2,100 surgeons, anesthesiologists and nurses about operating room communications. Their views—and the divergence among them—may shed light on how some surgical mistakes happen.

When the participants were asked to "describe the quality of communication and collaboration you have experienced" with other members of operating teams, surgeons were given the lowest rating for teamwork. Their worst assessment was from nurses, the group that got the highest rating.

"The study is somewhat humbling to me," said the lead author of the study, Dr. Martin A. Makary, a surgeon at Johns Hopkins who has been advocating a new approach to operating room communication. "There's a lot of pride in the surgical community. We need to balance out the captain-of-the-ship doctrine."

For the study, described in the current issues *Annals of Surgery* and *The Journal of the American College of Surgeons*, the researchers surveyed medical workers at 60 hospitals in 16 states. The survey was based on the Safety Attitudes Questionnaire that airlines use to improve cockpit management. The goal is to make sure all members of a team feel free to speak out if they feel a mistake is being made.

Many operating room mistakes, like sponges left in patients or the wrong body part being operated on, could be avoided through better communication, the researchers said. But this can mean getting over barriers of class, race, gender and even general outlook. Afterward, the researchers spoke with participants and found that "nurses often describe good collaboration as having their input respected, and physicians often describe good collaboration as having nurses who anticipate their needs and follow instructions."

Questions for Discussion

1. Why do process losses occur in hospital teams?
2. Using OB, how would you design a training program to build the intensive team routines necessary to avoid operating room errors?

The New York Times

"Working Together, Wherever They Are"

Steve Lohr, NYT, Oct. 5, 2005, p. G.1.

To glimpse the real effect of today's computer networks, it helps to travel far beyond the high-tech hothouse of Silicon Valley, away from the venture capitalists, inventors and billionaire-wannabe entrepreneurs. To go where Google is just a search engine, not an obsession, try Elkhart, Ind., home to Nibco Inc., a century-old maker and distributor of plumbing supplies. A private company, Nibco employs 3,000 workers and generates $500 million a year in sales. It faces stiff competition from Chinese producers.

Since the late 1990's, Nibco has pushed hard to increase productivity and improve customer service by using computer networks. The company first focused on its own operations, then established network links to its customers and suppliers. Now, Nibco's inventory, labor and administrative costs are down sharply, and 70 percent of all orders are digitally automated, twice the level of a few years ago.

The second round of Internet innovation appears to be here. Companies large and small experienced soaring productivity in the 90's as the Web made worlds of information available at the click of a mouse, and the Internet drastically reduced the cost of communicating and doing business with someone on the next floor or the next continent. That cost-cutting payoff continues to spread. But in the next wave, companies are embracing the potential of networked computing to let workers share their knowledge more efficiently as they nurture new ideas, new products and new ways to digitally automate all sorts of tasks. Companies are drawing on collaborative models that first blossomed in non-business settings, from online games to open-source software projects to the so-called wiki encyclopedias and blogs to speed up innovation. This networked collaboration is creating new opportunities and disrupting industries.

Open-source software is a pioneering example of the kind of collaborative work made possible by the Internet. Networks of far-flung programmers share code and ideas to constantly improve and debug their software. So the open-source Linux operating system is challenging Microsoft's windows, a product backed by one of the world's richest corporations. The open-source formula is being applied in one field after another. Projects range from Wikipedia, an open-source encyclopedia, to Biological Innovation for Open Society, or BIOS, an open source initiative in biotechnology. Corporations are rapidly adopting software tools intended to nurture collaborative work, including wikis, blogs, instant messaging, web-based conferencing and peer-to-peer programs.

For Mark Dickinson, a technical manager at the XRT Group, a software company, the payoff from using Web collaboration software is self-evident. With Microsoft's Live Meeting program, Mr. Dickinson can provide technical support to the large corporations that use XRT's cash management software without traveling from his office in King of Prussia, Pa. He can see what is on the computer screen in customers' data centers, tell data center teams what setting may be wrong, walk them through software upgrades—even, with permission, take control of their computers and make changes himself. In his job, Mr. Dickinson uses the web collaboration tool three or four times a day. "I can spend a few hours on a web conference instead of spending three days, including the travel time, for an on-site visit to a client," he said. "The productivity benefit is just obvious. Besides, I hate flying."

Dresdner Kleinwort Wasserstein, an investment bank, has been using wiki software, which lets users collaborate on web pages, to encourage teamwork among its traders and bankers around the world. The wiki software, from socialtext, a start-up, has replaced e-mail and conference calls for tasks like pricing international bond offerings. "It's a virtual work space for tapping the expertise and knowledge of more people," said P. J. Rangaswami, chief information officer of Dresdner Kleinwort. "Conference calls and e-mail just aren't suited for collaborative work."

Questions for Discussion

1. What is collaborative web-based software?
2. In what ways does this kind of IT facilitate the interactions between group members and increase team performance?

The New York Times

"Carmakers' Big Idea: Think Small"

Micheline Maynard, NYT, Feb. 5, 2006. p. 3.1.

No longer do the industry's two biggest companies, General Motors and Ford Motor, dominate the industry—not in profits, sales or buzz. The hottest action is now taking place among the next four companies: Chrysler, a unit of DaimlerChrysler of Germany, and the Japanese automakers Toyota, Honda and Nissan. As G.M. and Ford cut jobs, close plants and pledge yet again to introduce cars and trucks that Americans want to buy, their smaller rivals are in their strongest shape ever. The Next Four are adding jobs, opening plants filling showrooms with new models—and, most importantly, earning billions of dollars in profits that can contribute to even more growth. Although all the Next Four are part of big global companies, they have kept their size, costs and dealers in the United States relatively small and limited their brands and lineups, even as they explore new niches where they can pick up sales. For them, being small has added up to being almost as big as the two Detroit players.

"It's good to be small, because you can move quickly," said Ron Pinelli, president of the Autodata Corporation, an industry statistics firm in Woodcliff Lake, N.J. He said that "the whole large-company culture is a burden," one that both G.M. and Ford have vowed to shed. For inspiration, they can look to Chrysler, which once stood with them as one of the Big Three but is fast breaking away from the Detroit pack. Chrysler is already getting rid of its large-company mind-set—along with 46,000 jobs over the last five years. The latest example of its drive to do less with more is at a factory here in Dundee, Mich., 60 miles south of Detroit, where it is using a small number of workers to build four-cylinder engines for its small cars. The plant is run by the Global Engine Manufacturing Alliance, a partnership of Chrysler, Mitsubishi of Japan and Hyundai of South Korea. The companies will be able to share the half million engines the plant can build each year, allowing them all to invest smaller amounts, meet their needs for engines and enjoy economies of scale that they couldn't have achieved individually.

To get there, the three have negotiated a relatively small labor burden from the United Automobile Workers union: a contract as thin as a pocket calendar that does not call for dozens of narrowly defined jobs, as is common in many unionized auto plants, but has only one category, called team member, for hourly workers. Everyone learns every job—and a result is a work force that is self-starting and flexible.

Chrysler's efforts, as well as those of the others in the Next Four, show a new way of thinking in an industry that seemed paralyzed by its gargantuan roots.

The contrast between old and new is even clearer in the way jobs are assigned to workers at the Dundee plant. During their shifts—10 hours a day, four days a week—workers might be responsible for 18 to 20 spots on the assembly line, rather than be rigidly limited to one narrowly defined task. Indeed, each worker learns every job on the line, reflecting the plant's philosophy of "anyone, anywhere, anything, anytime." The workers, who are U.A.W. members, had to go through a rigorous application and training process, and had to be accepted by plant managers rather than just being assigned by the union. Because they are using an entirely new approach, the managers accepted only two workers from other Chrysler factories. Others came from parts makers or other companies with U.A.W. workers. Despite the intensity, Jimmie Pierce, 36, says the job is a godsend to him. He recently lost his previous job when the Lear Corporation, a parts supplier, closed its plant in Romulus, Mich. In his 12 years there, he said, he stuck to his assigned tasks, even if a problem popped up. "At Lear, someone else fixes it." said Mr. Pierce, a second-generation autoworker. At his new job, where he supervises a team of workers, he said that "you think of yourself more as part of a business."

Questions for Discussion

1. What kinds of process losses do teams avoid in a factory setting?
2. What are the specific sources of process gains that lead to lower costs and higher quality in a factory setting?
3. What other team concepts discussed in the chapter help explain higher factory efficiency?

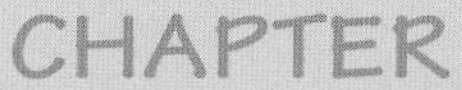

12 LEADERS AND LEADERSHIP

Learning Objectives

After studying this chapter, you should be able to:

- Describe what leadership is, when leaders are effective and ineffective, and the difference between formal and informal leaders.
- Identify the traits that show the strongest relationship to leadership, the behaviors leaders engage in, and the limitations of the trait and behavior models of leadership.
- Explain how contingency models of leadership and differentiate between four different contingency approaches.
- Describe why leadership is not always a vital process in some work situations because substitutes for leadership exist.
- Discuss transformational leadership and how it is achieved, explain how a leader's moods affects followers, and appreciate how gender may affect leadership style.

Opening Case

A SISTER ACT HELPS CLAIRE'S STORES TO SPARKLE

What's the sisters' approach to leadership?

Claire's stores, which sells cosmetics, jewelry, hair and body accessories, and gift items, was thriving in 2006 as it became the place of choice for teenage girls to hang out, socialize, and buy presents for their friends.[1] Claire's current success is largely due to the work of its two co-CEOs, Bonnie and Marla Schaefer, who took control of the store chain in 2002 after their then 86-year-old father and store founder, Rowland Schaefer, had a stroke. Their new leadership role had not been planned, indeed their father had refused to name a successor because he enjoyed being CEO, and as the family controls approximately 30 percent of the company's stock no one could make him! Even when the board asked them to assume leadership of the company, however, this was meant to be only temporary and would last only as long as it took them to recruit a new CEO. The two sisters, however, had other ideas.

Bonnie and Marla Schaefer are both sisters and co-CEOs of Claire's. Both women believe in delegating authority to the managers below them and have a participative approach to leadership.

Even though her father had fired her from her first job at Claire's because he thought she wasn't meeting job expectations, Bonnie, like her sister Marla, had spent most of her working life at Claire's. As the new leaders of the company, the sisters' first task was to decide how they would run the company together. When two people are at the helm, this frequently leads to conflict between them as they battle for control over decision making and power. The sisters were determined to avoid this leadership error and provide a united front to their subordinates—one based on a clear emphasis of the need to set goals and then work toward achieving them. They decided to take control over different areas of decision making. Bonnie would be in charge of real estate, store operations, and the company's international expansion. Marla would oversee product merchandising, investor relations, and human relations.[2] They were careful from the start to break down barriers between these different functions or departments, however, and to get all their subordinates to work together to stock and sell the products that Claire's customers would most want to buy.

Both women believe in delegating authority to the managers below them and have a participative approach to leadership. In the retail business this is vital because it allows merchandisers to work closely with store managers to decide on the right selection of products to offer customers.[3] It is also necessary in Claire's because Bonnie spends much of her time flying around the globe to spearhead international growth and to oversee the selection and opening of new stores.

Their goal-oriented approach works and they excel at creating a work situation that provides managers with the authority to get important things done so that nothing slips through the cracks. At the same time, they are highly supportive of their subordinates and have helped many of them develop the skills needed to manage in the fast-changing world of teenage fashion.

In any event, within one year of taking control, Claire's board of directors made their acting co-CEO titles permanent and, in the four years since they assumed leadership, Claire's profits have soared—as has its share price.[4] So, everyone is happy: Claire's managers, customers, employees, and investors—including their father.

Overview

When things go wrong in an organization, blame is most often laid at the leader's feet. Similarly, when organizations are doing particularly well, people tend to think that their leaders are doing an especially good job. The common belief that leaders "make a difference" and can have a major impact on people, groups, and whole organizations has prompted OB researchers to exert considerable effort to try to explain the nature of leadership. Researchers have focused primarily on two leadership issues: (1) Why do some members of an organization become leaders while others do not? and (2) Why are some leaders more successful or effective than others? As the opening case suggests, answering these questions is not easy because there are many different kinds of leaders and leadership approaches. While some approaches work in a particular situation, others do not.

This chapter addresses these two important issues and explores the nature of leadership in organizations. First, we define leadership and discuss the different types of leaders found in organizations. Second, we explore several different approaches to leadership that provide answers to the questions of why some people become leaders, and what makes some people able to perform at a higher level than others. We then consider the issue of substitutes and neutralizers for leadership—that is, factors that also help to motivate and coordinate employee behavior, and factors that can reduce leader effectiveness. Finally, we examine some new topics in leadership theory and research: transformational and charismatic leadership, the effect of a leader's mood on his or her subordinates, and gender and leadership. By the end of this chapter, you will understand how and why leaders so profoundly affect organizational behavior at all levels.

Introduction to Leadership

Although you can often recognize a leader when you see one in action, coming up with a precise definition of leadership is difficult. Even researchers often disagree about which characteristics best describe leadership but, in general, two are regarded as being the most important.[5] First, leadership involves *exerting influence* over other members of a group or organization. Second, leadership involves *helping a group or organization achieve its goals*. Combining these two key characteristics, we can define **leadership** as the exercise of influence by one member of a group or organization over other members to help the group or organization achieve its goals.[6] The **leaders** of a group or organization are the individuals who exert such influence. *Leader effectiveness* is the extent to which a leader actually does help a group or organization to achieve its goals.[7] An *effective* leader helps achieve goals; an *ineffective* leader does not.[8] Bonnie and Maria Schaefer have proved to be effective leaders at Claire's because they have worked hard to find ways to improve their company's performance.

LEADERSHIP
The exercise of influence by one member of a group or organization over other members to help the group or organization achieve its goals.

LEADER
An individual who is able to influence group or organizational members to help the group or organization achieve its goals.

Leaders influence and shape many aspects of organizational behavior that we have discussed in previous chapters: attitudes (Chapter 3), learning (Chapter 5), motivation

Tommye Jo Daves (right), a 60-year-old grandmother, was promoted and became the plant manager of Levi's factory in Murphy, North Carolina. She began as a seamstress at the plant in 1959 and rose to the top because her job knowledge and personal qualities earned her the trust and respect of the workforce.

(Chapters 6, 7, and 8), stress (Chapter 9), and work-group effectiveness (Chapters 10 and 11). Research has shown, for example, that leaders influence their subordinates' or followers' levels of motivation, performance, absenteeism, and turnover, and the quality of their decision making. (We use *followers* and *subordinates* interchangeably to refer to the members of a group or organization who are influenced by a leader).[9]

FORMAL LEADER
A member of an organization who is given authority by the organization to influence other organizational members to achieve organizational goals.

All leaders exert influence over members of a group or organization. Some leaders, however, have formal authority to do so while others do not. **Formal leaders** are those managers who are given the authority to influence other members in the organization to achieve its goals.[10] With this authority comes the responsibility to make the best use of an organization's resources, including its money and capital and the abilities and skills of its employees. Note that not all managers are leaders; some managers do not have subordinates who report to them.[11] For example, the accounting manager of a restaurant who is responsible for keeping the books is a manager but not a formal leader—this person could be an informal leader, however. Claire's is unusual in having two top formal leaders.

INFORMAL LEADER
An organizational member with no formal authority to influence others who nevertheless is able to exert considerable influence because of special skills or talents.

Informal leaders have no formal job authority to influence others but sometimes exert just as much influence in an organization as formal leaders—and sometimes even more. The ability of informal leaders to influence others often stems from special skills or talents they possess—skills the organization's members realize will help it achieve its goals. Eight waiters employed in a restaurant all have the same job of serving customers, for example, but the waiter who was the most experienced and had the best interpersonal skills became the informal leader of the group. He made sure that the other waiters provided good service, and he always stepped in to help settle arguments before they got out of hand. The other waiters listened to him because his advice about customer service helped them earn large tips and because his social skills made the restaurant a nice place to work.

In general, both formal leaders and informal leaders influence others in groups and organizations. The various approaches to leadership that we describe in this chapter seek to explain why some people become leaders and others do not and why some leaders are more effective than others.

Early Approaches to Leadership

Each of the various approaches to leadership we discuss in the next sections of this chapter complements the other—no one theory describes the *right* or *only* way to become a leader or be a good leader. Each of the theories focuses on a different set of issues, but taken together they provide a better understanding of how to become an effective leader. Two of the earliest perspectives on leadership were offered by the trait approach and the behavior approach.

The Leader Trait Approach

Early studies of leadership sought to identify *enduring personal traits* that distinguish leaders from followers and effective from ineffective leaders. Recall from Chapter 2 that traits are a person's particular tendencies to feel, think, and act in certain ways. The search for leadership traits began in the 1930s, and after nearly 300 studies, the list was narrowed to several traits that showed the strongest relationship to effective leadership[12]:

- *Intelligence* helps a leader solve complex problems.
- *Task-relevant knowledge* ensures that a leader knows what has to be done, how it should be done, and what resources are required for a group and organization to achieve its goals.
- *Dominance*, an individual's need to exert influence and control over others, helps a leader channel followers' efforts and abilities toward achieving group and organizational goals.
- *Self-confidence* both helps a leader influence followers and motivates them to persevere in the face of obstacles or difficulties.
- *Energy/activity levels*, when high, help a leader deal with the many demands he or she faces on a day-to-day basis.
- *Tolerance for stress* helps a leader deal with the uncertainty inherent in any leadership role.
- *Integrity* and *honesty* ensure that a leader behaves ethically and is worthy of his or her followers' trust and confidence.
- *Emotional maturity* ensures that a leader is not overly self-centered, can control his or her feelings, and can accept criticism.[13]

There is an important point to understand when viewing leadership using the trait approach. For some traits, it is not clear what comes first: *being in a leadership position* or *possessing the trait in question.* In other words, is it possession of the appropriate trait that leads a person to become a leader? Or, given what we learned in Chapter 2 that personality traits *can* change over the long term (several years), does being put in a leadership position result in a person developing leadership traits? The answer to this question is not clear or unambiguous. Individuals who possess the traits associated with effective leadership may be more likely to become effective leaders than those who do not. But many individuals who possess the appropriate traits may never become leaders, and many leaders who possess them are not effective. The difficulty of this question prompted researchers to look for other ways to understand effective leadership and search for other factors that contribute to it.

The Leader Behavior Approach

Rather than looking at the personal traits of leaders, in later years, researchers focused on what leaders actually do—that is, on the *specific behaviors* performed by effective leaders. Researchers at Ohio State University in the 1940s and 1950s were at the forefront of the leader behavior approach.[14] The Ohio State researchers realized one of the key ways in which leaders influence followers is through their concrete behaviors. The behavior approach seeks to identify leader behaviors that help individuals, groups, and organizations achieve their multiple goals.

The Ohio State researchers developed a list of over 1,800 specific, concrete behaviors they thought leaders might engage in such as setting goals for followers, telling followers what to do, being friendly, and making sure that followers are happy.[15] The researchers then developed scales to measure these behaviors and administered the scales to thousands of employees. Employees were asked to indicate the extent to which their leaders performed the various leader behaviors. After analyzing their responses, the researchers found that most leader behaviors involved either *consideration* or *initiating structure*. The Ohio State results have been replicated in many studies and in other countries such as Germany.[16]

CONSIDERATION
Behavior indicating that a leader trusts, respects, and values good relationships with his or her followers.

Consideration. Behaviors indicating that a leader trusts, respects, and values good relationships with his or her followers is known as **consideration**. Stanley Gault, a former CEO of Goodyear Tire and Rubber, demonstrated consideration on his very first day as CEO. He showed his followers that he trusted them. While moving into his luxurious office, he was offered a set of keys for the locked cabinets lining the office walls. Gault indicated that he didn't want the keys because he liked to keep things unlocked. The employee who offered Gault the keys urged him to reconsider because many people would be going in and out of his office every day and the cleaning staff would come in at night. Gault's response was that he didn't need the keys because, as he put it, "This company should be run on the basis of trust."[17] Other examples of consideration include a leader's being friendly, treating group members as his or her equals, and explaining to them why he or she has done certain things.

A leader who engages in consideration also shows followers that he or she cares about their well-being and is concerned about how they feel and what they think. David Pottruck, co-CEO of the brokerage firm Charles Schwab & Company, learned the importance of consideration by observing how subordinates react when their boss does *not* engage in consideration.[18] Early in his career, Pottruck adopted a very directed, competitive approach to leading and rarely engaged in consideration behaviors. Charles Schwab himself delivered a wake-up call to Pottruck when he let Pottruck know that people didn't like working with him and didn't trust him because he was forcing his initiatives on others and not soliciting their involvement.[19]

With the help of an executive coach, Pottruck began to alter his leadership style to incorporate consideration behaviors. Now, rather than forcing initiatives on others, Pottruck shows he respects his subordinates by explaining problems to them and soliciting their input. For example, when he came to the realization that Schwab might need to keep its branch offices open on Saturdays, he explained the need for this unpopular move to branch managers and also acknowledged the big imposition this might have on their lives and the lives of their subordinates. Rather than encountering resistance, the consideration behaviors Pottruck engaged in garnered enthusiasm and support for the initiative.[20] Pottruck now believes that consideration is a key contributor to a competitive advantage in the new Internet economy because it breeds collaboration and encourages teamwork.

INITIATING STRUCTURE
Behaviors that a leader engages in to make sure that work gets done and subordinates perform their jobs acceptably.

Initiating structure. Behaviors that a leader engages in to make sure the work gets done and subordinates perform their jobs acceptably are known as **initiating structure**. Assigning individual tasks to followers, planning ahead, setting goals, deciding how the work should be performed, and pushing followers to get their tasks accomplished are all initiating-structure behaviors.[21] In the opening case, CEOs, Bonnie and Marla Schaefer delegate authority to their subordinates. But, at the same time, from regular, structured meetings they can assess these managers' progress toward meeting current goals, and they can intervene and provide guidance and advice as needed.

Leaders at lower levels also engage in initiating structure. The informal leader of the group of waiters in the restaurant described earlier, for example, engaged in initiating structure by developing a system in which waiters serving very large tables would receive help from other waiters whose stations were not full. This leader also engaged in consideration by taking an interest in the personal lives of the other waiters and by having a cake made and throwing a small party to celebrate each of their birthdays.

Note that consideration and initiating structure are complementary but independent leader behaviors. They are *complementary* because leaders can engage in both types of behaviors. They are *independent* because knowing the extent to which a leader engages in consideration says nothing about the extent to which he or she engages in initiating structure and vice versa.

The Behavior Approach: Leader Reward and Punishing Behavior

In addition to engaging in consideration and initiating structure, leaders behave in other ways that have important effects on their followers. Recall from Chapter 5 that *reinforcement* can increase the probability of desirable behaviors and *punishment* can decrease the probability of undesirable behaviors occurring. In organizations, managers who are leaders administer reinforcements and punishments.

LEADER REWARD BEHAVIOR
A leader's positive reinforcement of subordinates' desirable behavior.

Leader reward behavior occurs when a leader positively reinforces subordinates' desirable behaviors.[22] Leaders who notice when their followers do a good job and acknowledge it with compliments, praise, or more tangible benefits like a pay raise or promotion are engaging in reward behavior. Leader reward behavior helps to ensure that employees perform at high levels. Gurcharan Das, while CEO of Vicks Vaporub's Indian subsidiary, recalls engaging in leader reward behavior when he gave annual raises to all employees who met at least 20 customers and 20 retailers or wholesalers during the year. Why did Das reward this behavior? It helped the employees keep in touch with the marketplace and come up with ways to improve the company's products and services.[23]

LEADER PUNISHING BEHAVIOR
A leader's negative response to subordinates' undesired behavior.

Leader punishing behavior occurs when a leader reprimands or otherwise responds negatively to subordinates who perform undesired behavior.[24] A factory foreman who docks the pay of any subordinate who fails to wear safety glasses on the job is engaging in leader punishing behavior.

Although punishing behavior can be an effective means of curtailing undesirable or potentially dangerous behavior in organizations (see Chapter 5), it is generally more effective to use reinforcement to encourage desired behavior than to use punishment to stop undesired behavior. Punishment can have unintended side effects such as resentment. The foreman mentioned previously would obtain more desirable organizational results by engaging in leader reward behavior, such as giving a bonus of some sort to subordinates who wear their safety glasses every day for a three-month period. Despite the research evidence, however, leaders often engage in punishing behavior.

Measuring Leader Behaviors

Considerable research has been done to develop scales to measure the leader behaviors described previously. The *Leadership Behavior Description Questionnaire* asks a leader's subordinates to indicate the extent to which their leader or supervisor engages in a number of different consideration and initiating-structure behaviors. The *Leadership Opinion Questionnaire*, completed by the leaders themselves, asks leaders to indicate which of a variety of consideration and initiating-structure behaviors they think result in good leadership.[25] Researchers have also developed measures of leader reward behavior and leader punishing behavior. Exhibit 12.1 is an example of one of these measures, which is completed by a leader's subordinates.

Some of the leadership models management consultants use to help managers learn how to be effective also employ scales to measure consideration and initiate structure. As we discuss in Chapter 18, an approach to organizational change designed to make managers more effective as leaders (Robert Blake and Jane Mouton's Managerial Grid) focuses on identifying the extent to which a company's leaders are concerned about people (consideration) and production (initiating structure).[26] Paul Hersey and Kenneth Blanchard's model, which is quite popular with consultants, also focuses on consideration and initiating-structure behaviors.[27]

What Is Missing in the Trait and Behavior Approaches?

Although the trait and behavior approaches to leadership are different from each other—one focuses on what effective leaders are *like*, and the other on what they *do*—they do have something in common: Each approach essentially ignores the situation in

EXHIBIT 12.1

A Measure of Leader Reward and Punishing Behavior

The subordinates of a leader are asked to indicate the extent to which they agree or disagree with each of the following statements on the following scale:

1 = Strongly disagree
2 = Disagree
3 = Slightly disagree
4 = Neither agree nor disagree
5 = Slightly agree
6 = Agree
7 = Strongly agree

1. My supervisor always gives me positive feedback when I perform well.
2. My supervisor gives me special recognition when my work performance is especially good.
3. My supervisor would quickly acknowledge an improvement in the quality of my work.
4. My supervisor commends me when I do a better than average job.
5. My supervisor personally pays me a compliment when I do outstanding work.
6. My supervisor informs his or her boss and/or others in the organization when I do outstanding work.
7. If I do well, I know my supervisor will reward me.
8. My supervisor would do all that she/he could to help me go as far as I would like to go in this organization if my work were consistently above average.
9. My good performance often goes unacknowledged by my supervisor.*
10. I often perform well in my job and still receive no praise from my supervisor.*
11. If I performed at a level below that which I was capable of, my supervisor would indicate his or her disapproval.
12. My supervisor shows his or her displeasure when my work is below acceptable standards.
13. My supervisor lets me know about it when I perform poorly.
14. My supervisor would reprimand me if my work were below standard.
15. When my work is not up to par, my supervisor points it out to me.

* For these items, scoring is reversed such that 1 = 7, 2 = 6, 3 = 5, 5 = 3, 6 = 2, 7 = 1.
Leader reward behavior = the sum of items 1–10
Leader punishment behavior = the sum of the items 11–15

Source: P. M. Podsakoff, W. D. Todor, R. A. Grover, and V. L. Huber, "Situational Moderators of Leader Reward and Punishment Behaviors. Fact or Fiction?" *Organizational Behavior and Human Decision Processes*, 1984, 34, pp. 21–63. Reprinted with permission of Academic Press, Inc.

which leadership takes place. Recall from Chapter 2 that the *interaction* of personal characteristics (such as traits and behaviors) with the organizational situation (including the amount of formal authority that leaders have and the nature of their subordinates) determines a person's behavior (for example, leadership and performance) in an organization.

The trait approach takes into account leaders' personal characteristics but ignores the situations in which they try to lead. However, certain leadership traits might result in effective leadership in some situations but ineffective leadership in others. Dominance, for example, may make a football coach a good leader for a football team. But the same trait in the head research scientist at a medical laboratory might not be effective because his or her subordinates are likely to be highly educated people who think independently and work best when left alone.

In a similar way, the behavior approach seeks to identify the behaviors responsible for effective leadership without considering how the situation affects behavior. The behavior approach implicitly assumes that regardless of the situation (such as a group's characteristics and composition or the type of task being done), certain leadership behaviors will result in high subordinate levels of satisfaction and performance. However, just as the situation can change how a leader's personal traits affect subordinates' responses, so, too, can it influence how subordinates respond to a leader's specific behaviors. Consider the performance of a group of carpenters who are building a complicated custom-built house. Their performance may increase if their leader engages in initiating structure by scheduling the work so the house is completely framed before the

EXHIBIT 12.2

The Nature of Leadership: The Role of Traits and Behaviors

Approach	Premise	Drawbacks
Trait approach	Effective leaders possess certain qualities or traits that help a group or an organization achieve its goals.	Some effective leaders do not possess all of these traits, and some leaders who possess these traits are not effective. The approach ignores the situation in which leadership takes place.
Behavior approach	Effective leaders perform certain behaviors, which may include consideration, initiating structure, reward behavior, and punishing behavior.	The relationship between these behaviors and subordinate performance and satisfaction is not necessarily clear-cut. The behavior approach ignores the situation in which leadership takes place.

roof is put on and by pushing employees to perform their tasks as quickly as possible. By contrast, the performance of a group of furniture assembly-line workers who have been performing the same tasks day in and day out for several years know exactly how to do their jobs. Not only is their leader's initiating-structure behavior unnecessary, it might actually lower their job satisfaction if they become annoyed by their leader constantly telling them what to do.

In sum, the trait and behavior approaches contribute to our understanding of effective leadership by indicating what effective leaders tend to be like and what they do (see Exhibit 12.2). A fuller understanding of leadership, however, can be gained only by also considering how the situation affects leadership.

CONTINGENCY THEORY OF LEADERSHIP
The theory that leader effectiveness is determined by both the personal characteristics of leaders and by the situations in which leaders find themselves.

Fiedler'S Contingency Theory of Leadership

The trait and behavior approaches ignore how the situation at hand influences a leader's effectiveness. Recognizing that effectiveness is determined by both (1) the characteristic of individuals and (2) the situations in which they find themselves, Fred Fiedler developed the **contingency theory of leadership**.[28] One of the most popular approaches to understanding leadership, Fiedler's theory sheds light on two important leadership issues: (1) why, in a particular situation, some leaders will be more effective than other leaders even though they have equally good credentials, and (2) why a particular leader may be effective in one situation but not in another.

Leaders who notice when their followers do a good job and acknowledge it with compliments and praise are engaging in reward behavior. Leader reward behavior encourages employees to perform at a high level.

Leader Style

Like the trait approach, Fiedler's theory acknowledges that personal characteristics influence the effectiveness of leaders. Fiedler was particularly interested in styles of leadership—how a person approaches being a leader. He identified two distinct leader styles—relationship-oriented and task-oriented styles—and proposed that all leaders are characterized by one style or the other.

Leaders who are *relationship-oriented* want to be liked by and get along well with their subordinates. Although they want their subordinates to perform at a high level, relationship-oriented leaders' first priority is developing good relationships with their followers. Their second priority is making sure that the job gets done (task accomplishment). Ken Franklin, who manages American-owned factories (*maquiladoras*) in Mexico's Bermúdez Industrial Park in Ciudad Juárez, has learned that a relationship-oriented style is particularly important when leading Mexican subordinates. Every morning at 6 o'clock he greets factory employees personally when they begin work.[29]

Leaders who are *task-oriented* want their subordinates to perform at a high level and accomplish all of their assigned tasks. Their first priority is task accomplishment, and they push subordinates to make sure that the job gets done. Having good relationships with their subordinates is their second priority.

According to Fiedler, a leader's style, whether relationship-oriented or task-oriented, is an enduring personal characteristic. Leader style cannot easily be changed: A relationship-oriented leader cannot be trained to be task-oriented and vice versa. A leader's style also cannot easily change with the situation. In other words, a leader will not be relationship-oriented in one situation and task-oriented in another; he or she will use the same style in all leadership situations.

Which style of leadership is most effective depends on the kind of situation the leader is dealing with. Because leaders cannot change their style, an organization must do one of two things to ensure that its leaders are able to help their subordinates and the organization as a whole attain important goals: *An organization must either assign leaders to situations in which they will be effective or change the situation to fit the leader.*

LEAST PREFERRED CO-EMPLOYEE SCALE
A questionnaire that measures leader style by scoring leaders' responses to questions about the co-employee with whom they have the most difficulty working.

Fiedler devised and used a unique scale to measure leader style: the **least preferred co-employee scale**. He asked leaders to think about their least preferred co-employee (LPC), or the co-employee with whom they have the most difficulty working. The leader was then asked to rate the LPC on a number of dimensions such as the extent to which the LPC was friendly, enthusiastic, and pleasant. Relationship-oriented leaders (also called *high LPC leaders*) described their least preferred co-employee in relatively positive terms. They were able to say some good things about the co-employee with whom they had the most difficulty working. They were able to set aside the work-related problems they had with the LPC and see that this person had merit as another human being. In contrast, task-oriented leaders (also called *low LPC leaders*) described their least preferred co-employee negatively. They believed their LPC had few redeeming qualities. Because they had difficulty working with the LPC, their overall impression of this person was very negative.

Fiedler theorized that the way in which leaders described their least preferred co-employee provided insight into their approach to leading. Specifically, relationship-oriented leaders would try to think positively about others—even the LPC—because a positive outlook fosters good relationships. Task-oriented leaders, on the other hand, would think negatively about others who were difficult to work with because their undesired behavior might hinder task accomplishment.

Situational Characteristics

Fiedler proposed that situations vary in their *favorability* for leading—that is, the extent to which the situation allows the leader to easily guide and channel subordinate behavior in the direction of high performance and goal attainment. When a situation is favorable for leading, it is easier for a leader to exert influence than it is when a situation is unfavorable. According to Fiedler, three characteristics determine how favorable situations are for leading: leader-member relations, task structure, and position power.

LEADER–MEMBER RELATIONS
The relationships between a leader and his or her followers.

Leader–member relations. When **leader–member relations**—the relationships between the leader and his or her followers—are good, followers appreciate, trust, and feel a certain degree of loyalty toward their leader, and the situation is favorable for leading. When leader–member relations are poor, followers dislike or distrust their leader, and the situation is unfavorable for leading. Consider the following situations: Robert Holkan, as head mechanic, leads a group of mechanics in a garage. He gets along well with the mechanics, and they often go out to lunch together. In Holkan's leadership situation, leader–member relations are good. Mary Lester is head of the English department of a small liberal arts college. The other professors in the department think Lester is a snob and a bit pretentious. Leader–member relations are poor in Lester's leadership situation.

TASK STRUCTURE
The extent to which the work to be performed by a group is clearly defined.

Task structure. **Task structure** is the extent to which the work to be performed by a group is clearly defined. When a group has specific goals that need to be accomplished and every group member knows how to go about achieving the goals, task structure is high. When group goals are vague or uncertain and members are not sure how to go about performing their jobs, task structure is low. Situations are more favorable for leading when task structure is high.

Task structure is high for head mechanic Robert Holkan because the garage has the clear goal of repairing customers' cars in a timely fashion and because the highly skilled mechanics generally know exactly what needs to be done on each car. Task structure is low for Mary Lester. Within the English department there is considerable turmoil about the relative emphasis on teaching and research. The English professors are split about which is more important, and there is considerable disagreement about how to evaluate professors' research and teaching performances. A result of the uncertainty about what the "work" of the department should be (teaching or research) is low task structure.

POSITION POWER
The amount of formal authority a leader has.

Position power. **Position power** is the amount of formal authority that a leader has. If a leader has the power to reward and punish subordinates by, for example, granting them pay raises and bonuses or docking their pay, then position power is high. If a leader can do little to reward or punish subordinates, then position power is low. A situation is more favorable for leading when position power is high.

At the garage, Robert Holkan has low position power because he has little control over rewards and punishments for the mechanics. The owner of the garage determines pay rates, benefits, and other rewards, and Holkan has little input into the process. Conversely, Lester has high position power as head of the English department. Each year, the department has a set amount of money for faculty raises, and Lester determines how to distribute the money among the faculty. She also determines who teaches which courses and the times at which all courses are taught. Members of the department are reluctant to disagree with her because they are afraid that she may assign them undesirable teaching times (a class, say, from 3 to 5 P.M. on Fridays).

The Contingency Model

All possible combinations of good and poor leader-member relations, high and low task structure, and high and low position power yield eight leadership situations. Fiedler applied the word *octant* to each type of situation (see Exhibit 12.3). According to Fiedler's

EXHIBIT 12.3

Flavorability of Situations for Leading

Source: Adapted from F. E. Fiedler, A *Theory of Leadership Effectiveness* (New York: McGraw-Hill, 1967). Reprinted with permission.

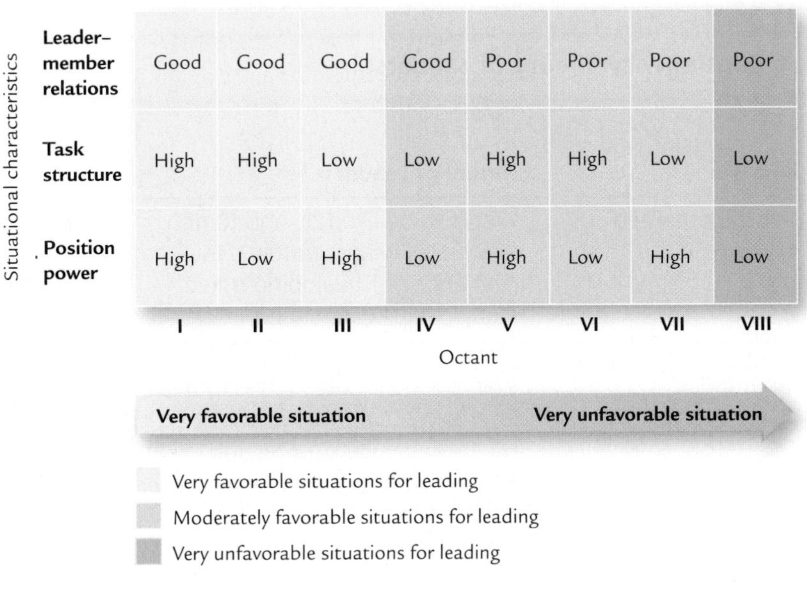

theory, octant I, II, and III situations are very favorable for leading; octant IV, V, VI, and VII situations are moderately favorable for leading; and an octant VIII situation is very unfavorable for leading.

Head mechanic Robert Holkan has good leader–member relations, high task structure, and low position power (octant II in Exhibit 12.3), a very favorable situation for leading. Professor Mary Lester, in contrast, has poor leader–member relations, low task structure, and high position power (octant VII in Exhibit 12.3), a moderately favorable situation for leading.

To determine whether Robert Holkan or Mary Lester will be the more effective leader, we need to look at Holkan's and Lester's leadership styles and the favorability of their situations. The impact of each of these factors on leader effectiveness depends, or is contingent upon, the other. To identify their leadership style, we ask both of them to describe their least preferred co-employee. Holkan describes his least preferred co-employee very negatively; he thinks this mechanic is basically stupid and difficult to get along with. This description indicates that Holkan is a task-oriented or low LPC leader. Lester describes her least preferred co-employee in positive terms. Even though she has trouble working with this professor, she thinks that he is intelligent and pleasant. This description indicates that Lester is a relationship-oriented or high LPC leader.

According to Fiedler's theory, task-oriented leaders are most effective in situations that are very favorable or very unfavorable, and relationship-oriented leaders are most effective in moderately favorable situations (see Exhibit 12.4). Thus, even though Holkan's and Lester's leadership situations are different as are their styles, they are actually equally effective leaders. Holkan is a task-oriented leader in a very favorable situation, and Lester is a relationship-oriented leader in a moderately favorable situation.

Why are task-oriented leaders most effective in very favorable and in unfavorable situations? And why are relationship-oriented leaders most effective in moderately favorable situations? Recall that the first priority of task-oriented leaders is task accomplishment and their second priority is good interpersonal relations. Fiedler suggests that when leaders and people in general are under stress, they concentrate on their first priorities. A very unfavorable situation for leading is stressful for most leaders, and task-oriented leaders will focus on getting the job done because that is their first priority. This focus is likely to be effective in such situations because it increases the chances that a group will at least accomplish its tasks. In very favorable situations, task-oriented leaders, realizing that the group will achieve its goals because the situation is so good, can

EXHIBIT 12.4

Fiedler's Contingency Theory of Leadership

Leader Style	Nature of Leader	Situations in Which Style Is More Effective
Relationship oriented	Wants to be liked by and to get along well with subordinates *First priority*: Developing good relationships with subordinates *Second priority*: Getting the job done	Moderately favorable for leading (octants IV, V, VI, and VII in Figure 12.2)
Task oriented	Wants subordinates to perform at a high level and accomplish all assigned tasks *First priority*: Getting the job done *Second priority*: Developing good relationships with subordinates	Very favorable or very unfavorable for leading (octants I, II, III, and VIII in Figure 12.2)

focus on their second priority—good interpersonal relations—because they know the job will get done. In moderately favorable situations, relationship-oriented leaders can focus on both interpersonal relations and task accomplishment.[30] Some leadership experts have questioned these explanations and Fiedler's model. Research studies provide some support for the model but also suggest that it (like most theories) needs modifying.[31]

In summary, Fiedler considers leadership styles to be relatively fixed or enduring. Leaders cannot be "taught" to be relationship-oriented or task-oriented, nor can a leader alter his or her style according to the situation. Instead, contingency theory holds that leaders must be assigned to situations in which they will be effective. If that won't work, the situation must be changed to fit the leader. In the first case, task-oriented leaders should be assigned to very unfavorable or to very favorable situations, while relationship-oriented leaders should be assigned to moderately favorable situations. In the second case, to improve the favorability of a situation for leading, it may be possible to increase the levels of task structure by giving a leader specific goals to be accomplished and guidelines for how to channel subordinates' behavior to reach those goals. Another alternative would be for the organization to improve the favorability of the situation by giving the leader the formal authority to make decisions about pay raises, bonuses, and promotions for subordinates—increase his or her power position, in other words.

Contemporary Perspectives On Leadership

Several newer theories or approaches to leadership—each of which deals with a different aspect of leadership—have been proposed in recent years. Like Fiedler's model, they are based on a contingency approach that takes into account both the characteristics of leaders and the situations in which they're trying to lead.

Path-goal theory describes how leaders can *motivate* their followers to perform at high levels and can keep them satisfied. The Vroom and Yetton model deals with a specific aspect of leadership: the extent to which leaders should *involve their subordinates in decision making*. Leader–member exchange theory takes into account the fact that leaders often do not treat each of their subordinates equally but instead develop *different kinds of relationships* with different subordinates. Each of these perspectives adds to an understanding of what makes leadership effective in organizations.

Path-Goal Theory: How Leaders Motivate Followers

PATH-GOAL THEORY
A theory that describes how leaders can motivate their followers to achieve group and organizational goals and the kinds of behaviors leaders can engage in to motivate followers.

Robert House, a widely respected leadership researcher, realized that much of what leaders try to do in organizations involves motivating their followers. House's **path-goal theory** describes how leaders can motivate their followers to achieve group and organizational goals and the kinds of behaviors they can engage in to accomplish that (see Exhibit 12.5).

EXHIBIT 12.5

Path-Goal Theory

Effective leaders motivate their followers to achieve group and organizational goals.

Effective leaders make sure that they have control over outcomes their subordinates desire.

Effective leaders reward subordinates for performing at a high level or achieving their work goals by giving them desired outcomes.

Effective leaders raise their subordinates' beliefs about their ability to achieve their work goals and perform at a high level.

In determining how to treat their subordinates and what behaviors to engage in, effective leaders take into account their subordinates' characteristics and the type of work they do.

Path-goal theory suggests that effective leaders follow three guidelines to motivate their followers. The guidelines are based on the expectancy theory of motivation (see Chapter 6). Effective leaders who follow these guidelines have highly motivated subordinates who are likely to meet their work goals and perform at high levels:

1. *Determine what outcomes subordinates are trying to obtain in the workplace*. For example, what needs are they trying to satisfy, or what goals are they trying to meet? After gaining this information, the leader must have control over those outcomes or over the ability to give or withhold the outcomes to subordinates.[32] The new manager of a group of five attorneys in a large law firm determined that salary raises and the opportunity to work on interesting cases with big corporate clients were the outcomes that her subordinates most desired. She already controlled the assignment of cases and clients, but her own boss determined salary raises. After realizing the importance of salary raises for the motivation of her subordinates, the manager discussed with her boss the importance of being able to determine her own subordinates' raises. The boss gave her sole authority to determine their raises as long as she kept within the budget. In this way, the manager made sure she had control over outcomes that her subordinates desired.
2. *Reward subordinates for performing at high levels or achieving their work goals by giving them desired outcomes*. The manager in the law firm had two important goals for her subordinates: completing all assignments within the budgeted hours and winning cases. When subordinates met these goals, they were performing at a high level. To motivate her subordinates to attain these goals, the manager made sure that her distribution of interesting monthly case assignments and semiannual raises reflected the extent to which her subordinates met these two goals. The subordinate who always stayed within the budgeted hours and won all of his or her cases in the last six months received not only the biggest raise but also the choicest assignments.
3. *Make sure the subordinates believe that they can obtain their work goals and perform at high levels*. Leaders can do this by showing subordinates the paths to goal attainment (hence the name *path-goal* theory), by removing any obstacles that might come up along the way, and by expressing confidence in their subordinates' capabilities. The manager in the law firm realized that one of her subordinates had low expectations. He had little confidence in his ability to stay within budget and to win cases no matter how hard he worked. The manager was able to raise this subordinate's expectations by showing him how to allocate his billable hours among the various cases he was working on and explaining to him the key ingredients to winning a case. She also told him to ask her for help whenever he came across a problem he thought might jeopardize his chances of winning a case. The subordinate followed her advice, and together they worked out ways to get around problems that came up on the subordinate's various cases. By clarifying the paths to goal attainment and helping to remove obstacles, the supervisor helped raise this subordinate's expectations and motivation, and he actually started to win more cases and complete them within the budgeted hours.

House identified four types of behavior that leaders can engage in to motivate subordinates:

- *Directive behavior* (similar to initiating structure) lets subordinates know what tasks need to be performed and how they should be performed.
- *Supportive behavior* (similar to consideration) lets subordinates know that their leader cares about their well-being and is looking out for them.
- *Participative behavior* enables subordinates to be involved in making decisions that affect them.
- *Achievement-oriented behavior* pushes subordinates to do their best. Such behavior includes setting difficult goals for followers, expecting high performance, and expressing confidence in their capabilities.

In determining how to motivate subordinates or which of these behaviors to engage in, a leader has to take into account the nature of his or her subordinates and the work they do. If a subordinate is under a lot of stress, a leader who engages in supportive behavior might be especially effective. Directive behaviors are likely to be beneficial when subordinates work on complex and difficult projects, such as the lawyer who was having trouble winning cases. As discussed earlier, when subordinates are performing easy tasks they are already proficient at, initiating structure or directive behaviors are not necessary and are likely to be resented; people don't like to be told how to do something they already do quite well. When it is important for subordinates to accept a decision that a leader needs to make, participative leadership behavior is likely to be effective, as the flowing OB Today suggests.

OB Today

Tammy Savage and the NETGENeration

Tammy Savage joined Microsoft's New York City sales office straight out of Cal State, Fresno, in 1993 when she was 22. A marketing whiz, Savage soon gained a reputation as an expert in understanding the needs of under-30 Internet users—the "Net Generation" or "NetGen." She became a central figure in the New York sales office's dealings with programmers back at Microsoft's Redmond, Washington, headquarters, and her knowledge of the NetGen led to her promotion. She became a manager in Microsoft's business development group, and she moved to Redmond.

Business development keeps a company's products alive and up to date with changing customer needs. Savage used her new more senior position to reevaluate the whole of Microsoft's business development efforts for the NetGen. Her conclusion was that Microsoft was missing the boat and risked losing the NetGens to rival companies like AOL and Yahoo! whose instant messenger services were already very popular. Savage's goal was to earn back the loyalty of the NetGen and thereby increase the popularity of Microsoft's own Internet service and instant messaging system. The goal was to come up with a product that the NetGen would just "have to have." Savage used her new power and position to begin a major research program to find out what needs NetGens were trying to satisfy and develop software to meet those needs.

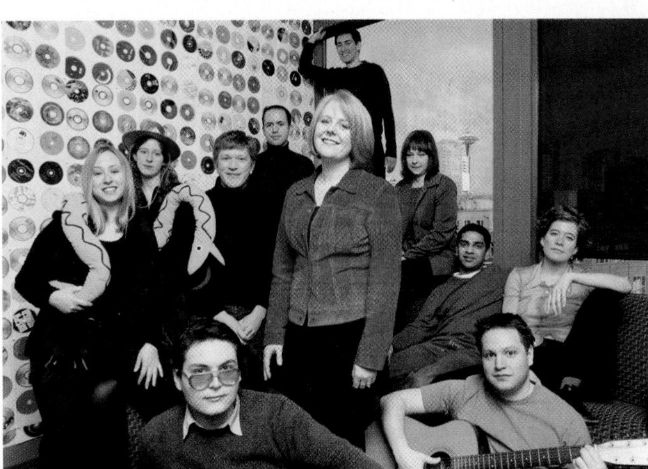

Microsoft manager Tammy Savage relied on a participative leadership model to motivate her team members because she knew they were highly competent and driven. Savage convinced them that by working as a team, they could quickly develop software to capture the NetGen market segment.

Savage presented her new ideas to Microsoft's top managers, including Bill Gates. She explained that the kinds of products NetGen customers wanted were not being made by Microsoft and that it risked losing an entire generation of Internet users if it could not provide a product that inspired them and met the principal needs they were satisfying—the need for online companionship and socialization. Microsoft's top brass heard her out; they knew she had a track record of success, yet they were not persuaded by her arguments. They could not understand why it was so important to NetGen that they have a product they could use to share their experiences and foster friendships on the web. Luckily for her, though, Microsoft Group VP Jim Allchin did understand what Savage was driving at. He was persuaded by her vision to develop a new generation of Microsoft Internet software that would attract young people.

Savage was made the manager and leader of a project team put together to develop the ideal NetGen web software. In early 2001, she began recruiting new college software graduates and "NetGeners" to join her team. From the beginning, she adopted the approach to leadership that Microsoft is well known for—a participative and achievement-oriented approach. Since she was recruiting people who were highly competent, showed a drive for achievement, and would have to work in teams where cooperation is vital, Savage knew she had to adopt its participative and achievement-oriented approach. Savage made it clear to team members that if they worked together to push the development of the product quickly along, they would see the results of their efforts right away. In other words, it was up to them to work together to find new ways to develop superior software quickly and take back the NetGen.

The result of Savage's team's efforts was the 3-*degrees* Windows peer-to-peer networking application that allowed users to listen to a shared play list, send digital photos, and initiate group chats with MSN messenger. The goal of this new kind of "relationship" software was to further the development of online relationships. Its users were able to build a "club," so to speak, of up to ten friends. The software allowed them to create a unique identity for the "club" through shared images, sounds, and animations called "winks." Whenever club members had something interesting to say, he or she could share it with the others and instant message everyone simultaneously. Members thus built online "togetherness" by sharing their music, feelings, and experiences with one another using the software.

When the 3-degrees team debuted the new software on Microsoft's internal website in 2002, its popularity soared. Even thousands of Microsoft employees got into the game, forming online clubs to get to know each other better. The question now is will it succeed with the NetGen?[33] When it debuted on the World Wide Web, it faced the challenge of getting users to switch from their current messaging systems such as AOL messenger and Windows messenger. Eventually, it became clear it was not going to build up a user base big enough for the new software to connect and the features of the program were folded into Windows messenger 7 in 2005. Nevertheless, the stunning growth of relationship-building sites like myspace.com shows that Savage's team's ideas were on the right track, and Microsoft is rushing to build the relationship aspect into its new Vista software suite.

In sum, path-goal theory enhances our understanding of effective leadership in organizations by specifying how leaders should motivate their followers. As we discussed in previous chapters, motivation is one of the key determinants of performance in organizations, and the ability to motivate followers is a crucial aspect of a leader's effectiveness.[34]

VROOM AND YETTON MODEL
A model that describes the different ways in which leaders can make decisions and guides leaders in determining the extent to which subordinates should participate in decision making.

The Vroom and Yetton Model: Determining the Level of Subordinate Participation in Decision Making

One of the most important things that leaders do in organizations is make decisions. Good decisions help the organization achieve its goals; bad decisions hinder goal attainment. The **Vroom and Yetton model**, developed in the 1970s by Victor Vroom and Philip Yetton, describes the different ways in which leaders can make decisions, and it offers guidelines regarding the extent to which subordinates should participate in decision making.[35]

As many leaders have learned, allowing subordinates to participate in decision making and problem solving can enhance leadership.[36] Participation helps to ensure that subordinates will accept a decision that affects them or requires their support. Participation may result in better decisions if, for example, subordinates have information pertaining to the decision that the leader does not have. Additionally, participation can help foster subordinates' growth and development and may result in higher performance levels and job satisfaction.[37]

There are, however, certain disadvantages to employee participation. The biggest disadvantage is time. Not only does decision making take longer when subordinates participate, but both the subordinates and the leader now spend time making the decision. Another disadvantage of participation is that subordinates may disagree among themselves about the appropriate course of action or even begin to question the way others are doing their jobs. In team situations, this can lead to conflict and lower performance.

Given the advantages and disadvantages of subordinates' participation in decision making, the Vroom and Yetton model seeks to specify when and to what extent leaders should allow their subordinates to participate. To identify the optimal amount of participation, the Vroom and Yetton model first requires leaders to determine whether an individual or a group decision needs to be made. Individual decisions pertain to a single subordinate. An example is the decision the law firm manager had to make about how to motivate a subordinate with low confidence in his ability. Group decisions pertain to a group of subordinates. An example is the decision the law firm manager had to make about how to distribute raises.

Leaders making either individual or group decisions can choose from four different decision-making styles, which vary in the extent to which subordinates participate in making the decision. They are as follows:

- Autocratic: The leader makes the decision without input from subordinates.
- Consultative: Subordinates have some input, but the leader makes the decision.
- Group: The group makes the decision; the leader is just another group member.
- Delegated: The leader gives exclusive responsibility to subordinates.

In leader–member exchange theory, the personal relationship between a leader and follower that develops over time may be warm and friendly or it may be cold and distant and the follower becomes part of the "in-group" or "out–group," respectively.

The Vroom and Yetton model then instructs leaders to choose among these alternative decision-making styles on the basis of their answers to a series of questions about the nature of the situation and the subordinates involved. The following criteria must be considered: The nature of the tasks being performed by employees, the level of task interdependence, the output being produced, and the characteristics of the employees involved, such as their skill levels. As such, the model adopts the same kind of contingency approach as Fiedler and House's, but it focuses on choosing the right leader *decision-making* style. Today, allowing subordinates to participate in decision making is a very important issue because so many companies have organized their employees into self-managed work teams (discussed in Chapter 10) with decision-making authority.[38]

Leader–Member Exchange Theory: Relationships Between Leaders and Followers

LEADER–MEMBER EXCHANGE THEORY
A theory that describes the different kinds of relationships that may develop between a leader and a follower and what the leader and the follower give to and receive back from the relationship.

Leaders do not treat all of their subordinates in exactly the same way and may develop different types of relationships with different subordinates. **Leader–member exchange theory** describes the different kinds of relationships that may develop between a leader and a follower and describes what the leader and the follower bring to and get out of the relationship. The theory focuses on the *leader–follower dyad*—that is, the relationship between the leader and the follower (a *dyad* is two individuals regarded as a pair).[39] Leader–member exchange theory proposes that each leader–follower dyad develops a unique relationship that stems from the unfolding interactions between the leader and the follower.

Although each relationship is unique, the theory suggests that two general kinds of relationships develop in leader–follower dyads (see Exhibit 12.6). In some dyads, the leader develops a special relationship with the subordinate, characterized by mutual trust, commitment, and involvement. In these dyads, the subordinate helps the leader, the leader helps the subordinate, and each has substantial influence over the other. The leader spends a lot of time with the subordinate, who is given latitude or freedom to use his or her own judgment on the job. In turn, the subordinate tends to be satisfied and to perform at a high level. Subordinates who develop this special kind of relationship with their leaders are said to be in the *in-group*.[40]

Other subordinates develop a more traditional relationship with their leaders. In these dyads, the leader relies on his or her formal authority and position in the organization to influence the subordinate, and the subordinate is expected to perform his or her job in an acceptable manner and to follow rules and the directives of the leader.[41] The subordinate has considerably less influence over the leader, and the leader gives the subordinate less freedom to use his or her own judgment. These dyads are characterized by an impersonal, distant, or cold relationship between the leader and the subordinate. Subordinates who develop this kind of relationship with their leaders are said to be in the *out-group*. They tend to be less satisfied and perform at lower levels than in-group subordinates.

EXHIBIT 12.6

Leader–Member Exchange Theory

The relationship between in-group followers and the leader is characterized by trust, commitment and involvement. The relationship between out-group followers and the leader is based on the formal authority of the leader and obedience to rules.

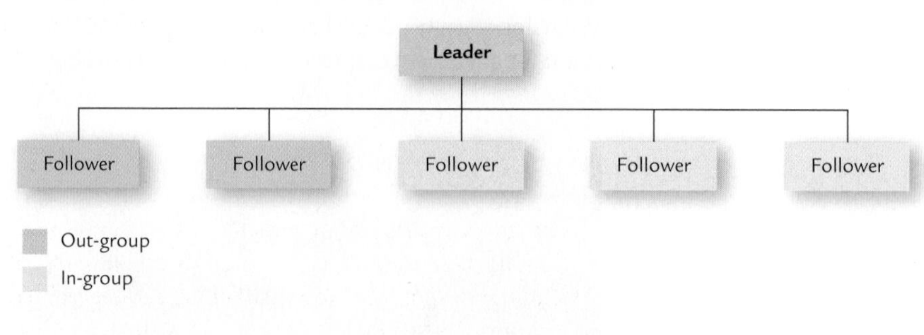

The relationship between a leader and his or her own supervisor is also a dyad that can be classified as an in-group or out-group relationship. Leaders who have high-quality relationships with their own supervisors are more likely to develop high-quality relationships with their subordinates. Furthermore, research conducted in Japan suggests that leaders who have high-quality relationships with their supervisors are more likely to advance quickly in an organization.[42]

Research suggests that it is desirable for leaders to develop special relationships with as many of their subordinates as they can because those who are in the in-group are more likely to perform at a higher level and exhibit loyalty than those in the out-group.[43] Research further suggests that a sharp distinction between the in-group and the out-group may not be desirable because subordinates in the out-group might resent their relatively inferior status and differential treatment.[44]

In summary, path-goal theory suggests that leaders need to focus on what outcomes motivate their followers and then to distribute those outcomes to subordinates when they attain their work goals and perform at high levels. It also suggests the need to tailor leadership styles to the characteristics of subordinates and the situation. The Vroom and Yetton model focuses on how much to allow subordinates to participate in decision making, which depends on the decision-making situation and the subordinates involved. Finally, leader–member exchange theory suggests that leaders should develop high-quality relationships with as many subordinates as possible. They should have as big an in-group and as small and out-group as possible.

Does Leadership Always Matter in Organizations?

By and large, research suggests that leaders *can* make a difference. Some researchers, however, have questioned whether leadership *always* makes a difference. Does it always help individuals, groups, and organizations perform at high levels, achieve their goals, and increase the organization's market share and profits? These researchers argue that although it might make people within the organization feel secure to think there is "someone" in charge, leadership may be more a figment of the imagination than a fact of organizational life.[45] These researchers suggest that leaders sometimes have little effect on the attitudes and behaviors of their followers. Sometimes, no matter what a leader does, employees are dissatisfied with their jobs or fail to perform highly. At other times, subordinates are satisfied with their jobs, attain or exceed their work goals, and perform at a high level without a leader's exerting much influence at all.

As an example of an employee of the latter type, consider Jason Jackson, a scriptwriter for a hit situation comedy on a major television network. Jackson prefers to work at home, where he has few interruptions. He stops by his office only a couple of times a week to pick up his mail. Jackson rarely sees his supervisor outside the quarterly planning and scheduling meetings that they both attend. Nevertheless, Jackson is very satisfied with his job and by all counts is a top performer. The show is in the top 10 and Jackson has received numerous industry awards for his scripts.

Jackson's case may be a bit extreme, but it does suggest in some situations leadership might not be very important. Two organizational behavior researchers, Steven Kerr and John Jermier, realized that leadership "substitutes" and "neutralizers" sometimes act to limit the influence that leaders have in organizations.[46]

Leadership Substitutes

LEADERSHIP SUBSTITUTE
Something that acts in place of a formal leader and makes leadership unnecessary.

A **leadership substitute** is something that acts in place of a formal leader and makes leadership unnecessary. Characteristics of the subordinate, the work, the group, and the organization all have the potential to act as substitutes for leadership. In Jackson's case, for example, both his personal characteristics and the nature of his work serve as leadership substitutes. Jackson is intelligent and skilled, and has a high level of intrinsic motivation.

(Recall from Chapter 6 that an employee who is intrinsically motivated enjoys his or her job and performs it well for its own sake.) Jackson loves writing and happens to be very creative. Because he is the way he is, Jackson does not need a supervisor to push him to write good scripts; his intrinsic motivation and capabilities ensure that he performs at a high level.

That Jackson's work tends to be interesting is an additional substitute for leadership: It contributes to his high performance and job satisfaction. It is not necessary for Jackson's supervisor to push him to perform, try to keep him happy, or even see him on a regular basis because of these powerful leadership substitutes. Fortunately, Jackson's supervisor realizes this and basically leaves Jackson alone, thereby freeing up some time to concentrate on his many other subordinates who *do* require leadership.

Leadership Neutralizers

Sidney Harman, CEO of Harman International Industries, realized that not seeing his subordinates on a day-to-day basis was leading them and his whole organization to imminent ruin. Harman International, located in California, manufactures audio equipment such as speakers for stereo systems. Although the company is located on the West Coast, Sidney Harman tried to lead the company from his office in Washington, D.C. How successful was he as a long-distance CEO? Not very. Harman International began to lose million of dollars. Fortunately, Harman acted quickly to turn around his company's performance. He moved to California, and by the next year, the company was making millions of dollars more than before.[47]

Why did Harman's move to California coincide with the dramatic change in his company's fortunes? Harman suggests that when he was 3,000 miles away he was unable to have as much influence on his subordinates as he needed. Not having their leader around on a day-to-day basis caused managers to tolerate and accept mediocre performance.[48] Essentially, the physical distance separating Harman from his subordinates neutralized his leadership efforts.

LEADERSHIP NEUTRALIZER
Something that prevents a leader from having any influence and negates a leader's efforts.

A **leadership neutralizer** is something that prevents a leader from having any influence and negates the leader's efforts. When neutralizers are present, there is a leadership void. The leader has little or no effect, and there is nothing to take the leader's place (there are no substitutes). Characteristics of the subordinate, the work, the group, and the organization can all serve as potential neutralizers of leadership. When subordinates lack *intrinsic* motivation and are performing boring tasks, for example, it is often necessary to use *extrinsic* rewards such as pay to motivate them to perform at a high level. Sometimes, however, the leaders of these subordinates do not have control over rewards like pay.

Elizabeth Williams, the leader of a group of ticket takers on a commuter railroad, had little at her disposal to motivate her subordinates' performances. The ticket takers' pay and benefits were based on seniority, and their employment contract specified they could be disciplined and dismissed only for a major infraction, such as coming to work intoxicated. Like Sidney Harman when he lived on the East Coast, Williams often did not see her subordinates. The ticket takers worked on the trains, but she did not. Because of those powerful neutralizers, Williams had little influence over her ticket takers, who often failed to collect tickets during rush hour because they didn't want to force their way through crowded passenger cars. Leadership neutralizers contributed to the railroad's losing money from lost ticket sales just as the transcontinental distance between Harman and his managers contributed to Harman International's losses in the early 1990s.

As these examples indicate, *substitutes* for leadership are actually *functional* for organizations because they free up some of a leader's time for other activities. But *neutralizers* are *dysfunctional* because a leader's influence is lacking. The fact that substitutes and neutralizers exist probably contributes to the perception that leadership is unimportant. Despite their existence, however, research suggests that leaders do in fact make a difference and can have positive effects on the attitudes and behaviors of their followers, as the following OB Today suggests.[49]

OB Today

No "One Size Fits All" Approach to Leadership

Many companies whose performance is falling significantly often search for a new leader or CEO who they believe will be able to solve its problems and turn around its performance. What is interesting about these CEOs is that they often have very different approaches to leadership—and not all of them are successful. There is no "one size fits all" approach when it comes to understanding what leaders do and what leadership is; neither is there just one way of solving a company's problems.

Take the example of Jacques Nasser, for example, an experienced global executive who was appointed as CEO of Ford Motors to turnaround its performance. Nasser was a brilliant, creative thinker who involved Ford in many different global projects to compete against efficient Japanese car companies. Nasser was a micromanager who sought to manage all major operating decisions and was reluctant to delegate authority to his top executives.[50] He had an achievement-oriented leadership approach based on setting his subordinates challenging difficult goals and then driving them to succeed. He created a tough performance-appraisal system to evaluate Ford's middle managers, one that sought to identify and weed out those he felt were poor performers.

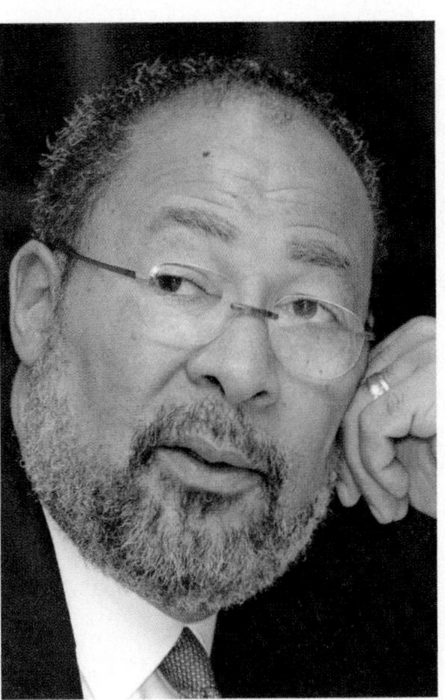

When Richard Parsons became CEO of Time Warner his participative approach to leadership encouraged Time Warner's competing managers to cooperate with each other across the organization.

By contrast, when struggling General Motors (GM) searched for a new leader, its selection was Rick Waggoner, a top executive known for being a team player and a "Type B" leader compared to hard-driving Nasser who was seen as a typical "Type A" leader. As a Type B leader, Waggoner's leadership style is participative—he recognizes the competence of his top executives and he delegates to them the authority they need to make the decisions in the areas and functions that they are in charge of. He lets people get on with their jobs and believes that "you've got to work well with people . . . you've got to be a good judge of talent."[51]

As it turned out, while Rick Waggoner is still the CEO of GM and his company's performance is improving, Jacques Nasser's approach didn't work for Ford. Its performance continued to slip and William Clay Ford, who has a consensus-building leadership style similar to Waggoner's, replaced him as CEO. He has delegated authority to his top managers to try to jumpstart Ford's turnaround; he has also abandoned Nasser's tough performance-appraisal system that discouraged managers from taking risks for fear of being fired for making mistakes.[52]

An example of a CEO who has adopted a leadership style that includes elements of both Nasser's and Waggoner's approach is Ellen Hancock, CEO of Exodus Communications, Inc., a prominent website-hosting company. Like Waggoner, Hancock is a strong believer in participation in decision making and gives the managers who report to her the authority to make important decisions in their areas of expertise. At the same, however, like

Nasser, Hancock is very goal oriented and excels at creating a work situation that provides managers with guidance so important things get done and nothing slips through the cracks. In addition, Hancock also is supportive of her subordinates and has mentored many women who want to succeed in the male-dominated world of high tech.[53]

A final example of the effect of different leadership approaches comes from Time Warner, the giant entertainment company.[54] In 2003, its visionary, achievement-oriented CEO, Gerald Levine retired and another Time Warner executive, Richard Parsons took over.[55] While both these CEOs believe in delegating authority to their managers, Parsons, unlike Levin, has a participative approach to leadership. When he became CEO, the diplomatic Parsons worked in a methodical way to encourage Time Warner's managers to cooperate with each other across the organization.[56] Levin's hard-driving approach had led these managers to compete with one another and turf battles between different business units were common. As a result, Time Warner's performance had fallen. Currently, Parson's approach is working for Time Warner and its performance has improved.[57]

The Romance of Leadership

Finally, it is worth noting that some researchers believe that the kinds of attribution errors and stereotypes discussed in Chapter 4 may sometimes lead people to perceive leaders in too positive or "romantic" a way. For example, perceptual biases can lead followers to attribute too much importance to a leader's personal style and too little importance to situational characteristics, like substitutes and neutralizers. In other words, followers may sometimes want to believe leaders have the ability to make a difference, and so they attribute qualities or powers to them they really don't possess. This is referred to as the *romance of leadership*.[58] Even if these beliefs aren't "real," they influence the way followers perceive a leader.[59] So leaders may be wise to conform to popular beliefs about what a successful leader should be "like"—for example, what they should wear, how they should behave toward subordinates, and how they should appear to the public.

You're the Management Expert

How to Lead Me

Each person has his or her own personality, values, beliefs, attitudes, and way of viewing the world. To help you gain insight into how different kinds of leadership approaches are likely to affect your *own* future work behaviors and attitudes, use the chapter material to think about the following issues:

1. What kind of personal characteristics should a leader possess to influence *you* to perform at the highest level you are capable of?
2. Which of the approaches to leadership described in the chapter would be (1) most likely, or (2) least likely, to influence and persuade you the most to perform at a high level? Why?
3. Which approach would *you* be most likely to adopt as a leader?

New Topics in Leadership Research

Given the prominence of the subject of leadership in scholarly literature and the popular press, it is not surprising there are always new developments, theories, and research on leadership. In this section, we explore some new topics of research: transformational and charismatic leadership, the effects of a leader's moods on his or her followers, and gender and leadership.

Transformational and Charismatic Leadership

Leadership researcher Bernard Bass has proposed a theory that looks at how leaders can sometimes dramatically affect their followers and organizations and literally transform them. Although several other theories focus on transformational and charismatic leadership, Bass's theory is highly thought of by other researchers, is relatively comprehensive, and incorporates ideas from some other well-known leadership approaches.[60]

TRANSFORMATIONAL LEADERSHIP Leadership that inspires followers to trust the leader, perform behaviors that contribute to the achievement of organizational goals, and perform at high levels.

According to Bass, **transformational leadership** occurs when a leader transforms, or changes, his or her followers in three important ways that together result in followers trusting the leader, performing behaviors that contribute to the achievement of organizational goals, and being motivated to perform at high levels (see Exhibit 12.7):

1. Transformational leaders increase subordinates' awareness of the importance of their tasks and the importance of performing them well.
2. Transformational leaders make subordinates aware of their needs for personal growth, development, and accomplishment.
3. Transformational leaders motivate their subordinates to work for the good of the organization rather than exclusively for their own personal gain or benefit.[61]

CHARISMATIC LEADER A self-confident, enthusiastic leader able to win followers' respect and support for his or her vision of how good things could be.

How do transformational leaders influence their followers and bring these changes about? Transformational leaders are **charismatic leaders**—leaders who have a vision of how good things *could be* in an organization in contrast to how things currently *are*.[62] Charismatic leaders clearly communicate this vision to their followers, and their excitement and enthusiasm induces their followers to enthusiastically support this vision.[63] To convey the excitement of their vision, charismatic leaders tend to have high levels of

EXHIBIT 12.7

Transformational Leadership

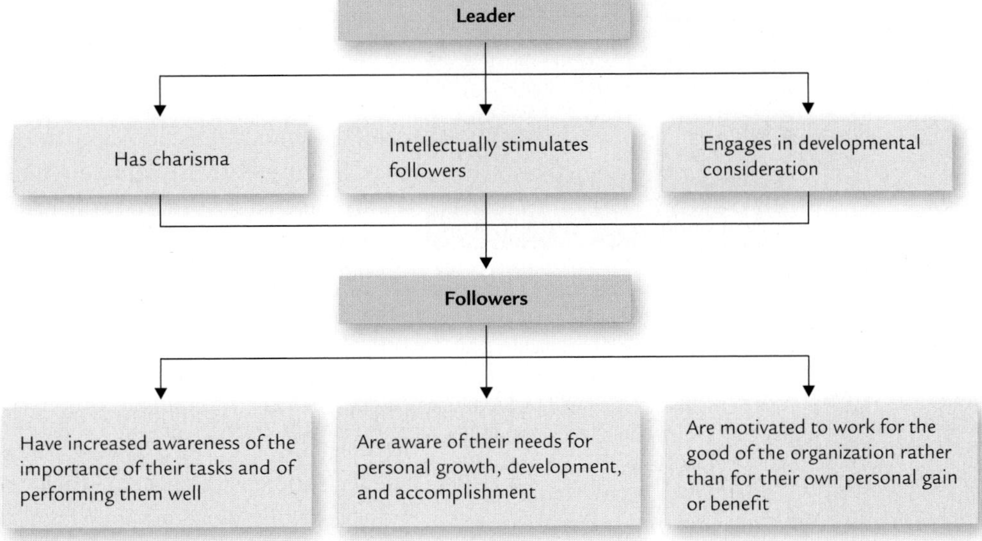

self-confidence and self-esteem, which further encourages their followers to respect and admire them.[64]

Transformational leaders influence their followers by intellectually stimulating them to become aware of problems in their groups and organization and view these problems from a new perspective—one consistent with the leader's vision.[65] Before the leader makes his or her influence felt, followers may not realize a problem exists, and if they do, they probably do not see the problem as something that directly concerns them. A transformational leader causes followers to view problems differently and feel some degree of responsibility for helping to solve them.[66]

DEVELOPMENTAL CONSIDERATION
Behavior by a leader that is supportive and encouraging toward followers and gives them opportunities to develop and grow on the job, such as
by acquiring new skills and capabilities.

Transformational leaders also influence their followers through developmental consideration.[67] **Developmental consideration** includes not only the consideration behavior discussed earlier in the chapter (which indicates a leader's concern for the well-being of his or her followers) but also behavior that supports and encourages followers and gives them opportunities to develop and grow on the job by acquiring new skills and capabilities.[68] Building trust is also an important aspect of transformational leadership.[69] Andrea Jung, CEO of Avon, is a transformational leader who has moved the company into the Internet age as illustrated in the following global view.

A Global View

Avon is Calling Everywhere

Pictured is Avon CEO Andrea Jung who has revolutionized the company's approach to selling its cosmetics and accessories by motivating its Avon sales reps to use the Internet and by recruiting new sales reps who match various age groups of its customers. Jung has also expanded Avon's global reach by recruiting an army of new sales reps around the world to sell its products.

If any company was in need of transformation it was Avon, the well-known, door-to-door selling cosmetics giant founded in 1886. Avon had over 3 million sales reps around the globe in 2000, but does door-to-door selling make sense in the Internet era when 75 percent of women in America work 9–5? After several years of declining sales, Avon recognized the need for change and appointed Andrea Jung as its CEO in 2000—its first woman CEO ever. Transforming the tradition-laden company would be a tough task for Jung.[70] She began by searching for a new vision for Avon.

In the early 2000s, Jung began to enthusiastically communicate her vision to Avon's 13,000 sales representatives who were anxious to learn about the company's new products and their new CEO. Jung let the sales representatives know that Avon's future success depended on their efforts and that they were at the heart of Avon. Jung preached about the importance of Internet sales and sought to help reps do more business online.[71] This was important because Avon's reps initially saw the Internet as a way of bypassing them and costing them their commissions. However, Jung worked hard to prove to them the company cared about them and that customers who purchased products online would likely end up being good prospects for personal selling in the future, once they had tried Avon's products. Jung's predictions proved to be correct. Internet sales actually increased—not decreased—the reps' commissions, and they now actively embrace the opportunities it has opened up for personal selling.

Moreover, Jung realized that a serious problem facing Avon was reaching beyond the typical 30-to-55-year-old woman who had always been its main customer. She decided to target the important 16-to-24-year-old segment and attract and build brand loyalty among young customers who will one day comprise its customer base. The potential of this market segment is enormous. The 17 million women in this segment have a total purchasing power of almost $100 billion a year and spend 20 percent of their income on beauty products.[72]

In 2003, a new Avon division called Mark began to distribute a new line of hip cosmetics designed specifically to meet the needs of this younger market segment. To meet the sales challenge of direct distribution to customers through a personal selling approach, Jung also decided to recruit a new generation of sales reps from the same demographic groups as younger customers. She hoped that being served by peers would enable Avon to gear up to the needs of this younger age group, and the company's sales reps would be trained to respond to them.

By 2004 Avon had 3.9 million reps located around the world and it reported record global profits on booming worldwide sales of its growing range of makeup, soaps, hair care, jewelry, and other products.[73] In 2005, however, Avon reported lower sales because its competitors had imitated its successful strategies and were growing their own new lines of products and advertising widely to increase their market share. In response Jung also increased advertising but emphasized to sales reps that they were still the key to achieving her vision of making Avon the number one "bricks and clicks" cosmetics shopping place for women around the globe.

TRANSACTIONAL LEADERSHIP
Leadership that motivates followers by exchanging rewards for high performance and noticing and reprimanding subordinates for mistakes and substandard performance.

Transformational leadership is often distinguished from transactional leadership. **Transactional leadership** occurs when a leader motivates followers purely by exchanging rewards for good performance and noticing and reprimanding subordinates for mistakes and substandard performance.[74] Transformational leaders, however, also may engage in transactional leadership. But they go one step further by actually *inducing* followers to support their vision and put aside their personal interests for the sake of the organization and take responsibility for solving its problems. Subordinates thereby grow and develop more than they would under exclusively incentive-based transactional-leadership styles.

Research on transformational leadership suggests that it is positively related to subordinate motivation, job satisfaction, and job performance.[75] One reason for this is that the characteristics of a transformational leader including a desire to be creative and take risks, to set ambitious goals for themselves, and to articulate a clear vision of what they want to achieve are appealing to their followers. In a sense, followers then model their behaviors on the transformation leader, buy into the vision, and develop a willingness to undertake the hard, stressful work that is necessary for creative, risk-taking work behavior.[76]

Several academic studies support the utility of this theory as do many popular books, such as *Built to Last*, that provide lucid accounts of transformation leaders establishing "big, hairy, audacious goals (BHAGs)" that serve as rallying points for their followers.[77] Challenging followers to achieve goals that they have not imagined could be achieved in order to attain the transformation leader's vision seems to be a common thread through many accounts of this form of leadership behavior. And the theory has gained support in research on managers across countries, levels in the hierarchy, and occupations. Moreover, evidenced suggests that it can be learned.[78]

Nothing succeeds like success, and research suggests that as a result transformational leaders may also be more likely to instill trust in their subordinates.[79] These leaders encourage and support their followers to be innovative and creative, they do not assign blame when things fail, and they just encourage employees to try again. And, when subordinates trust their leaders this can increase members' perceptions of procedural justice (see Chapter 6), which in turn, can lead employees to engage in organizational citizenship behaviors that can also raise performance (see Chapter 3).[80] In addition, by observing their leader, subordinates also learn how to lead in a transformational way, so the positive benefits of transformational leadership can cascade down an organization. All members of an organization come to buy into the vision the transformation leader creates, and this creates a strong organizational culture based on values and norms that help perpetuate such behaviors (this is discussed at length in Chapter 17).

Leader Mood

Megan Kelly and Rachel Feinstein are two bank tellers working for a medium-sized bank in New York City. They work different hours and have different supervisors but are close friends and frequently compare notes about their jobs and supervisors. Kelly recently complained to Feinstein that her boss, Bob Griffith, always seems so down. Even when everything is going smoothly on his shift, he rarely smiles and often looks as though the world is coming to an end. Although Griffith treats all the tellers on his shift fairly and is a capable supervisor, Kelly decides to try to switch to Feinstein's shift.

Part of the reason why Kelly requested a transfer to Feinstein's shift was some of the things that Feinstein told her about her boss, Santiago Ramirez. He almost always is in a good mood, and it is nice to be around him. He frequently jokes with the tellers, and smiles and laughs are as common on his shift as they are rare on Griffith's.

Kelly's experience (and probably your own) suggests that subordinates prefer to work for upbeat leaders than for those who are downbeat. Likewise, you might expect subordinates to work even harder when their leaders are happy and enthusiastic. Surprisingly, little research has been conducted on the effects that leader mood has on subordinates. Some preliminary research, however, suggests that leader mood may be an important factor when it comes to understanding why some leaders are more effective than others.

One recent study explored the effects of positive leader mood in a retail setting. The leaders were branch managers in a national chain. The researchers found that the managers who were in positive moods at work had stores that provided better customer service and had lower turnover rates than stores whose managers were not in positive moods. Although more research is needed, this initial study suggests that leader mood may be an important determinant of leader effectiveness.[81]

In addition to the moods a leader experiences, a leader's level of *emotional intelligence* (see Chapter 2) may also contribute to leader effectiveness. Emotional intelligence may help leaders develop a vision that is collective and shared throughout the organization and energize subordinates to enthusiastically work toward achieving it. It can also help leaders develop a meaningful identity for their organizations and instill an atmosphere of trust and cooperation. Finally, emotional intelligence can help leaders remain flexible in rapidly changing environments.[82]

Gender and Leadership

One common stereotype in organizations is that women are supportive, nurturing, and generally good at managing interpersonal relations. The male counterpart to the stereotype of the relationship-oriented woman is the notion that men are directive and focus on getting the job done—in other words, that men tend to be task-oriented. Judging from these stereotypes, you might expect that gender would have an effect on leadership. For example, you might expect female leaders to engage in more consideration behaviors than men, and male leaders engage in more initiating-structure behaviors than women.

Indeed, researchers have investigated this question. One recent review of the literature conducted by well-respected researcher Alice Eagly and a colleague found quite the opposite. It suggested that when men and women have leadership positions in organizations, they tend to behave in a similar manner. Men do not engage in more initiating structure just as women do not engage in more consideration.[83]

One difference did emerge, however. Women tended to lead in a more democratic style, and men tended to lead in a more autocratic style.[84] When leaders are democratic, they tend to involve their subordinates in decision making and seek their subordinates' input on a variety of matters. Autocratic leaders tend to discourage subordinate participation in decision making and like to do things their own way.

Why are women more democratic than men when they occupy leadership positions in organizations? Researchers have offered two potential explanations.[85] One is that women's interpersonal skills (they way they interact with other people) tend to be better than men's. To be democratic or participative, a leader needs to have good interpersonal skills. To encourage subordinates to express their opinions, for example, it is important for a leader to understand how subordinates feel. To reject subordinates' ideas or proposed solutions to problems and still maintain a good relationship with them requires a certain amount of sensitivity. Women may be more democratic as leaders than men simply because they are more skilled interpersonally.

The other potential explanation for the finding that women leaders tend to be more democratic than men is that women in leadership positions encounter more resistance from subordinates than do men in leadership positions. (Consistent with this reasoning is the tendency that people have to evaluate female leaders a bit more harshly than they evaluate male leaders.[86] Gender stereotypes (see Chapter 4) may lead members of an organization to readily accept men in leadership positions but to resist women taking on these same roles. For example, a 55-year-old male executive in an engineering firm who has always had a male supervisor throughout his professional career may resist having to report to a woman. His female supervisor, recognizing his resistance and resentment, might try to overcome it by involving the subordinate in decision making and seeking his input on a variety of matters. Given that women are assuming more leadership positions in organizations, it is important to understand whether and why they might be different from men when it comes to leading.

Interestingly enough, some recent research suggests that women may actually have better leadership skills in some respects. Some recent studies suggest that women leaders, when evaluated by co-employees, supervisors, and subordinates, receive somewhat higher ratings on skills like good communication and listening, work quality, and being able to motivate others.[87] Thus, to the extent that women are better listeners, less autocratic and more participative, more flexible, and more willing to admit they are wrong, watching and learning from women leaders may actually help men lacking one or more of these skills.[88] By the same token, watching how men network and seize opportunities to become leaders may help women advance further up the organizational hierarchy, where they are still significantly underrepresented.

Ethical Leadership

In the 2000s numerous CEOs and top managers who lead some of the largest U. S. companies have been accused of acting unethically, and many have also been convicted of acting illegally. In company after company leaders—such as Bernie Ebbers, the ex-CEO of WorldCom, and Ken Lay, Andrew Fastow, and Jeff Skilling, former leaders of bankrupt Enron—pursued their own interests at the interests of their employees and investors. And these people lost their jobs and their savings when these companies collapsed as a result of their criminal behaviors. To avoid this outcome companies are increasingly checking on the credentials of their leaders to ensure they are being managed by ethical, honest people. Many companies have been shocked to find that their CEOs "inflated" their résumés to obtain their jobs, often claiming college degrees or work experience they never received. As a result the ethics of the people who lead companies has come under increasing scrutiny.

Today the requirement that company leaders behave ethically and in a socially responsible way to protect the interests of their customers, investors, employees, and all those affected by their actions is more important than ever before. And one major reason for this is that leaders who are perceived as being ethical and fair in their dealings with others provide the role model for their subordinates to follow. As subordinates adopt high ethical standards so the perception of the need to behave in a fair and honest way cascades down the organization and a just, socially responsible culture emerges (we discuss this in more detail in Chapter 17). The way in which the CEO of one company, Whole Foods, created an ethical company illustrates many of the issues surrounding ethical leadership, and is profiled in the following OB in Action.

OB in Action

Whole Foods Markets Leads Through Ethics and Social Responsibility

The Whole Foods Markets supermarket chain, which specializes in the sale of organic and chemical- and drug-free meat, poultry, and produce, has enjoyed enormous success in the last decade. Despite the fact that it charges high prices for its premium produce, its store sales are growing fast. Indeed Whole Foods plans to double both the number of its present 170 stores by 2010 and its $4 billion revenue. All this from a company that was started by two hippies in Austin, Texas, in 1978 as a natural counter-culture food store. How and why has Whole Foods grown so rapidly? Because, says its founder and CEO John Mackey, of the way he chose to lead and manage his store chain from its beginning—in a manner based on the need to act ethically and in a social responsible way toward everybody involved in its business.

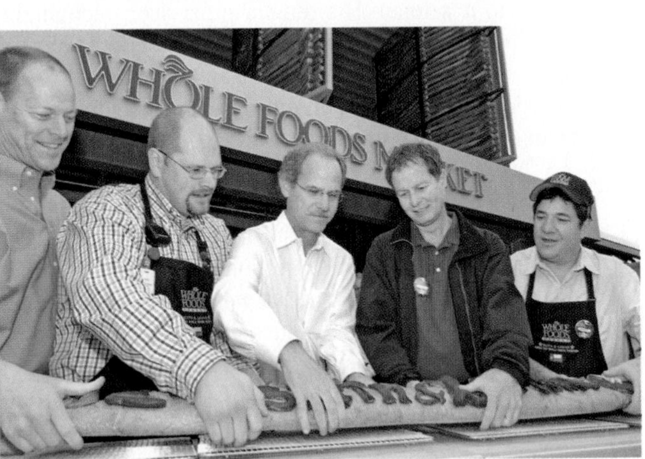

The founder and CEO of Whole Foods, John Mackey, says his company has grown so rapidly because he manages his store chain in an ethical way and all his employees behave in a socially responsible way toward everybody involved in its business.

Mackay started his business for three reasons—to have fun, to make money, and to contribute to the well-being of other people, customers. The company's mission is based on its members' collective responsibility to the well-being of all the various stakeholders who are involved with it. And, in order of priority at Whole Foods these are customers, team members, investors, suppliers, community, and natural environment. Mackay measures his company's success on how well it satisfies the needs of these stakeholders.

The ethical stance at the base of his business model is that Whole Food's customers are guaranteed that products are 100 percent organic, hormone free, or as represented. Similarly, Whole Foods insists that its suppliers behave in an ethical way so, for example, the beef it sells comes from cows pastured on grass not corn-fed in feed lots or the chicken it sells does not come from hens that have been confined in tiny cages that prevent them from even moving. His management approach to his employees, or team members as they are called, is also based on a unique ethical leadership position.

To pursue the company mission Mackey says that, "We put great emphasis at Whole Foods on the 'Whole People' part of this mission. We believe in helping support our team members to grow as individuals—to become 'Whole People.' We consciously use Maslow's hierarchy of needs model to help our team members to move up Maslow's hierarchy. As much as we are able, we attempt to manage through love instead of fear or greed. We allow tremendous individual initiative at Whole Foods and that's why our company is so innovative and creative."[89] Mackay claims all the stores in the chain are unique because in each one team members are constantly experimenting with new and better ways to serve customers and improve their well-being. As team members learn, they become self-actualized and this increase in their well-being translates into a desire to increase the well-being of other stakeholders. Mackay contrasts this supportive approach to leadership with the classical command and control, hierarchical rewards-based directive approach that he claims encourages the pursuit of personal rather than team- or organizational-based objectives.

Finally, Mackay's strong views on ethics and social responsibility also serve shareholders. Mackay does not believe the object of being in business is to primarily maximize profits for shareholders; he puts customers first. He believes, however, that when managers engage in ethical leadership, which satisfies the needs of customers and employees, investors' needs are simultaneously being satisfied because satisfied stakeholders behave in ways that lead to high profits—customers are loyal, and employees are committed. Indeed, since Whole Foods went public in 1992 and issued shares, the value of those shares has increased 25 times—something that has certainly increased the well-being of the company's owners![90] Clearly, ethical leadership has worked so far at Whole Foods.

Mackay's approach to leadership can be found in other successful companies such as Google and Southwest Airlines. At Southwest, for example, Coleen Barratt pursues an "employees first, customers second" approach because her belief is that, "If senior leaders regularly communicate with employees, if we're truthful and factual, if we show them that we care, and we do our best to respond to their needs, they'll feel good about their work environment and they'll be better at serving the passengers."[91]

TRUST
The willingness of one person or group to have faith or confidence in the goodwill of another person, even though this puts them at risk.

The issue of establishing trust between leaders and subordinates is a central concept in ethical leadership. **Trust** is the willingness of one person or group to have faith or confidence in the goodwill of another person, even though this puts them at risk (because the other might act in a deceitful way). For example, for employees to trust in their leaders they must believe that they will be rewarded for being cooperative and for working toward long-term organizational goals, even when this may hurt their short-run personal goals. Trust is also vital to establish good working relationships in groups and teams so that process gains can be achieved. Only if team members believe that other team members will also behave in an ethical way for example, they will not free ride or shirk, or that their leaders will "play favorites" so rewards are not linked to

EXHIBIT 12.8

Approaches to Understanding Effective Leadership

Approach	Focus
Trait approach	Specific traits that contribute to effective leadership
Behavior approach	Specific behaviors that effective leaders engage in
Fiedler's contingency model	Characteristics of situations in which different kinds of leaders (relationship oriented and task oriented) are most effective
Path-goal theory	How effective leaders motivate their followers
Vroom and Yetton model	When leaders should involve their subordinates in decision making
Leader–member exchange theory	The kinds of personal relationships that leaders develop with followers
Substitutes and neutralizers	When leadership is unnecessary and when a leader is prevented from having influence
Transformational and charismatic leadership	How leaders make profound changes in their followers and organizations
Leader mood	How leaders' feelings influence their effectiveness
Gender and leadership	Similarities and differences in men and women as leaders

performance, will members be motivated to cooperate. When ethical leadership helps establish trust and all parties work toward a common goal, the performance gains can be substantial.

Recap of Leadership Approaches

In this chapter, we have described several approaches to understanding effective leadership in organizations. These leadership approaches are complementary: each sheds light on a different aspect of, or set of issues pertaining to, effective leadership. The approaches are recapped in Exhibit 12.8.

Summary

Leaders at all levels in an organization help individuals, groups, and the organization as a whole achieve their goals and can thus have profound effects in organizations. The approaches to leadership covered in this chapter help explain how leaders influence their followers and why leaders are sometimes effective and sometimes ineffective. In this chapter, we made the following major points:

1. Leadership is the exercise of influence by one member of a group or organization over other members to help the group or organization achieve its goals. Formal leaders have formal authority to influence others by virtue of their job responsibilities. Informal leaders lack formal authority but influence others by virtue of their special skills or talents.
2. The trait approach to leadership has found that good leaders tend to be intelligent, dominant, self-confident, energetic, are able to withstand stress, honest, mature, and knowledgeable. Possessing these traits, however, does not guarantee that a leader will be effective, nor does the failure to have one or more of these traits mean that a leader will be ineffective.
3. A lot of the behaviors that leaders engage in fall into two main categories: consideration and initiating structure. Consideration includes all leadership behaviors that indicate that

leaders trust, respect, and value a good relationship with their followers. Initiating structure includes all the behaviors that leaders engage in to help subordinates achieve their goals and perform at a high level. Leaders also engage in rewarding and punishing behaviors.

4. Fiedler's contingency theory proposes that leader effectiveness depends on both leader style and situational characteristics. Leaders have either a relationship–oriented style or a task-oriented style. Situational characteristics, including leader–member relations, task structure, and position power, determine how favorable a situation is for leading. Relationship-oriented leaders are most effective in moderately favorable situations. Task-oriented leaders are most effective in extremely favorable or unfavorable situations. Leaders cannot easily change their styles, so Fiedler recommends changing situations to fit the leader or assigning leaders to situations in which they will be most effective.
5. Path-goal theory suggests that effective leaders motivate their followers by giving them outcomes they desire when they perform at a high level or achieve their work goals. Effective leaders also make sure their subordinates believe that they can obtain their work goals and perform at a high level, show subordinates the paths to goal attainment, remove obstacles that might come up along the way, and express confidence in their subordinates' capabilities. Leaders need to adjust the type of behavior they engage in (directive, supportive, participative, or achievement-oriented) to correspond to the nature of the subordinates they are dealing with and the type of work they are doing.
6. The Vroom and Yetton model specifies the extent to which leaders should have their subordinates participate in decision making. How much subordinates should participate depends on aspects of the decision that needs to be made, the subordinates involved, and the information needed to make a good decision.
7. Leader–member exchange theory focuses on the leader–follower dyad and suggests that leaders do not treat each of their followers the same but rather develop different kinds of relationships with different subordinates. Some leader–follower dyads have high-quality relationships. Subordinates in these dyads are members of the in-group. Other leader–follower dyads have low-quality relationships. Subordinates in these dyads form the out-group.
8. Sometimes, leadership does not seem to have much of an effect in organizations because of the existence of substitutes and neutralizers. A leadership substitute is something that acts in place of a formal leader. Substitutes make leadership unnecessary because they take the place of the influence of a leader. A leadership neutralizer is something that prevents a leader from having influence and negates a leader's efforts. When neutralizers are present, there is a leadership void—the leader is having little or no effect, and nothing else is taking the leader's place.
9. Transformational leaders increase their followers' awareness of the importance of their jobs and the followers' own needs for personal growth and accomplishment and motivate followers to work for the good of the organization. Leaders transform their followers by being charismatic, intellectually stimulating their followers, and engaging in developmental consideration. Transactional leadership occurs when leaders motivate their subordinates by exchanging rewards for high performance and reprimanding instances of low performance.
10. Leader mood at work and levels of emotional intelligence have the potential to influence leader effectiveness. Preliminary research suggests that when leaders tend to be in a good mood at work, their subordinates may perform at a higher level and be less likely to resign.
11. Women and men do not appear to differ in the leadership behaviors (consideration and initiating structure) that they perform in organizations. Women, however, appear to be more democratic or participative than men as leaders.
12. Ethical leadership helps develop trust among organizational members that translates into high performance and protects the well-being of all stakeholders.

Organizational Behavior in Action

Questions for Review

1. In what ways are the trait and behavior approaches to leadership similar?
2. Under what circumstances might leader-punishing behavior be appropriate?
3. Are Fiedler's contingency model and the trait approach consistent with one another or inconsistent? Explain.
4. How might a relationship-oriented leader who manages a restaurant and is in a very unfavorable situation for leading improve the favorability of the situation so that it becomes moderately favorable?
5. In what kinds of situations might it be especially important for a leader to focus on motivating subordinates (as outlined in path-goal theory)?
6. What might be some of the consequences of a leader having a relatively small in-group and a large out-group of subordinates?
7. Can organizations create substitutes for leadership to cut down on the number of managers they need to employ? Why or why not?
8. When might having a charismatic leader be dysfunctional for an organization?
9. Do organizations always need transformational leaders, or are they needed only some of the time? Explain.
10. How can managers practice ethical leadership, and encourage their subordinates to act ethically as well?

OB: Increasing Self-Awareness

Contemporary Leaders

Choose a public figure you are familiar with (you know the individual, you have read about the person in magazines and newspapers, or you have seen him or her on TV) who is in a leadership position. Pick someone other people in your class are likely to know. The person could be a leader in politics or government (at the national, state, or local level), a leader in your community, or a leader at the college or university you attend. For the leader you have selected, answer the following questions:

1. What traits does this leader appear to possess?
2. What behaviors does this leader engage in?
3. Is this leader relationship-oriented or task-oriented? How favorable is the leadership situation according to Fiedler's contingency model?
4. How does this leader try to motivate his or her followers?
5. To what extent does this leader allow his or her followers to participate in decision making?
6. Do any substitutes or neutralizers exist with regard to this leader? What are they?
7. Is this a transformational leader? Why or why not?
8. Does this leader engage in transactional leadership?

A Question of Ethics

Influence at Work

Influence and persuasion is a central part of a leader's job; leaders routinely attempt to influence employees to work hard and perform at a high level. Leadership can have a dark side if managers influence employees to behave in unethical ways, however. Think about the ethical issues involved in leadership and address the following questions:

1. What kinds of actions of a leader would you regard as being clearly unethical in their attempts to influence and persuade employees?
2. Do you think some kinds of leadership approaches are more ethical than others?
3. At what point does transformational leadership become unethical in an organizational setting?

Small Group Break-Out Exercise:

A Leadership Problem at HighandTall

Form groups of three to five people, discuss the following scenario, and discuss the questions; be prepared to share your discussions with your class:

You are the founding entrepreneurs of HighandTall Company, a fast-growing digital software company that specializes in home consumer electronics. Customer demand to license your software has boomed so much that in just two years you have added over 50 new software programmers to help develop a new range of software products. These people are young and inexperienced but are highly skilled and used to putting in long hours to see their ideas succeed. The growth of your company has been so swift that you still operate informally. As top managers you have been so absorbed in your own work that you have paid little attention to the issue of leading your growing company. You have allowed your programmers to find solutions to problems as they go along, they have also been allowed to form their own work groups, but there are signs that problems are arising.

There have been increasing complaints from employees that as managers you do not recognize or reward good performance and that they do not feel equitably treated. Moreover, there have been growing concerns that you are either too busy or not willing to listen to their new ideas and act on them. A bad atmosphere seems to be developing in the company and recently several talented employees have left.

You realize in hindsight that you have done a poor job of leading your employees and that you need to develop a common leadership approach to encourage employees to perform well and stay with your company.

1. Analyze this leadership situation to uncover the contingency factors that will be important in choosing a leadership approach. Examine the four approaches to leadership against these factors.
2. Which is the most effective leadership approach to adopt?
3. In what other ways could you influence and persuade your employees to perform well and stay with your company?

Topic for Debate

Leaders can have powerful effects on their subordinates and their organizations as a whole. Now that you have a good understanding of leadership, debate the following issue:

Team A. Managers can be trained to be effective leaders.

Team B. Managers either have what it takes to be an effective leader or they don't. If they don't, they cannot be trained to be effective leaders.

Experiential Exercise

Effectively Leading a Work Group

Objective

Your objective is to gain experience in effectively leading a group of employees who have varying levels of ability and motivation.

Procedure

Assume the role of Maria Cuellar, who has just been promoted to the position of supervisor of a group of four employees who create designs for wallpaper. The group's goal is to create imaginative and best-selling wallpaper designs. Cuellar is excited but apprehensive about assuming her first real leadership position. As a former member of this group, she has had ample opportunity to observe some of her new subordinates' (and former group members') on-the-job behaviors.

Each person brings different strengths and weaknesses to his or her job. Ralph Katten can turn out highly creative (and occasionally) best-selling designs if he tries. But often, he does not try; he seems to daydream a lot and not take his work seriously. Elisa Martinez is a hard employee who does an acceptable job; her designs are not particularly noteworthy but are not bad either. Karen Parker is new to the group and is still learning the ins and outs of wallpaper design. Tracy McGuire is an above-average performer; her designs are good, and she turns out a fair number of them.

1. Using the knowledge you have gained from this chapter (e.g., about the behavior approach, path-goal theory, and leader–member exchange theory), describe the steps Maria Cuellar should take to effectively lead this group of wallpaper designers. Should she use the same approach with each of her subordinates, or should her leadership approach differ depending on the subordinate involved?
2. The class divides into groups of three to five people, and each group appoints one member as spokesperson, to present the group's recommendations to the whole class.
3. Group members take turns describing the steps Cuellar should take to be an effective leader.
4. Group members compare and contrast the different leadership approaches that Cuellar might take and assess their advantages and disadvantages.
5. Group members decide what advice to give Maria Cuellar to help her be an effective leader of the four designers.

When the group has completed those activities, the spokesperson will present the group's recommendations to the whole class.

New York Times *Cases in the News*

The New York Times

"At LucasArts, No Playing Around in Quest to Be No. 1"

By Laura M. Holson, NYT, April 17 2006, p. C1.

In September 2004, Jim Ward met with the director George Lucas at his office at Skywalker Ranch near here. At the time, LucasArts, the video game company created by Mr. Lucas in 1982 and run by Mr. Ward, was in disarray. The division was making too many mediocre "Star Wars" games, it was rife with internal rivalries and it was in such lackluster financial shape that bonuses for employees were scrapped that year. Mr. Ward, a veteran Lucasfilm marketing executive who had been named president of LucasArts only four months earlier, was there to present Mr. Lucas with a business plan, but he had a few questions of his own. Most important, did Mr. Lucas have the desire to turn LucasArts into one of the top five video game publishers? Indeed, Mr. Lucas said, he did. "We can do this ourselves," Mr. Ward recalled Mr. Lucas telling him. "We will put our resources behind this."

LucasArts is not No. 5 yet. But last year it ranked No. 8 in sales, up from No. 13 a year earlier, according to the NPD Group. And, Mr. Ward, 46, is being credited with a turnaround. While No. 8 may seem low in an industry obsessed with No. 1, LucasArts got there selling a fraction of the games its competitors did. Analysts and others in the industry agree it is a promising turn for Lucas Arts and, in particular, Mr. Ward. But his most challenging days may be ahead. The video game industry has been in the doldrums for months; video game sales are lagging as consumers wait to buy the next generation of consoles, including the PlayStation 3. Sitting in his office overlooking the San Francisco Bay one recent morning, Mr. Ward reflected on what he and his team had done so far. It was at a town hall meeting in August 2004, the month before he met with Mr. Lucas, that he outlined his strategy in an auditorium filled with staff members. It seemed simple: LucasArts would make high-quality games, and deliver them on time and on budget. "I learned this from George," said Mr. Ward. "There are these countless meetings where he is rational, laid back. Back then he sets the bar so high you begin to think, like, this guy is out of his mind." To illustrate the point, Mr. Ward raised his right arm in the air, higher than the left. "I said, 'Gang, this is what we are doing,'" said Mr. Ward, slowly raising his left arm to meet the right. "Now they've learned that if they come remotely close to this, they can do amazing things."

Before joining Lucasfilm in 1997, Mr. Ward had distinguished himself for 13 years as an aggressive advertising executive working with the likes of Apple Computer, Nike and Microsoft. While working at the advertising firm of Wieden & Kennedy, he was involved in the introduction of Windows 95 for Microsoft. He and his colleagues recommended that Microsoft use the Rolling Stone's hit "Start Me Up" in its now famous campaign. Later, he was Wieden's global account director for Nike and part of the team that introduced Tiger Woods as a brand. Mr. Ward was recruited to Lucasfilm in 1997 to oversee the worldwide marketing of the last three movies in the "Star Wars" series, as well as all of Lucasfilm's DVD library. But by November 2003, Mr. Ward wanted more responsibility. Mr. Lucas and Ms. Chau agreed to let Mr. Ward "try out" at LucasArts even though he had no experience making video games. "When he talked to us we were thinking maybe, maybe not," said Ms. Chau. "But if he surrounded himself with people who knew the business, and he listened, this could be great." Mr. Ward was named president at LucasArts in May 2004.

Robbie Bach, president of the entertainment and devices division at Microsoft, who has known Mr. Ward since the start of Windows 95, said Mr. Ward sought advice from others on how best to revive LucasArts. "He did listen to a lot of people, but once he made a decision, he didn't waste time getting it done," said Mr. Bach. Along the way, he also developed a reputation for directness that could be a little rough. Mr. Riccitiello said that Mr. Ward "can run certain people over" with his big voice and strong point of view. "My sense is if you took the average executive with a 50- to 80-hour workweek, they spend about 50 percent of their time just being nice," said Mr. Riccitiello. "Jim doesn't deal with that. He picks up half a week right there."

In 2004, about one-quarter of nearly 400 employees at LucasArts lost their jobs, said several former employees. (Mr. Ward declined to discuss the layoffs. Currently there are 252 employees in the division.) He quickly sought to shake up the culture. "I needed to free them up and get rid of the politics so I could institute a team," said Mr. Ward. "I told them they either get on board or they don't." He began weekly meetings to encourage department heads to talk. He said he separated the quality-control department from product development to create "healthy tension," giving staff members more freedom to express their views.

Mr. Ward said he had successfully worked with creative people his entire career, and former LucasArts employees said he sought to inspire. But even Mr. Ward conceded that LucasArts developers were suspicious at first. "You've never run a video game company before," he said many of them told him. As a result he knew he needed someone to help who knew how to make games. So he promoted Peter Hirschmann, 34, to be vice president of product development. "The linchpin was to find a creative partner," Mr. Ward said. A former production assistant who worked with Steven Spielberg, Mr. Hirschmann was involved in developing that director's widely acclaimed Medal of Honor video games before joining LucasArts in 2002 as a producer. Mr. Ward got to know Mr. Hirschmann in early 2004, when he would pad down the hall to his office late at night to check on the progress of Star Wars: Battlefront, which Mr. Hirschmann was overseeing.

While Mr. Ward can be forceful, Mr. Hirschmann is more relaxed. He once hired an ice cream truck to deliver gelato to the staff. "Peter is a perfect counter to me," said Mr. Ward. At first Mr. Hirschmann was not interested in the job. "I saw a lot of baggage with it," said Mr. Hirschmann. "But Jim said, 'We are going to hit the reset button. We are going to reboot.' Then I thought, maybe this was doable." Their excitement was palpable on a recent afternoon, when Mr. Ward, Mr. Hirschmann and Haden Blackman, the project leader of a forthcoming "Star Wars" game, reviewed all of the company's recent projects. Mr. Blackman outlined a new storyline that delved deeper into Darth Vader's history. "There's a lot of pressure," said Mr. Ward. "I mean we're taking $20 million out of George's pocket," he said, tapping Mr. Hirschmann on the shoulder while referring to the potential cost of a video game for the next generation of consoles. Mr. Hirschmann and Mr. Blackman shot each other a knowing glance. "We feel the pressure, all right," Mr. Hirschmann said, laughing.

Questions for Discussion

1. What kind of a leader is Jim Ward, and what theory best describes his approach to leadership?
2. If you were his subordinate, how would Jim Ward expect you to behave?
3. Why does Peter Hirschmann complement Jim Ward at LucasArts?

The New York Times

"He Naps, He Sings, and He Isn't Michael Dell"

Gary Rivlin, NYT, September 11, 2005, p. 3.1.

There's an established drill, or so it sometimes seems, when a publicly traded company disappoints Wall Street. The chief executive blames high oil prices. Or it's the fault of unforeseen happenings in Asia, or of a software upgrade that didn't go as planned. But maybe Kevin B. Rollins, the chief executive of Dell, is so new to the job that he doesn't know any better. Mr. Rollins, 52, had been C.E.O. for barely a year when Dell, the computer maker, announced last month that it had fallen short of expectations—both its own and those of analysts. The company's profits did rise 28 percent in the second quarter, based largely on strong overseas sales, but total revenue came in several hundred million dollars short of projections.

Mr. Rollins, who became an executive after a career switch in his 40's, could have offered any number of excuses, not the least of which is Dell's own previous success. He might have also mentioned that Dell is wrestling with the same question facing other mature technology companies that ranked among the highest fliers of the 1990's: How to increase revenues when it is already so big? Despite all of this, Mr. Rollins blamed himself for Dell's disappointing earnings. "Frankly," he said during a conference call with analysts, "we executed poorly on managing overall selling prices"—in particular those machines sold to consumers.

If nothing else, Mr. Rollins, who succeeded the company's founder, Michael S. Dell, as chief executive in July 2004, is a different cut of C.E.O. Consider his reaction in 2001 when he came to believe that the corporate culture of Dell had been soured by greed. Mr. Rollins, then the company's second in command, blamed himself and fellow top executives for failing to set the right tone. To help set things right, he decreed that every Dell manager would submit to periodic evaluations by his or her underlyings—a policy still in place, though he endured the sting of people essentially telling him that he could be so supercilious and icy cold that his personality should be stored in a meat locker.

During that process, for instance, Paul D. McKinnon, a senior vice president who oversees human resources at Dell, remembers proclaiming Mr. Rollins aloof, a poor listener and a leader who at times could seem unapproachable. Another senior vice president, Paul D. Bell, who is responsible for the company's European, Middle Eastern and African operations, said that Mr. Rollins could be argumentative, maybe even bullheaded. Mr. Rollins chuckled as he recalled the first time he endured this twist on the standard employee review. "You mean when people said I was a little arrogant and maybe a lot opinionated?" he said, a slightly pinched smile on his face. He didn't seem defensive about what he had learned about himself so much as fascinated by the results of a social experiment in which he was the test subject.

"You tell your family about the things you learn and they go, 'Well, we knew that,' " he said. And with that, Mr. Rollins let loose another laugh. To the extent that he has any reputation at all, it is that of a button-down logistics expert, one of the operational geniuses most responsible for assembling a company so well run that academics study it, and even competitors admire the efficiency with which it spits out PC's and, increasingly, other products like printers, televisions and a cheaper alternative to the iPod. But when people meet him, they discover that he is more soft-spoken and reserved than a typical chief executive. Friends say he is also warmer and more easygoing than first impressions—if not also second and third impressions—might suggest. "A practiced extrovert" is the way Thomas J. Meredith, a good friend and the company's former chief financial officer, described him.

In the back-slapping world of big business, where deals are often consummated over glasses of bourbon or bottles of fine wine, Mr. Rollins also stands out. As a Mormon, he has never consumed an alcoholic beverage. He plays the violin several times a week, and occasionally performs publicly. He's a skier and a mountain biker, and he races motorcycles and fast cars, a pastime he occasionally shares with Joseph M. Tucci, chief executive of EMC, the computer storage device maker that has been a Dell partner since 2001. "He is very different once you get to know him," Mr. Tucci said. "He can come off as aloof, but he's far from it." Thirteen months ago, Dell Inc., the world's top computer maker, endured what is supposed to be one of the harder transitions for any corporation. Mr. Dell was chief executive for 20 years after he founded the company in his dorm room at the University of Texas in Austin. Though he gave up that title last year, he stayed on as chairman—a type of arrangement that can make the transfer of the day-to-day responsibilities to the new chief that much more difficult, said Samuel A. Culbert, a professor at the Anderson School of Management at the University of California, Los Angeles. "Usually this ends up being one big mess unless the founder gets the heck out of there," he said. Aside from Dell, there has been one notable exception to this in the technology world, added Professor Culbert, who has studied executive leadership for 35 years. It is Microsoft, where Bill Gates stepped aside as chief executive in 2000, after a quarter-century of running the company, but remained chairman (and added the new title of "chief software architect") after Steven A. Ballmer took over as C.E.O. In picking his successor, Mr. Dell "was fortunate to find the right guy," Professor Culbert said, "and then when he did, he was advanced enough as a human being to trust him and leave him alone and give him money and prestige and the freedom to do this job."

While Mr. Rollins and Mr. Dell are not particularly close on a personal level—they rarely socialize with each other, Mr. Dell said—they do work closely together, figuratively and literally. Their large wooden desks face one another in adjoining offices separated by a glass wall and a glass door. Mr. Tucci says he has visited those offices about 50 times and has never seen the door closed. "The way those two guys get along is not an act," Mr. Tucci said. "I can start a conversation with Michael, and two weeks later finish it with Kevin. They know what each other is thinking." Each also complements the other's talents. Mr. Dell is a skillful salesman and the resident technologist mapping new trends, Mr. Rollins takes responsibility for most everything else, from the speed at which the company's factories operate to employee morale.

"People always wonder how well a transition like this will work when the founder is staying very involved," Mr. Ballmer wrote in an e-mail message. But when people work together as well as Mr. Rollins and Mr. Dell do, he added, "it actually helps that the founder is staying involved, because you can continue to draw on each other's strengths." Mr. Ballmer has worked closely with both men, given the pre-eminence of both companies in the personal-computer universe. Mr. Rollins was living in Boston, a partner at Bain & company, the management consulting firm, when he was asked to fly to Austin in 1993 to meet with executives at Dell. He readily acknowledges that he was hardly thrilled about the assignment. "Texas is a lo-o-o-ng way from Boston, in many ways," he said. He had worked primarily with aerospace companies before his partners asked him to help what was then a modest-size computer company on pace to lose $100 million that year. Just before Mr. Rollins arrived, Dell announced that it would sell its computers at Wal-Mart stores, as well as continuing to sell directly to consumers over the Internet. Breaking into big-box retail outlets, Dell said, could bring in an additional $125 million in annual revenue—and rapidly build its brand name. Mr. Rollins promptly suggested that Dell scuttle the deal, telling a meeting of top Dell executives that the arrangement, over time, would prove to be a money loser. He apparently made a persuasive case. Within days Mr. Dell said he asked Mr. Rollins to end the company's agreements with retail chains. After that, Mr. Dell added, "very rapidly Kevin became a critical part of the senior management team"—although he was still technically a consultant.

Kevin Rollins naps. He admitted as much not long before Jeffrey R. Immelt, the chief executive of General Electric, one of Dell's top customers, was scheduled to speak to a group of Dell executives. Mr. Rollins reckoned that his famous visitor might have fun with the tale, so he broke the news that Mr. Immelt had called him on a recent vacation in Mexico and caught him in an afternoon snooze. Many people inside the company had the same reaction: "He naps?" The very idea seemed incongruous to those who work for him and see him put in 70- to 80-hour workweeks. (He still finds the time to run four or five miles several times a week and to pursue a long list of hobbies. And when he's in town, he attends church every sunday.) So, too, did the idea of Mr. Rollins putting on a cowboy hat, mounting a stage at a basketball arena and accompanying himself on the violin while belting out a song spoofing a computer industry foe. But he did that, too, at a Dell event. Among Mr. Rollins's gifts as chief executive, those around him say, is what Mr. Bell, head of Dell's European operations, calls his "tight messaging." So crisply does Mr. Rollins convey the Dell line, said Roger L. Kay the founder of Endpoint Technologies Associates, a research firm that monitors the personal computer industry, that it is "a little bit scary how everyone from the highest to the lowest employee is on message." Today Mr. Rollins's message is that everything is fine at Dell, despite a depressed stock price—now at $34.65, down 17 percent for the year. Dell may be the leading computer maker in the world, but it is No. 2 in Europe and No. 2 in Asia, leaving plenty of room for growth there. "As our big strategic initiatives capture share and profits, the profits we deliver will go up and our stock price will naturally rise," Mr. Rollins said. "We have a lot of room for growth for a long time before we have to ask what's the next vision thing. It's really a matter of execution."

THEREIN lies what Mr. Rollins hopes is his secret weapon. In early 2002, shortly after he learned what his closest underlings really thought of his style, he stood before 50 or so other top Dell executives and acknowledged that he needed to grow as a manager. "I could give the cold, calculated answer," he said in an interview recalling that meeting. "But I really wanted to be a more inspirational leader." The Dell way is to constantly tweak the system to make it more efficient. Just as Dell managers study the movements of workers on its assembly lines to maximize efficiency, they collectively decided to study themselves. For his part, Mr. Rollins read—particularly books about the country's founding fathers. He decided that he was too much like Alexander Hamilton—coolly efficient in his analysis but short on people skills—and too little like George Washington, whom Mr. Rollins cast as the kind of leader able to motivate people by helping them to better understand themselves. "Maybe I can't be a George Washington in terms of inspiration," he said, "but certainly I know I can always do better."

Questions for Discussion

1. What are the main elements of Kevin Rollins's leadership style?
2. How would you describe his personality or key personal strengths and weaknesses?
3. Given these factors, what approach to leadership do you think he has adopted? How successful has this approach been?

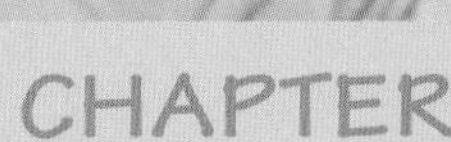

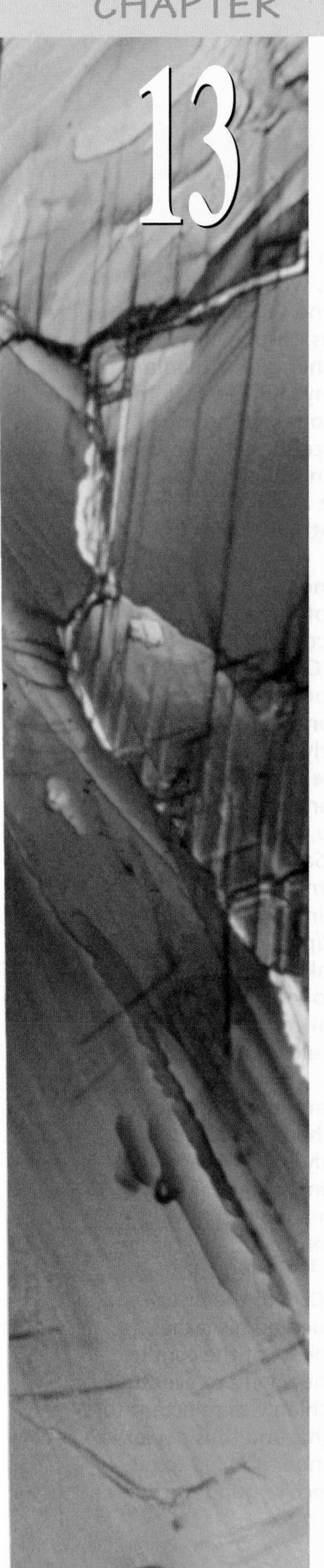

13 POWER, POLITICS, CONFLICT, AND NEGOTIATION

Learning Objectives

After studying this chapter, you should be able to:

- Understand the nature of power and explain why organizational politics exists and how it can help or harm an organization and its members.
- Differentiate between the main sources of formal and informal power people can use to engage in organizational politics as well as the sources of functional and divisional power.
- Discuss the nature of organizational conflict and the main sources of conflict in an organizational setting.
- Describe a model of the conflict process that illustrates how the conflict process works.
- Explain how negotiations can be used to manage the conflict process and resolve disputes between people and groups.

use. During his reign at the bank, the organization spent $310 million on itself—twice the amount it invested or lent to countries in Eastern Europe and the former Soviet Union.[8] Similarly, in 2004, Dennis Kozlowski, ex-CEO of Tyco, was accused of behaving illegally by diverting millions of dollars of Tyco's money for his personal use. His expenses included millions spent on a birthday party for his wife where Jimmy Buffet serenaded partygoers. Additional millions were spent to refurbish his New York apartment—reportedly, Kozlowski spent a whopping $6,000 on a new shower curtain alone! In 2005, Kozlowski was sentenced to up to 25 years in jail, with a minimum of eight.[9]

Managers who use (or, more correctly, abuse) power and politics to promote their own interests are likely to harm the interests of others—in these cases, countries that were to receive aid from the bank Attali was overseeing, and Tyco's stockholders.

On the other hand, there are ways in which power and politics can help organizations. First, when different managers or groups champion different solutions to a problem and use their power to promote these solutions, the ensuing debates over the appropriate course of action can help improve the quality of organizational decision making.[10] In other words, **political decision making**—decision making characterized by active disagreement over which organizational goals to pursue and how to pursue them—can lead to a more efficient use of organizational resources. Second, different managerial perspectives can promote the change that allows an organization to adapt to its changing environment. When **coalitions**, groups of managers who have similar interests, lobby for an organization to pursue new strategies or change its structure, the use of power can move the organization in new directions.[11]

POLITICAL DECISION MAKING
Decision making characterized by active disagreement over which organizational goals to pursue and how to pursue them.

COALITION
A group of managers who have similar interests and join forces to achieve their goals.

We will have more to say about organizational politics later in the chapter. For now, the main point is that power and politics can help an organization in two main ways: (1) Managers can use power to control people and other resources so that they cooperate to achieve an organization's current goals, and (2) Managers can also use power to engage in politics and influence the decision-making process to help promote new, more appropriate organizational goals. An organization has to guard continually and vigilantly against managers who might use power to harm the organization. Power-hungry managers are people to be feared and avoided. Nevertheless, power is necessary for the efficient functioning of organizations, and in any group of people, the question of how to distribute power and establish a power structure is an important one.[12]

An organization's power structure—partially revealed by its organizational chart—is the manifestation of the formal and informal sources of the power managers, functions, and divisions possess. The chart shows how the organization makes decisions and whose interests those decisions favor.[13]

To see how power can be acquired formally and informally, it is necessary to examine where organizational power comes from. When managers at the top of an organization understand the sources of power, it is easy for them to manage power and politics to gain the benefits while minimizing the negative effects. Indeed, a prerequisite of managerial success is the ability to analyze and chart an organization's power structure accurately. Such an analysis enables managers to develop coalitions and build a power base from which they can influence organizational decision making.

Sources of Individual Power

Most individuals in an organization have some ability to control the behavior of other individuals or groups, but some have more power than others. Where do individuals in an organization get their power from, and how do they get it? Researchers distinguish between the formal and informal power that individuals possess (see Exhibit 13.1).[14]

FORMAL INDIVIDUAL POWER
Power that originates from a person's position in an organization.

Sources of Formal Individual Power

Formal individual power is the power that stems from a person's position in an organization's hierarchy. When individuals accept a position in an organization, they accept the formal responsibility to carry out agreed-upon tasks and duties. In return, the organization

EXHIBIT 13.1

Sources of Individual Power

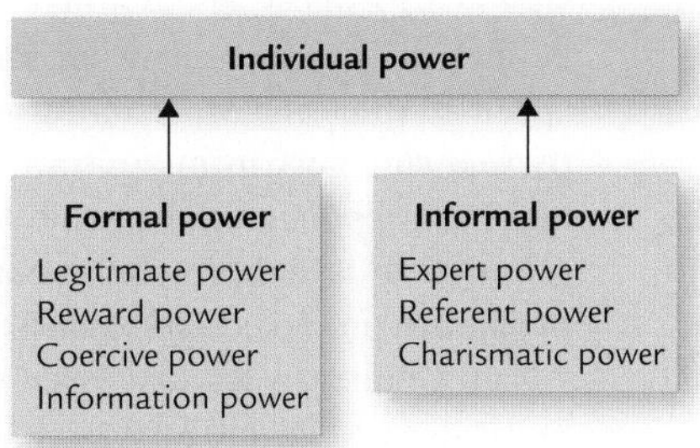

gives them formal authority to use its people and other resources to accomplish job-related tasks and duties. Rupert Murdoch and Sumner Redstone in the opening case possess the most formal power as the top executives of their respective media empires, which gives them authority over the managers below them, including their children who own billions of dollars in stock in these companies. Formal power is a reflection of an individual's *legitimate, reward, coercive*, and *information* power.

LEGITIMATE POWER
The power to control and use organizational resources to accomplish organizational goals.

Legitimate power. **Legitimate power** confers on an individual the legitimate authority to control and use organizational resources to accomplish organizational goals.[15] The legitimate power of a CEO, for example, is granted by an organization's board of directors, which, representing its owners' interests, gives the CEO authority over all organizational resources. The CEO, in turn, has the right to confer legitimate power upon managers further down in the organization's hierarchy. Continuing down through the hierarchy, upper-level managers give lower-level managers the authority to hire, fire, monitor, and oversee the behavior of subordinates. The CEO and lower-level managers also possess the power to withdraw authority from their subordinates, by firing, demoting, or otherwise stripping away a subordinate's authority to control organizational resources.

Legitimate power is the ultimate source of an individual's power in an organization. One day, a CEO like Jeff Immelt of GE or Carly Fiorino of HP may have a personal staff of five hundred people, a private jet, a chauffeur-driven limousine, and the right to use the company's New York penthouse. But if a CEO is removed from office by the board of directors, the next day, all of his or her authority and privileges are gone. The greater a manager's legitimate power is, the greater is the manager's authority and the more accountable and responsible is the person for his or her performance and use of organizational resources. This is why CEOs who perform poorly are often quickly replaced, as the former CEOs of Ford, Motorola, Lucent, McDonald's, and many other poorly performing companies have recently discovered.

REWARD POWER
The power to give pay raises, promotion, praise, interesting projects, and other rewards to subordinates.

Reward power. **Reward power** is the power to give pay raises, promotion, praise, interesting projects, and other rewards to subordinates. As long as subordinates value the rewards, a manager can use reward power to influence and control their behavior. In Chapter 5 (on learning), we discussed how important positive reinforcement could be in influencing behavior. In Chapters 6 and 7, we discussed how rewards can influence motivation.

The amount of rewards that an organization can give is limited. When extrinsic rewards such as raises and promotions are scarce, intrinsic rewards like praise and interesting job assignments can become more important. One challenge that managers face is motivating their subordinates when their abilities to confer tangible rewards is limited.

COERCIVE POWER
The power to give or withhold punishment.

Coercive power. **Coercive power** is the power to give or withhold punishment. Punishments range from suspension to demotion, termination, unpleasant job assignments, or even the withholding of praise and goodwill.

The ability to reward or punish subordinates gives supervisors great power, which is sometimes abused. As we discussed in Chapter 5, punishment has negative side effects and should be used with caution. It is for this reason that most organizations have clearly defined rules concerning when and how employees are to be rewarded or punished. Clearly specified rules and procedures that govern how coercive power and reward power are used prevent superiors from arbitrarily using their legitimate power to benefit their supporters and hurt opponents, or people they simply dislike or disagree with.[16] The function of review boards and promotion committees in organizations, for example, is to ensure that people are promoted on the basis of merit and *what* they know, not *whom* they know.

In Chapter 6 we discussed the importance of perceptions of equity in determining motivation in organizations. No matter what rewards or punishments people actually receive, they compare their rewards or punishments to those received by others. If they feel inequitably treated, they may perform poorly, be dissatisfied with their jobs, or quit. The ability to confer rewards and punishments fairly and equitably is a crucial managerial skill, and organizations usually provide managers with written guidelines to help them perform this function.

INFORMATION POWER
The power that stems from access to and control over information.

Information power. **Information power** is power stemming from access to and control over information.[17] The greater a manager's access to and control over information, the greater is his or her information power. The more information a manager possesses, the better able he or she is to solve problems facing subordinates. As a result, the greater is subordinates' dependence on the manager. Some managers are reluctant to share information with subordinates. They fear that if their subordinates know as much as they do, the power to control and shape their behavior will be lost.

Although individual managers sometimes benefit from keeping information to themselves, the most effective organizations are those in which organizational members share, not hoard, information. Indeed, in organizations that recognize the value of empowering employees, managers deliberately decentralize authority and make information easily accessible to everyone. This allows subordinates to assume more responsibility for the organization's performance and feel more motivated.[18]

Sources of Informal Individual Power

INFORMAL INDIVIDUAL POWER
Power that stems from personal characteristics such as personality, skills, and capabilities.

Several managers in a group or department may be at the same level in the organizational hierarchy or hold the same position, but some will have more power than others. Similarly, some lower-level managers may seem to have as much power and authority as higher-level managers—or even more. What accounts for this paradox? Power comes not only from an individual's formal position in an organization but also from a person's personality, skills, and capabilities. Power stemming from personal characteristics is **informal individual power**.[19] Researchers have identified several sources of it: *expert, referent*, and *charismatic* power.

Expert power. In any group, some individuals have skills or talents that allow them to perform at a higher level than others. In a group of engineers, there may be one or two individuals who always seem to find a simple or inexpensive design solution to a problem. In a group of salespeople, there may be a few individuals who always seem to land large new accounts. Group members often look to these individuals for advice, and in doing so, come to depend on them. This dependence gives these individuals expert power.

EXPERT POWER
Informal power that stems from superior ability or expertise.

Expert power is informal power that stems from superior ability or expertise in performing a task. Generally, people who possess expert power are promoted up the hierarchy of authority so that their informal power eventually becomes formal. Sometimes, however, individuals with expert power are mavericks: They have little ability or desire to assume formal authority over others. When that is the case, managers with formal power must take pains to develop good working relationships with subordinates who have expert power; otherwise, conflict may arise as formal leaders and informal leaders with expert power battle for control over people and resources.

REFERENT POWER
Informal power that stems from being liked, admired, and respected.

Referent power. People who gain power and influence in a group because they are liked, admired, and respected are said to possess **referent power**. Individuals who are high on the personality traits of agreeableness, extraversion, or even conscientiousness are often liked or admired (see Chapter 2). Willingness to help others may also lead to someone's being liked or admired. Fame is one sign that a person has acquired referent power. Why are famous film stars and athletes paid to endorse goods and services? Advertisers expect their referent power to attract their admirers to buy the companies' products. People with referent power are liked because of who they are, not just because of their expertise or their abilities to influence people, obtain resources, or achieve their own ends. Tennis star Serena Williams is one of these people. In 2004, William negotiated a contract with Nike paying her over $60 million for eight years of tennis product endorsements.

CHARISMATIC POWER
An intense form of referent power that stems from an individual's personality or physical or other abilities, which induce others to believe in and follow that person.

Charismatic power. Charismatic power is an intense form of referent power stemming from an individual's personality, physical strengths, or other abilities that induces others to believe in and follow that person.[20] In Chapter 12 we discussed how transformational leaders—leaders who possess charismatic power—often inspire awe and loyalty in their followers. These followers buy into the leader's vision and work with excitement and enthusiasm toward goals set by the leader.[21] When charismatic power exists, legitimate power, reward power, and coercive power lose their significance because followers give the charismatic leader the right to hold the reins of power and make the decisions that define the vision and goals of an organization and its members.

Many charismatic leaders can excite a whole organization and propel it to new heights, as have Bill Gates at Microsoft and Steve Jobs at Apple. But charismatic power can have a dark side, evident when followers of the charismatic leader blindly follow the leader and fail to take personal responsibility for their actions because they think the leader knows what is best for the organization. When charismatic power is abused by a leader who has a mistaken or evil vision, no checks or balances exist to resist the leader's directives, no matter how outrageous they may be. This appears to have happened at Enron, which became one of the seemingly most successful U. S. companies in record time. The company's success was attributed largely to the brilliance of its CEO Kenneth Lay and its CFO Andrew Fastow. Fastow and Lay's followers blindly followed the orders of their charismatic leaders. When fraud, rather than expertise and charisma, was shown to be the source of Enron's profits, the company imploded. Most of these employees lost their jobs, Fastow was jailed in 2004 for 10 years, and in 2006 Lay died of a heart attack before his long jail term began.

Some researchers have argued that charismatic leadership is an advantage only when a formal hierarchy of authority places some checks on the power of this person.[22] Thus,

You're the Management Expert

Identifying Who Has Power

Think about one of the organizations that you have worked for in the past or that you are currently employed by. Create a chart of the managers you come in contact with most often and the employees who seem to have the most influence in your department or organization. List the formal and informal sources of power of these people. Show on your chart how these people form a network that influences decision making. Which employees have the most influence? Which employees do you expect to be promoted the soonest? Why?

OB Today

Power Corrupts at WorldCom

In 2002, WorldCom, the giant telecommunications company, entered Chapter 11 bankruptcy after its was revealed that its top executives had deliberately overinflated revenues by $11 billion dollars. Not only its top executives (such as former CEO Bernie Ebbers) were implicated—so were eight of WorldCom's 11-member board of directors who were at the helm when the company booked these billions of dollars and provided $408 million in personal loans and lucrative pensions benefits to Ebbers. How could WorldCom's board of directors have failed in their oversight role?

Four of these eight board members had long-term personal and business ties to Ebbers and had been appointed to the board at his urging. Two of these four directors sat on WorldCom's compensation and stock option committee, which granted Ebbers these huge personal loans. At least one of these two directors reportedly also struck a deal with Ebbers whereby Ebbers gave him access to company aircraft for $1 a month plus a $400-an-hour usage fee, when the real cost of using such aircraft is hundreds of thousands of dollars a year. In return, this director agreed to Ebbers's huge severance package, which also ran into the hundreds of millions after he resigned.[23]

Former WorldCom CEO Bernie Ebbers was sentenced to 25 years in prison in July 2005 for using his power to oversee the $11 billion WorldCom fraud, the largest corporate fraud in U. S. history.

Small wonder then that in the fall of 2002, with these directors still collecting large fees and receiving huge perks from WorldCom, critics were calling for their removal from the board. They had not resigned voluntarily and legally the company cannot unilaterally replace them until WorldCom's next general meeting. However, WorldCom was able to fill three other vacancies with new directors, such as former U. S. Attorney General Nicholas Katzenbach and Dennis Beresford, a former chairman of the Financial Accounting Standards Board, who can ensure that these unethical directors can do no more harm to a company that has cost its shareholders billions of dollars and whose future is still in doubt.

Facing legal action, most of these directors have paid millions of dollars back to the company to avoid criminal prosecution. Former WorldCom boss Ebbers was sentenced to 25 years in prison in July 2005 for using his power as CEO to oversee the $11 billion WorldCom fraud—the largest corporate fraud in U. S. history. This is one of the toughest sentences ever imposed on an executive, and has become commonplace today. Even with possible time off for good behavior, Ebbers, currently in his 60s, will remain locked up until 2027, when he would be 85.

only when the power of a charismatic CEO is balanced by the power of the board of directors or a strong top management team is the CEO a force for good and someone who can stir people to work together to pursue common goals. In the 2000s, Michael Eisner, the former CEO of Walt Disney, came under scrutiny because critics argued he could control Disney's board of directors and so was making decisions that were often not in the company's best interests. Under pressure he eventually resigned, but what happened to WorldCom, whose charismatic but corrupt CEO took advantage of his control of the board of directors to behave unethically and illegally, is discussed in the following OB Today.

Sources of Functional and Divisional Power

Although formal individual power, particularly legitimate power, is the primary source of power in organizations, managers in particular functions or divisions can take advantage of other sources of power to enhance their individual power. A division or function becomes powerful when the tasks that it performs give it the ability to control the behavior of other divisions or functions, to make them dependent on it, and thereby increase its share of organizational resources (see Exhibit 13.2).[24]

Ability to Control Uncertain Contingencies

A contingency is an event or problem that could occur and must be planned for, by having people and resources in place to deal with it. A function or division has power over others if it can reduce the uncertainty they experience or manage the contingency or problem that is troubling them.[25] The marketing function, for example, often has power over the manufacturing function because it can forecast potential demand for a product (a contingency facing manufacturing). This ability to forecast demand reduces the uncertainty manufacturing faces by enabling it to plan production runs so as to minimize costs. Similarly, the public relations department and legal function are able to manage problems for other functions after those problems have occurred, and in doing so they reduce uncertainty for those functions and gain power over them. In general, functions or divisions that can solve the organization's problems and reduce the uncertainty it experiences are the ones that have the most power in the organization.[26] Today, the ability to control IT is one way to gain such power because it provides access to important relevant information.[27] However, IT must be used carefully to avoid provoking conflict between groups—and between customers and salespeople, as the following OB Today suggests.

Irreplacability

A function or division gains power when it is irreplaceable—that is, when no other function or division can perform its activities.[28] In one study of a French tobacco plant, for example, Michael Crozier found that the relatively low-status repair engineers had great power in the plant. The plant managers were very respectful toward them.[29] The source of the engineers' power, Crozier discovered, was their irreplacability. Although the engineering function was low in the formal hierarchy, the engineers as a group were the only employees who knew how to fix the plant's machines when they broke down. If they chose

EXHIBIT 13.2

Sources of Functional and Divisional Power

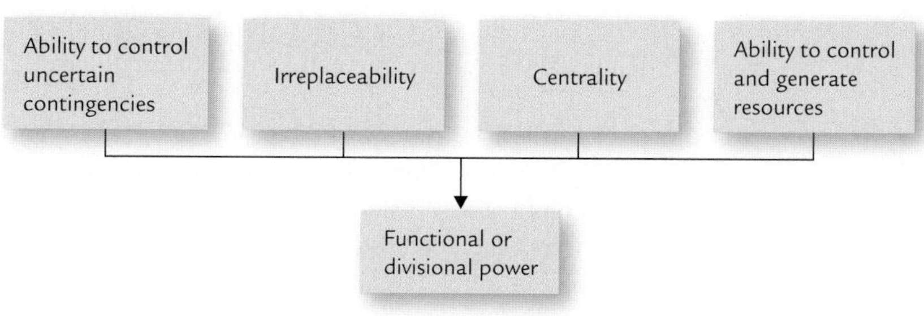

OB Today

Telemarketing Turns-Off Customers

In the 1990s, the use of telemarketing by companies such as phone service and credit card providers increased dramatically. Improvements in IT made it possible for specialist telemarketers to target customers and then to automatically dial their phone numbers repeatedly until they picked up the phone. At this point, a sales rep would come on the phone line to sell to the customer. To prevent such unwelcome intrusions, customers began to use services such as Caller ID and gadgets like TeleZapper, which blocks these automatic calls. Finally, in 2003 national legislation was passed that allows customers to register with the Federal Trade Commission to be put on a list that will make it illegal for telemarketers to make calls to their listed phone numbers.

Just as phone selling caused increasing conflict with customers in the 1990s, so has risen the frequency of face-to-face conflict with door-to-door salespeople.

Since telemarketing no longer reaches customers, companies have been forced to rethink their approach to sales and selling. Surprisingly, despite the fact we are living in a "wired world," some organizations have gone back to the old fashioned method of door–to–door selling. Hundreds of companies, like telephone providers AT&T and SBC, cable TV providers like Comcast, and countless regional utility companies, are sending out thousands of door-to-door sales reps to "connect" with people in the evenings at their homes.

Many people think it is their friends and neighbors knocking at their doors, but no, it's sales reps determined to get customers to switch their phone, cable, or utility service providers. People who have problems slamming the door in a sales rep's face, versus slamming down the phone, have been switching service only to regret it later. Just as phone selling caused increasing conflict with customers in the 1990s, so is face-to-face conflict with door-to-door salespeople on the rise. Provoking conflict with customers needs to be avoided since customer loyalty is vital for organizational effectiveness.

to, the engineers could cause problems for the manufacturing function. To maintain their status as irreplaceable employees, the engineers jealously hoarded their knowledge and refused to write it down.

All functions and divisions are irreplaceable to a certain degree. How irreplaceable they are depends on how easy it is to find a replacement for them.[30] For example, many organizations can assemble their products in low-cost foreign locations and thereby reduce the power of their domestic manufacturing functions relatively easily. Because it is difficult for an organization to gain access to high-quality research and development information, the R&D function in many companies is more irreplaceable than is the manufacturing.

Centrality

The power of a function or division also stems from its importance, or centrality, to the organization—that is, how central it is to the organization's operations and the degree to which it lies at the center of information flows.[31] Central functions, whose activities are needed by many other functions, have access to a lot of information, which gives them power in their dealings with others.[32] The product-development department, for example, has a high degree of centrality because R&D, engineering, marketing, and manufacturing all need product specifications in order to plan their activities. In the course of its dealings with other functions, product development acquires a lot of valuable information about many aspects of organizational activities—information that it can use to make other functions dependent on it.

Ability to Control and Generate Resources

The ability to control and generate resources for an organization is another source of functional and divisional power. The ability to control resources is, for example, a principal source of power for top managers such as Serge Weinberg.[33] These managers control the purse strings of the organization and have the ability to give or withhold rewards—money and funding—to functions and divisions. This ability is important because the more money a division is given, the more people it can hire and the more advanced facilities it can build so that it increases its chances of success. In contrast, when divisions are starved for funds, they cannot hire new skilled employees or buy new technology to increase their efficiency and this lack reduces their efficiency in the long run.

Although controlling resources is important, the ability to *generate* them is also important. The division whose goods and services provide the organization with the most profits will be the most important division in the organization. Very often, new CEOs and corporate headquarters staff are promoted from the divisions that have been most successful in generating resources. In the past, IBM's top managers came from its mainframe division, which generated most of the company's revenues and profits. Today, most of IBM's profits are being generated from computer services, so more top managers from this division are being promoted. Similarly, most of GM's top managers come from its most profitable car divisions.

To fully understand the power structure of an organization, a manager needs to analyze all sources of power. The sources of individual power, such as position in the hierarchy, are the most important determinants of power. But a manager must also take into consideration the sources of functional and divisional power when determining the relative power of functional and divisional managers in the organization.[34]

Organizational Politics: The Use of Power

Organizational politics are activities that managers engage in to increase their power. Once they acquire it, they can use power to influence decision making so that the organization pursues goals that favor their individual, functional, and divisional interests.[35]

One reason why many people engage in organizational politics is that jobs are a scarce resource.[36] The higher a manager rises in a hierarchy, the more difficult it is to continue to rise because fewer and fewer jobs are available at the upper levels. To compete for these scarce jobs and to increase their chances of promotion and share of organizational resources, employees try to increase their power and influence.[37] Without constant vigilance, organizational politics can get out of hand and prevent the organization from achieving its goals.[38] For this reason, it must try to manage the politics to promote positive effects and prevent negative ones.[39]

To understand how organizations can manage politics, we need to look at the tactics that managers use to increase their individual power and the power of their functions and divisions.[40]

Tactics for Increasing Individual Power

Managers can use many kinds of political tactics to increase their power, become experts at political decision making, and increase their chances of obtaining their goals.[41] In the following pages we describe some commonly used tactics (see Exhibit 13.3).

Tapping the sources of functional and divisional power. The way in which functions and divisions gain informal power suggests several tactics that managers can use to increase their individual power. First, managers can try to make themselves irreplaceable.[42] For example, they may develop specialized skills such as knowledge of computers or special relationships with key customers that allow them to solve problems or limit uncertainty for other managers in the organization. Second, managers may specialize in an area of increasing concern to the organization so that they eventually control a crucial contingency facing the organization.[43] Third, managers can try to make themselves more central in an organization by deliberately accepting responsibilities that bring them into contact with many functions or managers. Politically astute managers cultivate both people and information, and they are able to build up a personal network of contacts in the organization—contacts that they can use to pursue personal goals such as promotion.[44]

Recognizing who has power. Another way to increase individual power is to develop the ability to recognize who has power in the organization. With this knowledge a person knows whom to try to influence and impress. By supporting a powerful manager and being indispensable to him or her, it is possible to rise with that person up the organizational ladder. There are five factors to assess in order to determine the relative power of different managers in an organization.[45]

1. *Sources of Power*: Power has many sources in an organization. The power of a manager or subunit may come from legitimate authority, from the possession of scarce resources, or from expertise. A manager who assesses the source of various managers' power will learn whom to influence to obtain his or her objectives.
2. *Consequences of Power*: The people who have the most power can be identified by an assessment of who benefits the most from the decisions made in an organization. For example, managers compete for resources through the budgeting process, and obtaining access to scarce resources is a measure of how much power a manager has.
3. *Symbols of Power*: Many symbols of prestige and status are generally associated with power in an organization. Job titles, for example, are a prized possession; and titles such as "chief executive officer" and "president" confer great prestige on the officeholder.

EXHIBIT 13.3

Political Tactics for Increasing Individual Power

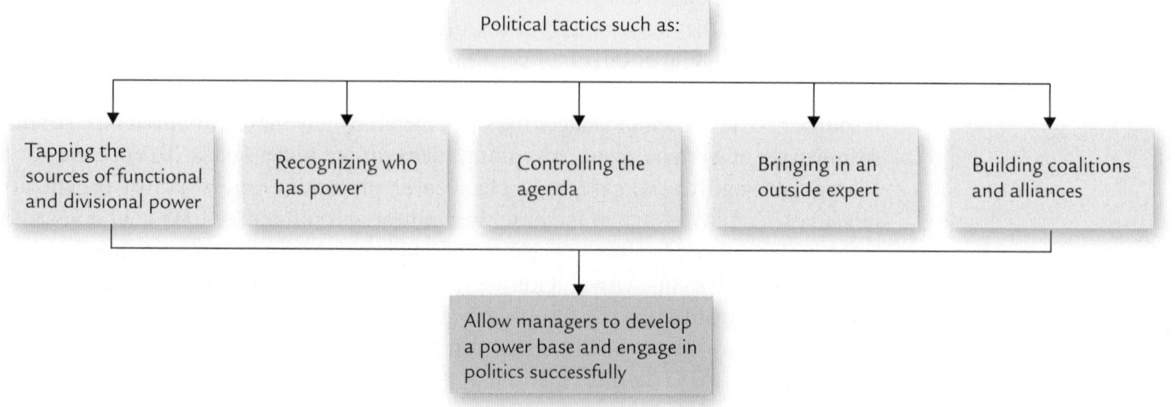

The use of a corporate jet or a chauffeured car, occupying a corner office with a wonderful view, and having a reserved parking place are other signs of power.

4. *Personal Reputations*: A person's reputation within an organization is likely to indicate the person's power to influence decision making.
5. *Representational Indicators*: The organizational roles a person or subunit plays and the responsibilities they possess are indications of power. A manager's membership on an influential committee, such as a company's operations committee, is a sign of the person's influence in organizational decision making. Managers who occupy central administrative roles have access to important information and derive power from this access. It strengthens their ability to make sound decisions and to alter the bargaining process in their favor.

By focusing on those five factors, a person new to an organization can assess which people or groups have the most power. Armed with this knowledge, the newcomer can make certain predictions about which groups will be favored by the decision-making process to receive a large share of organizational resources or be protected from cutbacks if resources are scarce.

Once managers have accurately assessed the power structure of an organization and have obtained some individual power, they can use several other tactics to enhance their power.

Controlling the agenda. An important tactic for influencing decision making is to control the agenda—that is, to determine what issues and problems decision makers will consider. The ability to control the agenda is one reason why managers like to be members of or in charge of committees. By controlling the agenda, managers can limit the consideration of alternatives in the course of decision making. Powerful managers, for example, can prevent formal discussion of any issue they do not support by not putting the issue on the agenda.

Bringing in an outside expert. When a major disagreement over goals emerges, as it often does when an organization is undergoing change or restructuring, managers know that every subunit is fighting to safeguard its own interests. Managers in charge of different functions want the ax to fall on functions other than theirs and want to benefit from whatever change takes place. Knowing that one function or one person's preferred alternative will be perceived by others as politically motivated and self-interested, a manager may bring in an outside expert who is considered to be a neutral observer. The manager then uses the "objective" views of this expert to support his or her position.

Building coalitions and alliances. Managers may form a coalition with other managers to obtain the power they need to influence the decision-making process in their favor. Many coalitions result from agreements to trade support: Function A agrees to support function B on an issue of interest to function B, and in return function B supports function A on an issue of interest to function A. Skills in coalition building are important in organizational politics because functional interests frequently change as the organizational environment changes. Because of such changes, coalitions must be actively managed by their members.

The ability to forge coalitions and alliances with the managers of the most important divisions provides aspiring top managers with a power base from which they can promote their personal agenda. Having many supporters enhances a manager's claims to power in the organization, but there is a downside to alliances: the possibility that individual members will request alliance support for their losing propositions. It is particularly important for top-level managers to build personal relationships with members of the board of directors. CEOs need the support of the board in any contest between top managers; without it CEOs might lose their jobs to another top-level manager. The way in which politics and power struggles have influenced Kodak is discussed in the following OB Today.

OB Today

Politics at Kodak

Eastman Kodak, whose little yellow film boxes have long been a part of the global photo scene, has experienced declining performance for years.[46] Kodak was slow to react to the threat of global competition in its central film-making business, and a successive series of political contests between its managers has stifled its attempts to restructure its activities. The problems have been going on for at least a decade.

In the early 1990s, Kay Whitmore, a Kodak veteran, was appointed as CEO. He gained the top job as the leader of a coalition of Kodak's most senior managers. Since any attempt of his to raise Kodak's performance would require massive cuts in some of Kodak's businesses, Whitmore was reluctant to make the drastic changes that Kodak needed to regain its competitiveness. So, in 1993, investors were delighted to hear about the appointment of Christopher Steffen as Kodak's new chief operating officer.

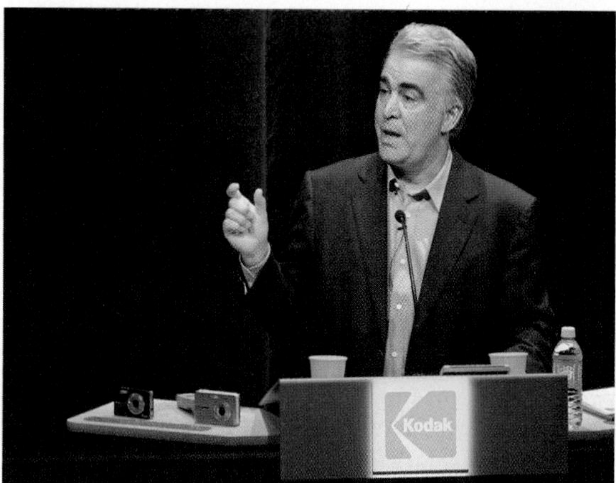

Kodak appointed Antonio Perez as its new CEO to reorganize the company and end the power battles between its top managers so it could aggressively pursue a digital imaging strategy. Intense competition in the digital imaging market is still hurting Kodak however, and the company is continuing to shrink.

Steffen has a reputation as a "turnaround artist" who performed miracles at Chrysler and Honeywell. Investors thought that an outsider would finally bring a breath of fresh air and fresh ideas to Kodak's inbred top management team. Investors were therefore shocked when Steffen announced his resignation from the company less than a week after his appointment, citing "differences with the company's approach to problem solving." Apparently he and the coalition of Kodak's top managers headed by CEO Whitmore had very different ideas about how to restructure the company and the speed at which restructuring should be done. Steffen wanted to massively reduce operating costs by closing several business units and laying off large numbers of employees. Whitmore's coalition resisted this and, as in the past, Kodak's entrenched management had the power to carry the day by firing Steffen.

After this event Kodak's stock plunged, and within months Whitmore was ousted by a concerned board of directors. He was replaced by George Fisher in 1994, the first outsider ever to lead Kodak. The hope was that Fisher would be able to change the way organizational politics worked at Kodak and that this would enhance the company's performance. Fisher made many changes, but he, too, had to fight against the no-change tactics used by Kodak's top brass to protect their interests. He never gained their support.[47]

Behind the scenes, another Kodak veteran, Dan Karp, was waiting to become its CEO. In 2000, supported by a coalition of Kodak's top managers, Karp became Kodak's new CEO and Fisher was out. Karp got the job because he had great support from other Kodak executives to expand its push into electronic imaging.[48] They backed his candidacy to protect their own jobs. By 2003 it became clear that Karp was still trying avoid the

radical restructuring necessary to save the troubled company. Karp was not the right person to take on this role, especially as he was obligated to many of Kodak's top managers who had lobbied for his appointment to the top job.

So, in 2003 Kodak's board of directors hired Antonio Perez, a former HP executive as its new president and COO, to reorganize the company. Perez did make the hard choices closing divisions and laying of many more thousands of managers and employees. In 2005, his success led to his appointment as Kodak's new CEO and he is responsible for implementing the new downsized streamlined company's new digital imaging strategy.[49] However, intense competition in the digital photography market, and declining film sales, has not allowed Perez to bring Kodak back to profitability—the best he has been able to do is to stem its losses, and its future is still uncertain.

Managing Organizational Politics

The exercise of power is an essential ingredient of organizational life, so it is important for an organization to manage organizational politics and harness it to support organizational interests. The management of organizational politics falls primarily to the CEO because only the CEO possesses legitimate power over all other managers. This power allows the CEO to control political contests so that they help rather than harm the organization. If the CEO is perceived as being weak, however, other top managers (who may possess their own stock of expert, referent, or charismatic power) will lobby for their own interests and compete among themselves for control of resources.

Power struggles, as in the opening case, sap the strength of an organization, waste resources, and distract the organization from achieving its goals. To avoid power struggles, an organization must have a strong CEO who can balance and manipulate the power structure so that no manager or coalition of managers becomes strong enough to threaten organizational interests. At the same time, a strong CEO should not fear to delegate significant responsibilities to managers below when they have demonstrated their personal success. When there is a balance of power, the decisions that result from the political process are more likely to favor the long-term interests of the organization.[50]

In summary, because power and politics influence many kinds of decision making in organizations, members need to be able to tell what's going on around them. They can do this by analyzing the sources of power at the functional, divisional, and organizational levels, and by identifying powerful people and observing their approach to leadership. To increase their chances of promotion most managers try to develop a personal power base to increase their visibility and individual power.

What is Organizational Conflict?

Organizational politics gives rise to conflict as one person or group attempts to influence the goals and decision making of an organization to advance its own interests—usually at the expense of some other person or group. **Organizational conflict** is the self-interested struggle that arises when the goal-directed behavior of one person or group blocks the goal-directed behavior of another person or group.[51]

ORGANIZATIONAL CONFLICT
The struggle that arises when the goal-directed behavior of one person or group blocks the goal-directed behavior of another person or group.

The effect of conflict on organizational performance has received considerable attention. In the past, researchers viewed conflict as always bad or dysfunctional for an organization because it leads to lower organizational performance.[52] According to this view, conflict occurs because managers have not designed an organizational structure that allows people, functions, or divisions to cooperate to achieve corporate objectives. The current view of conflict, however, is that, although it is unavoidable, it can often increase organizational performance if it is carefully managed and negotiated.[53]

Exhibit 13.4 illustrates the effect of conflict on organizational performance. At first, conflict can increase organizational performance because it exposes weaknesses in organizational

EXHIBIT 13.4

The Effect of Conflict on Organizational Performance

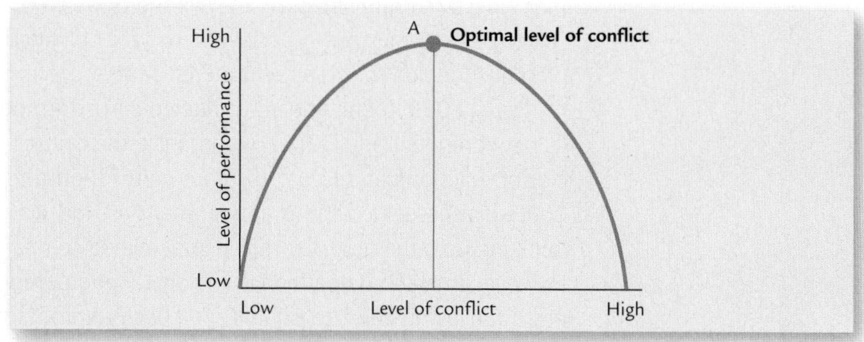

decision making and design and prompts the organization to make changes. Managers realign the organization's power structure and shift the balance of power in favor of the group that can best meet the organization's current needs. At some point—point A in Figure 13.4—an increase in conflict leads to a decline in performance because conflict between managers gets out of control, and the organization fragments into competing interest groups.[54]

The job of top managers is to prevent conflict from going beyond point A and to channel conflict in directions that increase organizational performance. Thus, managing conflict, like managing politics, is a way to improve organizational decision making and resource allocation, making the organization more effective.[55]

Sources of Organizational Conflict

Conflict, both between individuals and between groups, has many sources, and managers need to be aware of them so that when it occurs they can either control or resolve it. Three major sources of interpersonal and intergroup conflict are differentiation, task relationships, and scarcity of resources.[56]

Differentiation

Differentiation in an organization occurs when people and tasks are grouped or split up into functions and divisions to produce goods and services. The splitting of the organization into functions or divisions produces conflict because it makes the differences in functional orientations and status inconsistencies apparent.

Differences in functional orientations. Different functions commonly develop different orientations toward the organization's major priorities.[57] Their views of what needs to be done to increase organizational performance differ because their tasks, jobs, and goals differ. Manufacturing generally has a short-term, cost-directed efficiency orientation. Research and development is oriented toward long-term, technical goals, and sales is oriented toward satisfying customer needs. Thus, manufacturing may see the solution to a problem as one of reducing costs, research and development as one of promoting product innovation, and sales as one of increasing demand.

Because of differences in their functional orientations, functional groups can have differing views of the organization's priorities. These differences can lead to conflict that can do considerable harm, undermining the organization's cohesiveness and functional integration and reducing its performance.

Status inconsistencies. Over time, some functions or divisions come to see themselves as more vital than others to an organization's operations and believe that they have higher status or greater prestige in the organization.[58] In this situation, high-status functions make little attempt to adapt their behaviors to the needs of other functions, thus blocking the goals of other functions.[59] Similarly, functions that are most central and essential to a company's operations may come to see themselves as more important than other functions and attempt to achieve their goals at the expense of the less central functions.

Task Relationships

Task relationships generate conflict between people and groups because organizational tasks are interrelated and affect one another. Overlapping authority, task interdependence, and incompatible evaluation systems may stimulate conflict among functions and divisions.[60]

Overlapping authority. If two different functions or divisions claim authority for the same task, conflict may develop. Such confusion often arises when a growing organization has not yet fully worked out relationships between different groups.[61] As a result, functions or divisions fight for control of a resource and thus spawn conflict. At the individual level, too, managers can come into conflict over the boundaries of their authority, especially when one manager attempts to seize another's authority and resources. If a young manager starts to upstage his or her boss, for example, the boss may react by assigning the subordinate to relatively unimportant projects or by deliberately withholding the resources the person needs to do a good job. Something similar to this occurred at Gucci and is discussed in the following OB Today.

OB Today

Battle for Control Changes Gucci

Gucci, the Italian luxury fashion house, is one of the best-known companies in the world; its clothes, shoes, and accessories are bought and worn by the rich and famous everywhere.[62] The success of a luxury fashion house rests on its claim to offer customers products that are unique and different, and people who pay the incredibly high prices Gucci charges must feel they are part of the select crowd who can afford to wear its stylish creations.

Managers typically come into conflict when the areas of their authority are not defined and they compete to increase their power and status in an organization. This happened at Gucci, and led to the departure of its top designer, the brilliant gay Tom Ford.

Gucci's fortunes were saved in 1990, when its CEO Domenico De Sole invited the brilliant, Texas-born, gay clothes designer Tom Ford to become its principal clothes designer. With De Sole's backing, Ford designed new clothes collections that led to record sales, and Gucci once again became the fashion leader of the world. Together, the two men, known as "Tom and Dom" within Gucci and the fashion world, were admired and respected for their creative endeavors and design expertise.[63]

In 2004, however, the peace at Gucci was shattered when a huge conflict broke out at the top of Gucci about who should lead the company into the future. Gucci is a part of the huge French luxury goods company Pinault-Printemps-Redoute (PPR). The biggest shareholder of PPR is Francois-Henri Pinault, who appointed a top executive named Serge Weinberg to head the PPR Empire. In 2004,

Tom and Dom's contracts were due to expire, and Weinberg assumed responsibility for negotiating the conditions under which Ford and De Sole would run Gucci over the next decade.

Before Weinberg took over, De Sole and Ford had been given total control over Gucci and made all the important design and business decisions. Weinberg had no experience in high fashion and freely admitted that his main contact with high fashion had been through his wife who was a fashion model. Nevertheless, Weinberg was determined to exert his authority as the top executive of the whole PPR Empire over Gucci's top executives. He wanted the right to sign off on Tom and Dom's major business decisions; essentially, he wanted them to recognize his greater power, authority, and status. They on the other hand, wanted to protect their autonomy and feared Weinberg's interference would harm Gucci's performance.

Thus, the stage was set for a major power struggle between Tom and Dom, who felt Gucci's current success owed everything to their design talents, and Weinberg, who felt he had the right to decide under what conditions they should lead Gucci because he represented the interests of its owner.

For several months, Weinberg negotiated with Tom and Dom over who should have control of Gucci. Over time, the struggle escalated, and conflict arose because neither Weinberg nor Ford and De Sole would give in on the ultimate question of who should have the power to determine Gucci's future. Ultimately, Ford and De Sole announced they would leave Gucci when their contracts expired in 2004.[64] The fashion world was stunned and Weinberg was faced with the major problem of who to replace them with. Very often, when power struggles between managers escalate into conflict, it does no one any good. If these executives could only have found a way to negotiate and resolve their differences, perhaps by bringing in a neutral third party or mediator, the breakup might not have occurred.

Task interdependencies. The development or production of goods and services depends on the flow of work from one function to another; each function builds on the contributions of other functions.[65] If one function does not do its job well, the ability of the function next in line to perform is compromised, and the outcome is likely to be conflict.[66] For example, the ability of manufacturing to reduce costs on the production line depends on how well research and development has designed the product for cheap manufacture and how well sales has attracted large, stable customer accounts. When one function fails to perform well, all functions suffer.

The potential for conflict increases as the interdependence of functions or divisions increases. Thus, as task interdependence increases from pooled, to sequential, to reciprocal interdependence (see Chapter 11), the potential for conflict among functions or divisions is greater.[67]

Incompatible evaluation systems. Inequitable performance-evaluation systems that reward some functions but not others sometimes create conflict.[68] Typical problems include finding ways to jointly reward sales and production to avoid scheduling conflicts that lead to higher costs or dissatisfied customers. Also, the more complex the task relationships between functions are, the harder it is to evaluate each function's individual contribution to performance and reward it appropriately, which also increases the likelihood of conflict.

Scarcity of Resources

Competition for scarce resources produces conflict.[69] Conflict over the allocation of capital occurs among divisions and between divisions and corporate headquarters. Budget fights can be fierce when resources are scarce. Other organizational groups also have an interest in the way a company allocates scarce resources. Shareholders care about the size of the dividends. Employees want to maximize their salaries and benefits. Managers in competition for scarce resources may fight over whom should get the biggest pay raise.

Pondy's Model of Organizational Conflict

Because conflict of one kind or another is inevitable in organizations, it is an important influence on behavior. Louis Pondy developed one of the most widely accepted models of organizational conflict.[70] Pondy views conflict as a dynamic process that consists of five sequential stages (see Exhibit 13.5). No matter how or why conflict arises in an organization, managers can use Pondy's model to analyze a conflict and guide their attempts to manage it.

Latent Conflict

In the first stage of Pondy's model there is no actual conflict. The potential for conflict to arise is present, though latent, because of the sources of conflict that we just examined.

Perceived Conflict

The stage of perceived conflict begins when one party—individual or group—becomes aware that its goals are being thwarted by the actions of another party. Each party searches for the origins of the conflict, defines why the conflict is emerging, analyzes the events that led to its occurrence, and constructs a scenario that accounts for the problems it is experiencing with other parties. For example, the manufacturing function of a company may trace its production problems to defective inputs used in the assembly process. Manufacturing managers wonder why the inputs are substandard and after an investigation discover that the materials management function chose to buy inputs from the lowest-cost supplier instead of paying for high-quality inputs. This decision reduces input costs and improves materials management's performance but raises production costs and worsens manufacturing's performance. Manufacturing comes to see materials management as thwarting its goals and interests.

EXHIBIT 13.5

Pondy's Model of Organizational Conflict

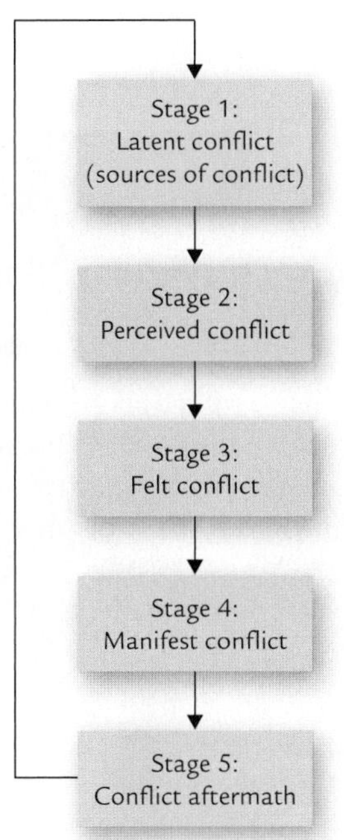

What usually happens at the stage of perceived conflict is that the conflict escalates as functions start to battle over the cause of the problem. In an attempt to get materials management to change its purchasing practices, manufacturing complains about materials management to the CEO or to anyone else who will listen. Materials management argues that low-cost inputs do not reduce quality and claims that manufacturing does not properly train its employees. Each party perceives the conflict and its causes differently.[71] Thus, although both functions share the same goal of superior product quality, they attribute the cause of poor quality very differently.

Felt Conflict

During the stage of felt conflict the parties in conflict develop negative feelings about each other. Typically, each group closes ranks, develops an us-versus-them attitude, and blames the other group for the problem. As conflict escalates, cooperation between groups declines, as does organizational effectiveness.[72] For example, it is almost impossible to speed new product development if materials management and manufacturing are fighting over the quality of inputs and final products.

As the parties in conflict battle and argue for their points of view, the significance of the disputed issue is likely to be blown out of proportion. Consider, for example, a relatively simple kind of conflict: conflict between roommates. Roommate A consistently neglects to put his dirty dishes in the dishwasher and clean the kitchen counters. To get the sloppy roommate to clean up, roommate B first makes a joke about the messy kitchen. If no change occurs in roommate A's behavior, roommate B starts to complain. If there is still no improvement, the roommates begin fighting and become so antagonistic toward one another that they not only cease to be friends but also begin looking for other living arrangements. The original problem was relatively minor, but when roommate A did nothing to solve it, the problem escalated into something that became increasingly difficult to manage. This may well have been the situation that developed at Gucci as both sides grew more and more antagonistic to the other as time went on.

Manifest Conflict

In the stage of manifest conflict, one party decides how to react to or deal with the party that it sees as the source of the conflict, and both parties try to hurt each other and thwart each other's goals.

Manifest conflict can take many forms. Open aggression or even violence between people and groups may occur. There are many stories and myths in organizations about boardroom fights in which managers actually came to blows as they sought to promote their interests. Infighting in the top-management team is a more indirect form of aggression that occurs as managers seek to promote their own careers at the expense of others in the organization. When Lee Iacocca was at Ford, for example, Henry Ford II decided to bring in the head of General Motors as the new Ford CEO. Within one year, Iacocca engineered the new CEO's downfall to clear his own path to the top. Eventually, he lost the battle when Henry Ford forced him out because he feared that Iacocca would take his power.

Manifest conflict between groups like teachers and parents, prisoners and guards, and unions and managers is also common. In the past in industrial disputes, for example, managers often obtained their goals by using tactics such as sabotage, strikebreaking, hiring new workers as permanent replacements for striking workers, and physical intimidation.

Manifest conflict also takes the form of a lack of cooperation between people or functions, a result that can seriously hurt an organization. If an organization's members do not cooperate, integration declines, and the organization is less likely to come together to achieve its goals. One particularly dysfunctional kind of manifest conflict occurs when parties accommodate or avoid managing a conflict. In this situation, one party might try to frustrate the goals of its opponent by passivity—that is, by doing

Arguing managers is one of the many forms that manifest conflict takes. On some occasions managers have been known to resort to loud shouting matches as they seek to exert control and win the decision-making battle.

nothing. Suppose there is a history of conflict between sales and production, but sales desperately needs to rush out an order for an important client. What might manufacturing do? One strategy is to agree informally to sales' requests and then do nothing. When sales comes banging on the door looking for its products, manufacturing says: "Oh, you meant *last* Friday, I thought you meant *this* Friday." In general, the stronger manifest conflict is, the more organizational effectiveness suffers because coordination and integration between managers and subunits decline. A particularly strong form of manifest conflict is illustrated in the following OB Today.

OB Today

When Partners Battle For Control of Their Company

CIC Inc. was founded by two partners, David Hickson and Glenn S. Collins III, in College Station, Texas. Each founder took a 50–50 stake in the small business. CIC's strategy was to maintain and service high-tech equipment like CT scanners, X-rays, and lasers, in hospitals and universities across the United States.[73] Hickson's and Collins's new venture proved very successful, business increased very rapidly, and by 2000 the company had over 200 employees. In the 1990s, CIC upgraded its service program so that all maintenance transactions could be handled electronically over the internet using the company's in-house software programs. Since CIC's new Internet service could save hospitals up to 20 percent of their maintenance costs, the savings would amount to millions of dollars a year. Hospitals flocked to join the program, and CIC's future looked bright indeed.

Imagine then the impact of the bombshell that occurred when Hickson, on vacation with his family, returned to College Station to find that in his absence, Collins had staged a coup. He found that he had been replaced as president by a CIC manager who was one of Collin's closest friends, that CIC managers and workers who had been loyal to Hickson had been fired, and that all the keys and security codes to CIC buildings had been changed. Hickson immediately sought and obtained a legal restraining order from a judge that allowed him back into the company and reinstated fired employees. The judge also issued an order preventing the two men from taking any actions that were not part of their normal job duties.

Apparently this extraordinary situation had occurred because the two owners had not been able to agree on the company's future direction—a problem that had resulted in a deteriorating personal relationship between them. Since they were equal partners, neither had power over the other to resolve the conflict. As a result, the conflict had become worse over time. Different camps had formed in the organization with different CIC managers being a member of one camp or the other, loyal either to Collins or Hickson.

In the months following this episode, it became clear that the two men would be unable to resolve the conflicts and problems between them. The only solution to the conflict seemed to be for one person to buy out the other, and they each searched for bank financing to do so. Finally, it was announced that Hickson had purchased Collin's share of the business. However, the problems between the two men were apparently not to be resolved there.[74] Collins immediately announced that he would use the money from his share of CIC to start another company that would essentially provide the same kind of service as CIC!

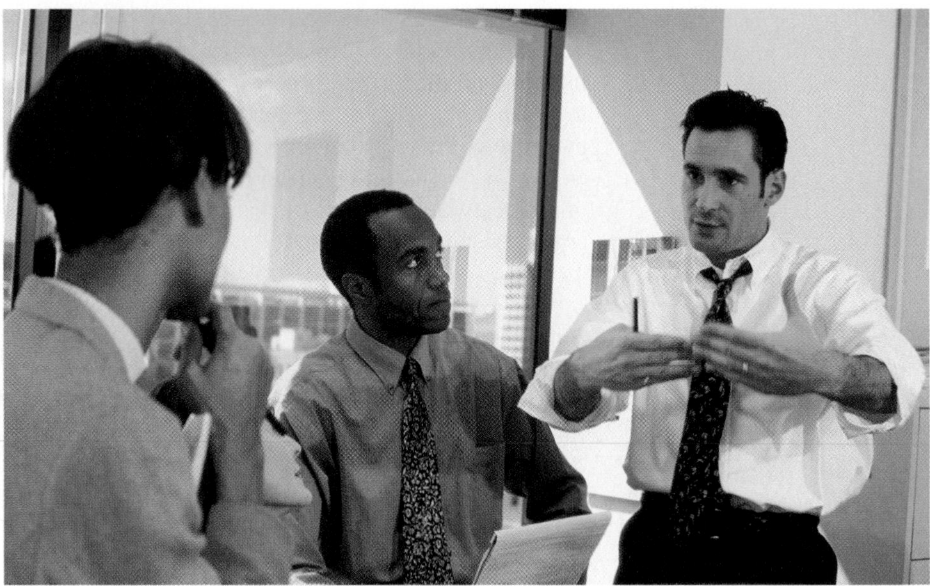

When conflicts arise, managers can help employees by framing a settlement both parties perceive to be a "win–win" situation.

Managers need to do all they can to prevent manifest conflict from becoming dysfunctional and to intervene as early as possible in this stage. If they cannot prevent the breakdown in communication and coordination that usually occurs in this stage, the conflict advances to the last stage: the conflict aftermath.

Conflict Aftermath

Sooner or later, conflict in an organization is resolved in one way or another—someone gets fired, a CEO tells a division to shape up, the organization gets reorganized, or the conflict becomes so bad that the organization fails. Regardless of the outcome, it is almost certain that the causes of the conflict will occur again in another context. Suppose that sales, still angry over the earlier "mix-up" with manufacturing, approaches manufacturing with a new request. How will these functions behave? Probably, their wariness and lack of trust will make it hard for them to agree on anything. Now suppose that after the earlier encounter sales and manufacturing were able to solve their dispute amicably through compromise and collaboration. In that case, when sales next has a special request for manufacturing, the two departments will be able to sit down together and work out a joint plan that suits the needs of both functions.

Every conflict episode leaves a conflict "aftermath" that affects the way both parties perceive and respond to future episodes. If conflict can be resolved by compromise or collaboration before it progresses to the manifest stage, the conflict aftermath will promote good future working relationships. But if conflict is not resolved until late in the process, the competition that takes place will result in a conflict aftermath that sours future working relationships and leads to an organizational culture poisoned by the presence of permanently uncooperative relationships like that at CIC.

Negotiation: Resolving Conflict

One of management's major responsibilities is to help parties in conflict—subordinates, functions, or divisions—cooperate in resolving their disputes. Indeed, much of a manager's time can be spent in managing conflict. If a company is to achieve its goals, managers must be able to resolve conflicts between employees and groups, and it is always best that conflict is settled by compromise between the parties in conflict.[75] Compromise is possible when each party is willing to engage in a give-and-take exchange and to make concessions until a reasonable resolution of the conflict is reached. When the parties to a conflict are willing to cooperate with each other to find a solution to the conflict that each finds acceptable, a company is more likely to achieve its goals.

NEGOTIATION
A process in which groups with conflicting interests meet together to make offers, counteroffers, and concessions to each other in an effort to resolve their differences.

Negotiation is a process in which groups with conflicting interests meet together to make offers, counteroffers, and concessions to each other in an effort to resolve their differences.[76] Negotiation is an important technique that managers can use to increase the chances of reaching compromise between individuals and groups in conflict.[77] Through negotiating and bargaining, the parties to a conflict try to come up with an acceptable solution by considering various ways to allocate resources. Sometimes, the parties believe that the more one party gains, the more the other loses. This makes them competitive and adversarial in the bargaining and negotiation process.[78] They "take a hard line," make unrealistic demands, and use all of their power to get what they want. Managers need to help the parties avoid viewing the conflict competitively—as a win-or-lose situation. Instead, they need to frame the situation so it can be viewed by both parties as a win-win situation. Negotiation is an important tool that managers can use to handle conflict in ways that lead to cooperative, functional outcomes rather than competitive, dysfunctional outcomes.

Individual-Level Conflict Management

The management of conflict between individuals is directed at changing the attitudes or behavior of those involved in the conflict.[79] If the conflict is due to a clash of personalities and the parties in conflict simply do not understand one another's point of view, the organization can help the people involved by bringing in outside help to give advice and counsel. Education and sensitivity and awareness training help people learn to understand and to deal with those who are not like themselves. If the conflict is due to work-force diversity—such as when a young person supervises older, more experienced workers or a female manager supervises an all-male work group—the organization can use education and training to help employees appreciate the differences in their attitudes and avoid or successfully resolve conflict.

If the conflict is due to a basic disagreement about how the work should be performed, or about the performance of the other party, managers can use a step-by-step negotiation approach to help resolve a dispute between employees. This is especially useful when the conflict has reached the felt and manifest conflict stage and the dispute is poisoning not just personal but also work-group relationships. The steps in the process are as follows[80]:

1. A manager meets with both the employees in conflict and forcefully outlines the way their behavior is affecting the way they perform their jobs and other members of the department. Each employee then is asked to express their thoughts and feelings about the conflict to open up the conflict so that the manager, and the employees, understand the facts of the conflict and each other's positions.
2. The manager summarizes the dispute between the employees in a written form, creating a report that carefully matches both sides of the case to identify the main factors that are in dispute. For example, if the dispute is about one employee not pulling his or her weight or performing substandard work, each employee's interpretation of the facts is balanced against the other.
3. The manager discusses the facts in the report with each employee separately acting as a neutral third party; the manager uses the fact-finding report to work out a solution each employee can accept, going back and forth between the employees until they can accept a common solution.
4. The manager meets with both employees to discuss the agreement and get their commitment to resolving the dispute. Each employee also agrees to meet with the manager should subsequent problems arise.

If the conflict cannot be negotiated successfully, another solution is to move people around. Managers can transfer employees to new positions where they will not meet each other, or where they can come to better appreciate the others' point of view. Job rotation and assignments to new teams or departments or even to new countries help people to develop fresh perspectives on issues in dispute. Promotion can also be used to change attitudes. Managers might deal with troublesome union shop stewards by making them supervisors. They might deal with troublesome manufacturing managers by promoting them sideways into a position in training, plant security, or elsewhere. In this way parties to the conflict are permanently removed from the conflict situation.[81] As a last resort, an organization can fire the people involved and replace them with others who have no history of dysfunctional conflict. Replacing managers from the CEO down to first-level supervisors is also a common method of eliminating conflict.

Group-Level Conflict Management

Group-level conflict management is aimed at changing the attitudes and behaviors of groups and departments in conflict.[82] Managers can physically separate work groups, deny them the opportunity to interact face to face, and thus eliminate the potential for direct conflict. Coordination between separate groups is then made possible by using integrating roles (see Chapter 16) and giving some people the full-time responsibility to coordinate the groups' activities while keeping them physically separate. Sometimes, managers can develop rules and standard operating procedures to coordinate the groups' activities or give them common goals, allowing them to achieve their goals simultaneously.

Often, however, these solutions provide only a temporary solution to the problem. If the underlying causes are not addressed, the conflict is never truly resolved, and the organization's performance may continue to suffer. Because few organizations can afford this outcome, most usually try to resolve the conflict at its source by negotiating at the group level.

THIRD-PARTY NEGOTIATOR
An outsider skilled in handling bargaining and negotiation.

MEDIATOR
A neutral third party who tries to help parties in conflict reconcile their differences.

ARBITER
A third party who has the authority to impose a solution to a dispute.

Direct negotiations between groups are held either with or without a **third-party negotiator**—an outsider who is skilled in handling bargaining[83] and negotiation. The third party facilitates the bargaining process and helps the parties in dispute find a solution to their problem.[84] Sometimes the common superior of the parties in conflict acts as the third party. If the third party plays the role of **mediator**, he or she takes a neutral stance and helps the parties to reconcile their differences. If the parties cannot find an equitable solution, the third party may act as **arbiter**, or judge, and impose a solution.

There are five basic forms that negotiation may take as groups can handle conflict with others: compromise, collaboration, accommodation, avoidance, and competition (see Exhibit 13.6).[85] The horizontal axis of Exhibit 13.6 measures the degree to which a person or group is concerned with obtaining its own goals. The vertical axis measures the extent to which the person or group is concerned with helping some other person or group to achieve its goals. Using this model, it is possible to compare the different ways of handling conflict during the felt stage.

EXHIBIT 13.6

Ways of Handling Conflict

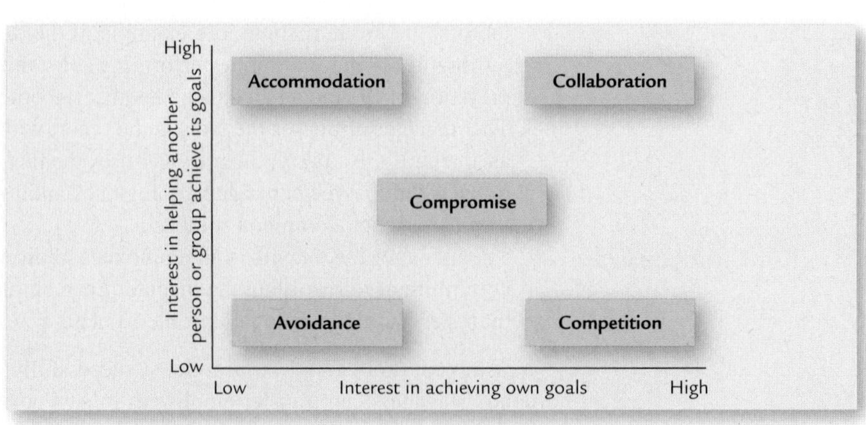

At the middle of the figure is *compromise*. Compromise usually involves bargaining and negotiation to reach a solution that is acceptable to both parties. Sometimes, the parties in dispute use *collaboration* to find a solution: Each side tries to satisfy not only its own goals but also the goals of the other side. Collaboration can benefit an organization because the parties work together to find a solution that leaves them both better off. Compromise and collaboration enable the parties in dispute to solve their differences.[86]

Accommodation is a style of handling conflict in which one party simply allows the other to achieve its goals. With *avoidance*, both parties refuse to recognize the real source of the problem and act as if there were no problem. Both of these conflict solutions are unsatisfactory from the organization's perspective and from the perspective of one or both of the parties in conflict. Accommodation means that one group uses its power to force the other to submit—to accommodate its demands, in other words. This solution is unlikely to lead to cooperation; furthermore, the weaker party is likely to become resentful and be on the lookout for any opportunity to get back at the stronger party. Similarly, avoidance means that the conflict will smolder, and the parties will remain uncooperative or uncommunicative.

Competition leads to the greatest and most visible conflict. Each party is looking out for its own interests and has little interest in understanding the other's position or taking the other's needs into account. When a conflict is handled competitively, or when accommodation or avoidance are typical styles of handling conflict, the conflict escalates to the next stage in Pondy's model.

Promoting Compromise

There are five specific tactics that managers can use to structure the negotiation and bargaining process to make compromise and collaboration more likely: emphasize common goals; focus on the problem, not the people; focus on interests, not demands; create opportunities for joint gain; and focus on what is fair.

Emphasize common goals. Common goals are goals that all parties agree on regardless of the source of their conflict. Increasing organizational effectiveness, increasing responsiveness to customers, and gaining a competitive advantage are just a few of the many common goals that members of a company can emphasize during bargaining. Emphasizing common goals help parties in conflict to keep in mind the big picture and the

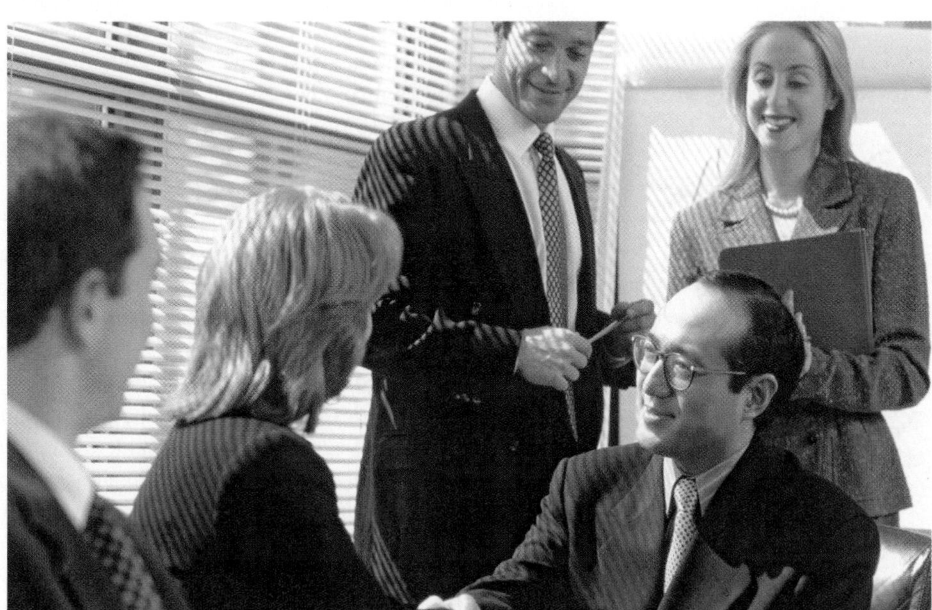

Once people in conflict focus on their joint interests, they are on the road toward achieving creative solutions that will benefit and satisfy each of them.

fact that they are working together to help the company succeed despite their disagreements.

Focus on the problem, not the people. People who are in conflict may not be able to resist the temptation to focus on the shortcomings and weaknesses of the other person or group. Now instead of attacking the problem itself, people start to attack one another. For example, they talk about the mistakes the other group has made in the past, and they criticize the personality of the other person or their personal habits. This approach is inconsistent with reaching a compromise through bargaining. All parties to a conflict need to remain focused on the problem or the source of the conflict and avoid the temptation to discredit each other personally.

Focus on interests, not demands. Demands are what a person wants; interests are why the person wants them. When two people are in conflict, it is unlikely that the demands of both can be met. Their underlying interests, however, can be met, and meeting them is what bargaining and negotiation is all about.

Create opportunities for joint gain. Once the parties to a conflict focus on their interests, they are on the road toward achieving creative solutions that will benefit them both. This win-win scenario means that rather than having a fixed set of alternatives from which to choose, the parties can come up with new alternatives that might even expand the resource "pie."

Focus on what is fair. Focusing on what is fair is consistent with the principles of equity theory. Equity theory emphasizes the fair distribution of outcomes based on the inputs or contributions that people make to companies. It is likely that parties in conflict will prefer different alternatives; each party wants the one that best serves his or her interests. Emphasizing fairness and equity will help the parties come to a mutual agreement about what the best solution is to the problem.

When managers pursue those five strategies and encourage other members of the company to do so, they are more likely to resolve their conflicts effectively through negotiation and bargaining. Then, managers can use conflict to help increase a company's performance and avoid destructive fights that harm the people involved in conflict as well as the organization.

Union–management negotiations. One of the most common types of negotiation and bargaining takes place between unions and management during contract talks. Suppose this year management is in a strong position because the economy is in recession. When management and the union sit down to negotiate, management crushes the union, which goes back to its members empty-handed. Next year, the economy has recovered, and the negotiations begin again. What will be the attitude of the union this time? Management probably will confront a no-holds-barred attempt to beat management and get everything the union thought it should have gotten last year.

When two parties are in continual negotiation with one another, they realize that, for the survival of the organization, they need to adopt a long-term perspective that emphasizes their joint objectives and minimizes differences. In a negotiation situation, such as management–union bargaining, it is important to note that two different processes go on simultaneously. First is *distributive bargaining*, in which the parties bargain over how to divide resources, deciding who gets what and how much.[87] Second is *attitudinal structuring*, in which the parties try to influence their opponent's attitudes. For example, either management or union negotiators might decide to act in an aggressive manner to increase their share of the resources, or perhaps act in a conciliatory manner to preserve long-term working relationships, save face, or demonstrate how much power they have should they choose to use it.[88]

Union and management negotiators often develop long-term relationships with one another and try to cooperate because they know that stalemate and attempts to destroy one another result in an antagonistic, destructive conflict aftermath in which everyone loses. Negotiation and bargaining is a difficult and delicate process in which the art of give-and-take and posturing for position is finely developed. Negotiations typically take place over a period of months as the parties discover what they can and cannot get. This is true of negotiations not only between management and unions but also between corporate headquarter managers and divisional managers, and between managers and subordinates as they discuss pay and promotions.

In summary, negotiation and bargaining is an important means to resolve and manage conflict in work and organizational settings. Conflict can never be eliminated because differences in interests and in attitudes, as well as competition over resources, are integral to the way organizations operate. For the outcome of conflict to be beneficial, an organization's members have to learn how to deal with conflict when it occurs and to adopt the appropriate way of resolving it. Managing conflict through negotiation is an important part of a manager's job and an important aspect of organizational behavior at all levels.

Summary

Understanding and managing power, politics, conflict, and negotiation is an integral part of a manager's job. Organizations are composed of people who come together to achieve their common goals. When resources are scarce, people and groups have to compete for them, and some achieve their goals while others do not. In an organization, managers have the primary responsibility to ensure that competition for resources is free and fair and that people who obtain power over resources do so because they possess skills and abilities that will, in the long run, benefit all members of the organization. Managers also have the responsibility to manage conflicts as they arise to ensure the long-term success of the organization and to maintain a balance of power to ensure that politics and conflict benefit rather than harm the organization. In this chapter, we made the following major points:

1. Power is the ability of one person or group to cause another person or group to do something they otherwise might not have done. Politics is activities in which managers engage to increase their power and to pursue goals that favor their individual and group interests. Power and politics can benefit or harm an organization.
2. Sources of formal individual power include legitimate power, reward power, coercive power, and information power. Sources of informal individual power include expert power, referent power, and charismatic power.
3. Sources of functional and divisional power include the ability to control uncertain contingencies, irreplacability, centrality, and the ability to control and generate resources.
4. Managers can use many kinds of political tactics to increase their individual power. These tactics include making oneself irreplaceable and central, controlling contingencies and resources, recognizing who has power, controlling the agenda, bringing in an outside expert, and building coalitions and alliances. Managing politics to obtain its positive effects requires a balance of power in an organization and a strong CEO who has the ability to keep powerful people and groups in check.
5. Conflict is the struggle that arises when the goal-directed behavior of one person or group blocks the goal-directed behavior of another person or group. Whether conflict benefits or harms an organization depends on how it is managed.
6. The three main sources of conflict are differentiation, task relationships, and the scarcity of resources. When conflict occurs, it typically moves through a series of stages. In Pondy's model of conflict, these stages are latent conflict, perceived conflict, felt conflict, manifest conflict, and the conflict aftermath.
7. Negotiation and bargaining are important means of managing and resolving conflict at both the individual and group level. The ability to negotiate an agreement is an important skill a manager needs to cultivate.

Exercises in Understanding and Managing Organizational Behavior

Questions for Review

1. In what ways can the use of power and politics help or harm an organization?
2. What are the principal sources of a manager's formal power and informal power? How does the way a manager exercises power affect subordinates?
3. Think of a manager you have worked under or a leader you have been in close contact with. What were the main sources of this person's individual power? What was your reaction to the way this person exercised power?
4. What are the main sources of functional and divisional power?
5. Why is it important to have a power balance in an organization?
6. In what ways can the manager of a function deliberately set out to gain power inside an organization?
7. Why may conflict be good or bad for an organization?
8. What are the main sources of conflict between functions?
9. Why is it important for managers to try to reduce manifest conflict and create a good conflict aftermath?
10. What are the main conflict resolution strategies?

Increasing Self-Awareness

Understanding Conflict and Politics

Think of the last time you came into conflict with another person or group, such as a manager you worked for or even a friend or family member. Then answer these questions:

1. Was this the first time you came into conflict with this party, or was the conflict one in a series of conflicts?
2. What was the source of the conflict? Did you and the other party see the source of the conflict differently? If so, why?
3. How would you describe the way you both reacted to the conflict?
4. Did the conflict reach the stage of manifest conflict? If it did not, how did you manage to avoid coming into manifest conflict? If it did, what form did the manifest conflict take?
5. How was the conflict resolved?
6. What kind of conflict aftermath resulted from the way you or the other party managed the conflict?
7. How well do you think you managed the conflict with the other party?
8. Given what you know now, how could you have handled the conflict more effectively?

A Question of Ethics

Power, Politics, and Negotiation

Managers routinely use organizational politics and negotiation to try to convince other managers to agree with their goals and follow the course of action they are championing. They may also seek ways to increase their personal power in an organization to further their own interests. Think about the ethical issues involved in politics, power, and negotiation and address the following issues:

1. At what point does it become unethical to use organizational politics to promote either personal interests or the interests of a function or division?
2. What is the role played by ethical values in the negotiation and bargaining process to ensure that outcomes are fair and equitable?

Small Group Break-Out Exercise

What Are the Sources of Conflict?

Form groups of three or four people and appoint one member as the spokesperson who will communicate your conclusions to the rest of the class.

Think of an organization you are all familiar with such as a local restaurant or supermarket store and discuss the way it operates. Using the material in the chapter:

1. Identify how *differentiation* might potentially give rise to conflict between different employees or groups in this organization (e.g., because of status inconsistencies).
2. Identify how *task relationships* might potentially result in conflict between different employees or groups in this organization (e.g., because of task interdependencies).
3. How does the way the organization operates, such as its hierarchy of authority and the way it groups activities into departments, help to prevent such conflict from arising?

Topic for Debate

Organizational politics and conflict are part of the fabric of behavior in organizations. Now that you understand how these processes work in organizations, debate the following issue.

Team A. The use of power by self-interested managers and groups has the potential to do an organization more good than harm.

Team B. The use of power by self-interested managers and groups has the potential to do an organization more harm than good.

Experiential Exercise

Managing Conflict Successfully

Objective

Your objective is to gain an appreciation of the conflict process and to understand the difficulties involved in managing conflict successfully.

Procedure

The class divides into groups of from three to five people, and each group appoints one member as spokesperson to report on the group's findings to the whole class. Here is the scenario.

You are a group of top managers that has been charged with resolving an escalating conflict between manufacturing and sales managers in a large company that manufactures office furniture. The company's furniture can be customized to the needs of individual customers, and it is crucial that sales provides manufacturing with accurate information about each customer's specific requirements. Over the last few months, however, manufacturing has been complaining that sales provides this information too late for it to make the most efficient use of its resources, that sales is increasingly making errors in describing each customer's special needs, and that sales demands unreasonably quick turnaround for its customers. For its part, sales is complaining about sloppy workmanship in the final product, which has led to an increased level of customer complaints, about increasing delays in delivery of the furniture, and about manufacturing's unwillingness to respond flexibly to unexpected last-minute customer requests. Problems are increasing, and in the last meeting between senior manufacturing and sales managers harsh words were spoken during a bitter exchange of charges and counter charges.

1. As a group, use the concepts discussed in this chapter (particularly Pondy's model) to analyze the nature of the conflict between manufacturing and sales. Try to identify the sources of the conflict and ascertain how far the conflict has gone.
2. Devise a detailed action plan for resolving the conflict. Pay particular attention to the need to create a good conflict aftermath. In devising your plan, be sure to analyze (a) the obstacles to resolving the conflict, (b) the appropriate conflict management techniques to use, and (c) ways to design a new control and reward system to help eliminate such conflict in the future.

When asked by your instructor, the spokesperson will describe your group's analysis of this conflict between functions and the action plan for resolving it.

New York Times *Cases in the News*

The New York Times

"New DaimlerChrysler CEO Targets Infighting and Intrigues"

By Neal E. Boudette and Steven Power, November 28, 2005, p. B.1.

DIETER ZETSCHE doesn't become chief executive of DaimlerChrysler AG until Jan. 1, but already he has started work on a vital task: softening the caustic corporate culture that marked the tenure of outgoing CEO Jurgen Schrempp.

In July, Mr. Schrempp, 61 years old, unexpectedly announced he would retire after 11 tumultuous years running the automaker. As his successor he named Mr. Zetsche, an occasional boardroom rival who engineered the dramatic turnaround of the company's U.S. arm, Chrysler Group. In September, Mr. Zetsche, 52 years old, moved from Chrysler to the company's Stuttgart headquarters and took control of the Mercedes division. After only a few days as Mercedes chief he signaled a big change, telling the unit's entire management staff in a memo that he "won't tolerate any infighting, intrigues or political games." The missive, Mr. Zetsche said in an interview during a gathering of Chrysler dealers in Las Vegas, was "a great chance to set the tone right from the beginning" and to make clear that under his leadership "what counts is performance," not internal alliances.

Such wasn't always the case under Mr. Schrempp. The prime mover behind the 1998 merger that created the German-American car maker, Mr. Schrempp epitomized the jet-setting, deal-making celebrity CEO of the 1990s. But when his strategy floundered and DaimlerChrysler's market value plunged, he came under sharp criticism from investors. At the company's April annual meeting, he faced hours of withering attacks on his strategy and leadership. That spectacle, people familiar with the matter said, contributed to his decision to retire with more than two years remaining on his contract. Trading big-shot CEOs like Mr. Schrempp for more down-to-earth team players is becoming more common in corporate boardrooms. Earlier this year, Hewlett-Packard Co. ousted the high-profile Carly Fiorina in favor of Mark Hurd, a low-key CEO from NCR Corp. Walt Disney Co. downshifted from the domineering Michael Eisner to Robert Iger, who is more of a consensus-builder.

During the go-go 1990s, high-octane, ego-driven CEOs were in vogue, says Judith Glaser, a management expert who examines executive personalities in a coming book called "The Leadership DNA." But over time, she says, the "me-centric" approach can morph into a bullying style and create a vindictive, politicized atmosphere in which subordinates battle each other to win the boss's favor. As a result, board members, employees and investors now find CEO hubris less appealing—especially if the company's performance falters, Ms. Glaser says. "There's definitely a trend from the 'I-centric' personalities to the 'we-centric.'"

So far, the CEO-elect has declined to give much detail about how he plans to proceed in the new job. His five years at Chrysler, however, indicate he is a hands-on, straight-talking manager willing to suffer a short-term setback for long-term benefit. In contrast to Mr. Schrempp, who distanced himself from operational matters and rarely mixed with ordinary employees, Mr. Zetsche has spent time in the last two months with Mercedes designers, offering suggestions to improve the styling of several models in development. Earlier this month he spoke at a gathering of Chrysler dealers—an audience Mr. Schrempp never addressed—and vowed to return to speak to the group as CEO.

Unlike a lot of new bosses, Mr. Zetsche says he isn't planning to replace the outgoing CEO's confidantes who continue to hold powerful posts at headquarters. These include Mr. Schrempp's wife, Lydia, who has a highly paid job in the office of the CEO. Mr. Zetsche said she will stay with the company, although she won't be part of his management team. And shortly after he was named CEO-elect, Mr. Zetsche approached Hartmut Schick, head of corporate communications, and asked him to remain in the post. Mr. Schick agreed. Though Mr. Zetsche acknowledged that "it's more usual" for a new boss to select his own key spokesman, he said he enjoyed a "totally open" relationship with Mr. Schick. Keeping him would also send a signal that he isn't intent on ousting Mr. Schrempp's team across the board.

Questions for Discussion

1. What kinds of power struggles and political battles exist inside DaimlerChrysler?
2. What is Dieter Zetsche's approach to managing power and politics?
3. What will be the biggest obstacles he faces in solving the company's problems?

The New York Times

"Fewer Corporate Chiefs Are also Serving as Chairmen."

By Claudia H. Deutsch, NYT, March 17, 2006, p. C.2.

Disney did it. So did Fannie Mae, Hewlett-Packard and Dell. Most companies in Britain do it. And now, more American companies are doing it, too: wresting board chairmanships away from chief executives. According to executive recruiting firm Russell Reynolds Associates, 29 percent of the companies in the S & P. have separated the jobs, up from 21 percent five years ago. Some, like Disney, we forced by shareholders to decouple the roles. Others, like Dell, did so to give a hard-working president a promotion to chief executive. Many others want to let a new chief executive grow into the job under the watchful eye of the former one, serving as chairman. The insurance industry may soon give companies a financial incentive to split the top jobs, too. "We always ask, Are you considering dividing the titles, and if not, why don't you?" said Lou Ann Layton, managing director incharge of national directors' and officers' liability insurance at Marsh Inc. Companies that do decouple the roles are starting to ask for discounts. "Our clients ask us about this every day," said Peter Tulupman, a spokesman for the American International Group.

Many shareholders say such splits are overdue. "When the same person fills both roles, the odds are much less that the board will challenge inappropriate decisions," said the New York State comptroller, Alan G. Hevesi, who oversees New York's pension funds. The Council of Institutional investors, which counts most large pension funds as members, has a policy that all boards should have an independent director as chairman. Directors themselves are jumping on the bandwagon. In a poll last year by Russell Reynolds that asked the question for the first time, 59 percent said they liked the idea of splitting the job of chairman and chief executive. "It is just harder to achieve independent oversight of a C.E.O. who's also the chairman," said Patricia C. Dunn, who became chairwoman of Hewlett-Packard when Carleton S. Fiorina, then chairwoman and chief executive, was ousted last year. Ms. Dunn retained the title after Mark V. Hurd was named chief executive.

And a few chief executives, wearied by the amount of time top jobs consume in this Sarbanes-Oxley era, welcome the split. Steven A. Raymund, the chairman and chief executive of Tech Data, plans to give up the chief executive slot as soon as the company finds a successor. "I want to stay involved in the company," Mr. Raymund, 50, said. "But I'm getting fatigued, and I want to do other things with my life." Charles A. Tribbett III, a Russell Reynolds managing director, said that more people aspiring to be chief executives were willing to accept the split, though most still found it unsettling. "Candidates still want both titles, but it's just not the deal breaker it was five years ago," he said.

Management specialists argue that too many corporate disasters can be traced to concentrating power at the top. James E. Schrager, a management professor at the Graduate School of Business of the University of Chicago, is certain that Ms. Fiorina's role as chairwoman and chief executive of Hewlett-Packard enabled her to push through the company's ill-starred acquisition of Compaq Computer. Mr. Hevesi and other Disney shareholders say that Michael D. Eisner, Disney's former chairman and chief executive, used his dual role to get a huge severance package for Michael S. Ovitz, whom he hired and then fired as his No. 2. Disney has since amended its guidelines to make separating the posts the norm.

Many shareholders prefer to keep the roles combined. Despite public outrage over the rich retirement package the board of General Elelctric granted to John F. Welch Jr., G.E.'s former chairman and chief executive, G.E. shareholders voted to let Jeffrey R. Immelt, who succeeded Mr. Welch, keep both titles. Peter O'Toole, a G.E. spokesman, said that the "presiding director" role of Ralph S. Larsen, who had never worked for G.E., conferred enough independence. Indeed, many companies now have "lead" or "presiding" directors overseeing committees that deal with compensation and other sensitive areas. "If there's a lead director who has the final say on meeting agendas or information flow, we're happy," said Patrick S. McGurn, executive vice president of Institutional Shareholder Services, which advises institutions on proxy matters. But that setup does not address perhaps the most compelling push to decouple the top two roles: the need, as corporations are under increasing scrutiny, to prove that the company takes governance seriously.

Splitting the roles "sends a signal to the outside world that the board really cares about governance," Ms. Dunn, the Hewlett-Packard chairwoman, said, "and to the senior-level staff that they are responsible for providing information to the board, not just to the C.E.O."

Questions for Discussion

1. What are (a) the advantages and (b) the disadvantages of separating the roles of chairperson and CEO?
2. Do you think politics and conflict will be higher or lower if these roles are split?
3. Which approach best serves shareholder interests?

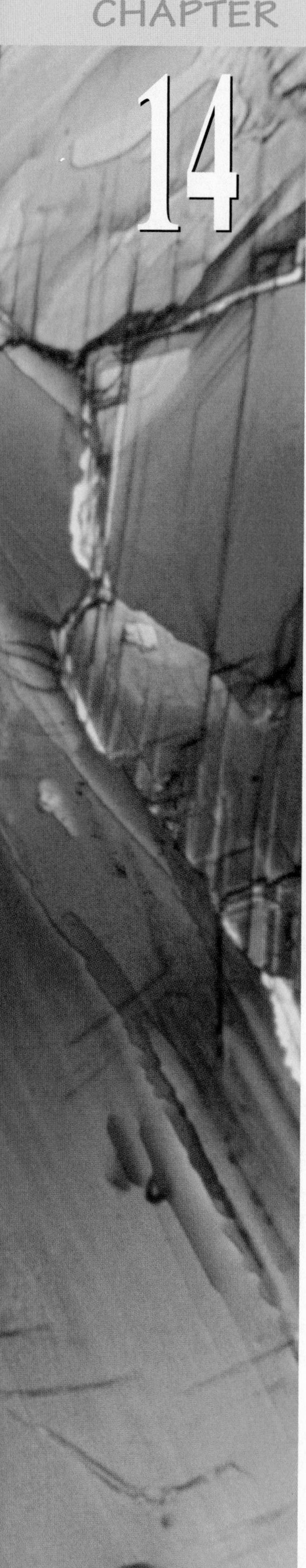

CHAPTER 14

COMMUNICATING EFFECTIVELY IN ORGANIZATIONS

Learning objectives

After studying this chapter, you should be able to:

- Describe the four main functions of communication and differentiate between different kinds of communications networks.
- Discuss the steps in the communications process and the requirements for successful communication to take place.
- Differentiate between the main kinds of barriers to communication and explain how they can reduce the effectiveness of communication.
- Identify the main kinds of communication media and explain how they vary along the dimension of information richness.
- Appreciate the importance of persuasive communication and describe how to create persuasive messages to influence others.

Opening Case

CHRYSLER'S TOM LASORDA KNOWS HOW TO TALK TO EMPLOYEES

Why is communication so important?

In the past, Chrysler (part of DaimlerChrysler's global empire) was often criticized for its failure to adequately communicate current problems and future plans to employees and the trade unions that represent many of them. Its "ivory tower approach" led top decision makers to remain isolated from what was going on in its car plants; and employees often felt they were kept in the dark as announcements about their company came from trained spokespeople reading carefully prepared script. This communication approach led to a wide gulf between Chrysler managers and employees—it contributed to the company's deteriorating performance during the 1990s.

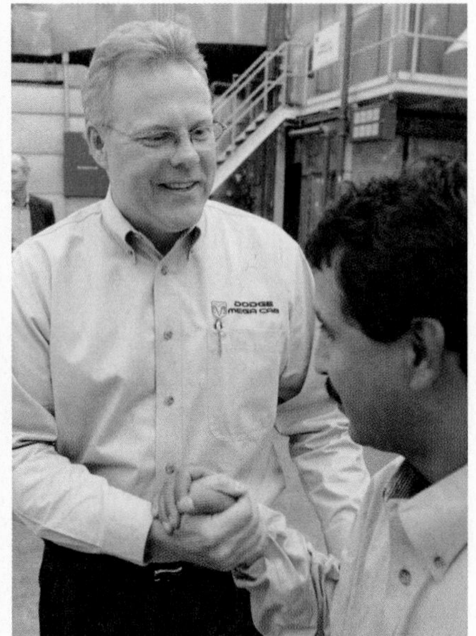

Tom LaSorda, CEO of Chrysler has first-hand knowledge of the concerns of auto workers today: his father and grandfather were both members of the United Auto Workers Union.

Chrysler has taken many steps to remedy this communication problem in the 2000s in order to bring managers and employees, at all levels of the company, closer together to deal with the major problems it faces. Chrysler's top executives recognized that only intense cooperation between employees and managers could produce the efforts needed to turnaround its performance and manage global competition. One step Chrysler took to encourage cooperation was to promote managers who understand the concerns and problems facing its workforce—and how to talk to employees. And who better could speak to workers than managers whose parents worked in Chrysler plants and who were raised in homes where events at the company were a major topic of conversation?

One of these managers is Tom LaSorda, whose father was the United Auto Workers (UAW) president of one of Chrysler's Canadian auto plants, and whose grandfather was also a union leader at that company. With his union roots, LaSorda has first-hand knowledge of what concerns auto workers at a time when thousands of them are losing their jobs because of intense global competition.[1] LaSorda remembers from his childhood when his father was laid off for six months when the economy collapsed; he also knows what it is to live from paycheck to paycheck, which most American families do.

Dieter Zetsche, the German-born former CEO of Chrysler, who engineered its recent turnaround, recognized LaSorda's unique skills—the background and experience that enables him to effectively communicate with employees, as well as his proven management skills. Zetsche is an extravert and showman, but he appreciated that down-to-earth LaSorda is at his best when interacting with ordinary people—like the employees in Chrysler's plants. Zetsche mentored LaSorda, and when his own success resulted in his being promoted to CEO of the whole of DaimlerChrysler, he decided LaSorda was the best choice as Chrysler's next CEO.[2]

How have LaSorda's skills in talking and relating to union employees and officials paid off? Analysts say that Chrysler has enjoyed more conciliatory dealings with employees and the UAW than GM or Ford. LaSorda has helped the UAW recognize the reality of global competition and that it is necessary to take a long-term view to help Chrysler and its employees prosper—despite the pain this will cause employees in the short run. So far, not only has the UAW agreed to a painful 24,000 layoffs in the last five years; it also has agreed to change work practices that resulted in high operating costs; and, it is working with the company to find ways to lower healthcare costs. These are all major factors hurting the competitiveness of Chrysler and the Big Three U. S. carmakers.

In return, LaSorda worked to improve the future prospects of those laid-off workers. Chrysler has provided major funding to allow new companies to open up car-parts operations near Chrysler's plants to provide new jobs; it provided new training, education, and severance benefits to laid-off employees; and it has behaved fairly to current employees. LaSorda has spent considerable time walking around Chrysler's plants talking with workers, meeting with UAW executives, and addressing union members at their annual meeting—the first Chrysler CEO ever to do so. As he says, "When you're running a business, you do what's best for *all*," and he hopes that in the long run this will translate into thousands of new well-paying auto jobs.[3] This will happen if Chrysler's innovative new cars (it will introduce ten new models in 2006) are popular, and U. S. car buyers once again become loyal Chrysler customers.[4]

Overview

As the work of Tom LaSorda at Chrysler suggests, communication is one of the most important processes that takes place in organizations; it has a major impact on individual, group, and organizational performance.[5] High-performing organizations have mastered the communication process; their members have the information they need when they need it to achieve the organization's goals. In contrast, the poor performance of many organizations is often the result of communication problems within the organization.

Given the sheer impact that communication has on individual, group, and organizational effectiveness, this chapter appropriately focuses on its nature.[6] First, we define communication, outline its implications for organizational behavior, and describe the functions that communication serves in organizations. Second, we examine common patterns of communication in organizations. Third, we describe a model of the communication process and discuss common communication problems and ways to avoid them. We then explore one of the key components of the communication process—the communication medium or method—in depth. Finally, we discuss the steps involved in persuasive communication. By the end of this chapter, you will understand why effective communication is so important in organizations.

What Is Communication?

One of the defining features of communication is the *sharing of information with other people*.[7] An accountant for Ernst & Young communicates with his boss by informing him about how quickly a large auditing project is going, when he asks to take his vacation at the beginning of June, and when he requests that his boss purchase a new software package to help in the preparation of complicated income tax forms.

The simple sharing of information is not enough for communication to take place, however. The second defining feature of communication is the *reaching of a common understanding*.[8] The sharing of information does not accomplish much in organizations unless people concur on what this information means. For example, suppose the accountant at Ernst & Young informs his supervisor that he has run into some problems on the auditing project and it will take longer to complete than was originally thought. The supervisor might assume that the audit is simply more complicated and time consuming than most others. The accountant, however, might suspect that the top-management team at the company it is auditing is trying to hide questionable, and perhaps illegal, accounting practices. In this situation, effective communication has not taken place. The supervisor does not understand the source and magnitude of the problems the auditor has encountered. In other words, a common understanding has *not* been reached. This reduces the effectiveness of both the auditor and the supervisor. The auditor doesn't get the supervisor's advice and help in handling the tricky situation, and the supervisor isn't living up to an important responsibility—namely, working closely with his employees on an unusual or especially difficult auditing project.

COMMUNICATION
The sharing of information between two or more individuals or groups to reach a common understanding.

In this case, **communication**—the sharing of information between two or more individuals or groups to reach a common understanding—hasn't occurred. Reaching a common understanding does *not* mean that people have to agree with each other. What it *does* mean is that people must have a relatively accurate idea of what a person or group is trying to tell them.[9] Communication is good or effective when members of an organization share information with each other and all parties involved are relatively clear about what this information means. Communication is ineffective when people either do not receive the information they need or are not quite sure what the information they do receive means.[10]

The Functions Of Communication

Effective communication is important in organizations because it affects practically every aspect of organizational behavior.[11] For example, members of an organization are likely to come to understand each other's personalities, attitudes, and values only when they communicate effectively with one another. Likewise, employees are motivated to perform at a high level when someone communicates clearly what is expected of them and expresses confidence in their ability to perform. Finally, leaders can influence and persuade their followers only when effective communication takes place.

When organizations experience problems such as unmotivated employees or excessively high turnover, poor communication is often partially to blame. A secretary may have low motivation to develop new bookkeeping skills or to take on the additional responsibility of planning conferences because he thinks he is in a dead-end job. In reality, no one has bothered to communicate to him that secretaries do have opportunities to advance in the company. Similarly, a software company that announces that a larger rival has purchased it may see its turnover rate triple, even though no layoffs and few internal changes will result from the change in ownership. The reason for the exodus is that its top managers have not clearly communicated to employees that their jobs are not at risk. Expecting the worst, the best performers (who have the most opportunities available to them elsewhere) will find other jobs.

Good communication prevents many problems like these from occurring and serves several other important functions in organizations: providing knowledge, motivating the organization's members, controlling and coordinating group activities, and expressing feelings and emotions (see Exhibit 14.1).

Providing knowledge. A basic function of communication is to give members of the organization the information they need to do their jobs effectively.[12] By providing knowledge about, for example, ways to perform tasks, and the decisions that have been made, an organization makes sure its members have the information they need to perform at high levels.

EXHIBIT 14.1

Functions of Communication

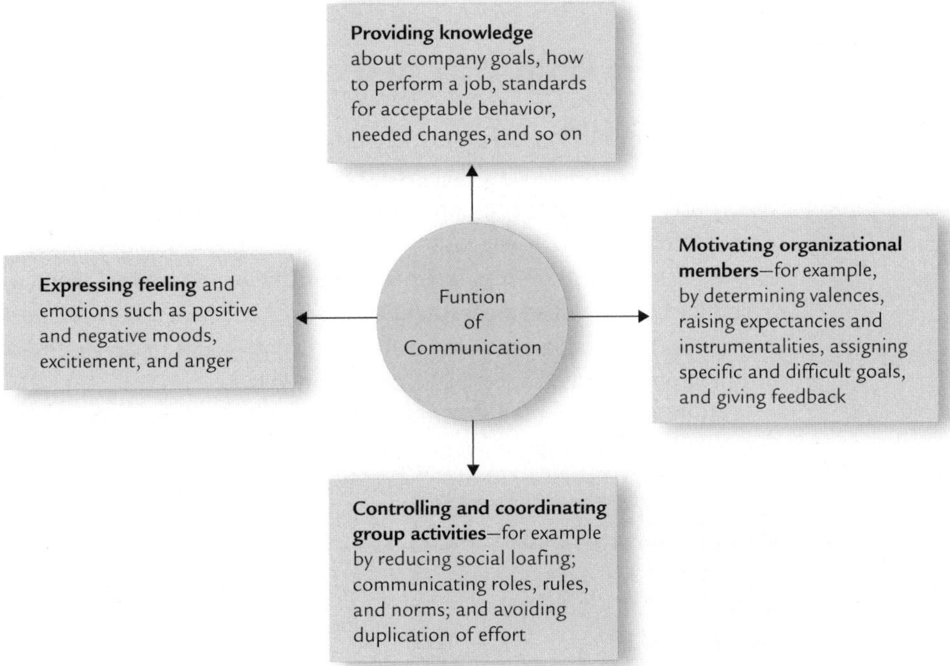

The importance of communication is most apparent when an employee has just started a new job. As you learned in Chapter 10, individuals starting new jobs face considerable uncertainty about what they are supposed to do, how they should go about doing it, and what the acceptable standards are. Communication from coworkers, supervisors, customers, clients, and others helps reduce this uncertainty and provides newcomers with the knowledge they need to perform their jobs effectively.

Communication is essential for the socialization of newcomers at all levels in an organization. When Mickey Drexler, the man who made Gap Inc. famous, became CEO of struggling clothes retailer J. Crew, he spent his first weeks on the job communicating with as many employees as he could to learn about the troubled company he was hired to help turn around. Drexler instituted a series of "town hall" meetings and talked to employees at all levels about J. Crew's problems.

The knowledge function also is important for even the most experienced members of an organization because things change. Just as the products or services an organization provides change in response to customers' desires, so does the nature of an employee's job responsibilities. Clearly communicating the new tasks, responsibilities, and policies required helps ensure that the members of the organization will continue to understand what needs to be done so it will achieve its goals.

The vast amount of information and knowledge available on the World Wide Web (WWW) today allows employees to access all kinds of data to help them perform their jobs and solve problems. On the other hand, employees can also plan vacations, shop for clothes, sell antiques, and make stock trades through the Internet on company time, which has raised ethical dilemmas for many organizations, as the following Managing Ethically suggests.

Motivating organizational members. As you learned in Chapters 6 and 7, motivation is a key determinant of performance in organizations, and communication plays a central role

Managing Ethically

What's the Right Way to Use the WWW?

A growing problem for more and more organizations is employee web surfing at work.[13] According to Dr. David Greenfield, who runs the Center for Internet Addiction based in West Hartford, Connecticut, pornographic websites are among the most common, non-work-related sites employees visit while they are supposed to be working.[14] The majority of the visits to pornographic websites occur during the normal workday. Similarly, the majority of stock trades made using online broker Charles Schwab are made from the workplace. It has been estimated that web surfing results in significant losses in productivity, with total costs tallying in the billions of dollars.[15]

This trend creates a number of ethical dilemmas for organizations. On the one hand, employees value their privacy, and access to the Internet is considered a perk on some jobs. On the other hand, when employees surf the WWW on company time, their job performances might suffer. Moreover, companies expose themselves to potential legal conundrums ranging from copyright infringement to hostile work environment charges, and sexual harassment allegations.[16]

It has been estimated that web surfing at work, at retail, stockbroking, and pornographic websites results in significant losses in employee productivity that cost companies billions of dollars.

The combined productivity losses and legal risks have led more organizations to actively monitor their employees' Internet activities and email messages.[17] According to an American Management Association survey of medium-to-large organizations in the United States, almost 75 percent of the companies surveyed indicated that they engage in some monitoring of employees' activities and communications.[18] Some organizations also install firewalls that prevent employees from accessing particular websites on the job. And when employees violate their organizations' Internet use policies, negative consequences often ensue. Thousands of companies have fired employees for visiting pornographic websites on the job. Hence, employees may want to think twice before they surf the WWW on company time.

in motivating members of an organization to achieve their goals. Expectancy theory (see Chapter 6) proposes, for example, that managers do the following:

- Determine what outcomes subordinates are trying to obtain from their jobs—that is, the valences of various outcomes.
- Make sure that employees perceive that obtaining these outcomes is contingent on performing at a high level—that is, make sure that instrumentalities are high.
- Make sure that employees believe that they can perform at a high level—that is, make sure that expectancies are high.

The only way that a manager can determine the valences of different outcomes for any given employee is by talking *and* listening to the employee to find out what the employee wants. Likewise, managers need to communicate with employees to assure them they are capable of performing at high levels and will be rewarded for doing so.

As another example of the role of communication in motivating employees, consider goal-setting theory (examined in Chapter 7). It suggests that employees will perform at a high level when they have specific and difficult goals and are given feedback concerning how they are doing. Managers use communication to let employees know what goals they should be striving for and how they are progressing in their efforts to achieve those goals.

Controlling and coordinating group activities. As you learned in Chapters 10 and 11, it is essential for groups to control their members' behaviors so that they perform their jobs in an acceptable fashion. Recall, for example, that a key challenge for self-managed work teams is to reduce social loafing—the tendency of people to exert less effort when working in groups than when working on their own. When a member of a group engages in social loafing, one of the primary ways that other members of the group can reduce it is by communicating to the loafer that his or her behavior has been observed and is not going to be tolerated. Groups and organizations exert control over their members by regularly communicating information about roles, rules, and norms to them. Similarly, as the interdependence between group members increases, the need for communication to coordinate their efforts in order to achieve group goals also increases.[19] For example, communication can help to eliminate duplication of effort in a team and to prevent one poorly performing member from keeping the other members from achieving the group's goals.

Expressing feelings and emotions. One of the most important functions of communication is to allow people to express their feelings and emotions.[20] These feelings and emotions can be general or specific and can originate from inside or outside the workplace.

Recall from Chapter 3 that *work moods* are the feelings people experience on a day-to-day basis as they perform their jobs. Often, individuals and groups can better achieve their goals if they can communicate their moods to others. The moods employees experience on the job influence their perceptions and evaluations of people and situations as well as their behavior.[21]

For example, when the manager of an electronics store snapped at a subordinate who was proposing an innovative way to increase customer traffic through the store and thus increase sales, the hurt look on the subordinate's face made the manager realize that such impatience was out of line. The manager decided to communicate his feelings to the subordinate, and he frankly told him that he was in a lousy mood and that they should wait until the next day to discuss what sounded like a promising proposal. This simple communication of feelings helped to prevent a minor incident from turning into a major problem.

Emotions such as excitement or anger are often stirred by specific events at work or at home, so it is often useful for individuals to communicate their emotions to others in the organization. An employee who has just learned she has received a promotion may be so elated she can't think straight enough to have an in-depth discussion with her supervisor about finding and training her successor. Simply communicating this fact to the supervisor and postponing the conversation for a while is the sensible thing to do. Similarly, as you learned in Chapter 9, an employee who is upset and angry about his spouse's terminal illness may feel a little bit better when he communicates his emotions to others and receives their social support.[22] Moreover, supervisors, co-employees, and subordinates will be more understanding of the employee's lack of enthusiasm or recent tendency to be overly critical when they realize the tremendous strain he is under. Communication of moods and emotions helps organizational members understand each other, and when people understand each other, they are better able to work together to perform well and achieve their goals.

In summary, communication is vital to ensure subordinates have all the information they need to perform their jobs and achieve their goals. Effective communication also lets subordinates know a leader is confident they can perform at high levels and that they will benefit from performing well. Communication is also vital to help subordinates understand the goals they should strive for and give them clear feedback about how they are performing.

Employees can also be encouraged to communicate effectively with each other to coordinate their activities, avoid duplication of effort, and limit social loafing. Finally, to avoid misunderstandings, managers use communication to express their own feelings and emotions to others, and should encourage their subordinates to do the same.

Communication Networks in Organizations

Communication in an organization—both between employees at different levels in the hierarchy, and between employees in different functions and departments—tends to occur in certain recurring patterns. The set of pathways through which information flows within a group or organization is called a **communication network**. Communication networks are found at both group and organizational levels.

COMMUNICATION NETWORK
The set of pathways through which information flows within a group or organization.

Group communication networks. As we discussed in Chapters 10 and 11, self-managed work teams, top-management teams, and other work groups play important roles in most organizations. Among the communication networks that can develop in such groups are the wheel, the chain, the circle, and the all-channel network (see Exhibit 14.2).

In a wheel network, most information travels through one central member of the group. This central member receives information from all other group members and is the sole sender of information to them; the other members of the group do not communicate directly with each other. Wheel networks are most common when there is *pooled task interdependence*—that is, when group members work independently and group performance is determined by summing up the performances of the members of the group. Examples of such groups are typing pools and groups of sales reps covering different

EXHIBIT 14.2

Group Communication Networks

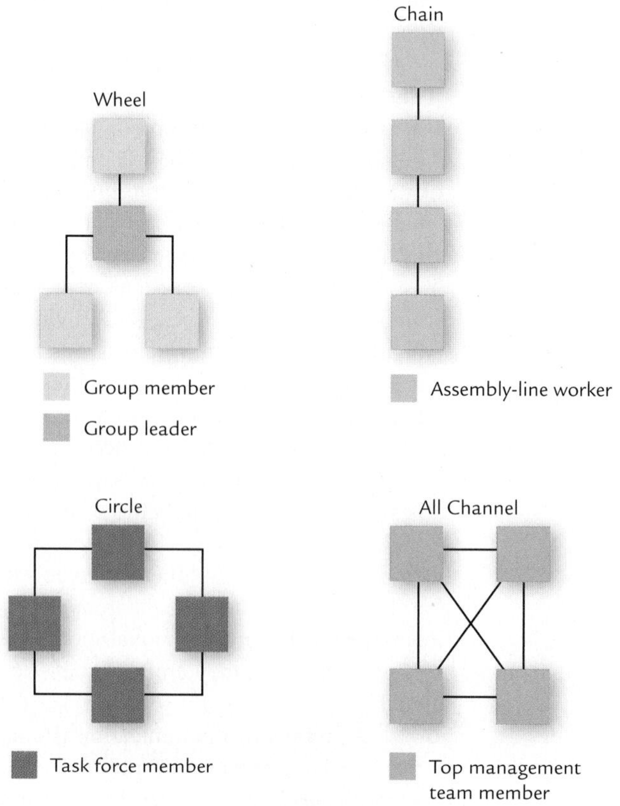

geographic regions—their members have little need to communicate directly with each other. Most communication flows to and from either the formal or the informal leader of the group. For these kinds of group tasks, the wheel is an effective communication pathway because it is fast and efficient.

In a chain network, communication flows in a predetermined sequence from one group member to the next. Chain networks are common when there is *sequential task interdependence,* and members are required to perform specific behaviors in a predetermined order. Examples of groups like this include all types of assembly-line work, where the finished product is the result of the sequential inputs of the group's members. While working on an assembly line, individuals are able to communicate only with others who are adjacent to them on the line. Chain networks also characterize communication up and down the hierarchy.

The circle network occurs in groups whose members communicate with others who are similar to them on some dimension ranging from experience, interests, or area of expertise to the location of their offices or even who they sit next to when the group meets. Employees tend to communicate with group members whose offices are located next to theirs, for example. Similarly, when groups sit at a round table, members tend to talk to those on either side of them.

In an all-channel network, every group member communicates with every other group member. All-channel networks are prevalent when there is *reciprocal task interdependence*—that is, when the activities of work-group members depend on one another. Each group member's behavior influences the behavior of every other member of the group. Examples of groups that use an all-channel communication network because of the complex nature of the work they perform include high-tech research and development teams, top-management teams, emergency room personnel, and surgical teams.

Organizational communication networks. Organization charts that summarize the formal reporting relationships in an organization reflect one type of organizational communication network. Formal reporting relationships emerge from the chain of command established by an organization's hierarchy. The hierarchy determines which subordinates report to a given supervisor, to whom that supervisor reports, and so on, up and down the chain of command. A simple organization chart is provided in Exhibit 14.3. When an organizational communication network is accurately described by an organization chart, communication flows up and down the hierarchy of the organization from subordinates to superiors and vice versa.

Newcomers to an organization may not see an organization chart until they have been on the job for several months. But when they see the chart, they are often surprised because the communication patterns that they have been observing bear little resemblance to the communication patterns specified by the chart. Lack of congruence between actual

EXHIBIT 14.3

A Simple Organization Chart

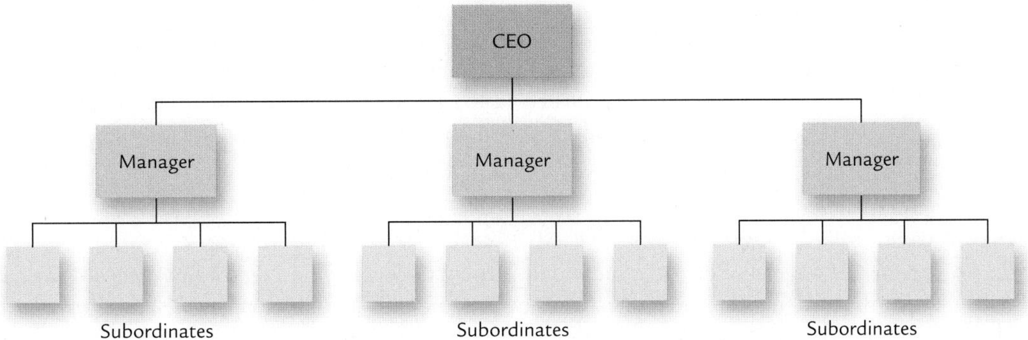

EXHIBIT 14.4

An Example of Actual Communication Patterns in an Organization

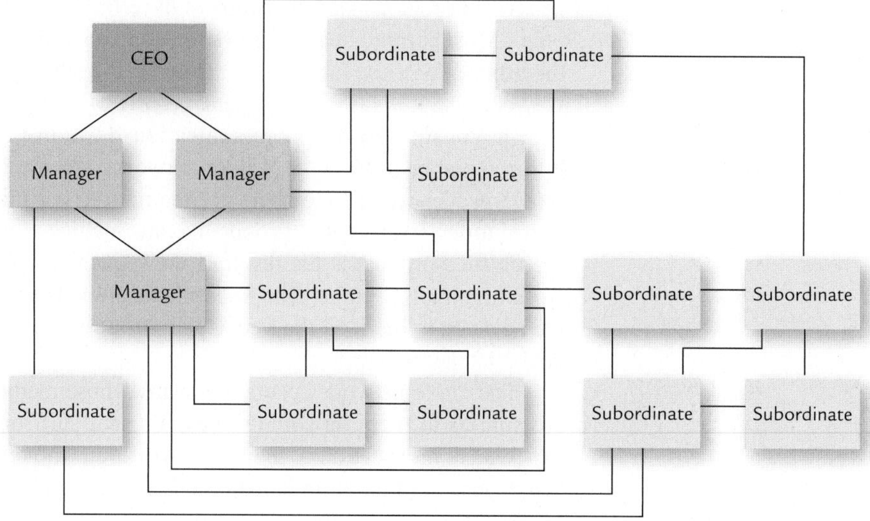

communication patterns and those specified in an organization chart is common. Communication in organizations often flows around issues, goals, projects, and problems rather than upward and downward from one formal reporting relationship to another. The roundabout flow ensures that members of the organization have access to the information they need to perform their jobs.

Actual communication patterns in an organization may look more like the informal network shown in Exhibit 14.4 than like the formal organization chart in Exhibit 14.3. Although the relationships shown on an organization chart are somewhat stable, actual communication patterns like in the network shown in Exhibit 14.4 are likely to change as conditions in the organization change. Members of an organization develop new patterns of communication as the type of information they need changes.[23]

Communication experts David Krackhardt and Jeffrey Hanson suggest that there are at least three informal communication networks in organizations: the advice network, the trust network, and the communication network. The *advice network* provides paths of communication for obtaining technical information. Examples might include determining the countries abroad that offer the lowest manufacturing costs and solving problems like how to fix a complicated machine when it breaks down. The *trust network* provides paths of communication for delicate information, such as information pertaining to conflicts, disagreements, and power struggles, as well as the handling of potential and actual crisis situations such as a product recall. The *communication network* provides paths of communication that are used on a day-to-day basis for ordinary work-related matters such as a change in accounting procedures or the upcoming company picnic.[24]

The Communication Process

SENDER
The individual, group, or organization that needs or wants to share information with some other individual, group, or organization.

Regardless of the nature of the communication network, effective communication involves a series of distinct steps shown in the model of the communication process presented in Exhibit 14.5 and described in the following paragraphs.[25] The model is cyclical since effective communication is a continually repeated process. However, the sender initiates the communication process, so we start by discussing the sender and the message.

The Sender and the Message

RECEIVER
The individual, group, or organization for which information is intended.

The **sender** is the individual, group, or organization that wants or needs to share information with some other individual, group, or organization to accomplish one or more of the four functions of communication described previously. The **receiver** is the individual,

EXHIBIT 14.5

The Communication Process

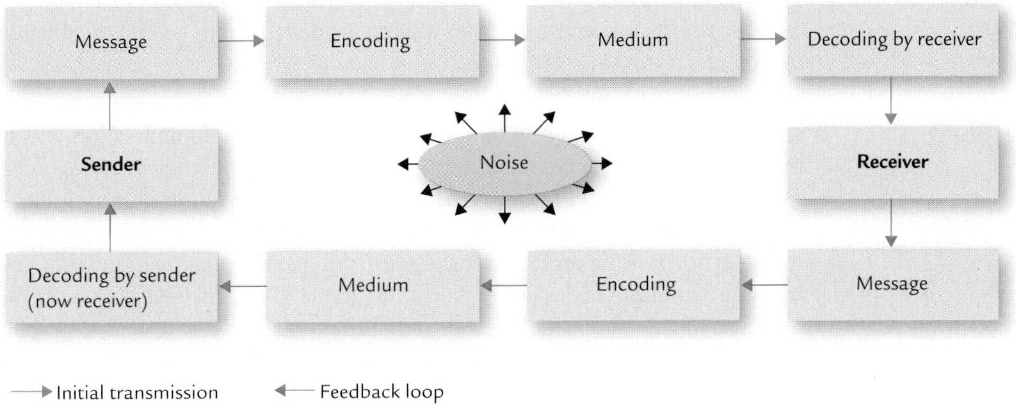

group, or organization for which the information is intended. For example, a supervisor may wish to send information to a subordinate about his or her performance, a task force on diversity may need to communicate to top management its assessment of the promotion barriers facing minorities, or the organization may need to communicate to the Environmental Protection Agency about what it's doing to comply with new waste disposal regulations.

MESSAGE
The information that a sender needs or wants to share with other people.

The **message** is the information that the sender needs or wants to share with other people. Effective communication depends on messages that are as clear and complete as possible. Clarity is important regardless of the content of the message, whether it relates to performance feedback, task-force findings and conclusions, or an organization's response to new government regulations. A message is *clear* when it contains information that is easily interpreted or understood. A message is *complete* when it contains all the information necessary to achieve a common understanding between the sender and the receiver. Sometimes, problems in the communication process crop up because the sender is vague or unsure about what the message should be. A supervisor, for example, might give vague feedback to a subordinate about performance on a recent assignment because the supervisor gave too little thought to how the subordinate actually performed or how his or her performance could improve in the future.

ENCODING
Translating a message into symbols or language that a receiver can understand.

Encoding

Once the sender has decided what the message is, the next step in the process is **encoding**, or translating the message into symbols or language the receiver can understand. A supervisor who puts ideas about how a subordinate is performing and ways that performance can be improved into words, a task force that summarizes the results of its investigations and weekly meetings into words and statistics such as the number of African Americans and women in top-management positions, and a member of an organization who shows a government inspector the organization's waste disposal operations—all of these are examples of the encoding of messages.

Although encoding ideas by putting them into words seems simple enough, some organizations are finding that their employees lack the basic writing and oral communication skills needed to do this and are taking action to improve encoding. First Bank Systems Inc., in Minneapolis, Minnesota, for example, helps employees ranging from clerks to managers improve their grammar through skills-upgrading classes. Smith Corona Corporation, located in New Canaan, Connecticut, teaches employees how to answer telephone calls.[26]

For communication to be effective, the sender must translate the message into a form that the receiver can understand. When ideas are translated into words, for example, the sender must take care to use words the receiver understands. Have you ever listened to a computer expert explain the workings of a new software package using terminology that meant nothing to you? His or her failure to communicate probably added to your confusion instead of providing you with the knowledge you needed. A visit to a doctor can also be an exercise in frustration if the doctor describes your problem and its treatment in words you can't understand.

JARGON
Specialized terminology or language that members of a group develop to aid communication among themselves.

Jargon. In both of those examples, a breakdown in communication occurs because of the use of **jargon**, specialized terminology or language that members of a profession, occupation, or other group develop to improve communication among themselves. Computer experts have their own jargon, as do physicians, lawyers, and people pursuing most occupations or professions. Jargon facilitates communication within an occupation because it simplifies encoding. Rather than having to describe a complex array of symptoms and their likely causes, a nurse can use a single medical term such as *gastroenteritis*, and other health care providers will know the ailment the nurse is referring to.

Messages encoded with jargon can lead to *effective* communication when senders and receivers are members of the same occupation or profession. Jargon becomes a problem only when the receiver of a jargon-laden message is outside the sender's profession or occupational group. In this case, the use of jargon leads to *ineffective* communication.

Sometimes even individual companies have their own jargon. For example, at the brewery Coors, newly developed beers are called "the liquid." At Microsoft, an employee's knowledge and ability are referred to as his or her "bandwidth." At Wal-Mart, training new employees to smile and offer a high level of customer service is known as being "Wal-Martized." And Intel executives "Intellize" new businesses they are trying to enter and compete in, such as telecommunications.[27]

The Medium

MEDIUM
The pathway through which an encoded message is transmitted to a receiver.

Once a message is encoded, it is transmitted to the receiver through some medium. The **medium** is the pathway through which an encoded message is transmitted to a receiver. (*Media* is the plural form.)

VERBAL COMMUNICATION
The sharing of information by means of words, either spoken or written.

Verbal communication. **Verbal communication** is the sharing of information by means of words, either spoken or written. For messages that are encoded into words, the media can include face-to-face oral communication, oral communication over the telephone, and written communication through the use of memos, letters, and reports that may also be electronically transmitted via email or fax machines.

Each medium of verbal communication has advantages and disadvantages. Although there are no clear-cut rules about when to use one rather than another, there are two guidelines for selecting a medium.

One guideline is to select a medium that the receiver monitors—a medium that the receiver pays attention to, in other words. People differ in their preferences for communication media. Mickey Drexler, CEO of J. Crew, prefers to use oral face-to-face communication. Ron Shaich, president of the Boston-based, fast-food chain Au Bon Pain, likes to see things in writing. The most effective forms of communication for people like Shaich are written memos, reports, and letters.[28] A sender who ignores receivers' individual preferences for media is asking for trouble. A receiver may not realize the importance of a message delivered in casual conversation over lunch if he or she expects the message to be delivered via a formal report. A receiver who is inundated with memos and letters and more accustomed to having important messages delivered orally might toss a letter containing an important message into the trash without ever reading it.

The second guideline to follow in selecting a medium is to try to select one that is appropriate to the message you are trying to convey and to use multiple media when necessary. Common sense suggests that if you are communicating a personal and important message to an individual (such as information about being fired, being promoted, receiving a raise, or being transferred to another unit), oral communication is called for, preferably face to face. Alternatively, if the message you are trying to communicate is involved and complex, such as a proposal to open a new factory in Singapore, written communication is appropriate. If the message is important, you might want to back up the written communication with oral communication as well.

NONVERBAL COMMUNICATION
The sharing of information by means of facial expressions, body language, and mode of dress.

Nonverbal communication. Words are not the only way people communicate. It is also important to realize that communication not only has a verbal component, it has a nonverbal component as well. **Nonverbal communication** is the sharing of information by means of facial expressions (smiles and grimaces), body language (posture and gestures), and even mode of dress (elegant business attire versus jeans and a T-shirt).[29] Research has shown that the receiver pays great attention to the way a message is delivered by the sender, to his or her tone of voice, stance, facial expressions, apparent moods and emotions, and so on. All these factors are used to help interpret the meaning in the message—and the meaning behind it. Thus a superior might simply say to a subordinate "please complete the assignment by five o'clock," but the nonverbal cues tell the subordinate the assignment should have already have been completed, the boss is mad, and unless the report is done by five o'clock there is going to be big trouble. Similarly, your coworker slamming his door in your face after a recent argument and the uniform worn by a police officer standing next to your illegally parked car all transmit encoded messages to you.

Indeed, an important nonverbal cue that affects the way a message is received includes the style of dress adopted by people in an organization or the way a particular person dresses. Some organizations, for example, insist on white button-down shirts and blouses, blue suits, and black shoes—something that often signifies a formal, hierarchical work setting. Increasingly, today many organizations encourage "business casual" dress or have informal dress days to communicate that employees and managers are partners who should trust one another. The way a particular person dresses can also signal much about the type of person he or she is, as the following OB in Action suggests.

In general, because people tend to have less control over their nonverbal than over their verbal communication, their facial expressions or body language often give them away when they wish to withhold some information. A sender who compliments someone he dislikes but fails to look the receiver in the eye, for example, is not concealing his insincerity. Nonverbal communication also can be useful for communicating support, acceptance, and a sense of camaraderie. Researchers have long noted the value of hugs as a form of communication. Hugs help reduce stress, raise self-confidence, and make people feel connected with those around them. Studies of newborns, the elderly, and children in orphanages have shown that touch is necessary for psychological well-being. Sometimes, a good hug at the right time can express powerful feelings and emotions. This was the case when retiring Supreme Court Justice William Brennan greeted his successor David Souter after Souter's confirmation hearings. According to Souter, "He hugged me and he hugged me, and he went on hugging me for a very, very long time."[30]

We have covered just some of the issues involved in selecting a communication medium. Given the importance of choosing the right medium and the difficulty of making the right choice, we focus on additional aspects of this step in the communication process later in this chapter, in the sections on information richness and the impact of technological advances on organizational communication.

DECODING
Interpreting or trying to make sense of a sender's message.

The Receiver: Decoding and the Feedback Loop

Just as senders have to translate their ideas or messages into a form that can be sent to the receiver, receivers have to make sense of the messages they receive. **Decoding** is interpreting

OB in Action

Dressing for Leadership Success

If you joined a new organization and on your first day entered a room full of employees, how would you tell which person was the leader? Increasingly, people who specialize in recruiting and selecting new CEOs and other top executives for major companies are coming to the conclusion that the old adage "the clothes maketh the man," and in business today, "the women as well," is a particularly good nonverbal clue as to who is in charge. Somehow, the leader is the person who always seems to wear the smartest, best-tailored suit that flatters his or her physique, or the nicest shirt or blouse, or the shiniest shoes, and best-looking briefcase.[31]

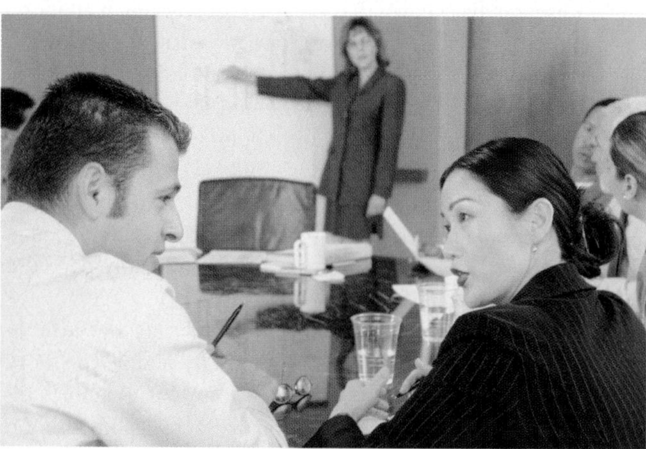

An important nonverbal cue that affects the way a message is received is the style of dress adopted by a particular person or group of people in an organization. CEOs often dress for success, but members of royal families have for centuries understood the advantages of being the most well-dressed of all.

Leaders have style, or at least they have learnt the importance of paying personal assistants (PAs) whose job it is to seek out and buy the clothes whose style makes the boss look best. Top executives such as Oracle CEO Larry Ellison, eBay's Meg Whitman, and of course Donald Trump who admits that he learnt the hard way the importance of wearing the right clothes, all employ PAs.[32] Of course good clothes cost more money, sometimes a lot more money; however, they keep their good looks for a longer time, they crease less, they clean better, and they can often last for years. And, the ultimate payoff is that when you look like a leader many people often will treat you like you are one and so over time this increases your chances of promotion.

or trying to make sense of a sender's message. For messages that are relatively clear-cut, such as information about a raise or about a specific goal, decoding can be straightforward. Some messages, however, are ambiguous. For example, what caused your boss's look of disgust when you told him your sales promotion was a flop? Was the look due to his displeasure with your performance or his concern over the dwindling sales of the product involved? Or was it just the result of one more piece of bad news that day? During decoding, the receiver tries to determine which interpretation of the message, of all the possible interpretations, is accurate.

When messages are ambiguous, the receiver may have difficulty with decoding or may think that the message means something other than what the sender intended. When messages are ambiguous, the likelihood increases that the receivers' own beliefs, attitudes, values, moods, perceptual biases, and so on will influence decoding.

You may be tempted to think that communication is largely complete once decoding has taken place. As indicated in Exhibit 14.5, however, only about half of the communication process has occurred up to this point—the initial-transmission half. Recall that communication is the sharing of information to reach a common understanding. Up until and including the point at which the receiver decodes the message, the communication process has largely been one of sharing information. Members of an organization know they have reached a common understanding and have communicated effectively by completing the feedback loop, the second half of the process illustrated in Exhibit 14.5.

After decoding the message, the receiver has to respond to it and start the feedback loop. The receiver must first decide what message to pass on to the original sender. Sometimes, the receiver's message is as simple as "I got your memo and agree that we need to meet to discuss this issue." At other times, the receiver may provide, in a long and detailed message, the information that the sender requested. Or, the receiver's response might be that he or she did not understand the message.

Once the receiver decides on a response, he or she *encodes* the message and transmits it, using a *medium* that the original sender monitors. The original sender *decodes* the response. If the original sender is confident that the receiver properly interpreted the initial message and a common understanding has been reached, the communication process is complete. However, if during decoding the original sender realizes that the receiver did not properly interpret or decode the message, the whole communication process needs to continue until both parties are confident that they have reached a common understanding.

The feedback loop in the communication process can be just as important as the initial transmission of the message because it confirms that the message has been received and properly understood. Thus, effective communicators do whatever they can to make sure they receive feedback. For example, an advertising executive hoping to convince a car company to use her firm to promote a new model may send a detailed proposal to the manager at the car company who will make the decision. In the letter accompanying the proposal, the advertising executive makes sure she will receive feedback by telling the manager that she will be calling him in two or three weeks to answer any questions he might have. During the phone conversation, the advertising executive makes sure that the manager has understood the key components of the proposal.

Barriers to Effective Communication

NOISE
Anything that interferes with the communication process.

Noise is anything that interferes with the communication process. Noise can include the use of jargon, poor handwriting, a broken answering machine, a heavy workload that prevents a receiver from reading a written report, a receiver's bad mood resulting in the misinterpretation of a message, or the operation of perceptual biases (see Chapter 4). One of the key challenges for managers is to eliminate as much noise as possible.

Noise is a general term, but there are specific communication problems that result in ineffective communication. Here, we examine six important potential communication problems in organizations and ways to overcome them so that individuals, groups, and organizations can communicate effectively and thus better achieve their goals: filtering and information distortion, poor listening, lack of or inappropriate feedback, rumors, workforce diversity, and differences in cross-cultural linguistic styles.

Filtering and Information Distortion

FILTERING
A sender's withholding part of a message because the sender thinks the receiver does not need or will not want to receive the information.

Filtering occurs when senders withhold part of a message because they think the receiver does not need the information or will not want to receive it. Nobody wants to be the bearer of bad news, and subordinates are particularly loath to pass negative information on to their bosses. However, if subordinates withhold negative information or filter it out of their messages, a supervisor may not even be aware of a problem until it's almost too late to resolve it. What was once a minor problem that could have been easily fixed now becomes a potential disaster. Supervisors also sometimes filter information in their communications with subordinates. As a result, subordinates may have more negative attitudes, be less effective, or experience more stress. Sometimes when an organization is making major changes, such as downsizing, supervisors fail to give their subordinates information about the changes, and the result is high levels of stress as subordinates become uncertain about their futures with the organization.

The magnitude of the filtering problem is underscored by the fact that subordinates are sometimes reluctant to convey negative information to their superiors even in crisis situations. A tragic example of this problem was the Air Florida plane that crashed into a bridge over the Potomac River after taking off from National Airport in Washington, D.C. Federal Aviation Administration (FAA) investigators determined that the crash resulted in part from the copilot's failure to tell the pilot about problems with engine power readings that were caused by ice on the engine sensors. Because of this and other instances of poor communication and filtering, the FAA now has mandatory assertiveness and sensitivity training for airline crew members to make sure that they communicate effectively and do not engage in filtering.[33]

INFORMATION DISTORTION
The change in meaning that occurs when a message travels through a series of different senders to a receiver.

Related to the problem of filtering is **information distortion**, the change in meaning that occurs when a message travels through a series of different senders to a receiver. Experiments (and the children's game "Telephone") have shown, for example, that a message that starts at one end of a chain of people is likely to become something quite different by the time it reaches the last receiver at the other end of the chain. In addition, senders may deliberately alter or distort a message to serve their own interests—to make themselves look good or to advance their own individual or group goals at the expense of organizational goals.

Filtering and information distortion can be avoided by establishing *trust* in an organization, as discussed earlier. One aspect of trust is the policy of *not* blaming the sender for bad news. When subordinates trust their supervisors, supervisors trust their subordinates, and coworkers trust each other, and when all members of an organization are confident that they will not be blamed for problems out of their control, filtering and distortion are much less likely to occur.

Poor Listening

Many people enjoy talking more than they enjoy listening to others. So, not surprisingly, poor listening is responsible for many communication problems in organizations. Consistent with this observation are findings from a recent study that suggests that

EXHIBIT 14.6

Barriers to Effective Communication

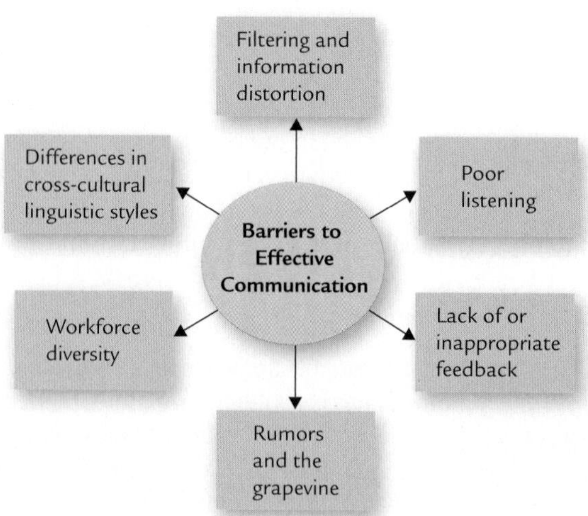

Someone with notoriously poor listening skills is Donald Trump, pictured here with Larry King who seems to be listening carefully as Trump relates his ambition to become President of the United States in a show televised in 1999.

managers think the voice mail they send is more important than the voice mail they receive and that senders generally think their messages are more important, urgent, and helpful than do the receivers.[34] In addition, people sometimes listen only to the part of a message they want to hear.

Members of an organization can do several things to become better listeners or receivers of messages. Being a good listener entails giving a sender your undivided attention, looking him or her in the eye, and not interrupting. Rather than thinking about what they are going to say next, good listeners focus on trying to understand what they are hearing and how the sender feels about it. Being a good listener also means asking questions and rephrasing key points to make sure you understand their meaning, avoiding distracting the sender (by glancing at the clock or tapping a pencil, for example), and accepting what the sender is telling you, even if it is not what you want to hear. It is especially important for supervisors to be good listeners when their subordinates are trying to communicating with them and avoid the natural tendency to pay more attention to the information coming from their superiors. The FAA's mandatory sensitivity training for airline crews, for example, may help pilots become better listeners. An interesting example of a manager who learned the importance of being a good listener is profiled in the following OB Today.

OB Today

The Consequences of Poor Listening Skills

In 1997, Marc Brownstein decided to return to his native city, Philadelphia, and assume the position of president of the small ad agency his father Bernie had founded—the Brownstein Group.[35] Months later, Marc Brownstein was confident that he had made the right decision and was leading the agency effectively because the Brownstein Group's revenues were up, it was gaining clients, and garnering more industry recognition.[36] Seeking to further enhance his leadership skills, Brownstein decided to enroll in a short executive-development course. One of his assignments for the course was to have his managers complete an anonymous questionnaire rating his job performance as president of the agency.[37]

Brownstein was shocked to learn that his managers did not think that he was an effective leader. While they thought that he meant well, managers complained about a breakdown in communication at the agency. They claimed that Brownstein failed to keep them informed about important matters like how the agency was doing and who its new clients were, and that he also often failed to give them feedback about how they were performing. Moreover, they claimed that Brownstein didn't seem to consider his subordinates' preferences when handing out assignments and that he was generally a poor listener. For example, when a manager would meet with him in his office, Brownstein would often interrupt him or her several times to take phone calls.[38]

Brownstein realized that he had to make some major changes quickly or he would lose talented employees. Turnover at the agency was already surprisingly high, and now he knew why. So he decided to change his communication style and schedule regular meetings with everyone on staff to open up the lines of communication. Any topic was fair game at these meetings, and Brownstein made a point of really listening to his managers. He focused his attention solely on what the person he was talking to was saying and put his phone calls on hold. His employees immediately sensed the change in his leadership style. Believing their contributions were now being appreciated, they more actively suggested ways to improve the agency's operations, including how it managed its clients[39] With the lines of communication opening up, Brownstein also began to understand what was really going on in his employees' minds. Above all, he learned that leaders need to pay attention to and listen to what their subordinates have to say—that the feedback they provide is just as important as the feedback their superiors give to them![40]

Lack of or Inappropriate Feedback

Sometimes communication breaks down because receivers either fail to provide feedback or provide feedback in an inappropriate manner. This barrier to effective communication is especially likely to occur when feedback is negative because negative feedback makes people feel uncomfortable. A manager at a bank, for example, may be reluctant to let one of her subordinates know that a loan application the subordinate worked closely on with a customer is going to be turned down. He or she may avoid broaching the issue, putting the subordinate in an embarrassing position if the bad news is divulged by the customer whose loan has been rejected. By developing good feedback skills, managers and employees at all levels in an organization will be more likely to respond in an appropriate manner to messages they receive, whether they're positive or negative.

Good feedback concentrates on the message being responded to, not on the sender's personality, attitudes, capabilities, or more general performance levels. Good feedback is specific and focuses on things the sender controls. When giving feedback, the receiver should try to put himself or herself in the original sender's shoes, understand how the sender feels, and relay the feedback in a manner that conveys the right message without unnecessarily hurting the sender's feelings.

Rumors and the Grapevine

RUMOR
Unofficial information on topics that are important or interesting to an organization's members.

A **rumor** is unofficial information on topics that are important or interesting to an organization's members. Rumors usually spread quickly and uncontrollably around communication networks and, once started, are often hard to stop. They are especially likely to spread when members of the organization are not informed about matters that have the potential to affect them personally, like perhaps a takeover attempt by another company, impending layoffs, or a scandal involving a top manager. Sensational rumors sometimes help relieve the everyday boredom of organizational life. These rumors often entail gossip about the personal lives and habits of the organization's various members.

How can companies halt the spread of inaccurate and sometimes damaging rumors and also provide employees with up-to-date, accurate information on issues that are important to them? One way is with an IT network consisting of computer monitors and/or television screens linked to the Internet, or via a company-owned satellite system that can beam information to employees working in many places. Wal-Mart, for example, has a state-of-the-art IT system that allows for the rapid communication of information to its thousands of stores.[41]

According to the Atlanta consulting firm KJH Communications, companies can use these systems to control the spread of rumors, communicate accurate information to large numbers of employees, and coordinate emergency efforts.[42] For example, when Jeff Imellt took over as CEO of GE, he appeared on GE's company-wide Intranet several times during his first months on the job to communicate to employees that they had no need to worry about the future of their jobs and organization. And when heavy fog in Memphis, Tennessee, halted delivery of thousands of Federal Express's overnight packages and letters, the company used its Intranet to keep employees informed and instruct them on what to do. Federal Express also uses its Intranet to communicate accurate information and halt the spread of unfounded rumors, such as those that sprang up when the company stopped making deliveries between European countries and laid off 4,000 European employees. American employees learned of these changes on Federal Express's computer monitors and were reassured that their own jobs were secure. The European employees who were actually let go were informed of the layoff face to face.

GRAPEVINE
A set of informal communication pathways through which unofficial information flows.

Rumors are often spread through the **grapevine**, a set of informal communication pathways through which unofficial information flows in an organization.[43] In any group, department, or division of an organization, some individuals seem to know everything about everyone and everything and pass along large quantities of unofficial information to others. Rumors that spread through the grapevine can be about the private or work lives of key members in the organization, the organization itself, or the future of the organization and its members. Although rumors that are spread through the grapevine are often inaccurate, sometimes information transmitted through the grapevine *is* accurate. For example, Mike O'Connell, a marketing manager in an airline company, told one of his co-employees over lunch that he was quitting his job, had given his supervisor two weeks' advance notice, and would be joining British Airways in London. By the end of the same work day, everyone in O'Connell's department knew of his plans even though he hadn't mentioned them to anyone else (nor had his supervisor).

Workforce Diversity

Increasing diversity might also become a barrier to effective communication when the members of a group or organization don't see eye to eye or fail to respect and appreciate each other's points of view. To counter this effect, many organizations are instituting diversity training programs so their employees can learn to communicate and work well together. For example, Federal Express has a voluntary four-and-a-half-day diversity training program available to its 5,500 managers to help them learn to understand and appreciate each others' points of view. Similarly, Pacific Gas & Electric has a mandatory four-hour diversity training for its 12,000 employees. Employees must find the training valuable because the classes often run long, sometimes up to six or eight hours.[44]

What goes on in a diversity training program? The training can be approached several different ways. One approach involves having a panel of minority members in the organization describe and share with their coworkers their own experiences and difficulties.

Another approach involves having members of an organization work for a period of time with people who are different from themselves. New recruits to the San Diego Police Department, for example, are assigned a one-week tour of duty working with citizens who are very different from them. A white woman might be sent to work with an all-male Hispanic teenage gang to gain some understanding of how these youths view society and learn how to communicate with them and other people who are very different from her. Regardless of how it is done, helping diverse groups and members in an organization get along so that they communicate effectively and work together to achieve their goals is imperative—especially as diversity within the workforce (and the world) continues to increase.

Differences in Crosscultural Linguistic Styles

LINGUISTIC STYLE
A person's characteristic way of speaking.

When people from different cultures interact, communication difficulties sometime arise because of differences in linguistic styles. **Linguistic style** is a person's characteristic way of speaking including tone of voice, volume, speed, use of pauses, directness or indirectness, choice of words, use of questions and jokes, and willingness to take credit for ideas.[45] Within a culture, linguistic styles can vary between, for example, different regions of a country or between men and women. Across cultures, however, linguistic style differences are typically much greater, and this can lead to many misunderstandings.

In Japan, for example, employees tend to communicate more formally and be more deferential toward their bosses than employees are in the United States. On the one hand, Japanese employees don't mind lengthy pauses in a conversation while they are thinking about something under discussion. On the other hand, American employees often find lengthy pauses in conversations uncomfortable and feel the need to fill the void by talking. Americans are also more likely to take individual credit for ideas and accomplishments in conversations, whereas Japan's more group-oriented culture makes individual credit-taking less likely.[46]

These cross-cultural differences can result in many communication difficulties. For instance, U.S. employees' tendencies to take credit for their ideas and accomplishments may cause Japanese employees to think they are being boastful when this is not the case. Lengthy pauses on the part of Japanese communicators may cause U.S. employees to feel that the Japanese aren't interested in the discussion. On the other hand, U.S. employees' tendencies to fill these pauses may cause the Japanese to think they are being pushy and not giving them a chance to think. Neither of these scenarios may be correct, but are merely products of different linguistic styles.

Cultures also differ in terms of the physical distance between speakers and listeners deemed appropriate for conversations at work.[47] For example, people in Brazil and Saudi Arabia favor closer physical distances than do people in the United States. Americans may feel uncomfortable when Brazilians stand "too" close to them during a conversation, while Brazilians may be wondering why Americans keep backing up and seem so standoffish.

Cross-cultural communication difficulties such as these can be overcome by understanding cross-cultural differences in linguistic styles. Before interacting with people from a different culture, members of an organization should try to learn as much as possible about the linguistic style of that culture. Expatriate managers who have lived in the country in question can often be a good source of information about its linguistic style because they have first-hand experience interacting with the culture's members. Learning about more general, cross-cultural differences is also often helpful because these differences are often linked to differences in linguistic styles.

Selecting an Appropriate Communication Medium

The communication difficulties that many companies experience demonstrate that sharing information to reach a common understanding is often more difficult than it appears to be. Choosing the right communication medium for any given message can help ensure that a message is received and properly understood, but selecting a medium involves trade-offs for both the sender and the receiver. One way to examine these trade-offs is by exploring the information richness of various media, their demands on the receiver's and the sender's time, and the paper trail they leave. In this section, we explore these issues and the implications of advances in information technology for communication in organizations.

Information Richness

INFORMATION RICHNESS
The amount of information a medium of communication can carry and the extent to which it enables senders and receivers to reach a common understanding.

Communication media differ in their **information richness**—that is, the amount of information they can carry and the extent to which they enable senders and receivers to reach a common understanding.[48] Media that are high in information richness are capable of transmitting more information and are more likely to generate a common understanding than are media that are low in richness. The various media available to organizational members can be categorized into four general groups based on their information richness (see Exhibit 14.7).[49]

Face-to-face communication. Face-to-face communication is the medium highest in information richness for at least two reasons. The first is that it provides the receiver not only with a verbal message but also with a nonverbal message conveyed by the sender's body language and facial expressions.[50] The nonverbal part of the communication gives receivers additional information they can use to decode the messages. When Joan Schmitt, an engineer for a construction firm, met with her supervisor Fred Johnston to discuss the plans for a Brazilian project the company was bidding on, Johnston got up from behind his desk to sit in a chair next to Schmitt's as she described her proposal. His action provided Schmitt with information: He respected her and wanted her to feel that they were on equal footing in their discussion of the bidding. Similarly, when Johnston mentioned that the newly hired and inexperienced son of the owner of the firm was to be a member of the team preparing the bid, his failure to look her in the eye and his pursed lips conveyed that he was not pleased with this situation.

The second reason why face-to-face communication is highest in information richness is that it allows receivers to give senders instant feedback. Senders can clarify ambiguous information immediately, and the communication process can be cycled through as many times as needed until a common understanding is reached.[51] At the engineering firm, Fred Johnston was quite familiar with the Brazilian clients for whom the bid was being prepared and thought it best they be more involved in the bidding process than was normally the case. He suggested, for example, that the clients have

EXHIBIT 14.7

The Information Richness of Communication Media

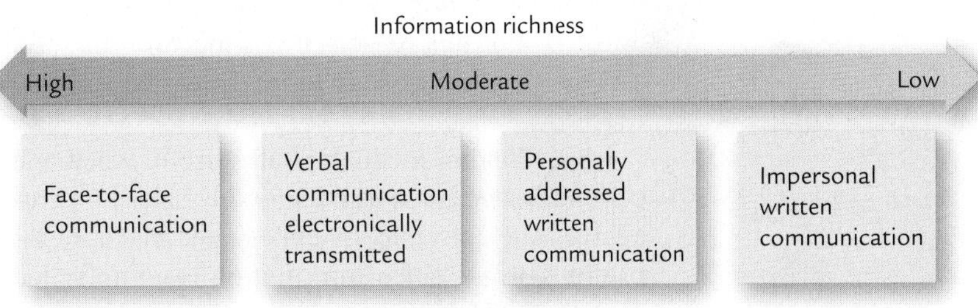

more input into materials specifications and quality parameters than was usual. Joan Schmitt was taken aback by Johnston's suggestion. She wasn't sure why it was important and how to carry it out. After a 20-minute discussion, however, Schmitt realized that what Johnston was suggesting was not unreasonable or difficult and that it made sense given the clients' desire to have more input into the details of the building's construction than was customary.

Verbal communication electronically transmitted. Verbal communication that is electronically transmitted over telephone lines is the communication medium next highest in information richness. Telephone conversations do not provide the receiver with nonverbal information from body language and facial expressions, but they still are a rich source of information. The receiver can hear the message, interpret the tone of voice in which it is delivered, hear clearly which parts of the message the sender emphasizes, and get a sense of the sender's general demeanor while communicating. Because this type of verbal communication is personally addressed to the receiver, the receiver is likely to pay attention to it. When Johnston was talking on the telephone with the Brazilian clients about the building they wanted, for example, he could sense their enthusiasm and was pleased that they sounded comfortable talking with him.

Telephone conversations also allow for instant feedback so misunderstandings can be cleared up quickly. Although not commonly used, video telephones allow callers to see the person they are talking to. As the use of broadband increases, computers are likely to serve as video telephones in the future.[52] Visual images add to the information richness of this medium.

Also in this category of electronic verbal media is communication using voice mail and answering machines, both of which allow receivers to gather information from the sender's tone of voice and inflections in the sender's verbal communication, but they do not permit immediate feedback. When using this medium to communicate with a receiver, the sender needs to make sure that the receiver monitors this medium by calling in frequently to receive messages.

Personally addressed written communication. Written communications (like letters and memos) addressed personally to the receiver are next in information richness. Personally addressing the communication helps to ensure the receiver will pay attention to it, and writing for one person allows the sender to tailor the message in such a way that the receiver is most likely to understand it. Feedback is not instantaneous, but this may not always be a disadvantage. In some situations, it is important for receivers to have time to reflect on a message and then formulate a response. E-mail is also included in this category of media. However, for communication to be effective receivers have to check periodically to see whether they have any electronic messages.

Impersonal written communication. Lowest in information richness is written communication that is not addressed to a particular receiver. This form of communication is used when a sender needs to communicate with a large number of receivers simultaneously, like when a company president wants to dispel rumors of an impending layoff. Because this type of medium is impersonal, receiving feedback is unlikely. For this reason, it is especially important for the sender to use language that all receivers will be able to interpret correctly, so that a common understanding will be reached.

This kind of medium is also useful when a large amount of information needs to be communicated, such as the monthly sales of a company's products by state, enrollment in a large state university by college and major, or the instructions for running a complicated printing press. When information is complicated (like the printing press instructions), some form of written communication is a necessity so that receivers can go back and review the information as needed.

Trade-Offs in the Choice of Media

In choosing a medium, one of the most significant trade-offs is between *information richness* and the *amount of time* it takes to communicate the message by using the medium. Oral, face-to-face communication, for example, has high information richness but can be very time consuming. When messages are important, and the sender is not certain that a written message will be understood, then taking the time to communicate orally is usually worthwhile. However, when a message is clear-cut and easy to understand, such as an announcement that a company will close at noon on the Friday before Memorial Day weekend, a written memo or letter may be most expedient.

Another trade-off that needs to be taken into account is the trade-off between *information richness* and the *need for a paper or electronic trail*—written documentation of a message, in other words. When messages are complicated and need to be referred to later, like those containing operating instructions or elaborate procedures, a paper or electronic trail is a clear advantage. Similarly, written communication is advantageous when a sender requires proof that a message was sent. A patient who is denied medical insurance coverage for a particular procedure and appeals the insurance company's decision wants to be able to prove that the insurance company was notified about the procedure and approved it.

Using New Information Technology

Recent advances in information technology (IT) have given members of organizations not only new ways to communicate with each other but also timely access to more information than ever before.[53] An organization must be careful not to overwhelm its employees with so much information that they spend more time reading e-mail and bulletin boards than doing their jobs.[54] Most employees in corporate America who use e-mail receive around 30 messages per day and spend about two hours a day responding and completing tasks related to the messages, according to Ferris Research based in San Francisco, and these figures are expected to increase significantly over the next few years.[55] Joseph Galli, who used to receive around 150 e-mails a day when he was president of Amazon.com suggests that e-mail should be used only for those tasks it is most suited for, such as sending data, memos, summaries, or relevant information. Other kinds of messages are more efficiently and effectively handled on the phone or in person. Also, Galli suggests that when it is important to express feelings such as congratulations for a job well done or motivate employees to excel, voice mail is superior to e-mail since feelings as well as words can be communicated.[56]

Despite these problems, IT has the potential to significantly reduce the costs of communicating information.[57] For example, at Aetna Life & Casualty Company, most training manuals, rate books, and other insurance documents (which used to be on paper) are now on computer. Aetna estimates that this change from paper to electronic communication saves about $6 million annually due to, for example, the elimination of costly storage fees for extra manuals and binders (around $2,000 a month) and the 4.5-cents-per-page cost of updating and changing employees' manuals when procedures are altered (often involving millions of pages).

Intranets. Communication information technology advances like the Internet have also dramatically altered the nature of communication in almost all organizations.[58] The United States has the most Internet users, but other countries in Europe and Asia also have high numbers of Internet users.[59] Many organizations, using the same technology that the Internet is based on, have created their own company-wide computer networks, called **intranets**, which use software to facilitate real-time online communication within an organization. Intranets contain a wide variety of information ranging from directories, manuals, and product specifications to delivery schedules, minutes of meetings, and current financial performance. They can be accessed by all members of the organization. Organizations use intranets to efficiently communicate information to their members as

INTRANET
A company-wide computer network.

OB in Action

Intranets Are Good for Business

Founded in 1996, Alteon Websystems quickly became a leading maker of the advanced hardware and software necessary to manage websites and e-businesses. It achieved its dominant position because of the way its managers developed one of the most effective systems of communication to speed up new product innovation in the Internet industry.[60]

From the beginning, demand for Alteon's products was so great that its managers were confronted with problems that required solutions that changed from week to week. Sales projections for its products were doubling on a monthly basis. How could the company find a way to allow its employees—both at different levels in the hierarchy and in its different departments—to communicate quickly and effectively to respond to such rapid and unpredictable changes? How could the communication process be changed so that Alteon's software engineers could communicate with manufacturing managers to develop and produce new products quickly and reliably?

Alteon's answer was to develop an in-house, web-based software platform, or Intranet, making it possible for its work groups, teams, and subunits like production, engineering, and sales to communicate quickly and effectively. For companies that rely mainly on written communication, it can take considerable time and many phone calls and e-mails before managers can agree on what to do. Using its state-of-the-art Intranet, however, all Alteon's salespeople could communicate with each other electronically and work together in real time on an ongoing basis to discuss the changing nature of customer needs.

When salespeople have decided what those needs are, they then use the Intranet to communicate them to the company's engineers, who then work together online to decide how to change the design of the company's hardware to meet those needs. Not only does this speed new product design, but also, because manufacturing managers are connected to the web-based Intranet, they knew about all the information and knowledge being developed in other parts of the organization. Using the company's Intranet they also offered their own inputs into the product-development process. The combined result of its improved communication was rapid, high-quality decision making that made Alteon a market leader.[61]

Interestingly enough, however, Alteon still recognized the need to encourage face-to-face, oral communication. Every Friday afternoon, its 240 employees gathered together for informal give-and-take sessions in which employees asked managers tough questions and then broke into groups to confront specific problems.[62] Any decisions and plans made in these groups were then inputted into the company's intranet and this information was communicated to all the company's employees everywhere. Today, an Intranet like the one Alteon developed is used by most companies seeking to keep abreast of fast-changing technology.

well as give them easy access to the information they need to do their jobs, when they need it, as discussed in the OB in Action.[63]

As the Alteon example suggests, Intranets enable employees to work together electronically to facilitate joint problem solving.[64] In real time, all of the members of one group, and even those of others, can see the messages being relayed back and forth via the Intranet and technology like instant messaging. The use of teleconferencing, which is relatively high in information richness because group members can see, as well as talk to, each other face-to-face in real time, has also grown in popularity as the use of broadband Internet connections has exploded.[65] The Japanese company Hitachi Limited, for example, uses teleconferencing to facilitate communication between its 29 research laboratories in Japan. Scientists and engineers in the different laboratories use teleconferencing to share knowledge and cooperate on joint research projects. Teleconferencing is also a good choice of medium when members of a group or organization are located in different countries.[66] HP and IBM are among the many companies that use teleconferencing to facilitate communication between managers in its foreign and domestic divisions. Nevertheless, when it comes to solving thorny problems, face-to-face communication is still often necessary because it is information rich.

In summary, research suggests that face-to-face communication works best when a message is important and there is a good chance that the receiver will have difficulty understanding it. Moreover, when messages are important and complex it is best to use multiple communication media such as face-to-face communication and written reports. On the other hand, written communication is appropriate when it is necessary to document that a message has been transmitted and when the message needs to be referred to more than once. Finally, in some situations, electronically transmitted oral or written communication is just as effective as face-to-face communication and can save time.

You're the Management Expert

How to Speed Product Development?

You have been called in by the top managers of a small, high-tech startup company to advise them how to solve a major communication problem. The company makes flat panel LCD displays that function both as computer monitors and as TV screens. The market is growing rapidly, and there is increasing demand for a wider variety of sizes of screens, and for screens with brighter displays that also offer a clearer picture when viewed at an angle. You have different teams of engineers working on the design of the different-sized screens, and even more teams working to design brighter displays that can be viewed from wider angles.

Recently, members of many of these teams have been complaining that they are not learning quickly enough about the technical advances being made by other teams. This is slowing down their progress, and many teams are falling behind the schedule you have set for launching your new displays in the marketplace. Currently, top managers are responsible for monitoring the progress of the various teams and disseminating new information to them. The managers hold regular meetings with the team leaders, and together they summarize any new information into technical e-mails that are sent to all team members. However, these methods of communication are obviously not sufficient.

Using the material in the chapter, design a new communications system for this company that will allow the teams to better share information and coordinate their actions to speed the product-development process.

Persuasive Communication

PERSUASIVE COMMUNICATION
The attempt by one person or group to transmit and share information with another person or group to get them to accept, agree with, follow, and seek to achieve the formers' goals and objectives.

In organizations, one person's ability to understand another is not the only objective of communication. Often a person wants to persuade and influence other people. **Persuasive communication** is an attempt by one person or group to transmit and share information with another person or group in order to get them to accept, agree with, follow, or otherwise achieve the objectives the communicator desires. When it comes to persuasive communication, not only is the accurate transfer of information necessary but also how it's "framed" or "packaged" so as to influence other people.

Persuasive communication is important in many different kinds of situations. We discussed in Chapter 12 how leaders attempt to influence and persuade their employees, but employees also attempt to influence their leaders. Some of the most important situations in which there is a need to communicate persuasively occur when one party lacks the power to direct the other party as he or she wishes. In this case, persuasion must be used. For example, managers in one functional department or group are often in a situation where they need to influence managers from other functional departments or groups. Since these managers have no power over one another, they have to influence and persuade their counterparts to follow or adopt their goals or objectives. Also, employees who work in a group often wish to influence their coworkers to follow their ideas. Since they have no legitimate power over their coworkers, they'll need to persuade them. Even employees who *do* have expert or referent power need to know how to persuade their coworkers to successfully influence them.

In each instance, communication becomes the vehicle through which attempts to influence and persuade others are made. Some studies have found that managers spend most of their time in meetings and committees where their primary goal is to provide accurate information about their plans and goals and elicit support for them. Small wonder then that people in organizations need to develop a competence in persuasive communication.

A Model of Persuasive Communication

To examine how persuasive communication competence is developed, we follow the steps in the communications model outlined previously but focus on how persuasive communication works. Recall that the two main parties involved in communication are known as the sender and the receiver. The sender's task is to influence the receiver's response to the message—that is, to persuade the receiver to agree with and act on the message. Five factors determine how persuasive a message will be: the characteristics of the sender, active listening, the content of the message, the medium or channel through which it is sent, and finally the characteristics of the receiver.

Characteristics of the sender. As you might expect, messages are always more persuasive when they are sent from those people who are *credible*, meaning that the receiver believes that the sender is in a position to know what is the appropriate objective. Leaders, of course, are credible because they have legitimate power they can use to gain the compliance of their employees. In addition, leaders who have expert and referent power are also credible and can use these qualities to secure the commitment of employees. Other factors that promote credibility are moral integrity and emotional intelligence. If the receiver believes the sender is an honest, trustworthy person, he or she is more likely to believe that the information he or she is receiving is true and should therefore be acted upon. People who have empathy—those who can understand and appeal to the feelings and emotions of others—can use empathy to gain credibility and influence others. Emotional intelligence can be used to good effect, but it can also be harmful, say, when a con artist takes advantage of his or her personal appeal to deliberately trick or deceive others.

People who are able to persuade others also often possess good speaking and listening skills. As speakers, they know how to use every word to effect. They don't speak too quickly, they marshal their arguments logically, and subtly come back to the same point again and again to make sure the key facts are being not only communicated but emphasized. Good speakers invite listeners to ask questions to clarify issues and generate feedback, interest, and support for their ideas. They use personal qualities such as their referent power or emotional intelligence to "emotionally charge" their words to convince others they *know* what they are doing, that their approach is the *right* one, and that it will *succeed*.

Active listening. The content of the message, that is, the information and arguments it contains, is also a crucial ingredient in the communication process. The receiver of the message, especially if he or she is an active listener, is always evaluating the meaning and implications of the information being given, looking for the theme behind it, and ambiguities or inconsistencies in the arguments.

A competent sender knows this and is careful not to offer the receiver a one-sided or incomplete account of why some issue is important. To gain credibility, the sender knows he or she needs to present all sides of an argument—even those contrary to his or her position. The sender can always later shift back to the major theme being communicated, using a few strong arguments to persuade and win over the receiver.

As you might expect, the content of a message can be greatly augmented by framing the argument with an emotional appeal that "it's in the best interests of everyone in our department and vital to the future of our company." In other words, the content of a message can be made much more persuasive when it appeals to the receiver's feelings and emotions as well as to his or her intellect.

Method of communication. In general, face-to-face communication and telephone conversations offer the greatest facility for persuasive communication, while formal written letters and memos and email are most suited for conveying factual, detailed information, which requires time and effort to digest and act upon. In practice, these electronic methods of communication might be used at the beginning of an "influence attempt" when managers and employees are collecting information to work out how to respond to some new development, such as a change in the work setting. The sender and receiver share such information and try to persuade the other as to the best course of action to pursue. In the hours or days before the final decision is made, the sender and receiver are likely to resort to a more persuasive approach. The exchange of emails declines and they start to use the telephone. Depending on the level of disagreement or complexity of the issue they are dealing with, face–to-face meetings then become the communication method of choice. These face-to-face meetings allow them to process the most information, both logically and emotionally, to arrive at the best decision.

Face-to-face communication is highest in information richness. Pictured is a shift meeting at a Mexican maquiladora plant that manufactures radios for Delco and GM. The supervisor and team members are exchanging messages to reach a common understanding of the day's work performance.

President Lyndon Johnson was a master at persuasive communication. He knew when to call Senators to gain their support, when to knock on their doors, or even when to cajole or threaten them.

People who are competent, persuasive communicators have a good understanding of how these different methods of communication should be used. They know when and when not to send an email, when it is time to make a phone call, and when it is vital to knock on the other person's door. Former President Lyndon Johnson was a master at this approach. To persuade senators to vote for his bills he would first send his aids to talk to them and give them written information. Later, he would call them on the telephone to discuss the issues and further his case. Then, in the days and hours before the final vote on a bill he would charge down to congress, locate the "swing-vote" senators, and literally push them against the wall into a corner. There he would put his hands on their shoulders, squeeze their arms, put his face close to theirs, and either cajole or threaten them until they agreed to do what he wanted. This physical approach is very common among powerful people, or people who know how to get their way. Failing to communicate persuasively can sometimes prove catastrophic, as the following OB Today on the space shuttle Columbia illustrates.

Characteristics of the receiver. What about the receiver? Because in any influence attempt, a receiver upon replying becomes a sender, much of the previous information applies to receivers, too. Receivers, for example, can learn to enhance their credibility, use their emotional intelligence, and select the best method to transmit a message back to the sender. However, there are certain characteristics of the receiver that come into play when persuasive communication takes place.

OB Today

A Failure in Communication

One day before the breakup and crash of the space shuttle Columbia in the Spring of 2003, senior NASA engineers worried that the shuttle's left wing might burn off and cause the deaths of its crew. But they never sent their warnings to NASA's top managers. After intense debate via phone and e-mail, the engineers, supervisors, and the head of the space agency's Langley research facility in Hampton, Virginia, decided against taking the matter to top NASA managers.[67]

The engineers suggested they should ask the U.S. Strategic Command to use its sophisticated ground-based imaging equipment to inspect the shuttle for damage that might have been caused by debris striking the left wing during launch. However, after asking for such help, a senior space agency official later withdrew the request before the NASA engineers had completed their analysis of how serious the tile damage problems might be. Once again, all this communication was handled by phone calls and e-mail.

Later, NASA top administrator Sean O'Keefe commented that he probably should have taken part in the decision to cancel the survey, but he had not been asked directly, face-to-face to participate, so he had just followed the debate through e-mail. Moreover, he said he had not known for most of the mission about the shuttle's problems.[68]

All these events point to the choice of the wrong method of persuasive communication. All the people involved in the investigation were communicating by e-mail and phone calls. NASA engineers knew all about the problems and risks involved and had reported them through e-mails. However, at no point had they asked for a face-to-face meeting with top managers where all the issues could be laid out on the table. Thus, even though a few NASA engineers knew there was the possibility of a potential disaster and had communicated this to middle managers electronically, this method did not persuade others, and the survey of the craft was not conducted.[69] Managers at all levels failed to request face-to-face meetings in which the engineers with first-hand knowledge could have been present to communicate their fears. The tragic event demonstrates the importance of managers knowing how to engage in and choose the right methods to communicate persuasively.

First, receivers who are themselves highly competent and have high self-esteem are less likely to be "taken in," or swayed, by logical or emotional arguments they believe are flawed. They are more likely to be able to "cut through the chaff" to determine if the sender is acting out of personal interest or in a way that will benefit others. Then, they can decide how to react to what the sender has said.

DEVIL'S ADVOCATE
A person willing to stand up and question the beliefs of more powerful people, resist influence attempts, and convince others that a planned course of action is flawed.

People with high self-esteem are very useful to have around because they are frequently the ones who will challenge the ideas or suggestions of a leader, or more senior manager, when they sense they are flawed. They act as what is known as the **devil's advocate**—a person willing to stand up and question the beliefs of more powerful people, resist influence attempts, and convince others that the planned actions are flawed. At this level, the issue of self-interest and the intent to persuade to personally benefit does come into play. Now, persuasive communication extends into the realm of organizational politics, a topic we discussed in the previous chapter.

In summary, the goal of persuasive communication is to sway and influence others by the kind of messages that are sent. Effective leaders, either managers, supervisors, or informal group leaders, understand the issues involved in persuasive communication and use them to promote individual, group, and organization goals.

Communication in Crisis Situations

Earlier we mentioned that communication in crisis or disaster situations poses particular problems for the organizational hierarchy. When a crisis arises, the unexpected nature of the emergency requires that managers have the ability to respond rapidly to it. And this typically involves working intensively with other managers in teams to find solutions to the problems that have arisen. In crisis situations then, the need to quickly set up teams often becomes the foundation of the communication network, and indeed, advance contingency planning for crisis situations often typically involves the prior selection of team members and decisions about where to locate them. Top-management team members must work together to make policy decisions and then communicate these decisions quickly to their subordinates, and so on down the organizational hierarchy so that information cascades out and all employees can develop the appropriate response.

Obviously, face-to-face communication provides the most effective communication channel in this situation because it provides for the transmission of rich information. However, this must be supplemented by getting experts into the crisis situation so they can rapidly evaluate the situation and transmit back accurate and relevant information to the top management team. Obviously, the quality of the team's decisions can only be as good as the quality of the information it receives.

Gathering accurate and timely information is especially important when two or more different organizations must cooperate to deliver a rapid response. The communication problem here, as we will discuss in depth in Chapter 16, is that a top manager from one organization has *no* authority over managers in a second organization—even lower-level managers. Thus, a rapid response is only possible if managers in different organizations can quickly agree on or arrive at a common definition of the situation. All too often, however, when confronted with major disasters such as the one that faced NASA and the response of U.S. government agencies to the devastation caused by Hurricane Katrina, there is a failure of communication. There are several reasons for this.

First, as we discussed in the last chapter managers often come into conflict when there are complex task interdependencies or when there are unclear reporting relationships, both of which are likely to emerge in crisis situations. Second, when confronted with the need to make crucial decisions many managers are inclined to "pass the buck" and leave the final decision to someone above them in the hierarchy. In this way they can avoid blame if something goes awry. Third, collecting good information simply takes time, and unless there has been effective advance planning, often involving dry runs and emergency simulations, it takes much longer for managers to diagnose and respond to the crisis or disaster. Some of these factors also seem to have played a role at NASA, and in the delayed response of the Federal Emergency Management Agency (FEMA) to Hurricane Katrina. In the FEMA case, the head of FEMA waited 48 hours to mobilize the huge relief effort, in large part because he wanted the green light from the White House. In addition to both the Governor of Louisiana and the Mayor of New Orleans, however, people in the field also failed to signal the level of emergency. Indeed, later reports suggested that one reason for Governor Kathleen Blanco's slow response was that she was inundated with e-mails from around the world from country leaders and others offering help, and from people whose relatives were trapped

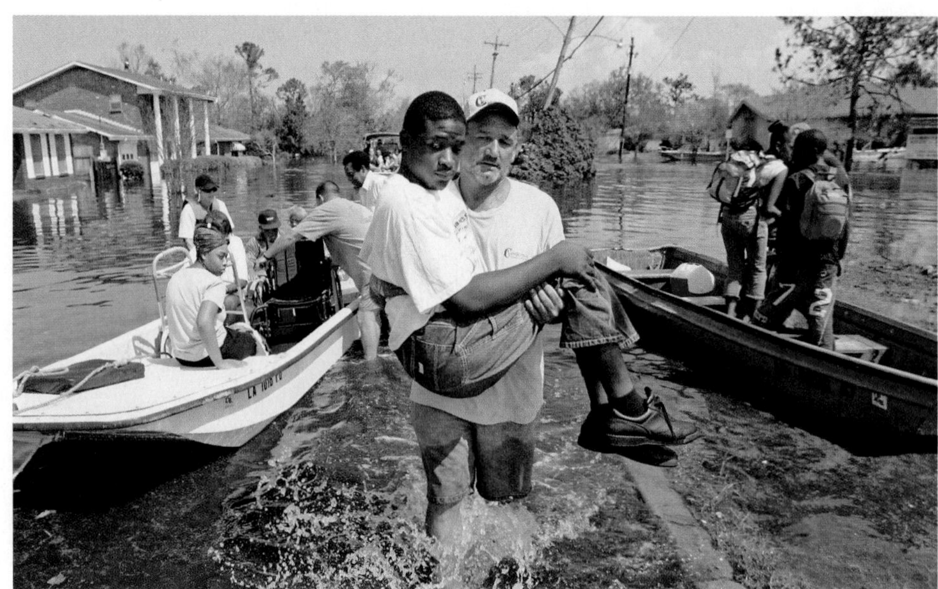

The former head of the federal Emergency Management Association (FEMA) waited 48 hours to mobilize the huge relief effort for New Orleans, in large part because he wanted the green light from his bosses at the White House.

in New Orleans. She was also engaged in political battles with other government agencies.[70]

Summary

Communication is one of the most important processes that takes place in organizations. Effective communication allows individuals, groups, and organizations to achieve their goals and perform at high levels, and it affects virtually every aspect of organizational behavior. In this chapter, we made the following major points:

1. Communication is the sharing of information between two or more individuals or groups in an organization to reach a common understanding. Communication serves four major functions in organizations: providing knowledge, motivating organizational members, controlling and coordinating individual efforts, and expressing feelings and emotions.
2. Four types of work-group communication networks are the wheel, the chain, the circle, and the all-channel. As the level of task interdependence increases in a group, so too does the need for communication between group members. When a group's task is characterized by pooled interdependence, the wheel network is likely to be used. When a group's task is characterized by sequential interdependence, a chain network is likely to be used. When a group's task is characterized by reciprocal interdependence, an all-channel network is likely to be used. An organization's actual communication network is seldom accurately depicted in its formal organization chart. Networks change as communication needs change within the organization or group.
3. The communication process entails a number of steps including the sender's encoding of the message, selection of a medium, decoding of the message by the receiver, and completing the feedback loop. Jargon (specialized language used by members of a group) facilitates communication within the group and hinders communication outside the group.
4. Filtering and information distortion, poor listening, lack of or inappropriate feedback, rumors, and cross-cultural differences in linguistic styles can all lead to ineffective communication in organizations. Communication can be improved by establishing trust and encouraging open communication, improving listening skills, developing good feedback skills, using company TVs to spread accurate information, and understanding cross-cultural differences in linguistic styles.
5. Communication media vary in information richness (the amount of information they can carry and the potential they have for enabling senders and receivers to reach a common understanding). Face-to-face communication is the medium highest in information richness. It is followed by verbal communication electronically transmitted, personally addressed written communication, and impersonal written communication. Other factors that affect the selection of a medium include how much of the sender's and receiver's time it takes and whether it leaves a paper or electronic trail.
6. Advances in information technology such as global computer networks like the Internet generally tend to contribute most to the knowledge function of communication. Given the vast array of information currently available to organizational members, organizations have to be careful that their members are not overloaded with information. Using electronic communication to replace face-to-face communication in work groups has certain disadvantages that tend to increase as the level of task interdependence between group members increases.
7. Persuasive communication is the use of information and messages to influence others to act in the way desired by the sender.

Exercises in Understanding and Managing Organizational Behavior

Questions for Review

1. Why is reaching a common understanding a necessary condition for communication to have taken place?
2. Why are members of an organization sometimes reluctant to express their feelings and emotions?
3. Why is feedback a necessary component of the communication process?
4. What jargon have you encountered? How did it hamper or help your understanding of messages being communicated to you?
5. Is filtering always dysfunctional? Why or why not?
6. Why do almost all organizations have grapevines?
7. Why are some people annoyed by the increasing use of voice mail in many organizations (instead of having secretaries and assistants take messages for people who are away from their desks)?
8. Is using a medium high in information richness always desirable? Why or why not?
9. How have advances in technology changed the ways that you communicate with other people on a day-to-day basis?
10. Should organizations have organization charts? If not, why not? If so, what should they be used for?

OB: Increasing Self-Awareness

Effective and Ineffective Communication

Think of two communication experiences you had in the last six months—one in which you felt that you communicated especially effectively with another individual or group (call it Communication Experience 1, or CE1) and one in which you felt that you had particularly poor communication with another individual or group (call it Communication Experience 2, or CE2). If you are currently employed, try to pick experiences that occurred at work. Describe both experiences, and then answer these questions:

1. Which of the functions of communication were served in CE1 and CE2? Which of the functions of communication should have been served in CE2 but were not?
2. Which parts of the communication process worked especially well in CE1? Which parts of the communication process failed in CE2?
3. Was any jargon used in either CE1 or CE2? If not, why not? If so, did the use of jargon lead to effective or ineffective communication?
4. Did any filtering take place in CE1 or CE2? Why or why not?
5. Were rumors or the grapevine involved in CE1 or CE2?
6. Describe the information richness of the communication media that were involved in CE1 and CE2.
7. Did either CE1 or CE2 involve the use of any advances in information technology? If so, how did these advances aid or hinder good communication?

A Question of Ethics

Communication is often used to influence other people and to persuade them to behave in ways that help an organization achieve its goals. Sometimes, however, influence and persuasion can be used for unethical purposes. Managers, for example, might persuade employees to overcharge customers for products such as legal or accounting services, or encourage employees to sell expensive products to customers who obviously cannot afford to buy them. On the other hand, employees might try to persuade their managers they are doing a good job by only communicating information that makes them look good and "hiding" the rest.

1. How can managers decide if their attempts to influence employees are ethical or unethical?
2. How can employees decide if their attempts to influence their managers or coworkers are ethical or unethical?
3. What kind of rules could be created in an organization to ensure attempts to influence and persuade others never become unethical?

Small Group Break-Out Exercise

Implementing IT in a Medical Clinic

After reading the following scenario, break up into groups of three or four people and discuss the issues involved. Be prepared to discuss your thinking with the rest of the class.

You have been called in by the doctors in a large medical clinic to advise them how to take advantage of their new information technology to improve organizational communication. Although the clinic does have an e-mail system, and doctors are connected into a local area network (LAN) that allows them to post information on bulletin boards and access shared patient records, in practice they rarely use them. Most communication takes place face-to-face when they meet each other in the coffee rooms or by playing telephone tag as they meet their busy schedules. As a communications expert your job is to get the doctors to appreciate the potential of their new IT.

1. What kinds of advantages can you tell the doctors they will obtain when they use the new IT?
2. How could you use persuasive communication to convince the doctors to use the new IT? Create an action plan to help the doctors learn how to use and appreciate the new IT.

Topic for Debate

Good communication is central to the functioning and effectiveness of all organizations. Now that you have a good understanding of communication in organizations, debate the following issue.

Team A. Advances in IT can make it easier for members of an organization to communicate with each other.

Team B. Advances in IT can make it more difficult for members of an organization to communicate with each other.

Experiential Exercise

Troubling Communication

Objective

Your objective is to gain experience in communicating effectively in a troublesome situation.

Procedure

The class divides into groups of three to five people and each group appoints one member as spokesperson to present the group's conclusions to the whole class. Here is the scenario.

One group member assumes the role of David Jimenez, the supervisor of a group of chemical engineers. Another group member assumes the role of Stuart Kippling, one of the chemical engineers. The remaining members of the group are observers. Once Jimenez and Kippling assume their roles, the observers take notes on the verbal and nonverbal communication they observe as well as instances of effective and ineffective communication between the two.

For the past several months, Kippling has been designing a prototype of a new waste-control processing device. He has just discovered that his device does not conform to a new Environmental Protection Agency (EPA) regulation that will go into effect in one year. This is a major setback. Although some of the design work can be salvaged, at least several weeks of work will be lost. Jimenez and Kippling are meeting in Jimenez's office to discuss the problem, why it occurred, and how it can be avoided in the future. Jimenez's position is that extrapolating from recent EPA regulations, requirements, and deliberations, Kippling should have been able to anticipate EPA's most recent ruling and take it into account in his design work, or at least he should have drawn up a contingency plan in case such a ruling was put into effect. Kippling's position is that there is no way he could have known what EPA was going to do.

1. Jimenez and Kippling assume their roles. They are meeting to discuss the problem, why it occurred, and how it can be avoided in the future. Jimenez is to meet with his boss in fifteen minutes to discuss the problem, so he and Kippling have only fifteen minutes to come to some kind of resolution of this matter.
2. When Jimenez and Kippling's meeting is finished, the observers should discuss the verbal and nonverbal communication they observed as well as what was particularly effective and ineffective.
3. The entire group determines which instances of communication between Jimenez and Kippling were especially effective and why and which instances of communication were especially ineffective and why.

When the group has finished those activities, the spokesperson will present the group's conclusions to the whole class.

New York Times *Cases in the News*

The New York Times

"Guess Who's Got His Back"

Michael Barbaro, NYT, May 1, 2006, p. F1.

RIGHT or wrong, it has somehow become conventional wisdom: Wal-Mart is bad for small businesses, outspending, outmaneuvering and outgrowing lesser rivals until they change their strategy or close their doors.

But for Sparky Electronics, a family-owned store in California that sells hard-to-find watch batteries and record-player needles, Wal-Mart is more ally than enemy, more lifeline than threat.

The 43-year-old store, which has a loyal customer base of handymen and contractors, wanted a Web site to reach consumers beyond its home in Fresno. But the big technology companies wanted up to $1,000 for a simple site, far more than the owner, Cheryl Cook, was willing to pay.

Then there was Wal-Mart. For $100, the retailer helped create sparkyelectronics.com, complete with the icon that sits above its store, an oversize electrified cartoon character. "The nice thing was that it did not cost us an arm and a leg," Ms. Cook said.

For thousands of independently owned convenience stores, restaurants and hair salons, the nation's largest—and most feared—retailer also happens to be a business partner. Through its Sam's Club division, a chain of 570 club stores, Wal-Mart helps them process credit-card transactions, build Web sites, pay employees and take out loans, all at bargain prices.

In that sense, Sam's Club is an oasis within the harsh climate of Wal-Mart. At Sam's, the very qualities that make Wal-Mart such a formidable competitor—its size and hard-nosed negotiating tactics with suppliers—have been unleashed on behalf of small businesses.

At Wal-Mart's request, for example, the health insurance company Extend Benefits Group waived a $500 fee for Sam's Club members who signed up for its plans. And the financial services company First Data, which processes credit-card payments, set aside 50 executives to work with Sam's members.

At a time when Wal-Mart is under assault by critics for, among other things, driving mom-and-pop stores out of business, Sam's looms as a relatively untapped public relations success story.

But that may be about to change. Wal-Mart's unusual plan to offer training to small businesses in urban areas where it wants to build stores, announced last month, will rely on the expertise of Sam's Club, which has provided such support to its members for two decades, executives said.

And Wal-Mart says marketing for Sam's Club, which has traditionally focused on its low prices and the good works of its blue-smocked employees, will soon focus on its relationship with small businesses.

It is a relationship that the company has invested heavily in. Sam's Club has exclusive hours for small businesses (7 a.m. to 10 a.m., five days a week), a designated online ordering system for small businesses (order by 5 p.m., pick up anytime the next day) and a team of sales representatives who even make house calls to small businesses.

Analysts estimate that small-business owners generate half of the $40 billion in annual sales at Sam's Club, though the company will not disclose such figures. Most businesses that use Sam's Club depend on it for routine purchases—cleaning supplies, hamburger patties, file folders, ink cartridges. Increasingly, however, they rely on Sam's Club for basic services that the retailer gets through a growing network of outside companies. Sam's Club's involvement in these services is limited. It negotiates the prices, but companies like Extend Benefits administer them, with Sam's Club closely monitoring customer service. Sam's Club generally derives little or no direct profit from its role. Rather, services like credit-card processing and health insurance generate good will for Sam's, and create an incentive to renew an annual membership.

Internal research shows that services increase loyalty to the retailer because members cannot secure the same discounts on their own. Customer Synergy Solutions, a consulting firm in Houston, was staggering under the weight of $2,600 in monthly health insurance premiums, partly because of back-to-back surgeries for one of its two employees. By switching to an Extend Benefits plan through Sam's Club, one with a Health Savings Account and a high deductible, rather than a small group plan, the company cut its premiums by $2,200 a month. The owners of K.C.'s County Store, in Nacogdoches, Tex., needed to process credit-card and debit-card payments in their two-month-old store. After researching five competing services, they chose First Data, another Sam's partner, because it charged the lowest rates. Some people join Sam's only for these services. Brett Hutton, the owner of Windoworks Etc., a residential window-washing company in Washington State, joined Sam's Club not for its cheap cleaning solution but to develop a cheap Web site, eastside windowcleaning.com, which would give his business more legitimacy.

"My office is my pickup and cellphone and laptop," he said. "There is nothing concrete, no storefront. The Web site becomes your storefront." The discounts that Sam's secures are, in many cases, considerable. First Data does not charge Sam's Club members its regular monthly service fee, which amounts to $60 a year, and gives them a free debit PIN pad—linked to a cash register—valued at $150. Extend Benefits not only eliminated a $500 administrative fee for Sam's Club members, it reduced a separate monthly fee for processing medical reimbursements from $5 to $2.50, or $30 a year. Brian Tenner, senior vice president for sales at Extend Benefits, said that Sam's Club was a tough negotiator. "That is what they are good at," he said, "They push back."

Every month, Wal-Mart's technology office produces a new list of businesses that have moved into the commercial area near a Sam's Club store, a list gleaned from public records like change-of-address forms. Two sales representatives, assigned to each club store, fan out to recruit those new businesses every week, knocking on doors rather than leaving telephone messages. Stores hold breakfasts for small-business members several times a year, often inviting one local company to make a presentation. And every manager at the company, from store managers to the chief executive, is required to work at a small business one day a year to better understand its needs. "There really is a small-town feel to it," said Judi Brenstein of Customer Synergy. She said she was on a first-name basis with the manager of her local Sam's Club, who has told her to call him, personally, if she needs anything.

Questions for Discussion

1. What kind of message is Sam's sending to small-business customers?
2. What are the main ways in which Sam's is communicating to business customers?
3. What has been their response and why has Sam's been successful?

The New York Times

"Guidant Consultant Advised Company to Release Data on Defects."

Barry Meier, NYT, March 9, 2006, p. C3.

A consultant to the Guidant Corporation told the company last year that he believed it had a clear ethical obligation to tell physicians about heart device defects, and urged the company to overhaul its practices, newly released court records show. In two lengthy memos written just before Guidant was swamped by controversy, the consultant, Dr. Richard N. Fogoros, also told company executives that their decision to withhold such data, while statistically defensible, was questionable. Guidant executives have said they did not publicize defibrillator flaws because they believed that patients faced greater risks from replacement surgery than from the units. But Dr. Fogoros wrote in one memo that Guidant, while believing it was acting in the patients' best interest, had violated a "sacred obligation" it had to doctors by interposing its medical judgment for theirs. He also noted that Guidant had a clear conflict of interest that would naturally lead it to disclose product failures only when "absolutely necessary."

"This conflict is not tacit; it is obvious for all to see," Dr. Fogoros wrote in a memo dated May 18, 2005, adding: "This means that when a tragedy occurs, our decisions will be viewed in the harshest light possible, without any objective consideration of the statistical niceties supporting our actions." The memos written by Dr. Fogoros are the latest internal Guidant records to emerge from a product liability lawsuit filed in a Texas state court by patients who received Guidant defibrillators. But the records may prove especially damaging to Guidant because they show a paid company consultant challenging the device maker's arguments. The documents are coming to light as the Senate Judiciary Committee plans a hearing tomorrow on possible new legislation that would make it a federal crime for a corporate executive to knowingly ship a defective product. A Minneapolis physician, Dr. Barry J. Maron, whose patient died after a defective Guidant defibrillator failed, is among those scheduled to testify.

Steven Tragash, a spokesman for Guidant, which is based in Indianapolis, said that the documents show "how seriously Guidant takes the very complex issue of how and when to communicate potential device risks to physicians—an issue that is being discussed and debated not only within Guidant but also throughout the industry." Dr. Fogoros, reached at his home yesterday, said that he had been asked not to comment on the documents because of active litigation. His memos, which make reference to Dr. Maron, were written last May, just after Guidant told the Minneapolis physician that his patient had had a type of Guidant defibrillator that had repeatedly short-circuited because of an electrical flaw. At that time, Dr. Maron and a colleague, Dr. Robert G. Hauser, urged Guidant to alert physicians about the device defect; the company had known about the defect for three years. When the company failed to do so, Dr. Maron and Dr. Hauser contacted other physicians and *The New York Times*, which published an article in late May about the device.

Since then, Guidant has recalled more than 100,000 implantable heart devices, including three models of defibrillators with similar electrical flaws that are tied to at least seven patient deaths. The company, which is based in Indianapolis, is also under investigation by the Justice Department and the Food and Drug Administration. A defibrillator is a device that uses electricity to disrupt a potentially fatal heart rhythm. Last May, soon after *The Times* article appeared, Dr. Fogoros, a cardiologist in Pittsburgh, vigorously defended Guidant's actions in an interview published on an Internet Web site, Medscape. "This data's been out there in public the whole time," he was quoted as saying about the device. But in internal memos written just two weeks earlier Dr. Fogoros took a critical view of Guidant's policies when it came to data disclosure, court records show. Those memos also predict, with an eerie accuracy, the crisis Guidant soon faced for failing to inform doctors about potentially life-threatening product failures.

In essence, Dr. Fogoros wrote that Guidant was caught between two conflicting impulses, doing what it thought was right for patients or allowing doctors to make that decision. He concluded that the company, by withholding data from doctors, was violating its basic ethical duty to be forthright with physicians. "Neither the doctor nor the patient consider themselves to have signed up to have Guidant dictate any treatment plans," he wrote in his May 18 memo.

Dr. Fogoros, who is still a company consultant, sent his memos to the chief medical officer of Guidant's heart device unit, Dr. Joseph M. Smith, records show. Guidant executives like Dr. Smith have defended their decision not to alert doctors earlier about heart device problems by saying that doing so would have led to unnecessary removal, exposing patients to surgical complications like infections. Implanted heart devices like defibrillators are normally replaced about every five years when their batteries wear out. A doctor's decision about whether to replace a problem device earlier is typically determined by how dependent an individual patient is on that unit. Dr. Fogoros wrote that he believed the device used by Dr. Maron's patient was highly reliable and that Guidant executives could defend their actions with statistics. But he added that it was in Guidant's best interest to overhaul its disclosure practices by "exposing our dirty laundry as well as our clean." He also predicted that the company's use of statistics to justify its actions would be met "with bitter derision towards our protests that we were only acting with the patients' best interests at heart."

The New York Times

"Anatomy of a Flawed Company"

Editorial, NYT, April 1, 2006, p. A14.

A manufacturer allowed its product engineers to keep faulty cardiac devices on the market without considering the medical impact and failed to alert doctors and patients when the devices started to malfunction. That is the damning conclusion of experts who evaluated how the company, the Guidant Corporation, reacted to evidence that some of its implanted defibrillators had short-circuited when they were supposed to stabilize the chaotic heartbeats of patients. At least seven patients died when their defibrillators failed to work.

The Guidant devices came under a cloud last May when *The Times* revealed that a college student had died when his defibrillator short-circuited and that the company had known about the flaw for three years but had never told doctors or patients. The company subsequently disclosed defects in other devices as well, recalled tens of thousands of flawed units and was hit with a barrage of lawsuits and investigations.

Now a panel of experts commissioned by the company has issued an independent verdict on the fiasco. It finds that Guidant's devices are generally reliable and among the best in the industry, but it faults the company's failure to protect patients from rare but life-threatening malfunctions. Indeed, it is astonishing how cavalier the company was. It left key decisions in the hands of low-level product performance engineers who were content if failure rates remained within predicted limits, regardless of the consequences for hapless patients. Its chief medical officer paid little attention to patient safety and learned about the failure problem late and inadvertently. Even after an improved version of the flawed defibrillator was developed, the company allowed some 4,000 of the older devices to be implanted in patients who weren't informed of the risks.

Guidant is now scrambling to put patient safety high in the decision-making process. Nobody knows how the company compares with others in the industry when it comes to handling defects. But it seems likely that all device manufacturers could benefit from the panel's advice that companies be far more forthcoming about publicizing defects and that a high priority be placed on preventing deaths from even rare malfunctions.

Questions for Discussion

1. Why should Guidant have communicated knowledge about its defective heart devices to doctors and patients?
2. What reasons did Guidant give to defend its decisions to withhold information?
3. What criteria can be used to decide when withholding information that is important to other people or groups is unethical?

Opening Case

DOLLS IN COMBAT: BARBIE VERSUS THE BRATZ

What were the mistakes made by Mattel's decision makers?

The rapid pace at which the world is changing is forcing all kinds of companies to speed up their decision making. Otherwise they will get left behind by competitors who do respond faster to changing customer fads and fashions. Nowhere is this truer than in the global toy industry, where in the doll business, worth over $10 billion a year in sales, vicious combat is raging.

The largest global toy company, Mattel, has earned tens of billions of dollars from the world's best-selling doll, Barbie, since it introduced her almost fifty years ago.[1] Mothers who played with the original dolls bought them for their daughters, and then granddaughters, and Barbie became an American icon. However, Barbie's advantage as best-selling global doll led Mattel's managers to make major errors in decision making in the 2000s.

Sales of Bratz dolls are increasing while sales of Barbie dolls are falling because the managers responsible for designing the dolls made different decisions about what young girls wanted from a doll in the 2000s.

Barbie and all Barbie accessories accounted for almost 50 percent of Mattel's toy sales in the 1990s, so protecting its star product was crucial. The Barbie doll was created in the 1960s when most women were homemakers, and her voluptuous shape was a response to a dated view of what the "ideal" woman should look like. Barbie's continuing success, however, led Bob Eckert—Mattel's CEO—and his top decision makers to underestimate how much the world had altered. Changing cultural views about the role of girls, women, sex, marriage, and women working in the last decades shifted the tastes of doll buyers. This led Mattel's managers to collectively buy into an "If it's not broken don't fix it" approach, so they continued to bet on Barbie's continuing success. In fact, given that Barbie was still the bestseller they thought it might be very dangerous to make major changes to her appearance because customers might not like it and stop buying her. Mattel's top managers decided not to rock the boat, they decided everything was fine with the brand, and no major changes in Barbie were planned.

So, Mattel was unprepared when a challenge came along in the form of a new kind of doll, the Bratz doll introduced by MGA Entertainment. Over the years many competitors to Barbie had emerged—selling dolls is very profitable—but no other doll had matched Barbie's appeal to young girls (or their mothers). The marketers and designers behind the Bratz line of dolls had spent a lot of time and money to discover what the new generation of girls, especially those aged 7–11, wanted from a doll. And it turned out that the Bratz dolls they designed met the desires of these girls. Bratz dolls have larger heads, have oversized eyes, wear lots of makeup, wear short dresses, and are multicultural to give each doll "personality and attitude."[2] The dolls were designed to appeal to a new generation of girls brought up in the fast-changing fashion, music, and television market/age that is relationship oriented. The Bratz dolls met the untapped needs of "tween" girls, and the new line took off. MGA quickly licensed the rights to make and sell the doll to toy companies overseas, and Bratz quickly became a serious competitor to Barbie.

Now Mattel's decision makers were in trouble; they had no choice but to change the assumptions behind their decision making and bring Barbie up to date. Furthermore, they had to learn to do what was necessary under intense pressure from a competitor that had everything to gain and nothing to lose—while Mattel faced the prospect of losing billions in Barbie sales. Mattel's designers must have been wishing they had been adventurous and made more radical changes earlier when they did not need to change. However, they decided to change Barbie's "extreme" vital statistics, they killed off her old-time boyfriend Ken and replaced him with Blaine, an Aussie surfer, and so on.[3]

They also recognized they had waited much too long to introduce their own new lines of dolls to meet the changed needs of tween and other girls in the 2000s. So they rushed out the "My Scene" line of dolls in 2002, which were obvious imitations of Bratz dolls. This new line has not matched the popularity of Bratz dolls. Mattel also introduced a new line called Flava in 2003 to appeal to even younger girls, but this line flopped completely. At the same time, the decisions that they made to change Barbie and her figure, looks, clothing, and boyfriends came too late—sales of Barbie dolls have continued to fall. This is serious stuff because Mattel's profits and stock price both hinge on Barbie's success.

Analysts argue that Mattel had not paid enough attention to organizational learning—that is, the need to stay up to date with changing customer needs and to introduce new and improved products that are necessary to keep a company on top of its market. Only time will tell if Mattel's decision makers can find ways to reverse the decline in doll sales. But, decision making at Mattel has changed forever: Managers recognize they must learn new ways of responding to a changing environment.

Overview

Making decisions is an essential part of behavior in organizations. Good decisions help individuals, groups, and organizations achieve their goals and perform well. Bad decisions hinder goal attainment and lower performance. Mattel's experience illustrates the way in which the quality of decision making can change quickly over time in a company. It suggests how complex the process of making good decisions can be and how factors at the individual and group level, like people's changing needs and desires, and a company's internal decision-making procedures that affect the way it views its environment can affect it. Decision making is one more important organizational behavior that needs to be understood.

In this chapter, we discuss how members of organizations make decisions. We examine the types of decisions that need to be made in organizations and the decision-making process. We explore some biases and problems in decision making. We look at the pros and cons of using groups instead of individuals to make decisions and some of the issues involved in group decision making. Finally, we discuss how a company can encourage organizational learning to both maintain and improve the quality of its decision making over time. By the end of the chapter, you will understand how decision making is a crucial determinant of whether or not individuals, groups, and organizations perform at high levels and achieve their goals.

Types of Decisions

In previous chapters, we discussed some of the choices that organizational members make everyday—decisions ranging from how managers should motivate and reward subordinates, to what is the best way for subordinates to communicate important information to their supervisors, to how group members should respond to a deviant coworker. Making such choices is the essence of decision making. In fact, **decision making** can be defined as the process by which members of an organization choose a specific course of action to respond to the opportunities and problems that confront them. Good decisions help an individual, group, or organization to be effective. Bad decisions hinder effectiveness and result in poor performance and negative attitudes at all organizational levels.

DECISION MAKING
The process by which members of an organization choose a specific course of action to respond to both opportunities and problems.

Decision making in response to *opportunities* occurs when members of an organization make choices or act in ways that result in benefits or gains. Such decisions range from those made by an upper-level manager in a successful electronics company trying to decide whether to market the firm's products in Europe, to a telephone operator at the same company deciding whether to take an online business course to expand his or her skills and opportunities. Individuals, groups, and entire organizations reach their full potentials only when they take advantage of opportunities to increase their efficiency and effectiveness. Many famous managers such as Andrew Grove, former CEO of Intel, and Steve Jobs, who was previously fired as CEO of Apple but is now its current CEO, suggest that successful companies often fail because they get complacent, fail to take advantage of opportunities, or misread the way the future of their industry is changing. Thus, managers at Intel and Apple are constantly on the lookout for new opportunities and spend a lot of time figuring out how to respond to them.[4]

Decision making in response to *problems* occurs when individual, group, or organizational goal attainment and performance are threatened. A doctor's goal to provide good medical care in a rural community is threatened when the doctor lacks the financial resources to purchase medical equipment. A production group's goal of winning the monthly quality contest is threatened when two of its members engage in social loafing. And an organization's goal of being profitable is threatened when the top-management team experiences communication problems. Through the decision-making process, organizational members choose how to respond to these and other kinds of problems.

Whether they are responding to a potential opportunity, or deciding how to solve a problem, two basic types of decisions are made in organizations: nonprogrammed decisions and programmed decisions.

Nonprogrammed Decisions

When members of an organization choose how to respond to new or novel opportunities and problems, they engage in **nonprogrammed decision making**.[5] Nonprogrammed decision making involves searching for the extra information that is needed to make the right choice.[6] Because the problem or opportunity has not been experienced before, members of the organization are uncertain about how they should respond, and thus they search for any information they can find to help them make their decision.

NONPROGRAMMED DECISION MAKING
Decision making in response to novel opportunities and problems.

Mike Castiglioni, the manager of a successful Italian restaurant called Ciao! in a small Texas town, for example, was confronted with a novel problem when a nationwide Italian restaurant chain, The Olive Garden, opened a new restaurant a few blocks away. The arrival of a strong competitor posed a novel problem for Mike; previously, Ciao! had been the only Italian restaurant in town. Similarly, staff members at Ciao! faced new potential employment opportunities when The Olive Garden advertised for waiters and waitresses.

As soon as he learned The Olive Garden was planning to open a restaurant, Mike tried to find out as much as he could about his new competitor—its lunch and dinner menus and prices, the kinds of customers it appeals to, the quality of its food, and so on. Mike also traveled to the nearby cities of Houston and Dallas and ate in several Olive Garden restaurants to sample the food and ambience and record customer traffic.

As a result of these search activities, Mike decided that the quality of the food he served at Ciao! was better and that the prices the two restaurants charged were similar. The Olive Garden, however, had a wider selection of menu items and offered a soup or salad with every entrée. Mike decided to expand his menu by adding three new items to the lunch menu and four to the dinner menu. He also decided to serve a house salad with all entrées, which would appeal to his health-conscious customers. As a result of his search for information, Mike Castiglioni was able to decide how to respond to the problem of competition in a successful way, and Ciao! continues to thrive despite its new competition.

Programmed Decisions

PROGRAMMED DECISION MAKING
Decision making in response to recurring opportunities and problems.

PERFORMANCE PROGRAM
A standard sequence of behaviors that organizational members follow routinely whenever they encounter a particular type of problem or opportunity.

Although members of an organization frequently make unprogrammed decisions, they also need to engage in **programmed decision making**—that is, making decisions in response to recurring opportunities and problems.[7] To make a programmed decision, the decision maker uses a **performance program**, a standard sequence of behaviors that organizational members follow routinely whenever they encounter a particular type of problem or opportunity.[8] Department stores develop performance programs that specify how salespeople should respond to customers who return items that have been worn and are defective. Grocery stores develop performance programs that indicate how clerks should respond when sale items are out of stock. Universities develop performance programs dictating how to deal with students who cannot complete their courses.

Organizations develop performance programs whenever the same kinds of opportunities or problems keep cropping up. Once a performance program is developed, members of the organization initiate the performance program almost automatically as soon as the opportunity or problem is encountered. They do not have to search for information or think about what they should do in response. Organizational rules (see Chapter 10) are types of performance programs developed to help members make programmed decisions.

Because of improvements in the local economy, Mike Castiglioni was faced with the recurring problem of Ciao!'s experienced waiters and waitresses being offered jobs at The Olive Garden and other new restaurants opening in town. Although the waiters and waitresses at Ciao! were generally satisfied with their jobs, they interviewed at some of the new restaurants to see whether they could earn more money, get better benefits, or working hours. Periodically, waiters or waitresses came to Mike and told him that they had been offered better benefits or working hours by one of his competitors. The first couple of times this happened, Mike needed to make a *nonprogrammed* decision because the problem was relatively novel. Accordingly, he searched for information to help him with his decision: How costly would it be to hire and train a new waiter or waitress? How important was it to have experienced waiters and waitresses who knew many of Ciao!'s regular customers? As a result of his search for information, Mike concluded that, whenever possible, he should try to retain as many of Ciao!'s waiters and waitresses as he could by matching the hourly rates, benefits, and working hours they were offered at other restaurants.

Once Mike had made this decision, whenever waiters or waitresses came to him and told him of better job offers they had received, he matched the offers whenever he could. Mike Castiglioni essentially had decided on a standard response to a recurring problem—the essence of *programmed* decision making and the use of performance programs.

As this example illustrates, performance programs often evolve from nonprogrammed decisions. Essentially, if what was once a novel problem or opportunity keeps recurring, it becomes something that requires a programmed decision, and the organization comes up with a standard response or performance program (see Exhibit 15.1).

EXHIBIT 15.1

Nonprogrammed and Programmed Decision Making

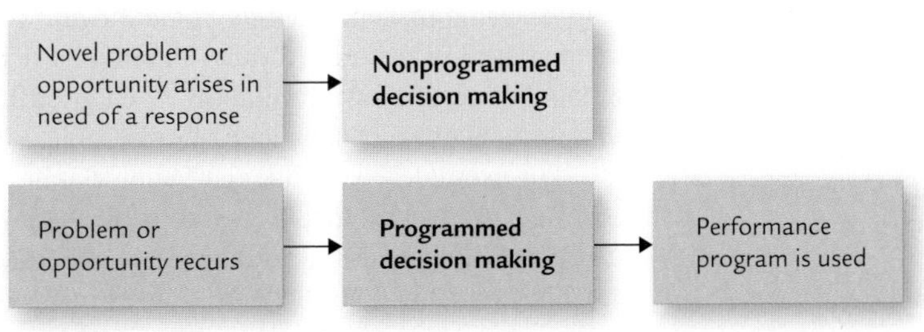

Performance programs save time because they make it unnecessary for organizational members to search for information to make a decision; instead, all they need to do is follow the performance program. Managers, however, must be able to realize when performance programs need to be changed and take the steps necessary to alter them. Organizations tend to be slow to change performance programs because doing things the way they have always been done in the past is often easier than devising and implementing new procedures.

The Decision-Making Process

When people think of decision making in organizations, the kinds of decisions they usually have in mind are nonprogrammed decisions involving a search for new and necessary information. Thus, in the remainder of this chapter, we focus on nonprogrammed decisions. Whenever we use the term *decision,* we are referring specifically to a *nonprogrammed* decision. Two widely studied models of the decision-making process are the classical decision-making model and James March and Herbert Simon's administrative decision-making model.

The Classical Model of Decision Making

CLASSICAL DECISION-MAKING MODEL A prescriptive approach based on the assumptions that the decision maker has all the necessary information and will choose the best possible solution or response.

The **classical decision-making model** is a *prescriptive model*—it describes how people *should* make decisions.[9] This model rests on two assumptions: (1) People have access to all the information they need to make a decision, and (2) people make decisions by choosing the best possible solution to a problem or response to an opportunity.[10] According to the classical model, a decision maker should choose how to respond to opportunities and problems by engaging in these four steps:[11]

1. Listing all alternatives from which a choice will be selected: These alternatives represent different responses to the problem or the opportunity.
2. Listing the consequences of each alternative: The consequences are what would occur if a given alternative were selected.
3. Considering his or her own preferences for each alternative or set of consequences and then ranking the sets from most preferred to least preferred.
4. Selecting the alternative that will result in the most preferred set of consequences.

According to the classical model, if members of an organization follow these four steps, they will make optimal decisions, given the decision maker's preferences.[12] Do members of an organization actually make decisions according to the classical model? If they do not, could they make better decisions if they did? The answer to both questions is "no" because of several basic problems with the classical model.

Sarah Hunter, a marketing manager at a food products company had to find ways to revive the sales of a line of frozen desserts. This is usual in ions whose outcomes were uncertain.

The classical model is unrealistic.[13] Its assumption that decision makers have all the information needed to make optimal decisions bears little resemblance to the conditions facing most organizations. Even if the decision makers did have all necessary information, they probably would not be able to use it all. This is because the cognitive abilities of decision makers are limited; often, they cannot take into account the large quantities of information available to them.

One way to consider the difficulties of the classical model is to compare the four steps previously described to actual decision making in organizations. With regard to the first step, decision makers often *do not know all the alternatives* they can choose from.[14] One of the defining features of nonprogrammed decisions is that they involve a considerable amount of search for information. Even after this search is complete, however, it is likely that decision makers are aware of only some of the possible alternatives.

For example, the challenge facing Sarah Hunter, a marketing manager at a Fortune 500 food products company, was to solve the problem of lackluster sales of a line of frozen desserts. Hunter's search for alternatives yielded three potential solutions to the problem: (1) The company could launch a series of newspaper and magazine advertisements with coupons; (2) the company could negotiate with major grocery store chains to give the desserts a more visible location (at eye level) in the frozen foods sections; or (3) the company could develop a series of expensive television ads airing during prime time. Hunter's information search failed to uncover other alternatives: (1) rename the products, (2) change the products' packaging, (3) reorient the packaging and marketing of some of the products to appeal to certain segments of the market (for example, pitch angel food cake to health-conscious adults and frozen yogurt bars to young children), and (4) dropping the line altogether.

In the second step of the classical model, decision makers list the consequences of each alternative. As in the first step, however, decision makers often *do not know all of the consequences* that will ensue if they choose a given alternative.[15] One reason it's hard to make decisions is that the decision maker often does not know what will happen if a given course of action is chosen. Sarah Hunter did not know whether coupons in newspapers and magazines would significantly boost sales because her company had experienced mixed success with this approach in the past. She knew that television ads were likely to increase sales, but it was not clear whether the increase in sales would be temporary or long lasting or be large enough to offset the high costs of purchasing air time in prime viewing hours.

As the third step in the classical model, decision makers must consider their own preferences for sets of consequences. Once again, the classical model assumes that decision makers are able to rank sets of consequences and know their own preferences.[16] However, decision makers *don't always know for sure what they want.* Stop and think about some of the important and difficult decisions you have had to make. Sometimes, these decisions were difficult to make precisely because *you weren't sure what you wanted.* A graduating senior with an accounting degree from the University of Wisconsin, for example, finds it hard to choose between a job offer from a Wisconsin bank and one from a major accounting firm in New York City because he doesn't know whether he prefers the security of staying in Wisconsin, where most of his family and friends are, to the excitement of living in a big city and the opportunity to work for a major firm. Similarly, Sarah Hunter did not know whether she preferred to dramatically improve frozen dessert sales or improve them just enough to maintain profitability and then move on to another product line.

Because of these problems with the first three steps in the classical model (1) *it is often impossible for an organization's members to make the best possible decisions,* and (2) *even if they make a good decision, the time, effort, and cost that was spent making it might not be worthwhile.*[17] Realizing this problem with the classical model, James March and Herbert Simon developed a more realistic account of decision making: the administrative decision-making model.[18]

March and Simon's Administrative Model of Decision Making

ADMINISTRATIVE DECISION-MAKING MODEL
A descriptive approach stressing that incomplete information, psychological and sociological processes, and the decision maker's cognitive abilities affect decision making and that decision makers often choose satisfactory, not optimal, solutions.

The classical model is prescriptive; it indicates how decisions *should* be made. In contrast, March and Simon's **administrative decision-making model** is *descriptive*—it explains how people *actually make* decisions in organizations.[19] March and Simon stress that incomplete information and the decision maker's cognitive abilities and psychological makeup affect decision making. Consequently, decision makers often choose *satisfactory*, not optimal, solutions.[20]

According to the administrative decision-making model, decision makers choose how to respond to opportunities and problems on the basis of a simplified and approximate account of the situation—the decision maker's definition of it, in other words. Decision makers do not take into account all information relevant to a problem or opportunity, nor do they consider all possible alternatives and their consequences.

Sarah Hunter did not consider renaming or changing the packaging of the frozen desserts, or reorienting them to appeal to certain segments of the market, or even recommending that the company drop the products altogether. She did not define the situation in those terms. She defined the situation in terms of increasing sales of existing products, not changing the products to make them more attractive to customers. In addition, the thought of dropping the line never entered her mind, although that is what the company ended up doing two years later.

Decision makers may follow some of the steps in the classical model, such as generating alternatives and considering the consequences of the alternatives and their own preferences. But the information they consider is based on their definition of the situation, which is the result of psychological and sociological factors. Psychological factors include the decision maker's personality, ability, perceptions, experiences, and knowledge. Sociological factors include the groups, organization, and organizational and national culture of which the decision maker is a member.

The alternatives Sarah Hunter considered and, more generally, her definition of the situation were based in part on two factors. One was her past marketing experiences: She had always worked on improving and maintaining sales of "successful" products. The other was the marketing department in which she worked. It was quite conservative. For example, it rarely made changes to product names and packaging, it had introduced few new products in the past 10 years, and it had not dropped an existing product in 12 years' time.

SATISFICING
Searching for and choosing an acceptable response or solution, not necessarily the best possible one.

Satisficing. Rather than making optimal decisions, organizational members often engage in **satisficing**—that is, they search for and choose *acceptable* responses to opportunities and problems, not necessarily the *best* possible responses.[21] One way that decision makers can satisfice is by listing criteria that would lead to an acceptable choice and picking an alternative that meets the criteria. When deciding among many job applicants to hire, for example, organizations often satisfice by listing criteria that an acceptable candidate should meet (such as having an appropriate degree from a college or university, job-related experience, and good interpersonal skills) and then choosing a candidate who meets the criteria. If organizations were to make the optimal hiring decision rather than a satisfactory one, they would have to pick the best candidate—the person with the best educational background, prior experience, and interpersonal skills. Often, it would be very difficult and time-consuming (if not impossible) to do this.

Ethical decision making. One criterion of a satisfactory decision in any organization is that it be *ethical*. Ethical decisions promote well-being and do not cause harm to members of an organization or to other people affected by an organization's activities. Although it is easy to describe what an ethical decision is, sometimes it is difficult to determine the boundary between ethical and unethical decisions in an organization. Is it ethical, for example, for a pharmaceutical company to decide to charge a high price for a lifesaving drug thus making it unaffordable to some people? On the one hand, it can be argued that the drug is costly to produce and the company needs the revenues to continue producing the drug as well as to research ways to improve its effectiveness. On the other hand, it can be argued that the company has a moral or ethical obligation to make the drug available to as many people as possible. In 2004, for example, Sheering Plough raised the price of its best-selling AIDS prevention drug by 500 percent, causing an uproar among doctors and patients who claimed that this would lead to great hardship for patients, many of whom would no longer be able to afford it. Sheering Plough simply said that it had been charging too low a price for its valuable drug and that it had the right to increase its price.

Some people deliberately make unethical decisions to benefit themselves or their organizations, but even decision makers who strive to be ethical are sometimes faced with difficult choices or ethical dilemmas. Under these circumstances, satisficing, or making acceptable decisions that are ethical, can be difficult. One example of blatantly unethical decision making by pharmaceutical companies occurred when six of them admitted they had conspired to artificially raise the price of vitamins, such as vitamins A, B^2, C, E, and beta carotene. Swiss giant Hoffman-La Roche agreed to pay $500 million in criminal fines, and German Company BASF paid a $225 million fine; the others were also fined large amounts.[22] How could this happen?

Senior managers from each of these company's vitamin divisions jointly made the decision to inflate their division's profits and to act unethically at the expense of consumers. In several meetings around the world, they worked out the details of the plot, which went undiscovered for several years. Many of the top managers involved have been prosecuted in their home countries, and all have been fired. BASF, for example, completely replaced its worldwide management team.[23]

What has been the end result of this fiasco for these companies? All have agreed to create a special "ethics officer" position within their organizations. The ethics officer is responsible for developing new ethical standards with regard to how decisions are made. The ethics officer is also responsible for listening to employees' complaints about unethical behavior, training employees to make ethical decisions, and counseling top managers to prevent further wrongdoing.[24]

BOUNDED RATIONALITY
An ability to reason that is constrained by the limitations of the human mind itself.

Bounded rationality. Unlike the classical model, which disregards the cognitive limitations of the decision maker, March and Simon acknowledge that decision makers are constrained by **bounded rationality**—an ability to reason that is limited by the limitations of the human mind itself. March and Simon's model assumes that bounded rationality is a fact of organizational life. Members of an organization try to act rationally and make good decisions that benefit the organization, but their rationality is limited by their own cognitive abilities.[25] It is often impossible for decision makers to simultaneously consider all the information relevant to a decision (even if it were available) and use all this information to make an optimal choice. Even though the information provided by advances in IT can help members of an organization make better decisions, rationality is always limited, or bounded, by the capabilities of the human mind. Thus, decision makers approach decisions on the basis of their own subjective definitions of the situation, and they usually satisfice rather than optimize.[26]

When members of an organization realize that decision making proceeds more often as described by March and Simon than as outlined in the classical model, they are better able to understand why both good and bad decisions are made in organizations and how decision making can be improved. Good decisions are often made when decision makers are able to identify and focus on the key aspects of the situation. Bad decisions may result from defining a situation improperly.

How did Sarah Hunter, in our earlier example, define the situation she was in? She believed that her challenge was to improve sales of an existing product rather than to change the product or evaluate whether it should be dropped. Her definition of the situation limited the potential solutions she considered. Only after trying two of those solutions and failing did she and her company realize the need to redefine the situation and recognize that the product line needed to be either dramatically changed or dropped.

In summary, it is important to realize that different members of an organization are going to define the same problem or opportunity in different ways, depending on their personalities, abilities, knowledge, expertise, and the groups they belong to. As a result, decision makers need to carefully examine how they define opportunities and problems and the implications these definitions have. To help improve decision making, it is important to focus on the information most relevant to the decision at hand and be cognizant of the sources of decision-making errors. We discuss these sources of error next.

Sources of Error in Decision Making

Given that decision makers often do not have all the information they need to make a good decision and are boundedly rational, it is not surprising that a variety of sources of error in decision making exist.[27] Some of these sources of error are pervasive and recurring.[28] Many decision makers succumb to these errors and make less than satisfactory decisions because of them.[29] Two major sources of error arise from (1) the shortcuts, or rules of thumb, people use to make decisions, which can lead to both good and bad decisions; and (2) the human tendency to throw good money after bad and continue involvement in unfruitful activities.

Heuristics and the Biases They May Lead To

Given the number and complexity of the many decisions that people have to make at work and in their personal lives, it is not surprising that they often try to simplify things or use certain rules of thumb to help them make decisions. The rules of thumb that help

HEURISTICS
Rules of thumb that simplify decision making.

people simplify decision making are called **heuristics**.[30] Heuristics are involved in much of the decision making that takes place in organizations; people tend to use them without even knowing they are doing so. Because they simplify matters, heuristics can aid in the decision-making process, but they can also lead to *biases*—systematic errors in decision making.[31] Three common rules of thumb are availability and representativeness heuristics, and anchoring and adjustment heuristics (see Exhibit 15.2). We discuss each of these next.

AVAILABILITY HEURISTIC
The rule of thumb that says an event that is easy to remember is likely to have occurred more frequently than an event that is difficult to remember.

Availability heuristic. When making decisions, organizational members often have to judge the frequency with which different events will occur and their likely causes. The **availability heuristic** reflects the tendency to determine the frequency of an event and its causes by how easy these events and causes are to remember (that is, how *available* they are from memory).[32] People tend to judge an event that is easy to remember as occurring more frequently than an event that is difficult to remember. Likewise, if a potential cause of an event comes to mind quickly, people are likely to think that it is an important causal factor.

The availability heuristic can aid decision making because events and causes that actually do occur frequently come easily to mind. However, factors other than frequency of occurrence also determine the availability of information that can be recalled. As a result, the availability heuristic can cause certain biases to enter into decision making. One such bias is the overestimation of the frequency of *vivid* or *extreme* events and their causes because they are easy to remember.[33] Another is the overestimation of the frequency of *recent* events and their causes because they also tend to be easy to remember.[34]

When Sarah Hunter was trying to decide how to increase sales of frozen desserts, for example, she remembered that one of her co-employees recently experienced dramatic success boosting fruit drink sales with a series of advertisements and coupons placed in magazines and Sunday newspaper supplements. The fact that the success was *recent* and *extreme* led Hunter to *overestimate* the extent to which this approach would increase the sales of her product line. This same bias led her to ignore instances in which the same kinds of advertisements and coupons failed to improve the sales of other products. As a result of the biases emanating from the availability heuristic, Hunter decided to place advertisements and coupons in magazines and Sunday supplements in the hope of increasing frozen dessert sales—a strategy that ultimately proved to be unsuccessful.

REPRESENTATIVENESS HEURISTIC
The rule of thumb that says similar kinds of events that happened in the past are a good predictor of the likelihood of an upcoming event.

Representativeness heuristic. The **representativeness heuristic** reflects the tendency to predict the likelihood of an event occurring from the extent to which the event is typical (or *representative*) of similar kinds of events that have happened in the past.[35] A manager in the United States trying to determine whether a domestically popular hand

EXHIBIT 15.2

Heuristics and the Biases They May Lead To

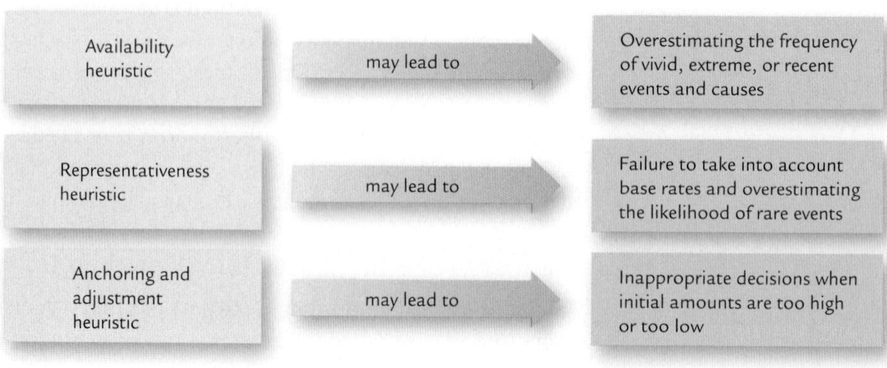

cream will sell in Spain, for example, compares the extent to which Spain is similar to foreign countries in which the cream has sold especially well or to countries in which the cream has not sold well. The manager decides not to export the hand cream to Spain because Spain is typical of the countries in which the product had bombed (the cream had bombed in other Spanish-speaking countries, for example).

The representativeness heuristic can sometimes be a good shortcut used to estimate the likelihood of an upcoming event because the fact that similar kinds of events happened in the past may be a good predictor of the upcoming event.[36] Sometimes, however, this heuristic can cause decision makers to disregard important information about the frequency of events. In such cases, the representativeness heuristic leads to biased decision making.

BASE RATE
The actual frequency with which an event occurs.

One source of bias emanating from the representativeness heuristic is the failure to take into account the **base rate**, or the actual frequency with which events occur.[37] The manager in the hand cream example should have considered the number of times the hand cream did not sell well in foreign countries. If he had, he would have found that the product sold well in *most* countries to which it was exported and that its failure in foreign markets was rare. Using this information in the decision-making process would have told the manager that chances that the cream would sell well in Spain were pretty high. However, the manager did not take this base-rate information into account. He decided not to export the hand cream to Spain, and missed out on a good opportunity. To avoid the pitfalls of the representativeness heuristic, it is important to take base rates into account because it is likely that common events (the hand cream's high sales in foreign countries) will occur again and that rare events (the product's failure in a few countries, some of which were Spanish-speaking) will not occur again.

ANCHORING AND ADJUSTMENT HEURISTIC
The rule of thumb that says that decisions about how big or small an amount (such as a salary, budget, or level of costs) should be can be made by making adjustments from some initial amount.

Anchoring and adjustment heuristic. The **anchoring and adjustment heuristic** reflects the tendency to make decisions based on adjustments from some initial amount (or *anchor*).[38] Decisions about salary increases are often made by choosing a percentage increase from an employee's current salary. Budget decisions are often made by deciding whether the current budget should be increased or decreased. Decisions about the degree to which costs must be cut are often based on the current level of costs. In situations like these, if the initial amounts are reasonable, then the anchoring and adjustment heuristic might be a good shortcut for decision making.

By using this heuristic, decision makers need to consider only the degree to which the current level needs to be changed. They do not, for example, need to determine a person's salary from scratch or build a budget from ground zero. But if the original amount from which a decision or adjustment is made is *not* reasonable, the anchoring and adjustment heuristic will lead to biased decision making. If employees' current salary levels are low in comparison to what they could be earning in similar kinds of jobs and companies, even a relatively large percentage increase (such as 15 percent) may still leave them underpaid. Likewise, if a department's budget is much too high, a 10 percent decrease will lead to the department's still being allocated more money than it really needs.

Many gamblers suffer from escalation of commitment because they chose to erroneously believe that betting more money will allow them to recoup the money they have just lost. This belief frequently leads to personal financial disaster.

Escalation of Commitment

A second source of error in decision making (in addition to biases) is **escalation of commitment**—the tendency of decision makers to invest additional time, money, or effort into what are essentially bad decisions or unproductive courses of action that are already draining the organization's resources.[39] Here is a typical escalation-of-commitment scenario: (1) A decision maker initially makes a decision that results in some kind of loss or negative outcome. (2) Rather than change the course of action contained in the initial decision, the decision maker commits more time, money, or effort to the course of action. (3) Further losses are experienced because of this escalation of commitment to a failing course of action. Escalation of commitment is graphically illustrated in Exhibit 15.3.

EXHIBIT 15.3

Escalation of Commitment

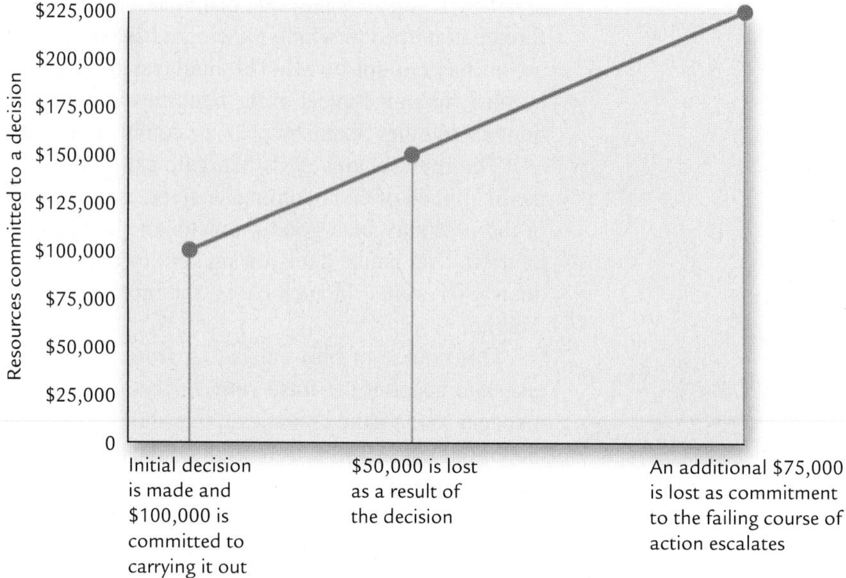

ESCALATION OF COMMITMENT
The tendency to invest additional time, money, or effort into what are essentially bad decisions or unproductive courses of action.

Sarah Hunter experienced escalation of commitment in her quest to improve sales of frozen desserts. First, she embarked on a series of magazine and newspaper ads. When this approach failed to boost sales and the money was spent, she decided to negotiate with grocery store chains to make the products more visible in their frozen foods sections. This was difficult to do, but she nonetheless persevered and was successful at getting it done. This strategy, however, also failed to boost sales. Instead of reassessing her original decision to try to boost frozen dessert sales, Hunter gave her boss a proposal for a series of expensive television advertisements. Luckily for the organization, the boss denied her request and halted her escalation of commitment.

Escalation of commitment is common in organizations (even at top-management levels) and in people's personal lives. Investors in stocks and real estate, for example, often continue to invest in losing ventures, pouring good money after bad. Why does escalation of commitment occur, even among presumably knowledgeable decision makers? There appear to be at least three causes of this type of faulty decision making:

1. *Decision makers often do not want to admit to themselves or to other people that they have made a mistake.*[40] Rather than reassess the wisdom of their original decision in light of the negative consequences they have experienced, decision makers commit more resources to the course of action in order to reconfirm the "correctness" of the original decision.
2. *Given the amount of money or resources that have been lost, decision makers erroneously believe that an additional commitment of resources is justified to recoup some of those losses.*[41] When the newspaper and magazine ads and the location change in the grocery stores failed to boost sales, what did Sarah Hunter do? She decided that after investing so much time, effort, and money into boosting sales, she had no alternative but to push ahead with the TV ads. The costs that she has already incurred, however, were **sunk costs**—costs that could not be recovered or affected by subsequent decision making. The sunk costs should not have entered into Hunter's decision making.
3. *Decision makers tend to take more risks when they frame or view decisions in negative terms (for example, as a way to recover money that has been lost) rather than in positive terms (for example, as a way to generate more money).*[42] When Sarah Hunter originally thought about TV ads, she decided against them because they were too risky; they would cost too much money given the uncertainty about whether or not they would boost sales. At that point, Hunter had spent no resources on boosting sales;

SUNK COSTS
Costs that cannot be reversed and will not be affected by subsequent decision making.

the TV ads were framed (in her mind) in positive terms: as a way to boost sales. But after her first two strategies failed, the TV ads were framed in negative terms: as a way to recover some of the time, effort, and money she had already spent unsuccessfully trying to boost sales. Once the decision was framed negatively, Hunter was willing to risk the high cost of the ads.[43]

Biases resulting from escalation of commitment and the use of heuristics can result in poor decision making at all levels in an organization. This problem is compounded by the fact that decision makers often use heuristics without being aware that they are doing so. Escalation of commitment also occurs without decision makers realizing that they are throwing good money after bad. No matter how knowledgeable a decision maker is, the potential for poor decision making as a result of biases and the escalation of commitment is always present.

Buyer's Remorse

BUYER'S REMORSE
An emotional condition in which a person or group feels doubt and regret about a decision that involve the purchase or winning of some high-priced product.

One of the outcomes of poor decision making, and one many individuals as well as groups and organizations often experience, is buyer's remorse. **Buyer's remorse** is an emotional condition in which a person or group feels doubt and regret about a decision that involves the purchase or winning of some high-priced product. It is frequently associated with the purchase of high-value products such as property, new machinery, or computers, or it may even be about the high-price paid to hire a new employee or manager or outside contractor.

The sense of doubt that the correct decision has been made is often brought about by the fear that a decision has been made too quickly, or without enough information being collected, for example, about the capacity of a computer, or the skills and experience of a new manager. Interestingly, the condition often arises after winning an auction because by definition the person must have been the one willing to pay the most so the doubt arises—have I paid too much? A top management team may wonder if they have paid too much for the oil rights to a section of ocean, or for the right to operate cell phones in a certain frequency range. A manager might wonder if they have really chosen the best person for the job or paid too much to obtain the lease of a new store. One of the cases at the end of the chapter explores this kind of reaction to decision making.

The Role of Information Technology

The use of IT can often help to reduce the effect of these biases and heuristics on decision making.[44] IT systems can generate much more information on which managers can base their decisions. Likewise, new software programs can generate improved tables and charts, making the data more meaningful to managers. This, in turn, can reduce the effects of the availability and representativeness biases.[45]

Additionally, because IT can be used to link managers at different levels and in different parts of the organization, there is less likelihood of their making errors. For example, the escalation-of-commitment bias is likely to become far less of a problem when more objective information is available that a serious problem does exist in the organization. Managers with different perspectives can simultaneously examine that information before deciding what to do.

IT can also turn many nonprogrammed decisions into programmed ones. For example, when salespeople can turn to online databases and software programs to access instant solutions for their customers, this frees up their time to make more sales calls or provide better-quality customer service. At all levels in the organization, the application of IT allows managers to spend more time making nonprogrammed decisions that can enhance organizational performance. The following A Global View profiles how the enterprise resource planning system designed and sold by the German IT company SAP can improve the quality of organizational decision making. An *enterprise resource planning (ERP) system* is a company-wide Intranet based on multimodule software that allows an organization to link and coordinate its functional activities and operations.

Global View

SAP's ERP System

SAP is the world's leading supplier of ERP software; it introduced the world's first ERP system in 1973. So great was the demand for its software that it had to train thousands of consultants from companies like IBM, HP, Accenture, and Cap Gemini to install and customize its software to meet the needs of companies in different industries around the world.[46]

The popularity of the ERP system is that it manages and connects all of a company's different functions. SAP's software has modules specifically devoted to each of a company's core functional activities such as marketing and manufacturing. Each module contains a set of functional "best practices," or rules, SAP has found works best to improve the function's efficiency and effectiveness.[47] SAP claims that when a company reconfigures its IT system to make the software work, it can achieve productivity gains of 30 to 50 percent, which for large companies can amount to billions of dollars in savings.

For each function, SAP has a software module that it installs on the function's Intranet. The function inputs its data into that module in the way specified by SAP. For example, the sales function inputs all the information about customer needs into SAP's sales module, and the materials management function inputs information about the product specifications it requires from suppliers into the materials management module. These modules give functional managers real-time feedback on the status of their particular functional activities. Essentially, each SAP module functions as an expert decision-making system that can reason through the information functional managers input into it. It then provides managers with recommendations for improvement. The magic of ERP does not stop there, however.[48]

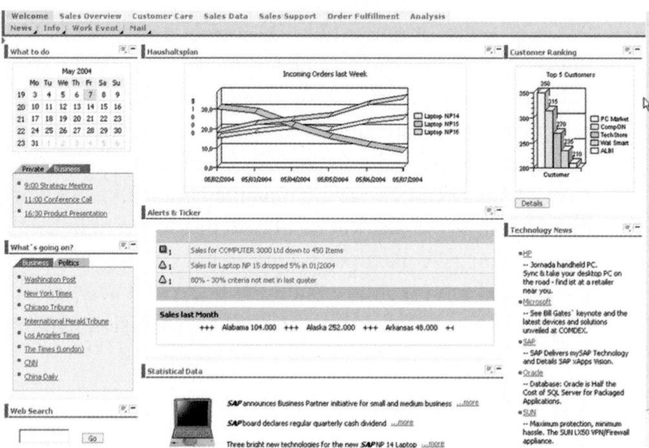

SAP, a German software developer, began producing planning programs over 30 years ago to help firms operate more efficiently. The software integrates their functional groups, taking some of the guesswork out of decision making.

SAP's ERP software also connects people across functions. Managers in all functions have access to the other functions' decision-making systems, and SAP's software is designed to alert them when their functional activities will be affected by decisions being made by managers in another function. Thus, the ERP system allows managers across the organization to better coordinate their decision making. This can be a big competitive advantage. Moreover, the software installed on the corporation's mainframe takes the information from all of the different functional expert systems and creates a company-wide overview of its operations. In essence, SAP's ERPs create a sophisticated top-level decision-making system that can reason through the huge volume of information being provided by the organization's functions.[49] It can then diagnose common problems and issues and recommend organization-wide solutions. Top managers armed with this information can then use these recommendations to improve the decisions they make in the changing environment the organization faces.

Group Decision Making

Frequently groups, rather than individuals, make decisions in organizations. These groups might have a formal leader or functional manager who oversees the decision-making process. Self-managed work teams also need to make decisions, however. In this section, we consider some of the potential advantages, disadvantages, and consequences of group decision making. (See Exhibit 15.4.)

Advantages of Group Decision Making

Advantages of using groups to make decisions include the availability and diversity of members' skills, knowledge, and expertise; enhanced memory for facts; greater ability to correct errors; and greater decision acceptance.

Availability and diversity of members' skills, knowledge, and expertise. When groups make decisions, each group member's skills, knowledge, and expertise can be brought into play. For certain kinds of decisions, an individual decision maker is very unlikely to have all the different capabilities needed to make a good decision. For example, when Jack Welch, General Electric's (GE) former CEO, needed to decide whether to invest $70 million to modernize GE's washing machine-manufacturing facilities near Louisville, Kentucky, or buy washing machines from another company and sell them under the GE brand name, he clearly did not have all the skills, knowledge, and expertise needed to make the decision by himself. He needed input from various managers about manufacturing costs, product development costs, and quality considerations. He also needed input from union representatives about whether GE's unionized employees would agree to needed changes in their jobs to cut costs if the company decided to go ahead with the modernization program. Relying on group decision making, Welch undertook the modernization program, which proved to be a wise choice.[50] Whenever a decision requires skills, knowledge, and expertise in several areas (such as marketing, finance, engineering, production, and research and development), group decision making has clear advantages over individual decision making.

This advantage of group decision making suggests that there should be *diversity* among group members (see Chapter 10). In addition to diversity in knowledge and expertise, it is often desirable to have diversity in age, gender, race, and ethnic backgrounds. Diversity gives a group the opportunity to consider different points of view. Traditionally, for example, groups that designed new automobiles for major car companies like GM and Ford were all male. Now, to develop popular world cars these companies realize it is vital to have women and designers from abroad on the team. They bring new, different, important cultural insights to the design process that result in a new car model that appeals to women and car buyers in other countries.[51] NutraSweet Corporation is another company

EXHIBIT 15.4

Advantages and Disadvantages of Group Decision Making

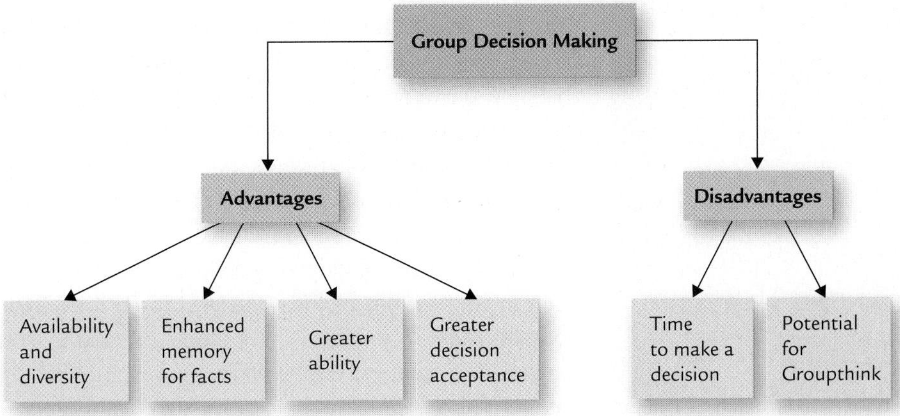

that values diversity. NutraSweet is attempting to improve its product's foreign sales and sales to African Americans and Hispanics, who have relatively high incidences of diabetes. Given this aim, NutraSweet views a diverse workforce as a practical business necessity. Another example of diversity working to help a company is profiled in the following OB Today.

Although diverse work groups can improve decision making, they can give rise to a problem: Group members who have different points of view because of their varied backgrounds sometimes find it hard to get along with each other. Many organizations are trying to respond to this challenge through diversity training programs, which aim to help members of an organization understand each other so they can work together effectively and make good decisions.

Enhanced memory for facts. When a decision requires the consideration of a substantial amount of information, groups have an advantage over individuals because of their memory for facts.[52] Most people engaged in the process of making a decision have experienced the frustrating problem of forgetting an important piece of information. Because a group can rely on the memory of each of its members, the problem of forgetfulness is minimized. Information that one member of the group forgets is likely to

OB Today

Gap Understands Diverse Customers Needs

Gap, the well-known clothing company, has always been responsive to the changing needs of its diverse customers, and it is careful to employ clothes designers and salespeople who reflect the demographics of its customers. It ran into major problems in the 1990s, however, when suddenly its designers lost contact with its customers and they chose to make lines of unusual or garish clothing that appealed to no one. Its profits plunged as sales fell in its Gap, Banana Republic, and Old Navy stores and investors felt it had lost sight of customers' needs.

Gap hired a new CEO, Mickey Pressler, an ex-Disney executive, to change Gap's decision-making process.[53] Pressler had learned at Disney how important it was to study customers' quickly changing needs. He restructured the design department by forming teams of diverse employees to investigate the changing needs and demographics of Gap's customers—to see which customer needs were being met and which were not. These teams discovered many things, and they quickly figured out how to meet the needs of Gap's traditional customers and its sales rose again. However, they also discovered that Gap was not adequately serving the needs of a major market segment—older women.[54] The 46 million baby-boom generation women born between 1946 and 1964 have vast spending power, indeed they are the people who give their children and grandchildren the money to shop at Gap's stores!

Pressler realized his diverse employee teams had discovered a profitable new sales opportunity and he formed a team charged with the task of making all the thousands of decisions involved in opening a new chain of Gap stores that would stock clothing targeted at the needs of older, female professional or casual customers who wanted to look good in clothes that fit their lifestyle. So Forth & Towne is Gap's new chain for female boomers, age 35 and up.[55] Five stores opened in 2005, and five additional stores are scheduled to open in 2006, with another 20 in 2007 if Gap finds that its decision making has worked, and its new chain proves popular.

be remembered by another. For example, even if Jack Welch had all the information he needed to decide whether General Electric should make or buy washing machines, it is highly unlikely he would be able to remember all of it when the time came to make the final decision. Having a group of GE managers and employees available to participate in the decision making helped to ensure that important information was not forgotten or overlooked.

Capability of error detection. No matter how experienced decision makers are, they all make mistakes. Some errors occur in the information-gathering stage or in the evaluation of alternatives. Other errors occur when the final decision is made. When a group makes a decision, errors made by some group members might be detected and corrected by others.[56] If, for example, a manager at GE made a mistake in calculating production costs at the new manufacturing facility that was being contemplated, there was always the chance that another manager would detect the error.

Greater decision acceptance. For a decision to be implemented, it is often necessary for several members of an organization to accept the decision. Suppose, for example, a grocery store manager decides to extend the store's operating hours from 18 to 24 hours a day by scheduling employees to work for longer periods of time (and not hiring any new employees). The employees must accept this decision for it to work. If none of the employees is willing to work the new 10 P.M. to 6 A.M. shift, the decision cannot be implemented.

The likelihood employees will accept a decision increases when they take part in the decision-making process. The successful implementation of GE's decision to invest $70 million to modernize its washing machine-manufacturing facilities, for example, depended on union leaders agreeing to changes in the employees' jobs.[57] By involving the union in the decision making, Jack Welch helped ensure that these employees would accept and support the decision to go ahead with the modernization plan.

Disadvantages of Group Decision Making

Group decision making has certain advantages over individual decision making (particularly when the decisions are complex, require the gathering and processing of a variety or large amount of information, and require acceptance by others for successful implementation). But there are also disadvantages to group decision making. Two of them are time and the potential for groupthink.

Time to make a decision. Have you been in the annoying situation of being in a group that seemed to take forever to make a decision that you could have made yourself in half the time? One of the disadvantages of group decision making is the amount of time it consumes. Groups seldom make decisions as quickly as individuals can. Moreover, if you multiply the amount of time a group takes to make a group decision by the number of people in the group, you can see the extent to which group decision making consumes the time and effort of organizational members.

For decisions that meet certain criteria, individual decision making takes less time than group decision making and is likely to result in a decision that's just as good. Organization's should use individual and not group decision making when (1) an individual is likely to have all the capabilities needed to make a good decision, (2) an individual is likely to be able to gather and accurately take into account all the necessary information, and (3) the acceptance of the decision by the organization's other members is either unnecessary or is likely to occur, regardless of their involvement in decision making.

GROUPTHINK
A pattern of faulty decision making that occurs in cohesive groups whose members strive for agreement at the expense of accurately assessing information relevant to the decision.

The potential for groupthink. **Groupthink** is a pattern of faulty decision making that occurs in cohesive groups whose members strive for agreement at the expense of accurately assessing information relevant to the decision.[58] Irving Janis coined the term *groupthink* in 1972 to describe a paradox that he observed in group decision making:

Groupthink often occurs in crisis situations when decision makers lack accurate information about events and process information according to the group's preferred assumptions and values. Some argue this occurred at NASA and resulted in the launch and subsequent destruction of the Challenger space shuttle.

Sometimes groups of highly qualified and experienced individuals make very poor decisions.[59] The decisions made by President Lyndon B. Johnson and his advisers between 1964 and 1967 to escalate the war in Vietnam, the decision made by President Richard M. Nixon and his advisers to cover up the Watergate break-in in 1972, the decision made by NASA and Morton Thiokol in 1986 to launch the *Challenger* space shuttle (which exploded after takeoff, killing all crew members)—all these decisions were influenced by groupthink. After the fact, the decision makers involved in these and other fiascoes are often shocked that they and their colleagues were involved in such poor decision making. Janis's investigations of groupthink primarily focused on government decisions, but the potential for groupthink in business organizations is just as likely. For example, the decision by Mattel's managers (see the Opening Case for this chapter) not to change Barbie or bring out new, contemporary lines of dolls to protect current Barbie sales can also be seen as an example of this decision-making error.

Recall from Chapter 11 that cohesive groups are very attractive to their members. The individuals in the group value their membership and strongly want to remain part of it. When groupthink occurs, members of a cohesive group unanimously support a decision favored by the group leader without carefully assessing its pros and cons.

This unanimous support is often based on members' exaggerated beliefs about the group's capabilities and moral standing. They think the group is more powerful than it is and could never make a decision that might be morally or ethically questioned. As a result, the group becomes closed-minded and fails to pay attention to information that suggests that the decision might not be a good one. Moreover, when members of the group do have doubts about the decision being made, they are likely to discount those doubts and not mention them to other group members. As a result, the group as a whole perceives that there is unanimous support for the decision, and group members actively try to prevent any negative information pertaining to the decision from being brought up for discussion.[60] Exhibit 15.5 summarizes Janis's basic model of the groupthink phenomenon. It is important to note that although groupthink occurs only in cohesive groups, many cohesive groups never succumb to this faulty mode of decision making.

A group leader can take the following steps specifically designed to prevent the occurrence of groupthink; these steps also contribute to good decision making in groups in general:[61]

- The group leader encourages all group members to be critical of proposed alternatives, to raise any doubts they may have, and to accept criticism of their own ideas. It is especially important for a group leader to subject his or her own viewpoint to criticism by other group members.

EXHIBIT 15.5

Groupthink

Source: Adapted from Irvin L. Janis, *Groupthink Psychological Studies of Policy Decisions and Fiascoes*, 2nd ed. Copyright © 1982 by Houghton Mifflin Company. Reprinted with permission.

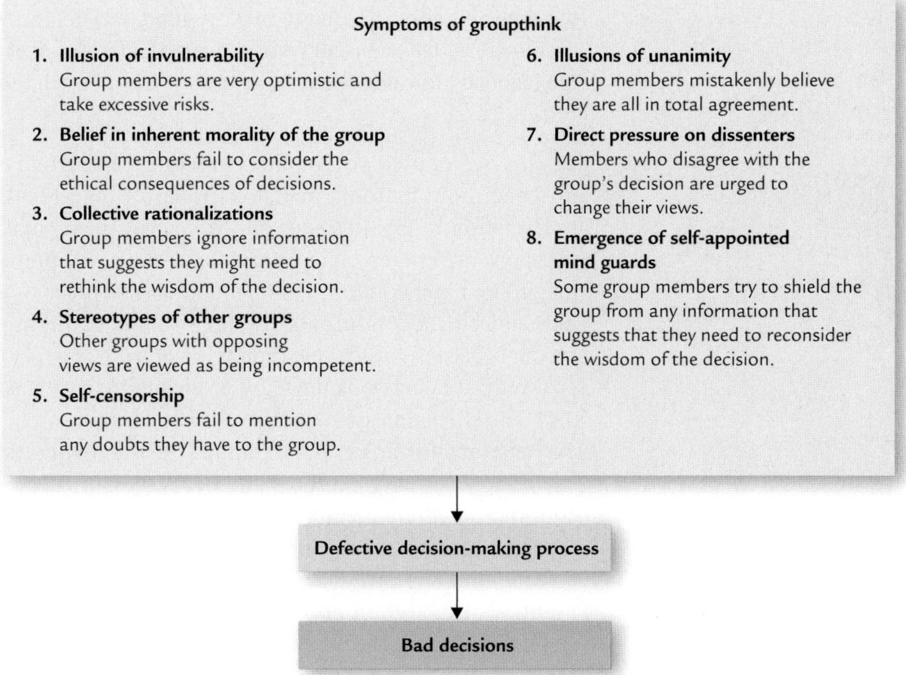

Symptoms of groupthink
1. Illusion of invulnerability
Group members are very optimistic and take excessive risks.
2. Belief in inherent morality of the group
Group members fail to consider the ethical consequences of decisions.
3. Collective rationalizations
Group members ignore information that suggests they might need to rethink the wisdom of the decision.
4. Stereotypes of other groups
Other groups with opposing views are viewed as being incompetent.
5. Self-censorship
Group members fail to mention any doubts they have to the group.
6. Illusions of unanimity
Group members mistakenly believe they are all in total agreement.
7. Direct pressure on dissenters
Members who disagree with the group's decision are urged to change their views.
8. Emergence of self-appointed mind guards
Some group members try to shield the group from any information that suggests that they need to reconsider the wisdom of the decision.
Defective decision-making process
Bad decisions

- The group leader refrains from expressing his or her own opinion and views until the group has had a chance to consider all alternatives. A leader's opinion given too early is likely to stifle the generation of alternatives and productive debate.
- The group leader encourages group members to gather information pertaining to a decision from people outside the group and to seek outsiders' perspectives on the group's ideas.
- Whenever a group meets, the group leader assigns one or two members to play the role of **devil's advocate**—that is, to criticize, raise objections, and identify potential problems with any decisions the group reaches. The devil's advocate should raise these problems even if he or she does not believe the points are valid.
- If an important decision is being made and time allows, after a group has made a decision, the group leader holds a second meeting. During the second meeting, members can raise any doubts or misgivings they might have about the course of action the group has chosen.

DEVIL'S ADVOCATE
Someone who argues against a cause or position in order to determine its validity.

Other Consequences of Group Decision Making

Three other consequences of group decision making are not easily classified as advantages or disadvantages: diffusion of responsibility, group polarization, and the potential for conflict.

Diffusion of responsibility. Group decisions are characterized by a diffusion of responsibility[62]—that is, the group as a whole rather than any one individual is accountable for the decision. If the decision was a good one, the group gets the credit; if the decision was a poor one, a single individual is not blamed.

Sometimes, when important decisions are made that entail considerable uncertainty, it can be very stressful for one individual to assume sole responsibility for the decision. Moreover, under these conditions, some people are inclined to make a decision they know will not come back to haunt them rather than the decision they think is best for the organization. When this is the case, diffusion of responsibility can be an advantage of group decision making.

Diffusion of responsibility can also be a disadvantage if group members do not take the time and effort needed to make a good decision because they are not held individually accountable. This consequence is related to the concept of social loafing (see Chapter 11), the tendency for individuals to exert less effort when they work in a group.

Group polarization. Another consequence of group decision making is that groups tend to make more extreme decisions than do individuals. This tendency is called group polarization.[63] By *extreme decisions* we mean making more risky or conservative decisions rather than taking a middle-of-the-road approach. For example, on the one hand, the group might commit a vast amount of resources to develop a new product that may or may not be successful. On the other hand, it might decide not to introduce any new products because of the uncertainty involved.

Why are decisions made by groups more extreme than decisions made by individuals? The diffusion of responsibility is one reason.[64] But there are at least two more explanations for group polarization. First, knowing that other group members have the same views or support the same decision can cause group members to become more confident of their positions.[65] Group members who initially supported committing a moderate amount of resources to the development of a new product may become more confident in the product's potential success after learning that other members of the group also feel good about the product. As a result of this increased confidence, the group makes the more extreme decision to commit a large amount of resources. Second, as a group discusses alternatives, members of the group often come up with persuasive arguments to support their favored alternative (say, for example, why the new product is "bound to be" a success).[66] As a result of these persuasive arguments, the group's confidence in the chosen alternative increases, and the decision becomes more extreme.

Potential for conflict. There is always the potential for conflict in decision-making groups. Group members differ in their knowledge, skills, and expertise as well as in their past experiences. These differences cause them to view opportunities and problems and responses to them in different ways. Moreover, certain group members may stand to benefit from one alternative being chosen over another, and self-interest may cause them to push for that alternative. Other group members may resent this pressure and disagree or push for an alternative that benefits them. Such conflict can be functional for groups and organizations when it forces them to evaluate the alternatives carefully. However, it can be dysfunctional when individual members become more concerned about winning the battle than making a good decision.

In summary, groups are used to make decisions when the decision requires a wide range of skills, knowledge, and expertise, or more information than a single individual could be expected to possess. Group decision making is time consuming, however, although IT can help reduce this problem. In addition, it is important to encourage group members to be critical of each other's ideas, to evaluate the different alternatives, and to follow the five steps that help prevent groupthink.

Decision Making in Crisis Situations

Earlier, we discussed how the psychologist Irvin Janis argued that many group interactions are characterized by a process known as groupthink that results in poor decision-making outcomes. Recall that groupthink occurs when a team of decision makers embarks on a course of action without questioning underlying assumptions. Typically, the team coalesces around a person or policy; it ignores or filters out information that can be used to question the policy and develops after-the-fact rationalizations for its decision. Commitment to mission or goals becomes based on an emotional, subjective rather than a cognitive, objective assessment of the "correct" course of action. The consequences are poor decisions.

You're the Management Expert

Solving Competition Between Teams

You're a management consultant who has been called in to help improve decision making at a large pharmaceutical company. The survival of the company depends on the number of successful new drugs developed by its research scientists. These scientists work in teams developing different kinds of drugs. Each team is committed to the success of its own drug project, and over time, they have become very competitive with one another. It has gotten to the point where each team has started to hoard information and knowledge that might actually be of use to other teams. The competition is reducing the quality of decision making and slowing down the drug development process.

Using the information in the chapter, suggest a program to improve the decision making process that both eliminates competition between teams and builds cooperation between them.

The phenomenon of groupthink may be especially likely to occur in crisis situations when decision makers lack first-hand, accurate information about events and so can process information according to their own preferred assumptions and values. Recall that Janis traced many past decision-making fiascoes to defective policymaking by government leaders who received social support from their in-group of advisers. For example, he suggested that President John F. Kennedy's inner circle suffered from groupthink when they collectively supported the decision to launch the Bay of Pigs invasion of Cuba, even though available information showed that it would be an unsuccessful venture and would damage U. S. relations with other countries. Some critics have pointed to the same process operating in the decision by the Bush government to invade Iraq despite the fact that available intelligence had not been able to uncover any evidence of weapons of mass destruction in Iraq at that time.

Janis has observed that groupthink-dominated groups are characterized by strong pressures toward uniformity, which make their members avoid raising controversial issues, questioning weak arguments, or calling a halt to soft-headed thinking. All these conditions are especially likely to be present in crisis situations where, as we noted in the last chapter, top decision makers may prefer to pass the buck so as to avoid assuming individual responsibility for decisions made. Instead, the group as a whole shares responsibility and this protects their collective interests, for no one person can be made the "scapegoat."

Thus, in crisis situations, it is especially important to use techniques like devil's advocacy, which requires the generation of a response plan to a crisis and then a critical analysis of the plan. When one member of the decision-making team assumes the role of devil's advocate and lists all the reasons why the response plan might fail, decision makers can become aware of the perils hidden in the recommended courses of action. Thus the people in charge of forming the top-level teams that respond to sudden crises might be well advised to build devil's advocacy into the decision-making process and employ one or more of the decision-making techniques discussed next.

Group Decision-Making Techniques

Several other techniques have been developed to help groups make good decisions that promote high levels of performance and positive attitudes and avoid some of the potential disadvantages of group decision making. In this section, we describe three of those techniques: brainstorming, the nominal group technique, and the Delphi technique. We also discuss some of the group decision-making techniques used in total quality management programs.

Brainstorming

BRAINSTORMING
A spontaneous, participative decision-making technique that groups use to generate a wide range of alternatives from which to make a decision.

Sometimes, groups do not consider as wide a range of alternative responses to opportunities and problems as they should. At other times, group members prematurely make a decision without adequately considering other alternatives. **Brainstorming** is a spontaneous, participative, decision-making technique that groups use to generate a wide range of alternatives from which to make a decision.[67] A typical brainstorming session proceeds like this:

1. Group members sit around a table, and one member of the group describes the problem or opportunity in need of a response.
2. Group members are encouraged to share their own ideas with the rest of the group in a free and open manner without any critical evaluation of the ideas.
3. Group members are urged to share their ideas no matter how far-fetched they may seem, to come up with as many ideas as they can, and to build on each others' suggestions.
4. One member of the group records the ideas on a chalkboard or flip chart as they are presented.

Although it seems that brainstorming groups would come up with a wide range of alternatives, research suggests that individuals working separately tend to generate more ideas than do brainstorming groups.[68] A group of marketing managers who brainstorm to come up with a catchy name for a new convertible sports car, for example, will in all likelihood come up with fewer ideas than will individual managers who dream up ideas on their own and then pool them. Why does this outcome occur? There are at least two reasons. First, even though members of brainstorming groups are encouraged to share even the wildest or strangest idea, and even though criticism is suppressed, group members tend to be inhibited from sharing all their ideas with others. Second, **production blocking** takes place. This loss of productivity has several causes.[69] Group members cannot give their full attention to generating alternatives because they are listening to other people's ideas. They forget some of their ideas while they are waiting for their turn to share them with the rest of the group. And only one person can speak at a time, so the number of ideas that can be presented is limited.

PRODUCTION BLOCKING
Loss of productivity in brainstorming groups due to various distractions and limitations inherent to brainstorming.

Electronic brainstorming can overcome some of these problems.[70] Group members can use personal computers to record their ideas while at the same time having access to alternatives generated by other group members on their computer screens. Electronic brainstorming is an effective means of preventing some of the production blocking that occurs when brainstorming groups meet face to face.[71]

The Nominal Group Technique

NOMINAL GROUP TECHNIQUE (NGT)
A decision-making technique that includes the following steps: group members generate ideas on their own and write them down, group members communicate their ideas to the rest of the group, and each idea is then discussed and critically evaluated by the group.

The **nominal group technique (NGT)** also can be used to overcome production blocking and is a way for groups that need to make a decision quickly to select an alternative.[72] Group members sit around a table, and one member of the group describes the problem or opportunity. Members are then given a certain amount of time (perhaps 20 or 30 minutes) to come up with ideas or alternative ways to respond to the problem or opportunity and write them down on a piece of paper. Because each member comes up with alternatives while brainstorming privately, the NGT avoids production blocking. Moreover, when the NGT is used, group members are encouraged to write down all their ideas no matter how bizarre they may seem. Doing this individually may help to overcome the inhibition that limits some brainstorming groups.

After writing down all of their ideas, members present them in a round-robin fashion: Each person seated at the table presents one idea at a time. One member records the ideas on a chalkboard or flip chart, and no discussion of the ideas takes place at this point. After all the ideas are listed, the group discusses them one by one. Members are allowed to raise questions and objections and critically evaluate each idea. After each alternative has been discussed, each member privately ranks all of the alternatives from most preferred to least preferred. The alternative that receives the highest ranking in the group is chosen, and the decision-making process is complete.

The NGT helps a group reach a decision quickly (sometimes in just a couple of hours), and it allows all of the ideas generated by the members to be considered. NGT is not feasible for complex decisions requiring the processing of large amounts of information and repeated group meetings. It is also not appropriate when it is important that all, or most, group members agree on the alternative chosen (a decision by a jury would be such an example).

The Delphi Technique

DELPHI TECHNIQUE
A decision-making technique in which a series of questionnaires are sent to experts on the issue at hand, though they never actually meet face to face.

When the **Delphi technique** is used, group members never meet face to face.[73] When a leader is faced with a problem or opportunity that needs to be responded to, the advice of experts in the area is sought through written communication. The leader describes the problem or opportunity and solicits their help by asking them to complete and return a questionnaire. After all the questionnaires have been returned, the leader compiles the responses and sends a summary of them to all group members, along with additional questions that need to be answered for a decision to be made. This process is repeated as many times as needed to reach a consensus or a decision that most of the experts think is a good one.

The Delphi technique has the advantage of not requiring group members who may be scattered around the country or the globe to meet face to face. Its principal disadvantages are that it can be time consuming, and it does not allow for group interaction. It also depends on the cooperation of the experts to respond promptly to the questionnaires and take the time needed to complete them carefully. These disadvantages can be overcome, to some extent, by using some of the new computer software being developed for work groups by companies like Microsoft.

Group Decision-Making Techniques Used in Total Quality Management

Total quality management (TQM)[74] is a philosophy and set of practices that have been developed to improve the quality of an organization's goods and services and the efficiency with which they are produced. Total quality management (which we discuss in detail in Chapter 18) includes two group decision-making techniques—benchmarking and empowerment—which can be used to improve group decision making in general. The objective of these techniques is to encourage group members to make suggestions and use their knowledge to come up with ways to reduce costs and waste and increase quality with the ultimate goal of pleasing the final customer. Benchmarking and empowerment can be used, for example, in manufacturing settings to reduce defects and recalls of new cars, in customer service departments to shorten the time it takes to respond to a customer complaint, and in accounting departments to make bills easier for customers to read.

Benchmarking. When groups make decisions, it is often difficult for group members to grasp exactly what they should be striving for or trying to achieve when they evaluate alternatives. A group's overall goal, for example, may be to increase performance and quality, but the level of performance or quality that the group should aim for may not be clear to group members. Benchmarking helps groups figure out what they should be trying to accomplish when making a decision. A benchmark is a standard against which something can be measured or judged.

BENCHMARKING
Selecting a high-performing group and using this group as a model.

Benchmarking involves selecting a high-performing group or organization that is currently providing high-quality goods or services to its customers and using this group or organization as a model. When a low-performing group needs to make a decision, members compare where their group is with where the benchmark group or organization is on some criterion of quality. They then try to determine how to reach the standard set by the group or organization being benchmarked. For example, when groups in express delivery organizations like DHL and UPS need to decide how to improve the quality of their services to customers, they sometimes use Federal Express's guarantee of next-day delivery and continuous tracking of letters and packages as benchmarks of what they should be striving for.

Empowerment. A guiding principle of total quality management is that performance and quality improvements are the responsibility of all organizational members. Employees are often in the best position to come up with ways to improve performance and quality. **Empowerment** is the process of giving these employees the authority to make decisions and be responsible for their outcomes. Empowerment often requires managers and other employees to change the ways they think about decision making. Rather than managers making the decisions and the rest of an organization's employees carrying them out, empowerment requires that the responsibility for decision making be shared throughout an organization.

EMPOWERMENT
The process of giving employees throughout an organization the authority to make decisions and be responsible for their outcomes.

Getting employees and managers to change the way they think about decision making in an organization can be difficult but also worth the effort. McDonald's, Federal Express, Citibank, and Xerox are among the growing list of companies using empowerment to improve group decision making.[75] Xerox has gone so far as to push its suppliers to use empowerment (and other TQM practices) to improve the quality of the parts Xerox buys from them.[76] For example, Trident Tools, located in Rochester, New York, supplies Xerox with electromagnetic components. Xerox helped train Trident employees to use TQM techniques like empowerment to improve the quality of Trident's parts. As a result of the training, groups of employees at Trident cut the number of steps in the company's materials-ordering process from 26 to 12, reducing the lead time needed to fill customer orders from 16 to 7 weeks. The employees also reduced the amount of time needed to design new components from 5 years to 16 months. The story of how managers at Plexus empowered the company's employees and created a learning organization is discussed in the following OB Today.

OB Today

How Plexus Decided It Could Make Flexible Manufacturing Pay Off

In the United States, over 2.3 million manufacturing jobs were lost to factories in low-cost countries abroad in 2003. While many large U. S. manufacturing companies have given up the battle, some companies like Plexus Corp., based in Neenah, Wisconsin, have been able to craft the decisions that have allowed them to survive and prosper in a low-cost manufacturing world.

Plexus started out making electronic circuit boards in the 1980s for IBM. In the 1990s, however, it saw the writing on the wall as more and more of its customers began to turn to manufacturers abroad to produce the components that go into their products, or even the whole product itself. The problem facing managers at Plexus was how to design a production system that could compete in a low-cost manufacturing world. U. S. companies cannot match the efficiency of foreign manufacturers in producing high volumes of a single product, such as millions of a particular circuit board used in a laptop computer. So Plexus's managers' decided to focus their efforts on developing a manufacturing technology, called "low-high," that could efficiently produce low volumes of many different kinds of products.

Plexus's engineers worked as a team to design a manufacturing facility in which products would be manufactured in four separate "focused factories." The production line in each factory is designed to allow the operations involved in making each product to be performed separately, although operations still take place in sequence. Workers are crosstrained so they can perform any of the operations in each factory. So, when work slows down at any point in the production of a particular product, a worker further along the line can step back to help solve the problem that occurred at the earlier stage on the line.

These workers are organized into self-managed teams empowered to make all of the decisions necessary to make a particular product in one of the four factories. Since each product is different, these teams have to quickly make the decisions necessary to assemble them if they are to do so cost effectively. The ability of these teams to make rapid decisions is vital on a production line because time is money. Every minute a production line is idle adds hundreds or thousands of dollars to the cost of production. To keep costs down, employees have to be able to react to unexpected contingencies and make nonprogrammed decisions, unlike workers on a conventional production line who simply follow a set performance program.

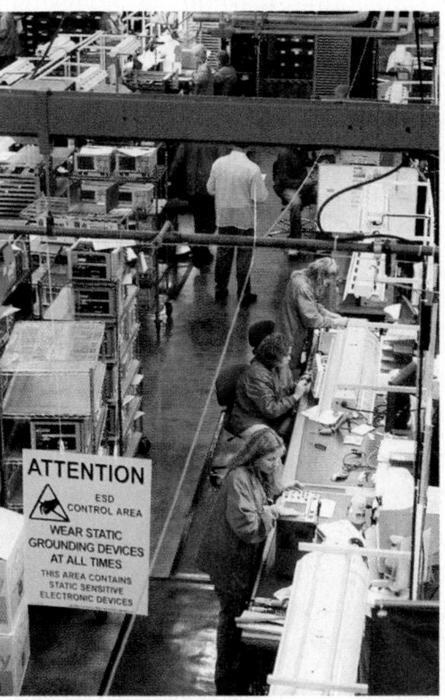

Other companies outsourced jobs to low-cost countries, but plexus, a Wisconsin-based circuit board maker, focused on teamwork, adaptation, and flexibility instead. Today, the company produces 2.5 times the number of circuit boards it did ten years ago when it had twice as many employees.

Team decision making also comes into play when the line is changed over to make a different product. Since nothing is being produced while this occurs, it is vital the changeover time be kept to a minimum. At Plexus, engineers and teams working together have reduced this time to as little as 30 minutes. Eighty percent of the time, the line is running and making products; only 20 percent of the time is it idle.[77] This incredible flexibility, developed by the members of the company working for years to improve the decisions involved in the changeover process, is the reason why Plexus is so efficient and can compete against low-cost manufacturers abroad. In fact, today, Plexus has about 400 workers, who can produce 2.5 times the product value that 800 workers could just a decade ago.

Quality is also one of the goals of the self-managed work teams. Employees know nothing is more important in the production of complex, low-volume products than a reputation for products that are reliable and have very low defect rates. By all accounts, both managers and workers are very proud of the way they have developed such an efficient operation. The emphasis at Plexus is on continuous learning to improve the decisions that go into the design of the production process.[78]

Organizational Learning

Because decision making takes place under uncertainty, and because of the errors that can affect decision making, it is not surprising that many of the decisions that managers and organizations make are mistakes and end in failure. Others, of course, allow an organization to succeed beyond managers' wildest dreams. Organizations survive and prosper when their members make the right decisions—sometimes through skill and sound judgment, sometimes through chance and good luck. For decision making to be successful over time, however, organizations must improve their abilities to make better decisions and reduce decision-making errors.

ORGANIZATIONAL LEARNING
The process through which managers seek to increase organization members' desire and ability to make decisions that continuously raise organizational efficiency and effectiveness.

One of the most important processes that can help managers make better decisions is organizational learning.[79] **Organizational learning** is a process managers seek out to improve the decision-making ability of employees and enhance organizational efficiency and effectiveness.[80] Because of the rapid pace of change in today's business environment, organizational learning is a vital activity that must be managed. This requires an understanding of how organizational learning occurs and the factors that can promote or impede it.

Types of Organizational Learning

EXPLORATION
Learning that involves organizational members searching for and experimenting with new kinds or forms of organizational behaviors and procedures to increase effectiveness.

EXPLOITATION
Learning that involves organizational members finding ways to refine and improve existing organizational behaviors and procedures to increase effectiveness.

LEARNING ORGANIZATION
An organization that purposefully takes steps to enhance and maximize the potential for explorative and exploitative organizational learning to take place.

James March, whose work on decision making was discussed earlier, proposed that two principal types of organizational learning strategies can be pursued to improve decision making: exploration and exploitation.[81] **Exploration** involves organizational members searching for and experimenting with new kinds or forms of behaviors and procedures to increase effectiveness. Learning that involves exploration might involve finding new ways to make and sell goods and services or inventing new ways to organize employees, such as developing crossfunctional or virtual teams.

Exploitation involves organizational members learning ways to refine and improve existing organizational behaviors and procedures to increase effectiveness. This might involve implementing a TQM program to promote the continuous refinement of existing operating procedures or developing an improved set of rules to enable a work group to more effectively perform its specific tasks.[82] Exploration is therefore a more radical learning process than exploitation although both are important for improved decision making that enhances the organization's effectiveness.[83]

A **learning organization** is an organization that purposefully takes steps to enhance and maximize the potential for explorative and exploitative organizational learning to take place.[84] How do managers create a learning organization, one capable of allowing its members to appreciate and respond quickly to changes taking place around it? By increasing the ability of employees at every level in the organization to question and analyze the way the organization performs its activities and to experiment with new ways to change it to increase effectiveness.

Principles of Organizational Learning

In order to create a learning organization, managers need to promote learning at the individual and group levels.[85] Some principles for creating a learning organization have been developed by Peter Senge and are discussed in the following paragraphs.[86] (See Exhibit 15.6.)

Personal mastery. At the individual level, managers need to do all they can to facilitate the learning of new skills, norms, and values so that individuals can increase their own personal ability to help build the organization's core competencies. Senge has argued that

EXHIBIT 15.6

Principles of Organizational Learning

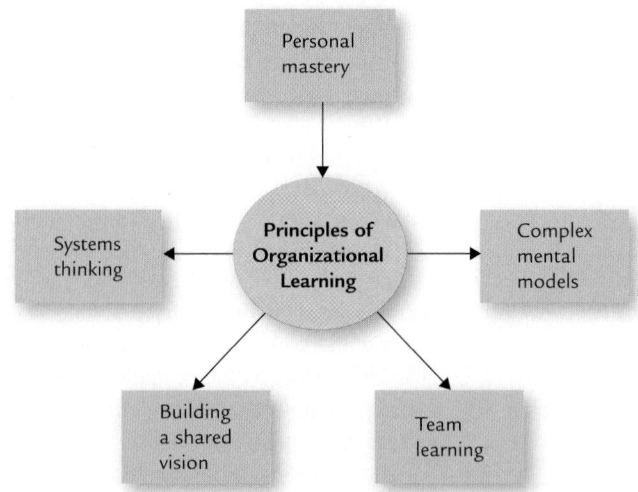

for organizational learning to occur, each person needs to develop a sense of *personal mastery*. Essentially, that means the organization should empower individuals to experiment and create and explore what they want. The goal is to give employees the opportunity to develop an intense appreciation for their work that translates into a distinctive competence for the organization.[87]

Complex mental models. As part of attaining personal mastery, and to give employees a deeper understanding of what is involved in a particular activity, organizations need to encourage employees to develop and use *complex mental models* that challenge them to find new or better ways to perform a task. As an analogy, a person might mow the lawn once a week and treat this as a chore that has to be done. However, suppose the person decides to study how the grass grows and to experiment with cutting the grass to different heights and using different fertilizers and watering patterns. Through this study, he or she notices that cutting the grass to a certain height and using specific combinations of fertilizer and water promote thicker growth and fewer weeds, resulting in a better-looking lawn that needs less mowing. What had once been a chore may become a hobby, and personal mastery is achieved. Looking at the task in a new way has become a source of deep personal satisfaction. This is the message behind Senge's principles for developing a learning organization. Namely, organizations must encourage each of their individual members to develop a taste for experimenting.[88]

A learning organization can encourage employees to form complex mental models and develop a sense of personal mastery by providing them with the opportunity to assume more responsibility for their decisions. This can be done in a variety of ways. Employees might be cross-trained so that they can perform many different tasks, and the knowledge they gain may give them new insights into how to improve work procedures. On the other hand, perhaps a specific task that was performed by several different employees can be redesigned or reengineered so that one employee, aided by an advanced information system, can perform the complete task. Again, the result may be an increase in the level of organizational learning as the employee finds new ways to get the job done.

Team learning. At the group level, managers need to encourage learning by promoting the use of various kinds of groups—such as self-managed groups or crossfunctional teams—so that individuals can share or pool their skills and abilities to solve problems. Groups allow for the creation of *synergy*—the idea that the whole is much more than the sum of its parts—which can enhance performance. In terms of Thompson's model of task interdependence discussed in Chapter 11, for example, the move from a pooled, to sequential, to reciprocal task interdependence will increase the potential for group-level learning because the group's members have more opportunities to interact and learn from one another over time. "Group routines" that enhance group effectiveness may develop from such interactions.[89] Senge refers to this kind of learning as *team learning,* and he argues that team learning is as, or even more, important than individual-level learning in promoting organizational learning. This is due to the fact that most important decisions are made in groups, like departmental and functional groups.

The ability of teams to bring about organizational learning was unmistakable when Toyota revolutionized the work process in a former GM factory in California. Large performance gains were achieved in the factory when Toyota's managers created work teams and empowered team members to take over the responsibility for measuring, monitoring, and controlling their own behavior to find ways to continuously increase performance.

Building a shared vision. Another one of Senge's principles for designing a learning organization emphasizes the importance of *building shared vision*. Building a shared vision involves creating an ongoing frame of reference or mental model that all of the organization's members use to frame problems or opportunities and that binds them to an organization. At the heart of this vision is likely to be the set of work values and norms that guide behavior in a particular setting.

Systems thinking. Senge's last principle of organizational learning, *systems thinking*, emphasizes that in order to create a learning organization, managers must recognize how learning at the individual and group levels affect each other. For example, there is little point in creating teams to facilitate team learning if an organization does not also take steps to give its employees the freedom to develop a sense of personal mastery. By encouraging and promoting organizational learning at each of these levels—that is, by looking at organizational learning as a *system*—managers can build and create a learning organization that facilitates an organization's ability to make high-quality decisions rapidly. The way in which Nike built a learning organization to respond to the changes constantly taking place around it is discussed in the following OB Today.

Leadership and Learning

While Phil Knight might encourage learning from employees below him in the hierarchy,

OB Today

Nike Creates a Learning Organization

Nike, headquartered in Beaverton, Oregon, is the biggest sports shoemaker in the world. In the 1990s, it seemed that its founder and CEO Phil Knight and his team of shoe designers could put no wrong foot forward, and all their design decisions led to the global acceptance of Nike's shoes and record sales and profits for the company. At the heart of Nike's business plan was its decision to design very expensive high-performance shoes that often sold for more than $100. Frequently, the shoes were touted by celebrities like Michael Jordan and Tiger Woods.[90]

Nike's designers and marketers are continually working to discover better ways to satisfy peoples' different needs for athletic and walking shoes. Their goal is to "thrill" customers and make buying a new pair of Nike shoes a major event—something worth the $120+ price Nike charges for its new shoes.

As time went on, however, and Nike's fortunes soared, some strange dynamics took place. The company's managers and designers became convinced they "knew best" what customers needed and that their choices and decisions about future shoe lines would unquestionably be well received by customers who would continue to flock to buy their new creations.

But things were changing in the sport-shoe environment. Many new competitors had entered the market, and they began to offer alternative kinds of sports shoes—shoes targeted at specific market segments like skateboarders, soccer players, or power walkers. Nike had no shoes in these market segments. Moreover, Nike also failed to notice that sports shoes were evolving into performance shoes for more everyday uses such as walking or backpacking. It also failed to take note of consumers' increasing preferences for dark blue and black shoes that wore well in cities and that could double as work and walking shoes.

By the end of the 1990s, Nike's sales and profits started to fall sharply. Many of its new lines of sports shoes were not well received by customers, and CEO Phil Knight knew he had to find a way to turnaround his company's performance. Realizing that his designers were starting to make poor decisions, he decided to bring in people from outside the company to try to change the way decisions were made. One of these was an executive named Gordon O. McFadden, who was brought in to lead the outdoor products division. He advised Knight to take over and purchase some of these small companies, such as North Face, to quickly widen Nike's product line. But Nike's managers and designers resisted this idea believing that they could still make the best decisions and that Nike should continue to grow its product lines from within. So, McFadden quit.[91]

By 2000, with sales still slumping, it became obvious that Nike would have to take over some competing shoe companies in order to grow successfully. One of the first of its acquisitions was ColeHann, the luxury shoemaker, and Nike's designers proceeded to revitalize its line of shoes by using their skills to make them more comfortable. Then, realizing it had to get into small markets, in 2002, Nike bought other small companies such as Hurley, the skate and surfboard apparel maker.

To try to overcome its past errors in its decision making, however, Knight decided on a new way to design shoes for specialized niche markets, like the skateboarding, golf, and soccer markets. Henceforth, rather than having Nike's designers all grouped together in one large design department, they would be split up into different teams. Each team would focus on developing unique products to match the needs of customers in its assigned market segment. The skate team, for example, was set up as a separate and independent unit, and its eleven designers and marketing experts were charged with coming up with a unique line of shoes for the sport. Similarly, because of poor sales, Nike separated golf products from the rest of the company and created an independent unit to develop new golf shoes, clubs, and other golfing products.[92]

What Nike was trying to accomplish with the change was to obliterate the company-wide, decision-making mindset that had resulted in its past decision-making errors. With many different teams, each working on different lines of shoes and other products, Nike was hoping to build diversity into its decision making and create teams of experts who were attuned to changing customer needs in their segments of the sports product market.

So far, it seems that Nike's new approach to decision making is working better. Many of its new products lines have been well-received, and its sales and profits have started to rebound. Nike has apparently learned from its mistakes. Indeed, Knight is trying to promote organizational learning—the process of helping the members of an organization to "think outside the box" and be willing to experiment, take risks, and be different. Knight's current willingness to delegate authority and empower the different units to take responsibility for their own product lines is one example of this.

apparently he does not encourage this from his top executives. In 2004, he appointed William Perez as CEO of Nike to take responsibility for its future strategic decision making.[93] However, just 13 months later in January 2006, the new CEO resigned claiming that Knight would not give him the autonomy to make those decisions and that he was constantly "micro-managing" his CEO and that he could not make any important decisions!

Encouraging organizational learning is a complex, difficult process precisely because it takes an organization and its decision makers on an uncharted route fraught with dangers and uncertainty. Yet uncertainty is at the heart of unprogrammed decision making and, as in the opening case, if decision makers are not prepared to make hard choices and meet customer needs, companies like Mattel can quickly lose out and see their profitability deteriorate.

By all accounts the best companies are those that encourage learning and nowhere is this clearer than at General Electric (GE), whose previous and current CEOs are on top of the learning game. GE's charismatic CEO Jeff Immelt has an approach to leadership that is

Jack Welch made organizational learning the basis of his approach to managing organizational behavior at GE. Welch continually employed new techniques such as total quality management and Six Sigma to challenge and motivate people to be innovative and creative.

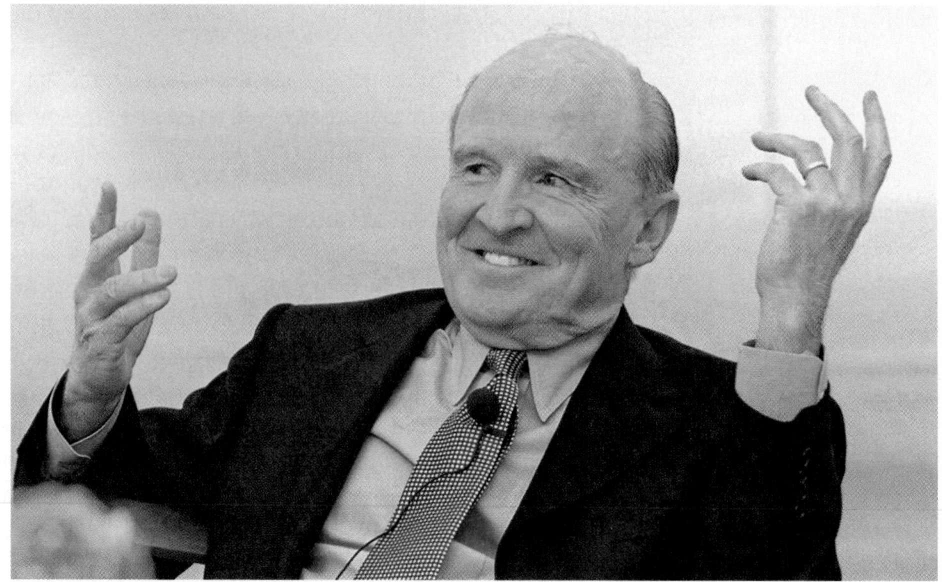

defined by his commitment to make GE a learning organization. Immelt has seen the importance of learning his entire career at GE, for his predecessor Jack Welch made organizational learning the foundation of his approach too. Welch was constantly employing new techniques such as total quality management, Six Sigma, and creating challenging evaluation and compensation systems to reward people for their innovative and creative ideas.

Immelt believes that in today's rapidly changing global environment the basis for successful decision making is not how much managers and employees know but how quickly they can learn new ways to respond. Consequently, Immelt makes organizational learning a cornerstone of his approach to leadership because he has seen the results of successful learning—continuous improvement in the way his company performs and flexibility that is the envy of companies many times smaller than GE.

At the center of learning in GE is its Crotonville "GE University," where every year thousands of GE's up and coming managers go through intensive learning programs designed to make them "learning managers." Furthermore, at GE promotion is based on a manager's perceived ability to learn quickly; this is a sign that a manager has leadership potential. Indeed, Immelt feels that continuous learning is a hallmark of all great CEOs who see encouraging and rewarding it as a main way of ensuring a company's continuing success.

One important way in which learning takes place is through benchmarking other companies. As discussed earlier, benchmarking is the process of choosing a company that possesses exceptional skills in performing a functional activity, such as marketing, materials management, or manufacturing, and then learning the specific routines and processes that enable it to perform at such a high level. Benchmarking gives a company's employees a goal or standard to achieve—GE benchmarks Toyota, Dell, and Procter & Gamble. From Toyota and Dell, the leaders, GE learns how to improve its manufacturing and materials management processes, and from P&G how to market new and existing products to customers in innovative ways. Leadership and learning go hand in hand today.

Summary

The decisions made by employees at all levels in organizations can have a major impact on levels of performance and well-being and on the extent to which individuals, groups, and whole organizations achieve their goals. In this chapter, we made the following major points:

1. Decision making is the process by which members of an organization choose how to respond to opportunities and problems. Nonprogrammed decision making occurs when members of an organization choose how to respond to novel opportunities and problems. Nonprogrammed decision making involves a search for information.

Programmed decision making occurs when members of an organization respond to recurring opportunities and problems by using standard responses (performance programs). This chapter focuses on nonprogrammed decision making.

2. The classical model of decision making is a prescriptive model that assumes that decision makers have access to all the information they need and will make the best decision possible. A decision maker using the classical model takes these four steps: (a) listing all alternatives, (b) listing the consequences of each alternative, (c) considering his or her preferences for each alternative or set of consequences, and (d) selecting the alternative that will result in the most preferred set of consequences. Decisions made according to the classical model are optimal decisions.
3. There are problems with the classical model because it is not realistic. Decision makers often do not know all the alternatives they can choose from, often do not know the consequences of each alternative, may not be clear about their own preferences, and in many cases lack the mental ability to take into account all the information required by the classical model. Moreover, the classical model can be very time consuming.
4. March and Simon's administrative decision-making model is descriptive; it explains how decisions are actually made in organizations. March and Simon propose that decision makers choose how to respond to opportunities and problems on the basis of a simplified and approximate account of the situation called the decision maker's definition of the situation. This definition is the result of both psychological and sociological processes. Rather than making optimal decisions, decision makers often satisfice, or make an acceptable decision, not necessarily an optimal decision. Satisficing occurs because of bounded rationality.
5. Heuristics are rules of thumb that simplify decision making but can lead to errors or biases. The availability heuristic reflects the tendency to determine the frequency of an event and its causes by how easy they are to remember (how available they are from memory). The availability heuristic can lead to biased decision making when the frequency of events and causes is overestimated because they are vivid, extreme, or recent. The representativeness heuristic reflects the tendency to predict the likelihood of an event from the extent to which the event is typical (or representative) of similar kinds of events that have happened in the past. Representativeness can lead to biased decision making when decision makers fail to take into account base rates. The anchoring and adjustment heuristic reflects the tendency to make decisions based on adjustments from some initial amount (or anchor). The anchoring and adjustment heuristic can lead to biased decision making when the initial amounts were too high or too low.
6. Escalation of commitment is the tendency of decision makers to invest additional time, money, or effort into losing courses of action. Escalation of commitment occurs because decision makers do not want to admit that they have made a mistake, view further commitment of resources as a way to recoup sunk costs, and are more likely to take risks when decisions are framed in negative rather than in positive terms.
7. The advantages of using groups instead of individuals to make decisions include the availability and diversity of members' skills, knowledge, and expertise; enhanced memory for facts; capability of error detection; and greater decision acceptance. The disadvantages of group decision making include the time it takes to make a decision and the potential for groupthink. Other consequences include diffusion of responsibility, group polarization, and the potential for conflict.
8. Group decision-making techniques used in organizations include brainstorming, the nominal group technique, and the Delphi technique. Two group decision-making techniques used in total quality management are benchmarking and empowerment.
9. Two main types of organizational learning that can lead to improved decision making are explorative and exploitative learning. Organizations can improve their members' ability to make high-quality decisions by encouraging them to develop personal mastery and complex mental models, through team learning, by building a shared vision, and through systems thinking.

Exercises in Understanding and Managing Organizational Behavior

Questions for Review

1. Do programmed decisions and the use of performance programs always evolve from what were originally nonprogrammed decisions? Why or why not?
2. For what kinds of decisions might the classical model be more appropriate than March and Simon's model?
3. How might the anchoring and adjustment heuristic affect goal setting?
4. Can the availability and the representativeness heuristics operate simultaneously? Why or why not?
5. How might decision-making groups fall into the escalation-of-commitment trap?
6. Why do members of diverse groups sometimes find it hard to make a decision?
7. In what ways can conflict in a decision-making group be both an advantage and a disadvantage?
8. Do all employees want to be empowered and make the decisions that their bosses used to make? Why or why not?
9. What is the relationship between the anchoring and adjustment heuristic and benchmarking?

OB: Increasing Self-Awareness

Analyzing Individual and Group Decisions

Think of two important decisions that you have recently made—one that you made individually and one that you made as a member of a group. Describe each decision. For each decision, answer these questions:

1. Was the process by which you made the decision more accurately described by the classical model or by March and Simon's model? Why?
2. In what ways were heuristics involved in making the decision?
3. Was escalation of commitment involved in making the decision?
4. Why did you make the individual decision on your own rather than in a group? Do you think a better decision would have been made if the decision had been made in a group? Why or why not?
5. Why did you make the other decision as a member of a group rather than on your own? Do you think that you could have made a better decision on your own? Why or why not?

A Question of Ethics

As the chapter discusses, the question of whether a decision is ethical or not is an important aspect of the decision-making process. In group decision making, sometimes the diffusion of responsibility can lead a group to make an extreme and unethical decision because the responsibility for it is spread over all group members. With this in mind, think about the following issues:

- To what extent to you believe each member of the group is aware that *collectively*, they might be making an unethical decision?
- What steps could be taken to make individual group members be more outspoken in suggesting a possible course of action is unethical?

Small Group Break-Out Exercise

Brainstorming

After reading the following scenario, break up into groups of three or four people and discuss the issues involved. Be prepared to discuss your thinking with the rest of the class.

You and your partners are trying to decide which kind of restaurant to open in a new shopping center in your city. The problem confronting you is that the city already has many restaurants that provide different kinds of food in all price ranges. Your challenge is to decide which type of restaurant is most likely to succeed. Using the brainstorming technique, follow these steps to make your decision:

1. As a group, spend 5 or 10 minutes generating ideas about the alternative kinds of restaurants you think will be most likely to succeed. Write down the alternatives.
2. Spend 5 to 10 minutes debating the pros and cons of the alternatives and try to reach a group consensus.

Topic for Debate

Decision making is one of the most important processes in all organizations. Now that you have a good understanding of decision making, debate the following issue.

Team A. Individuals generally make better decisions than groups.

Team B. Groups generally make better decisions than individuals.

Experiential Exercise

Using the Nominal Group Technique

Objective

Your objective is to gain experience in using the nominal group technique.

Procedure

The class divides into groups of three to five people, and each group appoints one member as spokesperson to report the group's experiences to the whole class. Here is the scenario.

Assume the role of a self-managed work team. The team is one of the best-performing teams in the company, and the members like and get along well with each other. Currently, team members are paid an hourly wage based on seniority. The company has decided to change the way in which members of all self-managed teams are paid and has asked each team to propose a new pay plan. One plan will be chosen from those proposed and instituted for all teams.

Use the nominal group technique to decide on a pay plan by following these steps:

1. Each team member comes up with ideas for alternative pay plans on his or her own and writes them down on a piece of paper.
2. Team members present their ideas one by one while one member records them on a piece of paper. There is no discussion of the merits of the different alternatives at this point.
3. Team members discuss the ideas one by one and raise any questions or objections. Critical evaluation takes place at this step.
4. Each team member privately ranks all the alternatives from most preferred to least preferred.
5. The team chooses the alternative that receives the highest ranking.

After the decision has been made, team members discuss the pros and cons of using the nominal group technique to make a decision like this one.

When your group has completed the exercise, the spokesperson will report back to the whole class on the decision the group reached as well as the group's assessment of the pros and cons of the nominal group technique.

New York Times *Cases in the News*

The New York Times

"Buyer's Remorse Is Causing Some Palpitations at Johnson & Johnson."

By Stephanie Paul, NYT, November 5, 2005, p. C1.

Johnson & Johnson's stumble in the purchase of the Guidant Corporation, the medical device maker, illustrates the perils of designing a corporate strategy around acquisitions. Until recently, Johnson & Johnson served as the rare example of a company that could execute such a strategy successfully. From 1995 to the end of last year, Johnson & Johnson bought 51 companies. Most of the acquisitions have been regarded as smart and successful, in part because the company prides itself on a slow, deliberative vetting process before making purchases. But like a new homeowner who has discovered a leak in the basement, Johnson & Johnson is experiencing buyer's remorse this time, particularly because Guidant is Johnson & Johnson's largest acquisition ever.

After the Federal Trade Commission approved the Guidant deal yesterday, Johnson & Johnson said it would not complete the $25.4 billion acquisition unless Guidant agreed to renegotiate the terms. In a statement, Johnson & Johnson cited product recalls of some Guidant heart devices and federal investigations of the company. The deal had been viewed as important to Johnson & Johnson's long-term strategy. It gave the company a chance to build a cardiac rhythm business, a fast-growing area. If Johnson & Johnson cannot persuade Guidant to agree on a lower price, some analysts expect Johnson & Johnson to look elsewhere to complete its strategy. The problem is other heart device makers may not want to do business with a company that just walked away from a deal. Johnson & Johnson's problems with the Guidant deal are not unique. Even before the deal began to unravel, questions had been raised about the wisdom of several other Johnson & Johnson purchases, as well as the way some companies have been integrated into the corporate family.

The deals illustrate the risk of aggressive buying. A medical product that looks promising on the surface can face regulatory problems or quickly turn into a lemon. And the seller always knows more than the buyer. While Johnson & Johnson has generally done a good job of taming the octopus—a far-flung collection of more than 200 operating companies with more than 115,000 employees—it has not always capitalized on the innovative abilities of the companies it acquires, according to Sydney Finkelstein, a management professor at the Tuck School of Business at Dartmouth. As an example, Mr. Finkelstein points to Johnson & Johnson's 1996 takeover of Cordis for $1.8 billion. While the acquisition was a chance for Johnson & Johnson to cement its early lead in the stent business, crucial Cordis talent, accustomed to an entrepreneurial approach, clashed with Johnson & Johnson's more top-down structure, he said. Some decided to leave the company.

"They tend not to be able to retain the innovative capability," Mr. Finkelstein said. "That resides in people." Because of the resulting delays in stent innovation, Johnson & Johnson left the door wide open for competitors, including Guidant, allowing other companies to capture the bulk of the stent market by 1998, according to Mr. Finkelstein. It took Johnson & Johnson several years to recover.

Retaining talent will be a major issue as Johnson & Johnson tries to renegotiate with Guidant. With many Guidant employees holding large amounts of stock, Johnson & Johnson runs the risk of angering vital Guidant employees if it pushes too hard, according to Jan David Wald, a financial analyst for A. G. Edwards & Sons who formerly worked for Guidant.

Questions for Discussion

1. What is buyer's remorse? Why is it a decision-making error?
2. Why did J&J's decision to buy Cordis run into problems? What can J&J learn from the Cordis acquisition that will help it devise a plan to motivate and retain Guidant employees?

The New York Times

"A Gamble on LCD TV's Meant Survival for Sharp"

By Martin Fackler, NYT, March 22, 2006, p. C1.

In corporate Japan, companies have long preferred to run with the pack. But some are now learning to act like lone wolves. Take Sharp, which for decades looked like other big Japanese electronics makers, producing every device under the sun from rice cookers to semiconductors. But when the company faced collapse eight years ago, its newly installed president, Katsuhiko Machida, jettisoned unprofitable products and bet Sharp's future on a single, then-unproven new product: flat-panel televisions using a screen technology called liquid-crystal display. The gamble paid off. Sharp now reaps record profits as a leader in the booming global market for L.C.D. televisions. "Survival today means innovating and doing things that no one else does," Mr. Machida said. "This is a lesson not only for Sharp but for all of Japan."

It is a lesson that the business world here has apparently taken to heart, as a wave of corporate revamping and innovation breathes new life into Japan's long-moribund economy. And as these lone wolves multiply, they may help Japan play a stronger role in global growth as the world's second-largest economy. Companies from supermarket chains to camera makers are moving away from traditional conformity. They have gotten more aggressive about containing costs after spending Japan's lost decade of stagnant economic growth closing factories, shrinking payrolls and writing off debt. More companies are also acting like Sharp, trying to set themselves apart from rivals with unique products and services. The changes are rewriting the rules of Japan's business culture, where for decades after World War II companies marched in lock step to advance the nation's economy. That collectivist system broke down when Japan's economy stalled and even contracted in the 1990's after the collapse of twin bubbles in the real estate and stock markets. "It's a new era for Japanese business," said John C. Beck, president of the business consulting company North Star Leadership and co-author of "Japan's Business Renaissance." "Japan has become much more entrepreneurial and innovative. Companies are taking new risks, going into new areas, making new products."

At Sharp, Mr. Machida said he had learned to take risks because the company had no choice. Sharp had thrived during the postwar years with products like hand-held calculators. But when Mr. Machida took the helm in 1998, weak domestic sales and cheaper Asian competition had plunged the 94-year-old company into its worse crisis since an earthquake flattened its original factory in 1923. As profit plummeted, Mr. Machida decided to shrink or halt production of semiconductors, computer monitors and tube televisions, which were major product lines where Sharp could no longer compete on price. Mr. Machida said he decided the only way to beat cheaper manufacturers was to stay ahead technologically. He said he chose flat-panel televisions to take advantage of L.C.D. technology that Sharp had originally developed in the 1970's for calculator screens. "The old way of doing things was just spreading us too thin," Mr. Machida said in an interview at Sharp's headquarters in this industrial city in western Japan.

Mr. Machida spent his first year as president making almost daily trips to Sharp offices and factory floors around Japan, exhorting employees to work extra hard to make his plan a success. "If we don't do this, Sharp has no future," Mr. Machida repeatedly said, according to employees. Many listened sullenly, unwilling to contradict their boss in public. Mr. Machida faced a particularly tough sell at Sharp's computer panel division, whose products he was scrapping. In town-hall-style meetings with 50 to 100 employees at a time, he said South Korean and Taiwanese manufacturers could make the same panels, and he challenged his engineers to raise the quality of L.C.D. screens high enough to work for televisions. He set technical goals, such as tripling the contrast ratio, a way of measuring picture sharpness, within three years. Employees said they were skeptical at first that L.C.D.'s could work, particularly for large televisions. But support quickly grew as they reached targets ahead of schedule. Sharp gained an early lead in L.C.D. televisions that it still strives to maintain. In October, it will open the first factory in the world to use so-called eighth-generation L.C.D. production technology, which increases production by using glass panels as large as a king-size bed but only as thick as a postcard. Sharp now competes in the global L.C.D. market with companies more than 10 times its size, like Sony and Samsung Electronics.

"We are constantly telling employees to push ahead," said Shigeaki Mizushima, head of Sharp's L.C.D. division. "We can't stand still for a moment."

Questions for Discussion

1. In what ways is Sharp's decision to go into the LCD-screen market an example of nonprogrammed decision making?
2. What kind of decisions did Mr. Machida make to promote organizational learning throughout Sharp? Why has Sharp succeeded so far?

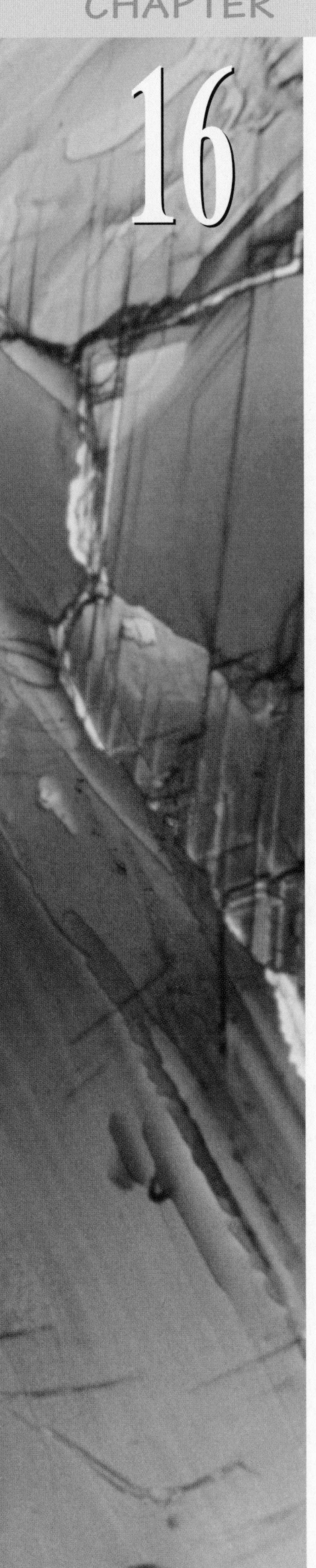

ORGANIZATIONAL DESIGN AND STRUCTURE

Learning Objectives

By the end of this chapter, you should be able to:

- Understand the relationship between organizational design and an organization's structure.
- Explain the main contingencies affecting the process of organizational design and differentiate between a mechanistic and an organic structure.
- Cite the advantages of grouping people into functions and divisions and distinguish between the main forms of organizational structure from which an organization can choose.
- Explain why coordination becomes a problem with the growth of an organization and differentiate between the three main methods it can use to overcome this problem and link its functions and divisions.
- Gain an understanding of the enormous impact modern information technology has had on the process of organizational design and structure both inside organizations and between them.

Opening Case

HOME DEPOT'S NEW MILITARY-STYLE STRUCTURE

How has Bob Nardelli changed his organization's structure?

The way in which Home Depot, the home improvement supply chain, has recently changed its organizational structure to better motivate and coordinate employees provides some good lessons in organizational behavior. The company's founders, Bernie Marcus and Arthur Blank, saw an opportunity to open a home improvement "superstore" and to offer a range and variety of products at low prices that no other home improvement store then in existence could match. They opened their first store in Atlanta, Georgia in 1979, and its huge success encouraged them to rapidly expand the number of their stores.[1] Because their young company was growing so quickly, they decided to give individual store managers considerable freedom to order and stock the kinds of products local and regional customers wanted to buy.

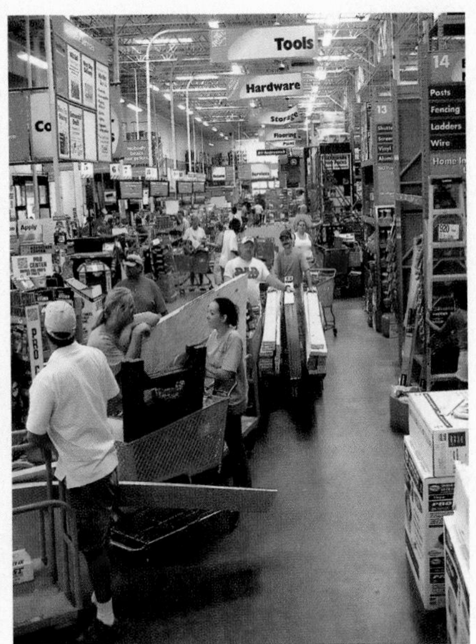

Home improvement stores Lowes and Home Depot have been fighting to expand their share of the market in the 2000s. Despite increasing performance, Bob Nardelli, Home Depot's CEO, resigned in January 2007 and left with a severance package valued at $210 million.

This decentralized approach to operating the store chain worked well until the huge profits Home Depot was earning attracted new competitors into the home improvement market, such as Lowe's. Lowe's managers had watched Home Depot's rapid growth and were convinced they could do better. In particular, they believed Home Depot's weakness was its poor-quality customer service and poor store layout, which was very similar to a warehouse. Lowe's managers designed stores so they easy for ordinary "unskilled" homeowners to shop in, they made sure lots of help was available, and they decided to stock a standardized range of products in all their stores to reduce costs. The result was that Lowe's quickly caught up with Home Depot in the 1990s; Home Depot's stock collapsed when investors feared it was downhill from here on.

Home Depot's founders decided it was time for a change; they searched for a new CEO to turnaround their company's performance. Bob Nardelli, a former GE top manager, was their choice. Nardelli had a reputation for finding ways to lower costs and overhead while giving customers what they wanted.[2] Nardelli also has a military background, and he understood the advantages of a centralized chain of command and uniform, standardized operating procedures to get the job done quickly and efficiently. Since 2002, Nardelli has worked to develop a military-style organization for Home Depot.[3] He has steadily recentralized authority over time and removed store managers' abilities to choose what products to stock for their individual stores. His goal was to streamline and centralize Home Depot's purchasing activities at its Atlanta headquarters to reduce costs. At the same time, he realized the need to attract customers by increasing the number of new, innovative products Home Depot stocks for them. Nardelli also created a sophisticated organization-wide IT system that provides store-by-store performance comparisons and each store manager knows how well their store is doing and where it ranks on this hierarchy. Now, top management has realtime, military-like information on how its "forces" are succeeding in the field.

Within eighteen months his new organizational structure worked—Home Depot's costs fell and its sales increased as customers responded to his new way of operating. This promising beginning convinced Nardelli that his new "mechanistic style" of organizing is the right one for increasing efficiency in the future. In fact, he has been busily recruiting ex-military officers, who understand his organizing approach, to help him. By 2005, Home Depot had recruited more than 17,000 ex-military personnel to manage its 1,600 stores and Nardelli's own personal assistant is an ex-marine staff Colonel.

Nardelli believes the home improvement business is not "rocket science," and that a company that focuses on keeping its costs low and giving its customers the most value will be the one that performs best in the long run. In 2006, however, Lowe's was continuing to perform well, and despite Home Depot's rapid recovery, it has its work cut out to remain the market leader—for, while its profits are up, Lowe's is still catching up.[4] In January 2007, despite 5 years of improved performance, declining stock price led Home Depot's board of directors to ask for Nardelli's resignation.

Overview

The Home Depot's experience suggests that the way an organization is designed has a major affect on the way employees behave and how well it operates. Moreover, with competition increasing in every market, like the home improvement market, it is imperative that companies continue to find new ways to operate efficiently and flexibly. In this chapter we first examine the nature of organizational design and structure, and we then discuss the main contingencies or changing conditions that affect the way a particular organization is designed. Second, we look at the different ways in which people and groups can be arranged to create an organizational structure that allows them to best achieve an organization's goals. Third, we examine the methods organizations use to coordinate and integrate people and groups to ensure that they work together well. Finally, we focus on the way new forms of information technology are changing the way organizations manage their activities.

ORGANIZATIONAL STRUCTURE
The formal system of task and reporting relationships that controls, coordinates, and motivates employees so that they cooperate and work together to achieve an organization's goals.

Designing Organizational Structure

ORGANIZATIONAL DESIGN
The process by which managers select and manage various dimensions and components of organizational structure and culture so that an organization can achieve its goals.

Organizing is the process of establishing the structure of working relationships among employees to allow them to achieve organizational goals effectively. **Organizational structure** is the formal system of task and job reporting relationships that determines how employees use resources to achieve the organization's goals.[5] **Organizational design** is the process of making the specific choices about how to arrange the tasks and job relationships that comprise the organizational structure.[6]

CONTINGENCY THEORY
Organizational structure should be designed to match the set of contingencies—factors or conditions—that cause an organization the most uncertainty.

According to **contingency theory**, an organization's structure needs to be designed to fit or match the set of contingencies—factors or conditions—that affect it the most and cause it the most uncertainty.[7] Since each organization faces a different set of contingencies, there is no "one best way" to design an organization: The best design is one that fits the organization's specific situation. Three important contingencies that factor into the design of organizational structure are: (1) the nature of the organization's environment, (2) advances in technology (increasingly, information technology), and (3) the characteristics of an organization's human resources.[8] Each of these is discussed in detail next, followed by the way they affect an organization's structure.

The Organizational Environment

We examined several forces in the environment that affect organizational behavior such as changes in the social, cultural, and global environment in Chapter 1. In general, the more quickly forces in the environment are changing, the greater the uncertainty within it, and the greater are the problems of quickly accessing resources the organization needs to perform well, like additional capital, plants, and equipment. In order to speed up the decision-making and communication processes related to obtaining resources, the most likely choice of design will be one that brings flexibility to the organization.[9] In this case, an organization is more likely to decentralize authority and empower its employees to make important operating decisions.[10] Since change is occurring everywhere in today's global environment, finding ways to structure organizations to empower self-managed teams and employees is on the rise.[11]

In contrast, if the environment is stable, resources are readily available, and uncertainty is low, then less coordination and communication among people and functions is needed to obtain resources. Organizational design choices can be made that bring more stability or formality to the structure. A more clearly defined hierarchy of authority and extensive body of rules and regulations is likely to be appropriate in this case.

Technology

TECHNOLOGY
The combination of skills, knowledge, tools, machines, computers, and equipment used in the design, production, and distribution of goods and services.

Technology is the combination of skills, knowledge, tools, machines, computers, and equipment that is used in the design, production, and distribution of goods and services. As a rule, the more complicated the technology that an organization uses, the more difficult it is to regulate and control it. Thus, in contingency theory, the more complicated the technology, the greater is the need for a flexible structure to allow an organization to respond to unexpected situations and provide its employees with the freedom to work out new solutions to the problems they encounter using it.[12] In contrast, the more routine the technology, the more appropriate is a formal structure because tasks are simple and the steps needed to produce goods and services have been worked out in advance.

What makes a technology routine or complicated? One researcher who investigated this issue, Charles Perrow, argued that two factors determine how complicated or nonroutine technology is: task variety and task analyzability.[13] *Task variety* is the number of new or unexpected problems or situations that a person or functional group encounters while performing tasks or jobs. *Task analyzability* is the degree to which programmed solutions are available to people or functional groups to solve the problems they encounter.

EXHIBIT 16.1

Three Contingencies Affecting Organizational Design

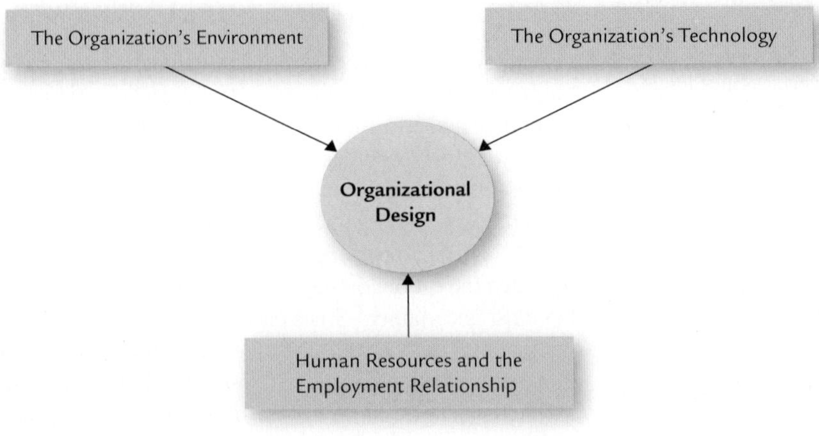

Nonroutine or complicated technologies are characterized by high task variety and low task analyzability; this means that many varied problems occur and that solving these problems requires significant nonprogrammed decision making. In contrast, routine technologies are characterized by low task variety and high task analyzability; this means that the problems encountered do not vary much and are easily resolved through programmed decision making.

Examples of nonroutine technology are found in the way scientists in a research and development laboratory develop new products or discover new drugs, or in the way emergency or operating room personnel cooperate to quickly respond to each patient's particular medical needs. Examples of routine technology include typical mass-production or assembly operations, where employees perform the same task repeatedly and the programmed solutions necessary to perform a task efficiently have already been identified and refined. Similarly, in service organizations such as fast-food restaurants, the tasks that crew members perform in making and serving the food are very routine.

The extent to which the process of actually producing or creating goods and services depends on people or machines is another factor that determines how nonroutine a technology is. The more the technology used to produce goods and services is based on the skills, knowledge, and abilities of people working together on an ongoing basis and not on automated machines that can be programmed in advance, the more complex the technology is. Joan Woodward, a professor who investigated the relationship between technology and organizational structure, differentiated among three kinds of technology on the basis of the relative contributions made by people or machines.[14]

SMALL-BATCH TECHNOLOGY
A method used to produce small quantities of customized, one-of-a-kind products based on the skills of people who work together in small groups.

Small-batch technology is used to produce small quantities of customized, one-of-a-kind products and is based on the skills of people who work together in small groups. Examples of goods and services produced by small-batch technology include custom-built cars, such as Ferraris and Rolls Royces, highly specialized metals and chemicals that are produced by the pound rather than by the ton, and the evaluation services performed by a small team of auditors hired to evaluate the accuracy of a firm's financial statements. Because small-batch goods or services are customized and unique, employees need to respond to each situation in a more unique fashion; a decentralized structure of authority allows them to respond flexibly. Such a structure is therefore appropriate with small-batch technology.

MASS-PRODUCTION TECHNOLOGY
A method of production using automated machines that are programmed to perform the same operations time and time again.

Woodward's second kind of technology, **mass-production technology**, is based primarily on the use of automated machines that are programmed to perform the same operations time and time again. Mass production works most efficiently when each person performs a

Skilled workers at Steinway and Sons wrap a 22-foot-long maple rim around the press that will shape it into the case for a Model D grand piano, an example of small-batch production in action. Roughly 200 people are involved in making and assembling the piano, which has 12,000 parts and costs about $ 60,000 to buy.

repetitive task. There is less need for flexibility; in this case, a formal organizational structure is preferred because it gives managers the most control over the production process. Mass production results in an output of large quantities of standardized products such as tin cans, Ford Tauruses, washing machines, and light bulbs, and services such as a car wash or dry cleaning.

CONTINUOUS-PROCESS TECHNOLOGY
A method of production involving the use of automated machines working in sequence and controlled through computers from a central monitoring station.

The third kind of technology that Woodward identified, **continuous-process technology**, is almost totally mechanized. Products are produced by automated machines working in sequence and controlled through computers from a central monitoring station. Examples of continuous-process technology include large steel mills, oil refineries, nuclear power stations, and large-scale brewing operations. The role of employees in continuous-process technology is not to produce individual products but instead to watch for problems that may occur unexpectedly and adversely affect the overall process. The possibility of a machinery or computer breakdown, for example, is a major hazard associated with continuous-process technology. If an unexpected situation does occur (like an explosion in a chemical complex), employees must be able to respond quickly and appropriately to prevent a disaster. In this case, the flexible response required will necessitate a flexible organizational structure.

As we discussed in previous chapters, new information technology is profoundly affecting how organizations operate. An IT-enabled organizational structure allows for new kinds of tasks and job-reporting relationships among electronically connected people that promotes superior communication and coordination. For example, one type of IT-enabled organizational relationship discussed in Chapter 15 is *knowledge management*, the sharing and integrating of expertise within and between functional groups and divisions in real time.[15] Unlike more rigid or bureaucratic organizing methods, new IT-enabled organizations can respond more quickly to changing conditions in the competitive environment.

Human Resources and the Employment Relationship

A third important contingency affecting an organization's choice of structure is the characteristics of its human resources and the nature of the employment relationship. In general, the more highly skilled an organization's workforce, the more people are required to work together in groups or teams to perform their tasks. In this case, an organization is more likely to use a flexible, decentralized structure. Also, the longer and better the employment relationship a company has with its employees, the more likely it is to choose a design structure giving them the freedom to make important decisions.[16] Highly skilled employees usually desire freedom and autonomy and dislike close supervision.[17] For example, no one needs to tell a scientist to report his or her results accurately and impartially or doctors and nurses to give patients the best care possible.

Moreover, when people work in teams like doctors and nurses and groups of research scientists do, they must be able to interact freely. A more flexible organizational structure makes this possible. When it comes to designing an organizational structure, both the work and the people who do it are important.

Organic and Mechanistic Structures

As the previous discussion suggests, an organization's environment, technology, and human resources are three main factors that influence the design of its structure. The greater the level of uncertainty in the environment of the organization, complexity of its technology, and skill of its workforce, the more likely managers are to design a flexible structure. In contingency theory, the term **organic structure** is used to describe an organizational structure that is designed to promote flexibility so that employees can initiate change and adapt quickly to changing conditions. In an organic structure, employees working in empowered teams assume the responsibility to make decisions as organizational needs dictate. Employees also are expected to continually develop skills in new kinds of tasks and to work together to find the best ways to perform a task. Shared work norms and values become the main means through which employees coordinate their activities to achieve organizational goals.

ORGANIC STRUCTURE
An organizational structure designed to promote flexibility so that employees can initiate change and adapt quickly to changing conditions.

In contrast, the more stable the organization's environment, the less complex and more well understood its technology, and the less skilled its workforce, the more likely are managers to design an organizational structure that is formal and controlling. In contingency theory, the term **mechanistic structure** is used to describe an organizational structure that is designed to induce employees to behave in predictable, accountable ways. In a mechanistic structure, decision-making authority is retained at the top of the organization, each employee performs a clearly defined task, and, each knows exactly what his or her area of responsibility is. The work process is coordinated by an extensive system of rules and regulations that link employee activities and make them ordered and predictable. How do you design an organization structure to be either flexible or formal? The way in which Bob Nardelli designed Home Depot's mechanistic structure is described in the opening case. In general, the way an organization's structure works depends on the organizing choices managers make about two principal issues:

MECHANISTIC STRUCTURE
An organizational structure designed to induce employees to behave in predictable, accountable ways.

- How to group jobs into functions and divisions
- How to coordinate or integrate jobs, functional groups, and divisions

Grouping Jobs into Functions and Divisions

As we note in Chapter 1, organizations are groups of people working together to achieve a wide variety of goals. One of the main reasons people work together is so that the organization can experience gains in productivity that result from the division of labor and specialization.[18]

FUNCTION
A group of people who perform the same types of tasks or hold similar positions in an organization.

The first issue in organizational design is to choose a division of labor or way to group different jobs together to best meet the needs of the organization's environment, technology, and human resources. Most organizations group jobs together according to their function, and thereby develop a functional structure. A **function** is a group of people working together who possess similar skills or use the same kind of knowledge, tools, or techniques to perform their jobs. A **functional structure** is an organizational structure composed of all the job specializations that an organization requires to produce its goods or services. For example, the salespeople in a car dealership belong to the sales function. Together, car sales, car repair, car parts, and accounting are the set of functions that allow an automotive dealership to sell and maintain cars. Consider how Michael Dell developed a functional

FUNCTIONAL STRUCTURE
An organizational structure that groups together people who hold similar positions, perform a similar set of tasks, or use the same kinds of skills.

You're the Management Expert

Which Work System Is the Best?

You're an expert on organizational design who has been called in to advise a new web-development company about how to organize its work activities. The company's goal is to design websites to suit the needs of specific clients, usually small- to medium-sized companies. This will require that the website developers work closely with each client. Once the site is built to the satisfaction of the client, it will have to be constantly updated to incorporate new software technology and to reflect changes in the client's business needs. The managers of the new company want to know if they should (1) design the work processes so that, using a sophisticated IT system, each employee working alone can make all the necessary decisions to satisfy a particular customer's request; or (2) use small-batch production and group employees into teams to develop several different websites at once. Which system do you think is likely to be most effective? Why?

EXHIBIT 16.2

Dell's Functional Structure

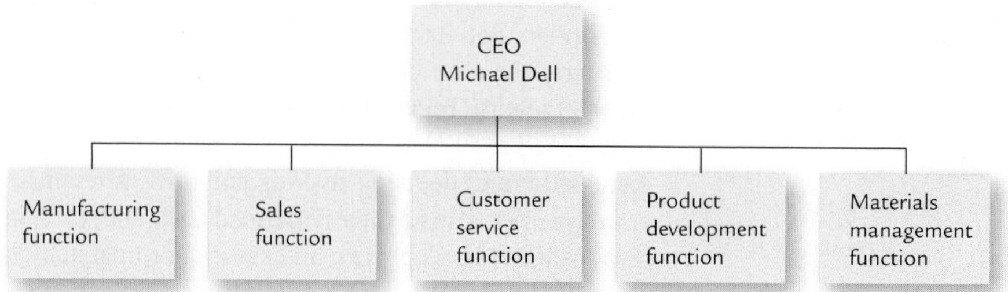

structure. To effectively control the activities of his employees as his company grew, Dell created the functional structure illustrated in Exhibit 16.2.

Dell groups all employees who perform tasks related to assembling personal computers into the manufacturing function and all employees who handle Dell's telephone sales into the sales function. Engineers responsible for designing Dell's computers are grouped into the product development function, and employees responsible for obtaining supplies of hard discs, chips, and other inputs are grouped into the materials management function. The functional structure suited the needs of Dell's growing company, especially as it battled with Compaq—now a part of HP—and Gateway for control of the personal computer market—a battle which it is currently winning hands down.[19]

If an organization subsequently grows and prospers, it often employs a second grouping by division and adopts a more complex form of divisional structure. A **division** is a group of functions created to specialize in making and selling a particular kind of good or service.[20]

DIVISION
A group of functions created to allow an organization to produce and dispose of a particular kind of good or service to customers.

Choosing a structure and then designing it so that it works as intended is a significant challenge. The ability to make the right kinds of organizing choices is often what differentiates effective from ineffective organizations. Organizational design is such an important decision because it affects the behavior of people in so many different ways. First, it affects employees' motivation to work hard and to develop supportive work attitudes. Second, it affects the likelihood that different groups, functions, or divisions will want to cooperate with one another, share resources, and work together effectively.[21] To be effective, an organization must decide how it wants its members to behave, what attitudes it wants to encourage, and what it wants its members to accomplish. Then, it can make design choices based on these goals.

Functional Structure

Advantages of a functional structure. A functional structure offers several advantages when it comes to managing an organization's activities. All organizations (even relatively small ones) group their activities by function, at least to some extent, to capture the benefits that result from the division of labor and specialization.

Coordination advantages. People grouped together according to similarities in their positions can easily communicate and share information with each other. As we saw in Chapter 13 on communication and Chapter 14 on decision making, people who approach problems from the same perspective can often make decisions more quickly and effectively than can people whose perspectives differ. A functional grouping also makes it easier for people to learn from one another's experiences. In this way, a functional structure helps employees improve their skills and thereby enhances individual and organizational performance.

Motivational advantages. Grouping by function improves an organization's ability to motivate employees. When employees are grouped together by function, supervisors are in a good position to monitor individual performance, reward high performance, and discourage social loafing. Functional supervisors find monitoring easy because they usually possess high levels of skill in the particular function. Grouping by function also allows group members to monitor and control one another's behavior and performance levels. Functional grouping can also lead to the development of norms, values, and group cohesiveness that promote high performance (see Chapter 11). Finally, grouping by function creates a career ladder to motivate employees: Functional managers and supervisors are typically employees who have been promoted because of their superior performances.

Disadvantages of a Functional Structure To manage the division of labor, most organizations develop a functional structure because of the coordination and motivation advantages associated with it. However, as an organization continues to grow and its activities become more diverse and complex, a functional structure may no longer allow it to coordinate its activities effectively. It may even hinder the organization for any one of the following three reasons:

1. When the range of products or services that a company produces increases, its various functions can begin to experience difficulties. Imagine the problems that would occur, for example, if a company started to make cars, then went into computers, followed by clothing, but used the same sales force to sell all three products. Most salespeople would not be able to learn enough about all three products quickly enough for the company to provide its customers good service.
2. Coordination problems may arise. As organizations attract customers with different needs, it may find it hard to service these different needs by using a single set of functions. The needs of individual customers, for example, are often very different from the needs of large corporate customers, although each still requires a high level of personalized service.
3. As companies grow, they often expand their operations nationally. Servicing the needs of different regional customers with a single set of manufacturing, sales, or purchasing functions becomes very difficult.

To cope with coordination problems such as these, organizations typically overlay their functional structures with divisional structures.

Divisional Structures: Product, Market, and Geographic

When a divisional structure overlays its functional groups, an organization can coordinate its activities more effectively. Organizations can choose from three kinds of divisional structure: product, market, and geographic structures (see Exhibit 16.3). Each is suited to a particular kind of coordination problem facing an organization.[22]

PRODUCT STRUCTURE
A divisional organizational structure that groups functions by types of product so that each division contains the functions it needs to service the products it produces.

Product structure. When an organization chooses to group people and functions so that it can produce a wide variety of different products, it moves to a **product structure**. Each product division contains the functions necessary to service the specific goods or products. Exhibit 16.3(a) shows the product structure used by a company like General Electric, which has many separate product-oriented divisions—for example, divisions responsible for producing light bulbs, aerospace products, and appliances. Each of these divisions has its own set of functions (such as accounting, marketing, and research and development).

What are the advantages of a product structure? It allows a company to increase its division of labor so that it can make and sell a wider range of products. Dell, for example, created product divisions when it began to sell new electronic goods like work stations, mini computers, printers, and PDAs in the 2000s. Each product division is responsible for the success of its new products, so the members of each division focus their energies on making those products a success. In 2006, Kodak announced it was splitting its consumer photographic products division into two parts. In the future, the digital imaging products group will manage growing sales of its digital cameras, printers, and accessories; the film

EXHIBIT 16.3

Three Types of Divisional Structure

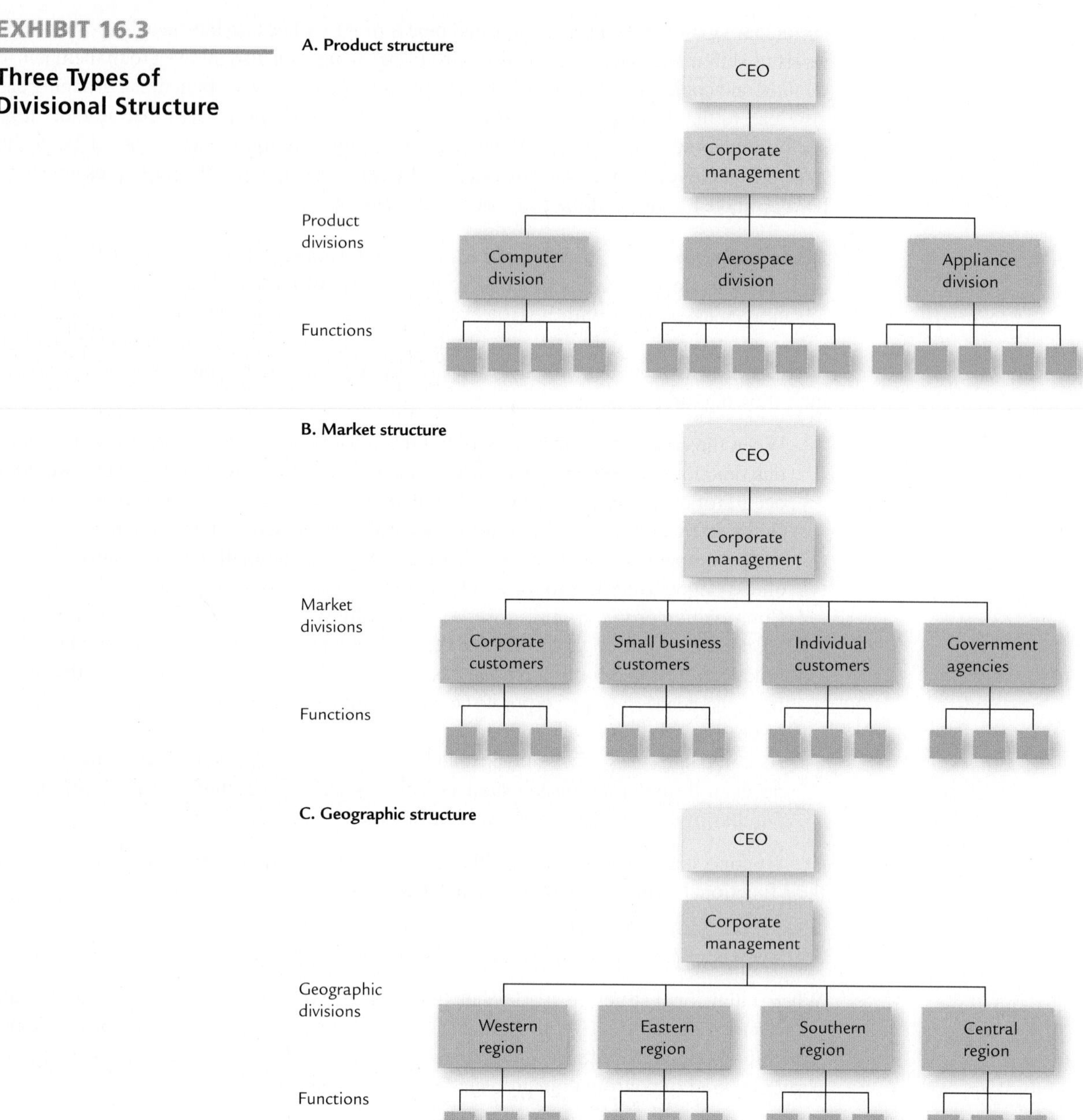

imaging products group will be responsible for Kodak's declining traditional chemical-based films and accessories.[23] Companies change their product divisions as the demand for their products rise and falls—the goal is to organize a company's resources to best meet customer needs.

MARKET STRUCTURE
A divisional organizational structure that groups functions by types of customers so that each division contains the functions it needs to service a specific segment of the market.

Market structure. Sometimes the most pressing problem facing an organization is to deliver products to customers in a way that best meets customer needs. To accomplish this goal, an organization is likely to choose a **market structure** and group functions into divisions to respond to the needs of particular types of customers. (See Exhibit 16.3B.) For example, companies like Staples and Office Max serves individual customers, but they also have large accounts with small-business customers and accounts with large companies and government agencies. Customers who buy large quantities of office supplies require special services and often demand special payment or delivery terms. To suit the specific needs of each group of customers, firms group their functions according to the type of customers' needs. That way, each market division can specialize in, and become more effective at, meeting them.

GEOGRAPHIC STRUCTURE A division organizational structure that groups functions by region so that each division contains the functions it needs to service customers in a specific geographic area.

Geographic structure. When organizations expand rapidly both at home and abroad, functional structures can become problematic because managers in one central location may find it increasingly difficult to deal with the different issues facing different regions. In these cases, a **geographic structure**, in which divisions are broken down by location, is often chosen (see Exhibit 16.3C). To achieve Federal Express's corporate mission of providing next-day mail service, CEO Fred Smith chose a geographic structure with regional divisions. Large retailers like Macy's, Neiman Marcus, and Brooks Brothers also use a geographic structure. Since retail customers' purchases can vary dramatically by region (more down parkas are likely to be sold in the Midwest than in California, for example) a geographic structure gives regional managers the flexibility they need to choose the range of products best suited to their customers.

If it adopts a *global geographic structure,* then an organization locates different divisions in each of the world regions in which it operates. Often, for example, products that appeal to U.S. customers do not appeal to customers in Europe, the Pacific Rim, or South America. The goal is to customize products to meet the needs of customers in those different world regions, and a global geographic structure allows an organization to do this.

Advantages of a Divisional Structure

A divisional structure—whether it's based on products, markets, or geography—has coordination and motivational advantages that overcome many of the problems associated with a functional structure as the size and complexity of an organization increases.

When a large company like GM has many different divisions, they are often housed in different buildings or locations. It becomes difficult for divisions to exchange information and coordinate their activities. Divisions may also start to compete and pursue their own goals at the expense of organizational goals. All these problems occurred at GM.

Coordination advantages. Because each division contains its own set of functions, functional groups are able to focus their activities on a specific kind of good, service, or customer. This narrow focus helps a division create high-quality products and provide high-quality customer service. Each product division, for example, has its own sales force that specializes in selling its particular product. This specialization enables salespeople to perform more effectively.

A divisional structure also facilitates communication between functions and can improve decision making, thereby increasing performance. Burlington Northern Santa Fe Railway began dividing up its shipping operations into product divisions by the commodities customers ship—cars, chemicals, food products, and so on. The change from a functional to a product structure allowed the company to reduce costs and make better use of their resources.[24]

Similar kinds of advantages can result from using a market structure. Grouping different functions together in a market division to serve one type of customer enables the functions to coordinate their activities and better serve their customers. For example, KPMG, the third largest accounting company in the United States, reorganized from a functional structure (in which people were organized into traditional functions like accounting, auditing, taxes, and consulting) to a market structure. Employees in each of these functional areas were grouped together to serve customers in different industries, like manufacturing, financial, and retail sectors, for example.[25] KPMG moved to a market structure to make better use of its human and other resources.

A geographic structure puts managers closer to the scene of operations than managers at central headquarters. Regional managers are well positioned to respond to the regional needs of customers and fluctuations in resources in those areas. Often they are able to find solutions to specific problems in those areas and use available resources more effectively than managers at headquarters can.

Finally, on an individual level, people who are grouped together into divisions are sometimes able to pool their skills and knowledge and brainstorm new ideas for products or improved customer service. As divisions develop a common identity and approach to solving problems, their cohesiveness increases, and the result is improved decision making.

Motivational advantages. Grouping into divisions offers organizations a wide range of motivational advantages as well. First, a divisional structure gives rise to a new level of management: **corporate management** (see Exhibit 16.3). The responsibility of corporate managers is to supervise and oversee the managers of the various divisions. Corporate managers coordinate and motivate divisional managers and reward them on the basis of the performance of their individual divisions. A divisional structure makes it easier for organizations to evaluate and reward the performance of individual divisions and their managers and reward them in a way that is closely linked to their performance.[26] Recall from Chapter 8 that a clear connection between performance and reward increases motivation. Corporate managers can also evaluate one regional operation against another and share ideas developed by one region with the others to improve performance.

CORPORATE MANAGEMENT
The set of managers whose responsibility is to supervise and oversee the divisional managers.

A second motivational advantage is that divisional managers enjoy a large measure of autonomy because they—not corporate managers—are responsible for operations. Their autonomy tends to promote positive work attitudes and boost performance. Another motivational advantage of a divisional structure is that regional managers and employees are close to their customers and more likely to develop personal relationships with them as a result. These relationships give the managers and employees an extra incentive to perform well. Finally, on an individual level, employees' close identification with their division can increase their commitment, loyalty, and job satisfaction.

Disadvantages of a Divisional Structure

Although divisional structures offer large, complex organizations a number of coordination and motivational advantages over functional structures, they have certain disadvantages as well. The disadvantages can be overcome with good management, but some of them are simply the result of the way a divisional structure works.

First, because each division has its own set of functions, the **operating costs** of managing an organization increase. The number of managers in an organization, for example, increases, because each division has its own set of sales managers, manufacturing managers, accountants, and so on. It also creates a completely new level of management that must be paid for—the corporate level of management.

OPERATION COSTS
The costs associated with managing an organization.

Second, as we discuss in the following, communication may suffer when a divisional structure is implemented. Because divisional structures normally have more managers and more levels of management than functional structures, communication can become more complex as various managers at various levels in various divisions attempt to exchange information with one another and coordinate their activities.

Third, divisions may start to compete for organizational resources and pursue their own goals at the expense of organizational goals. These conflicts reduce cooperation and can sometimes result in friction between divisions.

If these conditions exist, a company may decide to disband its division structure and split apart into separate companies that are easier to manage. For example, in 2006 Tyco, a large divisional company, decided that it would break into three independent companies that would operate in the electronics, healthcare, and security and fire protection industries.[27] Tyco's corporate managers believe that after the split the executives of each company will be able to develop a more competitive business model and choose a structure—for example, functional or product—that allows them to implement it more effectively. Additionally,

Tyco's corporate office will be closed down, which will result in savings in operating costs as corporate executives either leave the company or join one of the three new companies.

Managers must continually compare and evaluate the benefits and costs of using a functional or a divisional structure. When the benefits exceed the costs, they should move to a divisional structure. Even with a divisional structure, however, managers must find ways to operate that overcome some of the disadvantages inherent to it, and keep divisions and functions coordinated and motivated.

Matrix Structure

Moving to a product, market, or geographic divisional structure allows managers to respond more quickly and flexibly to the particular set of contingencies they confront. However, when the environment is dynamic and changing rapidly and uncertainty is high, even a divisional structure may not provide managers with enough flexibility to respond to quickly enough.[28] This can occur, for example, when information technology or the needs of customers are evolving rapidly. In this case managers must design the most flexible kind of structure available to their organization. This is called the *matrix structure.*

MATRIX STRUCTURE
An organizational structure that simultaneously groups people by function and by product team.

In a **matrix structure**, managers group people and resources in two ways simultaneously: by function and by product.[29] Employees are grouped by *functions* to allow them to learn from one another and become more skilled and productive. In addition, employees are grouped into *product teams* in which members of different functions work together to develop a specific product. The result is a complex network of reporting relationships among product teams and functions that makes the matrix structure very flexible. Each person in a product team reports to two bosses: (1) a functional boss, who assigns individuals to a team and evaluates their performance from a functional perspective, and (2) the boss of their product team, who evaluates his or her performance on the team. Thus, team members are known as *two-boss employees*.

Exhibit 16.4 illustrates a matrix structure. The vertical lines show the functions of an organization, and the horizontal lines show the product teams responsible for developing or manufacturing the organization's products. At the intersection of the lines are employees who report to both a functional boss and a product boss. The members of the teams are each developing a specific product. One team in Figure 16.4 is working on the Alpha computer workstation for small businesses; another team is working on the Beta workstation designed for large corporate customers.

Coordination advantages. Typically, a company uses a matrix structure (rather than an ordinary divisional structure) for three reasons:

1. It needs to develop new products very rapidly.
2. It needs to maximize communication and cooperation between team members.
3. Innovation and creativity are key to the organization's continuing success.[30]

Product teams permit face-to-face problem solving and create a work setting in which managers with different functional expertise can cooperate to solve nonprogrammed decision-making problems. Product team membership in a matrix structure is not fixed. Two-boss employees are transferred from team to team when their functional expertise is needed. For example, three electrical engineers work in the Alpha team to design the most efficient system to link the electronic components. When they solve the Alpha design problem, they may then move to the Beta team if it requires their expertise. The flexibility of a matrix structure allows an organization to make best use of its human resources.

Motivational advantages. To understand how the matrix structure influences motivation, it is important to understand that the members of the product teams are generally highly qualified and skilled employees with advanced degrees and expertise in their fields. The matrix structure provides a work setting giving employees freedom

EXHIBIT 16.4

A Matrix Structure

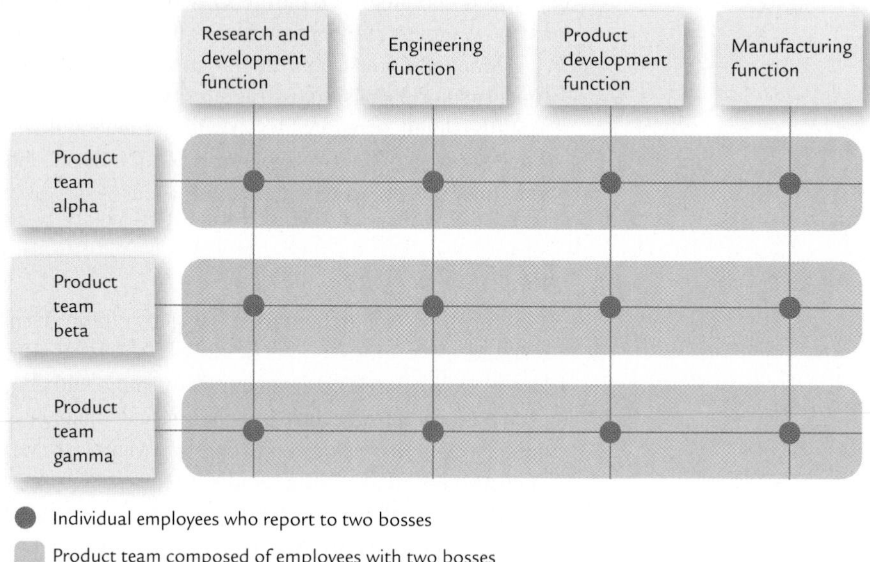

and autonomy over their work activities. As we saw in Chapter 7, job design is important in determining work attitudes and behaviors, and many people enjoy jobs with a high motivating-potential score. Matrix structures allow for such motivation and encourage work behaviors that enhance quality and innovation.

Disadvantages of a matrix structure. As you might expect, matrix structures have some disadvantages as well. Inherent to them are several properties that can cause job dissatisfaction. Matrix structures can increase role conflict and ambiguity (see Chapter 9), and high levels stress within them can sometimes ensue. Two bosses making conflicting demands on an employee can cause him or her to feel some role conflict; the very loose system of reporting relationships can make employees vulnerable to role ambiguity. The result is stress. Another source of discomfort for employees is that they might have trouble demonstrating their personal contributions to team performance because they move so often from team to team. For reasons such as these, some people dislike working within a matrix structure.[31]

As this discussion suggests, the matrix structure is associated with the most complex coordination and motivational issues. On the one hand, it has enormous coordination advantages; but on the other hand, it can cause complex motivational problems. The extent of these problems explains why only companies that depend for their survival on rapid product development designed to meet very specific customer needs use matrix structures. They are especially common in high-tech and biotechnology companies.

Summary

Large organizations are more complex than small organizations. They have a greater number and variety of functions and divisions because they produce a greater number and variety of goods and services. As organizations grow, they can implement one or more different organizational structures. Each structure offers coordination and motivational advantages and disadvantages, and each is suited to addressing a particular contingency or problem facing the organization. Most companies use a functional design to group organizational activities and then overlay it with a product, market, geographic, or matrix structure to manage the specific contingencies they face.

Coordinating Functions and Divisions

The first organizational design task is to group functions and divisions and create the organizational structure best suited to the contingencies an organization faces. The second organizational design task is to ensure that there is sufficient coordination or integration among functions and divisions so that the organization's resources are used effectively. Having discussed the ways in which organizational activities are divided up into functions and divisions, we now look at how the parts are put back together. We look first at the way in which the hierarchy of authority is used to coordinate functions and divisions so that they work together well. Then we focus on integration and examine the many different integrating mechanisms that can be used to coordinate functions and divisions.

Allocating Authority

AUTHORITY
The power that enables one person to hold another person accountable for his or her actions.

HIERARCHY OF AUTHORITY
An organization's chain of command that defines the relative authority of each level of management.

SPAN OF CONTROL
The number of employees who report to a specific manager.

As organizations grow and produce a wider range of goods and services, the size and number of their functions and divisions increase. To coordinate the activities of people, functions, and divisions, person must develop a clear hierarchy of authority.[32] **Authority** is the power vested in a person to make decisions and use resources to achieve organizational goals by virtue of his or her position in an organization. The **hierarchy of authority** is an organization's chain of command—the relative authority that each manager has—extending from the CEO at the top, down through the middle managers and first-line managers, to the nonmanagerial employees who actually make the goods or provide the services. In a hierarchy, each lower position is under the supervision of a higher one; as a result, authority links and integrates the activities of managers and employees across hierarchical levels. The term **span of control** refers to the number of subordinates who report directly to a manager.

Recall from the last section, for example, how the position of divisional manager emerges when an organization splits apart into divisions and how a corporate-level manager emerges to integrate the activities of divisional managers. Similarly, a hierarchy emerges inside each function to integrate the activities of employees within each function. As an organization grows and the problem of integrating activities within and between functions and divisions increases, the organization typically increases the number of levels in its hierarchy. As it does so, the span of control narrows.[33]

Compare the hierarchies shown in Exhibit 16.5(a) and 16.5(b). The CEO in Exhibit 16.5(a) supervises six different functions, so the CEO's span of control is six subordinates. There are three levels in the hierarchy—the CEO, the managers in charge of each function, and the employees who report to each functional manager. Suppose the CEO decides that he can no longer effectively monitor the activities of the six functions because they are growing so rapidly. One way of solving this problem is to create a new level in the hierarchy. To do this, the CEO adds a level to the hierarchy by creating the positions of operations manager and product development manager, as shown in Exhibit 16.5(b). Each of the new managers supervises three functions. These two managers and the CEO then work together as a team to integrate the activities of all six functions. The organization now has four levels in the hierarchy, the CEO's span of control narrows from six to two, and the span of control of the two new managers is three. Increasing the number of levels in an organization's hierarchy increases the coordination between the activities of different functions. Also, as the number of levels in the organizational hierarchy increases, the span of control narrows, so managers are better able to coordinate and motivate their subordinates.

Tall and flat hierarchies. The number of levels in a hierarchy varies from organization to organization. In general, the larger and more complex an organization is, the taller is its hierarchy. Tall organizations have many hierarchical levels relative to their size; flat organizations have few (see Exhibit 16.6).

Just as it becomes more difficult to coordinate the activities of different functions as their number increases, it becomes more difficult to achieve coordination between hierarchical levels when an organization's hierarchy becomes *too* tall. Communication and decision-making problems start to occur. As the number of managerial levels increases, the

EXHIBIT 16.5

Using the Hierarchy to Manage Intergroup Relations

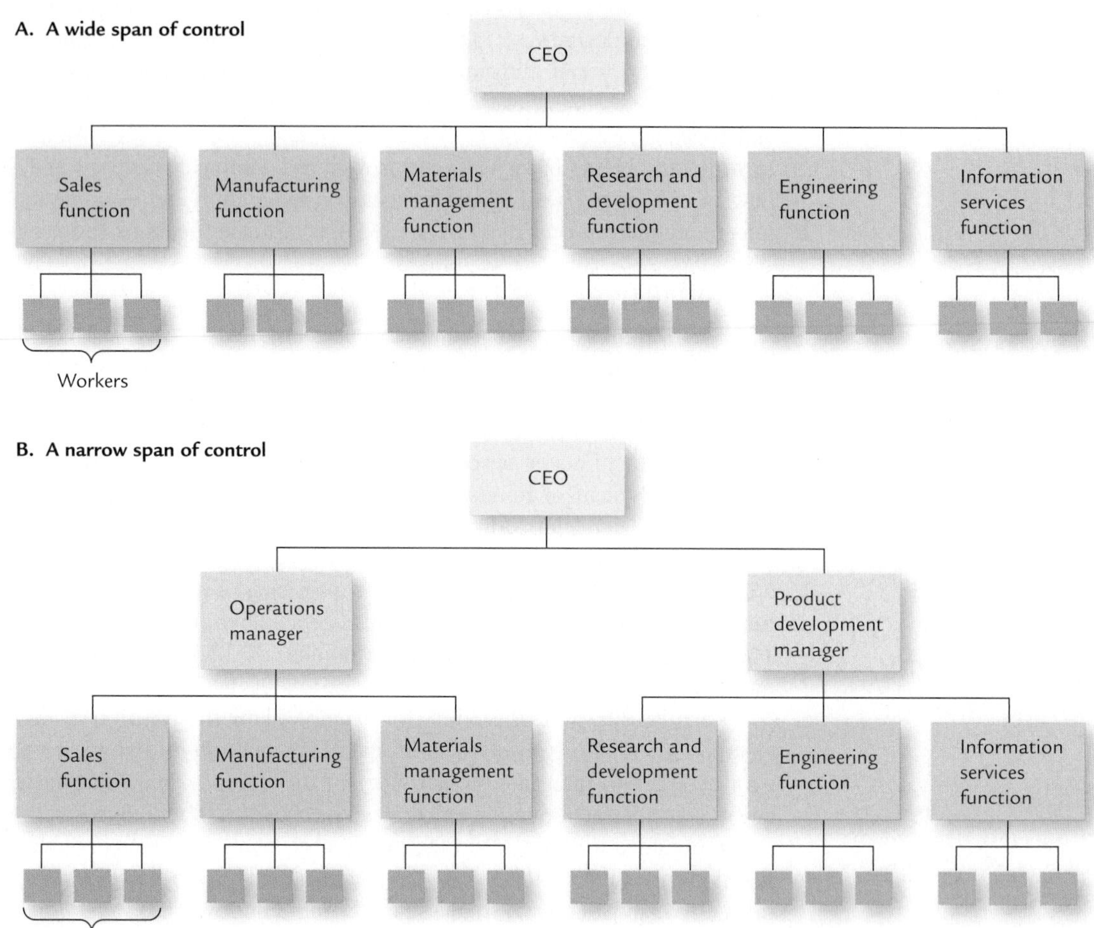

time it takes to send messages up and down the chain increases. The result is slower decision making. In addition, information passed from person to person is more likely to get distorted or filtered as messages become garbled and managers interpret them according to their own interests. These problems detract from the quality of decision making. In fact, all the communications problems discussed in Chapter 14 increase as an organization's hierarchy becomes taller and taller.

Colleen C. Barrett, the number two executive of Southwest Airlines, is well known for her efforts to empower employees and convince them they should feel free to go above and beyond their prescribed roles to provide customers better service.

The minimum chain of command. An important organizational design principle is the *principle of the minimum chain of command*. A minimum chain or command principle can help mitigate problems that ensue when the hierarchical structure becomes too tall. The principle states that an organization should operate with the fewest levels possible. Effective organizations should scrutinize their hierarchies to see whether the number of levels can be reduced—for example, whether one level can be eliminated and its responsibilities assigned to managers or employees above or below it.

This practice has become increasingly common in the United States as companies battling low-cost global competitors search for ways to cut costs. One manager who is constantly trying to empower employees and keep the hierarchy flat is Colleen C. Barrett, the number-two executive of Southwest Airlines.[34] At Southwest, she is well known for continually reaffirming the company's message that employees should feel free to go above and beyond their prescribed roles to provide customers better service. Southwest employees are encouraged not to look to their superiors for guidance but rather to themselves find

EXHIBIT 16.6

Examples of Flat and Tall Hierarchies

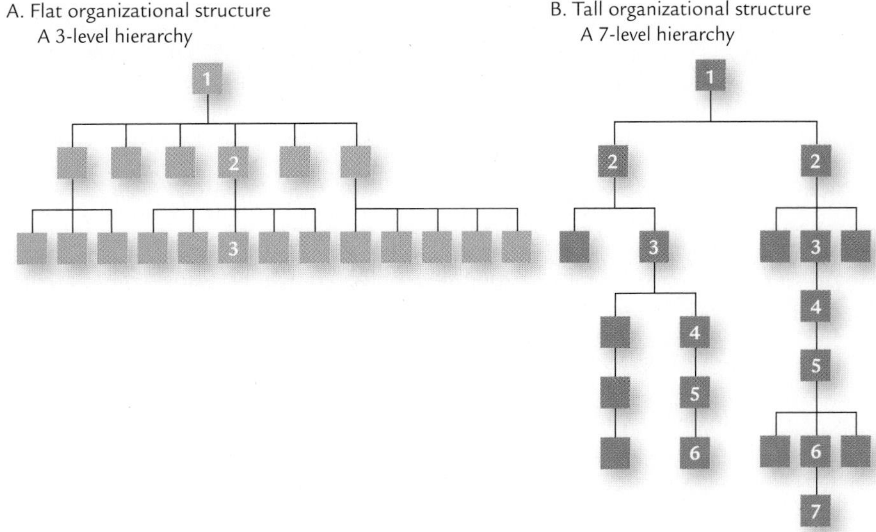

ways to do their jobs better. As a result, Southwest keeps the number of its middle managers to a minimum.

Centralization versus decentralization. Another way to keep the organizational hierarchy flat is to decentralize authority to lower-level managers and nonmanagerial employees.[35] When lower-level managers and non managerial employees have the responsibility to make important decisions, the problems of slow and distorted communication noted previously are kept to a minimum. This can increase motivation by making lower-level jobs more interesting and rewarding. Moreover, fewer managers are needed because their role is not to make decisions but to act as coach and facilitator and to help other employees make the best decisions.

Decentralizing authority allows an organization and its employees to behave in a flexible way even as the organization grows and becomes taller. This is why managers are so interested in empowering employees, creating self-managed work teams, establishing crossfunctional teams, and even moving to a product-team structure.

Although more and more organizations are taking steps to decentralize authority, too much decentralization has certain disadvantages. If divisions, functions, or teams are given too much decision-making authority, they may begin to pursue their own goals at the expense of the organization's goals. Managers in engineering design or R&D, for example, may become so focused on making the best possible product that they fail to realize that the best product may be so expensive, few people will be willing or able to buy it! Also, with too much decentralization, a lack of communication among functions or divisions may prevent synergies among them from materializing and organizational performance may suffer.

An organization must seek the balance between authority centralization and decentralization that best meets the major contingencies it faces. If an organization operates in a stable environment using well-understood technology, for example, then there is no pressing need to decentralize authority, and top-level managers can make most of the decisions.[36] However, in uncertain, changing environments like those in surrounding high-tech industries, companies are speeding new products to market. Employees and teams must be empowered to make important decisions so that the organization can keep pace with the changes taking place. These companies are more likely to prefer a higher degree of decentralization.

In summary, the design of the organizational hierarchy is one of the most important decisions an organization makes as it attempts to coordinate its functions and divisions and

OB Today

Microsoft Centralizes to Meet Google's Challenge

Microsoft has been racing to compete against companies like Yahoo! and especially Google, both of which are developing innovative web-based software products to attract broadband users. In the 2000s, the company has been hindered by its slow decision making, however, and its top managers decided that the source of the problem was that too much authority had been decentralized in the organization.

In 2005 Microsoft was composed of seven major business units, each of which was headed by a top executive who was in charge of the managers who led the hundreds of product teams working on related software applications in each business unit. This structure allowed each of the seven business units to make quick decisions internally; however, the problem was that many potential synergies between the business units—particularly in the area of developing integrated web-based applications—were going unnoticed. So, new products were not being developed and the result was that Google's lead was increasing.

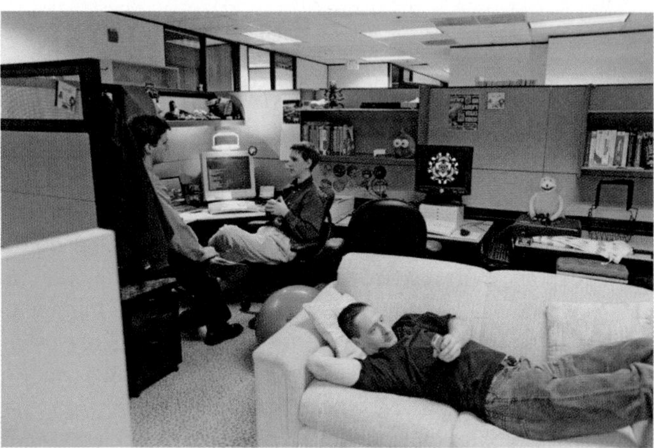

As the software programmer on the couch in the Googleplex suggests, Google strives to keep its structure as relaxed and flexible as possible to encourage people to cooperate and think "out of the box." Microsoft also strafed out this way but its very success led to so much growth it has to find new kinds of structure to achieve such cooperation and speed innovation+J174

Bill Gates, Steve Ballmer, and a team of other top Microsoft executives decided that a radical overhaul of the company's structure was necessary to change the way company-wide decisions were made and to speed organizational learning. The top-management team decided to consolidate and merge the activities of the seven different groups into three principal divisions, each of which would be headed by a top manager with a proven record of fast product innovation. The three divisions were the Microsoft Platform Products and Services Division responsible for the Windows platform, servers, and tools; the Microsoft Business Division responsible for its Office products and software for small and mid-sized businesses; and Microsoft Entertainment and Devices Division responsible for its Xbox console and games, mobile phones, and other hand-held products.[37]

The idea is that this reorganization will reduce the infighting and miscommunication that has been slowing product development between the seven different groups. To solve such problems, often Gates or Ballmer had to intervene and this slowed decision making. Now the head of each division could react faster, intervene, and solve problems as they arose because each division was more centralized. The result would be a faster flow of web-based products inside each group.

In the new structure, however, the three executives in charge of the divisions wield enormous power in the company. Although this reorganization has centralized control over product decision making it has also added another layer in Microsoft's hierarchy.

Thus, the danger exists that this new structure might make the company even more bureaucratized so that the potential gains will not be realized.[38] In 2006 it is still unclear whether or not Microsoft's new structure is working. Has the reorganization just created three new fiefdoms and more bureaucracy? Or will the change allow Microsoft to come out with its own Windows web-based offerings that will make Google's web-based products such as e-mail storing, desktop searching, and rumored web-based word processing less attractive to customers? Only time will tell, however. Delays in releasing its new Vista operating system does not bode well for its new structure—a more nimble Microsoft may still be a long way away.[39]

achieve its goals. Managers need to continually scrutinize the hierarchy to make sure it meets the organization's needs, and they must be prepared to change it if it does not. We discuss issues and problems in changing organizational structure in detail in Chapter 18.

Mutual Adjustment and Integrating Mechanisms

The organizational hierarchy is an important method of coordination because it links and allows the activities performed by employees at all levels of the organization to be controlled. If necessary, for example, the operations manager in Exhibit 16.5(b) can tell the sales, manufacturing, and materials management managers what to do and how to coordinate their activities. However, the operations manager cannot tell the product development manager what to do because the two managers are at the *same level in the hierarchy*. Furthermore, the operations manager cannot tell anyone in R&D, engineering, or information systems what to do even though they are at a lower hierarchical level because they do not report to him or her. These functions report to the product development manager, who is responsible only to the CEO. Ultimately, only the CEO, the person at the top of the hierarchy, has the authority to tell everyone in the organization what to do, and that is why an organization's top manager is so powerful.

Because managers at the same level or in different functions have no power over each other, organizations need to use tools other than the organizational hierarchy to coordinate their activities. One important form of coordination takes place through mutual adjustment and the use of integrating mechanisms. **Mutual adjustment** is the ongoing communication among different people and functions that is necessary for an organization to achieve its goals. Mutual adjustment makes an organization's structure work smoothly because it facilitates communication and the free flow of information between functions. Mutual adjustment, for example, prevents the emergence of different orientations that can cause significant communication and decision-making problems between functions and divisions.

MUTUAL ADJUSTMENT
The ongoing informal communication among different people and functions that is necessary for an organization to achieve its goals.

To facilitate mutual adjustment, organizations use various kinds of integrating mechanisms. **Integrating mechanisms** are organizing tools used to increase communication and coordination among functions and divisions. Here, we discuss several kinds of integrating mechanisms that facilitate mutual adjustment in the order of their importance.[40]

INTEGRATING MECHANISMS
Organizing tools used to increase communication and coordination among functions and divisions.

Direct contact. With direct contact, managers from different functions establish face-to-face working relationships that allow them to solve common problems informally without having to go through the formal channels of authority in the hierarchy. In a functional structure, for example, managers in sales try to develop good, informal working relationships with managers in manufacturing so that both can simultaneously make decisions to achieve their goals. Reaching agreement may not be easy because the goals of the two groups are not always identical. Manufacturing's goal is to keep costs at a minimum; to do this it is often necessary maintain production according to a particular schedule to smoothly manufacture goods in large batches. Sales's goal is to respond to the needs of customers; it often needs to ask manufacturing to change production schedules on short notice to accommodate unexpected customer requests. Because such sales-dictated changes raise manufacturing's costs, the potential for conflict arises. A high level of direct contact between sales and manufacturing managers, however, can lead to a give-and-take relationship that fosters cooperation between functions.

LIAISON ROLES
A permanent managerial position in which the manager's only role is to coordinate the activities of different divisions.

Liaison roles. Because organizations recognize that direct contact is important, they often establish **liaison roles** giving specific functional managers the *formal* responsibility of communicating with managers in another function to solve common problems. To facilitate communication, managers in liaison roles meet regularly to exchange information, and members of one function transmit requests to other functions through these liaison personnel. Over time, the personal working relationships that develop between the managers performing these roles enhance coordination throughout the organization.

Teams and task forces. Organizations often create teams and task forces composed of employees from different functions to facilitate communication and cooperation. While a team is a permanent group made up of representatives from two or more functions that meets regularly, a task force is a temporary, or ad hoc, group set up to solve a specific problem. An organization might set up a task force to study problems it expects to encounter as it expands its operations into another country, for example. After the task force comes up with a solution to the problem to which it is assigned, it disbands.

In contrast, an organization may use a team to increase coordination between functions like the product development team shown in Exhibit 16.7. Because product development is an ongoing activity, an organization is likely to create a permanent team composed of members from several functions whose job it is to constantly scrutinize new product ideas and make recommendations about the ones that should be funded.

The important role teams and task forces play to promote mutual adjustment cannot be overemphasized. It has been estimated that managers spend over 70 percent of their time in face-to-face meetings with other managers making decisions and solving problems that cannot be dealt with through the formal hierarchy or in any other way.[41]

Cross-functional teams. Recently, many organizations have implemented cross-functional teams to facilitate mutual adjustment. *Cross-functional teams* consist of people from different functions who are permanently assigned to work full-time on a team to bring a new good or service to the market.[42] Cross-functional teams are different from ordinary teams in several ways. Members of an ordinary team are full-time members of the same function or division; members of cross-functional teams are full-time members of different functions or divisions and report to the leader of the team. Exhibit 16.8 shows an example of a cross-functional team structure formed to facilitate mutual adjustment.

Hallmark Cards moved to a cross-functional team structure when it decided to organize its tasks according to specific types of cards—birthday cards, Christmas cards, Mother's Day cards, and so on. Rather than having card designers, artists, rhyme writers, and other

EXHIBIT 16.7

Using a Team to Increase Coordination Between Functions

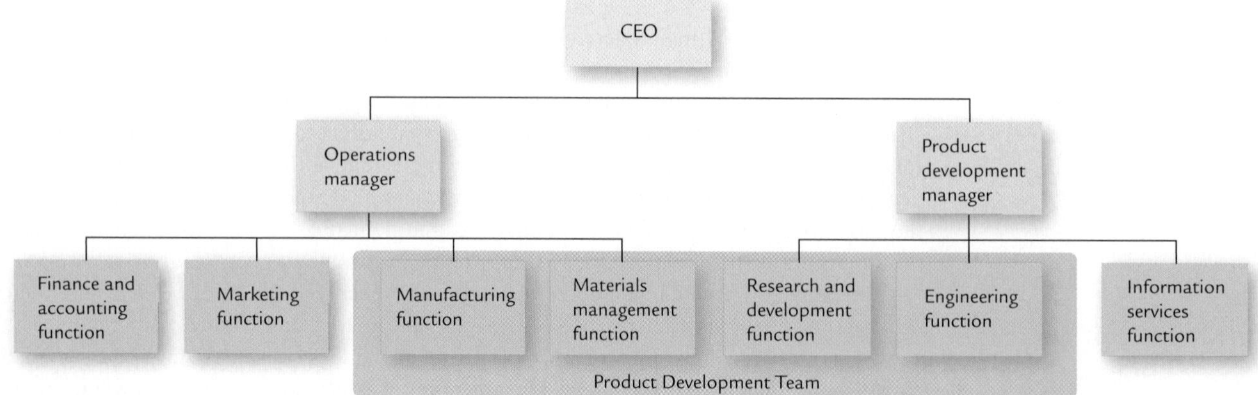

EXHIBIT 16.8

A Cross-Functional Team Structure

Cross-functional teams are composed of functional personnel who are assigned full-time to work in the team.

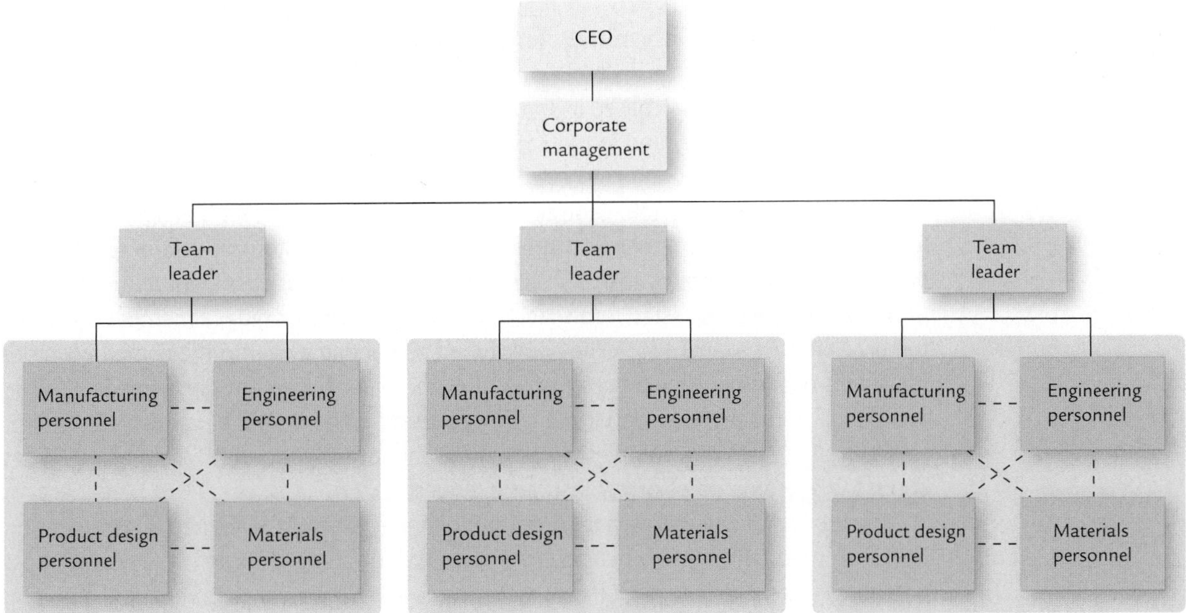

specialists work in separate functions, Hallmark assigned them to cross-functional teams to reduce the need to coordinate among functions. The new structure greatly speeded up product development. A new card used to take a year to get to the market; now it takes only a few months. Sun Life also provides a good example of a company that has used cross-functional teams with great success, as the following Global View discusses.

Standardization

STANDARDIZATION
The development of routine responses to recurring problems or opportunities.

The third principal tool that organizations can use to coordinate their activities and integrate functions and divisions is **standardization**—the development of programmed responses, performance standards, written rules, and standard operating procedures (SOPs) that specify how employees and functions should respond to recurring problems or opportunities. An organization can standardize activities at the input, conversion, and output stages.[43]

Standardizing inputs. Organizational inputs include the skills and capabilities of managers and employees, the quality of the raw materials and component parts used to make products, and the machinery and computers used in the production process. Organizations develop performance standards, such as quality or reliability specifications, used to evaluate and assess inputs before they are put into production. Japanese car companies, for example, are renowned for the stringent quality specifications that they require suppliers of car components such as engine blocks to meet. Increasingly, more global companies are recognizing that higher input standards result in higher-quality products.

Organizations can standardize the skills of their managers and employees by requiring them to have certain qualifications and experiences. An assembly-line employee might be required to have a high school diploma, an R&D scientist might be required to have a Ph.D. from a prestigious research university, and a CEO might be required to have shown that he or she has successfully managed similar kinds of businesses in the past.

Global View

Sun Life's New Product Team Structure

Canada Sun Life Financial, based in Toronto, Canada, is one of the largest insurance companies in North America, and in the 1990s, like most other insurance companies, it operated with an organizational a structure that was very rigid and bureaucratic.[44] Over the years it had developed a tall, centralized structure and upper-level managers made the final decisions about whether or not to offer prospective customers insurance and how much their policies should cost. Sun also operated with a functional structure. When a potential customer requested information about insurance coverage, a member of its customer service department took the application and handed it over to the company's order fulfillment department for processing. In turn, the order fulfillment department sent the application to the actuarial department that calculated the insurance premium. Only after several more steps were completed could Sun's salespeople inform a would-be customer about the outcome of his or her insurance request.

The process of channeling a request through many different levels in the hierarchy and across so many different functions took considerable time. Frequently, because most potential customers obtain multiple quotes from several insurance companies, the long time lag resulted in lost business. Customers simply "satisfice" and choose an insurance policy from one of the first two or three companies that give them an insurance quote quickly.

Sun Life realized it had to find a way to respond more quickly to its customers, especially because its competitors were acquiring other insurance companies and a number of dot.com companies had begun selling policies on the Internet. This new aggressive competition made Sun's managers realize that they had to change the way their company operated and do it fast. Sun needed a structure that would allow it to respond quickly and flexibly to the needs of customers; it knew it must empower front-line employees to quote and issue policies. Toward this end Sun decided on the following course of action: First, it discarded its functional structure and reorganized its 13 different functional groups into a series of crossfunctional product teams. Employees from sales, customer service, order fulfillment, and other functions became members of "service teams." Each team was also equipped with a sophisticated IT system that gave the team access to *all* the information needed to respond to a customer's request.[45] This empowered each team to perform all the steps necessary to process an insurance request; no longer was it necessary for subordinates to go to their managers for approval on policies—the team could make its own decisions.

When all the exchanges between departments were eliminated, Sun's managers were astonished by the way its new structure operated. Its new teams could work so quickly and flexibility that the time needed to process an insurance request fell by 75 percent! With such rapid service the company found it much easier to attract new customers and its business grew rapidly as a result. Sun Life soon realized that it could use IT in other ways to improve the way it coordinated its activities. As the company grew, for example, it began to offer a wider range of financial services such as pension management and investment and estate planning. Sun won a national award for the way it had transformed its organizational design to improve customer service—something that also resulted in record revenues and profits.[46]

Organizations that recruit and select employees who meet stringent criteria can be relatively confident that their employees will respond in appropriate ways to uncertain events. This is why organizations spend so much time recruiting and selecting employees.

Standardizing conversion processes. To standardize the conversion processes an organization uses to make the final product, organizations specify the kinds of behavior they expect from their employees. When these behaviors are specified, both individuals and groups are more likely to act consistently in ways that allow an organization to achieve its goals. The principal way in which organizations standardize behaviors is through the use of rules and SOPs. (See Chapter 10.)[47] Because rules and SOPs specify the series of actions or decisions that employees are expected to perform in a given situation, they standardize employee responses to the situation.

FORMALIZATION
The use of rules and standard operating procedures to control an organization's activities.

Formalization is the use of rules and SOPs to control an organization's activities. The more an organization can rely on formalization to specify required behaviors, the less it needs to use either direct supervision from the hierarchy or mutual adjustment. Formalization results in lower operating costs, once rules have been developed. They are also inexpensive to implement and cost the organization little to maintain. All that is required is that new employees be taught the appropriate rules to follow in certain situations. (Recall from Chapter 10 that socialization is the process by which employees learn organizational rules and SOPs.)

Although some rules are necessary to the smooth running of an organization, too many rules can give rise to a number of problems:

- Excessive formalization can "straitjacket" employees and prevent them from responding creatively and flexibly to new situations.
- Employees' inclination to obey rules without thinking about their consequences can reduce the quality of organizational decision making.
- Too much emphasis on the use of existing rules and procedures can make it especially difficult for an organization to make changes and develop new rules.

Despite these drawbacks, formalization is a powerful tool as the experience of siteROCK based in Emeryville, California suggests. siteROCK is in the business of hosting and managing other companies' websites and keeping them up and running and error free. A site that goes down or runs haywire is enemy number 1. The company is run by Dave Lilly, an ex-nuclear submarine commander. To maximize the performance of his employees and to increase their ability to respond to unexpected online events, Lilly decided the company needed a comprehensive set of rules and SOPs to cover all the major known problems that could crash a site.[48] He insisted that every problem-solving procedure be written down. siteROCK now has over 30 thick binders listing all the processes and checklists that employees need to follow when an unexpected event happens. Their job is to try to solve the problem using these procedures.

At siteROCK, these written rules and SOPs are also used to control employee behavior to achieve high levels of customer service. Because the goal is 100 percent reliability, detailed blueprints guide planning and decision making—not seat-of-the-pants solutions that might work 80 percent of the time but result in disaster the other 20 percent of the time. Before siteROCK employees are allowed in the control room each day, they must read over the most important rules and SOPs. At the end of a shift they spend 90 minutes doing paperwork that logs what they have done and detail any new or improved rules that they have come up with. siteRock's goal is simple: Use rules to achieve a quick resolution of complex issues. If the existing rules don't work, then employees must experiment. When they find a solution, it goes into the rule book to aid the future decision making of all employees in the organization. Clearly, siteROCK is making excellent use of rules to standardize its high-tech operations and is an exception to the rule that a company needs a decentralized approach to adjust to rapid technological change.

Standardizing Outputs. Finally, output standards are also an effective way to standardize behavior. Instead of specifying the behaviors the organization expects from its employees with rules and SOPs, the organization specifies what the final output of its employees must be for the organization to achieve its goals.[49]

Imagine, for example, how difficult it is for a manager to monitor the behavior of employees like salespeople or R&D scientists. It is impossible to watch a scientist to see how well he or she "does research." Likewise, the cost involved to have managers shadow salespeople and give them instructions would be exorbitant. So, organizations specify the level of performance they require from their employees and set standards—or performance goals—by which to measure actual employee outputs. In the case of salespeople, for example, an organization might set a sales target for how much each salesperson should sell each month or how many customers they should visit each day. Specifying the goals for researchers is more difficult because their work is so long term and complex, but an R&D function can be measured by the number of new products it develops or the number of new patents that it files. As we saw in Chapter 7, setting specific challenging goals can be an effective way to motivate employees.

By using specific goals and targets to measure the performance of individuals and groups, an organization increases the control it has over their activities. The more ways an organization can devise to measure its performance, the more effective it becomes.

New IT-Enabled Forms of Organizational Design and Structure

The increasing use of new information technology is changing the nature of organizational design and structure.[50] The principal reason is because IT changes companies and allows them to behave in more flexible, organic way. The effects of IT on organizational design can be seen both inside and between organizations.[51]

The Effects of IT Inside Organizations

In the last decade, information technology has had a dramatic effect on the way in which organizations group and coordinate their activities.[52] First, IT increases communication and coordination and promotes mutual adjustment among teams, functions, and divisions.[53] Second, IT permits the greater decentralization of decision making because employees have instant access to the information they need to make a decision.[54] A previous Global View showed how Sun Life used IT to reorganize from a functional structure to one based on crossfunctional product teams. Sun's new IT system gave teams the information they needed to handle each customer's specific request. As a result of using IT, organizations no longer need tall management hierarchies. They can operate with flatter structures that speed decision making and enable the organization to act in a more flexible and organic way.

Some organizations, especially those that provide complex services and employ highly trained workers, have gone one step further and created what has been called a virtual organization. A **virtual organization** is one in which employees are linked to an organization's centralized databases by computers, faxes, and videoconferencing and rarely see one another face-to-face, if ever.[55] These employees might only infrequently visit the physical premises of their companies; they receive their assignments electronically, report back to their superiors electronically, and operate autonomously.[56] Almost all their employees are out in the field, working anywhere around the globe working with clients to solve their problems. Large consultancy companies like EDS and Accenture operate in this fashion as the following OB Today illustrates. It provides an interesting example of how IT, by decentralizing authority to employees, can promote flexibility and allow a company to behave organically.

VIRTUAL ORGANIZATION
A company that operates largely using new information technology where people and functions are linked through company intranets and databases.

OB Today

Accenture's "Virtual" Organization

Accenture, a global management consulting company, has been one of the pioneers in using IT to revolutionize its organizational structure. Its managing partners realized that since only its consultants in the field could diagnose and solve clients' problems, the company should design a structure that facilitated creative, on-the-spot decision making. To accomplish this, Accenture decided to replace its tall hierarchy of authority with a sophisticated IT system to create a virtual organization.[57]

First, it flattened the organizational hierarchy, eliminating many managerial levels. Then, it went about setting up a shared organization-wide IT system that provides each of Accenture's consultants with the information and knowledge they need to make their own decisions. If the consultant still lacks specific knowledge to solve a client's problem, the system is designed to provide them with data from Accenture's thousands of consultants located around the globe who can provide them with expert backup help.[58]

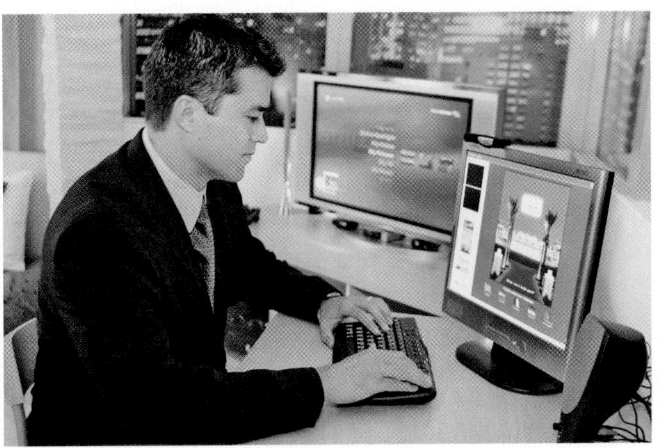

Accenture equips each of its consultants with a wireless laptop computer, then expert coordinators at its headquarters assemble all the client knowledge consultants feed into its corporate Intranet. They then send this knowledge wirelessly back to all consultants so they can work together to develop better client solutions.

To implement the change, Accenture first equipped every one of its consultants with a awireless laptop computer, and each consultant was linked to the others via a sophisticated corporate intranet, depending on the particular kind of client he or she served. For example, consultants who work with consumer product firms are linked together in one group, and those that work with brokerage companies are linked together in another. Often, the members of these groups e-mail their counterparts working at different client sites to see if any of them, say, have encountered a client problem similar to one they are presently facing and what they did to solve it. If members of the consultant's core group can't solve the problem, he or she can then communicate with members of other groups by tapping into Accenture's large information databases containing volumes of potentially relevant information. The consultant can also communicate directly with other company employees through a combination of phone, voice mail, e-mail, and teleconferencing in an attempt to gain access to more current information presently being gathered and applied at other client sites.[59]

Oftentimes, employees uncover useful information that can pertain to employees in very different areas of the firm. For example, if the project involves installing an enterprise-wide computer system, the consultant has quick access to the information of hundreds of others consultants who have dealt with the software in question but applied it in different

contexts. By utilizing these resources consultants stay abreast of the innovative practices being implemented within their own firm and within client firms.

Accenture found that the effects its virtual organization had on flattening the structure, decentralizing authority, and enlarging and enriching roles increased the creativity of its consultants and enhanced their performance. By providing employees with more information and enabling them to easily confer with other people, Accenture gave its consultants much more freedom to make decisions. Moreover, because they often work far away from Accenture's headquarters, the electronic connections have made consultants much more independent. They are able to make their own decisions, which has been a source of motivation. The end result for Accenture is that it now one of the best-known of all global consulting companies.[60]

The Effects of IT Between Organizations

Another innovation in organizational design—the use of outsourcing and networking structures between organizations—has largely been the result of information technology. Recall from Chapter 1 that *outsourcing* involves moving a functional activity that was done *inside* an organization to the *outside*, where another company performs it. Many companies have found that the use of the Internet and software platforms linking organizations together in real-time makes it easier and cheaper for them to send a specific kind of functional activity, such as making component parts, manufacturing the final product, or even managing the IT function itself, to other companies to perform For example, the U.S. military signed a 10 year $15 billion contract to let EDS, the computer services company, manage its vast array of computer networks and information systems. The move to outsource manufacturing to low-cost countries like China and Malaysia has been accelerating. Companies like Black and Decker, Sony, and Levi Strauss now contract with manufacturers abroad to produce most, if not all, of their products, which are then shipped to the markets in which they will be sold.

Some companies radically alter their organizational structures by focusing only on that one specific functional activity such as product design or research and development at which they excel and then outsource the rest of their other functional activities to other companies. In doing so, they operate within what is called a **network structure**.[61] Nike, for example, the largest and most profitable sports shoe manufacturer in the world, uses a network structure to make, distribute, and sell its shoes.[62] At the center of the network is Nike's product design and research function located in Beaverton, Oregon, where Nike's designers are constantly developing new, innovative sports shoe designs. However, that is almost all that Nike does in Beaverton, besides the corporation's administrative activities. All the other functional work that Nike needs to make and sell its shoes has been outsourced to companies around the world! Nike manages its relationships with the companies in its network through advanced IT. Its designers use sophisticated computer software systems to design its shoes, and all of the new product information, including its technical and manufacturing instructions and specifications, are stored electronically. When the designers have completed their work, they then relay the blueprints for the new products electronically to Nike's network of suppliers and manufacturers in Southeast Asia.[63] For example, instructions for the design of a new sole may be sent to a supplier in Taiwan, and instructions for the leather uppers to a supplier in Malaysia. These suppliers then produce the shoe parts, which are subsequently sent for final assembly to a manufacturer in China with whom Nike has established an alliance. From China, the shoes are shipped to distributors throughout the world and are marketed in each country by organizations that Nike contracts with.

NETWORK STRUCTURE
A structural arrangement whereby companies outsource one or more of their functional activities to other specialist companies.

The advantage of this network structure is that Nike can respond quickly and flexibly to changes in customer needs and tastes. If demand for a particular kind of shoe drops and demand for another soars, Nike can rapidly transmit new instructions to its network of manufacturers abroad to change their production plans. Moreover, because it does not have to coordinate many different functional activities, Nike can preserve its flat hierarchy and stay small and nimble. In essence, a network structure allows Nike and many other companies to act in an organic way.

Companies are increasingly recognizing the many opportunities outsourcing and networking afford when it comes to reducing costs and increasing flexibility. Clearly, managers have to carefully assess the relative benefits of having their own organization perform a functional activity or make a particular product versus forming an alliance with another organization to do it. As you can see, designing an organizational structure is becoming increasingly complex in today's rapidly changing global world.

Summary

Organizational structure affects how people and groups behave in an organization, it provides a framework that shapes employee attitudes and behavior. Organizations need to create a structure that allow them to coordinate and motivate people, functions and divisions effectively. This chapter makes the following major points:

1. Organizational structure is the formal system of task and job-reporting relationships that determines how employees use resources to achieve organizational goals. Organizational design is the process of making the specific organizing choices about tasks and job relationships that result in the construction of a particular organizational structure.
2. Contingency theory argues that an organization's structure needs to be designed to fit or match the set of contingencies—factors or conditions—that affect it the most and cause it the most uncertainty. Three important contingency factors are: the organizational environment, advances in technology (especially information technology), and an organization's human resources.
3. The greater the level of uncertainty in the environment, the more complex its technology; and the more highly skilled its workforce, the more likely managers are to design an organic structure—one that is flexible and that can change quickly. The more stable the environment, the less complex its technology; and the less skilled its workforce, the more likely an organization is to have a mechanistic structure—one that is formal, controlling and designed to induce employees to behave in predictable, accountable ways.
4. The main structures that organizations use to differentiate their activities and to group people into functions or divisions are functional, product, market, geographic, and matrix structures. Each of these is suited to a particular purpose and has specific coordination and motivation advantages and disadvantages associated with it.
5. As organizations grow, problems of coordinating activities between functions and divisions arise. Three methods organizations can use to solve coordination problems are to use the hierarchy of authority, mutual adjustment, and standardization.
6. To coordinate their activities, organizations develop a hierarchy of authority and decide how to allocate decision-making responsibility. Two important choices that they must make are how many levels to have in the hierarchy and how much authority to decentralize to managers throughout the hierarchy and how much to retain at the top.
7. To coordinate their activities, organizations develop mechanisms for promoting mutual adjustment (the ongoing informal communication and interaction among people and functions). Mechanisms that facilitate mutual adjustment include direct contact, liaison roles, teams and task forces, and crossfunctional teams.
8. Organizations that use standardization to coordinate their activities develop programmed responses and written rules that specify how people and functions are to coordinate their actions to accomplish organizational objectives. Organizations can standardize their input, throughput, and output activities.

Organizational Behavior in Action

Questions for Review

1. What is the relationship between organizational design and structure?
2. What contingencies would cause an organization to choose an organic rather than a mechanistic structure?
3. Why do organizations group activities by function?
4. Why do organizations move to some kind of divisional structure?
5. What kind of organizational structure would you expect to find in (a) a fast-food restaurant, (b) a company like General Electric or General Motors, (c) a biotechnology company?
6. What kind of structure does your college or business use?
7. Why is coordinating functions and divisions a problem for an organization?
8. What are the main issues in deciding on the design of an organization's hierarchy of authority?
9. Why is mutual adjustment an important means of integration in most organizations?
10. What kinds of organizational activities are easiest to standardize? Most difficult?

OB: Increasing Self-Awareness

Understanding Organizational Structure

Think of an organization that you are familiar with—a university, restaurant, church, department store, or an organization that you have worked for—and answer these questions:

1. What form of structure does the organization use to group people and resources? Draw a diagram showing the major functions. Why do you think the organization uses this form of structure? Would another form of structure (e.g., divisional) be more appropriate?
2. How many levels are there in the organization's hierarchy? Draw a diagram showing the levels in the hierarchy and the job titles of the people at each level. Do you think this organization has the right number of levels in its hierarchy? How centralized or decentralized is authority in the organization?
3. To what degree does the organization use mutual adjustment and standardization to coordinate its activities? What mechanisms does it use to increase mutual adjustment? Does it use teams or cross-functional teams? What kinds of rules and standard operating procedures does it use?

A Question of Ethics

How to Layoff Employees

You are the manager(s) charged with reducing high operating costs. You have been instructed by the CEO to eliminate 25 percent of the company's workforce, both managers and employees. You also must manage the layoff process and then find a new way to allocate authority in the company to increase efficiency.

Some managers charged with deciding which employees should be laid off might decide to keep the employees they like and who are obedient to them, rather than the ones who are difficult or the best performers. They might decide to lay off the most highly paid employees. When redesigning the hierarchy they might try to keep most power and authority in their hands. Think of the ethical issues involved in layoffs and organizational design and answer the following questions:

1. What ethical rules should managers use when deciding which employees to terminate?
2. What ethical rules can help managers to best allocate authority and design their hierarchies?
3. How can the use of ethical principles help managers make the layoff process less painful for employees?
4. What effects do you think the way the layoff is carried out will have on the employees who remain?

Small Group Break-out Exercise

Speeding Up Website Design

You have been called in as consultants by the top functional managers of a website design, production, and hosting company whose new animated website designs are attracting a lot of attention and a lot of customers. Currently, employees are organized into different functions such as hardware, software design, graphic art, and website hosting, as well as functions such as marketing and human resources. Each function takes its turn to work on a new project from initial customer request to final online website hosting.

The problem this company is experiencing is that it typically takes one year from the initial idea stage to the time that the website is up and running and the company wants to shorten this time by half to protect and expand its market niche. The managers believe their current functional structure is the source of the problem; it is not allowing employees to develop websites fast enough to satisfy customers' demands. They want you to suggest a better one.

1. Discuss ways in which you can improve the way the current functional structure operates to speed up website development.
2. Discuss the pros and cons of changing to a matrix structure to reduce website development time. Then, discuss the pros and cons of following Sony's approach and using crossfunctional teams to coordinate between functions.
3. Which of these structures do you think is most appropriate and why?

Topic for Debate

Different kinds of organizational structures lead people to behave in different ways. Now that you understand the kinds of choices that organizations face when they create their organizational structures, debate the following issues.

Team A. Today, the hierarchy of authority is more important than mutual adjustment in coordinating and motivating people and functions to achieve an organization's goals.

Team B. Today, mutual adjustment is more important than the hierarchy of authority in coordinating and motivating individuals and functions to achieve an organization's goals.

Experiential Exercise

Analyzing Organizational Structure

For this chapter you will analyze the structure of a real organization such as a department store, restaurant, hospital, fire station, or police department. In the next chapter you will identify the contingencies that have influenced the development of the organization's culture.

Objective

Your objective is to gain experience in analyzing and diagnosing an organization.

Procedure

The class divides into groups of from three to five people. Group members discuss the kind of organization the group will analyze and then explore the possibility of gaining access to the organization by using a personal contact or by calling and going to see the manager in charge of the organization. After the group gains access to the organization, each member of the group interviews one or more members of the organization. Use the following questions listed to develop an interview schedule to guide your interview of the organization's employees, but be sure to ask additional questions to probe more deeply into issues that you think are interesting and reveal how the organization's structure works.

After all of the groups complete the assignment, the instructor either will allocate class time for each group to make a presentation of its findings to the whole class or will request a written report.

1. Draw an organizational chart showing the major roles and functions in your organization.
2. What kind of structure does your organization use? Why does it use this structure? What are the advantages and disadvantages of this structure?
3. How does your organization integrate and coordinate its activities?
   a. Describe the organization's hierarchy of authority. Is it tall or flat? Is it centralized or decentralized? How wide a span of control does the top manager have?
   b. What integrating mechanisms does the organization use to coordinate its activities?
   c. To what degree does the organization standardize its activities, and how does it do this?
4. Summarizing this information, would you say the organization operates with a mechanistic or organic structure? Are there elements of both?

New York Times *Cases in the News*

The New York Times

"At Time Inc. the Big Heads Roll."

—David Carr, NYT, December 19, 2005, p. C.1.

TIME INC. was always the General Motors of the magazine industry. A huge company with a mass touch, the publisher of such Olympian-sounding brands as Time, Life and Money, it was both a chronicler and a symbol of American brawn that found a way year after year to come up with products that consumers wanted. With more than 150 publications, Time Inc. is still the General Motors of the magazine industry, but, of course, that has come to mean something different. The company that Henry Luce founded is confronted by profound secular changes in the marker and a flat-to-rotten advertising cycle that has left the once-patrician publishing house scrambling to make its numbers, reorganizing in fits and starts and, last week, cutting loose some of its more precious human assets.

Ann S. Moore, chairwoman and chief executive of Time Inc., moved with shocking swiftness, aiming at chiefs more than Indians, because that's where the money is. Jack Haire, chief of corporate sales and a 28-year employee of the company, was out, as was Richard Atkinson, a former chief financial officer who was in charge of the news and information group. Eileen Naughton, president of *Time Magazine* and one of the rising young stars in the business, was told to pack up, as were a number of other rising executives. On the editorial side, *Time Magazine's* bureau chiefs in Moscow, Beijing, Seoul and Tokyo were cut; to book the price of severing them in 2005, the company needed to move on managers who had no union protection. In all, more than 105 people out of 13,000 were let go—not a big number, but more cuts are coming.

It is a difficult time for print in general, but at Time Inc., magazines that depend on male readers are challenged in particular: Time is down 14.2 percent in advertising pages from 2004, while Sports illustrated is off a whopping 18.5 percent and Fortune is down 10.5 percent. Last August, Don Logan, the chairman of the media and communications group of Time Inc,'s parent company, Time Warner, Noticed that a division he used to run—and achieved profit growth in for 14 consecutive years—seemed to be tanking. He sent Ms. Moore a bluntly worded reminder that she needed to make her numbers.

Ms. Moore responded to the grim news and the pressure by naming Nora McAniff and John Squires, two executive vice presidents with very different but well-established publishing skills, as co-chief operating officers and then moving swifty to wipe out the layers of management underneath them. "The company was too top-heavy," Ms. Moore said on the phone last Friday. "You think that only weak people get caught up in a reorganization, but that was not the case here. These were good people, people I had worked with for years, but this is about taking chairs away from the table that don't make any sense any more." Reporters—myself included—have written for years about Time Inc.'s multiple layers of management: why should a single magazine have a president, a publisher and an executive in charge of sales?

"I am tired of all these little bets we have been coming up with." Ms. Moore said "We are big, and we need big bets. I think that as we have become more layered, the culture here has become risk-averse."

Questions for Discussion

1. What kinds of problems did Ann Moore identify with the way Time's organizational structure was working?
2. What changes did she make to the structure? Why will these changes improve Time's performance?

The New York Times

"Dow Jones Plans to Merge Online and Print Divisions."

Katharine Q. Seelye, NYT, February 23, 2006, p. C.6.

Dow Jones & Company, the publisher of *The Wall Street Journal*, announced yesterday that it would merge its print and online operations, putting them under the control of L. Gordon Crovitz, who had been president of the company's online unit.

"The Internet will not mean the end of the print medium," Mr Crovitz wrote in a memo yesterday. "But as people have many more choices about how, when and where they get their news, established media such as newspapers must adapt; we will be the first to adapt by developing a newspaper for this digital age." Like most newspapers, *The Journal* has struggled as readers and advertisers have moved to the Internet. Mr. Crovitz signaled his commitment to online operations yesterday, telling analysts in a conference call that "we don't compare ourselves to newspapers per se because that's only part of what we are."

The company is reorganizing around its three markets—consumer media, enterprise media and community media. It had been organized around its three methods of distributing information—print, online and community newspapers. "We have people in print who think about circulation, ad sales, producing and delivering newspapers and they're very print-focused because they grew up there," Mr. Zannino said in an interview. "They don't think about online. And we have a separate online organization that until today reported up to an entirely different management team."

His goal is to merge them so they sell print and digital ads at the same time and so they appeal to readers who, for example, read the paper and look at their BlackBerries at the same time, as he said he does.

"We'll run them like franchises, being somewhat agnostic about where people choose to get information from us," he said. "Well, not entirely agnostic. What we really want is for them to use us in all channels of distribution. When they do, we serve them better, they're happier and we get to generate more profit."

On the editorial side, he said there was already cooperation between the print and online staffs but he hoped to "take that up a notch." The two other markets around which the company is being restructured are enterprise media, consisting of the Dow Jones Newswires and its licensing services, and community media, overseeing the company's 15 daily and 19 weekly Ottaway community newspapers in nine states.

The New York Times

"Mellon Combines 2 Units Into a New Group"

NYT, January 4, 2006, p. C.4.

The Mellon Financial Corporation said yesterday that it had combined its Dreyfus Mutual Fund unit with its Institutional Asset Management group to create a new organization called Mellon Asset Management.

Mellon said that Ronald O'Hanley would lead the combined group, and that Stephen E. Canter would remain chief executive of Dreyfus Corporation. Mr. O'Hanley will report to Martin G. McGuinn, Mellon's chairman and chief executive. Mr. Canter, who previously reported to Mr. McGuinn, now reports to Mr. O'Hanley.

Mr. O'Hanley said the reorganization reflected a shift in the retail market, where investors increasingly buy through broker-dealers and advisers.

Mellon, based in Pittsburgh, has been criticized by some shareholders, in particular the hedge fund Highfields Capital, for a lagging stock price. Highfields, based in Boston, has urged that the company separate its asset management from its trust and processing businesses.

Mr O'Hanley said the arguments advanced by Highfields were illogical. "There are real benefits to both our clients and to our shareholders in keeping these businesses together," Mr. O'Hanley said. He said the major customer segment in both the investment management business and the processing business is the United States defined-benefit pension market. "There are not only the same institutions but also the same people in the institutions." Mr. O'Hanley said.

The New York Times

"ABN Amro Plans Reorganization to Shift Focus"

NYT, October 15, 2005, p. C.5.

The Dutch bank ABN Amro said yesterday that it planned to reorganize its operations to focus on midmarket corporate clients and said its chief operating officer would take over as finance chief next year.

The three main business units—consumer and commercial clients, wholesale clients, and private clients and asset management—will be broken into 10 units starting next year, giving clients access to more products, the company said.

ABN Amro said in February that it planned such a move and that it would focus on fewer corporate relationships.

"This is the next step in aligning our organization further with our strategy, enabling us to serve our clients even better by drawing on the untapped potential of the group," ABN Amro's chairman, Rijkman W. J. Groenink, said in a statement.

ABN's current chief operating officer, Hugh Y. Scott-Barrett, will take over as chief financial officer on Jan. 1. The current finance chief, Tom de Swaan, will retire on May 1.

Separately, the French bank Societe Generale said it planned to spin off its investment banking arm in the United States, SG Cowen & Company, next year through a stock offering.

"This flotation will allow SG Crown to pursue its development as an independent business and to finance its growth with direct access to capital markets," Jean-Pierre Muster, head of Societe Generale's investment banking arm, said in a statement.

Questions for Discussion

1. Why did each of the three companies discussed above change their organizational structure?
2. Using the types of organizational structure discussed in the chapter, (a) identify the structure that best describes their original structure, and (b) identify the structure that best describes the one they changed to.

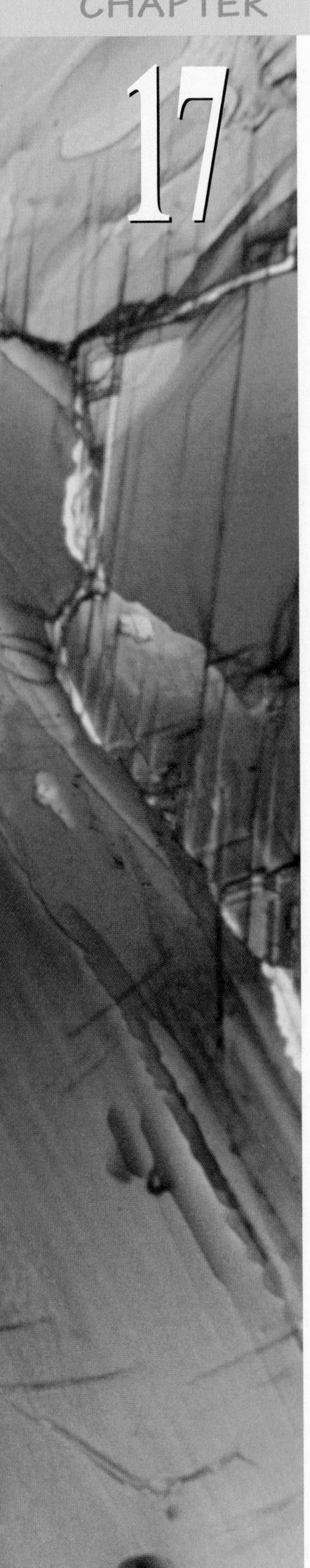

ORGANIZATIONAL CULTURE AND ETHICAL BEHAVIOR

Learning Objectives

After reading this chapter, you should be able to:

- Distinguish between values and norms and discuss how they are the building blocks of organizational culture.
- Appreciate how a company's culture is transmitted to employees through its formal socialization practices and through informal "on-the-job" learning.
- Discuss five main factors that shape organizational culture and explain why different organizations have different cultures.
- Appreciate how differences in national culture affect the culture of organizations within a particular society.
- Understand the importance of building and maintaining an ethical organizational culture.

Opening Case

OPENING CASE HOW TO BUILD A CREATIVE CULTURE

How does 3M's culture affect innovation?

3M is a company known worldwide for its organizational skills that promote creativity and the innovation of new products. 3M aims to achieve at least 25 percent of its growth each year from new products developed by its employees in the previous five years. To promote the creativity of its employees, 3M has developed cultural values and norms that strongly emphasize the need for employees to feel empowered, to experiment, and to take risks to come up with new product ideas. The company has many famous stories about employees who charged ahead and pursued their own product ideas—even when their managers doubted the success of their efforts. Take the case of Scotch tape.[1]

3M aims to achieve at least 25 percent of its growth each year from new products developed by its employees in the previous five years. To accomplish this it has developed an organizational culture based on values and norms that stress the need for employees to be innovative and creative.

The story of Scotch tape began when Dick Drew, a 3M scientist, visited an auto body shop in St. Paul, Minnesota.[2] Two-tone cars were popular then, and Drew watched as paint-shop employees improvised a method to keep one color of paint from being over sprayed onto the other using a paint shield made up of a combination of heavy adhesive tape and butcher paper. As they pulled their shield off when the paint was dry, however, it often took the other color paint with it. Employees joked with Drew that it would be a good idea if 3M could develop a product to make their task easier.

Dick went back to his boss and explained his idea for a new product—a tape with a weaker glue or adhesive, one that would not pull the paint off. His boss was not convinced this was a viable project, he told him to go back to work on developing an improved heavy-duty glue as he had been. Drew went back to his lab but decided that while he pursued his assigned project, he would also pursue his new idea. Over time, he began to divert more and more resources to his project and made repeated attempts to invent a weaker glue. Word of his efforts spread throughout 3M's labs, but his boss decided to turn a blind eye to his efforts; other people at 3M had done the same thing and they had had success. Within two years, Drew perfected his glue and developed "masking" tape. It was an instant success with paint-shop employees.

His boss realized they had a potential winner. Once it hit the market it soon became clear that masking tape had potentially thousands of other applications. Drew was now an organizational hero. He was given control of a major lab and the resources he needed to develop new kinds of tape for these varied uses. In 1930, for example, he invented clear cellophane tape; "Scotch" tape became one of 3M's most successful products.[3]

The fact that employees spend their time on projects of their own choosing is the source of many of 3M's cultural values and its success. 3M, for example, developed an informal norm that its researchers should spend 15 percent of their time to develop projects of their own choosing. It was this norm that brought about the development of other new products such as Post-It notes. To encourage more innovation and risk taking, 3M was careful to recognize its heroes—the people who invented its new products. 3M established its "Golden Step Program" which rewards successful product innovators with substantial monetary bonuses. Also, they become members of its "Carlton Hall of Fame," which gives them recognition throughout the company and access to a career ladder that can take them to the top. All these practices gained the loyalty and support of 3M's scientists and helped create a culture of innovation.

To speed innovation, 3M also realized the importance of creating organization-wide values to encourage employees to cooperate and share their ideas with one another. To avoid the problem of people in different functions focusing solely on their own tasks, 3M established a system of cross-functional teams made up of members from product development, process development, marketing, manufacturing, packaging, and other functions. So all the groups have a common focus, the teams work closely with customers. Customer needs, in other words, are the common denominator linking all of the teams. For example, one of 3M's cross-functional teams worked closely with disposable diaper manufacturers to develop the right kind of sticky tape for their needs. Clearly, all this attention to creating a culture of innovation that conveys to its employees the values of excellence and innovation has paid off for 3M.

Overview

3M attributes a large part of its success to a culture that encourages employees like Dick Drew to work hard, cooperate, be adventurous, and take risks in order to pursue their own ideas. In this chapter, we first define organizational culture and discuss the way it influences employees, work attitudes and behaviors. Then we discuss how employees learn about an organization's culture from the company's formal socialization practices and informal processes, like watching how things "get done." Five major building blocks of organizational culture are then discussed (1) the characteristics of people within the organization, (2) organizational ethics, (3) the employment relationship, (4) organizational structure, and (5) national culture. Finally, an issue that is especially important in the 2000s—how and why it is necessary for organizations to build and maintain an ethical culture is examined.

What Is Organizational Culture?

ORGANIZATIONAL CULTURE
The set of shared values, beliefs, and norms that influences the way employees think, feel, and behave toward each other and toward people outside the organization.

Organizational culture is the set of shared values, beliefs, and norms that influences the way employees think, feel, and behave toward each other and toward people outside the organization. In Schein's (1900) view, culture is "a pattern of shared basic assumptions a group learns as it solves its problems of external adaptation and internal integration, that is considered valid, is taught to new members as the correct way you perceive, think and feel in relation to those problems."[4] Just as an organization's structure can increase employee cooperation and motivation, so the values and assumptions in an organization's culture also can promote work attitudes and behaviors that increase organizational effectiveness.[5] This is because the organization's culture controls the way employees perceive and respond to their environment, what they do with information, and how they make decisions.[6]

VALUES
General criteria, standards, or guiding principles that people use to determine which types of behaviors, events, situations, and outcomes are desirable or undesirable.

What are organizational values, and how do they affect work attitudes and behavior? **Values** are general criteria, standards, or guiding principles that people use to determine

EXHIBIT 17.1

Terminal and Instrumental Values in an Organization's Culture

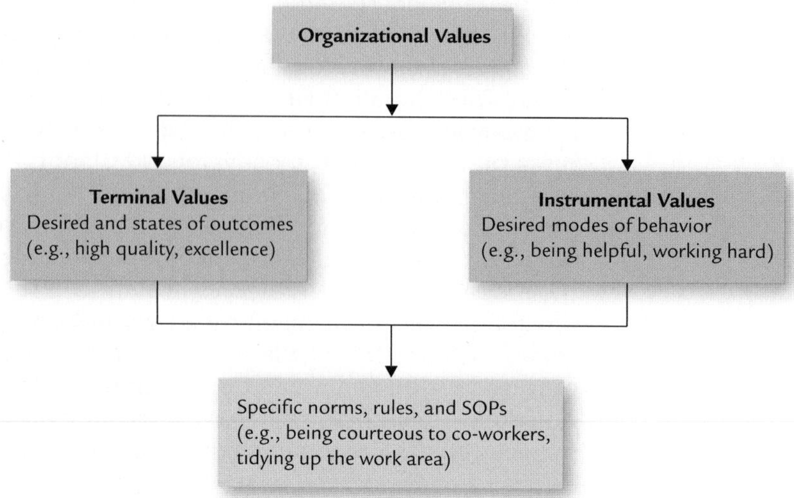

TERMINAL VALUES
A desired end state or outcome that people seek to achieve.

INSTRUMENTAL VALUE
A desired mode or type of behavior that people seek to follow.

which types of behaviors, events, situations, and outcomes are desirable or undesirable.[7] There are two kinds of values: terminal and instrumental (see Exhibit 17.1).[8] A **terminal value** is a desired end state or outcome that people seek to achieve. Organizations might adopt any of the following as terminal values, or guiding principles: quality, responsibility, innovativeness, excellence, economy, morality, and profitability. Large insurance companies, for example, may value profitability, but their terminal values are often stability and predictability because the company cannot afford to take risks. It must be there to pay off policyholders' claims.

An **instrumental value** is a desired mode or type of behavior. Modes of behavior that organizations advocate include working hard, respecting traditions and authority, being conservative and cautious, being frugal, being creative and courageous, being honest, taking risks, and maintaining high standards.

An organization's culture thus consists of the end states that the organization seeks to achieve (its *terminal values)* and the modes of behavior the organization encourages (its *instrumental values)*. Ideally, instrumental values help the organization achieve its terminal values. For example, computer companies like HP and Microsoft whose cultures emphasize the terminal value of innovativeness might attain this outcome by encouraging instrumental values like working hard, being creative, and taking risks. That combination of terminal and instrumental values leads to an entrepreneurial culture—one in which employees are challenged to take risks or go out on a limb to test their ideas.[9] On the other hand, insurance companies or accounting firms generally emphasize the terminal value of stability and predictability and try to attain this outcome by encouraging instrumental values that emphasize behaving cautiously, following the appropriate rules, and obeying instructions. The result will be a conservative culture.

To encourage members to adopt certain terminal and instrumental values and behave in certain ways as they pursue their goals, the organization develops specific norms. In Chapter 10 we defined a *norm* as a shared expectation for behavior. Norms are standards or styles of behavior that are considered acceptable or typical for a group of people. In essence, norms are informal rules of conduct that emerge over time to encourage employees to cultivate work attitudes and behaviors that are considered important to an organization. So, for example, the specific norms of being courteous, keeping one's work area clean, or being a "team player" will develop in an organization whose more general terminal or instrumental values include being helpful and hard working or cooperative.[10]

Norms are largely informal, so many of the most crucial values an organization has are also not written down. They exist only in the shared norms, beliefs, assumptions, and ways of thinking and behaving that people within an organization use to relate to each other and analyze and deal with problems.[11] For example, from one another, members learn how to perceive and respond to various situations in ways that are consistent with the organization's accepted values. Eventually, members choose and follow appropriate values without even realizing they are doing so.[12] Over time, they *internalize* the organization's values and the specific rules, norms, and SOPs that govern behavior; that is, organizational values become part of members' mindset and affect the way they perceive and respond to a situation.[13]

Values and norms work in a subtle, indirect fashion, yet have a powerful effect on behavior.[14] To get a feel for the effect of organizational values, consider how differences in behavior at Southwest Airlines and Value Line reflect differences in values. When Southwest Airlines was formed to compete against giant airlines like American and United, its CEO Herbert Kelleher and his second in command, Colleen Barrett, knew they had their work cut out for them. To compete they had to provide low-cost, high-quality airline service to customers. Kelleher and Barrett set out to develop terminal and instrumental values that would create a culture accomplishing this goal—and they succeeded. Today, Southwest's organizational culture is the envy of its competitors.

Southwest managers and employees are committed to the success of the organization. They do everything they can to help one another and provide customers with excellent service (a terminal value). Four times a year, Southwest managers work as baggage handlers, ticket agents, and flight attendants so they get a feel for the problems facing other employees. An informal norm makes it possible for employees to meet with Barrett (and Kelleher sometimes, although he has retired as CEO) every Friday at noon in the company's Dallas parking lot for a company cookout. Both managers have encouraged employees to be creative and to develop rules and norms to solve their own problems. To please customers, for example, employees dress up on special days like Halloween and Valentine's Day and wear "fun uniforms" every Friday. In addition, they try to develop innovative ways to improve customer service and satisfaction.

All employees participate in a bonus system based on the company's performances, and employees own over 20 percent of the airline's stock, which, not surprisingly, has consistently performed well. The entrance hall at Southwest Airline's headquarters at Love Field in Dallas is full of plaques earned by employees for their outstanding performance. Everybody in the organization cooperates to achieve Southwest's goal of providing low-cost, high-quality service, and Southwest's culture seems to be working to its advantage.

Former Southwest Airlines CEO Herb Kelleher (at left) and his second in command, Colleen Barrett, set out to develop terminal and instrumental values that would provide low-cost, high-quality airline service to customers. They created an organizational culture that accomplished this goal.

Contrast Southwest's culture with that of Value Line, Inc. Jean Buttner, publisher of the Value Line Investment Survey, fashioned an organizational culture that employees hate and no one envies. In her attempt to reduce costs and improve efficiency, Buttner created instrumental values of frugality and economy that soured employees' attitudes toward the organization. Among the other strict rules she created, employees were told to sign in by 9:00 A.M. every day and sign out when leaving. If they faked their arrival or departure time, they faced dismissal. Because at Value Line messy desks are considered signs of unproductivity, Buttner required department managers to file a "clean surfaces report" every day, certifying that employees have tidied their desks.[15] Buttner keeps salary increases as small as possible, and she has kept the company's bonus plan and health plan under tight rein.

Did promoting these terminal and instrumental values pay off? Many highly trained, professional workers left Value Line because of the hostile atmosphere produced by these "economical" values and work rules that debase employees. This turnover generated discontent among the company's customers. The relationship between employees and Buttner became so poor that employees reportedly put up a notice on their bulletin board criticizing Buttner's management style and suggesting that the company could use some new leadership. Buttner's response to this message was to remove the bulletin board. Clearly, Buttner did not create a culture of cooperation at Value Line.

The terminal and instrumental values that Kelleher and Buttner developed to manage their organizations elicited very different responses from their employees. The cultural values at Southwest led employees to perceive that they were appreciated by the organization and that the organization wanted to reward behavior that supported its goals. The cultural values at Value Line, on the other hand, alienated employees, reduced commitment and loyalty, and increased employee turnover.[16] Clearly, an organization's cultural values are important shapers of members' behaviors.[17] Shared cultural values provide a common reference point and smooth interactions among organizational members. People who share an organization's values may come to identify strongly with the organization, and feelings of self-worth may flow from their membership in it.[18] Employees of Southwest Airlines, for example, seem to value greatly their membership in the organization and are committed to it.

How Is an Organization's Culture Transmitted to Its Members?

The ability of an organization's culture to motivate employees and increase its effectiveness is directly related to the way in which members learn the organization's values. They learn the pivotal values and norms from an organization's formal socialization practices and from the signs, symbols, stories, rites, ceremonies, and organizational language that develop informally as an organization's culture matures. (See Exhibit 17.2).

Socialization and Socialization Tactics

As we discussed in Chapter 10, newcomers to an organization must learn the values and norms that guide existing members' behavior and decision making.[19] Newcomers are outsiders, and only when they have learned an organization's values and act in accordance with its norms will long-time members accept them as insiders. To learn an organization's culture, newcomers must obtain information about cultural values, and they do so formally by participating in an organization's socialization program. They do so informally by observing and working with other employees.

We discussed socialization in detail in Chapter 10. Recall Van Mannen and Schein's model for structuring the organization's socialization experience so newcomers learn its values. In turn, these values influence the way in which newcomers respond to a situation: Do they react passively and obediently to commands and orders? Are they creative and innovative in searching for solutions to problems? When organizations combine these tactics as suggested in Exhibit 10.1, there is some evidence that they can influence an individual's role orientation. Military-style socialization discussed in Chapter 10 is one such example (see p. 347). Dell has built a culture using socialization practices that are very instructive in this respect. The Texas-based computer maker has developed a lean organizational culture focused on cutting costs and providing excellent customer service to help

EXHIBIT 17.2

Ways of Transmitting Organizational Culture

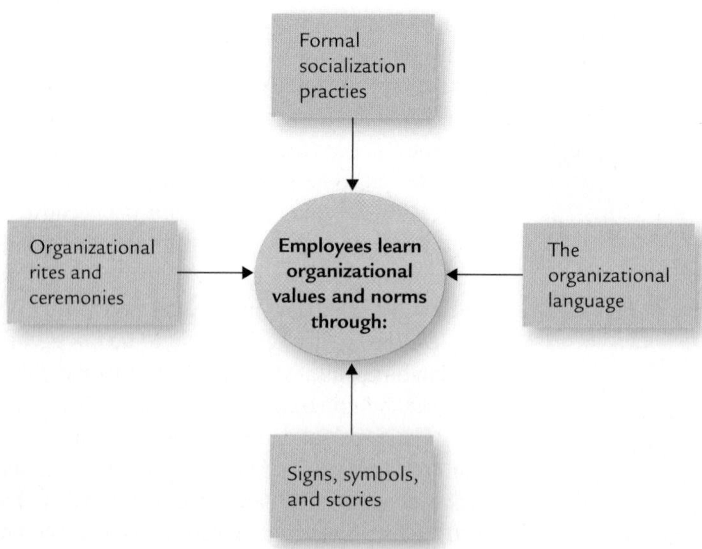

sell its products. How does Dell socialize its new employees so they learn the vales ands norms of its culture? In a very specific way: Just like the army, Dell has a "boot camp" to which it sends its employees for training.[20] For four weeks employees go to a Dell training center outside Austin, Texas, where they are educated about the basic software that operates Dell's products: MS office, WindowsNT, and Visual basic, the main programming language installed on the machines, are among the programs they study. At the end of the boot camp there is a mini project in which 6 to 9 people are given a real business problem facing Dell. They must arrive at a solution to the problem and then present their findings to a panel of instructors. During this training process new employees also learn the basic values and norms that guide Dell employees; they are also taught how to provide excellent customer service. Employees form many common bonds because they are all socialized together and trained in such a focused, concentrated way.[21]

After "boot camp," a week of shadowing is required: The new hire observes an experienced Dell employee performing the tasks that comprise his or her organizational role. The new hire is able to ask questions and absorb information quickly and effectively. In this way Dell's lean, cost-cutting organizational values are transmitted quickly to employees. The careful socialization process has become increasingly important at Dell because its rapid growth has required the company to recruit many new employees who must be brought quickly up to speed.[22]

Stories, Ceremonies, and Organizational Language

The cultural values of an organization are often evident in the stories, ceremonies, and language found in the organization.[23] At Southwest Airlines, for example, employees wearing costumes on Halloween, the Friday cookouts with top managers, and employees pitching in to help to speed aircraft turnaround as needed all reinforce and communicate the company's culture.

Organizations use several types of ceremonial rites to communicate cultural norms and values.[24] *Rites of passage* mark an individual's entry to, promotion in, and departure from the organization. The socialization programs used by the army and by Dell are rites of passage; so, too, are the ways in which an organization grooms people for promotion or retirement. *Rites of integration*, such as shared announcements of organizational success, office parties, and company cookouts, build and reinforce common bonds between members. *Rites of enhancement*, like awards dinners, newspaper releases, and employee promotions, give an organization the opportunity to publicly acknowledge and reward employees' contributions and thereby enhance their commitment to its values.

The stories and language of an organization are also important media for communicating culture. Stories (be they fact or fiction) about organizational heroes provide important clues about cultural values and norms. Such stories can reveal the kinds of behaviors that the organization values and the kinds of practices it frowns upon. Studying the stories and language can reveal the values that guide behavior.[25] At 3M, for example, to build cooperative team values and norms each team is headed by a "product champion," who takes the responsibility for building cohesive team relationships. Each team is also given a "management sponsor," one of 3M's top managers whose job it is to help the team get resources and provide support when the going gets tough. After all, product development is a very risky undertaking, and many projects do not succeed. Clearly, a team with a champion and a sponsor is more likely to experience success!

Because language is the principal medium of communication in organizations, the characteristic names or phrases a company uses to frame and describe events provide important clues about norms and values. Many organizations use technical languages to facilitate cooperation between their employees.[26] For example, because many 3M products are flat, such as Scotch tape, Post-It notes, floppy disks, sandpaper, and transparencies, the quality of "flatness" has come to be closely associated with 3M's terminal values. Flatness is often a winning theme in 3M's corporate language. At Microsoft, employees have developed a shorthand language of software-type phrases to describe communication problems. Technical languages are used by the military, sports teams, in hospitals, and in many other specialized work contexts.

The concept of organizational language encompasses not only spoken language but also how people dress, the offices they occupy, the company cars they drive, and how they formally address one another. In Microsoft and some other organizations casual dress is the norm. Indeed, in the last decade many large companies that used to emphasize conservative business-type clothing like Ford and IBM now encourage "business casual" clothing and "dress-down" days where employees can wear whatever they feel most comfortable in.

Like socialization practices, organizational language, ceremonies, and stories help people "learn the ropes" and the organization's cultural values. As the following OB Today shows, Wal-Mart uses many of these means to socialize its employees and enhance its organizational culture.

OB Today

Sam Walton and Wal-Mart's Culture

Wal-Mart, headquartered in Bentonville, Arkansas, is the largest retailer in the world. In 2003, it sold over $250 billion worth of products.[27] A large part of Wal-Mart's success is due to the nature of the culture that its founder, the late Sam Walton, established for the company. Walton wanted all his managers and workers to take a hands-on approach to their jobs and be totally committed to Wal-Mart's main goal, which he defined as total customer satisfaction. To motivate his employees, Walton created a culture that gave employees at all levels, who are called associates, continuous feedback about their performance and the company's performance.

To involve his associates in the business and encourage them to develop work behaviors focused on providing quality customer service, Walton established strong cultural values and norms for his company. Some of the norms associates are expected to follow include the "ten-foot attitude." The ten-foot attitude encourages associates, in Walton's word, to "promise that whenever you come within 10 feet of a customer, you will look him in the eye, greet him, and ask him if you can help him." The "sundown rule" states that employees should strive to answer customer requests by sundown of the day they are made. The Wal-Mart cheer ("Give me a W, give me an A," and so on), is used in all its stores.[28]

To encourage Wal-Mart's employees or "associates" to develop work behaviors focused on providing quality customer service, Walton established strong cultural values and norms for his company.

The strong customer-oriented values that Walton created are exemplified in the stories its members tell one another about Wal-Mart's concern for its customers. They include stories like the one about Sheila, who risked her own safety when she jumped in front of

a car to prevent a little boy from being struck; about Phyllis, who administered CPR to a customer who had suffered a heart attack in her store; and about Annette, who gave up the Power Ranger she had on layaway for her own son to fulfill the birthday wish of a customer's son.[29] The strong Wal-Mart culture helps to control and motivate employees to achieve the stringent output and financial targets the company has set for itself.[30]

A notable way Wal-Mart builds its culture is at its annual stockholders' meeting, an extravagant ceremony celebrating the company's success.[31] Every year Wal-Mart flies thousands of its highest performers to its annual meeting at corporate headquarters in Arkansas for a show featuring performers like exercise guru Richard Simmons and singers Reba McIntyre and Andy Williams. Wal-Mart feels that expensive entertainment is a reward its employees deserve and that it reinforces the company's high-performance values and culture. The proceedings are even broadcast live to all of Wal-Mart's stores so employees can celebrate the company's achievements together.[32] This is just one way Wal-Mart uses information technology to bolster its culture.[33] Online training programs and company announcements are electronically sent to all its stores on a regular basis so managers and employees know exactly what is happening at the company's many stores around the world.

Finally, organizational symbols often convey an organization's cultural values to its members and to others outside the organization.[34] In some organizations, for example, the size of peoples' offices, their location on the third floor or the thirty-third floor, the luxury of the furniture in them, and so on symbolize the cultural values an organization holds. Is the organization hierarchical and status-conscious, for example, or are informal, participative work relationships encouraged? At General Motors, the executive suite on the top floor of the Detroit headquarters is isolated from the rest of the building and open only to top GM executives. A private corridor and stairway link top managers' offices, and a private elevator connects them to a heated parking garage.

Sometimes, the very design of the building itself is a symbol of an organization's values. For example, the Walt Disney Company hired famed Japanese architect Arata Isozaki to design the Team Disney Building, which houses Disney's "imagineering unit" in Orlando, Florida. This building's contemporary and unusual design, featuring unusual shapes and bright colors, conveys the importance of imagination and creativity to the Walt Disney Company and to the people who work in it. When Louis Gerstner took control of IBM in the early 1990s when its sales were collapsing, one of his first actions was to build a brand-new, campus-style headquarters building similar to Disney's. He moved all IBM's managers to open-plan offices and suites in the new building. IBM's old high-rise skyscraper building, which Gerstner believed reduced teamwork and innovation and encouraged conservative thinking, was sold.

You're the Management Expert

A Culture of Cleanliness

You're the training expert for a fast-food restaurant chain that is opening up a location in a new city. One of your company's major priorities is food safety and cleanliness. The chain has never in its history had a case of food poisoning, and preserving this record is central to its culture. In fact, the chain insists its employees exhibit high personal hygiene and that they thoroughly clean and disinfect the restaurants each night upon closing. Your job is to instill these core values in the new hires quickly. How will you design your socialization program?

Factors Shaping Organizational Culture

Now that you have seen what organizational culture is and how members learn and become part of an organization's culture, some difficult questions can be addressed: Where does organizational culture come from? Why do different companies have different cultures? Why might a culture that for many years helps an organization achieve its goals suddenly harm the organization?

Organizational culture is shaped by the interaction of four main factors: the personal and professional characteristics of people within the organization, organizational ethics, the nature of the employment relationship, and the design of its organizational structure (see Exhibit 17.3). These factors work together to produce different cultures in different organizations and cause changes in culture over time.

Characteristics of People Within the Organization

The ultimate source of organizational culture is the people who make up the organization. If you want to know why cultures differ, look at their members. Organizations A, B, and C develop distinctly different cultures because they attract, select, and retain people who have different values, personalities, and ethics.[35] Recall the attraction-selection-attrition model from Chapter 2. People may be attracted to an organization whose values match theirs; similarly, an organization selects people who share its values. Over time, people who do not fit in leave. The result is that people inside the organization become more and more similar, the values of the organization become more and more pronounced and clearcut, and the culture becomes more and more distinct from that of similar organizations.[36]

The founder of an organization has a substantial influence on the organization's initial culture because of his or her personal values and beliefs.[37] Founders set the scene for the later development of culture because they not only establish the new organization's values but also hire its first members. Presumably, the people selected by the founder have values and interests similar to his or hers.[38] Over time, members buy into the founder's vision and perpetuate the founder's values in the organization.[39] This has certainly been the case at Microsoft and Dell, whose founders championed innovative and frugal values, respectively.

An important implication of this is that an organization's members become similar over time and come to share the same values. This, in fact, may actually hinder their abilities to adapt and respond to changes in the environment.[40] This happens when the organization's values and norms become *so* strong and promote *so* much group cohesiveness, members

EXHIBIT 17.3

Where an Organization's Culture Comes From

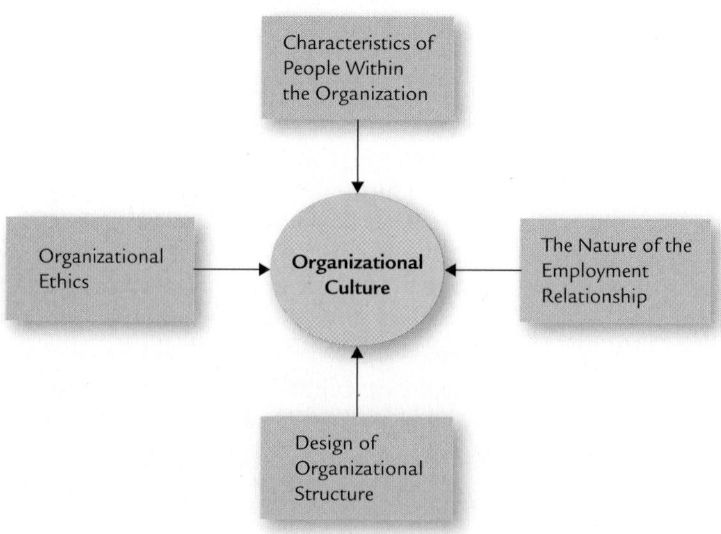

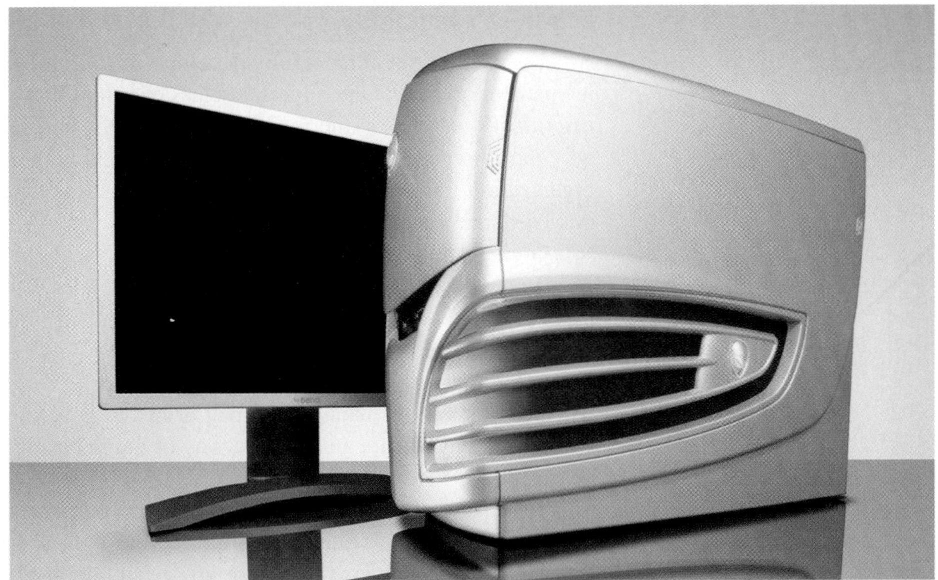

Computers are not just toys as this picture of a powerful Alienware desktop gaming computer suggests. Alienware, which was acquired by Dell in 2006, continues to push the limits of high-performance computing for gamers, creative professionals and the government space.

misperceive the environment.[41] Also, groupthink might appear as members reinforce one another's misperceptions and respond inappropriately to them. Groupthink has been a problem at many companies. Even though Microsoft has strong, cohesive values that bond its members, Bill Gates has worked hard to make it clear that employees should express their own personal views, even though they might differ from his and everyone else's in the organization. One example of how Gates's policy has worked to Microsoft's advantage occurred when the company started its Internet service, MSN. The company believed the popularity of its Windows platform would allow it to control the future development of the Internet, even though Netscape had introduced a popular browser. Two concerned Microsoft programmers working in its Internet division wrote a memo to top managers arguing that Microsoft would end up with *no* control over the Internet, given the pace at which it was developing. They also argued that Netscape's browser would become the dominant way people would access the Internet. The programmers argued that to compete with Netscape, Microsoft should rush to develop its own web browser.

After reading their memo, Gates convened a major organization-wide meeting. Top managers listened while all of the issues were aired and admitted they were wrong. The company then diverted most of its human talent to develop its own browser as quickly as possible. Within one year, the first version of Internet Explorer was ready, and Microsoft even went so far as to give it away free to users. This posed a major challenge for Netscape, which had been charging users for Netscape Navigator.

Successful companies like Microsoft certainly need a strong set of terminal values emphasizing innovation and hard work. However, they need to be careful their very success doesn't lead members to believe their company will always be the "best" in the business, or "invincible." Some companies have made this mistake. The old IBM of the 1980s believed its control of the mainframe market made it invincible; IBM employees laughed off the potential threat personal computers posed. The CEO of another dominant computer maker at that time, Digital Equipment, reportedly commented that "personal computers are just toys." Within a few years, Digital Equipment was experiencing huge losses.

The "people make the place" view of organizational culture explains how an organization develops the shared cultural values that can have such as powerful effect on the work attitudes and behaviors. The "people make the place" view also implies the culture of an organization must be managed by the people who control it to ensure that it does not lead to problems.[42] For this reason, some experts advocate that a company should have a board of independent-minded directors who aren't afraid to challenge top management and that CEOs and top managers should be changed regularly. We look at this issue later in the chapter when we discuss ethics.

Organizational Ethics

ORGANIZATIONAL ETHICS
The moral values, beliefs, and rules that establish the appropriate way for an organization and its members to deal with each other and with people outside the organization.

An organization can purposefully develop some kinds of cultural values to control the way its members behave. One important class of values that falls into this category stems from **organizational ethics**, the moral values, beliefs, and rules that establish the appropriate way for an organization and its members to deal with each other and people outside the organization. Ethical values rest on principles stressing the importance of treating everyone fairly and equally.

Organizations are constantly making choices about the right, or ethical, thing to do. A company like IBM, Target, or Sears might wonder whether it should have procedures in place giving advance notice to its employees about impending layoffs or plant closings. Traditionally, companies have been reluctant to do so because they fear employees will become hostile or apathetic and perform poorly. Similarly, a company has to decide whether to allow its managers to pay bribes to government officials in foreign countries where such payoffs are an accepted way of doing business, even though they may actually be illegal.[43]

To make these decisions, an organization purposefully implants ethical instrumental values in its culture.[44] Such ethics outline the right and wrong ways to behave when the action taken may help one person or group but hurt another.[45] Ethical values, and the rules and norms that reflect them, are an integral part of an organization's culture because they help to determine how its members will manage situations and make decisions.

The question is how are organizational ethics formed? Ethical values are a product of societal, professional, and individual ethics.[46] (See Exhibit 17.4.) We discuss each of the aspects next.

Societal ethics. The ethics of the country or society in which the organization exists are important determinants of its ethical values. Societal ethics are the moral values formalized in a society's legal system, in its customs and practices, and in the unwritten norms and values that its people follow in their daily lives. Most people automatically follow the ethical norms and values of the society in which they live because they have internalized them and made them their own.[47] When societal ethics are codified into law (rules), an organization is legally required to follow these laws in its dealings with people inside and outside of the organization.

One of top management's main responsibilities is to ensure that the organization's members obey the law. Indeed, in certain situations top managers can be held accountable for the conduct of their subordinates. One of the main ways top managers ensure ethical behavior on the part of their organizations is by instilling good values in their members.

EXHIBIT 17.4

Sources of Organizational Ethics

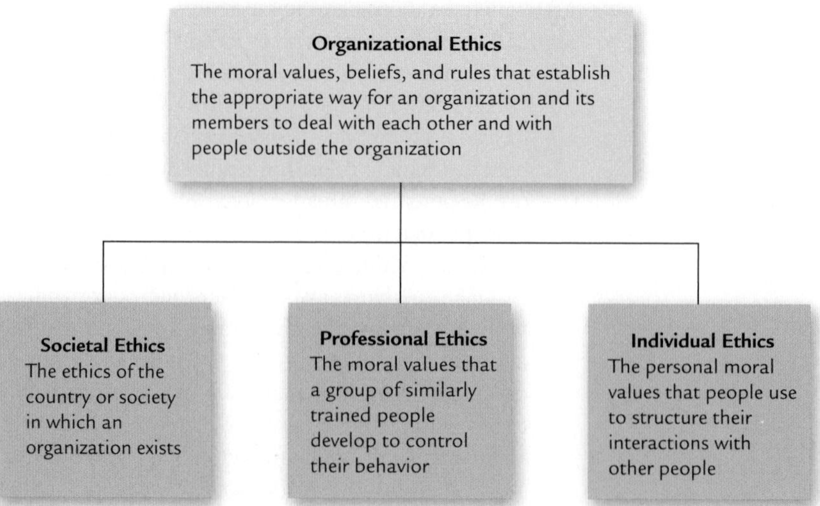

However, while some companies (like Johnson & Johnson and Merck) are well known for their ethical cultures, many organizations nonetheless act illegally, immorally, and unethically. These organizations frequently do little to develop ethical values for their employees to follow.

Professional ethics. Professional ethics are the moral values that a group of similarly trained people develop to control their performance of a task or use their resources.[48] People internalize the values and norms of their professions just as they do the values and norms of their societies. Generally, they follow these norms when deciding how to behave.[49] Some organizations have many types of professionals working for them—nurses, lawyers, researchers, doctors, and accountants—whose behavior is governed by professional ethics. These ethics help shape the organization's culture and determine how members deal with other people and groups. Medical ethics, for example, control how doctors and nurses do their jobs and help establish the culture of the organizations they work for. Professional ethics, for example, encourage doctors to act in best interests of their patients; performing unnecessary medical procedures for one's own financial benefit, for example, is considered unethical. Similarly, at companies like Merck and Johnson & Johnson, professional ethics induce scientists and technicians to behave ethically when preparing and presenting the results of their research.

Most professional groups have the authority to enforce the ethical standards of their profession. Doctors and lawyers, for example, can be barred from practicing their profession if they violate professional rules.

Individual ethics. Individual ethics are the personal moral values that people use to structure their interactions with other people. In many instances, personal ethics mirror societal ethics and originate in the law. But personal ethics are also the result of an individual's upbringing. They may stem from his or her family, friends, or membership in a church or other social organization. Because personal ethics influence how a person will act in an organization, an organization's culture is strongly affected by the people who are in a position to establish its ethical values. As we saw earlier, the founder of an organization plays a particularly important role when it comes to establishing the ethical norms and values of the organization.

The Employment Relationship

A third factor shaping organizational culture is the nature of the employment relationship a company establishes with its employees via its human resource policies and practices. Recall from Chapter 8 our discussion of the changing employment relationships between organizations and their employees: Human resource policies, like a company's hiring, promotion, and layoff policies along with pay and benefits, can influence how hard employees will work to achieve the organization's goals, how attached they will be to it, and whether or not they will buy into its values and norms.[50]

Whenever people must work together to accomplish a common goal the potential for miscommunication, competition, and conflict is always present. Well-designed human resource policies function as the "oil" preventing "people problems" from occurring and can align an employee's goals with his or her company's. They are also a good indicator of how the organization values its employees. Consider the effects of a company's promotion policy, for example. If a company pursues a policy of promoting "from within," employees who already work for the organization are recruited to fill higher-level positions. On the other hand, a company with a policy of promotion "from without" will fill its open positions with qualified outsiders. What impact will this have?

Promoting from within will bolster strong values and norms, build loyalty, and encourage employees to work hard to advance within the organization. Upward mobility is a major motivating factor for many people. Promoting from within also helps a company retain its highest-performing employees. If employees see no prospect of being promoted from within, they are likely to begin looking for opportunities elsewhere. As a result, values and norms emerge that lend themselves to employee turnover and a temporary relationship between companies and employees. This is what has happened at many companies in the high-tech sector, which has gone through great turmoil in recent years. An estimated one million U.S. tech employees lost their jobs following the burst of the dot.com bubble at the turn of the century. Companies like Apple Computer, Hewlett Packard, and IBM—well known for their strong corporate values, long-term employment, risk-taking initiatives, and employee commitment—were some of the corporations forced to lay off the most employees.

Another important human resource policy relates to the company's pay level and incentive systems. A company can choose to pay its employees above, below, or at the industry-average pay level. Some companies, Microsoft, Merck, and IBM among them, choose to pay their employees above the average-industry pay level. On one hand, above-average pay attracts the best-qualified employees. On the other hand, some companies pay below-average wages and accept a high level of employee turnover as normal. Similarly, there are many different kinds of incentive pay linked to individual, group, and company performance that affect employee work attitudes and behaviors. To retain their employees, many companies give them bonuses and company stock linked to their contributions or years of service. This tends to make employees feel like "owners" of the company. Companies like IBM, Microsoft, and Accenture believe incentives such as this encourage the development of values and norms that improve organizational effectiveness.[51] We saw how Jean Buttner's attempt to limit Value Line employees' benefits resulted in hostility and high turnover. We also saw how Herbert Kelleher, by establishing a company-wide stock-option system and encouraging employees to find better ways to make customers happy, fostered commitment and loyalty at Southwest Airlines. Indeed, evidence suggests that linking pay to performance creates a culture of committed and motivated employees who perform at high levels. The following OB Today shows how one company did just this.

OB Today

Bimba Changes Its Approach

The Bimba Manufacturing Company, based in Monee, Illinois, manufactures aluminum cylinders. Its owner Charles Bimba decided to sell the company to its employees by establishing an employee stock-ownership plan (ESOP). He kept 10 percent of the shares; the other 90 percent was sold to employees. Some of the employees' money came from an already existing profit-sharing plan; the rest was borrowed from a bank.[52]

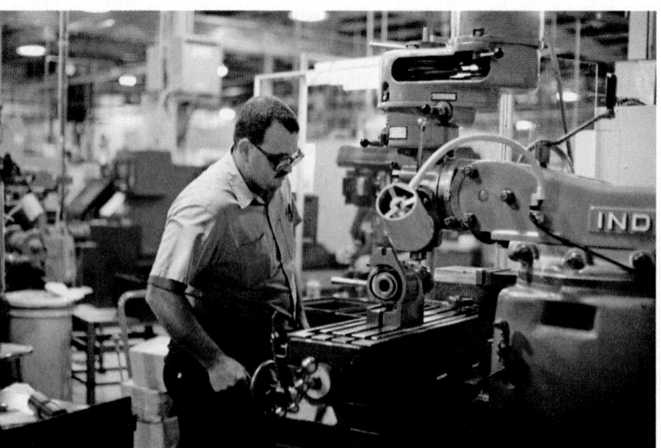

Before Bimba, Inc. employees purchased shares in their company, they merely followed managers' orders. Now these same employees think like owners. Teamwork and innovation have dramatically improved the aluminum cylinder maker's operations.

Changes in the company since the ESOP was introduced have been dramatic, and the orientation of the work force to the organization has totally changed. Previously, the

company had two groups of employees: managers who made the rules and workers who carried them out. Workers rarely made suggestions and generally just obeyed orders. Now, cross-functional teams composed of managers and workers meet regularly to discuss problems and find new ways to improve quality. These teams also meet regularly with customers to better meet their needs.

Because of the incentives provided by the new ESOP, management and workers have developed new working relationships based on teamwork to achieve excellence and high quality. Each team hires its own members and spends considerable time socializing new employees in the new culture of the organization. The new cooperative spirit in the plant has forced managers to relearn their roles. They now listen to workers and act as advisers rather than superiors.

So far, changing the company's property rights system has paid off. Both its sales and employment have doubled. Bimba has expanded to a new, larger facility, and it has opened facilities in both Europe and Asia. Furthermore, workers have repaid the entire loan they took out to finance the employee stock purchase.[53] In the words of one worker, the ESOP has led to "an intense change in the way we look at our jobs."[54] It has totally changed Bimba's corporate culture and the commitment of its work force.

Organizational Structure

As the Bimba story illustrates, redesigning human resource policies and introducing new training, promotion, and incentive systems can alter an organization's culture by changing its instrumental values and norms. Bimba's culture changed because it altered its organizational structure and empowered self-managed teams. At Bimba, this change eliminated the need for close supervision. Coordination is achieved by teams of employees who value cooperation and are motivated by the prospect of sharing in the wealth the organization generates.

We have seen how the values and norms that shape employee work attitudes and behaviors are derived from the organization's people, ethics, and HRM policies. A fourth source of cultural values comes from the organization's structure. Recall from Chapter 16 that *organizational structure* is the formal system of task and reporting relationships that an organization establishes to coordinate and motivate its employees. Because different structures give rise to different cultures, managers need to design a certain kind of organizational structure in order to create a certain kind of culture. Mechanistic structures, for example, give rise to totally different sets of norms, rules, and cultural values than do organic structures.

Recall from Chapter 16 that *mechanistic structures* are tall, highly centralized, and standardized, and *organic structures* are flat and decentralized and rely on mutual adjustment. In a tall, centralized organization, people have relatively little personal autonomy, and desirable behaviors include being cautious, obeying authority, and respecting traditions. Thus, a mechanistic structure is likely to give rise to a culture in which predictability and stability are desired end states. In a flat, decentralized structure, people have more freedom to choose and control their own activities, and desirable instrumental values include being creative or courageous and taking risks. Thus an organic structure is likely to give rise to a culture in which innovation and flexibility are desired terminal values.

An organization's structure can promote cultural values that foster integration and coordination. Out of stable task and role relationships, for example, emerge shared norms and rules that help reduce communications problems, prevent the distortion of information, and speed the flow of information. Moreover, norms, values, and a common organizational language can improve the performance of teams and task forces. It is easier for different functions to share information and trust one another when they share similar cultural values. One reason why product-development time is short and the organization is flexible in product team structures and matrix structures is that the reliance on face-to-face contact between functional specialists in teams forces those teams to quickly develop shared values and common responses to problems.

Whether a company is centralized or decentralized also leads to the development of different kinds of cultural values. By decentralizing authority and empowering employees an organization can establish values that encourage and reward creativity or innovation. In doing this, an organization signals them that it's "okay" to be innovative and do things their own way—as long as their actions are consistent with the good of the organization.

Conversely, in some organizations, it is important that employees do not make decisions on their own and that their actions be open to the scrutiny of superiors. In cases like this, centralization can be used to create cultural values that reinforce obedience and accountability. For example, in nuclear power plants, values that promote stability, predictability, and obedience to authority are deliberately fostered to prevent disasters.[55] Through norms and rules, employees are taught the importance of behaving consistently and honestly, and they learn that sharing information with supervisors, especially information about mistakes or errors, is the only acceptable form of behavior.[56]

Adaptive Cultures versus Inert Cultures

Adaptive cultures are those whose values and norms help an organization build momentum, grow, and change as needed to achieve its goals and be effective. Inert cultures are those that lead to values and norms that fail to motivate or inspire employees; they lead to stagnation and often failure over time. What leads to an adaptive or inert culture? Researchers have found that organizations with strong adaptive cultures like Whirlpool, GE, Toyota, Google, and IBM invest in their employees. They adopt human resource practices that demonstrate their commitment to their members by, for example, emphasizing the long-term nature of the employment relationship and trying to avoid layoffs. These companies develop long-term career paths for their employees and invest heavily in training and development to make them more valuable to the organization. In these ways, terminal and instrumental values pertaining to the worth of the people working within the organization encourage the development of supportive work attitudes and behaviors.

In adaptive cultures, employees often receive rewards linked directly to their performance and to the performance of the company as a whole. Sometimes, employee stock-ownership plans are developed. In an ESOP, workers as a group are allowed to buy a significant percentage of their company's stock. Workers who are owners of the company have an incentive to develop skills improving their performance levels. These employees are also more likely to search actively for ways to improve quality, efficiency, and performance. At Dell, for example, employees are able to buy Dell stock at a steep (15 percent) discount and build a sizable stake in the company over time.

However, some organizations develop cultures with values that do not include protecting and increasing the worth of their people as a major goal. Their employment practices are based on short-term employment needs and minimal investment in employees, who perform simple, routine tasks. Moreover, employees are not often rewarded based on their performance and therefore have little incentive to improve their skills to help the organization meet its goals. In a company with an inert culture and poor relationships with its employees, the instrumental values of noncooperation, laziness, and output restriction norms are common. Employees are content to be told what to do because they have little motivation to perform beyond the minimum requirements. Unfortunately, such a hierarchical structure and emphasis on close supervision produce a culture that doesn't readily adapt to a change. By contrast, an adaptive culture emphasizes entrepreneurship and respect for employees. Innovative organizational structures like crossfunctional teams that empower and motivate employees are likely to develop in such a culture. This puts the organization in a better position to adapt to the changing business climate.

An organization that seeks to manage and change its culture must take a hard look at all four factors that shape culture: the characteristics of its members (particularly the founder), its ethical values, human resource policies, and organizational structure. However, changing a culture can be difficult because of the ways these factors interact and affect one another.[57] Often, a major reorganization is necessary for a cultural change to occur, as we discuss in Chapter 18. The way Google creates a culture that makes it easy to adapt and change, and which encourages ongoing learning and creativity, is discussed in the following OB Today.

OB Today

How Goggle's Founders Created a Groovy Culture

Google, the web-based services company, whose fast-growing product line includes state-of-the-art search engines, e-mail, and chat, was started in 1995 when two Stanford graduates in computer science, Sergey Brin and Larry Page, collaborated to develop a new kind of search engine technology. They understood the shortcomings of existing search engines and by 1998 they had developed a superior engine that they felt was ready to go online. They raised $1 million from family, friends, and risk-taking "angel" investors to buy the hardware necessary to connect Google's software to the Internet.

At first, Google answered only 10,000 inquires a day—its plain home page is hardly very welcoming—but in a few months it was answering 500,000 inquires; by the end of 1999,3 million; end of 2000, 60 million; and in the spring of 2001 it reached 100 million per day![58] Today, Google has become the most-widely used search engine and the company has one of the top five most-used Internet web-sites. So quickly has Google's rise been that rivals like Yahoo! and Microsoft are struggling to catch up and prevent Google from providing all the services they offer, and doing it better and for free! (Google makes billions by selling advertising space on its widely used web-applications.)

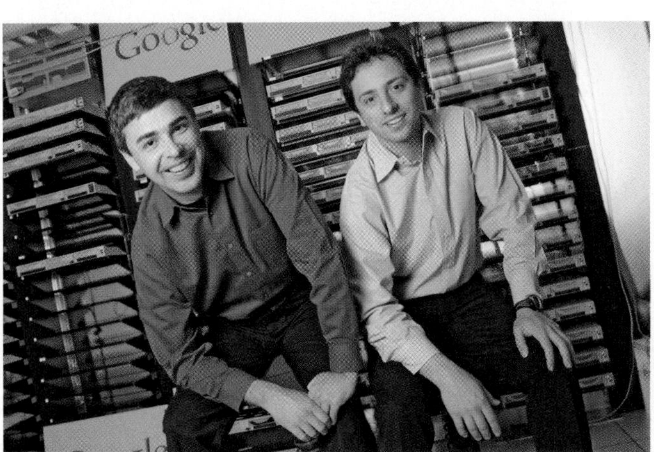

Pictured are Sergey Brin and Larry Page, the founders of Google, who started their company in 1995 to provide customers with a state-of-the-art search engine. Google has gone on to create a whole host of customer-friendly software products, many under development in "Google Labs" that have made it a star in the information technology world.

Google's explosive growth is largely due to the culture or entrepreneurship and innovation its founders cultivated from the start. Although in 2006 Google has grown to over 2,000 employees worldwide, its founders claim that it still maintains a small company feel because its culture empowers employees, who it calls staffers or "Googlers," to create the best software possible. Brin and Page created Google's entrepreneurial culture in several ways.

From the beginning, lacking space and seeking to keep operating costs low, Google staffers worked in "high-density clusters" that encourage intensive team interactions. Three or four employees, each equipped with a high-powered Linux workstation, sharing a desk, couch, and chairs shaped like large rubber balls, work together to improve its technology. Even when Google moved into more spacious surroundings at its modernistic "Googleplex" headquarters building, staffers continued to work in shared spaces and so its team atmosphere was perpetuated.

Google also designed its building so that staffers are constantly meeting each other in Google's funky lobby, in the Google Café where everyone eats together, in its state-of-the-art recreational facilities, and in its "snack rooms" equipped with bins packed with cereals, gummi bears, yogurt, and, carrots, and, of course make-your-own cappuccino. They also created many opportunities for employees to gather together at informal events such as a TGIF open meeting and a twice-weekly outdoor roller-hockey game where staffers are encouraged to bring down the founders.[59]

All this attention to creating what just might be the "grooviest" company headquarters in the world did not come about by chance. Brin and Page knew that Google's most important strength would be its ability to attract the best software engineers in the world and motivate them to perform well. Common offices, lobbies, cafes and so on bring all staffers into close contact with each other, develop collegiality, encourage them to share their new ideas with their colleagues, and encourage them to constantly improve its web-based applications and find new products to grow the company. Google also continually searches for new ideas emerging in the WWW, and in 2005 it bought a company that specializes in developing web-based personal word processing and storage. It will use the skills of these newcomers to develop products that will compete directly with Microsoft's PC-based software.

The freedom Google gives its staffers to pursue new ideas is a clear signal of its founders' desire to empower them to be innovative and to work to make Google the software powerhouse in the next decade. Also, to motivate staffers to innovate important new software applications, Google's founders reward their achievements by giving them stock in the company, which effectively makes staffers its owners as well. So successful have they been in designing Google's culture that in the mid-2000s, alienated by the growing bureaucracy at Microsoft, and the lack of opportunity to make real wealth (Microsoft no longer offers stock options but gives employees stock based on performance), Google has been attracting away many of its top software engineers who welcome the challenge of working for the visionary company.

Google's founders understand that building and maintaining a strong organizational culture is a prerequisite for successful, ongoing innovation.[60] In August 2004, Goggle went public and its shares, which were sold at $85 a share, were worth over $100 by the end of the first day of trading and rose to as high of $475 by January 2006. This made Brin and Page's stake in the company worth billions, and many of its employees are now multimillionaires. When Google went public, its founders also created two classes of stock, an ordinary class, and a special class that gives them the voting rights and power to control the future of their company. No outside company can take over Google. Its future is in their hands and those of its staffers, and what the company will become is something widely debated inside the company and beyond.

Traits of Strong, Adaptive Corporate Cultures

Several scholars have attempted to uncover the common traits that strong and adaptive corporate cultures share and to find out whether there is a particular set of values that dominates adaptive cultures that is missing from weak or inert ones. An early, but still influential, attempt is T. J. Peters and R. H. Waterman's account of the values and norms characteristic of successful organizations and their cultures.[61] They argue that organizations with strong cultures are characterized by three common value sets.

First, successful companies have values promoting a *bias for action*. The emphasis is on autonomy and entrepreneurship, and employees are encouraged to take risks—for example, to create new products—even though there is no assurance that these products will be winners. Managers are closely involved in the day-to-day operations of the company and do not simply make strategic decisions isolated in some ivory tower, and employees have a "hands-on, value-driven approach."

The second set of values stems from the *nature of the organization's mission*. The company must stick with what it does best and maintain control over its core activities. A company can easily get sidetracked into pursuing activities outside its area of expertise just because they seem to promise a quick return. Management should cultivate values so that a company sticks to its knitting, which means staying with the businesses it knows best. A company must also establish close relationships with customers as a way of improving its competitive position. After all, who knows more about a company's performance than those who use its products or services? By emphasizing customer-oriented values, organizations are able to learn customers' needs and improve their ability to develop products and services customers desire. All these management values are strongly represented in companies profiled in this chapter, such as 3M, Wal-Mart, and Google; they are also found in companies like IBM, Dell, and Toyota, which are sure of their mission and take constant steps to maintain it.

The third set of values bears on *how to operate the organization*. A company should try to establish an organizational design that will motivate employees to do their best. Inherent in this set of values is the belief that productivity is obtained through people and that respect for the individual is the primary means by which a company can create the right atmosphere for productive behavior. A similar philosophy pervades the culture of Japanese companies, as we discuss in the following paragraph,[62] Many U.S. companies, such as 3M and Google pay this kind of attention to their employees. An emphasis on entrepreneurship and respect for the employee leads to the establishment of a structure that gives employees the latitude to make decisions and motivates them to succeed. Because a simple structure and a lean staff best fit this situation, the organization should be designed with only the number of managers and hierarchical levels that are necessary to get the job done. The organization should also be sufficiently decentralized to permit employees' participation but centralized enough for management to make sure that the company pursues its mission and that cultural values are closely followed.

These three main sets of values are at the heart of a strong organizational culture, and management transmits and maintains them through transformational and ethical leadership. Managers need to establish the values and norms that will help them bring their organizations into the future. When this is accomplished, only those people who fit the values are recruited into the organization, and, through training, they become a part of the organization's culture.

Values From The National Culture

The values and norms of a nation have a profound impact on the culture of each and every organization operating or headquartered within it. Culture, whether organizational or national, is a product of the values and norms that people use to guide and control their behavior. On a national level, a country's values and norms determine what kinds of attitudes and behaviors are acceptable or appropriate. Members of a particular national culture are instilled with these values as they grow up. Norms and social guidelines dictate the way they should behave toward one another and, often, toward people of different cultures.

Recall from Chapter 1 that national culture is the particular set of economic, political, and social values that exist in a particular country. U.S. national culture, for example, is based on capitalistic economic values, democratic political values, and individualistic, competitive social values—all characterize the way people in the United States live and work. The culture of a U.S. company is distinct from the cultures of Japanese, French, or German companies, for example, because the values of these countries differ in significant ways.

Hofstede's Model of National Culture

Researchers have spent considerable time and effort identifying similarities and differences between the cultural values and norms of different countries. A model of national culture developed by Geert Hofstede argues that differences in the values and norms of different countries are captured by five dimensions of culture.[63]

Individualism versus collectivism. The dimension that Hofstede called individualism versus collectivism focuses on the values that govern the relationship between individuals and groups. In countries where individualism prevails, values of individual achievement, freedom, and competition are stressed. In countries where collectivism prevails, values of group harmony, cohesiveness, and consensus are very strong, and the importance of cooperation and agreement between individuals is stressed. In collectivist cultures, the group is more important than the individual, and group members follow norms that stress group rather than personal interests. Japan epitomizes a country where collectivist values dominate, and the United States epitomizes a country where individualist values prevail.[64]

Power distance. Hofstede used power distance to refer to the degree to which a country accepts the fact that differences in its citizens' physical and intellectual capabilities give rise to inequalities in their well-being. This concept also measures the degree to which countries accept economic and social differences in wealth, status, and well-being as natural. Countries that allow inequalities to persist or increase are said to have high power distance. Professionally successful workers in high-power-distance countries amass wealth and pass it on to their children. In these countries, inequalities increase over time; the gap between rich and poor, with all the attendant political and social consequences, grows very large. In contrast, countries that dislike the development of large inequality gaps between their citizens are said to have low power distance. These countries use taxation or social welfare programs to reduce inequality and improve the lot of the least fortunate members of society. Low-power-distance countries are more interested in preventing a wide gap between rich and poor and discord between classes.

Advanced Western countries like the United States, Germany, the Netherlands, and the United Kingdom score relatively low on power distance and are high on individualism. Poor Latin American countries like Guatemala, Panama, and Asian countries like Malaysia and the Philippines score high on power distance and low on individualism.[65] These findings suggest that the cultural values of richer countries emphasize protecting the rights of individuals and, at the same time, provide a fair chance of success to every member of society. But even among Western countries there are differences. Both the Dutch and the British see their countries as more protective of the poor and disadvantaged than Americans, who believe that people have the right to be rich as well as the right to be poor.

Achievement versus nurturing orientation. Countries that are achievement oriented value assertiveness, performance, success, and competition and are results oriented. Countries that are nurturing oriented value the quality of life, warm personal relationships, and service and care for the weak. Japan and the United States tend to be achievement oriented. The Netherlands, Sweden, and Denmark tend to be nurturing oriented.

Uncertainty avoidance. Just as people differ in their tolerance for uncertainty and willingness to take risks, so do countries. Countries low on uncertainty avoidance (such as the United States and Hong Kong) are easygoing, value diversity, and are tolerant of differences in what people believe and do. Countries high on uncertainty avoidance (such as Japan and France) tend to be rigid and intolerant. In high-uncertainty-avoidance cultures, conformity to the values of the social and work groups to which a person belongs is the norm, and structured situations are preferred because they provide a sense of security.

Differences in national culture help explain why the cultures of companies in one country tend to be different from those of companies in another. French and German organizations, for example, admire the entrepreneurial drive of U.S. managers and the American work ethic but treat their managers and workers in different ways than do U.S. organizations. French and German organizations are far less concerned with issues of equity and opportunity in their human resource policies. In France, for example, social class still determines the gender, ethnicity, and background of employees who will successfully climb the organizational ladder. Moreover, German and French companies employ far fewer foreign nationals in their management ranks than do U.S. companies. In the Unites States, the most talented employees are likely to be promoted regardless of their national origin.[66]

Long-term versus short-term orientation. The last dimension that Hofstede identified concerns whether citizens of a country have a long- or a short-term orientation toward life and work.[67] A long-term orientation is likely to be the result of values that include thrift and persistence. A short-term orientation is likely to be the result of values that express a concern for maintaining personal stability or happiness and for living in the present. Countries with long-term orientations include Japan and Hong Kong, well known for their high rate of per capita savings. The United States and France, which tend to spend more and save less, have a short-term orientation.

Exhibit 17.5 lists the ways people in ten countries score on Hofstede's five dimensions of national culture.

National cultures vary widely, as do the values and norms that guide the ways people think and act. When an organization expands into foreign countries, it employs citizens whose values reflect those of the national culture. The fact that national culture is a determinant of organizational culture poses some interesting problems for an organization seeking to manage its global operations.[68]

EXHIBIT 17.5

Culture Dimension Scores for 10 Countries

	Power Distance	Individualism	Achievement Orientation	Uncertainty Avoidance	Long-Term Orientation
United States	L	H	H	L	L
Germany	L	H	H	M	M
Japan	M	M	H	H	H
France	H	H	M	H	L
Netherlands	L	H	L	M	M
Hong Kong	H	L	H	L	H
Indonesia	H	L	M	L	L
West Africa	H	L	M	M	L
Russia	H	M	L	H	L
China	H	L	M	M	H

Note: H = top third, M = medium third, L = bottom third } among 53 countries and regions for the first four dimensions; among 23 countries for the fifth

Source: Adapted from G. Hofstede, "Cultural Constraints in Management Theories." *Academy of Management Executive,* 7 (1993):91.

If differences in values between countries cause differences in attitudes and behaviors between workers in different subsidiaries, an organization will find it difficult to obtain the benefits of global learning. Different parts of the company located in different countries may develop different orientations toward the problems facing the company and their own subcultures. They will become concerned more with their own local problems than with the global problems facing the company as a whole, and this will hinder organizational effectiveness.

Another major problem can occur when a company in one country seeks to cooperate with a company in a different country, perhaps via a joint venture. Differences in national values and norms can make such cooperation difficult for many reasons, as the problems that emerged when Pittsburgh-based Corning Glass, and Mexican glass-maker Vitro, formed a joint venture illustrate. Corning and Vitro formed their venture to share technology and market one another's glass products throughout North America and so take advantage of the North American Free Trade Agreement (NAFTA). At the signing of the joint venture, both companies were enthusiastic about the prospects for their alliance. Managers in both companies claimed they had similar organizational cultures. Both companies had top-management teams dominated by the family members of the founders; both were global companies with broad product lines; and both had been successful managing alliances with other companies in the past.[69] Nevertheless, within two years, Corning Glass terminated the joint venture, returning the $150 million Vitro had given it for access to its technology. Why had the venture failed? The cultures and values of the two companies were so different that Corning managers and Vitro managers could not work together.

Vitro, the Mexican company, did business the Mexican way, in accordance with values prevailing in Mexican culture. In Mexico, business is conducted at a slower pace than in the United States. Used to a protected market, Mexican companies are inclined to sit back and make their decisions in a "very genteel," consensual kind of way.[70] Managers typically come to work at 9 AM., spend two or more hours at lunch, often at home with their families, and then work late, often until 9 PM. Mexican managers and their subordinates are intensely loyal and respectful to their superiors. The corporate culture is based on paternalistic, hierarchical values, and most important decisions are made by small teams of top managers. This centralization slows down decision making because middle managers may come up with a solution to a problem but will not take action without top-management's approval. In Mexico, building relationships with new companies takes time and effort because trust develops slowly. Personal contacts that develop only slowly between managers in different companies are important for doing business in Mexico.

Corning, the American company, did business the American way, in accordance with values prevailing in American culture. Managers in the United States take short lunch breaks or work through lunch so they can leave early in the evening. In many American companies, decision-making authority is decentralized to lower-level managers, who make important decisions and commit their organization to certain courses of action. U.S. managers like to make decisions quickly and worry about the consequences later.

Aware of the differences in their approaches to doing business, managers from Corning and Vitro tried to compromise and find a mutually acceptable working style. Managers from both companies agreed to take long working lunches together. Vitro's managers agreed to forgo going home at lunchtime, and Corning's managers agreed to work a bit later at night so they could talk to each other and speed up the decision-making process. Over time, however, the differences in management styles and approaches to work became a source of frustration for both sets of managers. The slow pace of decision making was frustrating for Corning's managers. The pressure from Corning's managers to get everything done quickly was frustrating for Vitro's managers. In the end, the Americans withdrew from what had originally seemed to be a promising venture.[71] Corning's managers working in Mexico discovered that the organizational cultures of Vitro and Corning were not so similar after all, and they decided to go home. Vitro's managers also realized that it was pointless to prolong the venture when the differences were so great.

Corning and many other U.S. companies that have entered into global agreements have found that doing business in Mexico or in any other country is different from doing business at home. American managers living abroad should not expect to do business the American way. Because values, norms, customs, and etiquette differ from one country to another, expatriate managers must learn to understand the differences between their national culture and the culture of the host country, if they are to manage global organizational behavior successfully.

To prevent the emergence of different national subcultures within a global organization, an organization must take steps to create a global culture and organization-wide values and norms that foster cohesiveness among divisions. But what does that entail? Global information technology, networks, and teams can be used to transmit values to the organization's worldwide divisions. Via global networks, expatriate managers can move from one country to another, spreading the company's values and norms throughout its divisions. Indeed, the transfer of employees from one division to another helps them understand they are members of a global organization. Global teams—both real and virtual—formed of managers from different countries can also facilitate the development of shared values.

Many large companies attempt to develop a cohesive set of values and norms throughout their organizations by transferring their top managers to their global divisions. When Nissan, Honda, and Sony, for example, expand abroad, the entire top-management team of the new global division consists of Japanese managers whose job it is to disseminate the companies' values. The Japanese have been very successful at maintaining control of the organizational culture of their plants in the United States and England. Quality levels at Japanese auto plants in the United States are close to levels in Japan, in fact. Nevertheless, the cultural learning process works both ways, as the following Global View suggests.

Global View

A *Gaijin* Works to Turnaround Sony

Sony, the Japanese electronics maker, used to be renowned for using its innovation and engineering prowess to turn out blockbuster new products such as the Walkman and Trinitron TV. In the 1990s product engineers at Sony turned out an average of four new product ideas every day. Why? A large part of the answer was because of Sony's culture, called the "Sony Way," which emphasized communication and cooperation between groups of engineers across the company to foster innovation and change. Engineers were given considerable freedom to pursue their own ideas, and the managers of different product groups championed their own innovations; but problems arose with Sony's approach in the 2000s.

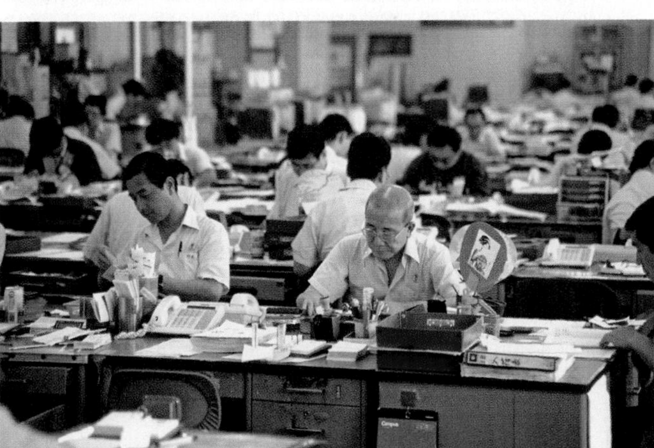

Many Japanese spend their entire working lives at the same company, and historically many Japanese companies have pursued a policy of lifetime employment, guaranteeing employees they will never be laid off in order to secure their loyalty and commitment.

Companies in Korea, Taiwan, and China began to innovate new technologies like digital LCD screens and flash memory

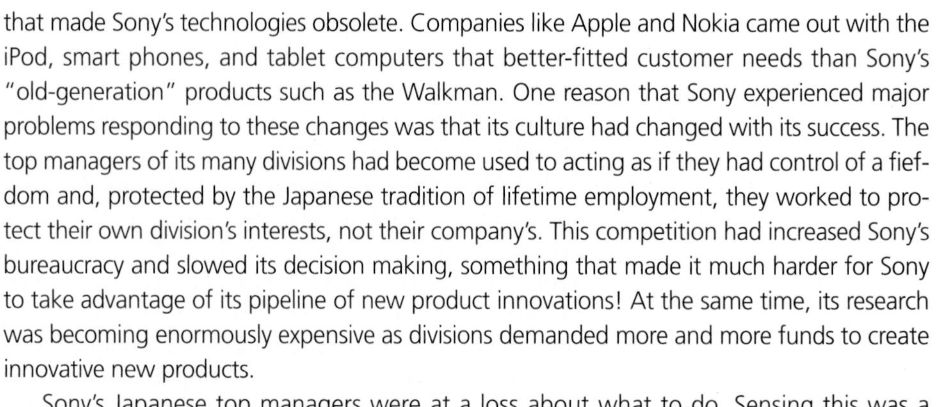

that made Sony's technologies obsolete. Companies like Apple and Nokia came out with the iPod, smart phones, and tablet computers that better-fitted customer needs than Sony's "old-generation" products such as the Walkman. One reason that Sony experienced major problems responding to these changes was that its culture had changed with its success. The top managers of its many divisions had become used to acting as if they had control of a fiefdom and, protected by the Japanese tradition of lifetime employment, they worked to protect their own division's interests, not their company's. This competition had increased Sony's bureaucracy and slowed its decision making, something that made it much harder for Sony to take advantage of its pipeline of new product innovations! At the same time, its research was becoming enormously expensive as divisions demanded more and more funds to create innovative new products.

Sony's Japanese top managers were at a loss about what to do. Sensing this was a crucial turning point in their company's history they turned to a *gaijin*—or a non-Japanese—executive to lead their company. Their choice was Sir Howard Stringer, a Welshman, who headed Sony's North American operations and had been instrumental in cutting costs and finding ways to increase the profits of Sony's U.S. division.

Stringer cannot speak Japanese, but luckily for him many of Sony's top executives do. And, now that he is in command he faces the problem of reducing costs in Japan where, like many Japanese companies, Sony has a policy of lifetime employment. He has made it clear that layoffs will be forthcoming as Sony must reduce its high operating costs. He has also made it clear that the politicking going on between Sony's different products groups must stop and managers must prioritize new products and only invest in those that have the highest chances of success, for it must reduce its huge R&D budget. Indeed, he wants to make engineering, not management, the focus once again at Sony and eliminate the tall, bloated hierarchy that has developed over time—by, for example, downsizing corporate headquarters. In Stringer's own words, the culture or "business of Sony has been management, not making products."[72] However, he has to accomplish this in Japan, which has a national culture known for its collectivist, long-term orientation, and for its distrust of gaijen or foreign values. And these same values operate inside Sony, so Stringer will have to be hard-headed and push Sony to make the best use of its resources.

Creating an Ethical Culture

We mention earlier that ethics–the moral values, beliefs, and rules that govern the way organizations and their members should act toward one another and people outside the organization—form an important part of an organization's cultural values. In an era when most companies' actions are being more intensively scrutinized by customers, investors, and government agencies, organizations and their employees cannot afford to engage in actions that will harm the company's reputation. Creating an ethical organizational culture has now become a major priority for many companies because failing to do so can be catastrophic.

One of the most important effects of ethical rules is to regulate and control the pursuit of unbridled self-interest. To understand why self-interest needs to be regulated, consider the "tragedy of the commons." The tragedy of the commons holds that it is rational for people to maximize their use of "common" land or resources (parks and open range are examples) because it's free. For example, cattle owners will all want to graze their herds on the open range to promote their individual interests. As a result, the land will almost certainly be overgrazed, and erosion will render it unusable. The rational pursuit of individual self-interests, in other words, will result in a collective disaster.

The same thing can happen in organizations: Left to their own devices, people will pursue their own goals at the expense of collective goals. Top managers, for example, may run the organization to their own advantage and to the detriment of shareholders, employees, and customers. Similarly, powerful unions may negotiate wages so high that in the long run, a company becomes uncompetitive.

Ethical values and rules control self-interested behavior that might threaten the collective interests of an organization and society in general. Ethical values establish desired end states—for example, equitable or "good" business practices—and the modes of behavior needed to achieve those end states, such as being honest or being fair. Ethical values in an organization's culture also reduce the need for people to always evaluate what is right or wrong. By automatically following an ethical rule, people are also more productive because they spend less time and effort trying to decide what course of action to take.[73]

Another important reason to act ethically is that when an organization follows accepted ethical rules, it gains a good reputation.[74] This is a valuable asset that entices people to do business with it, including customers, suppliers, and the best job applicants. On the other hand, organizations with unethical reputations breed hostility and mistrust. Although unethical organizations might reap short-term benefits, they are penalized in the long run because eventually people will refuse to deal with them. This has happened in the 2000s. People dumped companies like WorldCom/MCI and Qwest in droves because they "cooked their books" to inflate their profits. Unfortunately, even unethical behavior on the part of just a few individuals can harm the organization as a whole. Ethical rules, laws, and social customs were designed precisely because of this. Without them, organizations and societies would suffer.

Why Does Unethical Behavior Occur?

If there are good reasons for individuals and organizations to behave ethically, why do we see so many instances of unethical behavior?

Lapses in individual ethics. In theory, individuals learn how to behave ethically as they mature. People learn right from wrong from family members, friends, religious institutions, schools, professional associations, and other organizations. However, imagine that your father is a mobster, that your mother is a political terrorist, or your family belongs to a warring ethnic or religious group. Brought up in such an environment, you might be led to believe that any act—including murder—is acceptable if it benefits you, your family, or your friends. In a similar way, individuals within an organization may come to believe that any action that promotes or protects the organization is acceptable, even if it does harm to others.

This apparently happened at now-defunct accounting company Arthur Andersen, when its unscrupulous partners ordered middle managers to shred records of its dealings with Enron to hide evidence of its illegal accounting practices. Although middle managers knew this was wrong, they followed orders because of the power the firm's partners had over them. They were afraid they would lose their jobs if they did not behave unethically and shred the documents—and they were used to obeying orders. Nonetheless, in the end, their actions still cost them their jobs.

Ruthless pursuit of self-interest. We normally confront ethical issues when we weigh our personal interests against the effects our actions will have on others. Suppose you will be promoted to vice president of your company if you can secure a $100 million contract, but that to get the contract, you must bribe the contractor with $1 million. Your career and future will probably be assured if you perform this act. "What harm will it do?" you ask yourself. Bribery is common; if you don't pay the million dollars, you are certain that someone else will. So what do you do? Research suggests that people who believe they have the most at stake are the ones most likely to act unethically. Similarly, it has been shown that organizations that are doing badly economically and are struggling to survive are the ones most likely to commit unethical and illegal acts such as bribery, although many other organizations will do so if they are given the opportunity.[75]

Outside pressure. Many studies have found that the likelihood of unethical or criminal behavior increases when people feel outside pressure to perform. If company performance is deteriorating, for example, top managers may be pressured by shareholders to boost the corporation's performance. Fearful of losing their jobs, they may engage in unethical behavior to increase the value of the company's stock. If all outside pressures work in the same direction, it is easy to understand why unethical organizational cultures develop. Managers at all levels buy into unethical acts, and the view that the end justifies the means filters through the organization. If the organization's members pull together to disguise their unethical actions and protect one another from prosecution, the organization becomes increasingly defensive.

The social costs of unethical behavior are hard to measure but can be easily seen in the long run. They take the form of mismanaged organizations that become less innovative. Organizations like this spend less and less money developing new and improved products and more and more money on advertising or managerial salaries. When new competitors arrive who refuse to play the same game, the mismanaged organization begins to crumble.

Ways to Create an Ethical Culture

There are several ways to create an ethical organizational culture to help members resist the temptation to engage in illegal acts for personal gain. First, an organization can encourage people to act ethically by putting in place incentives for ethical behavior and disincentives to punish those who behave unethically. A company's top managers—the people who have the ultimate responsibility for ensuring an organization behaves ethically—must be proactive in establishing the company's ethical position. Managers create an ethical culture by making a personal commitment to uphold ethical values and transmit them to subordinates.

As a leader, a manager can promote the moral values that determine how employees will make decisions by establishing appropriate rules and norms of behavior that outline the organization's ethical position. It is also important for managers to demonstrate their commitment to following the rules via their own behavior. That includes being honest and acknowledging errors or omissions quickly and disclosing the facts accurately.

Second, organizations can design an organizational structure that reduces the incentives for people to behave unethically. The creation of authority relationships and rules that promote ethical behavior and punish unethical acts, for example, will encourage members to behave in a socially responsible way. The federal government, for example, has a set of uniform standards of conduct for executive branch employees to follow. These standards cover ethical issues like giving and receiving gifts, impartially assigning work to government contractors, and avoiding conflicts of interest when it comes to one's financial matters and outside work activities. These regulations cover five million federal workers.

WHISTLE-BLOWING
When an employee decides to inform an outside person or agency about illegal or unethical managerial behavior.

Third, an organization can develop fair and equitable human resource procedures towards the management of its diverse employees. This signals workers that they can expect to be treated in an ethical way, that they are working for an ethical organization, and that they should behave in a like manner. Fourth, organizations can put procedures into place giving subordinates access to upper-level managers to voice their concerns about unethical organizational behaviors they might observe. Ten percent of Fortune 500 companies now have ethics officers in their employment. An ethics officer is a manager responsible for training employees about ethical conduct and investigating claims of unethical behavior. Ethics committees within the organization can then make formal judgments depending upon the officer's findings. Ethical values, of course, flow down from the top of the organization but are strengthened or weakened by the design of the organizational structure and programs like these.

Pictured is Sherron Watkins, a former senior executive of the defunct Enron Corp., who revealed evidence about the fraud perpetrated by it is top managers to the FTC and other government agencies.

Organizations that lack avenues for employees to air their ethical concerns or fail to follow up on those concerns risk being exposed by whistle-blowers. **Whistle-blowing** occurs when an employee informs an outside person or organization, like a government agency, or newspaper or television reporter, about an organization's illegal or unethical behaviors (frequently on the part of its top managers). Employees typically become whistle-blowers when they feel powerless to prevent an organization from committing an unethical act or when they fear retribution from the company if they voice their concerns.[76]

Fifth, an organization can create a strong board of directors from outside the company with no ties to top management. The directors should oversee the actions of top managers, and, if they see any sign of wrongdoing or mismanagement, "nip it in the bud." In the 2000s, there have been many calls to strengthen the power of boards to scrutinize the decisions made by managers. One company forced to respond to this call is the Walt Disney Co., profiled in the following Ethics in Action.

Ethics in Action

Corporate Governance at Walt Disney

In the early 2000s, the performance of the Walt Disney Co. fell precipitously. By 2003, many analysts were wondering if Michael Eisner, who had been its CEO for the last 18 years, was still the right person to run the company. Eisner had a hands-on approach to running the business: he wanted to be involved in every major business decision, and he kept a tight reign on his managers. He was also criticized because, although 60 and due to retire in 2006, he had not laid out a succession plan that indicated which managers would assume the top roles at Disney after he stepped down. Such a plan is important because many companies flounder if a new CEO has not been groomed to take over the top job.

In addition, Eisner was criticized for creating a weak, captive board of directors that was unwilling to scrutinize and question his business decisions, some of which were major errors. Over the years, Eisner created a 16-member board of directors in the company, at least 8 of whom had personal ties to him. This did not serve Disney's stockholders well because Eisner's decisions often reduced the company's performance. For example, Eisner pushed through the merger of Disney with Capital/ABC and since the acquisition the poorly performing ABC network has dragged down Disney's stock price. In the meantime, over the 19 years he was CEO, Eisner received more than $800 million in stock options from the company and enjoyed all the lavish perks-corporate jets, penthouse suites, all-expenses paid trips that most CEOs of large companies receive today.

With its performance falling, Eisner came under increasing criticism for his autocratic management style, his lack of a succession plan for the company, and his creation of a weak board of directors, as well as the fact that that he is still paid vast sums of money despite his company's declining performance. Indeed, many analysts began to wonder if Eisner was behaving ethically as CEO, so in 2003 the company reorganized its board of directors. Two new special outside directors were appointed, one of whom chairs two board meetings a year that Eisner—who normally chairs these meetings—was not be permitted to attend. The board now had more freedom to assess Eisner's performance.

Many analysts claimed these changes were not enough because the majority of the board was still beholden to him. In 2004, Roy Disney, Walt Disney's nephew and a major stockholder, began a campaign to remove Eisner from his position as CEO and he lobbied board members for a change in leadership. Although unsuccessful in removing Eisner, in the fall of 2004 Eisner announced that he would not seek another term as CEO when his contract expires in 2006. The board then began an immediate search for Disney's next CEO and in 2005 named Robert Iger, Eisner's second in command and hand-picked successor, to be its next CEO when Eisner stepped down in September 2005, one year early.

For a while it appeared likely that Eisner might become Disney's new chairman and so retain substantial control of the company. Once again analysts wondered, is this the ethical thing to do? Wouldn't its shareholders be better served if Disney had an all-new team at the top? In any event, in December 2005 Disney announced it was negotiating to buy Pixar, the movie animation studio started by Steve Jobs, CEO of Apple. Eisner and Jobs had had many personal run-ins, and Steve Job's election to Disney's board effectively meant that Eisner was out of Disney for good. Indeed, some analysts started talking about Jobs being named CEO of Disney, and even a possible merger between Disney and Apple. Disney's performance under Iger has improved, however, and now that Jobs is on the board it is likely that the board will actively oversee the performance of top managers and ensure issues such as succession are resolved in ways that support the interests of Disney's shareholders.

EXHIBIT 17.6

Creating an Ethical Culture at MCI/WorldCom

In order to create an ethical culture at the old WorldCom, MCI's new managers took the following steps:

- Recruited a new CEO who was not at the company during the events at issue, and who brought a reputation for integrity and forthrightness in his leadership skills
- Recruited a new president and chief operating officer from outside the company who has more than 25 years of telecom experience
- Recruited a new chief financial officer, general counsel, and director of internal controls, all of whom came from outside the company
- Replaced its entire board of directors who were present at the time the fraud was discovered, thereby removing 100 percent of the directors who were participants in governance under the regime of the prior CEO Bernard J. Ebbers
- Recruited new and highly qualified independent directors
- Consented to the establishment (and continuation) of the Corporate Monitor program, which represents an unprecedented level of independent oversight of management activity
- Closed the finance and accounting department located in the company's former Clinton, Mississippi, headquarters where most of the fraudulent activities were conducted
- Hired more than 400 new finance and accounting personnel
- Retained a new outside auditor and commissioned a complete reaudit of the years 1999–2002 to document the company's actual performance as best as it can be reconstructed from available records and personnel
- Evaluated all corporate assets for value impairment, wrote off all goodwill, and wrote down asset-carrying values for property, plant, and equipment to achieve a realistic balance sheet
- Initiated a widespread and intensive review led by three new directors to identify wrongdoing that occurred and those who participated. Also funded a separate thorough investigation by the bankruptcy examiner and responded to his findings concerning wrongful activities of different types
- Terminated dozens of employees, including a number of senior officers, who either participated in inappropriate activities, who appeared to look the other way in the face of indications of suspicious activity, or who otherwise acted in a manner inconsistent with necessary standards of conduct
- Agreed to abolish use of stock options in favor of restricted stock with full expensing of the value of equity grants on the company's profit and loss statement
- Initiated a thorough review of internal controls to strengthen the company's systems and procedures for capturing and reporting financial data and a widespread program to create a much stronger system
- Put in place a new Ethics Pledge program pursuant to which senior officers including the CEO pledge to pursue ethics and integrity, compliance programs, and transparency and candor in financial reporting well beyond SEC requirements
- Established a new Ethics Office
- Commenced a training program for employees on their responsibilities under the federal securities laws, accounting issues that may signal inappropriate behavior or fraud, and ethical issues
- Consented to the Permanent Injunction
- Consented to a financial settlement with the SEC under which $500 million in cash and $250 million in stock will be paid into a trust for victims

Source: Academy of Management Executive: The Thinking Manager's Source. Copyright 1993 by Acad. of Mgmt. Reproduced with permission of Acad. of Mgmt. in the format Tetbook via Copyright Clearance Center.

Finally, just as pressures from those at the top of the organization can help prevent unethical behavior, so can pressures from people and groups outside the company.[77] Government agencies, industry councils, regulatory bodies, and consumer watchdog groups all play a role when it comes to making sure corporations follow the rules. In the last few years in particular, government regulators have very actively prosecuted managers at companies like WorldCom and Enron. WorldCom (now renamed MCI) later brought in new top managers who took many of the steps just discussed to rebuild that organization's ethical culture. The steps are summarized in Exhibit 17.6.[78]

In sum, there are many steps that can be taken to help strengthen managers' and employees' commitment to behave ethically. When ethical values are instilled, a strong adaptive culture develops, which, in turn, helps organizations achieve their goals.

Summary

Organizational culture is an important means through which organizations coordinate and motivate the behavior of their members. An organization can shape work attitudes and behaviors by the way it invests in and rewards its employees over time and by its attempts to encourage values of excellence. The chapter has made the following main points:

1. Organizational culture is the set of shared values, beliefs, and norms that influence the way employees think, feel, and behave toward each other and toward people outside the organization.
2. There are two kinds of organizational values: terminal (a desired outcome) and instrumental (a desired mode of behavior). Ideally, instrumental values help the organization to achieve its terminal values.
3. Culture is transmitted to an organization's members by means of (a) socialization and training programs and (b) stories, ceremonies, and language used by members of the organization.
4. Organizational culture develops from the interaction of four factors: the personal and professional characteristics of people within the organization, organizational ethics, the nature of the employment relationship between a company and its employees, and the design of its organizational structure. These factors work together to produce different cultures in different organizations and cause changes in culture over time.
5. Different organizations have different kinds of cultures because they attract, select, and retain different kinds of people. Because an organization's founder is instrumental in initially determining what kind of people get selected, a founder can have a long-lasting effect on an organization's culture.
6. Ethics are the moral values, beliefs, and rules that establish the right or appropriate ways in which one person or group should interact and deal with another person or group. Organizational ethics are a product of societal, professional, and individual ethics.
7. The nature of the employment relationship between a company and its employees causes the development of particular norms, values, and attitudes toward the organization.
8. Different organizational structures give rise to different patterns of interaction among people. These different patterns lead to the formation of different organizational cultures.
9. Adaptive cultures are those whose values and norms help an organization to build momentum, grow, and change as needed to achieve its goals and be effective. Inert cultures are those that lead to values and norms that fail to motivate or inspire employees. They lead to stagnation and often failure over time.
10. Another important determinant of organizational culture is the values of the nation in which a company is founded and has its home operations.
11. A company can help to build and sustain an ethical culture by establishing the right kinds of incentives and rules for rewarding ethical behavior, by establishing a strong board of directors, and by making sure employees follow the legal rules and guidelines established by government agencies and watched by consumer groups.

Organizational Behavior in Action

Questions for Review

1. What are the building blocks of organizational culture?
2. How do newcomers learn the culture of an organization?
3. Find a manager or person in charge of helping new employees "learn the ropes" and question this person about how their organization socializes its new members.
4. What four factors affect the kind of culture that develops in an organization?
5. In what ways can organizational culture increase organizational effectiveness?
6. Suppose you were starting a new restaurant. What kind of culture would help promote organizational effectiveness? How would you try to build such a culture?
7. How does national culture affect organizational culture?
8. Why is it important that an organization's members behave ethically? Why does unethical behavior occur?
9. How can you build and maintain an ethical culture?

OB: Increasing Self-Awareness

Understanding Culture

Pick an organization you are very familiar with such as a local school, church, or one in which you have worked for a long period of time. Use the chapter material to think about its culture and answer the following questions:

1. What are the terminal and instrumental values of the organization? How do they affect its members' attitudes and behaviors?
2. Identify the main beliefs and norms or organizational members. How do these norms relate to the organizations values? Is there a fit between them? Identify areas for improvement.
3. How does the organization socialize new members? Could the ways it helps newcomers learn the organization's culture be improved?
4. What kinds of organizational ceremonies does the organization have to help reinforce its values and norms?
5. Try to identify the source of the values and norms of your organization's culture; for example, do you think the people or the organization's rules and procedures have the most affect on organizational culture?

Small Group Break-Out Exercise

Developing a Service Culture

Form groups of three to five people and discuss the following scenario:

You are the owners/managers of a new five-star resort hotel opening up on the white sand beaches of the west coast of Florida. For your venture to succeed you need to make sure that hotel employees focus on providing customers with the highest-quality customer service possible. You are meeting to discuss how to create a culture that will promote such high-quality service, that will encourage employees to be committed to the hotel, and that will reduce the level of employee turnover and absenteeism, which are typically high in the hotel business.

1. What kinds of organizational values and norms encourage employees to behave in ways that lead to high-quality customer service?
2. Using the concepts discussed in this chapter (for example, people, employment relationship, socialization), discuss how you will create a culture that promotes the learning of these customer service values and norms.
3. Which factor is the most important determinant of the kind of culture you expect to find in a five-star hotel?

A Question of Ethics

When Is Culture too Strong

An organization's managers may attempt to influence employee attitudes and behaviors by building a particular kind of culture. The process of building a strong culture can have a dark side if managers create values and norms that ultimately cause employees to behave in unethical ways. In other words, sometimes a culture can become too strong and its members may all begin to act unethically and without regard to their effects of their actions on others. Think about the ethical issues involved in building organizational culture and address the following issues:

1. When and under what conditions can values and norms become so strong that they cause employees to act in unethical ways?
2. Think about the four main factors influencing organizational culture. How could they be used to create a culture that causes employees to act in unethical ways?
3. Why might differences in national culture lead to unethical behavior in a global organization?

Experiential Exercise

A Culture Problem at HighandTall

Form groups of three to five people, discuss the following scenario, and discuss the questions. Be prepared to share your discussions with you class:

You are the founding entrepreneurs of HighandTall Company, a fast-growing digital software company that specializes in home consumer electronics. Customer demand to license your software has boomed so much that in just two years you have added over 50 new software programmers to help develop a new range of software products. These people are young and inexperienced but are highly skilled and used to putting in long hours to see their ideas succeed. The growth of your company has been so swift that you still operate informally. You have been so absorbed in your own work that you have paid little attention to the issue of developing a culture for your growing company. Your programmers have been learning how your company works by observing you and by seeing what goes on in their own work groups. There are increasing signs that all is not well, however.

There have been increasing complaints from employees that as managers you do not recognize or reward good performance and that they do not feel equitably treated. Moreover, there have been growing concerns that you are either too busy or not willing to listen to their new ideas and act on them. A bad atmosphere seems to be developing in the company, and recently several talented employees have left.

You realize in hindsight that you have done a poor job of creating a culture that encourages employees to perform well and stay with your company.

1. What kinds of values and norms do you want to make the heart of your organization's culture?
2. Think about this work situation. How could you try to build an adaptive culture, based on these values and norms, for your organization? (Hint: Focus on the four sources of culture.)
3. In what other ways could you influence and persuade your employees to perform well and stay with your company?

New York Times *Cases in the News*

The New York Times

"For Trader Joe's, a New York Taste Test."

Julia Moskin, NYT, March 8, 2006. p. F1.

In an industrial park somewhere in Los Angels, the pieces of the puzzle come together. One crew, using rakes, turns 525 pounds of newly roasted peanuts trucked in from Texas. Another adds a heavy shower of dried whole chilies, lemon grass fibers, curry leaves and cane sugar imported from a producer in Thailand whose identity is a closely kept secret. "No one except us knows all the parts of the operation," said Matt Sloan, vice president for merchandising for the Trader Joe's food stores, whose popularity took off in California in the 1970's and whose first store in New York City is opening on March 17. "In that way it's like a conspiracy." Long before Trader Joe's went national, its inexpensive but unusual products—things like wild blueberry juice, Sicilian extra-virgin olive oil and frozen chicken-lemon grass spring rolls—inspired an intense following among American food lovers, rarely seen in the aisles of a supermarket.

The stores are small, the selection is uneven and the corporate culture can be described as dorky. But because its products are often not available anywhere else; because they mysteriously appear, disappear, then reappear on the shelves; or perhaps simply because they often taste very, very good, Trader Joe's has become tremendously popular among Americans who like to be entertained and educated by what they eat, as well as nourished by it. To protect its house-brand products, the company is notoriously secretive. But it opened slightly to this reporter recently, for the first time allowing an outsider into the daily critique conducted by the company's best-trained palates, a group known as "the testing panel." "The tasting panel is what takes us from having good products to having addictive products," said Doug Rauch, the president. Like Trader Joe's Thai Lime & Chili Peanuts, for example: rich, spicy, fragrant, sweet and not quite like anything else on the mass market. They represent the end of a long process of travel, research, argument and experimentation. "You can drive yourself crazy in this job, like a cat chasing its tail, and sometimes you never get there," said Lori Latta, who buys dried fruit and nuts for the company and has been on the tasting panel for 20 years.

More than a buyer, Ms. Latta adds in the skills of chef, advocate, food scientist and nutritionist. Her job, and those of the 14 other "category leaders," is to perpetually travel the world visiting all kinds of food businessess—restaurants, farmers' markets, artisanal pasta makers, street stalls and supermarkets—and then translate their finds to the stores. When a category leader was served an ideal tiramisu at a small restaurant on the Amalfi coast of Italy, he spent months working with the chef on a version that could be mass-produced, frozen, exported to the United States and sold for $6.99 in freezer cases from San Diego to Boston. But first it had to pass the tasting panel.

Once approved, new products line up next to the popular peanut-butter-stuffed pretzels, chocolate-covered espresso beans and green chili tamales, all of them additive-free, all-natural.

There is nothing quite like the chain anywhere else on the American food landscape. "Trader Joe's is radically different in many ways from other food retailers," said Stephen Dowdell, editor-in-chief of Progressive Grocer magazine. "The stores are small, they don't rely on national brands, you can't do price comparisons and they definitely don't offer one stop shopping. But every product has a story." The Polynesian-themed chain was established by Joe Coulombe in Pasadena, Calif., in the 1960's, in an attempt to rescue his convenience stores after 7-Eleven came to town. "We decided to go in the other direction—to appeal to people who are well-educated, well-traveled and underpaid," Mr. Coulombe said. (He sold his final interest in the company in 1989, but many of his innovations are still in place.) In the 1970's, he said, after the stores stopped selling things like Twinkies, magazines and batteries and focused on food and wine, the business took off. "For years, we were the country's largest importer of Dijon mustard. Of capers. Of arborio rice. Of everything like that you can think of."

Fans of the chain find such quirks endearing. All employees wear Hawaiian shirts at work, whether they are shelvers or the chief executive. "It helps us keep a sense of humor about what we do," said Mr. Sloan, who, like many senior staff members, began working for the company as a college student—that was in 1993—and never left.

One February afternoon at the headquarters in Monrovia, near Pasadena (yes, even the receptionists wear Hawaiian shirts), the tasting panel members, most well into their 40's or older, crowded cheerfully into the test kitchen. (This reporter was allowed in on condition that individual members—many of whom negotiate with vendors for changes in product not be quoted by name on the opinions they expressed.) The pasta buyer had boiled up six different Italian brands of whole-grain pasta and tossed them in plain olive oil.

The group fell silent and began chewing intently. Immediately, comments flew. "Interesting nutty flavors on No. 1." "This one has a cardboardy texture at the end." "What about the omega-3's on this one?" Eventually, a favorite was determined by a show of hands and a plan sketched for the step ahead: persuading the supplier to make refinements and solve problems. That kind of passionate, focused attention to food is clearly sensed by Trader Joe's customers. "This sounds crazy, but you feel like the company likes food even more than they like money," said Marcy Benfiglio, who lives near the branch in Larchmont, N.Y. "You don't feel that at the supermarket."

Questions for Discussion

1. Based on this description of Trader Joes, what do you think are the company's (1) terminal values?, and (2) instrumental values?
2. In what ways do you think its "dorky culture" is transmitted to its new employees? To its customers? Why has its culture helped it be successful?

The New York Times

"Sears Chairman Works to Emphasize Selling."

Michael Barbaro, NYT, April 13, 2006, p. C3.

The billionaire investor who pulled off the unlikely merger of Sears Roebuck and Kmart is undertaking another challenge: creating a business culture focused on selling. For 90 minutes on Wednesday, the investor, Edward S. Lampert, the normally reclusive chairman of Sears Holding, spoke expansively about the need to change attitudes and work habits at the merged company. One effort is already under way: assembling the company's top 500 managers here for marathon training sessions, where a film clip from "Miracle on Ice," about the United States hockey team that won the gold medal at the 1980 Winter Olympics, is used to promote team work and improve customer service.

"In the past, we had a situation where people worked here but could not get results," Mr. Lampert said during the first shareholder meeting for the newly formed retailer. "We need to invest in those people."

But one cultural change that analysts and investors wanted to see—the disclosure of a detailed plan for Sears—remained elusive. Investors and employees, he said, "must be comfortable with ambiguity and with failure." But he did give some hints about his plans, saying that Sears would upgrade its Lands' End clothing lines; that the popular Martha Stewart Everyday line of housewares, which analysts expected Sears to carry, would remain exclusive to Kmart; and that the company would not pay a dividend, but rather reinvest that money in operations. During an unusually candid question-and-answer session on Wednesday, Mr. Lampert, who is often criticized for sharing little information with stockholders, discussed a range of topics, talking at great length and, in many cases, not about Sears. He also acknowledged missteps since the merger, like the ill-fated Sears Essentials format, which failed because of what Mr. Lampert called a dozen mistakes, including how workers were deployed in the store and the mix of products.

But at a time when the company's revenue has slipped, the biggest emphasis Wednesday was on the employee culture at Sears and Kmart. One result of that emphasis is a program that allows workers at Sears stores who collect commissions to sell products across the store, not just in a niche area like refrigerators or dishwashers. Mr. Lampert acknowledged that critics might frown on his focus on culture. "How could a finance guy think that stuff matters," he asked. "It seems soft." But, citing examples of companies that have created strong cultures, he said "it's not soft at General Electric or Microsoft." He cited the example of Sears employees who used up to three coupons to buy a product at the store but were willing to pay full price at a rival, Target. "That's something to learn from," he said.

In a sign of how seriously Sears executives are taking corporate culture, the chief executive, Aylwin B. Lewis, said that he and Mr. Lampert had spent 90 days developing a relatively short vision-and-mission statement and defining its every word. The shift, Mr. Lewis said in an interview after the shareholder meeting, was more than just symbolic. In the last year, the company has replaced 35 percent of store managers at Sears and 25 percent of store managers at Kmart, saying they did not meet tough new standards. Typically, the turnover rate among store managers is 10 percent a year. "It's not the heartless whacking of people," Mr. Lewis said, "but telling them we are serious about our new standards."

Questions for Discussion

1. What do you think Edward Lampert means by a culture "focused on selling?"
2. Given his leadership approach, what kinds of terminal and instrumental values do you think he will use to create Sear's selling culture?
3. How successful do you think his approach will be with customers?

The New York Times

Excerpts From Report of the Columbia Accident Board

NYT, August 27, 2003, p. A18.

Following are excerpts from the report of the Columbia Accident Investigation Board, which was released yesterday. The full text is online at nytimes.com/Columbia.

The Board Statement

For all those who are inspired by flight, and for the nation where powered flight was first achieved, the year 2003 had long been anticipated as one of celebration—Dec. 17 would mark the centennial of the day the Wright Flyer first took to the air. But 2003 began instead on a note of sudden and profound loss. On Feb. 1, Space Shuttle Columbia was destroyed in a disaster that claimed the lives of all seven of its crew. . . .

It is our view that complex systems almost always fail in complex ways, and we believe it would be wrong to reduce the complexities and weaknesses associated with these systems to some simple explanation.

Too often, accident investigations blame a failure only on the last step in a complex process, when a more comprehensive understanding of that process could reveal that earlier steps might be equally or even more culpable. In this board's opinion, unless the technical, organizational and cultural recommendations made in this report are implemented, little will have been accomplished to lessen the chance that another accident will follow. . . .

Organizational Causes

. . . The organizational causes of this accident are rooted in the space shuttle program's history and culture, including the original compromises that were required to gain approval for the shuttle program, subsequent years of resource constraints, fluctuating priorities, schedule pressures, mischaracterizations of the shuttle as operational rather than developmental and lack of an agreed national vision.

Cultural traits and organizational practices detrimental to safety and reliability were allowed to develop, including reliance on past success as a substitute for sound engineering practices (such as testing to understand why systems were not performing in accordance with requirements/specifications); organizational barriers which prevented effective communication of critical safety information and stifled professional differences of opinion; lack of integrated management across program elements; and the evolution of an informal chain of command and decision making processes that operated outside the organization's rules.

In the board's view, NASA's organizational culture and structure had as much to do with this accident as the external tank foam. Organizational culture refers to the values, norms, beliefs and practices that govern how an institution functions. At the most basic level, organizational culture defines the assumptions that employees make as they carry out their work. It is a powerful force that can persist through reorganizations and the reassignment of key personnel. Given that today's risks in human space flight are as high and the safety margins as razor thin as they have ever been, there is little room for overconfidence. Yet the attitudes and decision making of shuttle program managers and engineers during the events leading up to this accident were clearly overconfident and often bureaucratic in nature. They deferred to layered and cumbersome regulations rather than the fundamentals of safety.

The shuttle program's safety culture is straining to hold together the vestiges of a once-robust systems safety program. As the board investigated the Columbia accident, it expected to find a vigorous safety organization, process and culture at NASA bearing little resemblance to what the Rogers Commission identified as the ineffective "silent safety" system in which budget cuts resulted in a lack of resources, personnel, independence and authority.

NASA's initial briefings to the board on its safety programs espoused a risk-averse philosophy that empowered any employee to stop an operation at the mere glimmer of a problem. Unfortunately, NASA's views of its safety culture in those briefings did not reflect reality. Shuttle program safety personnel failed to adequately assess anomalies and frequently accepted critical risks without qualitative or quantitative support, even when the tools to provide more comprehensive assessments were available.

Similarly, the board expected to find NASA's Safety and Mission Assurance organization deeply engaged at every level of shuttle management: the Flight Readiness Review, the Mission Management Team, the Debris Assessment Team, the Mission Evaluation Room and so forth. This was not the case. In briefing after briefing, interview after interview, NASA remained in denial. In the agency's eyes, "there were no safety-of-flight issues," and no safety compromises in the long history of debris strikes on the thermal protection system.

The silence of program-level safety processes undermined oversight; when they did not speak up, safety personnel could not fulfill their stated mission to provide "checks and balances." A pattern of acceptance prevailed throughout the organization that tolerated foam problems without sufficient engineering justification for doing so.

Connecting the parts of NASA's organizational system and drawing the parallels with Challenger demonstrate three things. First, despite all the post-Challenger changes at NASA and the agency's notable achievements since, the causes of the institutional failure responsible for Challenger have not been fixed. Second, the board strongly believes that if these persistent, systemic flaws are not resolved, the scene is set for another accident.

Therefore, the recommendations for change are not only not fixing the shuttle's technical system, but also not fixing each part of the organizational system that produced Columbia's failure. Third, the board's focus on the context in which decision making occurred does not mean that individuals are not responsible and accountable. To the countrary, individuals always must assume responsibility for their actions. What it does mean is that NASA's problems cannot be solved simply by retirements, resignations or transferring personnel.

The constraints under which the agency has operated throughout the shuttle program have contributed to both shuttle accidents. Although NASA leaders have played an important role, these constraint were not entirely of NASA's own making. The White House and Congress must recognize the role of their decisions in this accident and take responsibility for safety in the future.

Through its recommendations in Part 2, the board has urged that NASA's human spaceflight program adopt the characteristics observed in high-reliability organizations. One is separating technical authority from the functions of managing schedules and cost. Another is an independent safety and mission assurance organization. The third is the capability effective systems integration.

Perhaps even more challenging than these organizational changes are the cultural changes required. Within NASA, the cultural impediments to safe and effective shuttle operations are real and substantial, as documented extensively in this report. The board's view is that cultural problems are unlikely to be corrected without top-level leadership. Such leadership will have to rid the system of practices and pattern that have been validated simply because they have been around so long. Examples include the tendency to keep knowledge of problems contained within a center or program, making technical decisions without in-depth peer-reviewed technical analysis, and an unofficial hierarchy or caste system created by placing excessive power in one office. Such factors interfere with open communication, impede the sharing of lessons learned, cause duplication and unnecessary expenditure of resources, prompt resistance to external advice and create a burden for managers, among other undesirable outcomes. Collectively, these undesirable characteristics threaten safety. . . .

So did Ms. Hansen begin to yearn for the old days as a reporter? Not a bit. Instead, she learned an important lesson about the workplace; surface manifestations of a company's culture don't matter; what counts are its core values.

Ms. Hansen came to view the formality and strict rules at Bank One as little more a mild annoyance—and to appreciate what she saw as its principles of shared purpose, open communication and mutual respect among employees.

The money helped, too. "The new job required me to adapt my personality to the new circumstances," she said. "But I knew that in making these changes there would be a payoff. I've been able to achieve my personal goals. There's better money, excellent benefits. I'm saving to make a down payment on a mortgage and for the first time I'm debt free."

In March, Ms. Hansen began working at Banc One Capital Markets, a subsidiary of Bank One, as a research editor, a job that she called "a perfect fit."

There is a lesson in her experience for people looking for a job, or thinking of switching careers. It has always been accepted wisdom among workplace experts that employees thrive best in a company whose culture matches their personality. But as Ms. Hansen's shaky but ultimately successful transition shows, it is important for job candidates to peer below the surface to figure out what really matters to them.

Similarly, if you love what you are doing, maybe you should stay put, even if more lucrative offers beckon. Christine Bracco, 31, an executive assistant for the Anschutz Entertainment Group, a sports and entertainment company in Los Angeles, says she never felt more professionally fulfilled than when she worked from 1997 to 2000 as an executive assistant at Scholastic, the Manhattan publisher that specializes in children's books.

Ms. Bracco, a certified teacher, strongly identified with its mission to educate children and improve literacy. And she said she felt that management cared about employees, treating them to lectures and workshops by authors and educators, giving them perks like a rooftop restaurant and an on-site library. The management kept employees informed through the company's newsletter and Intranet site.

Though she left Scholastic to move to California in 2000, she is hoping a return is not out of the question, especially if the company opens an office there, as she has heard it plans to do.

Of course, in this sagging economy, people desperate for work can be forgiven for ignoring potential employers' culture altogether. "You don't think about it if you're just concerned about survival," said Randall S. Hansen, the publisher of Quintessential Careers, an online job site.

"Any offer is a good one if it allows you to pay the bills or ensure you won't be homeless," said Dr. Hansen, who is no relation to Joyce Hansen.

But the economy is starting to show signs of life. Last week, surveys from May showed that factory activity exceeded expectations and job cuts by employers declined sharply. If the economy rebounds this summer, as some expect, people looking for work might find they have more flexibility to take a close look at the companies that want to hire them.

Sometimes, of course, it is obvious where you belong and where you don't. An environmental activist would not have to scratch much below the surface to realize she would not enjoy working for an oil company with a spotty record on pollution.

Job seekers should think hard about what, exactly, in a company's culture is important to them and what is not, experts say. For some, a rooftop restaurant or large office with a north–south exposure might matter a lot. Others might prefer a laid-back environment, and some value opportunities for advancement and to make more money.

Dr. Hansen offered a basic test: "You want to be happy going to work. You don't want to be one of those people who spend Sundays thinking. 'Oh my God, I can't face my job tomorrow.' "

There are many ways to learn about a company's culture, from doing online research to chatting with employees off the premises.

Benjamin Dattner, president of Dattner Consulting and an adjunct assistant professor of organizational psychology at New York University, says you can pick up clues by making a casual visit. "Are people sitting in the reception area responded to? Ask people to flat-out describe what it's like to work there and what types of people are happiest."

Job hunters should be aware that employers, too, are intent on finding the right match. In fact, because they are hiring fewer people than they were a few years ago, they are paying closer attention to the personalities of applicants to make sure they share the company's values and goals, according to Herbert Greenberg, chief executive of Caliper Human Strategies, a job-aptitude assessment company in Princeton, N. J.

Caliper charges $265 for its personality and job-aptitude test, a two-hour exam used by companies like FedEx and Avis, and it says that business has increased 20 percent over the last year.

Another method that has been gaining favor recently for scrutinizing job candidates, Dr. Hansen says, is something called the situational interview, which uses role-playing techniques to gauge applicants' responses to situations they might encounter on the job.

For all the emphasis on finding the right fit, employers should not lose sight of the value of a diversity of viewpoints, workplace experts say. Sometimes, new hires with contrarian ideas can shake things up in a positive way.

"They're coming from a fresh perspective," Dr. Dattner said. "They can ask, 'Why do we do it this way? Let's try it that way.' "

Questions Discussion

1. In what ways does the accident board attribute the *Columbia* disaster to Nasa's culture?
2. How could Nasa's culture *and* structure be changed to ensure such a tragedy never happens again?

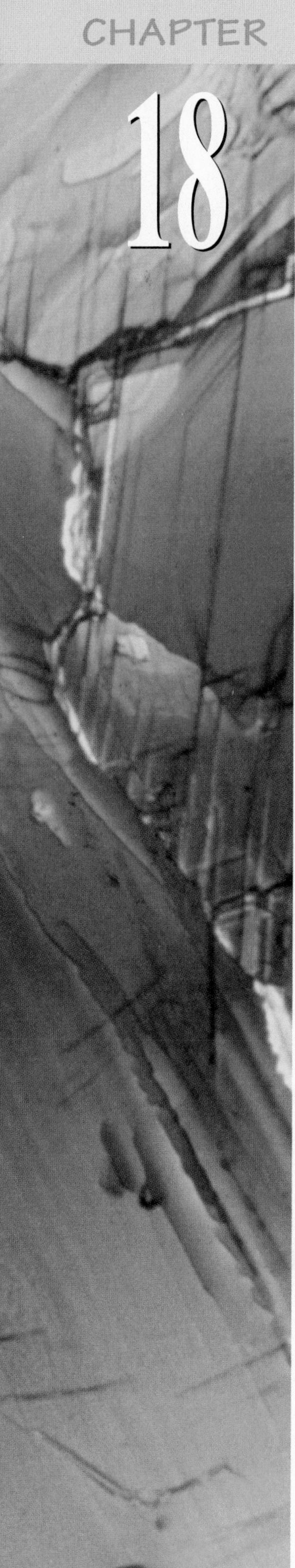

ORGANIZATIONAL CHANGE AND DEVELOPMENT

Learning Objectives

After reading this chapter, you should be able to:

- Appreciate the forces that lead to organization change and the various impediments to change that arise during the change process.
- Distinguish between evolutionary and revolutionary change and identify the main types of each of these kinds of change process.
- Discuss the main steps involved in action research and identify the main issues that must be addressed to manage the change process effectively.
- Understand the process of organization development and how to use various change techniques to facilitate the change process.

Opening Case

ANNE MULCAHY TRANSFORMS XEROX

What is Mulcahy's approach to change?

In 2001, Xerox, the well-known copier company, was near bankruptcy. A combination of aggressive Japanese competitors selling low-price copiers, and a shift toward digital copying that made the old light-lens copying process that Xerox had pioneered obsolete, was leading to plummeting sales. Xerox was losing billions of dollars and its board desperately searched for a new CEO who could change the way the company operated and revitalize its product line.[1] The person they chose to transform the company was Anne Mulcahy, a 26-year Xerox veteran who had begun her career as a salesperson, transferred into human resource management, and then used her leadership abilities to work her way up to become its president.

As a part of her efforts to change Xerox and turn the company around, Ann Mulcahy implemented an approach called "Focus 500." This requires Xerox's top 200 executives to go out into the field and visit its top 500 customers and develop an ongoing relationship with them.

The biggest challenge Mulcahy faced was how to save billions of dollars by reducing Xerox's huge operating costs while at the same time investing billions of dollars in R&D to innovate new kinds of copiers. Only by simultaneously achieving both of these objectives could she save the company. To find solutions to the problem, she focused her efforts on involving and listening to Xerox's employees and customers. Mulcahy began a series of "town hall" meetings with Xerox employees and told them that tough times were ahead and that layoffs would be necessary in the short run.[2] At the same time she emphasized that only their suggestions, creative responses, and hard work to find ways to reduce costs could help save the company.

To help discover how the company should best invest its R&D budget, she made reaching out to customers her other main priority. From the top down she insisted that managers, engineers, and salespeople must work with customers to find out what they wanted most from copiers. She implemented an approach called "Focus 500" that requires Xerox's top 200 executives to go out into the field and visit its top 500 customers and to develop an ongoing relationship with them. She reinforced this as a major priority by such means as issuing standing orders that even if Xerox executives were in important meetings, they should immediately go to the phone and meet the needs of their assigned customers.

By listening closely to both employees and customers, Mulcahy, and Xerox's managers, researchers, and engineers gained new insights that have transformed its product line. Mulcahy decided to focus the R&D budget on producing two new major kinds of product, a new line of digital color copying machines for use by medium and large businesses, and low-end copiers that offer a print quality, speed, and price that even Japanese competitors cannot match.[3] Xerox also invested in developing an efficient sales and service network to support its new copiers and manage customer relationships. At the same time, Xerox has cut 26 percent from corporate overhead, and 29 percent from R&D since 2000, and has reduced its workforce from 95,000 to 55,000.

Bt 2005 it seemed that Mulcahy and her managers did choose the right turnaround plan to save the company. Their risky gamble on two new main lines of copiers, and a painful downsizing and reorganization have paid off. Xerox is now the leader in the high-end and low-end of the digital copying market and over two-thirds of Xerox revenues now come from products and services developed since 20001. Xerox's profits are still not high, however, because of intense price competition in copiers from companies like Lexmark, Canon, and HP. However, it now can build from a position of strength, and its employees who have worked so hard to turn around the company see that their efforts have paid off, and that their jobs and futures seem secure. Indeed, by 2006 the company was hiring 1,000 new workers each quarter as demand for its products increased.[4]

One other outcome of Mulcahy's change strategy has been to build a new company culture based on the use of total quality management that emphasizes the continuous improvement or work processes. Xerox's lower costs have been achieved by its employees' never-ending efforts to find better, more reliable, and more efficient ways of performing the thousands of specific tasks involved in making and selling copiers. The result has also been an increase in the quality of its copiers, which is vital to its customers. Xerox's new adaptive culture emphasizes the values of customer service and commitment to employees. Mulcahy's hope is that Xerox will once again take its place as one of the most admired companies in the world.

Overview

Xerox, like other companies facing the digital revolution, needed to transform itself and change in order to survive and prosper. In an era when technology is advancing rapidly, most organizations are confronting the need to learn new ways to reduce costs and offer better goods and services to customers. The need to change is a fact of life that most organizations have to deal with. Indeed, in today's environment, organizations cannot afford to change only when their performance is deteriorating; they need to continuously predict and anticipate the need for change.

There are many reasons why organizations change and many types of change they can pursue, like restructuring, reengineering, "e-engineering," innovation, and total quality management. In this chapter, we complete our analysis of organizational behavior by examining the nature and process of organization change. We look at forces for and resistance to change, and we examine different types of changes that occur in organizations. We also look at "action research," a method organizations can use to plan, implement, and ease the change process. We examine various techniques that managers can use to overcome resistance to change and facilitate the process.[5] By the end of this chapter you will understand why managing change successfully is a vital part of organizational behavior.

Forces for and Resistance to Organization Change

ORGANIZATION CHANGE
The movement of an organization away from its present state and toward some desired future state to increase its effectiveness.

Organization change is the movement of an organization away from its present state and toward some desired future state to increase its effectiveness. Why does an organization need to change the way it performs its activities? The business environment is constantly changing, and the organization must adapt to these forces in order to survive.[6] Exhibit 18.1 lists the most important forces for and impediments to change that confront an organization and its managers.

EXHIBIT 18.1

Forces for and Impediments to Change

Forces for Change	Impediments To Change
Competitive forces	*Organizational impediments*
	Power and conflict
Economic and political forces	Differences in functional orientation
	Mechanistic structure
Global forces	Organizational culture
Demographic and social forces	*Group impediments*
	Group norms
	Group cohesiveness
Ethical forces	Groupthink and escalation of commitment
	Individual impediments
	Uncertainty and insecurity
	Selective perception and retention
	Habit

Forces for Change

Recall from Chapter 16 that many environmental forces have an impact on the organization and that recognizing the nature of these forces is one of a manager's most important tasks.[7] If managers are slow to respond to competitive, economic, political, global, and other forces, the organization will lag behind its competitors and its effectiveness will be compromised.

Competitive forces. Organizations are constantly striving to achieve a competitive advantage.[8] Competition is a force for change because, unless an organization matches or surpasses its competitors in at least one competitive area (either in terms of efficiency, quality, innovation, or responsiveness), it will not survive.[9]

To excel in the area of *efficiency* or *quality*, an organization must constantly adopt the latest technology as it becomes available. The adoption of new technology usually brings a change to task relationships as employees learn new skills or techniques to operate the new technology.[10] Later in this chapter we discuss total quality management and reengineering, two change strategies that organizations can use to achieve superior efficiency or quality.

To excel in the area of *innovation* and obtain a technological advantage, a company must skillfully manage the process of innovation, another source of change. (We discuss innovation later in the chapter.) Central to the ability to capture and sustain a competitive advantage is the ability to excel in the most important area of all: *responsiveness to customers.*

Economic, political, and global forces. As we saw in Chapter 1, economic and political forces continually affect organizations and compel them to change how and where they produce goods and services. Economic and political unions between countries are becoming an increasingly important force for change.[11] The North American Free Trade Agreement (NAFTA) paved the way for cooperation among Canada, the United States, and Mexico. Many organizations in these countries have taken advantage of NAFTA to find new markets for their products and new sources of inexpensive labor and inputs.

The European Union (EU)—an alliance of European countries that traces its origin to the end of World War II—includes over twenty members eager to exploit the advantages of a large protected market. Poland and many other formerly communist countries of Eastern Europe, and Georgia and other former republics of the Soviet Union, have now joined the European Union to foster their own economic and political development. Many more countries such as Turkey are seeking entry as well.

Japan and other fast-growing Asian countries like Malaysia, Thailand, and China—recognizing that economic unions protect member nations and create barriers against foreign competitors—have moved to increase their presence in countries abroad. Numerous Japanese companies, for example, have opened manufacturing plants in the United States, Mexico, and in European countries such as Spain, Poland, and the United Kingdom to capitalize on the advantages the European Union and trade agreements like NAFTA offer. Toyota, Honda, and Nissan have all opened large car plants in England to supply cars to EU member countries, for example. These firms are also taking advantage of the low labor costs in England (compared to those in France, Germany, or Japan), and the products made in England are not subject to EU import tariffs. Similarly, in the Far East, Pacific Rim countries like Japan, Thailand, Taiwan, Malaysia, and Singapore all face the problem of how to develop an economic union of their own as the world divides into three distinct economic spheres: North America, Europe, and Asia.

No organization can afford to ignore the effects of global economic and political forces on its activities. The rise of low-cost foreign competitors, the development of new technology that can erode a company's competitive advantage, and the failure to exploit low-cost inputs abroad all spell doom for an organization competing in the global marketplace.[12]

Other global challenges organizations face include the need to help their managers who work abroad adjust to a variety of national cultures and understand the economic, political, and cultural values of the countries in which they are located.[13] Toyota, for example, has realized the importance of sending its Japanese car designers and engineers to work with their counterparts in other countries. This helps the company meet the needs of customers in overseas markets as well as spread its Kaizen manufacturing methods to its other divisions.

Demographic and social forces. Managing a diverse work force is one of the biggest challenges to confront organizations in the 2000s.[14] We discussed in previous chapters how changes in the composition of the work force and the increasing diversity of

Here, a class of adults is shown attending a class on English as a second language. While such classes are on the increase, so are classes for adults to study Spanish as a second language as immigration from Mexico and central America continues to rise.

employees have presented organizations with many challenges and opportunities. Increasingly, changes in the demographic characteristics of the work force have led managers to alter their styles of managing employees in an effort to learn how to best understand, supervise, and motivate minority and female members. This includes abandoning the stereotypes they unwittingly held in the past when making promotion decisions. It also means understanding the importance of equity in the recruitment process and acknowledging that employees today are looking for a better balance between work and leisure. As more and more women have entered the work force, companies have had to accommodate the needs of dual-career and single-parent families. This might include providing employees with child and eldercare and allowing them to keep flexible work schedules to better manage their busy lives.[15]

Many companies have helped their employees keep up with changing technology by supporting advanced education and training for them. Increasingly, organizations are coming to realize that the ultimate source of competitive advantage and organizational effectiveness lies in fully utilizing the skills of their members, by, for example, empowering their employees to make important decisions.[16] As we discuss later in this chapter, reengineering and total quality management are change strategies that aim to alter how an organization views its activities and the employees who perform them.

Ethical forces. While it's important for an organization to change in response to demographic and social forces, it also is important for them to do so in an ethical way—especially in the face of increasing government, political, and social scrutiny.[17] Many companies have created the role of ethics officer, a person to whom employees can report ethical lapses on the part of the organization's managers or turn to for advice when faced with ethical business dilemmas. Organizations are also trying to promote ethical behavior by giving employees direct access to important decision makers and by protecting whistle-blowers who expose ethical problems.

Many organizations need to make changes to allow managers and employees at all levels to report unethical behavior so that the organization can move quickly to eliminate this behavior and thereby protect the organization, its members, and customers from reputational harm.[18] Similarly, if organizations operate in countries that pay little attention to human rights or the well-being of employees, they have to learn how to change these standards—at least within their own organizations—to protect their foreign employees. The story given in the following Ethics in Action of how U. S. sporting good makers have battled accusations about their products being produced in third-world sweatshops illustrates this issue.

Impediments to Change

From customer design preferences to the issue of where clothes should be produced and whether economic or political unrest will affect the availability of raw materials, the forces of change bombard organizations from all sides. Effective organizations are agile enough to adjust to these forces. But many internal forces make the organization resistant to change.[19]

In the last decade, many of America's best-known (and formerly strongest and most successful) companies—Chrysler, Ford, Xerox (profiled in the opening case), Kodak, Delta, HP, and Macy's among them—have seen their fortunes decline. Some, like Macy's, went bankrupt; others like Ford, Delta, and Kodak are still in deep financial trouble. But some companies, like Chrysler and Xerox, seem to have reversed the decline and embarked upon a recovery. How did such former powerhouses lose their effectiveness? The main explanation for such decline is almost always an organization's inability to change in response to changing environmental conditions like increased competition. Research suggests that one of the main reasons for some organizations' inability to change is **organizational inertia**, or the tendency to maintain the status quo.[20] Impediments to change that cause inertia are found at the organization, group, and individual levels.[21] (See Exhibit 18.1.)

ORGANIZATIONAL INERTIA
The tendency of an organization to maintain the status quo.

Ethics in Action

Nike, Reebok, Adidas, and the Sweatshops

More products are increasingly being manufactured in poor, third-world countries today, but the behavior of the companies who outsource their production to subcontractors in these countries has increasingly been called into question. Nike, a giant in the sportswear industry, was one of the first companies to experience this when it came to light how employees working abroad for Nike's subcontractors were being treated. Indonesian employees were stitching together shoes in hot, noisy factories for only 80 cents a day, or about $18 a month.[22] Employees in Vietnam and China fared better; they could earn about $1.60 a day. Critics charged that at least a $3-a-day wage was needed for these workers to make a living.

Female employees work in a huge factory to sew clothing for sale in the United States. More and more companies are policing the conditions under which such employees labor as stories about 100-hour work weeks with few breaks are reported in the media.

These facts surrounding Nike's subcontracting practices abroad generated an outcry in the United States. Nike was roundly attacked for its practices, which resulted in a sales backlash for the company. Phil Knight, Nike's billionaire owner, was asked how, when his own net worth was over $3 billion, he could defend paying a worker 80 cents a day. As criticism mounted, Knight was forced to reevaluate Nike's labor practices. The company subsequently announced that henceforth all of the factories producing its shoes and clothes would be independently monitored and inspected. Then, after Reebok, a competitor criticized for similar labor practices, announced it was raising wages in Indonesia by 20 percent, Nike raised its wages by 25 percent, to about $23 a month.[23] Small though this may seem, it was a boon to employees in these countries.

In Europe, Adidas, another sportswear company, had largely escaped such criticism. But soon reports arose that a Taiwan-based Adidas subcontractor in El Salvador was employing girls as young as 14 in its factories and making them work for over 70 hours a week. They were only allowed to go to the restroom twice a day, and if they stayed in the restroom longer than three minutes, they were penalized a day's wages.[24] Adidas moved swiftly to avoid the public relations nightmare that Nike had experienced. It announced that, henceforth, its subcontractors would also be required to abide by more strict labor standards. Thus, throughout the industry companies were forced to reevaluate the ethics of their labor practices and promise to keep a vigilant watch on their subcontractors in the future.

In the 2000s, companies like Nike have worked hard to correct such abuses.[25] In 2005 Nike employed over 100 inspectors who visit several hundred factories a year and evaluate their working conditions, and, if problems are found, work to correct them.[26] These

new procedures have had a major impact; many reports of abuses now come directly to Nike, which then takes action so complaints about working conditions have fallen.[27] Moreover, the movement to protect the rights of employees manufacturing clothing abroad has spread to include all types of other products and other retailers and wholesalers. A particularly good example of a company's description of its ethical position on the treatment of overseas employees can be found at Gap's website.[28]

Organization-Level Resistance to Change

Many forces inside an organization make it difficult for the organization to change in response to changing conditions in its environment.[29] The most powerful organization-level impediments to change include power and conflict, differences in functional orientation, mechanistic structure, and organizational culture.

Power and conflict. Change usually benefits some people, functions, or divisions at the expense of others. When change causes power struggles and organizational conflict, an organization is likely to resist it.[30] Suppose that a change in purchasing practices will help the materials management group in an organization achieve its goal of reducing input costs but that it will harm manufacturing's ability to reduce manufacturing costs. Materials management will push for the change, but manufacturing will resist it. The conflict between the two functions will slow down the process of change and perhaps prevent it from occurring at all.

Many large companies have experienced resistance to change on the part of their functional groups. In the 1990s, for example, managers in IBM's mainframe computer division were the most powerful in the corporation. To preserve their established position, prestige, and power in the organization, these managers fought off attempts to redirect IBM's resources to produce workstations and network computers that customers desperately wanted. This failure to change in response to customer demands severely hampered IBM's speed of response to its competitors. As a result, the company lost billions of dollars. It was not until a new CEO took over operations and ruthlessly laid off thousands of mainframe managers and diverted resources toward making and servicing network computers that the company's fortunes began to change.

Differences in functional orientation. Differences in functional orientation are another major impediment to change and source of organizational inertia. Different functions and divisions often see the source of a problem or issue differently as a result of their own viewpoints. This "tunnel vision" increases organizational inertia because the organization must spend time and effort to secure agreement about the source of a problem before it can even consider how the organization needs to respond to the problem.

Mechanistic structure. Recall from Chapter 16 that tall hierarchies, centralized decision making, and the standardization of behavior through rules and procedures characterize mechanistic structures. In contrast, organic structures are flat and decentralized and rely on mutual adjustment between people to get the job done.[31] Which structure is likely to be more resistant to change?

Mechanistic structures are more resistant to change. People who work within a mechanistic structure are expected to act in certain ways and do not develop the initiative to adjust their behavior to changing conditions. The extensive use of mutual adjustment and decentralized authority in an organic structure, on the other hand, fosters the development of skills that enable employees to be creative, responsive, and find solutions to new problems. A mechanistic structure typically develops as an organization grows and is a principal source of inertia, especially in large organizations.

Organizational culture. The values and norms in an organization's culture can be another source of resistance to change. Just as role relationships result in a series of stable expectations between people, so values and norms cause people to behave in predictable ways. If organizational change disrupts taken-for-granted values and norms and forces people to change what they do and how they do it, resistance is likely to ensue. Many organizations develop conservative values that support the status quo and make managers reluctant to search for new ways to compete. As a result, if the environment changes and a company's products become obsolete, the company has nothing to fall back on; failure is therefore likely.[32] Sometimes, values and norms are so strong that even when the environment is changing and it is clear that a new strategy needs to be adopted, managers cannot do so because they are wed to the ways they presently do business.

Group-Level Resistance to Change

As we discussed in Chapters 10 and 11, groups perform much of an organization's work, and several group characteristics can produce resistance to change. Here we consider four: group norms, group cohesiveness, groupthink, and escalation of commitment.

Group norms. Many groups develop strong informal norms that specify appropriate and inappropriate behaviors and govern the interactions between group members (see Chapter 10). Often, change alters task and role relationships in a group; and when it does, it disrupts group norms and the informal expectations that members have of one another. As a result, members of a group may resist change because a whole new set of norms may have to be developed to meet the needs of the new situation.

Group cohesiveness. Group cohesiveness, or the attractiveness of a group to its members, affects group performance (see Chapter 11). Although some level of cohesiveness promotes group performance, too much cohesiveness can actually reduce performance because it stifles opportunities for the group to change and adapt. A highly cohesive group may resist attempts by management to change what it does or even who its members are. Group members may unite to preserve the status quo and to protect their interests at the expense of other groups.

Groupthink and escalation of commitment. Groupthink is a pattern of faulty decision making that occurs in cohesive groups when members discount negative information in order to agree with each other. Escalation of commitment worsens this situation. This occurs when members realize that their course of action is wrong, but continue to pursue it regardless. Groupthink and escalation can make changing a group's behavior very difficult.

Individual-Level Resistance to Change

Individuals within an organization may be inclined to resist change because of uncertainty, selective perception, and force of habit.[33]

Uncertainty and insecurity. People tend to resist change because they feel uncertain and insecure about what its outcome will be.[34] Employees might be given new tasks; role relationships may change; some employees might lose their jobs while others might be promoted. Employees' resistance to the uncertainty and insecurity surrounding change can cause organizational inertia. Absenteeism and turnover may increase as change takes place, and employees may become uncooperative, attempt to delay or slow down the change process, or passively resist it.

Selective perception and retention. Perception and attribution play a major role in determining work attitudes and behaviors (see Chapter 4). There is a general tendency for people to selectively perceive information that is consistent with their existing views (or schemas) of their organizations. Thus, when change takes place, employees tend to focus only on how it will personally affect them or their function or division. If they perceive few benefits, they may reject the change. Not surprisingly, it can be difficult for an organization to develop a common platform to promote change across an organization and get people to see the need for it.

Habit. Habit, people's preference for familiar actions and events, is another impediment to change. The difficulty of breaking bad habits and adopting new styles of behavior indicates how hard it is for people to change their habits. Why are habits hard to break? Some researchers have suggested that people have a built-in tendency to return to their original behaviors—a tendency that stymies change.

Lewin's Force-Field Theory of Change

FORCE-FIELD THEORY
The theory that organizational change occurs when forces for change strengthen, resistance to change lessens, or both occur simultaneously.

As you have seen, a wide variety of forces make organizations resistant to change, and a wide variety of forces push organizations toward change. Researcher Kurt Lewin developed a theory about organizational change. According to his **force-field theory**, these two sets of forces are always in opposition in an organization.[35] When the forces are evenly balanced, the organization is in a state of inertia and does not change. To get an organization to change, managers must find a way to increase the forces for change, *reduce* resistance to change, or do both simultaneously. Any of these strategies will overcome inertia and cause an organization to change.

Exhibit 18.2 illustrates Lewin's theory. An organization at performance level P1 is in balance: Forces for change and resistance to change are equal. Management, however, decides that the organization should strive to achieve performance level P2. To get to level P2, managers must *increase* the forces for change (the increase is represented by the lengthening of the up-arrows), *reduce* resistance to change (the reduction is represented by the shortening of the down-arrows), or both. If managers pursue any of the three strategies successfully, the organization will change and reach performance level P2.

Before we look in more detail at the techniques that managers can use to overcome resistance and facilitate change, we need to look at the types of change they can implement to increase organizational effectiveness.

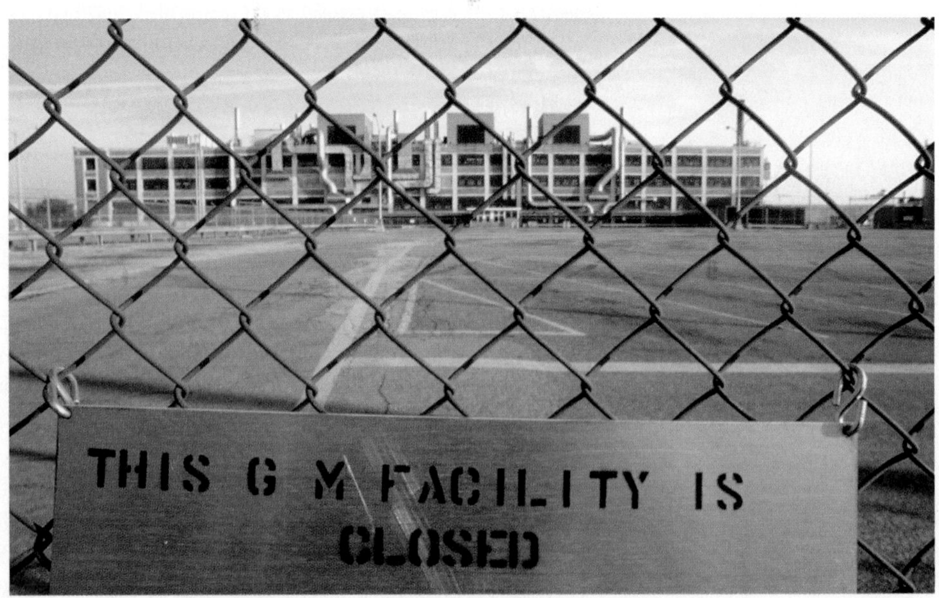

One of GM's many plants that have either closed or are due for closure over the next several years as the company shrinks its manufacturing capabilities due to the success of Japanese competitors. At the same time, Japanese carmakers have opened dozens of new plants in the United States.

EXHIBIT 18.2

Lewin's Force-Field Theory of Change

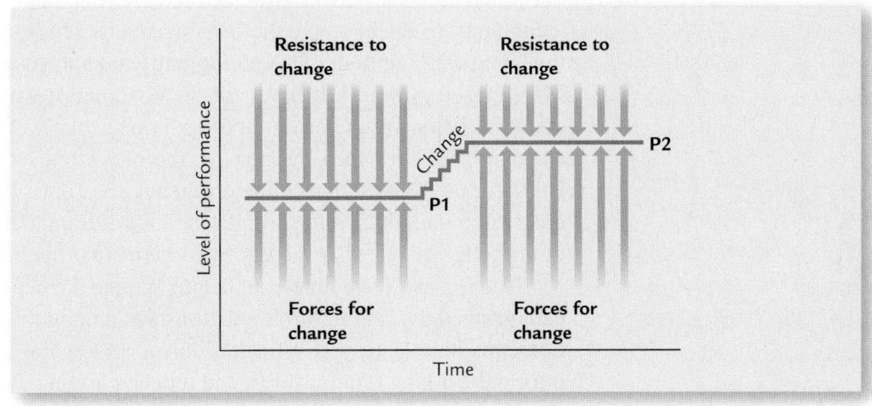

Evolutionary and Revolutionary Change in Organizations

Managers continually face choices about how best to respond to the forces for change. There are several types of change that managers can adopt to help their organizations achieve desired future states.[36] In general, types of change fall into two broad categories: evolutionary change and revolutionary change.[37]

EVOLUTIONARY CHANGE
Change that is gradual, incremental, and narrowly focused.

Evolutionary change is gradual, incremental, and narrowly focused. Evolutionary change is not drastic or sudden but a constant attempt to improve, adapt, and adjust strategy and structure incrementally to accommodate changes taking place in the environment.[38] Socio-technical systems theory and total quality management, or kaizen, are two instruments of evolutionary change. Such improvements might entail utilizing technology in a better way or reorganizing the work process.

Some organizations, however, need to make major changes quickly. Faced with drastic, unexpected changes in the environment (for example, a new technological breakthrough) or with an impending disaster resulting from mismanagement, an organization might need to act quickly and decisively. In this case, revolutionary change is called for.

REVOLUTIONARY CHANGE
Change that is rapid, dramatic, and broadly focused.

Revolutionary change is rapid, dramatic, and broadly focused. Revolutionary change involves a bold attempt to quickly find new ways to be effective. It is likely to result in a radical shift in ways of doing things, new goals, and a new structure for the organization. The process has repercussions at all levels in the organization—corporate, divisional, functional, group, and individual. Reengineering, restructuring, and innovation are three important instruments of revolutionary change.

Evolutionary Change I: Socio-Technical Systems Theory

SOCIO-TECHNICAL SYSTEMS THEORY
Ideas about how organizations should choose specific kinds of control systems that match the technical nature of the work process.

Socio-technical systems theory was one of the first theories that proposed the importance of changing role and task or technical relationships to increase organizational effectiveness.[39] The theory emerged from a study of changing work practices in the British coal-mining industry.[40]

After World War II, new technology that changed work relationships between miners was introduced into the British mining industry. Before the war, coal mining was a small-batch, or craft, process. Teams of skilled miners dug coal from the coalface underground and performed all the other activities necessary to transport the coal to the surface. Work took place in a confined space where productivity depended on close cooperation between team members. Employees developed their own routines and norms to get the job done and provided one another with social support to help combat the stress of their dangerous and confining working conditions.

This method of coal mining, called the "hand got method," approximated small-batch technology (see Chapter 16). To increase efficiency, managers decided to replace it with the "long wall method." This method utilized a mechanized, mass-production technology. Miners used powered drills to cut the coal, and it was then transported to the surface on conveyer belts. Tasks became more routine as the work process became programmed and standardized. On paper, the new technology promised impressive increases in efficiency. But after its introduction, mine efficiency rose only slowly and absenteeism among miners, which had always been high, increased dramatically. Consultants were called to the mines to figure out why the expected gains in efficiency had not occurred.

The researchers pointed out that to operate the new technology efficiently, management had changed the task and role relationships among the miners. The new task and role relationships had destroyed informal norms and social support, disrupted long-established informal working relationships, and reduced group cohesiveness. To solve the problem, the researchers recommended linking the new technology with the old social system by recreating the old system of tasks and roles and decentralizing authority to work groups. When managers redesigned the production process, productivity improved and absenteeism fell.

This study illustrates the need to fit, or "jointly optimize," the workings of an organization's technical and social systems. The lesson learned from socio-technical systems theory is that when managers change task and role relationships, they must gradually adjust the technical and social systems so that group norms and cohesiveness are not disrupted. By taking a gradual approach like this, an organization can avoid group-level resistance to change.

Evolutionary Change II: Total Quality Management

TOTAL QUALITY MANAGEMENT (TQM) OR KAIZEN
An ongoing and constant effort by all of an organization's functions to find new ways to improve the quality of the organization's goods and services.

Total quality management (TQM) or **kaizen** is an ongoing and constant effort by all of an organization's functions to find new ways to improve the quality of the organization's goods and services.[41] In many companies, the initial decision to adopt a TQM approach signals a radical change in the way they organize their activities. Once TQM is adopted by an organization, it generally leads to continuous, incremental change, and all functions are expected to cooperate with each other to improve quality.

First developed by a number of American business consultants, such as W. Edwards Deming and Joseph Juran, total quality management was eagerly embraced by Japanese companies after World War II. For Japanese companies, with their tradition of long-term working relationships and cooperation between functions, the implementation of the new TQM system was an incremental step. Shop-floor employees in Japan, for example, had long been organized into **quality circles**—groups of employees who met regularly to discuss the way work was performed in order to find new ways to improve performance.[42]

QUALITY CIRCLES
Groups of employees who meet regularly to discuss the way work is performed in order to find new ways to increase performance.

Changes frequently inspired by TQM include altering the design or type of machines used to assemble products and reorganizing the sequence of an organization's activities to provide better service to customers. As in socio-technical systems theory, the emphasis in TQM is on the fit between technical and social systems. Changing crossfunctional relationships to help improve quality is very important in TQM. Poor quality often originates at crossover points or after handoffs—that is, when people turn over the work they are doing to people in different functions. The job of intermediate manufacturing, for example, is to assemble inputs to make the final product. Coordinating the design of the various inputs so that they fit together smoothly and operate effectively together is one area that TQM focuses on. Members of the different functions work together to find new ways to reduce the number of inputs needed or to suggest design improvements to help the inputs to be assembled more easily and reliably.

TQM and kaizen can help increase product quality and lower costs, as we saw earlier with Xerox. The results of TQM activities can also dramatically affect an organization's responsiveness to its customers, as Citibank found out. Citibank is one of the leading global financial institutions and has established the goal to become *the* premier institution in the twenty-first century. To achieve this lofty goal the company started to use TQM to increase its responsiveness to customers. It recognized that, ultimately, its customer base and loyalty determine a bank's future success. As the first step in its TQM effort, Citibank focused upon identifying the factors that dissatisfy its customers. When it analyzed the complaints, it found that most of them centered around the time it took to complete a customer's request—like responding to an account problem or getting a loan. So, Citibank's managers began to examine how they handled each kind of customer request.

For each distinct kind of request, they formed a crossfunctional team of people whose job was to break down a specific request into the steps between people and departments needed to fulfill the request. These teams found that oftentimes many steps in the process were unnecessary and could be done away with if the right information systems tools were used. They also found that very often delays occurred because employees simply did not know how to handle the request. They were not being given the right kind of training to deal with them. As a result, Citibank decided to implement an organization-wide TQM program.

Managers and supervisors at the company were charged with reducing the complexity of the work process and finding the most effective way to process requests. They were also charged with teaching employees how to answer each specific request. The results were remarkable. For example, in the loan department the TQM program reduced the number of handoffs necessary to process a request by 75 percent; average time taken to respond to a customer dropped from several hours to thirty minutes. By 2000, over 100,000 employees had been trained worldwide in the new TQM processes. And Citibank could easily measure TQM's effectiveness by the increased speed with which it was handling a higher volume of custom requests from its growing number of global customers in over 100 countries.[43] Another company regarded by many as the global leader in TQM is Toyota, profiled in the following Global View.

Global View

Toyota's Commitment to Continuous Improvement

Toyota has long been known as a company that has constantly strived to change its production systems to enhance efficiency, quality, and customer responsiveness. It pioneered the system of "lean production," a form of reengineering the work process that resulted in dramatic improvements in the quality of its vehicles. And Toyota has always pursued total quality management or Kaizen, a change strategy that involves a continuous incremental improvement of work procedures. Using kaizen, production-line employees are made responsible for finding ways to improve work procedures to drive down costs and drive up quality. Individually, and in quality groups or circles, employees suggest ways to improve how a particular Toyota car model is made. Over time, from their thousands of suggestions, incremental innovations made to the car assembly process result in major improvements to the final product. Employees receive

At this Toyota plant TQM was used to redesign the machines used to assemble products and reorganize the sequence of tasks used to assemble a product. The result was an increase in efficiency and quality.

cash bonuses and rewards for finding ways to improve work procedures, and the result has been a continuous increase in car quality and reduced manufacturing costs.

In the 2000s, however, under the leadership of Toyota's new president, Jujio Cho, the company sought to increase the speed of change to further improve its efficiency and quality to gain an edge over its major competitors like GM, Ford, and DaimlerChrysler. It has begun a series of new kinds of change programs, each directed at improving some aspect of its operations, which Toyota hopes will bring both incremental and radical changes to the way it operates.

Some incremental change programs involve strengthening its kaizen program such as *pokayoke*, or mistake-proofing. This initiative concentrates on the stages of the assembly process that have led to most previous quality problems; employees are required to double- and triple-check a particular stage to discover defective parts or to fix improper assembly operations that lead to subsequent customer complaints. Another program is "CCC21," which involves working with the company's suppliers to find ways to reduce the costs of Toyota's car components by 30 percent—something that will result in billions of dollars in savings. Toyota has also introduced a new manufacturing process called GBL, which uses a sophisticated new assembly process to hold a car body firmly in place during production. This allows welding and assembly operations to be performed more accurately, resulting in better quality cars. GBL has also enabled Toyota to build factories that can assemble several different kinds of models on the same production line with no loss in efficiency or quality. This is a major competitive advantage. The company's global network of plants can now quickly change over the kinds of cars they are making depending upon buyers' demands for various models at different points in time.

Other radical change efforts have focused on revamping Toyota's development and design process to keep up with changing customer needs and demographics—for example, the age of the average Toyota car buyer has been steadily increasing. Despite Toyota's climbing global sales (which exceeded $160 billion in 2006), the company was criticized for failing to understand how the market was changing. Analysts blamed the problem on centralized decision making at the company and a culture that had long been dominated by Toyota's cautious and frugal Japanese designers. Rather than designing innovative, flexible vehicles customers were increasingly demanding, Toyota continued to focus on cutting costs and increasing the quality of its vehicles. When the company's U. S. designers, for example, argued with designers in Tokyo that an eight-cylinder pickup truck was what Toyota needed to keep pace with GM and Ford, they were ignored. Headquarters also turned a deaf ear to the call to manufacture other new kinds of vehicles appealing to younger customers. Slow sales of small pickups and compact cars soon showed that both these design changes were necessary, however.

To quickly get an improved design process into gear, President Cho championed two new change techniques to radically alter the design process: PDCA and Obeya. Obeya is based on frequent brainstorming sessions between engineers, designers, production managers, and marketers designed to speed new model cars to the market. PDCA—or "plan," "do," "check," "action,"—is a program designed to empower the company's designers outside of Japan to intervene in the car development process and champion designs that meet the needs of local customers. The result of promoting a flexible, decentralized car design process was the speedy introduction of the rugged eight-cylinder Tundra pickup truck and the angular, Scion xB compact in the United States, as well as the Yaris, Toyota's best-selling European car. The Yaris was designed in Europe, and its success there led to its subsequent introduction in Japan, where it also sold well.

Toyota's mastery of the need to manage change has made it by far the most profitable of the major carmakers. With all its new change processes operating at full speed, Toyota replaced Ford as the world's second largest carmaker in 2004 and seems likely to replace GM as the world's biggest carmaker before 2010.

More and more companies are embracing the continuous, incremental type of change that results from the implementation of TQM programs. Many companies have found, however, that implementing a TQM program is not always easy because it requires employees and managers to adopt new ways of looking at their roles in the organization. Managers must be willing to decentralize decision making, empower employees, and become facilitators rather than supervisors. The "command and control" model gives way to an "advise and support" model. It is also important that employees, as well as managers, share in the increased profits that successful TQM programs can provide. In Japan, for example, performance bonuses frequently account for 30 percent or more of employees' and managers' salaries, and salaries can fluctuate widely from year to year because organizational performance changes.

Despite the success that organizations like Toyota, Citibank, Harley-Davidson, and Xerox have had with TQM, many other organizations do not achieve the increases in quality and cost reductions associated with TQM and abandon their programs. One reason TQM can fail is because top managers underestimate the degree of commitment from people at all levels in an organization necessary to implement the program. A second reason is the long timeframe necessary for TQM efforts to yield results. Unfortunately, TQM is not a quick fix that can turn an organization around overnight.[44] It is an evolutionary process that bears fruit only when it becomes a way of life in an organization as it has become at Toyota, which is perhaps the world's leader in championing the kaizen process.

Revolutionary Change I: Reengineering

Reengineering involves the "fundamental rethinking and radical redesign of business processes to achieve dramatic improvements in critical, contemporary measures of performance such as cost, quality, service, and speed."[45] Change resulting from reengineering requires managers to go back to the basics and dissect each step in the work process. Instead of focusing on an organization's *functions*, the managers of a reengineered organization focus on business processes—just as Toyota did when reengineering its car development and design process.

BUSINESS PROCESS Any activity that is vital to the quick delivery of goods and services to customers or that promotes high quality or low costs.

A **business process** is any activity (such as order processing, inventory control, or product design) vital to the quick delivery of goods and services to customers, or a process that promotes high quality or low costs. Business processes are not the responsibility of any one function; they involve activities across functions. Because reengineering focuses on business processes and not functions, a reengineered organization always adopts a new approach to organizing its activities.

Organizations that take up reengineering ignore the existing arrangement of tasks, roles, and work activities. Management starts the reengineering process with the customer (not with the product or service) and asks the question: "How can we reorganize the way we do our work, our business processes, to provide the best-quality, lowest-cost goods and services to the customer?" Frequently, when companies ponder this question, they discover better ways to organize their activities. For example, a business process that currently involves members of ten different functions working sequentially to provide goods and services might be performed by one person or a few people at a fraction of the cost after reengineering. Because reengineering often results in such changes, job enlargement and enrichment (discussed in Chapter 7) are common results of reengineering. Individual jobs become increasingly complex, and people are grouped into crossfunctional teams as business processes are reengineered to reduce costs and increase quality, like what happened at Chrysler, which is discussed in the following OB Today.

Reengineering and TQM are highly interrelated and complementary. After revolutionary reengineering has taken place and the question "What is the best way to provide customers with the goods or service they require?" has been answered, evolutionary TQM takes over. The focus for the organization then becomes: "How can we now continue to improve and refine the new process and find better ways of managing task and role relationships?" Successful organizations examine both questions simultaneously, and they continuously attempt to identify new and better processes for meeting the goals of

OB Today

Chrysler Adopts a Crossfunctional Team Structure

After almost going bankrupt in the early 1990s, Chrysler's managers realized they needed to radically reengineer their organizational structure to reduce costs and speed the development of new cars that customers would want to buy. Chrysler became the first U. S. car company to pioneer the use of crossfunctional teams and new information technology to lower manufacturing costs and speed[46] the introduction of new products.[46] Chrysler's decision to use crossfunctional teams linked to a sophisticated computer network came about in the following way.

In 1988, Chrysler acquired American Motors (AMC) and its seven hundred design engineers. Rather than distributing these engineers among Chrysler's different engineering functions—transmissions, brakes, engines, and so on—Chrysler made a radical decision. It chose to keep the engineers together and have all seven hundred of them work together in a crossfunctional team devoted to redesigning the Jeep Grand Cherokee, infamous among consumers for its poor reliability.

The Daimler Chrysler PT Cruiser introduced in 1999 was the first of several new models that help the company transform itself and catch up with Japanese car makers. Nevertheless, in 2006 Chrysler, like GM and Ford, had to cut back on production by some 70,000 vehicles as customers turned to fuel-efficient cars which are still mainly produced by the Japanese.

The seven hundred engineers from all areas of design engineering worked together on a single huge work floor. They were joined by marketing, finance, purchasing, and other functional experts who gave them information about customers' needs, input costs, and so on. All of the information communicated between functional specialists was recorded and exchanged electronically through sophisticated computer systems so that each member of the team knew what the others were doing. Top management then gave the team a target price for the car and told them to design it to fit within that price range. The result was astounding. The new design was finished just in two years, and the Jeep Cherokee was an instant success when it was introduced in 1992. Chrysler was so pleased with the results the crossfunctional team achieved that it decided to change the entire structure of the company from one that revolved around functions to one that utilized these crossfunctional teams.

In the new structure, functional personnel are assigned to one of four major teams—the small car, large car, minivan, or Jeep/truck team—and each team has its own vice president. Chrysler also built a $1 billion technology center with separate floors to house each team. Its crossfunctional team structure allows Chrysler's functional experts to meet and share ideas to speed the development process. It also allows for the intense interaction among people necessary for successful innovation and product development.

Chrysler's turnaround and new skills in lean production attracted the attention of Daimler, the maker of the Daimler Benz car. Daimler wanted to combine Chrysler's low-cost skills with its engineering excellence and the companies merged to form Daimler Chrysler in 1998.[47] The merger resulted in many new problems, but by 2004 the merger seemed to be working. There has been an outpouring of new, innovative vehicles like the Chrysler Crossfire, Pacifica, PT Cruiser Convertible, its best-selling 300Cl, and the redesigned Sebring and new Aspen SUV planned for 2007.[48]

increased efficiency, quality, and responsiveness to customers.[49] Hallmark Cards, based in Kansas City, Missouri, provides many lessons for managers seeking to put such a plan for change into action.

Hallmark sells 55 percent of the 8 billion birthday, Christmas, and other kinds of cards sold each year in the United States.[50] However, in the last decade Hallmark experienced great competition from smaller and more agile card companies that pioneered new kinds of specialty greeting cards and sold them—often at discount prices—in supermarkets and discount stores. To keep Hallmark on top of its market its managers decided to examine how they were currently performing work activities and what improvements could be made.

Top management began this evaluation by organizing a hundred managers into teams to analyze Hallmark's competitors, the changing nature of customer needs, the organizational structure the company was using to coordinate its activities, and the way it was developing, distributing, and marketing its cards—its basic business processes, in other words. What the teams found startled managers from the top down and showed there was a desperate need for change.

Managers discovered that although Hallmark had the world's largest creative staff—over 700 artists and writers who design over 24,000 new cards each year—it was taking over three years to get a new card to market. Once an artist designed a new card and a writer came up with an appropriate rhyme or message, it took an average of three years for the card to be produced, packaged, and shipped to retailers. Information on changing customer needs, a vital input into decisions about what cards should be designed, took many months to reach artists. That delay made it difficult for Hallmark to respond quickly to its competitors.

Armed with this information, the hundred team managers presented top management with a hundred recommendations for changes that would allow the company to do its work more quickly and effectively. The recommendations called for a complete change in the way the company organized its basic business processes. Hallmark began by completely restructuring its activities. Previously the company had relied on a functional structure. Artists worked separately from writers, and both artists and writers worked separately from materials management, printing, and manufacturing personnel. Twenty-five handoffs between employees were needed to produce the final product, and 90 percent of the time work was simply sitting in somebody's in- or out-basket. Taking the advice of the teams, Hallmark changed to a crossfunctional team structure. People from different functions—artists, writers, editors, and so on—were grouped into teams responsible for producing a specific kind of card, such as Christmas cards, get-well cards, or new lines of specialty cards.

To eliminate the need for handoffs between departments, each team is now responsible for all aspects of the design process. To reduce the need for handoffs within a team, all team members work together from a card's inception to plan the steps in the design process, and all are responsible for reviewing the success of their efforts. To help each team evaluate its efforts and give it the information it needs about what customers want, Hallmark introduced a computerized point-of-sales merchandising system in each of its Hallmark Card stores. This gives each team instant feedback on what and how many kinds of cards are selling at any given point in time. Each team can now continuously experiment with new card designs to attract more customers.

The effects of these changes have been dramatic. Not only are cards introduced in less than one year, but some reach the market in a matter of months. Quality has increased as each team focuses on improving its cards, and costs have fallen because the new work system is so efficient. The message is clear Managers must continually analyze their business processes to ensure they are aligned with changing customer needs and business practices. Every company must adopt the state-of-the-art kaizen and IT applications that are the key to success today.

E-Engineering. In fact, the term E-engineering has been coined to refer to companies' attempts to use all kinds of information systems to improve their performances. In previous chapters, there have been many examples of how the use of Internet-based software systems can change the way a company's strategy and structure operates. New information systems can be employed in all aspects of an organization's business and for all kinds of reasons.[51] For example, Cypress Semiconductor's CEO, T. J. Rodgers, uses the company's online management-information system to continually monitor his managers' activities and help him keep the organizational hierarchy flat. Rodgers claims that he can review the goals of all his 1,500 managers in about four hours, and he does so each week.[52] We have already discussed how companies like Citibank and Toyota use Internet-based systems to streamline their operations and to better link themselves to their customers. The importance of E-engineering is only likely to increase in the future as it changes the ways a company organizes people and tasks and links them together to improve its performance.

Revolutionary Change II: Restructuring

Organizations experiencing a rapid deterioration in performance may try to turn things around by restructuring. An organization that resorts to restructuring usually attempt to simplify its organizational structure by eliminating divisions, departments, or levels in the hierarchy, and downsizing employees to lower operating costs. It also contracts with other companies to perform its manufacturing, customer service, and other functional activities.

When William F. Malec, for example, took over as the head of the federally administered Tennessee Valley Authority (TVA), the organization had over fourteen levels in its hierarchy of 37,000 employees, and its customers had experienced an average increase in their utility rates of over 10 percent per year. Describing TVA as a top-heavy bureaucracy, Malec quickly moved to slash costs and restructure the organization; he reduced the levels in the hierarchy to nine and the employees to 18,500, and he froze utility rates for ten years. Another example of restructuring that illustrates the important role played by outsourcing is discussed in the following Global View insight.

Why does restructuring become necessary, and why may an organization need to downsize or outsource its operations? Sometimes, an unforeseen change in the environment occurs: Perhaps a shift in technology makes the company's products obsolete, or a worldwide recession reduces demand for its products. Sometimes an organization has excess capacity because customers no longer want the goods and services it provides because they are outdated, low quality, offer little value, or the customer service related to them is poor, as at eMachines. Sometimes organizations downsize because they have grown too tall and bureaucratic and their operating costs have become much too high. Organizations even restructure, at times, when they are in a strong position simply to stay on top in the face of competition. Microsoft, for example, is constantly changing its structure to realign its resources with the changing computing environment. In 2003, for example, the company broke its MSN division into two distinct units, one to handle its internet customers, and one to handle its growing Internet activities like X-Box gaming.[53] Then, recall from Chapter 11 that in 2006 the company reorganized to three major operating groups focusing on furthering its web-based Windows operating, applications, and gaming activities.

All too often, companies are forced to downsize and lay off employees because they do *not* continually monitor the way they operate—and do not make the incremental adjustments to their strategies and structures allowing them to contain costs and adapt.[54] Paradoxically, because they have not paid attention to the need to reengineer themselves,

Global View

eMachines Merges with Gateway

In 2001, eMachines, a low-price computer maker whose machines sold for less than $800, was going bankrupt. The main problem? Low product quality because of eMachines' inefficient manufacturing operations and poor service from its customer service reps, who seemed unable to help customers fix problems with their new computers. Wayne Inouye, a Japanese American who has been in charge of Best Buy's computer-retailing division, was put in charge of turning around the company or shutting it down if he could not.

To turnaround the company, Inouye adopted a radical approach to change. He decided to outsource the company's manufacturing, sales, and customers service operations. Henceforth, eMachines' computers would be assembled at low-cost global locations in countries like China or Malaysia, and software specialists in Bangalore, India, would handle its customer service operations. Furthermore, while eMachines used to sell most of its computers online or by advertising, in the future Inouye decided to sell his computers through retail partners such as Best Buy.

After outsourcing all these activities, Inouye focused his company's efforts on marketing, constantly monitoring what kinds of new features customers want from their computers and how much they are willing to pay for them. eMachines is electronically linked to its retailers and its managers have real-time information on which kinds of computers are selling and why. Using this information they can then redesign computers and then electronically ship new computer specifications to their overseas manufacturers. In this way, the computers coming off the assembly line match customers' current needs thereby increasing eMachine's sales. The results of all these changes were astounding. In 2003 the company's sales exceeded $1 billion, and it replaced Gateway to become the number three leading PC maker, only to be bought out by this company in 2004 so Gateway could now adopt eMachine's successful business practices.

they are forced into a position where restructuring becomes the only way they can survive to compete in an increasingly cutthroat environment.

Restructuring, like reengineering, TQM, and other change strategies, generates resistance to change. Often, the decision to downsize will require the establishment of new task and role relationships. Because this change may threaten the jobs of some employees, they resist the changes taking place. Many plans to introduce change, including restructuring, take a long time to implement and fail because of the high level of resistance encountered at all levels of the organization.

Revolutionary Change III: Innovation

Restructuring is often necessary because advancing technology makes the technology an organization is currently using to produce goods and services (or the goods and services themselves) obsolete. For example, advancing technology has made computers much more powerful and cheaper to manufacture. This in itself has changed the type of computers customers want. Laptops are rapidly becoming more popular than home PCs, for example. If organizations are to avoid falling behind in the competitive race to produce new goods and services, they must take steps to introduce new products or develop new technologies to produce them reliably and at a low cost. Innovation, as we discussed in Chapter 15, is the successful use of skills and resources to create new technologies or new goods and services so that an organization can change and better respond to the needs of customers.[55] Innovation can result in spectacular success. Apple Computer changed the face of the computer industry when it introduced its personal computer. Honda changed the face of the small motorbike market when it introduced small 50cc motorcycles. Mary Kay changed the way cosmetics are sold to customers when it introduced at-home cosmetics parties and personalized selling.

Although innovation does bring about change, it is also associated with a high level of risk because the outcomes of research and development activities are often uncertain.[56] It has been estimated that only from 12 to 20 percent of R&D projects result in products that make it to the market.[57] Thus innovation can lead not only to the changes organizations want—the introduction of profitable new technologies and products—but also to the kinds of changes they want to avoid—technologies that are inefficient or products that customers *don't* want. In the 2000s, for example, cell phone users have increasingly demanded new features such as calendars, color screens, word processing, games, and even digital cameras built into their phones. Companies like Motorola and Nokia that were slow to build-in these new features have seen their sales fall, and companies like Sanyo and Sony that moved quickly to introduce these features have prospered.

Innovation is one of the most difficult instruments of change to manage.[58] Recall from Chapter 16 that when organizations rely on innovation as the source of their competitive advantage, they need to adopt organic, flexible structures such as matrix or crossfunctional team structures giving employees the freedom to experiment and be creative.[59] Like with reengineering, the need for functions to coordinate their activities and to work together is important for successful innovation, and companies that rely on innovation have to facilitate the change effort and support the efforts of their members to be creative. For example, the term *skunk works* was coined at Lockheed Corporation when that company set up a specialized unit, separate from its regular functional organization, to pioneer the development of the U-2 spy plane. Ford copied the skunk works model to develop a new version of the Mustang and other cars. To try to increase the success rate of innovation and new product development, many high-tech organizations have developed the role of **product champion**, an expert manager appointed to head a new product team and see a new product from its inception to sale.[60] Many of the techniques for managing change that we discuss in the next section were developed to help facilitate innovation. Of all the instruments of revolutionary change, innovation offers the best prospect for long-term success but also poses the most risk.

PRODUCT CHAMPION
An expert manager appointed to head a new product team and lead a new product from its beginning to commercialization.

Managing Change: Action Research

No matter what type of evolutionary or revolutionary change an organization adopts, managers face the problem of getting the organization to change. Kurt Lewin, whose force-field theory argues that organizations are balanced between forces for change and resistance to change, has a related perspective on how managers can bring change to their organizations (see Exhibit 18.3).

In Lewin's view, implementing change is a three-step process: (1) unfreezing the organization from its present state, (2) making the change, and (3) "refreezing" the organization in the new desired state so that its members do not revert to their previous work attitudes and role behaviors.[61] Lewin warns that resistance to change will quickly cause an organization and its members to revert to their old ways of doing things unless the organization actively takes steps to refreeze the organization with the changes in place. It is not enough to make some changes in task and role relationships and expect the changes to be

EXHIBIT 18.3

Lewin's Three-Step Change Process

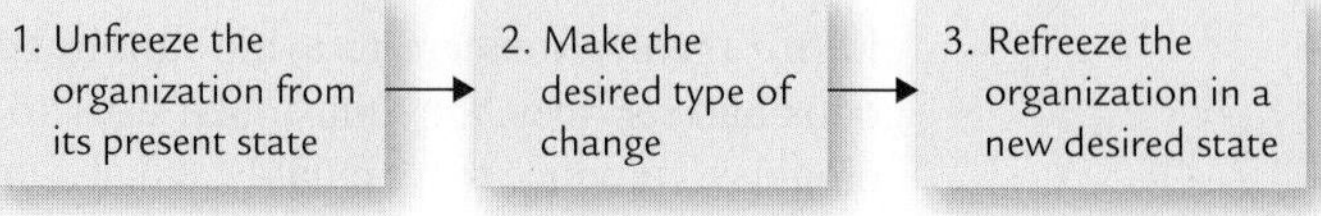
1. Unfreeze the organization from its present state
2. Make the desired type of change
3. Refreeze the organization in a new desired state

EXHIBIT 18.4

The Steps in Action Research

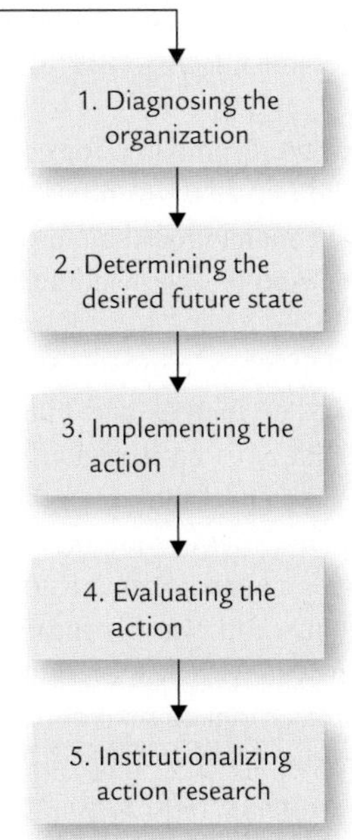

ACTION RESEARCH
A strategy for generating and acquiring knowledge that managers can use to define an organization's desired future state and to plan a change program that allows the organization to reach that state.

successful and endure. To get an organization to remain in its new state, managers must actively manage the change process.[62]

Action research is a strategy for generating and acquiring knowledge that managers can use to define an organization's desired future state and to plan a change program enabling it to reach that state.[63] The techniques and practices of action research help managers unfreeze an organization, move it to its new desired position, and refreeze it again so that the benefits of the change are retained. Exhibit 18.4 identifies the main steps in action research.

Diagnosis of the Organization

The first step in action research requires managers to recognize the existence of a problem that needs to be solved and acknowledge that some type of change is needed. In general, recognition of the need for change arises because someone in the organization thinks there is a gap between desired performance and actual performance. Perhaps customer complaints about the quality of goods or services have increased. Perhaps profits have recently fallen or operating costs have escalated. Or perhaps turnover among managers or employees has been excessive. In the first stage, managers need to analyze what is going on and why problems are occurring. Recall that slow sales of its small pickup trucks and the aging of its typical car buyer caused managers at Toyota to reevaluate the organization's present state.

Diagnosing the organization can be a complex process. Like a doctor, managers have to distinguish between symptoms and causes. For example, there is little point in introducing new technology to reduce production costs if the problem is that demand is falling because customers do not like the design of the product. Toyota needed to introduce new change programs to address just this problem. Managers have to carefully collect information about the organization to diagnose the problem correctly and get employees committed to the change process. At this early stage it is important for managers to collect information from people at all levels in the organization and from outsiders such as customers and suppliers. Questionnaire surveys given to employees, customers, and suppliers, and interviews with employees and managers can provide information essential to a correct diagnosis.

Determining the Desired Future State

After identification of the present state, the next step is to identify where the organization needs to be—its desired future state. This step also involves a difficult planning process as managers work out various alternative courses of action that could move the organization to where they would like it to be. Identifying the desired future state involves deciding what the organization's strategy and structure should be. For example, should the organization focus on reducing costs and increasing efficiency? Or are improving quality and responsiveness to customers the key to future success? What is the best kind of structure for the organization to adopt to realize organizational goals—a product structure or perhaps a crossfunctional team structure?

Implementing Action

Implementing action is the third step of action research.[64] It is a three-step process. First, managers need to identify possible impediments to change that they will encounter as they go about making changes. These include impediments at the organization, group, and individual levels.[65] Suppose managers choose to reengineer the company from a functional to a crossfunctional team structure to speed product development and reduce costs. They must anticipate the obstacles they will encounter when they "unfreeze" the organization and make the changes. Functional managers, for example, might strongly resist efforts to change the company because their power and prestige in the organization might suffer. Similarly, members of each function who have grown accustomed to working with the same people and to stable task and role relationships will resist being assigned to a new team where tasks and roles have to be worked out again and new interpersonal relationships have to be forged.

The more revolutionary the change that is adopted, the greater will be the problem of implementing it. Managers need to find ways to minimize, control, and coopt resistance to change. They also need to devise strategies to bring the organization's members on board and foster their commitment to the change process. Moreover, they must look to the future and seek ways to refreeze the changes they have made.

The second step in implementing action is deciding who will be responsible for actually making the changes and controlling the change process. The choices are to employ **external change agents**—outside consultants who are experts in managing change—or **internal change agents**—managers from within the organization who are knowledgeable about the situation—or some combination of both.[66]

EXTERNAL CHANGE AGENT
An outside consultant who is an expert in managing change.

INTERNAL CHANGE AGENT
A manager from within an organization who is knowledgeable about the situation to be changed.

The principal problem with using internal change agents is that other members of the organization may perceive them as being politically involved in the changes and biased toward certain groups. External change agents, in contrast, are likely to be perceived as being less influenced by internal politics (although recall from Chapter 13 that one political tactic is to bring in an outside expert to provide support for one's own view of what needs to be changed). Another reason for employing external change agents is that as outsiders, they have a detached view of the organization's problems and can distinguish between the "forest and the trees." Insiders can be so involved in what is going on within the organization that they cannot see the true source of the problems. Management consultants, such as those from McKinsey & Co. and Accenture, are frequently brought in by large organizations to help the top-management team diagnose the organization's problems and suggest solutions. Many consultants specialize in certain types of organizational change, like restructuring, reengineering, or implementing total quality management.

The third step in implementing action is deciding which specific change strategy will most effectively unfreeze, change, and refreeze the organization. Specific techniques for implementing change are discussed later in this chapter. The types of change that these techniques give rise to fall into two categories: top-down and bottom-up.[67]

TOP-DOWN CHANGE
Change that is implemented by managers at a high level in the organization.

Top-down change is change that is implemented by managers at a high level in the organization. The result of radical organizational restructuring and reengineering is top-down change. Managers high up in the organization decide to make a change, realizing full well that it will reverberate at all organizational levels. The managers choose to manage and solve problems as they arise at the divisional, functional, or individual levels during the process.

BOTTOM-UP CHANGE
Change that is implemented by employees at low levels in the organization and gradually rises until it is felt throughout the organization.

Bottom-up change is change that is implemented by employees at low levels in the organization and gradually rises until it is felt throughout the organization. When an organization wants to engage in bottom-up change, the first step in the action research process—diagnosing the organization—becomes pivotal in determining the success of the change. Managers involve employees at all levels in the change process to get their input and lessen their resistance. By reducing the uncertainty employee's experience, bottom-up change facilitates unfreezing and increases the likelihood that employees will retain the new behaviors they learn during the change process. In contrast, top-down change proceeds rapidly, forces employees to keep up with the pace of change, and troubleshoots problems as they arise.

In general, bottom-up change is easier to implement than top-down change because it provokes less resistance. Organizations that have the time to engage in bottom-up change are generally well-run organizations that pay attention to change, are used to change, and change often. Poorly run organizations, those that rarely change or postpone change until it is too late, are frequently forced to engage in top-down restructuring simply to survive. For example, Lucent did not have the luxury of being able to use bottom-up change when its performance declined precipitously in the early 2000s. Lucent's new CEO Patricia Russo had to take immediate action to reduce costs and develop new products that would turn around the company when she took over in 2003.[68] Russo slashed the number of Lucent's product development teams from 14 to 5, closing 9 of Lucent's operating divisions in the process. She also focused its resources on developing fewer, but more advanced, products. In contrast, even though Microsoft dominates its competitors, Bill Gates constantly seeks change to improve his organization's performance. Even though

Chairman of the French telecommunications equipment-maker Alcatel, Serge Tchuruk and Lucent CEO Patricia Russo attend a press conference in Paris in 2006 where they announced their agreement to merge. The merger will create the world's second largest telecommunications company, and Russo will become its CEO.

Microsoft was earning record profits, in 2006, Gates announced new initiatives to develop new web-based Windows software for all kinds of digital devices including smartphones, tablet PCs, and MP3 players. He also established three new operating divisions to develop these products to stay on top of the industry.[69]

Organizations that change the most are able to exploit the advantages of evolutionary bottom-up change because their managers are always open to the need for change and constantly use action research to find new and better ways to operate and increase effectiveness. Organizations in which change happens rarely are likely candidates for revolutionary top-down change. Because their managers do not use action research on a continuing basis, they attempt change so late that their only option is some massive restructuring or downsizing to turn their organization around.

Evaluating the Action

The fourth step in action research is evaluating the action that has been taken and assessing the degree to which the changes have accomplished the desired objectives. Armed with this evaluation, management decides whether more change is needed to reach the organization's desired future state or whether more effort is needed to refreeze the organization in its new state.[70]

The best way to evaluate the change process is to develop measures or criteria to help managers assess whether the organization has reached its desired objectives. When criteria developed at the beginning of action research are used consistently over time to evaluate the effects of the change process, managers have ample information to assess the impact of the changes they have made. They can compare costs before and after the change to see whether efficiency has increased. For example, they can survey employees to see whether they are more satisfied with their jobs. They can survey customers to see whether they are more satisfied with the quality of the organization's products. As part of its kaizen effort, managers at Toyota carefully survey their customers to make sure that the quality and features of the company's new car models meet their expectations. That information helped them to evaluate the success of their change effort.

Assessing the impact of change is especially difficult because the effects may emerge slowly. The action research process that we have been describing may take several years to complete. Typically, reengineering and restructuring take months or years, and total quality management, once under way, never stops. Consequently, managers need valid and reliable measures that they can use to evaluate performance. All too often poorly performing organizations fail to develop and consistently apply criteria to evaluate their performance.

You're the Management Expert

Bringing Change to a Restaurant

You are the change agent called in to help a local restaurant find out why its sales are not increasing. The restaurant's major problem is a low level of repeat business—customers just don't seem to return often. After visiting the restaurant several times posing as a customer, you discover that there seems to be a high level of conflict between the chefs in the kitchen and the waiters, and a high level of conflict between the waiters themselves. The chefs are also playing favorites with the waiters to get a share of their tips; waiters who give the chefs a cut of their tips get better food for their customers than those who do not, and their customers are served quicker. Unfortunately, customers notice the strife between employees and react to it negatively. That means smaller tips for both waiters and chefs and fewer repeat customers for the restaurant. Draw up a plan for changing this situation and develop some before-and-after measures to evaluate how well your plan is succeeding.

For those organizations, the pressure for change often comes from the outside when shareholders complain about poor profits, customers complain about their products, or regulatory bodies investigate their practices.

Institutionalizing Action Research

The need to manage change is so vital in today's quickly changing environment that organizations must institutionalize action research—that is, make it a required habit or a norm adopted by every member of the organization. The institutionalization of action research is as necessary at the top of the organization (where the top management team plans the organization's future strategy) as it is on the shop floor (where employees meet in quality circles to find new ways to increase efficiency and quality). Because change is so difficult and requires so much thought and effort to implement, members at all levels of the organization must be rewarded for being part of successful change efforts. Top managers can be rewarded with stock options and bonus plans linked to organizational performance. Lower-level members can be rewarded through an employee stock-ownership plan and by performance bonuses and pay linked to individual or group performance. Indeed, tangible rewards are one way of helping to refreeze the organization in its new state because, as we discussed in Chapter 8, pay is an important motivation tool for helping people learn and sustain desired organizational behaviors.

Organization Development

ORGANIZATIONAL DEVELOPMENT (OD)
A series of techniques and methods that managers can use in their action research program to increase the adaptability of their organization.

Organization development (OD) is a series of techniques and methods that managers can use in their action research program to increase the adaptability of their organization.[71] In the words of organizational theorist Warren Bennis, OD refers to a "complex educational strategy intended to change beliefs, attitudes, values, and structure of organizations so that they can better adapt to new technologies, markets, and challenges and the dizzying rate of change itself."[72] The goal of OD is to improve organizational effectiveness and help people reach their potentials and realize their goals. As action research proceeds, managers need to continually unfreeze, change, and refreeze managers' and employees' attitudes and behaviors. Many OD techniques have been developed to help managers do this. We first look at OD techniques to help managers unfreeze an organization and overcome resistances to change. We then look at OD techniques to help managers change and refreeze an organization in its new desired state.

OD Techniques to Deal with Resistance to Change

Resistance to change occurs at all levels of an organization. It manifests itself as organizational politics and power struggles between individuals and groups, differing perceptions of the need for change, and so on. Tactics that managers can use to reduce resistance to change include education and communication, participation and empowerment, facilitation, bargaining and negotiation, manipulation, and coercion.[73]

Education and communication. One of the most important impediments to change is uncertainty about what is going to happen. Through education and communication, internal and external agents of change can inform members of the organization about the change and how it will affect them.[74] Change agents can communicate this information in formal group meetings, by memo, in one-on-one meetings, and, increasingly, through electronic means such as e-mail and videoconferencing. Wal-Mart, for example, has a state-of-the-art videoconferencing system. Managers at corporate headquarters put on presentations that are beamed to all Wal-Mart stores so that both managers and employees are aware of the changes taking place.

Even when plant closures or massive layoffs are planned, it is still best—from both an ethical and a change standpoint—to inform employees about what will happen to them as downsizing occurs. Many organizations fear that disgruntled employees may try to hurt the organization as it closes or sabotage the closing process. More often, however, employees are cooperative until the end. As organizations become more and more aware of the benefits offered by incremental change, they are increasing communication with the work force to gain employees' cooperation and to overcome their resistance to change.

Participation and empowerment. Inviting employees to participate in the change process is becoming a popular method of reducing resistance to change. Participation complements empowerment by increasing employees' involvement in decision making and giving them greater autonomy to change their work procedures. In addition, to encourage employees to share their skills and talents, organizations are opening up their books to inform employees about the organization's financial condition. Some organizations use ESOPs to motivate and reward employees and to harness their commitment to change. Wal-Mart, for example, has an ESOP for all of its store employees and encourages their continual input regarding decision making. Participation and empowerment are two key elements of most TQM programs.

Facilitation. Both managers and employees find change stressful because established task and role relationships alter as it takes place. As we discussed in Chapter 9, there are several things organizations can do to help their members manage stress: Provide them with training to help them learn how to perform new tasks, and allow them time off from work to recuperate from the stressful effects of change. Companies like Microsoft and Apple Computer, for example, give their most talented programmers time off from ordinary job assignments to think about ways to create new kinds of products. Other companies offer senior managers sabbaticals to "recharge their batteries" following stressful events.

Many companies employ psychologists and consultants to help employees handle the stress associated with change. During organizational restructuring, especially when large layoffs are common, many organizations employ consultants to help employees deal with the stress and uncertainty of being laid off and having to find new jobs. Some companies pay consultants to help their CEOs manage the stress associated with being forced to downsize their employees.

Bargaining and negotiation. Bargaining and negotiation are important tools that help managers manage conflict (see Chapter 13). Because change causes conflict, bargaining can counter resistance to change. By using action research, managers can anticipate the effects of change on interpersonal and intergroup relationships. Managers can use this knowledge to help different people and groups negotiate their future tasks and roles and reach compromises that will lead them to accept change. Negotiation also helps individuals and groups understand how change will affect others so that the organization as a whole can develop a common perspective on why change is taking place and why it is important.

Manipulation. When it is clear that change will help some individuals and groups at the expense of others, senior managers need to intervene in the bargaining process and manipulate the situation to secure the agreement, or at least the acceptance, of various people or groups to the results of the change process.[75] As we discussed in Chapter 13, powerful managers have considerable ability to resist change, and in large organizations infighting among divisions can slow or halt the change process unless it is carefully managed. Politics and political tactics like cooptation and building alliances become important as ways of overcoming the opposition of powerful functions and divisions that feel threatened by the changes taking place.

Coercion. The ultimate way to eliminate resistance to change is to coerce the key players into accepting change and threaten dire consequences if they choose to resist. Employees and managers at all levels can be threatened with reassignment, demotion, or even termination if they resist or threaten the change process. Top managers attempt to use the legitimate power at their disposal to quash resistance to change and to eliminate it. The advantage of coercion can be the speed at which change takes place. The disadvantage is that it can leave people angry and disenchanted and can make the refreezing process difficult.

Managers should not underestimate the level of resistance to change. Organizations work because they reduce uncertainty by means of predictable rules and routines that people can use to accomplish their tasks. Change wipes out the predictability of rules and routines and perhaps spells the end of the status and prestige that accompany some positions. It is not surprising that people resist change and that organizations themselves, because they are made up of people, are so difficult to change.

OD Techniques to Promote Change

Many OD techniques are designed to make changes and to refreeze them. These techniques can be used at the individual, group, and organization levels. The choice of techniques is determined by the type of change. In general, the more revolutionary a change is, the more likely is an organization to use OD techniques at all three levels. Counseling, sensitivity training, and process consultation are OD techniques directed at changing the attitudes and behavior of individuals. Different techniques are effective at the group and organization levels.

Counseling, sensitivity training, and process consultation. Recall from Chapter 2 that the personalities of individuals differ and that the differences lead individuals to interpret and react to other people and events in a variety of ways. Even though personality cannot be changed significantly in the short run, people can be helped to understand that their own perceptions of a situation are not necessarily the correct or the only possible ones. People can also be helped to understand that they should learn to tolerate differences in perception and to embrace and accept human diversity. Counseling and sensitivity training are techniques that organizations can use to help individuals to understand the nature of their own and other people's personalities and to use that knowledge to improve their interactions with others.[76] The highly motivated, driven boss, for example, must learn that his or her subordinates are not disloyal, lazy, or afflicted with personality problems because they are content to go home at five o'clock and want unchallenging job assignments. Instead, they have their own set of work values, and they value their leisure time. Traditionally, one of OD's main efforts has been to improve the quality of the work life of organizational members and increase their well-being and satisfaction with the organization.

Trained professionals such as psychologists counsel organizational members who are perceived by their superiors or peers to have certain problems in appreciating the viewpoints of others or in dealing with certain types of organizational members. Through counseling they learn how to more effectively manage their interactions with other people in the organization. Recall from Chapter 1, for example, that one challenge facing growing numbers of white male managers is learning how to manage female and minority employees effectively. Similarly, a female manager might receive counseling because her peers find her too aggressive or ambitious and her drive to succeed is poisoning work relationships in a group.

SENSITIVITY TRAINING
An OD technique that consists of intense counseling in which group members, aided by a facilitator, learn how others perceive them and may learn how to deal more sensitively with others.

Sensitivity training is an intense type of counseling.[77] Members who have problems dealing with others meet in a group with a trained facilitator to learn more about how they and other group members view the world. Group members are encouraged to be forthright about how they view themselves and others, and through discussion they learn the degree to which others perceive them as similar or different from themselves. By examining the source of differences in perception, members can reach a better understanding of the way others perceive them and become more sensitive when dealing with others.

Participation in sensitivity training is a very intense experience because a person's innermost thoughts and feelings are brought to light and dissected in public. This process makes many people very uncomfortable, so certain ethical issues may be raised by an organization's decision to send "difficult" members for sensitivity training in the hope that they will learn more about themselves.

PROCESS CONSULTATION
An OD technique in which a facilitator works closely with a manager on the job to help the manager improve his or her interaction with other group members.

Is a manager too directive, too demanding, or too suspicious of subordinates? Does a manager deliberately deprive subordinates of information in order to keep them dependent? **Process consultation** provides answers to such questions. Process consultation bears a resemblance to both counseling and sensitivity training.[78] A trained process consultant, or facilitator, works closely with a manager on the job, to help the manager improve his or her interaction with other group members. The outside consultant acts as a sounding board so that the manager can gain a better idea about what is going on in the group setting and can discover the interpersonal dynamics that are affecting the quality of the relationships within the group.

Process consultation, sensitivity training, and counseling are just three of the many OD techniques that have been developed to help individuals learn to change their attitudes and behavior in order to function more effectively. It is common for many large organizations to provide their higher-level managers with a yearly budget to be spent on individual development efforts such as these or on more conventional executive education programs.

TEAM BUILDING
An OD technique in which a facilitator first observes the interactions of group members and then helps them become aware of ways to improve their work interactions.

Team building and intergroup training. To manage change within a group or between groups, change agents can employ three different kinds of OD techniques. **Team building**, a common method of improving relationships within a group, is similar to process consultation except that all the members of a group participate together to try to improve their work interactions.[79] For example, group members discuss with a change agent (who is a trained group facilitator) the quality of the interpersonal relationships between team members and between the members and their supervisor. The goal of team building is to improve the way group members work together—to improve the interaction in the group to achieve process gains and reduce process losses. Team building does *not* focus on what the group is trying to achieve, but, rather, on the members' relationships.

Team building is important when reengineering reorganizes the way people from different functions work together. When new groups are formed, team building can help group members quickly establish task and role relationships so that they can work effectively together. Team building facilitates the development of functional group norms and values and helps members develop a common approach to solving problems.

The change agent begins the team-building process by watching group members interact and identifying the way the group currently works. Then the change agent talks with some or all of the group members one on one to get a sense of the problems that the group is experiencing or just to identify where the group process could be improved. In a subsequent team-building session that normally takes place at a location away from the normal workplace, the change agent discusses with members the observations he or she has made and asks for their views on the issues brought to their attention. Ideally, through this discussion team members develop a new appreciation about the group dynamics that affect their behavior. Group members may form small task forces to suggest ways of improving the

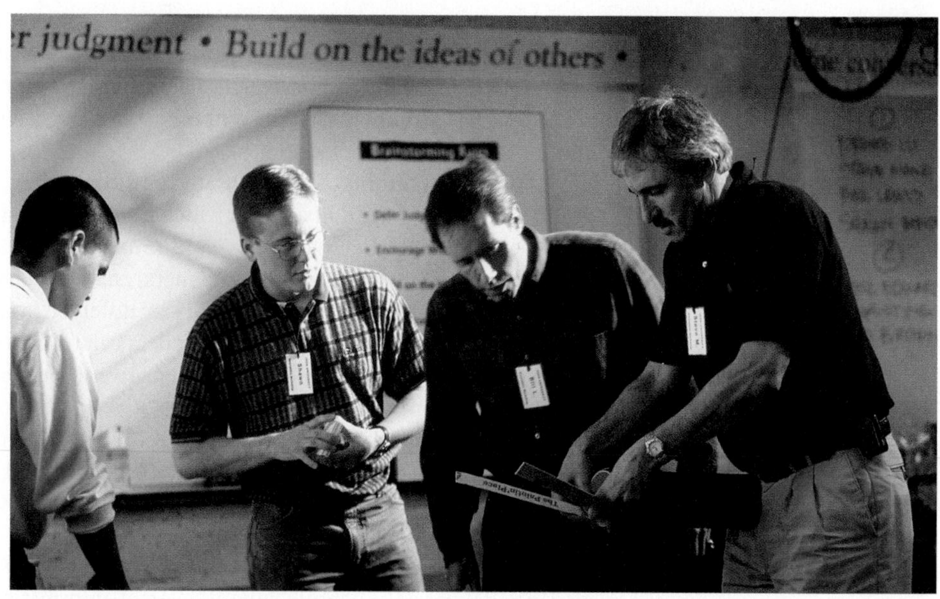

Team building is used to improve the interactions and relationships between group members to achieve process gains and reduce process losses. Frequently, a team is assigned to work on a specific project where members have to negotiate the role and task relationships necessary to get the job done efficiently.

group process or to discuss specific ways of handling problems that have been arising. The goal is to establish a platform from which group members themselves, with no input from the change agent, can make continuous improvements in the way the group functions.

INTERGROUP TRAINING
An OD technique that uses team building to improve the work interactions of different functions or divisions.

Intergroup training takes team building one step further and uses it to improve the ways different functions or divisions work together. Its goal is to improve organizational performance by focusing on a function or division's joint activities and output. Given that crossfunctional coordination is especially important in reengineering and total quality management, intergroup training is an important OD technique that organizations can exploit to implement change.

ORGANIZATIONAL MIRRORING
An OD technique in which a facilitator helps two interdependent groups explore their perceptions and relations in order to improve their work interactions.

A popular form of intergroup training is called **organizational mirroring**, an OD technique designed to improve the effectiveness of interdependent groups.[80] Suppose that two groups are in conflict or simply need to learn more about each other, and one of the groups calls in a consultant to improve cooperation between the two. The consultant begins by interviewing members of both groups to understand how each group views the other and uncover possible problems the groups are having with each other. The groups are then brought together in a training session, and the consultant tells them that the goal of the session is to explore perceptions and relations in order to improve their work relationships. Then, with the consultant leading the discussion, one group describes its perceptions of what is happening and its problems with the other group, while the other group sits and listens. Then the consultant reverses the situation—hence the term *organizational mirroring*—and the group that was listening takes its turn discussing its perceptions of what is happening and its problems, while the other group listens.

As a result of this initial discussion, each group appreciates the other's perspective. The next step is for members of both groups to form task forces to discuss ways to deal with the issues or problems raised. The goal is to develop action plans that can be used to guide future intergroup relations and provide a basis for follow-up. The change agent guiding this training session needs to be skilled in intergroup relations because both groups are discussing sensitive issues. If the process is not managed well, intergroup relations can be further weakened by this OD technique.

ORGANIZATIONAL CONFRONTATION MEETING
An OD technique that brings together all of the managers of an organization to confront the issue of whether the organization is effectively meeting its goals.

Total organizational interventions. A variety of OD techniques can be used at the organization level to promote organization-wide change. One is the **organizational confrontation meeting**.[81] At this meeting, all of the managers of an organization meet to confront the issue of whether the organization is effectively meeting its goals. At the first stage of the process, again with facilitation by a change agent, top management invites free and open discussion of the organization's situation. Then the consultant divides the managers into groups of seven or eight, ensuring that the groups are as heterogeneous as possible and that no bosses and subordinates are members of the same group (so as to encourage free and frank discussion). The small groups report their findings to the total group, and the sorts of problems confronting the organization are categorized. Top management uses this statement of the issues to set organizational priorities and plan group action. Task forces are formed from the small groups to take responsibility for working on the problems identified, and each group reports back to top management on the progress that has been made. The result of this process is likely to be changes in the organization's structure and operating procedures. Restructuring, reengineering, and total quality management often originate in organization-wide OD interventions that reveal the kinds of problems that an organization needs to solve.

Summary

Organizational change is an ongoing process that has important implications for organizational performance and for the well-being of an organization's members. An organization and its members must be constantly on the alert for changes from within the organization and from the outside environment, and they must learn how to adjust to change quickly and effectively. Often, the revolutionary types of change that result from restructuring and reengineering are necessary only because an organization and its managers ignored or were unaware of changes in the environment and did not make incremental changes as needed. The more an organization changes, the easier and more effective the change process becomes. Developing and managing a plan for change are vital to an organization's success. In this chapter, we made the following major points:

1. Organizational change is the movement of an organization away from its present state and toward some future state to increase its effectiveness. Forces for organizational change include competitive forces, economic, political, and global forces, demographic and social forces, and ethical forces. Organizations are often reluctant to change because resistance to change at the organization, group, and individual levels has given rise to organizational inertia.
2. Sources of organization-level resistance to change include power and conflict, differences in functional orientation, mechanistic structure, and organizational culture. Sources of group-level resistance to change include group norms, group cohesiveness, and groupthink and escalation of commitment. Sources of individual-level resistance to change include uncertainty and insecurity, selective perception and retention, and habit.
3. According to Lewin's force-field theory of change, organizations are balanced between forces pushing for change and forces resistant to change. To get an organization to change, managers must find a way to increase the forces for change, reduce resistance to change, or do both simultaneously.
4. Types of changes fall into two broad categories: evolutionary and revolutionary. The main instruments of evolutionary change are socio-technical systems theory and total quality management. The main instruments of revolutionary change are reengineering, restructuring, and innovation.
5. Action research is a strategy that managers can use to plan the change process. The main steps in action research are (1) diagnosis and analysis of the organization, (2) determining the desired future state, (3) implementing action, (4) evaluating the action, and (5) institutionalizing action research.
6. Organizational development (OD) is a series of techniques and methods to increase the adaptability of organizations. OD techniques can be used to overcome resistance to change and to help the organization to change itself.
7. OD techniques for dealing with resistance to change include education and communication, participation and empowerment, facilitation, bargaining and negotiation, manipulation, and coercion.
8. OD techniques for promoting change include, at the individual level, counseling, sensitivity training, and process consultation; at the group level, team building and intergroup training; and at the organization level, organizational confrontation meetings.

Organizational Behavior in Action

Questions for Review

1. What are the main forces for and impediments to change?
2. How do evolutionary change and revolutionary change differ?
3. What is the main purpose of total quality management?
4. What is a business process, and why is reengineering a popular instrument of change today?
5. Why is restructuring sometimes necessary for reengineering to take place?
6. Which type of change is likely to encounter the greatest resistance?
7. What are the main steps in action research?
8. What is organizational development, and what is its goal?
9. In what ways can team building and intergroup training promote organizational effectiveness?

OB: Increasing Self-Awareness

Coping with Change

Imagine that you are the manager of a design group that is soon to be reengineered into a crossfunctional team composed of people from several different functions that have had little contact with each other.

1. Discuss the resistance to change at the organizational and individual levels that you will likely encounter.
2. Using action research, chart the steps that you will use to manage the change process.
   a. How will you diagnose the work group's present state?
   b. How will you determine the crossfunctional team's desired future state?
   c. What will be the most important implementation choices you will face? For example, how will you manage resistance to change?
   d. What criteria will you use to evaluate the change process?
3. How might you use team building and other organizational development techniques to implement the change?

A Question of Ethics

Managing the Change Process

Some people find change a very difficult thing for reasons described in the chapter. Managers often find it difficult also to change an organization's culture because they cannot get people to develop new kinds of work attitudes or to adopt new kinds of values and norms—such as those involved in implementing kaizen.

Sometimes, kaizen requires both people and groups to change their work attitudes and behaviors in important ways, often ways they do not wish, and they resist the changes being made. Also, there have been cases where organizations actively involve employees in the change process by, for example, suggesting ways to change their jobs and perform them more effectively. Then, after the change process has taken place they proceed to layoff employees. Think about the ethical issues involved in this situation and address the following issues:

1. What kinds of techniques should managers be allowed to use to change employee attitudes and behavior before their actions would be considered unethical?
2. Under what conditions it is ethical to terminate employees as a result of implementing an organizational change program?
3. What kind of guarantees should managers offer employees to enlist their support if they suspect layoffs may be necessary?

Small Group Break-Out Exercise

Practicing Kaizen

Form groups of three to five people and discuss the following scenario:

You are a group of software engineers meeting to discuss how to implement a kaizen program to reduce the number of mistakes made in the developing and writing of computer code. Presently, your employees are each responsible for a different section of the code and they typically just hand off their work to the person next in line—which is the point where errors often creep in. You are contemplating introducing a computer-aided design process that will make each employee's code-writing activities visible to everyone else *and* that will alert employees when changes they make impact other employees code-writing activities. This will likely cause considerable conflict among employees because it will complicate their work activities.

1. How can you manage the change process to reduce employees' likely resistance to the changes that will take place in the work process?
2. What kind of reward system could you devise to motivate employees to contribute and make suggestions for improving the new system?

Topic For Debate

Organizational change alters role and task relationships at all levels of an organization. Now that you understand the nature and process of organizational change, debate the following issue:

Team A. Changing people's attitudes and behavior is easier than changing organizational structure and culture.

Team B. Changing organizational structure and culture is easier than changing people's attitudes and behavior.

Experiential Exercise

Analyzing Forces for and Impediments to Change

Objectives

Your objective is to understand the complex problems surrounding organizational change.

Procedure

The class divides into groups of from three to five people. Each member of the group assumes the role of supervisor of a group of manufacturing employees who assemble mainframe computers. Here is the scenario.

The employees' jobs are changing because of the introduction of a new, computer-controlled manufacturing technology. Using the old technology, employees stationed along a moving conveyor belt performed a clearly defined set of operations to assemble the computers. The new, computerized technology makes it possible to produce many different models of computers simultaneously.

To operate the technology effectively, employees have to learn new, more complex skills, and they also have to learn how to work in teams because the new technology is based on the use of flexible work teams. In the new work teams, the employees themselves, not a supervisor, will be responsible for product quality and for organizing work activities. The new role of the supervisor will be to facilitate, not direct, the work process. Indeed, a major part of the change to flexible work teams involves introducing a total quality management program to improve quality and reduce costs.

1. Chart the main impediments to change at the organization, group, and individual levels that you, as internal change agents, are likely to encounter as you assign employees to flexible work teams.
2. Discuss some ways to overcome resistance to change in order to help the organization move to its future desired state.
3. Discuss the pros and cons of top-down change and bottom-up change, and decide which of them should be used to implement the change in the work system.
4. Which specific organizational development techniques might be most useful in helping to implement the change smoothly?

New York Times *Cases in the News*

The New York Times

"Ford Eliminating up to 30,000 Jobs and 14 factories."

Micheline Maynard, NYT, January 24, 2006, A1.

The Ford Motor Company said Monday that it would close as many as 14 factories and cut up to 30,000 jobs over the next six years. It was the latest move in a fundamental restructuring of Detroit's traditional auto companies, hit hard by foreign competitors, who have taken more than 40 percent of the American market. The moves by Ford, the second-largest automaker in the United States, come two months after General Motors, the industry leader, said it would close all or part of a dozen factories and eliminate a similar number of jobs. Including cuts that took place at the Chrysler Corporation, the Big Three automakers have eliminated or announced plans to eliminate nearly 140,000 jobs since 2000, including salaried positions. That is about one-third of their North American payroll, a rollback to a work force size not seen since the end of World War II.

While the Big Three are visibly shrinking, their combined moves do not spell the end of automotive manufacturing in the United States. But the geographic footprint has largely shifted south, where a new auto industry is flourishing. Japanese, German and South Korean companies now employ 60,000 people, or about the same number by which Ford and G.M. have said they will shrink. But foreign makers are creating a younger, cheaper work force, sidestepping Detroit's unemployed and the higher pay and benefits packages that Detroit workers were getting. The United Automobile Workers union, which represents workers in the United States, said the announcement by Ford was "deeply disappointing and devastating" for its members. The cutbacks signal a new reality for auto workers—one in which $30-an-hour wages and generous benefits are no longer a guarantee.

The cuts at Ford are taking place under a turnaround plan it is calling the Way Forward, marking its second attempt to revamp the company in the last four years. Ford's goal is to become as nimble as Toyota and Honda, cutting through layers of bureaucracy that have stymied the development of innovative vehicles like hybrid electric cars. It also highlights Ford's American roots and aims to create clearer identities for its Ford, Lincoln and Mercury brands. Rising gas and steel prices and strong competition from abroad have intensified the challenge to Ford and G.M., already burdened by rising health care costs and a legacy of promising rich pension packages and other retirement benefits. More important, both companies have failed to find the right formulas to satisfy the American car buyer. The result has been a swift slide in market share. Ford, which held about 25 percent of the car market in 2000, held only 17.4 percent in 2005.

Monday's cuts at Ford affect about a third of its hourly payroll in North America, where it has 87,000 workers. The company is also cutting another 4,000 salaried employees, or about 10 percent of its white-collar force, and has pledged to reduce its executive ranks by 12 percent. Foreign manufacturers, who now sell more than 4 of every 10 cars and trucks in the United States, have created tens of thousands of jobs at new factories from Ontario to Ohio, across the South and in Mexico. Because of their growth, there has been no net loss in American automotive jobs over the last 10 years. In fact, those foreign companies, which collectively employed about 60,000 workers at the North American plants last year, are expanding their factories. Later this year, Toyota will open a new truck plant in San Antonio, and it is building another factory in Ontario.

While foreign automakers have hired some former Detroit workers, most of their workers have no automotive experience and were chosen through rigorous screening processes that stress physical endurance and a bent for working in teams. With a smaller market share, Ford has its plants in North America operating at only three-quarters capacity, sparking the company's decision Monday to close assembly plants in Wixom, Mich., outside Detroit; Hapeville, Ga., outside Atlanta; and Hazelwood, Mo., a suburb of St. Louis.

Ford's chief executive, William Clay Ford Jr., called the cuts "a painful last resort." But he said the company's plan contained "the vision and strategic focus to rebuild the business." "With it," Mr. Ford said, "we will retake the American roadway." Mr. Ford, who unveiled the earlier transformation program in 2002, shortly after he installed himself as chief executive, said that plan had achieved its goals but was not enough in the face of stiff foreign competition. "We will not stand for business as usual," Mr. Ford said. But Ford held out hope for some workers, saying that it planned to create a new factory somewhere in North America to build small cars at a low cost. Ford executives declined to say when the plant would be built—or whether it planned to employ unionized workers in the United States or Canada.

Questions for Discussion

1. What are the main problems confronting Ford?
2. What kind of change strategies is Ford adopting to turnaround its performance?
3. How will these changes help to improve performance?

The New York Times

"When Terry Met Jerry, Yahoo!"

Richard Siklos, NYT, January 29, 2006, 3.1.

WHEN Yahoo Inc. announced nearly five years ago that Terry S. Semel, then a former leader of the Warner Brothers motion picture studio, would become its chairman and chief executive, the reaction both outside and within Yahoo was not exactly one of wild encouragement. Despite a hugely successful career running companies that make movies, television shows and music, Mr. Semel was immediately labeled an "old media" guy. Worse, he was a Hollywood guy, and had barely touched a computer during the nearly two decades he oversaw Warner Brothers. At Yahoo, where the collapse of the dot-com bubble and the evaporation of online advertising had just helped sink the company's market value from a peak of $127 billion to just $12.6 billion when he joined, the reception wasn't warm. Mr. Semel, then 58, had neither geek credit like that of Yahoo's co-founders, Jerry Yang and David Filo, nor Silicon Valley venture-capitalist swagger. Mr. Semel looked like a self-assured but unassuming guy who originally hailed from Queens, which he was.

The story line at Yahoo is much different today. Having lost $98 million on revenue of $717 million in the year when Mr. Semel joined it. Yahoo earned $1.2 billion last year on sales of $5.3 billion. Dollars aside, Yahoo has the widest global reach of any Internet site. It counts more than 420 million registered users around the world, and it owns the most-used e-mail, instant-messaging and music Web sites on the planet. In the United States alone, Yahoo attracted 103 million unique visitors in December, making it the country's most-visited Web destination, according to Nielsen NetRatings.

"It's a 21st-century media company." Mr. Semel said in a recent interview. "The difference between the more traditional media companies and companies like Yahoo is all about technology, and the two—technology and media—totally marry each other." As he looks back over his five years running Yahoo, Mr. Semel makes no pretense of being a techno-guru, and he is often asked weather he really understands technology. "I'm never going to be a technologist, but I have to be conversant," he said, adding: "I was never an actor or a director or a singer—I had to understand the process well enough to help make decisions."

By the time he was hired, Yahoo already had the foundation for success—most notably its number of worldwide users, more than 200 million, who did everything from checking business news and sports scores to sending e-mail and instant messages, listening to music and shopping. But beyond the powerful brand and a company full or whizzes, there was no clear business strategy. The first thing Mr. Semel did was to steamline 44 business units into 4. That helped to set corporate priorities. "Terry's relentless focus on focus is probably the most important thing we as a team or as a company are doing." Mr. Yang said.

Mr. Semel's first big decision—and probably his shrewdest—was to make advertising its mainstay business. At some of his earliest meetings at Yahoo, Mr. Semel recalled, some executives were advocating that the business instead pour its efforts into trying to extract monthly fees from its registered users. "He was very early on in thinking, 'if we can keep the users growing and we can keep growing usage, we will be able to monetize this and we will be able to create value,'" said Mary Meeker, the Internet analyst as Morgan Stanley. "It sounds like mom and apple pie, but that was something a lot of people did not get in 2001."

Mr. Semel was also keen to develop other revenue streams, including music services, games and premium e-mail accounts. Its absence in the dial-up Internet access business, where AOL and Microsoft had pole positions, seemed, in those days, a glaring disadvantage. Mr. Semel addressed this with his second smart move: establishing a partnership with SBC, now AT&T, to sell Yahoo brand high-speed connections over souped-up phone lines. Yahoo later added Verizon, British Telecom and Rogers Communications in Canada, and now has 9.6 million subscribers, according to Morgan Stanley estimates. Each subscription generates an average of $3 a month for Yahoo. Vital to its focus on advertising was Yahoo's decision, in 2003, to develop its own search business—built on the rapid-fire acquisitions of Inktomi and Overture, which itself had just bought AltaVista—to compete with Google. That freed Yahoo from having to license Google's search technology. "We hardly went to sleep after we started to understand their business." Mr. Semel said of Overture's service of placing sponsored links alongside relevant search results. (Overture has been rechristened as Yahoo Search Marketing.)

Two years after introducing its own search engine, Yahoo trails only Google in that field. But it has also had to acknowledge that it is less effective than its rival at instantly matching relevant ads to search results. And Yahoo's share of the search market slipped to 30 percent in December from 32 percent in the same month a year earlier, while Google's share rose to 40 percent from 35 percent, according to ComScore Media Metric. Improving the financial return on search advertising, Mr. Semel says, is in the works. Although search represents only 5 percent of activity on the Web, this is no small matter: the higher profit margins generated by Google's AdWords business are a big reason that Google's $128 billion market capitalization now dwarfs Yahoo's. (History will decide whether Google or, for that matter, Yahoo warrants their starry valuations in a market where the stocks of media companies with much higher revenues are being shunned by investors.) Still, Mr. Semel contends that Yahoo's ability to blend brand and search advertising will set it apart as the Web continues its swift evolution. Susan L. Decker, Yahoo's finance chief, notes that most search advertisers are already online one way or another and tend to be small or midsized companies. But, she said, many major corporations are still spending only a small percentage of their marketing budgets online.

Without content that people want, of course, advertising is moot. Yahoo has gained attention in the past year for developing original programming, based out of a new Yahoo Media complex in Santa Monica, Calif. Columnists have been hired for its news sites, reporters are hatching multimedia presentations and the inevitable online reality show is in the works. Yahoo wants to be the largest online video hub, streaming everything from news clips and movie trailers to Howard Stern stunts and NASA missions. Last year, it streamed four billion music videos, enough to fill the schedules of a lot of MTV channels.

Mr. Semel and his Yahoo colleagues are most eager to encourage their registered users, who represent roughly 40 percent of the one billion people now online globally, to create their own content. Yahoo executives say that social networks, blogs, message boards and sites where users from around the world share materials—like the recent Yahoo acquisitions Flickr, a photo sharing business, and Del.icio.us. where people swap information on favorite Web sites and other things—are the keys to a fast emerging media market:

Across Yahoo's overflowing campus of purple cubicles in Sunnyvale, Calif., teams are working on a range of products—with names like Yahoo360, Y!Q, Yahoo MindSet, MyWeb 2.0 and Yahoo Answers—that use Web-searching as a ribbon for tying together virtual communities. MyWeb 2.0, for example, bills itself as a "social search engine" that lets users tag search results they may want to come back to and to share those results with cyberfriends.

Jeff Weiner, Yahoo's senior vice president for search and marketplace, came up with the acronym FUSE to sum up Yahoo's social networking ambitions: to "find, use, share and expand all human knowledge." This sounds awfully high-minded for a company whose logo ends in an exclamation point, but it underscores another difference between old and new in a cynical age: "People come to work trying to change things," Mr. Weiner said. They also come to work knowing that the Internet is a field of dreams without barriers to entry. If you don't build it, someone else will—most likely Google. Technology is what allows Yahoo to start these services and to tie them together on a global scale. "Almost from the first day I came to Yahoo," Mr. Semel said, "I realized that every strategy we were considering had to be related to the quality of our technology."

Questions for Discussion

1. What problems did Terry Semel identify as obstacles to improving Yahoo!'s performance?
2. What kinds of change strategy has Mr. Semel been using to turnaround Yahoo!'s performance? How successful has he been?

Appendix

Research Methods in Organizational Behavior

Overview

Research methods is a broad term that refers to the set of techniques used to acquire knowledge or learn about something of interest. In organizational behavior, research methods are the techniques used to learn about how individuals and groups respond to and act in organizations and how organizations respond to their environments.

An understanding of research methods is important for several reasons:

1. It allows researchers, managers, and other members of organizations to learn about why people feel and behave as they do in organizations.
2. It helps people to solve problems in organizations and, more generally, come up with ways to increase performance and well-being.
3. It can help managers and other members of an organization use findings from research done by others to improve conditions in their organizations.
4. It can help members of an organization properly evaluate advice and recommendations provided by others such as consultants.
5. It allows people to evaluate the various theories of organizational behavior.[1]

Our discussion of research methods proceeds as follows. We present a general model of the scientific process used to learn about organizational behavior. We discuss how researchers develop theories to explain some aspect of organizational behavior and how theories can be evaluated. We move on to the actual testing of theories. We discuss the different types of research designs that are used throughout the scientific process. We conclude with a discussion of ethical considerations.

The Scientific Process

A basic model of the scientific process is provided in Exhibit A.1.[2] Because the model is cyclical, we could start describing the process at any point. For convenience, we start at point A, the observation of organizational behavior. At point A, a researcher notices something about organizational behavior that she or he wishes to learn more about. The researcher may observe, for example, that levels of absenteeism are higher in some groups than in others, that employees performing some jobs experience much higher levels of stress than do those performing other jobs, or that some employees put forth much more effort than others.

After making observations like these, the researcher tries through induction to come up with a general explanation for what she or he has observed (point B in Exhibit A.1). *Induction* is the process that researchers use to come up with general ways to account for or explain specific observations or instances of organizational behavior. Researchers who observed that individuals varied in the amounts of effort they exerted on the job, for example, tried to come up with some general explanations for what they observed. The outcome was theories of work motivation.

Once a researcher has a general explanation to account for a phenomenon, then, through deduction, she or he makes specific predictions that seem likely to be true if the general explanation was a good one. *Deduction* is the process of making specific predictions (point C in Exhibit A.1) from general explanations. A general explanation for absenteeism (arrived at through induction), for example, might be that employees are most likely to be absent from their jobs when they are dissatisfied and have a lot of personal responsibilities in addition to their work responsibilities. Having made this general explanation from induction, the researcher might use deduction to predict that nurses who are dissatisfied with their jobs and have children will have higher levels of absence from work during a year than will nurses who are satisfied and do not have children.

EXHIBIT A.1

The Scientific Process

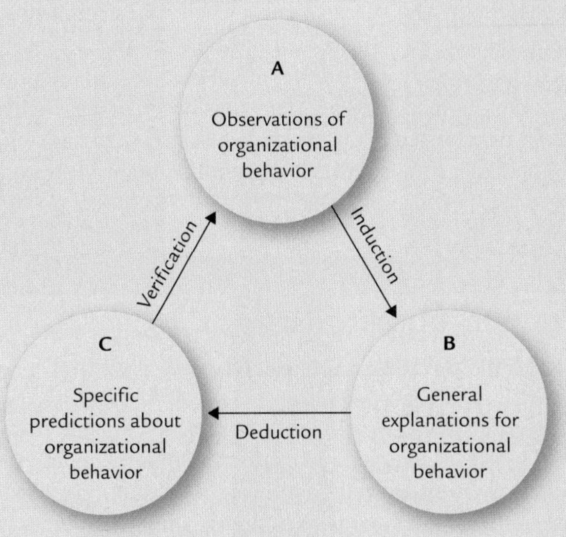

Once a researcher has made a prediction, the next step in the scientific process is to test this prediction and determine the extent to which it is true. *Verification* is the process by which researchers determine whether their predictions are accurate by making specific observations about organizational behavior. The researcher might ask 150 nurses employed by a large hospital to complete a questionnaire that includes measures of job satisfaction and also asks them how many children they have. The researcher might also ask the hospital to supply the number of days each nurse is absent for one year. These observations allow the researcher to verify whether his or her predictions are accurate. Verification completes the cycle of the scientific process and the researcher is back at point A in Exhibit A.1.

Because human behavior in organizations is complex and determined by many factors, it is often the case that at least part of the predictions researchers make are not verified or found to be accurate by observations of actual organizational behavior. When this occurs, a new cycle of induction and deduction begins. Researchers cycle through the process again and try to come up with another general explanation for what they observed, make predictions from this explanation, and then test these predictions through verification.

Research in organizational behavior, as in all fields of study, is a cooperative undertaking. Several different researchers might all be studying the same phenomenon and learning from each other's research. One researcher who studies absenteeism, for example, might come up with a new explanation for absenteeism. Based on this explanation, another researcher might make certain predictions and test them in several organizations. Some of these predictions might be verified, and others might not be. A third researcher then might seek to modify the original explanation to account for these new observations.

Researchers cooperate with each other or learn and build from each other's research in several ways. Researchers who already know each other often share ideas and research findings informally as well as ask for each other's advice. At professional meetings and conferences researchers present their work to other researchers who are interested in the same topic. And researchers write up their ideas and findings and publish them in journals and books for others to read.

Coming Up With General Explanations: The Role of Theory Building

A *theory* is a general explanation of some phenomenon. Theories are arrived at through induction. When researchers build theories, they are moving from point A to point B in the scientific process shown in Exhibit A.1. Theories summarize and organize what researchers have already learned about some phenomenon as well as provide direction for future research. Theories can never be proved to "be correct" because there is always the possibility that a future study will not support the theory. When research findings are consistent with or support a theory, confidence in the theory increases. Above all else, theories should be useful. Theories should help us understand organizational behavior as well as provide direction for future research in organizational behavior.

Four basic criteria that researchers can use to determine how useful a theory is are correspondence, coherence, parsimony, and pragmatism.[3] *Correspondence* is the extent to which a theory is congruent with what is actually observed in organizations. One way to determine correspondence is to see whether predictions derived from the theory are verified or found to be accurate. *Coherence* is the extent to which the logic in the theory is straightforward and the theory is free of any logical contradictions. *Parsimony* is the extent to which a theory is free of concepts or relationships that are not necessary to provide a good explanation. Suppose there are two theories of absenteeism, one includes five concepts and the other ten, and each does an equally good job of explaining absenteeism. The simpler theory is preferred because of its greater parsimony. *Pragmatism* is the extent to which a theory stimulates further research. A minimal condition for pragmatism is that the theory is able to be tested. No matter how eloquent a theory is, if no one is able to test it, the theory is not very useful at all.

Developing Specific Predictions: Formulating Hypotheses

Once a theory is in place, researchers need to make specific predictions based on the theory; in other words, through deduction, move from point B to point C in Exhibit A.1. Specific predictions in organizational behavior are often stated in the form of hypotheses. A *hypothesis* is a statement about the relationship between two or more variables.[4] A *variable* is a dimension along which some aspect of individuals, groups, or organizations differs or varies. Variables pertaining to individuals include age, gender, job satisfaction, organizational commitment, motivation, and job performance. Variables pertaining to groups include group size, group norms, and group cohesiveness. Variables pertaining to organizations include organizational structure, technology, and culture.

Some hypotheses simply state that two or more variables are related to each other. Other hypotheses state how variables affect each other—that is, they describe a causal relationship between variables. Ultimately, researchers always prefer to be able to state their hypotheses in causal

EXHIBIT A.2

A Causal Relationship

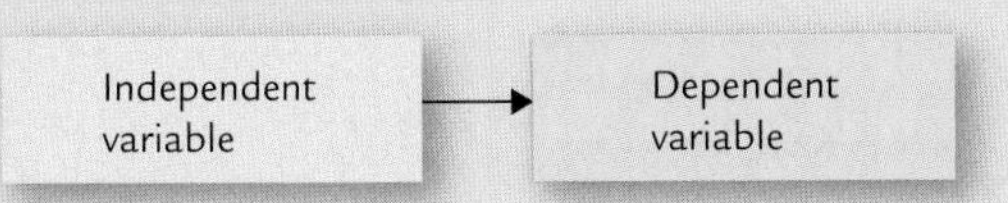

terms; causal relationships provide explanations for *why* things happen. When hypotheses are not stated in causal terms, the reason often is that the researcher is very uncertain about what causal relationship to expect or knows that she or he will not be able to conduct research to test a causal relationship.

When hypotheses do describe a causal relationship between variables, the variables can be categorized into four types: independent variables, dependent variables, mediator variables, and moderator variables. An *independent variable* is a variable that causes another variable to change when it varies or changes. The variable that changes in response to the independent variable is called the *dependent variable* (see Exhibit A.2). A hypothesis might state, for example, that when the payment of production workers changes from an hourly basis to a piece-rate basis, levels of performance or production increase. In this example, the method of pay is the independent variable, and performance is the dependent variable.

Sometimes independent variables do not directly affect dependent variables but rather operate through a third variable. A *mediator variable* is a mechanism through which an independent variable has an effect on a dependent variable (see Exhibit A.3). In organizational behavior, mediator variables often refer to something that is hard to observe directly, such as motivation. In our previous example, a mediator of the relationship between method of pay and performance may be motivation. Method of pay impacts motivation such that employees are more motivated to perform at a high level when their pay is based on their performance rather than on an hourly rate. When motivation increases, performance increases (assuming all else is equal).

A *moderator variable* is a variable that, when it changes, it also changes the nature of the relationship between the independent and the dependent variables (see Exhibit A.3). When the moderator variable changes, for example, it can turn strong positive relationships into weaker positive relationships, into negative relationships, or into no relationship at all. Positive, negative, and no relationship is depicted graphically in Exhibit A.4. An example of a moderator of the relationship between method of pay and performance is financial need. A hypothesis might state that there is a strong, positive relationship between method of pay and performance for employees who have high financial needs and a weak positive relationship for employees who have low financial needs.

EXHIBIT A.3

Mediator and Moderator Variables

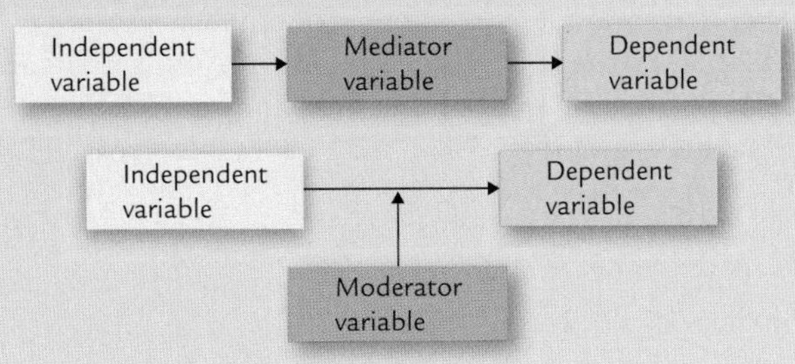

Testing Hypotheses: Operationalizing Variables

Once researchers have specific predictions or hypotheses, they then have to test them through the process of verification—that is, they must move from point C to point A in the scientific process illustrated in Exhibit A.1. In order to test hypotheses, researchers need to find ways to measure the variables in the hypotheses. Many of the variables of interest in organizational behavior are abstract. Job satisfaction, motivation, stress, culture, and organizational structure, for example, are abstract terms that are sometimes hard to define, let alone measure. Nevertheless, finding measures for these variables is necessary in order to test hypotheses.

As a first step, researchers need to have clear conceptual definitions of the variables or be certain about what exactly they are trying to measure. Then they need to find ways of *operationalizing*, or measuring, these variables. A specific measure of a variable is sometimes called an *operational definition* of the variable.

There are two important criteria by which to judge whether a good operational definition or measure of a variable is being used in a research study: reliability and validity. *Reliability* is the extent to which a measure of a variable is free of error. Suppose you are weighing people but the scale you are using is not reliable. Each time you weigh them their weight varies by three or four pounds even though their actual weight has not changed. Your measure of weight lacks reliability because it contains a significant amount of error.

Measures of job satisfaction, performance, and other organizational behavior variables need to be reliable in order for researchers to be able to have good tests of their hypotheses. For some organizational behavior variables, such as job satisfaction, reliable measures have already

EXHIBIT A.4

Relationships Between Independent Variables (IV) and Dependent Variables (DV)

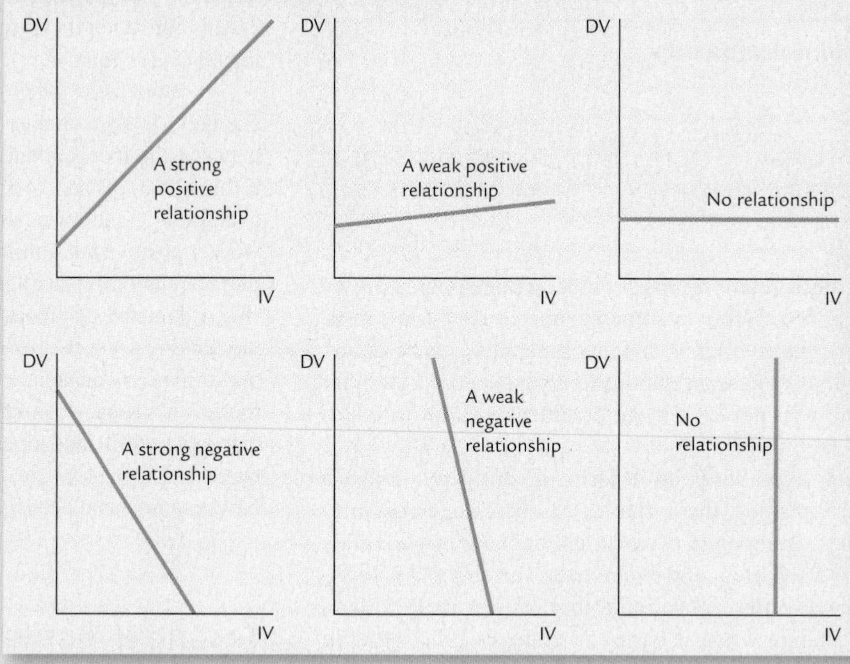

been created in the past and used in many research studies. These measures typically ask employees to answer a number of questions about their current jobs. Sample items from two of these measures are provided in Exhibit 3.9 in Chapter 3. When using an existing measure of a variable, researchers should always determine how reliable or free of error the measure is in their own particular study.

There are several ways to assess the reliability of a measure. For example, if a questionnaire measure of job satisfaction asks employees to answer ten questions about their current job, each of the questions should be assessing job satisfaction. One way to determine whether the measure is reliable is to assess the extent to which each person's answers to the questions are consistent with each other. If each question taps job satisfaction, but on some questions people indicate that they are very satisfied and on others that they are very dissatisfied, then there is a lot of error in the measure and it is not reliable. This technique assesses *internal consistency reliability*.

Another way of determining reliability is assessing the extent to which repeated measures of a variable agree with each other (assuming that the variable itself has not changed). This technique assesses *test-retest reliability*. For example, the height of adults should not change from day to day, and a way to assess the reliability of a measure of height is to use the measure to determine people's height on several different days and assess the extent to which the measures of height are the same from day to day.

The second criterion by which to judge an operational definition or measure is validity. *Validity* is the extent to which an operational definition of a variable is actually measuring the variable in question. Given that many of the variables in organizational behavior research are abstract, it is essential that measures of variables are valid or that the measures are actually measuring what the researcher wants to measure. A measure of job satisfaction, for example, is not valid if it is simply measuring the extent to which people tend to have a positive outlook on life in general and not how they feel about their current jobs. Reliability is a necessary but not sufficient condition for validity. In order for a measure to be valid, at a minimum the measure has to be free of error. However, the measure also has to be tapping into the right variable.

Determining the validity of measures in organizational behavior is an ongoing and complicated process. Researchers cannot be sure from one research study that their measures are valid. Only through repeated use of measures can researchers be confident in the validity of their measures. Moreover, there are multiple indicators of validity. One indicator is the extent to which experts in an area think that the measure is adequately gauging the variable in question. Another indicator is the extent to which the measure is related to measures of other variables in expected ways and is different from other measures of different variables. Only through using a measure many times and relying on multiple indicators of validity can researchers be confident in the validity of their measures.

Research Designs

The design of a specific research study is geared toward what the researcher wishes to accomplish from the study.

Different research designs or ways of conducting research are well suited to different stages in the research process. Here, we discuss three types of research designs: qualitative research, cross-sectional research, and experimental research.[5] Qualitative research can help researchers move from point A to B and from point B to C in the scientific process (see Exhibit A.1). Cross-sectional and experimental research can help researchers move from point B to C and from point C to A. Each research design can be helpful in other ways as well. Cross-sectional research, for example, sometimes helps researchers move from point A to point B.

Qualitative Research

One hallmark of qualitative research is the careful *observation* of actual behavior in organizations. Researchers watch what members of an organization do and listen to what they say in the hopes of getting an accurate picture of what naturally occurs in an organization. Researchers keep careful records of what they have observed. Qualitative research can provide researchers with a rich description of organizational life and the many factors that affect it.

There are two basic ways of doing qualitative research: participant observation and direct observation. In *participant observation*, the researcher actually becomes a member of the organization that he or she is observing, and often other members of the organization do not realize that the newest member of the department or team is conducting research. Participant observation gives the researcher the opportunity to experience first hand what it is like to be a member of the organization, and it helps the researcher gain the confidence and trust of other members of the organization. In *direct observation*, the researcher enters an organization as an observer and records what he or she sees (often as it occurs). Direct observation can be less time-consuming than participant observation.

Because qualitative research entails detailed observations, it is often conducted in one or a few organizations. A key question that arises from this kind of research design pertains to the *generalizability* of the findings—the extent to which what researchers discover in one organization is true of other organizations.

Cross-Sectional Research

When using a cross-sectional design, researchers develop and test specific hypotheses about relationships between variables. To do so, they must develop or use existing measures of variables that are both reliable and valid. Questionnaires and interviews are often used to gather measures of variables. Although qualitative designs are well suited for making observations and coming up with general explanations for them, cross-sectional designs are well suited for testing specific hypotheses because the researcher is actually collecting measures of variables. However, researchers cannot test hypotheses that state causal relationships between variables by using cross-sectional designs because they have no control over the many other factors that might impact a dependent variable in addition to the independent variable. Hence, with cross-sectional designs, researchers can test only hypotheses that state that certain variables are related to each other.

Experimental Research

The hallmark of experimental research designs is the controlled *manipulation*, or changing, of an independent variable to determine what effect it has on a dependent variable. There are two types of experimental research designs: true experiments and quasi-experiments.

True experiments are the only kind of research design that allows researchers to test causal hypotheses and draw conclusions about causal relationships. True experiments allow researchers to do this by controlling for everything else that might affect a dependent variable besides changes in the independent variable. Two features of true experiments provide this control: a control group and random assignment of participants to the experimental and the control groups.

Suppose a researcher is interested in the relationship between method of pay and performance and decides to do an experiment. The researcher hypothesizes that switching from an hourly pay plan to a piece-rate pay plan results in an increase in performance. He or she takes a group of employees who are currently being paid on an hourly rate and switches them to a piece-rate plan and measures their performance before and after the change. Performance does increase after the change. Can the researcher conclude that the change in pay plan caused the change in performance? No, and the reason is that the researcher did not control for other things—in addition to the change in pay plan—that might have been responsible for a change in performance, such as the fact that the employees have gained more job experience and thus their performance would have increased regardless of the change in pay plan.

By having a *control group*—a group of participants for whom the researcher does not change the independent variable (in this case, the pay plan)—the researcher is able to control for, or take into account, other things besides the pay plan that might affect performance because the control group also will be exposed to these things. By randomly assigning participants to the experimental and control groups, the researcher guarantees that these groups start out at an equivalent position. Because the experimental and control groups start out in equivalent positions (because of random assignment), the *only* difference between the groups is the change in pay plan. Thus, if the performance level of the control group stays the same but rises for the experimental group, the researcher can confidently conclude that the change in pay plan caused the change in performance. Conversely, if the performance levels of both groups stay the same or increase, then the change in pay plan is not having the hypothesized effect.

For practical reasons it is very difficult to conduct true experiments in real organizations. Manipulating variables like pay and randomly assigning employees to experimental and control groups are often very disruptive to the ongoing activities of an organization, and few managers are willing to tolerate these disruptions. Partially for this reason, true experiments are often conducted in laboratory settings at universities using college students as participants rather than employees. The logic behind this practice is that if a researcher is studying some fundamental aspect of human functioning like motivation, she or he should be able to observe its operation in a laboratory with students or in an organization with employees. Although this assumption makes sense, it might also be the case that conditions in organizations are so different from conditions in the lab (or that some differences between employees and college students are so fundamental) that results from the lab do not generalize to the field or to real organizations. In other words, what might occur in the laboratory might not occur in an organization and vice versa. To be on the safe side, researchers need to supplement laboratory research with field research whenever possible.

Similar to a true experiment, *quasi-experiments* also involve the manipulation of an independent variable. The major difference is that in a quasi-experiment a researcher does not have a control group or does not randomly assign participants to experimental and control groups. Quasi-experiments are often a practical necessity when researchers want to conduct experiments in real organizations. For example, a researcher might find an organization that currently operates six factories that employ a hundred employees each. The organization wants to experiment with changing from an hourly pay plan to a piece-rate pay plan. Management decides to make the change in three of the factories and leave the other three (to be used as a control group) on the existing hourly plan. In this quasi-experiment, there is a control group but no random assignment because of the practical problem that all employees in a single factory need to be working under the same pay system.

Because of the lack of a control group or random assignment, researchers cannot test causal hypotheses or arrive at causal conclusions from quasi-experiments. Nevertheless, quasi-experiments can provide valuable insights into organizational behavior.

Tradeoffs in the Choice of Research Designs

By this time, it should be clear to you that multiple tradeoffs affect the choice of a research design. Qualitative designs have the advantage of providing researchers with a rich account of the many factors that influence organizational behavior. True experiments have the advantage of allowing researchers to test causal relationships. Researchers cannot come to causal conclusions from qualitative designs, and they might be neglecting important organizational behavior variables in true experiments. No one design is preferable over another, and each one is well suited to different stages in the scientific process. Moreover, research on any topic in organizational behavior benefits from research using all three types of designs.

Ethical Considerations in Organizational Behavior Research

Researchers have ethical obligations to research participants. There is disagreement about the exact nature of these obligations, but here are some guidelines that many researchers would agree with:[6]

1. The researcher should obtain the informed consent of research participants. When consent is *informed*, participants know that they are taking part in a research study and do so voluntarily. Obtaining informed consent becomes troublesome in a participant observation design because an integral feature of this design is that members of an organization do not realize that research is actually being conducted.
2. Participants should not be harmed in any way by the research being conducted.
3. Participants' rights to privacy should be respected.
4. Participants in a control group should not be denied treatment that the researcher knows would benefit them. This guideline is most clearly relevant to medical research. However, there are instances when it might be relevant to organizational behavior research, such as the case when a researcher knows that a certain type of training benefits employees yet gives only some of the employees the training (that is, those in the experimental group).
5. Participants should be debriefed. Once researchers have completed a study, they should let participants know what the study was about, and they should be available to answer questions.
6. Data should be treated confidentially.

Summary

Only through conducting research on organizational behavior can progress be made in understanding how individuals and groups respond to and act in organizations and how organizations respond to their environments.

References

CHAPTER 1

1. www.Amazon.com, "About Amazon.com" 2006.
2. Ibid.
3. H. Fayol, *Industrial and General Administration* (London: Pitman, 1949); P. F. Drucker, *Management Tasks, Responsibilities, Practices* (New York: Harper and Row, 1974).
4. www.flysouthwest.com, 2006.
5. www.ddir.com, 2006.
6. http://seattletimes.nwsource.com/html/obituaries/2001211576_dicks23m.html
7. H. Mintzberg, *The Nature of Managerial Work* (New York: Harper and Row, 1963).
8. R. L. Katz, "Skills of an Effective Administrator," *Harvard Business Review*, September–October (1974): 90–102.
9. T. Donaldson, "Taking Ethics Seriously—A Mission Now More Possible," *Academy of Management Review* 28 (2003): 363–67.
10. E. Soule, "Managerial Moral Strategies—In Search of a Few Good Principles," *Academy of Management Review* 27 (2002): 114–25.
11. R. C. Soloman, *Ethics and Excellence* (New York: Oxford University Press, 1992).
12. D.L. Swanson, "Towards an Integrative Theory of Business and Society: A Research Strategy for Corporate Social Performance," *Academy of Management Review* 24 (1999): 506–22.
13. L. K. Trevino, "Ethical Decision Making in Organizations: A Person-Situation Interactionist Model," *Academy of Management Review* 11 (1986): 601–17.
14. T.M. Jones, "Convergent Stakeholder Theory," *Academy of Management Review* 24 (1999): 206–22.
15. www.consumerreports.com, 2006.
16. www. yahoo.com, 2006.
17. H. Mintzberg, "The Case for Corporate Social Responsibility," *Journal of Business Strategy* December (1983): 3–15; J. J. Chrisman and A. B. Carroll, "Corporate Responsibility-Reconciling Economic and Social Goals," *Sloan Management Review* 25 (1984): 59–65.
18. G.R. weaver, L. Trevino, and P.L. Cochran, "Corporate Ethics Programs as Control Systems: Influences of Executive Commitment and Environmental Factors," *Academy of Management Journal* 42 (1999): 41–58.
19. H. Mintzberg, "The Case for Corporate Social Responsibility," *Journal of Business Strategy* Winter (1973): 3–15.
20. "Companies Strengthen their Codes of Ethics," www.yahoo.com, January 8th, 2006.
21. www.mci.com, 2006; www.kpmg.com, 2006.
22. B.R. Agle and R.K. Mitchell, "Who Matters to CEOs? An Investigation of Stakeholder Attributes and Salience," *Academy of Management Journal* 42 (1999): 507–26.
23. T. M. Jones, "Ethical Decision Making by Individuals in Organizations: An Issue Contingent Model," *Academy of Management Review* 16 (1991): 366–95; G. R. Shea, *Practical Ethics* (New York: American Management Association, 1988).
24. Bohr, J. "Deadly Roses," *The Battalion* February 13 (2006): 3.
25. L. I. Kessler, *Managing Diversity in an Equal Employment Opportunity Workplace* (Washington, DC: National Foundation for the Study of Employment Policy, 1990); W. B. Johnson and A. H. Packer, *Workforce 2000: Work and Employees in the 21st Century* (Indianapolis: Hudson Institute, 1987); M. Galen and A. T. Palmer, "White, Male and Worried," *Newsweek* January 31 (1994) 50–55.
26. Workforce 2020, Hudson Institute, Hudson.org, 2006.
27. Ibid.
28. M. Fine, F. Johnson, and M. S. Ryan, "Cultural Diversity in the Workforce," *Public Personnel Management* 19 (1990): 305–19.
29. W. E. Hopkins and S. A. Hopkins, "Effects of Cultural Recomposition on Group Interaction Processes," *Academy of Management Journal* 45 (2002): 1029–46.
30. P. M. Elsass and L. M. Graves, "Demographic Diversity in Decision Making Groups," *Academy of Management Review* 22 (1997): 946–72.
31. T. Cox, Jr., *Cultural Diversity in Organizations* (San Francisco: Berrett Koehler, 1994).
32. D. Jamieson and J. O'Mara, *Managing Workforce 2000: Gaining the Diversity Advantage* (San Francisco: Jossey-Bass, 1991).
33. C. Muir, "Can We All Get Along? The Interpersonal Challenge at Work," *Academy of Management Executive* 14 (2000): 143–45.
34. R. C. Orlando, "Racial Diversity, Business Strategy, and Firm Performance: A Resource-Based View," *Academy of Management Journal* 43 (2000): 164–78.
35. www.uboc.com, 2006.
36. G. Colvin, "The 50 best Companies for Asians, Blacks, and Hispanics," *Fortune* July 19 (1999): 53–57.
37. Union Bank of California Honored By U.S. Labor Department For Employment Practices, Press Release, September 11, 2000.
38. G. A. Gilbert and J. M. Ivancevich, "Valuing Diversity: A Tale of Two Organizations," *Academy of Management Executive* 25 (2000): 93–106.
39. M. C. Higgins, "Reconceptualizing Mentoring at Work: A Developmental Network Perspective," *Academy of Management Review* 26 (2001): 264–89.
40. P. Dass and B. Parker, "Strategies for Managing Human Resource Diversity: From Resistance to Learning," *Academy of Management Executive* 13 (1999): 68–81.
41. C. K. Prahalad and Y. L. Doz, *The Multinational Mission: Balancing Local Demands and Global Vision* (New York: Free Press, 1987); C. A. Bartlett and S. Ghoshal, *Transnational Management* (Homewood, IL: Irwin, 1992).
42. A. K. Gupta and V. Govindarajan, "Cultivating a Global Mindset," *Academy of Management Executive* 16 (2002): 116–27.

43. S. A. Zahra, "The Changing Rules of Global Competitiveness in the 21st Century," *Academy of Management Executive* 13 (1999): 36–43.
44. P. J. Dowling and R. S. Schuler, *International Dimensions of Human Resource Management* (Boston: PWS-Kent, 1990).
45. N. Adler, *International Dimensions of OB* (Boston: Kent, 1991).
46. L. Van Dyne and A. Soon, "Organizational Citizenship Behavior of Contingent Workers in Singapore," *Academy of Management Journal* 41 (1998): 692–704.
47. T. W. Malnight, "Emerging Structural Patterns Within Multinational Corporations: Towards Process Based Structures," *Academy of Management Journal* 44 (2001): 1187–211.
48. G. Hofstede, "The Cultural Relativity of Organizational Practices and Theories," *Journal of International Business Studies* Fall (1983): 75–89.
49. www.ikea.com, 2006.
50. Ibid.; K. Kling and I. Goteman, "IKEA CEO Anders Dahlvig on International Growth and IKEA's Unique Corporate Culture and Brand Identity," *Academy of Management Executive* 17 (2003): 38–46.
51. www.forbes.com, 2006.
52. C. A. Bartlett and S. Ghoshal, *Managing Across Borders* (Boston: Harvard Business School Press, 1989).
53. Ibid.
54. E. Kelley, "Keys to Effective Virtual Global Teams," *Academy of Management Executive* 15 (2001): 132–34.
55. www.yahoo.com, 2006.
56. T. W. Malone and J. F. Rockart, "Computers, Networks, and the Corporation," *Scientific American* 263 (1991): 128–37.
57. R. Forrester and A. B. Drexler, "A Model for Team Based Organizational Performance," *Academy of Management Executive* August (1999): 36–49.
58. T. H. Davenport and L. Prusak, *Information Ecology* (Oxford: Oxford University Press, 1997).
59. C. K. Prahalad and V. Ramaswamy, "Co-opting Customer Competence," *Harvard Business Review* January–February (2000): 79–90.
60. www.myspace.com, 2006; www.Youtube.com, 2006; www.flickr.com, 2006, rottentomatoes.com, 2006.
61. Murdock.com, *Newsweek* February 13th (2006): 44.
62. D. M. Rousseau and Z. Shperling, "Pieces of the Action: Ownership and the Changing Employment Relationship," *Academy of Management Review* 28 (2003): 553–71.
63. D. P. Lepak, "The Human Resource Architecture: Toward a Theory of Human Capital Allocation and Development," *Academy of Management Review* 24 (1999): 31–49.
64. R. J. Trent and R. M. Monczka, "Pursuing Competitive Advantage Through Integrated Global Sourcing," *Academy of Management Executive* 16 (2002): 66–81; S. J. Freeman and K. S. Cameron, "Organizational Downsizing: A Convergence and Reorientation Framework." *Organizational Science* 4 (1993): 10–29.
65. S. L. Robinson and M. S. Kraatz, "Changing Obligations and the Psychological Contract: A Longitudinal Study," *Academy of Management Journal* 37 (1994): 137–53.
66. E. W. Morrison and S. L. Robinson, "When Employees Feel Betrayed: A Model of How Psychological Contract Violation Develops," *Academy of Management Review* 22 (1997): 226–57.
67. A. Yuan, Z. Guorong, and D. T. Hall, "International Assignments for Career Building: A Model of Agency Relationships and Psychological Contracts," *Academy of Management Review* 27 (2002): 373–92.
68. W. A. Randolph and M. Sashkin, "Can Organizational Empowerment Work in Multinational Settings?" *Academy of Management Executive* 16 (2002): 102–16.
69. "Dell to Hire 5,000 people in India," www.yahoo.com, January 30, 2006.
70. F. W. Taylor, *Shop Management* (New York: Harper, 1903); F. W. Taylor, *The Principles of Scientific Management* (New York: Harper, 1911).
71. L. W. Fry, "The Maligned F. W. Taylor: A Reply to His Many Critics," *Academy of Management Review* 1 (1976): 124–29.
72. J. A. Litterer, *The Emergence of Systematic Management as Shown by the Literature from 1870–1900* (New York: Garland, 1986).
73. D. Wren, *The Evolution of Management Thought* (New York: Wiley, 1994), 134.
74. L. D. Parker, "Control in Organizational Life: The Contribution of Mary Parker Follett," *Academy of Management Review* 9 (1984): 736–45.
75. P. Graham, *M. P. Follett—Prophet of Management: A Celebration of Writings from the 1920s* (Boston: Harvard Business School Press, 1995).
76. M. P. Follett, *Creative Experience* (London: Longmans, 1924).
77. E. Mayo, *The Human Problems of Industrial Civilization* (New York: Macmillan, 1933); F. J. Roethlisberger and W. J. Dickson, *Management and the Employee* (Cambridge, MA: Harvard University Press, 1947).
78. D. W. Organ, "Review of Management and the Employee, by F. J. Roethlisberger and W. J. Dickson," *Academy of Management Review* 13 (1986): 460–64.
79. D. Roy, "Banana Time: Job Satisfaction and Informal Interaction," *Human Organization* 18 (1960): 158–61.
80. For an analysis of the problems in determining cause from effect in the Hawthorne studies and in social settings in general, see A. Carey, "The Hawthorne Studies: A Radical Criticism," *American Sociological Review* 33 (1967): 403–16.
81. D. McGregor, *The Human Side of Enterprise* (New York: McGraw-Hill, 1960).
82. Ibid., 48.

CHAPTER 2

1. M. Fong, "Woven in China'," *The Wall Street Journal,* April 11, 2005: B1, B4.
2. G. Heiman, "Innovation, Not Quotas," www.washingtonpost.com, April 8, 2005: A25.
3. "Your Partner in Finding *Solutions*." www.standardtextile.com, March 20, 2006.
4. G. Helman, "Company Overview," *Standard Textile,* March 20, 2006, http://www.standardtextile.com/ company.asp.
5. M. Fong, "Woven in China'," *The Wall Street Journal,* April 11, 2005: B1, B4.
6. Ibid.

7. Ibid.
8. G. Heiman, "Innovation, Not Quotas," www.washingtonpost.com, April 8, 2005: A25.
9. Ibid.
10. M. Fong, "Woven in China'," *The Wall Street Journal,* April 2005: B1, B4.
11. P. T. van den Berg and J. A. Feij, "Complex Relationships Among Personality Traits, Job Characteristics, and Work Behaviors," *International Journal of Selection and Assessment* 11(4 December 2003): 326–49.
12. R. Ilies and T. A. Judge, "On the Heritability of Job Satisfaction: The Mediating Role of Personality," *Journal of Applied Psychology* 88(4 2003): 750–59.
13. A. Tellegen, D. T. Lykken, T. J. Bouchard et al., "Personality Similarity in Twins Reared Apart and Together," *Journal of Personality and Social Psychology* 54 (1988): 1031–39.
14. Ibid.
15. J. M. George, "The Role of Personality in Organizational Life: Issues and Evidence," *Journal of Management* 18 (1992): 185–213.
16. R. D. Arvey, T. J. Bouchard, N. L. Segal, and L. M. Abraham, "Job Satisfaction: Environmental and Genetic Components," *Journal of Applied Psychology* 74 (1989): 187–92; A. P. Brief, M. J. Burke, J. M. George, B. Robinson, and J. Webster, "Should Negative Affectivity Remain an Unmeasured Variable in the Study of Job Stress?" *Journal of Applied Psychology* 73 (1988): 193–98; J. L. Holland, *Making Vocational Choices: A Theory of Careers* (Upper Saddle River, NJ: Prentice Hall, 1973); R. J. House, W. D. Spangler, and J. Woycke, "Personality and Charisma in the U.S. Presidency: A Psychological Theory of Leader Effectiveness," *Administrative Science Quarterly* 36 (1991): 364–96.
17. M. R. Barrick, M. K. Mount, and J. P. Strauss, "Conscientiousness and Performance of Sales Representatives: Test of the Mediating Effects of Goal Setting," *Journal of Applied Psychology* 78 (1993): 715–22.
18. A. Davis-Blake and J. Pfeffer, "Just a Mirage: The Search for Dispositional Effects in Organizational Research," *Academy of Management Review* 14 (1989): 385–400.
19. R. C. Carson, "Personality," *Annual Review of Psychology* 40 (1989): 227–48; D. T. Kenrick and D. C. Funder, "Profiting from Controversy: Lessons from the Person-Situation Debate," *American Psychologist* 43 (1988): 23–34; D. C. Rowe, "Resolving the Person-Situation Debate: Invitation to an Interdisciplinary Dialogue," *American Psychologist* 42 (1987): 218–27.
20. E. Olson, "Adventures as a Team Sport," *The New York Times* 23(3): 9.
21. "Investor Relations ~ Alaska Communications System: Board of Directors," *ACS* (March 20, 2006), http://www.acsalaska.com/ALSK/en-US/Board+of+Directors/Liane+Pelletier.htm.
22. E. Olson, "Adventures as a Team Sport," *The New York Times* 23(3): 9.
23. Ibid.
24. "Investor Relations ~ Alaska Communications System: Welcome to ALSK.com," *ACS* (March 20, 2006), http://www.acsalaska.com/ALSK/en-US.
25. "Alaska Communications," *Corporate Spotlight* (March 21, 2006), http://www.redcoatpublishing. com/spotlights/sl_08_05_Alaska.asp.
26. G. G. Marcial, "Heading North To Alaska Communications," *Business Week Online* (June 27, 2005), http://www.businessweek.com.
27. E. Olson, "Adventures as a Team Sport," *The New York Times* 23(3): 9.
28. B. Schneider, "The People Make the Place," *Personnel Psychology* 40 (1987): 437–53.
29. J. Schaubroeck, D. C. Ganster, and J. R. Jones, "Organization and Occupation Influences in the Attraction-Selection-Attrition Process," *Journal of Applied Psychology* 83 (1998): 869–91.
30. "Who Hires at Small Concerns? Often, It Is the Head Honcho," *Wall Street Journal*, November 17, 1992, A1.
31. J. M. Digman, "Personality Structure: Emergence of the Five-Factor Model," *Annual Review of Psychology* 41 (1990): 417–40.
32. Ibid.; R. R. McCrae and P. T. Costa, "Validation of the Five-Factor Model of Personality Across Instruments and Observers," *Journal of Personality and Social Psychology* 52 (1987): 81–90; R. R. McCrae and P. T. Costa, "Discriminant Validity of NEO-PIR Facet Scales," *Educational and Psychological Measurement* 52 (1992): 229–37.
33. J. Sandberg, "Case Study," *Newsweek*, January 24, 2000, 31–36.
34. J. M. George and A. P. Brief, "Personality and Work-Related Distress." In B. Schneider and B. Smith (Eds.), *Personality and Organization* (Mahwah, NJ: Erlbaum, 2004 pp. 193–219).
35. M. J. Simmering, J. A. Colquitt, R. A. Noe, and C. O. L. H. Porter, "Conscientiousness, Autonomy Fit, and Development: A Longitudinal Study," *Journal of Applied Psychology* 88(5 2003): 954–63.
36. M. R. Barrick and M. K. Mount, "The Big Five Personality Dimensions and Job Performance: A Meta-Analysis," *Personnel Psychology* 44 (1991): 1–26; Barrick, Mount, and Strauss, "Conscientiousness and Performance of Sales Representatives."
37. J. O'C. Hamilton, "Roger Salquist," *BusinessWeek, Reinventing America*, 1992: 186.
38. L. A. Witt and G. R. Ferris, "Social Skills as Moderator of the Conscientiousness—Performance Relationship: Convergent Results Across Four Studies," *Journal of Applied Psychology* 88(5 2003): 809–20.
39. J. M. George and J. Zhou, "When Openness to Experience and Conscientiousness Are Related to Creative Behavior: An Interactional Approach," *Journal of Applied Psychology* 86 (2001): 513–524.
40. "A Gallery of Risk Takers," *BusinessWeek, Reinventing America*, 1992: 183.
41. I. M. Kunii, "Making Canon Click," *Business Week* 16 (September 2002): 40–42; www.canon.com (March 22, 2006).
42. I. M. Kunii, "Making Canon Click," *Business Week* 16 (September 2002): 40–42.
43. S. Ballmer, "Repeat Performers," *Business Week Online* (January 13, 2003), www.businessweek.com/@@ X9eC1IQQvgmr3QcA/magazine/content/03_0;

F. Mitarai, "Market-Leading Value Creation through Strength in Innovative Technologies" (January 24, 2004), www.canon.com/about/greeting/index.html; "Corporate Philosophy–Kyosei" (January 24, 2003), www.canon.com/about/philosophy/index.html.
44. Kunii, "Making Canon Click," *Business Week* 16 (September 2002): 40–42.
45. Ibid.
46. I. Rowley, "Can Canon Keep Printing Money?" *Business Week Online* (September 5, 2005), www.businessweek.com.
47. M. A. Burke, A. P. Brief, and J. M. George, "The Role of Negative Affectivity in Understanding Relationships Between Self-Reports of Stressors and Strains: A Comment on the Applied Psychology Literature," *Journal of Applied Psychology* 78 (1993): 402–12.
48. Barrick and Mount, "The Big Five Personality Dimensions and Job Performance"; J. M. George, "Mood and Absence," *Journal of Applied Psychology* 74 (1989): 317–24; J. M. George, "Time Structure and Purpose as a Mediator of Work-Life Linkages," *Journal of Applied Social Psychology* 21 (1991): 296–314.
49. J. B. Rotter, "Generalized Expectancies for Internal vs. External Control of Reinforcement," *Psychological Monographs* 80 (1966): 1–28; P. Spector, "Behavior in Organizations as a Function of Employees' Locus of Control," *Psychological Bulletin* 91 (1982): 482–97.
50. M. Snyder, "Self-Monitoring of Expressive Behavior," *Journal of Personality and Social Psychology* 30 (1974): 526–37; M. Snyder, "Self-Monitoring Processes." In L. Berkowitz (Ed.) *Advances in Experimental Social Psychology* 12 (New York: Academic Press, 1979): 85–128.
51. T. A. Judge, A. Erez, J. E. Bono, and C. J. Thoresen, "The Core Self-Evaluations Scale: Development of a Measure," *Personnel Psychology* 56 (2003): 303–31.
52. J. Brockner, *Self-Esteem at Work* (Lexington, MA: Lexington Books, 1988).
53. D. C. Ganster, J. Schaubroeck, W. E. Sime, and B. T. Mayes, "The Nomological Validity of the Type A Personality Among Employed Adults," *Journal of Applied Psychology* 76 (1991): 143–68; R. H. Rosenman, "Current and Past History of Type A Behavior Pattern." In T. Schmidt, J. M. Dembrowski, and G. Blumchen (Eds.), *Biological and Psychological Factors in Cardiovascular Disease* (New York : Springer-Verlag, 1986) pp. 15–40.
54. R. A. Baron, "Personality and Organizational Conflict: Effects of the Type A Behavior Pattern and Self-Monitoring," *Organizational Behavior and Human Decision Processes* 44 (1989): 281–97.
55. D. C. McClelland, Human Motivation (Glenview, IL: Scott, Foresman, 1985); D. C. McClelland, "How Motives, Skills, and Values Determine What People Do," *American Psychologist* 40 (1985): 812–25; D. C. McClelland, "Managing Motivation to Expand Human Freedom," *American Psychologist* 33 (1978): 201–10.
56. D. C. McClelland, "Achievement and Entrepreneurship: A Longitudinal Study," *Journal of Personality and Organizational Behavior* 1 (1965): 389–92.
57. L. Goldberg, "Continental Executive Is Still a Pilot," *Houston Chronicle*, February 26, 2000 1C, 3C; Continental Airlines News Release, September 20, 1999; www.continental .com/corporate.
58. L. Goldberg, "Continental Executive Is Still a Pilot."
59. D. G. Winter, *The Power Motive* (New York: Free Press, 1973).
60. R. J. House, W. D. Spangler, and J. Woycke, "Personality and Charisma in the U.S. Presidency: A Psychological Theory of Leader Effectiveness," *Administrative Science Quarterly* 36 (1991): 364–96.
61. M. J. Stahl, "Achievement, Power, and Managerial Motivation: Selecting Managerial Talent with the Job Choice Exercise," *Personnel Psychology* 36 (1983): 775–89.
62. Ibid.
63. D. C. McClelland and D. H. Burnham, "Power Is the Great Motivator," *Harvard Business Review* 54 (1976): 100–10.
64. D. S. Ones and C. Viswesvaran, "Job-Specific Applicant Pools and National Norms for Personality Scales: Implications for Range-Restriction Corrections in Validation Research," *Journal of Applied Psychology* 88(3 2003): 570–77.
65. L. M. Hough, N. K. Eaton, M. D. Dunnette, J. D. Kamp, and R. A. McCloy, "Criterion-Related Validities of Personality Constructs and the Effect of Response Distortion on Those Validities," *Journal of Applied Psychology* 75 (1990): 581–95.
66. D. Lubinski and R. V. Dawis, "Aptitudes, Skills, and Proficiencies." In M. D. Dunnette and L. M. Hough (Eds.), *Handbook of Industrial and Organizational Psychology*, 2nd ed., vol. 3. (Palo Alto, CA: Consulting Psychologists Press, 1992), 1–59.
67. Ibid.
68. J. C. Nunnally, *Psychometric Theory*, 2nd ed. (New York: McGraw-Hill, 1978); T. G. Thurstone, "Primary Mental Abilities and Children," *Educational and Psychological Measurement* 1 (1941): 105–16.
69. K. R. Murphy, B. E. Cronin, and A. P. Tam, "Controversy and Consensus Regarding the Use of Cognitive Ability Testing in Organizations," *Journal of Applied Psychology* 88(4 2003): 660–71.
70. Ibid.
71. J. F. Salgado, N. Anderson, S. Moscoso, C. Bertua, F. de Fruyt, and J. P. Rolland, "A Meta-Analytic Study of General Mental Ability Validity for Different Occupations in the European Community," *Journal of Applied Psychology* 88(5 2003): 1068–81; J. F. Salgado, N. Anderson, S. Moscoso, C. Bertua, and F. de Fruyt, "International Validity Generalization of GMA and Cognitive Abilities: A European Community Meta-Analysis," *Personnel Psychology* 56 (2003): 573–605.
72. J. A. LePine, "Team Adaptation and Postchange Performance: Effects of Team Composition in Terms of Members' Cognitive Ability and Personality," *Journal of Applied Psychology* 88(1 2003): 27–39.
73. M. D. Dunnette, "Aptitudes, Abilities, and Skills." In M. D. Dunnette (Ed.), *Handbook of Industrial and Organizational Psychology* (Chicago: Rand McNally, 1976), 473–520.
74. E. A. Fleishman, "The Description and Prediction of Perceptual-Motor Skill Learning." In R. Glaser (Ed.), *Training Research and Education* (Pittsburgh, PA: University of Pittsburgh Press, 1962)pp. 137–176; E. A. Fleishman, "On the Relation Between Abilities, Learning, and Human Performance," *American Psychologist* 27 (1972): 1017–32.

75. H. M. Chipuer, M. Rovine, and R. Plomin, "LISREL Modeling: Genetic and Environmental Influences on IQ Revisited," *Intelligence* 14 (1990): 11–29; N. L. Pedersen, R. Plomin, J. R. Nesselroade, and G. E. McClearn, "A Quantitative Genetic Analysis of Cognitive Abilities During the Second Half of the Life Span," *Psychological Science* 3 (1992): 346–53.
76. "Think About It: Your Brainpower May Be Vastly Underused on the Job," *Wall Street Journal*, May 11, 1997, p. A1.
77. R. Merle, "Technology Workers See No Sizzle in What They Do," *Wall Street Journal*, April 26, 2000, p. T2.
78. "Drug Tests Keep Paying Off, But Continued Gains Are Tougher," *Wall Street Journal,* April 5, 1998, p. A1.
79. L. McGinley, " 'Fitness' Exams Help to Measure Worker Acuity," *Wall Street Journal*, April 21, 1992, pp. B1, B6.
80. D. Goleman, *Emotional Intelligence* (New York: Bantam Books, 1994); J. D. Mayer and P. Salovey, "The Intelligence of Emotional Intelligence," *Intelligence* 17 (1993): 433–42; J. D. Mayer and P. Salovey, "What Is Emotional Intelligence?" In P. Salovey and D. Sluyter (Eds.), *Emotional Development and Emotional Intelligence: Implications for Education* (New York: Basic Books, 1997) pp. 3–34; P. Salovey and J. D. Mayer, "Emotional Intelligence," *Imagination, Cognition, and Personality* 9 (1989–1990): 185–211.
81. D. Goleman, *Emotional Intelligence* (New York: Bantam Books, 1994); J. D. Mayer and P. Salovey, "The Intelligence of Emotional Intelligence," *Intelligence* 17 (1993): 433–42; J. D. Mayer and P. Salovey, "What Is Emotional Intelligence?" In P. Salovey and D. Sluyter (Eds.), *Emotional Development and Emotional Intelligence: Implications for Education* (New York: Basic Books, 1997)pp. 3–34; P. Salovey and J. D. Mayer, "Emotional Intelligence," *Imagination, Cognition, and Personality* 9 (1989–1990): 185–211.
82. A. Farnham, "Are You Smart Enough to Keep Your Job?," Fortune, January 15,1996, pp. 34–48; M. E. P. Seligman, *Learned Optimism* (New York: A. A. Knopf, 1990).
83. K. Law, C. Wong, and L. Song, "The Construct and Criterion Validity of Emotional Intelligence and Its Potential Utility for Management Studies," *Journal of Applied Psychology* 89 (2004): 483–496.
84. "Leading by Feel," *Harvard Business Review* 82(1) (January 2004): 27–37.
85. J. M. George, "Emotions and Leadership: The Role of Emotional Intelligence," *Human Relations*, 2000, 53, 1027–1055; R. S. Rubin, D. C. Munz, and W. H. Bommer, "Leading From Within: The Effects of Emotion Recognition and Personality on Transformational Leadership Behavior," *Academy of Management Journal* 48(5 2005): 845–858.
86. J. Zhou and J. M George, "Awakening Employee Creativity: The Role of Leader Emotional Intelligence," *The Leadership Quarterly* 14 (2003): 545–68.
87. A. Farnham, "Are You Smart Enough to Keep Your Job?"
88. Ibid.
89. Ibid.
90. A. Jung, "Leading by Feel: Seek Frank Feedback," *Inside the Mind of the Leader* (January 2004): 31.
91. "Christine A. Poon Appointed A Vice Chairman of Johnson & Johnson," *Johnson & Johnson* (March 20, 2006), www.jnj.com.
92. M. Austria Farmer, "The Power Who Leads a Billion-Dollar Business," *Diversity Inc. Magazine Cover Store, July 2003,* www.diversityinc.com.
93. Ibid.
94. Ibid
95. Ibid.
96. W. Arthur, Jr., W. Bennett, Jr., P. S. Edens, and S. T. Bell, "Effectiveness of Training in Organizations: A Meta-Analysis of Design and Evaluation Features," *Journal of Applied Psychology* 88(2 2003): 234–45.
97. J. Pfeffer, "A Blueprint for Success," *Business 2.0* (April 2005): 66.
98. L. Conley, "Cultural Phenomenon," *Fast Company* (April 2005): 75–77.
99. "China's people problem," *The Economist* (April 16, 2005): 53–54.

CHAPTER 3

1. J. Guyon, "The Soul of a Moneymaking Machine," *Fortune* (October 3, 2005): 113–20; "Valero's Bill Greehey To Focus On Role As Chairman," *Velero Energy Corporation* (October 31, 2005), http://www.valero.com/NR/exeres/AD148F57-B714-4C01-A208-8812D4A75D9.htm.
2. R. Barker, "Valero's Sweet Spot," *Business Week Online* (October 24, 2005), www.businessweek.com; "Valero Energy Cooperation Reports Fourth Quarter and Full Year 2005 Earnings," *Valero Energy Coporation* (January 31, 2006), http://www.valero.com/NewsRoom/News+Releases/NR_20060131.htm; "Valero Receives Several Top Honors," *Valero Energy Corporation* (December 30, 2005), http://www.valero.com/NewsRoom/News+Releases/NR_20051230.htm.
3. J. Guyon, "The Soul of a Moneymaking Machine," *Fortune* (October 3, 2005): 113–20.
4. Ibid.
5. Ibid.
6. Ibid.
7. Ibid.
8. Ibid.
9. "Fortune 100 Best Companies to Work for: Full List," CNN Money.com (March 23, 2006), http:// money.cnn.com/magazines/fortune/bestcompanies/full_list); "About the 2005 Speakers," *Great Place to Work-Conference* (March 22, 2006), http://www.greatplacetowork-conference.com/conference/speakers,php?id=86; "Valero Jumps to No. 3 on Fortune's List of 'America's 100 Best Companies to Work For' in America," *Valero Energy Corporation* (January 9, 2006), http://www.valero.com /NewsRoom/News+Releases/NR_20060109.htm; "Bill Greehey, Chairman of the Board," *Valero Energy Corporation* (March 22, 2006), http://www.valero.com/NewsRoom/ Executive+Team/.
10. "Fortune 100 Best Companies to Work for: Valero Energy," *CNN Money.com* (March 23, 2006), http://money.cnn .com/magazines/fortune/bestcompanies/snapshots/1521.html.
11. W. R. Nord, A. P. Brief, J. M. Atieh, and E. M. Doherty, "Work Values and the Conduct of Organizational Behavior," In B. M. Staw and L. L. Cummings (Eds.), *Research in Organizational Behavior*, vol. 10 (Greenwich, CT: JAI Press, 1988), 1–42.

12. M. Rokeach, *The Nature of Human Values* (New York: Free Press, 1973).
13. Ibid.
14. Nord, Brief, Atieh, and Doherty, "Work Values and the Conduct of Organizational Behavior"; A. Malka and J. A. Chatman, "Intrinsic and Extrinsic Work Orientations as Moderators of the Effect of Annual Income on Subjective Well-Being: A Longitudinal Study," *Society for Personality and Social Psychology, Inc.* 29 (6 June 2003): 737–46.
15. T. L. Beauchamp and N. E. Bowie (Eds.), *Ethical Theory and Business* (Englewood Cliffs, NJ: Prentice-Hall, 1979).
16. Rokeach, *The Nature of Human Values*.
17. R. E. Goodin, "How to Determine Who Should Get What," *Ethics* (July 1975): 310–21.
18. D. C. Johnston, "Kodak to Reduce Its Work Force by Up to 15,000," *New York Times,* January 23, 2004: C5; M. York, "With More Layoffs at Kodak, Rochester's Corporate Identity Erodes," *New York Times,* January 25, 2004.
19. T. M. Jones, "Ethical Decision Making by Individuals in Organizations: An Issue Contingent Model," *Academy of Management Journal* 16 (1991): 366–95; G. F. Cavanaugh, D. J. Moberg, and M. Velasquez, "The Ethics of Organizational Politics," *Academy of Management Journal* 6 (1981): 363–74.
20. T. M. Jones, "Ethical Decision Making by Individuals in Organizations: An Issue Contingent Model," *Academy of Management Journal* 16 (1991): 366–95; G. F. Cavanaugh, D. J. Moberg, and M. Velasquez, "The Ethics of Organizational Politics," *Academy of Management Journal* 6 (1981): 363–74.
21. L. K. Trevino, "Ethical Decision Making in Organizations: A Person–Situation Interactionist Model," *Academy of Management Review* 11 (1986): 601–17; W. H. Shaw and V. Barry, *Moral Issues in Business,* 6th ed. (Belmont, CA: Wadsworth, 1995).
22. Jones, "Ethical Decision Making by Individuals in Organizations: An Issue Contingent Model," *Academy of Management Journal* 16 (1991): 366–95.
23. M. S. Frankel, "Professional Codes: Why, How, and with What Impact?" *Ethics* 8 (1999): 109–15; J. Van Maanen and S. R. Barley, "Occupational Communities: Culture and Control in Organizations," In B. Staw and L. Cummings, (Eds.), *Research in Organizational Behavior,* vol.6, (Greenwich, CT: JAI Press, 1984): 287–365; D. Denby, "The Lies of the Party," *Fortune* (January 26, 2004): 99–108; M. France, "White-Collar Crime: Heiress in Handcuffs," *Business Week* (November 24, 2003): 32–40; R. Lowenstein, "The Rigases Tried Desperately to Maintain Control of Their Cable Company Adelphia," *The New York Times Magazine* (February 1, 2004): 27–42, 62.
24. A. S. Watermann, "On the Uses of Psychological Theory and Research in the Process of Ethical Inquiry," *Psychological Bulletin* 103 (3 1988): 283–98; R. B. Schmitt, "Companies Add Ethics Training: Will It Work?" *Wall Street Journal,* November 4, 2002, pp. B1-B3.
25. Frankel, "Professional Codes"; Van Maanen and Barley, "Occupational Communities"; Denby, "The Lies of the Party"; France, "White-Collar Crime"; Lowenstein, "The Rigases Tried Desperately to Maintain Control of Their Cable Company Adelphia"; G. Colvin, "Get Ready: It's Going to Be a Trying Year," *Fortune* (February 10, 2004), www.furtune.com/fortune/subs/columnist/0,15704,575738,00.html.
26. Watermann, "On the Uses of Psychological Theory and Research in the Process of Ethical Inquiry"; Schmitt, "Companies Add Ethics Training."
27. S. N. Mehta, "ENRON 'Employees Are the Best Line of Defense,' " *Fortune* (October 14, 2003), www.fortune.com/fortune/subs/print/0,15935,518339,00.html.
28. "2 Entries for Whistleblower" (February 9, 2004), http://dictionary.reference.com; M. P. Miceli and J. P. Near, "Whistleblowing: Reaping the Benefits," *Academy of Management Review* 8 (3 1994): 65–72.
29. Watermann, "On the Uses of Psychological Theory and Research in the Process of Ethical Inquiry"; Schmitt, "Companies Add Ethics Training."
30. Ibid.
31. Ibid.
32. "Sarbanes-Oxley Act of 2002," *CPE Online* (February 7, 2004), www.cpeonline.com/cpenew/sarox.asp.
33. Ibid.
34. Ibid.
35. Watermann, "On the Uses of Psychological Theory and Research in the Process of Ethical Inquiry"; Schmitt, "Companies Add Ethics Training."
36. "National Whistleblower Center: About the Center" (February 9, 2004), www.whistleblowers.org/html/about_the_whistleblow.htm; S. M. Kohn, "National Whistleblower Center: Corporate Whistleblowers" (February 9, 2004), www.whistleblowers.org/html/corporate_whistleblowers.htm.
37. M. Fishbein and I. Ajzen, "Attitudes and Opinions," *Annual Review of Psychology* 23 (1972): 487–544.
38. D. Watson and A. Tellegen, "Toward a Consensual Structure of Mood," *Psychological Bulletin* 98 (1985): 219–35.
39. D. Watson, *Mood and Temperament* (New York: Guilford Press, 2000).
40. Ibid.
41. J. M. George and A. P. Brief, "Feeling Good-Doing Good: A Conceptual Analysis of the Mood at Work-Organizational Spontaneity Relationship," *Psychological Bulletin* 112 (1992): 310–29.
42. C. M. Pearson and C. L. Porath, "On the nature, consequences and remedies of workplace incivility: No time for 'nice'? Think again," *Academy of Management Executive* 10(1 2005): 7–18.
43. R. Chao, "Not-So-Nice Costs," *The Wall Street Journal* (January 2006): B4.
44. C. M. Pearson and C. L. Porath, "On the nature, consequences and remedies of workplace incivility: No time for 'nice'? Think again," *Academy of Management Executive* 10(1 2005): 7–18.
45. J. M. George, "Trait and State Affect," In K. R. Murphy (Ed.), *Individual Differences and Behavior in Organizations* (San Francisco: Jossey-Bass, 1996), 145–74; J. Zhou and J. M. George, "Awakening Employee Creativity: The Role of Leader Emotional Intelligence," *The Leadership Quarterly* 14 (2003): 545–68.
46. J. M. George, "Mood and Absence," *Journal of Applied Psychology* 74 (1987): 317–24; J. M. George, "State or Trait: Effects of Positive Mood on Prosocial Behaviors at Work," *Journal of Applied Psychology* 76 (1991): 299–307.

47. George, "State or Trait."
48. J. M. George and K. Bettenhausen, "Understanding Prosocial Behavior, Sales Performance, and Turnover: A Group Level Analysis in a Service Context," *Journal of Applied Psychology* 75 (1990): 698–709.
49. A. M. Isen and R. A. Baron, "Positive Effect as a Factor in Organizational Behavior," In B. M. Staw and L. L. Cummings (Eds.), *Research in Organizational Behavior*, vol. 13 (Greenwich, CT: JAI Press, 1991), 1–53; J. P. Forgas (Ed.), *Feeling and Thinking: The Role of Affect in Social Cognition* (Cambridge, UK: Cambridge University Press, 2000); J. P. Forgas, "Mood and Judgment: The Affect Infusion Model," *Psychological Bulletin* 117 (1995): 39–66; A. M. Isen, "Positive Effect and Decision Making," In M. Lewis and J. M. Haviland-Jones (Eds.), *Handbook of Emotions,* 2nd ed. (New York: Guilford Press, 2000), 417–35; R. C. Sinclair, "Mood, Categorization Breadth, and Performance Appraisal: The Effects of Order of Information Acquisition and Affective State on Halo, Accuracy, Informational Retrieval, and Evaluations," *Organizational Behavior and Human Decision Processes* 42 (1988): 22–46.
50. L. L. Martin and A. Tesser (Eds.), *Striving and Feeling: Interactions Among Goals, Affect, and Self-Regulation* (Mahwah, NJ: Erlbaum, 1996).
51. A. M. Isen, K. A. Daubman, and G. P. Nowicki, "Positive Affect Facilitates Creative Problem Solving," *Journal of Personality and Social Psychology* 52 (1987): 1122–31; A. M. Isen, M. M. S. Johnson, E. Mertz, and G. R. Robinson, "The Influence of Positive Effect on the Unusualness of Word Associations,"*Journal of Personality and Social Psychology* 48 (1985): 1413–26.
52. J. M. George and J. Zhou, "Understanding When Bad Moods Foster Creativity and Good Ones Don't: The Role of Context and Clarity of Feelings," *Journal of Applied Psychology* 87 (2002): 687–697. G. Kaufmann and S. K. Vosburg, "Paradoxical Mood Effects on Creative Problem-Solving," *Cognition and Emotion* 11 (1997): 151–70; L. L. Martin and P. Stoner, "Mood as Input: What We Think About How We Feel Determines How We Think," In L. L. Martin and A. Tesser (Eds.), *Striving and Feeling: Interactions Among Goals, Affect, and Self-Regulation* (Mahwah, NJ: Erlbaum), 279–302.
53. Martin and Stoner, "Mood as Input."
54. N. H. Frijda, "The Laws of Emotion," *American Psychologist* 43(5, May 1988): 349–58; J. L. Tracy, R. W. Robins, and K. H. Lagattuta, "Can Children Recognize Pride?" *Emotions* 5(3), (2005): 251–57; P. Ekman and R. J. Davidson (Eds.), *The Nature of Emotion: Fundamental Questions* (New York: Oxford University Press, 1994); J. L. Tracy and R. W. Robins, "Show Your Pride: Evidence for a Discrete Emotion Expression," *Psychological Science* 15(3 2004): 194–97.
55. J. L. Tracy and R. W. Robins, "Show Your Pride: Evidence for a Discrete Emotion Expression," *Psychological Science* 15(3 2004): 194–97; B. Azar, "The faces of pride," *Monitor on Psychology* (March 2006): 24–25; P. Ekman, "An argument for basic emotions," *Cognition and Emotion* 6: 169–200; P. Ekman, E. R. Sorenson, and W. V. Friesen, "Pan-cultural elements in facial displays of emotion," *Science* 164: 86–88.
56. J. L. Tracy and R. W. Robins, "Show Your Pride: Evidence for a Discrete Emotion Expression," *Psychological Science* 15(3 2004): 194–97; B. Azar, "The faces of pride," *Monitor on Psychology* (March 2006): 24–25; J. L. Tracy, R. W. Robins, and K. H. Lagattuta, "Can Children Recognize Pride?" *Emotions* 5(3 2005): 251–57.
57. J. P. Forgas, "Affect in Social Judgments and Decisions: A Multi-Process Model," In M. Zanna (Ed.), *Advances in Experimental and Social Psychology*, vol. 25, (San Diego, CA: Academic Press, 1992): 227–75; J. P. Forgas and J. M. George, "Affective Influences on Judgments and Behavior in Organizations: An Information Processing Perspective," *Organizational Behavior and Human Decision Processes* 86 (2001): 3–34; J. M. George, "Leadership and Emotions: The Role of Emotional Intelligence," *Human Relations* 52 (2000): 1027–55; W. N. Norris, *Mood: The Frame of Mind*, (New York: Springer-Verlag, 1989).
58. B. Morris, "What a Life," *Fortune* (October 6, 2003): 50–62.
59. "VIRGIN AMERICA: On the Record: Fred Reid," *SFGate.com* (March 19, 2006), http://www.sfgate.com/cgi-bin/article.cgi?file=/chronicle/archive/2006/03/19/BUG6VHOI
60. A. Sewer, "Do Branson's Profits Equal His *Joie de Vivre?*" *Fortune* (October 2005): 57.
61. B. Morris, "What a Life," *Fortune* (October 6, 2003): 50–62.
62. "Virgin Group eyes Bally Total Fitness: NY Post," *Reuters* (March 21, 2006), http://today.reuters.com.
63. Morris, "What a Life."
64. Ibid.
65. Ibid.
66. J. M. George, "Affect Regulation in Groups and Teams," In R. G. Lord, R. J. Klimoski, and R. Kanfer, (Eds.), *Emotions in the Workplace: Understanding the Structure and Role of Emotions in Organizational Behavior* (San Francisco, CA: Jossey-Bass, 2002) pp. 183–217; A. R. Hochschild, "Ideology and Emotion Management: A Perspective and Path for Future Research," In T. D. Kemper, (Ed.), *Research Agendas in the Sociology of Emotions* (Albany: University of New York Press, 1990): 117–42; J. M. Diefendorff and R. H. Gosserand, "Understanding the Emotional Labor Process: A Control Theory Perspective," *Journal of Organizational Behavior* 24 (2003): 945–59.
67. J. M. Diefendorff and E. M. Richard, "Antecedents and Consequences of Emotional Display Rule Perceptions," *Journal of Applied Psychology* 88 (2 2003): 284–94.
68. T. D. Kemper, "Social Models in the Explanation of Emotions," In M. Lewis and J. M. Haviland-Jones, (Eds.), *Handbook of Emotions, 2nd ed.* (New York: Guilford Press, 2000): 45–58.
69. T. D. Kemper, "Social Models in the Explanation of Emotions." In M. Lewis and J. M. Haviland-Jones, (Eds.), *Handbook of Emotions, 2nd ed.* (New York: Guilford Press, 2000): 45–58.
70. D. R. Middleton, "Emotional Style: The Cultural Ordering of Emotions," *Ethos* 17 (2 1989): 187–201; A. R. Hochschild, "Ideology and emotion management."
71. J. A. Morris and D. C. Feldman, "The Dimensions, Antecedents, and Consequences of Emotional Labor," *Academy of Management Review* 21 (4 1996): 986–1010.

72. S. L. Wilk and L. M. Moynihan, "Display Rule 'Regulators': The Replationship Between Supervisors and Worker Emotional Exhaustion," *Journal of Applied Psychology* 90(5, September 2005): 917–27; S. Burling, "Faking Happiness Makes You Sad," *The Houston Chronicle* (November 28, 2005): D1.
73. T. Matthews, "The Inn at Little Washington," *Wine Spectator Online* (September 30, 2001),www.winespectator.com/Wine /Archives/Show_Article/0,1275,3363,00.html; J. Lustig, "Virginia: A Dream Dinner at the Inn at Little Washington," *NewYorkmetro.com* (March 26, 2001), www.newyorkmetro .com/travel/guides/52weekends/locations/Virginia.htm.
74. T. Raz, "A Recipe for Perfection," *Inc.* (July, 2003): 36–38.
75. Ibid.
76. Ibid.
77. Ibid.
78. J. A. Fuller, J. M. Stanton, G. G. Fisher, C. Spitzmüller, S. S Russell, and P. C. Smith, "A Lengthy Look at the Daily Grind: Time Series Analysis of Events, Mood, Stress, and Satisfaction," *Journal of Applied Psychology* 88 (6 2003): 1019–33; C. J. Thoresen, S. A. Kaplan, A. P. Barsky, C. R. Warren, and K. de Chermont, "The Affective Underpinnings of Job Perceptions and Attitudes: A Meta-Analytic Review and Integration," *Psychological Bulletin* 129 (6 2003): 914–25.
79. G. R. Jones and J. M. George, "The Experience and Evolution of Trust: Implications for Cooperation and Teamwork," *Academy of Management Review* 23 (1998): 531–46.
80. R. Axelrod, *The Evolution of Cooperation* (New York: Basic Books, 1984); P. Bateson, "The Biological Evolution of Cooperation and Trust," In D. Gambetta (Ed.), *Trust: Making and Breaking Cooperative Relations* (New York: Basil Blackwell, 1988), 14–30; L. G. Zucker, "Institutional Theories of Organization," *Annual Review of Sociology* 13 (1997): 443–64.
81. R. Galfor and A. S. Drapeau, "The Enemies of Trust," *Harvard Business Review* (February 2003): 89–95.
82. G. Korentz, "Hate Your Job? Join the Club," *Business Week* (October 6, 2003): 40.
83. "U.S. Job Satisfaction Keeps Falling, The Conference Board Reports Today," *The Conference Board* (February 28, 2005), http://www.conference-board-org/utilities/pressPrinterFriendly.cfm?press_ID=2582; J. Bachman, "Employee morale falls, survey says," *The Houston Chronicle* (August 29, 2005): D3.
84. E. Alt Powell, "Fewer People Means Doing More with Less," *The Houston Chronicle* (January 23, 2006): D1, D4.
85. J. M. George, "The Role of Personality in Organizational Life: Issues and Evidence," *Journal of Management* 18 (1992): 185–213; P. T. van den Berg and J. A. Feij, "Complex Relationships Among Personality Traits, Job Characteristics, and Work Behavior," *International Journal of Selection and Assessment* 11 (December 4, 2003): 326–40; R. Ilies and T. A. Judge, "On the Heritability of Job Satisfaction: The Mediating Role of Personality," *Journal of Applied Psychology* 88 (4, 2003): 750–59; T. A. Judge, A. Erez, J. E. Bono, and C. J. Thoresen, "The Core Self-Evaluation Scale: Development of a Measure," *Personnel Psychology* 56 (2003): 303–31.
86. J. M. George, "Time Structure and Purpose as Mediator of Work-Life Linkages," *Journal of Applied Social Psychology* 21 (1991): 296–314.
87. R. D. Arvey, T. J. Bouchard, N. L. Segal, and L. M. Abraham, "Job Satisfaction: Environmental and Genetic Components," *Journal of Applied Psychology* 74 (1989): 187–92.
88. A. P. Brief, *Attitudes In and Around Organizations* (Thousand Oaks, CA: Sage, 1998).
89. "Mothers Want Flexibility Most," *Houston Chronicle* (September 23, 2003): 3B.
90. "Mothers Want Flexibility Most," *Houston Chronicle* (September 23, 2003): 3B.
91. Ibid.
92. J. Zhou and J. M. George, "When Job Dissatisfaction Leads to Creativity: Encouraging the Expression of Voice," *Academy of Management Journal* 44 (4, August 2001): 682–96.
93. K. Brooker, "The Pepsi Machine," *Fortune* (February 6, 2006): 68–72.
94. T. DeAngelis, "The 'Who Am I' Question Wears a Cloak of Culture," *APA Monitor* (October 1992): 22–23.
95. Ibid.
96. S. Shellenberger, "More Job Seekers Put Family Needs First," *Wall Street Journal*, November 15, 1991, pp. B1, B6.
97. "100 Best Companies to Work for 2004," *Fortune* (February 10, 2004), www.fortune.com/fortune/ bestcompanies.
98. "Biotech Firm Offers Remedy for Parents," *Houston Chronicle*, June 13, 2000, p. 10C.
99. R. W. Rice, K. Markus, R. P. Moyer, and D. B. McFarlin, "Facet Importance and Job Satisfaction: Two Experimental Tests of Locke's Range of Affect Hypothesis," *Journal of Applied Social Psychology* 21 (1991): 1977–87.
100. D. Milbank, "More Business Graduates Snap Up Jobs in Rust Belt That Promise Them Clout," *Wall Street Journal*, July 21, 1992: pp. B1, B6.
101. Ibid.
102. F. Herzberg, *Work and the Nature of Man* (Cleveland: World, 1966).
103. N. King, "Clarification and Evaluation of the Two-Factor Theory of Job Satisfaction," *Psychological Bulletin* 74 (1970): 18–31; E. A. Locke, "The Nature and Causes of Job Satisfaction," In M. Dunnette (Ed.), *Handbook of Industrial and Organizational Psychology* (Chicago: Rand McNally, 1976), 1297–349.
104. D. B. McFarlin and R. W. Rice, "The Role of Facet Importance as a Moderator in Job Satisfaction Processes," *Journal of Organizational Behavior* 13 (1992): 41–54; R. A. Katzell, "Personal Values, Job Satisfaction, and Job Behavior," In H. Borow (Ed.), *Man in a World of Work* (Boston: Houghton Mifflin, 1964).
105. T. Lee, "What Kind of Job Are You Likely to Find?" *National Business Employment Weekly* (Spring 1992): 5–6.
106. McFarlin and Rice, "The Role of Facet Importance as a Moderator in Job Satisfaction Processes."
107. F. J. Landy, "An Opponent Process Theory of Job Satisfaction," *Journal of Applied Psychology* 63 (1978): 533–47.
108. B. M. Staw and J. Ross, "Stability in the Midst of Change: A Dispositional Approach to Job Satisfaction," *Journal of Applied Psychology* 71 (1985): 469–80.

109. R. W. Griffin, "Effects of Work Redesign on Employee Perceptions, Attitudes, and Behaviors: A Long-Term Investigation," *Academy of Management Journal* 34 (1991): 425–35.
110. D. J. Weiss, R. V. Dawis, G. W. England, and L. H. Lofquist, *Manual for the Minnesota Satisfaction Questionnaire, Minnesota Studies in Vocational Rehabilitation*, vol. 22, Industrial Relations Center, University of Minnesota, 1967.
111. R. B. Dunham and J. B. Herman, "Development of a Female Faces Scale for Measuring Job Satisfaction," *Journal of Applied Psychology* 60 (1975): 629–31; T. Kunin, "The Construction of a New Type of Attitude Measure," *Personnel Psychology* 8 (1955): 65–78.
112. P. C. Smith, L. M. Kendall, and C. L. Hulin, *The Measurement of Satisfaction in Work and Retirement* (Chicago: Rand McNally, 1969).
113. M. T. Iaffaldano and P. M. Muchinsky, "Job Satisfaction and Performance: A Meta-Analysis," *Psychological Bulletin* 97 (1985): 251–73.
114. T. A. Judge, C. J. Thoresen, J. E. Bono, and G. K. Patton, "The Job Satisfaction-Job Performance Relationship: A Qualitative and Quantitative Review," *Psychological Bulletin* (2001): 376–407.
115. D. R. Dalton and D. J. Mesch, "On the Extent and Reduction of Avoidable Absenteeism: An Assessment of Absence Policy Provisions," *Journal of Applied Psychology* 76 (1991): 810–17; D. R. Dalton and C. A. Enz, "Absenteeism in Remission: Planning, Policy, and Culture," *Human Resource Planning* 10 (1987): 81–91; D. R. Dalton and C. A. Enz, "New Directions in the Management of Employee Absenteeism: Attention to Policy and Culture," In R. S. Schuler and S. A. Youngblood (Eds.), *Readings in Personnel and Human Resource Management* (St. Paul: West, 1988), 356–66; "Expensive Absenteeism," *Wall Street Journal*, July 7, 1986, p. 1.
116. G. E. Hardy, D. Woods, and T. D. Wall, "The Impact of Psychological Distress on Absence from Work," *Journal of Applied Psychology* 88 (2 2003): 306–14.
117. R. M. Steers and S. R. Rhodes, "Major Influences of Employee Attendance: A Process Model," *Journal of Applied Psychology* 63 (1978): 391–407.
118. George, "Mood and Absence."
119. W. H. Mobley, "Intermediate Linkages in the Relationship Between Job Satisfaction and Employee Turnover," *Journal of Applied Psychology* 62 (1977): 237–40.
120. George and Brief, "Feeling Good-Doing Good"; D. W. Organ, *Organizational Citizenship Behavior: The Good Soldier Syndrome* (Lexington, MA: Lexington Books, 1988).
121. Ibid.
122. Organ, *Organizational Citizenship Behavior*.
123. "Finding Motivation in the Little Things," *Wall Street Journal*, November 2, 1992, p. B1.
124. "We Caught You Doing Something Right," *Texas A&M University Human Resources Newsletter*, October 1992, p. 6.
125. N. Schmitt and A. G. Bedeian, "A Comparison of LISREL and Two-Stage Least Squares Analysis of a Hypothesized Job Satisfaction-Life Satisfaction Reciprocal Relationship," *Journal of Applied Psychology* 67 (1982): 806–17.
126. A. Cortese, "Bored to Death at Work–Literally," *Business Week* (July 1, 2002): 16.
127. N. J. Allen and J. P. Meyer, "Affective, Continuance, and Normative Commitment to the Organization: An Examination of Construct Validity," *Journal of Vocational Behavior* 49 (1996): 252–76.
128. Ibid.
129. S. Alexander, "Life's Just a Bowl of Cherry Garcia for Ben & Jerry's," *Wall Street Journal*, July 15, 1992, p. B3.
130. Allen and Meyer, "Affective, Continuance, and Normative Commitment to the Organization"; J. E. Mathieu and D. M. Zajac, "A Review and Meta-Analysis of the Antecedents, Correlates, and Consequences of Organizational Commitment," *Psychological Bulletin* 108 (1990): 171–94.
131. R. Cropanzano, D. E. Rupp, and Z. S. Byrne, "The Relationship of Emotional Exhaustion to Work Attitudes, Job Performance, and Organizational Citizenship Behaviors," *Journal of Applied Psychology* 88 (1 2003): 160–69.
132. Allen and Meyer, "Affective, Continuance, and Normative Commitment to the Organization"; Mathieu and Zajac, "A Review and Meta-Analysis of the Antecedents, Correlates, and Consequences of Organizational Commitment," *Psychological Bulletin* 108 (1990): 171–94.
133. Allen and Meyer, "Affective, Continuance, and Normative Commitment to the Organization: An Examination of Construct Validity"; J. E. Mathieu and D. M. Zajac, "A Review and Meta-Analysis of the Antecedents, Correlates, and Consequences of Organizational Commitment," *Psychological Bulletin* 108 (1990): 171–94.

CHAPTER 4

1. "Hotel to Pay $8 Million in Settlement," March 22, 2000, *Houston Chronicle*, March 22, 2000, p. 3A.
2. M. France and T. Smart, "The Ugly Talk on the Texaco Tape," *Business Week*, (November 18, 1996): 58; J. S. Lublin, "Texaco Case Causes a Stir in Boardrooms," *Wall Street Journal*, November 22, 1996, pp. B1, B6; T. Smart, "Texaco: Lessons from a Crisis-In-Progress," *Business Week* (December 2, 1996): 44.
3. "Ford, Settling Bias Case, Will Hire More Women, Minorities," *Houston Chronicle*, February 19, 2000, p. 8C.
4. C. Salter, "A Reformer Who Means Business," *Fast Company* (April 2003): 102–11.
5. Ibid.; A. Zimmerman, "Wal-Mart Appeals Bias-Suit Ruling," *Wall Street Journal*, August 8, 2005: B5; C. H. Deutsch, "Chief of Unit Files Lawsuit Accusing G. E. of Racial Bias," *The New York Times*, May 18, 2005: C3.
6. C. Daniels, "GM Tried: How to Love a Bad Report Card," *Fortune* (July 10, 2000): 189.
7. A. Zimmerman, "Wal-Mart Appeals Bias-Suit Ruling," *Wall Street Journal*, August 8, 2005: B5; C. H. Deutsch, "Chief of Unit Files Lawsuit Accusing G.E. of Racial Bias," *The New York Times*, May 18, 2005: C3.
8. J. C. Peoples, "Diversity Practices That Work: The American Worker Speaks," The National Urban League www.nul.org.
9. Ibid.; A. Fisher, "How You Can Do Better On Diversity," *Fortune* (November 15, 2004): 60.

10. A. Fisher, "How You Can Do Better On Diversity," *Fortune* (November 15, 2004): 60.
11. J. C. Peoples, "Diversity Practices That Work: The American Worker Speaks," The National Urban League www.nul.org; A. Fisher, "How You Can Do Better On Diversity," *Fortune* (November 15, 2004): 60.
12. W. B. Swann, Jr., J. T. Polzer, D. C. Seyle, and S. J. Ko, "Finding Value in Diversity: Verification of Personal and Social Self-Views in Diverse Groups," *Academy of Management Review* 29 (1), (2004): 9–27.
13. J. Pfeffer, "Recruiting for the Global Talent War," *Business 2.0* (August 2005): 56.
14. Ibid.
15. S. T. Fiske and S. E. Taylor, Social Cognition (Reading, MA: Addison-Wesley, 1984).
16. J. S. Bruner, "Going Beyond the Information Given," In H. Gruber, G. Terrell, and M. Wertheimer (Eds.), Contemporary Approaches to Cognition (Cambridge, MA: Harvard University Press, 1957); Fiske and Taylor, Social Cognition; G. R. Jones, R. Kosnik, and J. M. George, "Internalization and the Firm's Growth Path: On the Psychology of Organizational Contracting," In R. W. Woodman and W. A. Pasmore (Eds.), Research in Organizational Change and Development (Greenwich, CT: JAI Press, 1993): 105–35.
17. Fiske and Taylor, Social Cognition.
18. A. B. Fisher, "When Will Women Get to the Top?" Fortune (September 21, 1992): 44–56; S. Hamm, "Why Women Are So Invisible," *Business Week* (August 25, 1997): 136.
19. D. J. Schneider, "Social Cognition," *Annual Review of Psychology* 42 (1991): 527–61.
20. Fiske and Taylor, Social Cognition.
21. K. D. Elsbach, "How to Pitch a Brilliant Idea," *Harvard Business Review* (September 2003): 117–23.
22. "Security Ordeal for Qantas Boss," CNN.com (January 10, 2006).
23. Ibid.
24. N. Alster, "When Gray Heads Roll. Is Age Bias at Work?" *The New York Times* (January 30, 2005): BU3.
25. R. King, "If Looks Could Kill," Business 2.0 (December 2001): 24–26; J. Simons, "Living in America," *Fortune* 7 (January 2002): 92–94; M. Conlin, "Taking Precautions—Or Harassing Workers?" *Business Week* 3 (December 2001): 84; A. Salkever, "The INS Hurts Uncle Sam Most of All: By Detaining Hundreds of the Foreign Muslims It Lured into West Coast Offices, the Agency Succeeded Only Harming U.S. Security," *Business Week* Online (January 23, 2003).
26. D. C. McClelland and J. W. Atkinson, "The Projective Expression of Needs: The Effect of Different Intensities of the Hunger Drive on Perception," *Journal of Psychology* 25 (1948): 205–22.
27. Ibid.
28. Ibid.
29. Ibid.
30. Ibid.
31. Ibid.
32. M. Freudenheim, "Help Wanted: Older Workers Please Apply," *The New York Times*, March 23, 2005: A1.
33. Ibid.
34. L. Corghan, "Don't Let 'Rampant' Age Bias Bring You Down in Job Hung," *The Houston Chronicle* (August 29, 2005): D1.
35. C. J. Thoresen, S. A. Kaplan, A. P. Barsky, and K. de Chermont, "The Affective Underpinnings of Job Perception and Attitudes: A Meta-Analytic Review and Integration," *Psychological Bulletin* 129 (6): 914–45.
36. J. M. George and A. P. Brief, "Feeling Good-Doing Good: A Conceptual Analysis of the Mood at Work-Organizational Spontaneity Relationship," *Psychological Bulletin* 112 (1992): 310–29; A. M. Isen and R. A. Baron, "Positive Affect as a Factor in Organizational Behavior," In B. M. Staw and L. L. Cummings (Eds.), *Research in Organizational Behavior* 13 (Greenwich, CT: JAI Press, 1991), 1–54.
37. J. Merritt, "Wanted: A Campus That Looks Like America," *Business Week* 11 (March 2002): 56–58.
38. R. Leery and R. M. Kowalski, "Impression Management: A Literature Review and Two-Component Model," *Psychological Bulletin* 107 (1990): 34–47.
39. Ibid.
40. C. N. Alexander Jr. and G. W. Knight, "Situated Identities and Social Psychological Experimentation," Sociometry 34 (1971): 65–82; Fiske and Taylor, Social Cognition; K. J. Gergen and M. G. Taylor, "Social Expectancy and Self–Presentation in a Status Hierarchy," *Journal of Experimental Social Psychology* 5 (1969): 79–92.
41. C. Stephenson, "Business Etiquette's More Than Minding Peas, Queues," *The Bryan-College Station Eagle*, February 8, 1993, pp. A1, A3.
42. Leery and Kowalski, "Impression Management."
43. Fiske and Taylor, Social Cognition.
44. Ibid.; R. M. Kanter, Men and Women of the Corporation (New York: Basic Books, 1977).
45. P. R. Sackett, C. M. Hardison, and M. J. Cullen, "On Interpreting Stereotype Threat as Accounting for African American-White Differences on Cognitive Tests," American Psychologist 59(1), (January 2004): 7–13; P. R. Sackett, C. M. Hardison, and M. J. Cullen, "On the Value of Correcting Mischaracterizations of Stereotype Threat Research," *American Psychologist* 59 (1 1995): 47–48.
46. C. M. Steele and J. A. Aronson, "Stereotype Threat Does Not Live by Steele and Aronson (1995) Alone," *American Psychologist* 59 (1), (January 2004): 47–48; J. Aronson, M. Lustina, C. Good, K. Keough, C. M. Steele, and J. Brown, "When White Men Can't Do Math: Necessary and Sufficient Factors in Stereotype Threat," *Journal of Experimental Social Psychology* 35 (1999): 29–46; Sackett, Hardison, and Cullen, "On Interpreting Stereotype Threat as Accounting for African American-White Differences on Cognitive Tests"; C. M. Steele and J. Aronson, "Stereotype Threat and the Intellectual Test Performance of African Americans," *Journal of Personality and Social Psychology* 69 (1995): 797–811.
47. Sackett, Hardison, and Cullen, "On Interpreting Sterotype Threat as Accounting for African American-White Differences on Cognitive Tests"; Sackett, Hardison, and Cullen, "On the Value of Correcting Mischaracterizations of Stereotype Threat Research."
48. Steele and Aronson, "Stereotype Threat Does Not Live by Steele and Aronson (1995) Alone"; Aronson, Lustina, Good, Keough, Steele, and Brown, "When

White Men Can't Do Math"; Sackett, Hardison, and Cullen, "On Interpreting Stereotype Threat as Accounting for African American-White Differences on Cognitive Tests"; Steele and Aronson, "Stereotype Threat and the Intellectual Test Performance of African Americans."

49. S. H. Mehta, "America's 50 Best Companies for Minorities: What Minority Employees Really Want," *Fortune* (July 10, 2000): 181–86.
50. Ibid.
51. Ibid.
52. "Chartbook on Work and Disability," Access to Disability Data (April 6, 2006), http://www.infouse.com/disabilitydata/workdisability/1_1.php; L. Myers, "Gap Widens Between Working-Age People With and Without Disabilities in the Workforce, Reports Shows," *ChronicleOnline* (October 5, 2005), http://www.news. cornell.edu/stories/Oct05/Disab .work.rpt.html; "Rehabilitation Research and Training Center on Disability Demographics and Statistics (StatsRRTC): 2004 Disability Status Reports United States," Cornell University www.DisabilityStatistics.org.
53. M. Conlin, "The New Workforce," *Business Week* (March 20, 2000): 64–68.
54. "Chartbook on Work and Disability," Access to Disability Data (April 6, 2006), http://www.infouse.com/disabilitydata/workdisability/1_1.php; L. Myers, "Gap Widens Between Working-Age People With and Without Disabilities in the Workforce, Reports Shows," *ChronicleOnline* (October 5, 2005), http://www.news. cornell.edu/stories/Oct05/Disab.work.rpt.html; "Rehabilitation Research and Training Center on Disability Demographics and Statistics (StatsRRTC): 2004 Disability Status Reports United States," Cornell University www.DisabilityStatistics.org; A. Stein Wellner, "The Disability Advantage," *Inc. Magazine* (October 2005): 29–31.
55. J. Williams, "A Kind Act Indeed," *Business Week* (March 20, 2000): 74.
56. A. Stein Wellner, "The Disability Advantage," *Inc. Magazine* (October 2005): 29–31.
57. "Habitat International: Our Products," (April 6, 2006), http:www.habitatint.com/products.htm; "Habitat International Home Page," (April 6, 2006), http://www.habitatint.com.
58. A. Stein Wellner, "The Disability Advantage," *Inc. Magazine* (October 2005): 29–31.
59. "Habitat International: Our People," (April 6, 2006), http://www.habitatint.com/people/htm.
60. A. Stein Wellner, "The Disability Advantage," *Inc. Magazine* (October 2005): 29–31.
61. Ibid.
62. Ibid.
63. Ibid.
64. E. Bonabeau, "Don't Trust Your Gut," *Harvard Business Review* (May 2003): 116–23.
65. S. A. Fisicaro, "A Reexamination of the Relation Between Halo Errors and Accuracy," *Journal of Applied Psychology* 73 (1988): 239–44.
66. E. D. Pulakos and K. N. Wexley, "The Relationship Among Perceptual Similarity, Sex, and Performance Ratings in Manager-Subordinate Dyads," *Academy of Management Journal* 26 (1983): 129–39.
67. A. B. Fisher, "When Will Women Get to the Top?"; L. Himelstein and S. A. Forest, "Breaking Through," *Business Week* (February 17, 1997): 64–70; S. Hamm, "Why Women Are So Invisible."
68. E. S. Browning, "Computer Chip Project Brings Rivals Together, but Cultures Clash," *Wall Street Journal*, May 3, 1994, pp. A1, A8.
69. R. K. Merton, Social Theory and Social Structure (New York: Free Press, 1957).
70. R. Rosenthal and L. F. Jacobson, Pygmalion in the Classroom (New York: Holt, Rinehart and Winston, 1968).
71. C. O. Wood, M. P. Zanna, and J. Cooper, "The Nonverbal Mediation of Self-Fulfilling Prophecies in Interracial Interaction," *Journal of Experimental Social Psychology* 10 (1974): 109–20.
72. R. Galford and A. Seibold Drapeau, "The Enemies of Trust," *Harvard Business Review* (February 2003): 889–95.
73. F. Heider, The Psychology of Interpersonal Relations (New York: Wiley, 1958); L. Ross, "The Intuitive Psychologist and His Shortcomings: Distortions in the Attribution Process," In L. Berkowitz (Ed.), *Advances in Experimental Social Psychology* 10 (New York: Academic Press, 1977).
74. E. E. Jones and R. E. Nisbett, "The Actor and the Observer: Divergent Perceptions of the Causes of Behavior," In E. E. Jones, D. E. Kanouse and H. H. Kelley et al. (Eds.), Attribution: Perceiving the Causes of Behavior (Morristown, NJ: General Learning Press, 1972).
75. J. A. Knight and R. R. Vallacher, "Interpersonal Engagement in Social Perception: The Consequence of Getting into the Action," *Journal of Personality and Social Psychology* 40 (1981): 990–99; M. Zuckerman, "Attribution of Success and Failure Revisited, or: The Motivational Bias Is Alive and Well in Attribution Theory," *Journal of Personality* 47 (1979): 245–87.
76. D. T. Miller and M. Ross, "Self-Serving Biases in Attribution of Causality: Fact or Fiction?" *Psychological Bulletin* 82 (1975): 213–25.
77. Fiske and Taylor, Social Cognition.
78. J. M. Burger, "Motivational Biases in the Attribution of Responsibility for an Accident: A Meta-Analysis of the Defensive-Attribution Hypothesis," *Psychological Bulletin* 90 (1981): 496–512; Fiske and Taylor, Social Cognition.
79. J. A. Hall and S. E. Taylor, "When Love Is Blind: Maintaining Idealized Images of One's Spouse," *Human Relations* 29 (1976): 751–61.
80. E. R. Robinson and J. Hickman, "The Diversity Elite," *Fortune* (July 19, 1999): 62–70; C. Y. Chen and J. Hickman, "America's 50 Best Companies for Minorities," *Fortune* (July 10, 2000): 190–200; J. Hickman, "America's 50 Best Companies for Minorites," *Fortune* (July 8, 2002): 110–20.
81. Hickman, "America's 50 Best Companies for Minorites."
82. Robinson and Hickman, "The Diversity Elite"; Chen and Hickman, "America's 50 Best Companies for Minorities."
83. J. Dreyfuss, "Valley of Denial," *Fortune* (July 19, 1999): 60–61.
84. E. Robinson, "Father Figure at the Front Door," *Fortune* (July 19, 1999): 66.
85. K. Hynes, "PwC's Toni Riccardi: Her Seat at the Table Makes Others Accountable," *DiversityInc* (March/April 2003)" 65–70.

86. "Pricewaterhouse Coopers 2004 Press Releases—Chief Diversity Officer," (April 6. 2006), http://www.pwc-global.com.
87. Y. Cole, "Corporate Recruitment Matters: How to Attract Top Candidates of Color," *DiversityInc* (November/December 2002): 53–56.
88. Y. Cole, "The Diversity Director: An Evolving Position with a Hand in All Business Aspects," *DiversityInc* (March/April 2003): 72.
89. Hynes, "PwC's Toni Riccardi."
90. S. Gelston, "The '90s Work Force Faces Diverse Challenges," Boston Herald, January 25, 1994, p. N18.
91. M. Lee, "Diversity Training Brings Unity to Small Companies," Wall Street Journal, September 2, 1993, p. B2.
92. Y. Cole, "Learning from the Winners," *DiversityInc* (November/December 2002): 12–27.
93. E. L. Hinton, "When Words Go Too Far: How to Handle Offensive Talk at the Office," *DiversityInc* (November/December 2002): 58–59.
94. Ibid.
95. Rutkowski and Associates, Employment Law Update, September 1991, 1–12.
96. E. Klee, L. Hayes, and G. W. Childress, "A Kentucky Response to the ADA," *Training & Development* (April 1994): 48–49.
97. "Racial Differences Discourage Mentors," *Wall Street Journal*, October 29, 1991, p. B1.
98. C. Comeau-Kirschner, "Navigating the Roadblocks," *Management Review* 88 (5 May 1999): 8.
99. D. Leonhardt, "The Saga of Maytag's Lloyd Ward," *Business Week* (August 9, 1999): Business Week Archives.
100. D. Foust, "Will Coke Go Better with Carl Ware?" *Business Week* (January 24, 2000): Business Week Archives.
101. A. T. Palmer, M. McBride, D. Rocks, and L. Woellert, "Poverty in America: Finally There's Some Good News," *Business Week* (October 18, 1999): Business Week Archives.
102. "A Mentor for the Asking: Bernadette Williams Wants to Provide Minority Women with Experienced Guides to the Tech Biz," *Business Week* (December 6, 1999): Business Week Archives.
103. S. Wellington, M. Brumit Kropf, and P. R. Gerkovich, "What's Holding Women Back?" *Harvard Business Review* (June 2003): 18–19.
104. Y. Cole, "The Truth About Mentoring, Especially Between Races: Supportive Relationships Add Real Value," DiversityInc (November/December 2002): 44–46.
105. Y. Cole, "Learning from the Winners," *DiversityInc* (November/December 2002): 12–27.
106. S. M. Shafer, "Sexual Harassment Exists at All Levels, Army Says," *The Bryan-College Station Eagle*, September 12, 1997, p. A4.
107. "2 Academies Faulted on Treatments of Women," *The New York Times* (August 26, 2005): A11.
108. "Chevron Settles Claims of 4 Women at Unit as Part of Sex Bias Suit," *Wall Street Journal*, January 22, 1995, p. B12; J. Muller, "Ford: The High Cost of Harassment," *Business Week* (November 15, 1999): 94–96.
109. R. L. Paetzold and A. M. O'Leary-Kelly, "Organizational Communication and the Legal Dimensions of Hostile Work Environment Sexual Harassment," In G. L. Kreps (Ed.), Sexual Harassment: Communication Implications (Cresskill, NJ: Hampton Press, 1993).
110. A. M. O'Leary-Kelly, R. L. Paetzold, and R. W. Griffin, "Sexual Harassment as Aggressive Action: A Framework for Understanding Sexual Harassment," paper presented at the annual meeting of the Academy of Management, Vancouver, Canada, August 1995.
111. "Chevron Settles Claims of 4 Women at Unit as Part of Sex Bias Suit."
112. J. Muller, "Ford: The High Cost of Harassment," *Business Week* (November 15, 1999): 94–96.
113. S. Olafson, "Dow Fires Workers for E-Mail Abuse," *Houston Chronicle*, August 22, 2000, p. 13A; A. Carrns, "Bawdy E-Mails Were Funny Till Times' Parent Fired 22," *Houston Chronicle*, February 6, 2000, p. 3D.; M. Conlin, "Workers, Surf at Your Own Risk," *Business Week* (June 12, 2000): 105–6.
114. "What Productivity Revolution?" *Business Week* (June 12, 2000): 106.
115. R. Ilies, N. Hauserman, S. Schwochau, and J. Stibal, "Reported Incidence Rates of Work-Related Sexual Harassment in the United States: Using Meta-Analysis to Explain Reported Rate Disparities," *Personnel Psychology* 56 (2003): 607–31.
116. T. M. Glomb, L. J. Munson, C. L. Hulin, M. E. Bergman, and F. Drasgow, "Structural Equation Models of Sexual Harassment: Longitudinal Explorations and Cross-Sectional Generalizations," *Journal of Applied Psychology* 84 (1999): 14–28.
117. K. T. Schneider, S. Swan, and L. F. Fitzgerald, "Job-Related and Psychological Effects of Sexual Harassment in the Workplace: Empirical Evidence from Two Organizations," *Journal of Applied Psychology* 82 (1997): 401–15.
118. T. M. Glomb, W. L. Richman, C. L. Hulin, et al., "Ambient Sexual Harassment: An Integrated Model of Antecedents and Consequences," *Organizational Behavior and Human Decision Processes* 71 (September 1997): 309–28.
119. E. Jensen and J. Lippman, "NBC's Problem: Gifted Executive Who Drank," *Wall Street Journal*, December 13, 1996, pp. B1, B19.
120. S. J. Bresler and R. Thacker, "Four-Point Plan Helps Solve Harassment Problems," *HR Magazine* (May 1993): 117–24.
121. "Du Pont's Solution," Training (March 1992): 29; Jensen and Lippman, "NBC's Problem," *Wall Street Journal*, December 13, 1996, pp. B1, B19; J. S. Lublin, "Sexual Harassment Moves Up Agenda in Many Executive Education Programs," *Wall Street Journal*, December 2, 1991, pp. B1, B4; "Navy Is Teaching Sailors What Proper Conduct Is," *The Bryan-College Station Eagle*, April 19, 1993, p. A2.
122. "Training New Workers to Avoid Sexual Harassment Is a Summer Priority," *Wall Street Journal*, June 29, 1999, p. A1.
123. Ibid.

CHAPTER 5

1. B. Nussbaum, "How to Build Innovative Companies," *BussinessWeek* (August 1, 2005): 61–68.
2. Ibid.
3. Ibid.
4. Ibid; L. Tischler, "Join the Circus," *Fast Company* (July 2005): 52–58.

5. B. Nussbaum, "How to Build Innovative Companies," *BussinessWeek* (August 1, 2005): 61–68.
6. J. Weber, " 'Mosh Pits' Of Creativity," *BusinessWeek* (November 7, 2005): 98–100.
7. Ibid.
8. B. Nussbaum, "How to Build Innovative Companies," *BussinessWeek* (August 1, 2005): 61–68.
9. Ibid.
10. Ibid; L. Tischler, "Join the Circus," *Fast Company* (July 2005): 52–58; J. Weber, " 'Mosh Pits' Of Creativity," *BusinessWeek* (November 7, 2005): 98–100.
11. W. C. Hamner, "Reinforcement Theory and Contingency Management in Organizational Settings." In H. Tosi and W. C. Hamner (Eds.), *Organizational Behavior and Management: A Contingency Approach* (Chicago: St. Clair Press, 1974).
12. B. F. Skinner, *Contingencies of Reinforcement* (New York: Appleton-Century-Crofts, 1969).
13. F. Luthans and R. Kreitner, *Organizational Behavior Modification and Beyond* (Glenview, IL: Scott, Foresman, 1985).
14. J. L. Komaki, "Applied Behavior Analysis and Organizational Behavior: Reciprocal Influence of the Two Fields." In B. M. Staw and L. L. Cummings (Eds.), *Research in Organizational Behavior*, vol. 8 (Greenwich, CT: JAI Press, 1986), 297–334.
15. H. M. Weiss, "Learning Theory and Industrial and Organizational Psychology." In M. D. Dunnette and L. M. Hough (Eds.), *Handbook of Industrial and Organizational Psychology,* 2nd ed., vol. 1 (Palo Alto, CA: Consulting Psychologists Press, 1990), 171–221.
16. S. Overman, "When It Comes to Managing Diversity, a Few Companies Are Linking Pay to Performance," *HRMagazine* (December 1992): 38–40.
17. J. D. Shaw, M. K. Duffy, A. Mitra, D. E. Lockhart, and M. Bowler, "Reactions to Merit Pay Increases: A Longitudinal Test of Signal Sensitivity Perspective," *Journal of Applied Psychology* 88(3 2003): 538–44.
18. Weiss, "Learning Theory and Industrial and Organizational Psychology."
19. "Working at Lincoln," (December 15, 2003), www.lincolnelectric.com/corporate/career/default.asp; "About Lincoln," (December 15, 2003), www.lincolnelectric.com/corporate/about/about.asp; "Our History—A Century of Excellence, A Future of Innovation," (December 15, 2003), www.lincolnelectric .com/corporate/about/history.asp; "Lincoln Electric Vision and Missions," (December 15, 2004), www.lincolnelectric .com/corporate/about/ visions.asp.
20. J. P. Houston, *Fundamentals of Learning and Memory*, 3rd ed. (New York: Harcourt Brace Jovanovich, 1986); Weiss, "Learning Theory and Industrial and Organizational Psychology."
21. R. D. Arvey and J. M. Ivancevich, "Punishment in Organizations: A Review, Propositions, and Research Suggestions," *Academy of Management Review* 5 (1980): 123–32.
22. A. D. Stajkovic and F. Luthans, "Behavioral Management and Task Performance in Organizations: Conceptual Background, Meta-Analysis, and Test of Alternative Models," *Personnel Psychology* 56 (2003): 155–94.
23. Luthans and Kreitner, *Organizational Behavior Modification and Beyond*; F. Luthans and A. D. Stajkovic, "Reinforce for Performance: The Need to Go Beyond Pay and Even Rewards," *Academy of Management Executive* 13(2 1999): 49–56.
24. Luthans and Stajkovic, "Reinforce for Performance."
25. Stajkovic and Luthans, "Behavioral Management and Task Performance in Organizations"; Luthans and Stajkovic, "Reinforce for Performance"; G. Billikopf Encina and M. V. Norton, "Pay Method Affects Vineyard Pruner Performance," www.cnr.berkeley.edu/ucce50/ag-labor/7research/7calag05.htm.
26. A. D. Stajkovic and F. Luthans, "A Meta-Analysis of the Effects of Organizational Behavior Modification on Task Performance, 1975–95," *Academy of Management Journal* 40(5 1997): 1122–49.
27. A. D. Stajkovic and F. Luthans, "Differential Effects of Incentive Motivators on Work Performance," *Academy of Management Journal* 4(3 2001): 580–90.
28. Ibid.
29. "In California Garment: Workers Have Rights," (October 2002), www.dir.ca.gov, www.workitout.ca.gov.
30. A. Bandura, *Social Learning Theory* (Upper Saddle River, NJ: Prentice Hall, 1977); A. Bandura, *Self-Efficacy: The Exercise of Control*, (New York: W. H. Freeman and Co., 1997).
31. Bandura, *Social Learning Theory* (Upper Saddle River, NJ: Prentice Hall, 1977); Bandura, *Self-Efficacy: The Exercise of Control*, (New York: W. H. Freeman and Co., 1997).
32. Bandura, *Social Learning Theory*; T. R. V. Davis and F. Luthans, *Organizational Behavior Modification and Beyond.* Glenview, IL: Scott Foresman, 1985.
33. "Fact Sheet," The Ritz-Carlton (July 28, 2003), www. ritzcarlton.com/corporate/about_us/fact_sheet.asp; "The Ritz Carlton: Fact Sheet," April 12, 2006), http://www. ritzcarlton.com/corporate/about_us/fact_sheet.asp; "Puttin' On The Glitz In Miami," *BusinessWeek Online* (April 12, 2006), http://www. businessweek.com/print/ magazine/content/ 04_08/c3871141.htm?chan=mz.
34. In T. Gutner, "Dividends," *Business Week Online* (July 28, 2003). No
35. "Gold Standards," The Ritz-Carlton (July 28, 2003), www.ritzcarlton.com/corporate/about_us/fact_sheet.asp.
36. Ibid.
37. P. Hemp, "My Week as a Room-Service Waiter at the Ritz," *Harvard Business Review* (June 2002): 50–62.
38. Ibid.
39. "Fact Sheet"; "Press Release: The Ritz-Carlton Company Repeats as Most Prestigious Luxury Hotel Brand in 2006 Survey of the Luxury Institute," *The Ritz-Carlton Press Room* (April 12, 2006), http://www.ritzcarlton.com/ corporate/press_room/releases/luxury_institute_06.html.
40. J. Zhou, "When the Presence of Creative Coworkers Is Related to Creativity: Role of Supervisor Close Monitoring, Developmental Feedback, and Creative Personality," *Journal of Applied Psychology* 88(3 2003): 413–22.
41. A. P. Goldstein and M. Sorcher, *Changing Supervisor Behavior* (New York: Pergamon Press, 1974); Luthans and Kreitner, *Organizational Behavior Modification and Beyond*.

42. A. Bandura, "Self-Reinforcement: Theoretical and Methodological Considerations," *Behaviorism* 4 (1976): 135–55.
43. M. Moravec, K. Wheeler, and B. Hall, "Getting College Hires on Track Fast," *Personnel* (May 1989): 56–59.
44. T. J. Maurer, E. M. Weiss, and F. G Barbeite, "A Model of Involvement in Work-Related Learning and Development Activity: The Effects of Individual, Situational, Motivational and Age Variables," *Journal of Applied Psychology* 88(4 2003): 707–24.
45. M. E. Gist and T. R. Mitchell, "Self-Efficacy: A Theoretical Analysis of Its Determinants and Malleability," *Academy of Management Review* 17 (1992): 183–211.
46. A. Bandura, "Self-Efficacy Mechanism in Human Agency," *American Psychologist* 37 (1982): 122–47.
47. A. Bandura and E. A. Locke, "Negative Self-Efficacy and Goal Effects Revisited," *Journal of Applied Psychology* 88(1 2003): 87–89.
48. Bandura, "Self-Efficacy Mechanism in Human Agency."
49. D. Eden and A. B. Shani, "Pygmalion Goes to Boot Camp: Expectancy, Leadership, and Trainee Performance," *Journal of Applied Psychology* 67 (1982): 194–99.
50. Bandura, "Self-Efficacy Mechanism in Human Agency."
51. C. Rogers, "Experimental Learning," *tip.psychology.org/rovers.html*, (June 26, 2003); M. K. Smith, "David A. Kolb on Experiential Learning," www.infed.org/biblio/b-explrn.htm (June 26, 2003).
52. T. M. Amabile, "A Model of Creativity and Innovation in Organizations." In B. M. Staw and L. L. Cummings, *Research in Organizational Behavior*, vol. 10 (Greenwich, CT: JAI Press, 1988), 123–67.
53. Ibid.
54. Ibid.
55. J. L. Adams, *Conceptual Blockbusting: A Guide to Better Ideas*, 4th ed. (Cambridge, MA: Perseus Publishing, 2001).
56. P. Lewis, "A Perpetual Crisis Machine," *Fortune* (September 19, 2005): 58–71.
57. Ibid.; "Samsung's Digital World," (April 12, 2006), http://www.samsung.com/.
58. P. Lewis, "A Perpetual Crisis Machine," *Fortune* (September 19, 2005): 58–71; B. Nussbaum, "How to Build Innovative Companies," *BusinessWeek* (August 1, 2005): 61–68.
59. P. Lewis, "A Perpetual Crisis Machine," *Fortune* (September 19, 2005): 58–71.
60. B. Nussbaum, "How to Build Innovative Companies," *BusinessWeek* (August 1, 2005): 61–68.
61. P. Lewis, "A Perpetual Crisis Machine," *Fortune* (September 19, 2005): 58–71.
62. Ibid.
63. F. B. Barron and D. M. Harrington, "Creativity, Intelligence, and Personality," *Annual Review of Psychology* 32 (1981): 439–76; R. W. Woodman, J. E. Sawyer, and R. W. Griffin, "Toward a Theory of Organizational Creativity," *Academy of Management Review* 18 (1993): 293–321.
64. R. W. Woodman and L. F. Schoenfeldt, "Individual Differences in Creativity: An Interactionist Perspective." In J. A. Glover, R. R. Ronning, and C. R. Reynolds (Eds.), *Handbook of Creativity* (New York: Plenum Press, 1989), 77–92.
65. Ibid.
66. Barron and Harrington, "Creativity, Intelligence, and Personality."
67. Amabile, "A Model of Creativity and Innovation in Organizations."
68. Amabile, "A Model of Creativity and Innovation in Organizations"; Woodman, Sawyer, and Griffin, "Toward a Theory of Organizational Creativity."
69. Amabile, "A Model of Creativity and Innovation in Organizations."
70. Ibid.
71. Ibid.
72. Ibid.
73. Ibid.
74. J. M. George and J. Zhou, "When Openness to Experience and Conscientiousness Are Related to Creative Behavior: An Interactional Approach," *Journal of Applied Psychology* 86 (3 2001): 513–24.
75. J. Zhou and J. M. George, "Awakening Employee Creativity: The Role of Leader Emotional Intelligence," *The Leadership Quarterly* (July 24, 2003).
76. P. Senge, *The Fifth Discipline: The Art and Practice of the Learning Organization* (New York: Doubleday, 1990).
77. J. Goldenberg, R. Horowitz, A. Levav, and D. Mazursky, "Finding Your Innovation Sweet Spot," *Harvard Business Review* (March 2003): 120–29.
78. Senge, *The Fifth Discipline: The Art and Practice of the Learning Organization*.
79. M. J. Grawitch, D. C. Munz, E. K. Elliott, and A. Mathis, "Promoting Creativity in Temporary Problem-Solving Groups: The Effects of Positive Mood and Autonomy in Problem Definition on Idea-Generating Performance," *Group Dynamics: Theory, Research, and Practice* 7(3 2003): 200–13; M. J. Grawitch, D. C. Munz, and T. J. Kramer, "Effects of Member Mood States on Creative Performance in Temporary Workgroups," *Group Dynamics: Theory, Research, and Practice* 7(1 2003): 41–54.
80. S. E. Prokesch, "Unleashing the Power of Learning: An Interview with British Petroleum's John Browne," *Harvard Business Review* (September–October 1997): 148.
81. J. S. Brown and P. Duguid, "Balancing Act: How to Capture Knowledge Without Killing It," *Harvard Business Review* (May–June 2000): 73–80.
82. Ibid.
83. Ibid.

CHAPTER 6

1. J. Goodnight, "Welcome to SAS" (August 26, 2003): www.sas.com/corporate/index.html; "SAS Press Center: SAS Corporate Statistics,"(April 18, 2006), http://www.sas.com/bin/pfp.pl?=fi.
2. "SAS Continues Annual Revenue Growth Streak" (August 28, 2003): www.sas.com/news/ prelease/ 031003/news1.html; "SAS Press Center: SAS Corporate Statistics," (April 18, 2006), http://www.sas.com/bin/ pfp.pl?=fi.
3. "SAS Press Center: SAS Corporate Statistics," (April 18, 2006), http://www.sas.com/bin/pfp.pl?=fi.
4. "Worklife" (August 26, 2003): www.sas.com/corporate/worklife/index.html; "SAS Makes FORTUNE'S '100 Best

Companies to Work For’,” (April 18, 2006), http://www.sas.com/news/feature/12jan06/fortune.html.

5. “Saluting the Global Awards Recipients of Arthur Andersen’s Best Practices Awards 2000” (September 6, 2000): www.fortune.com; J. N. Gangemi, “Teaching the Benefits of Balance,” *BusinessWeek Online* (September 20, 2005), http://www.businessweek.com/print/bschools/content/sep2005/bs20050920_2005-bs001.h.
6. J. Pfeffer, “SAS Institute: A Different Approach to Incentives and People Management Practices in the Software Industry” (January 1998): Harvard Business School Case HR-6.
7. Ibid.
8. “Worklife” (August 26, 2003): www.sas.com/corporate/worklife/index.html.
9. Pfeffer, “SAS Institute”; N. Stein, “Winning the War to Keep Top Talent” (September 6, 2000): www.fortune.com.
10. “SAS Makes FORTUNE’S ‘100 Best Companies to Work For’,” (April 18, 2006), http://www.sas.com/news/feature/12jan06/fortune.html.
11. Goodnight, “Welcome to SAS”; “By Solution” (August 26, 2003): www.sas.com/success/solution.html.
12. S. H. Wildstrom, “Do Your Homework, Microsoft,” *BusinessWeek Online* (August 8, 2005), http:// www.businessweek.com/print/magazine/content/05-b3946033-mz006.htm?chan.
13. G. P. Latham, and M. H. Budworth, “The Study of Work Motivation in the 20th Century.” In L. L. Koppes (Eds.), *Historical Perspectives in Industrial and Organizational Psychology* (Hillsdale, NJ: Laurence Erlbaum Associates Inc., 2006).
14. F. J. Landy and W. S. Becker, “Motivation Theory Reconsidered.” In B. M. Staw and L. L. Cummings (Eds.), *Research in Organizational Behavior*, vol. 9 (Greenwich, CT: JAI Press, 1987), 1–38.
15. J. P. Campbell and R. D. Pritchard, “Motivation Theory in Industrial and Organizational Psychology.” In M. D. Dunnette (Ed.), *Handbook of Industrial and Organizational Psychology* (Chicago: Rand McNally, 1976), 63–130.
16. R. Kanfer, “Motivation Theory and Industrial and Organizational Psychology.” In M. D. Dunnette and L. M. Hough (Eds.), *Handbook of Industrial and Organizational Psychology*, vol. 1 (Palo Alto, CA: Consulting Psychologists Press, 1990), 75–170.
17. Ibid.
18. A. K. Kirk and D. F. Brown, “Latent Constructs of Proximal and Distal Motivation Predicting Performance Under Maximum Test Conditions,” *Journal of Applied Psychology* 88 (1 2003): 40–49.
19. A. P. Brief and R. J. Aldag, “The Intrinsic-Extrinsic Dichotomy: Toward Conceptual Clarity,” *Academy of Management Review* 2 (1977): 496–99.
20. C. Hymowitz, “Recruiting Top Talent in China Takes a Boss Who Likes to Coach,” *The Wall Street Journal* (April 26, 2005): B1.
21. Brief and Aldag, “The Intrinsic-Extrinsic Dichotomy.”
22. N. Nicholson, “How to Motivate Your Problem People,” *Harvard Business Review* (January 2003): 57–65.
23. L. Hales, “An Environmental Problem Slipping Through the Quacks,” *washingtonpost.com* (August 27, 2005), http://www.washingtonpost.com/wp-dyn/content/article/2005/08/26/AR2005082601888.
24. M. Conlin and P. Raeburn, “Industrial Evolution,” *Business Week* (April 8, 2002): 70–72.
25. Ibid.
26. “Masters of Design: William McDonough,” *Fastcompany.com* (April 18, 2006), http://www.fastcompany.com/magazine/83/mod_mcdonough.html; “William McDonough, FAIA,” (April 18, 2006), www.mcdonough.com.
27. “Masters of Design: William McDonough,” *Fastcompany.com* (April 18, 2006), http://www.fastcompany.com/magazine/83/mod_mcdonough.html.
28. Ibid.
29. “Designing the Future,” *MSNBC.com* (April 18, 2006), http://www.msnbc.msn.com/id/7773650/site/newsweek/?artid=1130.
30. A. H. Maslow, *Motivation and Personality* (New York: Harper & Row, 1954); C. P. Alderfer, *Existence, Relatedness, and Growth: Human Needs in Organizational Settings* (New York: Free Press, 1972).
31. Maslow, *Motivation and Personality*; J. P. Campbell and R. D. Pritchard, “Motivation Theory in Industrial and Organizational Psychology.” In M. D. Dunnette (Ed.) *Handbook of Industrial and Organizational Psychology* (Chicago: Rand McNally, 1976), 63–130.
32. V. Anderson, “Kudos for Creativity,” *Personnel Journal* (September 1991): 90–93.
33. Maslow, *Motivation and Personality*; Campbell and Pritchard, “Motivation Theory in Industrial and Organizational Psychology.”
34. C. P. Alderfer, “An Empirical Test of a New Theory of Human Needs,” *Organizational Behavior and Human Performance* 4 (1969): 142–75; Alderfer, *Existence, Relatedness, and Growth*; Campbell and Pritchard, “Motivation Theory and Industrial and Organizational Psychology.”
35. Kanfer, “Motivation Theory and Industrial and Organizational Psychology.”
36. V. H. Vroom, *Work and Motivation* (New York: Wiley, 1964).
37. Ibid.
38. Ibid.
39. Ibid.
40. Ibid.
41. Campbell and Pritchard, “Motivation Theory in Industrial and Organizational Psychology”; T. R. Mitchell, “Expectancy-Value Models in Organizational Psychology.” In N. T. Feather (Ed.), *Expectations and Actions: Expectancy-Value Models in Psychology* (Hillsdale, NJ: Erlbaum, 1982), 293–312.
42. T. J. Maurer, E. M. Weiss, and F. B. Barbeite, “A Model of Involvement in Work-Related Learning and Development Activity: The Effects of Individual, Situational, Motivational, and Age Variables,” *Journal of Applied Psychology* 88 (4 2003): 707–24.
43. N. Shope Griffin, “Personalize Your Management Development,” *Harvard Business Review* (March 2003): 113–19.
44. P. A. Galagan, “Training Keeps the Cutting Edge Sharp for the Andersen Companies,” *Training & Development* (January 1993): 30–35.
45. M. J. Stahl and A. M. Harrell, “Modeling Effort Decisions with Behavioral Decision Theory: Toward an Individual

Differences Model of Expectancy Theory," *Organizational Behavior and Human Performance* 27 (1981): 303–25.

46. Campbell and Pritchard, "Motivation Theory in Industrial and Organizational Psychology"; Kanfer, "Motivational Theory and Industrial and Organizational Psychology."
47. J. S. Adams, "Toward an Understanding of Inequity," *Journal of Abnormal and Social Psychology*, 67: 422–36.
48. Ibid.
49. Ibid.
50. Ibid.
51. Ibid.
52. R. Cropanzano, B. Goldman, and R. Folger, "Deontic Justice: The Role of Moral Principles in Workplace Fairness," *Journal of Organizational Behavior* 24 (2003): 1019–24.
53. J. Greenberg, "Approaching Equity and Avoiding Inequity in Groups and Organizations." In J. Greenberg and R. L. Cohen (Eds.), *Equity and Justice in Social Behavior* (New York: Academic Press, 1982), 389–435; J. Greenberg, "Equity and Workplace Status: A Field Experiment," *Journal of Applied Psychology* 73 (1988): 606–13; R. T. Mowday, "Equity Theory Predictions of Behavior in Organizations." In R. M. Steers and L. W. Porter (Eds.), *Motivation and Work Behavior* (New York: McGraw-Hill, 1987), 89–110.
54. J. A. Colquitt, J. Greenbery, and C. P. Zapata-Phelan, "What is Organizational Justice? A Historical Overview." In J. Greenberg and J. A. Colquitt (Eds.), *Handbook of Organizational Justice* (Mahwah, NJ: Erlbaum, 2005), 12–45; J. Greenberg, "A Taxonomy of Organizational Justice Theories," *Academy of Management Review* 12 (1987): 9–22.
55. Y. R. Chen, J. Brockner, and J. Greenberg, "When Is It 'A Pleasure to Do Business with You?' The Effects of Relative Status, Outcome Favorability, and Procedural Fairness," *Organizational Behavior and Human Decision Processes* 92 (2003): 1–21; J. A. Colquitt, J. Greenbery, and C. P. Zapata-Phelan, "What is Organizational Justice? A Historical Overview." In J. Greenberg and J. A. Colquitt (Eds.), *Handbook of Organizational Justice* (Mahwah, NJ: Erlbaum, 2005), 12–45; J. A. Colquitt, "On the Dimensionality of Organizational Justice: A Construct Validation of a Measure," *Journal of Applied Psychology* 86(3 2001): 386–400; J. A. Colquitt, D. E. Conlon, M. J. Wesson, C. O. L. H. Porter, and K. Yee Ng, "Justice at the Millennium: A Meta-Analytic Review of 25 Years of Organizational Justice Research," *Journal of Applied Psychology* 86(3 2001): 425–45; J. A. Colquitt and J. C. Shaw, "How Should Organizational Justice Be Measured?" In J. Greenberg and J. A. Colquitt (Eds.) *Handbook of Organizational Justice* (Mahwah, NJ: Erlbaum, 2005): 115–41; R. J. Bies, "Are Procedural Justice and Interactional Justice Conceptually Distinct?" In J. Greenberg and J. A. Colquitt (Eds.) *Handbook of Organizational Justice* (Mahwah, NJ: Erlbaum, 2005): 88–106; M. L. Ambrose and A. Arnaud, "Are Procedural Justice and Distributive Justice Conceptually Distinct?" In J. Greenberg and J. A. Colquitt (Eds.) *Handbook of Organizational Justice* (Mahwah, NJ: Erlbaum, 2005): 60–78.
56. L. J. Skitka and F. J. Crosby, "Trends in the Social Psychological Study of Justice," *Personality and Social Psychology Review* 7 (4 2003): 282–85.
57. J. A. Colquitt, J. Greenbery, and C. P. Zapata-Phelan, "What is Organizational Justice? A Historical Overview." In J. Greenberg and J. A. Colquitt (Eds.), *Handbook of Organizational Justice* (Mahwah, NJ: Erlbaum, 2005), 12–45; J. A. Colquitt, "On the Dimensionality of Organizational Justice: A Construct Validation of a Measure," *Journal of Applied Psychology* 86(3 2001): 386–400.
58. R. Folger and M. A. Konovsky, "Effects of Procedural and Distributive Justice on Reactions to Pay Raise Decisions," *Academy of Management Journal* 32 (1989): 115–30; J. Greenberg, "Organizational Justice: Yesterday, Today, and Tomorrow," *Journal of Management* 16 (1990): 399–432; M. L. Ambrose and A. Arnaud, "Are Procedural Justice and Distributive Justice Conceptually Distinct?" In J. Greenberg and J. A. Colquitt (Eds.) *Handbook of Organizational Justice* (Mahwah, NJ: Erlbaum, 2005): 60–78.
59. E. E. Umphress, G. Labianca, D. J. Brass, E. Kass, and L. Scholten, "The Role of Instrumental and Expressive Social Ties in Employees' Perceptions of Organizational Justice," *Organization Science* 14 (6 November–December 2003): 738–53.
60. M. L. Ambrose and M. Schminke, "Organization Structure as a Moderator of the Relationship Between Procedural Justice, Interactional Justice, Perceived Organizational Support, and Supervisory Trust," *Journal of Applied Psychology* 88 (2 2003): 295–305.
61. J. A. Colquitt, "On the Dimensionality of Organizational Justice: A Construct Validation of a Measure," *Journal of Applied Psychology* 86(3 2001): 386–400; J. A. Colquitt and J. C. Shaw, "How Should Organizational Justice Be Measured?" In J. Greenberg and J. A. Colquitt (Eds.) *Handbook of Oraganizational Justice* (Mahwah, NJ: Erlbaum, 2005): 115–41.
62. J. A. Colquitt, "On the Dimensionality of Organizational Justice: A Construct Validation of a Measure," *Journal of Applied Psychology* 86(3 2001): 386–400; J. A. Colquitt and J. C. Shaw, "How Should Organizational Justice Be Measured?" In J. Greenberg and J. A. Colquitt (Eds.) *Handbook of Oraganizational Justice* (Mahwah, NJ: Erlbaum, 2005): 115–41.
63. Ibid.
64. J. A. Colquitt, "On the Dimensionality of Organizational Justice: A Construct Validation of a Measure," *Journal of Applied Psychology* 86(3 2001): 386–400.
65. Greenberg, "Organizational Justice: Yesterday, Today, and Tomorrow"; E. A. Lind and T. Tyler, *The Social Psychology of Procedural Justice* (New York: Plenum, 1988).
66. J. A. Colquitt, "On the Dimensionality of Organizational Justice: A Construct Validation of a Measure," *Journal of Applied Psychology* 86(3 2001): 386–400; R. J. Bies, "Are Procedural Justice and Interactional Justice Conceptually Distinct?" In J. Grenberg and J. A. Colquitt (Eds.) *Handbook of Organizational Justice* (Mahwah, NJ: Erlbaum, 2005): 88–106.
67. R. J. Bies, "The Predicament of Injustice: The Management of Moral Outrage." In L. L. Cummings and B. M. Staw (Eds.), *Research in Organizational Behavior*, vol. 9 (Greenwich, CT: JAI Press, 1987), 289–319; R. J. Bies and D. L. Shapiro, "Interactional Fairness Judgments: The

Influence of Causal Accounts," *Social Justice Research* 1 (1987): 199–218; J. Greenberg, "Looking Fair vs. Being Fair: Managing Impressions of Organizational Justice." In B. M. Staw and L. L. Cummings (Eds.), *Research in Organizational Behavior*, vol. 12 (Greenwich, CT: JAI Press, 1990), 111–57; T. R. Tyler and R. J. Bies, "Beyond Formal Procedures: The Interpersonal Context of Procedural Justice." In J. Carroll (Ed.), *Advances in Applied Social Psychology: Business Settings* (Hillsdale, NJ: Erlbaum, 1989), 77–98; J. A. Colquitt, "On the Dimensionality of Organizational Justice: A Construct Validation of a Measure," *Journal of Applied Psychology* 86(3 2001): 386–400.

68. J. A. Colquitt, "On the Dimensionality of Organizational Justice: A Construct Validation of a Measure," *Journal of Applied Psychology* 86(3 2001): 386–400; J. A. Colquitt and J. C. Shaw, "How Should Organizational Justice Be Measured?" In J. Greenberg and J. A. Colquitt (Eds.) *Handbook of Oraganizational Justice* (Mahwah, NJ: Erlbaum, 2005): 115–41.
69. J. A. Colquitt, D. E. Conlon, M. J. Wesson, C. O. L. H. Porter, and K. Yee Ng, "Justice at the Millennium: A Meta-Analytic Review of 25 Years of Organizational Justice Research," *Journal of Applied Psychology* 86(3 2001): 425–55; J. A. Colquitt, J. Greenbery, and C. P. Zapata-Phelan, "What is Organizational Justice? A Historical Overview." In J. Greenberg and J. A. Colquitt (Eds.), *Handbook of Organizational Justice* (Mahwah, NJ: Erlbaum, 2005), 12–45; D. E. Conlon, C. J. Meyer, and J. M. Nowakowski, "How Does Organizational Justice Affect Performance, Withdrawal, and Counterproductive Behavior?" In J. Greenberg and J. A. Colquitt (Eds.) *Handbook of Organizational Justice* (Mahwah, NJ: Erlbaum, 2005): 303–22; R. H. Moorman and Z. B. Byrne, "How does Organizational Justice Affect Organizational Citizenship Behavior?" In J. Greenberg and J. A. Colquitt (Eds.), *Handbook of Organizational Justice* (Mahwah, NJ: Erlbaum, 2005): 357–75.
70. B. Morris, "The Best Place to Work Now," *Fortune* (January 23, 2006): 78–86; "Genentech: A Biotech Research and Information Company: About Us," (April 18, 2006), http://www.gene.com/gene/about/index.jsp?hl=en&q-Genetech&btnG=Google+Search; "Genentech: About Us – Awards & Recognition," (April 18, 2006), http://www. gene.com/gene/about/corporate/awards/index.jsp.
71. "Genentach: Newsroom—Corporate Information—Genentech Fast Facts," (April 18, 2006), http://www.gene.com/gene/news/kits/corporate/fastFacts.jsp; A. Weintraub, "No Apologies for Genentech's Prices," *BusinessWeek Online* (March 21, 2006), http://www.businessweek.com/print/technology/content/mar2006/tc20060321_073434.htm.
72. B. Morris, "The Best Place to Work Now," *Fortune* (January 23, 2006): 78–86.
73. Ibid.
74. Ibid.
75. J. Greenberg, "Reactions to Procedural Injustice in Payment Distributions: Do the Means Justify the Ends?" *Journal of Applied Psychology* 72 (1987): 55–61.
76. J. A. Colquitt, D. E. Conlon, M. J. Wesson, C. O. L. H. Porter, and K. Yee Ng, "Justice at the Millennium: A Meta-Analytic Review of 25 Years of Organizational Justice Research," *Journal of Applied Psychology* 86(3 2001): 425–45; D. E. Conlon, C. J. Meyer, and J. M. Nowakowski, "How Does Organizational Justice Affect Performance, Withdrawal, and Counterproductive Behavior?" In J. Greenberg and J. A. Colquitt, *Handbook of Organizational Justice* (Mahwah, NJ: Erlbaum, 2005): 303–22; J. A. Colquitt, J. Greenbery, and C. P. Zapata-Phelan, "What is Organizational Justice? A Historical Overview." In J. Greenberg and J. A. Colquitt (Eds.), *Handbook of Organizational Justice* (Mahwah, NJ: Erlbaum, 2005), 12–45.
77. D. E. Conlon, C. J. Meyer, and J. M. Nowakowski, "How Does Organizational Justice Affect Performance, Withdrawal, and Counterproductive Behavior?" In J. Greenberg and J. A. Colquitt, *Handbook of Organizational Justice* (Mahwah, NJ: Erlbaum, 2005): 303–22; R. H. Moorman and Z. B. Byrne, "How does Organizational Justice Affect Organizational Citizenship Behavior?" In J. Greenberg and J. A. Colquitt (Eds.), *Handbook of Organizational Justice* (Mahwah, NJ: Erlbaum, 2005): 357–75.
78. Ibid; D. E. Warren, "Constructive and Destructive Deviance in Organizations," *Academy of Management Review* 28(4 2003): 622–32; B. E. Litzky, K. A. Eddleston, and D. L. Kidder, "The Good, the Bad, and the Misguided: How Managers Inadvertently Encourage Deviant Behaviors," *Academy of Management Perspectives* (February 2006): 91–103.
79. Ibid; D. S. Ones, "Employee Silence: Quiescence an Acquiescence as Responses to Perceived Injustice," *International Journal of Selection and Assessment* 10, (2002): 1–4.

CHAPTER 7

1. R. D. Hof, "Why Tech Will Bloom Again," *Business Week Online* (August 25, 2003): www.businessweek.com; "Google Corporate Information: Quick Profile," (April 24, 2006), http://www.google.com/corporate/ facts.html.
2. B. Elgin, "Managing Google's Idea Factory," *BusinessWeek* (October 3, 2005): 88–90; "Google Corporate Information: Company Overview," (April 24, 2006), http://www.google.com/corporate/index. html.
3. K. H. Hammonds, "Growth Search," *Fast Company* (April 2003): 74–81.
4. J. Kerstetter, "Still the Center of This World," *Business Week Online* (August 25, 2003): www.businessweek.com; "Google Corporate Information: Quick Profile," (April 24, 2006), http://www.google.com/corporate/facts.html.
5. K. H. Hammonds, "Growth Search," *Fast Company* (April 2003): 74–81.
6. "Google Corporate Information: Google Milestones," (April 24, 2006), http://www.google.com/corporate/history.html.
7. Ibid.
8. B. Helm, "Google's Giant Stride," *BusinessWeek Online* (April 21, 2006), http://www.businessweek.com/ print/technology/content/apr2006/tc20060420_217866.htm.

9. "Google Corporate Information: Google Offices," (April 24, 2006), http://www.google.com/corporate/ address.html.
10. "Google Corporate Information: Company Overview," (April 24, 2006), http://www.google.com/corporate/index.html; "Google Corporate Information: Our Philosophy," (April 24, 2006), http://www.google.com/corporate/tenthings.html; "Google Corporate Information: Features Overview," (April 24, 2006), http://www.google.com/corporate/features.html.
11. K. H. Hammonds, "Growth Search," *Fast Company* (April 2003): 74–81.
12. B. Elgin, "Managing Google's Idea Factory," *Business Week* (October 3, 2005): 88–90.
13. Ibid.
14. "Google Corporate Information: The Google Culture," (April 24, 2006), http://www.google.com/corporate/culture.html.
15. B. Elgin, "Managing Google's Idea Factory," *Business Week* (October 3, 2005): 88–90.
16. Ibid.
17. G. P. Latham and M. H. Budworth, "The Study of Work Motivation in the 20th Century." In L. L. Koppes (Ed.), *Historical Perspectives in Industrial and Organizational Psychology* (Hillsdale, NJ: Laurence Erlbaum Associates Inc, 2006).
18. F. W. Taylor, *The Principles of Scientific Management* (New York: Harper and Brothers, 1911).
19. R. W. Griffin, *Task Design: An Integrative Approach* (Glenview, IL: Scott, Foresman, 1982).
20. A. C. Filley, R. J. House, and S. Kerr, *Managerial Process and Organizational Behavior* (Glenview, IL: Scott, Foresman, 1976); C. R. Walker, "The Problem of the Repetitive Job," *Harvard Business Review* 28 (1950): 54–58.
21. Griffin, *Task Design*.
22. P. Gogoi, "Thinking Outside the Cereal Box," *Business Week* (July 28, 2003): 74–75; "Hamburger Helper Announces 'Better Tasting' Product Line," General Mills (June 17, 2003): www.generalmills.com; "NASCAR Driver Bill Lester Featured on Honey Nut Cheerios Package," *General Mills* (July 16, 2003): www.generalmills.com; "General Mills: Company," (April 25, 2006), http://www.generalmills.com/corporate/company/index.aspx.
23. P. Gogoi, "Thinking Outside the Cereal Box" *Business Week* (July 28, 2003): 74–75; "Hamburger Helper Announces 'Better Tasting' Product Line," *General Mills* (June 17, 2003): www.generalmills.com; "NASCAR Driver Bill Lester Featured on Honey Nut Cheerios Package," *General Mills* (July 16, 2003): www.generalmills.com.
24. Ibid.
25. "General Mills: Leadership Biographies," (April 25, 2006), http://www.generalmills.com/corporate/media_center/biography_detail.aspx?itemID=4898.
26. Latham and Budworth, "The Study of Work Motivation in the 20th Century."
27. J. R. Hackman and G. R. Oldham, "Motivation Through the Design of Work: Test of a Theory," *Organizational Behavior and Human Performance* 16 (1976): 250–79; J. R. Hackman and G. R. Oldham, *Work Redesign* (Reading, MA: Addison-Wesley, 1980); A. N. Turner and P. R. Lawrence, *Industrial Jobs and the Worker* (Boston: Harvard School of Business, 1965).
28. Hackman and Oldham, "Motivation Through the Design of Work"; Hackman and Oldham, Work Redesign.
29. Hackman and Oldham, *Work Redesign*.
30. Ibid.
31. M. W. Brauchli, "When in Huangpu . . . ," *Wall Street Journal*, December 10, 1993, p. R3.
32. Y. Fried and G. R. Ferris, "The Validity of the Job Characteristics Model: A Review and Meta-Analysis," *Personnel Psychology* 40 (1987): 287–322.
33. B. T. Loher, R. A. Noe, N. L. Moeller, and M. P. Fitzgerald, "A Meta-Analysis of the Relation of Job Characteristics to Job Satisfaction," *Journal of Applied Psychology* 70 (1985): 280–89.
34. G. R. Salancik and J. Pfeffer, "A Social Information Processing Approach to Job Attitudes and Task Design," *Administrative Science Quarterly* 23 (1978): 224–53.
35. S. Nolen, "Contingent Employment." In L. H. Peters, C. R. Greer, and S. A. Youngblood (Eds.), *The Blackwell Encyclopedic Dictionary of Human Resource Management* (Oxford: Blackwell Publishers, 1997): 59–60.
36. Ibid.
37. Ibid.
38. R. W. Griffin, "Objective and Social Sources of Information in Task Redesign: A Field Experiment," *Administrative Science Quarterly* 28 (1983): 184–200; J. Thomas and R. Griffin, "The Social Information Processing Model of Task Design: A Review of the Literature," *Academy of Management Review* 8 (1983): 672–82.
39. "About Hydro" (September 5, 2003): www.hydro.com; "Hydro Fact Sheet," http://www.hydro.com/en/press_room/facts/index.html; "Socially Responsible Business Operations," (April 24, 2006), http:// www.hydro.com/en/global_commitment/society/index.html.
40. C. Fishman, "The Way to Enough: Norsk Hydro's Work-Life Experiments Test a Radical Idea: A Company Can Compete on the Basis of Balance," *Fast Company* (July/August 1999): 160–74; A. Sains, "Is Norway's Oil Patch at Last Open to Outsiders?" *Business Week* (Online), June 14, 1999; A. Sains, "What Happened to Norway's Gusher," *Business Week (Online)*, November 16, 1998; www.hydro.com/en/about/index.html; "Living Industrial History Through 100 Years," *Business Week* (April 24, 2006), http://www.hydro.com/en/about/history/ index.html.
41. "Social Responsibility" (September 5, 2003): www.hydro.no/en/about/global_commitment/socail_resp/index.html; E. Reiten, "Dear Shareholder" (September 5, 2003): www.hydro.no/en/investor_ relations/financial_rep/2002_annual_report/share_letter.html; "Our Values," (April 24, 2006), http:// www.hydro.com/en/about/our_values/index.html.
42. "Sustainable Development Good for Environment—and Bottom Line" (September 5, 2003): www.americas.hydro.com; "Talking Environment with Suppliers" (September 5, 2003): www.hydro.no/en/about/global_commitment/environment.
43. E. Bull-Hansen and T. Aasland, "Hydro on Dow Jones Sustainability Index for Fifth Year" (September 5, 2003): www.hydro.com/en/press_room/news/archive/2003_09/dowjones_sustainindex_en.html.
44. "Welcome to the Dow Jones Sustainability Indexes," *Dow Jones Sustainability Indexes* (September 5, 2003):

www.sustainability-indexes.com; "Frequently Asked Questions," *Dow Jones Sustainability Indexes* (September 5, 2003): www.sustainability-indexes.com; "Corporate Sustainability," *Dow Jones Sustainability Indexes* (September 5, 2003): www.sustainability-indexes.com.

45. "Hydro Fact Sheet," (April 24, 2006), http://www.hydro.com/en/press_room/facts/index.html; "Socially Responsible Business Operations," (April 24. 2006), http://www.hydro.com/en/global_communications/society/index.html.
46. Fishman, "The Way to Enough."
47. H. Tajfel and J. C. Turner, "The Social Identity Theory of Intergroup Behavior." In S. Worschel and W. G. Austin (Eds.), *Psychology of Intergroup Relations* (2nd ed.; Chicago: Nelson-Hall, 1985), pp.7–24.
48. B. E. Ashforth and F. Mael, "Social Identity Theory and the Organization," *Academy of Management Review* 14 (1989): 20–39; Tajfel and Turner, "The Social Identity Theory of Intergroup Behavior."
49. M. E. Brown, "*Identification and Some Conditions of Organizational Involvement," Administrative Science Quarterly* 14 (1969): 346–55; Tajfel and Turner, "The Social Identity Theory of Intergroup Behavior"; Ashforth and Mael, "Social Identity Theory and the Organization."
50. K. H. Hammonds, "Growth Search," p. 76.
51. Latham and Budworth, "The Study of Work Motivation in the 20th Century."
52. "Learning to Live With Offshoring," *Business Week* (January 30, 2006): 122.
53. Ibid.
54. "Offshoring: Spreading the Gospel," (March 6, 2006), http://www.businessweek.com/print/magazine/content/06_10/b3974074.htm?chan=gl.
55. "Offshoring: Spreading the Gospel," (March 6, 2006), http://www.businessweek.com/print/magazine/content/06_10/b3974074.htm?chan=gl; "Genpact: Management Team," (April 25, 2006,) http://www. genpact.com/aboutus.asp?key=1&page=team.htm&submenu=0; "Genpact," (April 25, 2006), http://www.genpact.com/genpact/aboutus?key=1; "Genpact: Growth History," (April 25, 2006), http://www.genpact.com/genpact/aboutus.asp?key=1&page=growth.htm.
56. "Offshoring: Spreading the Gospel," *BusinessWeek Online* (March 6, 2006), http://www.businessweek. com/print/magazine/content/06_10/b3974074.htm?chan=gl.
57. "Genpact: Management Team," (April 25, 2006,) http://www.genpact.com/aboutus.asp?key=1&page=team.htm&submenu=0; "Genpact," (April 25, 2006), http://www.genpact. com/genpact/aboutus?key=1; "Genpact: Growth History," (April 25, 2006), http://www.genpact.com/genpact/aboutus.asp?key=1&page=growth.htm.
58. "Offshoring: Spreading the Gospel," *BusinessWeek Online* (March 6, 2006), http://www.businessweek. com/print/magazine/content/06_10/b3974074.htm?chan=gl.
59. Ibid.
60. E. A. Locke and G. P. Latham, *A Theory of Goal Setting and Task Performance* (Upper Saddle River, NJ: Prentice Hall, 1990).
61. J. J. Donovan and K. J. Williams, "Missing the Mark: Effects of Time and Causal Attributions on Goal Revision in Response to Goal-Performance Discrepancies," *Journal of Applied Psychology* 88 (3 2003): 379–90.
62. N. Nicholson, "How to Motivate Your Problem People," *Harvard Business Review* 81 (1 January 2003): 57–65.
63. Locke and Latham, A *Theory of Goal Setting and Task Performance;* M. E. Tubbs, "Goal Setting: A Meta-Analytic Examination of the Empirical Evidence," *Journal of Applied Psychology* 71 (1986): 474–83.
64. P. C. Earley, "Supervisors and Shop Stewards as Sources of Contextual Information in Goal Setting: A Comparison of the U.S. with England," *Journal of Applied Psychology* 71 (1986): 111–17; M. Erez and I. Zidon, "Effect of Goal Acceptance on the Relationship of Goal Difficulty to Performance," *Journal of Applied Psychology* 69 (1984): 69–78; G. P. Latham and H. A. Marshall, "The Effects of Self-Set, Participatively Set and Assigned Goals on the Performance of Government Employees," *Personnel Psychology* 35 (1982): 399–404; T. Matsui, T. Kakkuyama, and M. L. Onglatco, "Effects of Goals and Feedback on Performance in Groups," *Journal of Applied Psychology* 72 (1987): 407–15; B. J. Punnett, "Goal Setting: An Extension of the Research," *Journal of Applied Psychology* 71 (1986): 171–72.
65. A. Bandura and E. A. Locke, "Negative Self-Efficacy and Goal Effects Revisited," *Journal of Applied Psychology* 88 (1 2003): 87–99.
66. F. K. Lee, K. M. Sheldon, and D. B. Turban, "Personality and the Goal-Striving Process: The Influence of Achievement Goal Patterns, Goal Level, and Mental Focus on Performance and Enjoyment," *Journal of Applied Psychology* 88 (2 2003): 256–65.
67. P. J. Sauer, "Open-Door Management," *Inc.* (June, 2003): 44.
68. J. M. Jackman and M. H. Strober, "Fear of Feedback," *Harvard Business Review* (April 2003): 101–6.
69. E. A. Locke, K. N. Shaw, L. M. Saari, and G. P. Latham, "Goal Setting and Task Performance: 1969–1980," *Psychological Bulletin* 90 (1981): 125–52.
70. P. M. Wright, J. M. George, S. R. Farnsworth, and G. C. McMahan, "Productivity and Extra-Role Behavior: The Effects of Goals and Incentives on Spontaneous Helping," *Journal of Applied Psychology* 78 (1993): 374–81.
71. P. C. Earley, T. Connolly, and G. Ekegren, "Goals, Strategy Development, and Task Performance: Some Limits on the Efficacy of Goal Setting," J*ournal of Applied Psychology* 74 (1989): 24–33; R. Kanfer and P. L. Ackerman, "Motivation and Cognitive Abilities: An Integrative/Aptitude-Treatment Interaction Approach to Skill Acquisition," J*ournal of Applied Psychology* 74 (1989): 657–90.
72. Kanfer and Ackerman, "Motivation and Cognitive Abilities."
73. J. Zhou, "When the Presence of Creative Coworkers Is Related to Creativity: Role of Supervisor Close Monitoring, Developmental Feedback, and Creative Personality," J*ournal of Applied Psychology* 88 (3 2003): 413–22.
74. H. Levinson, "Management by Whose Objectives?" *Harvard Business Review* (January 2003): 107–16.
75. S. J. Carroll and H. L. Tosi, *Management by Objectives: Applications and Research* (New York: Macmillan, 1973); P. F. Drucker, *The Practice of Management* (New York: Harper & Row, 1954); C. D. Fisher, L. F. Schoenfeldt, and J. B. Shaw, *Human Resource Management*

(Boston: Houghton Mifflin, 1990); R. Rodgers and J. E. Hunter, "Impact of Management by Objectives on Organizational Productivity," *Journal of Applied Psychology* 76 (1991): 322–36.

76. Fisher, Schoenfeldt, and Shaw, *Human Resource Management*.

CHAPTER 8

1. S. Greenhouse, "How Costco Became the Anti-Wal-Mart," *New York Times* (July 17, 2005): BU1, BU8.
2. Ibid.
3. Ibid.
4. "Costco Wholesale Corporation Reports Second Quarter and Year-to-Date Operating Results Fiscal 2006 and February Sales Results," *Costco Wholesale Investor Relations: News Release* (April 28, 2006), http://phx. corporate-ir.net/phoenix.zhtml?c=83830&p=irol-newsArticle&ID=824344&highlight=; "Costco Wholesale Corporation Reports March Sales Results and Plans for Membership Fee Increase," Costco Wholesale Investor Relations: News Release (April 28, 2006), http://phx.corporate-ir.net/phoenix.zhtml?c= 83830&p=irol-newsArticle&ID=839605&highlight=; "Wal-Mart Stores Post Higher January Sales," *BusinessWeek Online* (February 2, 2006), http://www.businessweek. com/print/investor/conent/feb2006/pi2006022_ 0732_pi004.htm.
5. S. Greenhouse, "How Costco Became the Anti-Wal-Mart," *New York Times* (July 17, 2005): BU1, BU8.
6. "Corporate Governance," *Costco Wholesale Investor Relations* (April 28, 2006), http://phx.corporate-ir.net/phoenix.zhtml?c=83830&p=irol-govhighlights.
7. S. Greenhouse, "How Costco Became the Anti-Wal-Mart," *New York Times* (July 17, 2005): BU1, BU8; S. C., "Because Who Knew a Big-Box Chain Could Have a Generous Soul," *INC. Magazine* (April 2005): 88.
8. S. Holmes and W. Zellner, "Commentary: The Costco Way," *BusinessWeek Online* (April 12, 2004), http://www.businessweek.com/print/magazine/content/04_15/b3878084_mz021.htm?chan . . . ; M. Herbst, "The Costco Challenge: An Alternative to Wal-Martization?" *LRA Online* (July 5, 2005), http://www.laborreseach.org/print.php?id=391.
9. S. Greenhouse, "How Costco Became the Anti-Wal-Mart," *New York Times* (July 17, 2005): BU1, BU8.
10. Ibid.
11. M. Herbst, "The Costco Challenge: An Alternative to Wal-Martization?" *LRA Online* (July 5, 2005), http://www.laborreseach.org/print.php?id=391.
12. S. Greenhouse, "How Costco Became the Anti-Wal-Mart," *New York Times* (July 17, 2005): BU1, BU8.
13. Ibid.
14. B. Einhorn, "Move Over, India," *Business Week* (August 11, 2003): 42–43.
15. L. M. Shore and J. A-M. Coyle-Shapiro, "Editorial: New Developments in the Employee-Organization Relationship," *Journal of Organizational Behavior* 24 (John Wiley & Sons, Ltd. 2003): 443–50.
16. Ibid.
17. D. M. Rousseau and J. McLean Parks, "The Contracts of Individuals and Organizations," *Research in Organizational Behavior* 15 (JAI Press, Inc. 1993): 1–43; S. L. Robinson, "Trust and Breach of the Psychological Contract," *Administrative Science Quarterly* 41 (Cornell University, 1996): 547–99; S. L. Robinson et al., "Changing Obligations and the Psychological Contract: A Longitudinal Study," *Academy of Management Journal* 37 (1994): 137–52; I. R. MacNeil, "Relational Contract: What We Do and Do Not Know," *Wisconsin Law Review* (1985): 483–525.
18. L. Schurer Lambert, J. R. Edwards, and D. M. Cable, "Breach and Fulfillment of the Psychological Contract: A Comparison of Traditional and Expanded Views," *Personnel Psychology* 56 (2003): 895–934.
19. Rousseau and Parks, "The Contracts of Individuals and Organizations"; Robinson, "Trust and Breach of the Psychological Contract"; Robinson et al., "Changing Obligations and the Psychological Contract"; MacNeil, "Relational Contract."
20. Shore and Coyle-Shapiro, "Editorial."
21. J. Aselage and R. Eisenberger, "Perceived Organizational Support and Psychological Contracts: A Theoretical Integration," *Journal of Organizational Behavior* 24 (2003): 491–509; D. M. Rousseau, *Psychological Contracts in Organizations* (Thousand Oaks, CA: Sage, 1995).
22. Ibid.
23. S. L. Premack and J. P. Wanous, "A Meta-Analysis of Realistic Job Preview Experiments," *Journal of Applied Psychology* 70 (1985): 706–19; J. P. Wanous, "Realistic Job Previews: Can a Procedure to Reduce Turnover Also Influence the Relationship Between Abilities and Performance?" *Personnel Psychology* 31 (1978): 249–58; J. P. Wanous, *Organizational Entry: Recruitment, Selection, and Socialization of Newcomers* (Reading, MA: Addison-Wesley, 1980).
24. Aselage and Eisenberger, "Perceived Organizational Support and Psychological Contracts"; Rousseau, Psychological Contracts in Organizations.
25. Ibid.
26. Rousseau and Parks, "The Contracts of Individuals and Organizations": Robinson, "Trust and Breach of the Psychological Contract"; Robinson et al., "Changing Obligations and the Psychological Contract"; MacNeil, "Relational Contract."
27. R. Cropanzano, D. E. Rupp, and Z. S. Byrne, "The Relationship of Emotional Exhaustion to Work Attitudes, Job Performance, and Organizational Citizenship Behaviors," *Journal of Applied Psychology* 88 (1 2003): 160–69.
28. Rousseau and Parks, "The Contracts of Individuals and Organizations"; Robinson, "Trust and Breach of the Psychological Contract"; Robinson et al., "Changing Obligations and the Psychological Contract"; MacNeil, "Relational Contract."
29. D. N. Sull, "Mangaging By Commitments," *Harvard Business Review* (June 2003): 82–91.
30. Rousseau and Parks, "The Contracts of Individuals and Organizations"; Robinson, "Trust and Breach of the Psychological Contract"; Robinson et al., "Changing Obligations and the Psychological Contract"; MacNeil, "Relational Contract."
31. M. Kripalani, "Calling Bangalore: Multinations Are Making It a Hub for High-Tech Research," *Business Week* (November 25, 2002): 52–53.

32. B. Stone, "Men at Overwork: The Good News Is We're More Productive. The Bad News? They Don't Need as Many of Us," *Newsweek* (August 11, 2003): 38–39.
33. S. Armour and M. Kessler, "USA's New Money-Saving Export: White-Collar Jobs," *USA Today* (August 5, 2003): 1B-2B.
34. "Outsourcing Jobs: Is it Bad?" *Business Week* (August 25, 2003): 36–38; K. Madigan, "Yes . . . " *Business Week* (August 25, 2003): 36–38; M. J. Mandel, ". . . No" *Business Week* (August 25, 2003): 36–38.
35. Rousseau and Parks, "The Contracts of Individuals and Organizations"; Robinson, "Trust and Breach of the Psychological Contract"; Robinson et al., "Changing Obligations and the Psychological Contract"; MacNeil, "Relational Contract."
36. Ibid.
37. Ibid.
38. "The Human Cost of Cheaper Towels," *The Economist* (April 23, 2005): 30.
39. S. Lohr, "I. B. M. to Lay Off Over 10,000 In Struggle to Keep Up Profits," *New York Times* (May 5, 2005): A1, C7.
40. L. Hawkins, Jr., N. E. Boudette, and K. Maher, "GM, Amid Industry Overhaul, Cuts Health Benefits for Retirees," *The Wall Street Journal* (October 18, 2005): A1, A8.
41. A. Geller, "Workers Play Role of 'GM Gypsies'," *The Houston Chronicle* (May 6, 2006): D1, D4.
42. Ibid.
43. Ibid.
44. Ibid.
45. N. Shirouzu, "Ford May Go Deeper With Job Cuts," *The Wall Street Journal* (July 22, 2005): A6.
46. C. D. Fisher, L. F. Schoenfeldt, and J. B. Shaw, *Human Resource Management* (Boston: Houghton Mifflin, 1990).
47. J. M. Jackman and M. H. Strober, "Fear of Feedback," *Harvard Business Review* (April 2003): 101–06.
48. Fisher, Schoenfeldt, and Shaw, *Human Resource Management.*
49. Ibid; G. P. Latham and K. N. Wexley, *Increasing Productivity Through Performance Appraisal* (Reading, MA: Addison-Wesley, 1982).
50. R. Henkoff, "Make Your Office More Productive," *Fortune* (February 25, 1991): 72–84.
51. R. S. Schuler, *Managing Human Resources* (New York: West, 1992).
52. T. A. DeCotiis, "An Analysis of the External Validity and Applied Relevance of Three Rating Formats," *Organizational Behavior and Human Performance* 19 (1977): 247–66; Fisher, Schoenfeldt, and Shaw, *Human Resource Management.*
53. Schuler, *Managing Human Resources.*
54. N. Nicholson, "How to Motivate Your Problem People," *Harvard Business Review* (January 2003): 56–65.
55. H. Lancaster, "Performance Reviews Are More Valuable When More Join In," *Wall Street Journal*, July 9, 1996, p. B1.
56. Ibid.
57. Ibid; J. S. Lublin, "Turning the Tables: Underlings Evaluate Bosses," *Wall Street Journal*, October 4, 1994, p. B1; J. S. Lublin, "It's Shape-Up Time for Performance Reviews," *Wall Street Journal*, October 3, 1994, p. B1; S. Shellenbarger, "Reviews from Peers Instruct—and Sting," *Wall Street Journal*, October 4, 1994, pp. B1, B4.
58. Lublin, "Turning the Tables."
59. Shellenbarger, "Reviews From Peers Instruct—and Sting."
60. W. C. Borman and D. W. Bracken, "360 Degree Appraisals." In C. L. Cooper and C. Argyris (Eds.), *The Concise Blackwell Encyclopedia of Management* (Oxford, UK: Blackwell Publishers, 1998), 17; D. W. Bracken, "Straight Talk About Multi-Rater Feedback," *Training and Development* 48 (1994): 44–51; M. R. Edwards, W. C. Borman, and J. R. Sproul, "Solving the Double-Bind in Performance Appraisal: A Saga of Solves, Sloths, and Eagles," *Business Horizons* 85 (1985): 59–68.
61. "Problems With Your Boss?" ImproveNow.com. (September 23, 2003), www.improvenow.com.
62. A. Harrington, "Workers of the World, Rate Your Boss!" *Fortune* (September 18, 2000): 340, 342.
63. Ibid; J. Montgomery, "They Mean It When They Ask, 'Is Everything All Right Here?' " *Wall Street Journal*, February 6, 2000, p. 6D.
64. E. E. Lawler III, *Pay and Organization Development* (Reading, MA: Addison-Wesley, 1981).
65. J. D. Shaw, M. K. Duffy, A. Mitra, D. E. Lockhard, and M. Bowler, "Reactions to Merit Pay Increases: A Longtitudinal Test of a Signal Sensitivity Perspective," *Journal of Applied Psychology* 88 (3 2003): 538–44.
66. A. Bennett, "Paying Workers to Meet Goals Spreads, but Gauging Performance Proves Tough," *Wall Street Journal* (September 10, 1991, pp. B1, B8.
67. M. Conlin, "Give Me That Old-Time Economy," *Business Week* (April 24, 2000): BusinessWeek.Online; G. Hardesty, "Dot-compensation Makes Some Green," *Houston Chronicle*, May 21, 2000.
68. "Just Deserts," *The Economist* (January 29, 1994): 71.
69. Lawler, *Pay and Organization Development.*
70. Ibid.
71. J. F. Lincoln, *Incentive Management* (Cleveland: Lincoln Electric Company, 1951); R. Zager, "Managing Guaranteed Employment," *Harvard Business Review* 56 (1978): 103–15.
72. Lawler, *Pay and Organization Development.*
73. Fisher, Schoenfeldt, and Shaw, *Human Resource Management;* B. E. Graham-Moore and T. L. Ross, *Productivity Gainsharing* (Upper Saddle River, NJ: Prentice Hall, 1983); A. J. Geare, "Productivity from Scanlon Type Plans," *Academy of Management Review* 1 (1976): 99–108.
74. J. Labate, "Deal Those Workers In," *Fortune* (April 19, 1993): 26.
75. D. Duston, "Women Tend to Pay More in Marketplace, Author Claims," *Bryan-College Station Eagle*, May 18, 1993, p. A1; F. C. Whittelsey, *Why Women Pay More* (Washington, DC: Center for Responsive Law, 1993).
76. Fisher, Schoenfeldt, and Shaw, *Human Resource Management.*
77. D. J. Treiman and H. I. Hartmann, *Women, Work, and Wages: Equal Pay for Jobs of Equal Value* (Washington, DC: National Academy Press, 1981).
78. A. Borrus, "A Battle Royal Against Regal Paychecks," *Business Week* (February 24, 2003): 127; "Too Many Turkeys," *The Economist* (November 26, 2005): 75–76; G. Morgenson, "How to Slow Runaway Executive Pay," *The New York Times* (October 23, 2005): 1, 4.

79. M. Conlin, "Going Sideways on the Corporate Ladder," *Business Week* (September 30, 2002): 39.
80. Useem, and E. Florian, "Have They No Shame?" *Fortune* (April 23, 2003): 57–64; G. Morgenson, "How to Slow Runaway Exeuctive Pay," *The New York Times* (October 23, 2005): 1, 4; "Too Many Turkeys," *The Economist* (November 26, 2005): 75–76.
81. S. Greenhouse, "How Costco Became the Anti-Wal-Mart," *The New York Times* (July 17, 2005): BU1, BU8.
82. J. H. Greenhaus, *Career Management* (New York: Dryden Press, 1987).
83. A. Malka and J. A. Chatman, "Intrinsic and Extrinsic Work Orientations as Moderators of the Effect of Annual Income on Subjective Well-Being: A Longtiduinal Study," *Society for Personality and Social Psychology, Inc.* 29 (6 June 2003): 737–46.
84. N. Shope Griffin, "Personalize Your Management Development," *Harvard Business Review* (March 2003): 113–19.
85. M. J. Driver, "Careers: A Review of Personal and Organizational Research." In C. L. Cooper and I. Robertson (Eds.), *International Review of Industrial and Organizational Psychology* (New York: Wiley, 1988).
86. Ibid.
87. Ibid.
88. C. Hymowitz and G. Stern, "At Procter & Gamble, Brands Face Pressure and So Do Executives," *Wall Street Journal,* May 10, 1993, pp. A1, A8.
89. Driver, "Careers: A Review of Personal and Organizational Research."
90. Ibid.
91. Greenhaus, *Career Management.*
92. M. B. Arthur, "The Boundaryless Career: A New Perspective for Organizational Inquiry," *Journal of Organizational Behavior*, 15 (1994): 295–306; M. B. Arthur and D. M. Rousseau, *The Boundaryless Career: A New Employment Principle for a New Organizational Era* (New York: Oxford University Press, 1996a), 237–55; "Introduction: The Boundaryless Career as a New Employment Principle." In M. B. Arthur and D. M. Rousseau (Eds.) *The Boundaryless Career: A New Employment Principle for a New Organizational Era* (New York: Oxford University Press, 1996b): 3–20; L. T. Eby et al., "Predictors of Success in the Era of the Boundaryless Career," *Journal of Organizational Behavior* 24 (2003): 689–708.
93. S. C. de Janasz, S. E. Sullivan, and V. Whiting, "Mentor Networks and Career Success: Lessons for Turbulent Times," *Academy of Management Executive* 17 (4 2003): 78–91.
94. Greenhaus, Career Management.
95. J. L. Holland, *Making Vocational Choices: A Theory of Careers* (Upper Saddle River, NJ: Prentice Hall, 1973); M. B. Barrick, M. K. Mount, and R. Gupta, "Meta-Analysis of the Relationship Between the Five-Factor Model of Personality and Holland's Occupational Types," *Personnel Psychology* 56 (2003): 45–74.
96. J. Chamberlin, "Study Offers Clues on Why Women Choose Medicine over Engineering," *Monitor on Psychology* (September 2003): 13.
97. Ibid.
98. Ibid.
99. J. P. Wanous, "Realistic Job Previews: Can a Procedure to Reduce Turnover Also Influence the Relationship Between Abilities and Performance?" *Personnel Psychology* (1978): 249–58; J. P. Wanous, *Organizational Entry: Recruitment, Selection and Socialization of Newcomers* (Reading, MA: Addison-Wesley, 1980).
100. Greenhaus, *Career Management.*
101. Ibid.
102. G. Dreher and R. Ash, "A Comparative Study of Mentoring Among Men and Women in Managerial, Professional, and Technical Positions," *Journal of Applied Psychology* 75 (1990): 525–35; T. A. Scandura, "Mentorship and Career Mobility: An Empirical Investigation," *Journal of Organizational Behavior* 13 (1992): 169–74; W. Whitely, T. W. Dougherty, and G. F. Dreher, "Relationship of Career Mentoring and Socioeconomic Origin to Managers' and Professionals' Early Career Success," *Academy of Management Journal* 34 (1991): 331–51.
103. D. B. Turban and T. W. Dougherty, "The Role of Protégé Personality in Receipt of Mentoring and Career Success," *Academy of Management Journal* 37 (1994): 688–702.
104. L. Clyde Jr., "Would You Make a Good Protégé?", National Business Employment Weekly: Managing Your Career (Spring-Summer 1993): 15–17.
105. Greenhaus, *Career Management*.
106. T. P. Ference, J. A. F. Stoner, and E. K. Warren, "Managing the Career Plateau," *Academy of Management Review* 2 (1977): 602–12.
107. B. T. Abdelnor and D. T. Hall, *Career Development of Established Employees* (New York: Center for Research in Career Development, Columbia University, 1981); J. M. Bardwick, "Plateauing and Productivity," *Sloan Management Review* 24 (1983): 67–73.
108. Abdelnor and Hall, *Career Development of Established Employees;* J. Sonnenfeld, "Dealing with the Aging Workforce," *Harvard Business Review* 56 (1978): 81–92.
109. Ference, Stoner, and Warren, "Managing the Career Plateau."
110. J. Fierman, "Beating the Midlife Career Crisis," *Fortune* (September 6, 1993): 52–62.
111. J. Pfeffer, "SAS Institute: A Different Approac to Incentives and People Management Practices in the Software Industry," *Harvard Business School Case* HR-6 (January 1998).
112. S. Clifford, "Saying No to Retirement," *Inc. Magazine* (September 2005): 27–29; "Demographic Profile of American Baby Boomers," (May 5, 2006), http://www. metlife.com/Applications/Corporate/WPS/CDA/PageGenerator/0,P8895~AP,0. . . ; "Baby boomer," www.wikipedia.org (May 2, 2006), http://en. wikipedia.org/wiki/Baby_boomer; "The Baby Boomer Generation—Trends, Research, Discussion and Comment," *Aging Hipsters: The Baby Boomer Generation* (May 2, 2006), http://www.aginghipsters.com.
113. P. Coy, "Old. Smart. Productive." *BusinessWeek* (June 27, 2005): 78–86; T. Gutner, "When You Still Want to Work," *BusinessWeek* (July 25, 2005): 102–3; S. Clifford, "Saying No to Retirement," *Inc. Magazine* (September 2005): 27–19.
114. P. Coy, "Old. Smart. Productive." *BusinessWeek* (June 27, 2005): 78–86.
115. Ibid.
116. Ibid.

117. Ibid.
118. G. Graham, "Would You Lie for Your Boss or Would You Just Rather Not?" *Bryan-College Station Eagle*, October 24, 1993, p. C3.
119. L. S. Gottfredson, "Dilemmas in Developing Diversity Programs." In S. E. Jackson and Associates (Eds.), *Diversity in the Workplace: Human Resources Initiatives* (New York: Guilford Press, 1992).
120. Ibid.

CHAPTER 9

1. C. Daniels, "The Last Taboo," *Fortune*, October 28, 2002, 135–44; B. Hindo, "Turning the Tide," *BusinessWeek*, September 26, 2005, 64–66.
2. In E. LaFreniere (Ed.), "Attitudes in the American Workplace VII, The Seventh Annual Labor Day Survey," The Marlin Company by Harris Interactive, 1–11.
3. K. Duran, "Vacation? What Exactly Is That?" *The Houston Chronicle*, December 5, 2005, D5.
4. R. Konrad, "Sleepless in America," *The Houston Chronicle*, May 15, 2005, D8.
5. Ibid.
6. Ibid.
7. J. Scott, "Burnout Bites Workers and Employers," *The Houston Chronicle*, February 17, 2006, D1, D4.
8. C. Krischer Goodman, "Saying No to Extra Work," *The Houston Chronicle*, April 18, 2005, D5.
9. C. Hymowitz, "Doing More with Less, Avoiding Shoddy Work and Burned-Out Staff," *In the Lead*, February 25, 2003, B1.
10. Ibid.
11. Ibid.
12. In E. LaFreniere (Ed.), "Attitudes in the American Workplace VII, The Seventh Annual Labor Day Survey."
13. Ibid.
14. Ibid.
15. "Bad Jobs Are a Problem Europe-wide," *hazards magazine*, October 22, 2003, www.hazards.ord/workedtodeath/wordedtodeath3.htm.
16. J. A. Fuller, J. M. Stanton, G. G. Fisher, C. Spitzmiller, and S. S. Russell, "A Lengthy Look at the Daily Grind: Time Series Analysis of Events, Mood, Stress, and Satisfaction," *Journal of Applied Psychology* 88 (6 2003): 1019–33.
17. "Negative Feelings Afflict 40 Million Adults in U.S.," *Wall Street Journal*, November 26, 1993, p. B1.
18. R. S. Lazarus, *Psychological Stress and Coping Processes* (New York: McGraw-Hill, 1966); R. S. Lazarus and S. Folkman, *Stress, Appraisal, and Coping* (New York: Springer, 1984); R. S. Lazarus, "Psychological Stress in the Workplace," *Journal of Social Behavior and Personality* 6 (7 1991): 1–13.
19. Lazarus and Folkman, *Stress, Appraisal, and Coping*.
20. J. Cole, "Fight Workplace Violence: Safeguard Yourself and your employees," *Fortune Small Business*, October 21, 2003, www.fortune.com/fortune/print/0,15935,360655,00.html; S. Gold and L. Hart, "Factory Worker Kills 5, Self in Plant Shooting," *Miami Herald*, July 9, 2003, 3A; D. M. Halbfinger, "Factory Killer Had a Known History of Anger and Racial Taunts," *New York Times*, July 10, 2003, NYTimes.com.
21. T. DeAngelis, "Psychologists Aid Victims of Violence in Post Office," *APA Monitor* (October 1993): 1, 44–45.
22. R. C. Clay, "Securing the Workplace: Are Our Fears Misplaced?" *Monitor on Psychology* (October 2000): 46–49; Washington Post, "Mail Workers Not More Inclined to 'Go Postal,' Workplace Report Says," *Houston Chronicle*, September, 1, 2000, 8A; T. DeAngelis, "Psychologists Aid Victims of Violence in Post Office."
23. "Workplace Violence: OSHA Fact Sheet," *U.S. Department of Labor: Occupational Safety and Health Administration*, 2002, www.osha.gov.
24. Ibid.
25. Clay, "Securing the Workplace: Are Our Fears Misplaced?"; Washington Post, "Mail Workers Not More Inclined to 'Go Postal,' Workplace Report Says."
26. T. Molloy, "Ex-Postal Worker Kills 5, Herself at Mail Center," *The Houston Chronicle*, February 1, 2006, A3.
27. Clay, "Securing the Workplace: Are Our Fears Misplaced?"
28. "Workplace Violence: OSHA Fact Sheet."
29. Ibid.
30. M. J. Burke, A. P. Brief, and J. M. George, "The Role of Negative Affectivity in Understanding Relations Between Self-Reports of Stressors and Strains: A Comment on the Applied Psychology Literature," *Journal of Applied Psychology* 78 (1993): 402–12; D. Watson and L. A. Clark, "Negative Affectivity: The Disposition to Experience Aversive Emotional States," *Psychological Bulletin* 96 (1984): 465–90.
31. H. Cooper, "Carpet Firm Sets Up an In-House School to Stay Competitive," *Wall Street Journal*, October 5, 1992, A1, A5.
32. J. Seligmann, T. Namuth, and M. Miller, "Drowning on Dry Land," *Newsweek*, May 23, 1994, 64–66.
33. D. Watson and J. W. Pennebaker, "Health Complaints, Stress, and Distress: Exploring the Central Role of Negative Affectivity," *Psychological Review* 96 (1989): 234–54.
34. Ibid.
35. D. Watson and A. Tellegen, "Toward a Consensual Structure of Mood," *Psychological Bulletin* 98 (1985): 219–35.
36. C. Maslach, *Burnout: The Cost of Caring* (Upper Saddle River, NJ: Prentice Hall, 1982).
37. R. T. Lee and B. E. Ashforth, "On the Meaning of Maslach's Three Dimensions of Burnout," *Journal of Applied Psychology* 75 (1990): 743–47.
38. Seligmann, Namuth, and Miller, "Drowning on Dry Land."
39. Ibid.
40. D. Jansen, "Winning: How the Olympian Quit Trying Too Hard—and Finally Won," *USA Weekend*, July 15–17, 1994, 4–5.
41. G. E. Hardy, D. Woods, and T. D. Wall, "The Impact of Psychological Distress on Absence from Work," *Journal of Applied Psychology* 88 (2 2003): 306–14.
42. A. B. Fisher, "Welcome to the Age of Overwork," *Fortune*, November 30, 1992, 64–71.
43. "Stress Busters: Employers Fight Anxiety as Staffs Shrink and Work Increases," *Wall Street Journal*, December 1, 1992, A1.
44. "A Nurse Shortage May Be Easing, but Stress Persists," *Wall Street Journal*, January 5, 1993, A1.
45. Y. Wijers-Hasegawa, "JPN Rise in Work-Related Suicides," *IWW-news*, May 10, 2003, www.japantimes.co.jp/cgi-bin/

getarticle.p15?nn20030510b3.htm, B. Lafayette De Mente, "Asian Business Codewords," May 2003, www.apmforum.com/columns/boye51.htm.
46. A. Stevens, "Suit over Suicide Raises Issue: Do Associates Work Too Hard?" *Wall Street Journal*, April 15, 1994, B1, B7.
47. "Japan Wakes Up to Fatal Work Ethic," *Japan Forum*, June 15, 2003, http://forum.japanreference.com/showthread.php?s=&threadid=2886.
48. Ibid.
49. J. Ryall, "Japan Wakes Up to Fatal Work Ethic," *Scotland on Sunday*, June 15, 2003, www.scotlandonsunday.com/international.cfm?id=660412003.
50. "Bad Jobs Are a Problem Europe-Wide."
51. S. Shellenbarger, "Keeping Workers by Reaching Out to Them," *Wall Street Journal*, June 1, 1994, B1.
52. J. M. George and A. P. Brief, "Feeling Good-Doing Good: A Conceptual Analysis of the Mood at Work-Organizational Spontaneity Relationship," *Psychological Bulletin* 112 (1992): 310–29.
53. T. H. Holmes and M. Masuda, "Life Change and Illness Susceptibility." In B. S. Dohrenwend and B. P. Dohrenwend (Eds.), *Stressful Life Events: Their Nature and Effects* (New York: Wiley, 1974), 45–72; T. H. Holmes and R. H. Rahe, "Social Readjustment Rating Scale," *Journal of Psychosomatic Research* 11 (1967): 213–18.
54. R. S. Bhagat, S. J. McQuaid, H. Lindholm, and J. Segovis, "Total Life Stress: A Multimethod Validation of the Construct and Its Effect on Organizationally Valued Outcomes and Withdrawal Behaviors," *Journal of Applied Psychology* 70 (1985): 202–14; A. P. Brief, M. J. Burke, J. M. George, B. Robinson, and J. Webster, "Should Negative Affectivity Remain an Unmeasured Variable in the Study of Job Stress?," *Journal of Applied Psychology* 73 (1988): 193–98; B. S. Dohrenwend, L. Krasnoff, A. R. Askenasy, and B. P Dohrenwend, "Exemplification of a Method for Scaling Life Events: The PERI Life Events Scale," *Journal of Health and Social Behavior* 19 (1978): 205–29; J. H. Johnson and I. G. Sarason, "Recent Developments in Research on Life Stress." In V. Hamilton and D. M. Warburton (Eds.), *Human Stress and Cognition: An Information Processing Approach* (New York: Wiley, 1979), 205–36.
55. R. L. Kahn and P. Byosiere, "Stress in Organizations." In M. D. Dunnette and L. M. Hough (Eds.), *Handbook of Industrial and Organizational Psychology*, 2nd ed., vol. 3 (Palo Alto, CA: Consulting Psychologists Press, 1992), 571–650; S. Jackson and R. Schuler, "A Meta-Analysis and Conceptual Critique of Research on Role Ambiguity and Role Conflict in Work Settings," *Organizational Behavior and Human Decision Processes* 36 (1985): 16–78.
56. Ibid.
57. Kahn and Byosiere, "Stress in Organizations."
58. Fisher, "Welcome to the Age of Overwork."
59. J. A. Byrne, "The Pain of Downsizing," *Fortune*, May 9, 1994, 60–68.
60. Fisher, "Welcome to the Age of Overwork."
61. L. W. Winik, "What You May Not Know About Workers in America Today," *Parade Magazine*, October 26, 2003, 10.
62. J. M. Brett and L. K. Stroh, "Working 61 Plus Hours a Week: Why Do Managers Do It?" *Journal of Applied Psychology* 88 (1 2003): 67–78.
63. Fisher, "Welcome to the Age of Overwork."
64. Seligmann, Namuth, and Miller, "Drowning on Dry Land."
65. A. P. Brief and J. M. Atieh, "Studying Job Stress: Are We Making Mountains Out of Molehills?" *Journal of Occupational Behaviour* 8 (1987): 115–26.
66. Ibid; R. L. Kahn, *Work and Health* (New York: Wiley, 1981); S. V. Kasl and S. Cobb, "Blood Pressure Changes in Men Undergoing Job Loss: A Preliminary Report," *Psychosomatic Medicine* 32 (1970): 19–38.
67. J. Brockner, "The Effects of Work Layoffs on Survivors: Research, Theory, and Practice." In B. M. Staw and L. L. Cummings (Eds.), *Research in Organizational Behavior* (Greenwich, CT: JAI Press, 1988) pp. 213–255.
68. J. Fierman, "Beating the Midlife Career Crisis," *Fortune*, September 6, 1993, 52–62.
69. M. Davis, "Anadarko to Jettison 400 Jobs: Senior Managers Depart in Wave," *Houston Chronicle*, August 1, 2003, 1C.
70. L. A. Johnson, "Study: 1 in 5 Laid Off in Recent Recession," *Houston Chronicle*, July 28, 2003, 9A.
71. Ibid.
72. B. Rose, "Part-Time Work, Full-Time Worries," *Houston Chronicle*, April 7, 2003, 10D.
73. Ibid.
74. Ibid.
75. "Extended Mass Layoffs in the Fourth Quarter of 2005 and Annual Averages for 2005," *News United States Department of Labor*, www.bls.gov/mls/, May 10, 2006.
76. Ibid.
77. Brief and Atieh, "Studying Job Stress"; L. Levi, "Psychological and Physiological Reaction to and Psychomotor Performance During Prolonged and Complex Stressor Exposure," *Acta Medica Scandinavica*, 191 Supplement no. 528, (1972): 119; M. Timio and S. Gentili, "Adrenosympathetic Overactivity Under Conditions of Work Stress," *British Journal of Preventive and Social Medicine* 30 (1976): 262–65.
78. R. Ilies, N. Hauserman, S. Schwochau, and J. Stibal, "Reported Incidence Rates of Work-Related Sexual Harassment in the United States: Using Meta-Analysis to Explain Reported Rate Disparities," *Personnel Psychology* 56 (2003): 607–31.
79. K. Pope, "Keyboard Users Say Makers Knew of Problems," *Wall Street Journal*, May 4, 1994, B1, B5.
80. B. Schreiner, "Hot Water over Bathroom Breaks," *Houston Chronicle*, August 28, 2002, 21A.
81. Ibid.
82. J. M. George, T. F. Reed, K. A. Ballard, J. Colin, and J. Fielding, "Contact with AIDS Patients as a Source of Work-Related Distress: Effects of Organizational and Social Support," *Academy of Management Journal* 36 (1993): 157–71; J. Barling, E. K. Kelloway, and R. D. Iverson, "High-Quality Work, Job Satisfaction, and Occupational Injuries," *Journal of Applied Psychology* 88 (2 2003): 276–83.
83. "Cargo Pilots Say They Are Flying Tired, and Seek Tougher Schedule Rules," *Wall Street Journal*, April 5, 1994, A1.
84. "Workplace Injuries May Be Far Worse Than Government Data Suggest," *Wall Street Journal*, February 2, 1993, A1.
85. J. A. Krug, "Why Do They Keep Leaving?" *Harvard Business Review* (February 2003): 14–15.

86. Ibid.
87. Ibid.
88. Y. Cole, "Work-Life in a Down Economy: Morale Boost or Revenue Flush?" *DiversityInc* (March/April 2003): 96–101.
89. Ibid.
90. S. Shellenbarger, "Single Parenting Boosts Career Stress," *Wall Street Journal*, June 1, 1994, B1.
91. S. Shellenbarger, "The Aging of America Is Making 'Elder Care' a Big Workplace Issue," *Wall Street Journal*, February 16, 1994, A1, A8.
92. "Sandwich Generation Caught in Demographic Trap," *Management Issue*, May 10, 2006, http://www.management-issues.com/display_page.asp?section= research&id=1221.
93. S. Shellenbarger, "The Aging of America Is Making 'Elder Care' a Big Workplace Issue," *Wall Street Journal*, February 16, 1994, A1, A8; "Sandwich Generation Caught in Demographic Trap," *Management Issue*, May 10, 2006, http://www.management-issues. com/display_page.asp?section=research&id=1221.
94. A. M. Ryan, B. J. West, and J. Z. Carr, "Effects of the Terrorist Attacks of 9/11/01 on Employee Attitudes," *Journal of Applied Psychology* 88 (4): 647–59.
95. "Credibility of Witness Is Attacked at Tyco Trial," *New York Times*, October 21, 2003, C5; "First Trails Monday in Series of Corporate Scandals," *CNN.com./LAW CENTER*, September 28, 2003, www.cnn.com/2003/LAW/09/28/white.collar.tirals.ap/; "Enron 'Bribed Tax Officials'," *BBC NEWS*, February 17, 2003, www.bbc.co.uk/1/hi/in_depth/business/2002/scandals.
96. L. M. Sixel, "Counselors Help Survivors Deal with Grief," *The Houston Chronicle*, March 29, 2005, A1.
97. J. E. Brody, "Experts Offer Ways to Alleviate Stress," *Houston Chronicle*, April 20, 2003, 4E.
98. Ibid.
99. Ibid.
100. L. M. Sixel, "Counselors Help Survivors Deal with Grief," *The Houston Chronicle*, March 29, 2005, A1.
101. Ibid.
102. L. A. Mainiero and D. E. Gibson, "Managing Employee Trauma: Dealing with the Emotional Fallout from 9/11," *Academy of Management Executive* 17(3 2003): 130–43.
103. Ibid.
104. C. Haberman, "As Opposed to Numbness, Pain Is Good," *New York Times, October 21, 2003:* C20.
105. M. A. Schuster, B. D. Stein, L. H. Jaycox, R. L. Collins, G. N. Marshall, M. N. Elliott, A. J. Zhou, D. E. Kanouse, J. L. Morrison, and S. H. Berry, "A National Survey of Stress Reactions after the September 11, 2001, Terrorist Attacks," *The New England Journal of Medicine* 345(20), November 15, 2001, 1507–12, "Feds Eye Engines in Air Crash," *CNN.com/U.S.*, November 12, 2001, www.cnn.com/2001/US/11/12/newyork.crash.
106. S. Folkman and R. S. Lazarus, "An Analysis of Coping in a Middle-Aged Community Sample," *Journal of Health and Social Behavior* 21 (1980): 219–39; S. Folkman and R. S. Lazarus, "If It Changes It Must Be a Process: Study of Emotion and Coping During Three Stages of a College Examination," *Journal of Personality and Social Psychology* 48 (1985): 150–70; S. Folkman and R. S. Lazarus, "Coping as a Mediator of Emotion," *Journal of Personality and Social Psychology* 54 (1988): 466–75.
107. Ibid.
108. Ibid.
109. D. Dunn, "For Globetrotting Execs en Famille," *Business Week*, January 11, 1993, 132–33.
110. A. Lakein, *How to Get Control of Your Time and Your Life* (New York: Peter H. Wyden, 1973); J. C. Quick and J. D. Quick, *Organizational Stress and Preventive Management* (New York: McGraw-Hill, 1984).
111. E. Alt Powell, "Time Management Can Produce Rewards," *The Atlanta Journal-Constitution* ATC.com (October 23, 2003) www.ajc.com/business/ap/ap_s. . . /AP.V9597.AP-On-the-Money.htm.
112. Ibid.
113. S. Shellenbarger, "Multitasking Makes You Stupid: Studies Show Pitfalls of Doing Too Much at Once," *Wall Street Journal*, February 27, 2003, B1.
114. Ibid.
115. Ibid.
116. W. L. French and C. H. Bell Jr., *Organizational Development: Behavioral Science Interventions for Organization Improvement* (Upper Saddle River, NJ: Prentice Hall, 1990).
117. S. Shellenbarger, "Work and Family: Men Find More Ways to Spend Time at Home," *Wall Street Journal*, February 12, 1992, B1.
118. S. Forster, "Companies Say Yoga Isn't a Stretch: Physical, Emotional Benefits Are Praised as More Firms Look to Cut Health Costs," *Wall Street Journal*, October 14, 2003, D4.
119. Ibid.
120. Ibid.
121. Quick and Quick, *Organizational Stress and Preventive Management.*
122. S. Begley, "Dalai Lama and MIT Together Investigate Value of Meditation," *Wall Street Journal*, September 19, 2003, B1.
123. Ibid.
124. S. Cohen and T. A. Wills, "Stress, Social Support, and the Buffering Hypothesis," *Psychological Bulletin* 98 (1985): 310–57; I. G. Sarason, H. M. Levine, R. B. Basham, and B. R. Sarason, "Assessing Social Support: The Social Support Questionnaire," *Journal of Personality and Social Psychology* 44 (1983): 127–39.
125. "Stress Busters."
126. B. Ash, "Companies Say Yes to Child-Care Services," *Bryan-College Station Eagle*, May 29, 1994, C5.
127. M. D. Fefer, "Babes in Work Land," *Fortune*, April 18, 1994, 31–32.
128. S. Shellenbarger, "Firms Help Employees Work with Sick Kids," *Wall Street Journal*, May 11, 1994, B1.
129. "Work-Family Problems Get Their Own Managers," *Wall Street Journal*, April 14, 1992, B1.
130. "Training Workers to Be Flexible on Schedules," *Wall Street Journal*, February 10, 1993, 1; "Workplace Flexibility Is Seen as Key to Business Success," *Wall Street Journal*, November 23, 1993, A1.
131. "Training Workers to Be Flexible on Schedules."
132. J. Aley, "The Temp Biz Boom: Why It's Good," *Fortune*, October 16, 1995, 53–55.
133. N. B. Kurland and D. E. Bailey, "Telework: The Advantages and Challenges of Working Here, There, Anywhere, and Anytime," *Organizational Dynamics* (Autumn 1999): 53–68.

134. Ibid.
135. P. J. Knight and J. Westbrook, "Comparing Employees in Traditional Job Structures vs. Telecommuting Jobs Using Herzberg's Hygienes & Motivators," *Engineering Management Journal* (March 1999): 15–20.
136. M. Igbaria and T. Guimaraes, "Exploring Differences in Employee Turnover Intentions and Its Determinants Among Telecommuters and Non-Telecommuters," *Journal of Management Information Systems* (Summer 1999): 147–64.
137. T. L. Dixon and J. Webster, "Family Structure and the Telecommuter's Quality of Life," *Journal of End User Computing* (Fall 1998): 42–49.
138. "Annual Survey Shows Americans Are Working From Many Different Locations Outside Their Employers Office," International Telework Association & Council—News—Press Release, May 10, 2006, http://www.workingfromanywhere.org/news; "ITAC, The Telework Advisory Group For WorldatWork," May 10, 2006, http:www.workingfromanywhere.org; "Virtual Business Owners Community,—FAQ Center: Telecommuting / Telework," May 10, 2006, http://www. vsscyberoffice .com/vfaq/25.html.
139. R. Eisenberger, P. Fasolo, and V. Davis-LaMastro, "Perceived Organizational Support and Employee Diligence, Commitment, and Innovation," *Journal of Applied Psychology* 75 (1990): 51–59; R. Eisenberger, R. Huntington, S. Hutchinson, and D. Sowa, "Perceived Organizational Support," *Journal of Applied Psychology* 71 (1986): 500–7; M. L. Ambrose and M. Schminke, "Organization Structure as a Moderator of the Relationship Between Procedural Justice, Interactional Justice, Perceived Organizational Support, and Supervisory Trust," *Journal of Applied Psychology* 88 (2 2003): 295–305.
140. D. N. Sull, "Managing By Commitments," *Harvard Business Review* (June 2003): 82–91.
141. J. M. George, T. F. Reed, K. A. Ballard, J. Colin, and J. Fielding, "Contact with AIDS Patients as a Source of Work-Related Distress: Effects of Organizational and Social Support," *Academy of Management Journal* 35 (1996): 157–71.
142. B. Oliver, "How to Prevent Drug Abuse in Your Workplace," *HRMagazine* (December 1993): 78–81.
143. R. A. Wolfe and D. F. Parker, "Employee Health Management: Challenges and Opportunities," *Academy of Management Executive* 8 (2 1994): 22–31.
144. U.S. Department of Health and Human Services, *1992 National Survey of Worksite Health Promotion Activities: A Summary Report* (Washington, DC: U.S. Department of Health and Human Services, 1992).
145. Wolfe and Parker, "Employee Health Management."
146. I. M. Augstums, "Best Company Perk? Employees' Time Off," *The Houston Chronicle*, January 9, 2006, D4.

CHAPTER 10

1. "Whirlpool Corporation Today," May 10, 2006, http://www.whirlpoolcorp.com/about/default.asp.
2. "Future Growth through Global Presence," May 10, 2006, http://www.whirlpoolcorp.com/about/vision_and_strategy/globalplatform.asp; "Whirlpool to shed factories and jobs," *The Houston Chronicle,* May 11, 2006, D1; D. Cameron, "Whirlpool to cut 4,500 jobs in plant closures," *MSNBC.com,* May 10, 2006, http://www.msnbc.msn.com/id/12722969.
3. C. Salter, "Whirlpool Finds Its Cool," *Fast Company*, June 2005, 73–75.
4. Ibid; "How Whirlpool Defines Innovation" *BusinessWeek Online*, March 6, 2006, http://www.businessweek.com/innovate/content/mar2006/id20060306_287425.htm; "Global Cooperation and Teamwork Procedure an Award Winning Product," May 10, 2006, http://www.whirlpoolcorp.com/news/features/home.asp?news.id=9&action=print; "2004 World Technology Awards Winners & Finalists," *The World Technology Network,* May 10, 2006, http://www.wtn.net/2004/bio141.html; C. Salter, "A Jones for Design," *FastCompany*, May 10, 2006, http://www.fastcompany.com/design/2005/jones-qa.html; M. Arndt, "Creativity Overflowing," *BusinessWeek Online,* May 8, 2006, http://www.businessweek.com/magazine/content/06_19/b3983061.htm?campaign_id=search; "Online Extra: Whirlpool's Future Won't Fade," *BusinessWeek Online*, May 8, 2006, http://www. businessweek.com/magazine/content/06_19/b3983067. htm?campaign_id=search.
5. "Global Cooperation and Teamwork Procedure an Award Winning Product," May 10, 2006, http:// www.whirlpoolcorp.com/news/features/home.asp?news.id=9&action=print.
6. C. Salter, "Whirlpool Finds Its Cool," *Fast Company*, June 2005, 73–75; C. Salter, "A Jones for Design," *FastCompany*, May 10, 2006, http://www.fastcompany.com/design/2005/jones-qa.html.
7. "Global Cooperation and Teamwork Procedure an Award Winning Product," May 10, 2006, http://www.whirlpoolcorp.com/news/features/home.asp?news.id=9&action=print.
8. C. Salter, "Whirlpool Finds Its Cool," *Fast Company*, June 2005, 73–75.
9. Ibid; C. Salter, "A Jones for Design," *FastCompany*, May 10, 2006, http://www.fastcompany.com/design/2005/jones-qa.html.
10. C. Salter, "A Jones for Design," *FastCompany*, May 10, 2006, http://www.fastcompany.com/design/2005/ jones-qa .html.
11. Ibid; C. Salter, "Whirlpool Finds Its Cool," *Fast Company*, June 2005, 73–75.
12. Ibid.
13. "Online Extra: Whirlpool's Future Won't Fade," *BusinessWeek Online*, May 8, 2006, http://www.businessweek.com/magazine/content/06_19/b3983067.htm?campaign_id=search.
14. *Toward Phenomenology of Groups and Group Membership*, H. Sondak, M. Neale, and E. Mannix (Eds.), (Oxford: Elsevier Science, 2003); W. A. Kahn, Book Review of Toward Phenomenology of Groups and Group Membership, *Administrative Science Quarterly* (June 2003): 330–32.
15. H. Moon, D. E Conlon, S. E Humphrey, N. Quigley, C. E. Devers, and J. M. Nowakowski, "Group Decision Process

and Incrementalism in Organizational Decision Making," *Organizational Behavior and Human Decision Processes* 92 (2003): 67–79.

16. B. Dumaine, "The Trouble with Teams," *Fortune,* September 5, 1994, 86–92.
17. M. E. Shaw, *Group Dynamics*, 3rd ed. (New York: McGraw-Hill, 1981).
18. T. M. Mills, *The Sociology of Small Groups* (Upper Saddle River, NJ: Prentice Hall, 1967).
19. J. A. Pearce II and E. C. Ravlin, "The Design and Activation of Self-Regulating Work Groups," *Human Relations* 11 (1987): 751–82.
20. B. W. Tuckman, "Developmental Sequences in Small Groups," *Psychological Bulletin* 63 (1965): 384–99; B. W. Tuckman and M. C. Jensen, "Stages of Small Group Development," *Group and Organizational Studies* 2 (1977): 419–27.
21. R. G. LeFauve and A. C. Hax, "Managerial and Technological Innovations at Saturn Corporation," *MIT Management* (Spring 1992): 8–19.
22. R. S. Peterson and K. Jackson Behfar, "The Dynamic Relationship Between Performance Feedback, Trust, and Conflict in Groups: A Longitudinal Study," *Organizational Behavior and Human Decision Processes* 92 (2003): 102–12.
23. C. J. G. Gersick, "Time and Transition in Work Teams: Toward a New Model of Group Development," *Academy of Management Journal* 31 (1988): 9–41; C. J. G. Gersick, "Marking Time: Predictable Transitions in Task Groups," *Academy of Management Journal* 32 (1989): 274–309.
24. L. L. Thompson, *Making the Team: A Guide for Managers* (Upper Saddle River, NJ: Prentice Hall, 2000).
25. G. R. Jones, "Task Visibility, Free Riding, and Shirking: Explaining the Effect of Structure and Technology on Employee Behavior," *Academy of Management Review* 9 (1984): 684–95.
26. C. Gibson and F. Vermeulen, "A Healthy Divide: Subgroups as a Stimulus for Team Learning Behavior," *Administrative Science Quarterly* 48 (2003): 202–39.
27. W. B. Swann, Jr., J. T. Polzer, D. C. Seyle, and S. J. Ko, "Finding Value in Diversity: Verification of Personal and Social Self-Views in Diverse Groups," *Academy of Management Review* 29 (1 2004): 9–27.
28. F. Warner, "In a Word, Toyota Drives for Innovation," *Fast Company*, (August 2002): 36–38.
29. J. Stuart Bunderson and K. M. Sutcliffe, "When to Put the Brakes on Learning," *Harvard Business Review* (February 2003): 20–21.
30. A. Fisher, "How to Battle the Coming Brain Drain," *Fortune* (March 21, 2005): 121–28.
31. Ibid.
32. Ibid.
33. Ibid; "Northrop Grumman Corporation-Defining the Future," May 11, 2006, http//www.northropgrumman.com.
34. "General Electric: Our Company," May 11, 2006, http://www.ge.com/en/company/; A. Fisher, "How to Battle the Coming Brain Drain," *Fortune* (March 21, 2005): 121–28.
35. A. Fisher, "How to Battle the Coming Brain Drain," *Fortune* (March 21, 2005): 121–28.
36. Ibid.
37. Ibid.
38. T. C. Brown, "The Effect of Verbal Self-Guidance Training on Collective Efficacy and Team Performance," *Personnel Psychology* 56 (2003): 935–64.
39. A. Bandura, *Self-Efficacy: The Exercise of Control* (New York: W. H. Freeman and Company, 1997).
40. Ibid.
41. Ibid.
42. Ibid.
43. Ibid.
44. Ibid.
45. C. F. Bond Jr. and L. J. Titus, "Social Facilitation: A Meta-Analysis of 241 Studies," *Psychological Bulletin* 94 (1983): 265–92; Shaw, *Group Dynamics*.
46. Ibid.
47. B. Dumain, "Who Needs a Boss?" *Fortune,* May 7, 1990, pp. 52–60.
48. Ibid.
49. B. Burlington, "The Coolest Small Company in America," *Inc. Magazine* (January 2003): 64–74.
50. "Zingerman's Mail Order," www.zingermans.com, September 9, 2003, www.zingerman.com/AboutUs.pasp.
51. E. Levine, "Movable Feasts for the Holidays," *BusinessWeek* Online, December 7, 1998, www.buinessweek.com/@@JAsbxYQQBa@r3QcA/archives/1998/b36071553.arc.htm.
52. Burlington, "The Coolest Small Company in America,"; www.zingermans.com, May 11, 2006, http://www.zingermans.com/index.pasp.
53. Burlington, "The Coolest Small Company in America."
54. "Six Steps to Selecting Superior Cheese," www.zingermans.com (2003).
55. "A Guide to Getting Along: ZCoB Procedures for Dealing with Conflict or Dissatisfaction with a Co-Worker," *Zingerman's Staff Guide* (2002), www.images. inc.com/freetools/zing_train/zing_guide.pdf.
56. "3 Steps to Great Finance," Zingerman's *Staff Guide* (2002), www.images.inccom/freetools/zing_train/zing_finance.pdf.
57. Burlington, "The Coolest Small Company in America."
58. J. R. Hackman, "Group Influences on Individuals in Organizations." In M. D. Dunnette and L. M. Hough (Eds.), *Handbook of Industrial and Organizational Psychology*, 2nd ed., vol. 3 (Palo Alto, CA: Consulting Psychologists Press, 1992), 199–267.
59. Ibid.
60. D. C. Feldman, "The Development and Enforcement of Group Norms," *Academy of Management Review* 9 (1984): 47–53.
61. Hackman, "Group Influences on Individuals in Organizations."
62. E. P. Hollander, "Conformity, Status, and Idiosyncrasy Credit," *Psychological Review* 65 (1958): 117–27.
63. M. Dalton, "The Industrial Ratebuster: A Characterization," *Applied Anthropology* 7 (1948): 5–18.
64. Hackman, "Group Influences on Individuals in Organizations."
65. C. L. Jackson and J. A. LePine, "Peer Response to a Team's Weakest Link: A Test and Extension of LePine and Van Dyne's Model," *Journal of Applied Psychology* 88 (3 2003): 459–75.
66. C. J. Nemeth and B. M. Staw, "The Trade-Offs of Social Control and Innovation in Groups and Organizations,"

Advances in Experimental Social Psychology 22 (1989): 175–210.

67. Ibid.
68. M. J. Grawitch, D. C. Munz, and T. J. Kramer, "Effects of Member Mood States on Creative Performance in Temporary Workgroups," *Group Dynamics: Theory, Research, and Practice* 7 (1 2003): 41–54; M. J. Grawitch, D. C. Munz, E. K. Elliott, and A. Mathis, "Promoting Creativity in Temporary Problem-Solving Groups: The Effects of Positive Mood and Autonomy in Problem Definition on Idea-Generating Performance," *Group Dynamics: Theory, Research, and Practice* 7 (3 2003): 200–13.
69. M. Williams and Y. Ono, "Japanese Cite Need for Bold Change, but Not at the Expense of 'Stability,' " *Wall Street Journal*, June 29, 1993, A10.
70. G. R. Jones, "Psychological Orientation and the Process of Organizational Socialization: An Interactionist Perspective," *Academy of Management Review* 8 (1983): 464–74.
71. J. Van Mannen and E. H. Schein, "Towards a Theory of Organizational Socialization." In B. M. Staw, (Ed.), *Research in Organizational Behavior*, vol. 1 (Greenwich, CT: JAI Press, 1979), 209–64.
72. G. R. Jones, "Socialization Tactics, Self-Efficacy, and Newcomers' Adjustments to Organizations," *Academy of Management Review* 29 (1986): 262–79.
73. Ibid; Van Mannen and Schein, "Towards a Theory of *Organizational Socialization*."
74. www.intercotwest.com/disneyland; M. N. Martinez, "Disney Training Works Magic," *HRMagazine* (May 1992): 53–57.

CHAPTER 11

1. www.microsoft.com, 2006.
2. O. Thomas, "Microsoft Employees Feel Maligned," www.money.cnn.com, March 10 2006.
3. J. Nightingale, "Rising Frustration with Microsoft's Compensation and Review System." www.washtech.org, March 10, 2006.
4. Ibid.
5. "Microsoft's Departing Employees." www.yahoo.news.com, May 6 2006.
6. I. D. Steiner, Group Process and Productivity (New York: Academic Press, 1972).
7. R. A. Guzzo and G. P. Shea, "Group Performance and Intergroup Relations in Organizations." In M. D. Dunnette and L. M. Hough (eds.), *Handbook of Industrial and Organizational Psychology*, 2nd ed., vol. 3 (Palo Alto, CA: Consulting Psychologists Press, 1992), 269–313; I. D. Steiner, Group Process and Productivity.
8. Guzzo and Shea, "Group Performance and Intergroup Relations in Organizations."
9. P. B. Paulus and H. C. Yang, "Idea Generation in Groups: A Basis for Creativity in Organizations," *Organizational Behavior and Human Decision Processes* (May 2000): 76–87.
10. L. Thompson and L. F. Brajkovich, "Improving the Creativity of Organizational Work Groups," *Academy of Management Executive*, February 2003, vol. 17, 96–112.
11. C. Daniels, "This Man Wants to Help You. Seriously," *Fortune* (June 26, 2000): 327–33.
12. www.secondcity.com.
13. Daniels, "This Man Wants to Help You. Seriously."
14. Ibid., 328.
15. www.rollingstones.com, 2006.
16. A. Serwer, "Inside the Rolling Stones Inc." *Fortune*, September 30, 2002, 58–72.
17. www.rollingstones.com, 2006.
18. L. R. Offermann and R. K. Spiros, "The Science and Practice of Team Development: Improving the Link," *Academy of Management Journal*, April 2001, vol. 44, 376–393.
19. P. C. Earley, "Social Loafing and Collectivism: A Comparison of the United States and the People's Republic of China," *Administrative Science Quarterly* 34 (1989): 565–81; J. M. George, "Extrinsic and Intrinsic Origins of Perceived Social Loafing in Organizations," *Academy of Management Journal* 35 (1992): 191–202; S. G. Harkins, B. Latane, and K. Williams, "Social Loafing: Allocating Effort or Taking It Easy," *Journal of Experimental Social Psychology* 16 (1980): 457–65; B. Latane, K. D. Williams, and S. Harkins, "Many Hands Make Light the Work: The Causes and Consequences of Social Loafing," Journal of Personality and Social Psychology 37 (1979): 822–32; J. A. Shepperd, "Productivity Loss in Performance Groups: A Motivation Analysis," *Psychological Bulletin* 113 (1993): 67–81.
20. George, "Extrinsic and Intrinsic Origins of Perceived Social Loafing in Organizations"; G. R. Jones, "Task Visibility, Free Riding, and Shirking: Explaining the Effect of Structure and Technology on Employee Behavior," *Academy of Management Review* 9 (1984): 684–95; K. Williams, S. Harkins, and B. Latane, "Identifiability as a Deterrent to Social Loafing: Two Cheering Experiments," *Journal of Personality and Social Psychology* 40 (1981): 303–11.
21. M. A. Brickner, S. G. Harkins, and T. M. Ostrom, "Effects of Personal Involvement: Thought-Provoking Implications for Social Loafing," *Journal of Personality and Social Psychology* 51 (1986): 763–69; S. G. Harkins and R. E. Petty, "The Effects of Task Difficulty and Task Uniqueness on Social Loafing," *Journal of Personality and Social Psychology* 43 (1982): 1214–29; N. L. Kerr and S. E. Bruun, "Dispensability of Member Effort and Group Motivation Losses: Free-Rider Effects," *Journal of Personality and Social Psychology* 44 (1983): 78–94.
22. N. L. Kerr, "Motivation Losses in Small Groups: A Social Dilemma Analysis," *Journal of Personality and Social Psychology* 45 (1983): 819–28.
23. J. M. Jackson and S. G. Harkins, "Equity in Effort: An Explanation of the Social Loafing Effect," *Journal of Personality and Social Psychology* 49 (1985): 1199–206.
24. B. Latane, "Responsibility and Effort in Organizations." In P. S. Goodman (ed.), *Designing Effective Work Groups* (San Francisco: Jossey-Bass, 1986); Latane, Williams, and Harkins, "Many Hands Make Light the Work"; Steiner, Group Process and Productivity.
25. M. E. Shaw, Group Dynamics, 3rd ed. (New York: McGraw-Hill, 1981).

26. K. Lovelace, D. L. Shapiro, and L. R. Weingart, "Maximizing Cross-Functional New Product Teams' Innovativeness and Constraint Adherence: A Conflict communications Perspective," *Academy Management Journal*, August 2001, vol. 44, 779–94.
27. S. Harkins and J. Jackson, "The Role of Evaluation in Eliminating Social Loafing," Personality and Social *Psychology Bulletin* 11 (1985): 457–65; N. L. Kerr and S. E. Bruun, "Ringelman Revisited: Alternative Explanations for the Social Loafing Effect," *Personality and Social Psychology Bulletin* 7 (1981): 224–31; Williams, Harkins, and Latane, "Identifiability as a Deterrent to Social Loafing."
28. Brickner, Harkins, and Ostrom, "Effects of Personal Involvement"; Harkins and Petty, "The Effects of Task Difficulty and Task Uniqueness on Social Loafing."
29. R. Rapaport, "To Build a Winning Team: An Interview with Head Coach Bill Walsh," *Harvard Business Review* (January–February 1993): 111–20.
30. Latane, "Responsibility and Effort in Organizations"; Latane, Williams, and Harkins, "Many Hands Make Light the Work"; Steiner, Group Process and Productivity.
31. www.gsk.com, 2006.
32. Ibid.
33. J. D. Thompson, *Organizations in Action* (New York: McGraw-Hill, 1967).
34. G. Stewart and M. R. Barrick, "Team Structure and Performance: Assessing the Mediating Role of Intrateam Process and The Moderating Role of Task Type," *Academy of Management Journal*, April 200, vol. 43, 135–49.
35. Ibid.
36. Steiner, Group Process and Productivity.
37. www.levistrauss.com, 2006.
38. R. T. King "Jeans Therapy: Levi's Factory Employees are Assigned to Teams and Moral Takes a Hit." *Wall Street Journal*, 1998, May 20th, A1.
39. www.levistrauss.com, 2004, press release.
40. www.hickorysprings.com, 2006.
41. J. Bailey, "With Price Increases Rare, Small Firms Struggle to Survive," *Wall Street Journal*, September 4th, 2001, B2.
42. G. S. Van Der Vegt, E. Van De Vliert, and A. Oosterhof, "Informational Dissimilarity and Organizational Citizenship Behavior: The Role of Intra-team Interdependence and Team Identification," *Academy of Management Journal*, December 2003, vol. 46, 715–28.
43. L. Festinger, "Informal Social Communication," *Psychological Review*, 57 (1950): 271–82; Shaw, Group Dynamics.
44. D. Cartwright, "The Nature of Group Cohesiveness." In D. Cartwright and A. Zander (eds.), Group Dynamics, 3rd ed. (New York: Harper & Row, 1968) L. Festinger, S. Schacter, and K. Black, Social Pressures in Informal Groups (New York: Harper & Row, 1950); Shaw, Group Dynamics.
45. D. A. Harrison, K. H. Price, J. H. Gavin, and A. T. Florey, "Time, Teams and Task Performance: Changing Effects of Surface- and Deep-Level Diversity on Group Functioning," *Academy of Management Journal*, October 2002, vol. 45, 1029–46.
46. J. A. Chatman and F. J. Flynn, "The Influence of Demographic Heterogeneity on the Emergence and Consequences of Cooperative Norms in Work Teams," *Academy of Management Journal*, October 2001, vol. 44, 956–75; A. E. Randel and K. S. Jaussi, "Functional Background Identity, Diversity, and Individual Performance in Cross-Functional Teams," *Academy of Management Journal*, December 2003, vol. 46, 775.
47. B. Beersma, J. R. Hollenbeck, S. E. Humphrey, H. Moon, D. E. Conlon, and D. R. Ilgen, "Cooperation, Competition, and Team Performance: Toward a Contingency Approach," *Academy of Management Journal*, October 2003, vol. 46, 591.
48. D. Knight, C. C. Durham, and A. Edwin, "The Relationship of Team Goals, Incentives, and Efficacy to Strategic Risk, Tactical Implementation, and Performance," *Academy of Management Journal*, April 2001, vol. 44, 236–339.
49. J. S. Bunderson and K. M. Sutcliffe, "Comparing Alternative Conceptualizations of Functional Diversity in Management Teams: Process and Performance Effects," *Academy of Management Journal*, October 2002, vol. 45, 875–94.
50. G. Chen and R. J. Klimoski, "The Impact of Expectations on Newcomer Performance in Teams as Moderated by Work Characteristics, Social Exchanges, and Empowerment," *Academy of Management Journal*, October 2003, vol. 46, 591–608.
51. Shaw, Group Dynamics.
52. J. R. Hackman, "Group Influences on Individuals in Organizations." In Dunnette and Hough (eds.), *Handbook of Industrial and Organizational Psychology*, 2nd ed., vol 2 (Palo Alto, CA: Consulting Psychologists Press, 1992), 199–267.
53. Shaw, Group Dynamics.
54. R. O. Crockett and S. Baker, "Suddenly, Mobile Phones Aren't Moving So Fast," *Business Week* (November 6, 2000): BusinessWeek Online; S. Baker, I. Resch, and R. O. Crockett, "Commentary: Nokia's Costly Stumble," *Business Week* (August 14, 2000): BusinessWeek Online.
55. www.nokia.com, 2006.
56. Ibid.
57. Ibid.
58. Ibid.
59. S. Finkelstein and D. C. Hambrick, "Top management Team Tenure and Organizational Outcomes: The Moderating Role of Managerial Discretion," *Administrative Science Quarterly* 35 (1990): 484–503.
60. I. L. Janis, *Victims of Groupthink*, 2nd ed. (Boston: Houghton Mifflin, 1982).
61. C. J. Collins and K. D. Clark, "Strategic Human Resource Practices, Top Management Team Social Networks, and Firm Performance: The Role of Human Resource Practices in creating Organizational Competitive Advantage," *Academy of Management Journal*, December 2003, vol. 46, 740–52.
62. V. U. Druskat and J. V. Wheeler, "Managing From the Boundary: The Effective Leadership of Self-Managing Work Teams," *Academy of Management Journal*, August 2003, vol. 46, 435–58.
63. J. A. Pearce II and E. C. Ravlin, "The Design and Activation of Self-Regulating Work Groups," *Human Relations* 11 (1987): 751–82.
64. A. R. Montebello and V. R. Buzzotta, "Work Teams That Work," *Training and Development* (March 1993): 59–64.

65. J. R. Hackman and G. R. Oldham, Work Redesign (Reading, MA: Addison-Wesley, 1980).
66. B. Dumain, "Who Needs a Boss?," *Fortune* (May 7, 1990): 52–60; Pearce and Ravlin, "The Design and Activation of Self-Regulating Work Groups."
67. A. B. Henley and K. H. Price, "Want a Better Team? Foster a Climate of Fairness," *Academy of Management Executive*, August 2002, vol. 16, 153–55.
68. J. St Bunderson, "Team Member Functional Background and Involvement in Management Teams: Direct Effects and The Moderating Role of Power Centralization," *Academy of Management Journal*, August 2003, vol. 46, 458–75.
69. B. L. Kirkman and D. L. Shapiro, "The Impact of Cultural Values on Job Satisfaction and Organizational Commitment in Self-Managing Work Teams: The Mediating Role of Employee Resistance," *Academy of Management Journal*, June 2001, vol. 44, 557–70.
70. Dumain, "Who Needs a Boss?"
71. T. D. Wall, N. J. Kemp, P. R. Jackson, and C. W. Clegg, "Outcomes of Autonomous Workgroups: A Long-Term Field Experiment," *Academy of Management Journal* 29 (1986): 280–304.
72. R. D. O'Keefe, J. A. Kernaghan, and A. H. Rubenstein, "Group Cohesiveness: A Factor in the Adoption of Innovations Among Scientific Work Groups," *Small Group Behavior* 6 (1975): 282–92; C. A. O'Reilly and K. H. Roberts, "Task Group Structure, Communication, and Effectiveness in Three Organizations," *Journal of Applied Psychology* 62 (1977): 674–81.
73. R. T. Keller, "Cross-Functional project Groups in Research and New Product Development: Diversity, communications, Job Stress, and Outcomes," *Academy of Management Journal*, June 2001, vol. 44, 547–56.
74. J. B. White and O. Suris, "How a 'Skunk Works' Kept the Mustang Alive—on a Tight Budget," *Wall Street Journal*, September 21, 1993, A1, A12.
75. Ibid.
76. B. L. Kirkman, B. Rosen, C. B. Gibson, P. E. Tesluk and S. O. McPherson, "Five Challenges to Virtual Team Success: Lessons From Sabre, Inc.," *Academy of Management Executive*, August 2002, vol. 16, 67–80.
77. J. Lipnack, "Virtual Teams," *Executive Excellence* 16(5 May 1999): 14–15.
78. D. L. Duarte and N. T. Snyder, Mastering Virtual Teams (San Francisco: Jossey-Bass 1999); K. A. Karl, "Book Review: Mastering Virtual Teams," *Academy of Management Executive* (August 1999): 118–19.
79. Ibid.
80. Steve Lohr, "Working Together, Wherever They Are," *New York Times*, October 5, 2005, G1.
81. B. Geber, "Virtual Teams," *Training* 32(4 April 1995): 36–40; T. Finholt and L. S. Sproull, "Electronic Groups at Work," *Organizational Science* 1 (1990): 41–64.
82. B. L. Kirkman and D. L. Shapiro, "The Impact of Cultural Values on Job Satisfaction and Organizational Commitment in Self-Managing Work Teams: The Mediating Role of Employee Resistance," *Academy of Management Journal*, June 2001, vol. 44, 557–70.
83. www.hp.com, 2006.
84. Geber, "Virtual Teams."
85. Ibid.
86. Ibid.
87. G. R. Jones and J. M. George, "The Experience and Evolution of Trust: Implications for Cooperation and Teamwork," *Academy of Management Review*, July 1998, vol. 23, 531–47.
88. Geber, "Virtual Teams."
89. E. J. Hill, B. C. Miller, S. P. Weiner, and J. Colihan, "Influences of the Virtual Office on Aspects of Work and Work/Life Balance," *Personnel Psychology* 31 (1998): 667–83; S. G. Strauss, "Technology, Group Process, and Group Outcomes: Testing the Connections in Computer-Mediated and Face-to-Face Groups," *Human Computer Interaction* 12 (1997): 227–66; M. E. Warkentin, L. Sayeed, and R. Hightower, "Virtual Teams versus Face-to-Face Teams: An Exploratory Study of a Web-based Conference System," *Decision Sciences* 28(4 Fall 1997): 975–96.
90. Geber, "Virtual Teams."

CHAPTER 12

1. www.claires.com, 2006.
2. D. Foust, "A Sister Act That's Wowing Them," *BusinessWeek*, March 13, 2006, 28–30.
3. Ibid.
4. www.claires.com, 2006.
5. G. Yukl, "Managerial Leadership: A Review of Theory and Research," *Journal of Management* 15 (1989): 251–89.
6. G. Yukl, *Leadership in Organizations*, 2nd ed. (New York: Academic Press, 1989).
7. W. Shen, "The Dynamics of the CEO-Board Relationship: An Evolutionary Perspective," *Academy of Management Review*, July 2003, vol. 28, 466–77.
8. D. A. Waldman, G. G. Ramirez, R. J. House, and P. Puranam, "Does Leadership Matter? CEO Leadership Attributes and Profitability Under Conditions of Perceived Environmental Uncertainty," *Academy of Management Journal*, February 2001, vol. 44, 134–44.
9. L. Coch and J. R. P. French, "Overcoming Resistance to Change," *Human Relations* 1 (1948): 512–32; G. Graen, F. Dansereau Jr., T. Minami, and J. Cashman, "Leadership Behaviors as Cues to Performance Evaluation," *Academy of Management Journal* 16 (1973): 611–23; G. Graen and S. Ginsburgh, "Job Resignation as a Function of Role Orientation and Leader Acceptance: A Longitudinal Investigation of Organizational Assimilation," *Organizational Behavior and Human Performance* 19 (1977): 1–17; R. J. House and M. L. Baetz, "Leadership: Some Empirical Generalizations and New Research Directions." In B. M. Staw and L. L. Cummings (eds.), *Research in Organizational Behavior*, vol. 1 (Greenwich, CT: JAI Press, 1979), 341–423; N. R. F. Maier, *Problem Solving and Creativity in Individuals and Groups* (Belmont, CA: Brooks-Cole, 1970); K. N. Wexley, J. P. Singh, and G. A. Yukl, "Subordinate Personality as a Moderator of the Effects of Participation in Three Types of Appraisal Interviews," *Journal of Applied Psychology* 58 (1973): 54–59.
10. House and Baetz, "Leadership."
11. Yukl, "Managerial Leadership."
12. Stogdill, *Handbook of Leadership*; House and Baetz, "Leadership."

13. B. M. Bass, *Bass and Stogdill's Handbook of Leadership: Theory, Research, and Managerial Applications*, 3d ed. (New York: Free Press, 1990); House and Baetz, "Leadership"; S. A. Kirpatrick and E. A. Locke, "Leadership: Do Traits Matter?" *Academy of Management Executive* 5(2 1991): 48–60; G. Yukl, *Leadership in Organizations*; Yukl and Van Fleet, "Theory and Research on Leadership in Organizations."
14. E. A. Fleishman, "The Description of Supervisory Behavior," *Personnel Psychology* 37 (1953): 1–6; A. W. Halpin and B. J. Winer, "A Factorial Study of the Leader Behavior Descriptions." In R. M. Stogdill and A. E. Coons (eds.), *Leader Behavior: Its Description and Measurement* (Columbus: Bureau of Business Research, Ohio State University, 1957).
15. E. A. Fleishman, "Performance Assessment Based on an Empirically Derived Task Taxonomy," *Human Factors* 9 (1967): 349–66.
16. D. Tscheulin, "Leader Behavior Measurement in German Industry," *Journal of Applied Psychology* 56 (1971): 28–31.
17. P. Nulty, "The Bounce Is Back at Goodyear," *Fortune* (September 7, 1992): 70–72.
18. G. G. Marcial, "Goldman & Schwab," *Business Week* (October 2, 2000): BusinessWeek Online; www.schwab.com.
19. "The Top 25 Managers–Managers to Watch"; "David S. Pottruck and Charles R. Schwab, Charles Schwab Corp.," *Business Week* (January 8, 2001): BusinessWeek Online.
20. Ibid.
21. E. A. Fleishman and E. F. Harris, "Patterns of Leadership Behavior Related to Employee Grievances and Turnover," *Personnel Psychology* 15 (1962): 43–56.
22. P. M. Podsakoff, W. D. Todor, R. A. Grover, and V. L. Huber, "Situational Moderators of Leader Reward and Punishment Behaviors: Fact or Fiction?," *Organizational Behavior and Human Performance* 34 (1984): 21–63; P. M. Podsakoff, W. D. Todor, and R. Skov, "Effects of Leader Contingent and Noncontingent Reward and Punishment Behaviors on Subordinate Performance and Satisfaction," *Academy of Management Journal* 25 (1982): 810–21.
23. G. Das, "Local Memoirs of a Global Manager," *Harvard Business Review* (March–April 1993): 38–47.
24. Podsakoff, Todor, Grover, and Huber, "Situational Moderators of Leader Reward and Punishment Behaviors"; Podsakoff, Todor, and Skov, "Effects of Leader Contingent and Noncontingent Reward and Punishment Behaviors on Subordinate Performance and Satisfaction."
25. E. A. Fleishman, *Leadership Opinion Questionnaire* (Chicago: Science Research Associates, 1960).
26. R. R. Blake and J. S. Mouton, *The New Managerial Grid* (Houston: Gulf, 1978).
27. P. Hersey and K. Blanchard, *Management of Organizational Behavior: Utilizing Human Resources* (Upper Saddle River, NJ: Prentice Hall, 1982).
28. F. E. Fiedler, *A Theory of Leadership Effectiveness* (New York: McGraw–Hill, 1967); F. E. Fiedler, "The Contingency Model and the Dynamics of the Leadership Process." In L. Berkowitz, (ed.), *Advances in Experimental Social Psychology* (New York: Academic Press, 1978).
29. M. Mofflet, "Culture Shock," *Wall Street Journal*, September 24, 1992, R13–R14.
30. House and Baetz, "Leadership."
31. Ibid.; L. H. Peters, D. D. Hartke, and J. T. Pohlmann, "Fiedler's Contingency Theory of Leadership: An Application of the Meta-Analysis Procedures of Schmidt and Hunter," *Psychological Bulletin* 97 (1985): 274–85.
32. T. J. Maurer, H. R. Pierce, and L. M. Shore, "Perceived Beneficiary of Employee Development Activity: A Three-Dimensional Social Exchange Model," *Academy of Management Journal*, July 2002, vol. 27, 432–45.
33. www.microsoft.com, 2006; www.msn.com, 2006.
34. J. C. Wofford and L. Z. Liska, "Path-Goal Theories of Leadership: A Meta-Analysis," *Journal of Management* 19 (1993): 857–76.
35. V. H. Vroom and P. W. Yetton, *Leadership and Decision-Making* (Pittsburgh: University of Pittsburgh Press, 1973).
36. J. Templeman, "Bob Eaton Is No Lee Iacocca—but He Doesn't Need to Be," *Business Week* (November 9, 1992): 96.
37. V. U. Druskat and J. V. Wheeler, "Managing From the Boundary: The Effective Leadership of Self-Managing Work Teams," *Academy of Management Journal*, August 2003, vol. 46, 435–58.
38. D. I. Jung and B. J. Avolio, "Effects of Leadership Style and Follower's Cultural Orientation on Performance in Group and Individual Task Conditions," *Academy of Management Journal*, April 1999, vol. 42, 208–19.
39. R. M. Dienesch and R. C. Liden, "Leader–Member Exchange Model of Leadership: A Critique and Further Development," *Academy of Management Review* 11 (1986): 618–34; G. Graen, M. Novak, and P. Sommerkamp, "The Effects of Leader-Member Exchange and Job Design on Productivity and Satisfaction: Testing a Dual Attachment Model," *Organizational Behavior and Human Performance* 30 (1982): 109–31.
40. G. Graen and J. Cashman, "A Role-Making Model of Leadership in Formal Organizations: A Development Approach." In J. G. Hunt and L. L. Larson (eds.), *Leadership Frontiers* (Kent, OH: Kent State University Press, 1975), 143–65.
41. C. A. Schriesheim, L. Neider, and T. A. Scandura, "Delegation and Leader-Member Exchange: Main Effects, Moderators, and Measurement Issues," *Academy of Management Journal*, June 98, vol. 41, 298–319.
42. M. Wakabayashi and G. B. Graen, "The Japanese Career Progress Study: A Seven-Year Follow-Up," *Journal of Applied Psychology* 69 (1984): 603–14.
43. H. J. Klein and J. S. Kim, "A Field Study of the Influence of Situational Constraints, Leader-Member Exchange, and Goals," *Academy of Management Journal*, February 1998, vol. 41, 88–96.
44. W. E. McClane, "Implications of Member Role Differentiation: Analysis of a Key Concept in the LMX Model of Leadership," *Group and Organization Studies* 16 (1991): 102–13; Yukl, *Leadership in Organizations*; Yukl and Van Fleet, "Theory and Research on Leadership in Organizations."
45. J. R. Meindl, "On Leadership: An Alternative to the Conventional Wisdom." In B. M. Staw and L. L. Cummings (eds.), *Research in Organizational Behavior*, vol. 12 (Greenwich, CT: JAI Press, 1990), 159–203.

46. S. Kerr and J. M. Jermier, "Substitutes for Leadership: Their Meaning and Measurement," *Organizational Behavior and Human Performance* 22 (1978): 375–403.
47. L. Killian, "California, Here We Come," *Forbes* (November 23, 1992): 146–47.
48. Ibid.
49. P. M. Podsakoff, B. P. Niehoff, S. B. MacKenzie, and M. L. Williams, "Do Substitutes for Leadership Really Substitute for Leadership? An Empirical Examination of Kerr and Jermier's Situational Leadership Model," *Organizational Behavior and Human Decision Processes* 54 (1993): 1–44.
50. D. Hakim, "Type B Chief Guides GM on a Course to revival," *New York Times*, November 25, 2001, 3.1.
51. Ibid.
52. www.ford.com, 2006.
53. B. Elgin, "Making Her Own Luck," *Business Week* (November 20, 2000): EB48–EB56.
54. www.timewarner.com, 2006.
55. M. Peers, "Tuning Up; Unflamboyant CEO Parsons Calms Infighting, Cuts Debt," *Wall Street Journal*, December 11, 2003, B.1.
56. J. L. Roberts, "Prime Time for Parsons," *Newsweek*, December 22 2003, 43–44.
57. www.timewarner.com, 2006
58. R. J. Meindl, "On Leadership: An Alternative to the Conventional Wisdom," *Research in Organizational Behavior* 1990, 12, 159–203.
59. W. L. Gardner and B. J. Avolio, "The Charismatic Relationship: A Dramaturgical Perspective," *Academy of Management Journal*, January 1998, vol. 23, 32–59.
60. B. M. Bass, *Leadership and Performance Beyond Expectations* (New York: Free Press, 1985).
61. J. E. Bono and T. A. Judge, "Self-Concordance at Work: Toward Understanding the Motivational Effects of Transformational Leaders," *Academy of Management Journal*, October 2003, vol. 46, 554–72; Bass, *Bass and Stogdill's Handbook of Leadership*; Yukl and Van Fleet, "Theory and Research on Leadership in Organizations."
62. J. A. Conger and R. N. Kanungo, "Behavioral Dimensions of Charismatic Leadership." In J. A. Conger, R. N. Kanungo, and Associates, *Charismatic Leadership* (San Francisco: Jossey-Bass, 1988).
63. G. Chen and R. J. Klimoski, "The Impact of Expectations on Newcomer Performance in Teams as Mediated by Work Characteristics, Social Exchanges, and Empowerment," *Academy of Management Journal*, October 2003, vol. 46, 591–608.
64. Ibid.; D. A. Waldman, "CEO Charismatic Leadership: Levels-of-Management and Levels-of-Analysis Effects," *Academy of Management Journal*, April 1999, vol. 24, 266–86.
65. J. C. Pastor, J. R. Meindl, and M. C. Mayo, "A Network Effects Model of Charisma Attributions," *Academy of Management Journal*, April 2002, vol. 45, 410–21.
66. Bass, *Leadership and Performance Beyond Expectations*; Bass, *Bass and Stogdill's Handbook of Leadership*; Yukl and Van Fleet, "Theory and Research on Leadership in Organizations."
67. T. Dvir, D. Eden, B. Avolio, and B. Shamir, "Impact of Transformational Leadership on Follower Development and Performance: A Field Experiment," *Academy of Management Journal*, August 2003, vol. 45, 735–45.
68. Ibid.
69. C. Caldwell, R. Litz, and W. R. Nord, "Building Trust Through Effective Governance—Three Perspectives of Organizational Leadership," *Academy of Management Review*, October 2003, vol. 28, 667–74.
70. N. Byrnes, "Avon: The New Calling," *Business Week* (September 18, 2000): 136–48; C. Hawn, "Tag Team," *Forbes* (January 11, 1999): 184–86; J. Pellet, "Ding-Dong Avon Stalling," *Chief Executive* (June 2000): 26–31; P. Sellers, "Big, Hairy, Audacious Goals Don't Work—Just Ask P&G," *Fortune* (April 3, 2000): 39–44.
71. Ibid.
72. www.avon.com, 2006
73. Ibid.
74. Bass, *Leadership and Performance Beyond Expectations*.
75. Bass, *Bass and Stogdill's Handbook of Leadership*; B. M. Bass and B. J. Avolio, "Transformational Leadership: A Response to Critiques." In M. M. Chemers and R. Ayman (eds.), *Leadership Theory and Research: Perspectives and Directions* (San Diego: Academic Press, 1993), 49–80; B. M. Bass, B. J. Avolio, and L. Goodheim, "Biography and the Assessment of Transformational Leadership at the World Class Level," *Journal of Management* 13 (1987): 7–20; J. J. Hater and B. M. Bass, "Superiors' Evaluations and Subordinates' Perceptions of Transformational and Transactional Leadership," *Journal of Applied Psychology* 73 (1988): 695–702; R. Pillai, "Crisis and the Emergence of Charismatic Leadership in Groups: An Experimental Investigation," *Journal of Applied Psychology* 26 (1996): 543–62; J. Seltzer and B. M. Bass, "Transformational Leadership: Beyond Initiation and Consideration," *Journal of Management* 16 (1990): 693–703; D. A. Waldman, B. M. Bass, and W. O. Einstein, "Effort, Performance, and Transformational Leadership in Industrial and Military Service," *Journal of Occupational Psychology* 60 (1987): 1–10.
76. D. I. Jung and B. J. Avolio, "Opening the Black Box: An Experimental Investigation of the Mediating Effects of Trust and Value Congruence on Transformational and Transactional Leadership," *Journal of Organizational Behavior*, December 2000, 949–64.; B. M. Bass and B. J. Avolio, "Transformational and Transactional Leadership:1992 and Beyond," *Journal of European Industrial Training*, 1990, January, 20–35.
77. J. Porras and J. Collins, *Built to Last: Successful Habits of Visionary Companies* (New York: HarperCollins, 1994).
78. J. Barling, T. Weber, and E. K. Kelloway, "Effects of Transformational Leadership on Attitudes and Financial Outcomes: A Field Experiment," *Journal of Applied Psychology*, December 1996, 827–32.
79. T. Dvir, D. Even, and B. J. Avolio, "Impact of Transformational Leadership on Follower Development and Performance," *Academy of Management Journal*, August 2002, 735–44.
80. R. Pillai, C. A. Schriesheim, and E. S. Williams, "Fairness Perceptions and Trust as Mediators for Transformational and Transactional Leadership: A Two-Sample Study," *Journal of Management* 25 (1999): 897–933.
81. J. M. George and K. Bettenhausen, "Understanding Prosocial Behavior, Sales Performance, and Turnover: A

Group-Level Analysis in a Service Context," *Journal of Applied Psychology* 75 (1990): 698–709.
82. J. M. George, "Emotions and Leadership: The Role of Emotional Intelligence," *Human Relations* 53(8 2000): 1027–55.
83. A. H. Eagly and B. T. Johnson, "Gender and Leadership Style: A Meta-Analysis," *Psychological Bulletin* 108 (1990): 233–56.
84. Ibid.
85. Ibid.
86. A. H. Eagly, M. G. Makhijani, and B. G. Klonsky, "Gender and the Evaluation of Leaders: A Meta-Analysis," *Psychological Bulletin* 111 (1992): 3–22.
87. R. Sharpe, "As Leaders, Women Rule," *Business Week* (November 20, 2000): 75–84.
88. P. Gogoi, "Teaching Men the Right Stuff," *Business Week* (November 20, 2000): 84.
89. www.wholefoodsmarket.com, 2006. John Mackey's Blog: 20 Questions with Sunni's Salon.
90. D. McGinn, "The Green Machine," *Newsweek*, March 21, 2005, E8–E10.
91. S. Shim, "Getting Grads on LUV, Colleen," *Biz Ed*, March/April, 2003, 20.

CHAPTER 13

1. www.Viacom.com, 2006; www.cbs.com, 2006, www.newscorp.com, 2006.
2. J. L. Robers, "A Mogul in Full," *Newsweek*, April 24, 2006, 43–45.
3. www.newscorp.com, 2005.
4. J. L. Roberts, "Murdock Family Values," *Newsweek*, August 8, 2005, 36–38.
5. R. A. Dahl, "The Concept of Power," *Behavioral Science*, 1957, 2, 210–15; R. M. Emerson, "Power Dependence Relations," *American Sociological Review*, 1962, 27, 31–41.
6. J. Pfeffer, *Power in Organizations* (Boston: Pitman, 1981).
7. A. M. Pettigrew, *The Politics of Organizational Decision Making* (London: Tavistock, 1973); R. H. Miles, *Macro Organizational Behavior* (Santa Monica, CA: Goodyear, 1980).
8. "Making Ends Meet," *The Economist*, April 7, 1993, 3.
9. "Tyco Executives Get Up to 25 Years In Jail," www.msnbc.com, Septemper 19, 2005.
10. S. K. Kearns, "When Goliaths Clash: Managing Executive Conflict to Build a More Dynamic Organization," *Academy of Management Executive*, November 2003, vol. 17, 162–65.
11. J. G. March, "The Business Firm As a Coalition," *Journal of Politics*, 1962, 24, 662–78; D. J. Vrendenburgh and J. G. Maurer, "A Process Framework of Organizational Politics," *Human Relations*, 1984, 37, 47–66.
12. W. Shen and A. A. Cannella Jr., "Power Dynamics Within Top Management and Their Impacts on CEO Dismissal Followed by Inside Succession," *Academy of Management Journal*, December 2002, vol. 45, 1195–207.
13. P. H. Thornton, "The Rise of Corporation in a Craft Industry: Conflict and Conformity in Institutional Logics," *Academy of Management Journal*, February 2002, vol. 45, 81–102.
14. This section draws heavily on J. R. P. French, Jr., and B. Raven, "The Bases of Social Power." In D. Cartwright, ed., *Studies in Social Power* (Ann Arbor: University of Michigan, Institute for Social Research, 1959), 150–67.
15. M. Weber, *The Theory of Economic and Social Organization* (New York: Free Press, 1947).
16. Ibid.
17. Pettigrew, *The Politics of Organizational Decision Making*; G. Yukl and C. M. Falbe, "Importance of Different Power Sources in Downward and Lateral Relations," *Journal of Applied Psychology*, 1991, 76, 416–23.
18. J. A. Conger and R. N. Kanungo, "The Empowerment Process: Integrating Theory and Practice," *Academy of Management Review*, 1988, 13, 471–81.
19. French and Raven, "The Bases of Social Power."
20. M. Weber, *Economy and Society* (Berkeley: University of California Press, 1978); H. M. Trice and J. M. Beyer, "Charisma and Its Routinization in Two Social Movement Organizations," *Research in Organizational Behavior*, 1986, 8, 113–64.
21. B. M. Bass, "Leadership: Good, Better, Best," *Organizational Dynamics*, 1985, 13, 26–40.
22. Weber, *Economy and Society*.
23. J. Hall, "WorldCom Board Expected to be Wiped Clean," www.Reuters.com, October 8, 2002.
24. This section draws heavily on D. J. Hickson, C. R. Hinings, C. A. Lee, R. E. Schneck, and D. J. Pennings, "A Strategic Contingencies Theory of Intraorganizational Power," *Administrative Science Quarterly*, 1971, 16, 216–27; and C. R. Hinings, D. J. Hickson, J. M. Pennings, and R. E. Schneck, "Structural Conditions of Interorganizational Power," *Administrative Science Quarterly*, 1974, 19, 22–44.
25. Hickson, Hinings, Lee, Schneck, and Pennings, "A Strategic Contingencies Theory of Intraorganizational Power."
26. M. Gargiulo, "Two Step Leverage: Managing Constraint in Organizational Politics," *Administrative Science Quarterly*, 1993, 38, 1–19.
27. M. M. Montoya-Weiss, A. P. Massey, and M. Song, "Getting It Together: Temporal Coordination and Conflict Management in Global Virtual Teams," *Academy of Management Journal*, December 2001, vol. 44, 1251–63.
28. Ibid.
29. M. Crozier, "Sources of Power of Lower Level Participants in Complex Organizations," *Administrative Science Quarterly*, 1962, 7, 349–64.
30. T. Welbourne and C. O. Trevor, "The Roles of Departmental and Position Power in Job Evaluation," *Academy of Management Journal*, August 2000, vol. 43, 761–72.
31. Ibid; J. D. Bunferson, "Team Member Functional Background and Involvement in Management Teams: Direct Effects and the Moderating Role of Power Centralization," *Academy of Management Journal*, August 2003, vol. 46, 458–75.
32. A. M. Pettigrew, "Information Control as a Power Resource," *Sociology*, 1972, 6, 187–204.
33. G. R. Salancik and J. Pfeffer, "The Bases and Uses of Power in Organizational Decision Making," *Administrative Science Quarterly*, 1974, 19, 453–73; J. Pfeffer and G. R. Salancik, *The External Control of Organizations: A*

Resource Dependence View (New York: Harper and Row, 1978).

34. K. S. Jehn and E. A. Mannix, "The Dynamic Nature of Conflict: A Longitudinal Study of Intragroup Conflict and Group Performance," *Academy of Management Journal*, April 2000, vol. 44, pp. 238–252.
35. D. A. Schuler, K. Rehbein and R. D. Cramer, "Pursuing Strategic Advantage Through Political Means: A Multivariate Approach," *Academy of Management Journal*, August 2000, vol. 45, pp. 659–673.
36. T. Burns, "Micropolitics: Mechanisms of Institutional Change," *Administrative Science Quarterly*, 1961, 6, pp. 257–281.
37. E. Jennings, The Mobile Manager (New York: McGraw-Hill, 1967).
38. R. S. Meyers, "Managing With Power," Academy of Management Executive, May 1992, vol. 6, pp. 104–107.
39. M. D. Lord, "Constituency Building as the Foundation for Corporate Political Strategy," *Academy of Management Executive*, February 2003, vol. 17, pp. 112–125.
40. T. G. Pollock, H. M. Fischer and J. B. Wade, "The Role of Power and Politics in the Repricing of Executive Options," *Academy of Management Journal*, December 2002, vol. 45, pp. 1172–1183.
41. This discussion draws heavily on Pfeffer, Power in Organizations, Ch. 5.
42. Hickson, Hinings, Lee, Schneck, and Pennings, "A Strategic Contingencies Theory of Intraorganizational Power."
43. K. M. Eisenhardt and L. J. Bourgeois, III, "Politics of Strategic Decision Making in High-Velocity Environments: Toward a Midrange Theory," *Academy of Management Journal*, December 1988, vol. 31, pp. 737–71.
44. B. Townley, "The Role of Competing Rationalities in Institutional Change," *Academy of Management Journal*," February 2002, vol. 45, pp. 163–180.
45. This section draws heavily on Pfeffer, Power in Organizations, Ch. 2.
46. www.kodak.com, 2006.
47. G. Jones, "Kodak: We Push the Button, You Do the Rest," In C.W. L. Hill and G.R. Jones, "Strategic management: An Integrated Approach, 6th ed. Boston: Houghton Mifflin, 2004.
48. "Kodak Forms 15-member Senior Management Team," *Business Wire*, October 14, 1999.
49. www.kodak.com, 2006.
50. B. Gray and S. S. Ariss, "Politics and Strategic Change Across Organizational Life Cycles," *Academy of Management Review*, October 1985, vol. 10, pp. 707–724.
51. J. A. Litterer, "Conflict in Organizations: A Reexamination," *Academy of Management Journal*, 1966, 9, pp. 178–186; S. M. Schmidt and T. A. Kochan, "Conflict: Towards Conceptual Clarity," Administrative Science Quarterly, 1972, 13, pp. 359–370; Miles, *Macro-Organizational Behavior*.
52. Miles, Macro-Organizational Behavior.
53. S. P. Robbins, Managing Organizational Conflict: A Nontraditional Approach (Englewood Cliffs, N.J.: Prentice-Hall, 1974); L. Coser, The Functions of Social Conflict (New York: Free Press, 1956).
54. A. C. Amason, "Distinguishing the Effects of Functional and Dysfunctional Conflict on Strategic Decision Making . . . ," *Academy of Management Journal*, February 1996, vol. 39, pp. 123–149.
55. B. Kabanoff, "Equity, Equality, Power, and Conflict," *Academy of Management Review*, April 1991, vol. 16, pp. 416–442.
56. This discussion owes much to the seminal work of the following authors: Lou R. Pondy, "Organizational Conflict: Concepts and Models," *Administrative Science Quarterly*, 1967, 2, pp. 296–320; and R. E. Walton and J. M. Dutton, "The Management of Interdepartmental Conflict: A Model and Review," *Administrative Science Quarterly*, 1969, 14, pp. 62–73.
57. S. W. Floyd, "Strategizing Throughout the Organization: Managing Role Conflict in Strategic Renewal," *Academy of Management Review*, January 2000, vol. 25, pp. 154–178.
58. M. K. Duffy, J. D. Shaw and E. M. Stark, "Performance and Satisfaction in Conflicted Interdependent Groups: When and How Does Self-Esteem Make a Difference?" *Academy of Management Journal*, August 2000, vol. 43, pp. 772–783.
59. M. Dalton, Men Who Manage (New York: Wiley, 1959); Walton and Dutton, "The Management of Interdepartmental Conflict."
60. Walton and Dutton, "The Management of Interdepartmental Conflict"; J. McCann and J. R. Galbraith, "Interdepartmental Relationships," in P. C. Nystrom and W. H. Starbuck, eds., Handbook of Organizational Design (New York: Oxford University Press, 1981).
61. R. E. Nelson, "The Strength of Strong Ties: Social Networks and Intergroup Conflict in Organizations," *Academy of Management Journal*, June 1989, vol. 32, pp. 377–402.
62. www.gucci.com, 2006.
63. A. Galloni, J. Carreyrou, and C. Rohwedder, "Stripped of Stars at Top, Will Gucci Still Be Gucci?" *Wall Street Journal*, 2003, November 5, pp. A.1, A.14.
64. C. Horyn, "Struggling to Design the Future at Gucci," *New York Times*, 2004, Jan 10th, p. C.1.
65. J. D. Thompson, Organizations in Action (New York: McGraw-Hill, 1967).
66. K. S. Jehn and E. A. Mannix, "The Dynamic Nature of Conflict: A Longitudinal Study of Intragroup Conflict and Group Performance," *Academy of Management Journal*, April 2000, vol. 44, pp. 238–252.
67. Walton and Dutton, "The Management of Interdepartmental Conflict," p. 65.
68. Ibid., p. 68.
69. Pondy, "Organizational Conflict," p. 300.
70. Ibid., p. 310.
71. S. W. Floyd, "Strategizing Throughout the Organization: Managing Role Conflict in Strategic Renewal," Academy of Management Review, January 2000, vol. 25, pp. 154–178.
72. G. Labianca, D. J. Brass and B. Gray, "Social Networks and Perceptions of Intergroup Conflict: The Role of Negative Relationships and . . . ," *Academy of Management Journal*, February 1998, vol. 41, pp. 55–68.
73. CIC Corp. website www.cicagency.com.
74. B. Fannin, "CIC Workers Ask Judge to Void Noncompliance Pact." *The Eagle*, October 23rd, 1997.p.1.

75. P. S. Nugent, "Managing Conflict: Third-Party Interventions for Managers," *Academy of Management Executive*, February 2002, vol. 16, pp. 139–141.
76. J. Z. Rubin and B. R. Brown, The Social Psychology of Bargaining and Negotiation (New York: Academic Press, 1975).
77. J. F. Brett, "Stairways to Heaven: An Interlocking Self-Regulation Model of Negotiation," *Academy of Management Review*, July 1999, vol. 24, pp. 435–452.
78. J. T. Polzer, E. A. Mannix and M. A. Neale, "Interest Alignment and Coalitions in Multiparty Negotiation," *Academy of Management Journal*, February 1998, vol. 41, pp. 42–55.
79. E. E. Neilsen, "Understanding and Managing Intergroup Conflict." In J. F. Veiga and J. N. Yanouzas, eds., The Dynamics of Organizational Theory (St. Paul, Minn.: West, 1979), pp. 290–296; Miles, Macro-Organizational Behavior.
80. T. L. Stanley, "When Push Comes to Shove: A Manager's Guide to Resolving Disputes," Supervision, 2003, vol. 64, p. 6.
81. P. S. Nugent, "Managing Conflict: Third-Party Interventions for Managers," *Academy of Management Executive*, February 2002, vol. 16, pp. 139–141.
82. Neilsen, "Understanding and Managing Intergroup Conflict."
83. C. Bendersky, "Organizational Dispute Resolution Systems: A Complementarities Model," *Academy of Management Review*, October 2003, vol. 28, pp. 643–657.
84. R. E. Walton, "Third Party Roles in Interdepartmental Conflict," *Industrial Relations*, 1967, 7, pp. 29–43.
85. K. Thomas, "Conflict and Negotiation Processes in Organizations." In M. D. Dunnette and L. M. Hough, eds., Handbook of Industrial and Organizational Psychology, 2nd ed., vol 3 (Palo Alto, Calif.: Consulting Psychologists Press, 1992), pp. 651–717.
86. R. L. Pinkley and G. B. Northcraft, "Conflict Frames of Reference: Implications for Dispute Processes and Outcomes," *Academy of Management Journal*, February 1994, vol. 37, pp. 193–206.
87. R. E. Walton and R. B. McKersie, A Behavioral Theory of Labor Relations (New York: McGraw-Hill, 1965).
88. Ibid.

CHAPTER 14

1. K. Naughton, "The Blue-Collar CEO," *Newsweek*, December 5, 2005, 4–6.
2. www.daimlerchrysler.com, 2005.
3. K. Naughton, op. cit.
4. www.chrysler.com, 2006.
5. L. W. Porter and K. H. Roberts, "Communication in Organizations." In M. D. Dunnette (ed.), *Handbook of Industrial and Organizational Psychology* (Chicago: Rand McNally, 1976), 1553–89.
6. J. K. Barge and C. Oliver, "Working With Appreciation in Managerial Practice," *Academy of Management Review*, January 2003, vol. 28, 124–43.
7. C. A. O'Reilly and L. R. Pondy, "Organizational Communication." In S. Kerr (ed.), *Organizational Behavior* (Columbus, OH: Grid, 1979) pp.71–106.
8. Ibid.
9. K. L. Ashcraft, "Perspectives on Organizational Communications: Finding Common Ground," *Academy of Management Review*, October 2001, vol. 26, 666–69.
10. D. A. Hofmann and A. Stetzer, "The Role of Safety Climate and Communication in Accident Interpretation: Implications for Learning From Negative Events," *Academy of Management Journal*, December 1998, vol. 41, 644–58.
11. N. Phillips and J. L. Brown, "Analyzing Communication in and Around Organizations: A Critical Hermeneutic Approach," *Academy of Management Journal*, December 1993, vol. 36, 1547–77.
12. P. P. Le Breton, *Administrative Intelligence-Information Systems* (Boston: Houghton Mifflin, 1963); W. G. Scott and T. R. Mitchell, *Organization Theory* (Homewood, IL: Irwin, 1976).
13. R. Breeden, "Small Talk, Surfing the Net—At Work," *Wall Street Journal*, Oct 21, 2003, A24.
14. M. Conlin, "Employees, Surf at Your Own Risk," *Business Week* (June 12, 2000): 105–6.
15. Ibid.
16. L. Armstrong, "Someone to Watch Over You," *Business Week* (July 10, 2000): BusinessWeek Online.
17. "Internet Filters Curb Web Surfing," *Industrial Distribution*, 2003, 92, 36.
18. Ibid.
19. O. W. Baskin and C. E. Aronoff, *Interpersonal Communication in Organizations* (Santa Monica, CA: Goodyear, 1989).
20. F. Fearing, "Toward a Psychological Theory of Human Communication," *Journal of Personality* 22 (1953–1954): 73–76; Scott and Mitchell, *Organization Theory*.
21. J. M. George, "Mood and Absence," *Journal of Applied Psychology* 74 (1989): 317–24; J. M. George, "State or Trait: Effects of Positive Mood on Prosocial Behaviors at Work," *Journal of Applied Psychology* 76 (1991): 299–307; J. M. George and A. P. Brief, "Feeling Good-Doing Good: A Conceptual Analysis of the Mood at Work Organizational Spontaneity Relationship," *Psychological Bulletin* 112 (1992): 310–29.
22. S. Cohen and T. A. Wills, "Stress, Social Support, and the Buffering Hypothesis," *Psychological Bulletin* 98 (1985): 310–57; J. M. George, T. F. Reed, K. A. Ballard, J. Colin, and J. Fielding, "Contact with AIDS Patients as a Source of Work-Related Distress: Effects of Organizational and Social Support," *Academy of Management Journal* 36 (1993): 157–71.
23. V. Anand and C. C. Manz, "An Organizational Memory Approach to Information Management," *Academy of Management Review*, October 1998, vol. 23, 796–810.
24. D. Krackhardt and J. R. Hanson, "Informal Networks: The Company," *Harvard Business Review* (July–August 1993): 104–11.
25. E. M. Rogers and R. Agarwala-Rogers, *Communication in Organizations* (New York: Free Press, 1976).
26. "Employers Struggle to Teach Their Employees Basic Communication Skills," *Wall Street Journal*, November 30, 1993, A1.
27. "Corporate Jargon: If You Don't Know the Inside Skinny, It Can Be a Jumble," *Wall Street Journal*, February 15, 1994, A1.

28. "Managing Your Boss," *Harvard Business Review*, Video Series No. 4.
29. J. T. Malloy, *Dress for Success* (New York: Warner Books, 1975).
30. J. Sandberg, "People Are Hugging a Lot More Now and Seem to Like It," *Wall Street Journal*, March 15, 1993, A1, A5.
31. Ibid.
32. C. Gallo, "Leaders Must Look the Part," www.businessweek.com, March 11, 2006.
33. J. Carey, "Getting Business to Think About the Unthinkable," *Business Week* (June 24, 1991): 104–6.
34. Briefings from the Editors, "The New Communications: Don't Fax Me, I'll Fax You," *Harvard Business Review* (March–April 1993): 8–9.
35. www.brownsteingroup.com, 2004.
36. "Ultimate Vision," *ADWEEK* Eastern Edition (November 10, 1997): 54.
37. www.brownsteingroup.com; "Pennsylvania," *ADWEEK* Eastern Edition (September 9, 1996): 57; H. Stout, "Self-Evaluation Brings Change to a Family's Ad Agency," *Wall Street Journal*, January 6, 1998, B2.
38. H. Stout, "Self-Evaluation Brings Change to a Family's Ad Agency."
39. Ibid.
40. M. Anderson, "Renaissance Woman," *Adweek*, May 14, 2001, 5.
41. www.walmart.com, 2006.
42. N. Templin, "Companies Use TV to Reach Their Employees," *Wall Street Journal*, December 7, 1993, B1, B16.
43. Baskin and Aronoff, *Interpersonal Communication in Organizations*.
44. A. Rossett and T. Bickham, "Diversity Training: Hope, Faith, and Cynicism," *Training* (January 1994): 41–45.
45. D. Tannen, "The Power of Talk," Harvard Business Review (September–October 1995): 138–48; D. Tannen, *Talking from 9 to 5* (New York: Avon Books, 1995).
46. Ibid.
47. Ibid.
48. R. L. Daft, R. H. Lengel, and L. K. Trevino, "Message Equivocality, Media Selection, and Manager Performance: Implications for Information Systems," *MIS Quarterly* 11 (1987): 355–66; R. L. Daft and R. H. Lengel, "Information Richness: A New Approach to Managerial Behavior and Organization Design." In B. M. Staw and L. L. Cummings (eds.), *Research in Organizational Behavior* (Greenwich, CT: JAI Press, 1984), pp. 212–235.
49. R. L. Daft, *Organization Theory and Design* (New York: West, 1992).
50. J. D. Ford and L. W. Ford, "The Role of Conversations in Producing Intentional Change in Organizations," *Academy of Management Review*, July 1995, vol. 20, 541–71.
51. Ibid.
52. S. P. Weisband and S. K. Schneider, "Computer-Mediated Communication and Social Information: Status Salience and Status Differences," *Academy of Management Journal*, August 1995, vol. 38, 1124–52.
53. R. W. Collins, "Communications Policy and Information Technology: Promises, Problems and Prospects," *Academy of Management Review*, October 2003, vol. 28, 673–76.
54. E. Licking, "Innovations," *Business Week* (November 6, 2000): BusinessWeek Online; International Editorials, "The Mobile Net Requires a New Ethos," *Business Week* (May 22, 2000): BusinessWeek Online.
55. Ibid.
56. Ibid.
57. R. W. Collins, "Communications Policy and Information Technology: Promises, Problems and Prospects" *Academy of Management Review*, October 2003, vol. 28, 673–76.
58. Ibid.
59. Ibid.
60. www.alteonwebsystems.com, 2000.
61. B. Riggs, "Smarter Networks," *Informationweek*, (April 12, 1999): 6.
62. M. Borden, "When Big Growth Happens to Small Companies," *Fortune* (March 6, 2000): 385.
63. A. L. Sprout, "The Internet Inside Your Company," *Fortune* (November 27, 1995): 161–68.
64. S. G. Straus and J. E. McGrath, "Does the Medium Matter? The Interaction of Task Type and Technology on Group Performance and Member Reactions," *Journal of Applied Psychology* 79 (1994): 87–97.
65. S. G. Straus, S. P. Weisband, J. M. Wilson, "Human Resource Management Practices in the Networked Organization: Impacts of Electronic Communication Systems." In C. L. Cooper and D. M. Rousseau (eds.), *Trends in Organizational Behavior*, Vol. 5 (New York: John Wiley & Sons 1998): 127–54.
66. M. C. Boudreau, K. D. Loch, D. Robey, and D. Straud, "Going Global: Using Information Technology to Advance the Competitiveness of the Virtual Transnational Organization," *Academy of Management Executive*, November 1998, vol. 12, 120–29.
67. F. Morring, "Culture Shock Nasa Considers a Test Flight to Validate Fixes Set by Columbia Board," *Aviation Week*, Sept 1, 2003, 22.
68. M. L. Wald, "Management Issues Looming in Shuttle Inquiry," *Wall Street Journal*, Aug 6, 2003, A.11.
69. K. Chang and S. Coledad, "Some Recommended Changes Are Already Occurring," *New York Times*, Aug 27, 2003, A.16.
70. D. Simpson, "E-Mails Show How Katrina Swamped La. Gov." www.yahoo.com, 2005, December 10.

CHAPTER 15

1. www.mattel.com, 2006.
2. "Doll Wars," *Business Life*, May 2005, 40–42.
3. www.mattel.com, 2006.
4. A. Grove, "How Intel Makes Spending Pay Off," *Fortune* (February 22, 1993): 56–61.
5. J. G. March and H. A. Simon, *Organizations* (New York: Wiley, 1958); H. A. Simon, *The New Science of Management Decision* (New York: Harper & Row, 1960).
6. March and Simon, *Organizations*.
7. Ibid.; Simon, *The New Science of Management Decision*.
8. Ibid.
9. M. K. Stevenson, J. R. Busemeyer, and J. C. Naylor, "Judgment and Decision-Making Theory." In M. D. Dunnette and L. M. Hough, eds., *Handbook of Industrial and Organizational Psychology*, 2nd ed., vol. 1 (Palo Alto, CA: Consulting Psychologists Press, 1990), 283–374.

10. W. Edwards, "The Theory of Decision Making," *Psychological Bulletin* 51 (1954): 380–417; H. A. Simon, "A Behavioral Model of Rational Choice," *Quarterly Journal of Economics* 69 (1955): 99–118.
11. Ibid.
12. Edwards, "The Theory of Decision Making"; Stevenson, Busemeyer, and Naylor, "Judgment and Decision-Making Theory."
13. Simon, "A Behavioral Model of Rational Choice."
14. March and Simon, *Organizations*.
15. Ibid.
16. Ibid.
17. Edwards, "The Theory of Decision Making"; March and Simon, *Organizations*; Simon "A Behavioral Model of Rational Choice."
18. March and Simon, *Organizations*; Simon, "A Behavioral Model of Rational Choice."
19. Stevenson, Busemeyer, and Naylor, "Judgment and Decision-Making Theory."
20. March and Simon, *Organizations*; Simon, "A Behavioral Model of Rationale Choice."
21. March and Simon, *Organizations*.
22. "Hoffman-La Roche and BASF Agree to Pay Record Criminal Fines for Participating in International Vitamin Cartel," U. S. Department of Justice News Release, March 21, 1999.
23. J. R. Wilke, and S. Warren, "Vitamin Firms Settle U. S. Charges. Agree to Pay $ 725 Million in Fines," *Wall Street Journal*, May 21, 1999, A3.
24. "Defining the Role of Ethics Monitor," www.businessweek .com, February 13, 2006.
25. Simon, *The New Science of Management Decision*.
26. Ibid.
27. P. C. Nutt, "Why Decisions Fail," *Academy of Management Journal*, February 2003, vol. 17, 130–33.
28. C. M. Fiol and E. J. O'Connor, "Waking Up! Mindfulness in the Face of Bandwagons," *Academy of Management Review*, January 2003, vol. 28, 54–71.
29. P. C. Nutt, "Surprising but True: Half the Decisions in Organizations Fall," *Academy of Management Executive*, November 99, vol. 13, 75–91.
30. M. H. Bazerman, *Judgment in Managerial Decision Making* (New York: Wiley, 1994); D. Kahnman and A. Tversky, "Subjective Probability: A Judgment of Representativeness," *Cognitive Psychology*, 3 (1972): 430–54; A. Tversky and D. Kahneman, "Judgment Under Uncertainty: Heuristics and Biases," *Science* 185 (1974): 1124–31.
31. Bazerman, *Judgment in Managerial Decision Making*; Tversky and Kahneman, "Judgment Under Uncertainty."
32. Ibid.
33. Ibid.
34. Bazerman, *Judgment in Managerial Decision Making*.
35. Ibid.; Tversky and Kahneman, "Judgment Under Uncertainty."
36. L. A. Burke and M. K. Miller, "Taking the Mystery Out of Intuitive Decision Making," *Academy of Management Executive*, November 1999, vol. 13, 91–100.
37. Ibid.
38. Tversky and Kahneman, "Judgment Under Uncertainty."
39. B. M. Staw, "The Escalation of Commitment to a Course of Action," *Academy of Management Review* 6 (1981): 577–87; B. M. Staw and J. Ross, "Understanding Behavior in Escalating Situations," *Science* 246 (1986): 216–220.
40. Staw and Ross, "Understanding Behavior in Escalation Situations."
41. Ibid.
42. D. Kahneman and A. Tversky, "Prospect Theory: An Analysis of Decision Under Risk," *Econometrics* 47 (1979): 263–91; Staw and Ross, "Understanding Behavior in Escalation Situations."
43. S. B. Sit-in and L. R. Weingarten, "Determinants of Risky Decision-Making Behavior: A Test of the Mediating Role of Risk Perceptions . . . ," *Academy of Management Journal*, December 1995, vol. 38, 1573–93.
44. R. W. Collins, "Communications Policy and Information Technology: Promises, Problems and Prospects," *Academy of Management Review*, October 2003, vol. 28, 673–76.
45. G. P. Huber, "A Theory of the Effects of Advanced Information Technologies on Organizational Design, Intelligence, and Decision Making," *Academy of Management Review*, January 1990, vol. 15, 47–72.
46. www.sap.com, 2006.
47. P. S. Goodman and E. D. Darer, "Exchanging Best Practices Through Computer-Aided Systems," *Academy of Management Executive*, May 1996, vol. 9, 7–20.
48. G. Jones, "SAP and the Enterprise Resource Planning Industry." In C.W.L. Hill and G.R. Jones, *Strategic Management: An Integrated Approach* (Boston, Mass.: Houghton Mifflin, 2004.
49. Ibid.
50. Z. Schiller, "GE's Appliance Park: Rewire, or Pull the Plug?" *Business Week* (February 8, 1999): 30.
51. J. Martin, "Detroit's Designing Women," *Fortune* (October 18, 1993): 10–11.
52. D. W. Johnson and F. P. Johnson, *Joining Together: Group Theory and Group Skills* (Boston: Allyn and Bacon, 1994); V. Villasenor, *Jury: The People vs. Juan Corona* (New York: Bantam, 1977).
53. www.gap.com, 2006.
54. A. Merrick, "Gap's Greatest Generation," *Wall Street Journal*, September 18, 2005, A1.
55. www.gap.com, 2006.
56. M. Shaw, "A Comparison of Individuals and Small Groups in the Rational Solution of Complex Problems," *American Journal of Psychology* 44 (1932): 491–504; R. Ziller, "Group Size: A Determinant of the Quality and Stability of Group Decision," *Sociometery* 20 (1957): 165–73.
57. Schiller, "GE's Appliance Park."
58. Ibid.
59. I. L. Janis, *Groupthink*, 2nd ed. (Boston: Houghton Mifflin, 1982).
60. Ibid.
61. Ibid.
62. J. M. Darley and B. Latane, "Bystander Intervention in Emergencies: Diffusion of Responsibility," *Journal of Personality and Social Psychology* 8 (1968): 377–83; M. E. Shaw, *Group Dynamics* (New York: McGraw-Hill, 1981).
63. S. Moscovici and M. Zavalloni, "The Group as a Polarizer of Attitudes," *Journal of Personality and Social Psychology* 12 (1969): 125–35; Shaw, *Group Dynamics*.

64. M. A. Wallach, N. Kogan, and D. J. Bem, "Group Influence on Individual Risk Taking," *Journal of Abnormal and Social Psychology* 65 (1962): 75–86; M. A. Wallach, N. Kogan, and D. J. Bem, "Diffusion of Responsibility and Level of Risk Taking in Groups," *Journal of Abnormal and Social Psychology* 68 (1964): 263–74.
65. L. Festinger, "A Theory of Social Comparison Processes," *Human Relations* 7 (1954): 117–40.
66. A. Vinokur and E. Burnstein, "Effects of Partially Shared Persuasive Arguments on Group-Induced Shifts: A Group Problem-Solving Approach," *Journal of Personality and Social Psychology*, 29 (1974) 305–15; Shaw, *Group Dynamics*.
67. A. F. Osborn, *Applied Imagination* (New York: Scribners, 1957).
68. T. J. Bouchard Jr., J. Barsaloux, and G. Drauden, "Brainstorming Procedure, Group Size, and Sex as Determinants of the Problem-Solving Effectiveness of Groups and Individuals," *Journal of Applied Psychology* 59 (1974): 135–38.
69. M. Diehl and W. Stroebe, "Productivity Loss in Brainstorming Groups: Toward the Solution of a Riddle," *Journal of Personality and Social Psychology* 53 (1987): 497–509.
70. R. B. Gallupe, L. M. Bastianutti, and W. H. Cooper, "Unblocking Brainstorms," *Journal of Applied Psychology* 76 (1991): 137–42.
71. Ibid.
72. D. H. Gustafson, R. K. Shulka, A. Delbecq, and W. G. Walster, "A Comparative Study of Differences in Subjective Likelihood Estimates Made by Individual, Interacting Groups, Delphi Groups, and Nominal Groups," *Organizational Behavior and Human Performance* 9 (1973): 280–91.
73. N. Dalkey, *The Delphi Method: An Experimental Study of Group Decisions* (Santa Monica: CA: Rand Corporation, 1969).
74. S. M. Young, "A Framework for the Successful Adoption and Performance of Japanese Manufacturing Practices," *Academy of Management Review* 17 (1992): 677–700; M. Walton, *The Deming Management Method* (New York: Perigee Books, 1990).
75. "How Does Service Drive The Service Company?" *Harvard Business Review* (November–December 1991): 146–58.
76. A. Gabor, "Rochester Focuses: A Community's Core Competences," *Harvard Business Review* (July–August 1991): 116–26.
77. W. M. Bulkeley, "Plexus Strategy: Smaller Runs of More Things," *Wall Street Journal*, October 8, 2003, B1, B.12.
78. www.plexus.com, 2006.
79. B. Hedberg, "How Organizations Learn and Unlearn." In W. H. Starbuck and P. C. Nystrom, eds., *Handbook of Organizational Design*, vol. 1 (New York: Oxford University Press, 1981), 1–27.
80. P. M. Senge, *The Fifth Discipline: The Art and Practice of the Learning Organization* (New York: Doubleday, 1990).
81. J. G. March, "Exploration and Exploitation in Organizational Learning." *Organizational Science*, 1991, vol. 2, 71–87.
82. M. J. Benner and M. L. Tushman, "Exploitation, Exploration, and Process Management: The Productivity Dilemma Revisited," *Academy of Management Review*, April 2003, vol. 28, 238–57.
83. T. K. Lant and S. J. Mezias, "An Organizational Learning Model of Convergence and Reorientation," *Organizational Science*, 1992, vol. 5, 47–71.
84. M. Dodgson, "Organizational Learning: A Review of Some Literatures," *Organizational Studies*, 1993, vol. 14, 375–94.
85. A. S. Miner and S. J. Mezias, "Ugly Duckling No More: Pasts and Futures of Organizational Learning Research," *Organizational Science*, 1990, vol. 7, 88–99.
86. P. Senge, *The Fifth Discipline: The Art and Practice of the Learning Organization* (New York: Doubleday, 1990).
87. P. M. Senge, "Taking Personal Change Seriously: The Impact of Organizational Learning on Management Practice," *Academy of Management Executive*, May 2003, vol. 17, 47–51.
88. P. Senge, "The Leader's New Work: Building Learning Organizations," *Sloan Management Review*, Fall 1990, 7–23.
89. Miner and Mezias, "Ugly Ducking No More."
90. www.nike.com, 2004.
91. D. Shook, "Why Nike Is Dragging Its Feet," *Business Week*, March 19, 2001pp. 35–37.
92. B. Stone, "Nike's Short Game," *Newsweek*, January 26, 2004, 40–41.
93. "It's Still Knight's Nike," www.businessweek.com, February 26, 2006.

CHAPTER 16

1. www.homedepot.com, 2006.
2. Ibid.
3. "Renovating Home Depot," www.businessweekonline.com, March 6, 2006.
4. H. R. Weber, "Profits Are Up, Sales Are Not," www.businessweek.com, May 16, 2006.
5. G. R. Jones, *Organizational Theory, Design, and Change: Text and Cases* 5th ed.(Upper Saddle River, NJ: Prentice Hall, 2007).
6. J. Child, *Organization: A Guide for Managers and Administrators* (New York: Harper and Row, 1977).
7. P. R. Lawrence and J. W. Lorsch, *Organization and Environment* (Boston: Graduate School of Business Administration, Harvard University, 1967).
8. R. Duncan, "What Is the Right Organizational Design?" *Organizational Dynamics* (Winter 1979): 59–80.
9. T. Burns and G. R. Stalker, *The Management of Innovation* (London: Tavistock, 1966).
10. P. W. Beamish, "Sony's Yoshihide Nakamura on Structure and Decision Making," *Academy of Management Executive*, 1999, vol. 13, 12–17.
11. Jones, op. cit. Ch.5; T. W. Malnight, "Emerging Structural Patterns Within Multinational Corporations: Towards Process-Based Structures," *Academy of Management Journal*, 2001, vol. 44, 1187–2013.
12. G. DeSanctis, J. T. Glass, and I. M. Morris, "Organizational Designs for R&D," *Academy of Management Executive*, 2002, vol. 16, 55–67.
13. C. Perrow, *Organizational Analysis: A Sociological View* (Belmont, CA: Wadsworth, 1970).
14. J. Woodward, *Management and Technology* (London: Her Majesty's Stationery Office, 1958).

15. Ibid.
16. E. Gedajlovic and D. M. Shapiro, "Ownership Structure and Firm Profitability in Japan," *Academy of Management Journal*, 2002, vol. 45, 565–67.
17. P. K. Mills and G. Ungson, "Reassessing the Limits of Structural Empowerment: Organizational Constitution and Trust as Controls," *Academy of Management Review*, 2003, vol. 28, 143–54.
18. R. H. Hall, *Organizations: Structure and Process* (Englewood, Cliffs, NJ: Prentice-Hall, 1972); R. Miles, *Macro Organizational Behavior* (Santa Monica, CA: Goodyear, 1980).
19. www.dell.com, 2006.
20. Jones, op.cit. Ch.6.
21. J. Child, *Organization: A Guide for Managers and Administrators* (New York: Harper and Row, 1977).
22. Jones, op.cit, Ch. 6.
23. "Kodak to Divide Photography Unit," www.photonics.com, December 18, 2005.
24. D. Machalaba, "Burlington Northern Executives Retire, Raising Speculation About CEO Search," *Wall Street Journal*, June 2, 1994, B8.
25. L. Berton and M. Selz, "Peat Marwick Cuts U.S. Staff of Professionals," *Wall Street Journal*, June 2, 1994, A4.
26. M. V. Russo, "The Multidivisional Structure as an Enabling Device: A Longitudinal Study of Discretionary Cash as a Strategic Resource," *Academy of Management Journal*, 1991, vol. 34, 718–34.
27. B. Pfister, "Tyco to Split into 3 Cos." www.yahoo.com, January 13, 2006.
28. G. deSanctis, J. T. Glass, and I. M. Morris, "Organizational Designs for R&D," *Academy of Management Executive*, 2002, vol.16, 55–67.
29. S. M. Davis and P. R. Lawrence, *Matrix* (Reading, MA: Addison-Wesley, 1977); J. R. Galbraith, "Matrix Organization Designs: How to Combine Functional and Project Forms," *Business Horizons* 14 (1971): 29–40.
30. L. R. Burns, "Matrix Management in Hospitals: Testing Theories of Matrix Structure and Development," *Administrative Science Quarterly*, 1989, 34, 349–68.
31. S. M. Davis and P. R. Lawrence, "Problems of Matrix Organization," *Harvard Business Review*, May–June 1978, 131–42.
32. P. Blau, "A Formal Theory of Differentiation in Organizations," *American Sociological Review* 35 (1970): 684–95.
33. Ibid
34. S. McCartney, "Airline Industry's Top-Ranked Woman Keeps Southwest's Small-Fry Spirit Alive," *The Wall Street Journal*, November 30, 1995, B1.
35. P. M. Blau and R. A. Schoenherr, *The Structure of Organizations* (New York: Basic Books, 1971).
36. Jones, *Organizational Theory*.
37. www.microsoft.com, 2005, press release.
38. A. Linn, "Microsoft Organizes to Compete Better," www.yahoo.com, September 26, 2005.
39. www.microsoft.com, 2006.
40. J. Galbraith, *Designing Complex Organizations* (Reading, MA: Addison-Wesley, 1973).
41. H. Mintzberg, *The Nature of Managerial Work* (New York: Harper and Row, 1973).
42. R. Parthasarthy and S. P. Sethi, "The Impact of Flexible Automation on Business Strategy and Organizational Structure," *Academy of Management Review*, 1992, vol. 17, 86–108.
43. Mintzberg, *The Structuring of Organizations*, Ch. 1.
44. www.sunlife.com, 2003.
45. www.sunlife.com, "company history," 2003.
46. IT World Canada, Press Release, 2003, June 4.
47. Thompson, *Organizations in Action*.
48. B. Elgin, "Running the Tightest Ships on the Net," *Business Week*, January 29, 2001, 125–26.
49. M. Rokeach, *The Nature of Human Values* (New York: Free Press, 1973).
50. T. Dewett, and G. R. Jones, "The Role of Information Technology in the Organization: A Review, Model, and Assessment," *Journal of Management*, 2001, vol. 27, 313–46.
51. J. Child and R. G. McGrath, "Organizations Unfettered: Organizational Form in an Information Intensive Economy," *Academy of Management Journal*, 2001, vol. 44, 1135–49.
52. G. DeSanctis and P. Monge, "Introduction to the Special Issue: Communication Processes for Virtual Organizations," *Organization Science*, 1999, 10, 693–703.
53. D. Constant, L. Sproul, and S. Kiesler, "The Kindness of Strangers; The Usefulness of Electronic Ties for Technical Advice," *Organization Science*, 1996, 7, 119–35.
54. G. G. Dess and A. Rasheed, "The New Corporate Architecture," *Academy of Management Executive*, 1995, vol. 9, 7–19.
55. J. Fulk and G. Desanctis, "Electronic Communication and Changing Organizational Forms," *Organizational Science*, 1995, vol. 6, 337–49.
56. Y. P. Shao, S. Y. Liao, and H. Q. Wang, "A Model of Virtual Organizations," *Academy of Management Executive*, 1998, 12, 120–28.
57. A. Williams, "Arthur Andersen-IT Initiatives Support Shifts in Business Strategy," *Informationweek*, September 11, 2000, 14–18.
58. T. Davenport and L. Prusak, *Information Ecology*. (London: Oxford University Press, 1997).
59. www.accenture.com, 2006.
60. www.yahoo.com, 2006.
61. A. Grandori, "An Organizational Assessment of Interfirm Coordination Modes," *Organizational Studies*, 1997, 18, 897–925.
62. www.nike.com, 2006.
63. G. S. Capowski, "Designing a Corporate Identity," *Management Review*, June 1993, 37–38.

CHAPTER 17

1. G. R. Jones, *Organizational Theory, Design, and Change*, 5th ed. (Upper Saddle River, New Jersey: Pearson, 2007).
2. www.3M.com, 2006.
3. www.3M.com, 2006.
4. G. M. Spreitzer and W. R. Nord, "Organizational Culture: Mapping the Terrain," *Academy of Management Review*, 2003, vol.28, 3, 514–16. (Book review); E. H. Schein, "Organizational Culture," *American Psychologist*, February 1990, 109–19.

5. G. R. Jones, "Transaction Costs, Property Rights, and Organizational Culture," *Administrative Science Quarterly*, 1983, vol. 28, 456–87; L. Smircich, "Concepts of Culture and Organizational Analysis," *Administrative Science Quarterly*, 1983, vol. 28, 339–58.
6. S. D. N. Cook and D. Yanow, "Culture and Organizational Learning," *Journal of Management Inquiry*, 1993, vol. 2, 373–90.
7. J. M. George, and G. R. Jones, "Experiencing Work: Values, Attitudes, and Moods," *Human Relations*, 1997, 50, 393–416; G. R. Jones, and J. M. George, "The Experience and Evolution of Trust: Implications for Cooperation and Teamwork," *Academy of Management Review*, 1998, 3, 531–46.
8. M. Rokeach, *The Nature of Human Values* (New York: The Free Press, 1973).
9. A. R. Jassawalla and H. C. Sashittal, "Cultures that Support the Product-Innovation Process," *Academy of Management Executive*, 2002, vol. 16, 42–55.
10. J. R. Detert, "A Framework for Linking Culture and Improvement Initiatives in Organizations," *Academy of Management Review*, 2000, vol. 25, 850–64.
11. M. J. Hatch, "The Dynamics of Organizational Culture," *Academy of Management Review*, 1993, vol. 7, 657–95.
12. D. M. Cable, L. Aiman-Smith, P. W. Mulvey, and J. R. Edwards, "The Sources and Accuracy of Job Applicants Beliefs about Organizational Culture," *Academy of Management Journal*, 2000, vol. 43, 1076–86.
13. P. L. Berger and T. Luckman, *The Social Construction of Reality* (Garden City, N.Y.: Anchor Books, 1967).
14. E. H. Schein, "Culture: The Missing Concept in Organization Studies," *Administrative Science Quarterly*, 1996, vol. 41, 229–40.
15. A. Bianco, "Value Line: Too Lean, Too Mean," *Business Week*, 16 March, 1992, 104–6.
16. J. P. Walsh and G. R. Ungson, "Organizational Memory," *Academy of Management Review*, 1991, vol. 1, 57–91.
17. K. E. Weick, "Organizational Culture as a Source of High Reliability." California Management Review, 1984, vol. 9, pp. 653–669.
18. A. Etzioni, A Comparative Analysis of Organizations (New York: The Free Press, 1975).
19. G. R. Jones, "*Psychological Orientation and the Process of Organizational Socialization:* An Interactionist Perspective." Academy of Management Review, 1983, vol. 8, pp. 464–474.
20. C. Johnson, "The best of Both Worlds, *HRMagazine*, September, 1999, pp. 12–14.
21. "J. Cone, "How Dell Does It," Training & Development, June, 2000, pp. 58–70.
22. A. Chen & M. Hicks, "Going Global? Avoid Culture Clashes," *PC Week*, April3, 2000, p. 65.
23. H. M. Trice and J. M. Beyer, "Studying Organizational Culture Through Rites and Ceremonials." *Academy of Management Review*, 1984, vol. 9, pp. 653–669.
24. H. M. Trice and J. M. Beyer, The Cultures of Work Organizations (Englewood Cliffs, N.J.: Prentice Hall, 1993).
25. Trice and Beyer, "Studying Organizational Culture Through Rites and Ceremonials."
26. A. M. Pettigrew, "On Studying Organizational Cultures." *Administrative Science Quarterly*, 1979, vol. 24, pp. 570–582.
27. www.walmart.com, 2006.
28. "Associates Keystone to Structure," *Chain Store Age*, December, 1999. p. 17.
29. www.walmart.com, 2006.
30. M. Troy, "The Culture Remains the Constant," *Discount Store News*, 1998, June 8, pp. 95–98.
31. S. Voros, "3D Management," Management Review, January, 2000, pp. 45–47.
32. M. Ramundo, "Service Awards Build Culture of Success," *Human Resources Magazine*, August 1992, pp. 61–63.
33. "Neurosis, Arkansas-style," Fortune, April 17, 2000, p. 36.
34. H. M. Trice and J. M. Beyer, "Studying Organizational Cultures Through Rites and Ceremonials," *Academy of Management Review*, 1984, vol. 9, pp. 653–670.
35. B. Schneider, "The People Make the Place." *Personnel Psychology*, 1987, vol. 40, pp. 437–453.
36. J.E. Sheriden, "Organizational Culture and Employee Retention," *Academy of Management Journal*, 1992, vol. 35, pp. 657–692.
37. E. H. Schein, "The Role of the Founder in Creating Organizational Culture." *Organizational Dynamics*, 1983, vol. 12, pp. 13–28.
38. J. M. George, "Personality, Affect, and Behavior in Groups." *Journal of Applied Psychology*, 1990, vol. 75, pp. 107–116.
39. E. Schein, Organizational Culture and Leadership, 2d ed. (San Francisco: Jossey-Bass, 1992).
40. M. Hannan and J. Freeman, "Structural Inertia and Organizational Change." *American Sociological Review*, 1984, vol. 49, pp. 149–164.
41. C. A. O'Reilly, J. Chatman, D. F. Caldwell, "People and Organizational Culture: Assessing Person-Organizational Fit," *Academy of Management Journal*, 1991, vol. 34, pp.487–517.
42. George, "Personality, Affect, and Behavior in Groups"; D. Miller and J. M. Toulouse, "Chief Executive Personality and Corporate Strategy and Structure in Small Firms," *Management Science*, 1986, vol. 32, pp. 1389–1409.
43. T. M. Jones, "Ethical Decision Making by Individuals in Organizations: An Issue Contingent Model," *Academy of Management Review*, 1991, 2, pp. 366–395.
44. T. L. Beauchamp and N. E. Bowie, eds., Ethical Theory and Business (Englewood Cliffs, N.J.: Prentice-Hall, 1979); A. MacIntyre, After Virtue (Notre Dame, Ind.: University of Notre Dame Press, 1981).
45. T. J. Peters and R. H. Waterman, Jr., In Search of Excellence: Lessons from America's Best-Run Companies (New York: Harper and Row, 1982).
46. B. Victor and J. B. Cullen, "The Organizational Bases of Ethical Work Climates." *Administrative Science Quarterly*, 1988, vol. 33, pp. 101–125.
47. L. Kohlberg, "Stage and Sequence: The Cognitive—Development Approach to Socialization." In D. A. Goslin, ed., Handbook of Socialization Theory and Research (Chicago: Rand McNally, 1969), pp. 347–380.
48. M. S. Frankel, "Professional Codes: Why, How, and with What Impact?" *Journal of Business Ethics*, 1989, vol. 8, pp. 109–115.
49. J. Van Mannen and S. R. Barley, "Occupational Communities: Culture and Control in Organizations." In B. Staw and L. Cummings, eds., *Research in Organizational*

Behavior, vol. 6 (Greenwich, Conn.: JAI Press, 1984), pp. 287–365.
50. A. Sagie and D. Elizur, "Work Values: A Theoretical Overview and a Model of their Affects," *Journal of Organizational Behavior*, 1996, 17, pp. 503–514.
51. G. R. Jones, "Transaction Costs, Property Rights, and Organizational Culture: An Exchange Perspective." *Administrative Science Quarterly*, 1983, vol. 28, pp. 454–467.
52. www.bimba.com, 2006.
53. www.bimba.com, 2006.
54. "ESOP Binges Change in Corporate Culture." *Employee Benefit Plan Review*, July 1992, pp. 25–26.
55. C. Perrow, Normal Accidents (New York: Basic Books, 1984).
56. H. Mintzberg, The Structuring of Organizational Structures (Englewood Cliffs, N.J.: Prentice Hall, 1979).
57. G. Kunda, Engineering Culture. (Philadelphia: Temple University Press, 1992).
58. Company History, www.google.com, 2006.
59. Google, www.businessweek.com, April 27th, 2004.
60. The Google Culture, www.google.com, 2006.
61. T. J. Peters and R. H. Waterman, In Search of Excellence: Lessons from America's Best-Run Companies (New York: Harper & Row, 1982).
62. W. G. Ouchi, Theory Z: How American Business Can Meet the Japanese Challenge (Reading, Mass.: Addison-Wesley, 1981).
63. G. Hofstede, B. Neuijen, D. D. Ohayv, and G. Sanders, "Measuring Organizational Cultures: A Qualitative and Quantitative Study Across Twenty Cases," *Administrative Science Quarterly*, 1990, 35, pp. 286–316.
64. W. G. Ouchi, Theory Z: How American Business Can Meet the Challenge of Japanese Management (Reading, Mass.: Addison-Wesley, 1981).
65. G. Hofstede, "The Cultural Relativity of Organizational Practices and Theories," *Journal of International Business Studies*, Fall 1983, pp. 75–89.
66. "Big-Company CEOs Exemplify Diversity," *HR Magazine*, August 1994, pp. 25–26.
67. Hofstede, Neuijen, Ohayv, and Sanders, "Measuring Organizational Cultures."
68. G. Hofstede, "The Cultural Relativity of Organizational Practices and Theories," *Journal of International Business Studies*, Fall 1983, pp. 75–89.
69. www.corning.com, 2006; www.vitro.com, 2006.
70. A. DePalma, "It Takes More Than a Visa to Do Business in Mexico," *New York Times*, June 26, 1994, p. F5.
71. www.corning.com, 2006.
72. "A Good Knight for Sony," Newsweek, March 25th 2005, p. 49.
73. T. M. Jones, "Instrumental Stakeholder Theory: A Synthesis of Ethics and Economics." *Academy of Management Review*, 1995, vol. 20, pp. 404–437.
74. J. Dobson, "Corporate Reputation: A Free Market Solution to Unethical Behavior." *Business and Society*, 1989, vol. 28, pp. 1–5.
75. M. S. Baucus and J. P. Near, "Can Illegal Corporate Behavior Be Predicted? An Event History Analysis." *Academy of Management Journal*, 1991, vol. 34, pp. 9–36.
76. J. B. Dozier and M. P. Miceli, "Potential Predictors of Whistle—Blowing: A Prosocial Behavior Perspective," *Academy of Management Review*, 1985, vol. 10, pp. 823–836; J. P. Near and M. P. Miceli, "Retaliation Against Whistle—Blowers: Predictors and Effects," *Journal of Applied Psychology*, 1986, vol. 71, pp. 137–145.
77. D. Collins, "Organizational Harm, Legal Consequences and Stakeholder Retaliation." *Journal of Business Ethics*, 1988, vol. 8, pp. 1–13.
78. www.mci.com, 2006.

CHAPTER 18

1. www.xerox.com, 2006.
2. "She Put the Bounce Back Into Xerox," www.businessweek .com., March 1, 2005.
3. F. Arner, "How Xerox Got Up to Speed," www.businessweek .com, March 2, 2006.
4. www.xerox.com, 2006.
5. J. P. Kotter, L. A. Schlesinger, and V. Sathe, *Organization* (Homewood, IL: Irwin, 1979), 487.
6. C. Argyris, R. Putman, and D. M. Smith, *Action Science* (San Francisco: Jossey-Bass, 1985).
7. R. M. Kanter, *The Change Masters: Innovation for Productivity in the American Corporation* (New York: Simon & Schuster, 1984).
8. C. W. L. Hill and G. R. Jones, *Strategic Management: An Integrated Approach*, 7th ed. (Boston: Houghton Mifflin, 2007).
9. Ibid.
10. G. R. Jones, *Organizational Theory, Design, and Change: Text and Cases*, 5th ed. (Upper Saddle River, NY: Prentice Hall, 2007).
11. C. W. L. Hill, *International Business*, 4th ed (Chicago, IL: McGraw-Hill, 2005).
12. C. A. Bartlett and S. Ghoshal, *Managing Across Borders* (Boston: Harvard Business School Press, 1989).
13. C. K. Prahalad and Y. L. Doz, *The Multinational Mission: Balancing Local Demands and Global Vision* (New York: Free Press, 1987).
14. D. Jamieson and J. O'Mara, *Managing Workforce 2000: Gaining a Diversity Advantage* (San Francisco: Jossey-Bass, 1991).
15. T. H. Cox and S. Blake, "Managing Cultural Diversity: Implications for Organizational Competitiveness," *Academy of Management Executive*, August 1991, 49–52.
16. S. E. Jackson and Associates, *Diversity in the Workplace: Human Resource Initiatives* (New York: Guilford Press, 1992).
17. W. H. Shaw and V. Barry, *Moral Issues in Business*, 6th ed. (Belmont, CA: Wadsworth, 1995).
18. T. Donaldson, *Corporations and Morality* (Englewood Cliffs, NJ: Prentice-Hall, 1982).
19. S.K. Piderit, "Rethinking Resistance and Recognizing Ambivalence: A Multidimensional View of Attitudes Toward an Organizational Change," *Academy of Management Review*, 2000, vol. 25, 4, 783–95.
20. M. Hannan and J. Freeman, "Structural Inertia and Organizational Change," *American Sociological Review*, 1989, 49, 149–64.
21. L. E. Greiner, "Evolution and Revolution as Organizations Grow," *Harvard Business Review*, July–August 1972, 37–46.
22. "Nike Battles Backlash From Overseas Sweatshops," *Marketing News*, November 9, 1998, 14.

23. J. Laabs, "Mike Gives Indonesian Employees a Raise," *Workforce*, December, 1998, 15–16.
24. W. Echikson, "It's Europe's Turn to Sweat About Sweatshops," *Business Week*, July 19, 1999, 96.
25. www.nike.com, 2006
26. "Nike's New Game Plan for Sweatshops," www.businessweek.com, March 5, 2005.
27. Ibid.
28. http://www.gapinc.com/public/SocialResponsibility/sr_ethic_prog.shtm, 2006.
29. R. M. Kanter, *When Giants Learn to Dance: Mastering the Challenges of Strategy* (New York: Simon and Schuster, 1989).
30. J. P. Kotter and L. A. Schlesinger, "Choosing Strategies for Change," *Harvard Business Review*, March-April 1979, 106–14.
31. T. Burns and G. M. Stalker, *The Management of Innovation* (London: Tavistock, 1961).
32. P. R. Lawrence and J. W. Lorsch, *Organization and Environment* (Boston: Harvard Business School Press, 1972).
33. R. Likert, *The Human Organization* (New York: McGraw-Hill, 1967).
34. C. Argyris, *Personality and Organization* (New York: Harper and Row, 1957).
35. This section draws heavily on K. Lewin, *Field Theory in Social Science* (New York: Harper and Row, 1951).
36. L. Chung-Ming and R. W. Woodman, "Understanding Organizational Change: A Schematic Perspective," *Academy of Management Journal*, 1995, vol. 38, 2, 537–55.
37. D. Miller, "Evolution and Revolution: A Quantum View of Structural Change in Organizations," *Journal of Management Studies*, 1982, 19, 11–151; D. Miller, "Momentum and Revolution in Organizational Adaptation," *Academy of Management Journal*, 1980, 2, 591–614.
38. C. E. Lindblom, "The Science of Muddling Through," *Public Administration Review*, 1959, 19, 79–88; P. C. Nystrom and W. H. Starbuck, "To Avoid Organizational Crises, Unlearn," *Organizational Dynamics*, 1984, 12, 53–65.
39. E. L. Trist, G. Higgins, H. Murray, and A. G. Pollock, *Organizational Choice* (London: Tavistock, 1965); J. C. Taylor, "The Human Side of Work: The Socio-Technical Approach to Work Design," *Personnel Review*, 1975, 4, 17–22.
40. E. L. Trist and K. W. Bamforth, "Some Social and Psychological Consequences of the Long Wall Method of Coal Mining," *Human Relations*, 1951, 4, 3–38; F. E. Emery and E. L. Trist, *Socio-Technical Systems* (London: Proceedings of the 6th Annual International Meeting of the Institute of Management Sciences, 1965), 92–93.
41. W. Edwards Deming, *Out of the Crisis* (Cambridge, MA: MIT Press, 1989); M. Walton, *The Deming Management Method* (New York: Perigee Books, 1990).
42. J. McHugh and B. Dale, "Quality Circles," In R. Wild, ed., *International Handbook of Production and Operations Research* (London: Cassel, 1989), pp. 123–156.
43. www.citigroup.com, 2006.
44. S. M. Young, "A Framework for the Successful Adoption and Performance of Japanese Manufacturing Techniques in the United States," *Academy of Management Review*, 1992, 17, 677–700.
45. M. Hammer and J. Champy, *Reengineering the Corporation* (New York: HarperCollins, 1993).
46. "Man with a Plan," *Business Week*, October 4, 1999, 34–37.
47. www.daimlerchrysler.com, 2006.
48. www.Chrysler.com, 2006.
49. A. M. Pettigrew, R. W. Woodman, and K. S. Cameron, "Studying Organizational Change and Development: Challenges for Future Research," *Academy of Management Journal*, 2001, vol. 44, 4, 697–714.
50. "Facts About Hallmark," www.hallmark.com, 2000.
51. J. Child and R. G. McGrath, "Organizations Unfettered: Organizational Form in an Information-Intensive Economy," *Academy of Management Journal*, 2001, vol. 44, 6, 1135–49.
51. www.cypress.com, 2006.
53. www.microsoft.com, 2006.
54. W. McKinley, "Some Anticipated Consequences of Organizational Restructuring," *Academy of Management Review*, 2000, vol. 25, 4, 735–53.
55. Jones, *Organizational Theory*; R. A. Burgelman and M. A. Maidique, *Strategic Management of Technology and Innovation* (Homewood, IL: Irwin, 1988).
56. G. R. Jones and J. E. Butler, "Managing Internal Corporate Entrepreneurship: An Agency Theory Perspective," *Journal of Management*, 1992, 18, 733–49.
57. E. Mansfield, J. Rapoport, J. Schnee, S. Wagner, and M. Hamburger, *Research and Innovation in the Modern Corporation* (New York: Norton, 1971).
58. K. J. Klein and J. Speer, "The Challenge of Innovation Implementation," *Academy of Management Review*, 1996, vol. 21, 4, 1055–71.
59. R. A. Burgelman, "Designs for Corporate Entrepreneurship in Established Firms," *California Management Review*, 1984, 26, 154–66.
60. D. Frey, "Learning the Ropes: My Life as a Product Champion," *Harvard Business Review*, September–October 1991, 46–56.
61. Lewin, *Field Theory in Social Science*, 172–74.
62. M. Crossan, "Altering Theories of Learning and Action: An Interview with Chris Argyris, *Academy of Management Executive*, 2003, vol. 17, 2, 40–47.
63. This section draws heavily on P. A. Clark, *Action Research and Organizational Change* (New York: Harper and Row, 1972); L. Brown, "Research Action: Organizational Feedback, Understanding and Change," *Journal of Applied Behavioral Research*, 1972, 8, 697–711; N. Margulies and A. P. Raia, eds., *Conceptual Foundations of Organizational Development* (New York: McGraw-Hill, 1978).
64. W. L. French and C. H. Bell, *Organizational Development* (Englewood Cliffs, NJ: Prentice-Hall, 1990).
65. L. Coch and J. R. P. French, "Overcoming Resistance to Change," *Human Relations*, 1948, 1, 512–32.
66. French and Bell, *Organizational Development*.
67. Ibid.
68. www.lucent.com, 2006.
69. www.microsoft.com, 2006.
70. W. L. French, "A Checklist for Organizing and Implementing an OD Effort." In W. L. French, C. H. Bell, and R. A. Zawacki, *Organizational Development and Transformation* (Homewood, IL: Irwin, 1994), 484–95.
71. Kotter, Schlesinger, and Sathe, *Organization*, p. 487.

72. W. G. Bennis, *Organizational Development: Its Nature, Origins, and Perspectives* (Reading, MA: Addison-Wesley, 1969).
73. Kotter and Schlesinger, "Choosing Strategies for Change."
74. S. Fox and Y. Amichai-Hamburger, "The Power of Emotional Appeals in Promoting Organizational Change Programs," *Academy of Management Executive*, 2001, vol. 15, 4, 84–95.
75. S. Myeong-Gu, "Overcoming Emotional Barriers, Political Obstacles, and Control Imperatives in the Action-Science Approach to Individual and Organizational Learning," *Academy of Management Learning and Education*, 2003, vol. 2, 1, 7–22.
76. E. H. Schein, *Organizational Psychology* (Englewood Cliffs, NJ: Prentice-Hall, 1980).
77. R. T. Golembiewski, "The Laboratory Approach to Organization Change: Schema of a Method." In Margulies and Raia, eds., *Conceptual Foundations of Organizational Development*, 198–212; J. Kelley "Organizational Development Through Structured Sensitivity Training," Ibid., 213–28.
78. E. H. Schein, *Process Consultation* (Reading, MA: Addison-Wesley, 1969).
79. M. Sashkin and W. Warner Burke, "Organization Development in the 1980s," *Journal of Management*, 1987, 13, 393–417; D. Eden, "Team Development: Quasi-Experimental Confirmation Among Combat Companies," *Group and Organization Studies*, 1986, 5, 133–46; K. P. DeMeuse and S. J. Liebowitz, "An Empirical Analysis of Team Building Research," *Group and Organization Studies*, 1981, 6, 357–78.
80. French and Bell, *Organization Development*.
81. R. Beckhard, "The Confrontation Meeting," *Harvard Business Review*, March-April 1967, 159–65.

APPENDIX

1. E. F. Stone, *Research Methods in Organizational Behavior* (Santa Monica, CA.: Goodyear, 1978).
2. C. G. Hempel, *Aspects of Scientific Explanation* (New York: Free Press, 1965); Stone, *Research Methods in Organizational Behavior*.
3. A. Kaplan, *The Conduct of Inquiry* (New York: T. Y. Crowell, 1964).
4. M. Cohen and E. Nagel, *An Introdution to Logic and Scientific Method* (New York: Harcourt, Brace, 1934); F. Kerlinger, *Foundations of Behavioral Research* (New York: Holt, Rinchart and Winston, 1973); Stone, *Research Methods in Organizational Behavior*.
5. Some of the material in this section draws from the following sources: T. D. Cook and D. T. Campbell, "The Design and Conduct of Quasi-Experiments and True Experiments in Field Settings." In M. D. Dunnette, ed., *Handbook of Industrial and Organizational Psychology* (Chicago: Rand McNally, 1976), 223–326; P. J. Runkel and J. E. McGrath, *Research on Human Behavior* (New York: Holt, Rinehart and Winston, 1972); Stone, *Research Methods in Organizational Behavior*.
6. S. W. Cook, "Ethical Issues in the Conduct of Research in Social Relations." In C. Selltiz, L S. Wrightsman, S. W. Cook, eds., *Research Methods in Social Relations* (New York: Holt, Rinehart and Winston, 1976); H. C. Kelman, *A Time to Speak: On Human Values and Social Research* (San Francisco: Jossey Bass, 1968), Runkel and McGrath, *Research on Human Behavior*; Stone, *Research Methods in Organizational Bahavior*.

Photo Credits

Chapter 1 p. 2: Mark Richards; p. 7: Jeff Geissler/Bloomberg/Landov; p. 10: Dick's Drive-In Restaurants; p. 15: Jade-Snow Moy/Bloomberg News/Landov; p. 17: Charles Krupa/AP Wide World Photos; p. 21: Ingvar Andersson/AP Wide World Photos; p. 25: LUCAS JACKSON/Reuters/Landov LLC; p. 28: A. Ramey/PhotoEdit Inc.

Chapter 2 p. 40: © epa/Corbis; p. 43: Joerg Sarbach/AP Wide World Photos; p. 45: Courtesy of Alaska Communications Systems; p. 49: AFP/Paul Buck/Agence France Presse/Getty Images; p. 51: Koji Sasahara/AP Wide World Photos; p. 58: Landov LLC; p. 61: Rocco Forte Hotels

Chapter 3 p. 72: J. Pat Carter/AP Wide World Photos; p. 77: AP Wide World Photos; p. 79: © Michael Goldman/Masterfile; p. 81: AP Wide World Photos; p. 84: Jeff Greenberg/PhotoEdit Inc.; p. 86: Corbis Royalty Free; p. 89: © 2006 SAS Institute Inc. All rights reserved; p. 96: HARRISON MCCLARY/Bloomberg News/Landov LLC

Chapter 4 p. 108: Walter Hodges/Getty Images Inc./Stone Allstock; p. 112: Mark Richards; p. 115: Marcio Jose Sanchez/AP Wide World Photos; p. 121: Dennis Brack/Black Star; p. 123: Habitat International Inc.; p. 124: © Michael Mahovlich/Masterfile; p. 132: Mark Richards; p. 134: Mark Douet/Getty Images Inc./Stone Allstock

Chapter 5 p. 146: AP Wide World Photos; p. 150: Gerhard Westrich/Laif/Aurora/Aurora & Quanta Productions, Inc.; p. 152: The Image Works; p. 158: David Grossman/The Image Works; p. 159: Alan Klehr/Churchill & Klehr Photography; p. 160: Jim Pickerell/The Stock Connection; p. 163: Taxi/Getty Images; p. 165: Ki Ho Park/Kistone Photography

Chapter 6 p. 180: Courtesy of SAS Institute, Inc.; p. 183: David Walega; p. 185: Courtesy of MBDC; p. 189: David R. Frazier/PhotoEdit Inc.; p. 192: Michael Newman/PhotoEdit Inc.; p. 195: Michael Newman/PhotoEdit Inc.; p. 199: Michael Newman/PhotoEdit Inc.; p. 200: Paul Sakuma/AP Wide World Photos

Chapter 7 p. 210: Rick Wilking/Corbis/Reuters America LLC; p. 213: Getty Images Inc.; p. 215: AP Wide World Photos; p. 217: © Ariel Skelley/CORBIS; p. 226: © Masterfile/Masterfile; p. 227: Mark Richards; p. 230: Norsk Hydro; p. 232: Gautam Singh/AP Wide World Photos

Chapter 8 p. 246: Tim Boyle/Getty Images, Inc.; p. 249: © Pierre Tremblay/Masterfile; p. 251: AP Wide World Photos; p. 252: AP Wide World Photos; p. 263: © Michael Goldman/Masterfile; p. 267: Diane Bondareff, Pool/AP Wide World Photos; p. 271: MTPA Stock/Masterfile Stock Image Library; p. 274: Ann Heisenfelt/AP Wide World Photos

Chapter 9 p. 284: Digitalvision/AGE Fotostock America, Inc.; p. 287: William Thomas/Getty Images, Inc.; p. 290: PhotoAlto/AGE Fotostock America, Inc.; p. 292; Corbis/Bettmann; p. 298: AP Wide World Photos; p. 302: The Galveston County Daily News, Chad Greene/AP Wide World Photos; p. 310: Corbis/Bettmann;

Chapter 10 p. 322: Whirlpool Corporation; p. 326: Masterfile Stock Image Library; p. 329: AGE Fotostock America, Inc.; p. 332: Digital Vision/AGE Fotostock America, Inc.; p. 333: Getty Images Entertainment; p. 337: Peter Smith/Zingerman's Delicatessan; p. 345: PhotoAlto/AGE Fotostock America, Inc.; p. 348: A. Ramey/PhotoEdit Inc.

Chapter 11 p. 356: Rex Rystedt Photography; p. 360: Digitalvision/AGE Fotostock America, Inc.; p. 361: David J. Phillip/AP Wide World Photos; p. 365: Pixtal/AGE Fotostock America, Inc.; p. 370: Digitalvision/AGE Fotostock America, Inc.; p. 373: Masterfile Corporation/Zefa; p. 378: ADEK BERRY/AFP/Getty Images; p. 381: Corbis/Bettmann

Chapter 12 p. 390: Debi Fox Photography, Washington D.C./Claire's Stores; p. 392: Michael A. Schwarz Photography, Inc.; p. 397: Javier Larrea/AGE Fotostock America, Inc.; p. 403: John W. Clark; p. 405: image100/AGE Fotostock America, Inc.; p. 409: © CHRIS PIZZELLO/Reuters/Corbis; p. 412: Getty Images, Inc./Liaison; p. 416: Bob Daemmrich/The Image Works

Chapter 13 p. 428: PA/Topham/The Image Works; p. 434: Mary Altaffer/AP Wide World Photos; p. 436: Dion Ogust/The Image Works; p. 440: Andrew Harrer/Bloomberg News/Landov LLC; p. 443: UPPA/Topham/The Image Works; p. 446: Bruce Ayres/Getty Images Inc./Stone Allstock; p. 448: Image State/Alamy Images; p. 451: J. Stockshooter/AGE Fotostock America, Inc.

Chapter 14 p. 460: Dario Lopez-Mills/AP Wide World Photos; p. 464: ANDREAS POLLOK/Getty Images, Inc./Taxi; p. 472: © Reuters/CORBIS; p. 475: WIREIMAGESTOCK/WireImageStock/Masterfile Stock Image Library; p. 485: Bob Daemmrich/The Image Works; p. 486: © Bettmann/CORBIS. All Rights Reserved; p. 486: NASA/John F. Kennedy Space Center; p. 488: Eric Gay/AP Wide World Photos

Chapter 15 p. 498: Imagination Photo Design; p. 502: Vstock/AGE Fotostock America, Inc.; p. 507: Ric Francis/AP Wide World Photos; p. 514: NASA/AP Wide World Photos; p. 521: Plexus Corporation; p. 524: Rick Bowmer/AP Wide World Photos; p. 526: AP Wide World Photos

Chapter 16 p. 534: Virginia Hart/AP Wide World Photos; p. 537: Lisa Quinones/Black Star; p. 543: Paul Sancya/AP Wide World Photos; p. 548: Courtesy of Southwest Airlines; p. 550: © Catherine Karnow/CORBIS; p. 557: Jeff Christensen/Reuters Limited

Chapter 17 p. 566: 3M; p. 569: LM Otero/AP Wide World Photos; p. 572: Gilles Mingasson/Getty Images; p. 575: Alienware; p. 578: Jean-Marc Giboux/Getty Images, Inc.; p. 581: Kim Kulish/Corbis/Bettmann; p. 587: Mark Richards; p. 590: Martin H. Simon/Corbis/SABA Press Photos, Inc.

Chapter 18 p. 602: Getty Images News; p. 605: Jeff Greenberg/Omni-Photo Communications, Inc.; p. 607: AP Wide World Photos; p. 610: Bob Krist/Corbis/Bettmann; p. 613: Al Behrman/AP Wide World Photos; p. 616: Getty Images News; p. 623: © OLIVER WEIKEN/epa/Corbis; p. 628: Mark Richards

Name Index

C

D

N

O

P

T

Company Index

Subject Index

D

H

I

J

P

T